D0162637

FORENSIC SCIENCE

and LAW

Investigative Applications in Criminal, Civil, and Family Justice

FORENSIC SCIENCE and LAW

Investigative Applications in Criminal, Civil, and Family Justice

Edited by

Cyril H. Wecht
John T. Rago

Editorial Coordinator

Benjamin E. Wecht

Taylor & Francis
Taylor & Francis Group

Boca Raton   London   New York

A CRC title, part of the Taylor & Francis imprint, a member of the
Taylor & Francis Group, the academic division of T&F Informa plc.

Published in 2006 by
CRC Press
Taylor & Francis Group
6000 Broken Sound Parkway NW, Suite 300
Boca Raton, FL 33487-2742

International Standard Book Number-10: 0-8493-1970-6 (Hardcover)
International Standard Book Number-13: 978-0-8493-1970-9 (Hardcover)
Library of Congress Card Number 2005051076

Library of Congress Cataloging-in-Publication Data

Forensic science and law : investigative applications in criminal, civil, and family justice / edited by Cyril H. Wecht, John T. Rago.
    p. cm.
Includes index.
Includes bibliographical references and index.
ISBN 0-8493-1970-6 (alk. paper)
    1. Evidence, Expert--United States. 2. Forensic sciences--United States. 3. Criminal investigation--United States. I. Wecht, Cyril H., 1931- II. Rago, John T.

KF8961.F665 2005
347.73'67--dc22   2005051076

Taylor & Francis Group
is the Academic Division of T&F Informa plc.

Visit the Taylor & Francis Web site at
http://www.taylorandfrancis.com

**and the CRC Press Web site at
http://www.crcpress.com**

Preface

As a practicing forensic scientist for more than 40 years, I have spent the majority of my life seeking social truth and justice through the application of scientific methods and legal principles to some of the world's greatest mysteries. Over that period of time, I have watched forensic science undergo dramatic progress, most recently in the areas of DNA collection and analysis and computer-simulated reconstruction of crime scenes. Unfortunately, and despite what such popular TV shows as *CSI* and *Crossing Jordan* might suggest, too few professionals are equipped with the knowledge necessary to fully unleash the promise of science in civil, criminal, and family legal matters. Such recent real-life dramas as the O.J. Simpson investigation and trial and the unsolved murder of JonBenet Ramsey provide ample confirmation of this fact.

What's more, the academic community has been slow and splintered in its response to the need to prepare a broader base of professionals for the study and implementation of this critical body of knowledge. As a result, the field of forensic science, along with its role in our various systems of justice, has reached a crucial juncture.

As educators, we can no longer ignore the need for the legal and scientific communities to work in greater unity toward the apprehension and prosecution of the perpetrators of crime or of those who cause injuries to others, nor toward the exoneration of the wrongfully convicted. Forensic science has already made a great impact on our systems of justice, but if we are to become truly effective in our collective "search for the truth," we must inform and involve other professionals and their specialties as well.

Forensic Science and Law — like the Cyril H. Wecht Institute of Forensic Science and Law, out of which it grew — was designed, in large part, to communicate the wide range of methods and approaches for achieving civil, criminal, and family justice. But more importantly, it is an undertaking that brings together the words and thoughts of professionals from multiple disciplines who stand united in the goal of speaking truth to power. It is a book that should engender in all of its readers — whether students or teachers, scientists or lawyers — an appreciation of the need to integrate our skills and understanding of this multidisciplinary approach to applying science to law.

The application of forensic science to the justice system can have profound results. But if we are to fully harness the promise of forensic science in the administration of justice, today's students — along with professionals who have dedicated their lives to public service and education — must seek out opportunities for growth in this rapidly emerging body of work. It is our sincere hope that this book represents one such opportunity.

Cyril H. Wecht, M.D., J.D.
Coroner, County of Allegheny, Pennsylvania
Advisory Board Chairman,
The Cyril H. Wecht Institute of Forensic Science and Law
Adjunct Professor of Law, Duquesne University School of Law

Objective truth is a difficult conquest. No study of any single body of intellectual activity — the problems of chemistry, physics, biology, mathematics, philosophy, psychology, or the history of social economy, *inter alia* — can, in and of itself, achieve the level or degree of truth necessary to comprehend the full range of human conduct. The substance of this textbook represents an attempt to respond to this limitation by identifying new pedagogical and professional methods that shed critical light on our pursuit of objective truths. It breathes forth the conviction that law and forensic science, viewed in the context of each other, harmonize and call for a climate of genuine interdisciplinary study. And at the heart of this convergence resides the authors' collective belief that the combined study of forensic science and law will continue to lead to the revelation of new knowledge and certain objective truths in a variety of our social settings and institutions.

If the primary task of education is to instill respect for truth in all its forms, these writings are designed to encourage students (and their professors) to contemplate the emerging presence and broad appeal of forensic scientific and legal studies at all levels of education. By sharing the same coefficient of reality, forensic science and law animate our pursuit of truth. Free of bias or prejudice, the product of this marriage of thought convincingly reveals to us that just as all life rebels against death, so, too, does all truth in every facet of life, and its social arrangements rebel against contradiction.

The origin for this work is grounded in ancient traditions. Aristotle has described human beings as "rational animals," positing that we are driven to identify methods by which we can achieve an abstract notion of truth and concrete conditions of objective truth. The combination of forensic scientific and legal studies achieves this objective and much more. This textbook represents the authors' efforts to reveal the fruits of these shared objectives — a revelation that begins with an understanding of the contextual relationship of certain foundations in criminal, civil, and family justice, before moving on to a variety of forensic scientific applications. Of particular importance is a close examination of the critical role played by the rules of evidence and the use of experts in attaining these shared objectives.

The law is predicated upon the "reasonable man" standard for approaching much of its fact-finding obligation; however, "reason" can give rise to misunderstanding. "Rational" thought, on the other hand — the predicate analytical approach of science — has its appeal, but is similarly flawed since science is neither the whole of mankind nor the key to unlocking all of its objective truths. Stated simply, no single discipline or combined schools of thought will definitely and exhaustively elucidate the mystery of human existence in search of objective truth...but we can think of few better and more proven places to begin than at the intersection of forensic science and law.

John T. Rago, J.D.
Assistant Professor of Law, Duquesne University School of Law
Executive Director, The Cyril H. Wecht Institute of Forensic Science and Law

About the Editors

Cyril H. Wecht is a medical–legal and forensic science consultant, author and lecturer, who also serves as coroner of Allegheny County (Pittsburgh), Pennsylvania. He administers a governmental department which is responsible for investigating all sudden, suspicious, violent, and unexplained deaths within its jurisdiction. As a medical–legal expert, he has performed approximately 14,000 autopsies and has supervised, reviewed, or been consulted on approximately 30,000 additional post-mortem examinations.

Dr. Wecht is a clinical professor at the University of Pittsburgh schools of Medicine, Dental Medicine, and Public Health; an adjunct professor at Duquesne University's schools of Law, Pharmacy, and Health Sciences; and a distinguished professor at Carlow University, as well as chairman of the Advisory Board of The Cyril H. Wecht Institute of Forensic Science and Law, which he founded at the Duquesne University School of Law in 2000. He has served as president of the American College of Legal Medicine and the American Academy of Forensic Science, as well as chairman of the boards of trustees of both the American Board of Legal Medicine and the American College of Legal Medicine Foundation.

Dr. Wecht is the author of more than 475 professional publications; an editorial board member of 18 national and international medical–legal and forensic scientific publications; and editor of 35 books, including the 5-volume set, *Forensic Sciences* (Matthew Bender), and two 3-volume sets, *Handling Soft Tissue Injury Cases* and *Preparing and Winning Medical Negligence Cases* (both published by Michie).

Dr. Wecht frequently appears as a guest on national TV and radio shows to discuss various medical–legal and scientific subjects, including medical malpractice, alcohol and drug abuse, the assassinations of President John F. Kennedy and Senator Robert F. Kennedy, the death of Elvis Presley, and the O.J. Simpson and JonBenet Ramsey cases. These cases, along with many others, are discussed in his popular non-fiction books, *Cause of Death* (Penguin), *Grave Secrets* (Penguin), *Who Killed JonBenet Ramsey?* (Onyx), *Mortal Evidence* (Prometheus Books), and *Tales from the Morgue* (Prometheus Books).

Formerly chairman of the Department of Pathology and president of the medical staff at St. Francis Central Hospital in Pittsburgh, Dr. Wecht received his medical degree from the University of Pittsburgh and his law degree from the University of Maryland. He is certified by the American Board of Pathology in anatomic, clinical, and forensic pathologies, and is a fellow of the College of American Pathologists, the American Society of Clinical Pathologists, and the National Association of Medical Examiners.

John T. Rago is an assistant professor of law at the Duquesne University School of Law, where he also serves as the executive director of The Cyril H. Wecht Institute of Forensic Science and Law and director of the Law School's Post-conviction DNA Project. In addition to this work and his teaching in the area of criminal law and procedure, Professor Rago maintains a faculty appointment to the Duquesne University Bayer School of Natural and Environmental Sciences, where he teaches graduate courses on Wrongful Convictions, Foundations in American Law, and Constitutional Criminal Procedure. Professor Rago, whose work is focused, in large part, on the subjects of innocence reform and wrongful convictions, also serves as an appointed member to the Innocence Project's Policy Group of the Cardozo School of Law in New York.

In his role with the Wecht Institute, Professor Rago directs a multidisciplinary educational initiative that collaborates with his faculty colleagues in the university's schools of Law, Nursing, Natural and Environmental Sciences, Pharmacy, Business and College of Liberal Arts, to offer graduate degree and professional certificate programs in forensic science and law to a diverse group of students.

The institute's interdisciplinary work, consisting of scholarship, teaching, consulting, and curricular design, has served as the impetus for the creation of six degree programs at the university and articulation agreements (shared academic programming under development) with several colleges and universities throughout the region. The institute has hosted five major national symposia in as many years, and along with Duquesne University and the Duquesne University School of Law, is recognized in the forensic science community as a leader among the nation's academic institutions in providing an interdisciplinary approach to the study of the forensic sciences in context with the law.

Before joining the Law School's administration as associate dean in 1993, followed by his appointment to the School's faculty in 2001, Professor Rago was in private practice and served as a law clerk in both the federal and state courts. He is admitted to practice before the Pennsylvania Supreme Court, the United States Supreme Court, the U.S. Court of Appeals for the Third Circuit, and the U.S. District Court for the Western District of Pennsylvania. He holds degrees from Duquesne University's College of Arts and Sciences and Law School.

A lifelong Pittsburgh resident, Professor Rago and his wife, Ann, have three children — Annie J., Emily J., and John Henry.

Contributors

The Honorable Ruggero J. Aldisert
Senior Circuit Court Judge
U.S. Court of Appeals
    for the 3rd Circuit
Santa Barbara, California, USA

Bruce A. Antkowiak, J.D.
Assistant Professor of Law
Duquesne University
    School of Law
Pittsburgh, Pennsylvania, USA

Scott D. Batterman, Ph.D.
Engineering Consultant
Batterman Engineering, LLC
Cherry Hill, New Jersey, USA

Steven C. Batterman, Ph.D.
Professor Emeritus
University of Pennsylvania
Philadelphia, Pennsylvania, USA;
Engineering Consultant
Batterman Engineering, LLC
Cherry Hill, New Jersey, USA

Jagdeep S. Bhandari, J.D., Ph.D.
Professor of Law
Florida Coastal School of Law
Jacksonville, Florida, USA

Vanessa S. Browne-Barbour, J.D.
Associate Dean, Associate
    Professor of Law
Duquesne University School of Law
Pittsburgh, Pennsylvania, USA

Ann Wolbert Burgess,
    D.N.Sc., RN, CS, FAAN
Professor
Connell School of Nursing
Boston College
Chestnut Hill, Massachusetts, USA

Nicholas P. Cafardi, J.D., J.C.L.
Dean Emeritus and Katarincie
    Professor of Legal Process
Duquesne University School of Law
Pittsburgh, Pennsylvania, USA

Deborah L. Chaklos, M.S.
Scientist
Firearms and Toolmarks Section
Allegheny County Coroner's Office
Forensic Science Laboratory Division
Pittsburgh, Pennsylvania, USA

Carole E. Chaski, Ph.D.
Executive Director
Institute for Linguistic Evidence
Georgetown, Delaware, USA

Suzanne Edgett Collins,
    RN, M.P.H., J.D., Ph.D.
Associate Professor
Department of Nursing
University of Tampa
Tampa, Florida, USA

Laura Ann Ditka, J.D.
Deputy District Attorney and Supervisor,
    Child Abuse Unit
Office of the Allegheny County
    District Attorney
Pittsburgh, Pennsylvania, USA

Frederick W. Fochtman, Ph.D.
Director and Chief Forensic Toxicologist
Allegheny County Coroner's Office
Forensic Science Laboratory Division;
Director
Master's in Forensic Science and Law
Duquesne University
Pittsburgh, Pennsylvania, USA

Neal H. Haskell, Ph.D., B.C.E.
Forensic Entomology Consultant
Professor of Forensic
    Science and Biology
Saint Joseph's College
Rensselaer, Indiana, USA

Sarah Eckel Hinton, J.D.
Law Clerk
United States District Court, for the
    Western District of Pennsylvania, USA

Robert M. Huston, B.S.
Allegheny County Coroner's Office
Forensic Sciences Branch
Pittsburgh, Pennsylvania, USA

Steven Koehler, Ph.D.
Forensic Epidemiologist
Allegheny County Coroner's Office
Pittsburgh, Pennsylvania, USA

Margaret K. Krasik, J.D.
Associate Professor of Law
Duquesne University School of Law
Pittsburgh, Pennsylvania, USA

Michelle N. Kuehner, B.A., B.S.
Scientist
Firearms and Toolmarks Section
Allegheny County Coroner's Office
Forensic Science Laboratory Division
Pittsburgh, Pennsylvania, USA

Patrick Lavelle, J.D.
Attorney
DuBois, Pennsylvania, USA

Henry C. Lee, Ph.D.
Chief Emeritus
Connecticut Department of
    Public Safety
Division of Scientific Services
Branford, Connecticut, USA

Michael J. Machen, J.D.
Chief Public Defender
Office of the Public Defender
Pittsburgh, Pennsylvania, USA

Matthew R. Marlin, Ph.D.
Professor of Economics
Duquesne University
Pittsburgh, Pennsylvania, USA

Kellen McClendon, J.D.
Associate Professor of Law
Duquesne University
    School of Law
Pittsburgh, Pennsylvania, USA

Kenneth C. McCrory, CPA, CFE
Principal
McCrory and McDowell, LLC
Pittsburgh, Pennsylvania, USA

Thomas C. Meyers, M.S.
Serologist/Criminalist/DNA
    Technical Leader
Allegheny County Coroner's Office
Pittsburgh, Pennsylvania, USA

John E. Murray, Jr., J.D., S.J.D.
Chancellor and Professor of Law
Duquesne University School of Law
Pittsburgh, Pennsylvania, USA

Richard F. Paciaroni, J.D.
Partner
Construction Practice Group
Kirkpatrick and Lockhart,
    Nicholson Graham, LLP
Pittsburgh, Pennsylvania, USA

Timothy M. Palmbach, J.D., M.S.
Director and Associate Professor
Forensic Science Program
University of New Haven
West Haven, Connecticut, USA

Mark M. Pollitt, M.S.
President
Digital Evidence Professional
    Services, Inc.
Ellicott City, Maryland, USA

John T. Rago, J.D.
Assistant Professor of Law
Duquesne University School of Law
Executive Director
The Cyril H. Wecht Institute of Forensic
    Science and Law
Pittsburgh, Pennsylvania, USA

Katherine M. Ramsland, Ph.D.
Assistant Professor
Department of Social Science
DeSales University
Center Valley, Pennsylvania, USA

Kathleen J. Reichs, Ph.D., DABFA
Professor
Department of Sociology and
    Anthropology
University of North
    Carolina–Charlotte
Charlotte, North Carolina, USA;
Responsable-Anthropologie
    Judiciaire, Laboratoire de Sciences
    Judiciaires et de Médecine Légale,
Montréal, Québec

L. Kathleen Sekula, Ph.D., APRN
Associate Professor of Nursing,
    Program Director
Graduate Forensic Nursing Program
Duquesne University
    School of Nursing
Pittsburgh, Pennsylvania, USA

Raymond F. Sekula, J.D., L.L.M.
Professor of Law
Duquesne University School of Law
Pittsburgh, Pennsylvania, USA

Jack W. Snyder, M.D., J.D., Ph.D.
Associate Director
Division of Specialized Information
    Services
Bethesda, Maryland, USA

Michael N. Sobel, D.M.D., DABFO
Clinical Associate Professor
Dental Public Health
University of Pittsburgh
    School of Dental Medicine
Chief Forensic Odontologist
Allegheny County Coroner's Office
Pittsburgh, Pennsylvania, USA

James E. Starrs, L.L.M.
Professor of Law and Professor of
    Forensic Sciences
George Washington University
Washington, District of Columbia, USA

S. Michael Streib, J.D., M.B.A.
Professor of Law
Duquesne University School of Law
Pittsburgh, Pennsylvania, USA

Kevin J. Stubblebine, J.D.
Senior Associate
Construction Practice Group
Kirkpatrick and Lockhart
    Nicholson Graham
Pittsburgh, Pennsylvania, USA

Robert D. Taylor, J.D., M.Div., J.D.
Professor of Law
Duquesne University School of Law
Pittsburgh, Pennsylvania, USA

Thomas W. Vastrick
Forensic Document Examiner
Altamonte Springs,
Florida, USA

Pamela M. Woods, M.S.
Scientist
Allegheny County Coroner's Office
Forensic Science Laboratory Division
Trace Evidence Section
Pittsburgh, Pennsylvania, USA

Mark D. Yochum, J.D.
Professor of Law
Duquesne University School of Law
Pittsburgh, Pennsylvania, USA

Cyril H. Wecht, M.D., J.D.
Advisory Board Chairman
The Cyril H. Wecht Institute of Forensic
    Science and Law
Pittsburgh, Pennsylvania, USA

Victor W. Weedn, M.D., J.D.
Visiting Professor
Duquesne University
    Bayer School of Natural and
    Environmental Sciences
Pittsburgh, Pennsylvania, USA

Michael Welner, M.D.
Chairman
The Forensic Panel
Associate Clinical
    Professor of Psychiatry
New York University
    School of Medicine
New York, New York, USA

Contents

Part I: Overview

1. Ancient Tradition — The Relationship of Science and Law 3
   Robert D. Taylor
   The Pleistocene Epoch: The Regime of Fire over Ice...................... 4
   The Neolithic Period: The Stellar Regime 5
   The Newtonian Age: The Machine Regime 6
   The Present and the Future: The Age of Chaos........................... 8
   Notes 8

2. Logic in Forensic Science.. 11
   The Honorable Ruggero J. Aldisert
   The Language of Logic 12
      Argument 12
      Conclusion 12
      Premise 12
      Inference... 13
      The Distinction between Deductive and Inductive Reasoning 14
   Logic in the Forensic Sciences Is Neither All Deductive nor All Inductive. 14
      Deductive Reasoning 15
      Inductive Reasoning 21
   Fallacies 26
      Formal Fallacies....................................... 26
      Informal (Material) Fallacies 27
      Argumentum ad Nauseum 32
   How Logic Will Help You 33
   Notes 33

3. Forensic Science and Law — Revealing Truth and Freedom in a Single Light... 35
   John T. Rago
   Introduction..................................... 35
   The Learning Moment of Postconviction DNA Testing: Forensic Science
      and Law at Work.. 37
   Innocence Reforms: The Race Begins 37
   With a Reading of *The Blooding*, a Scientific Revolution Is Unleashed
      in American Criminal Justice: The Story of Kirk Noble Bloodsworth.... 39
   The Evidence Is In....................................... 43
   Have You Reached Your Verdict?........................... 44
   We Are Not Sure, Your Honor 45
   The Legal Profession and Public Policy Begin to Respond to the Ageless
      Errors of Our Ways 46
   Notes 49

Part II: Foundations of Law

4. Criminal Law and Procedure 67
   Bruce A. Antkowiak
        The Historical Perspective 68
        The Philosophical Basis of the American Criminal Justice System 71
             The Need for Clearly Defined Criminal Laws 73
             The Jury Trial 74
             The Presumption of Innocence and Proof beyond a Reasonable Doubt   75
             Other Aspects of the American System Influenced
                  by the Philosophy of the Enlightenment 80
        Sources of Criminal Law.. 82
        The Constitution and Criminal Procedure 85
             Search and Seizure: The 4th/14th Amendments 85
             The Requirements of a Valid Search Warrant 86
             Some Common Exceptions to the Warrant Requirement 88
             Custodial Interrogations: the 5th/14th Amendments 91
        Making the Case Ready for Trial 92
             Preserving Evidence for Trial 92
             Preserving and Producing Evidence in Discovery 93
        When the System Fails: Wrongful Convictions 96
        Notes 99

5. Forensic Science and the Family.................................... 109
   Vanessa S. Browne-Barbour and Margaret K. Krasik
        Introduction... 109
             Fundamentals of Family Law 109
             Domestic Violence 111
             Child Custody 114
             Syndromes 115
             Parentage Testing 119
        Elder Law Basics: Planning for Autonomy............................ 121
             Intestacy: The Default System for Identifying Heirs
                  to a Decedent's Property 122
             Probate: The Default System for Administering
                  and Distributing Decedents' Property 123
             Guardianship: The Default System for Personal Decision
                  Making in the Case of Incompetency............................ 124
             Planning Ahead to Avoid the Default System, Part 1: Using Wills
                  and Other Basic Legal Instruments to Achieve Financial
                  Autonomy 125
             Planning Ahead to Avoid the Legal Default System, Part 2:
                  Using Powers of Attorney Health Care and Living Wills to Plan
                  for Personal Autonomy 127
        Conclusion 130
        Sources for Part II: Elder Law..................................... 130
        Notes 130

6. The Civil Justice System 139

Nicholas P. Cafardi

    Civil and Criminal Justice 139
    The Elements of the Civil Justice System 140
        Civil Claims 140
    The Court System 140
        The State Court System 141
        The Federal Court System 141
        Finding the Right Court 142
        Personal Jurisdiction 142
        Venue 143
    The Phases of a Civil Justice Proceeding 143
        The Pretrial Phase 144
        The Trial Phase 146
        The Post Trial Phase 147
    Further Reading 148
    References 148

7. Discovery in Civil Cases 151

S. Michael Streib

    Introduction 151
    History and Purpose 151
    Overview of Civil Discovery 152
    Forms of Discovery 153
        Depositions 153
        Requests to Produce or Examine Documents and Things 154
        Interrogatories 154
        Request for Admissions 155
    Postscript 155

8. Contract Law — Forensic Agreements 157

John E. Murray, Jr.

    Introduction 157
    Economic Organization 157
    Agreements vs. Forensic Agreements 158
    The Discipline of Forensic Agreements — Contract Law 158
    The Evidence — Objective Manifestations 159
    Where Is "The Contract"? 160
    What Do the Terms Mean? Interpretation 161
    Breach — Material or Immaterial 162
    Contract Remedies — Putting Humpty Dumpty Together
      Again — The Purpose of Contract Law 162
    Conclusion 164

9. Fundamental Principles of Tort Law 165

Kellen McClendon

    Introduction 165

What Is a Tort?.. 165
The Interests Protected by Tort Law 165
Three General Categories of Tort Liability 165
Fault 166
Cause of Action 166
Intentional Torts.. 167
Preliminary Considerations...................................... 167
Against Person 170
Against Property 179
Recklessness 187
Definition... 187
Interest Protected 187
Elements to the Cause of Action and Defense to the Cause of Action . 187
Negligence.. 189
Initial Definitions 189
Interest Protected 191
Elements of the Cause of Action................................. 191
Defenses to a Cause of Action for Negligence..................... 208
Additional Matters 213
Strict Liability and Absolute Liability 216
Strict Liability... 217
Absolute Liability 217
Nuisance 218
Notes 219

10. Product Liability 231
Patrick Lavelle
In the Beginning, There Was Warranty............................. 231
From Warranty to Strict Liability 232
Product Defects... 234
Important Issues in Strict Liability 236
References... 237

11. Forensic Medicine and Medical Negligence — Initial Case Investigation
Applications 239
Suzanne Edgett Collins
Medical Negligence Litigation..................................... 239
Medical Errors and Adverse Events: A Fertile Field.............. 239
Medical Negligence Litigation and Forensic Medicine:
A Necessary Alliance 240
The Social and Legal Context of Medical Malpractice 241
Medical Negligence as a Subset of Medical Malpractice.............. 242
Brief Overview: Elements of and Defenses to Medical Negligence 243
The Critical Analysis of Potential Medical Negligence Cases 246
Initial Case Investigation 246
Information Organization Is Essential 247

A Changing Landscape: Reform Initiatives Focused on Medical
    Malpractice 250
References.. 252

12. Construction Law 255
Richard F. Paciaroni and Kevin J. Stubblebine
    Introduction.. 255
    The Legal Need for Forensic Engineers............................... 256
    The Role of the Forensic Engineer 256
        The Big Picture 256
        The Process 258
        Primary Tasks.. 260
    Attributes of an Effective Forensic Engineer 262
        Qualifications/Expertise of a Construction
            Forensic Engineer.. 262
    Considerations for Lawyers Investigating Construction
        Failures 264
        Types of Investigations 264
        Protection of Evidence 264
        Coordination of Expert Investigations 265
        Managing the Expert 265
    Types of Construction Failures....................................... 266
        Safety Failures.. 267
        Functional Failures 268
        Ancillary Failures... 268
    Causes of Construction Failures...................................... 268
        Defective Design 269
        Defective Construction 269
        Defective Materials.. 269
        Improper Operation and Maintenance................................. 270
        Poor Planning/Poor Management/Owner Interference 270
        Unforeseeable Factors 270
    Case Studies of Infamous Construction Disasters...................... 270
        Kansas City Hyatt Regency Hotel Walkway Collapse 271
        The Hartford Civic Center Collapse 272
        The L'Ambiance Plaza Collapse...................................... 273
        Willow Island Cooling Tower Collapse.............................. 274
    Notes 277
    Further Reading 278
    Appendix A: The Eight (8) Phases of a Failure Investigation 279

Part III: Bridging the Foundations

13. Experts and the Admissibility of Evidence Concerning Scientific,
    Technical, and Other Specialized Areas of Knowledge 285
Raymond F. Sekula and Sarah Eckel Hinton

An Overview of the Rules of Evidence Concerning
    Witnesses in General 286
Expert Testimony 287
    Expert Qualifications 287
    Subject Matter 287
Notes 293
Further Reading 294

Part IV: Foundations of Forensic Science

Section A: Evidence and the Physical Sciences

14. A Critical Analysis of Selected Features of Fingerprinting 299
    James E. Starrs
    Introduction: The Coverage 299
    Preposterous Claims 300
    The Fingerprint as an "Unforgeable Signature" 301
    More Fuel for the Defense Flame: The CSI Effect 305
    Fingerprinting Testimony beyond the Expert's Qualifications 307
    The Uniqueness Dilemma 308
    The Infallibility Equation 310
    Objectivity is the Watchword of Science 312
    A Method without Uniform Standards 312
    Remedial Recommendations 313
    Who's in Charge? 314
    Notes 314
    SWGFAST Glossary 317

15. Trace Evidence Examination 323
    Pamela M. Woods
    Introduction 323
    Collection of Trace Evidence 325
    Packaging and Labeling Evidence 327
    Questioned Materials and Known Materials 327
    Defining Trace Evidence 328
    Fiber Examination 329
    Glass Evidence 329
    Paint Evidence 330
    The Importance of Trace Evidence Collection 331
    Endnotes 331

16. Firearm and Toolmark Identification 333
    Deborah L. Chaklos and Michelle N. Kuehner
    Introduction 333
    Introduction to Firearms 334
    Introduction to Ammunition 336

Firearms Identification.. 338
  Theory of Firearms Identification.................................... 338
  Barrel Manufacturing Process 338
  Marks Produced on Bullets and Cartridge Cases: Class and
    Individual Characteristics 339
Laboratory Examination of Firearms and Fired Components........... 343
  Laboratory Examination of Firearms 344
  Laboratory Examination of Fired Ammunition Components.......... 345
National Integrated Ballistic Information Network (NIBIN) 346
Other Types of Examinations 347
  Serial Number Restoration 347
  Detection of Primer Gunshot Residue (PGSR)....................... 348
  Distance Determination/Detection of Gunshot Residue on Clothing.. 350
Glossary of Terms.. 353
References and Resources.. 354

17. The Investigation of Fire and Explosions 357
Robert M. Huston
  Principles of Ignition and Combustion................................ 357
  Processing the Fire Scene 358
  The Nature and Role of Explosions 360
  Processing the Explosion Scene 361
  Fire and Explosions and Death Investigations 362
  Special Fire Investigation Scenarios 362
  References... 363

18. Questioned Document Examination.................................... 365
Thomas W. Vastrick
  Introduction.. 365
  Handwriting: Background Information 366
  Forgery... 370
  Handwriting: Known Specimens 373
  Distorted Handwriting.. 375
    Disguise.. 375
    Outside Influences 376
  Handwriting: The Comparison Process 377
  Alterations to Documents... 377
  Indented Writing 382
  Charred Documents 382
  Office Machine Examinations... 383
  Counterfeit Document Examination 383

Section B: Evidence and the Biological Sciences

19. Forensic Pathology 387
Cyril H. Wecht and Victor W. Weedn
  Pathology and Forensic Pathology 387

Coroners and Medical Examiners 390
Medical–Legal Death Investigation....................................... 392
The Value of Forensic Pathologists to Society 394
   Forensic Pathology and Criminal Justice............................ 395
   Forensic Pathology and Public Health 395
   Forensic Pathology and Homeland Security......................... 396
   Forensic Pathology Education and Research 396
Forensic Pathology and the Federal Government 397
Forensic Science and the Forensic Pathologist 398
References... 399

20. Forensic Toxicology 401
   Frederick W. Fochtman
   Postmortem Forensic Toxicology....................................... 401
   Human Performance Toxicology 403
   Alcohol in the Body and Its Effects.................................... 403
   Drugs and Driving.. 404
   Forensic Drug Testing.. 405
   References... 407

21. Serology 409
   Thomas C. Meyers
   The Role of the Forensic Serologist 409
   Identification of Blood.. 410
   Catalytic Tests 410
      Crystal Tests... 411
      Immunological Tests 412
   Blood Stain Pattern Interpretation 413
   Identification of Semen and Saliva 414
      Semen 414
      Saliva 416
   References... 417

22. DNA Analysis 419
   Victor W. Weedn
   Historical Backdrop... 419
   What Is DNA?.. 420
   Biological Evidence 421
      Rapes/Sexual Assaults... 422
      Other Crimes 422
   Specimen Collection.. 422
   Trace DNA 423
   Analytic Methods... 423
      RFLP... 423
      PCR 423
      STRs... 424
      Amelogenin 425

	Y-STRs	425
	mtDNA	425
	New Techniques	426
	Databases	426
	Field Testing	427
	QA/Accreditation	427
	Legal Challenges	428
	References	428

23. **The Science of Forensic Entomology** 431
Neal H. Haskell

	Forensic Entomology as a Concept	431
	Historical Perspective of Forensic Entomology	432
	Current Forensic Entomology	433
	Time Since Death	434
	Case Study on Time Since Death Estimation	435
	Determination of Victim Origin by Known Insect Species Distribution	437
	Colonization of Areas on Remains to Identify Sites of Trauma	438
	Other Applications of Forensic Entomology	438
	Entomology in Civil Litigation	439
	Conclusions	440
	References	440

24. **Forensic Odontology** 443
Michael N. Sobel

	Introduction	443
	Basic Concept of Forensic Odontology	445
	Dental Identification	445
	Identification Case Example 1	446
	Identification Case Example 2	447
	Mass Casualty Management	447
	Bite Mark Evidence	448
	Bite Mark Case Example	449
	Patterned Mark Case Example	449
	Human Abuse Evidence	450
	Abuse Case Example	451
	Analysis of Dental Evidence	451
	Tooth Fragment Case Example	451
	Developing Applications	451
	UV Light Case Example	452
	Conclusion	452
	References	453

25. **Forensic Anthropology** 455
Kathleen J. Reichs

| | Introduction | 455 |
| | Stage I: Field Recovery | 457 |

Stage II: Laboratory Analysis: The Biological Profile 457
    Age 457
    Sex... 458
    Race 458
    Stature 458
    Individuation 459
Stage II: Laboratory Analysis: Time and Manner of Death 459
    Time of Death 459
    Manner of Death... 459
Stage III: Report/Court Testimony 461
Conclusion 461
References... 462

Section C: Evidence and the Social and Applied Sciences:
An Overview **465**
    Jagdeep S. Bhandari
    Notes 472

26. Behavioral Science and the Law 475
    Michael Welner and Katherine M. Ramsland
    Introduction... 475
    Criminal Matters 476
        Competency.. 476
        Criminal Responsibility 478
        Presentencing 480
        Corrections 481
        Behavioral Profiling 483
        Psychological Autopsy................................ 484
    Civil Matters 485
        Involuntary Hospitalization and Treatment 485
        Emotional Injury.................................... 486
        Elders and the Incapacitated......................... 487
        Child Custody and Domestic Relations 488
    Workplace Matters... 489
        Harassment and Discrimination...................... 489
        The ADA and Disability, and Fitness for Duty 489
        Workplace Risk...................................... 490
    Practice Issues 490
        Ethics.. 490
        Psychological Testing................................ 493
        Working with the Psychiatrist and Psychologist 493
    Notes 493

27. Digital Forensics 495
    Mark M. Pollitt
    Introduction... 495
    What Is Digital Evidence?.................................. 495
    A Brief History of Digital Forensics 496

Digital Evidence as a Process... 498
Acquisition 500
Examination... 500
Analysis 501
Presentation 501
The Future 502
Notes 502

28. Forensic Linguistics, Authorship Attribution, and Admissibility.............. 505
Carole E. Chaski
Language, Metalinguistic Ability, and Linguistic Expertise 505
The Forensic Context 505
Linguistics: The Scientific Approach to Language 506
The Scope of Forensic Linguistics as an Application of Linguistics....... 508
Authorship Evidence and Expertise 509
Authorship Evidence and Admissibility Hearings........................ 514
Appendix A.. 518
Linguistic Profiling.. 518
The Anthrax Letters: A Linguistic Analysis 519
Endnotes.. 520
References... 521

29. Forensic Accounting.. 523
Kenneth C. McCrory
Introduction: The Role of the Forensic Accountant...................... 523
The Difference between Accountants as Auditors and
Forensic Accountants.. 524
What Forensic Accountants Bring to the Legal Process 524
Services the Forensic Accountant Provides 526
Business Damages.. 526
Fraud 529
Bankruptcy... 531
Valuations.. 531
Divorce Proceedings.. 533
Personal Damages.. 534
Murder and Arson for Profit 537
How to Use Forensic Accountants 538
Conclusion 538
Reference... 539

30. Forensic Economics in Instances of Wrongful Death and Injury.............. 541
Matthew R. Marlin
Introduction to Forensic Economics 541
Economic Estimates and Valuation.. 542
Earning Capacity, Earnings, and Mitigating Earnings.................... 543
Earning Capacity... 543
Earnings 543
Mitigation 545

Fringe Benefits.. 546
Medical Insurance 547
Pension Plans... 547
Social Security 548
Work Life, Retirement, and Life Expectancy.......................... 548
Work Life Expectancy 548
Retirement 550
Life Expectancy 551
Household Services 551
The Concept of Household Services 551
Hours Spent Producing Household Services 552
Hourly Value of Household Services............................. 553
Personal Consumption or Maintenance 554
Present Value 555
The Concept of Present Value 555
The Appropriate Interest (Discount) Rate 556
Summary.. 557
Notes 558
Appendix A: Ethics and the Forensic Economist 559
National Association of Forensic Economics 559
Statement of Ethical Principles and Tenets of Practice.............. 559

31. Forensic Engineering and Science.................................... 561
Steven C. Batterman and Scott D. Batterman
Introduction... 561
Accident Reconstruction 562
Biomechanics of Injury 564
Engineering Failures 566
Tacoma Narrows Bridge, November 17, 1940 567
Kansas City Hyatt Regency Skywalk Collapse, July 17, 1981 567
Space Shuttle Failures Challenger Explosion, January 28, 1986,
and Columbia Breakup, February 1, 2003 567
Collapse of the World Trade Center (WTC) Towers, September 11,
2001; Remarks on the Murrah Federal Building, Oklahoma City,
July 19, 1995.. 568
Products Liability... 569
Failure Modes and Effects Analysis (FMEA) 570
Fault-Tree Analysis (FTA) 570
Product Safety Audit (PSA) 570
Slips and Falls 570
Conclusion 571
Bibliography 572

Part V: Topics in the Practice of Forensic Science

32. Crime Scene Management.. 577
Henry C. Lee and Timothy M. Palmbach
Introduction... 577

Crime Scene Management Components.. 577
   Manpower Management.. 578
   Evidence Management... 580
Information Management... 582
   Information from Victims.. 583
   Information from Witnesses.. 583
   Information from Suspects 584
   Information from Databases.. 584
Technology Management 586
Management of Logistics 587
   Command Posts... 587
   Media Relations.. 588
   Interagency Liaison.. 588
   Resource Allocation 589
   Technology/Procedures... 589
Selecting an Appropriate Crime Scene Investigation Model.............. 590
   Traditional 590
   Crime Scene Technicians 591
   Scene-of-the-Crime/Major Crime Squad 591
   Laboratory Based Crime Scene Scientists 591
   Collaborative Team Approach 592

33. The Roles of Public Attorneys in the Practice of Forensic Science 593
Laura Ann Ditka and Michael J. Machen
The Role of the Prosecutor in the Practice of Forensic Science........... 593
   Determination of Criminal Occurrence....................................... 593
   Determination of Criminal Mechanism....................................... 595
   Suspect Identification 596
The Role of the Public Defender in the Practice of Forensic Science 596
   The Responsibility and Structure of a Public Defender's Office........ 596
   Forensic Science in the Public Defender's Office 597
   A Case Study in Forensic Consultation 598
Notes 599

34. Forensic and Legal Nursing.. 601
L. Kathleen Sekula and Ann Wolbert Burgess
Overview and History of Forensic Nursing............................... 601
Guidelines for Practice.. 604
Practice/Specialty Areas 605
   Sexual Assault Nurse Examiner.. 605
   Pediatric Sexual Assault Nurse Examiner 607
   Sexual Assault Response Team... 607
   Forensic Clinical Nurse Specialist.. 608
   Forensic Psychiatric Nurse.. 609
   Forensic Correctional Nurse... 615
   Nurse Coroner/Death Investigator 617
   Legal Nurse Consultant/Nurse as Expert Witness/Nurse Attorney 618
Education 621

Research 622
Professional Organizations and Journals 623
References 623
Appendix A 626
    Violence 626
    Rape 627

35. Forensic Science and Public Health — The Role of Enabling Statutes,
    Reporting Obligations, and Privacy Laws 629
Jack W. Snyder
    Pennsylvania Enabling Statutes 631
    Reporting of Diseases (Including Cancer) 632
        Pennsylvania's Electronic Disease Reporting Project (PA-NEDSS) 634
        PA-NEDSS Functionality 634
    Reporting of Drugs 635
    Reporting of Impaired Drivers 635
        Impaired Vision 635
        Epilepsy 636
        Other Disqualifications 636
    Reporting Procedure 637
    Reporting of Errors 637
    Reporting of Health Care Institutions and Practitioners 637
    Reporting of Crimes and Criminal Activities 638
        What Is a "Reported" Crime? 639
        Compliance and Prevention 639
    Reporting of Abortions 641
    Reporting of Child Care and Abuse 641
        Child Abuse Reporting Statutes 642
    Public Health Surveillance Laws 649
    The Clash between Compliance with Reporting Obligations and
        Compliance with Privacy Laws 653
    References 654

36. Forensic Science and Public Health — The Role of Forensic Epidemiology 655
Steven Koehler
    Introduction 655
    The Emergence of a New Science 656
    Forensic Consulting 657
    Expert Witnesses 657
    Coroners'/Medical Examiners' Offices and Health Departments 658
    Two Different Worlds 659
    Examples of Forensic Epidemiology 659
    Conclusion 661
    References 661

37. Lawyers, Ethics, and the Forensic Professional 663
  Mark D. Yochum
    Introduction.. 663
    Authority to Enforce Rules of Lawyers' Ethics against the
      Nonlawyer Forensic Professional..................................... 663
    Issues with Respect to the Confidentiality of Information
      Learned in the Forensic Process 667
    Conflicts of Interest... 670
    Fees 672

Index... 675

Overview

I

Ancient Tradition — The Relationship of Science and Law

1

ROBERT D. TAYLOR

Forensic science and law, law and science![1] What exactly is this relationship like or to what shall it be compared? Is this relationship something like oil and water, which do not mix? Or is it more like husband and wife in the ideal marriage, where the two become one flesh? Or is it simply an estranged relationship heading for either a quick or a contested divorce? Or might it perhaps simply be a matter of attempted seduction? Or is this couple merely dating and exploring whether or not a long term relationship is in their mutual interest? Have there been any children yet? Is this family, if such it be, a functional or dysfunctional one? Many questions rightfully assail us at this juncture.

But overriding all our questions such as these is the contemporary experience that in entering the field of forensic science and law one is entering upon a totally new, cutting-edge relationship between science and law. It is, however, the purpose of this reflective essay to suggest that this is not the case. Quite to the contrary, one is entering into a very ancient and certainly always profound interaction between science and law.

What we wish to do here is to acquaint both the student entering upon this career path and the seasoned practitioner as well with this very ancient and constant interaction between science and law. Indeed, Western civilization itself has emerged from the interaction of four very fundamental relationships toward the universe: namely, religion, philosophy, science, and law. To change our metaphor concerning this interaction, we may consider these four to be the very roots from which the trees of the civilization of the Western world have grown. It is very important then that students and experienced practitioners alike not lose sight of this thick forest of growth while engaging and studying the countless details of its individual scientific and legal trees. For without such an overarching or foundational picture, it will be difficult, if not impossible, to attain coherent public knowledge which is the vaunted claim of science and, instead, we will continue to have that pathetic state of affairs whereby we know more and more about less and less until we know everything about nothing at all essential. We would have a world in even

3

more fragments than our world currently is — in short, we would have a world fissured and fractured further by the jargon of scientific and legal experts.

What we intend in this essay will hopefully serve as a modest antidote to fragmented thinking and as a brief meditation on three constitutive moments in the long history of interaction among science, law, philosophy, and religion but particularly among science and law. The three periods that will serve as the occasions for our reflections are the Pleistocene epoch, the Neolithic period, and the Newtonian age: three constitutive moments of this fourfold interaction. Our essay will then conclude with a series of present-day questions confronting both students and professionals in this hybrid field of forensic science and law. Without confronting these living questions, the vision set forth here would mean that we only understand the past to be merely of antiquarian value and fail to see it as a repository of real wisdom that can give us needed guidance in our fissured and fractured world.

The Pleistocene Epoch: The Regime of Fire over Ice

The Pleistocene epoch is that period of widely alternating temperature changes characterizing the encroaching and receding glaciers that covered our planet like white paint poured over our earthly sphere. This epoch and its changeable conditions, which both shaped and elicited a response from our prototypical ancestors or progenitors, lasted for some two million years.[2] Now imagine yourself huddled in a cave, nearly freezing to death along with other members of your little clan. Weather conditions have been such as to produce violent storms, including terrifying sky-to-ground bolts of lightning. In a flash, one of those high energy bolts from out of the heavens ignites a leafless tree outside the entrance to your cave. Warily, you and some younger and braver members of your clan approach this blazing tree and feel the strange radiations emerging from it and warming your frozen body. After much gaping and playing around with limbs torn from the tree, you and your companions carry some burning limbs and broken sticks into the cave. Behold! With this and further experimentation (protoscience), the domestication of fire has begun and with it the long journey out of the cave and into the future of Western civilization.[3]

Now, this experience would certainly have been a religious one as well as a scientific and technological one. After all, the sky gods must have sent the lightning, so fire must be a gift from the gods. Of course, this is still a long way from the time when fire would ignite the many altars of religious sacrifice around the world. But religion has begun here along with the technology and science of fire. But what of law? How did law likely come onto the scene in such circumstances as depicted here?

To understand the emergence of law, we will speculate (since we are without writing, which was not yet invented) based upon the role of the fire keeper so often found among many tribal peoples. These keepers of the fire were responsible for keeping alive the fires necessary for both survival and religious ceremonial purposes. Now place yourself back in your cave with your small clan of members desperately depending upon keeping their life-saving fire alive. Here one would confront issues that are legal-like, quasi-legal issues that might have led to disputes among the members of the clan. How so? Questions like the following: What should be done to the person or persons that negligently or otherwise fail to keep the fire alive and fed? Who should be allowed near the life-quickening fire when it is a scarce resource? The elderly? The men? The women? The sick or pregnant? How should the persons responsible for keeping the life-sustaining fire alive be determined? And who should decide these matters anyhow? So around the fire, quite literally, along with the science of the domestication of fire and the religious experiences accompanying it, there emerge matters of law and order as well. An ancient interaction indeed!

The Neolithic Period: The Stellar Regime

While the above is speculative (though probable), when we enter the period of the neolithic age we are on more solid ground because of abundant monumental archeological and textual evidence. The emergence of the so-called city states along alluvial plains of some of the great rivers of the world, such as the Tigris, the Euphrates, and the Nile, was both a cause and a consequence of the neolithic revolution. During the course of this revolution, (1) plants and animals were domesticated; (2) massive projects such as irrigation and building construction were undertaken; (3) large food surpluses were kept in storage; (4) a form of organized government oversight occurred; and above all (5) writing was invented and records of commercial, legal, medical, and astronomical events were diligently kept. In short, the constitutive building blocks of civilization were put in place. And yet again, we see the interaction of religion, science, and law. And to this interaction we now turn.

The central figures in this interaction were the astronomers. Now that writing had been invented, the long term observations of heavenly bodies could be recorded and handed down to future would-be scanners of the heavens. And why was this burgeoning science of astronomy so important? Its critical nature lay in the fact that the astronomers, on the basis of their heavenly observations, constructed the calendars that were so essential to neolithic societies. In fact, the calendar — accurate or inaccurate — could determine the very matters of life and death. This is the case because calendars told one when to plant and when to harvest, when to sow and when to reap. In addition, the calendars determined liturgical-religious matters and other political matters of state as well, such as, for example, the time to go to war. To be wrong with respect to the coordination of calendar and season could result in planting too soon or harvesting too late: and this, in turn, could make the difference as to whether or not the crop would die of frost, rot, or drought. And when surplus food supply was threatened this, in turn, placed the entire society in jeopardy. So important was the office of astronomer that a chief astronomer could be appointed prime minister of state. One should recall here the "magi" in the New Testament who read earthly political events from a spectacular stellar phenomenon. Reading the sky was to read matters having to do directly with events on the earth. But where might law be in relation to this embryonic science of astronomy?

The answer to this question is manifold. In the first place, the calendars that were created on the basis of stellar observations could be likened to the first legal statute books. After all, what is it that a legal statute does? It tells or commands one with respect to *what* one has to do and *when* one has to do it. Do not even our electronic gadgets, which serve as reminders concerning our many agenda, do likewise? With calendars setting or commanding a society's agenda, we have an example of a prototypical legal code for ancient neolithic cultures. Secondly, it is from astronomical observations that our ancestors conceived of the idea of order and, thus, of law and order. The mythologist Joseph Campbell tells us that:

> ... having remarked a mathematically calculable regularity in the passage of the planets through the constellations of the fixed stars, these first systematic observers of the heavens conceived — in that specific period, in that place, for the first time in human history — the grandiose idea of a mathematically determined cosmic order of greater and lesser, ever-revolving cycles of celestial manifestation, disappearance, and renewal, with which it would be prudent for man to put himself in accord. Hence the relationship even now of religious festivals to astronomically based calendars; also, the notion of laws and mandates handed down from on high. Hence, too, the imitation of heavenly circumstance in the costumes and procedures of royal courts: solar crowns, star-bedecked robes; monarchs and their queens revered as gods and, vice versa, deities revered as kings and queens.[4]

And immediately connected to this idea of order is the derivative one of attempting to imitate below on the earth the order conceived of in the heavens. In fact, the mantra — as above, so below — supplied a sort of unified field theory of governance in the ancient Near East. Memory of this is still sedimented in the Lord's prayer which says, "Your Kingdom come, Your will be done on earth as it is in heaven." Accordingly, some neolithic societies regarded cosmic imitation and cosmic maintenance to constitute the very essence of human governance. Imitating or living the sky was the governing principle of many ancient societies.[5] And even our very English word "disaster" contains the sedimentation of this ancient wisdom of this neolithic understanding as well. For the very etymology of this word "dis-aster" (dis = separation, aster = star) implies that in separation from the stars, our very well-being itself is at stake. It is instructive to note here before leaving this point that current astronomy does not find such calm and ordered tranquillity in the universe, but rather conceives it as a violent universe with stars as nuclear reactors and black holes as infinite sink holes. One wonders if we on earth do not project our own societal happenings into the heavens rather than reading out straightforwardly what is already there in the heavens!

So here, once again, we see the interaction of science, law, and religion as shaping forces of the Western world. So that a change in any one of these always had an impact on the others. This is most familiar to us in the birth of the modern world, starting with Copernicus (1473–1543) and ending with Sir Isaac Newton (1642–1727).

The Newtonian Age: The Machine Regime

The accomplishment of Copernicus is well known. His astronomy decentered the earth, putting the sun in its rightful place at the center of our solar system. But with Isaac Newton, perhaps the greatest scientist of all time, we enter upon the age of Enlightenment, that world view which gave a distinctive shape to modernity. And yet, once again, we see a strong connection between science and law — science and the idea of law as the proper governance of society. With his three laws of motion and his universal theory of gravitation, Newton unified celestial and terrestrial mechanics, the law of the heavens and the earth. As a result, the universe came to be looked upon as a vast clockwork of motion that was able to be both predicted and retrodicted as well. An all-embracing deterministic mechanism unified by one universal force, gravity, produced a regularity and an order that prevailed throughout the universe under the aegis of strict lawfulness. And for those taking their cue from the truth of Newtonian physics, the task for those who govern was to learn about and to reproduce this same regularity and order in society, which itself came to be seen as a social mechanism or social clockwork paralleling or imitating the same regularities which were now seen to pervade the solar system and indeed the universe. This understanding of what could be called Newtonian governance is illustrated in the title of a poem written by John Theophilus Desaguliers (1683–1744). The title reads: "The Newtonian System of the World, the Best Model of Government." In this allegorical poem, the poet compares society to the solar system which is "coerc'd" by law which "[d]irects, but not destroys" society's liberty. Such law only regulates how fast or slowly the society revolves and with what order.[6] We might add here that the entire scheme of jurisprudence based on rights, duties, privileges, and immunities — called Hohfeldian jurisprudence — is an extension of Newtonian thinking into legal thinking. According to the Hohfeldian view, law can be looked upon as a mechanical system of rights, duties, privileges, and immunities, which interlock in a system of cause and effect. It is no surprise that a contemporary view of legal education understands the study of law to be tantamount to the learning of social engineering. A lawyer is a social engineer learning to design, maintain, and repair the social clockworks that run society. Legal concepts were understood through the Newtonian concepts of forces acting on individuals yielding a pattern of ordered motion through space and time.[7] To this day, as a result of Newtonian thinking in law, we still understand law to be but a force that operates on society as a cause producing an effect.

As gravity is to celestial and terrestrial bodies, so law is to social bodies (institutions) and individuals as well. Even Adam Smith's invisible economic hand can be looked upon as the economist's equivalence of gravity. Individuals and social bodies each had their own motion, and law was the means of bringing about a unification and harmony of ordered motion rather than motion which is chaotic and conflicting. Corresponding to gravity, which in its most recent manifestations is looked upon as a field of force operating throughout the universe, an equivalent legal force field is conceived, ideally, to be operating throughout the social realm. And lawyers and natural scientists alike can be analogized to natural and social engineers seeking the unifying laws behind the natural and the social universes. The behavior of matter and the behavior of human beings are both understood as law governed, and the natural sciences (physics supremely) and the social sciences (law supremely) become the quest for law and its ordering manifestations. Many natural and social scientists still work with models and metaphors rooted in the Newtonian mechanistic world view. Even the very contemporary theory of human rights (which can be likened to the directional vectors of Newtonian mathematical mechanics) roots in this world view. So yet once again, we witness the interaction between science and law. And at times, this interaction even becomes a rivalry for supremacy competing for dominance in the sociopolitical consciousness of citizens who pay the bills each of these enterprises accrue.

The Present and the Future: The Age of Chaos

Here our presentation will be very brief. But it is to be noted that with the birth of the Einsteinian scientific age of the Special and General Theories of Relativity and quantum physics, at least with respect to the very fast (approximating the speed of light) and the very tiny (particle physics), we enter a world that is anything but predictable in any Newtonian sense. And along with this world, "chaos theory" is born. And correlatively, our social world grows likewise ever more chaotic and turbulent. It seems that as a society decays, its laws and regulations multiply. And correspondingly, there is little of our social, political, legal, and economic world that remains predictable and stable. So yet once again, science and law, science and governance, seem to dance with one another as they always have from time immemorial. Whether or not this world of improbable probabilities bespeaks the fact that our species is at entropy or at the point of new creation remains to be seen. But in the interface of the science of forensics and law, we are confronted by questions, the answers to which will determine and give shape to their relationship in the future — whether it is to be one of happy harmony, bitter conflict, or eventually even indifference, or with one simply outrunning the other. We conclude this essay on this very ancient and noble heritage between science and law with a series of questions directed at both those who are new to this field as well as at its seasoned practitioners.

The technology that undergirds forensic science is expensive. Consequently, does this not simply give only the rich and/or government access to the better tools of the applied sciences while at the same time cutting out the poor? Should we have specialized judges and/or jurors who are scientifically educated and thus cannot be flummoxed by it? What about science's own past fixations, for example, the now rejected theories of ether and phlogiston? Clearly, today's supposed truths can become tomorrow's rejected casualties. Might this not end up whipsawing law from one scientific pillar to another scientific post? From what scientific domains, subject matters, and concepts should law draw and from which should it not? And by whom is this to be determined? What happens when law loses touch with the ordinary common sense of average people and simply becomes a battle of experts each with their specialized jargon and model-building displays? Should all technological intrusions into law be assumed guilty until proven innocent? Technology is itself not neutral but has social, political, economic, and psychological consequences. What are they? Who benefits? What is the downside?

Let us recall that our founding fathers thought that all significant power could be contained within the realm of law. Are we entering on a way where this "faith" is no longer true, and is law about to be cabined by science and technology? Will the virtual become a substitute for the real? These are but some of the questions that will confront both newcomers and seasoned practitioners in the domain of forensic science and law as we move more deeply into this ancient but also constant and ever future interaction between the natural sciences and law. Whom we let answer these and similar questions and the answers they give may well determine whether we move more seriously toward a deeper liberty or toward still another form of tyranny.

Notes

1. There have been many relationships between law and other subject matters, for example, law and religion, law and rhetoric, law and business, law and ethics, law and economics, law and

anthropology, law and literature, law and philosophy — to name but a few. We are prone to regard the relationship of law and science as the most recent due in part to our abysmal ignorance of the long history of science.

2. See *The Times Atlas of World History*. New Jersey: Hammond; 1992, p. 36.

3. For a very full treatment as well as a lengthy bibliography concerning the domestication of fire in the civilizing process, see the fascinating book by Goudsblom Johan. *Fire and Civilization*. New York: Penguin Press; 1992.

4. Campbell Joseph, *The Mythic Image*. Princeton University Press, New Jersey; 1974, p. 74.

5. For very readable and intriguing studies of this and other matters refer to the books by Williamson, R.A. *Living The Sky: the Cosmos of the American Indian*. Boston: Houghton Mifflin Company; 1984 and Krupp, E. C. *Echoes of Ancient Skies: The Astronomy of Lost Civilizations*. New York: Oxford University Press; 1983.

6. Portions of this poem are found in a volume by Fairchild Hoxie Neale entitled *Religious Trends in English Poetry*. Columbia University Press, New York; 1939, vol. I, pp. 356–358.

7. For a full treatment of this theme refer to the article by Shapiro, B.J. Law and Science in Seventeenth Century England. *Stanford Law Rev* 1969; 21: 727–766.

Logic in Forensic Science* 2

RUGGERO J. ALDISERT[1-5]

"Elementary deduction, my dear Watson." Sherlock Holmes is talking to his famous colleague, John H. Watson, M.D., late of the British Army Medical Department. This statement, or variations thereof, runs throughout Sir Arthur Conan Doyle's classic novels and short stories.

Forensic science in the courtrooms and public safety organizations is generally considered a modern phenomenon, with the development of the great profession of forensic pathology and the availability of university-trained criminalists, crime scene specialists, toxicologists, and laboratory Ph.Ds. And, to be sure, forensic scientists are now the most popular heroes of current television, if you look at the skyrocketing ratings of shows such as Law and Order, Crossing Jordan, CSI: Crime Scene Investigation, CSI: Miami, CSI: New York, and NCIS.

But the first popular forensic scientist appeared over 100 years ago when Sherlock Holmes arrived on the scene in 1901. In the first novel, *A Study in Scarlet*, when Dr. Watson was looking for a man to share lodgings, a friend referred him to Holmes, who was then working in the chemical laboratory of a hospital. The friend said, "I believe he is well up in anatomy, and he is a first class chemist; but, as far as I know, he has never taken any systematic medical classes." Watson later tells us that "[s]ometimes, [Holmes] spent his day at the chemical laboratory, sometimes in the dissecting rooms ... and [he] has a good practical knowledge of British law." That is a pretty good resumé for any forensic specialist.

But essentially he has been referred to as "Holmes the Deductive Machine." And the success of all the stories came from "the aptitude of Holmes' deductions drawn from clues which, with scrupulous fairness, are always laid before the reader."[6]

With Holmes as a backdrop, I have several theses I intend to defend on these pages:

- A professional in forensic science can use logic and still be wrong.
- But a professional who does not use logic can never be right.
- Most professionals in forensic sciences use deductive and inductive reasoning every day without realizing they are applying the canons of logic.

* © 2005 by Ruggero J. Aldisert. Adapted from *Logic for Lawyers: A Guide to Clear Thinking*, 3rd ed., National Institute of Trial Advocacy, Notre Dame, IN.; 1997.

Those who master the technique of reasoning are not always certain what it is. Certainly, they learn how to do it, at least some of it. They pick up idiosyncratic signals somewhere and even a playbook. They learn how to go through the process, and occasionally, they learn *why* they do it. Others do not know exactly what is being done. They learn the exercise. They go through the motions. But most are a little shy on theory.

This chapter is a modest attempt to fill that void. It is directed to "the what" of formal reasoning, or, if you will, logic, a term I use interchangeably with reasoning. Our purpose here is to explain, in very broad strokes, the basics of logic and its application to your profession, to describe the mental processes we utilize in reflective thinking.[7]

The purpose, quite frankly, is to get you thinking about thinking, or to suggest that if using reflective thinking was good enough for Sherlock Holmes, it should be good enough for you.

It is also a plea to avoid making conclusions on the basis of a hunch or intuition. Judge Joseph C. Hutcheson of the U.S. Court of Appeals for the Fifth Circuit was fond of saying that decisions may emerge from four separate processes: "first the cogitative, of and by reflection and logomachy; second, aleatory, of and by the dice; third, intuitive, of and by feeling or 'hunching'; and fourth, asinine, of and by an ass." Whatever decision making technique you may choose to make in your personal life, when it comes to your profession, you have one option only — reflective thinking.

The Language of Logic

Let us start with some definitions.

Argument

An argument is any group of propositions where one proposition is claimed to follow from the others, and where the others are treated as furnishing grounds or support for the truth of the one. An argument is not a mere collection of propositions, but a group with a particular, rather formal, structure.

It is important that you understand this basic concept. Disabuse yourself right now of the notion that when I discuss an argument on the pages that follow, I am talking about a quarrel.

Conclusion

The conclusion of an argument is the *one* proposition that is arrived at and affirmed on the basis of the *other* propositions of the argument.

Premise

The premises of an argument are the *other* propositions which are assumed or otherwise accepted as providing support or justification for accepting the *one* proposition which is the conclusion. Thus, in the three propositions that follow in the universal affirmative deductive categorical syllogism, the first two are *premises* and the third, the *conclusion*:

All men are mortal.
Socrates is a man.
Socrates is mortal.

There are four standard form categorical propositions, or premises, each of which has a name and a letter (A, E, I, or O) that logicians traditionally use for identification. We can represent each standard form categorical proposition by way of a statement using the letters S and P to represent the Subject and Predicate of the proposition. The four standards forms are as follows:

A: Universal Affirmative Proposition
         All S is P: Every member of the first class is also a member of the second class.
E: Universal Negative Proposition
         No S is P: No member of the first class is also a member of the second class.
I: Particular Affirmative Proposition
         Some S is P. Some members (at least one) of the first class are also members
         of the second class.
O: Particular Negative Proposition
         Some S is not P: Some members (at least) of the first class are not members of
         the second class.

The letters A, E, I, and O emanate from the Latin *Affirmo* (affirm) and *Nego* (deny). Logicians describe the three propositions in the All-men-are-mortal syllogism as AII.[8]

It is important to recognize that premise and conclusion are relative terms. Because many arguments contain more than one syllogism (*polysyllogisms*), any premise can serve as a major premise in one argument after having been the conclusion of a previous argument. Premises and conclusions require each other. A proposition standing alone is neither a premise nor a conclusion. Only when it occurs as an assumption in an argument is a proposition a premise; moreover, the conclusion that you draw every day in forensic science is valid only when it is the proposition that is arrived at and claimed to follow other premises in the argument.

Inference

An inference is a process in which one proposition (a conclusion) is arrived at and affirmed on the basis of one or more other propositions, which were accepted as the starting point of the process. Professor Stebbing observes that inference "may be defined as a mental process in which a thinker passes from the apprehension of something given, the datum, to something derived, the conclusion, related in a certain way to the datum, and accepted only because the datum has been accepted."[9]

Inference, then is "any passing from knowledge to new knowledge."[10] A logical inference is a process in which the thinker passes from one proposition to another that is connected with the former in some way. But for the passage to be valid, it must be made according to the laws of logic that permit a reasonable movement from one proposition to another. The passage cannot be a mere speculation, intuition, or guessing. The key to a logical inference is the reasonable probability that the conclusion flows from the evidentiary datum because of past experiences in human affairs.

A nickel-plated revolver was used in a bank holdup by a ski-masked robber who got away with $10,000 in marked money. A nickel-plated revolver, a ski mask, and $10,000 in marked money was found in the apartment of Dirty Dan, its sole occupant. The inference permissible is that our friend Dan was the bank robber.

A moment is necessary to discuss the difference between *inference* and *implication*. These terms are obverse sides of the same coin. We *infer* a conclusion from the data; the data *imply* the conclusion. Professor Cooley explains:

> When a series of statements is an instance of a valid form of inference, the conclusion will be said to *follow* from the premises, and the premises to *imply* the conclusion. If a set of premises implies a conclusion, then, whenever the premises are accepted as true, the conclusion must be accepted as true also . . . .[11]

Or, as Professor Brennan put it: "In ordinary discourse, [implication] may mean 'to give a hint,' and [inference], 'to take a hint.' Thus when my hostess yawns and looks at her watch, I *infer* from her behavior that she would like me to go home. Her yawn and look *imply* that this is her desire."[10] Drawing a proper inference is critical in the practice of your profession.

The Distinction between Deductive and Inductive Reasoning

For our purposes, I suggest that whether an inference is deductive or inductive depends upon the nature of the relationship between the given proposition and the inferred proposition. What is recommended here is a simplified, convenient formula for use by your profession, a clean cut approach that should satisfy all your needs, even though certain distinguished logicians, who teach to a broader census, may quarrel with the neatness, or oversimplification of this formula. Here is how I approach the dichotomy at this time:

- When conclusions are reached from the general to the particular, we call it deductive reasoning.[12]
- When conclusions are reached by reasoning from a number of particulars to the general, or from one particular to another particular, we call it induction.

The fundamental difference between these two types of argument is that in deductive arguments, if the premises are true, the conclusion is absolutely true. In inductive reasoning, we say the conclusion that follows from the premises is merely more probable than not. This is a distinction *with* a difference. The two types of reasoning will be treated in modest detail in the following pages.

Logic in the Forensic Sciences Is Neither All Deductive nor All Inductive

Forensic science is made up of particulars. Its raw materials are the particular facts found at the crime scene, in the autopsy room, or in the laboratory. From these facts, you infer certain conclusions. To be sure, where the starting forensic science principles are clear and the application of the facts to the principle equally plain, the argument often sounds solely in deductive reasoning. Where forensic principles are not clear, and the sole question is application of facts to the principles, both inductive and deductive reasoning are used.

This being so, what form of reasoning do we discuss first? Here we have a chicken-or-the-egg question. Forensic science develops from particulars to broader precepts, a classic process of inductive reasoning that we call inductive generalization. Yet, to understand induction, it is best to first learn deduction. Hence, we put the deductive cart before the inductive horse with some introductory observations on deductive reasoning.

Deductive Reasoning

Deductive reasoning is a mental operation that a forensic scientist, lawyer, or judge must employ every working day. Formal deductive logic is an act of the mind in which, from the relation of two propositions to each other, we infer, that is, we understand and affirm a third proposition. In deductive reasoning, the two propositions which imply the third proposition, the *conclusion*, are called *premises*.

Logical Form

The broad proposition that forms the starting point of deduction is called the *major premise*; the second proposition is called the *minor premise*. They have these titles because the major premise represents the *all*; the minor premise represents something or someone included in the all.

In each argument, the major premise is a broad principle or concept that qualifies as a universal proposition. By *universal*, we mean that the proposition applies to all members of its class without restriction ("*Any* manufacturer who ... is liable"). Words suggesting a universal proposition (or distributed term) include "every," "any," "all," "each," "always," "everywhere," "in every instance," "no," "never," "nowhere," and "under no circumstances."

Had the assertion applied only to a restricted, or partial class, it would be called a *particular* proposition. ("*Some* manufacturers who ... are liable.") Words suggesting a particular proposition (or undistributed term) include "some," "certain," "one," "this," "that," "sometimes," "not everywhere," "sometimes not," "occasionally," "once," and "somewhere."

The subject *term* of a universal proposition is said to be *distributed*. In our example, we speak of "*any* manufacturer." The assertion concerns all manufacturers in the stated class without restriction. Hence, the subject is distributed.

The subject *term* of a particular proposition is said to be *undistributed*. In our example, we know that "some manufacturers who ... are liable," but we would not know which of the some; hence, the subject is undistributed.

Fundamentally, you cannot assert a valid major premise in a deductive syllogism with a particular proposition. It must be universal. It must be the all. It must be the entire class.

Truth

But this is only part of the study of logic. In addition to logical form, the premises must be true.

Examine the following deductive syllogism for logical form:

All men are mortal.
Socrates is a man.
Therefore, Socrates is a mortal.

All forensic scientists have green blood.
Cyril H. Wecht is a forensic scientist.
Therefore, Cyril H. Wecht has green blood.

How about the logical validity of the second syllogism? Does it follow the rule of Socrates is a man? Of course it does. What is wrong with it then?

This introduces the second major ingredient of a valid and sound argument. The premises must be true. The problem with the second syllogism is not its logical validity, but the nonsense contained in the major premise.

The validity of a syllogism and the soundness of the argument's structure deal only with relations between the premises. Validity deals only with form. It has absolutely nothing to do with content. Arguments, therefore, may be logically valid, yet absolutely nonsensical. Assuming a valid form, the essence of an argument must always be a search for the truth or falsity of the premises. Remember, in deductive logic, the conclusion *must* follow from the premises. Watch out for GIGO: garbage in, garbage out.

Logical argument is a means of determining the validity and truth of a purported conclusion. We do this by following well established canons of a logical order in a deliberate and intentional fashion. Here we concentrate on logical validity. We will leave the truth up to you.

Logical Validity

In forensic science, you must think and reason logically. You must follow a thinking process that emancipates you from impulsively jumping to conclusions, or frees you from an argument supported only by strongly felt emotions or superstitions. That which John Dewey said for school teachers in generations past is still vital and important today: "[Reflective thought] converts action that is merely appetitive, blind, and impulsive into intelligent action."[13]

The classic means of deductive reasoning is the *syllogism.* Aristotle, who first formulated its theory, offered this definition: "A syllogism is a discourse in which, certain things being stated, something other than what is stated follows of necessity from their being so."[14] He continued: "I mean by the last phrase that they produce the consequence, and by this, that no further term is required from without to make the consequence necessary."[15] From this definition, we can say that a syllogism is a form of implication in which two propositions jointly imply a third.[15]

Special rules of the syllogism serve to inform exactly under what circumstances one proposition can be inferred from two other propositions. Consider again the familiar classic affirmative categorical deductive syllogism:

All men are mortal.
Socrates is a man.
Therefore, Socrates is mortal.

This is a *universal affirmative categorical deductive syllogism*, an argument having three propositions — two premises and a conclusion. A categorical syllogism contains exactly three terms or class names, each of which occurs in two of the three constituent propositions. The class names of an affirmative categorical deductive syllogism are illustrated in the following definitions:

- The major term is the predicate term of the conclusion, and of the major premise.
- The minor term is the subject term of the conclusion, and of the minor premise.
- The middle term does not appear in the conclusion, but must appear in each of the other two propositions.
- The major premise is the premise containing the major term.
- The minor premise is the premise containing the minor term.

Because the first proposition contains the major, or larger term, it is named the *major premise*, the larger precept laid down. It must be universal to be valid. Because the second contains the minor, or the smaller term, it is called the *minor premise*, the lesser statement laid down. Because it follows from the major to the minor premise, the third proposition is called the *conclusion*. In the standard form categorical syllogism as used in law, the major premise is stated first, the minor premise second, and finally, the conclusion. Returning to our classic Socrates-is-a-man (affirmative categorical deductive) syllogism:

Major Premise:	All men are mortal.
Major Term:	Mortal.
Middle Term:	All men.
Minor Premise:	Socrates is a man.
Minor Term:	Socrates.
Middle Term:	Man.
Conclusion:	Therefore, Socrates is a mortal.
Minor Term:	Socrates.
Major Term:	Mortal.

Before confusion sets in, some helpful hints can be derived from the foregoing rules: the middle term ("All men") may always be known by the fact that it does not occur in the conclusion. In science, the major term ("mortal") is often the predicate of the conclusion. The minor term ("Socrates") is always the subject of the conclusion.

Yet, in ordinary writing and speaking, the formal three propositions (two premises and a conclusion) arrangement is seldom observed, except perhaps in teaching children. Good girls get a star on their forehead; Lisa is a good girl; Lisa gets a star on her forehead. Normally, we would say that Lisa got a star on her forehead because she was a good girl. We would omit the major premise completely because it would be generally understood. A large body of propositions can be presumed to be common knowledge, and many writers or speakers save themselves time and energy by not repeating well known and perhaps trivially true propositions that their hearers or readers can well be expected to supply for themselves.

In formal argument, when one of the premises or the conclusion is not expressed, the argument is called an enthymeme. Such an argument is said to be stated incompletely, partly being "understood" or "only in the mind." Many arguments are enthymematic because either a premise or the conclusion is obvious and is understood (or is believed to be obvious and understood). Most often, the omitted premise is the major premise and is called an enthymeme of the First Order ("Lisa is a good girl; Lisa gets a star on her forehead"). Less commonly, the minor premise is unexpressed, and the enthymeme is of the Second Order ("All good girls get stars; Lisa gets a star").

As stated before, often the argument is compressed to a single sentence. Thus, in writing for the Court in *Roe v. Wade*, Justice Blackmun declared:

> This right of privacy, whether it be founded in the Fourteenth Amendment's concept of personal liberty and restrictions upon state action, as we feel it is, or, as the District Court determined, in the Ninth Amendment's reservation of rights to the people, is broad enough to encompass a woman's decision whether or not to terminate her pregnancy.

Implicit in this enthymematic statement of reasons was the following syllogism:

> *Major Premise:* The right of privacy is guaranteed by the Fourteenth (or Ninth) Amendment.
> *Minor Premise:* A woman's decision to terminate her pregnancy is protected by the right of privacy.
> *Conclusion:* Therefore, a woman's decision whether to terminate her pregnancy is protected by the Fourteenth (or Ninth) Amendment.

I emphasize this because in most aspects of forensic science — from police investigations, crime scene operations, laboratory testing, and autopsy reports, there is a truncated expression of the categorical deductive syllogism — in which either an affirmative universal proposition or a negative universal proposition is omitted.

Returning to Sherlock Holmes in *The Study in Scarlet*, upon meeting Watson, the great detective immediately said that the good doctor had recently returned from Afghanistan. Some time later, Holmes was talking to him:

> "Those rules of deduction laid down in that article which aroused your scorn are invaluable to me in practical work. Observation with me is second nature. You appeared to be surprised when I told you, on our first meeting, that you had come from Afghanistan."
>
> "You were told, no doubt."
>
> "Nothing of the sort. I knew you came from Afghanistan. From long habit the train of thoughts ran so swiftly through my mind that I arrived at the conclusion without being conscious of intermediate steps. There were such steps, however. The train of reasoning ran, 'Here is a gentleman of a medical type, but with the air of a military man. Clearly an army doctor, then. He has just come from the tropics, for his face is dark, and that is not the natural tint of his skin, for his wrists are fair. He has undergone hardship and sickness as his haggard face says clearly. His left arm has been injured. He holds it in a stiff and unnatural manner. Where in the tropics could an English army doctor have seen much hardship and got his arm wounded? Clearly in

Afghanistan.' The whole train of thought did not occupy a second. I then remarked that you came from Afghanistan, and you were astonished."[6]

We have an enthymeme here. This is an affirmative universal categorical syllogism in which Holmes omits the major premise that would read: "All gentlemen who are of a medical type, but with the air of a military man etc., etc., are from Afghanistan." He began his analysis with the minor premise stating the above quoted description of Watson, and then stated the conclusion that Watson had been in Afghanistan.

We emphasize enthymemes so much because each of you in your forensic science work use them so often in stating a conclusion.

Applying Canons of Deductive Reasoning to Forensic Science

Let us apply some of these concepts to the following scenario: The time is 1960. Jonathan Carstairs, a leading New York financier, well known philanthropist, husband to a member of the Social Register, and father of three adult children, had decided to leave his long time mistress, Florence Talmadge. He offered a substantial financial settlement, including a condominium. The girlfriend, twenty-five years his junior, kept a diary in which she expressed how disturbed she was at his plan to leave her and recounted that she told him that if he left, she would go to the newspapers and publicly disclose their long time affair. One evening, in response to a call, the police arrived at her apartment and found her body. She had been shot in the face. Carstairs was present and was taken into custody. Quoting the lead homicide detective, Conrad Fletcher, news accounts related that Carstairs had been with her at the time of the shooting and that he called the police who promptly brought him down to the station house. His only statement was: "She did not have to do it." The police administered a paraffin test on his hands. The result showed the presence of blue flecks, which is a sign of nitrates. The detective said that the test results showed that Carstairs had discharged a firearm — as firing a pistol will produce nitrates on the hand or hands that held the pistol. They booked him on a murder charge. A 0.32 caliber Remington automatic pistol was recovered in the apartment. Fingerprints were found on the pistol, which were later identified by a technician as those of Carstairs and the deceased. The police discovered the spent bullet, which the crime laboratory described as a Remington 140-grain, 0.32 special cartridge. The autopsy report revealed that the bullet entry was in the back of the mouth and took a downward path 10 mm until it smashed into the vertebral column and exited. There were traces of orange tattooing on both inside cheeks and soot near the entry wound.

At trial, the lead detective, Fletcher, was the People's first witness:

"We conclude that the decedent was standing at this point," he said, indicating to the jury with a pointer a particular place on the diagram. "The shooter was standing right here, about six to eight feet from the decedent." Fletcher indicated to the center of the fifteen foot wide living room.

"You determined the location of the decedent from the position of the body. How did you decide where the shooter was standing?"

"Two reasons. First, from the location where the spent cartridge was found." Fletcher indicated a point against the wall to the shooter's left, about midway between the two positions. "Second, and I am reading from the police report now: 'At the station house before we permitted the suspect to go to the wash room, we carefully examined his clothing, hands and arms for traces of blood or tissue.'"

"And you say the shooter was holding the pistol with two hands. How do you reach that conclusion?"

"It was from information I received from our technician who conducted the paraffin tests on the defendant."

"And what was the information you received from the technician? If the court please, before an objection is raised, I seek this information not for the truth of the statement but only on the basis of how this witness reached his conclusion. The People will present the technician as a witness to verify."

"No objection, subject to a motion to strike if not verified."

"As a result of a paraffin test, nitrate residue was found on both of Carstairs' hands, leading to the conclusion that he was holding the pistol with both hands as he fired. After we conducted the test, we permitted him to wash his hands. For some reason his hands were dirty at the time of the arrest."

"You have personal knowledge that a paraffin test was made that evening."

"Yes, it was a quiet night, and I remember that was the only paraffin test made during my tour."

"So, six to eight feet away with both hands on the pistol, is that your testimony detective?"

"Yes."

The defense is that Talmadge committed suicide, and from the foregoing, it is obvious that the outcome of the trial will depend on expert testimony from forensic scientists.

First, the detective determined the location of the shooter on the basis of the location of the spent cartridge. Fletcher reached the conclusion of six to eight feet from the victim because the cartridge was found against the wall about midway between the body and the two positions.

To give credence to this conclusion, Detective Fletcher would have to support it by means of a categorical affirmative deductive syllogism, something like this:

In some instances, when you fire from a 0.30 caliber Remington automatic pistol, the ejected 140 grain 0.32 Remington special cartridge will land three or four feet forward and more than four feet to the left of the shooter.

The shooter fired a 0.30 caliber Remington automatic pistol.

Therefore, the 140 grain 0.32 Remington special cartridge landed three or four feet forward and more than four feet to the left of the shooter.

The problem here is that Detective Fletcher did not prove that all ejected cartridges would land at this spot. The validity of his reasoning could be challenged in court by a factual defense, or by an objection by defense counsel that as an expert his reasoning was all wet.

The same criticism may be lodged about the paraffin test. The detective could not possibly begin his argument (yes, it is an argument in the logical sense) by asserting as a major premise:

All the nitrate blue flecks found on a hand in the paraffin wax test are the result of discharging a firearm.
Carstairs had blue nitrate flecks on his hand found in the paraffin test.
Therefore, Carstairs discharged a firearm.

The difficulty here, too, is that a man could have ammonium nitrate fertilizer on his hand, and it would show the same effects as discharging a firearm. The evidence here showed that Carstairs' hands were dirty at the time he was arrested. He could have been using plant fertilizer containing ammonium nitrate on the plants in Talmadge's balcony. This would have produced the same result. Or, a man could have urine on his fingers, and if administered the same test as the police did here, it would test the same way. Thus, the major premise does not state the truth. Watch GIGO: garbage in, garbage out.

Take a few moments to reflect on some of the other particulars in the Carstairs case. Detective Fletcher concluded that the shooter was six or eight feet from the victim. The autopsy report showed a downward trajectory of 10 mm from bullet entry to exit. Reason this though. How high above the floor would the pistol have to be to cause this trajectory? Is this inductive or deductive? The police will contend that the statement: "She didn't have to do it" incriminates Carstairs, as it shows motive — he wanted to silence her from going public. The defense will argue that this meant that she did not have to shoot herself. How would you reason this out?

Inductive Reasoning

Deductive reasoning and adherence to the "Socrates-is-a-man" type of syllogism is only one of the major components of reflective thinking. Inductive reasoning is equally important. In legal logic, it is often used to fashion either the major or the minor premise of the deductive syllogism. Often, it is unquestionable that a principle of forensic sciences qualifies as the controlling major premise. Such a principle is a proven scientific matter, with which the facts (minor premise) are compared, so as to reach a decision (conclusion). This is standard deductive reasoning.

But often no clear rule is present, and it becomes necessary to draw upon collective scientific experience to fashion a proper major premise from existing results in a number of cases. This is done by one of the two major categories of inductive reasoning known as inductive generalization. Specifically, from a number of similar particulars, a universal is fashioned.

Difference between Deductive and Inductive Reasoning

In general logic, there are fundamental differences between the two types of reasoning.[16] In deduction, the connection between a given piece of information and another piece of information concluded from it is a *necessary* connection. A deductive argument is one whose conclusion is claimed to follow from its premises with absolute necessity. If its premises are valid, the conclusion is valid. If the conclusion is valid, the premises are valid. Thus, in a valid deductive argument, if the premises are true, the conclusion *must* be true.

An inductive argument, however, is one whose conclusion is claimed to follow from its premises only with *probability* and not absolute necessity. All that is represented is that the conclusion is more probable than not. In induction, the connection between given pieces of information and another piece inferred from them is *not* a logically necessary connection. Its premises do not provide *conclusive* support for the conclusion; they provide only *some* support for it. Inductive arguments may be evaluated, for better or for worse, by the degree of likelihood or probability which their premises confer upon the conclusion. In a valid inductive argument, the conclusion is not necessarily an absolute truth; by induction, we reach a conclusion that is only *more probably* true than not.

Thus, the core of the difference between deductive and inductive reasoning lies in the strength of the claim that is made about premises and their conclusion. In the deductive argument, the claim is that if the premises are true and valid, then the conclusion is true and valid. In the inductive argument, the claim is merely that if the premises are true, the conclusion is more probably true than not:

- In forensic science and law, deductive reasoning moves from the general (universal) to the particular.
- In forensic science and law, inductive reasoning moves from the particular to the general (universal) (induced generalization by enumeration of instances), or from the particular to the particular (analogy).

Inductive Generalization

For an introductory look at the process of induction, let us start with the major premise, "All men are mortal." The premise, in general form, resulted from the process of enumeration, as it was created by enumerating billions of particulars to create a general statement. This is an example of inductive generalization:

Adam is a man and Adam is a mortal.
Moses is a man and Moses is a mortal.
Tiberius is a man and Tiberius is a mortal.
George Washington is a man and George Washington is a mortal.
Abraham Lincoln is a man and Abraham Lincoln is a mortal.
My father was a man and he was a mortal.
Therefore, all men are mortal.

It should be clear that the truth of the conclusion drawn from this inductive process is not guaranteed by the form of the argument — not even when all the premises are true and no matter how numerous they are. We always run the risk of the fallacy of hasty generalization when we generalize from too small a number of particular instances.

We can say, however, that the creation of a major premise by the technique of *inductive enumeration*, although not guaranteed to produce an absolute truth, does produce a proposition more likely true than not. This is the classic reasoning from a group of particulars to the general. This premise (which is the conclusion reached by inductive reasoning) is then, of course, always subject to modification as new cases are decided.

Formulating a generalization, that is, enumerating a series of tight results from individual encounters to create a working rule of science, is at best a logic of probabilities. We accept the result, not because it is an absolute truth, like a proposition in mathematics, but because it gives our results a certain hue of credibility. The process is designed to yield workable and tested premises, rather than truths.

From this, you can see the interrelationship in forensic science between inductive and deductive argument. Inductive enumeration is one use of inductive reasoning to reach a conclusion that embodies a general class. The inductive conclusion then becomes the major premise in a deductive argument to reach the conclusion urged in your work.

Analogy

Closely akin to reasoning by generalization is reasoning by *analogy*. This is reasoning from one particular to another particular. Although I find it convenient to classify analogy as a type of inductive reasoning, not all logicians agree, many suggesting that there is a difference between argument by enumeration and argument by analogy.[17] I place both processes under the heading of inductive reasoning because each process begins with an examination of particular instances. Moreover, as we shall see later, the strength of analogy is sometimes measured by an enumeration of relevant resemblances. In both forms, the conclusion from the premises is represented as more probable than not. No further representation is made.

For our purposes, the specific room to which analogies should be assigned in the house of logic is not as important as understanding the criteria to be applied to analogies. Pursuant to the method of analogy, one proceeds from certain relevant resemblances and differences between the facts in a given case and those in another single case or a relatively small group of cases. The relation between enumeration and analogy is close. Both use probability in reasoning. The force of an induced generalization by enumeration is measured by the *quantity* of instances. The force of analogy depends upon the *quality* of the positive and negative resemblances.

Forensic experts in the courtroom are often vulnerable to attacks on their reasoning by analogy. A proper analogy should identify the number of respects in which the compared cases, or fact scenarios, resemble one another (let us call these resemblances positive analogies) and the number of respects in which they differ (negative analogies). In analogy, unlike the method of enumeration, the *quantity* of cases is not significant. Instead, what is important is *similarity* in the facts. We ask the question whether the compared facts resemble, or differ from, one another in relevant respects.

The distinction between enumeration and analogy is reflected in John Stuart Mill's question: "Why is a single instance, in some cases, sufficient for a complete induction, while in others, myriads of concurring instances, without a single exception known or presumed, go such a very little way toward establishing a universal proposition?"[18] Indeed, "[w]hoever can answer this question knows more of the philosophy of logic than the wisest of the ancients, and has solved the problem of Induction."[18]

To refer again to the all-men-are-mortal syllogism, we can also use the process of analogy to conclude that Plato is a man:

Socrates is a man and possesses physiological characteristics X, Y, and Z.
Plato possesses physiological characteristics X, Y, and Z.
Therefore, Plato is a man.

With this background in mind, let us now turn to more practical examples to highlight the important interrelationships between inductive and deductive reasoning, as well as inductive generalization and reasoning by analogy.

Examples of Inductive Generalization in Forensic Science and the Interrelationship between Inductive and Deductive Reasoning

Certain conclusions can be reached about gunshot wounds, which may determine the range from gun muzzle to target — contact, near contact, intermediate, and distant. Each has individual characteristics. As you review this, consider the evidence in the Carstairs case introduced above.

- *Contact Wounds:* Here the muzzle is held against the surface of the body at the time the firearm is discharged. For all contact wounds, we can say that soot, powder, vaporized metals from the bullet, primer and cartridge case, and carbon dioxide are deposited in and along the wound tract.
- *Near Contact Wounds:* The muzzle is not in contact with the skin but is a short distance away. It does not produce the same effect as intermediate range wounds. For example, there is no tattooing, but the entrance wound is surrounded by a wide zone of powder soot overlaying seared blackened skin. The soot in the seared area is baked into the skin and cannot be completely wiped away.
- *Intermediate Range Wounds:* The muzzle is held away from the body at the time of discharge but close enough that powder grains expelled from the muzzle along with the bullet produce powder tattooing on the skin. For handguns, tattooing begins at a distance of approximately 10 mm. Tattooing consists of numerous reddish brown to orange–red punctuate lesions surrounding the wound of entrance, which indicates that the individual was alive at the time she was shot. If she were dead before she was shot, these marks would have a moist gray or yellow appearance rather than the color of an ante mortem wound. Powder soot is also present, and for handguns will appear within a range from muzzle to wound of 20–30 cm.
- *Distant Gunshot Wounds:* The only marks on the body are produced by the mechanical action of the bullet perforating the skin.

These benchmarks did not come from on high. They were not the product of original theoretical concepts. Rather, they resulted from the cumulative experience of hundreds, if not thousands, of pathologists over the years who compared their autopsy findings on bodies with testimony regarding distance between handgun and victim adduced at a like number of Criminal Courts. These benchmarks are inductive generalizations from thousands of particulars:

Soot and tattooing appeared near the wound where the muzzle to target distance was 14 mm in case A.
Soot and tattooing appeared near the wound where the muzzle to target distance was 14 mm in case B.
And so on and so forth from case C to case AAAA.
Soot and tattooing appeared near the wound where the muzzle to target distance was 14 mm in case AAAA.

Therefore, we may conclude that soot and tattooing will appear near *all* wounds where
the muzzle to target distance is 14 mm.

And the same experience was recorded for various ranges to produce the established
benchmarks for each. Keep in mind, however, the quality of the conclusion bears a close
relation to the highest number of particular instances.

Thus, in forensic science, we see the interrelationship between inductive and deductive reasoning. By means of inductive generalization — moving from particulars to the
general — we arrive at what will become the major premise in deductive reasoning.
Each of the types of gunshot wounds described above that show the different ranges
from muzzle to wound become the major premise in a categorical deductive syllogism.
For example:

In all cases, where soot, powder, vaporized metals from the bullet, primer and cartridge
case, and carbon dioxide are deposited in and along the wound tract, we have a
contact wound.
In this case, we have soot, powder, vaporized metals from the bullet, primer and cartridge case, and carbon dioxide deposited in and along the wound tract.
Therefore, in this case, we have a contact wound.

Examples of Analogy and the Interrelationship between Analogy and Induced Generalizations

But it did not start out this way. Before an induced generalization came about — arguing
from particulars to the general — the forensic scientist had to rely on *analogy*, rather than
generalization. He or she had to compare the similarities and differences between one case
and another.

Thus, beginning with case A, we had the target distance of 14 mm, a 140 grain
Remington special cartridge, and numerous reddish brown to orange–red punctuate
lesions that surrounded the wound of entrance.

Then comes case B, in which we did not know the target distance but did have a
140 grain Remington special cartridge, and numerous reddish brown to orange–red
punctuate lesions that surrounded the wound of entrance. Using analogy, we can
argue that the target distance was around 14 mm. Let us examine how analogy is used
in the following:

In case XXXX+1, we know that the range from the pistol to the target was 10 feet, that
there was no soot or tattooing in or near the wound, and that the only marks on
the body were those produced by the mechanical action of the bullet perforating
the skin.
In case XXXX+2, we know that the range from the pistol to the target was 5 feet, that
there was no soot or tattooing in or near the wound, and that the only marks on
the body were those produced by the mechanical action of the bullet perforating
the skin.
In case XXXX+3, we do not know the range, but we do know that there was no soot or
tattooing in or near the wound, and that the only marks on the body were those
produced by the mechanical action of the bullet perforating the skin. From this,

we can reason from particulars to a particular and analogize that the target range could be between 10 feet as in XXXX+1 and 5 feet as in XXXX+2.

Reasoning by analogy reveals how forensic science is dynamic. As new firearms and ammunition are developed, new guidelines will appear through experience. In toxicology, chemicals become more and more complex and new controlled substances appear. For example, Methamphetamine is increasingly cooked in kitchens in homemade laboratories by different "cooks." In many urban areas, amateur "cooks" change cocaine powder to rock or crack cocaine.

Analogies will be drawn, and will evolve from repetition-induced generalizations. When I first started to try cases in criminal court in 1948 (yes, that is a long time ago), the test used by the police to show that an accused had recently discharged a firearm was to coat liquid paraffin on the hand to determine whether blue flecks would appear, revealing the presence of nitrate. But there were problems with this method, as we showed in the previous excerpt from the Carstairs murder example.

Modern police departments use new techniques such as a qualitative colorimetric chemical test to show the presence of barium, antimony, and lead. These metals originate in the primer of a cartridge and appear only upon the discharge of a firearm. When the primer is struck by the firing pin, these metals are deposited on the back of the firing hand as discrete particulate matter. The colormetric chemical test is a specific test, as distinguished from the nonspecific test for nitrates and nitrites. Only firing a handgun will produce this phenomenon on the hands. Handling ammonium nitrate fertilizer will not show the presence of barium, antimony, and lead. Nor will urine. This brings us to our discussion of logical fallacies.

Fallacies

In ordinary speech, the word fallacy is used in many ways. A perfectly proper use of the word is to designate any mistaken idea or false belief: "Any team that Joe Torre coaches will be a winning team." "All lawyers are thieves, all doctors, quacks."

In ordinary usage then, fallacy can be used to describe a false or erroneous idea. Because we are talking about reflective thinking, I use the term as a word of art. I use it to refer to the logical *form* (formal fallacy) or *content* or *context* (informal or material fallacy) of a syllogism.

Nevertheless, the terms "fallacy" or "fallacious" are often used to describe a premise in a syllogism as false or untrue. Thus, you will find many people, including judges and lawyers, sometimes using the expressions in the lay sense to describe something that is not supported by the facts. Notwithstanding its popular or lay use, logicians use the term "formal fallacy" in a narrower sense to describe a type of incorrect argument, and "informal or material fallacy" to describe a falsity or error in the contents of premises.

Formal Fallacies

Again, this chapter does not pretend to be a handbook on logic, and because I have concentrated on the "Soctrates-is-a-man" type of syllogism, my discussion will be limited to fallacies in the affirmative categorical deductive syllogism.

A formal fallacy is any violation of any of the six rules of the categorical syllogism, or the rules of the hypothetical or disjunctive-alternative syllogism. It is an argument whose conclusion could be false even if all its premises are true. It can be detected merely by examining the *form* (hence its name) or structure of the argument.

In categorical arguments, there are six possible fallacies:

1. Four terms instead of three
2. Undistributed middle term
3. Illicit major term
4. Illicit minor term
5. Negative premises
6. Particular premises

For our purposes, I will discuss one of these only: the fallacy of the undistributed middle.[19] You will recall that the middle term is the subject of the major premise ("All men" in "All men are mortal"). The middle term has to be a distributed term that describes a general class. This would include words like "every," "any," "all," "each," "always," "everywhere," "in every instance," "no," "never," "nowhere," "under no circumstances." With a distributed term, you get a universal proposition.

I refer back to the old paraffin test to determine the presence of nitrates or nitrites on the hands of an accused as a proof that he or she had recently discharged a firearm.

> *Some* blue flecks found in the paraffin are nitrates that blew back on the hand after the discharge of a hand gun.
> *Carstairs' hands showed blue flecks (nitrates).*
> Therefore, the blue flecks blew back on Carstairs' hands after the discharge of a hand gun.

This is an invalid argument because for it to work, the middle term had to be distributed. It had to be "*All* blue flecks." As it stands, it is the fallacy of the undistributed middle. It could not be distributed because nitrates on the hand could have come from urine or from ammonium nitrate fertilizer.

Informal (Material) Fallacies

What are informal fallacies and how do we detect them? For our purposes, perhaps the best answer comes from Professors Copi and Burgess-Jackson:

> By definition these fallacies cannot be detected merely by examining the form or structure of the argument in which they occur. How, then, can they be detected? There are two ways. One is by examining the *context* in which the argument is made. Who, for example, is trying to establish the claim, and for what purpose(s)? Who is the audience for the argument? What assumptions do the parties share? Are there any ground rules for the discussion? The context (con-text) is the complete set of circumstances which the argument (the "text") is made.
>
> The second way is by examining the *content* or substance of the argument. This requires attention to the way the argument is expressed in language, to the meaning of words, and to such things as ambiguity, vagueness, and nonliterality. Content has to do with *what* is being said and *how* it is being said, not in

the form of what is said. In short, sometimes, we reason fallaciously because our arguments are structurally defective (formal fallacies); sometimes, we commit fallacies because we violate contextual rules of argument (the first type of informal fallacy); and sometimes, we commit fallacies because we misunderstand or misuse language (the second type of informal fallacy).[20]

Although it is difficult to condense into a single definition all that is encompassed by informal fallacies, two basic tenets of logic provide keys to their understanding:

- Logical reasoning presupposes that the terms shall be clearly and unambiguously defined and, as used in the premises and the conclusion, signify a uniform, fixed and definite meaning throughout.
- Logic demands that the conclusion be not assumed, but derived from the premises.

Two groups generally come within the ambit of irrelevance and distraction. These are arguments that miss the central point at issue or rely principally upon emotions, feelings, and ignorance to defend a thesis.

Fallacy of Irrelevance

I begin with the fallacy of irrelevant evidence. This argument misses the central point at issue and is sometimes called the fallacy of missing the point. Over the years, I have often asked counsel at oral argument to discuss an issue that interests the court. Often, lawyers treat me with the response: "But that's not the point, your honor!" My rejoinder is: "Why don't you assume that it is, and please discuss it."

How you come out in a case often depends on how you go in. And too often counsel choose to "go in" with an argument favorable to them, but miss the point that is objectively critical to the decision.

The fallacy of irrelevance, or *ignoratio elenchi*, is an argument purporting to establish a particular conclusion but is instead directed to proving another conclusion. It occurs whenever we advance as an argument something that has nothing to do with the point at issue. The method can make appeals to emotions, but not every case of *ignoratio elenchi* involves such an appeal. We can use cold, antiseptic, or neutral language and still commit the fallacy. Often, we see the fallacy of the straw person in which the arguer knocks down a misstated argument and concludes that the original argument was bad. The name comes from the supposition that a straw person would be light and flimsy, and therefore much easier to demolish than a real person.

Not every argument of irrelevant conclusion is premeditated or deliberate. It may be the result of involuntary confusion on the part of a lawyer or judge. But it also may be consciously adopted as a stratagem to deceive an adversary or the court.

Fallacies of Distraction

These are somewhat self-explanatory, and I list them out for you to consider and have in your repertoire to avoid in your work:

- *Argumentum ad misericordium,* or the appeal to pity
- *Argumentum ad verecundiam,* or the appeal to prestige
- *Argumentum ad hominem,* or the appeal to personal ridicule

- *Argumentum ad populum,* or the appeal to the masses
- *Argumentum ad antiquitam,* or the appeal to age
- *Argumentum ad terrorem,* or the appeal to terror
- *Argumentum ad ignorantiam,* or the appeal to ignorance

Miscellaneous Informal Fallacies

The informal fallacies that I now discuss are not readily susceptible to categorization. In an extremely rudimentary attempt at classification, I will describe the first group under the rubric of "context" in the sense of the form or structure in which these fallacious arguments are made. The other group can be described as "content" or "linguistic." Both groups have one characteristic in common: The fallacies take place in context and content of the argument's premises and not the argument's logical form.

Dicto Simpliciter (Fallacy of Accident).

General rules usually have their exceptions. This is especially true in law. The informal fallacy I discuss here relates to general rules and exceptions to these rules. It is called the fallacy of accident, *dicto simpliciter,* and it occurs when we apply the general rule to special circumstances. The application of the general rule is inappropriate because of the situation's "accidents," or exceptional facts. To commit the fallacy of accident is to apply the general rule to exceptions to the rule. In the law of evidence, for example, there are many exceptions to the hearsay rule: a dying declaration, a statement against interest or a statement of personal or family history. To apply the general hearsay rule to these exceptions is to commit the fallacy of accident or *dicto simpliciter.*

The Converse Fallacy of Accident (Hasty Generalization).

The converse fallacy of accident is the reverse of *dicto simpliciter.* It occurs when we move carelessly or too quickly to a generalization. It occurs when we construct a general rule from an inadequate number of incidents. Watch out for this fallacy when you seek to create a principle of forensic science by inductive generalization. It is the bugaboo of inductive reasoning and often appears. Also called the fallacy of selected instances, it results from enumerating instances without obtaining a representative number to establish an inductive generalization. The fallacy appears when one or two decisions are used to make a quantum leap to a conclusion that these decisions form a rule with general application. The error lies in failing to obtain an adequate number of instances.

False Cause.

The fallacy of false cause is an argument that treats as the cause of a thing something that is not really its cause. It appears very often in your work and takes at least two forms.

In one form, it is to mistake what is not the cause of a given effect as the real cause (*non causa pro causa*). The events could be so correlated because they were both caused by a third, unexamined event, although neither caused the other.

In the other, more prevalent form, is the suggested inference that one event is the cause of another merely because the first occurs earlier than the other (*post hoc ergo propter hoc*) (after this, therefore in consequence of this). The *post hoc* fallacy consists of reasoning from sequence to consequence. It is reasoning from what happened in sequence to the assumption of a causal connection. We commit this fallacy whenever we argue that because a certain event was preceded by another event, the preceding event was the cause of the latter. This is the fallacy of inferring causation from temporal succession only.

Non Sequitur (**It Does Not Follow**).   You all know this one. We can consider the *non sequitur* (it does not follow) as a separate fallacy. It is an argument that contains a conclusion that does not necessarily follow from the premises or any antecedent statement offered in its support. It is sometimes called the fallacy of the consequent because it always exhibits a lack of a logical connection between the premises and their conclusion.

The difference between the *post hoc* and the *non sequitur* fallacies is that the *post hoc* fallacy lacks a causal connection; the *non sequitur* fallacy lacks a logical connection.

Petitio Principii (**Begging the Question**).   This fallacy is really a first-class rascal because it sneaks up on us so often. It is a species of question begging that assumes as true what is to be proved. It is to assume the truth of what one seeks to prove in the effort to prove it.

The rascal bears many names, *petitio principii*, arguing in a circle, circular reasoning, putting the bunny in the hat, failing to prove the original proposition asserted, and using the original premise as a proof of itself. In order to prove that A is true, B is used as a proof, but since B requires support, C is used in defense of B, but C also needs a proof and is substantiated by A, the proposition which was to be proved in the first place. Thus, that which was to be proved in the first place is affirmed ultimately in defense of itself.

We see this fallacy often. A conclusion, or some proposition that follows from the conclusion alone, appears tacitly or explicitly among the supporting premises. It is essentially a fallacy of the proof, rather than the logical form.

In entertainment, this was used as the basic ingredient in the long-running George Burns and Gracie Allen radio show:

Gracie: Gentlemen prefer blondes.
George: How do you know that?
Gracie: A gentleman told me so.
George: How did you know he was a gentleman?
Gracie: Because he preferred blondes.

We may put the fact that we want to prove, or its equivalent, under another name. It occurs when we define a sleeping pill "as a medicine that has a soporific effect." Or Yogi Berra's famous quips: "It isn't over until it's over"; or, "You can observe a lot just by watching." Where the inference takes several steps, the fallacy is called circular reasoning, or arguing in a circle.

Linguistic Fallacies

Categorical syllogism Rule 1 insists that the argument contains exactly three terms and that each term be used in the same sense throughout the argument. When different senses are utilized, linguistic fallacies occur. Some of these are fallacies of ambiguity (equivocation and amphibology). Others are known as fallacies of composition, division, and vicious abstraction.

Equivocation.   When we confuse the several meanings of a word or phrase, we use the word or phrase equivocally. When we do this in the context of an argument, we commit the fallacy of equivocation. This fallacy refers to the use of terms which are ill defined, vague, and signify a variety of ideas, none of which can be made clear or precise either by definition or by the context. When we confuse the different meanings a single word or phrase may have, or use a word or a phrase in different senses in the same context, we are using it equivocally. The fallacy is committed whenever we allow the meaning of a term to shift between the premises of our argument and our conclusion.

Any of the three terms of the syllogism may be subject to a shift in meaning, but it is usually the middle term which is used in one sense in one premise and in another sense in the other. Sometimes, this is called the fallacy of the ambiguous middle. Avoidance of this fallacy is critical. Again, it is important to keep in mind Rule 1 of the categorical syllogism:

> A valid categorical syllogism must contain exactly three terms, each of which is used *in the same sense* throughout the argument.

Fallacy of Amphibology.   In equivocation, ambiguity comes from changing meanings of the word; in amphibology, ambiguity comes from the grammatical structure. The double meaning lies not in the word but in the syntax or grammatical construction of a sentence or sentences. Professor Brennan furnishes an excellent example:

> I give and bequeath the sum of $5,000 to my cousins Ruth Henning and Sylvia Woodbury.[10]

You know that counsel for the beneficiaries are going to claim that each is entitled to $5000; the estate lawyer will argue that the total sum is not $10,000 but $5000.

A statement is amphibolous when its meaning is unclear because of the loose or awkward way in which its words are combined. Amphibology differs from equivocation in two important respects. Amphibologies arise in an argument where meaning is muddled by slovenly syntax — bad grammar, poor punctuation, dangling participles, and misplaced modifiers. At trial of a drunken driver, the arresting officer's testimony was summarized. "When the officer arrested the driver, the officer said he did not know what he was doing." This is an example of amphibology derived from a relative pronoun with more than one referent. Logicians uniformly cite the classic example: "He said, 'Saddle me the ass.' And they saddled him." In World War II, we had posters urging all to "Save Soap and Waste Paper."

Fallacy of Composition.   The fallacy of composition consists of reasoning improperly from a property of a member of a group to a property of the group itself. It is to argue that something is true of a whole which can safely be said of its parts taken separately. The confusion is usually an inference that proceeds from the specific to the general and argues from attributes of parts of the whole to attributes of the whole itself.

"The defendant in this case is a very wealthy man because he owns a Jaguar." "There are muggings all over Philadelphia. I read about three that happened on Market Street." In our personal lives, we experience this often. For example, you visit Chicago for an overnight stopover. The taxi driver is surly; the room clerk is a snob; the waitress at breakfast is impatient. You leave Chicago, return home, and say, "That Chicago is a terrible town. All the people are horrid!" Stereotypical images are also improperly formed by this fallacy. "Members of the Mafia break the law; therefore, all Americans of Italian origin are law breakers."

Fallacy of Division.   The fallacy of division is the converse of the fallacy of composition and takes two forms: the inference that properties of the whole are also properties of parts making up the whole and that properties of a collection are also properties of the members of that collection.

We take separately what we ought to take jointly. The same confusion is present as in composition, but this time, the inference proceeds in the opposite direction, from the whole to its parts. It argues that what is true of the whole must be true of its parts.

"The Pittsburgh Symphony is the best in the country; therefore, the concertmaster is the best violinist in the land." "Italy has the best pasta in the world. Therefore, if you eat pasta at Giovanni's in Rome, you will eat the best dish of pasta in the world." "The New York Yankees is the best team in baseball. Thus, the Yankee first baseman is the best first baseman in baseball."

Fallacy of Vicious Abstraction.   The removal of a statement from its context, thereby changing the meaning of an argument, is known as the fallacy of vicious abstraction. Statements may be easily and critically altered merely by dropping something out of context. A general rule is confidently stated in an attorney's brief without any mention of exceptions. Counsel may cite to the court: "No deviations will be permitted from a discovery order."

The Sahakians illustrate this fallacy with some examples, each followed by the correct, complete statement:

> "St. Paul said, 'Money is the root of all evil.'" ("The *love* of money is the root of all evil.")
>
> "Ralph Waldo Emerson said: 'Consistency is the hobgoblin of little minds.'" ("Foolish consistency is the hobgoblin of little minds.")[21]

Argumentum ad Nauseum

I simply had to include this one, a fallacy more understandable than explainable. The *argumentum ad nauseum* is the unnecessarily long report or a windbag presentation where the advocate seeks to sustain his position by repetition piled upon repetition rather than by succinct, effective reasoned proof, or logical development.

We see this everyday in life — brought to us by TV commercials, advertising executives, public relations specialists, and political consultants. Is it not obnoxious to look at a TV news program every night of the week and see an identical commercial shown earlier displayed again? Or to watch a football game and be treated to the same commercial four times in one hour? I am not convinced that such repetition encourages critical consumer existence.

Lewis Carroll's bellman said it all in the "Hunting of the Snark":

> "'Just the place for a Snark!' the Bellman cried,
> As he landed his crew with care;

Supporting each man on the top of the tide
By a finger entwined in his hair.

Just the place for a Snark! I have said it twice:
That alone should encourage the crew.
Just the place for a Snark! I have said it thrice:
What I tell you three times is true."[22]

How Logic Will Help You

And so I conclude. My thesis has been straightforward. I do not say that knowledge of these materials is absolutely essential to being a practitioner of forensic medicine. A person may reason correctly without knowing a single rule of syllogism; conversely, a person may know all the details of logic and not be able to discover truths that are necessary. A guide to logical reasoning, or logic in forensic science, is tautologically speaking, simply a guide.

But what I do suggest is that an understanding of what I have said here should assist you:

- To develop clarity and consistency in the practice of your profession
- To avoid errors in analyzing
- To avoid errors in preparing and presenting a written or oral report
- To detect errors in the reasoning process mounted by any adversary
- To think and reason about difficult matters
- To avoid the pitfalls of both formal and informal fallacies
- And most importantly, to develop and improve the specific mental discipline which the study and practice of your profession demands and requires

A final word. Logical reasoning and avoidance of fallacies do not always guarantee a solution. But there is one guarantee that I will make. The more knowledgeable you are in the precepts of deductive and inductive reasoning, the better you will perform your duties in forensic science, the more effective you will be when you appear as a witness in a courtroom, and the more you will surmount the cross examination you will receive:

Q.   So is it fair to say that the conclusions you reach today are based on your experience and the hunches and intuitions you acquired in your work?

A.   No. My conclusions are reached from the data I collected which I then applied to time-tested scientific principles through precepts of deductive and inductive reasoning. There was no hunch. No guess work.

So there you have it.

Happy thinking!

Notes

1. Chief Judge Emeritus, U.S. Court of Appeals for the Third Circuit.

2. Aldisert, R. J.; *Logic for Lawyers: A Guide to Clear Legal Thinking;* 3rd ed., National Institute of Trial Advocacy; Notre Dame; 1997.

3. Aldisert, R.J.; *Winning on Appeal: Better Briefs and Oral Argument;* 2nd ed., National Institute for Trial Advocacy; Notre Dame; 2003.

4. Aldisert, R.J.; *The Judicial Process: Text, Materials and Cases;* 2nd ed., West Publishing Co., St. Paul; 1996.

5. Aldisert, R.J.; *Opinion Writing;* West Publishing Co., St. Paul; 1990.

6. Doyle, A.C.; *A Treasury of Sherlock Holmes;* International Collectors Library; Garden City, New York; 1955; v.

7. For a comprehensive discussion of the materials presented here, see Ref. 2.

8. For a detailed discussion of A, E, I, and O and how they are applied to propositions, see Copi, I.M and Cohen, C.; *Introduction to Logic;* 9th ed.; Prentice Hall; Englewood Cliffs; 1994; pp. 210, 214.

9. Stebbing, L.S.; *A Modern Introduction to Logic;* 6th ed.; Harper & Bros.; New York; 1948; pp. 211–212.

10. Brennan, J.G.; *A Handbook of Logic;* Harper & Bros.; New York; 1957; p. 1, pp. 2–3, p. 190.

11. Cooley, J.C.; *A Primer of Formal Logic;* Macmillan; New York; 1949; p. 13.

12. This is but a rule of thumb. There are times when a valid deductive argument may have universal propositions for its conclusion as well as for its premises. Especially where *polysyllogisms* are involved. In these circumstances, the conclusion of the first syllogism (*prosyllogism*) becomes the major premise for the second (*episyllogism*). See Ref. 2, pp. 64–66.

13. Dewey, J.; *How We Think;* D.C. Heath; Boston; 1933; p. 17.

14. See Ref. 9 (quoting *Anal. Priora* 24b).

15. See Ref. 9 (quoting *Anal. Priora,* 18).

16. As I now proceed to explain the difference between deductive and inductive reasoning, I do so with a pronounced caveat. This is a relatively short chapter on reasoning employed in the forensic sciences. It is neither a presentation on *general* reasoning, nor is it an introduction to the general study of logic. Our formulations of definitions are guided by Max Radin's comment that the test of a definition is whether it is useful. I therefore acknowledge that our explanations may be considered by some logicians to be simplistic, if not precisely accurate when viewed against the universal cosmos of logic.

17. See, for example, Ref. 10, p. 154 ("Current logicians, however, tend to regard all inductions as following the first pattern, that is, as inferences to generalizations [rather than from particular to particular.]"). Compare with Ref. 8, p. 433 ("Because of the great similarity between argument by simple enumeration and argument by analogy, it should be clear that the same types of criteria apply to both.").

18. Mill, J.S.; *A System of Logic: Ratiocinative and Inductive;* 8th ed.; Longmans, Green, and Co., New York; 1916; p. 206.

19. For a more complete discussion, see Ref. 2.

20. Copi, I.M. and Burgess-Jackson, K.; *Informal Logic;* 3rd ed.; Prentice Hall, Upper Saddle River; 1996; p. 98.

21. Sahakian, W.S. and Sahakian, M.L.; *Ideas of the Great Philosophers;* Barnes and Noble Everyday Handbooks; New York; 1966; pp. 15–16.

22. Carroll, L.; *The Complete Works of Lewis Carroll;* Random House; New York; 1936; p. 757.

Forensic Science and Law — Revealing Truth and Freedom in a Single Light

3

JOHN T. RAGO[1]

"But the student should not imagine, that enough is done, if he has so far mastered the general doctrines of the common law, that he may enter with some confidence into practice. There are other studies, which demand his attention. He should addict himself to the study of philosophy, of rhetoric, of history, and of human nature. It is from the want of this enlarged view of duty, that the profession has sometimes reproached . . . with a deficiency in liberal and enlightened policy."

— Joseph Story, "The Value and Importance of Legal Studies"[2]

Introduction

Many first year law students hear these words when they begin their legal education. The message should be mandatory "thinking" for all students in every discipline and at all levels of education. Genuine interdisciplinary study is a vital passage to the full promise of a liberal and professional education. More to the point, nowhere is Justice Story's observation witnessed as truer than in the offspring of the intellectual marriage of forensic science and law.

At a time when the intersection of law and forensic science reveals new and important tools in our search for factual truth, it should not be lost on anyone that our legal, academic, scientific, and governmental institutions and organizations nationwide are hard at work building bridges between programs and professions. Their shared pedagogical and philosophical aim is profoundly simple and aimed at the core value of our Republic . . . the preservation of freedom grounded in our search for the certainty of factual truth. While neither law nor forensic science, nor any discipline for that matter, is the whole of life in this intellectual journey, the product of their combined study, at a minimum, has become highly relevant and self-evident in its various applications to criminal, civil, and family justice pursuits.

Forensic science methodologies and applications across disciplines, particularly when viewed in terms of the results they provide in legal investigations and fact finding, are revealing themselves as a powerful energy in a variety of expeditions in search of justice. Such a force is plainly manifest in law and other disciplines, but its intellectual force of forensic science and law has yet to reach its angle of repose. Remarkable developments have occurred in the forensic science community in recent years — changes that have inspired a nation to explore new scientific, legal, and academic methods for finding factual truth. A recent survey of education literature suggests that there are more than 200 academic institutions with undergraduate, graduate, and certificate programs in forensic science. This relatively recent ascendancy of forensic science and law education in the applied, social, and natural sciences has created new challenges and opportunities for all levels of academic life. Forensic science in its entire splendor has struck a popular chord in our curricula and culture as well as in our governmental, legal, and scientific institutions; it reminds us that truth and freedom are intimately related and reciprocally necessary values in a free and democratic society.

This message is nowhere more apparent, nor more compelling, than in the stories of the 163[3] men and women who have been exonerated since 1989[3] as a result of postconviction DNA testing — a fraternity of wrongfully convicted individuals that is sure to grow in years ahead. Their stories, and particularly the story of one such historic individual which follows, sustain the conviction that throughout curricula in the applied, social, and natural sciences, forensic science and law must be studied and made to harmonize in the interest of protecting the core values of a free and democratic society — truth and freedom.

> "And it must follow, as the night the day, thou canst not then be false to any man."
>
> — William Shakespeare, The Tragedy of Hamlet[4]

Truth is the basis of our freedom.[5] It is a "*liberum iudicium*," a free judgment, said St. Thomas, who saw in reason and truth the ultimate foundation of freedom.[6] In *Centesimus Annus*, Pope John Paul II wrote:

> "[I]f there is no ultimate truth to guide and direct political activity, then ideas and convictions can easily be manipulated for reasons of power . . . . In a world without truth, freedom loses its foundation and man is exposed to the violence of passion and to manipulation, both open and hidden."[7]

Two years later, in his Encyclical letter, *Veritas Splendor*, Pope John Paul II further articulated his belief in the intimate relationship of truth and freedom by the opening words in his address to the Bishops of the Catholic Church on certain fundamental moral teachings of the Church with the following apostolic blessing:

> "The Splendor of Truth shines forth in all the works of the Creator and, in a special way, in man, created in the image and likeness of God (cf. Gen 1:26). Truth enlightens man's intelligence and shapes his freedom, leading him to know and love the Lord. Hence the Psalmist prays: "Let the light of your face shine on us, O Lord" (Ps 4:6)."[8]

In this context, the words of the Gospel, *veritas liberabit vos* — "the truth shall make you free"[9] — express, beyond the religious mystery to which they speak,[10] a profoundly philosophical and political reality: that truth and freedom are intimately related values.[11] Far from being mutually opposed, they are reciprocally necessary and are incapable of existing independently of each other.[12] Accepting this as true brings us face to face with the critical problem facing American criminal justice.

The Learning Moment of Postconviction DNA Testing: Forensic Science and Law at Work

> "Our procedure has always been haunted by the ghost of the innocent man convicted. It is an unreal dream."
>
> — Judge Learned Hand, *United States v. Garsson*[13]

The intrinsic and moral relationship of truth and freedom in American criminal justice is as apparent as the besieged condition in which we currently find it. It is arguable, perhaps even probable, that the quality of our criminal justice system has never fallen under such an ominous shadow of doubt.[14] For the past decade, in one case after another, conclusive evidence produced by postconviction deoxyribonucleic acid (DNA) testing has established, beyond all doubt, the tragic reality that we are convicting factually innocent individuals.[15] Since the first exoneration of a death row inmate in 1992,[16] the innocence of 163 individuals, indisputably authenticated by DNA evidence, has been established, largely through the work of innocence projects nationwide.[17] This "learning moment of extraordinary revelation" — words frequently used by Professor Barry Scheck to characterize the clarity of thought provided by postconviction DNA exonerations – makes us recall the fundamental value of American criminal justice: It is far worse to convict an innocent man than to let a guilty man go free.[18]

The principles of criminal responsibility "are deeply rooted in our moral sense of fitness that punishment entails blame and that, therefore, punishment may not justly be imposed where the person is not blameworthy."[19] But there is growing doubt in the moral force of the criminal law, doubt that is made evident by the nature of our errors and the likelihood of a large number of wrongful convictions that remain undiscovered. These conditions strike at the very heart of our standard of proof, which is, at best, weakened by these revelations.[20]

Findings of wrongful convictions are beginning to focus a harsh light on the questions of why and how often factually innocent people are convicted.[21] Postconviction DNA exonerations give us a scientific truth from which we can examine, with complete confidence, those flaws in our system that allow these injustices to occur.[22] The "learning moment," it appears, is answering old questions while asking new ones. The data set of the growing class of wrongfully convicted individuals provides a remarkable opportunity to re-examine, with a greater insight than ever before, the strengths and weaknesses of our criminal justice system and how they bear on the central question of factual innocence.

Innocence Reforms: The Race Begins

DNA has forced Lady Justice to look in the mirror and blanch. Of the 163 individuals exonerated with the help of innocence projects and the efforts of like-minded people nationwide, 15[23] had been sentenced to death while 42 of the exonerated had been convicted of murder.[24] Many of these individuals would have almost certainly faced execution if death penalty had been available in the jurisdictions in which they were tried.[25] The lessons that we are learning from their convictions are the product of the cymbal-crash arrival of DNA in criminal justice.

The tempo of DNA's arrival is both welcome and worrisome as we find ourselves toiling over what to do about innocence reforms while under the crushing weight of time that is not on our side. Until recently, public policy was slow to respond to the failures made evident by these exonerations.

Our first race begins with the effort to both preserve and locate biological materials[26] that may lead to the discovery of countless other wrongfully convicted individuals[27] and to the apprehension of the real perpetrators of unsolved crimes.[28] The race continues with the effort to discover how to transfer the lessons learned from DNA postconviction exonerations to postconviction, non-DNA cases — cases representing approximately 80% of the serious felonies — in which there is no biological material.[29] Yet another leg of this important race is the identification of the best possible methods for utilizing the lessons of postconviction DNA testing in pretrial proceedings in DNA and non-DNA cases. Although legal conventions do not always live up to their promise, the rules of criminal procedure and state and federal constitutions mandate that a defendant be entitled to have access to physical evidence prior to trial.[30]

Although we appreciate the impact of DNA in establishing the innocence of the wrongfully convicted, at a bare minimum, is there any alternative but to recognize that the lessons taught by the exonerations have raised the bar for the government to establish, pretrial, *prima facie* findings of criminal culpability in non-DNA cases to avoid the problem of the wrongfully accused? This leads us to the fourth and final leg of our race — one that likely poses the most important and difficult pursuit of all. The demonstrable examples of our repeated errors[31] (p. 361–64) cannot help but cast genuine doubt over our ability to fairly and consistently find the truth, and, more fundamentally, undermine our faith in the fairness of criminal justice. Indeed, there are powerful arguments to support the belief that we are seeing just the beginning of a long line of very deep and very disturbing injustices. This marathon effort to stem the loss of confidence in our system of criminal justice will test our will for innocence reforms against the economic, social, and political conditions of the day,[32] for innocence reform initiatives, like all public initiatives, are tied to malleable public values.

Unless we start these races and win them, the 163 "ghosts" whom we know, and certainly many others whom we have yet to meet, will walk the land, not as our inspiration for reforms, but as harbingers of the retreat of true freedom in our lifetimes, urged along by a series of failures that threaten a genuine crisis in confidence in our system of criminal justice and the rule of law. Whether our confidence in the quality of criminal justice is compromised by ignorance, anger, or apathy, once we surrender our belief in facts and truths, and our belief in standards for distinguishing facts and truths from fictions and falsehoods, we destroy that confidence and, consequently, subvert our freedom. The truth is found by conscientious attempts to discover a reality that exists independent of our biases, prejudices, perceptions, and attitudes concerning attributes such as race, ethnicity, gender, or class. If we deny this, we deny the foundation upon which our freedom rests. The consequences are clear. If we are successful with reforms, in five years, we should look back at our current crisis of confidence as a story of adaptations and extinctions. Without meaningful reforms, public confidence in American criminal justice will simply continue its steep descent into disorder, irregularity, and disorientation.

Our democracy rests directly on our faith in the ability to separate those who are guilty from those who are not.[33] Nearly everyone understands that the administration of criminal justice is in human hands and that, despite the safeguards that surround the accused at trial, errors do occur.[34] *A priori*, understanding that we may never achieve the flawless administration of criminal justice is not the same as countenancing the conviction of factually innocent people. But there can be no "innocence calculus," suggesting a "permissible" margin of error in criminal convictions. In practice, we know that we make mistakes. In theory, we must not accept them. If society fails to accept this syllogism as true, then the principle on which America rests is false.

Whether or not criminal law's most celebrated and sacred rubrics, the "presumption of innocence" and "proof beyond a reasonable doubt,"[35] have become metaphoric or remain as effective safeguards of the truth is a difficult question to answer. DNA makes it an even more difficult question to avoid. As deeply disquieting as these exonerations are, the consequences that we face if we fail to correct our mistakes are apparent and even more disturbing.

There are individuals who live their lives without reflection.[36] Most assuredly, wrongfully convicted and wrongfully accused individuals are not among them. Their suffering is our learning moment — and the lesson is clear — that all Americans should reflect on our freedom as a timeless rather than a timely exercise.

We know that freedom is not restless. It is not supposed to be. The exercise of our freedom is not haphazard or disorderly. On the contrary, freedom makes itself felt as a principle of order, orientation, and regularity. It enables us to utilize our circumstances to further those values to which we dedicate our lives for our own benefit and the benefit of those whom we serve. It follows that the absence of freedom — the diminution or dilution of truth from the sum total of the economic, social, and political conditions necessary for the concrete exercise of our freedom — disturbs the order and regularity in our lives and unsettles our fundamental beliefs.

As America has grown intolerant of corporate greed, political arrogance, and pious deceptions, our reactions have been sharp and heartfelt. Indeed, many have stopped investing, stopped voting, and stopped believing. These experiences teach us that the obfuscation of truth in our lives triggers a range of responses, from angst to anger and confusion to contempt. More importantly for our purposes, they also reveal that there will be consequences if our faith in the quality of American criminal justice remains in decline.

With a Reading of *The Blooding*,[37] a Scientific Revolution Is Unleashed in American Criminal Justice: The Story of Kirk Noble Bloodsworth[38]

Current forensic DNA identification methodologies owe much to the nascent writings of Francis Crick, a graduate student at Cambridge University, and Dr. James D. Watson, a young biochemist, who, in 1953, jointly published a short paper in the journal *Nature* proposing that DNA, or deoxyribonucleic acid, the molecule seemingly responsible for heredity, had a double helix structure.[39] In 1985, DNA fingerprinting, or DNA profiling,[40] was "first described" by Sir Alec Jeffreys, "an English geneticist" in the field of forensic identification science.[41] "Dr. Jeffreys found that certain regions of DNA contained DNA sequences that were repeated over and over again next to each other."[42] In the process, "he also discovered that the number of repeated sections present in a sample could differ from individual to individual."[42] These DNA repeat regions became known as "variable number of random repeats" (VNTR).[43]

Dr. Jeffreys's methods were first used for identification purposes in the United Kingdom in an immigration case.[44] Shortly thereafter, these methods were used to solve a double homicide in Leicestershire that involved the tragic murders of two teenage girls, otherwise known as the Narborough Murders.[45]

On the afternoon of July 25, 1984, nearly one year prior to Dr. Jeffreys's revolutionary work, a world-shattering event of a different sort shocked the small, semirural community of Fontana Village located a few miles outside of the City of Baltimore.[46] It was the day that the police found the body of nine-year-old Dawn Hamilton in a wooded area near a spot known as Becky's Pond.[46] She had been brutally raped and murdered.[46] In another world, just a few miles away from where Dawn Hamilton's body lay, a 23-year-old honorably discharged Marine was struggling to make a life for himself while trying to mend a breaking marriage.[46] It was also the day that Kirk Noble Bloodsworth's life began its fall into an unimaginable nightmare.

By all accounts, Kirk Bloodsworth was a hard working individual.[46] He never had any trouble with the law.[46] He grew up as a member of a proud family of watermen from the Eastern Shore who had been in the fishing industry for nearly 150 years.[46] Bloodsworth's fishing, family, and faith were staples in his life.[46]

A few weeks earlier, Wanda Bloodsworth had left her marital home in Cambridge, MD, and returned to the town of Essex to live with her sister.[46] On July 3, Bloodsworth, determined to rejoin his wife, hitchhiked his way to this small Baltimore County town.[46] He moved into his sister-in-law's home with the hope of saving his distressed marriage.[46] Over the next several weeks, Bloodsworth and his wife fought often.[46]

On the morning of July 25, Chris Shipley, age 10, and his friend, eight-year-old Jackie Poling, were fishing under the bright midmorning sun.[47] (p. 273–88) Jackie was especially proud of the snapping turtle that he caught with his simple fishing string,[47] (p. 273–88) and offered to show his catch to a man — later described by the boys to the police as being tall and skinny, with curly blonde hair and a mustache, and wearing a muscle tee-shirt and shorts — who was then walking by them.[48] The stranger obliged the boy's request.[46] He approached the two youngsters, peering down at Jackie's quarry with his back to the sun that was shining directly behind and above him.[46] From a short distance, a young girl's voice called out the boys' names.[46] Looking up, the three saw nine-year-old Dawn Hamilton approaching them along the path that ran beside the pond.[46] Her aunt had sent her to look for her cousin, Lisa.[46] The boys told Dawn that Lisa had not been there and returned to their fishing.[46] Almost immediately, the man stepped forward and offered to join Dawn in her search.[46] Dawn thanked the man and they disappeared down the path and into the woods.[46] A woman in a nearby yard saw them passing by and heard Dawn calling out for Lisa.[46] She also heard the man telling Dawn that he and Lisa were playing hide and seek.[46] That was the last time that anyone would hear Dawn's voice.[46]

By midafternoon, nearly five hours after Dawn and the skinny man with curly blonde hair and a mustache vanished down the wooded trail, Dawn's seminaked body was found facedown on the ground.[47] (p. 273–88) Her skull had been crushed.[47] (p. 273–88) A porous rock was resting near her lifeless body.[47] (p. 273–88) The physical evidence of her struggle was apparent, though the scene of the crime itself did not seem to be particularly disturbed.[47] (p. 273–88) Her pants and underwear were found hanging on a tree branch at a slight distance from her body.[47] (p. 273–88) A herringbone patterned print appeared across her neck causing investigators to speculate initially that the impression was made by a tennis shoe.[49] A large but otherwise nondescript rock was found next to the young girl's body.[50] She had been violated by a stick.[51] In addition, a belt loop from a man's pair of pants, a red gum wrapper, and a shoeprint were found.[47] (p. 273–88)

Not surprisingly, every local television, radio, and print medium repeatedly led with the story of Dawn's rape and murder.[46] Heartbreaking and horrifying pictures of Dawn ran on the front page of the *Baltimore Sun*.[46] The image of the smiling little girl appeared above the fold next to a photograph of two men carrying the young girl away from the crime scene in a closed body bag.[46] The community's outrage was palpable.[46] Based upon a description of the man given by the two young boys, a police artist was able to create a composite sketch of the killer.[46] A "hotline" was set up, and, by August 3, a total of 286 telephone calls were received.[52] One of those calls was from an anonymous woman who said that the sketch looked like someone named "Kirk" who worked at a local furniture store.[46] In response to police questioning, the storeowner expressed great surprise.[46] She told the officers that she had never had a better worker than Bloodsworth.[46] Store records established that, on the evening before the murder, Bloodsworth had worked a 12-hour shift until 10:30 P.M and that July 25 was his scheduled day off.[46] The storeowner also told the police that Bloodsworth had left work one day in early August, never to return, complaining that he was not feeling well.[46]

Meanwhile, at or about the same time, Bloodsworth had moved out of his sister-in-law's home and was staying at the Pilot Motel on Maryland State Route 40.[46] He called his mother-in-law to explain that he had enough with Wanda's behavior and was returning to Cambridge, MD.[46] Back in Cambridge, Bloodsworth discussed his failed marriage with friends, telling them that he felt that he had done a terrible thing by leaving his wife without paying off their bills.[46] That day, Wanda inexplicably filed a missing-person report.[46]

On August 8, with the investigation continuing at a breakneck pace, the police went to Cambridge to locate and question Bloodsworth.[46] Prior to interviewing Bloodsworth, the investigation team consulted with the Federal Bureau of Investigation (FBI) Behavioral Science Unit, hoping to create a profile of the killer.[47] (p. 273–88) The profilers suggested a simple test.[47] (p. 273–88) The team investigating the murder was told to clear the interrogation room of everything but a few artifacts looking like several critical pieces of evidence found at the murder scene.[47] (p. 273–88) The items were to be placed on the table in front of Bloodsworth for the simple purpose of gauging Bloodsworth's reaction.[47] (p. 273–88)

Detectives Robert Capel and William Ramsey prepared for Bloodsworth's interrogation.[46] A pair of panties and shorts, similar to those worn by Dawn Hamilton, as well as a nondescript rock with a "red" mark on its side, were momentarily placed on a table in Bloodsworth's line of sight.[46] Bloodsworth showed no reaction to the materials placed in front of him other than to recall later, for friends, what he had seen in the interrogation room.[53]

Bloodsworth cooperated with the police on the condition that they would not force him to go back to Wanda.[54] Bloodsworth told the investigators that he could not be certain of where he had been on July 25 because that was his day off.[46] He did, however, adamantly tell the detectives that he had never been to Fontana Village and that he had nothing to do with the murder of Dawn Hamilton.[46] The police took several Polaroid pictures of Bloodsworth and sent him on his way.[46]

The next day, back in Baltimore County, the mothers of two young eyewitnesses brought their sons to the police station to look at a photospread.[46] A series of Polaroids was shown to Chris and Jackie.[46] Jackie could not identify anyone, and Chris thought that Bloodsworth looked like the man, but that his hair color was wrong — it was too red.[46] The investigators felt that they had enough to secure a warrant for Bloodsworth's arrest.[46] On August 9, Bloodsworth was arrested at his cousin's home in Cambridge for the rape and murder of Dawn Hamilton.[46] Bloodsworth was furious.[46]

As he prepared to leave the police station for processing following his arrest and interrogation, Bloodsworth was scornful of the officer who suggested that he might want to shield his face from the news cameras.[46] Bloodsworth later acknowledged that not covering his face was a terrible decision.[46] He walked defiantly through a gauntlet of news cameras and reporters, refusing to hide his face from anyone because he knew that he had done nothing wrong.[46] Meanwhile, the police informed several of their witnesses that an arrest had been made.[47] (p. 273–88) The witnesses were told not to watch television because a line-up was imminent, and it would be better if they did not see the accused until they were at the precinct station.[47] (p. 273–88) The witnesses watched the news.[47]

On August 13, Jackie and Chris were again brought to the police station by their mothers, this time to participate in a line-up identification.[47] (p. 273–88) Both boys appeared to be extremely nervous.[47] (p. 273–88) Six individuals were placed in the line-up. Bloodsworth was number six.[47] (p. 273–88) Jackie identified Number 3, a police officer, as the perpetrator.[47] (p. 273–88) Chris shook his head (indicating a "Number") when he was asked if he could identify anyone.[47] (p. 273–88) Detective Capel testified at trial that, once outside of the line-up room, Chris regained his composure.[47] (p. 273–88) "He said he knew all the time that it was Number 6, but he did not want the man to hear his voice because the man could tell it was him because it was a little kid's voice."[47] (p. 273–88) Nearly four weeks later, Jackie returned to the station with his mother, who explained that her son was too afraid to name the real killer.[47] (p. 273–88) She indicated that he said "Number 6" was the real killer.[47] (p. 273–88) At trial, Jackie did not identify Bloodsworth as the man he saw on July 25.[55] Chris made a positive, in-court identification, as did the woman who was the last to see Dawn and the man with curly blonde hair walking down the wooded path.[47] (p. 273–88) Eyewitness testimony was elicited from five individuals claiming to have seen Bloodsworth with the girl on July 25.[47] (p. 273–88) One individual claimed to have seen Bloodsworth alone as early as 6:00 A.M.[46]

Bloodsworth's trial evidence was largely the same evidence, although less developed, that the police used to establish the probable cause for Bloodsworth's arrest.[56] Tests were conducted on the girl's underwear, but the testing methods at the time were inadequate for the purpose of detecting and identifying biological material belonging to the assailant.[47]

With no physical evidence linking Bloodsworth to the crime, and despite the availability and testimony of numerous alibi witnesses, the jury returned a verdict within two hours of the beginning of their deliberations.[47] (p. 273–88) Bloodsworth was convicted on March 8, 1985, of sexual assault, rape, and first-degree premeditated murder.[47] (p. 273–88) Baltimore County Judge J. William Hinkel sentenced Bloodsworth to death.[47] (p. 273–88) His fate was sealed, apparently, because he looked like someone who might have committed the crime.[57]

Nearly two years later, Bloodsworth won a second trial when his defense counsel discovered that the government had withheld the potentially exculpatory evidence of another potential suspect.[58] Richard Gray was listening to police communications on his scanner on the day that Dawn Hamilton was killed and purportedly went into the woods to search for her in response to what he had heard on his scanner.[46] He found her panties and shorts hanging on a tree.[46] Police records indicated that Gray was sitting in his parked car approximately 180 feet from Dawn Hamilton's body when he responded to the transmitted information. The police also discovered a pair of panties belonging to a young girl in Gray's car.[46] Gray said that he had found the undergarment in the same woods two days earlier and had decided to keep it for his daughter who would use the panties on one of her dolls.[46] Police records also noted that Gray had what appeared to be a red mark, perhaps a bloodstain, on his shirt.[46] The stain was never tested.[46]

On the day before the jury was to begin its deliberations on Bloodsworth's second trial, his lawyer, yet again, discovered that potentially exculpatory material was withheld from his client.[46] On the day that Dawn Hamilton was killed, police records indicated that a man by the name of David Rehill voluntarily checked into a local psychiatric hospital for an evaluation.[46] His appearance was disheveled and he had scratch marks across his face.[46] He was sweating profusely while he told the treating physician that he had had some trouble with a little girl that day.[46] Bloodsworth's attorney called Rehill to the stand, but Rehill asserted his right against self-incrimination.[47] (p. 273–88) Rather than seeking a continuance to conduct a thorough investigation of this late-found evidence, Bloodsworth's attorney made the fatal decision to let the case proceed to the jury.[47] (p. 273–88) This time, Bloodsworth was sentenced to two life terms to run consecutively without the possibility of parole.[47]

Having already served in excess of two years on death row, Bloodsworth was now relegated, but not resigned, to spending the rest of his life in jail for a crime that he did not commit.[46] He fought off numerous attempted rapes and beatings.[46] He wrote more than 3000 letters to everyone and anyone who would listen to his claim of innocence.[46]

Bloodsworth had nothing but time on his hands, and he used his time wisely.[46] An avid reader, Bloodsworth received a book written by the son of a Pittsburgh police officer in the mail.[59] Joseph Wambaugh's *The Blooding* was the true crime story of the first use of DNA evidence in a criminal investigation.[60] The story resonated with Bloodsworth.[46]

The Evidence Is In

The Blooding is the story of the Narborough Village murders of 1983 and 1986.[61] Fifteen-year-old Lynda Mann had been savagely raped and strangled.[61] Her body was found lying along a shady footpath near the English village of Narborough.[61] Although a massive 150-person dragnet was launched, the case remained unsolved.[61] Three years later, the killer struck again, raping and strangling teenager Dawn Ashforth, virtually on the same path where Lynda Mann was so brutally murdered.[61] As the story unfolded, Bloodsworth learned that it took four years, a scientific breakthrough, and the blooding[62] of more than 4,000 men before the real killer, Colin Pitchfork, was apprehended[61] (p. 238). For the first time in history, a police force took blood samples from every male in the vicinity and later compared the samples to evidence recovered from the crime scene.[63]

The story played over and over in Bloodsworth's mind, as did Wambaugh's brief but fascinating portrayal of Dr. Jeffreys's work.[61] Armed with his newly found information and a new lawyer, Bloodsworth was able to persuade the prosecution for permission to conduct DNA testing of the victim's shorts and underwear.[47] (p. 273–88) Fortunately, and somewhat remarkably, the physical evidence from Bloodsworth's trial was kept in the trial judge's chamber closet.[46]

With the emergence of new forensic identification methods unavailable to Bloodsworth at the time of his first trial, Bloodsworth's lawyer, Robert E. Morin,[64] moved to have the evidence released for more sophisticated testing.[46] The prosecution consented to the motion.[46] In April 1992, the victim's panties and shorts, a stick found inside Dawn's body, reference blood samples taken from the victim and Bloodsworth, and an autopsy slide were sent to Dr. Edward Blake of Forensic Science Associates (FSA) for polymerase chain reaction (PCR) testing.[65]

The FSA conducted its tests and issued a report on May 17, 1993. The report revealed that the biological sample (semen) on the autopsy slide was insufficient for testing.[47] It also stated that a small semen stain had been found on the panties[47] — and that the majority of DNA associated with the epithelial fraction[66] had the same genotype as the semen did due to the low level of epithelial cells present in the stain.[47] (p. 273–88) The final report did not surprise Bloodsworth.[47] (p. 273–88) FSA concluded that Bloodsworth's DNA did not match any of the evidence received for testing.[47] (p. 273–88) Consistent with their protocols, FSA secured a fresh reference sample of Bloodsworth's blood for retesting and, on June 3, FSA reaffirmed its previous findings.[47] (p. 273–88) Bloodsworth could not be responsible for the stain on Dawn Hamilton's underwear.[47] (p. 273–88) On June 25, the FBI independently validated FSA's conclusion.[47] (p. 273–88) Bloodsworth did not murder Dawn Hamilton.

Based upon the FSA and FBI assays, prosecutors relented and joined Bloodsworth in his pardon petition.[46] On June 28, 1993, a Baltimore County circuit judge ordered Bloodsworth's release from prison.[46] Bloodsworth received a pardon from the Governor of Maryland six months later.[46] Bloodsworth had served almost nine years of his sentence, including two years on death row.[67]

For nearly 18 years, not a day went by that Bloodsworth did not wonder how two different juries could put an innocent man in prison.[46] He struggled — and continues to do so — with the pain of watching his father grow old without the life savings spent for his son's lawyers and other defense costs.[46] Worst of all, he misses the chance to talk with his mother, who died five months before he walked out of prison a free and innocent man.[46]

Have You Reached Your Verdict?

"DNA is ... God's signature and God's signature is never a forgery and his checks don't bounce."

— Eddie Joe Lloyd, false confession case[68]

In the 1996, National Institute of Justice (NIJ) monograph, Convicted by Juries, Exonerated by Science: Case Studies in the Use of DNA Evidence To Establish Innocence After Trial,[69] the U.S. Department of Justice examined the Bloodsworth case along with 27 other cases in which individuals, convicted after jury trials and sentenced to long term imprisonment, successfully challenged their convictions using DNA tests on biological evidence.[70] The report provided an extraordinary set of data collected by the FBI since it began forensic DNA testing in 1988.[71] In 1996, NIJ supplemented these data by conducting a nationwide telephone survey of 40 public and private DNA laboratories that performed DNA tests.[69] The survey sought answers to two critical questions: First, from the time that the laboratories began DNA testing, how many cases had they handled? Second, of that number, what percentage yielded results that excluded defendants as sources of the DNA evidence or were inconclusive?[69]

Of the laboratories surveyed, 19 yielded sufficient data.[69] The nineteen included thirteen at the state and local levels, four in the private sector, one military laboratory, and the FBI's laboratory.[69] For the most part, DNA testing at the various laboratories had begun only a few years prior to the 1995–1996 survey.[69] Twelve began testing between 1990 and 1992.[72] Three of the four private laboratories began in 1986 or 1987, while the FBI started DNA testing in 1988.[69]

The 19 laboratories reported that, since they had begun testing, they had received evidence in 21,621 cases for DNA analysis, with the FBI accounting for 10,060 cases.[69] Three of the four private laboratories averaged 2400 each; the state and local laboratories averaged 331 each.[69]

In about 23% of the 21,621 cases, DNA test results excluded suspects, according to the respondents.[69] Approximately 16% of the cases yielded inconclusive results, often because the test samples had deteriorated or were too small.[69] Inconclusive results aside, test results in the balance of the cases did not exclude the suspect.[69]

In the 10,060 cases tested during this period by the FBI, DNA examination results indicated that about 20% tested inconclusive and 20% resulted in exclusions; the other 18 laboratories (11,561 cases) reported about 13% inconclusive and 26% exclusions.[69]

Private laboratory and FBI pretrial exclusion statistics have remained constant since the FBI began pretrial DNA testing in 1988.[69] Plainly speaking, these results suggest that, in cases in which biological material is recovered from the victim or from the crime scene and is subjected to testing — after there is an arrest, after there is an indictment or criminal information charged, and after there is a finding of the probable cause that the suspect committed a rape or a murder — the primary suspect is excluded in ~26% of these cases. Of course, it does not necessarily follow that 26% of the people in prison are innocent, but the lingering question is apparent. In this class of exclusions, what would have happened if these individuals had gone to trial? What would have been the false conviction rate for these individuals?[73] Hypothetically speaking, if we assume an error rate of one quarter of 1% just for this category of crimes, is there any doubt that there are thousands of factually innocent Americans who could prove their innocence with DNA? With more than two million individuals in jail for serious felonies, is this an extravagant claim?[74]

We Are Not Sure, Your Honor

"[Since] Galileo . . . [the man of] reason . . . must approach nature . . . in the character of . . . an appointed judge who compels the witnesses to answer questions which he has himself formulated."

— Immanuel Kant, Critique of Pure Reason[75]

Forensic sciences generally, and DNA in particular, are not panaceas for all that ails the criminal justice system. On the contrary, there are a host of forensic assays in dispute, such as microscopic hair and fiber comparisons, fingerprinting, psychological profiles, bullet lead comparisons, bite mark comparisons, glass comparisons, questioned documents, arson, and explosives, to mention only a few. That said, the matching probabilities of DNA have been conclusively established.[76] Unlike other forensic identification methods, DNA has proved, beyond reproach, the remarkable degree of fallibility that exists in the basic fact-finding processes on which we rely in criminal cases.[77]

We are in a race against time and, perhaps, political indifference, to find these wrongfully convicted Americans. Armed with an unimpeachable truth, we respond in confusion. Law students are reminded of the value of the rule of law, whereas philosophy students are told that disinterested and objective truths are not to be trusted.[78] Death penalty advocates call for moratoriums.[79] A few governors listen, but most will not return the advocates' calls.[80] While one California prosecutor voluntarily begins an arduous review of a generation of cases in which DNA evidence may reveal the convictions of factually innocent individuals,[81] across the country another prosecutor refuses to release a man convicted by his office because he believes that the DNA testing results of five independent laboratories are flawed.[82] Perhaps worst of all, months before he is welcomed by the warm applause of a group of admiring law students, an innocent Kirk Bloodsworth is yelled at by a Maryland "neighbor" who alights from his porch, points out at Bloodsworth, and repeatedly screams that a "child murderer" is in the neighborhood.[83]

In the face of the clarity that DNA provides to a fact finder, it is paradoxical that *habeas corpus*,[84] "the basis of all our freedoms,"[85] could not save the life of a man who discovered new and powerful evidence of his factual innocence simply because his lawyer missed a filing deadline by three days.[86] Justice may be a process and not a result,[87] but what process allows our jurisprudence to stand on the premise that, while it may be unconstitutional to execute a factually innocent individual, it may also be constitutional for a factually innocent individual to be in jail?[88] Perhaps, the best that can be said is that the actual innocence standard for federal habeas relief is unresolved, apparently because we have yet to believe that truth is the progress of science.[89]

The Legal Profession and Public Policy Begin to Respond to the Ageless Errors of Our Ways

> "I have long urged that the State or community assume the risks of official wrongdoing and error instead of permitting the losses resulting from such fault or mistake to be born by the injured individual alone. Among the most shocking of such injuries are erroneous criminal convictions of innocent people."
>
> — Edwin M. Borchard, Convicting the Innocent[90]

The flight of innocence reforms may have arrived on the wings of DNA, but they have floated through the ages in the foregoing words from Professor Borchard's 1932 classic study of 65 cases of wrongful convictions.[90] Interestingly, but not surprisingly, many of the convictions that Professor Borchard reviewed rested on the same flawed foundations revealed by postconviction DNA testing.[91] The legal profession's belated, but no less sincere, response to wrongful convictions appeared in an aptly title article written by Andrew Taslitz, "Convicting the Guilty and Acquitting the Innocent: The ABA Takes a Stand,"[92] which reflects the action taken in 2004 by the American Bar Association House of Delegates that adopted five new policy recommendations based on findings by the Criminal Justice Section regarding the improvement of the criminal justice system's accuracy in convicting the guilty and acquitting the innocent.[92] (p. 18)

Clearly, the most significant movements in our federal public policy on this subject are found in the Innocence Protection Act that was subsequently subsumed by the Justice For All Act of 2004.[93] On October 30, 2004, President George W. Bush signed into law one of the most sweeping criminal justice reform measures in modern history. Born of the union of forensic science and law, this Act's impact on criminal justice, including but certainly not limited to the expansion of the information science of DNA and exoneration through postconviction DNA testing, will be profound once it is fully funded.

The Justice For All Act and its treatment of the information science of DNA represents the most significant piece of criminal justice reform legislation, perhaps in our lifetime. In short order, the Act is designed to:

> "(1) eliminat[e] the backlog of DNA samples collected from crime scenes and convicted offenders; (2) expand[...] the Combined DNA Index System (CODIS); (3) improv[e] and expand[...] the DNA testing capacity of federal, state and local crime laboratories; (4) increas[e] research and development of new DNA testing technologies; (5) develop[...] new training programs for the collection and use of DNA evidence; (6) extend[...] the statute of limitations for crimes where the suspect is linked to the crime through DNA evidence; (7) provid[e] post-conviction DNA testing and the preservation of biological evidence."[94]

The Act further establishes a National Forensic Science Commission and "authorizes grants to states for improving the quality of legal education representation, including investigative and expert services, provided to indigent defendants in state capital cases."[94]

The policy underpinnings of this Act are, perhaps, best reflected in a statement issued by Senator Patrick Leahy of Vermont, viewed by many as one of several principal proponents of innocence reforms. This statement was issued in anticipation of the passage of the Justice For All Act in the 108th Congress:

> "On February 1, 2000, I came to the floor to call attention to the growing national crisis in the administration of capital punishment. I noted that since the reinstatement of capital punishment in the 1970s, 85 people had been found innocent and released from death row. And I urged Senators on both sides of the aisle, both those who supported the death penalty and those who opposed it, to join in seeking ways to minimize the risk that innocent persons will be put to death. A few days later, I introduced the Innocence Protection Act of 2000.
>
> That was more than four years ago. During that time, many more innocent people have been freed from death row — the total is now 117, according to the Death Penalty Information Center. During that time, the Republican

Governor of Illinois commuted all the death sentences in his State to life in prison, having lost confidence in a system that exonerated more death row inmates than it executed. During that time, we learned about problems at the Houston crime lab so serious that the city's top police official called for a moratorium on executions of the inmates who were convicted based on evidence that the lab handled or analyzed. And during that time, the bipartisan, bicameral coalition supporting the Innocence Protection Act has continued to grow.

Earlier this week, the House of Representatives passed the Justice For All Act of 2004, a wide-ranging criminal justice package that includes the Innocence Protection Act. The House bill also includes the Debbie Smith Act and the DNA Sexual Assault Justice Act, which together authorize more than $1 billion over the next five years to eliminate the DNA backlog crisis in the Nation's crime labs and fund other DNA-related programs. Finally, the House bill includes crime victims' rights and provisions that I sponsored with Senators Feinstein and Kyl, and which already passed the Senate earlier this week. Today, at long last, the Senate is poised to pass the Justice For All Act and to send this important legislation to the President. I hope he will sign it, despite his Justice Department's continued efforts to kill this bill. The reforms it enacts will create a fairer system of justice, where the problems that have sent innocent people to death row are less likely to occur, where the American people can be more certain that violent criminals are caught and convicted instead of the innocent people who have been wrongly put behind bars for their crimes, and where victims and their families can be more certain of the accuracy, and finality, of the results.

This bill has been many years in the making, and there are many people to acknowledge and thank. Let me begin by thanking Kirk Bloodsworth, Debbie Smith, the Justice Project, and through them all the crime victims and the victims of a flawed criminal justice system who have made these changes possible. Without their commitment and dedication, these straightforward reforms simply would not have happened. Kirk and Debbie sat patiently, hour after hour, through our committee's work on this bill, and their presence was strong and eloquent testimony of the need for this legislation.

. . .

The Justice For All Act is the most significant step we have taken in many years to improve the quality of justice in this country. DNA is the miracle forensic tool of our lifetimes. It has the power to convict the guilty and to exonerate the innocent. And as DNA has become more and more available, it also has opened a window on the flaws of the death penalty process. This is a bill to put this powerful tool into greater use in our police departments and our courtrooms. It also takes a modest step toward addressing one of the most frequent causes of wrongful convictions in capital cases, the lack of adequate legal counsel. These reforms, to put it simply, will mean better, faster, fairer criminal justice."[95]

The policies adopted in the aforementioned ABA position paper, the evolving posture of our public policy, and the learning moment of those individuals and organizations on the front line of innocence reforms in light of our experience with wrongful convictions, leave us with a clear challenge and the moment to meet them.[96] However, we have had these moments and missed opportunities before. It is unsettling that, after more than 70 years, Professor Borchard's work says something to us that we can be sure was not his intention. His book, *Convicting the Innocent*, much like history, teaches us that, in spite of the lessons of the past, and the learning moments of the present, we are prone to fall back into the same errors, preferring to live our lives as "the man on the street"[97] and unwilling to undertake the difficult and laborious task of reconciling truth and freedom in our system of criminal justice. Professor Borchard probably had more faith in our rule of law than perhaps the rule of law was entitled to.

It is worth repeating that, "[i]n a world without truth, freedom loses its foundation and man is exposed to the violence of passion and to manipulation, both open and hidden."[98] Every time truth is separated from freedom in our lives, freedom has been voided of its very meaning. Inversely, the truth cannot flourish outside a climate of freedom.

Truth and freedom indeed are intimately related values.
If you are not yet certain of this in your life, just ask Kirk Bloodsworth.

Notes

1. Assistant Professor of Law, Duquesne University School of Law; Executive Director, The Cyril H. Wecht Institute of Forensic Science and Law, Duquesne University School of Law.

2. J. Story, Miscellaneous Writings of Joseph Story 527 (1852).

3. Innocence Project, Case Files, at http://www.innocenceproject.org/case/display_cases.php?sort=year_exoneration (last visited Oct. 11, 2005) [hereinafter Innocence Project, Case Files].

4. W. Shakespeare, The tragedy of Hamlet, Prince of Denmark, act 1, scene 1.

5. The author wants to thank his dear friend, Kirk Noble Bloodsworth, for his tireless efforts in seeing that his injustice will be everyone's learning moment. *Bloodsworth's story is contained in a compelling book titled, Bloodsworth: The True Story of the First Death Row Inmate Exonerated by DNA* (by T. Junkin, Algonquin Books of Chapel Hill, 2004.) The author wishes to acknowledge the *Dickinson Law Review* for providing the opportunity to share these views. (The author and Dickinson Law Review share a copyright to the article "Truth or Consequences" and Postconviction DNA Testing: Have You Reached Your Verdict (107 *Dick. L. Rev.* 845). Portions of this chapter appear therein.

6. St. Thomas Aquinas, Summa Theologica pt. I, q. 83, arts. 1, 3 (Fathers of the Eng. Dominican Province trans., Benzinger Bros., Inc. 1947) (n.d.).

7. Encyclical Letter of Pope John Paul II on the Hundredth Anniversary of Rerum Novarum, Centesimus Annus para. 46 (May 1, 1991) [hereinafter Centesimus Annus]. In this passage, the Pope reveals his belief that an authentic democracy is possible only on the basis of respect for the rule of law. Id. [Authors's note: The term "Id." is used to refer to the source listed in the immediately preceding endnote, or to the immediately preceding source within the same endnote. See generally, The Bluebook, A Uniform System of Citation 40–41 (1996).]

8. www.usccb.org/profile/tdocs/veritatis.htm

9. John 8:32.

10. Then said Jesus to those Jews who believed: "If ye continue in my word, then are ye my disciples indeed; and ye shall know the truth, and the truth shall make you free." Id. The impression on Jesus followers produced by these words was to press them into "continuance" in the faith, since only then were they His real disciples, see John 15:3–15:8, and then would experimentally "know the truth," and "by the truth be made (spiritually) free." 3 R. Jamieson, A.R. Fausset, and D. Brown, Jamieson-Fausset-Brown Bible Commentary (Hendrickson Publishers, 1974) (1871).

11. This sense of freedom and truth, or more precisely, the sociological, economic, political, and philosophical sense of freedom and truth, refers to the sum total of all of the conditions necessary for the actual exercise of our freedom. "A thing is said to be done freely according as it is under the control of the doer," as expressed by St. Thomas. "*Secundum hoc aliqui libere fieri dicitur, quod est in postetate facientis.*" *St. Thomas Aquinas, Quaestiones Disputatae de Veritate* [Disputed Questions on Truth] q. 24, art. 1 (n.d.), reprinted in Selected Writings of St. Thomas Aquinas 121 (R.P. Goodwin trans., 1965).

12. If innocence is the offspring of truth and freedom, it finds itself in a perilous condition as a legal presumption within our criminal justice system. We are well served to revisit its ancestry. The presumption of innocence was identified for the first time in the case of *Coffin v. United States*, 156 U.S. 432 (1895). The Court, citing Greenleaf on Evidence, traced the ancient origin of the "presumption of innocence" to Deuteronomy, and quoted Mascardius Do Probationibus, to show that the presumption was substantially grounded in the laws of Sparta and Athens. Id at 454. In this light, the Coffin Court also referred to Roman Law traditions, citing the following extracts from the Code of Justinian and Digest of Justinian:

> "Let all accusers understand that they are not to prefer charges unless they can be proven by proper witness or by conclusive documents, or by circumstantial evidence which amounts to indubitable proof and is clearer than day." Id.
> "The noble (divus) Trajan wrote to Julius Frontonus that no man should be condemned on a criminal charge in his absence, because it was better to let the crime of a guilty person go unpunished than to condemn the innocent." Id.
> "In all case of doubt the most merciful construction of facts should be preferred." Id.
> "In criminal cases the milder construction shall always be preserved."
> "In cases of doubt it is no less just than it is safe to adopt the milder construction."
> Id (citations omitted). Finally, the Coffin Court wrote that many of the fundamental and humane maxims of Roman law are preserved in canon law. Id at 455.

13. 291 F. 646, 649 (S.D.N.Y. 1923).

14. In his testimony before the Senate Committee on the Judiciary on June 18, 2002, Professor James S. Liebman identified five findings that could reasonably serve to diminish public confidence in criminal justice. Protecting the Innocent: Proposals to Reform the Death Penalty: Hearing Before the Senate Comm. on the Judiciary, 107th Cong. 22–26 (2002) (statement of J.S. Liebman, Simon H. Rifkind Professor of Law, Columbia Law School). The list is not conclusive. First, he noted that state death penalty verdicts are "fraught with reversible error." Id. Of the 5826 state capital verdicts that were reviewed by state and federal courts, an astounding sixty-eight percent "were found to contain reversible error and had to be sent back for retrial." Id. In addition to identifying several contributing political problems relating to an elected and partisan-appointed bench, Professor Liebman also noted that "suppression of evidence of innocence or mitigation, misinstruction of juries, and biased judges and jurors" account for a large number of these errors. Id. A third finding by Professor Liebman suggests that "the review process is so overwhelmed by the number of serious capital mistakes that it cannot catch them all." Id. Fourth, in noting that "the capital reversal rate is over 50%,"

Professor Liebman argued that "the death penalty system cannot achieve its law enforcement goals." Id. Finally, Professor Liebman cited the paucity of adequately trained and compensated capital defense lawyers as "[t]he single most common reason for capital reversals at the state post-conviction and federal habeas stages of review." Id. For a complete view of the supporting text for these summary statements taken from Professor Liebman's acclaimed study, see J.S. Liebman *et al.*, A Broken System, Part II: Why There Is So Much Error in Capital Cases, and What Can Be Done About It (2002). See also *United States v. Quinones*, 196 F. Supp. 2d 416, 418 (S.D.N.Y. 2002), rev'd, 313 F.3d 49 (2d Cir. 2002); Edward Connors *et al.*, U.S. Dep't of Justice, Convicted by Juries, Exonerated by Science: Case Studies in the Use of DNA Evidence To Establish Innocence After Trial (1996).

15. What is factual innocence? There are many kinds of errors that can take place during a trial resulting in a miscarriage of justice that do not involve factually innocent individuals. Consider capital murder. The conviction of an individual when a killing was done in self-defense, or when the accused is insane, or when the defendant's due process rights were violated, are three such examples. Convicting the "wrong" person for a crime is a miscarriage of a different sort. Convicting the wrong person, the factually innocent person, is best understood by the example of convicting a person for a crime that never happened. See generally M.L. Radelet et al., In Spite of Innocence: Erroneous Convictions in Capital Cases (1992). Most cases of wrongful convictions surface from the mid to late 1980s, a period when forensic DNA technology was not readily accessible or well developed. The earliest case involves a conviction in 1979; the most recent is a conviction in 1991. See Innocence Project, Case Files, supra note 3. For a view of the running list of post-conviction DNA exonerations, see id.

16. Kirk Noble Bloodsworth was wrongfully convicted in March of 1985 for the brutal sexual assault and killing of a nine-year-old girl. Connors et al., supra note 14, at 35–36. He was released from prison in June 1993 and pardoned the following December. Id. Bloodsworth has the fortunate, yet sorrowful, distinction of being the first individual in the United States to be exonerated of a crime that placed him on death row. Id.

17. For the current number of exonerated individuals and their case profiles, see Innocence Project, Case Files, supra note 3. For a current contact list of the 67 existing innocence projects in 50 states, Canada, and Australia, see D. Berry and S. Berry, Truth in Justice: Innocence Projects Contact List, at http://www.truthinjustice.org/ipcontacts.htm (last visited Apr. 29, 2005).

18. In re Winship, 397 U.S. 358, 372 (1970) (Harlan, J., concurring). Interestingly, without exception, DNA allows for neither error, perhaps rendering obsolete Lord Blackstone's venerable maxim. 2 William Blackstone, Commentaries 352. For an interesting dialogue on this subject, see J. Reinman and E. van den Haag, *On the Common Saying That It Is Better That Ten Guilty Persons Escape Than That One Innocent Suffer: Pro and Con*, Soc. Phil. & Pol'y, Spring 1990, at 226.

19. S.H. Kadish, Why Substantive Criminal Law — A Dialogue, 29 *Clev. St. L. Rev.* 1 (1980).

20. *Winship*, 397 U.S. at 364 (Harlan, J., concurring).

21. In their book, *Actual Innocence*, Professor Barry Scheck, Peter Neufeld and Jim Dwyer identify 12 leading factors in the first 74 of the 163 DNA exonerations of factually innocent individuals. J. Dwyer, P. Neufeld, and B. Scheck, *Actual Innocence* 361–64 (2000). They are, in descending order: mistaken identifications (81%), serology inclusions (51%), police misconduct (50%), prosecutorial misconduct (45%), defective or fraudulent science (34%), microscopic hair comparison (35%), bad lawyering (32%), false confessions (22%), false witness testimony (20%), informants/snitches (19%), other forensic inclusions (7%), and DNA inclusions (1%). Id. The authors note that serology inclusion refers to A-B-O and protein blood

typing of semen, saliva, and bloodstains. Other forensic inclusions refer to the comparisons of fingerprints, fibers, and other physical evidence. Id.

22. Presently, legislation is in place in 39, and pending in four states, that provides for post-conviction access to DNA testing. See Innocence Project, Browse Legislation, at http://www.innocenceproject.org/legislation/display_legislation.php (last visited Apr. 29, 2005) [hereinafter Innocence Project, Browse Legislation]. The quality of these statutes in terms of providing adequate relief and safeguards varies from state to state. Some of the limiting language in these statutes include sunset provisions, restrictive time provisions, and laboratory restrictions. See Id. Those states that have yet to establish their policy on this subject include Alabama, Alaska, Hawaii, North Dakota, South Dakota, Vermont, and Wyoming. See Id. For a list of the states that provide for post-conviction DNA testing, see Id.

23. Frank Smith was exonerated posthumously. See Innocence Project, Case Files, supra note 3.

24. For individual profiles, including the crimes for which these individuals were charged and their sentences, see Id.

25. There are currently 38 states with the death penalty: Alabama, Arizona, Arkansas, California, Colorado, Connecticut, Delaware, Florida, Georgia, Idaho, Illinois, Indiana, Kansas, Kentucky, Louisiana, Maryland, Mississippi, Missouri, Montana, Nebraska, Nevada, New Hampshire, New Jersey, New Mexico, New York, North Carolina, Ohio, Oklahoma, Oregon, Pennsylvania, South Carolina, South Dakota, Tennessee, Texas, Utah, Virginia, Washington, and Wyoming. Death Penalty Info. Ctr., State by State Death Penalty Information, at http://www.deathpenaltyinfo.org/state (last visited Oct. 11, 2005); see also Cornell Law Sch., Cornell Death Penalty Project, at http://www.lawschool.cornell.edu/library/death (last visited Apr. 4, 2003). In addition, both the U.S. federal courts and military courts may impose the death penalty. Death Penalty Info. Ctr., supra. Of these jurisdictions, New Hampshire, New Jersey, New York, South Dakota, Kansas, and the U.S. military have had no executions since 1976. Id.

There are currently 12 states without the death penalty: Alaska, Hawaii, Iowa, Maine, Massachusetts, Michigan, Minnesota, North Dakota, Rhode Island, Vermont, West Virginia, and Wisconsin. Id. In addition, the District of Columbia does not provide for the death penalty. Id. The death penalty statutes in New York and Kansas were declared unconstitutional in 2004. Id.

26. In the Survey of DNA Crime Laboratories, 2001, the U.S. Department of Justice collected data from 110 of the 120 known, publicly operated forensic crime labs that perform DNA testing. G.W. Steadman, Survey of DNA Crime Laboratories, 2001, at 1 (U.S. Dep't of Justice, N.C.J. 191191, 2002), available at http://www.ojp.usdoj.gov/bjs/pub/pdf/sdnacl01.pdf. The survey is a follow-up to the initial survey of DNA crime laboratories in 1998. Id. The survey included questions about each laboratory's budget, personnel, workloads, procedures, equipment, and other topics. Id. Numerical tables present workloads in terms of known subject cases, unknown subject cases, and convicted offender DNA samples. See Id. at 1–7. The report compares findings to the baseline data from the initial survey. See id. Highlights include the following: (1) "In 2000 DNA crime laboratories received about 31,000 subject cases, an increase from almost 21,000 cases in 1999." Id. at 1. (2) "Forty-five percent of public laboratories reported contracting a private laboratory to do forensic DNA testing in 2000." Id. (3) "At the beginning of 2001, 81% of DNA crime laboratories had backlogs totaling 16,081 subject cases and 265,329 convicted offender samples." Id.

27. For a discussion of reform proposals concerning retention, preservation, and record-keeping in cases involving biological material, see George H. Ryan, Ill. Comm'n on Capital Punishment, Report of the Governor's Commission on Capital Punishment (2002) (containing recommendations for specific improvements to the capital punishment system in Illinois),

available at http://www.idoc.state.il.us/ccp/ccp/reports/commission_report/complete_report.pdf.

28. See, for example, Fed. Bureau of Investigation, U.S. Dep't of Justice, The FBI's Combined DNA Index System Program CODIS (1998), available at http://www.fbi.gov/hq/lab/codis/brochure.pdf.

"The FBI Laboratory's COmbined DNA Index System (CODIS) blends forensic science and computer technology into an effective tool for solving violent crimes. CODIS enables federal, state, and local crime labs to exchange and compare DNA profiles electronically, thereby linking crimes to each other and to convicted offenders." Id at 2.

"CODIS began as a pilot project in 1990 serving 14 state and local laboratories. The DNA Identification Act of 1994 (Public Law 103 322) formalized the FBI's authority to establish a national DNA index for law enforcement purposes. In October 1998, the FBI's National DNA Index System (NDIS) became operational. CODIS is implemented as a distributed database with three hierarchical levels (or tiers) — local, state, and national. NDIS is the highest level in the CODIS hierarchy, and enables the laboratories participating in the CODIS Program to exchange and compare DNA profiles on a national level. All DNA profiles originate at the local level (LDIS), then flow to the state (SDIS) and national levels. SDIS allows laboratories within states to exchange DNA profiles. The tiered approach allows state and local agencies to operate their databases according to their specific legislative or legal requirements." Id. at 2.

"Ultimately, the success of the CODIS program will be measured by the crimes it helps solve. CODIS's primary metric, the "Investigations Aided" is defined as a case that CODIS assisted through a hit (a match produced by CODIS that would not otherwise have been developed.)" id at 4.
"As of August 2005, CODIS has produced over 25,100 hits assisting in more than 27,000 investigations." Fed. Bureau of Investigation, U.S. Dep't of Justice, CODIS: Measuring Success, at http://www.fbi.gov/hq/lab/codis/success.htm (last visited Oct. 11, 2005). For a list of the "cold hits" on a state-by-state basis, see Fed. Bureau of Investigation, U.S. Dep't of Justice, CODIS: Investigations Aided, at http://www.fbi.gov/hq/lab/codis/aidedmap.htm (last visited Oct. 11, 2005).

29. See Steadman, supra note 26. For a frank and laudable opinion on the fallibility of the fact-finding process evidenced by post-conviction DNA testing, see *United States v. Quinones*, 196 F. Supp. 2d 416 (S.D.N.Y. 2002), rev'd, 313 F.3d 49 (2d Cir. 2002).

30. See, for example, Fed. R. Crim. P. 16(a)(1)(c)–(d); Pa. R. Crim. P. 573(b)(1); *Brady v. Maryland*, 373 U.S. 83 (1963). For a discussion on pretrial testing and exclusion rates, see also Connors et al., supra note 14.

31. See Dwyer, Neufeld and Scheck, supra note 21, at 361.

32. The report of the Illinois Commission on Capital Punishment (Ryan Report), commissioned by former Governor G.H. Ryan, is one of several state-inspired initiatives seeking to introduce reforms in criminal justice largely as a result of the successful application of DNA fingerprinting and the resulting exonerations. Cornell Law Sch., supra note 25; see, for example, Ryan, supra note 27. The Ryan Report contains 85 reform proposals designed to ensure that the Illinois capital punishment system is "fair, just and accurate." See id. The types of reforms necessary to ensure the integrity of the "truth-finding" process on behalf of the wrongfully accused in noncapital cases raise separate but compatible policy imperatives as those identified in the Commission's report. The Ryan Report provides considerable weight and insight to a variety of reforms that will serve the "truth-finding" process; however, it tends to confuse the separate (though not entirely separate) debate over the death penalty with

"innocence reforms." Clearly, without regard to an individual's ideological position, no one would countenance that a factually innocent person should be incarcerated. It remains inescapable, however, that the added dimension of the death penalty debate at worst polarizes and at least compromises consideration of true innocence reforms. See supra note 22.

33. Writing in dissent in *Victor v. Nebraska*, 511 U.S. 1 (1994), which held that an instruction defining reasonable doubt did not violate the Due Process Clause, Justice Blackmun observed that "democracy rests... [upon] a faith which springs fundamentally from the requirement that unless guilt is established beyond all reasonable doubt, the accused shall go free." Id. at 28. (Blackmun, J., dissenting).

34. *In re* Winship, 397 U.S. 358, 363–64 (1970). See generally Henry L. Chambers, Jr., Reasonable Certainty and Reasonable Doubt, 81 *Marq. L. Rev.* 655 (1998); W.S. Laufer, The Rhetoric of Innocence, 70 *Wash. L. Rev.* 329 (1995); L.M. Solan, Refocusing the Burden of Proof in Criminal Cases: Some Doubt About Reasonable Doubt, 78 *Tex. L. Rev.* 105 (1999).

35. The origin of the traditional definition of "beyond a reasonable doubt," which served for more than a century as the basis for many reasonable doubt jury instructions, is found in *Commonwealth v. Webster*, 59 Mass. (1 Cush.) 295 (1850). Writing for the Court, Chief Justice Shaw of the Massachusetts Supreme Court opined:
"[W]hat is reasonable doubt? It is a term often used, probably pretty well understood, but not easily defined. It is not mere possible doubt; because every thing relating to human affairs, and depending on moral evidence, is open to some possible or imaginary doubt. It is that state of the case, which, after the entire comparison and consideration of all the evidence, leaves the minds of jurors in that condition that they cannot say they feel an abiding conviction, to a moral certainty, of the truth of the charge." Id. at 320.

36. William James wrote:
"[M]an is the only metaphysical animal. To wonder why the universe should be as it is presupposes the notion of its being different, and a brute, which never reduces the actual to fluidity by breaking up its literal sequences in his imagination, can never form such a notion. He takes the world simply for granted, and never wonders at it at all."
2 W. James, *The Principles of Psychology* 465–67, (Dover Publications, 1950), (1890).

37. J. Wambaugh, *The Blooding* (1989).

38. It is important to point out that voluminous newspaper articles and original trial transcripts were reviewed by the author in order to create a comprehensive and accurate look at the circumstances surrounding Dawn Hamilton's murder. See Record, *Bloodsworth v. State*, 512 A.2d 1056 (Md. 1986) (No. 71); see also *Bloodsworth*, 512 A.2d 1056 (Md. 1986) (discussing record); *Bloodsworth v. State*, 543 A.2d 382 (Md. Ct. Spec. App. 1988) (discussing evidence in second trial). While the facts herein are generally contained in numerous other sources — as Bloodsworth's case has been widely examined, see R. Hiaasen, The Second Life of Kirk Bloodsworth, *Balt. Sun*, July 30, 2000, at 7A — several important differences from the "popularized" account of Bloodsworth's ordeal arise in certain critical areas — namely, the actual crime scene and evidence collected from the crime scene. The original newspaper articles and the notes of transcript materials remain in Bloodsworth's possession. In addition, this narrative is supported by extensive personal interviews with Bloodsworth, Interviews with Kirk Noble Bloodsworth in Pittsburgh, PA. (Jan. 17–18, Feb. 22–23, Mar. 1, 2003), and several phone interviews, Telephone Interviews with Kirk Noble Bloodsworth (Mar. 8–9, 2003). Additional information and facts have been taken from Dwyer, Neufeld, and Scheck, supra note 21. Bloodsworth is the first American to be exonerated from death row based on DNA evidence. Id. at 360–61; see also Connors et al., supra note 14, at 35–36; Innocence Project, Case Files, supra note 3. He has given numerous interviews and consistent details of his tragic account to

various innocence projects and media since his release in 1992. See, for example, G. Small, Nine-Year Prison 'Nightmare' Ends as Former Convicted Killer is Released; DNA Test Leads to Exoneration, *Balt. Sun*, June 29, 1993, at 1A; Kirk Noble Bloodsworth Case Chronology, *Balt. Sun*, June 29, 1993, at 7A.

39. A.J. Jeffreys et al., Hypervariable 'Minisatellite' Regions in Human DNA, 314 *Nature* 67 (1985) [hereinafter Jeffreys et al., Minisatellite]; A.J. Jeffreys et al., Individual-Specific "Fingerprints" of Human DNA, 316 *Nature* 76 (1985) [hereinafter Jeffreys et al., Fingerprints].

40. Jeffreys et al., Minisatellite. Also, for an extensive review on forensic DNA typing and the biology and technology behind STR (short tandem repeat) markers, see J. M. Butler, Forensic DNA Typing (2001). The following effort to identify DNA typing technologies and the steps taken in processing a DNA sample are offered from this source simply for general reference. With respect to DNA identification and testing techniques, evolving DNA identification-typing technologies over the past 15 years have produced varying results in terms of the speed, analysis, costs, and power of discrimination. Id. at 3. The first genetic tool used for distinguishing between individuals is the A-B-O blood grouping. With only four possible genotype groups, A, B, AB, and O, this quick and affordable test is useful for exclusions, but has relatively little value for the purpose of establishing an inclusion. Id. at 3–4. Mitochondrial DNA (mtDNA), which is inherited strictly from one's mother, was first sequenced in 1981. Id. at 4–5. It has the "lowest power of discrimination" and the "longest sample processing time"; however, it remains useful as an identification tool in cases where the biological material is severely degraded because it can work with small samples and can be efficiently amplified. Id. at 5. Also, for a timeline of DNA identification methods, see Id. at 9. RFLP (restriction fragment length polymorphism) multi and single locus probes represent another technology that is a "highly discriminating testing technique." Id. at 4. First utilized by the FBI in 1988, the slow processing speed of this technology led to its abandonment by the FBI and most major laboratories in 2000. Id. at 9. Finally, STR testing, developed in 1993, id., is viewed by many as the optimal testing method.

> "STR (short tandem repeat) markers have a high power of discrimination and rapid analysis speed that can be analyzed three or more at a time. Multiple STRs can be examined in the same DNA test or "multiplexed." Multiplex STR's are valuable because they can produce highly discriminating results and can successfully measure sample mixtures and biological materials containing degraded DNA molecules. In addition, the detection of multiplex STR's can be automated, which is an important benefit as the demand for DNA testing increases."

Id. at 4.

The steps in a DNA sample process (STR) are also described in Butler's treatise:

> "DNA is first extracted from its biological source material and then measured to evaluate the quantity of DNA recovered. After isolating the DNA from its cells, specific regions are copied with a technique known as the polymerase chain reaction (PCR). PCR produces millions of copies for each starting DNA molecule permitting minute amounts of DNA to be examined. Multiple STR regions are examined simultaneously to increase the informativeness of the DNA test. The resulting PCR products are then separated and detected to characterize the STR region being examined. The separation methods include slab jel and capillary electrophoresis aided by fluorescent detection methods." Id. at 5 and 6.

> "The resulting DNA profile for a sample, which is a combination of individual STR genotypes, is compared to other samples. In the case of a forensic investigation, these other samples would include known reference samples such as the victim or a suspect that are compared to the crime scene evidence. If there is no match between the

questioned sample and the known sample, then the samples may be considered as having originated from different sources. The term for the failure to match two DNA profiles is 'exclusion.'" Id. at 5–6.

In *Harvey v. Horan*, 285 F.3d 298 (4th Cir. 2002), Judge Luttig explained the power of current DNA testing in his concurring opinion. Id. at 305 n.1 (Luttig, J., concurring).

> "The current standard STR test examines 13 independent regions of DNA ("loci"), although testing at just 8–10 loci usually is sufficient to distinguish between any two persons who are not identical twins. In fact, researchers have found that the probability that any two unrelated individuals match at nine specific loci (the "matching probability") is approximately 1 in 740 billion. Because the standard test probes 13 loci (not 8 or 9), it should be correspondingly more powerful. Even the most conservative estimates have placed this matching probability as high as 1 in 100 billion. It is also worth noting that some current generation STR systems have matching probabilities on the order of 1 in 1 quadrillion. For purposes of understanding the magnitude of these figures of probability, it is estimated that there are only 6 billion persons on the planet." Id. (Lutting, J., concurring) (citations omitted).

41. Butler, supra note 40, at 2; see also Jeffreys et al., Fingerprints, supra note 39, at 318; P. Gill, A.J. Jeffreys, and D.J. Werrett, Forensic Application of DNA "Fingerprints," 318 *Nature* 577 (1985).

42. Butler, supra note 40, at 2–3.

43. Id at 3. Dr. Jeffreys examined VNTRs through a technique called RFLP, restriction fragment length polymorphism, involving "the use of a restriction enzyme to cut the regions surrounding the VNTR." Id. at 3. This early DNA testing method was used to solve the Narborough Murders. Id. at 3 (referencing the Narborough murders as a "double homicide"); see also Wambaugh, supra note 37.

44. K.F. Kelly et al., Method and applications of DNA Fingerprinting: A Guide for the Non-Scientist, 1987 *Crim. L. Rev.* 105, 108 ("The first reported use of DNA identification was to prove a familial relationship. A Ghanaian boy was refused entry into the United Kingdom (U.K.) for lack of proof that he was the son of a woman who had the right of settlement in the United Kingdom. Immigration authorities contended that the boy could be the nephew of the woman, not her son. DNA testing showed a high probability of a mother–son relationship. The U.K. Government accepted the test findings and admitted the boy."); L. Bouwer Hansen, comment, Stemming the DNA Tide: A Case for Quality Control Guidelines, 16 *Hamline L. Rev.* 211, pp. 213–214 (1992).

45. In 1986, police asked Dr. Jeffreys

> "to verify a suspect's confession that he was responsible for two rape-murders in the English Midlands. Tests proved that the suspect had not committed the crimes. Police then began obtaining blood samples from several thousand male inhabitants in the area to identify a new suspect, Colin Pitchfork. In a 1987 case in England, Robert Melias became the first person convicted of a crime (rape) on the basis of DNA evidence."

> R.R. Belair, Forensic DNA Analysis: Issues (U.S. Dep't of Justice, N.C.J. 128567, 1991). In one of the first uses of DNA in a criminal case in the United States, in November 1987, the State of Florida convicted Tommy Lee Andrews of rape after DNA tests matched his DNA from a blood sample with semen traces found in a rape victim. *Andrews v. State*, 533 So. 2d 841 (Fla. Dist. Ct. App. 1988).

46. See sources cited supra note 38.

47. See Dwyer, Neufeld and Scheck, supra note 21, at 273–88.

48. Id. In his own words, Kirk Bloodsworth has never been "skinny." See sources cited supra note 38. Bloodsworth weighed more than 200 pounds ever since he was a young teenager. See sources cited supra note 38. At the time, Bloodsworth's hair and mustache were "fire-engine red." See sources cited supra note 38.

49. See Dwyer, Neufeld and Scheck, supra note 21, at 273–88. The actual nature of the agent that left an imprint on Dawn Hamilton's neck was never established. Id.

50. See Dwyer, Neufeld and Scheck, supra note 21, at 273–88. Although the investigators suspected that the rock was used by the killer to cause Dawn Hamilton's fatal head injuries, forensic testing did not conclusively identify the rock as an instrument used in her death. Id. No rock fragments were found in or about her skull. Id.

51. See Dwyer, Neufeld and Scheck, supra note 21, at 273–88. This report, though accurate, is inconsistent with many stories on the crime scene evidence that suggest that the stick was found near her body. See sources cited supra note 38.

52. See Dwyer, Neufeld, and Scheck, supra note 21, at 273–88. According to Bloodsworth, neither he nor his attorneys heard the taped message from the anonymous tipster. Id. He reported that he was told by the police that all of the hotline tapes had been mistakenly erased. Id

53. See sources cited supra note 38. Pursuant to the profilers' direction, the items placed in the room were quickly removed from Bloodsworth's view. See sources cited supra note 38. The intended effect of the items placed in the room never materialized. See sources cited supra note 38. Bloodsworth did not react to the items placed in his plain view, although at trial Detective Capel testified that there was no "immediate reaction, but it was a long-term reaction. He remembered everything we put on the table." See sources cited supra note 38. In fact, there is nothing in the record that suggests that Bloodsworth had any prior knowledge of the crime scene or recollection of the child's clothing or the rock other than repeating to others what he had seen placed before him during his interrogation.

54. See sources cited supra note 38. Bloodsworth stated to investigators and at trial that his disappearance from his job and his life in Essex was due to his wife's repeated indiscretions and his inability to cope any longer with his failed marriage. He did not want to face her. See sources cited supra note 38.

55. See sources cited supra note 38. Jackie also failed to identify Bloodsworth as the perpetrator in Bloodsworth's second trial. See sources cited supra note 38.

56. The following summary represents the prosecutor's principal evidence at trial and Bloodsworth's reaction to that evidence (in parentheses) to this day: (1) An anonymous hotline caller told police that a guy named Kirk, who worked at a local furniture store, looked like the police composite. Another anonymous caller said that she saw Bloodsworth with the girl earlier in the day. See sources cited supra note 38. (Neither Bloodsworth nor his attorney ever heard the taped messages taken by the hotline. The police stated that the tapes were mistakenly erased. See sources cited supra note 38.) (2) A witness identified Bloodsworth from a police sketch compiled by five witnesses. The five witnesses testified that they had seen Bloodsworth in the area, both alone and with the little girl. One of the witnesses, James Keller, said that, while leaving for work at 6:00 A.M. on July 25, he saw Bloodsworth in the area. See sources cited supra note 38. (In the same building where Keller lived, Faye McCullouch, a defense witness, gave conflicting testimony of the man whom she saw at or about the same time that morning, opining that it was not Bloodsworth whom she saw, but another individual. The defense offered other alibi witnesses who gave contrary testimony to the State's evidence of Bloodsworth's whereabouts that day. In one case, an alibi witness testified that Bloodsworth did not leave his home until after

1:00 P.M. on July 25. See sources cited supra note 38.) (3) Bloodsworth told acquaintances he had done something "terrible" that would affect his marriage. See sources cited supra note 38. (Bloodsworth testified that the "terrible thing" he did was that he forgot to take his wife to the taco salad bar for dinner and that he left her without paying off their marital debts. See sources cited supra note 38.) (4) In his first police interrogation, Bloodsworth mentioned a "bloody rock," even though no weapons were known of at the time. See sources cited supra note 38. (Bloodsworth's statements to his friends about evidence "at the scene" was based upon his recollection of the materials placed before him at his first custodial interrogation. See sources cited supra note 38.) (5) Testimony was offered that a shoe impression found near the victim's body was made by a pair of shoes found in a Cambridge home where Bloodsworth was staying. See sources cited supra note 38. (The shoeprint matched the sole of a pair of shoes that were in the house where Bloodsworth stayed for one evening when he returned to Cambridge. The shoes were owned by an individual living there who wore a size eight shoe. Bloodsworth's shoe size is an eleven. No casting of the footprint was taken from the crime scene. See sources cited supra note 38.)

57. There are numerous stories in the *Baltimore Sun* concerning Bloodsworth's investigation, trial, and posttrial experiences. See sources cited supra note 38. For a particularly informative passage, see Small, supra note 38.

58. See *Bloodsworth v. State*, 512 A.2d 1056 (Md. 1986).

59. See sources cites supra note 38. To this day, Bloodsworth does not know who sent this "life-saving" book to him. See sources cited supra note 38.

60. Wambaugh, supra note 37, at 138–40, 230–40. In his author's note, Joseph Wambaugh observed "this was the first murder case resolved by genetic fingerprinting." Id. at i.

61. See Wambaugh, supra note 37, at 1–15, 138–40, 230–40.

62. "Blooding" was the term used in the story for the voluntary taking of blood from 4,000 individuals with the hope of finding a DNA match with the biological materials taken from the victims' bodies. Wambaugh, supra note 37 at 138–40.

63. Wambaugh, supra note 37, at 238–40. In addition to describing the ongoing investigation of the appalling crimes, there is another relevant thread that runs through the book in terms of the causes underlying wrongful convictions. This is the story of another local youth who falsely confessed to committing both murders. Id at 127–33. His innocence was later established beyond doubt. Id.

64. R.E. Morin is now a federal judge for the District Court of the District of Columbia. See, for example, S. Levine, Md. Man's Exoneration Didn't End Nightmare; First Death Row Inmate Cleared by DNA Pours Emotions Into Activism, *Wash. Post, Feb.* 24, 2003, at B2.

65. See sources cited supra note 38; see also Dwyer, Neufeld and Scheck, supra note 21, at 273–88.

66. Epithelial describes the healing tissue that forms a thin protective layer on exposed bodily surfaces and forms the lining of internal cavities, ducts, and organs. *Tabor's Cyclopedic Medical Dictionary 2000* (C.L. Thomas et al. eds., 1993).

67. See sources cited supra note 38. Bloodsworth remarried to Brenda Ewell and is busy trying to rebuild his life. See sources cited supra note 38. In this respect, oddly enough, he is one of the lucky ones as so many of the 163 wrongfully convicted individuals have found re-entry into society to be an unhappy and endless struggle. See sources cited supra note 38. Bloodsworth is active with several national organizations doing work on behalf of wrongfully convicted individuals. See sources cited supra note 38. He currently serves as a consultant to the Justice Project and the Duquesne University School of Law Innocence Project. See sources cited supra note 38.

68. The Montel Williams Show: Falsely Accused: Rebuilding Your Life (Paramount Pictures Oct. 7, 2002). E.J. Lloyd was convicted in a Michigan court for first degree felony murder in 1985. Id. Lloyd was sentenced to life without parole. See Innocence Project, Case Files, supra note 3. He was exonerated in 2002. Id.

69. Connors et al., supra note 14, at 35–36.

70. The study from the National Institute of Justice described the similarities in these cases:

"The 28 cases in this study were tried in 14 States and the District of Columbia. The States are Illinois (5 cases), New York (4 cases), Virginia (3 cases), West Virginia (3 cases), Pennsylvania (2 cases), California (2 cases), Maryland, North Carolina, Connecticut, Kansas, Ohio, Indiana, New Jersey and Texas. Many cases share a number of descriptive characteristics, as noted below." Id. at 44.

"The 28 cases shared several common themes in the evidence presented during and after trial." Id. at 47.

"All cases, except for homicides, involved victim identification both prior to and at trial. Many cases also had additional eyewitness identification, either placing the defendant with the victim or near the crime scene (e.g., in *Bloodsworth*, five witnesses testified that they had seen the defendant with the nine-year-old victim on the day of the murder)." Id. at 47.

"Many defendants presented an alibi defense, frequently corroborated by family or friends. For example, Edward Honaker's alibi was corroborated by his brother, sister-in-law, mother's housemate, and trailer park owner. The alibis apparently were not of sufficient weight to the juries to counter the strength of the eyewitness testimony."
Id. at 47. These 28 individuals served an average of seven years in prison. Id. at 34–76.

71. Following Dr. Jeffreys's development of multi-loci RFLP probes in 1985, DNA testing became a public business in 1986 with the creation of Cellmark and Lifecodes. Butler, supra note 40, at 9. In 1988, the FBI began testing biological evidence for state and local jurisdictions with single-locus RFLP probes. Id. In 1990, the population statistics data set used with RFLP methods was called into question. Id. PCR testing methods emerged. Id. In 1992, the FBI started conducting its casework methods through PCR testing. Id. The FBI began mtDNA testing in 1996, the same year that multiplex STR kits became available. Id. In 1998, the FBI launched the Combined DNA Index System (CODIS). Id. In 1999, as multiplex STR (short tandem repeat) kits became validated for use in labs nationwide, the FBI converted its testing methods. Id. In 2000, the FBI and many private and public laboratories stopped running RFLP analyses and converted to multiplex STR's. Id. This history, in part, reflects the vital role of the National Institute of Justice and the FBI in advancing the use of DNA identification technology and its acceptance in the legal community.

72. Connors et al., supra note 14, at 35–36. Testing methods also varied: seven of the laboratories reported using RFLP testing; four used PCR testing; and eight utilized both types of tests. Id.

73. Id. The figure of 26% is fairly characterized as a conservative number. Id. For statistical purposes, the exclusion of multiple suspects in a single case is counted by the FBI as a single exclusion. Id.

74. P.M. Harrison and A.J. Beck, Prison and Jail Inmates at Midyear 2004, at 1 (U.S. Dep't of Justice, N.C.J. 208801, 2005) ("At midyear 2004 the Nation's prisons and jails incarcerated 2,131,180 persons.... Since midyear 2003 the total incarcerated population has increased 2.3%."), available at http://www.ojp.usdoj.gov/bjs/abstract/pjim04.htm. Approximately 600,000 prisoners are serving time for serious felonies. See generally, Id. at 1–6.

75. I. Kant, *Critique of Pure Reason* 20 (N.K. Smith trans., St. Martin's Press 1964) (1787).

76. See sources cited supra notes 39–40.

77. *United States v. Quinones*, 196 F. Supp. 2d 416, 420 (S.D.N.Y. 2002), rev'd, 313 F.3d 49 (2d Cir. 2002).

78. See generally R. Rorty, Objectivity, Relativism, and Truth (1991). For an interesting commentary on Rorty, supra, see R.A. Posner, *Overcoming Law*, pp. 444–63 (1995).

79. A court-appointed, independent panel completed a two-year study on race and gender bias and prejudice in the Pennsylvania courts. S. Kalson, Moratorium on Death Penalty Urged; Study Commission Finds Widespread Gender, Racial Bias in Pennsylvania Judicial System, *Pittsburgh Post-Gazette*, Mar. 5, 2003, at A1. Based on its findings, the panel, *inter alia*, recommended a death penalty moratorium. Id.

80. One day after the panel recommendation was issued, supra note 79, Governor Edward G. Rendell rejected the panel's position. S. Kalson, Rendell Rejects Death Penalty Ban, *Pittsburgh Post-Gazette*, Mar. 6, 2003, at B3.

81. In the summer of 2000, the Office of the District Attorney for the County of San Diego, in a project headed by Deputy District Attorney George W. ("Woody") Clarke, became one of the first to review voluntarily past cases involving biological materials in order to determine if DNA evidence could provide exonerating information. A. Roth, San Diego DA To Use DNA Tests To Recheck Convictions; Bold Plan Aims to See None Are Wrongfully Imprisoned, *San Diego Union-Trib.*, June 4, 2000. A number of prosecutors nationwide have voluntarily taken his lead. See, for example, S. Pfeifer, O.C. Pioneering a D.A. — Defender Project on DNA Law: As 'Innocence Projects' To Root Out Wrongful Convictions Spring Up Nationwide, This One Pairs Traditional Adversaries, *L.A. Times*, July 28, 2000, at A1.

82. Bruce Godschalk served 15 years of his 22 year sentence before DNA evidence exonerated him. Innocence Project, Case Files, supra note 3. District Attorney Bruce Castor, Jr., of Montgomery County, Pennsylvania, rejected the results of the DNA tests, choosing instead to believe his detectives and his tape-recorded confession. Id. Godschalk was released after five independent testing laboratories reached conclusive and consistent results. See *Commonwealth v. Godschalk*, 679 A.2d 1295 (Pa. Super. Ct. 1996) (denying Godschalk's petition for DNA testing and citing overwhelming evidence and defendant's confession).

    In *Commonwealth v. Reese*, 663 A.2d 206 (Pa. Super. Ct. 1995), the court established a qualified right to post-conviction DNA testing of previously untested biological material. Id. at 210. Pennsylvania now has a post-conviction DNA testing statute. See 42 Pa. Cons. Stat. § 9543.1 (2001). The provision was signed into law on July 10, 2002. Act of July 10, 2002, P.L. 745, 2002 Pa. Laws 109 (codified at 42 Pa. Cons. Stat. § 9543.1). The statute applies to individuals "serving a term of imprisonment or awaiting execution" except individuals convicted after January 1995 who did not request DNA testing at trial. 42 Pa. Cons. Stat. § 9543.1(a). The petitioner must make a prima facie case showing that the identity was at issue. See id. § 9543.1(c)(3). The Commonwealth and applicant must mutually select the laboratory to do the test, or, if they are unable to agree, the court will choose the laboratory. See id. § 9543.1(e)(1). An applicant can file for post-conviction relief within sixty days from when the DNA test results were obtained. See id. § 9543.1(f)(1). The applicant must assert "actual innocence of the offense" in order to meet the standard for post-conviction DNA tests. See id. § 9543.1(c)(3)(ii)(A). In a capital case, the motion must "assert the applicant's actual innocence of the charged or uncharged conduct constituting an aggravating circumstance ... if the applicant's exoneration of the conduct would result in vacating a sentence of death," or must assert that the outcome of the DNA testing would establish a "mitigating circumstance." See id. § 9543.1(c)(3)(ii)(B)–(C). Unless indigent, the applicant must pay for the test. See id. §9543.1(e)(2). A preservation of evidence requirement becomes effective upon the receipt of a motion or a notice of a motion requesting DNA testing. See id. § 9543.1(b)(2). There are no provisions to overcome any procedural bars or provisions that address compensation. See also Innocence Project, Browse Legislation, supra note 22.

83. Hiassen, supra note 38. Bloodsworth had been circulating a petition for an environmental group when this individual charged at Bloodsworth and yelled for all who could hear that a child murderer was in the neighborhood. Id.

84. Prisoners in state custody have long had the ability to file habeas corpus petitions alleging that their convictions or sentences were obtained or imposed in violation of federal law. See generally *Brown v. Allen*, 344 U.S. 443 (1953). Under the "exhaustion doctrine," state prisoners must usually present their federal claims to the relevant state court before seeking relief in federal court. See generally Ex parte Royall, 117 U.S. 241 (1886).

85. Habeas Corpus: Hearing Before the Subcomm. on Civil and Constitutional Rights of the House Comm. on the Judiciary, 103d Cong. 492–495 (1994) [hereinafter Habeas Corpus Hearing] (statement of former United States Attorneys General Benjamin Civiletti, Nicholas deB. Katzenbach, Edward H. Levi, and Elliot Richardson, on behalf of the Emergency Committee to Save Habeas Corpus).

86. In a prepared joint statement presented at a congressional hearing on habeas corpus reform, several former attorneys general referenced the case of *Coleman v. Thompson*, 501 U.S. 722 (1991):

"In the *Coleman v. Thompson* case in 1991, a death row inmate with strong new evidence of actual innocence — evidence so powerful and disturbing that Time magazine featured it as a cover story — was denied an opportunity to even have his new evidence heard in federal court, because his lawyer had unwittingly missed a filing deadline by three days. The Court ruled that the mistake of the otherwise competent lawyer ... barred any habeas review of the evidence. Mr. Coleman was executed."

Habeas Corpus Hearing, supra note 85, at 494.

87. "[W]hat we have to deal with is not the petitioners' innocence or guilt but solely the question whether their constitutional rights have been preserved." *Moore v. Dempsey*, 261 U.S. 86, 87–88 (1923).

88. See *Harvey v. Horan*, 285 F.3d 298 (4th Cir. 2002), in which Judge Luttig perceived post-conviction DNA tests as a protected, though diminished, liberty interest in the context of federal habeas applications in order to establish a predicate for other constitutional violations. Id. at 320 (Luttig, J., dissenting). See also Seth F. Kreimer and David Rudovsky, Double Helix, Double Blind: Factual Innocence and Postconviction DNA Testing, 151 U. Pa. L. Rev. 547, 590 n. 184 (2002), for a thorough discussion of the Supreme Court's view, as presented in *Herrera v. Collins*, 506 U.S. 390 (1993), on the subject of actual innocence in the context of a habeas application.

"Chief Justice Rehnquist's majority opinion assumed "for the sake of argument" that a "truly persuasive" showing would have that effect; however, it concluded that no such showing had been made. In this proposition, he was joined by separate concurring opinions by Justice O'Connor, writing for herself and Justice Kennedy, and by Justice White. The dissent by Justice Blackmun, joined by Justices Stevens and Souter, would have held that a "truly persuasive demonstration of 'actual innocence'" "would make execution of the petitioner unconstitutional, and remanded for investigation of petitioner's claim on that standard. Only Justices Scalia and Thomas would have found no due process concerns presented by newly discovered evidence of innocence." Kreimer and Rudovsky, supra, at 590 n. 184.

89. Kreimer and Rudovsky, supra note 88, at 590 n.184. Kreimer and Rudovsky offer an exceptionally insightful article on the status of post-conviction DNA testing, the practices and policies of prosecutors, and the doctrinal bases for a constitutional right to post-conviction DNA disclosure. See generally Id.

90. E.M. Borchard, *Convicting the Innocent: Errors of Criminal Justice*, at vii–viii (1932).

91. Quoting Dean Wigmore on the subject of eyewitness identification, Borchard wrote:

    "Dean Wigmore has suggested a more scientific method, based on the psychology of recognition, for effecting identifications. He proposes the use of talking film, by which body, motions, and voice of the subject shall be recorded in numerous poses, the pictures then to be presented to viewers, in perhaps a series of perhaps twenty-five similar films, selected from a classified stock of one hundred types of men and women on file, the viewers to indicate recognition by the pressure of an electric button. When it is realized how unreliable the haphazard methods of identification have frequently proved to be, it will be apparent that more scientific methods of identification must be devised."

    Id. at 367–68 (citing J. H. Wigmore, *Evidence — Corroboration By Witness' Identification of an Accused on Arrest*, 25 *Ill. L. Rev.* 550, 552 (1931)).

92. A.E. Taslitz. Convicting the Guilty and Acquitting the Innocent: The ABA Takes a Stand, 19-WTR *Crim. Just.* 18 (2005).

93. 118 Stat. 2260 (2004).

94. A helpful summary of the provisions of the Justice For All Act appears on the web site for the American Society of Law Medicine and Ethics. This particular report by Attorney Noble can be found at Grant No. 1 RO1-HG002836-01, available at http://www.aslme.org/dna_04/spec_reports/justice_for_all.pdf. Also, see generally http://www.aslme.org/dna_04/reports/index.php.

95. Press Release, U.S. Senator Patrick Leahy: The Justice For All Act of 2004 (October 9, 2004), available at http://leahy.senate.gov/press/200410/100904B.html. For the entire text of this statement and many more on the topic of innocence, please see Senator Leahy's web site at http://www.leahy.senate.gov.

96. First introduced in 2000, the Innocence Protection Act is a comprehensive package of criminal justice reforms aimed at reducing the risk that innocent persons may be executed. See Innocence Protection Act of 2000, S. 2690, 106th Cong. Most urgently, the bill would: (1) "ensure that wrongfully convicted persons have an opportunity to establish their innocence through DNA testing," (2) "ensur[e] competent legal services in capital cases," (3) "compensat[e] the unjustly condemned," and (4) provide the public with annual reports regarding the administration and effects of capital punishment laws. Id. ß ß 101, 201, 301–302, 404.

    On February 4, 2003, Senators Patrick Leahy, Gordon Smith, and Susan Collins and Congressmen Bill Delahunt and Ray LaHood made the following joint statement on the widely acclaimed Innocence Protection Act (IPA):

    "Three years ago, we joined together to introduce the Innocence Protection Act, a balanced, bipartisan package of sensible criminal justice reforms aimed at reducing the risk that innocent persons may be executed — and ensuring that inmates who have been wrongfully convicted have access to the evidence that can establish their innocence.

    The bill would achieve these goals in two principal ways: first, by ensuring that eligible inmates are not denied access to DNA testing that can establish their innocence; and second, by helping states improve the quality of legal representation in capital cases so that fewer defendants are wrongfully convicted in the first place.

This legislation gained enormous momentum during the last Congress, with 32 Senators and 250 Representatives — well over half the House–signed on in support. Hearings were held in each House, and a version of the bill was reported out of the Senate Judiciary Committee in July.

Many of the bill's cosponsors are supporters of the death penalty. Many others oppose it. But all are united in the belief that a just society cannot condone the execution or wrongful incarceration of the innocent."

Press Release, U.S. Senator Patrick Leahy, Joint Statement by Senators Patrick Leahy, Gordon Smith and Susan Collins, and Congressmen Bill Delahunt and Ray LaHood: The Innocence Protection Act (Feb. 4, 2003), available at http://leahy.senate.gov/press/200302/020403b.html.

On March 11, 2003, the Bush administration announced a five-year, $1 billion program to increase and improve the use of DNA in criminal justice. Dan Eggen, $1 Billion Proposed for DNA Testing, Wash. Post, Mar. 12, 2003, at A3. The impact on the IPA of the DNA budget and policy proposals remains unclear. The first allocation for fiscal year 2004, which begins on October 1, 2003, requires congressional approval. Id. The first year's expenditures include the following items: $92 million to reduce the estimated 700,000 untested DNA samples in state and federal rape, homicide, and kidnapping cases, and samples taken from convicted criminals; $90.4 million for federal, state, and local crime lab improvements, in part, to process the DNA testing more quickly and efficiently; $24.8 million for research and development and to create a National Forensic Science Commission to conduct continuing studies on efficiency and use; $17.5 million for training and other assistance for police, prosecutors, defense attorneys, judges, and other law enforcement officials who collect DNA; $5 million to cover post-conviction DNA testing for inmates who contend that they were wrongly convicted; and $2 million for education and training of law enforcement for use in missing persons cases. Id. States receiving these funds will be required to develop plans that ensure prompt and accurate testing methods and that discourage frivolous claims. Id. While generally well received, the plan has been criticized by Professor Barry Scheck and various innocence projects around the country as a step in the right direction but providing far too little support for the wrongfully convicted. Richard Willing, Bush To Boost Criminal DNA Tests, U.S.A Today, Mar. 11, 2003, at 1A.

97. Thomas D. Langan, The Meaning of Heidegger: A Critical Study of an Existentialist Phenomenology 42 (1959).

98. Centesimus Annus, supra note 7, para. 46.

Foundations of Law

II

Criminal Law and Procedure[1]

4

BRUCE A. ANTKOWIAK

At midnight on December 31, 2002, millions of people across the country celebrated New Year's Eve with friends and family.

It may be said with relative certainty, however, that 2,033,331 people in the United States did not join in New Year's revelry. They would sing no songs and sip no champagne. If any thoughts came to mind as the old year passed, they would probably parallel the thoughts of Oscar Wilde:

> I know not whether Laws be right,
> Or whether Laws be wrong;
> All we know who lie in gaol is that the wall is strong;
> And that each day is like a year, a year whose days are long.[2]

The 2,033,331 people were in federal, state, or county jails in America.

Another group, over 2½ times that number (approximately 4,748,306 people), probably celebrated a subdued New Year's as well, for they were under the scrutiny of federal or state governments as persons on probation or parole.[3] In both instances, the number of people in prison and on probation and parole on December 31, 2002, was more than the number whose celebrations were similarly subdued at the end of 2001. For yet another year, America increased the number of people it officially labeled "criminals."

To say that these people are where they are simply because they are "bad people" who universally deserve either incarceration, restrictions on their freedom, or worse, is simplistic and, on occasion, simply wrong. The question of how these people came to be where they are (and the process that exposes everyone within the country to the risk of similar restriction) is a question to be answered by an understanding of the system which put them there: the criminal justice system.

The Historical Perspective

Americans certainly did not invent crime and the criminal justice system that deals with it. Although a complete historical analysis of the phenomenon of crime and the systems societies have created to deal with it is far beyond the scope of this chapter, placing the American system in historical context is critical to an appreciation of the features that typify our system today.

While the vast and increasing numbers of people in American prisons and on parole and probation would make us think that ours is a world filled with a new breed of violent and dangerous people, a brief review of the history of this so-called "civilized world" will bring the sharp realization that the world has never been a gentle place. Indeed, it has been anything but that.

The English writer and historian, Colin Wilson, observes:

> If we are to understand the history of the past 3000 years we have to make an effort of imagination, and try to forget this notion of being protected by the law. In ancient Greece, the problem was not simply the brigands who haunted the roads and the pirates who infested the seas; it was the fact that the ordinary citizen became a brigand or pirate when he felt like it, and no one regarded this as abnormal.[4]

Wilson variously refers to "the warrior tradition" as one which typified much of life in the organized world for centuries.[4] (p. 167) This tradition manifested itself at an early stage; in fact, there is "no way of knowing when piracy and banditry became common in Europe; but it was probably toward the end of the third millennium B.C." (p. 168)

At that time, the first walled cities appeared, suggesting that warfare among peoples was not an exceptional state of human nature but, rather, its rule. That rule existed even in the days before written history. Wilson quotes the Greek historian Thucydides writing in the fifth century B.C., that, in times ancient to him, the world was commanded by leaders of powerful bands of raiders who plundered towns and villages with such a pervasive violent nature that all Greeks were required to carry weapons in defense of their homes and persons.[4] (p. 169)

To be sure, ancient civilizations tried as best they could to deal with the sort of "warrior mentality" that was both the stuff of myth and legend and a very dangerous current reality to people living in those times. They did so by developing criminal justice systems.

From the outset, an understanding of those systems required an understanding of some basic philosophical choices made for or by the populace of those cultures. As Herbert Johnson has written, the cultures of biblical Israel, Athens, and Rome had various approaches to the question of crime and criminal justice dictated largely by the philosophical conceptions upon which those cultures were based.[5]

The Israel of biblical times centered its view of civilization on its conception that it represented the decedents of Abraham, a chosen people who occupied a unique position of relationship with an all powerful God, Yahweh:

> Rules of behavior as well as the structure of criminal laws and punishments reflected this profound religious influence. Wrongful conduct was offensive on two grounds: one, it destroyed the bonds of society and caused dissension

among the people of Israel and, two, the wrong of any member of God's chosen people could easily bring divine wrath down upon the entire nation. National rectitude was essential to the survival of a culture so closely tied to their jealous and all knowing deity.[5] (p. 23–24)

In contrast, the citizens of Athens, while not disregarding the potential threat of retribution from the gods, were more concerned with the threat coming from a temporal tyrant. Democracy was seen as the key to prosperity for them, and their criminal justice would reflect it.

The Roman theory was one "founded upon the concept of the citizen soldier as the key to Roman dominance in the world."[5] (p. 24) The system of criminal justice they founded was geared to protecting the Roman citizen "from unjust prosecution" and also to give that citizen "a clear understanding of his rights and responsibilities to the state."[5] (p. 24)

These philosophies were reflected in the different treatments the cultures gave to the crime of homicide.

The Israelis of biblical times differed from what Professor Johnson calls the pattern of other near eastern civilizations. That pattern simply permitted a murderer or his family to pay compensation to the family of the deceased victim given that, in such primitive societies, manpower was scarce.[12] (p. 24) The law of the Israelis demanded that the one who killed should be put to death, a principle that derived from the:

> theological connection between the blood of the victim and the spirit of God. Yahweh was believed to possess the blood of a man, which in turn contained the spirit given to the individual by the creator. In shedding human blood, a murderer took what rightfully belonged to Yahweh, and only his death and the shedding of his blood was adequate compensation.[5] (p. 24)

Athenian law made the punishment for homicide, whether it was an intentional or unintentional killing, expulsion from Athens and its surrounding countryside.[5] (p. 24) A killer returning from exile would be tried at a seaside location, or a special court would hear the evidence of his guilt from a boat anchored off shore, with the potential punishment either being a re-imposition of exile or death.

The Romans provided for death as the penalty for intentional homicide and, according to Professor Johnson, "life was held more cheaply in Roman society" than in Athens. This was so even for Roman citizens.

A critical feature of Roman law was the law found in the Twelve Tables, stone tablets that, while not intended as a complete recitation of Roman law, set forth much of its principles in systematic ways.[6] The Twelve Tables made law less mystical, not derived from revelation, but more the product of the Roman citizenry itself. It was publicly stated and more accessible as a guide for the average citizen's course of conduct.[7]

Wilson's treatise argues in large measure that the adventurer (the pirate) of early history typified a mindset that remained in various manifestations for centuries, and was largely unchecked by penal systems developed over time. He tracks the history of England as one in which organized criminal conduct (through the medium of gangs of robbers) was hardly uncommon, even leading to circumstances in the years 1347 and 1348 in which the city of Bristol was taken over by a brigand who, at the same time robbing ships in the harbor, issued his own edicts as if he were a conquering ruler.[7] (p. 24)

Even in the Victorian age, Wilson indicates that things did not become markedly more genteel:

> What is so hard for us to grasp is that the whole of society, from top to bottom, operated upon principles that would seem ferociously cruel to a modern citizen of the western world. Our present concern for children and animals would have struck an early Victorian as ludicrous, while Dr. Johnson would simply have condemned it as a dangerous sentimentality.[7] (p. 164)

But things had to change. Pirates and rogues were hardly the stuff of nation-states or the components of sound economic order. Advancements in trade, science, and communications could not flourish where simple life tasks exposed innocent people to the oppression of the brigand. The chronicle of human history, which is a chronicle that runs parallel with the history of systematic and organized violence of one person against another, took a turn, according to Colin Wilson, when it simply became intolerable for such lawlessness to be the order of the day in the face of the rise of great nations seeking to impose their own brand of order on themselves and others.

> Society became more stable because it *had* to become more stable. The old chaos could no longer be tolerated in this world of increasingly powerful nation: the England of Cromwell, the France of Loues XIV, the Spain of Charles II, the Prussia of Frederick William-and later of Frederick the Great, the Russia of Peter the Great, the Sweden of Charles the XII, these changes were reflected in English Puritanism, in German Lutheranism, in French Protestantism-with its roots in Calvinism ... society *had* to learn to become more orderly.[4] (p. 423–24)

The order that society needed to be imposed would not, however, come from a new and even more powerful central tyrannical ruler. Rather, it would come from a source of power largely overlooked in the history of human kind to that point: the common man. Wilson writes:

> When we look over the past eight thousand years, it is clear that the most irritating characteristic of human beings is their passivity. The mass of people accept whatever happens to them as cows accept the rain. It is true even of the great rulers and generals; we have seen how, again and again, they achieve some triumph, relax for a brief period, then begin to feel oddly bored and dissatisfied, and look around for fresh adventures. There is no evidence that Alexander the Greek really wept when he had no more worlds to conquer; but whoever invented the story had a profound understanding of human psychology. So for more than 7000 years of civilized history, the human urge to escape boredom found its way into armed aggression, while the common people huddled together and waited for the storm to pass over. Then came the crusades, which taught the upper classes of Europe that the world was not quite static after all. Luther's revolt against the Catholic Church taught the common people the same wisdom. Then a series of catastrophes — like the Thirty Years War, the war of the Spanish succession, the wars of Frederick

the Great — made Europe aware that it ought to be looking actively for peace, while the rise of science and industry showed the world that there were interesting alternatives to *war*. The old cow-like spirit was vanishing. The British civil war under Cromwell and the French revolution taught the common people that they could also influence the course of history.[4] (p. 441–42).

This lesson was not lost upon the people of America. They drew upon the philosophy of the time (the Enlightenment) to fashion for themselves a political system that was not only meant to serve the needs of the "common man," but derived its legitimacy from him.

The Enlightenment was a philosophical period which drew its strength from scientific method and the elevation of the rule of reason. Men such as John Locke and the French writer Montesquieu embraced a concept of secular humanism that rejected the notion that governments, like religion, derived their authority from a divine source. Instead, they argued that the legitimacy of the government was based upon its ability to fulfill the needs of the society which created it through reason and analytical thought.[5] (p. 115–16)

Reason was a capacity possessed by more than just members of a royal family. Reason dictated that power began with the individuals through whose consent a legitimate government would take form. The statement in the preamble of the U.S. Constitution "We the People" is not a matter of poetic elegance; rather, it is a clear expression of the Enlightenment theory that the federal government being created (like the state governments then in existence) based its legitimacy upon the fact that the governed had consented to the creation of a collective agency that would perform for them certain tasks they could not do individually.[5] (p. 140–41)

The individuals who created the government did so with a specific purpose in mind. Because the government was not to be given the free reign that it would have if it ruled by divine right, it was necessary for those same individuals to build into the structure of the government such checks on its power that the government, once created, would not become a Frankenstein-like monster that would enslave the people whose consent created it.

American writers and thinkers embraced this concept in both establishing the Constitution of the United States and in setting down the basic rules of the administration of a criminal justice system that still affects us today.

Like the ancient systems we have noted, it is impossible to understand the parameters of our system without understanding its basic philosophy. That philosophy is derived from the thinking of the Enlightenment and places at its core the importance of individual sovereignty and liberty, seeing government as a tool created by the individual and, ultimately, limited by the individual's capability to withdraw or alter the nature of their consent.

The Philosophical Basis of the American Criminal Justice System

In a prior work, I have written extensively on the thinking that underlies the forming of our government.[8] In a short summary, the U.S. political system has as the basis of its political faith "the doctrine of the sovereignty of the people."[9] David Jayne Hill has written that:

> the one original idea in the American Constitution was the conception of liberty as a strictly personal prerogative to be secured by fundamental public law. I say as a *personal* prerogative, because liberty had previously been regarded as something belonging to the people in the mass, as a trophy extorted from royalty; but the American conception was that liberty is something inherent in each individual as moral personalities; not a concession made to the people by a government.[10]

With the individual at the center of a political universe, the authors of the federal Constitution constructed a system which is a most inefficient form of government. This inefficiency is the product of the doctrine of separation of powers, which divides federal authority among a legislature, an executive, and an independent judiciary, and the doctrine of federalism, which recognizes the independent sovereignty of states and the federal government and the fact that they will, at times, compete with each other for the exercise of political power. Together, these produce a far less effective government than one which features a single monarch wielding absolute power.

But this quite inefficient way to govern people was also a quite intended effort on the part of the Framers of the Constitution to allow for the government to do that which the people consented it to do, and not become so empowered that it would turn around on the people who created it and take from them the liberty in a variety of areas they had withheld in their original grant of power.[11]

Layered on top of the structural protections of liberty found in separation of powers and federalism were the protections specifically spelled out in the Bill of Rights. While the Federalist party at the time felt that a specific guarantee of liberties was not necessary, given the structural protections of liberty found in the Constitution itself, the Antifederalists, particularly Thomas Jefferson, argued that the explicit protection of liberties was necessary since the machine created in the Constitution might, in operation, occasionally produce outcomes violative of the basic rights of individuals and, as such, a greater hedge against those accesses would be necessary. (*supra* note 8 at 29, footnote 81).

But it is not only the Bill of Rights to which we may look for protection from the government. It is the entire Constitution that speaks of the primacy of individual rights and the limit on collective authority.

The excursion into the political theory behind the creation of the American government is far more than a historical or academic exercise. No serious student of the criminal justice system of the United States can appreciate any of its key features without understanding that it springs from a government based upon a fundamental theory that individual rights and liberties are the paramount concern of this political system. Government is, indeed, best which does only what the collective group of individuals, by their consent, have deemed that it should do. As government does not proceed from the will of a supreme being but proceeds from the body of the people, it does not have an ecclesiastical mandate to do whatever it thinks is right. It is to act in defined terms and in confined ways to achieve those specific goals that the Constitution, as the first and greatest product of democracy, has deemed it should do.

This will mean that the catching of criminals and their incarceration is not the only or ultimate goal of the Criminal Justice System. Rather, the ultimate goal of the criminal justice system in the universe governed by our Constitution is to do justice. Justice comes, we believe, by adherence to a set of procedures that we have deemed appropriate to interdict and punish a certain spectrum of criminal activity without, at the same time, so unduly restricting the freedom of individuals that citizens will live in a society free of crime but not free in any other sense. The manifestations of this philosophy are seen throughout our system today.

The Need for Clearly Defined Criminal Laws

Blackstone, writing in the 1750s, expressed the view that legitimacy in the criminal law occurred when the individual transferred from himself the sovereign power to impose punishment on others for wrongs committed against him. This led to a system that the criminal himself had to respect because it was "founded upon the principle that the law by which they suffer was made by their own consent; it was part of the original contract into which they entered, when they first engaged in society; it was calculated for, and had long contributed to their own security."[12] This meant that the government had "exactly the same power, and no more, over its members, as each individual member had naturally over himself or others."[12] To insure this limitation, when that government passed laws making certain acts criminal, it was required to be precise so that penalties would not be uncertain and arbitrary[12] (*supra* note 12, Book IV, Section 3, Chapter 1). The whole method of passing laws, and affixing precise punishments to them, was to be very rational, almost scientific, and drawn with a clear eye that the lawgiver was not speaking from a position of divine authority. It was vintage Enlightenment philosophy.[13]

In America, a fundamental principle of the protections of due process of law contained both in the Fifth and Fourteenth Amendments to the U.S. Constitution is that statutes neither be vague nor so broad that in their sweep they prohibit constitutionally protected activity as well as acts that society can punish.[14] In actuality, the requirement that laws be precisely drawn fulfills three separate constitutional principles, all of which flow from the overriding principle of the supremacy of individual liberty.

First, a law which is unclear does not give the individual proper notice and ability to conform their conduct to the legitimate requirements of the law. Individuals have the right to know when the collective entity of which they are a part has drawn a line over which they have consented not to cross.

Second, laws that allow for the almost unlimited discretionary application by members of the executive branch (the police) allow that executive branch officer to "make a law" and not just "execute" the law. Under a system of separation of powers, it is the legislature that makes laws. To so change the system that the executive is now the entity that creates restrictions it then enforces is to violate that bedrock principle that limits government in the first place.

Finally, where laws allow Courts and executive branch officers too broad a discretion to apply them, those officials may well take into account invidious criteria for their application (such as race, gender, or other prohibited categories) and invite violations of the equal protection clause of the Fourteenth Amendment.

Another manifestation of the need for precision in the writing and the administration of criminal laws is contained in a series of U.S. Supreme Court cases beginning in 1995 and continuing through the present day. In what has become known as the *Apprendi* line of cases, named after *Apprendi vs. New Jersey*,[15] the Supreme Court of the United States has held that any aspect of a criminal law (other than a person's history of prior convictions) that would operate to increase the maximum penalty affixed by the legislature is an element of the crime that must be proven to a jury beyond a reasonable doubt or be the subject of the defendant's specific plea of guilty before such additional punishment can be meted out.[16]

All of these principles requiring precision demonstrate that the government is not free to simply imprison people because of a generic sense that they are "bad" or that they somehow deserve moral sanction. Rather, the governed have given their consent to the imposition of criminal laws only when the governing body draws those laws with precision, dictates various elements to be proven, and lets the persons against whom the laws that are being enforced know exactly where the line is that they must not cross.

The Jury Trial

Once the legislative body has adequately defined the crime, the final determination as to whether the crime was committed is turned over, not to a body of governmental officials, but to a committee of the governed: the jury.

Even before enactment of the Constitution, the jury trial had become an important protection from false accusations of crime for colonial Americans. A great deal of faith was placed in the common law jury as a means of providing this important protection of liberty.[5] (p. 132)

Indeed, down through time, writers of great documents setting forth the rights of individuals have consistently included the right to trial by jury in all such compilations. The right to trial by jury can, indeed, be found in every document significant to the notion of American independence and justice. It finds voice in the Magna Carta, Declaration of Independence, all of the state Constitutions that were enacted between 1776 and 1786 (in fact, it was the only right common to all such documents), and the body of the Constitution of the United States where it is found in Article III and three of the Bill of Rights (the Fifth Amendment by way of the Grand Jury, Sixth Amendment for juries in criminal cases, and Seventh Amendment for juries in civil cases) (*supra* note 8, and authorities noted therein).

This institution that Alexander Hamilton called "the very palladium of free government"[17] was and is far more than just a personal right of a defendant facing trial. It is, moreover, a part of the very structure of the governmental system itself. The jury represents the recognition on the part of the Framers that control of the government by a mere wish or hope is not likely to produce a government effectively limited enough to not infringe upon the rights and dignities of the individual.

Rather, there are times when a committee of the governed, from whose consent the basic legitimacy of government arises, must assemble to authorize the creature they have made to exercise power that is on the frontier of the grant of authority we have given to the many to rule over the one.

In a criminal case, the accused faces a charge crafted by the legislature, prosecuted by the executive, and administered over by the courts. The individual is arrayed against a three-headed governmental entity and faces either the loss of life or liberty at the hands of so formidable an opponent. Into this mix is interjected a group of citizens to sit in judgment of the individual. It sits to protect his individual liberties and to make a committee of the people a part of the governmental process, reminding the governmental players that, on occasion, they must go back to the governed for approval for certain ominous actions they otherwise intend to take.[8] (p. 28–31)

Although we often see courts as the ultimate entity for the protection of personal freedom, the traditions surrounding the jury trial do not hold the courts in such an elevated position. Historically, writers viewed the judiciary as simply a branch of the executive, not to be trusted with respect to providing a buffer between the individual and the whims of the executive branch (*supra* note 8, footnote 83). Grand Juries, for example, were impaneled to specifically interpose a group of citizens between the executive branch officers and the person under investigation, with no reliance being placed on the Court itself to filter out the frivolous charge (*supra* note 8, footnote 84).

Professor Amar has drawn parallels between the jury and militia, with the militia operating as a check on paid professional armies and juries operating to "thwart overreaching by powerful and ambitious government officers."[18]

In essence, juries manifest direct democracy.[8] (p. 34) They are an extremely inefficient method of determining the truth, but efficiency is not a goal given the preeminence of all others. A jury trial system is *meant* to be "inefficient" when compared with other systems of finding facts, and it is inefficient for the reason that through its deliberative process, the state is put to its proof in a way that limits its ability to disregard individual liberties in the name of law enforcement. Although jury trials in America are the exception and not the rule (*supra* note 8, footnote 102), the place of the jury is a reflection of the underlying philosophy of a criminal justice system that believes that outcomes determined by an omnipotent government are, by definition, unjust.

The Presumption of Innocence and Proof beyond a Reasonable Doubt

Consistent with the overall philosophy of our system, the government faces the hurdle of having to prove the guilt of an accused to a nongovernmental body (a jury), and the government must do so to the highest standard known to the law: proof beyond a reasonable doubt. The U.S. Supreme Court has repeatedly held that it is a fundamental requirement of due process of law that a person cannot be convicted of a crime unless the jury is convinced that the government has proven each of the elements of that offense beyond a reasonable doubt.[19]

The specifics of this requirement have however, never been completely spelled out. The Supreme Court has held that proof beyond a reasonable doubt is something that can be expressed in a variety of ways, as long as the jury is made to clearly understand that each juror must come "to reach a subjective state of near certitude of the guilt of the accused."[20]

Defining this concept in terms understandable by a group of nonlawyers and judges, however, is no easy task. One Court, guilty perhaps of one of the great understatements of all time, discussed the difficulties of defining "reasonable doubt" in this way:

> Reasonable doubt is not an easy concept to understand and it is all the more difficult to explain. Moreover, given the concerns about crime that are so prevalent in today's society, common sense suggests that it is particularly difficult for lay jurors to understand that they must acquit a criminal defendant if the

> prosecution does not establish guilt beyond a reasonable doubt, even if they feel that the defendant is probably guilty. Jurors may well be reluctant to free someone accused of a serious and violent crime "merely" because the government didn't prove beyond reasonable doubt what they feel "in their hearts" is probably true. Yet, due process is satisfied by nothing less than a juror's understanding that he or she may not vote to convict a defendant based upon a mere belief "that the defendant is probably guilty."[21]

Leaving the concept undefined risks, at best, draining it of the meaning the Constitution imparts to it and, at worst, allowing it to be manipulated into a perversion of the system the Constitution would forbid. The task of defining proof beyond a reasonable doubt is aided by the recognition that it is not the product of recent scientific discovery but is a matter rich in the history of our law.

The history of the reasonable doubt instruction underscores both the difficulties in defining it and the importance it holds in the criminal system.[22] Part of that history requires an appreciation that the concept of proof beyond a reasonable doubt is inextricably intertwined with the equally ancient yet continually vital concept that any system based on Enlightenment theory would, and has, embraced: that persons accused of crime must be presumed innocent. As the Supreme Court has held:

> The reasonable doubt standard plays a vital role in the American scheme of criminal procedure. It is a prime instrument for reducing the risk of convictions resting on factual error. The standard provides concrete substance for the presumption of innocence — that bedrock "axiomatic and elementary" principle whose "enforcement lies at the foundation of the administrative of our criminal law."[23]

It is, indeed, impossible to speak about the reasonable doubt standard without also speaking about the presumption of innocence. The Court, in *Coffin vs. United States*, traced that concept back to the Book of Deuteronomy, the laws of ancient Sparta and Athens, and through the formative stages of English common law.[24] Professor Sheppard, in an excellent historical piece, traces the origin of the reasonable doubt standard effectively to periods in the 17th and 18th centuries, and finds its first important formulation in the three categories of knowledge philosophers of the day had identified.[25]

Those categories of knowledge were physical knowledge, that which a person learns from the information immediately supplied by the senses; mathematical knowledge, facts that are susceptible of the precise proofs of geometry and the other "hard" sciences; and, finally, moral knowledge, that which is derived from testimony and second hand reports of other data.

Although this third category of knowledge was not based on immediate sensory impressions, and although it could not call upon immutable laws of the universe for confirmation, Professor Shapiro has indicated that moral knowledge was still susceptible of "moral certainty." Such certainty, ascertainable in areas of history, law, and many of the natural sciences, was predicated upon the belief that certain types of things were knowable to the degree that "no one without a prejudice would dissent from it."[25] (p. 7–8) Put another way, knowing something to a moral certainty would be to know it to an extent that no reasonable person could doubt its existence.

While the phraseology of this test would eventually evolve into a question of whether the evidence was sufficient to satisfy the juror's conscience as to the defendant's guilt,[26] (pp. 7–8) the reasonable doubt concept was one founded on the transposition of the "moral certainty" concept of philosophers into a standard of proof for lawyers and juries. The standard, while clearly not requiring geometric precision, was nonetheless rigorous, that is, as rigorous as matters based upon human testimony could be. In this realm, while mathematical certainty was not possible,

> ... we ought not to treat everything as merely a guess or a matter of opinion. Instead, in this realm there are levels of certainty, and we reach higher levels of certainty as the quantity and quality of the evidence available to us increases. The highest level of certainty in this empirical realm in which no absolute certainty is possible is what traditionally was called "moral certainty," a certainty there was no reason to doubt.[27]

The standard of proof beyond a reasonable doubt sprung from a fundamental desire to describe a state of certainty about the existence of past events that a reasonable person would feel having properly assessed all the evidence. As with any state of certainty, part of describing where you are now is to chart the path from whence you came. In the criminal field, the starting point for any juror's path must be the presumption of innocence. The state of believing that there is now proof beyond a reasonable doubt is a state to which one may come only having been moved there by compelling evidence that reason cannot ignore. That movement is through a continuum that ranges from the presumption of innocence, past suspicion, past preponderance, and, finally, to that state of "near certitude" the Constitution requires.

Although reasonable doubt instructions found their way into some of the earliest trials in the Americas,[25] (p. 24) one of the more influential instructions on reasonable doubt appeared in *Commonwealth vs. Webster*.[28] Chief Justice Shaw of the Massachusetts Supreme Judicial Court gave the following explanation of the concept of reasonable doubt:

> What is reasonable doubt? It is a term often used, probably pretty well understood, but not easily defined. It is not mere possible doubt; because everything relating to human affairs, and depending on moral evidence, is open to some possible or imaginary doubt. It is that state of the case, which, after the entire comparison and consideration of all the evidence, leaves the minds of jurors in that condition that they cannot say they feel an abiding conviction, to a moral certainty, of the truth of the charge. The burden of proof is upon the prosecutor. All the presumptions of law independent of evidence are in favor of innocence; and every person is presumed to be innocent until he is proved guilty. If upon such proof there is reasonable doubt remaining, the accused is entitled to the benefit of it by an acquittal. For it is not sufficient to establish a probability, though a strong one arising from the doctrine of chances, that the fact charged is more likely to be true than the contrary; but the evidence must establish the truth of the fact to a reasonable and moral certainty; a certainty that convinces and directs the understanding, and satisfies the reason and judgment, of those who are bound to act conscientiously upon it. This we take to be proof beyond reasonable doubt.

This instruction is much in the mode of trying to describe a state of certainty, a "state of the case...which...leaves the minds of the jurors" in the condition the Court sought to describe. The problem is, however, as scholars have noted, that gradually and without overt rejection of the original notion, the law began to view the matter not as defining the state of believing a fact proven beyond a reasonable doubt, but as one defining a reasonable doubt as if it were a tangible object bouncing about a courtroom. The change in approach was substantive and ominous, since by defining it as a thing, the question became whether there was a reasonable doubt in the case, a question that inevitably shifted the burden to the defendant to put one there. Such a shift seriously threatened the meaning of the presumption of innocence.

As the U.S. Supreme Court would say almost 120 years later in *In re: Winship*, reasonable doubt and the presumption of innocence are wholly intertwined concepts.[29] To evolve language about reasonable doubt from its original conception as proof to a "moral certainty" did not just affect reasonable doubt: it threatened a reversal of the presumption of innocence.

Professor Sheppard has argued that, from the beginning, the controversy over the reasonable doubt standard has revolved around four questions:

1. What is the role of the juror, that is, how much independence should they exercise in reaching a verdict?
2. How should the juror go about analyzing the problem of reaching a verdict?
3. To what degree must the juror be convinced in order to convict?
4. What language can best express the resolution of these three concepts.[25] (p. 1169)

His conclusion about the history and current state of these issues is troubling:

> Despite its later prominence as a shield against wrongful conviction, the instruction was not devised to protect more fully the innocent. Rather it was pursued as a means of more easily convicting the accused. Toward this end, a fundamental purpose of the instruction was to constrain the juror, to prevent the juror from acting with excessive independence in determining innocence. From such dark beginnings, the manner in which these ends have been pursued has been accelerated in the light of cultural and linguistic shifts, marked especially by changes in understanding the nature and meaning of "reason." The instruction has moved from a standard incorporating three elements — a form of non-metaphysical consideration, a form of moral reasoning, and a measure of sufficiency in the evidence — to being only a standard of sufficiency. As a result of these changes, the legal consequences of the instruction have changed. Over time, the burden upon the juror who would acquit has grown, and so the evidence necessary for the state to convict has lessened. This change in the burden of proof has profound implications for the prosecutor's burden of persuasion. The new understanding of reasonable doubt can reverse the operation of the presumption of innocence.[25]

This reversal, with its serious implications for a system that has civil liberties as its central article of faith, has been occasioned by an erosion of the idea that a conviction required the prosecution to leave a juror in a state of overall satisfaction about guilt (i.e., a feeling that it would simply not be reasonable to doubt the conclusion of guilt based on the evidence), to one that required the juror to articulate what specific reason he or she had to doubt the finding of guilt sought by the state. Such a shift would, in many ways, place the burden on a defendant to "put a reasonable doubt" into the case, or, at least, specifically point one out to the jury.

Once courts began to try to define reasonable doubt as a thing, instead of telling a jury how it ought to feel if the prosecution had proven its case to them to a degree of certainty captured by the phrase "beyond a reasonable doubt," the role of the juror changed, and not necessarily for the better:

> Over time, the loss of our understanding of moral certainty and the increasing acceptance of articulability as a basis for reasonableness underscored a great shift in thinking about judgment by a juror. The courts have moved the jurors' goal from a vote for the state if the state can convince them of a fact to a vote for the state unless the defense can convince them of a certain type of doubt. This shift highlights two fundamental concerns regarding the role of the juror, and our beliefs about that role.[25] (p. 1239)

This change threatens the presumption of innocence because, for a juror to acquit where reasonable doubt is defined as a thing that cannot be in a case where conviction results, the juror "would seem to be obliged to say precisely what the doubt with the state's case is and why it is reasonable. A mere declaration that the juror is not convinced does not seem enough; it lacks the specificity suggested."[25] As the state is not obligated to articulate or prove such a doubt, a natural shift of the burden to a defendant in that regard would be inevitable.[30]

It does not have to be thus. The process of a trial should be seen, in simplest terms, as the effort on the part of the prosecution to change the juror's mind. The juror must begin believing that the defendant is innocent, that is, as the law sees him. To presume someone innocent does not mean just to pretend that we think he is innocent; we must hold it as an article of civil faith. If, however, through the presentation of lawful and credible evidence, the state is able to change the jurors' minds and convince them that their initial belief in the defendant is wrong to the degree that reason does permit any feeling of doubt as to the matter, then a conviction should follow.[31]

The current state of instructions on reasonable doubt in many jurisdictions, however, does not do this and has earned much criticism. One author has gathered extensive evidence in this regard. First, the standard of proof beyond a reasonable doubt is not self-explanatory, and juries, left unguided as to its meaning, apply an enormously wide range of understandings of this critical principle in a way that will undoubtedly affect the verdict.[32] Moreover, judges and jurors have very different ideas as to what the standard of proof beyond a reasonable doubt means, and even within the community of judges, there is a considerable range of debate as to how certain an individual ought to be before they feel that the proof is beyond a reasonable doubt.[32] (p. 5–6)

Again, from the *Victor* Court and others, all that the Supreme Court has said is that the language must reflect to the jury that they must have a subjective state of near certitude of guilt before a conviction may be had, but misunderstandings on a jury's part about this standard have undoubtedly led to defendants being erroneously convicted under a standard of proof that is far less than what due process would otherwise require.[32] (p. 6–7)

Various Courts use different formulations.[33] A very common formulation is to analogize the level of proof beyond a reasonable doubt to the level at which a person would feel able to act without hesitancy in a matter of importance in their own lives. Although some have criticized this standard as being too subjective to the individual juror,[32] (p. 12–13) it does recast the focus of the inquiry from a reasonable doubt *as a thing* to prove beyond a reasonable doubt *as producing a state of certainty.* It also provides at least some guidance to jurors in fixing upon an idea that conveys the critical importance of an overall sense of near certitude, rather than one that converts "proof beyond a reasonable doubt" to "absence of a specific reason to doubt."

For present purposes, it is critical to understand that our system, by embracing the presumption of innocence and reasonable doubt as core principles, has made a thoughtful decision that the government's power to imprison people for crimes that the government believes they have committed must be limited. Altering that standard does more than just make it easier to imprison or execute just one more alleged miscreant. It speaks unfaithfully of the overall conception of the government our Constitution promised us.

Other Aspects of the American System Influenced by the Philosophy of the Enlightenment

The philosophy of the American political system of elevating the rights of the individual and limiting government to the performance of certain and specific tasks spelled out in the Constitution is also demonstrated in a variety of other procedural rights that the American criminal justice system has embraced.

Although the investigatory system of justice described by Professor Shapiro as the Romano-Canon inquisition process put great evidentiary weight upon a confession and, accordingly, authorized (if not encouraged) torture to get one,[25] (p. 118–119) the Fifth Amendment to the U.S. Constitution provides that individuals may not be compelled to give testimony against themselves. Confessions are traditionally a key element of proof in a case, but the police tactics of obtaining one are curtailed. The Courts have held that interrogation of a suspect while in custody threatens the protection of the Fifth Amendment, since officers may well either use tactics to coerce the statement, or simply expose the suspect to dangers that the Courts have called "inherently coercive" in that environment.[34] *Miranda* warnings[35] are required whenever an individual is in police custody and the police seek to question them, but their invocation is not a talisman that, once having been announced, gives the police the right to conduct an interrogation. Rather, the individual who receives these warnings must knowingly, intelligently, and voluntarily waive their rights before a statement can be admitted.

The efforts of law enforcement to get a suspect to talk to them are also quite certainly thwarted by the presence of a lawyer whose ethical duty is to protect the suspect against conviction. For many years, the U.S. Supreme Court has recognized that the Sixth Amendment to the U.S. Constitution and, ultimately, the Fourteenth Amendment as well, require that an accused in a criminal proceeding be afforded the right to counsel.[36] As the Court held in *Gideon*:

> Governments, both state and federal, quite properly spend vast sums of money to establish machinery to try defendants accused of crime. Lawyers to prosecute are everywhere deemed essential to protect the public's interest in an orderly

society. Similarly, there are few defendants charged with crime, few indeed, who fail to hire the best lawyers they can get to prepare and present their defenses. That government hires lawyers to prosecute and defendants who have the money hire lawyers to defend are the strongest indications of the widespread belief that lawyers in criminal courts are necessities, not luxuries. The right of one charged with crime to counsel may not be deemed fundamental and essential to fair trials in some countries, but it is in ours. From the very beginning, our state and national constitutions and laws have laid great emphasis on procedural and substantive safeguards designed to assure fair trials before impartial tribunals in which every defendant stands equal before the law. This noble ideal cannot be realized if the poor man charged with crime has to face his accusers without a lawyer to assist him.[37]

Criminal defense lawyers, often a ridiculed and despised group, thus perform a function as old and as dignified as the Constitution itself. They do not help the government get convictions, and the Constitution and ethics that bind them as attorneys require that they do not.

These defense lawyers quite often invoke another procedural rule the U.S. Supreme Court has enacted to enforce the provisions of the Fourth Amendment and serve the ancient purposes of the philosophy of the limited government that pervades the nation.

Where evidence is seized in violation of the Fourth Amendment to the U.S. Constitution, it is to be excluded regardless of whether the trial occurs in federal or state courts.[38] Although the rules regarding search and seizure are subject to many exceptions, and although many believe that (particularly in federal court) the protections of the exclusionary rule have been substantially eroded, the rule remains a vital part of the criminal procedure.

It operates to tell the government that it cannot introduce against the defendant otherwise relevant and incriminating evidence that has been seized illegally. If our system was solely concerned with a search for the theoretical "truth," such a rule could never exist. However, since the system serves more complicated goals that involve assuring that the government never, even in the name of law enforcement, grows so big as to suppress freedom and crime in the same breath, the basis of the rule becomes quite understandable.

There are many other rules that limit the ability of the government to obtain a conviction. The rules of evidence, discussed otherwise in this book, place limits on the admission of certain kinds of information in a trial that we otherwise rely upon on a daily basis in our own lives. Another regards a defendant's right to confront the witnesses. The U.S. Supreme Court has steadfastly protected the defendant against the admission of statements of others, including his alleged co-conspirators, where the defendant has not had the chance to crossexamine them.[39]

Although it is common to think of the purposes of a criminal justice system in terms of the traditional goals of sentencing (deterrence, incapacitation, retribution, and rehabilitation),[40] it would be a mistake for a student to believe that those purposes are pursued by the criminal justice system without regard to the means used to achieve them. The system has its goals but, like all systems created in our political society, it reflects a belief that greater purposes are at work that do not make those goals the final measure of success. The system reflects an underlying theory that a limited government is, while certainly inefficient when compared to other options, a safer government to have for people who put their principal emphasis on the freedom of the individual.

Although the ebbs and flows of societal events tend to increase or decrease citizens' fears about internal crime or external terrorism, the philosophy of those who wrote the Constitution, and the words of that fundamental law that remain essentially unchanged since 1789 continue to reflect the philosophy of the Enlightenment. Until and unless a thoughtful decision is made by the nation to abandon that philosophy, and the law that has been promulgated because of it, our criminal justice system will have to deal with the need to accept the fact that efficient means to "fight crime" are often inconsistent with an effort to keep the people more free.

Sources of Criminal Law

Consistent with the need to have criminal laws defined so that the people who consented to their passage may understand them, the sources of criminal law today are the various statutes enacted by each state and the U.S. Government. Those statutes set forth definitions of crimes, defenses, and other aspects of the criminal process in ways courts may apply them when a charge under any particular section is brought against the citizen.

Although state laws vary considerably, many states have adopted as a model for their statutes a work first published in 1962 by a collection of renowned criminal law scholars under the auspices of the American Law Institute. This publication, the Model Penal Code, has been revised and amended a number of times, and it forms a pattern for many of the state laws dealing with a wide variety of crimes. The Model Penal Code itself declares the general purposes of its effort to define a criminal offense as follows:

A. To forbid and prevent conduct that unjustifiably and inexcusably inflicts or threatens substantial harm to individual or public interest
B. To subject to public control persons whose conduct indicates that they are disposed to commit crimes
C. To safeguard conduct that is without fault from condemnation is criminal
D. To give fair warning of the nature of the conduct declared to constitute an offense
E. To differentiate on reasonable grounds between serious and minor offenses.[41]

The Code and actual criminal codes of various jurisdictions define crimes in terms of elements and defenses, and, in part, in terms of relative burdens of proof.

The Supreme Court of the United States has made it clear that any aspect of a criminal offense that would work to increase the potential maximum punishment faced by an individual is an element of the offense that has to be proven by the prosecution beyond a reasonable doubt.[42] An element of the offense cannot be decided by the judge alone and presented to the jury as something they must accept.[43]

In broad terms, the elements of any criminal offense involve some voluntary act and a requisite state of mind with which the act is done. This harkens back to Blackstone's consideration that "as a vicious will without a vicious act is no civil crime, so, on the other hand, an unwarrantable act without a vicious will is no crime at all." (see Blackstone Book IV §21 in *supra* note 7). The Model Penal Code, in Sections 2.01 and 2.02 set forth these requirements, indicating that a person cannot be guilty unless their conduct is based on a voluntary act or omission, and done with purpose, knowledge, recklessness, or criminal negligence.

A useful illustration of these principles may be found in a state law defining homicide.

In the Commonwealth of Pennsylvania, where a person's acts or omissions are the legal cause of a death of another, there are five separate degrees of criminal homicide for which they may be liable.

Murder of the first degree is a criminal homicide committed by an intentional killing, that is, a killing by means of "poison, or by lying in wait, or by any other kind of willful deliberate and premeditated killing."[44]

Murder of the second degree occurs when a criminal homicide is committed while a defendant "was engaged as a principle or an accomplice in the perpetration of a felony."[45] This is the so-called felony murder rule, which holds an individual liable when a homicide is committed by them or their confederate while they are engaged in attempting to commit or fleeing from a robbery, rape, other sexual assault, arson, burglary, or kidnapping.

Murder of the third degree under Pennsylvania law is simply defined as "all other kinds of murder."[46] The distinction between murder and manslaughter in Pennsylvania is the concept of malice, which must be found in each of the three grades of murder in order for the offense to rise to that level.

In first-degree murder, it is the intentional and premeditated nature of the act that supplies malice. In second-degree murder, the malice requirement is supplied by the defendant's commission of a dangerous felony that provides the setting for an innocent person to die. The kinds of murder that would be typified by third-degree murder (and be distinct from the other two) are the types of murder where the individual acts with a willful and wanton disregard that he has created an unjustified and extremely high risk that his conduct will result in death or serious bodily injury to another person. Such an act would be typified, for example, by a person who fired a gun into a crowded bar. Regardless of whether it was his specific intention to kill one of the patrons, such an act could only be perceived as constituting the sort of malicious disregard that would warrant a finding of third-degree murder, at a minimum.[47]

The final two offenses that may constitute criminal homicide under the law of Pennsylvania are voluntary and involuntary manslaughter. These offenses are unjustified killings without malice. A voluntary manslaughter conviction may be obtained where the defendant intentionally takes the life of another but does so under either "a sudden and intense passion resulting from serious provocation" (either by the individual killed or by another person that the defendant tries to kill) but, in the process, accidentally kills another; or, where the defendant kills a person under the belief that his actions are justified by self-defense but, in fact, his belief is unreasonable.[48]

Note that in voluntary manslaughter, the defendant's conduct is as intentional as it is in first-degree murder. The distinguishing feature is that in voluntary manslaughter cases, the defendant's conduct has some element to it (the provocation or the unreasonably mistaken belief) that negates the malice element of murder.

Involuntary manslaughter is a death resulting from the defendant's performance of an unlawful act in a reckless or grossly negligent manner.[49] This does not, however, equate the civil negligence standard to the criminal law. The concept of criminal negligence and recklessness requires a higher degree of culpability for an individual to be guilty of the offense of involuntary manslaughter. The law here endeavors to draw a distinction between a civil wrong compensable to the party damaged by a monetary award and the state's lawful justification in seeking a penalty extracted in terms of months or years of a defendant's life for conduct that crosses the line into the criminal realm.

Federal laws also have specific statutory elements.[50]

One issue regarding federal criminal statutes that comes as a surprise to many jurors and students is the occasionally odd element not otherwise present in a similar offense under state law. The federal statute prohibiting extortion, otherwise known as the Hobbs Act, 18 U.S.C. §1951, for example, makes it a crime for an individual "to obstruct delay or affect interstate commerce" by robbery or extortion. This statute has been applied to prohibit a wide variety of conduct, including violence during a labor dispute,[51] bank robbery,[52] and political corruption.[53] Despite the apparent breadth of this statute, the key element in any prosecution under it is proof of some effect on interstate commerce.

The reason for this is that Congress does not have a general grant of authority to pass whatever criminal laws it likes. Rather, the U.S. Congress must draw its authority for any statute from a Constitutional grant of authority. For the Hobbs Act, this grant is the clause under Article 1, Section 8, that allows the United States to pass laws regulating commerce among the several states. While Hobbs Act prosecutions do not require a devastating effect on commerce,[54] the Supreme Court has indicated at least some willingness to draw a tighter ring around congressional authority to pass laws pursuant to the Commerce Clause.[55] The point is that federal statutes must find a Constitutional "hook" of authority to be valid; a limited government of delegated powers must operate in that way.[56]

Many statutory schemes also define certain defenses that an individual may raise when charged with certain types of crimes. Although a state may not relieve the prosecution from its burden of proving an essential element of a crime beyond a reasonable doubt,[57] a state may Constitutionally place a burden on a defendant to offer certain affirmative defenses that are separate from the elements of the offense itself.[58] Where, for example, insanity is not an element of the crime, the burden may be placed on a defendant.[59] The establishment of other defenses, such as voluntary intoxication, self-defense, and duress, may be placed upon the defendant as well.[60]

An interesting example of this is the defense of entrapment.

Under federal law, once a defendant offers some evidence indicating that the government or one of its operatives induced him to commit a crime when he was not otherwise predisposed to do so, the burden will shift to the government to prove his predisposition beyond a reasonable doubt.[61] In this regard, the defendant may even claim at trial the alternative defenses that he did not commit one or more elements of the crime but that, if he did, he was entrapped to do so; there is no rule in criminal proceedings that a defendant be consistent in his pleading.[62]

By contrast, states such as Pennsylvania have placed the burden of proving entrapment on a defendant. Pursuant to Title 18 Pa.C.S. §313, a defendant bears the burden of proving, to a preponderance of the evidence (i.e., that it is more likely than not) that the government or one of its agents either knowingly made a false representation that was designed to induce his belief that the conduct he engaged in was not prohibited, or that those agents employed some methods of persuasion or inducement that created a substantial risk that a person other than one ready to commit a crime would commit it. In Pennsylvania, the subjective predisposition of the defendant is not an issue. If the defendant proves that the government agents committed acts that would otherwise constitute entrapment, he is entitled to an acquittal, regardless of whether he himself was predisposed to commit the crime.

The Constitution and Criminal Procedure

Obviously, to prove its case against a defendant, the government needs evidence. Besides the testimony of witnesses, the government often seeks, and many times is required by the nature of the case to offer, a wide variety of physical evidence it has obtained during its investigation.

In some cases, the admission of that evidence may be challenged by a defendant who claims that it was obtained in violation of his rights under the Fourth and Fourteenth Amendments to the U.S. Constitution. If the defendant successfully proves that the seizure of that evidence was accomplished by an unexcused violation of his rights under those Amendments, he/she may invoke the exclusionary rule and require that this evidence, although entirely relevant to the prosecution, be excluded from the trial of the case. In many cases, this may cripple or effectively terminate the ability of the state to prosecute.[63]

The exclusionary rule was established in federal courts in 1914 in *Weeks vs. United States*.[64] In *Mapp vs. Ohio*,[65] the Court extended the exclusionary rule via the Fourteenth Amendment to the states. It applies in various circumstances to both the seizure of physical evidence and the obtaining of statements and confessions.

Search and Seizure: The 4th/14th Amendments

Libraries are filled with books that discuss at considerable length and breadth the multitude of issues that arise in a case involving the Constitutional protections against illegal searches and seizures. The scope of the present chapter is wholly insufficient for an in-depth look at this complex issue. What is attempted here, rather, is an effort to provide the student with a structure for thinking about Fourth Amendment issues. No thorough analysis of any Fourth Amendment issue can be done, however, without consultation of a variety of texts that systematically discuss the issue.[66]

Let us consider a framework for the analysis of the Fourth Amendment by asking one overall question: Under what circumstances will the exclusionary rule be invoked to preclude the use of relevant evidence in the trial of the criminal case? Generally, it will be invoked when the following circumstances have been shown to exist.

When the Search/Seizure Has Been Performed by the Government or Persons Acting at the Direction of the Government

The Fourth Amendment is a restriction on the power of the government. The Fourteenth Amendment, which applies the Fourth Amendment to the states, is also a Constitutional protection that interposes itself between a citizen and a government, not between two private citizens. Accordingly, the Fourth/Fourteenth Amendment only applies to searches that are conducted by the government or persons acting in active consort with the government, that is, their agents, whether formal or not.[67]

The Actions of the Government Agent Must Constitute a Search or Seizure

The Fourth Amendment protects the privacy of citizens. Where that privacy has been invaded by the government, a search has occurred. Whether government actions constitute a search for these purposes is determined by whether a citizen has an actual subjective expectation of privacy and whether society is prepared to recognize that expectation as objectively reasonable.[68]

Where a citizen exposes incriminating evidence to the public, where they abandon property, or where they allow the government to search in an area, the expectations of privacy are either not subjectively present or not objectively justifiable; in those circumstances, the government agents have not conducted a search and those items they have seized are not subject to suppression.[69]

Garbage left out for collection at a curb, for example, may be seized under the Fourth Amendment as there is no legitimate expectation of privacy in it once it is put out there.[70] Where a person leaves incriminating evidence in their dining room with the blinds open and the room is visible from the public area near the street, their expectation of privacy and the officer's observation of that incriminating evidence is not subject to Fourth Amendment scrutiny.[71] However, in *Kyllo vs. United States*,[72] the Court held there was a legitimate expectation of privacy in the interior of the home, where, to get incriminating evidence about the defendant's activities in the home, a government official had to use a thermal imaging device to detect heat emanating from it.

The Search Must Violate the Privacy Interests of the Person Who Seeks Its Suppression

Just as the Fourth Amendment protects a citizen only against the actions of the government, only the citizen whose rights have been violated may obtain the relief of the exclusionary rule. Regardless of the degree to which a search may violate the Fourth Amendment, unless a defendant shows that he has "standing" to challenge the search, the evidence obtained as a result of it will come in against him. A defendant cannot invoke a violation of the Constitutional rights of someone else as part of his exclusionary rule argument.

Standing is conferred where a defendant has both a subjective expectation of privacy in the area searched or the items seized, and where society recognizes that expectation is reasonable.[73]

The Search Must Neither Be Supported by a Valid Warrant nor Be Justified under an Accepted Exception to the Warrant Requirement

The Requirements of a Valid Search Warrant

The Fourth Amendment reads as follows:

> The right of the people to be secure in their persons, houses, papers and effects against unreasonable searches and seizures shall not be violated, and no Warrant shall issue, but upon probable cause, supported by oath or affirmation, and particularly describing the place to be searched, and persons or things to be seized.

The U.S. Supreme Court has interpreted the Fourth Amendment to stand for the proposition that searches without a warrant are *"per se* unreasonable," and may be valid only under a few specifically defined exceptions.[74] Thus, when a search has been accomplished by the government, the first question is whether a validly issued warrant has supported it.

The requirements of a proper warrant are that a neutral and detached magistrate (i.e., an impartial member of the judicial branch) must have assessed a showing by the police (made through a sworn affidavit) that establishes probable cause to believe that in a specifically described place specifically delineated things which are an evidence of a crime will be found.[75]

The affidavit, or other sworn testimony that the judicial officer is to review, must establish probable cause, which has been defined as a fair probability that contraband or evidence of a crime will be found in a particular place.[76] Probable cause may be based upon the personal knowledge of the officer, facts or circumstances supplied by other officers, or by any information for which the police can supply the magistrate with information to establish that it is reasonably trustworthy. Overall, the evidence must be such as to permit a belief by a prudent person that an offense has been committed and that evidence of it will be found in the place to be searched.[77]

The judicial officer is required to consider the affidavit of the policeman in a practical and common sense manner, but must make an independent assessment as to whether probable cause exists; he must not simply take the officer's opinion to substitute for facts.[78] The information supplied by the officer must establish probable cause to believe that evidence of the crime will be found *at the time* the warrant is executed; this means that the information contained in the affidavit must not be stale.[79] The nature of the items searched for is an important consideration in determining whether the evidence is stale. Although it may not be reasonable to believe that a small amount of drugs will still be in a place when the latest information about its whereabouts is several weeks old, the presence of body parts or blood residue may indicate that information otherwise slightly out dated can still be relied upon for a finding of probable cause.

The final consideration regarding warrants is that they must be particular in two respects: First, the warrant must particularly describe the place to be searched so that it does not become a general authorization that allows the police to search wherever they please.[80] A warrant becomes particular enough where the executing officers are able, with a reasonable effort, to ascertain and identify the place that is intended.[81]

Second, the warrant must be particular in describing the things to be seized and in limiting the discretion of the officer on the scene; otherwise, the actual decision as to what is to be seized will be made by an executive branch officer and not a member of the judiciary, as the Fourth Amendment requires.[82]

Where a warrant has been issued, an attack on it may either allege that the warrant was insufficiently particular as to the place to be searched or things to be seized, or that the affidavit contained an insufficient showing of probable cause. Deference will be paid to the magistrate's determination in this regard, however, and it is often necessary for a defendant to mount a challenge that various information within the warrant was false and that, with that evidence excised, the affidavit would be insufficient.

The defendant bears the burden of proving that material information contained in the affidavit was false and included there knowingly or with reckless disregard for the truth.[83] Mere innocent mistakes in an affidavit or, for that matter, in the warrant itself, will not necessarily lead to the suppression of evidence obtained as a result of its execution.

In *United States vs. Leon*,[84] the Supreme Court held that even where the affidavit was subsequently found to have insufficient evidence to support probable cause, if the officers were found to have acted in good faith reliance that the warrant was proper, the exclusionary rule remedy will not be applied.[85] This, according to the Supreme Court, is because the exclusionary rule's deterrent effect against police misconduct would have no real effect in a case where the officers acted in good faith.

However, where the police do not have reasonable grounds for believing that they are relying on a valid warrant, such as:

- Where the affidavit filed in support of it contains intentionally or recklessly false information;
- Where the issuing authority does not act in a neutral and detached manner;
- Where the probable cause is so completely deficient that no reasonable officer could have believed that a valid warrant could be issued on that basis; or
- Where the warrant was in some other way so facially deficient that no officer could possibly have believed it was valid;

the good faith exception will not apply.[86]

Finally, the general Fourth Amendment requirement of reasonableness extends to the manner in which the police execute the warrant. Generally, police have to comply with the so-called "knock and announce" requirements, with the officers announcing their authority and purpose before entering so that the resident may have a reasonable opportunity to surrender the premises without the necessity of a forcible entry.[87] The Supreme Court has held that, while the knock and announce principle is inherent within the Fourth Amendment requirements, Courts must analyze on a case-by-case basis whether the information known to the officer at the time of the execution of the warrant justifies the officer in foregoing the knock and announcing his entry in favor of a quick and decisive incursion, or in assessing how long the officers must wait after knocking before forcing entry.[88] However, the knock and announce requirement may not be the subject of a generic exception in a class of cases where, for example, the police are engaged in a felony drug investigation.[89]

Another issue that regards the execution of a warrant is the propriety of the detention of occupants during the search. Generally, the Supreme Court has permitted such detention and reasonable force that may be required under the circumstances to effectuate it.[90]

Some Common Exceptions to the Warrant Requirement

The U.S. Supreme Court has identified a variety of circumstances in which a search may be valid even though it is not conducted pursuant to a warrant issued by a neutral and detached magistrate. Some of the major warrantless search exceptions are as follows:

Search Incident to a Valid Arrest. Where the police have conducted a valid arrest of an individual, they may conduct a warrantless search of the entirety of his person and the area under his immediate control without the necessity of obtaining a warrant.[91] The immediate area is one defined in which the arrestee might gain possession of a weapon or destroy evidence.[92] The reason for this exception is essentially officer safety, but it is also meant to ensure that evidence is not destroyed, because the defendant is now within the custody of the police, and it is essentially within their ready view.[93]

The Protective Sweep. Where the police effect an arrest inside a residence, they may not conduct a full search of the residence unless they have a valid warrant that authorizes that sort of search. However, they may conduct a limited "protective sweep," if they have a reasonable belief based on specific facts that other individuals who pose a danger to them may be in the residence.[94] The search is designed to find people, and it must not last longer than is necessary to dispel the officer's reasonable suspicion that dangerous persons may be lurking in the area.[95]

Exigent Circumstances. Related to the protective sweep concept is the limited exception that allows the police to intrude into an area where exigent circumstances and probable cause both exist. Exigent circumstances are those in which the police believe that an individual is in immediate danger or that evidence is immediately likely to be destroyed.[96] Where the police believe that a violent crime has occurred, they may enter the place based on exigent circumstances if they also reasonably believe that victims or dangerous persons may be present there.[97] Officers may also enter a burning building or any other place in which a physical hazard is present.[98] Once at the scene of a fire, investigators may stay back to investigate the cause, but once that cause is established, a warrant has to be secured to obtain a further search of evidence of arson.[99]

This discussion should not lead the student to believe that there is a general "crime scene" exception to the Fourth Amendment. The U.S. Supreme Court has addressed this matter on at least three occasions.

In *Mincey vs. Arizona,*[100] the police investigated the defendant's apartment, the scene of a gunfight with an undercover narcotics officer. Homicide detectives arrived and conducted a four-day warrantless search of the apartment, seizing between 200 and 300 items. All the while, the defendant had been removed from the apartment and was in the hospital. Although the Arizona court recognized a "murder scene exception" to the warrant requirement, the Supreme Court disagreed. Whatever emergency situation may have justified the initial entry of the premises, the removal of the defendant to the hospital and the absence of anyone else in the apartment removed that exigency. Moreover, the seriousness of the offense was irrelevant to determining whether exigent circumstances truly exist; the proper inquiry was whether evidence may be lost or destroyed regardless of the nature of the underlying offense.

In *Thomson vs. Louisiana,*[101] a woman killed her husband and then attempted suicide by swallowing an amount of pills. Before losing consciousness, she contacted her daughter who summoned the police. After the mother was taken to the hospital, homicide detectives arrived and conducted a warrantless and general exploratory search for evidence, lasting two hours. The Supreme Court of the United States held that although the length of time was much shorter than in *Mincey*, it was still a warrantless intrusion subject to the Fourth Amendment requirements. The mere fact that the owner of the residence sought medical assistance did not mean that she had immediately surrendered her expectation of privacy in her home. The evidence was suppressed.

Finally, in *Flippo vs. West Virginia,*[102] the Supreme Court again rejected the existence of a "murder scene exception." In *Flippo*, the defendant called the police to say that he and the others had been attacked. When the police arrived, the defendant, exhibiting wounds on his head and legs, met the police outside his cabin. After the defendant was taken to the hospital, the officers searched for evidence of footprints or forced entry. For 16 hours, the

officers took photographs and searched the cabin. In the defendant's subsequent prosecution for the murder of his wife, the defendant sought the suppression of the evidence.

Although the state courts disagreed, the U.S. Supreme Court reaffirmed *Mincey* and
held that only if the police believe that a person is in need of immediate aid may they make
an entry into the residence without the aid of a warrant. As the entire investigation was conducted without a warrant, it was unreasonable under the Fourth Amendment principles.

Vehicle Searches. The U.S. Supreme Court has held that the police do not need a search
warrant to search an automobile when they have a probable cause to believe it contains
contraband or other evidence of a crime.[103]

The automobile exception to the warrant requirement is based upon the fact that automobiles are inherently mobile, creating what the Court found to be exigency, making it
impractical to obtain a warrant for them.[104] The automobile exception applies even in
cases where the car is already at the police station or in an impound lot.[105]

Consent Searches. Although it may be argued that a consent search is not really an
exception of the warrant requirement at all, but a different class of permissible government
intrusion, when an individual voluntarily gives the police consent to search an area in
which they have a justifiable expectation of privacy, they will not be heard thereafter to
complain that the police found something of interest.[106]

The voluntariness of the consent is to be considered under the totality of circumstances.[107] A consent is not voluntary if it is given only where the police falsely assert
that they actually have a warrant, and the consent is nothing more than a defendant's
nodding agreement to an authority the police claim already exists.[108] A proper consent
also cannot be given where a defendant is illegally in the custody of the police where,
for example, there was no probable cause to arrest him.[109]

The Plain View Exception. An important warrantless exception that often times applies
during the course of the execution of another kind of search is the plain view exception.
Where an officer is lawfully executing an arrest or a search warrant, or is otherwise lawfully
at a place he has a right to be without violating the Fourth Amendment's rights of an individual, and he sees evidence the incriminating character of which is immediately apparent
to him, he may seize it without having to run to a magistrate to get a warrant.[110]

The Terry Stop Doctrine. In an important development particularly significant to on-
street confrontations, the Supreme Court has held that a brief seizure of a person and a pat
down of their outer clothing to ensure that the individual is not armed is permissible if the
officer's information, while short of probable cause, still constitutes a reasonable suspicion
to believe that criminal activity is afoot.[111] This is the so-called *Terry* stop.

If, during the officer's pat down of the suspect it becomes immediately apparent to the
officer that the item he is touching is contraband or evidence of crime, he may seize it on
what is generally called the plain touch or plain feel exception.[112]

Use of Dogs to Detect Contraband/Evidence. The U.S. Supreme Court has held that the
use of a dog to sniff a parcel to detect the presence of contraband is not in itself a search under
the Fourth Amendment standards although inquiry about whether the circumstances leading
up to the detention of the parcel and its owner is still subject to such Constitutional

scrutiny.[113] A vehicle stopped legitimately for a traffic violation, for example, may be subjected to a dog sniff without a further probable cause or reasonable suspicion.[114]

Caveat: State Courts May Interpret Their Constitutions to Provide Greater Protections Than the Fourth Amendment

Finally, of necessity, the discussion in this segment has related to the federal law of search and seizure. Although all states must conform their state constitutional principles to the minimum standards set by the U.S. Supreme Court in interpreting the Fourteenth Amendment, they are free to provide citizens with a greater protection under the auspices of their own state constitution. Investigators working in a given state must examine those areas of state law that may provide greater protection to citizens and conform their activities to higher standards.[115]

Custodial Interrogations: the 5th/14th Amendments

As our historical review of the criminal process has indicated, confessions have always been considered as matters of great importance in determining who was responsible for a criminal act and the degree to which they were culpable. Again, however, our Constitution interposes a limitation on the government's ability to obtain this sort of evidence. That limitation is, in substantial part, the Fifth Amendment privilege against compulsory self-incrimination.

The Supreme Court of the United States has developed rules that presume, in general terms, that once a person is "in custody," questioning of that individual may occur in circumstances where either active compulsion, overt coercive interrogation, or simply an inherently coercive environment may put at risk the Fifth Amendment privilege the individual otherwise enjoys.[116]

In an effort to limit the use of coercion in such circumstances, while still allowing an individual to make a statement about their own culpability, the Supreme Court in *Miranda* developed a set of rules that have become so generally known in popular culture.[117] In simplest terms, the suspect must be told that:

1. They have the right to remain silent.
2. What they choose to say can be used against them in Court.
3. They have a right to an attorney (invoking the Sixth Amendment right to counsel).
4. If they cannot afford an attorney, one would be provided to them by the Court.

Although common, the nature of *Miranda* warnings are sometimes badly misunderstood. The police do not have to give *Miranda* warnings to make an arrest legitimate. Rather, *Miranda* warnings only have to be given where the police have someone in custody and wish to question him.[118] To exclude statements and other evidence derived from those statements, the record must indicate that there was both *custody* and *police interrogation* without a knowing, intelligent, and voluntary waiver of *Miranda* warnings.

Custody means the deprivation by the police of a person's freedom of movement in a significant way viewed objectively as one that would indicate that either a formal arrest has taken place or that a person's freedom of movement has been restricted to the same degree that it would have been a formal arrest occurred.[119]

Besides custody, the police have to engage in interrogation to trigger the necessity of *Miranda* warnings. This includes, of course, specific questioning of a suspect and those actions that the police know "are reasonably likely to elicit an incriminating response from the suspect."[120] Interrogation may be found when the police employ some sort of psychological trick or device that is designed to elicit an incriminating response.[121]

However, the Supreme Court has indicated that routine police processing or booking questions are not considered to be interrogation because they are not designed to produce incriminating responses and are only necessary for maintaining police records.[122]

A suspect who invokes his *Miranda* rights and declines to make a statement has the right to insist that the police scrupulously honor that invocation.[123] Particularly when the individual makes a clear request for counsel, law enforcement officers must stop their interrogation until counsel has been obtained or unless the suspect subsequently waives that right through a knowing, intelligent, and voluntary act.[124]

Besides *Miranda*, the Constitution generally prohibits confessions and statements that are involuntary. If, based on a review of all the circumstances, it is found that the actions of law enforcement officers overbore the will of the accused, the statement cannot be admitted for any purpose.[125]

Making the Case Ready for Trial

Preserving Evidence for Trial

Although much of the work of a professional criminalist is done at crime scenes or in laboratories, that work has a meaning only to the extent that it could ultimately be used as evidence in the trial of the case. The gathering of physical evidence, its processing and testing, and its preservation for use at trial, are all critical aspects of the criminalist's duty to assist in the fair disposition of a case.

Although these matters will be more appropriately discussed in detail in that section of this work dealing with the rules of evidence, a criminalist must understand that getting evidence in accord with Constitutional principles is only one of the major considerations to be kept in mind while trying to find the truth at the heart of a puzzling crime.

The fruits of a criminalist's work, that is, the physical evidence they have obtained, must be authenticated before a court will accept it for a jury's consideration. Authentication means that a court must be satisfied that the object the criminalist identifies as an item relevant to the prosecution in the courtroom is, in fact, what the criminalist claims it to be. Rule 901 of the Federal Rules of Evidence, for example, states the following:

> The requirement of authentication or identification as a conditioned precedent to admissibility is satisfied by evidence sufficient to support a finding that the matter in question is what its proponent claims.

Although some things may be self-authenticating (i.e., certain types of sealed documents and certified copies of public records),[126] bloodstains, fingerprint lifts, and most other types of physical or scientific evidence are not. They must be independently authenticated, and one of the most common ways is by testimony of a witness who has knowledge that the item is what it claims to be. In the context of criminal evidence, this sometimes is referred to as proof of the chain of custody. As a noted text on the law of evidence has stated:

> Chain of custody requires testimony of continuous possession by each individual having possession, together with testimony by each that the object remained

in the substantially same condition during its presence in his possession. All possibility of alteration, substitution or change of condition need not be eliminated, for example, normally an object may be placed in a safe to which more than one person had access without each person being produced.[127]

Similarly, an actual break in the chain of custody will not result in exclusion of the evidence if the chain of custody established to have occurred, viewed as a whole, supports the improbability of alterations, substitution, or change of condition.[127] The more an exhibit is indistinguishable from others of its kind, or the more likely it is that some change in its basic condition could have occurred, the more important will be the chain of custody proof; however, courts have generally assumed that evidence will be properly preserved in the absence of a showing that something unusual occurred that altered it or subjected it to tampering.[128]

A defendant is always free to argue to the jury that even though the court has admitted the exhibit under a preliminary standard of admissibility, the jury should not accept it as the authentic exhibit if that determination is necessary to their finding of proof beyond a reasonable doubt. It is often said in this context that the Court is to determine, as a preliminary matter, the admissibility of an exhibit, leaving to the jury the determination as to its weight for matter of proof purposes.[129]

Good police work, like good laboratory work, involves careful handling of the exhibits. Virtually every police laboratory or department has established procedures for the marking, identification, securing, and preservation of the exhibits so that a chain of custody issue is not likely to arise. Still, concerns about the handling of various laboratory exhibits have arisen in recent years, and continued vigilance by criminalists in this area is required.[130]

Preserving and Producing Evidence in Discovery

Although police and criminalists are, in one sense, members of the prosecution team, they must remember that when they gather evidence, they are also gathering it under obligations imposed by court rules and the Constitution that ultimately lead to the defendant and his attorney obtaining the results of their efforts.

The Federal government, for example, has procedural rules that govern the disclosure of information to a defendant in the pretrial stage. Generally, the purpose of such rules is to insure that trials are conducted with a modicum of fairness. A defendant is not to be ambushed at trial by evidence that completely surprises him and for which he was unprepared. The Federal Rules of Criminal Procedure serve as a good model for rules that provide for the disclosure of such information.

Under Rule 16, a defendant is entitled to the following information prior to trial:

1. Any relevant oral statement he made either before or after his arrest in response to interrogation by a person he knew to be a government agent.
2. Any recorded statement the defendant has given, any written record concerning the substance of any oral statement he has made before or after arrest interrogation, and any testimony he has given before a Grand Jury.
3. A copy of his prior criminal record.[131]
4. Books, papers, documents, data, photographs, tangible objects, buildings, places, or other such tangible items if they are material to the preparation of his defense, if

the government intends to use them in its case in chief at trial, or the item belonged to or was obtained from the defendant.

5. Results or reports of physical or mental examinations as well as any scientific test or experiment if the matter is within the government's possession, the attorney for the government knows or should have known that the items existed, and the item is material to the preparation of the defense or where the government intends to use it in its case in chief at trial. Related to this is the requirement that upon the defendant's request, the government gives him a written summary of any testimony the government intends to use in its in chief from an expert. That summary must describe the expert's opinion, the basis for his opinion, and his qualifications.

Once the government has fully complied with its discovery obligations, it may request that the defendant provide it with certain things in return. The government may request that the defendant provide any tangible objects he intends to use in his case in chief, the results of any examinations or scientific test he has performed in which he intends to use in his case in chief and the substance of any expert testimony he intends to offer.

Both sides have a continuing duty to disclose evidence that is otherwise called for under the rule and if there is a special reason why one side or the other believes it should not have to give up this information, the rules provide for that party to seek a protective order from the Court to limit or somehow restrict discovery.

The Constitutional dimension of the obligation of the police and prosecutors to turn over evidence helpful to the defendant begins with the Supreme Court's decision in *Brady vs. Maryland*.[132] In *Brady*, the Supreme Court held that where the state suppresses evidence favorable to the accused, a violation of due process occurs where the evidence is material to either guilt or punishment, regardless of whether the failure to disclose it was in good faith or bad faith. Although this rule would certainly apply to evidence that would directly exculpate a defendant (in *Brady* itself, for example, the prosecution failed to disclose that Brady's companion had confessed to the killing with which he was charged), the rule has been expanded to include evidence that would tend to impeach the credibility of government witnesses.[133]

The obligation to make sure that a *Brady* violation does not occur is borne squarely by the prosecutor since the prosecutor is in a far superior position to determine the existence of such information and disclose it pursuant to the Constitutional mandate. This point was made dramatically in *Kyles vs. Whitley*,[134] in which the Court held that "the prosecutor remains responsible for gauging the cumulative effect of the failure to disclose favorable evidence regardless of any failure by the police to bring favorable evidence to the prosecutor's attention.[135]

The Court also rejected the notion that a defendant must always make a specific request for such information before the obligation is triggered. Rather, the obligation exists, and the filing of a specific request for certain material simply heightens the specific inquiry the prosecutor must make; the obligation on the prosecutor to inquire and, where he finds such information, to disclose it, is constant and absolute.[136]

In *Strickler vs. Greene*, the Court reaffirmed its position that the prosecutor bears the burden of learning of evidence known to others within the prosecution team, including investigating officers.[137] This, again, goes to issues of evidence directly exculpatory and that which is exculpatory because it impeaches the credibility of government witnesses.

Where such evidence has not been disclosed, and when it could reasonably have put the whole case in such a different light that the verdict against the defendant is one in which confidence is no longer possible, cases that have already been the subject of conviction may be reversed and new trials ordered.[138]

Given the compelling nature of the prosecutor's obligation, the prosecutor will not hesitate to disclose information wherever it is possible that it would fit the *Brady* standard. Indeed, the Supreme Court has observed that a prudent prosecutor will resolve all doubts in favor of disclosure and "that is as it should be."[139]

The obligations of the *Brady* doctrine manifest themselves in various specific ways for the criminalist. Courts have discussed issues of fingerprints, photographs, and other physical evidence in terms of whether a due process violation has occurred by the way they were handled, mishandled, or destroyed during an investigation, thereby depriving the defendant of access to them.

In *Commonwealth vs. Phoenix*, the Court held that there was no violation where a bloody fingerprint was destroyed while investigators were attempting to lift other prints off a paper bag.[140] The criminalist was faced with a decision to either try to raise other latent prints or preserve the bloody print. After photographing the bloody print in its original state, the print was destroyed in an attempt to get other prints from the bag, thereby denying the defense the opportunity to examine it. The Court concluded that the action was reasonable and stated that the mere possibility that there would be information from the original print was not enough to establish a Constitutional violation.

In *State vs. Hawkins*, the Court held that there was no Constitutional violation where serological testing rendered the defendant's bloody palm print on a flashlight unusable for further analysis.[141] The print was photographed according to established procedures but, because of the blood testing, the print was rendered unusable for further fingerprint analysis. The Court advised, similar to the prior case, that the choices faced by the state rendered it impossible that they could preserve both the print and the testing of the blood which constituted it.

Fingerprints that have no evidentiary value either because they are smeared or because they have insufficient points to support a proper comparison need not generally be preserved in the absence of a showing of bad faith on the part of the prosecution in destroying them.[142]

However, in *Scoggins vs. State*, the prosecution was dismissed where the state lost latent fingerprints of the defendant allegedly taken from items in the drug laboratory, along with the equipment from which the prints were lifted.[143] The state police accidentally had the evidence destroyed, and the fingerprints, being the only real evidence the state had in its case, could not be admitted. The defendant was discharged.

Similarly, in *Sparks vs. State*, a murder conviction was reversed when a defendant successfully claimed that the victim had gone after her with a gun and the police mishandled the gun in such a way so as to have lost evidence such as blood, hair, or fingerprints that could otherwise have been obtained from the weapon.[144] The state's ineffective handling of this important piece of evidence cost it its prosecution.

Photographs are used by police investigators for a variety of purposes. Sometimes, photographs of the defendant and various others are used as photo arrays to assist an individual seeking to identify the perpetrator. In *State vs. Baur*,[145] the Court reversed a conviction where the police lost or destroyed the photographs used in a photographic

array. There, a witness had identified the defendant, and there was no other independent basis to verify the reliability of that identification. As the defense attorney was
not able to use the photographic array to seek to impeach the witness, the conviction
was reversed.

This is not always the case, however, in that, where there is less of a showing of
materiality, the loss or destruction of a photo array will not necessarily constitute a
Brady violation.[146]

Photographs taken of a crime scene before the commission of the crime are generally
not found to be so material to a case as to require a reversal where they are lost or
destroyed.[147]

However, surveillance photographs taken of the crime in progress may help to identify
the accused and are extraordinary material to both the prosecution and the defense. Their
destruction may well lead to a reversible error.[148]

Various Courts have held that *Brady* violations have occurred when evidence regarding
blood or semen has been destroyed in circumstances where the defendant was materially
prejudiced. In *Davis vs. Pitchess*,[149] and *Ex parte Geeslin*,[150] the Court found *Brady*
violations where semen samples taken during the investigation were destroyed prior to
the time the defense had the opportunity to examine them. In both cases, the results
could well have been exculpatory.

In *Cheung vs. Maddock*,[151] the prosecution was found to have violated the *Brady* doctrine when it failed to disclose medical reports that a key government witness had a blood
alcohol test value twice the legal limit. Such information could have easily affected the
credibility of that witness and his ability to identify the shooter.

In *In re Brown*,[152] a *Brady* violation was also found to have occurred when the defendant claimed intoxication, the state had proof of PCP in his system but concealed the
results of that test upon request from the defense. The violation was found even though
the prosecutor was not personally aware of the results of the test. As discussed previously,
the prosecutor cannot defend based on the fact that the police or laboratory technicians
knew something that she did not; if the item not disclosed was material, a reversal of
the prosecution can occur.

In these cases, many of the problems the prosecution encountered could have been
remedied if the flow of information between the investigating officers, criminalists, and
the prosecutors had been complete. The *Brady* doctrine, at its heart, tries to serve as a
truth determining function, and is a faithful part of a system influenced by a philosophy
that does not grant to the government an assumption that the government is always
right. All who are part of the system have an obligation to insure that their actions
are well documented and made available so that the trial process can function as was
intended.

When the System Fails: Wrongful Convictions

Throughout this chapter, we have tried to recall how the basic philosophy of the system
affects the specific aspects of the criminal justice in America. The philosophy of the
Enlightenment, with its emphasis on individual liberty and its effort to establish a
limited government that does not become a weapon to invade the province of individual

choice, conflicts with the notion that large numbers of people are denied their freedom when, in truth, they have done nothing wrong at all.

And yet, there is a growing body of evidence that our criminal justice system fails at an alarmingly high rate by condemning to death or to prison persons who are actually innocent of the offense with which they have been charged.

As of the date of the publication of his article in 2003,[153] Professor Rago was able to document that from the late 1970s forward, 127 people had been exonerated as result of postconviction DNA testing; in a number of cases, the individuals were on death row.[154]

A 1996 study of wrongful convictions published by the Department of Justice collected FBI data showing that during 1989–1996, and including approximately 10,000 sexual assault cases, the person who was initially arrested as the perpetrator was ruled out approximately 25% of the time by DNA testing.[155] These statistics represent provable instances in which persons who were actually innocent were formally placed at risk of the loss of their liberty by the criminal justice system.

Other studies have reported that although it is not possible to accurately fix the number of innocent people who have been wrongfully convicted, estimates of the total number of wrongful convictions range from 0.5%, to 8%, to a general public estimate of 13%.[156] Wrongful convictions, in fact, have been studied since the early 1930s.[157] Professor Huff, in a 2003 publication, noted that DNA testing has provided a barometer to test convictions and that approximately 18,000 criminal cases where biological evidence was available, DNA excluded prime suspects 25% of the time. He suggests that a 25% error rate, even if it is exaggerated by a few points, is still extremely significant.[158]

All in all, given the number of convictions in a base year, the most conservative estimates would indicate that approximately 7,700 innocent people were convicted of serious crimes in 2000 and, if the 8% estimate derived in studies from Illinois is correct, then more than 123,000 people have been wrongfully convicted.[159] Professor Bedau has written that the numbers derived from capital cases and DNA exonerations represent only a small percentage of all criminal cases within the system and gives some indication that wrongful convictions are likely to occur in cases where such evidence is not available to be tested against rigorous scientific standards.[160]

Virtually every article listed in this section details at length the possible causes of wrongful convictions. Most agree that the data indicate that the single most important factor in leading to wrongful convictions is a misidentification by an eye witness.[161] In addition, these studies regularly cite to alleged unethical police and prosecutorial behavior, including *Brady* violations and other acts of misconduct.[162] Line-up procedures that are impermissibly suggestive, ineffective assistance of trial counsel, the use of false or coerced confessions, the reliance upon unreliable jailhouse informants, plea bargaining in which the defendant pleas in fear of a conviction of a more serious crime for a more serious penalty, and other factors, are also identified.[163] All of these have led to calls for and implementation of moratoriums on the death penalty,[164] but the concerns, as indicated earlier, go far beyond cases that have landed the defendant on death row.[165]

Debate about such statistical projections is proper and, indeed, giving an accurate estimate of the number of wrongly convicted persons may ultimately prove to be an impossibility. Ultimately, however, the system needs to face the reality that the occurrence of factually innocent people being convicted, imprisoned, and, sometimes, executed, is not such an aberration that we may blissfully assume that a critical review of our processes and procedures to seek justice is not required. Perhaps we will make the societal choice that the current extent of wrongful convictions is a price we are willing to pay for a law enforcement system we wish to fund at current levels, and from which we expect a large number of convictions. Perhaps we would choose otherwise.

In making those judgments, we need to assess the matter from many perspectives, not the least of which is the perspective of the person suffering the wrongful conviction. Certainly, the terror of their situation must call to mind more of the laments of Oscar Wilde:

> We were as men who through a fen
> Of filthy darkness grope:
> We did not dare to breathe a prayer,
> Or to give our anguish scope:
> Something was dead in each of us,
> And what was dead was Hope.[166]

It is not simply, though, that those victimized by wrongful conviction will rightfully challenge the legitimacy of the laws and system that put them there. It is an issue which, as Professor Huff noted, is something that must cut across racial and political boundaries:

> In societies that value the freedom of their citizens and have done so much to protect that freedom, it is arguable that being convicted of a crime that one did not commit, and being incarcerated with criminals or even put to death, represents one of the worst nightmares imaginable. And yet, when we consider the two major types of error — false positives and false negatives — we find much more preoccupation with the question of the guilty going free, probably because of the public safety implications of freeing a criminal, who might victimize others. The irony, of course, is that these two errors are inversely related, and every time we convict an innocent person we leave the actual offender free to continue victimizing citizens. Therefore, although the issue of wrongful conviction is generally portrayed as a so-called liberal issue focusing on the rights of the accused, it is every bit as much an issue that affects public safety and should be of equal concern to so-called law and order conservatives.[167]

This author may add that it should also be of concern to every citizen who, after a study of the history and philosophical underpinnings of this country, knows that a system powerful enough to regularly imprison significant numbers of innocent people is a system inconsistent with a design of those who first planned and executed it. Although any system based upon human judgment and reason is fallible, and although mistakes inevitably will be made, it would seem to be a most basic article of faith in this country that doing all we could to insure that those mistakes were not made and to correct them as readily as possible, would be a high commandment of our collective civic faith.

Adherence to this civic faith does not require that we embrace a tolerance of lawlessness and invite a return to the rule of the brigand. The phenomenon of crime in our society was a circumstance well known to those who crafted the Constitution. Power was amply afforded to the government to deal with it in a way that would permit our democracy to function in an ordered system of liberty without sacrificing the fundamental liberty interests that would make a "crime-free" world devoid of basic human freedom. The argument that our liberties must be sacrificed in the name of law enforcement is false. As the Supreme Court said when faced with a similar argument in 1866:

> Such a doctrine leads directly to anarchy or despotism, but the theory of necessity on which it is based is false; for the government, within the Constitution, has all the powers granted to it, which are necessary to preserve its existence....[168]

Good law enforcement and civil liberties can co-exist. The hope of our nation is that they will be a joint reality.

Notes

1. The author acknowledges the research help received in this matter from Duquesne Law School Students Steven Toprani, Lucas Repka, Sarah Cottrill, and Bryan Brantly. He expresses particular appreciation to his former research assistant Matthew Debbis, a brilliant and passionate scholar who is fast becoming an outstanding practitioner of criminal law.

2. *The Ballad of Reading Gaol*, Oscar Wilde, in Mark Zimmerman, Encylopedia of the self, available at http://emotionalliteracyeducation.com/class_books_online/rgao110.htm

3. All statistics are from the U.S. Department of Justice, Office of Justice Programs Reports: Prisoners in 2002 (July 2003) and Probation and Parole in the U.S. 2002 (August 2003). By mid-year 2003, the total number of incarcerated persons increased to 2,078,570 according to a report published in May 2004 by the same Office of the Justice Department.

4. *A Criminal History of Mankind*, Colin Wilson (New York, NY: G.P. Putnam's Sons 1984), at 163. [hereinafter, *Wilson*].

5. *History of Criminal Justice*, H.A. Johnson (Cincinnati, OH: Anderson Publishing Co. 1988) pp. 23–24. [hereinafter, *Johnson*].

6. *The Historical and Institutional Context of Roman Law*, George Musourakis (Ashgate 2003), pp. 121–124.

7. The societal differences reflected here also manifested themselves in laws other than homicide. In one of the seminal works of the legal system, Blackstone's *Commentaries on the law of England*, the history of punishments of various offenses are set forth. In Book IV, Chapter 15, Blackstone indicates that the crime of rape under Jewish law "was punished with death, in case the damsel was betrothed to another man; and in case she was not betrothed, then a heavy fine of 50 shekels was to be paid to the damsel's father, and she was to be the wife of the ravisher all the days of his life; without that power of divorce, which was in general permitted by the mosaic law." It is not possible to appreciate this sort of formulation without having a concurrent understanding of the place of women in such a setting.

8. *See*, Bruce Antkowiak, *The Ascent of an Ancient Palladium: The Resurgent Importance of Trial by Jury and the Coming Revolution in Pennsylvania Sentencing*, 13 *Widener L.J.* 11 (2003), at 25–30. [hereinafter, *Antkowiak*].

9. *Democracy in America*, Alexis DeTocqueville (1945), at p. 55.

10. *A Machine That Would Go of Itself*, Michael Kammen (Alfred Knopf, Inc. 1987), at 207. See also, Wilson, *supra* note 4 at 443–44.

11. James Madison, in the Federalists' Papers, particularly Federalist Paper Number 51, called the division of government horizontally into hemispheres of federal and state governments, and then a division of the federal government vertically into the three co-equal branches, a "double security" for the rights of the individual. The U.S. Supreme Court has recognized this principle numerous times. In *United States vs. Lopez*, 514 U.S. 549 (1995), the Court explicitly invoked Madison's idea, calling the unique contribution of the framers of the constitution to political science and political theory their "insight ... that freedom was enhanced by the creation of two governments, not one." 514 U.S. 549 at 576 (Kennedy J. concurring). Justice Scalia, in *Printz vs. United States*, 521 U.S. 898, 935 (1997), wrote that federalism was "one of the Constitution's structural protections of liberty." In cases involving the Court's striking down of federal laws on the basis that they violate protections of state's sovereignty found in the Tenth Amendment, the preservation of federalization was necessary to uphold an internal structure of government intended "to prevent the exercise of tyranny against individuals." See, *New York vs. United States*, 505 U.S. 144, 206 (1992) (White J. dissenting).

12. Book IV, Chapter 1.

13. Professor Johnson has opined that the philosophy that criminal laws should be clear and plainly understood was a primary tenet of the writings of Montesquieu. The benefits of such clarity were to allow individuals within society to precisely measure whether committing the crime would be worth it to them in the long run with a hoped for outcome that they would conform their conduct to the requirements of the law without testing its ability to detect them. Moreover, clear criminal statutes were meant to reduce judicial discretion which writers of the time believed would simply be the avenue through which unequal application of the law would flow. Johnson, *supra* note 5, at 118–19.

14. See, *City of Houston vs. Raymond Wayne Hill*, 482 U.S. 451 (1987); and *Chicago vs. Morales* 527 U.S. 41 (1999).

15. 530 U.S. 506 (1995), and extended discussion of same in Antkowiak, *supra* note 8.

16. For example, in *Apprendi*, the individual had committed an assault on another but, at the time of sentencing, the state sought to prove that this was an incident of a hate crime. As the hate crime determination was simply made by the judge at sentencing instead by the jury during trial, and as it vastly increased the maximum penalty, the Supreme Court struck down the statute as unconstitutional.

17. *The Federalist Papers*, No. 83, at 562 (Jacob E. Cooke Ed., 1961).

18. *Supra* note 8 at footnote 87, citing to a brilliant article by Akhil Reed Amar, *The bill of rights as a constitution*, 100 *Yale L.J.* 1131, 1183 (1991). To illustrate this, it is worthy of note that while the Fourth Amendment to the Constitution of the United States. will permit a search of a home where government officials alone have authorized it (an officer from the executive branch obtains judicial approval for the search), to actually charge a citizen with a crime and place him at the risk of loss of his liberty, two bodies of citizens (a grand and petit jury) were needed to accomplish that attempted incarceration. *Supra* note 8.

19. *In re: Winship*, 397 U.S. 358 (1970); *Victor vs. Nebraska*, 511 U.S. 1 (1994).

20. *Jackson vs. Virginia*, 443 U.S. 307, 315 (1979).

21. *United States vs. Hernandez*, 176 F.3d 719, 728 (3d Cir. 1999); citing, *Sullivan vs. Louisiana*, 508 U.S. 275, 278 (1993).

22. By adopting this standard, society clearly makes a judgment as to the degree to which it weighs the injustice of letting an actually guilty person go free versus the injustice of convicting a group of people who are truly innocent. The system, being a creation of human beings, is

bound to error. The question is simply how much error and of what type the system is willing to accept. See, Scott Sundby, *The reasonable doubt rule and the meaning of innocence*, 40 *Hast Law J* 457, 460–461 (1989).

23. *In re: Winship*, 397 U.S. at 363, citing *Coffin vs. United States*, 156 U.S. 432, 453 (1895).

24. 156 U.S. 432, 453 (1895).

25. Stephen Sheppard, *The metamorphoses of reasonable doubt: How changes in the burden of proof have weakened the presumption of innocence.* 78 *N.D. L. Rev.* 1165, 1171–81 (May 2003) [hereinafter, Sheppard]. See also, Professor Barbara Shapiro's important work: *Beyond Reasonable Doubt and Probable Cause: Historical Perspectives on the Anglo-American Law of Evidence*, (University of California Press 1991) [hereinafter, Shapiro].

26. *Supra* note 25 at 13. See also, The challenge of explaining reasonable doubt, Hirsham M. Ramadan, Vol. 40, *Crim Law Bull* No. 1, 15 (2004), at p. 15.

27. *Supra* note 25, at 41. Professors Shapiro and Sheppard disagree on whether the modern evolution of the instruction on reasonable doubt is really one that was proposed by prosecutors who feared that then existing instructions were far too defense oriented. Shapiro, *supra* note 25, at 21, Sheppard, *supra* note 25, at 1169.

28. 59 Mass. 295, 320 (1850).

29. Professor Sheppard put it this way:

From the very beginning, the reasonable-doubt instruction was intertwined with the presumption of innocence. The state held the burden of persuasion, who must prove or disprove guilt, and the burden of proof established whether the state had met its obligation, by setting how sufficiently the state had proved the defendant's guilt. These two separate obligations are merged in the claim that the government must prove the defendant's guilt beyond a reasonable doubt. Therefore, even though the two standards are usually subject to separate instructions, when the Supreme Court adopted the reasonable-doubt standard as an interpretation of due process, it also enshrined the standard of a presumption of innocence as a constitutional requirement.

Of course, the relationship between these standards is somewhat more complex. As the whole of a case grows more complex, and as certain defenses require proffers and rebuttals or counter-rebuttals, the effect of shifting burdens of persuasion on the underlying burden of proof may grow even more strained. These interrelationships are especially keen in the relationship between the separate instructions on reasonable doubt and the presumption of innocence, especially in the light of verdicts that must stand on circumstantial evidence to infer conclusions for which no direct evidence is available. Thus, the difficulty that jurors have in applying the reasonable-doubt standard has given rise to concerns that juror confusion regarding the burden of proof may affect juror application of the presumption of innocence. Sheppard, *supra* note 25, at 1238.

30. Professor Sheppard also identifies a second problem with such a change in the juror's role as a moral one. By so confining their role to searching the record for a reasonable doubt as opposed to reaching an overall judgment as to the level of certainty they feel as to the issue of guilt, the jury is asked to perform a highly moral task of condemnation without being allowed to exercise a full range of moral choice. Such, Sheppard argues, is itself immoral. *Supra* note 30 at 1242.

31. By adopting this standard, society clearly makes a judgment as to the degree to which it weighs the injustice of letting an actually guilty person go free versus the injustice of convicting a group of people who are truly innocent. The system, being a creation of human beings, is bound to error. The question is simply how much error and of what type the system is willing to accept. See, Scott Sundby, *The reasonable doubt rule and the meaning of innocence.* 40 *Hast Law J* 457, 459–60 (1989).

32. Ramadan, *supra* note 26, footnote 4, at 4–5.

33. Indeed, the 7th Circuit Court of Appeals has apparently determined not to define the term of reasonable doubt while other Courts leave the precise formulation solely in the hands of the trial courts. *Supra* note 26 in 4–5.

34. *See, New York vs. Quarles*, 467 U.S. 649, 654 (1984).

35. *Miranda vs. Arizona*, 384 U.S. 436 (1966).

36. *Johnson vs. Zerbst*, 304 U.S. 458 (1938); and *Gideon vs. Wainwright*, 372 U.S. 335 (1963).

37. *Gideon*, 372 U.S. at 344.

38. *Weeks vs. United States*, 232 U.S. 383 (1914); and *Mapp vs. Ohio*, 367 U.S. 643 (1961).

39. *Lily vs. Virginia*, 527 U.S. 116 (1999); *Crawford vs. Washington*, 541 U.S. 36 (2004).

40. See, *Sentencing, Sanctions and Corrections*, Kittrie et al. (Foundation Press 2d. Edition 2002) page 56; Blackstone Book IV, §11; and, The American Law Institute Model Penal Code: Sentencing (April 11, 2003).

41. Model Penal Code Section 1.02 (2003).

42. *Apprendi vs. New Jersey*, 530 U.S. 506 (1995).

43. *United States vs. Gaudin*, 515 U.S. 506 (1995).

44. Title 18 Pa.C.S. §2502(a).

45. Title 18 Pa.C.S. §2502(b).

46. Title 18 Pa.C.S. §2502(c).

47. See also, Model Penal Code Section 210.2, 1 (official draft and revised comments 1980).

48. Title 18 Pa.C.S. §2503.

49. Title 18 Pa.C.S. §2504.

50. In both federal and state law cases, excellent sources for understanding the elements of any crime are published jury instructions which judges use to delineate for a trial jury the various elements they must find beyond a reasonable doubt before convicting a defendant. See *Pennsylvania Suggested Standard Jury Instruction — Criminal*, Pennsylvania Bar Institute (2004); *Federal Jury Practice and Instructions*, K.F. O'Malley, J.E. Grenig, and W.C. Lee (2004).

51. *United States vs. Enmons*, 410 U.S. 396 (1973).

52. *United States vs. Culbert*, 435 U.S. 371 (1978).

53. *McCormick vs. United States*, 500 U.S. 257 (1991).

54. See, generally, *United States vs. Farrish*, 122 F.3d 146 (2d Cir. 1997) (a *de minimis* effect is sufficient).

55. See, *United States vs. Lopez*, 514 U.S. 549 (1995) (firearms statute struck down where it prohibited the possession of firearm in a school where the Court found that there was no nexus between interstate commerce and the offense charged).

56. Another example of federal authority is the federal mail fraud statute. 18 U.S.C. §1341. This statute also has an extremely broad scope, punishing frauds, swindles, and political corruption of various types. The authority for this statute is the Constitutional ability of Congress to establish a post office and necessary for proof of a mail fraud is proof that the U.S. mails were used to further the scheme otherwise concocted by the defendant. Related laws make it an offense to use interstate carriers to facilitate the fraud, but those acts are passed under the commerce clause. See, §1343.

57. *Mullaney vs. Wilbur*, 421 U.S. 684, 703–04 (1975); *Sandstrom vs. Montana*, 442 U.S. 510, 524 (1979); *Patterson vs. New York*, 432 U.S. 197, 212–16 (1977).

58. *Martin vs. Ohio*, 480 U.S. 228, 234 (1987).

59. *Leland vs. Oregon*, 343 U.S. 790, 799 (1952).

60. *See, Martin, supra; United States vs. Bailey*, 444 U.S. 394, 410–11 (1980); *Szuchon vs. Lehman*, 273 F.3d 299, 320 (3d Cir. 2001).

61. *Jacobson vs. United States*, 503 U.S. 540 (1992); *Sorrells vs. United States*, 287 U.S. 435 (1932).

62. *Mathews vs. United States*, 485 U.S. 58 (1988).

63. The remedy he seeks goes beyond just suppressing the particular thing obtained directly as the result of the alleged illegality. A defendant will claim that other evidence obtained subsequent to the unlawful intrusion has been tainted by it and should also be suppressed under the fruit of the poisonous tree doctrine. *Wong Sun vs. United States*, 371 U.S. 471 (1963). If an initial illegality has occurred, the government must show that subsequent evidence was either obtained in circumstances so attenuated by time or events that the initial illegality was purged, that the evidence was truly discovered from a source independent of the illegal search, or that the evidence would have been inevitably discovered by normal, lawful police procedures. *Segura vs. United States*, 468 U.S. 796 (1984); *Murray vs. United States*, 487 U.S. 533 (1988); *Nix vs. Williams*, 467 U.S. 431 (1984).

64. 232 U.S. 383 (1914).

65. 367 U.S. 643 (1961).

66. Two excellent texts in this regard are *Search and Seizure*, Third Edition, Wayne R. LaFave (2004) and the *Annual Review of Criminal Procedure, Georgetown Law J* (2003). These texts have been consulted extensively by the author in preparing this section of the chapter.

67. *Walter vs. United States*, 447 U.S. 649 (1980); *New Jersey vs. TLO*, 469 U.S. 325 (1985) (vice-principal found to be state agent while carrying out state required policies); *United States vs. Souza*, 223 F.3d 1197 (10th Cir. 2000) (UPS employee found to be state agent when government officials repeatedly encouraged her to open a package and assisted her in doing so); *United States vs. Knoll*, 16 F.3d 1313 (2d Cir. 1994) (private citizens found not to be state agents when they stole documents and turned them over to a government agent to review as the agent did not encourage the individuals to engage in this action before hand).

68. *Katz vs. United States*, 389 U.S. 347 (1967).

69. An officer simply does not have to avert his eyes when he sees some incriminating evidence while in a location that he has a right to occupy. See, *Katz*, 389 U.S. at 351.

70. *California vs. Greenwood*, 486 U.S. 35 (1988).

71. *United States vs. Taylor*, 90 F.3d 903 (4th Cir. 1996).

72. 533 U.S. 27 (2001).

73. *Minnesota vs. Carter*, 525 U.S. 83 (1998) (a defendant lacked standing where he is simply a short-term guest entirely for commercial purposes in a residence); *Rawlings vs. Kentucky*, 448 U.S. 98 (1980) (a defendant lacked standing to challenge drugs seized from his female friend's purse); and *Rakas vs. Illinois*, 439 U.S. 128 (1978).

74. *Katz*, 389 U.S. at 357.

75. *Coolidge vs. New Hampshire*, 403 U.S. 443 (1971); *Warden vs. Hayden*, 387 U.S. 294 (1967).

76. *Illinois vs. Gates*, 462 U.S. 213 (1983).

77. *Beck vs. Ohio*, 379 U.S. 89 (1964); *Wong Sun vs. United States*, 371 U.S. 471 (1963).

78. *Aguillar vs. Texas*, 378 U.S. 108 (1964); *Giordenello vs. United States*, 357 U.S. 480 (1958).

79. *Emery vs. Holmes*, 824 F.2d 143 (1st Cir. 1987); *United States vs. Zimmerman*, 277 F.3d 426 (3d Cir. 2002).

80. *Maryland vs. Garrison*, 480 U.S. 79 (1987); *Andresen vs. Maryland*, 427 U.S. 463 (1976).

81. *Andresen*, 427 U.S. at 480; *Steele vs. United States*, 267 U.S. 498 (1925).

82. *Andresen*, 427 U.S. at 480; *United States vs. Morris*, 977 F.2d 677 (1st Cir. 1992) (warrant found insufficiently particular where it authorized the seizure of "any other object that is in violation of the law"); *United States vs. Brown*, 984 F.2d 1074 (10th Cir. 1993) (warrant found insufficient where it authorized the seizure of other items the officers determined to be stolen once they proceeded with the search).

83. *Franks vs. Delaware*, 438 U.S. 154 (1978).

84. 468 U.S. 897 (1984).

85. 468 U.S. 897 (1984) at 925–26.

86. Franks, 438 U.S. 154; *Lo-Ji Sales vs. New York Inc.*, 442 U.S. 319 (1979); Leon, 468 U.S. at 923; Zimmerman, 277 F.3d at 437; *United States vs. Reilly*, 76 F.3d 1271 (2d Cir. 1996).

87. See, *Miller vs. United States*, 357 U.S. 301 (1958). *Groh vs. Ramirez*, 540 U.S. 551 (2004) (Good faith defense inapplicable where warrant wholly insufficient).

88. *Wilson vs. Arkansas*, 514 U.S. 927 (1995); United States vs. Banks, 124 S.Ct. 521, 540 U.S. 31 (2003).

89. *Richards vs. Wisconsin*, 520 U.S. 385 (1997).

90. *Michigan vs. Summers*, 452 U.S. 692 (1981); *Muehler vs. Mena*, 1965 (2005) U.S. 125 S.Ct. (decided March 22, 2005).

91. *New York vs. Melvin*, 453 U.S. 454 (1981); *Chimel vs. California*, 395 U.S. 752 (1969).

92. *Chimel*, 395 U.S. 752 (1969).

93. One may also wonder if this can be called a "search" at all since the person arrested has a far less expectation of privacy than one who is not.

94. *Maryland vs. Buie*, 494 U.S. 325 (1990).

95. *Buie*, 494 U.S. at 335.

96. *Cupp vs. Murphy*, 412 U.S. 291 (1973); *Warden vs. Hayden*, 387 U.S. 294 (1967).

97. *Mincey vs. Arizona* 437 U.S. 385 (1978); *United States vs. Holloway*, 290 F.3d 1331 (11th Cir. 2002).

98. *Michigan vs. Clifford*, 464 U.S. 287 (1984).

99. *Clifford*, 464 U.S. at 293–97; *Michigan vs. Tyler*, 436 U.S. 499 (1978).

100. 437 U.S. 385 (1978).

101. 469 U.S. 17 (1985).

102. 528 U.S. 11 (1999).

103. *United States vs. Ross*, 456 U.S. 798 (1982); *Chambers vs. Maroney*, 399 U.S. 42 (1970).

104. See, *Pennsylvania vs. Labron*, 518 U.S. 938 (1996); *United States vs. Chadwick*, 433 U.S. 1 (1977).

105. See, *Chambers vs. Mareney*, 399 U.S. 42 (1970); *Florida vs. Myers*, 466 U.S. 380 (1984).

106. *Schneckloth vs. Bustamonte*, 412 U.S. 218 (1973); *United States vs. Matlock*, 415 U.S. 164 (1974); *United States vs. Bunnell*, 280 F.3d 46 (1st Cir. 2002).

107. *United States vs. Mendenhall*, 446 U.S. 544 (1980).

108. *Bumper vs. North Carolina*, 391 U.S. 543 (1968).

109. *Florida vs. Royer*, 460 U.S. 491 (1983).

110. *Coolidge vs. New Hamphire*, 403 U.S. 444 (1971); *Thompson vs. Louisiana*, 469 U.S. 17 (1984); *Horton vs. California*, 496 U.S. 128 (1990) (the discovery need not be inadvertent); *Arizona vs.*

Hicks, 480 U.S. 321 (1987) (plain view doctrine does not justify a further inspection of a stereo so that the officer could get the serial number when the inspection of that stereo was not justified by any warrant or other exception of the warrant requirement).

111. *Terry vs. Ohio*, 392 U.S. 1 (1968).

112. *Minnesota vs. Dickerson*, 508 U.S. 366 (1993).

113. *United States vs. Place*, 462 U.S. 696 (1983).

114. *Illinois vs. Caballes*, 125 S.Ct. 834 (2005).

115. See, for example, *Commonwealth vs. Edmonds*, 526 Pa. 374, 586 A.2d 887 (1991) (Pennsylvania Supreme Court refuses to accept the good faith exception to the warrant requirement recognized in the *Leon* decision); *Commonwealth vs. White*, 543 Pa. 45, 669 A.2d 896 (1995) (Pennsylvania Supreme Court refuses to accept that all automobiles seized in Pennsylvania may be searched without the benefit of a warrant); *Commonwealth vs. Martin*, 534 Pa. 136; 626 A.2d 556 (1993) (Treating dog sniffs as searches under State Constitution). In all of these cases, Pennsylvania Courts assert that their State Constitution affords greater protection of the right of personal privacy than the federal counterpart.

116. *New York vs. Quarles*, 467 U.S. 649 (1984).

117. *Miranda vs. Arizona*, 384 U.S. 436 (1966). The principles of *Miranda* were reaffirmed by the U.S. *Supreme Court in Dickerson vs. United States*, 530 U.S. 428 (2000).

118. *Illinois vs. Perkins*, 496 U.S. 292 (1990).

119. *California vs. Beheler*, 463 U.S. 1121 (1983); *Berkemer vs. McCarty*, 468 U.S. 420 (1984) (person detained pursuant to a routine traffic stop was not in custody); *Minnesota vs. Murphy*, 465 U.S. 420 (1984) (routine interview between an individual and their probation officer is not custodial); *Michigan vs. Sumners*, 452 U.S. 692 (1981) (routine detention of an individual during the execution of a lawful search warrant does not, simply by itself, establish the need for *Miranda* warnings).

120. *Rhode Island vs. Innis*, 446 U.S. 291, 301 (1980).

121. *Arizona vs. Mauro*, 481 U.S. 520 (1987).

122. *Pennsylvania vs. Muniz*, 496 U.S. 582 (1990).

123. *Michigan vs. Mosley*, 423 U.S. 96 (1975).

124. *Edwards vs. Arizona*, 451 U.S. 477 (1981).

125. *Haynes vs. Washington*, 373 U.S. 503 (1963); *Colorado vs. Connelly*, 479 U.S. 157 (1986).

126. See, Rule 902 of Federal Rules of Evidence.

127. Graham, *Handbook of Federal Evidence* (St. Paul, MN: West Publishing Co. Fifth Edition 2001), at Section 901.1, pp. 658–660.

128. *United States vs. Briley*, 319 F.3d 360 (8th Cir. 2003); *United States vs. Myers*, 294 F.3d 203 (1st Cir. 2002).

129. *United States vs. Matta-Ballesteros*, 71 F.3d 754 (9th Cir. 1995).

130. Report of the U.S. Department of Justice, Office of the Inspector General, FBI Crime Laboratory (1997), finding "significant instances of testimonial errors, substandard analytical work, and deficient practices."

131. This element in particular demonstrates how the rules anticipate that the individual really being informed by way of pretrial discovery is the defendant's attorney. Presumably, an individual has a fairly good idea of what their prior criminal record has been; their attorney may not be able to discern the details of that record simply by talking to his client. He may well need the information otherwise available through this rule.

132. 373 U.S. 83 (1963).

133. See, *Giglio vs. United States*, 405 U.S. 150 (1972).

134. 514 U.S. 419 (1995).

135. 514 U.S. 421 (1995).

136. 514 U.S. 506 (1995).

137. 527 U.S. 263 (1999).

138. See, *Banks vs. Dretke*, 540 O.S. 668 124 S.Ct. 1256 (2004); Slutzker v. Johnson 393 F.3d 373 (3rd Cir. 2004).

139. Kyles, 514 U.S. at 509.

140. 409 Mass. 408, 567 N.E. 2d 193 (1991).

141. 131 Idaho 396, 958 P.2d 22 (1998).

142. See, *Torres vs. Mullin*, 317 F.3d 1145 (10th Cir. 2003); *Johnson vs. Lecureux*, 859 F.2d 922 (6th Cir. 1998); *AZ vs. Tucker*, 157 Ariz. 433, 759 P.2d 579 (1988).

143. 111 N.M. 122, 802 P.2d 631 (1991).

144. 104 Nev. 316, 759 P.2d 180 (1988).

145. 123 Wis.2d 444, 368 N.W. 2d 59 (1985).

146. See, *Nieves vs. Kelly*, 990 F.Supp. 255 (S.D. N.Y. 1997).

147. See, *State vs. Holden*, 126 Idaho 755, 890 P.2d 341 (1995); *State vs. Harris*, 407 N.W. 2d 456 (Min. 1987).

148. See, *Brown vs. Barlett*, 993 92 Cir. 0324 (S.D.N.Y. 1993); *State vs. Goodson*, 277 SE. 2d 602 (S.C.1981).

149. 388 F. Supp. 105 (C.D. Cal. 1974).

150. 505 So. 2d 1246 (Ala. 1986).

151. 32 F. Supp. 2d 1150 (N.D. Cal. 1998).

152. 17 Cal. 4th 873, 952 P.2d 715 (1998).

153. John Rago, *Truth or consequences and post-conviction DNA testing: have you reached your verdict*, 107 *Dickinson Law Review* 845 (2003). [hereinafter *Rago*].

154. Professor Rago's source for this number, the Innocence Project website founded in 1992 by Barry Sheck and Peter Neufeld at the Cardozo School of Law in New York identified the number of persons exonerated as 157 as of April 1, 2005. See, www.innocenceproject.org.

155. *Convicted by Juries, Exonerated by Science: Case Studies in the Use of DNA Evidence to Establish Innocence After Trial*, National Institute of Justice 1996, cited in Rago, *supra* note 153, at 868.

156. See, H. Patrick Furman, *Wrongful Convictions and the Accuracy of the Criminal Justice System*, 32 *Colorado Lawyer 11*, 11–12 (2003), (citing numerous studies).

157. *Supra* note 156 at 12.

158. C. Ronald Huff, *Wrongful Conviction: Causes and Public Policy Issues*, 18 Criminal Justice 15 (American Bar Association 2003).

159. Id. See also, Furman, *supra* note 156, at 12.

160. Hugo A. Bedau, *Causes and Consequences of Wrongful Convictions*, 86 Judicature 115 (2002).

161. Bedau, *supra* note 160, at 16. See also, Furman, *supra* note 156, at 12; Huff, *supra* note 158, at 18.

162. Note the strange course of the case of *Commonwealth vs. Smith*, 532 Pa. 177, 615 A.2d 321 (1992), in which an individual was convicted twice for the murder of a mother and two young children. The conviction was reversed and the case dismissed by the Pennsylvania Supreme Court on the grounds that the prosecution intentionally withheld exculpatory physical evidence, improperly placing the defendant twice in jeopardy for the same offense.

163. Bedau, *supra* note 160, at 117–18; Furman, *supra* note 156, at 15–23; Huff, *supra* note 156, at 15–19; Rago, *supra* note 153, at 871.

164. See, Keith A. Findley, *Learning from our mistakes: a criminal justice commission to study wrongful convictions*, 38 *California Western Law Review*, 333 (2002) (discussing the Illinois moratorium in detail).

165. Professor Furman has identified a further area in which a troubling statistical pattern has emerged. This area questions whether the incidents of wrongful conviction are a function of the race of the individual who is accused:

> Wrongful convictions that have been exposed through the use of DNA evidence have received a disproportionate share of publicity, perhaps because of the newness of the technology or because of the often-incontrovertible nature of the exculpatory evidence. However, most cases are not susceptible to re-evaluation with DNA technologies for many reasons, because there is no biological material capable of being tested or retesting does not answer the relevant questions. Issues concerning the accuracy of the criminal justice system grow even more troubling when race is considered. Any criminal justice system needs to periodically examine itself to determine whether race (or gender, wealth, ethnicity, or any other offender or victim characteristic) is improperly entering into the determination of guilt and innocence or into sentencing decisions. There has been a fair amount of research and scholarship into this question in the limited context of capital punishment, the general context of the criminal justice system, and the context of wrongful convictions.

—Furman, *supra* note 156, at 13 (footnotes omitted).

Professor Furman goes on in his article to identify that scholarship and the conclusion that a disproportionate number of wrongful felony convictions involve black or Hispanic defendants; indeed, 57% of the wrongful convictions proven involve a defendant who is a member of minority group (*supra* note 156 at 13).

The same FBI statistics quoted at the beginning of this chapter reveal that as of December 31, 2002, black males outnumbered white males and Hispanic males among inmates in incarceration with sentences of more than one year. U.S. Department of Justice, Bureau of Justice Statistics Bulletin, *Prisoners in 2002* (July 2003), page 9. See also, Comment, *the Race effect on wrongful convictions*, 29 *William Mitchell Law Rev* 845 (2003). According to this same study, 10.4% of black males between the ages of 25 and 29 were in prison as of this date as compared with 2.4% of Hispanic males and 1.2 of white males in the same age group. Similarly, by the end of 2002, 42% of all adults on parole were black as compared to 39% white and 18% Hispanic. In contrast, those who receive probation were predominantly white, with 55% of the adults on probation white compared to 31% black and 12% Hispanic.

Perhaps these statistics do not evidence a racial bias of the system. Statistics, any statistics, count outcomes. They do not critically analyze the complex processes that create those outcomes. Still, the outcomes suggest at least a *prima facie* basis for concern and a significant argument for a more detailed study of this sensitive but crucial area.

166. Ballad of Reading Gaol., Supra note 2.

167. Huff, *supra* note 158, at 15.

168. Ex parte Milligan, 71 U.S. 2 (1866).

Forensic Science and the Family

5

VANESSA S. BROWNE-BARBOUR AND MARGARET K. KRASIK

Introduction

Increasingly, courts, lawyers, and litigants are relying on forensic science to assist in resolving disputes in family law matters. For example, where the paternity of a child is at issue, medical professionals and laboratory technicians may provide reports and testimonial evidence concerning the statistical probability of paternity based upon results from DNA and other tests, using, among other things, blood and body tissue samples. Various health-care professionals may also provide vital evidence in cases involving domestic violence, elder abuse, child abuse, child sexual abuse, and rape trauma. For example, forensic psychiatrists and psychologists may provide the court with comprehensive written reports and testimonial evidence regarding the existence and the effects of domestic violence in particular cases. In divorce litigation, forensic experts may evaluate DNA evidence for proof of infidelity, whereas forensic economists may be retained to assess and testify concerning the value of the marital estate that will be divided. In custody disputes, forensic psychologists and other health-care professionals may provide the court with opinions and recommendations based upon their evaluation of the child, the parents, and other parties involved in the child's life. This chapter introduces several fundamental principles of family law and examines how forensic science increasingly serves as an invaluable resource in resolving numerous issues concerning domestic relations.

Fundamentals of Family Law

Family law, also known as the law of domestic relations, governs the creation, maintenance, dissolution, and postdissolution of family relationships.[1] Considering the significant demographic changes during the past century, what constitutes a family unit varies from household to household.[2] The traditional family unit comprises a husband, wife, and their children who share the same residence.[3] A nontraditional family comprises a group of individuals, who may or may not be related by blood, sharing the same residence as a family unit.[4] Presently, nearly one third of all children in the United States live in a single parent household.[5]

In family law matters, an ever present, interested third party of any family unit is the state.[6] Under both its general police powers and the ancient doctrine of *parens patriae*, a state has both a right and an obligation to protect the welfare of its citizens and, thus, maintains an interest in family relationships.[7] In the United States, historically, states have jurisdiction over domestic relations and are accorded broad discretion in such matters.[8] States regulate domestic relations through statutes enacted by state legislatures or by common law in the form of decisions rendered by state courts. With respect to marriage, generally, states are free to place reasonable restrictions on who may marry and to prescribe licensure procedures that must be followed before marriage.[9] For example, many states have laws that prohibit individuals from marrying persons related to them within certain degrees of consanguinity, that is, one who is closely related by blood.[10] These statutes expressly state that individuals are prohibited from marrying their mother, father, sister, brother, aunt, uncle, and, in some states, their first cousin.[11] The majority of states also impose minimum age restrictions on who may marry.[12]

Marriage may be defined as a "legal union of a man and a woman as husband and wife."[13] Marriage is a contractual relationship and gives rise to a status with certain legally protected rights and obligations in which states maintain an interest.[14]

"The marriage contract, once entered into, becomes a relation, rather than a contract, and invests each party with a status toward the other, and society at large, involving duties and responsibilities that no longer matter for private regulation but concern the commonwealth. And in this aspect, marriage is a civil and social institution, *publici juris*, being the foundation of the family and the origin of domestic relations, which is of the utmost importance to civilization and social progress; hence, the state is deeply concerned about maintaining its purity and integrity."[14]

Under the Full Faith and Credit Clause of the U.S. Constitution,[15] each state is required to recognize the laws and judicial decisions of all other states, unless such laws are repugnant to public policy in that state.[16] In 1996, Congress enacted the Defense of Marriage Act,[17] which defines marriage under federal law as a union between a man and a woman, as husband and wife and also provides that states are not required to recognize same-sex marriages of a sister state.[18] Although activists in several states propose changes in restrictions on same-sex marriages, currently no state recognizes, either by statute or constitution, same-sex marriages. In fact, many states expressly prohibit same sex marriages by defining marriage as a union between a man and a woman.[19]

In addition to regulating marriage, states are also free to establish procedures for obtaining a divorce or dissolution of marriage, and resolution of issues related to divorce.[20] Legal issues incident to divorce may include determinations of child custody and support, alimony or spousal support, and distribution of marital property. In almost every state and the District of Columbia, no-fault divorce laws allow parties to obtain a divorce without having to prove that one party to the marriage was at fault.[21] Many states, however, have retained several fault-based grounds for divorce, such as adultery, bigamy, desertion, and cruel and inhumane treatment.[22] In divorce cases where adultery is alleged, DNA evidence may be evaluated and offered to prove infidelity.[23] Where cruel and inhumane treatment is alleged, various health-care and law enforcement professionals may evaluate the case and provide testimony and written reports to establish the occurrence of extreme mental and physical violence.[24]

Currently, whether based on fault or no-fault, in the United States, researchers project that nearly 50% of recent marriages will likely end in divorce.[25]

Domestic Violence

Domestic violence is an insidious societal problem that affects individuals regardless of age, socioeconomic status, race, religious beliefs, educational background, culture, nationality, or sexual orientation.[26] The abuse and control of domestic violence may also victimize the elderly, adolescent dating partners, and the disabled.[27] In considering what constitutes domestic violence, one may immediately think of an exertion of physical force that results in bodily contact of another.[27] Domestic violence, however, involves physical contact, rape threats, harassment, emotional abuse, and stalking by an abusive spouse, intimate partner, or date to control their partners.[28] A domestic violence abuser may use power over finances to control the economically dependent victim, and children, if any, may also be used to manipulate the abused.[27] Domestic violence encompasses violence between intimate partners and includes violence or a reasonable fear of physical injury or harm inflicted by one member on another member of the same household.[28] (p. 597–98) Thus, multiple factors, including, psychological, familial, social, and other factors affect the abuser's ability to exert control over the abused.[27]

Apart from the obvious negative consequences, domestic violence presents legal issues in the areas of family, criminal, tax, insurance, and estate planning law.[27] Further, harm caused by domestic violence has created a public health crisis and places a strain on economic productivity in the U.S.[27] The National Institute of Justice reports that domestic violence costs $67 billion annually for medical and mental health costs and other victim services, property damage and loss, police and fire services, and lost worker productivity.[27] Domestic violence related medical and mental health costs are estimated at nearly $4.1 billion each year.[29] Although women account for only 39% of violence related visits to hospital emergency rooms, approximately 84% of these women suffered injuries from an intimate partner.[30] Moreover, intimate partner violence results in short- and long-term costs for treatment of physical injuries and illnesses, as well as psychological symptoms.[31]

In an effort to prevent violence and reduce crime, Congress passed the Crime Bill in 1994, which included a provision entitled Violence Against Women Act (VAWA).[32] The VAWA was enacted specifically "to protect the civil rights of victims of gender motivated violence and to promote public safety, health, and activities affecting interstate commerce by establishing a Federal civil rights cause of action for victims of crimes of violence motivated by gender."[33] The VAWA authorized funding for additional prosecutors and also funded specialized domestic violence training for health care and social services professionals, prosecutors, and law enforcement officers.[34] The VAWA further provided an increase in counseling services and shelters for victims of domestic violence.[34] The Act also provided an effective program to educate the public about domestic violence and authorized funding for more extensive research on the causes of domestic violence.[34] Importantly, the Act provided interstate pursuit and enforcement of perpetrators of gender motivated violence.[34]

Shortly after its enactment, the constitutionality of the VAWA was challenged in a case involving the alleged rape of a female student by two members of the varsity football team at Virginia Polytechnic Institute (VPI) in the fall of 1994.[35] The female student filed a suit in a federal district court against the two alleged rapists and VPI contending that (1) the attack violated § 13981 of VAWA and (2) VPI's handling of the complaint violated Title IX of the Education Amendments of 1972.[35] (p. 604) The alleged rapists filed a motion to dismiss for failure to state a cognizable claim and on the grounds that § 13981 was unconstitutional.[35] (p. 604) The trial court dismissed the plaintiff's VAWA claims.[35] (p. 604–05) The U.S. Court of Appeals for the Fourth Circuit, following a rehearing *en banc*, affirmed that § 13981 was unconstitutional.[35] (p. 627) The U.S. Supreme Court affirmed the holdings of the lower courts determining that Congress exceeded its authority in enacting § 13981.[35] (p. 627) Thus, the Commonwealth of Virginia, and not Congress, had the authority to provide a civil remedy for the alleged claims.[35] (p. 627) Subsequent to the Court's decision in *Morrison*, the Violence Against Women Civil Rights Restoration Act of 2000 was introduced in Congress to amend the VAWA.[36]

Although men are also victims of domestic violence, it is estimated that 90–95% of the victims of reported cases of domestic violence in the United States are women.[37] In fact, a woman is battered every 15 seconds in the U.S.[38] and nearly one out of four women report being raped or physically assaulted by an intimate partner.[39] Women are 5–8 times more likely to be victimized by an intimate partner, and among those who were raped or physically assaulted since attaining the age of 18 years, 76% were abused by a current or former husband or boyfriend, a cohabiting partner, or a date.[40] Intimate partners include a current or former boyfriend or a husband, a cohabiting partner, or a date.[41]

In 1992 and 1993, a report from the U.S. Department of Justice Bureau of National Statistics reveals that women suffer approximately 3.8 million assaults and 500,000 rapes each year.[27] More recent national estimates on domestic violence incidents suggest that intimate partners physically assault at least 2 million women each year.[27] Further, annually, approximately 324,000 pregnant women suffer from acts of violence from an intimate partner.[27] From 1996 through 2001, the National Domestic Violence Hotline received approximately 700,000 calls for assistance with issues related to domestic violence,[42] which is the most frequently reported crime based on statistical data collected by the Federal Bureau of Investigation.[43] Although these statistics are alarming, the view of several scholars is that domestic violence is the most underreported crime.[44] Consequently, if all incidences of domestic violence were reported, the increase in its total number would likely be significant.

In the United States, from 1976 through 1996, approximately 31,600 women were murdered by an intimate partner.[45] In 1999 alone, 1,218 were murdered by their intimate partners.[46] Women between the ages of 20 and 29 years have the greatest risk of being killed by an intimate partner.[47] Most of these murders occur when the battered woman attempts to leave the abusive relationship or seeks legal assistance to prevent future harm.[27] Divorced and separated women represent only 10% of all women, yet, as a group, they constitute 75% of all battered women and are battered 14 times more often than women who continue live to with their intimate partner.[48] Additionally, between 1981 and 1998, intimate partners used firearms most often to commit homicide against battered women.[49]

Studies indicate that there are certain risk factors associated with persons who engage in intimate partner violence.[49] With respect to intimate male partners, drug and alcohol abuse and unemployment are associated with increased risk for committing physical, sexual, and emotional abuse.[49] Research on intimate partner violence indicates that men had consumed alcohol in 45% of the cases, and women had consumed alcohol in 20% of the cases.[49] Comparatively, a significant proportion of intimate male partners who engage in domestic violence report that they experience more aggression, more depression, lower self-esteem, and more hostility toward women than do nonviolent intimate male partners.[49] Violent intimate male partners are also more likely to suffer from certain personality disorders such as antisocial or narcissistic behaviors, dependency and attachment issues, and schizoidal or borderline schizoidal personalities.[49] Typically, however, the perpetrator of domestic violence blames the victim and claims the victim provoked the violent acts.[27]

Although the law provides legal remedies, such as filing criminal charges, tort claims, and divorce, many domestic violence victims are unwilling or unable to avail themselves of these alternatives.[50] Consequently, states have enacted domestic abuse statutes that provide domestic violence victims with an additional legal recourse for protection from abuse.[50] Although domestic abuse statutes are civil in nature and are designed primarily to prevent domestic violence,[50] certain provisions make it a felony offense to intentionally inflict a physical injury upon one's spouse or a member of one's household.[50] In many jurisdictions, the victim may obtain an *ex parte* protection from an abuse order that, among other things, excludes the abuser from the residence and prohibits contact with the victim for a limited period of time pending a court hearing on the abuse charges. Further, the federal Safe Homes for Women Act of 1994 makes it a crime for a person to travel across a state border with the purpose of injuring, harassing, or intimidating one's spouse or intimate partner.

Health-care professionals may be among the first to identify and treat injuries caused by domestic violence.[51] Physicians, nurses, emergency medical specialists, other health-care professionals, and social services providers should receive the necessary training to enable them to identify domestic violence and sexual assaults and provide the requisite treatment and referrals.[51] The American Medical Association (AMA) has adopted comprehensive diagnostic and treatment guidelines related to domestic violence, child sexual and physical abuse, elder abuse, and neglect.[52] AMA guidelines provide that physicians have an ethical duty to diagnose and treat victims of domestic violence.[53] Certain states have statutes that require treating physicians to report to law enforcement or other appropriate authority incidents of criminal and intimate partner abuse.[54] Due to privacy concerns, however, absent consent of a victim who is competent or a state statute compelling disclosure, the AMA, however, does not require physicians to report the abuse to law enforcement or other agencies.[55] Nevertheless, physicians and other health care providers who fail to report incidents of domestic violence to law enforcement or other protective agencies may be liable civilly in negligence.[56] Acknowledging the need to become more involved, the Joint Commission on the Accreditation of Health care Organizations mandates that all hospitals develop and implement protocols that will assist them in the identification, evaluation, and treatment of intimate partner violence victims.[57]

Similarly, in a position statement on maltreatment, domestic violence, and neglect, the Emergency Nurses Association (ENA) states that emergency nurses are advocates for victims of domestic violence and have a duty to identify and report suspected cases of domestic violence, maltreatment, and neglect.[58] The ENA position statement makes patient safety and confidentiality a priority.[58] (p. 3) The position statement also acknowledges the importance of emergency nurses making appropriate documentation of domestic violence abuse, including photographs, body maps of injuries, drawings, and, importantly, detailed reports in legible handwriting.[59] Proper documentation by nurses and other health care providers is crucial to assist prosecutors in preparing and presenting cases, as well as assisting courts in deciding domestic violence cases.[60] Since victims often deny patterns and escalation of abuse, the victim's "survival may depend on the astute observations, assessments, and interventions by emergency nurses and other health care providers."[60]

Further, the ENA position statement advocates support for numerous objectives: concerning domestic violence, maltreatment, and neglect. Among these objectives are:

A. Development of protocols to improve identification, treatment, intervention, and prevention of abuse
B. Mandatory professional development and education that emphasizes the importance of documentation
C. Increased funding for outreach programs and public education
D. Allocation of adequate funding for research, advocates, shelters, and other services[61]

Generally, health care providers must develop routine protocols that enable them to gather, preserve, document, and testify concerning forensic evidence of domestic violence.[62]

Child Custody

In the evolving law of domestic relations, the U.S. Supreme Court has "long recognized that a parent's interests in the nurture, upbringing, companionship, care, and custody of children are generally protected by the Due Process Clause of the Fourteenth Amendment" of the U.S. Constitution.[63] Historically, however, the father had the absolute right and responsibility to the custody, care, and services of his children.[64] This presumption was primarily based upon the paternal preference rule in English common law[64] and existed in ancient Roman law.[65] The father also possessed absolute authority to make decisions relating to the child's medical, religious, and educational matters.[66] The basis of this feudalistic paternal preference rule is a natural and legal presumption that the father as "the author of their being feels for them with tenderness which will secure their happiness more certainly than any other tie on earth,"[67] as well as the law of private property.[68] By early nineteenth century, however, courts began to reject the harshness of the paternal preference rule, in part, as a result of the rule's complete disregard of a fit mother's right to nurture her child.[69]

After rejecting the paternal preference rule, courts began to apply the tender years' presumption in custody disputes and awarded mother custody of young children, usually less than seven years of age.[70] The underlying rationale for the tender years' presumption is that mothers are better suited for nurturing infants and very young children.[71] Subsequently, courts rejected all gender classifications, including the tender years' presumption, as the determining factor in custody disputes between parents on the basis that, among other reasons, such a presumption violates the Equal Protection Clause of the Fourteenth Amendment.[72] Thus, in deciding child custody issues, courts seek to promote the best interest of the child.[73] In the United States, some scholars have concluded that for most of the twentieth century courts have employed maternal preference rules to implement a best interest analysis in deciding custody matters.[74]

In the United States, whether by statute or case law, courts seek to award custody based on the best interest of the child in custody cases.[75] "The priority of the child's interests over those of the competing adults is premised on the assumption that when a family breaks up, children are usually the most vulnerable parties and thus most in need of the law's protection."[76] To ascertain the best interest of the child, the Uniform Marriage and Divorce Act (UMDA) requires a court to evaluate all relevant factors, including, the interrelationship between the child, his parents, his siblings, and other individuals who may significantly affect the child's best interest, and the wishes of the child and his or her parents.[77] Similarly, in the American Law Institute's principles governing family dissolution, the best interest standard requires consideration of a broad range of factors, including the fitness of the parents to care for the child, emotional attachments between the child and parents, the mature and reasonable preference of the child, and all other factors relevant to the welfare of the child.[78]

Best interest determinations require a case-by-case evaluation of these and other factors with respect to individual circumstances and needs of a particular child.[79] In California, for example, the Family Code requires courts to consider all relevant factors, including the child's "health, safety, and welfare" and any evidence of domestic violence in determining a best interest analysis in custody matters.[80] Similarly, in Pennsylvania, a best interest of the child analysis is "based on a consideration of all factors that legitimately affect the child's physical, intellectual, moral, and spiritual well-being."[81]

Since the best interests of the child determinations in custody disputes should seek to protect the health, safety, and welfare of the child, courts should consider the presence of domestic violence in the home. Thousands of children witness intimate partners commit acts of domestic violence each year.[82] Men who commit acts of violence against their intimate partner are likely to commit violent acts against children.[83] Children who experience or witness domestic violence are at an increased risk of committing and becoming victims of intimate partner violence and also are at risk for long-term mental and physical health issues.[84] These long-term mental and physical problems include alcohol and substance abuse.[84] In light of the findings concerning the harmful effects of exposure to domestic violence has on children, courts must calculate the presence of domestic violence as a relevant factor in deciding custody.[85]

In custody matters, courts frequently rely upon written reports and testimony of various experts in determining the best interest of the child. Forensic experts, including physicians, psychologists, psychiatrists, nurses, and social workers may provide testimony and written reports to assist courts in making best interests analyses. Among the various issues on which forensic experts prepare comprehensive reports to advise courts are:

1. Aspects related to parental fitness, such as neglect and abuse, and chemical or alcohol dependency and abuse
2. Domestic violence history
3. Parent's ability to meet the child's physical and emotional needs
4. Evaluation of the primary caretaker and psychological parent
5. Willingness of the custodial parent to foster a positive relationship with the noncustodial parent
6. Living and child care arrangements[86]

Syndromes

A syndrome is "a number of symptoms occurring together and characterizing a specific disease or conditions."[87] Posttraumatic stress disorder, most commonly associated with combat soldiers and prisoners of war, develops as a result of a severe traumatic stressor such as experiencing domestic violence, sexual and physical abuse as a child, or being held as a hostage.[88] The most common traumatic events resulting in posttraumatic stress disorder in women are rape, sexual molestation, being threatened with a weapon, physical attacks, and experiencing psychic abuse as a child.[89] For men, the most common traumatic events leading to posttraumatic stress disorder are combat exposure, rape, experiencing physical abuse, or neglect as a child.[90]

Posttraumatic stress disorder is an anxiety disorder resulting from exposure to traumatic life-threatening events and may lead to abnormal behaviors.[91] Many scholars and courts view rape trauma syndrome, battered women's syndrome, and battered child syndrome as specific types of posttraumatic stress disorder.[92] In contrast, other scholars contend that rape trauma syndrome is a set of behaviors in response to the rape and, unlike posttraumatic stress syndrome, is not abnormal behavior.[93] The pervasive presence in our society of domestic violence against women supports research indicating that the largest class of posttraumatic stress disorder sufferers is women who have experienced assaults.[94]

Rape Trauma Syndrome

According to the U.S. Department of Justice statistics for the years 1992 through 2000, there were approximately 140,990 rapes, 109,230 attempted rapes, and 152,680 sexual assaults committed each year against a person 12 years or older.[95] The victims were female in 94% of the rapes, 91% of all attempted rapes, and 89% of the sexual assaults.[96] These statistics clearly are underrepresentative since most rapes and sexual assaults are not reported and most victims do not seek treatment for their injuries.[97] Personal privacy, fear of reprisal, perceived police bias, and desire to protect the offender are among the reasons victims give for failing to report rapes and sexual assaults.[98]

Rape trauma syndrome, so named by Drs. Ann Burgess and Lynda Holmstrom in 1974,[99] is an "acute stress reaction" to rape or attempted rape and is characterized by certain physical, psychological, and behavioral responses.[100] Rape trauma syndrome, which affects both men and women, consists of two phases: (1) an acute phase that is characterized by the emotional disorganization and physical effects of the rape and (2) a re-organization phase that is a long-term rape recovery process.[101]

The acute phase is characterized by three kinds of reactions:[102] The first reactions are impact reactions immediately following the rape, including the victim's perception of the rape and the initial responses of others toward the victim.[102] Emotional reactions are the second type of reactions in the acute phase of rape trauma syndrome.[103] Generally, emotional reactions fall within one of two categories.[104] In the first category, the victim tends to be emotionally expressive, exhibiting feelings of anxiety, anger, and fear "through such behavior as crying, sobbing, smiling, restlessness, and tenseness."[105] In contrast, in the second category, the victim masks or hides her emotions beneath a controlled, calm composure.[106] Other emotional reactions may include feelings of shame, embarrassment, and self-blame.[107] The somatic category is the third type of reactions in the acute phase and involves the physical manifestations of the rape.[108] Evidence of physical trauma include bruises, soreness, tension headaches, fatigue, itching, vaginal discharge, chronic vaginal infections, and sleep disturbances.[108] As described, the acute phase of rape trauma syndrome is represented in the emotional disorganization and physical injuries experienced by the rape victim.[109]

The re-organization phase of rape trauma syndrome is a long-term process during which the victim employs various coping mechanisms in an effort to restore some semblance of order to her life.[110] During this phase, the victim may attempt to cope by changing her contact information, such as address and telephone number, in an effort to feel safe.[110] Victims also may experience sleep disturbances such as dreams and nightmares.[110] Additionally, rape victims may develop traumatophobia that manifests itself in various types of feelings of fear.[111] For example, a victim who was attacked from behind may develop a fear of having anyone behind them.[111] Other common phobias include fear of having sexual relations and fear of being alone.[111] Studies suggest that counseling and a strong support system may improve a victim's chance of recovery from rape trauma syndrome.[112]

In addressing the need to treat victims suffering from rape trauma, many hospitals staff sexual assault nurse examiners (SANE) who are specially trained to conduct thorough physical examinations and gather forensic evidence of the crime.[113] SANE use special kits containing sterile swabs to collect bodily fluids, fingernail scrapings, and hair.[114] SANE also may take photographs and provide comprehensive written documentation.[115] Evidence gathered may assist in prosecution of the rape or assault charges.[116] Specifically, the physician who examined the rape victim may testify that, among other things, penetration occurred and that the victim's physical injuries were caused by forced sexual intercourse.[117]

More than one half of U.S. states and the District of Columbia have held that evidence of rape trauma syndrome is admissible.[118] Evidence of rape trauma syndrome has been offered, among other things, to (1) establish the rape; (2) prove the reliability and relevance of the syndrome; (3) rehabilitate the credibility of the victim; and (4) assist in the victim's defense to explain culpable behavior.[119] Although evidence of rape trauma syndrome may be offered to prove rape, such evidence generally is inadmissible for that purpose to avoid misleading the jury.[120]

Extensive research suggests that the majority of women who are raped will suffer from posttraumatic stress disorder symptoms.[121] Rape trauma sufferers may experience acute symptoms such as paranoia, extreme fearfulness, anxiety, nightmares, and other sleep disturbances.[122] Rape trauma victims may also experience nausea, fatigue, headaches, an inability to concentrate on work or school, and episodes of crying.[122] Additionally, rape trauma sufferers may experience certain physiological responses such as hyperalertness, arousal, and startle responses.[122]

Chronic symptoms of sexual assault trauma include depression, eating disorders, devalued self-esteem, guilt, recurrent gynecological and gastrointestinal ailments, chronic fatigue, and habitually troubled relationships.[122] Women who have a history of sexual or physical assault may be more likely to engage in behavior that is detrimental to their health, such as chemical dependency, smoking, and high-risk sexual encounters.[122] Since research suggests that women who suffer physical or sexual assaults are more likely to seek help from their primary physicians rather than law enforcement officers, lawyers, or mental health professionals, primary physicians should be trained to screen for domestic violence, including rape and sexual assaults.[122]

Battered Spouse Syndrome

Battered spouse syndrome is used interchangeably with battered woman syndrome, battered wife syndrome, and battered person syndrome,[123] and is a subcategory of post-traumatic stress disorders.[124] Battered spouse syndrome may be defined as a "constellation of medical and psychological conditions of a woman [or man] who has suffered physical, sexual, or emotional abuse at the hands of a spouse or lover."[125] In addition to the physical injuries suffered, a battered spouse, most often a woman, may experience traumatic psychological harm.[126] Symptoms of traumatic psychological harm include amnesia, re-experiencing trauma through flashbacks, lack of emotional reactions, angry or hostile reactions, and depression.[126]

The relationship between perpetrator and victim of domestic violence is complex, yet frequently falls within one of several clear and predictable patterns of behavior. Relying on a psychosocial theory of learned helplessness, Dr. Lenore Walker, a noted psychologist, identified one pattern of battering behavior as a "cycle of violence" that consists of three recurring phases.[127] The cycle of violence consists of varying "levels of positive and negative emotional engagement, coercion, and physical aggression."[127] The first phase is the tension building phase during which the perpetrator becomes increasingly abusive toward the abused by exerting control, engaging in verbal and physical intimidation and isolating the abused from friends and family.[128] During the tension building phase, the abused engages in a futile attempt to placate the batterer to prevent the abuse from escalating.[129]

In phase two, the acute battering phase, the batterer escalates the level of violence that may range from open hand slaps to closed fist punches, from kicks to beatings, and from threats with deadly weapons, such as knives and guns, to actual use of the same.[130] It is during this acute battering phase that the victim suffers more severe injuries, forced sexual intercourse, and sometimes death.[131] The final stage of the battering cycle is known as the honeymoon phase during which the batterer apologizes, professes his love, and promises to seek counseling.[132]

During the honeymoon phase, the batterer continues to control and manipulate the victim and may even blame the victim for the batterer's violent behavior.[133] Typically, the victim remains in the relationship for numerous reasons, including the fact that she is completely economically, emotionally, and socially dependent on the batterer.[134] For fear of deportation, battered women who are undocumented immigrants frequently remain in an abusive relationship until their legal status issues are resolved.[135] Additional explanations as to why the victim remains in the relationship are fear of retaliation, escalation in the abuse, and fear that the batterer, legally or illegally, will gain custody of the children.[136] Another identifiable pattern of battering is separation abuse.[136] When the victim of abuse attempts to leave the relationship or seeks legal recourse, the batterer will threaten or retaliate with violence.[136] As previously noted, most murders of battered women occur when the battered woman attempts to leave the abusive relationship or seeks legal assistance to prevent future harm.[27] Thus, the victim remains in the relationship of dependence and fear, and the battering cycle continues and even intensifies.[137]

According to Walker, there are three primary symptom clusters psychologists use to measure whether a person exposed to trauma has developed posttraumatic stress syndrome: cognitive disturbances, high arousal symptoms, and high avoidance symptoms.[138] First, cognitive disturbances involve, among other things, repetitive intrusive memories, memory disturbances, and repressed memories of the battering experiences.[138] Second, high arousal symptoms may include high anxiety, nervousness, jumpiness, and panic attacks, during which the battered person experiences neurochemical, physiological, and physical changes.[139] Third, high avoidance symptoms are evidenced by denial, depression, withdrawal from established social circles, minimizing the danger of the situation, or repressing the battering incidents.[139]

Although battered spouse syndrome is not a true defense, evidence that the defendant in a criminal trial is a victim of domestic violence may be relevant and admissible in support of the defense of duress, insanity, or self-defense.[140] The purpose of offering evidence on battered spouse syndrome is to assist the trier of fact, either court or jury, as to whether the use and the degree of force were reasonable under the circumstances in light of the battered person's state of mind at the time of the event.[141] Evidence that the defendant suffered from battered spouse syndrome may be admissible as mitigating evidence for purposes of sentencing and also may assist in the prosecution of the alleged batterer.[142]

Expert testimony may assist the court by providing general information on clinical and scientific knowledge concerning the effects of domestic violence.[143] Experts may also testify regarding the specific effects of domestic violence on the defendant based upon the expert's psychological or psychiatric evaluation of the battered spouse.[143] In certain jurisdictions, a forensic psychologist may determine (1) whether the person is a battered spouse, (2) whether the abuse suffered has caused the development of battered spouse syndrome, and (3) the impact of the battering on the person's state of mind at the relevant time.[144] Further, expert testimony may dispel common myths and misperceptions the court or jury may have about battering, batterers, and battered spouses.[145] Currently, expert testimony on battering and its effect are admissible in varying degrees and purposes in all 50 states and the District of Columbia.[146]

Parentage Testing

Absent use of assisted reproductive technologies involving donated ova or a mix-up in the hospital nursery, generally there is no question as to the maternity of a child. Such is not the case, however, with respect to the paternity of a child. Whether a child is born during a marriage or out of wedlock, both mother and father have a legal duty to support the child. Further, in cases involving a nonmarital child, the marital status should not affect the child's legal right to the care and support of his or her father, and the father has a corresponding right and obligation to care for and support his child. With respect to a nonmarital child who receives federal funds for care and support, federal laws require the child's paternity to be established for child support enforcement purposes.[147] In the United States, there are approximately 250,000 children for whom paternity must be established each year.[148]

There are various means by which parentage, most often paternity, may be established. In 1973, the Uniform Parentage Act (UPA) was promulgated to set forth procedures for establishing paternity of children and provide for equality under the law without regard for whether the child was born during, outside of, or in the absence of marriage.[149] In light of significant advancements in scientific technologies concerning establishment of paternity and assisted reproduction, the UPA was replaced with the UPA of 2000, and subsequently amended in 2002.[150] The revised UPA, among other things, includes provisions for establishing paternity, genetic testing, and paternity registry.[151]

Historically, under a common law doctrine known as the presumption of legitimacy, a child born during marriage was presumed to be the child of the husband.[152] The presumption of legitimacy doctrine served to protect the family unit and to prevent the child from being illegitimate.[152] This presumption could only be rebutted by showing that the husband was impotent and incapable of fathering children or that the husband did not have access to his wife to engage in sexual intercourse during the relevant time of conception of the child at issue.[153] Absent proof of either of these two, the presumption stood, and the child was considered to be a child of the marriage.[153]

In *Michael H. v. Gerald D.*, the U.S. Supreme Court upheld a California statute that codified the common law presumption of legitimacy that a "child born to a married woman living with her husband is presumed to be a child of the marriage."[154] In *Michael H.*, blood tests indicated a 98.07% probability that a man with whom the wife had an adulterous affair was determined to be the natural father of a child born during the marriage.[155] The Court affirmed the state court's denial of the natural father's request for visitation with the child and upheld the state statute concerning presumption of legitimacy.[156] The evidence indicated that the husband was capable of fathering children and had access to his wife during the relevant time period.[157] Thus, the natural father was unable to rebut the presumption of legitimacy. The Court found that "the conclusive presumption expresses the State's substantive policy and furthers it, excluding inquiries into the child's paternity that would be destructive of family integrity and privacy."[158] The Court further determined that there was neither authority nor "deeply rooted traditions" to support the natural father's claim that he has a fundamental right to visitation with a child he fathered as a result of an adulterous affair with the mother, particularly where the marriage remains intact.[159] Consequently, the denial of the natural father's request for visitation with his child was affirmed.[160]

There are various means by which parentage may be established. Pursuant to the UPA, parentage for a woman may be established by giving birth to a child, adopting a child, or by a court adjudicating that the woman is the mother of a child.[161] The UPA further provides that a man may become a parent by (1) voluntary acknowledgement, (2) an unrebutted legal presumption, (3) adoption of a child, (4) consent to one's spouse to participate in assisted conception, or (5) by court adjudication.[162] Early paternity proceedings were quasi-criminal hearings and required the mother to establish paternity of the putative father beyond a reasonable doubt.[163] The underlying policy for these proceedings was to enforce the father's legal obligation to support his child and relieve the public treasury from the burden of support.[164]

Evidence admissible in a trial to establish paternity may range from the physical resemblance between the child and the alleged father to results from genetic tests on blood and tissue samples.[165] Genetic tests consist of "an analysis of genetic markers to exclude or identify a man as the father or a woman as the mother of a child."[166] Genetic testing to establish parentage includes tests on deoxyribonucleic acid (DNA) and "blood-group antigens, red-cell antigens, human-leukocyte antigens, serum enzymes, serum proteins, or red-cell enzymes."[167]

A paternity index is a ratio obtained by calculating the likelihood of paternity of a man based on the results of genetic tests of the mother, child, and putative father and comparing the results with the likelihood that the man is not the father of the child based on the same data.[168] The probability of paternity is "the measure, for the ethnic or racial group to which the alleged father belongs, of the probability that the man in question is the father of the child, compared with a random, unrelated man of the same ethnic or racial group, expressed as a percentage incorporating the paternity index and a prior probability."[169] With recent advances in technology, parentage may be established or disestablished conclusively through genetic marker tests yielding a probability of parentage, most often paternity, of 99.9%.[170]

Presently, genetic marker tests of DNA samples are used more frequently than serology to establish paternity.[171] DNA is found in blood "skin, tissue, sweat, bone, the root and shaft of hair, earwax, mucus, urine, semen, and vaginal or rectal cells."[172] DNA determines the physical characteristics of humans, such as height, bone structure, and eye and hair color.[172] No two people, except identical twins, have the same DNA.[173] Among the techniques employed to examine genetic markers in DNA are polymerase chain reaction (PCR), single-strand conformation polymorphism (SSCP), and restriction fragment length polymorphisms (RFLPS).[174] Thus, forensic science and technology can assist in establishing or disproving paternity.

As a condition of receiving federal funds, states developed and implemented procedures to establish paternity by voluntary acknowledgement.[175] The mother and the genetic father sign a voluntary acknowledgement under penalty of perjury.[176] Pursuant to the UPA, even the presumption of legitimacy may be overcome by a voluntary acknowledgement of paternity, provided that the presumed father signs a denial of paternity.[176] Another means by which paternity may be established is the doctrine of equitable estoppel.[177] Pursuant to the doctrine of estoppel, parties may be barred from denying the paternity of a child where (1) the mother holds out her child as being the child of one man or (2) a parental relationship has developed with the child.[178] The policy underlying this doctrine is to protect the child from trauma and interference with an established parent–child bond.[179] Finally, in certain jurisdictions, the subsequent marriage of the mother and the father shortly after the birth of the child is a legally effective means of establishing the parentage of the child.[180] Thus, establishing parentage assists courts in their efforts to determine the best interests of the child and in obtaining support for the child's reasonable health, welfare, and educational needs.[181]

Elder Law Basics: Planning for Autonomy

Elder law, seen as an area of specialized practice for lawyers, spans a wide and diverse array of legal issues. The elderly, and those who anticipate being elderly, encounter the same legal problems as do other citizens. They have concerns about employment, housing and real estate matters, domestic relations problems, insurance, access to credit, contractual disputes, and even criminal matters! Nevertheless, elders commonly feel a heightened sense of anxiety about a cluster of issues that arise from worries about financial and physical security in old age.[182]

Most elders, if asked, would say that they value maintaining their autonomy — their ability to act relatively independently — in personal and financial matters. They have concerns about loss of their physical ability to care for themselves (and each other), to arrange for shelter and medical care, and to make health care wishes known and respected. They are equally worried about being able to conserve and use assets to provide for themselves in later days and, if possible, to pass some kind of legacy on to family and loved ones. Many of the elderly look to lawyers and other professionals to help them achieve these objectives.

A discussion of some of the basics of elder law — those legal principles and rules of broad interest and application to most elderly Americans — then can center on asking what the "default" scenario is. That is, how does the law address these important physical and financial questions when an individual has *not* planned ahead or taken any action to address them? How does the law fill in the blanks in personal planning for financial and physical security?

Intestacy: The Default System for Identifying Heirs to a Decedent's Property

Most of the elderly expect or hope that they will be owners of property — real estate, cash, personal belongings, investments — at the time of their deaths. Many people nevertheless die without writing a will to control disposition of that property to survivors. The legal default position is supplied by the law of *intestate succession*, also called the law of descent and distribution. In the United States, *intestate succession* is a matter of state law; therefore, the details of the law will vary from state to state, although there is a great deal of similarity among the various state systems.

Under the law of intestate succession, all the property of a decedent's *probate estate* (i.e., property that the decedent owned during life and that did not otherwise pass to another person) must be distributed to those persons whom the statute defines as the *intestate heirs*. In all states, these heirs include the decedent's surviving spouse. In certain instances, especially where there are no surviving lineal descendants of the decedent and no surviving parents of the decedent, the spouse will even take the entire estate.[183] The spouse is thus given a favored position under most intestate distribution schemes. He or she is also virtually always the only intestate heir who is not a blood relative of the decedent.

After the surviving spouse, the "issue" or "lineal descendants," of the decedent take as heirs. This category includes children, grandchildren, great-grandchildren, and in fact a theoretically indefinite number of generations who might be alive at the death of the intestate person. This category under most state laws *does not include stepchildren* and foster children, but usually *does include* children who are adopted into the family, and also includes children (and grandchildren, etc.) who are nonmarital children — that is, children born out of wedlock.

If an intestate dies survived by multiple generations of lineal descendants, intestate laws commonly mandate a scheme for distribution among the generations based on a principle of *representation*:

Example A(1): Alice, a widow, died intestate possessing a probate estate of $50,000. She was survived by her son Bob and his two children, and her daughter Carol and her three children.

> Under most intestate laws, Bob and Carol would be Alice's intestate heirs, and they would split the estate equally. The grandchildren would take nothing, since an earlier generation would have priority to take a share.

Example A(2): Assume that Alice's daughter, Carol, predeceased her, and Alice was survived only by Bob, Bob's two children, and Carol's three children.

> Under most intestate laws, Bob would take half of his mother's estate, and Bob's children would still take nothing, but Carol's children would take the other half of Alice's estate, taking their deceased mother's share by representation.

If an intestate is not survived by a spouse or lineal descendants, the law names as heirs the following relatives, ancestors, or collaterals, who take in the following order of priority: parents; brothers and sisters; grandparents; uncles and aunts; children and grandchildren of uncles and aunts. In some states, even more distant relatives, sometimes called "laughing heirs," may be the ones who inherit the estate.[184] All state laws provide for the possibility that a decedent will not be survived by anyone who qualifies as an heir. In such a case, the statutes provide that the decedent's property will *escheat* to the State, as the heir of last resort.

These state laws — the "default" system of intestate succession — are based on assumptions about what most decedents' wishes would be if they had expressed them. Most people want their spouses and children and other blood relatives to inherit their property. The intestate succession system is, however, a "one size fits all"[185] arrangement. Every decedent is treated the same. Alice, of Example A, might have preferred that Bob inherit her entire estate if Carol did not survive her, or she might have preferred that her property goes directly to her five grandchildren. Unfortunately, unless Alice planned ahead and took steps to avoid the default system of intestate succession, her estate will be distributed according to the generally applicable rules.

Probate: The Default System for Administering and Distributing Decedents' Property

When a property owner dies holding title to and owning property, the "default" legal rules require that this *estate* go through the *probate* process. *Probate* is the official judicial process by which a decedent's property is collected and managed and then distributed to those entitled to distribution. Generally, all estates, whether intestate or testate (i.e., pursuant to a valid will) must go through probate. A *personal representative* (who acts as an *administrator* or *executor*) must be appointed.[186] That person then collects assets, pays debts, and makes an official accounting concerning the estate, finally distributing the property as required by law. Appointment of a personal representative is necessary to accomplish important tasks such as transferring title of the decedent's real property to the new owner. The personal representative is entitled to compensation for performing this role, and the compensation is payable out of the decedent's estate. In addition, accounting and other expenses and fees may be payable out the estate.

The probate process can sometimes be avoided if the decedent's estate is not large and the state law provides an alternative, more informal procedure for administration of small estates. Often, however, the probate process is unavoidable unless the decedent had planned ahead and taken steps to eliminate the necessity of a probate or to minimize the cost. Without such preplanning, probate will be necessary to settle the decedent's final financial matters.

Guardianship: The Default System for Personal Decision Making in the Case of Incompetency

In American law, competent adults have personal autonomy and the right to self-determination. That is, competent adults have a right to make their own choices about all manner of personal matters relating to things such as housing, health care, employment, business arrangements, use of property, travel, personal association, and any other matter of personal preference and choice. Adults are presumed to be competent to do so, but often in some cases, when a person reaches advanced age, an adult's mental competency may suffer decline.

Guardianship laws — again a matter of individual state law — provide the default system under which the law addresses the status of persons whose ability to make choices may be in decline. Under guardianship statutes, the State exercises its *parens patriae* power, that is, the power to act for any of its citizens who do not have the ability to take care of themselves. Once it is determined that an adult is unable to make responsible decisions about personal and financial matters, under guardianship law a judicial process is invoked to appoint a *guardian* as a surrogate to make those decisions on behalf of the incompetent person.

The core of the guardianship process is the determination of incompetency or mental incapacity. Although varying from state to state, the determination always involves medical as well as lay testimony concerning a person's ability to handle financial and personal affairs, including such matters as making medical treatment decisions. The law provides for due process protections for those who are subject to incapacity determinations, including appointment of a lawyer and requirements of notice and opportunity for the person who is the target of the proceedings to appear and defend against the proposed finding.

In the past, when a person was declared incompetent or incapacitated, and a guardian was appointed, the person lost all power to make personal decisions. Under most modern guardianship statutes, however, the court may make a finding that only a *limited guardianship* is necessary.[187] Using this approach, a court individualizes its finding to fit the particular characteristics and needs of a particular incapacitated individual and grants to the guardian only those powers necessary to compensate for the incapacitated person's weaknesses. Thus, if a person is found to be incapable of handling financial matters, but retains the ability to make personal medical and housing decisions, the guardian will be given powers only as to financial affairs. Guardians may be appointed to be those of the estate or of the person or both, and the particular powers they have as such may be tailored by the court's order to any given individual situation.

Guardianship, once established, continues as long as the incapacitated person remains so, although all statutes provide that guardianship may be terminated where it is shown that capacity has been recovered. The person who serves as a guardian, in the meantime, has a legal duty to use the powers for the benefit of the incapacitated person, and to also account to the court during the duration of the guardianship. The process of instituting and administering a guardianship can be very costly and can constitute a major drain on the financial assets of the incapacitated person.

Planning Ahead to Avoid the Default System, Part 1: Using Wills and Other Basic Legal Instruments to Achieve Financial Autonomy

To avoid having the law's default system of intestacy determine the final disposition of an individual's property, and to avoid the expense of having a guardian appointed to manage financial affairs when incapacity occurs, the elderly (and others) can use some basic legal techniques. These include wills, trusts and other *inter vivos* property arrangements, and powers of attorney.

Wills: Written Testamentary Dispositions of Property

All states permit adults to execute written *wills* that determine the disposition of property on death. If a person executes a valid will, he or she is then said to die *testate*, and the intestate succession scheme is overridden. State laws vary, but generally the essential elements of a valid will include a writing that (1) expresses *testamentary intent* that the instrument be effective on the *testator's* death to pass property interests to named beneficiaries (2) is signed and witnessed or otherwise executed in whatever way a particular will statute specifies.

Using a will gives the elderly person the ability to treat family members differently, according to individual needs and preferences, and to make testamentary gifts to persons other than family members. Seen from a more negative perspective, the will statutes allow testators to disinherit most family members if that is what the testator wants to do. Nevertheless, surviving spouses *cannot* be disinherited completely under virtually all state laws. They are given a forced share, or a right to elect to take against a will or equivalent testamentary dispositions. Other family members who might be intestate heirs, however, may be disinherited. Thus, an elderly person can plan to make a final disposition to family members or nonfamily beneficiaries that is specifically tailored to the testator's wishes and the beneficiaries' situations, going beyond the "one size fits all" intestate succession scheme.

Trusts and Other Will Substitutes

Other basic legal techniques and tools allow elders to make property arrangements that address, and sometimes combine, *inter vivos* (i.e., lifetime) financial management aspects with mandates as to disposition of property on death. These include *trusts, joint property arrangements*, and *powers of attorney for financial matters*. Often called *will substitutes*, they have some of the effects of that primary means of testamentary disposition, the will.

A trust is created when a *settlor* (property owner) transfers assets to a trustee who holds the legal title to the property and has a duty to manage and use the property for the benefit of a *beneficiary*, who is said to hold the equitable, or beneficial, title to the property. Creating a trust involves executing a written trust instrument and selecting a trustee, who may be an individual or a corporate entity, such as a bank. The provisions of the trust control how the income and principal of the trust are to be distributed, and usually provide for management of the property during the life of the settlor and distribution of the property on the death of the settlor. Trusts can be revocable or irrevocable: A revocable trust, often called a living trust, can be changed or terminated anytime by the settlor. An irrevocable trust may not be changed by the settlor.

Given these characteristics, trusts are effective planning and management devices. If an elderly person transfers assets to a trustee, he or she has essentially handed over responsibility for management of the property. The settlor can retain the right to collect the income of the trust, and can provide that the trustee distributed amounts from the principal if the settlor needs funds. Finally, the trust can provide that when the settlor dies, named beneficiaries receive the funds. Assuming that the settlor is competent to execute the trust instrument, subsequent mental incapacity will not affect the arrangement. To the extent that financial matters are under the control of a trustee, it may be possible to avoid appointment of a guardian to manage the elder's financial affairs. Trustees receive compensation, but such costs may well be less than those associated with guardianship. Finally, it can be said that:

- Trust provisions will control distribution of property on the settlor's death
- Such property will not be part of the probate estate
- Probate process and intestate succession laws generally will not apply

Other so-called will substitutes include joint ownership of real and personal property and joint accounts. If an owner of real property changes title to the property, for instance, by deeding her solely owned property to herself and another as *joint tenants with right of survivorship*, that property will not pass through the probate estate. On the death of one of the joint owners, that person's interest in the property passes by operation of law under the terms of the deed to the surviving owner. Thus, an owner can assure that a certain person takes ownership of particular property on her death by using joint tenancy arrangements.

A variety of joint accounts can also be used to hold money during one's life and to transfer it on death. *Joint accounts* and *trust accounts* allow contributors of funds to specify other persons as co-owners of the funds during their lives or on the death of the contributor.[188] Sometimes, the accounts can be set up as convenience accounts, allowing another person to essentially act as an agent of the elderly person who contributes funds. If and when the elder finds it inconvenient or impossible to take care of financial matters, the agent has authority to use the money for the elder's benefit. For small amounts of money and in some limited circumstances, joint accounts may be useful to provide assurance that the elder has some help with financial tasks. Under the terms of such accounts and the applicable statutes, the disposition of the funds on the contributor's death is specified.

Powers of Attorney for Financial Matters

One of the most effective tools the elderly can use to ease their burdens and concerns in the present and in the future is the *power of attorney*. This document is a written instrument by which a person, known for these purposes as a *principal*, appoints an *agent* to act for her in a potentially wide variety of matters.[189] Powers of attorney are also a subject of state law, which will normally set out the requirements for making such a document legally effective. These include signing, witnessing, various declarations of and notices to the principal and the agent, and perhaps filing with a state office. The statutes also delineate which powers principals may delegate to agents. All statutes permit such common grants of authority as power to enter in real estate transactions, to manage cash, investments or checking and, other bank accounts, to enter into contractual arrangements, and to pay bills and deal with creditors. The specific powers of an individual agent are determined by what the principal includes in a specific power of attorney document. The document constitutes notice to all that the agent has authority to act in the stead of the principal as to those matters.

Historically, the law provided that if an adult competent person executed a power of attorney, the agent's authority existed only as long as the principal remained competent and did not lose mental capacity. The law has changed and has made the power of attorney an even more valuable planning technique. Presently, applicable state laws generally provide that powers of attorney, as long as they are executed pursuant state law, are considered *durable.* This *durability* actually means that the agent's power will continue even if the principal becomes mentally incompetent. If the state law does not provide that powers of attorney are automatically deemed durable, the principal can explicitly provide in the document for durability of the agent's authority.

It is immediately obvious that the *durable power of attorney for financial matters* is an important tool for elders to use in planning for future financial autonomy in the face of the possibility of declining competence. It may also be a way to avoid guardianship. A durable power of attorney, executed of course while the principal is mentally competent to do so, can give an agent (perhaps a family member or friend, perhaps a professional) authority over essentially all of that person's financial affairs. If that principal later becomes mentally incapacitated, a court is likely to decide that even though an elderly person may have become mentally incapacitated, appointment of a guardian is not necessary because there is already a representative — the agent — who has authority to conduct the incapacitated person's financial affairs. The trouble and expense of judicial guardianship proceedings is avoided.

As long as the principal remains competent, he may revoke the power of attorney. In addition, the agent, under law, has a fiduciary obligation to the principal, can only use the powers for the benefit of the principal, and has specific responsibility to report and account to the courts concerning the discharge of the agent's responsibilities.

A durable financial power of attorney is also useful for the elderly and others who do not experience mental incapacity, but who have physical deficits or some other impediment to management of their financial affairs. In other words, it can be used as a convenience, and not just as a document to come into effect out of necessity borne of mental incapacity. A power of attorney can give an agent power to act concurrently with the principal, to act when the principal loses mental capacity, or even to come into effect *only* in the event of mental incapacity. It is a document with a great deal of flexibility and is usually inexpensive to obtain. It is a private arrangement that is an effective way of avoiding the need to resort to the public process of guardianship.

To plan for their future financial autonomy, the elderly might use other legal techniques, such as lifetime giving, insurance, and various contractual arrangements. Wills, joint property arrangements, and powers of attorney for financial matters are probably the most commonly used and effective techniques.

Planning Ahead to Avoid the Legal Default System, Part 2: Using Powers of Attorney Health Care and Living Wills to Plan for Personal Autonomy

One of the major topics of concern for the elderly is their ability to make end-of-life decisions concerning life-sustaining or extraordinary medical care. Generally, adult American patients have the right to receive medical treatment only after they have given informed consent, which signifies that their consent to medical treatment is not effective unless they know and understand all the risks and benefits that are attached to a particular medical treatment, as well as to its alternatives. Often, with elderly patients, this issue arises as the concern over patients' "right to die" or their choice to agree to or reject extraordinary medical treatment at the end of their lives. Worries over the uncertainty that will prevail if an elderly person becomes mentally incapacitated and unable to make health and medical decisions are real. To preserve the person's rights to give informed consent and to refuse treatment, the law provides a default system — primarily guardianship — to cover the scenario. Nevertheless, planning ahead in the area of personal decision making can be just as effective as it can be in the financial arena.

As stated before, if a person becomes mentally incapacitated, the default system of the law provides that a guardian may be appointed. Where necessary, the court will appoint a *guardian of the person* of such an individual, and give that person the power to make decisions on such matters as choice, approval, refusal, and withdrawal of medical treatment. Generally, as stated earlier, a competent adult has the right to choose or refuse medical treatment, even life-sustaining treatment.[190] Historically, the law has said that family members and even spouses do *not* have authority by virtue of a family relationship to give consent or make treatment decisions. Rather, the law would require appointment of a guardian or surrogate, and charge the guardian with making the treatment decision. Of course, that guardian will often be a spouse or relative.

In many such cases, the incapacitated person, although competent, had never expressed an opinion about such matters in writing. In some such instances, courts will say that the guardian must apply a *substitution of judgment* standard, making whatever decision the evidence shows would have been made by the incapacitated person. The court will consider evidence of what the patient would have wanted, including prior statements. In other instances, the courts would say that the guardian must make the decision that is in the *best interests of the patient*.

In many cases, the guardians appointed are family members who may or may not have any knowledge of what the wishes of the patient would have been. In many cases, family members may disagree among themselves and with the person appointed as guardian as to what the decision should be. In all cases, of course, appointment of a guardian involves judicial proceedings, expense, and time.

Faced with this difficult issue, elders can use two legal techniques — *the advance directive for health care*, often known as the *living will*, and the *durable power of attorney for health care* — to eliminate a lot of uncertainty and to plan for such end-of-life decisions.

Advance Directives for Health Care: Moving Toward Personal Choice at the End of Life

In decisions like those in the *Quinlan*[192] and *Cruzan*[252] cases, state and federal courts have recognized the constitutional right of privacy extending to the choice of medical treatment and the right to have that choice exercised by a surrogate when an individual has become mentally incompetent. A *living will* is a legal document that embodies the expresses of an individual with regard to life-sustaining and other treatment decisions that may be made when the individual is incompetent.

Where state law recognizes living wills, adults may execute these and specify the treatments that they do and do not want to receive. For instance, a typical state statute would permit persons to plan ahead and execute a declaration that generally *refuses* life-prolonging treatment *or* generally *requests* life-prolonging treatment. These laws will go further and allow a person to address specifics; that is, the person executing the living will can express an opinion on particular kinds of treatments, for example, tube feeding, antibiotics, kidney dialysis, pain relief, mechanical respiration, or cardiac resuscitation.[193] Under these laws, the declarant can address different types of treatments and can sometimes appoint a surrogate, a person who has the authority to make the treatment decisions, even if the specific treatment option has not been covered in the living will.

Where there is a living will, it should not be necessary to have a guardian appointed to make these medical treatment decisions on behalf of a mentally incapacitated person. Statutes generally require health-care professionals to comply with the mandates expressed in the *living will* and may even provide penalties for failure to do so. It is more likely that a choice made pursuant to the directives in a living will are consistent with the wishes of the patient. The document itself evidences what the choices are. In addition, if a surrogate is also appointed by the declarant before incapacitation, they both should have and would have discussed the issues in order to provide a foundation for the treatment decision.

One significant limitation may exist in the law of living wills that may decrease their effectiveness. Many statutes make living wills effective only if the declarant who executed the will is suffering from a terminal disease or is permanently unconscious. It is clear that there are many conditions (e.g., Alzheimer's disease) that do not fit this description. For incapacitated patients with severe conditions that are neither terminal nor involve permanent unconsciousness, a living will may not be legally effective under the statute. The declarant might include a statement of her wishes in the event she is overtaken by a grave condition that is not terminal and does not equate with permanent unconsciousness, but technically those wishes may not have the force of law.

Living wills must generally be in writing and, to be effective, must be made known to caregivers before they will be bound by them. Living wills can also be revoked at any time, should the declarant change her mind, and this can be done without formality. Living wills may not cover all possible eventualities, but they are an important tool that will allow elderly persons to have some confidence that they will retain their autonomy to make health care treatment decisions.

Powers of Attorney for Health Care

Powers of attorney as described before for use regarding financial matter may also be used to delegate health care decision making powers to an agent. Because living wills might operate only in specifically defined scenarios, such as terminal illness, many areas where health care decisions have to be made may be neglected. A power of attorney can be used to appoint an agent to make special decisions and everyday decisions involving health, medical, and personal issues. For instance, elders who want to prepare for possible mental incapacitation may consider executing a durable power of attorney that addresses problems such as housing decisions involving choices of nursing homes, personal care homes, or other facilities; medical treatment decisions not covered by a living will; Medicaid, Medicare, or disability issues; and other details of day-to-day living and routine aspects of health care.

It is less clear under the law of some states whether broad powers as to personal life decisions can be given to an agent in the same way financial powers can be given.[194]

Nevertheless, durable powers of attorney for health care are often used, and, in unclear cases, an elderly person's wishes as stated in such a document can be an important factor. Also, it is not always strictly necessary to execute separate durable powers of attorney for financial matters and health care. The powers could be combined in one instrument and one agent could be appointed to exercise all of those powers for the elderly person. Often, however, the principal would prefer to have two different people exercise the different kinds of power, and two documents would be used.

Conclusion

Those who have concerns about the loss of independence and decision making ability later in life due to mental incapacity or otherwise, and who wish to preserve some measure of autonomy and self-determination with respect to financial and health matters, may avoid the operation of the legal default systems that exist to fill in the blanks. Intestate succession, probate, and guardianship procedures can be made unnecessary if such people take advantage of a variety of legal techniques that can give the elderly person more flexibility and control over personal decision making, even in the face of a possible loss of physical or mental capacity.

Sources for Part II: Elder Law

American Bar Association. *The American Bar Association legal guide for older Americans: the law every American over fifty needs to know.* New York, NY: Times Books, 1998.

Dayton, A. Kimberley et al. *Elder Law; Readings, Cases, and Materials.* 2d ed. Cincinnati: Andersen Pub. Co., 2003.

Dobris, Joel C. et al. *Estates and Trusts; Cases and Materials.* 2d ed. New York: Foundation Press, 2003.

Fleming, Robert B. *Elder Law Answer Book.* New York, NY: Aspen Publishers, 2000.

Frolik, Lawrence A., Richard L. Kaplan. *Elder Law in a Nutshell.* 3d ed. St. Paul, MN: Thomson West, 2003.

Helewitz, Jeffrey A. *Elder Law.* Albany, NY: West/Thomson Learning, 2001.

Hunt, L. Rush, et al. *Understanding Elder Law: Issues in Estate Planning, Medicaid, and Long-term Care Benefits.* L. Rush Hunt (Ed.). Chicago: American Bar Association, 2002.

Sabatini, Charles P. Competency: refining our legal fictions, in *Older Adults Decision-Making and the Law.* Michael Smyer, K. Warner Schaie, and Marshall B. Kapp (Eds.) New York NY: Springer Pub. Co., 1996.

Notes

1. See Lynn D. Wardle, et al., *Fundamental Principles of Family Law*, at 4 (Buffalo, NY: William S. Hein & Co. 2002).
2. See *Troxel v. Granville*, 530 U.S. 57, 63–64 (2000).
3. See Wardle et al., *supra* n. 1, at 14–15 (discussing family and commenting that the term family has "many meanings and levels of meaning.")
4. See *supra* n. 3 at 4.

5. See *Troxel*, 530 U.S. at 64; U.S. Dept. of Commerce, Bureau of Census, Current Population Reports, *America's Families and Living Arrangements: Population Characteristics*, at 6–7 (2001).

6. See John DeWitt Gregory, et al., *Understanding Family Law*, 1–4 (New York, NY: Mathew Bender, 2d ed. 1998 reprint) (quoting *Simms v. Simms*, 175 U.S. 162, 167 (1899) ("Within the states of the Union, the whole subject of the domestic relations of husband and wife, parent and child, belongs to the laws of the state, and not to the laws of the United States."); *Maynard v. Hill*, 125 U.S. 190, 205 (1888) ("Marriage, as creating the most important relation in life, as having more to do with the morals and civilization of a people than any other institution, has always been subject to the control of the legislature. That body prescribes the age at which parties may contract to marry, the procedure or form essential to constitute marriage, the duties and obligations it creates, its effects upon the property rights of both, present and prospective, and the acts which may constitute grounds for dissolution.")

7. See *Berman v. Parker*, 348 U.S. 26, 32 (1954) (explaining that states' general police powers include, but are not limited to, '[p]ublic safety, public health, morality, peace and quiet, law and order....'). See also *Dictionary of Modern Legal Usage* 638 (Oxford, UK: Oxford University Press, 2d ed. 2001) (defining *parens patriae* literally as "father of a country" and refers to the king or queen as guardian of social interest and those in need of care.)

8. See *Barber v. Barber*, 62 U.S. (21 How.) 582 (1858) (recognizing, in dicta, limitations on the jurisdiction of federal courts to hear domestic relations cases).

9. See *Zablocki v. Redhail*, 434 U.S. 374, 386–87 (1978).

10. See 23 *Pa. Cons. Stat. Ann.* § 1304 (e) (West 2001); Uniform Marriage and Divorce Acts ("UMDA") §§ 203 and 205.

11. See, for example, 23 *Pa. Cons. Stat. Ann.* § 1304(e).

12. See 23 *Pa. Cons. Stat. Ann.* § 1304(b) (West 2001).

13. See Bryan A. Garner, editor, *Handbook of Family Law Terms*, St. Paul, MN: West Group, 2001 at 373, *Black's Law Dictionary Series* (St. Paul, MN: West Group, 1999).

14. See *In re Moorehead's Estate*, 137 A. 802, 806 (Pa. 1927) (quoting *Coy v. Humphreys*, 125 S.W. 877, 879 (Mo. App. 1910) (emphasis added).

15. "Full Faith and Credit shall be given in each State to the public Acts, Records and judicial Proceedings of every other State. And the Congress may by general Laws prescribe the Manner in which such Acts, Records and Proceedings shall be proved, and the Effect thereof." U.S. Const. art. IV, § 1.

16. *Williams v. North Carolina (Williams I)*, 317 U.S. 287 (1942); *Williams v. North Carolina (Williams II)*, 325 U.S. 226 (1945).

17. See 1 U.S.C. § 1; 28 U.S.C. § 1738C.

18. See Wardle et al., *supra* n. 1, at 213.

19. See, e.g., 23 *Pa. Cons. Stat. Ann.* § 1102 (West 2001) (declaring that same gender marriages are void); 23 *Pa. Cons. Stat. Ann.* § 1704 (stating that as a matter of "strong and long standing public policy of this Commonwealth," same sex marriages are void, even if valid in the state where the union is created).

20. See *Ankenbrandt v. Richards*, 504 U.S. 689, 693 (1992) (reaffirming the existence of the domestic relations exception and that it restricts federal court jurisdiction to issue divorce, custody and alimony decrees).

21. See Wardle et al., *supra* n. 1, at 677 (identifying Arkansas as the only state without modern no-fault divorce laws).

22. See Wardle, Supra n.1 at 672–75; 23 *Pa. Cons. Stat. Ann.* section 3301(a) (West 2001) (fault based grounds for divorce available to the "innocent and injured" spouse).

23. See Mary R. Anderlik and Mark A. Rothstein, 28 *Am. J.L. & Med.* 215, 221 (2002) (commenting on the use of DNA tests on garments as evidence of infidelity).

24. See Garner, *supra* n. 13, at 146.

25. See U.S. Dept. Commerce, Bureau of Census, *Number, Timing, and Duration of Marriages and Divorces: 1996*, at 17 (2002).

26. See *Domestic and family violence*, available at http://ohr.gsfc.nasa.gov/family/domestic/whatis.htm (visited 08/13/2004).

27. See Roberta L. Valente, Esq., *Domestic Violence and the Law*, available at http://www.abanet.org/cle/clenow/dv/domviol.html (visited 05/04/2004).

28. See American Bar Association ("ABA") Commission on Domestic Violence, *Five Ways to Eliminate Domestic Violence*, ¶ 1, (providing recommendations on eliminating domestic violence and a list of domestic violence coalitions with telephone contact numbers for each state, the District of Columbia, Puerto Rico, and the Virgin Islands), http://www.abanet.org/domviol/victims.html (visited May 5, 2004); Nancy Ver Steegh, *Yes, no, and maybe: informed decision making about divorce mediation in the presence of domestic violence*, 9 Wm. & Mary J. Women & L. 145, 151(2003).

29. See Center for Disease Control, Intimate Partner Violence: Fact Sheet ("CDC Intimate Partner Violence Fact Sheet"), available at http://www.cdc.gov/ncipc/factsheets/ipvfacts.htm (visited 08/13/2004).

30. See National Domestic Violence Hotline, *Domestic Violence Information: National Statistics* ("NDVH Domestic Violence Information"), available at http://www.ndvh.org/dvInfo.html (visited 08/13/2004), citing *Violence by Intimates: Analysis of Data on Crimes by Current or Former Spouses, Boyfriends, and Girlfriends*, U.S. Dept. of Justice (March 1998).

31. See CDC Intimate Partner Violence Fact Sheet, *supra* n. 37.

32. See 34 U.S.C. §13981 (2000).

33. See 34 U.S.C. §13981(a).

34. See U.S. Dept. of Health and Human Services, Administration for Children and Families: *Domestic Violence Fact Sheet* ("DHHS Domestic Violence Fact Sheet"), available at http://www.acf.dhhs.gov/programs/opa/facts/domsvio.htm (visited 08/13/2004).

35. See *U.S. v. Morrison*, 529 U.S. 598, 602–03 (2000).

36. See Violence Against Women Civil Rights Restoration Act of 2000, H.R. 5021, 106th (2000).

37. See *Domestic and Family Violence*, supra *n. 26, citing Bureau of Justice Statistics (1994); Victoria L. Lutz, et al., Special Issue, Model of Collaboration in Family Law, Domestic Violence and Parent Education*, Necessary measures and logistics to maximize the safety of victims of domestic violence attending parent education programs, *42 Fam. Ct. Rev. 363, 369 (April 2004).*

38. See *Domestic and Family Violence*, *supra* n. 26.

39. See CDC Intimate Partner Violence Fact Sheet, *supra* n. 29.

40. See *NDVH Domestic Violence Information*, *supra* n. 30.

41. See *Domestic and Family Violence*, *supra* n. 26.

42. See Emergency Nurses Association Position Statement: *Domestic Violence, Maltreatment and Neglect* ("ENA Position Statement") (rev'd. 2003), available at http://www.ena.org/about/position/domesticviolence.asp (visited 08/13/2004), citing Press Release: *National Domestic Violence answers 700,000th call for help*, available at www.ndvh.org.

43. See Katherine M. Reihing, *Protecting Victims of Domestic Violence and Their Children After Divorce: The American Law Institute's Model*, 37 Fam. & Conciliation Courts Rev. 393, 393 (July 1999).

44. See, for example, Sarah M. Buel, *Effective Assistance of Counsel for Battered Women Defendants: A Normative Construct*, 26 Harv Women's L.J. 217 (Spring 2003); *NDVH Domestic Violence Information*, *supra* n. 30.

45. See *NDVH Domestic Violence Information*, *supra* n. 30.

46. See *ENA Position Statement*, *supra* n. 42.

47. See *CDC Intimate Partner Violence Fact Sheet*, *supra* n. 29.

48. See Reihing, *supra* n. 43 at 393.

49. See *CDC Intimate Partner Violence Fact Sheet*, *supra* n. 37.

50. See 28 C.J.S. Domestic Abuse and Violence, § 3, §§ 5–6, 17.

51. See *NDVH Domestic Violence Information*, *supra* n. 30.

52. See American Medical Association ("AMA"), available at www.americanmedicalassociation. org; James T. R. Jones, *Battered spouses' damage actions against non-reporting physicians*, 45 *Depaul L. Rev.* 191, 199–200 (1996), citing American Medical Association, Council on Ethical and Judicial Affairs, *Physicians and domestic violence: ethical considerations*, 267 *Jama* 3190, 3190 (1992).

53. See Jones, *supra* n. 52 at 199–200.

54. See Jones, *supra* n. 52 at 201.

55. See *supra* n.1 at 200.

56. See Jones, *supra* n. 52 at 220.

57. See Jones, *supra* n. 52 at 199–200.

58. See *ENA Position Statement*, *supra* n. 42.

59. See *supra* n. 58 at 2. See also U.S. Dept. of Justice, NIJ/OJP, National Institute of Justice Research in Brief, *Documenting Domestic Violence: How Healthcare Provides Can Help Victims* (Sept. 2001) ("*NIJ/OJP Brief on Domestic Violence*.")

60. See *ENA Position Statement*, *supra* n. 42, at 2.

61. See *supra* n. 60 at 4. The ENA also supports the U.S. Department of Health and Human Services Healthy People 2010 goals concerning the prevention of violence and abuse. *supra* n. 60 at 3, citing U.S. Dept. of Health and Human Services, *Tracking Healthy People 2010* (Nov. 2000), Washington, D.C.: U.S. Government Printing Office.

62. See *ENA Position Statement*, *supra* n. 42.

63. See *Troxel*, 530 U.S. at 77, Souter, J., concurring.

64. See *Ex parte Devine*, 398 So.2d 686, 688 (Ala. 1981).

65. See Cynthia Starnes, *Swords in the Hands of Babes: Rethinking Custody Interviews After Troxel*, 2003 *Wis. L. Rev.* 115, 119–120 (2003).

66. See Danaya C. Wright, *The Crisis of Child Custody: a History of the Birth of Family Law in England*, 11 *Colum. J. Gender & L.* 175, 184 (2002).

67. See *Ex parte Devine*, 398 So.2d at 688. When father lost custody of his child permanently, frequently, it was for some economic reason that benefited the child. See Wright, *supra* n. 64, at 184.

68. See Wright, *supra* n. 66, at 184.

69. See *Ex parte Devine* at 689, *quoting*, W. Forsyth, *A Treatise on the Law Relating to the Custody of Infants in Cases Of Difference Between Parents or Guardians* 66 (1850).

70. See, for example, *Ex parte Devine*, 398 So.2d at 689, *citing Helms v. Franciscus*, 2 Bland Ch. 544 (Md. 1830). In England, "by a series of statutes culminating with Justice Talfourd's Act, 2 and 3 Vict. C. 54 (1839), Parliament affirmatively extended the rights of mothers, especially as concerned the custody of young children." *supra* n. 105.

71. See *Ex parte Devine*, 398 So.2d at 689.

72. See Lucy S. McGough, *Starting over: the heuristics of family relocation decision making*, 77 *St. John's L. Rev.* 291, 296–98 (Spring 2003), *citing* Sanford N. Katz, *"That they may thrive" goal of child custody: reflections on the apparent erosion of the tender years presumption and the emergence of the primary caretaker presumption*, 8 *J. Contemp. Health L. & Pol'y*, 123, 126 (1992). See also *Ex parte Devine*, 398 So.2d 686 (finding the tender years presumption to be a violation of the Fourteenth Amendment); *Johnson v. Johnson*, 564 P.2d 71 (Alaska 1977) (rejecting the tender years presumption as an impermissible criterion in custody and requiring court to engage in best interest analysis). In rejecting the tender years' presumption, some courts have adopted the primary caretaker presumption that

overwhelmingly results in mothers being awarded custody their children. See, for example, Wright, *supra* n. 66.

73. See *Ali Principles of the Law of Family Dissolution: Analysis and Recommendations* ("ALI Principles of Family Dissolution") § 1(a) (2002), as adopted and promulgated by The American Law Institute, Washington, D.C. (May 16, 2000). Given the broad discretion of courts in custody determinations, criticisms of the best interests test include (1) the lack of predictability, (2) opportunity to apply test to express biases, for example, race, religion, unconventional behaviors, and (3) creation of unrealistic standard for courts. *supra* n. 72. See also Thomas Foley, Student Note, *extending comity to foreign decrees in international custody disputes between parents in the United States and Islamic Nations*, 41 Fam. Ct. Rev. 257, 259 (April 2003).

74. See ALI Principles of Family Dissolution, *supra* n. 73.

75. See McGough, *supra* n. 74, at 298.

76. See, for example, ALI Principles of Family Dissolution at § 2.02, cmt. b. These principles seek to achieve what is in the child's best interests and fairness to parents, which is intertwined with the child's interests. *supra* 75.

77. See, Uniform Marriage and Divorce Act (UMDA) § 402. Other relevant factors listed in the UMDA for determining the best interest of the child include his adjustment to home, school and community, and the physical and mental health of all of the parties involved in the custody dispute. See *supra* n. 76.

78. See ALI Principles of Family Dissolution at § 2.08 cmt. n. Other relevant factors may include the conflict level of the parents, geographic distance between parents, daily schedules of parents and child, and cost and difficulty in transporting the child. *Id.*

79. See, for example, *Wheeler v. Mazur*, 793 A.2d 929, 933–34 (Pa. Super. Ct. 2002).

80. See *Cal Fam. Code* § 3011 (West 1994).

81. See, for example, *Wheeler v. Mazur*, 793 A.2d at 933–34.

82. See *CDC Intimate Partner Violence Fact Sheet*, supra *n. 29.*

83. See *ABA Commission on Domestic Violence Impact Report*, *supra* n. 28.

84. See *CDC Intimate Partner Violence Fact Sheet*, *supra* n. 29.

85. See *ABA Commission on Domestic Violence Impact Report*, *supra* n. 29.

86. See Florence M. Fass and Robin W. Levine, *Custody and Visitation Issues for the New Matrimonial Practitioner*, 277 PLI/Est. 251, 255–267 (1999).

87. See *Webster's New World Dictionary* at 1358 (New York, NY: Simon & Schuster, Inc. 3rd College Ed. 1988).

88. See Kathy Luttrell Garcia, *Battered Women and Battered Children: admissibility of Evidence of Battering and its Effects to Determine the Mens rea of a Battered Woman Facing Criminal Charges for Failing to Protect a Child from Abuse*, 24 J. JUV. L. at 112, citing Am. Psychiatric Ass'n Diagnostic and Statistical Manual, Vol. IV, Diagnostic Code 309.81 at 425 (1994).

89. See Susan A. Angell, Ph.D., M.S.W., *Acute and Chronic Symptomatology of Sexual Trauma: Treatment Issues*, NCP Clinical Quarterly 4(3/4): Summer/Fall 1994.

90. See National Center for PTSD Fact Sheet, *Epidemiological Facts about PTSD* ("PTSD Fact Sheet"), available at http://www.ncptsd.org/facts/general/fs_epidemiological.html (visited Aug. 13, 2004).

91. See Arthur H. Garrison, *Rape Trauma Syndrome: a Review of a Behavioral science theory and its Admissibility in Criminal Trials*, 23 Am. J. Trial Advoc. 591, 630–32 (2000).

92. See Garcia, *supra* n. 88, at 112; Garrison, *supra* n. 91, at 630–41.

93. See Garrison, *supra* n. 91, at 602, 630–31.

94. See Kelly R. Chrestman, Ph.D., et al., *Enhancement of Primary Care Treatment for Women Trauma Survivors, NCP Clinical Quarterly* 6(4): Fall 1996.

95. See Callie Marie Rennison, Ph.D., *Rape and Sexual assault: reporting to police and medical attention, 1992–2000*, U.S. Department of Justice, Bureau of Justice Statistics (Aug. 2002), Table 1.

96. See *supra* n. 95 at 1, Table 1.

97. See *supra* n. 95 at 2, Tables 2–4.

98. See *supra* n. 95 at 3.

99. See Garrison, *supra* n. 91, at 59, citing Ann Wolbert Burgess & Lynda Lytle Holmstrom, *Rape Trauma Syndrome*, 131 *Am. J. Psychiatry*, Sept. 1974, at 982–83.

100. See Garrison, *supra* n. 91, at 594–95.

101. See Garrison, *supra* n. 91, at 594–95, 627.

102. See *supra* n. 91 at 594–95.

103. See *supra* n. 91 at 595–96.

104. See *supra* n. 91 at 596.

105. See *supra* n. 91 at 596, quoting Ann Wolbert Burgess & Lynda Lytle Holmstrom, *Rape Trauma Syndrome*, 131 *Am. J. Psychiatry*, Sept. 1974, at 982–83.

106. See Garrison, *supra* n. 91, at 596.

107. See *supra* n. 91 at 596–97.

108. See *supra* n. 91 at 596.

109. See Garrison, *supra* n. 91, at 596–97.

110. See *supra* n. 91 at 597.

111. See *supra* n. 91 at 598.

112. See *supra* n. 91 at 597.

113. See C. M. Dougherty, MTF, Clinical Forensic Medicine: *Nursing*, at 1123–27 (Edison Corp. 2000).

114. See U.S. Dept. of Justice, OJP, *Understanding DNA Evidence: A Guide for Victim Service Providers* ("*Understanding DNA Evidence*"), April 2001, available at http://www.ojp.usdoj.gov/ovc/publications/bulletins/dna_4_2001/dna2_4_01.html.

115. See U.S. Department of Justice, OJP, *Understanding DNA Evidence: A Guide for Victim Service Providers*, April 2001, available at http://www.ojp.usdoj.gov/ovc/publications/bulletins/dna_4_2001/dna2_4_01.html.

116. See Dougherty, *supra* n. 113, at 1123–27.

117. See 23 C.J.S. Criminal Law § 1067.

118. See Garrison, *supra* n. 89 at 628–29.

119. See *supra* at 628.

120. See 23 C.J.S. Criminal Law § 1067.

121. See *Marylene Cloitre*, Ph.D., *Practical and Theoretical Considerations in the Treatment of Sexually Revictimized Women*, NCP Clinical Quarterly 4(3/4): Summer/Fall 1994;

122. See Angell, *supra* n. 89.

123. See *People v. Brown*, 16 Cal.Rptr.3d 447, 452, 94 P.3d 574 (Cal. 2004) (noting that the "theory of the 'battered woman syndrome' originated in the works of psychologist Lenore Walker.")

124. See Lenore E.A. Walker, *Battered Women Syndrome and Self-Defense*, 6 *Notre Dame J.L. Ethics & Pub. Pol'y* 321, 327 (1992).

125. See Garner, *supra* n. 13, at 71.

126. See U.S. Dept. of Justice, NIJ and ABA Joint Research Report, *Legal Interventions in Family Violence: Research Findings and Policy Implications* ("NIJ/ABA Joint Report on Family Violence"), at 65 (1998).

127. See Walker, *supra* n. 124, at 330–32; Lenore Walker, Ph.D., *The Battered Woman* (New York, NY: Harper and Row 1979); *People v. Brown*, 16 Cal. Rptr.3d at 452 (finding evidence on domestic violence admissible); See also, NIJ/ABA Joint Report on Family Violence, *supra* n. 126, at 65.

128. See Garcia, *supra* n. 88, at 105–06; Walker, *supra* n. 124, at 330–32; NIJ/ABA Joint Report on Family Violence, *supra* n. 87, at 65.

129. See Jones, *supra* n. 52, at 192 n. 5; Walker, *supra* n. 124, at 330–32.

130. See Garcia, *supra* n. 88, at 106; Walker, *supra* n. 124, at 330–32; Jones, *supra* n. 52, at 192 n. 5.
131. See *supra* n. 85, at 139 n. 5; Walker, *supra* n. 124, at 330–32.
132. See Garcia, *supra* n. 88, at 106–07; Walker, *supra* n. 124, at 330–32.
133. Walker, *supra* n. 124, at 330–32.
134. Walker, *supra* n. 124, at 330–32; NIJ/ABA Joint Report on Family Violence, *supra* n. 126, at 65.
135. See NDVH Domestic Violence Information, *supra* n. 30.
136. See NIJ/ABA Joint Report on Family Violence, *supra* n. 126, at 65.
137. See Garcia, *supra* n. 88, at 108–09.
138. See Walker, *supra* n. 124, at 327.
139. See Walker, *supra* n. 124, at 328.
140. See NIJ/ABA Joint Report on Family Violence, *supra* n. 126, at 65.
141. See Walker, *supra* n. 172, at 321–25; 23 C.J.S. Criminal Law § 1067.
142. See NIJ/ABA Joint Report on Family Violence, *supra* n. 126, at 65.
143. See *supra* n. 126 at 65–66.
144. See Walker, *supra* n. 126, at 323.
145. See *supra* n. 26 at 66.
146. See *supra* n. 26 at 68–69.
147. See, for example, Child Support and Establishment of Paternity Act of 1974, 42 U.S.C. §§ 651–665 (1994) (requiring establishment of paternity); Omnibus Budget Reconciliation Act of 1993 42 U.S.C. § 666 (West 2001) (requiring procedures for acknowledgement of paternity); Personal Responsibility and Work Opportunity Reconciliation Act of 1996, 42 U.S.C. § 601 (West 2001).
148. See U.S. Dept. of Justice, FBI, *Issues in the Use of Genetic Technologies in Forensics*, at 7 (2003).
149. See UPA of 1973.
150. See UPA of 2000, as amended in 2002.
151. See *supra* n. 26 42 U.S.C. §§ 654 and 666.
152. See *Michael H. v. Gerald D.*, 491 U.S. 110, 124 (1989). See also Paula Roberts, *Biology and beyond: the case for Passage of the New Uniform Parentage act*, 35 *Fam. L. Q.* 41, 57 (2001) (commenting that the presumption of legitimacy applies where child is born within 300 days of "termination of the marriage death, annulment, decree of separation, or divorce.)"
153. See 491 U.S. 124–25.
154. See *supra* n. 26 at 113.
155. See *supra* n at 114.
156. See 491 U.S. 110.
157. See *supra* n. 26 at 115–16.
158. See *supra* n. 26 at 120.
159. See *supra* n. 26 at 124–25.
160. See 491 U.S. 110.
161. See UPA § 201(a)(1)–(a)(4).
162. See UPA § 201(b)(1)–(b)(6).
163. See Roberts, *supra* n. 152, at 43–44.
164. See *supra* n. at 45.
165. See, for example, Roberts, *supra* n. 152, at 65–66; *Com.ex rel. Borscious v. Fern*, 613 A.2d 17 (Pa. Super. Ct. 1992); *Mitchell v. Hopson*, 545 A.2d 371 (Pa. Super. Ct. 1988).
166. See UPA § 102(10).
167. See UPA § 102(10)(B).
168. See UPA § 102(15).
169. See UPA § 102(17).

170. See Roberts, *supra* n. 152, at 65–66; Donald C. Hubin, Daddy dilemmas: untangling the puzzles of paternity, 13 *Cornell J.L. & Pub. Pol'y* 29, 75 (2003).

171. See U.S. Dept. of Justice, FBI, *Issues in the Use of Genetic Technologies in Forensics*, at 7 (2003).

172. See *Understanding DNA Evidence, supra* n. 114.

173. See *supra* n. 164 Kamrin T. MacKnight, The Polymerase Chain Reaction (PCR): The second generation of DNA analysis methods takes the stand, 20 *Santa Clara Computer & High Tech. L. J.* 95, 98–99 (2003).

174. See UPA § 102 cmt; MacKnight, *supra* n. 174; Randi B. Weiss, et al., *The Use Of Genetic Testing In The Courtroom*, 34 *Wake Forest L. Rev.* 889, 899–904 (1999).

175. See, Roberts, *supra* n. 152, at 57–58, 61–62; UPA § 301 *et seq.*

176. See Roberts, *supra* n. 152, at 57–58.

177. See *supra* n. 152 at 59–60.

178. See, for example, *Lynn v. Powell*, 809 A.2d 927 (Pa. Super. Ct. 2002) (estoppel doctrine applies to bar man from denying paternity once he accepts it); *Hamilton v. Hamilton*, 795 A.2d 403 (Pa. Super. Ct. 2002) (same).

179. See, for example, *McConnell v. Berkheimer*, 781 A.2d 206 (Pa. Super. Ct. 2001).

180. See, for example, 23 Pa.C.S. § 5102(b)(1) (2001); Roberts, *supra* n. 152, at 57.

181. See 14 C.J.S. Children Out-of-Wedlock § 70.

182. Fleming, Robert B. *Elder Law Answer Book.* New York, NY: Aspen Publishers, 2000, 1–2.

183. For example, the Pennsylvania law provides that where there are no "issue" (lineal descendants) and no parents of the decedent surviving, the spouse takes all. 20 *Pa. Cons. Stat. Ann.* s 2102(1).

184. See Fleming, *supra* n. 182, at 7–14.

185. Dobris, Joel C. et al. *Estates and Trusts; Cases and Materials.* 2d ed. New York: Foundation Press, 2003, p. 63.

186. See Dobris, *supra* n. 186, at 994–995.

187. Dayton, A. Kimberley, et al. *Elder Law; Readings, Cases, and Materials.* 2d ed. Cincinnati, Andersen Pub. Co., 2003, p.317–319.

188. For instance, a typical Multiple Party Account statute recognizes arrangements such as Joint Accounts and Trust Accounts. 20 *Pa. Cons. Stat. Ann. Sections*, Chapter 63.

189. Hunt, L. Rush, et al. *Understanding Elder Law: Issues in Estate Planning, Medicaid, and Long-term Care Benefits.* L. Rush Hunt, Chicago, American Bar Association, 2002, p. 35–43.

190. See generally, Sabatini, Charles P. Competency: refining our legal fictions, in Older adults Decision-Making and the Law. Michael Smyer, K. Warner Schaie, Marshall B. Kapp (Eds.) New York, NY: Springer Pub. Co., 1996.

191. *In re* Quinlan, 70 N.J. 10, 355 A.2d 647 (1976).

192. *Cruzan v. Director, Missouri Dep't of Health*, 497 U.S. 261 (1990).

193. See 20 Pa. Cons. Stat. Ann. Sec. 5404.

194. Frolik, Lawrence A. & Richard L. Kaplan. *Elder Law in a Nutshell.* 3d ed. St. Paul, MN, Thomson West, 2003, pp. 41–42.

The Civil Justice System 6

NICHOLAS P. CAFARDI

Civil and Criminal Justice

When we speak of "the civil justice system," we are really drawing a distinction between two major systems of justice: the civil and the criminal. All of the proceedings in the courts of the United States and the 50 states are either civil proceedings or criminal proceedings. Although this chapter will deal with the civil justice system (as opposed to the criminal justice system), it is important that we understand the difference between these two major systems of justice.

The criminal justice system deals with the administration of criminal law or the law of crimes. In a criminal law proceeding, the parties are the prosecuting unit of government (local, state, or federal) that brings the criminal charges and the accused (or the defendant) against whom the charges are brought. A criminal justice proceeding begins when a person is accused by the government of the commission of a crime. This accusation can occur either through a grand jury indictment or through the prosecutor deciding to charge someone with the commission of a crime by filing an "information" against them.[1] A crime is simply an act prohibited by criminal law.

Once a person is accused, it is the state's burden to prove, in a trial, that the elements of a crime are present. The elements of a crime always involve two items: the required mental state, called the *mens rea*, which is Latin for a "criminal mind," and the criminal act, or *actus reus* in Latin. The applicable criminal statute will specify the *mens rea* or criminal mental state that must be proven by the government (e.g., purposely, knowingly, recklessly, negligently),[2] and it will also specify which acts make up the crime (*actus reus*).

If both of these elements of a crime are proven in a trial, the defendant is found guilty. As a result of a finding of guilt, or a conviction, the convict will be fined, sentenced to prison or to a suspended sentence, or will be punished with some combination of these. If the items required for a crime are not proven by the government, then the accused is found "not guilty" (never "innocent") and may never be retried for the same crime. The defining elements of the criminal justice system are an accusation of a crime by the government, a trial at which guilt is either proven or not, and the final disposition of the accusation, as either proven ("guilty") or not ("not guilty").

Because the government, at the local, state, or federal level is always a party to any criminal justice proceeding, criminal justice is a public form of justice. The public, represented by the government, is always a party.

The Elements of the Civil Justice System

The civil justice system is really a system of private justice. In the legal systems of continental Europe, the civil justice system is actually referred to as "private law." This is in contrast to "public law" such as the criminal law where the government, or the public, is always a party.

In the civil justice system, the parties are private individuals or companies or corporations who are either suing or being sued. Units of government can sue or be sued in the civil justice system, but that does not change its basically private (as opposed to public) character. In a civil justice proceeding, the parties are the plaintiff and the defendant, and it is the plaintiff's burden to prove the elements of a civil claim against the defendant. If the elements of a civil claim are proven, the defendant will have to pay the plaintiff money damages and can be enjoined by the court to do or to refrain from doing something, to the plaintiff's benefit. These elements highlight the broad distinction between the civil justice system and the criminal justice system: Criminal justice deals with alleged crimes and can lead to fines or prison; civil justice deals with civil claims and can lead to money damages and injunctions.

Civil Claims

Civil claims are the basis of every lawsuit in the civil justice system, and they fall into two broad categories that the common law developed from the ancient English writ system,[3] namely (1) claims arising from a tort and (2) claims arising from a contract. Later sections of this chapter will deal, in more detail, with what constitutes a tort claim or a contractual claim. Briefly, a tort is a civil (as opposed to a criminal) injury.[4] The plaintiff has been harmed in its person or property by some action or omission of the defendant. The most common tort is negligence. A contractual claim alleges that the defendant has failed to perform or has improperly performed a contractual obligation that the defendant has with the plaintiff.[5] Civil justice proceedings are proceedings that deal either with torts or with contracts. There are other branches of civil justice that deal with admiralty law — or the law of the sea, bankruptcy law, divorce and custody law, and the law of estates and trusts (decedent's property issues). These separate branches of the civil justice system all follow the broad procedural rules of civil justice that we will see in this chapter, although they may have some special rules for their unique proceedings.

The Court System

Before we get into the actual phases of a civil justice proceeding, we need to look at the structure of the court system, because the first question that a plaintiff must ask in pursuing a civil justice claim against a defendant is: "What court do I go to in order to file my claim against the defendant?" Each state, along with the District of Columbia, has its own court system, broadly referred to as state courts. Parallel to the state court system is the federal court system, the court system of the United States. The state and federal court systems cover the nation and very often they have overlapping jurisdiction to hear civil claims.

The State Court System

The courts of the 50 American states are primarily courts of *general subject matter jurisdiction*, which means that the court can hear *any* claim the plaintiff has against the defendant. In general, the state court system is divided into four types of courts:

1. Courts of Last Resort — typically referred to as State Supreme Courts, for example, the Supreme Court of Pennsylvania
2. Intermediate Appellate Courts
3. Trial Courts of General Subject Matter Jurisdiction
4. Trial Courts of Limited Subject Matter Jurisdiction

The highest state court — the court of last resort — is officially named the Supreme Court in 43 of the 50 American states. One notable exception is New York, where the court of last resort is known as the Court of Appeals, and the trial court is called the Supreme Court. Courts of last resort hear cases that can be classified as either mandatory or discretionary. Mandatory cases encompass those appeals that must be heard and decided on the merits. Discretionary cases cover those cases in which the party wishing to go before the highest state court must file a petition (which itself must be accepted in order for the case to reach the court of last resort). Intermediate appellate courts hear those cases that are appealed from the state trial courts — the courts of general jurisdiction. These intermediate appellate courts, such as the Superior Court of Pennsylvania, will review the trial court proceedings and amend any errors made by the trial court in the application of the law. The trial courts of general subject matter jurisdiction, such as the Allegheny County Court of Common Pleas, are the major courts of record in each state, and have jurisdiction to hear virtually every type of case, hence the name "general" jurisdiction. All suits brought in the state court system will initially be heard by a court of general subject matter jurisdiction, except for those cases reserved for courts of limited subject matter jurisdiction, which typically function at the lowest levels of the state court system. A common example of a state court of limited subject matter jurisdiction is the traffic court, which can only hear traffic cases or the magistrate court, which can only hear minor (usually limited by a dollar amount) civil claims.

The Federal Court System

The federal court system is composed primarily of three tiers: the federal district courts acting as trial courts, the circuit courts handling the appeals from the district court and the U.S. Supreme Court functioning as a court of last resort. In addition to the district courts, Congress has created special courts to handle specific disputes. These courts include the Tax Court, the Court of Claims, the Court of Customs and Patent Appeals, and so on. The Supreme Court of the United States stands sovereign as the highest court in the land, before which cases may be brought by way of appeal, by writ of *certiorari*,[6] or through the original jurisdiction of the court.

The lower federal courts (i.e., the levels below the U.S. Supreme Court) are courts of *limited subject matter jurisdiction*. They can only hear claims that are within the limited subject matter authority that Congress has granted them, under Article III, Section 2, of the U.S. Constitution. Congress has granted the federal courts subject matter jurisdiction in two major subject areas: federal question jurisdiction and diversity jurisdiction. Federal question jurisdiction involves the litigation of a claim that "arises under" a federal statute, a federal treaty or the U.S. Constitution. "Arises under" has been generally interpreted to mean that plaintiff's claim must be based on a right created by a federal law, treaty or the Constitution.[7] Federal diversity jurisdiction involves the litigation of a claim in which the plaintiff and the defendant are citizens of different states (hence, they are "diverse") and where the amount claimed is above the statutory threshold, currently set at $75,000.[8] So cases litigated in the federal court system will fall into one of these two broad subject matter categories: (1) cases involving a federal statute or the federal Constitution — federal question cases and (2) cases between citizens of different states — diversity suits.

Finding the Right Court

In bringing its claim, the first thing the plaintiff must decide is in which court to bring it. This decision will involve concepts of jurisdiction and venue. Jurisdiction is of two types: *subject matter jurisdiction* over the "matter" or the topic of the plaintiff's claim and *personal jurisdiction* over the defendant, the party being sued. We have already seen a notion of subject matter jurisdiction in our explanation of the court system. The state courts (except for the lowest level of limited jurisdiction courts such as traffic court, which can only hear traffic cases) are courts of general subject matter jurisdiction. They are able to hear any claim against a defendant over whom they have personal jurisdiction. The federal courts, on the other hand, can only hear claims within the limited subject matter jurisdiction given them by Congress, namely, federal question claims and diversity claims.

Personal jurisdiction is another type of jurisdiction that must exist before a court can hear a claim. It must exist in addition to the court's jurisdiction over the subject matter of the claim. Personal jurisdiction means just what it says, *jurisdiction over the person against whom the claim is made*, over the defendant.

Personal Jurisdiction

Personal jurisdiction, or jurisdiction of the court over the person who is being sued, the defendant, must be based on some relationship that the defendant has with the state where the plaintiff has brought the claim.[9] Even the federal courts rely on the defendant's relationship with the state where the federal court is located to determine if the federal courts have personal jurisdiction over the defendant.

Personal jurisdiction of the courts over the defendant can occur in one of four ways: The first and most basic is presence. The defendant is physically present in the state, and while present, is served with notice of the lawsuit. Physical presence in the state gives the state the ability to hear any claim against the defendant.[9] The second basis for personal jurisdiction is domicile. The defendant is domiciled in, or is a citizen of the state. Domicile, like presence, allows the state to hear any claim against the defendant.[10] Every state has personal jurisdiction over its citizens, people who have their domicile within the state. The third basis for personal jurisdiction is consent.[11] This consent can occur either before or after the claim is brought. Preclaim personal jurisdiction is usually contractual. The defendant has agreed to jurisdiction in a named state as part of a larger contract. This type of consent gives the state only the jurisdiction to hear contract-related claims. Post-claim consent to personal jurisdiction occurs when the defendant shows up in the state to defend against the claim. This type of personal jurisdiction is also limited to the claims stated. The fourth basis for personal jurisdiction is contacts. A state can exercise personal jurisdiction over a defendant who has had "sufficient contacts" with the state.[12] Personal jurisdiction based on the defendant's contacts with the state is limited to those claims arising from the defendant's activities within the jurisdiction or directed at the jurisdiction.[12]

Applying the rules of personal jurisdiction to corporations as opposed to individuals requires some adaption of the four basic concepts of personal jurisdiction: presence, domicile, consent, or contacts. Since the only way a corporation can be present is through corporate activities, a corporation's systematic and continuous activities in a state subject it to that state's general jurisdiction.[13] General jurisdiction covers any claim against the corporation and is not limited to claims arising from state-directed activities. A corporation really has no domicile in the way that a physical person does, but, through a related concept, a state in which a corporation has been incorporated has general jurisdiction over it. As can individuals, corporations can agree or consent to jurisdiction by showing up and defending or by prior contractual agreement. The contacts analysis as a basis for a state's jurisdiction over a corporation applies in the same way that it does to individuals. Jurisdiction will be based on the corporation's contacts with the state. Limited contacts will result in limited jurisdiction, that is, jurisdiction limited to claims relating to the defendant's contacts with the state; systematic and continuous business contacts with a state will result in general jurisdiction in that state over the corporation.

Venue

"Venue" is the territorial determination of which court (of those that have both personal jurisdiction over the defendant and subject matter jurisdiction over the claim) should hear the plaintiff's claim.[14] It tells us in which specific branch of the court to file the action. Within the state court system, it tell us in which county to file a suit. In the federal court system, it specifies in which federal district to file a suit. "Venue" is really a choice of court statute. In the state court system, the venue usually lies where the defendant resides or where the actions or omissions complained of by the plaintiff occurred. In the federal system, the venue is proper where the defendant resides, where the actions or omissions complained of occurred, or where personal jurisdiction over the defendant can be obtained.[14]

The Phases of a Civil Justice Proceeding

In a civil justice proceeding, the plaintiff is claiming that it has suffered some form of legally cognizable injury (a tort or a contractual injury) because of the action or inaction of the defendant. Note that we are using the word "proceeding." This is the case because there is more to the civil justice system than simply the trial of the plaintiff's claim. There are actually three major phases of a civil justice proceeding: (1) the pretrial phase (sometimes also called the "discovery" phase), (2) the actual trial phase, and (3) the appellate or the post trial phase.

The Pretrial Phase

Notice

Once the claim is filed in the appropriate jurisdiction, the defendant must be notified.[15] The best form of notice is personal service of process on the defendant. A process server actually hands to the defendant (or for corporations, a corporate official) a copy of the summons, or notice of the lawsuit. For out-of-state defendants, most states now allow for service by certified or registered mail. Whatever form the service takes, it must be of the type reasonably guaranteed to ascertain that the defendant has actual notice of the proceeding against it.

Complaint

Although service of a summons (notice of suit) on the defendant is all that is required to commence a legal action, eventually, the defendant must receive a copy of the actual complaint, specifying the nature of the claim against it. There are two basic types of complaints, those based on fact pleading and those based on notice pleading. Factual pleading requires that the complaint be reasonably detailed in setting forth the facts and legal basis for the plaintiff's claim. Notice pleading simply requires that the complaint give the defendant adequate notice of the claim being made against it. It is not as detailed as factual pleading. The Federal Rules of Civil Procedure, on which most state rules are modeled, requires only notice pleading.[16]

Preliminary Objections

After the complaint is filed and before it is answered, the defendant can object to the complaint by means of preliminary objections. Preliminary objections may raise issues of jurisdiction, venue, improper service or notice, or insufficiency of the pleading, that is, the pleading fails to state a legally cognizable claim against the defendant. This is sometimes called "failing to state a cause of action."[17]

These objections are then ruled on by the court. Certain substantive preliminary objections, particularly those that point to a lack of jurisdiction, or to a complaint that fails to state a claim upon which relief may be granted, may be fatal to the lawsuit. Others may raise only procedural defects, in which case the plaintiff will probably be given leave to amend his complaint, properly serve the defendant, or join any parties which the court deems indispensable.

Answer

Assuming the plaintiff is not out of court by this point; the next step is the defendant's answer. The answer must respond to the complaint and raise all affirmative defenses, such as *res judicata*, collateral estoppel, and the statute of limitations. If these defenses are not raised in the answer, they are waived, and cannot be raised at trial unless the plaintiff explicitly or implicitly consents to them.

Res judicata, sometimes also called "claim preclusion," is an affirmative defense that precludes a plaintiff from relitigating a claim that it has brought in a prior lawsuit and lost.[18] *Res judicata* covers not only the prior claim, but any related claims that the plaintiff ought to have brought in the prior lawsuit.

Collateral estoppel, sometimes also called "issue preclusion" is an affirmative defense that precludes a plaintiff from relitigating an issue that it raised in a prior lawsuit and lost.[18] (p. 209) Issues are different from claims in that claims are time bound, that is, they must be alleged to have happened within a specific time frame. Issues are not time bound, and the same issue can be raised in a subsequent lawsuit in which the claim, although similar to a prior claim, is not barred by *res judicata* because the time frame alleged is different. In such situations, where the claim is new, because it occupies a different time frame from the earlier, similar claim, issue preclusion, or collateral estoppel, works to prevent the plaintiff from relitigating an issue on which it has lost in a prior suit.

For example, suppose that Mr. Smith sues Mr. Brown for trespassing on his property during September 2004. Mr. Brown's defense is that he has an easement, granted by a prior owner, to cross Mr. Smith's property, and therefore is not guilty of trespass. Mr. Brown prevails. Then, Mr. Smith sues him again for trespassing on his property during September 2005. *Res judicata* will not work here, because Mr. Smith's claim, although similar, is not the same. The first claim asserts trespass in 2004, the second in 2005. The time frame is different. But collateral estoppel does work here. Once the issue of Mr. Brown's easement is litigated and Mr. Smith loses it, it can be raised as an affirmative defense every time Mr. Smith brings a new claim against Mr. Brown for trespass. This is because throughout the changes in time and in claims, the issue remains the same (i.e., whether Mr. Brown has a legal right to cross Mr. Smith's property), and that issue has already been litigated and lost by Mr. Smith. Thus, Mr. Smith is collaterally estopped from litigating it again.

The statute of limitations is a law requiring that claims be filed in a timely fashion. In most states, the time frame on tort claims is a two year statute from the time of the injury and a four year statute on contractual issues. Claims brought after the statute of limitations on the claim has run are held to be barred by the statute.

Discovery

Once the answer is filed, discovery may begin.[19] Discovery commences with a case management conference, wherein the parties meet and discuss the possibility of a settlement, or an alternative resolution of their dispute. If there is to be no settlement or arbitration, the parties will develop a discovery plan during the case management conference and turn in a written report to the court hearing the case. Next, the parties will submit to each other pretrial disclosures, which include the names of witnesses they intend to use, and a list of documents and exhibits they expect to offer in evidence. During the course of discovery, opposing parties will serve interrogatories (written questions requiring written responses) on each other, and request that certain admissions be made which are germane to the facts of the case (also in writing). Parties may also depose (examine orally) other parties and nonparties alike, and request production of documents and items relevant to the cause of action. Although Pennsylvania courts do not normally set a time limit on discovery, the federal courts do.

Summary Judgment

Upon completion of discovery, either side may move for a summary judgment.[20] This is a form of judgment on the pleadings, which means that if after examining the complaint, answer, and all discovery documents, the court concludes that a necessary element of the plaintiff's cause of action or the defendant's affirmative defense is lacking, that cause of action or defense will no longer be a triable issue before the court. Summary judgment can either be partial (i.e., the case proceeds in the absence of the particular claim or defense disposed of) or final, resulting in a complete dismissal of the case.

After discovery, and assuming no summary judgment or settlement has yet occurred, the trial phase of the cause of action begins.

The Trial Phase

The Trier of Fact and the Trier of Law

In the trial phase, the facts of the case are determined by the presentation of evidence to the trier of fact. In a trial with a jury, the trier of fact is the jury. Based on the evidence presented to them, the jury determines the facts of the case. Not every civil justice proceeding has a jury, however. The case may, at the request of the defendant, be tried only in front of a judge. The judge's role in a trial is normally to decide issues of the applicable law. In a trial without a jury, the judge is both the trier of fact (i.e., the judge determines what the facts are) and the determiner of the applicable law.

Opening Statements

A trial commences with an opening statement, first by the plaintiff, then by the defendant, in which each sets forth in a broad outline form their version of the facts and the applicable law.

The Plaintiff's Case in Chief

Next comes the plaintiff's case in chief, in which the plaintiff presents evidence to the trier of fact that proves the plaintiff's claim against the defendant. Witnesses can be:

- *Fact Witnesses:* Those who see or witness certain facts that tend to prove the plaintiff's claim and they can so testify to the trier of fact;
- *Expert Witnesses:* Those who have a certifiable expertise in the area of the litigation and they can testify, within their expertise, on the meaning of the evidence to the trier of fact.

Very often, in civil justice proceedings, these experts are forensic experts. During the plaintiff's case in chief, the defendant may crossexamine the plaintiff's witnesses.

Defense Motions

Following the plaintiff's case in chief, the plaintiff rests. At this point, the defendant may move to the court that, as a matter of law, the plaintiff has failed to prove any cognizable legal claim. If the court agrees, the plaintiff's case is dismissed.[21]

Defendant's Case in Chief

If the court does not grant defendant's motion to dismiss, then the trial proceeds to the next phase: defendant's case in chief. Here the defendant presents witnesses to prove that the defendant is not liable to the plaintiff on the plaintiff's claim. These witnesses may be crossexamined by the plaintiff.

Plaintiff's Motions

At the end of the defendant's case in chief, the plaintiff may move for judgment in his/her favor as a matter of law. If this motion is granted, the trial ends. If the motion is not granted, then the plaintiff can call rebuttal witnesses as can the defendant.

Closing Arguments

Following rebuttal, the case ends with closing arguments. The plaintiff goes first, followed by the defendant, but the plaintiff then ends with a final close to the trier of fact.

Instructions to the Jury and Verdict

If the trier of fact is a jury, after closing arguments, the judge instructs the jury on the law of the case. Following the judge's instructions, the jury returns to deliberate and reach a verdict. In civil trials, unlike criminal trials, a unanimous verdict is *not* constitutionally required, nor is a jury of 12. In federal court, juries can be as small as six-person juries, but the federal courts do, as a matter of law, require unanimity of civil jurors.

The Post Trial Phase

Post Trial Motions

Once a verdict or judgment is reached, the parties have a limited amount of time (10 days in federal court) to make motions to the trial court against the verdict. These are a motion for judgment as a matter of law,[22] which argues that, despite the facts as found, the losing party is entitled to judgment as a matter of law; or a motion for a new trial[23] because of some error or misconduct in the trial or because of the discovery of new evidence.

The Appeal

After the trial phase of a civil justice proceeding, the losing party may appeal the judgment of the trial court. This is the appeals or posttrial phase of a civil proceeding. Once the trial court has issued a final judgment, the losing party can appeal to the first level of an appeals court. In the state system, this is the intermediate appeals court. In the federal system, it is the circuit court. In the post trial phase of the civil justice process, the parties are no longer the plaintiff and the defendant, but the appellant, the party bringing the appeal, and the appellee, the party against whom the appeal is brought.

On appeal of a trial court's judgment, the appellate court does not rehear the case. The trial court is the finder of fact, and whichever facts have been established in the record at trial will remain the facts of the case throughout all levels of appeal. Most appeals argue that the law was applied improperly to the facts at the trial level, or that the facts established at trial were not legally sufficient to support the trial court's judgment, or that the trial court used incorrect legal principles to decide the case. For this reason, appellate court decisions, while they will include recitals of the facts, function principally as examinations of legal principles and the application of those principles to the facts of the case. An appeals court hears no witnesses and cannot establish facts that differ from those established at trial. What an appeals court can do is scrutinize, re-apply, and perhaps even change what were determined to have been the guiding legal principles at the trial level.

After the first level of appeal, sometimes called the intermediate level of appeal, the state courts and the federal courts have a final level of appeal, to the highest level of state court, usually called the state supreme court, and to the U.S. Supreme Court. The U.S. Supreme Court and most state supreme courts are "certiorari" courts. This means that the right to appeal to them after an unfavorable decision by the lower appeals court is not mandatory, but discretionary, in which the party wishing to go before the highest state court must file a petition (which itself must be accepted in order for the case to reach the court of last resort). Discretionary appeals courts hear only those cases which they choose to hear. The court's decision to hear or not to hear an appeal is usually based on areas where the court believes that the law needs clarification, or where a novel principle of law needs either to be adopted or rejected. Mandatory courts of last resort, on the other hand, must hear those appeals which the applicable law mandates that they hear, and in which they have no discretion as to hearing the case or not. In a number of states, for example, although the highest level of appeals court is discretionary in matters of civil justice, state law often makes it mandatory that they hear certain types of criminal justice appeals, as, for example, capital or death penalty cases.

Further Reading

Garner, B.A., Ed.; *Black's Law Dictionary*, West Group, St. Paul, MN, 2000.
Wright, C.A.; *Law of Federal Courts*, West Publishing, St. Paul, MN, 1994.
Hazard, G.C. Jr.; Michele Tartufo, *American Civil Procedure*, Yale University Press, NH, 1993.
Shreve, G.R. and Raven-Hansen, P.; *Understanding Civil Procedure*, Matthew Bender, New York, NY, 1994.
Resnick, J.; *Processes of the Law*, Foundation Press, New York, NY, 2004.
Kane, M.K.; *Civil Procedure in a Nutshell*, Thomson West, St. Paul, MN, 2003.

References

1. Federal Rules of Criminal Procedure 6 and 7 (2002).

2. Model Penal Code Section 2.02 (2) (a).

3. Sward, E.E.; The history of the civil trial in the United States. 51 *U. Kan. L. Rev.* 347, 349 (2003).

4. Prosser, W. and Keeton, P.W.; *Prosser and Keeton on Torts.* § 1 (St. Paul, MN: West Publishing Co. 5th ed., 1985).

5. Murray, J.E.; *Murray on Contracts* § 2 (Deyton, OH: Lexis Nexis Group 4th ed., 2001).

6. *Black's Law Dictionary* 179 (St. Paul, MN: West Publishing Co. 7th ed., 2001).

7. 28 U.S.C. § 1331 (2002).

8. 28 U.S.C. § 1332 (2002).

9. *Pennoyer v. Neff*, 95 U.S. 714 (1877).

10. *Milliken v. Meyer, Administratrix*, 311 U.S. 457 (1940).

11. *Hess v. Pawloski*, 274 U.S. 352 (1927).

12. *International Shoe Co. v. State of Washington*, et al., 326 U.S. 310 (1945).

13. *Perkins v. Benguet Mining Co.* et al., 342 U.S. 437 (1952).

14. 28 U.S.C. § 1391.

15. *Mullane v. Central Hanover Bank and Trust Co.*, 70 U.S. 437 (1950); Federal Rules of Civil Procedure 4 (2002).

16. Federal Rules of Civil Procedure 5 (2002).

17. Federal Rules of Civil Procedure 12 (2002).

18. *Black's Law Dictionary* 209, 1052 (St. Paul, MN: West Publishing Co. 7th ed., 2000).

19. See Federal Rule of Civil Procedure 26 (2002).

20. See Federal Rule of Civil Procedure 56 (2002) .

21. See Federal Rule of Civil Procedure 5(a) (2002).

22. Federal Rule of Civil Procedure 50(b) (2002).

23. Federal Rule of Civil Procedure 59(a)(1).

Discovery in Civil Cases

7

S. MICHAEL STREIB

Introduction

Some lawyers like to tell the jury at the beginning of their opening statement that the evidence the jury will hear is similar to the pieces of a jigsaw puzzle, and the purpose of the opening statement is to describe what the puzzle will look like after all the pieces are assembled. The analogy to a jigsaw puzzle also serves to explain the role of discovery.

We have all seen or done jigsaw puzzles, and we know how long they can take. Imagine that you are given one and then given a short time limit for putting it together. If you have done that puzzle before, you would be better able to perform the task; but if you have no experience with the puzzle, you will probably be left with quite a few pieces that you could not put together. If the purpose of the contest is to see how quickly you think and respond under pressure, we do not want you to see it beforehand. If, on the other hand, our purpose is to fully and accurately assemble the puzzle in the allotted time, then we would be well served by letting you examine and work on it ahead of time.

The evidence each side produces at trial is in a sense like the pieces of a puzzle. Further, the purpose of a trial (contrary to what may be suggested by the media and the entertainment industry) is not sport and gamesmanship, it is the ascertainment of truth. That purpose is, therefore, best served by allowing the adversaries to examine all of the facts, or the pieces of the puzzle, before the trial so that they can be assembled in the most accurate and coherent fashion in the time available. Discovery is the name for the process by which the parties obtain access to the pieces of the puzzle, or the information possessed by each other and by third parties, prior to the trial.

History and Purpose

Discovery has not always been an important part of the civil litigation process. Many years ago, parties to a dispute had very limited obligations to disclose the facts in their possession. The opposing party generally had to try and obtain those facts through whatever private investigation that party could afford. As a result, many facts were learned for the first time at trial, and lawyers have pejoratively referred to that system as "trial by assassination."

Since at least the 1930s, discovery has become a critical part of the civil litigation process. Through the obligations discovery places on litigants and third parties to disclose the information, documents, and objects known or available to them before trial, the parties to the lawsuit are able to preview and analyze the evidence they will use and encounter in the courtroom. Today's abundant, and sometimes overzealous, use that is made of the discovery process has led lawyers to now pejoratively describe the current civil litigation system as "trial by annihilation." Regardless, however, that "annihilation" seems much more conducive to the ascertainment of truth than was the "assassination" that occurred when you were limited in your pretrial factual development by the resources you could devote to private investigation.

The obligations imposed by discovery serve several purposes in addition to its principal use in allowing parties to fully develop and examine the evidence before trial. Through discovery, a party can: a) preserve evidence and testimony that may no longer be available at the time of trial; b) make a record of witness recollections that will fade while the case awaits trial; and c) reduce (or even eliminate) the factual disagreements that were thought to exist before all the facts were known by both sides. (The latter, in turn, may enable the court to dispose of some or all of the case before trial by a process known as summary judgment.) Finally, as a practical matter, the obligation to disclose information to the opposition serves the very valuable function of facilitating and promoting settlement, as it places both sides in a much better position to assess the risks and rewards of entrusting the outcome of the dispute to a jury or a judge who will have less familiarity with the matter than the parties themselves.

Overview of Civil Discovery

Although the discovery process itself is generally found in rules of court, it is not a process in which the courts play a large role. It is a system that operates in large part without court intervention and is conducted by the parties themselves, absent some disagreement regarding the obligations imposed by the rules of court. That is, the only time the court will become involved is when there are disagreements over things such as the extent of the disclosure that is required or the timing of that disclosure.

This limited involvement by the court is primarily a function of the predetermined time limits for disclosure set forth in the various rules, the ability of the parties to modify or expand those time limits themselves if necessary, and most importantly, the broad scope of what can be inquired into or discovered.

Typically, the subject matter that can be inquired into on discovery is not bounded by the formal rules of evidence that apply in the courtroom. It certainly includes all of the evidence and testimony that could be introduced under those evidentiary rules, but it also includes anything that, although not itself admissible evidence, is "reasonably calculated" to lead to the discovery of what may be admissible evidence or testimony. In other words, the scope of discovery generally includes any facts that are related to the matters in dispute (including the credibility of potential witnesses), provided that the disclosure of those facts is not protected by some privilege. Common examples of privileges are those that exist between doctors and patients or attorneys and clients, or the privilege that protects lawyers from having to disclose their strategies, thought processes, impressions, or "work product."

Forms of Discovery

The basic forms of discovery, or discovery tools, are interrogatories (which are written questions); requests to produce or examine documents and things (including, in some cases, people); depositions (which involve the taking of testimony under oath outside of the courtroom); and requests that a party admit certain facts which may originally have been in dispute. These discovery tools need not be used in any particular order (although they often are), can be used as frequently as necessary, and involve differing effort, expense, and anticipated result.

Depositions

As noted, depositions are a procedure whereby the sworn testimony of a person is taken before trial. Specifically, the witness (called a "deponent") appears before an officer who is authorized to administer oaths. After taking an oath, the deponent gives answers to questions posed by counsel for the parties to the litigation. The questions asked of the witness and the witness' answers are recorded and, when the deposition is concluded, a written transcript of those questions and answers is prepared.

Depositions generally take place in a lawyer's office and are conducted much less formally than are proceedings in court. They can be taken of any person (including the parties themselves) that has nonprivileged information bearing on the matters in dispute in the litigation.

Depositions are not public proceedings, and the only persons usually present for the deposition are a court reporter, the witness, counsel for the parties to the litigation, and perhaps the parties themselves or an expert retained by them to assist in technical or scientific matters.

Although there are depositions that are specifically taken so that the witness need not personally appear at trial (i.e., the transcript is read at trial or a video recording of the testimony is played), the purpose of discovery depositions is not to act as a substitute for the witness attending the trial and giving live testimony. To the contrary, a deposition is usually taken to see whether the deponent is a witness one of the parties will call at the trial.

Depositions allow the parties and their attorneys to see, first hand, the potential impact of a witness' testimony before experiencing it at trial. They get to hear what the deponent or potential witness has to say, and they are able to observe the deponent's appearance, demeanor, attitude, and responsiveness to questions. Further, the attorneys can probe the full extent of the witness' potential testimonial contribution by asking for any nonprivileged information that is within the broad scope of discovery, and can commit or pin the deponent down under oath as to all of his or her observations, recollections, understandings, and opinions. These benefits make depositions a very important and attractive discovery tool.

At the same time, however, depositions are a very expensive procedure. The party taking the deposition must pay for the costs of the transcript of the deponent's testimony and for the time that party's attorney spent preparing for and taking the deposition. Further, the other party will usually want to purchase a copy of the deposition transcript (which is somewhat less expensive than the original) and will in all probability also be paying an attorney for attendance at the deposition. Accordingly, although depositions are a very important and powerful discovery tool, the expense involved in taking them is a major consideration, and it is best to be as prepared as practicable before committing those resources. It is for this reason that litigants often use other discovery tools to educate themselves before beginning the deposition process.

Requests to Produce or Examine Documents and Things

While depositions enable litigants to learn about potential witnesses and their testimony before trial, requests to produce or examine documents and other things, such as any personal or real property that may have bearing on the dispute, enable litigants to learn about the nontestimonial evidence that they or their opponents may wish to use at trial. These requests are thus another very important discovery device.

Requests to produce or examine documents and things can be made of the other party or parties to the litigation and are usually permitted to be made of third party witnesses as well. Often, if not most of the time, the party making the request does not know exactly what documents or things are in the possession or control of the person to whom the request is directed. In such instances, the request is framed by describing a category of documents or things with sufficient specificity and particularity as will enable the responding party or person to produce the requested items without undue burden or expense. For example, in a simple automobile accident case, one could ask for all "documents" (which would no doubt be defined in the request to include photographs, diagrams, etc.) that describe, discuss, or relate to the accident that occurred at Maple and Main Streets on January 1, 2005.

As mentioned before, a request for examination can include an examination of a person, either physically or mentally. Basically, only parties are a proper subject of this sort of request, and then only when their physical or mental condition is an issue in the litigation.

A request to produce or examine documents and things is not nearly as financially burdensome on a party as is a deposition, and it certainly is a very powerful tool for learning about the evidence that is available in the case. As a result, a request for production or examination of documents and things often precedes the taking of a deposition, as the information that can be rather easily obtained through that request helps to insure that all pertinent questions are posed to the witness at the deposition.

Interrogatories

Interrogatories are written questions submitted by one party to the litigation to another party to the litigation. They are not generally submitted to nonparty witnesses. The party to whom they are submitted responds with written answers that are given under oath and that are, for the most part, composed with a great deal of input and assistance from counsel.

A big advantage of interrogatories is that they are relatively inexpensive to prepare. A second advantage of interrogatories is that the responding party has a duty to disclose the information that he, she, or it knows and the information they can obtain through reasonable investigation. The drawbacks are that the answers are not spontaneous, but carefully crafted by, or with considerable assistance from, counsel for the responding party. In fact, answers to interrogatories are often specifically drafted and designed to disclose as little as is necessary in responding to the questions. As a result, interrogatories are often the first discovery device employed, with follow-up and elaboration left for a deposition, and are perhaps most useful for obtaining general types of information or the organizational knowledge of an entity.

Request for Admissions

These are essentially statements of fact or law that one party to the litigation composes and sends to the other parties to the litigation. The recipient of these requests is required to admit or deny the statement, and if denied, to explain the reasons for the denial. The admissions which the responding party makes in response to these requests are binding upon them for purposes of that litigation, and a failure to respond at all within the allotted time period is treated as an admission.

This particular discovery device is especially well suited for narrowing the issues that need to be resolved at trial. In fact, the factual issues can sometimes be narrowed to the point where a trial is no longer necessary and the dispute can be resolved by the court as a matter of law.

Postscript

The above is merely an overview of the discovery process and devices. There are, of course, many more details and complications involved in the process that are beyond the scope of this discussion. Some of those other matters involve objections that are lodged to discovery requests and sanctions that can be imposed by the court upon persons who do not comply with their discovery obligations. Those are primarily matters for lawyers, but it should be kept in mind by the parties and their witnesses, as well as by the lawyers, that very severe sanctions can be imposed for dishonestly fulfilling discovery responsibilities.

That is, if an extrajudicial system for exchanging information is to function properly and successfully, the persons participating in it must act honestly and responsibly. Those parties who seek to avoid that burden by hiding or destroying evidence behave unethically and dishonestly. If caught, they may find that the court will adjudicate the case against them and enter judgment in favor of their opponent as a sanction for that behavior. In other words, the price that is to be paid for the information a litigant wants to receive from his opponent is candor and honesty in responding to his or her opponent's request for that same type of information.

Contract Law — Forensic Agreements

8

JOHN E. MURRAY, Jr.

Introduction

Contract law may seem far removed from the fascinating search for clues at a crime scene by forensic scientists. The reality, however, is that, in any significant case involving an alleged breach of contract, the meticulous pursuit of evidence is the critical foundation to determine the rights and duties of the parties. In this sense, contract law may be characterized as the law of "forensic agreements." To appreciate how lawyers and courts pursue forensic agreements, it is essential to have a preliminary understanding of the nature of "contract" and "agreement."

Economic Organization

"Contract" is a social institution that is found in every society. One of the phenomena of every society is the concept of economic exchange — one party giving something of economic value to another party in return for something of economic value. The fundamental requirement of economic exchange is individual ownership of property. Unless I own the property I want to exchange for other property, the other party will not be willing to enter into the exchange. Without a legal system, I cannot "own" anything. I can possess something but I may lose it by force to someone who is stronger. A legal system protects my ownership of property just as it protects your ownership of your property. Once such ownership is recognized, it is possible for parties to exchange their property. Each of us has "rights" in the property because the legal system recognizes such rights.

Basic economic exchanges of property may occur without the social institution of contract. The farmer may exchange the wheat he has grown for a calf owned by another farmer. This primitive form of exchange is called bartering. Millions of exchanges, however, will not occur under a barter system. Hauling wheat to the other farmer's location with the mere hope that the farmer might exchange a calf for the wheat deters exchanges. Unless the wheat farmer has some assurance that the deal will be made, he will be reluctant to travel that distance and go to the trouble of transporting his wheat. If, however, the two farmers assure each other that the exchange will occur in the future with the knowledge that the law will stand behind such assurances, that reluctance will disappear. The enforcement of assurances or promises made between two parties that each other's promises will be enforced was a critical factor in societal development. Without it, modern civilization would be impossible. Now the deal can be made even before the wheat is grown or before the calf is born. The parties can make promises to each other that they will exchange wheat for the calf, and those promises will be enforceable at law. The fact that the parties know the promises are legally enforceable is a very strong inducement to perform their respective promises.

Agreements vs. Forensic Agreements

One of the distinctive qualities of human beings is their ability to make agreements. An ordinary definition of "agreement" suggests harmonization of thought — coming to the same conclusion or the same mind on a particular subject or topic. We can agree on virtually any thought — the correct spelling of a word, or the correct date when a historical event occurred such as the death of Abraham Lincoln in 1865, or when a particular member of a family was born or married. This kind of agreement would certainly not be called a "contract."

When we think of "contract," we think of something to be done or not to be done in the *future.* "Contract" suggests a plan to be carried out. Two parties agree on a planned course of conduct. Yet, there are innumerable agreements on future conduct that are not contracts. We make agreements about everything. A parent agrees to collect a child at the end of a school day; friends agree to go to dinner or a baseball game; a "doctor's appointment" implies a promise by the physician that he will be available at a certain time to treat the patient, and the patient's promise that she will arrive at that time. The total number of agreements made in any given day are in billions. We live by agreements we make with employers, telephone and energy companies, and so many other necessary services in our lives. Every time we buy anything, we make an agreement. Corporations and governments make agreements as do self-employed owners of businesses. Among the billions of agreements made, which agreements involve the law? Another way of asking the same question is, among all agreements made, which of them qualify as *forensic agreements*? Forensic agreements are contracts because they are agreements enforceable at law. They are "contracts" and the particular field of law that explores all of the issues of contracts is "contract law."

The Discipline of Forensic Agreements — Contract Law

We look to contract law to determine which agreements are "forensic," that is, how does the law decide that certain agreements are enforceable at law while others are not enforceable at law? What are the elements of a contract? How do you make a contract? How do you breach a contract? What does the law prescribe as a remedy for breaching a contract? These basic questions raise innumerable additional questions such as whether a contract must be evidenced in writing or, more recently, by an electronic record. When there is a failure to perform a contract, are there degrees of such failures? Some breaches are minor, while other breaches are major. Contract law separates "material" from "immaterial" breaches. What is the difference in effect between these two types of breaches? Can you ever be excused from performing a contract?

We are so used to making promises and receiving promises in exchange for every thing and every service we need or desire in our daily lives that we take contracting for granted. We never give a second thought to innumerable contracts we make because in the overwhelming majority of cases, the parties carry out their promises. They perform as the promised to perform. It is relatively rare for a party to fail to perform her promise. The overwhelming majority of the contracts made between businesses are also made and performed without difficulty. Some promises, however, are not kept. It is not always due to one party deliberately refusing to perform his promise, though that sometimes occurs.

There may be a question as to whether there is a contract at all where one party claims that he never made an offer or accepted an offer from the other party. The parties may agree that they have a contract, but they may disagree about the parties' respective rights and duties under their contract. There may be language in their contract that gives rise to a difference of opinion as to what that language means. This is a question of interpretation that arises in many contract cases. Sometimes, the parties do not include all of the terms of a contract, and the court must decide whether the missing terms are fatal to finding a contract. At other times, the written evidence of the contract does not mention a particular matter which the other party insists was intended to be included in the contract, and the other party disagrees and the court must decide whether such evidence is admissible. The duty of a party under a contract may be conditional, that is, some fact or event must occur before that duty becomes activated. There may be a dispute over whether the conditioning event has occurred.

The Evidence — Objective Manifestations

The forensic evidence of contract law is found in the outward (objective) manifestations of the parties — their words and conduct. A court will not recognize an agreement as a contract simply because one of the parties states that he intended his words to be a contract. Similarly, a court will not accept a party's subjective statement that he did not intend to make a contract if his words or actions would be reasonably interpreted to form a contract. Where, for example, two parties negotiated the purchase and sale of a farm, the owner claimed that he was only joking and did not intend to form a contract. The court reconstructed the facts of the transaction. The critical fact was whether the owner *appeared* to be serious when he promised to sell the farm. The test applied by the court was whether a reasonable person hearing what the owner said and reading the words written on the paper describing the purchase and sale would have understood that the owner was serious in agreeing to sell the farm. It did not matter what the owner subjectively thought he was communicating. Rather, it was what a reasonable person would have understood by the owner's communication. The court held that there was a contract because the buyer was reasonable in understanding the owner to be serious in promising to sell the farm.

Contract law requires constant interpretation by courts. To make a contract, one party must make an *offer* which the other party must *accept* to form the contract. There are innumerable cases dealing with whether the language or conduct of the parties indicated that an offer and acceptance occurred. Absent an offer, there is nothing to accept and an offer without an acceptance is not a contract because there is no agreement, no "mutual assent." Where a seller of goods advertises its products for sale, typically this is not an offer because there is no promise or commitment to sell the goods to any particular party. It simply states that certain goods or services are available. There is no commitment to sell them to a specific person. A given advertisement, however, can be an offer if it contains language of promise or commitment to do something or refrain from doing something in the future and requires something in exchange from one or more parties. The classic example is an advertisement that contains a promise to pay a certain sum to any member of the public who provides information leading to the arrest and conviction of a felon. The offeree is not identified when the offer is made, but he or she is identifiable. The offer is not seeking an acceptance through a typical return promise. Rather, it is seeking an act — a performance — providing the critical information. The party who performs that act accepts the offer and forms a contract, traditionally called a "unilateral" contract as contrasted with a "bilateral" contract, the more typical contract where an offer contains a promise and is accepted by a promise.

Where Is "The Contract"?

There is a tendency to think of "the contract" as the document, the paper on which the words are written. The document or documents, however, are only *evidence* of the contract. Where someone says, "Hand me the contract," she is really saying, "Hand me the evidence of the contract." Spoken words are also evidence of the contract and the parties' conduct is evidence of the contract. Written evidence of a contract may be found in one document or innumerable documents. A dispute over a contract for the sale of goods or services may require a careful consideration of purchase orders, acknowledgment forms, letters, e-mails, formal documents, or any number of other written or printed terms.

A major source of objective evidence of what the parties intended is provided where the parties have contracted in the past and entered into a new contract on the same terms as the old contract. If the new contract contains a word, phrase, sentence, or paragraph that becomes the subject of dispute, the court will allow evidence of the meaning of such words if the parties have had occasions to act on those same words in the prior contract. How the parties dealt with each other in the past may provide the court with strong evidence of what they intended the same words to mean in the new contract.

The strongest source of evidence of the parties' intent may be found where the parties have begun to perform the present contract. Suppose, for example, that the contract states that the buyer of goods must make monthly payments by the 15th of each month in a 48 month contract. For the first 13 months, the buyer has made payments ranging from the 15th to the 30th of each month. In fact, the buyer has made payments by the 15th only on two occasions. The other 11 payments have been later in the month. This is strong evidence that the seller did not intend payments by the 15th to be essential and a court will find no breach because of this "course of performance" evidence based on how the parties, themselves, have performed the contract to this point.

What Do the Terms Mean? Interpretation

Where there is no dispute over whether the parties intended to be bound to a contract, there are thousands of cases dealing with the meaning of the terms of the contract. Although it may appear simple to discover the meaning of any word through a dictionary, the same word may have different meanings. Where, for example, a contract between an American buyer and a Canadian seller for equipment is priced at $400,000, did the parties mean American dollars or Canadian dollars? The objective evidence may indicate that the parties may have intended a given word to have a meaning different from its ordinary meaning. In a famous case, the contract required a meat product to have a protein content of "50%." The delivered product had a protein content between 49.5 and 49.96%. The buyer claimed a breach of contract. The court, however, considered expert evidence of trade usage — a regularly observed method or practice of dealing in this trade — which indicated that merchants in this trade viewed the term "50%" as including a protein content of 49.5% and higher as equal to 50%. Sometimes, a word has a technical meaning that differs from an ordinary definition. Courts will interpret the word according to that technical meaning if the parties appear to have intended that meaning. This is in keeping with the general purpose of fulfilling the intentions of the parties to the contract. Courts do not make contracts for the parties. Based on the objective evidence, courts are supposed to discover the agreement (or lack of agreement) that the parties intended.

The evidence of an alleged contract may be incomplete. A number of terms may not have been expressed in the contract documents. There may be no time or place of the delivery of goods or the time for performing a service. Even the price term may be missing. If, however, courts can otherwise determine that the parties intended to be bound by a contract and the court has an adequate basis for providing a remedy for its breach, the court will supply the missing terms on a reasonable basis, essentially what reasonable parties would have intended the missing term to be.

Although a court must often consider numerous documents in a contract dispute, the parties' intention may be found in other documents that were not intended as contract documents. In the 17th century, the English Parliament enacted a statute requiring certain types of contracts to be evidenced by a signed writing to avoid fraud and perjury by parties alleging that contract were made without such evidence. The "statute of frauds" inherited from England became part of the contract law of the United States. At the present time, state statutes of frauds require contracts for the sale of land or the sale of goods over a certain price must be evidenced in writing. Most states require contracts that cannot possibly be performed within one year from the making must be in writing, Contracts to answer for the debt of another are unenforceable without written evidence. The minutes of a corporation's board of directors meeting evidencing a contract the corporation had allegedly made were sufficient for a court to find that document as sufficient evidence of a contract to make it enforceable against the corporation. Recent statutes allow electronic records to meet the requirement of a "writing." Electronic records may be found in e-mails, voice mails, or other electronic sources to make contracts enforceable. Just as such electronic evidence may be collected in a criminal case, its collection in a contracts case may be essential.

The gathering of factual evidence is critical in contracts cases to determine whether any contract was made and the intended meaning of the terms of the contract. Where a large building or bridge or other structure collapses, evidence of the design, engineering plans, and other contract documents are often critical in determining where the fault lies for the collapse. In a case involving the one of the largest civil verdicts in history of over $10 billion, the essential issue was whether an "agreement in principle" for the merger of a major oil company constituted a binding contract, or whether the parties did not intend to be bound until a final, formal document was executed. This is a question of intention which, again, can only be discerned through a meticulous investigation of all of the objective evidence, including but not limited to any documentary evidence. The jury returned the huge verdict in this case after considering all of this evidence and concluding that the parties intended to be bound when they executed the "agreement in principle" rather than a final more formal document.

Breach — Material or Immaterial

Where one party claims the other party breached the contract, a court will first determine whether *any* breach occurred. Again, this will require the court to clearly set forth the respective rights and duties of the parties, which involves interpretation of the contract to determine such rights and duties. Assuming a breach has occurred, the court will determine whether the breach is material or immaterial. A material breach deprives the other party of substantially what was bargained for. An immaterial breach is a failure to perform as required, but does not interfere substantially with what the other party was entitled to receive. In the construction of a building, for example, there may be some relatively minor deficiencies that constitute immaterial breaches. A structural defect that creates a safety hazard or makes the building unusable for its intended purpose, however, is a material breach. Although even an immaterial breach requires the breaching party to compensate the other party for any loss, it does not discharge the contract. The other party must continue to perform even though that party is entitled to any damages (money) it can prove because of the breach. Courts must consider all of the objective evidence to make these often difficult determinations.

Contract Remedies — Putting Humpty Dumpty Together Again — The Purpose of Contract Law

It is important to consider the purpose of contract law. Contracts ought to be performed in accordance with the parties' manifested intentions. Unless performance is legally excused as where it is impossible or highly impracticable to perform the contract for reasons beyond the control of the party that did not perform, a failure to perform is a breach. The other party, the "aggrieved" party, is injured by such a breach. The purpose of contract law is to remedy this breach by placing the injured party in the position that party would have been in had the contract been performed. Such a remedy fulfills the expectations of the aggrieved party. In the U.S. legal system, this purpose is fulfilled through compensation in the form of damages (money) except in rare cases. An obvious example is a breach of a contract for the sale of goods where the seller fails to deliver the goods or delivers goods that do not conform to the contract. Unless the seller "cures" the breach, the buyer can make a reasonable substitute purchase of the same or similar goods from another supplier, that is, the buyer can "cover" by making the substitute purchase. If the price of the substitute goods is higher than the original contract price, the buyer recovers the difference between the higher price and the contract price. Thus, where a buyer must "cover" at a price of $25,000 and the contract price was $20,000, the buyer is entitled to damages of $5000. The result is that buyers receive the goods they expected to receive at a net price of $20,000, the price they originally contracted to pay. The buyers' expectations have been fulfilled.

Where a remedy of money damages will not place the aggrieved party in the same position they should have been in had the contract been performed, courts will resort to requiring the other party to perform. Here there is no "adequate remedy at law," that is, the recovery of damages in a court of law will not fulfill the buyers' expectations. For example, in the sale of a unique item such as a famous painting, there is no adequate substitute for such a painting. The buyer cannot "cover" since there is no substitute for the painting the buyer contracted to purchase. A contract for the sale of land breached by the seller will also allow this extraordinary remedy since land is unique, at least in location. A court will order a breaching seller to deliver the painting to the buyer for the original contract price. In such a case, a court sits as a court of equity since it is ordering a party to specifically perform their promise. Even if the subject matter is not truly unique as where ordinary products become scarce, a court will order a seller to deliver because the goods cannot be procured elsewhere. Courts will not, however, force a party to perform a personal service contract since that would be unconstitutional. If a famous athlete refuses to perform his contract, a court will not order him to perform. It is, however, possible to prevent the athlete from performing for another team through issuance of an injunction precluding such a performance.

In determining how to fulfill the aggrieved party's expectations, courts will consider various kinds of objective evidence. Damage calculations in complicated commercial cases can be difficult. Damages must be proved with reasonable certainty, and this may require considerable expert evidence from a number of different sources. Where a contract is breached and it is impossible to determine the expectation damages with reasonable certainty, it may be possible for an aggrieved party to recover any amount it has expended in reliance on the contract or any benefits already conferred on the other party to preclude unjust enrichment by providing the aggrieved party with restitution. Determining the actual loss to the aggrieved party and the reasonable value of any benefit already conferred on the breaching party often requires a meticulous examination of the objective evidence.

One cogent example of the difficulty of determining damages with reasonable certainty involves a contract to create a facility for a new business that is supposed to be completed by a certain date. The builder's breach delays the construction by several months, depriving the owner of the profits it would have earned during that period. The typical reaction to this situation in older cases was to apply what came to be called the "new business" rule that would not allow the owner to collect any damages for lost profits because they could not be proved with the requisite "reasonable certainty." These courts contrasted the situation with an established business which had closed for remodeling and the remodeling construction was delayed by several months. The established business could present clear evidence of prior profits during similar past periods to prove its current loss. Many modern courts, however, have taken a different position with respect to the proof of lost profits for a new business. Objective expert evidence of similar businesses, the location of the new business and numerous other factors, including demographic and weather conditions, will be admissible to allow the new business owner to prove lost profits with reasonable certainty.

Conclusion

Forensic science raises visions of forensic experts collecting myriad forms of evidence for analysis at a crime scene surrounded by yellow police tape. The general purpose is to discover objective evidence to determine the identity and guilt of one or more felons. In the civil law where an injured party seeks compensation for an injury to person or property such as an auto accident, the "tort scene" is similar to a crime scene to determine which party was negligent. Where the claim is for breach of contract, the "contract scene" requires the collection of all of the relevant objective evidence, the documents, the spoken words, any trade usage, course of dealing or course of performance, expert analysis from experts in many disciplines, and any other relevant objective evidence. It requires the same meticulous examination of such evidence to assure a clear understanding of the parties' agreement and an appropriate judicial remedy to assure that the intention of the parties as manifested in that agreement are fulfilled.

Fundamental Principles of Tort Law

9

KELLEN McCLENDON

Introduction

What Is a Tort?

In one of the leading works on torts, *Prosser and Keeton on Torts*,[1] the authors begin their answer to this question by observing that "a really satisfactory definition of a tort is yet to be found."[1] (§1, p. 1) Torts have been around long enough, however, such that the same authors are able to "broadly" define a tort as "a civil wrong, other than breach of contract, for which the court will provide a remedy in the form of an action for damages."[1] (§1, p. 2) This definition is one that is pretty much accepted and is similar to the definitions that many other scholars and courts have ascribed to the word.[2] The author of an early 1900 treatise on torts defined a tort as "a breach of a duty (other than a contractual or quasi-contractual duty) which gives rise to an action for damages."[3] Most courts have defined the word tort in a similar fashion. The U.S. Supreme Court, referring to the *Prosser and Keeton* definition, has adopted the same definition.[4]

The Interests Protected by Tort Law

Tort law protects various tangible and intangible human interests. The 1965 version of the *Restatement (Second) of Torts* (hereinafter referred to as "the *Restatement*") defines "interest" as "the object of any human desire."[5] The tangible interests can be divided into personal physical interests and certain property interests. Examples of these types of interests include the interests in being free from bodily injury (a personal physical interest) and the interest in being free from damage to property (a property interest). The intangible interests are those such as freedom from injury to reputation misrepresentation.

Three General Categories of Tort Liability

In the effort to protect these interests, the tort law imposes liability on the person or the entity that causes damages to these interests. The person or the entity that causes the injury is said to have committed a tort; that person or entity is referred to as a tortfeasor. There are three general categories of tort liability: (1) fault-based liability, (2) strict liability, and (3) absolute liability. Intentional torts, negligence, and recklessness fall within the fault-based category of liability.

Fault

Because "fault" is at the basis of this category of liability, we need to have some understanding of fault. Unfortunately, fault is one of those words that we may come to understand less as we seek to understand it more. *Webster's Ninth New Collegiate Dictionary* uses the following words, among others, to explain fault: "weakness," "failing," "a moral weakness less serious than a vice," "a physical or intellectual imperfection or impairment," and "mistake."[6] *Prosser and Keeton on Torts* say this about fault:

> [I]f we say that all liability rests on "fault," then the "fault" must be "legal" or "social" fault, which may but does not necessarily coincide with personal immorality. The law finds "fault" in a failure to live up to an ideal standard of conduct which may be beyond the knowledge or capacity of the individual, and in acts which are normal and usual in the community, and without moral reproach in its eyes. It will impose liability for good intentions and for innocent mistakes.... "[F]ault" has come to mean no more than a departure from the conduct required of the actor by society for the protection of others, and it is the public and social interest which determines what is required.[1] (§4, p. 22 — footnotes omitted)

Courts have defined or explained "fault" in a variety of ways. Some of the more helpful judicial definitions or explanations are as follows:

- "Fault connotes some form of active participation in creating the injuries for which the plaintiff seeks to recover"[7]
- "Fault ... encompasses many acts which are not morally wrong, but are merely violative of laws or of legal duties"[8]

If we place fault at one end of the spectrum of tort liability, at the opposite end of the spectrum, we will find liability that is not based upon fault — in other words, tort liability that is based upon activity that is *supposedly* faultless. This fault-free activity is any activity for which courts and legislature have decided to impose liability even though the activity is *supposedly* free of fault. According to *Prosser and Keeton*, during the first half of the twentieth century courts demonstrated a "willingness" (1) to eliminate fault as an "absolute requirement for liability" and (2) "to consider and entertain the contention that the law is, or should be, primarily a question of which interest is to prevail even where no one is at 'fault' ..."[1] (§4, p. 23).

Whether the activity is fault based or fault-free, if there is injury to the interest to be protected, the person who committed the tort may be liable to the injured party.

Cause of Action

In our legal system, a person whose tort interests have been harmed can remedy the harm by way of what is known as a cause of action. Over the centuries, law has established

various causes of action by which we can remedy tortious harm. What is a cause of action?
Cause of actions has been defined as follows:

- [A] "cause of action" involves an assertion of particular legal rights arising out of a definable factual transaction.[9]
- "Cause of action," ... means operative facts which give rise to plaintiff's right to judicially assert action against defendant.[10]
- A cause of action is that single group of facts which is claimed to have brought about an unlawful injury to the plaintiff and which entitles the plaintiff to relief .... A right of action at law arises from the existence of a primary right in the plaintiff, and an invasion of that right by some delict [wrong, injury, offense, violation of a public or private duty] on the part of the defendant. The facts which establish the existence of that right and that delict constitute the cause of action.[11]
- A statement of facts sufficient to constitute a cause of action means a narrative of events, acts, and things done or omitted which show a legal liability of the defendant to the plaintiff.[12]
- [A] "cause of action" is an invasion of a legal right and damages therefrom ....[13]

Each cause of action has elements, of which each has to be proven by the plaintiff. Otherwise, it is said that the plaintiff has not made out her cause of action. The word "element" has been defined as "[t]he ultimate undecomposable parts which unite to form anything."[14] In other words, the elements to a cause of action are those things that constitute (a) the wrong done to the plaintiff and (b) the basis for the plaintiff being entitled to recover money damages from the defendant. If the plaintiff cannot prove all of the elements, he has not made out his cause of action.

Intentional Torts

There are several "intentional torts." They are assault, battery, false imprisonment, intentional infliction of emotional distress, trespass to land, trespass to chattels, and conversion. Assault, battery, false imprisonment, and intentional infliction of emotional distress are referred to as personal torts; trespass to land, trespass to chattels, and conversion are referred to as property torts. Because each intentional tort is different from the others, their elements are different except for three that are common to all of the intentional torts. Those three elements are act, intent, and causation. A word of caution is in order here. When we discuss the specific elements of each of the intentional torts, we will see that beyond the basic nature of intent, the intent element for the intentional tort causes of action (except for the cause of action for assault and the cause of action for battery) is different for each of the intentional tort causes of action.

Preliminary Considerations

Act

Section 2 of the *Restatement* defines act as "an external manifestation of the actor's will"[5] (§2). The comments to Section 2 point out that the act has to be volitional as opposed to an involuntary movement of the body[5] ($2 cmt. a). The comments provide the following example regarding the relationship between the act and the actor's will:

> [I]f A, finding himself about to fall, stretches his hand out to seize some object, whether a fellow human being or a mere inanimate object, to save himself from falling, the stretching out of his hand and the grasping of the object is an act . . ., since the defendant's mind has grasped the situation and has dictated a muscular contraction which his rapidly formed judgment leads him to believe to be helpful to prevent his fall. While the decision is formed instantaneously, nonetheless the movement of the hand is a response to the will exerted by a mind which has already determined upon a distinct course of action. The exigency in which the defendant is placed, the necessity for a rapid decision, the fact that the decision corresponds to a universal tendency of mankind, may be enough to relieve the defendant from liability, but it is not enough to prevent his grasping of the object from being his act.
>
> — *Restatement*[5] ($2 cmt. b)

Intent

As with many words, there are various definitions of intent. Perhaps the best definition of intent is that of Prosser and Keeton:

> [Intent] is a *state of mind* . . . about the consequences of an act (or omission) and not about the act itself, and . . . it extends not only to having in the mind a purpose (or desire) to bring about given consequences but also to having in mind a belief (or knowledge) that given consequences are substantially certain to result from the act.[15]

There are several aspects to this definition: The first aspect is that intent is a *state of mind*. In other words, intent takes place in the mind. The second aspect is that the state of mind is *about the consequences of an act (or mission) and not about the act itself.* We have already considered what constitutes an act. An act and consequences are not the same thing. What are "consequences"? *Webster's Ninth New Collegiate Dictionary* defines consequence as "something produced by a cause or necessarily following from a set of conditions."[6] (p. 279) *Prosser and Keeton on Torts* points out that "[a]n act is to be distinguished from its consequences."[1] ($8, p. 34) Comment "c" of Section 2 of the *Restatement* explains the difference in the following words:

> The word "act" includes only the external manifestation of the actor's will. It does not include any of the effects of such manifestation, no matter how direct, immediate, and intended.
>
> Thus, if the actor, having pointed a pistol at another, pulls the trigger, the act is the pulling of the trigger and not the impingement of the bullet upon the other's person. So too, if the actor intentionally strikes another, the act is only the movement of the actor's hand and not the contact with the other's body immediately established.
>
> — *Restatement*[5] ($2 cmt. c)

Intent can be effectuated in two ways: First, intent can be brought about by a "purpose or desire." Thus, if the tortfeasor has an end to be attained, he has a purpose in mind. Or if the tortfeasor has a wish or need, he has a desire. Under either circumstance, the tortfeasor's state of mind is more definite than is the case if her intent is effectuated in the second of the two ways by which intent can be effectuated. In this second way, the tortfeasor does not have a purpose or desire, but has a belief or the knowledge that certain consequences are substantially certain to result from his act. The tortfeasor's state of mind is not as definite, but it is definite enough that the law will consider the tortfeasor's actions to have been intentional.

Except for the cause of action for assault and the cause of action for battery, the intent element of each of the intentional tort causes of action is different for each of the intentional tort causes of action.

Causation

The other element that is common to every intentional tort cause of action is causation. Indeed, causation is an element to every cause of action in tort. Once again, we need to begin with a definition. Causation is a process by which one thing brings about another thing; the process by which one thing "produces an effect"; the process by which one thing "brings about an effect or a result."[6] (p. 217) If I throw a rock at you and it hits you, my act of throwing the rock at you was the cause of the rock impacting your body. This aspect of causation is referred to in one of several ways: (1) factual cause, (2) actual cause, (3) cause-in-fact, and (4) logical cause.[16]

The second aspect of causation is referred to in one of two ways: (1) proximate cause or (2) legal cause. Only the first aspect of causation has to be proven to satisfy the causation element of the intentional tort causes of action.[17] Both aspects, however, have to be proven to satisfy the causation element of all the other tort causes of action — that is, the tort causes of action that are based on negligence, strict liability, and absolute liability.[18]

Why is it that only the factual cause aspect has to be proven for the intentional tort causes of action? The answer to this question is that because the intentional torts are the more egregious of the torts — that is, because the tortfeasor intends to cause harm — the intentional tortfeasor should not benefit from the policy that is at the base of the proximate cause/legal cause concept.[17]

Let us consider the respective purpose that these two aspects of causation serve. Factual cause serves the purpose of proving that the defendant's act was indeed the thing that brought about the plaintiff's harm.[19] Proximate cause/legal cause is a policy concept by which the courts will limit or completely cut off liability if the events that led to the plaintiff's harm are so extraordinary that no person could have foreseen the results.[20] The plaintiff in an intentional tort case has to prove factual cause, but not proximate cause/legal cause; or, stated another way, the defendant in an intentional tort case cannot benefit from the liability-limiting aspect of proximate cause/legal cause.[17] Thus, an intentional tortfeasor's liability is potentially limitless; the intentional tortfeasor cannot make use of proximate cause to limit her liability. When we get to negligence, we will see that the negligent tortfeasor's liability can be limited by the concept of proximate cause/legal cause.

The Definition of, the Interest Protected by, and the Elements of the Causes of Action for the Intentional Torts

Remember that the intentional torts against persons are (1) assault, (2) battery, (3) false imprisonment, (4) intentional infliction of emotional distress; and the intentional torts against property are (1) trespass to land, (2) trespass to chattels, and (3) conversion.

Against Person

Assault

Definition.   Assault has been defined in a variety of ways. Michigan has defined assault as "(1) an intentional, unlawful threat or offer to do bodily injury by force (2) under circumstances that create a well-founded fear of imminent peril (3) coupled with the ability to carry out the act if not prevented."[21] "Under the Ohio law, an assault is 'the willful threat or attempt to harm or touch another offensively, which threat or attempt reasonably places the other in fear of such contact.'"[22] For Pennsylvania, an assault is an act intended "to cause an imminent apprehension of a harmful or offensive bodily contact."[23] Virginia defines assault as "an act intended to cause either harmful or offensive contact with another person or apprehension of such contact, and that creates in that other person's mind a reasonable apprehension of an imminent battery."[24] As you notice, two of these definitions have the word "fear" in them. The other two do not have the word "fear" as part of the definition. Instead, the other two use the word "apprehension." Are "fear" and "apprehension" synonymous?

Although some courts use "fear" and "apprehension" synonymously, a better view is that from the perspective of the tort of assault, "fear" and apprehension" are not necessarily the same thing. As has been stated by the Montana Supreme Court, "apprehension is not the same thing as fear."[25] The *Restatement (Second) of Torts* is also of the view that "fear" and "apprehension" are not necessarily synonymous. In the words of the *Restatement*, "The apprehension which is sufficient to make the actor liable may have no relation to fear…"[5] (§24 cmt. b). The *Restatement* illustrates this point with the following hypothetical:

> A, a scrawny individual who is intoxicated, attempts to strike with his fist B, who is the heavyweight champion pugilist of the world. B is not at all afraid of A, is confident that he can avoid any such blow, and in fact succeeds in doing so. A is subject to liability to B.
>
> — *Restatement*[5] (§24 illus. 1)

Fear is apprehension, but not all apprehension is fear. In other words, apprehension is not limited to fear. One dictionary definition of apprehension is "the act or power of perceiving or comprehending"[9] (p. 97). Anticipation is a useful word by which to understand apprehension.

Interest Protected.   The interest that is protected by a cause of action for assault is "[t]he interest in freedom from apprehension of a harmful or offensive bodily contact."[1] (§10)

Elements of the Cause of Action

- **The *Restatement***

Section 21 of the *Restatement* provides that "[a]n actor is subject to liability to another for assault if (a) he acts intending to cause a harmful or offensive contact with the person of the other or a third person, or an imminent apprehension of such a contact and (b) the other is thereby put in such imminent apprehension."[5] (§21) Breaking this section apart, we see that for there to be a cause of action, there must be (1) an act, (2) intent to cause (a) a harmful or offensive contact with another person or (b) apprehension of such a contact, (3) causation, (4) apprehension of such a contact. In addition to these elements, a plaintiff seeking to recover in a cause of action for assault has to prove that she did not consent to the assault. *Restatement*[5] (§21, cmt. c) states that:

> [W]here the privilege [to commit an intentional tort] is based upon the consent of the other affected by the actor's conduct, there is a distinction between consent to invasions of the interests of personality, in which the burden is upon the plaintiff to prove absence of consent, and consent to all other legally protected interests, including the possessory and proprietary interest in land and chattels, in which the burden of proving the consent is upon the defendant.

General damages are presumed and are thus not an element — if the other elements to the cause of action are proven.[1] (§7, page 31, fn 18):

> [I]n assault, battery, false imprisonment, and trespass to land . . . the action may be maintained without proof of damages.

Of course, if the plaintiff has suffered specific damages, he can recover those damages upon proof thereof.

Note that a person can be liable for an assault if she intends to do one or the other of two things: (1) to cause "a harmful or offensive contact" or (2) to cause "an imminent apprehension of such a contact." Thus, if a tortfeasor starts out with the intent to cause a harmful or offensive contact (i.e., the intent to cause a battery) is unsuccessful in doing so, but nonetheless causes apprehension of such a contact, he could be found liable for assault.[26] What is meant by harmful? What is meant by offensive? A harmful contact is "any physical impairment of the condition of another's body, or physical pain or illness."[5] (§15) "A bodily contact is offensive if it offends a reasonable sense of personal dignity."[5] (§19)

Another important matter arising from Section 21 is the phrase "imminent apprehension." The drafters of the *Restatement* (Second) of Torts used the phrase "imminent apprehension" in the black letter[27] portion of Section 21, but used a reversed and slightly different phrase in the comments to the section. The black letter portion of Section 21 (1) provides that "(1) [a]n actor is subject to liability to another for assault if (a) he acts intending to cause a harmful or offensive contact with the person of the other or a third person, or an *imminent apprehension* of such a contact and (b) the other is thereby put in such *imminent apprehension*."[5] (§21, emphasis added) Comment b to Section 21 (1), on the other hand, states in part that for a person to be liable for assault, "it is only necessary that his act should cause an *apprehension of an immediate contact*, whether harmful or merely offensive."

When you compare and contrast the italicized phrases, you can see that they are saying different things. In the phrase *imminent apprehension* imminent describes apprehension, which is the subject of the phrase and imminent (the time aspect of the phrase) is the descriptor of the subject of the phrase. An *imminent apprehension* is an apprehension that will occur in a short span of time. On the other hand, in the phrase *apprehension of an immediate contact*, contact is the subject of the phrase, and immediate (the time aspect of the phrase) is one of the descriptors of the subject of the phrase.

What all of this boils down to is that the apprehension has to be of a contact that is "ready to take place."[28] In other words, imminent should describe contact not apprehension. This conclusion is borne out by a part of the black letter portion and a part of the comments of Section 29 of the *Restatement*. Subsection (1) of Section 29 states that a person is liable for an assault if she puts another person "in apprehension of an imminent contact"[5] (§29 (1)). Comment b of Section 29 explains it in the following words:

> The apprehension created must be one of *imminent contact*, as distinguished from any contact in the future. "Imminent" does not mean immediate, in the sense of instantaneous contact, as where the other sees the actor's fist about to strike his nose. It means rather that there will be no significant delay. It is not necessary that one shall be within striking distance of the other, or that a weapon pointed at the other shall be in a condition for instant discharge. It is enough that one is so close to striking distance that he can reach the other almost at once, or that he can make the weapon ready for discharge in a very short interval of time[5] (§29 cmt. b, emphasis added).

- **Case Law**

California: Citing the *Restatement*, the California Court of Appeal has held that to prove a cause of action for assault,

> a plaintiff must prove (1) the defendant intentionally did an act that made the plaintiff reasonably believe she was about to be touched in a harmful or offensive manner and, for offensive touching, (2) a reasonable person in the plaintiff's situation would have been offended by the touching. "Words do not make the actor liable for assault unless together with other acts or circumstances they put the other in reasonable apprehension of an imminent harmful or offensive contact with his person."[29]

Colorado: The Colorado Court of Appeals has held that:

> [t]he elements of assault are that: (1) the defendant acted either with the intent of making a contact with the person of the plaintiff or with the intent of putting the plaintiff in apprehension of such a contact; (2) the plaintiff was placed in apprehension of an imminent contact with his or her person by the conduct of the defendant; and (3) such contact was or appeared to be harmful or offensive.[30]

North Carolina: In North Carolina, "[t]he elements of assault are intent, offer of injury, reasonable apprehension, apparent ability, and imminent threat of injury.

[A] [p]laintiff establishes a cause of action for assault upon proof of these technical elements without proof of actual damage."[31]

Iowa: The U.S. District Court for the Northern District of Iowa summarized Iowa's law regarding a cause of action for assault in the following words:

> A person commits an assault when, without justification, the person does any of the following:
>
> (1) Any act which is intended to cause pain or injury to, or which is intended to result in physical contact which will be insulting or offensive to another, coupled with the apparent ability to execute the act.
>
> (2) Any act which is intended to place another in fear of immediate physical contact which will be painful, injurious, insulting, or offensive, coupled with the apparent ability to execute the act.[32]

Additional Matters.   There are other aspects of assault that deserve particular comment. Because assault involves apprehension, if the plaintiff does not apprehend or is incapable of it — there can be no assault. In a 1993 North Carolina case, the court ruled out that the defendant who was alleged to have pointed a gun at a group of people, one of whom was a four-month-old child, who was asleep, could not be liable for assault because the child could not have apprehended any imminent harmful or offensive contact because he was asleep or was too young.[33] A cause of action for assault cannot be defeated by proof that the plaintiff is "abnormally sensitive."[5] (§27, cmt. a) Nor can a cause of action for assault be defeated by proof that the actions that caused the apprehension were conditional. Section 30 of the *Restatement* provides several illustrations to demonstrate this point; two of those illustrations are as follows:

> A owes B a sum of money. B points a gun at A, saying, "If you do not pay me my money, I will have your life." B is subject to liability to A.
>
> — *Restatement*[5] (§30 illus. 3.)

> A standing near B, draws back his hand and threatens to knock B down if he does not stop talking. A is subject to liability to B.
>
> — *Restatement*[5] (§30 illus. 5.)

Words alone are not enough to constitute an assault; the words must be accompanied by "other acts or circumstances."[5] (§31) "[M]ere words do not constitute assault . . . [;] some overt act is required."[5] (§31)

> "[I]t is not necessary that [the tortfeasor] have or that he believe that he has the ability to inflict the harmful or bodily contact which his act apparently threatens."[5] (§33)

This point is demonstrated by the following illustration:

> "A, knowing a pistol to be unloaded, points it at B and threatens to shoot him. B believes the pistol to be loaded. A is subject to liability to B."
>
> — *Restatement*[5] (§33 illus. 1.)

Some of the intentional torts do not require the plaintiff to prove pecuniary or physical loss.[34] Nominal damages are provided in the absence of proof of actual loss.[34] Assault is one of those torts.[34]

Two final points need to be made about the cause of action for assault: A plaintiff who sues on a theory of assault, in addition to the other elements that she has to establish, has to prove that she did not consent to the assault.[35] Finally, the *Restatement* points out that damages — in the sense of pecuniary or physical harm — are not an element for a cause of action in assault.[36] (see also *Restatement* §§21, and 907 cmt. b)

Battery

Definition.   Whereas assault may be said to affect the mind, battery affects the rest of the body. The Appellate Court of Illinois has defined battery as "the willful touching of another by the aggressor or a substance or force put in motion by the aggressor." The U.S. Disctrict Court for the Eastern District of Wisconsin has stated that "Under Wisconsin law a battery ... is ... an intentional contact with another, which is unpermitted."[37] In Louisiana, a battery is "[a] harmful or offensive contact with a person, resulting from an act intended to cause the plaintiff to suffer such a contact.[38] In a similar refrain, the Federal District Court for the Western District of Michigan has stated that, under Michigan law, a "[b]attery is the willful and harmful or offensive touching of another person against [his or her] will."[39]

Interest Protected.   The interest that is protected by a cause of action for battery is "freedom from intentional and unpermitted contacts with the plaintiff's person"[1] (§9). The interest that is protected "extends to any part of the body, or to anything which is attached to it and practically identified with it."[1] (§9, footnotes omitted) "The interest in the integrity of [the] person includes all those things which are in contact with the person".[1] (§9) As we will see, the cause of action for battery protects against "harmful bodily contacts" and "offensive bodily contacts"[5] (§§13, 18).

Elements of the Cause of Action

- **The *Restatement***

Section 13 of the *Restatement* provides that a person is liable for battery if:

> (a) he acts intending to cause a harmful or offensive contact with the person of the other or a third person, or an imminent apprehension of such a contact, and
> (b) a harmful contact with the person of the other directly or indirectly results.

Section 18 of the *Restatement* provides that a person is liable for battery if:

> (a) he acts intending to cause a harmful or offensive contact with the person of the other or a third person, or an imminent apprehension of such a contact, and
> (b) an offensive contact with the person of the other directly or indirectly results.

As you can see, there are two types of contacts for which the *Restatement* provides liability: harmful contact and offensive contact. A contact with the body of another person is harmful if it results in "impairment of the condition of another's body, or physical pain of illness"[5] (§15). A contact with the body of another person is offensive if it "offends a reasonable sense of personal dignity"[5] (§19).

The *Restatement* points out that damages — in the sense of pecuniary or physical harm — are not an element for a cause of action in battery.[40]

- **Case Law**

Mississippi: In 2001, the Mississippi Supreme Court has discussed the elements to a cause of action for battery in the following manner:

> An assault occurs where a person (1) acts intending to cause a harmful or offensive contact with the person of the other or a third person, or an imminent apprehension of such contact, and (2) the other is thereby put in such imminent apprehension. A battery goes one step beyond an assault in that a harmful contact actually occurs.[41]

New York: A statement often found in the decisions of New York courts regarding the elements for a cause of action for battery is that "'[t]he elements of a cause of action [to recover damages] for battery are bodily contact, made with intent, and offensive in nature.'"[42]

Ohio: Citing the *Restatement*, the Ohio Supreme Court has stated that "[a] person is subject to liability for battery when he acts intending to cause a harmful or offensive contact, and when a harmful contact results.[43]

Pennsylvania: "As traditionally stated, the elements of the tort of battery are 'a harmful or offensive contact with a person, resulting from an act intended to cause the plaintiff or a third person to suffer such a contact, or apprehension that such a contact is imminent.'"[44]

West Virginia: In West Virginia, the elements for the cause of action in battery are the same as found in the *Restatement*. In *West Virginia Fire & Casualty Co. v. Stanley*,[45] the West Virginia Supreme Court declared:

> [T]he *Restatement* . . . §13 . . . sets out the following elements of the tort of battery:
>> An actor is subject to liability to another for battery if (a) he acts intending to cause a harmful or offensive contact with the person of the other or a third person, or an imminent apprehension of such a contact, and (b) a harmful contact with the person of the other directly or indirectly results.
>> Also, this Court [has] held . . . that "[i]n order to be liable for a battery, an actor must act with the intention of causing a harmful or offensive contact with a person."

- **An Additional Matter Regarding the Elements to a Cause of Action for Battery**

As with a cause of action for assault, a plaintiff who sues on a theory of battery, in addition to the other elements that he has to establish, has to prove that he did not consent to the assault.[46] Finally, the *Restatement* points out that damages — in the sense of pecuniary or physical harm — are not an element for a cause of action in battery.[36] (see also *Restatement* §§18 and 907, cmt. b)

False Imprisonment

Definition.   False imprisonment has been defined by the Kentucky Court of Appeals as "being any deprivation of the liberty of one person by another or detention for however short a time without such person's consent and against his will, whether done by actual violence, threats, or otherwise."[47]

   Prosser and Keeton on Torts explains the word "imprisonment" in the following words:

> "[i]mprisonment," although it seems originally to have meant stone walls and iron bars, no longer signifies incarceration; the plaintiff may be imprisoned when restrained in the open street, or in a traveling automobile, or when confined in an entire city, or compelled to go ... with the defendant. The older idea of confinement has persisted, however, in the requirement that the restraint be a total one, rather than a mere obstruction of the right to go where the plaintiff pleases.
> — Prosser and Keeton,[1] (§11.)

Interest Protected.   According to *Prosser and Keeton*, false imprisonment "protects the personal interest in freedom from restraint of movement."[1] (§11) This statement of the interest protected is in accord with the *Restatement*. The title of the subject matter under which false imprisonment is listed in the *Restatement* is "The Interest in Freedom from Confinement."[48]

Elements of the Cause of Action

* **The *Restatement***

Section 35 of the *Restatement* sets for the following as the elements to a cause of action for false imprisonment:

> (1) An actor is subject to liability to another for false imprisonment if
> (a) he acts intending to confine the other or a third person within boundaries fixed by the actor, and
> (b) his act directly or indirectly results in such a confinement of the other, and
> (c) the other is conscious of the confinement or is harmed by it

Restatement, §35. Subsection (2) of Section 35 goes on to point out that:

> [a]n act which is not done with the intention stated in Subsection (1, a) does not make the actor liable to the other for a merely transitory or otherwise harmless confinement, although the act involves an unreasonable risk of imposing it and therefore would be negligent or reckless if the risk threateneed bodily harm.

   The confinement that is this tort protects against is one that "within the boundaries fixed by the defendant" and is "complete."[5] (§36) There is no confinement if there is a "reasonable means of escape" that is known to the plaintiff.[5] (§36) The confinement can result from "actual or apparent physical barriers."[5] (§38) "overpowering physical force or by submission to physical force,"[5] (§39) "duress other than threats of physical force,"[5] (§40A) or "asserted legal authority."[5] (§41) If the plaintiff is unaware of the confinement, there is no cause of action for false imprisonment.[5] (§42)

   As with a plaintiff asserting a claim for either assault or battery — a plaint asserting a claim for false imprisonment does not have to prove actual damages. In other words, actual damages are not an element of the cause of action for false imprisonment. If a plaintiff establishes her cause of action for false imprisonment, she can recover nominal damages in the absence of the proof of actual damages.

- **Case Law**

California: In California, the law states that "[t]he elements of a tortious claim of false imprisonment are: (1) the nonconsensual, intentional confinement of a person, (2) without lawful privilege, and (3) for an appreciable period of time, however brief."[49]

Michigan: The Michigan Court of Appeals has held that "[t]he elements of false imprisonment are '[1] an act committed with the intention of confining another, [2] the act directly or indirectly results in such confinement, and [3] the person confined is conscious of his confinement."[50]

Minnesota: The Minnesota Supreme Court has said that "the elements [of the cause of action] of false imprisonment consist of the following elements: (1) words or acts by defendant intended to confine the plaintiff, (2) actual confinement, and (3) awareness by plaintiff that he or she is being confined."[51]

Ohio: The Ohio Court of Appeals has determined that "[c]laims for false arrest and false imprisonment require proof of the same essential elements. A false arrest and false imprisonment claim is made by showing (1) the intentional detention of the person and (2) the unlawfulness of the detention. To establish a claim for false imprisonment, one must prove by a preponderance of the evidence that he was intentionally detained or confined without lawful privilege and against his consent. False imprisonment is not concerned with good or bad faith or malicious motive."[52]

Rhode Island: "'To establish . . . [a] cause of action [for false imprisonment], a plaintiff [in Rhode Island] must show more than that (1) the defendant intended to confine him, (2) the plaintiff was conscious of the confinement, (3) the plaintiff did not consent to the confinement, and (4) the confinement was not otherwise privileged.' The plaintiff must also show that he or she was detained without legal justification."[53]

- **An Additional Matter Regarding the Elements to a Cause of Action For False Imprisonment**

As with the cause of action for assault and the cause of action for battery, a plaintiff who sues on a theory of false imprisonment, in addition to the other elements that she has to establish, has to prove that she did not consent to the assault.[35] Finally, the *Restatement* points out that damages — in the sense of pecuniary or physical harm — are not an element for a cause of action in battery.[54]

Intentional Infliction of Emotional Distress

Definition.   One definition of intentional infliction of emotional distress is that which is representative of how courts define the tort and that which relies upon Section 46 of the *Restatement*. "extreme and outrageous conduct intentionally or recklessly caus[ing] severe emotional distress to another."[55]

Interest Protected.   *Prosser and Keeton on Torts* provides a backdrop to understanding the interest protected by the tort of intentional infliction of emotional distress:

> Notwithstanding early recognition of a cause of action for assault, the law has been slow to accept the interest in peace of mind as entitled to independent legal

protection, even as against intentional invasions. Not until comparatively recent decades has the infliction of mental distress served as the basis of an action, apart from any other tort.[1] (§12)

Prior to the acceptance of intentional infliction of emotional distress as a tort, "[v]arious reasons [had] been advanced for [the] reluctance to redress mental injuries."[56] It was argued that courts did not have the ability to place a "value" on "[m]ental pain or anxiety."[56] Emotional distress "was regarded as something 'metaphysical,' 'too subtle and speculative to be capable of admeasurement by any standard known to the law.'" Another view that was offered in opposition to the tort was that recognition of the tort would open the flood gates to "fictitious claims" and lawsuits the bases of which would be "trivialities and mere bad manners."[56] Those early objections to the recognition of intentional infliction of emotional distress have pretty much been laid to rest as evidenced by the fact that the majority of states[57] and the *Restatement* recognize the tort.[5] (§§46–48)

Elements of the Cause of Action

- **The *Restatement***

Section 46 of the *Restatement* sets forth the following as the elements to a cause of action for intentional infliction of emotional distress:

§46. Outrageous Conduct Causing Severe Emotional Distress

(1) One who by extreme and outrageous conduct intentionally or recklessly causes severe emotional distress to another is subject to liability for such emotional distress, and if bodily harm to the other results from it, for such bodily harm.[5]

In parsing this section, we see that the plaintiff would have to prove that (1) the defendant's conduct was intentional or reckless, (2) the conduct was extreme and outrageous, and (3) the conduct would cause severe emotional distress. As you can see, Section 46 further provides that bodily harm is not a required element, but if it results from emotional distress, the plaintiff would be permitted to prove bodily harm. "The liability clearly does not extend to mere insults, indignities, threats, annoyances, petty oppressions, or other trivialities."[5] (§46, cmt. d) The nature of extreme and outrageous conduct is summed up in these words from the comments to Section 46:

Liability has been found only where the conduct has been so outrageous in character, and so extreme in degree, as to go beyond all possible bounds of decency, and to be regarded as atrocious, and utterly intolerable in a civilized community. Generally, the case is one in which the recitation of the facts to an average member of the community would arouse his resentment against the actor, and lead him to exclaim, "Outrageous!"[5] (§46, cmt. d)

- **Case Law**

Connecticut: In Connecticut, the elements of a cause of action for intentional infliction of emotional distress are as follows:

(a) defendant intended to inflict emotional distress, or knew or should have known that emotional distress was a likely result of [its] conduct; (b) defendant['s] conduct was extreme and outrageous; (c) defendant['s] conduct caused the plaintiff's distress; and (d) the emotional distress suffered by the plaintiff was severe. The standard in Connecticut for conduct reaching the level of "extreme and outrageous" is defined as "that which exceeds all bounds usually tolerated by a decent society, of a nature which is especially calculated to cause, and does cause, mental distress of a very serious kind."[59]

Hawaii: "In Hawaii, the elements of a claim for intentional infliction of emotional distress . . . are: (1) that the conduct allegedly causing the harm was intentional or reckless, (2) that the conduct was outrageous, and (3) that the conduct caused extreme emotional distress to another."[60]

Illinois:

> To prove a cause of action for intentional infliction of emotional distress, the plaintiff must establish three elements: (1) Extreme and outrageous conduct; (2) Intent or knowledge by the actor that there is at least a high probability that his or her conduct would inflict severe emotional distress and reckless disregard of that probability; and (3) Severe and emotional distress.[61]

North Carolina: A claim for intentional infliction of emotional distress exists "when a defendant's "conduct exceeds all bounds usually tolerated by decent society" and the conduct 'causes mental distress of a very serious kind.'" To make out a *prima facie* showing for intentional infliction of emotional distress, the plaintiff must show the following: (1) that the defendant engaged in extreme and outrageous conduct, (2) which was intended to cause and did cause (3) severe emotional distress. "The tort may also exist where defendants' actions indicate a reckless indifference to the likelihood that they will cause severe emotional distress."[62]

Wyoming: "To recover under the tort of intentional infliction of emotional distress, the plaintiff must prove that the defendant acted in an extreme and outrageous manner and that the defendant intentionally or recklessly caused the plaintiff severe emotional harm."[63]

Against Property

Trespass to Land

Definition. In a 1959 decision of the Oregon Supreme Court, trespass to land was defined as "any intrusion which invades the possessor's protected interest in exclusive possession [of her land], whether that intrusion is by visible or invisible pieces of matter or by energy which can be measured only by the mathematical language of the physicist."[64] A 2001 decision of the South Carolina Court of Appeals includes within its definition the intentional characteristic of trespass to land: "[trespass to land is] any intentional invasion of the plaintiff's interest in the exclusive possession of his property."[65] The *Restatement* defines a person in possession of land as one who

> (a) is in occupancy of land with intent to control it, or (b) has been but no longer is in occupancy of land with intent to control it, if, after he has ceased his occupancy without abandoning the land, no other person has obtained possession as stated in Clause (a), or (c) has the right as against all persons to immediate occupancy of land, if no other person is in possession as stated in Clauses (a) and (b).[5] (§157)

Interest Protected.   The cause of action for trespass to land protects a person's "right of exclusive possession" of his land.[66] *Prosser and Keeton* say this about the interest that is protected by the tort of trespass to land: "In the bundle of rights, privileges, powers, and immunities that are enjoyed by an owner of real property, perhaps the most important is the right to the exclusive 'use' of the real property."[1] (§13, p. 67)

Elements of the Cause of Action

- **The *Restatement***

Section 158 of the *Restatement* sets for the following as the elements to a cause of action for trespass to land:

> §158. Liability for Intentional Intrusions on Land
>
> One is subject to liability to another for trespass, irrespective of whether he thereby causes harm to any legally protected interest of the other, if he intentionally
> (a) enters land in the possession of the other, or causes a thing or a third person to do so, or (b) remains on the land, or (c) fails to remove from the land a thing which he is under a duty to remove.[67]

To be in "possession" of land, one must (a) be "in occupancy of land with intent to control it," or (b) ha[ve] been but no longer is in occupancy of land with intent to control it . . . or (c) has the right as against all persons to immediate occupancy of land ....[5] (§157) To "enter" means "not only coming upon land, but also remaining on it, and, in addition, to include the presence upon the land of a third person or thing which the actor has caused to be or to remain there."[1] (§158, cmt. b) What constitutes a thing can lead to an interesting debate as to how big and perceptible the thing has to be. One case in which the debate was evident was the 1959 case of *Martin v Reynolds Metals Company* in which the court held that "the intrusion of the fluoride particulates . . . constituted a trespass," provided that — unlike a trespass in which the thing that made entry onto the land was perceptible to the naked eye — proof of "actual damages" or "interference . . . with a legitimate use of the [land]" was required.[68] As used in the title to Section 158, the word "intrusion" means "that the possessor's interest in the exclusive possession of his land has been invaded by the presence of a person or thing upon it without the possessor's consent."[1] (§158, cmt. c) As with other intentional torts, damages are not an element of the cause of action.[69] In the absence of actual damages, a plaintiff may recover nominal damages in a cause of action for trespass to land,[69] which can occur either on the surface or beneath the surface of land.[70] The trespass can result from the defendant entering the land, from the defendant "[c]ausing entry of a thing, or from the defendant "[c]ausing entry of a third person."[71] That a person initially is legally on land will not prevent her from being a trespasser if the basis of her legally being on the land terminates.[72] The failure to leave, after expiration of the consent or privilege to be on the land will constitute a trespass.[72] Finally, take note that "[t]he intent required . . . is simply an intent to be at the place on the land where the trespass allegedly occurred."[1] (§13, p.73)

- **Case Law**

Iowa: In Iowa, "[o]ne is subject to liability to another for trespass, irrespective of whether he thereby causes harm to any legally protected interest of the other, if he intentionally

(a) enters land in the possession of the other, or causes a thing or a third person to do so, or (b) remains on the land."[73]

Michigan: A 1999 Michigan Court of Appeals decision states the elements to a cause of action for trespass to land points out that actual damages are not an element to a cause of action for trespass to land:

> Recovery for trespass to land in Michigan is available only upon proof of an unauthorized direct or immediate intrusion of a physical, tangible object onto land over which the plaintiff has a right of exclusive possession. Once such an intrusion is proved, the tort has been established, and the plaintiff is presumptively entitled to at least nominal damages.[74]

Minnesota: In a 1978 case, the Minnesota Supreme Court adopted the following statements as to the elements of a cause of action for trespass to land:

> The two essential elements of trespass to realty are right of possession in plaintiff and wrongful and unlawful entry upon such possession by defendant. Though title of the plaintiff may be an issue, it is not essential that it should be. It affects the measure of damages. It is not essential that the plaintiff have title and as against any one but the true owner it is sufficient if he has the possession. Actual possession of realty is prima facie evidence of ownership in fee in the absence of evidence showing a superior title, and in such case is sufficient proof of title to sustain an action for damages to the freehold.[75]

South Carolina: Finally, "[t]o constitute actionable trespass [in South Carolina] ... there must be an affirmative act, invasion of land must be intentional, and harm caused must be the direct result of that invasion."[76] In addition,

> The gist of trespass is the injury to possession, and generally either actual or constructive possession is sufficient to maintain an action for trespass.

For a trespass action to lie, "the act must be affirmative, the invasion of the land must be intentional, and the harm caused by the invasion of the land must be the direct result of that invasion."[76] (citations omitted)

Trespass to Chattels

Definition.   A useful starting point for the definition of trespass to chattels is seen in the following statement from the Texas Court of Appeals: "To interfere wrongfully with the use or possession of property is a trespass to chattels."[77] This definition, however, needs to be expanded upon, especially in light of the fact that trespass to chattels can be confused with the tort of conversion. As *Prosser and Keeton on Torts* puts it: "Trespass to chattels [is the] little brother to conversion."[1] (§14, p. 86) A 2000 decision from the Alabama Supreme Court puts into focus the similarities and differences between trespass to chattels and conversion:

> Conversion, as a cause of action, is closely similar to an action for trespass to chattels, see Wint v. Alabama Eye & Tissue Bank, 675 So.2d 383, 384–85

(Ala 1996) (quoting Roberts and Cusimano, Alabama Tort Law Handbook, §29.0, p. 598 (1990)), but these actions differ in that the tort of conversion requires a more extensive interference with the plaintiff's possession. *Restatement*, §222 cmt. a, reads:

> "Normally any dispossession is so clearly a serious interference with the right of control that it amounts to a conversion; and it is frequently said that any dispossession is a conversion. There may, however, be minor and unimportant dispossessions, such as taking another man's hat by mistake and returning it within two minutes upon discovery of the mistake, which do not seriously interfere with the other's right of control, and so do not amount to conversion. In such a case the remedy of the action of trespass remains, and will allow recovery of damages for the interference with the possession."[78]

It is also useful to know what a chattel is. In a 2005 decision, the Washington Supreme Court provided the following explanation: The sixth edition of *Black's Law Dictionary* defines a chattel as "[a]n article of personal property, as distinguished from real property. A thing personal and moveable. It may refer to animate as well as inanimate property." [The eighth edition], of Black defines chattel as "[m]oveable or transferable property," and a chattel personal as a "tangible good or an intangible right (such as a patent)." If a patent (a governmental grant of a right) can be a chattel, then surely a stock option can be a chattel as well.[79]

In a 2003 decision involving damage caused by spam, the California Supreme Court noted that:

> A series of federal district court decisions . . . has approved the use of trespass to chattels as a theory of spammers' liability to [Internet service providers (ISP's)], based upon evidence that the vast quantities of mail sent by spammers both overburdened the ISP's own computers and made the entire computer system harder to use for recipients, the ISP's customers. In those cases . . . the underlying complaint was that the extraordinary quantity of [unsolicited commercial bulk e-mail] impaired the computer system's functioning.[80] (emphasis in original deleted)

Possession for purposes of chattels has been defined as "the physical control of the chattel."[5] (§216)

Interest Protected.   The interest that is protected by a cause of action for trespass to chattels is the plaintiff's right to be free from injury to the personal property to which he/she has a possessory right[81] and "physical condition of the chattel.[82]

Elements of the Cause of Action

- **The *Restatement***

Section 217 of the *Restatement* lays the foundation for the elements to a cause of action for trespass to chattels. Section 217 provides that "[a] trespass to a chattel may be committed by intentionally (a) dispossessing another of the chattel, or (b) using or intermeddling with a chattel in the possession of another."[5] (§217) Based upon Section 216 of the *Restatement* "physical control" is the essential characteristic of possession.[5] (§216) In the words of Section 216: "a person who is in 'possession of a chattel' is one who has physical control of the chattel with the intent to exercise such control on his own behalf, or on behalf of another."[5] (§216) Dispossession may result from one of five following acts:

A. Taking a chattel from the possession of another without the other's consent
B. Obtaining possession of a chattel from another by fraud or duress
C. Barring the possessor's access to a chattel
D. Destroying a chattel while it is in another's possession
E. Taking the chattel into the custody of the law

The *Restatement* defines intermeddling as "intentionally bringing about a physical contact with the chattel."[5] (§217, cmt. e)

Sections 218–220 of the *Restatement* set forth the elements to this cause of action from the respective perspectives of (1) persons "in possession" of chattels,[5] (§218) (2) persons "entitled to immediate possession,"[5] (§219) and persons "[e]ntitled to future possession."[5] (§220)

Section 218 of the *Restatement*[5] sets for the elements to a cause of action in favor of a person "in possession" of a chattel and provides the following:

§218. Liability To Person In Possession

One who commits a trespass to a chattel is subject to liability to the possessor of the chattel if, but only if, (a) he dispossesses the other of the chattel, or (b) the chattel is impaired as to its condition, quality, or value, or (c) the possessor is deprived of the use of the chattel for a substantial time, or (d) bodily harm is caused to the possessor, or harm is caused to some person or thing in which the possessor has a legally protected interest

Section 219 of the *Restatements*[5] in turn sets forth the elements for a cause of action in favor of a person "entitled to immediate possession" of a chattel and provides the following:

§219. Liability To Person Entitled To Immediate Possession

One who commits a trespass to a chattel is subject to liability to another who is, or may by demand become, entitled to the immediate possession of the chattel if, but only if, (a) the chattel is impaired as to its condition, quality, or value, or (b) the person entitled to immediate possession is deprived of the use of the chattel for a substantial time, or (c) bodily harm is thereby caused to the person entitled to immediate possession, or harm is caused to some person or thing in which he has a legally protected interest

Section 220 provides for a cause of action for a person "entitled to future possession" of a chattel: "One who commits a trespass to a chattel is subject to liability to another who is entitled to the future possession of the chattel for harm thereby caused to such other's interest in the chattel"[5] (§220).

Finally, Section 222 of the *Restatement* discusses what damages are available to a plaintiff in a cause of action for trespass to chattels. According to Section 222, a defendant in a trespass to chattels cause of action may be liable for nominal damages, actual harm to the chattel, and for any decrease in the value of the chattel.[5] (§222, cmt. a) A comment to Section 218, however, states that "the interest of a possessor of a chattel in its inviolability ... is not given legal protection by an action for nominal damages for harmless intermeddlings with the chattel."[5] (§218, cmt. e) As we will see in the discussion of conversion, the nature of the damages is a distinguishing factor between a cause of action for trespass to chattels and a cause of action for conversion.

- **Case Law**

California: In a 2000 federal district court case out of California, the court (citing the California case law) had the occasion to observe (in a case involving the Internet) that trespass to chattels "lies where an intentional interference with the possession of personal property has proximately cause injury." Trespass to chattels "although seldom employed as a tort theory in California" was recently applied to cover the unauthorized use of long distance telephone lines. Specifically, the court noted "the electronic signals generated by the [defendants'] activities were sufficiently tangible to support a trespass cause of action." ... To prevail on a claim for trespass based on accessing a computer system, the plaintiff must establish that (1) the defendant intentionally and without authorization interfered with the plaintiff's possessory interest in the computer system; and (2) the defendant's unauthorized use proximately resulted in damage to the plaintiff.[83]

New York: A federal district court in New York explained what the New York law required a plaintiff to prove to establish a cause of action for trespass to chattels:

> Under the principle of law that allows recovery for a trespass to chattels, it is necessary that the defendant have acted for the purpose of interfering with the chattel, or what is almost the same thing, that he have acted with knowledge that such would be the result of his conduct. Trespass is an intentional harm at least to this extent; while the trespasser, to be liable, need not intend or expect the damaging consequence of his intrusion, he must intend the act which amounts to or produces the unlawful invasion, and the intrusion must at least be the immediate or inevitable consequence of what he willfully does, or which he does so negligently as to amount to willfulness.[84]

North Carolina: The North Carolina Supreme Court has held that "[t]he basis of a trespass to chattel cause of action lies in 'injury to possession.'" In expanding upon this statement, the court further held that:

> [a] successful action for trespass to chattel requires the party bringing the action to demonstrate that she had either actual or constructive possession of the personalty or goods in question at the time of the trespass, and that there was an unauthorized, unlawful interference or dispossession of the property.
>
> In order to satisfy the first element of a trespass to chattel cause of action, [a plaintiff] must have been in either actual or constructive possession of the property at the time [the] alleged trespass was committed. Actual possession consists of exercising dominion over, making ordinary use of, or taking the

profits from the land in dispute. Constructive possession is a legal fiction existing when there is no actual possession, but there is title granting an immediate
right to actual possession. The key to assessing possession under a trespass to
chattel claim is determining if there is a right to present possession whenever
so desired.[85]

Ohio: As is often the case, some courts adopt the wording of the applicable section of the
Restatement when declaring what the elements are for a cause of action. The Ohio Court of
Appeals did this in a 1999 decision:

> According to Section 218 of the *Restatement* 2d, Torts, a trespasser to chattel is
> liable "if, but only if," one of the following occurs: (a) he dispossesses the other
> of the chattel, or (b) the chattel is impaired as to its condition, quality, or value,
> or (c) the possessor is deprived of the use of the chattel for a substantial time, or
> (d) bodily harm is caused to the possessor, or harm is caused to some person or
> thing in which the possessor has a legally protected interest."[86]

Conversion

Definitions. Conversion has been defined as "the unauthorized assumption and
exercise of the right of ownership over goods or personal chattels belonging to
another, to the alteration of the condition or the exclusion of the owner's rights."[87]
Conversion has also been defined as "'the wrongful or unauthorized exercise of dominion
or control over a chattel."[88] From these definitions, we can see that important aspects of
conversion are (1) right of ownership, (2) alteration of the condition of the chattel, and
(3) the exercise of dominion or control. "Ownership" has been defined as "not a single
concrete entity but a bundle of rights and privileges as well as of obligations."[89] Alteration
of the condition of the chattel seems obvious enough such that resort to a legal definition is
not necessary. To exercise "dominion" over a chattel is to exercise possession or control
over the chattel.[90] "Possession" in regard to a chattel is "the physical control of the
chattel"[5] (§216).

Interest Protected.   The interest that is protected by a cause of action for conversion is
the right to be free from one person's "serious interference"[5] (§15, p. 90) with or exercise
of dominion over another person's chattels.[5] (§222A, cmt. a)

Elements of the Cause of Action

- **The *Restatement***

The elements of the cause of action for conversion is set forth in various sections of the
Restatement of which Section 222A provides the following:

> (1) Conversion is an intentional exercise of dominion or control over a chattel
> which so seriously interferes with the right of another to control it that the actor
> may justly be required to pay the other the full value of the chattel. (2) In deter-
> mining the seriousness of the interference and the justice of requiring the actor
> to pay the full value, the following factors are important: (a) the extent and

duration of the actor's exercise of dominion or control; (b) the actor's intent to assert a right in fact inconsistent with the other's right of control; (c) the actor's good faith; (d) the extent and duration of the resulting interference with the other's right of control; (e) the harm done to the chattel; (f) the inconvenience and expense caused to the other.

Section 223 of the *Restatement* points out that conversion can be committed in one of several ways. A person may, for example, be liable for conversion because he dispossessed another of his chattel,[91] or altered or destroyed another person's chattel.[5] (§223, 226) If found to have committed conversion, a defendant may be liable to the person who was in possession of the chattel[5] (§224A) and the person who was entitled to immediate possession.[5] (§225)

What makes conversion so interesting and perhaps is the biggest difference between it and trespass to chattels is the damages aspect of conversion. As specified in Section 222A of the *Restatement*, a defendant liable for conversion has to pay the full value of the chattel that was converted. In a successful conversion suit, the defendant in effect ends up buying the converted chattel.[5] (§222a, cmt. c) Conversion is one of the intentional torts in which the plaintiff has to prove actual damages.[92]

Finally, according to the *Restatement*, consent is not an element of a plaintiff's cause of action for conversion.[93]

- **Case Law**

California: The case law in California holds that "[t]he elements of a conversion are the plaintiff's ownership or right to possession of the property at the time of the conversion; the defendant's conversion by a wrongful act or disposition of property rights; and damages."[94] Furthermore, "[i]t is not necessary that there be a manual taking of the property; it is only necessary to show an assumption of control or ownership over the property, or that the alleged converter has applied the property to his own use."[94]

Kentucky: The Kentucky Supreme Court has cited with approval, the following statement of the elements to a cause of action for conversion:

> The elements necessary to prove a conversion claim established in case law are: (1) the plaintiff had legal title to the converted property; (2) the plaintiff had possession of the property or the right to possess it at the time of the conversion; (3) the defendant exercised dominion over the property in a manner which denied the plaintiff's rights to use and enjoy the property and which was to the defendant's own use and beneficial enjoyment; (4) the defendant intended to interfere with the plaintiff's possession; (5) the plaintiff made some demand for the property's return which the defendant refused; (6) the defendant's act was the legal cause of the plaintiff's loss of the property; and (7) the plaintiff suffered damage by the loss of the property.[95]

Missouri: In a 1999 Missouri Court of Appeals case, the court stated that "[c]onversion is the unauthorized assumption and exercise of the right to ownership over personal property of another to the exclusion of the owner's rights,"[96] and went on to declare that "[t]here are three elements which must be established to prove conversion: (1) plaintiff was the owner of the property or entitled to its possession; (2) defendant took possession of the property with the intent to exercise some control over it; and (3) defendant thereby deprived plaintiff of the right to possession."[96]

New York: The Appellate Division of the New York Supreme Court has held that "to establish a cause of action for conversion, a plaintiff must establish legal ownership of a specific identifiable piece of property and the defendant's exercise of dominion over or interference with the property in defiance of the plaintiff's rights."[97] That court has further held that "[i]ntent to possess another's property is not an essential element of conversion. It is not even necessary that a converter take physical possession of the property. 'Any wrongful exercise of dominion by one other than the owner is a conversion.'"[97]

Recklessness

Definition

The New Jersey Supreme Court has pointed out that recklessness is a tort that lies somewhere between the intentional torts and negligence.[98] As that court stated: "By recklessness we mean conduct that 'involves a greater degree of fault than negligence but a lesser degree of fault than intentional wrongdoing .... The ordinary meaning of the word [recklessness] is a high degree of carelessness. It is the doing of something which in fact involves a grave risk to others ....'"[99]

Interest Protected

The interest that a cause of action for recklessness protects is the interest to be free from injury caused by reckless conduct.

Elements to the Cause of Action and Defense to the Cause of Action

Restatement

According to Section 500 of the *Restatement*, an "actor's conduct is in reckless disregard of the safety of another if he does an act or intentionally fails to do an act which is his duty to the other to do, knowing or having reason to know of facts which would lead a reasonable man to realize, not only that his conduct creates an unreasonable risk of physical harm to another, but also that such risk is substantially greater than that which is necessary to make his conduct negligent."[5] (§500)

Comment a of Section 500 of the *Restatement* points out that there are two types of recklessness.[5] (§500)

> [In the first type] the [defendant] knows, or has reason to know ... of facts which create a high degree of risk of physical harm to another, and deliberately proceeds to act, or to fail to act, in conscious disregard of, or indifference to, that risk. [In the Second type], the [defendant] has such knowledge, or reason to know, of the facts, but does not realize or appreciate the high degree of risk involved, although a reasonable man in his position would do so.[5] (§500)

Section 501 of the *Restatement* provides that:

> (1) Except as stated in Subsection (2) and in §503, the rules which determine the actor's liability to another for reckless disregard of the other's safety are the same as those which determine his liability for negligent misconduct.
>
> (2) The fact that the actor's misconduct is in reckless disregard of another's safety rather than merely negligent is a matter to be taken into account in determining whether a jury may reasonably find that the actor's conduct bears a sufficient causal relation to another's harm to make the actor liable therefore.[5] (§501)

Thus, based upon the *Restatement*, a plaintiff has to prove duty, breach of duty, causation, and damages.

According to Section 503 of the *Restatement*, contributory negligence is not a defense to a cause of action for recklessness.[5] (§503) The plaintiff's reckless disregard of her own safety is a defense to the plaintiff's cause of action for recklessness.[5] (§503)

- **Case Law**

Arizona: In a 1991 case, the Arizona Court of Appeals, citing Section 501 of the *Restatement* stated that "[t]he rules by which liability for wanton misconduct is determined are the same as those by which liability for simple negligence is decided."[100] Going further, the court went on to point out that the Arizona Supreme Court had held that "a plaintiff's ordinary contributory negligence does not apply to defeat his recovery when his injury was the result of the willful, wanton or reckless conduct of the defendant [and that] . . . when the plaintiff's contributory negligence was itself willful, wanton or reckless, it may be balanced against the wanton negligence of the defendant so as to bar the plaintiff's recovery."[100]

California: Citing Section 501 of the *Restatement* and California case law, the federal district court for the Northern District of California pointed out that the causation rules of the intentional torts govern the causation element of a cause of action for recklessness rather than the causation rules of negligence.[101] The court held that "[p]roximate cause is a requirement for a finding of negligence, but is not required in the field of intended torts, which rules apply to recklessness as well."[101]

Colorado: In the context of a cause of action for recklessness, the Colorado Court of Appeals while determining whether the defendant owed the plaintiff a duty applied Section 501 of the *Restatement*; in doing so, it stated the following:

> Once an actor's conduct is determined to be reckless, his or her liability for the harm resulting from such behavior is determined by the same rules that determine the liability of a negligent actor. Thus, a plaintiff must still plead and prove facts demonstrating the existence of the basic elements of duty, breach, proximate cause, and damages in order to state a claim upon which relief can be granted.[102]

An Additional Matter

In addition to the causation element of a cause of action for recklessness being different from that for a cause of action for negligence, the two causes of action also differ with regard to damages. The Florida District Court of Appeal explained the rationale for applying punitive damages to a recklessness cause of action in the following words:

> To merit an award of punitive damages, the defendant's conduct must transcend the level of ordinary negligence and enter the realm of willful and wanton misconduct, which the courts define as conduct that is of a gross and flagrant character, evincing reckless disregard of human life, or of the safety of persons exposed to its dangerous effects, or there is that entire want of care which would raise the presumption of a conscious indifference to consequences, or which shows wantonness or recklessness, or a grossly careless disregard of the safety and welfare of the public, or that reckless indifference to the rights of others which is equivalent to an intentional violation of them.[103]

"Under Pennsylvania law, only the first type of reckless conduct described in comment a to Section 500, is sufficient to create a jury question on the issue of punitive damages."[104]

Negligence

Initial Definitions

Over the years, negligence has been defined in a variety of ways. In the famous 1928 case of *Palsgraf v. Long Island Railroad Company,* negligence was defined as "the absence of care, according to the circumstances."[105] The *Restatement* defines negligence as "conduct which falls below the standard established by law for the protection of others against unreasonable risk of harm. It does not include conduct recklessly disregardful of an interest of others."

The definition that will be the basis of this discussion is that negligence is conduct that falls below the standard of care established by law for the protection of others against unreasonable risks of harm.[106]

Let us take a few moments and analyze this definition by taking it as a whole and breaking it down into its components. What then are the components of negligence? To begin with, negligence is *conduct.* Conduct is "the act, manner, or process of carrying on."[107] Knowing that negligence is conduct allows us to distinguish intent, which is a state of mind.[108]

The conduct that negligence is concerned with falls below *the standard of care.* A standard is "something established by authority, custom, or general consent as a model or example [;] something...established by authority as a rule for the measure of quantity, weight, extert, valve, or quality."[109] Care is "a disquieted state of blended uncertainty, apprehension, and responsibility"; or "painstaking or watchful attention."[110] In general, the standard of care is based upon the so-called reasonable person standard. This concept in the form of a question can be expressed as: "What would a reasonable person do under the circumstances that existed at the time of the incident?"

Standards of care are established by law. What is meant by "established by law?" According to the *Restatement* (§285), standards of care "may be"

(a) established by a legislative enactment or administrative regulation which so provides, or

(b) adopted by the court from a legislative enactment or an administrative regulation which does not so provide, or

(c) established by judicial decision, or

(d) applied to the facts of the case by the trial judge or the jury, if there is no such enactment, regulation, or decision.

Compare and contrast what the *Restatement* and some courts have said about who establishes standards of care. In a 1932 decision of the Court of Appeals of the Second Circuit, Judge Learned Hand declared that when all is said and done, standards of care are established by the courts.[111] In so holding, Judge Hand said the following:

There are, no doubt, cases where courts seem to make the general practice of the calling the standard of proper diligence; we have indeed given some currency to the notion ourselves. Indeed in most cases reasonable prudence is in fact common prudence; but strictly it is never its measure; a whole calling may have unduly lagged in the adoption of new and available devices. It never may set its own tests, however persuasive be its usages. Courts must in the end say what is required; there are precautions so imperative that even their universal disregard will not excuse their omission.[112]

In a 1985 case, the Arizona Supreme Court, which held that the standard of care for manufacturers is not to be set by the manufacturers,[113] put it this way:

Volkswagen argues that case law already recognizes that in negligent design cases a manufacturer is not liable absent a showing that he failed to conform to the standard of care in design followed by other manufacturers. We do not agree. . . .

Special groups will be allowed to create their own standards of reasonably prudent conduct only when the nature of the group and its special relationship with its clients assure society that those standards will be set with primary regard to protection of the public rather than to such considerations as increased profitability. We do not believe that automobile manufacturers fit into this category. This is no reflection upon automobile manufacturers, but merely a recognition that the necessities of the marketplace permit manufacturers neither the working relationship nor the concern about the welfare of their customers that the professions generally permit and require from their practitioners.[113] (citations omitted)

Standards of care are established for *the protection of others against unreasonable risks of harm.* A risk is a "[p]ossibility [or probability] of loss or injury . . . the chance of loss . . . ."[6] (p.1018) Take note that the risks spoken of in the definition of negligence are unreasonable risks. Unreasonable is defined, among other ways as "not governed by reason."[6] (p. 1293) We, therefore, need to know what is reason, which has been defined, among other ways, as "a rational ground or motive.[6] (p. 981) The law of negligence does not protect against reasonable risks.

In the section to follow, we will consider the elements to a *cause of action* for negligence. As with other torts, the *definition* of negligence is not the same thing as the *cause of action* for negligence. You can be as negligent as you want to as long as your negligence does not cause injury to another. It has often been stated that "[p]roof of negligence in the air, so to speak, will not do."[114] In other words, if a plaintiff proves only that the defendant was negligent — without proving that the defendant's negligence caused injury — a cause of action for negligence has not been established, and the defendant will bear no liability.

Interest Protected

The interest protect by a cause of action in negligence is the freedom from personal injury or property damage caused by negligence.[115]

Elements of the Cause of Action

The Restatement

Section 281 of the *Restatement* is entitled "Statement of the Elements of a Cause of Action for Negligence;" it provides the following:

> The actor is liable for an invasion of an interest of another, if:
> (a) the interest invaded is protected against unintentional invasion, and
> (b) the conduct of the actor is negligent with respect to the other, or a class of persons within which he is included, and
> (c) the actor's conduct is a legal cause of the invasion, and
> (d) the other has not so conducted himself as to disable himself from bringing an action for such invasion.[116]

Case Law: in General

The courts typically state that there are four elements to a cause of action for negligence: (1) a duty, (2) a breach of that duty, (3) causation, and (4) damages.[117] Some courts have expressed the elements in different ways. For example, the Louisiana Court of Appeal has held that a cause of action for negligence consists of five elements:

> (1) that the defendant's conduct was a cause-in-fact of the plaintiff's injuries (the cause-in-fact element); (2) that the defendant's conduct failed to conform to the appropriate standard (the breach element); (3) that the defendant had a duty to conform his conduct to a specific standard (the duty element); (4) that the defendant's conduct was a legal cause of the plaintiff's injuries (the scope of liability or scope of protection element); and (5) that the plaintiff suffered actual damages (the damages element).[118]

Another example is the view of the Texas Court of Appeals, which has held that "Texas law requires proof of three familiar elements to sustain a cause of action for negligence: (1) a legal duty owed by one party to another; (2) a breach of that duty; and (3) damages proximately caused by the breach."[119] When all of this is boiled down, the result is that when we analyze the statements of those courts that express the cause of action as being more or less than four, we really end up with four elements: (1) duty, (2) breach of the duty, (3) causation,[120] and (4) damages. A third example is seen in the words of the Court of Appeals of Indiana: To sustain an action for negligence, a plaintiff must establish: "(1) a duty owed by the defendant to conform her conduct to a standard of care arising from her relationship with the plaintiff; (2) a breach of that duty; and (3) an injury proximately caused by the breach of that duty."[121]

The Elements Considered Individually

Duty.   What is a duty? One helpful place to start is to think of it as an obligation. The Arizona Supreme Court has said that "a duty in the parlance of tort law" is "a legal obligation to protect [a person or thing] from injury or harm."[122] In a like manner, the South Carolina Court of Appeals has declared that "[in general, duty is defined as the obligation to conform to a particular standard of conduct toward another."[123] The U.S. District Court for the Northern District of Ohio has similarly equated duty with obligation: "Duty, as used in Ohio tort law, refers to the relationship between the plaintiff and the defendant from which arises an obligation on the part of the defendant to exercise due care toward the plaintiff."[124] Other courts have taken a different approach to the definition of duty. For instance, the California Supreme Court has held that duty is "an expression of the sum total of those considerations of policy which lead the law to say that the particular plaintiff is entitled to protection."[125]

Now that we know what a duty is, we need to ascertain why it is that one person has a duty to another person. In the eyes of the law, it is not enough simply to say that there should be a duty? The law requires more. The burden is on the plaintiff to prove that the defendant had a duty not to be negligent toward the plaintiff.[126]

How does one go about proving that there is a duty on the defendant to protect the plaintiff from injury? In general, there are two ways in which a duty arises, "by operation of law and ... out of a contractual relationship...."[127] The former can come about in several ways or based upon several concepts. Foreseeability is one of those "by operation of law" concepts by which the existence of a duty can be proven. To foresee is "to see ... beforehand"[6] (p. 483). In 1928, what has come to be one of the most famous tort case was handed down by the New York Court of Appeals. That case was *Palsgraf v. Long Island Railroad Co.*[128] In *Palsgraf*, a woman standing at one end of a railroad platform was injured by a set of weighing scales that fell on her as a result of the explosion of a package of fireworks that was being carried by a passenger who, with the help of one of the employees of the railroad company, was attempting to board a train as it was moving out of the train station.[129] The majority of the court found that the defendant railroad company did not owe a duty to the plaintiff to protect her against the misfortune that befell her, deciding the case on the basis of duty.[130] In coming to this conclusion, the court said, among other things: "The risk reasonably to be perceived defines the duty to be obeyed, and risk imports relation; it is risk to another or to others within the range of apprehension."[131]

As demonstrated in the following quote, the Tennessee Court of Appeals allows foreseeability to be used in its state as a basis for establishing duty:

> If the injury which occurred could not have been reasonably foreseen, the duty of care does not arise, and even though the act of the defendant in fact caused the injury, there is no negligence and no liability. The plaintiff must show that the injury was a reasonably foreseeable probability, not just a remote possibility, and that some action within the [defendant's] power more probably than not would have prevented the injury.[132]

An interesting discussion of the role that foreseeability plays in establishing duty was provided by the Minnesota Supreme Court in a case in which the issue was whether "the operator of a commercial parking ramp owe[d] a duty to a ramp customer to protect her from trespassing rapist."[133]

> In this case we inquire whether the duty to protect should be extended to . . . a commercial parking ramp. As to business enterprises generally, the law has been cautious and reluctant to impose a duty to protect. A mere merchant-customer relationship is not enough to impose a duty on the merchant to protect his customers. . . .
>
> Whether a duty is imposed depends, therefore, on the relationship of the parties and the foreseeable risk involved. Ultimately, the question is one of policy. . . .
>
> This leads us then to the case at hand. We have a large commercial parking ramp facility in a downtown metropolitan area. Several hundred cars, for a fee, are parked within the structure. The interior, with its many levels, its supporting pillars, its stairwells, its relatively low ceilings, and its rows of unoccupied parked cars, provides places in which to hide or to lurk, especially if the interior is dimly lit. Anyone from the street may enter the structure unobserved by the ramp attendant. The place is relatively deserted, with people present only momentarily to either leave or retrieve their car. The cars, left unattended, attract thieves and vandals, and criminal activity, though generally of the property sort, is not uncommon.
>
> These general characteristics of a parking ramp facility, it seems to us, present a particular focus or unique opportunity for criminals and their criminal activities, an opportunity which to some degree is different from that presented out on the street and in the neighborhood generally. We do not think the law should say the operator of a parking ramp owes no duty to protect its customers. Some duty is owed.
>
> We hold that the duty should be defined and explained to the jury along the following lines: The operator or owner of a parking ramp facility has a duty to use reasonable care to deter criminal activity on its premises which may cause personal harm to customers. The care to be provided is that care which a reasonably prudent operator or owner would provide under like circumstances. Among the circumstances to be considered are the location and construction of the ramp, the practical feasibility and cost of various security measures, and the risk of personal harm to customers which the owner or operator knows, or in the exercise of due care should know, presents a reasonable likelihood of happening. . . .
>
> The likelihood of harm is, of course, an important factor. Here, for example, the defendants point out there had never been a sexual assault in the ramp prior to plaintiff's case, an important consideration. On the other hand, in this instance, it would appear that the jury might consider the likelihood of the appreciable increase in criminal activity breeding crimes of violence.[134]

The fact that something is foreseeable has not always persuaded courts to find that a duty exists. An example of this is seen in a 1984 Pennsylvania Supreme Court's decision in which a woman was abducted from the parking garage adjacent to and part of the complex in which her apartment building was located; she was later raped. The woman sued the owners of the complex, asserting that the owners were negligent in not protecting her from the criminal acts of those who abducted and raped her.[135] At one point in its opinion, the court stated that "[t]he criminal can be expected anywhere, any time, and has been a risk of life for a long time. He can be expected in the village, monastery and the castle keep."[136] Nonetheless, the court refused to allow foreseeability to be used as the basis for what it saw as an expansion of a landlord's duty to his or her tenant and held that owners did not have a duty to protect the plaintiff. In so holding, the court said that "[t]o impose a general duty [under the facts of this case] would effectively require landlords to be insurers of their tenants safety: a burden which could never be completely met given the unfortunate realities of modern society."[136]

In a 1989 case, the California Supreme Court, in the context of a negligent infliction of emotional distress (NIED) case, declared its concern that "the limitless exposure to liability that the pure foreseeability test of 'duty'" could bring about in the absence of some check on the use of foreseeability as a basis for establishing duty.[137] The court characterized the use of foreseeability as the test for duty in NIED cases as "arbitrary and unacceptable,"[138] and further declared that "foreseeability of the injury alone is not a useful 'guideline' or a meaningful restriction on the scope of the NIED action."[138]

That the use of foreseeability as a basis for establishing duty (especially in the context of NIED) is a controversial matter, witness what the Alaska Supreme Court had to say about the Thing decision:

> The [defendant] urges us to restrict NIED claims by applying the Dillon factors as strict requirements rather than guidelines, the approach taken by the California Supreme Court in *Thing v. La Chusa*, We decline to adopt the Thing approach. Rather, we believe that courts "should apply the concepts of foreseeability and duty to negligent infliction of emotional distress actions, with a view toward a policy favoring reasonable limitations on liability."
>
> . . .
>
> We believe that both justice and the policy favoring reasonable limitations on liability can be served with a less restrictive approach than that taken by the Thing court. . . . We believe, however, that one who is thrust, either voluntarily or involuntarily, into such dramatic events and who makes a sudden sensory observation of the traumatic injuries of a close relative in the immediate aftermath of the event which produced them is no less entitled to assert a claim for his or her emotional injuries than one who actually witnessed the event.[139]

Yet another of the "by operation of law" concepts that can give rise to a duty is relationship. In Texas, a doctor's duty is based upon the relationship concept: "The question of duty is a question of law, which a court must decide before reaching the standard of care. If there is no prior relationship between the physician and the patient, there must be some affirmative action on the part of the physician to treat the patient to create such a relationship."[140] New York also recognizes the relationship concept as a basis for establishing the existence of a duty: "In analyzing questions regarding the scope of an individual actor's duty, the courts look to whether the relationship of the parties is such as to give rise to a duty of care, whether the plaintiff was within the zone of foreseeable harm and whether the accident was within the reasonably foreseeable risks.[141] Ohio is another state in which a duty can arise out of relationship between the parties (along with foreseeability). In the words of the Ohio Supreme Court: "a defendant's duty to a plaintiff depends upon the relationship between the parties and the foreseeability of injury to someone in the plaintiff's position."[142]

Another aspect of relationship as being a basis for establishing duty is the "special relationship" theory. A 2001 decision of the North Carolina Court of Appeals explains this approach to duty:

"Actionable negligence presupposes the existence of a legal relationship between parties by which the injured party is owed a duty by the other, and such duty must be imposed by law." Thus, the preliminary question is whether defendant owed a duty of care to plaintiff under the circumstances. Traditionally, courts have distinguished between negligence claims based on affirmative acts and those based on omissions.... In cases involving omissions, negligence may arise where a "special relationship" exists between the parties. A helpful description of the category of cases in which an affirmative duty to act is imposed upon a defendant as a result of a special relationship is set forth in [*Prosser and Keeton*]:

> During the last century, liability for [omissions] has been extended still further to a limited group of relations, in which custom, public sentiment and views of social policy have led the courts to find a duty of affirmative action. In such relationships the plaintiff is typically in some respect particularly vulnerable and dependent upon the defendant who, correspondingly, holds considerable power over the plaintiff's welfare. In addition, such relations have often involved some existing or potential economic advantage to the defendant. Fairness in such cases thus may require the defendant to use his power to help the plaintiff, based upon the plaintiff's expectation of protection, which itself may be based upon the defendant's expectation of financial gain.... There is now respectable authority imposing the same duty upon a shopkeeper to his business visitor, upon a host to his social guest, upon a jailor to his prisoner, and upon a school to its pupil.

Thus, where the alleged negligence is premised on a defendant's failure to protect a plaintiff from a harm that the defendant did not directly create, as in the instant case, the defendant may be held liable if a special relationship existed between the parties sufficient to impose upon the defendant a duty of care.[143]

The California Court of Appeal has explained what a special relationship is in the following words:

In cases where the alleged duty requires taking action to protect someone from the conduct of others, courts have also considered factors involving the relationship between the parties and the connection between the defendant and the injury-producing event. These include whether the defendant induced the victim's reliance on a promise that defendant would protect or warn the victim, the extent to which a defendant created the peril or increased the risk of harm to potential victims, and the existence of a dependency relationship between the plaintiff and defendant. When the balance of all relevant factors weigh in favor of imposing a duty to protect someone from the conduct of others, a "special relationship" is said to exist. "Special relationship" is thus "simply a label expressing the conclusion that the facts, considered in light of the pertinent legal considerations, support the existence of a duty of care."[144]

An example of a special relationship that can result in the imposition of a duty is the relationship between the owner of land and a person who comes onto the land. In 1976, the New York Court of Appeals decided a case that discusses (1) the category of persons who go onto the land of another, (2) the respective duties owed to those persons, and (3) the alternative to the special relationship theory.[145] One of the issues in the case was what was the plaintiff's status when he went onto the defendant's property: was he a trespasser, a licensee, or a business invitee?[146] If the plaintiff was a business guess, the defendant's duty would have been "'to keep the premises in a reasonably safe condition for the use of a person such as the plaintiff coming on the premises."[146] If the plaintiff was a licensee, the defendant's duty would have been "to make sure that if there were any dangerous conditions existing on the roadway that they should let him know.'"[147] If the plaintiff was a trespasser, the defendant's duty would have been "'not to do any willful or wanton or aggressive act with respect to his safety. . . .'"[147] In other words, high duty would have been owed to the plaintiff if he were a business invitee, a lower duty would have been owed to him if he were a licensee, and the lowest duty would have been owed to him if he were a trespasser.

The court decided to abandon the special relationship theories and replace them with the foreseeability approach to duty:

> Rather than to demand continued attempts to fit a plaintiff into one of the three rigid categories, the court pauses instead to reflect, to reconsider the necessity for such classification and to state today that the distinctions need no longer be made. . . . New York courts are not unmindful of the adoption of the single standard of care in several of our sister States. . . . While we have demonstrated our inclination to correlate the duty of care owed plaintiff with the risk of harm reasonably to be perceived, regardless of status, and concurrently consider the question of foreseeability, we have not, until today, abandoned the classifications entirely and announced our adherence to the single standard of reasonable care under the circumstances where by foreseeability shall be a measure of liability. To be sure, this standard of reasonable care should be no different than that applied in the usual negligence action.[148]

Another of the "by operation of law" concepts that can give rise to a duty is what has come to be known as the BPL formula. This concept was first expressed in the famous New York case of *United States v. Carroll Towing Co.*[149] In the *Carroll Towing Co.* case, the court had to decide, among other things, whether the owners of a barge that had sunk would have to bear some of the responsibility for its having sunk.[150] To answer that question, the court had to determine whether the owner had a duty to have someone on board the barge to watch over it.[150] In concluding that the owner of the barge had such a duty, the court said the following:

> [T]here is no general rule to determine when the absence of a bargee or other attendant will make the owner of the barge liable for injuries to other vessels if she breaks away from her moorings. However, in any cases where he would be so liable for injuries to others obviously he must reduce his damages proportionately, if the injury is to his own barge. It becomes apparent why there can be no such general rule, when we consider the grounds for such a liability. Since there are occasions when every vessel will break from her moorings, and since, if she does, she becomes a menace to those about her; the owner's duty, as in other similar situations, to provide against resulting injuries is a function of three variables: (1) The probability that she will break away; (2) the gravity of the resulting injury, if she does; (3) the burden of adequate precautions. Possibly it serves to bring this notion into relief to state it in algebraic terms: if the probability be called P; the injury, L; and the burden, B; liability depends upon whether B is less than L multiplied by P: i.e., whether B is less than PL. Applied to the situation at bar, the likelihood that a barge will break from her fasts and the damage she will do, vary with the place and time; for example, if a storm threatens, the danger is greater; so it is, if she is in a crowded harbor where moored barges are constantly being shifted about. On the other hand, the barge must not be the bargee's prison, even though he lives aboard; he must go ashore at times. We need not say whether, even in such crowded waters as New York Harbor a bargee must be aboard at night at all; it may be that the custom is otherwise . . . and that, if so, the situation is one where custom should control.[151]

The BPL formula is an economic or cost approach to the question of whether a duty is owed as seen in the words of the Court of Appeals of North Carolina:

> [T]he basic approach to negligence law outlined by Judge Learned Hand in *United States v. Carroll Towing Co.* essentially defines negligence [sic] as the unreasonable balancing of the cost of safety measures against the risk of accidents. (explaining that 'if the probability [of an accident] be called P; the injury, L; and the burden [of adequate precautions], B; liability depends upon whether B is less than L multiplied by P: i.e., whether $B < PL$').[152]

Res ipsa loquitur and negligence *per se* are two tort concepts that also fall within the circumstance in which a duty arises by operation of law.

Recall that a duty may also "arise out of a contractual relationship."[153] According to a 2004 decision of the Michigan Supreme Court, a duty "may and frequently does arise out of a contractual relationship, the theory being that accompanying every contract is a common-law duty to perform with ordinary care the thing agreed to be done, and that a negligent performance constitutes a tort as well as a breach of contract."[154] A 1967 decision of that court brings this theory into focus:

> Actionable negligence presupposes the existence of a legal relationship between parties by which the injured party is owed a duty by the other, and such duty must be imposed by law. The duty may arise specifically by mandate of statute, or it may arise generally by operation of law under application of the basic rule of the common law, which imposes on every person engaged in the prosecution of any undertaking an obligation to use due care, or to so govern his actions as not to unreasonably endanger the person or property of others. This rule of the common law arises out of the concept that every person is under the general duty to so act, or to use that which he controls, as not to injure another.
>
> Such duty of care may be a specific duty owing to the plaintiff by the defendant, or it may be a general one owed by the defendant to the public, of which the plaintiff is a part. Moreover, while this duty of care, as an essential element of actionable negligence, arises by operation of law, it may and frequently does arise out of a contractual relationship, the theory being that accompanying every contract is a common-law duty to perform with ordinary care the thing agreed to be done, and that a negligent performance constitutes a tort as well as a breach of contract. But it must be kept in mind that the contract creates only the relation out of which arises the common-law duty to exercise ordinary care. Thus in legal contemplation the contract merely creates the state of things which furnishes the occasion of the tort. This being so, the existence of a contract is ordinarily a relevant factor, competent to be alleged and proved in a negligence action to the extent of showing the relationship of the parties and the nature and extent of the common-law duty on which the tort is based.[155]

The Virginia Supreme Court has expressed a similar view:

> To establish a cause of action for negligence, the duty alleged to have been tortiously breached must be a common law duty, not a duty arising between the parties solely by virtue of a contract . . . . Before any duty of care can arise to control the conduct of third persons, there must be a special relationship between the defendant and either the plaintiff or the third person. We have recognized a special relationship between a defendant and a plaintiff in cases involving a common carrier and its passenger, a business proprietor and its invitee, and an innkeeper and its guest. However, these are not exclusive examples of a special relationship.[156]

It seems then that relationship is the theory that undergirds the view that a contract can give rise to a tort-law duty.

Breach of Duty.   Simply put, a breach is a "break," or "an infraction or violation of a law, obligation, tie, or standard."[157] In terms of tort law, a breach of duty is "conduct below the applicable standard of care."[158] "A breach of duty occurs when [a] [d]efendant fail[s] to exercise reasonable care under the circumstances."[159]

Causation.   Causation is a process by which "A" brings about "B". In tort law, causation is the process by which the actions of one person or entity bring about harm to another person or entity. It should come as no surprise that a defendant should not be liable if what he did or did not do was not the cause of the plaintiff's loss.

There are two "aspects" to causation. In an unpublished opinion, the Ohio Court of Appeals has explained these two aspects in the following words:

> In determining whether a negligent party may be held liable for a plaintiff's injuries, courts must examine two aspects of causation: actual causation and proximate causation. First, a court must determine whether the negligent party was the cause in fact of the plaintiff's injuries; that is, whether the plaintiff would have suffered injury but for the defendant's negligent act. In Anderson v. St. Francis-St. George Hosp., Inc. the court described the cause in fact test as follows:
>
>> The standard test for establishing causation is the sine qua non or "but for" test. Thus, a defendant's conduct is a cause of the event (or harm) if the event (or harm) would not have occurred but for that conduct; conversely, the defendant's conduct is not the cause of the event (or harm) if the event (or harm) would have occurred regardless of the conduct.
>
> Once the court determines that the defendant's negligent act constitutes the "but for" cause of the plaintiff's injuries, the court must examine whether the defendant's negligence was the proximate or legal cause of the plaintiff's injuries. We note that it is a basic and well-settled concept that negligence is without legal consequence unless the negligent act is a proximate cause of the plaintiff's injury.
>
> The rule of proximate cause "requires that the injury sustained shall be the natural and probable consequence of the negligence alleged; that is, such consequence as under the surrounding circumstances of the particular case might, and should have been foreseen or anticipated by the wrongdoer as likely to follow his negligent act." In Mussivand [v. David], the court described the proximate cause test as follows:
>
>> [I]n order to establish proximate cause, foreseeability must be found. * * * If an injury is the natural and probable consequence of a negligent act and it is such as should have been foreseen in the light of all the attending circumstances, the injury is then the proximate result of the negligence. Thus, liability for negligence extends to those injuries that the defendant should have foreseen.
>
> Accordingly, for liability to attach to a negligent defendant, the plaintiff must establish that: (1) her injury would not have occurred but for the defendant's negligence; and (2) her injury was a natural and probable result of the defendant's negligence, i.e., the defendant knew or should have known that his negligent act would cause injury.[160]

- **Actual Cause, Cause-in-Fact, Factual Cause**

The first aspect of causation is referred to in one of three ways: actual cause, cause in fact, or factual cause (hereinafter referred to as actual cause).[161] One way to understand this aspect of causation is to view it as "logical cause." Along this line, one commentator has characterized cause-in-fact as "a logical cause and effect relationship between the conduct complained of and the harm for which liability is sought."[162] If the defendant's negligence is not the cause of the plaintiff's injury, the defendant is not liable to the plaintiff.[163] The 1919 Massachusetts Supreme Judicial Court case of *Ford v. Trident Fisheries Co*[164] demonstrates the nature of actual cause. A sailor on a fishing trawler was thrown overboard when the ship rolled while on a fishing voyage.[165] There was no cry of help heard by those on board the ship, and no one saw the sailor fall overboard.[165] Unfortunately, the sailor disappeared immediately after he fell overboard.[165] One of the plaintiff's theories of liability was "the boat which was lowered to pick up the [sailor] was lashed to the deck instead of being suspended from davits and . . . to launch it the lashings had to be cut; that the [person], who manned [the rescue boat] had, had only one oar . . . ."[165]

The court concluded that the circumstances of the rescue boat did not cause the sailor's death because even if the rescue boat had been "properly suspended" and equipped with two oars, the sailor could not have been rescued — because the sailor "disappeared when he fell [into the ocean]."[165] In other words, the circumstances surrounding the rescue boat did not bring about the sailor's death; a speedily launched rescue boat and a properly equipped rescuer would have done no good, because the sailor immediately sank below the surface of the water.

- **The Theories by Which Actual Cause Can Be Proven**

Over the years, two theories have been developed for proving that a defendant's negligence was the actual cause of the plaintiff's injuries. One of those theories is referred to as the "but-for" theory and the other as the "substantial factor theory."[166]

1. The But-For Theory
    As stated in *Prosser and Keeton*[1]: "An act or omission is not regarded as a cause of an event if the particular event would have occurred without it."[1] (§41, p. 265) This rule is also known as the *sine qua non* rul.[1] (§41, p. 266) Translated, *sine qua non* means "without which not" or "that without which the thing cannot be."[167] Synonymous terms for "but for" might be "except for" or in the absence of. "An example of applying the "but-for" theory might be as follows: "Except for the defendant having failed to have his brakes checked, he would have been able to stop his car prior to his car having collided with my client's car. The collision would not have occurred without the defendant having failed to have his brakes inspected."

2. The Substantial Factor Theory
    The substantial factor theory comes into play when there has been more than one cause to an event. "[T]wo causes concur to bring about an event, and either one of them, operating alone, would have been sufficient to cause the identical result."[1] (§41, p. 266) *Prosser and Keeton* provides the following examples of the circumstances in which the substantial factor rule should be applied:

    > Two motorcycles simultaneously pass the plaintiff's horse, which is frightened and runs away; either one alone would have caused the fright.

A stabs C with a knife, and B fractures C's skull with a rock; either wound would be fatal and C dies from the effect of both. The defendant sets a fire, which merges with a fire from some other source; the combined fires burn the plaintiff's property, but either one would have done it alone. In such cases, it is quite clear that each cause has in fact played so important a part in producing the result that responsibility should be imposed upon it; and it is equally clear that neither can be absolved from that responsibility upon the ground that the identical harm would have occurred without it, or there would be no liability at all.[1] (§41, p. 267, footnotes omitted)

A 1995 decision of the Idaho Court of Appeals explains the substantial factor theory in the following words:

[U]se of "but for" terminology in a jury instruction on actual causation is improper where there are multiple independent forces that may have caused or contributed to the harm. The Court there held that in multiple causation cases the jury must be instructed that proximate cause is established if the jury finds that the defendant's negligence was a "substantial factor" in causing the plaintiff's injury. ... The substantial factor test was adopted to allow recovery in circumstances where the defendant's negligence may have concurred with another cause to bring about the injury, even though it could not be established that the damage to the plaintiff would not have occurred "but for" the defendant's negligence. In other words, substantial factor is a more liberal standard, allowing recovery in situations where a strict "but for" analysis might relieve the defendant of liability.[168]

The California Court of Appeals, in a 2003 decision, expressed the view that "[t]he substantial factor standard has gained favor as a clearer rule of causation and one which subsumes the 'but for' test ...."[169] This is a view that appears to be espoused by the *Restatement*. Section 431 of the *Restatement* states in part that "[t]he actor's negligence conduct is a legal cause of harm to another if (a) his conduct is a substantial factor in bringing about the harm ...."[5] (§431). Subsection (1) of Section 432 of the *Restatement* goes on to state that "[e]xcept as stated in Subsection (2), the actor's negligence conduct is not a substantial factor in bringing about harm to another if the harm would have been sustained even if the actor has not been negligent."[5] (§432)

- **Proximate Cause/Legal Cause[170]**

In discussing this second aspect of causation, let me begin by pointing out that the authors of *Prosser and Keeton*[1] consider the term "proximate cause" to be "an unfortunate term."[1] (§41, p. 264) Indeed, the authors of *Prosser and Keeton* go on to make the following declaration:

The word "proximate" is a legacy of Lord Chancellor Bacon, who in his time committed other sins. The word means nothing more that near or immediate; and when it was first taken up by the courts it had connotations of proximity in time and space which have long since disappeared. It is an unfortunate word, which places an entirely wrong emphasis upon the factor of physical or mechanical closeness. For this reason, "legal cause" or perhaps even "responsible cause" would be more appropriate term[1]($41, p. 273).

One of the best ways to understand proximate cause/legal cause is found in some other observations of the authors of *Prosser and Keeton*:

> Once it is established that the defendant's conduct has in fact been one of the causes of the plaintiff's injury, there remains the question whether the defendant should be legally responsible for the injury. Unlike the fact of causation, with which it is often hopelessly confused, this is primarily a problem of law. It is sometimes said to depend on whether the conduct has been so significant and important a cause that the defendant should be legally responsible. But both significance and importance turn upon conclusion in terms of legal policy, so that they depend essentially on whether the policy of the law will extend the responsibility for the conduct to the consequences which have in fact occurred.... This is not a question of causation, or even a question of fact, but quite far removed from both; and the attempt to deal with it in such terms has led and can lead only to utter confusion.
>
> The term "proximate cause" is applied by the courts to those more or less undefined consideration which limit liability even where the fact of causation is clearly established.[1] ($pp. 272–273)

From this quotation, we learn that proximate cause/legal cause comes into play only after the actual cause has been established. In addition, proximate cause/legal cause is a public policy matter; it is a matter for the court to decide whether the defendant who was the actual cause of the plaintiff's injury should be held liable. In other words, are there any factors from a public policy perspective that relieve the defendant of liability even though the defendant was the actual cause of the plaintiff's injury? The Supreme Court of Wisconsin applies six public policy factors to determine whether a court should refuse to hold a defendant liable even though she was the actual cause of the plaintiff's injury.[171] Those factors are:

> (1) [t]he injury is too remote from the negligence; or (2) the injury is too wholly out of proportion to the culpability of the negligent tort-feasor; or (3) in retrospect it appears too highly extraordinary that the negligence should have brought about the harm; or (4) because allowance of recovery would place too unreasonable a burden on the negligent tort-feasor; or (5) because allowance of recovery would be too likely to open the way for fraudulent claims; or (6) allowance of recovery would enter a field that has no sensible or just stopping point.[172]

The Tennessee Court of Appeals has said that "[l]egal or proximate cause is 'a policy decision made by the legislature or the courts to deny liability for otherwise actionable conduct....'"[173] The Supreme Court of Illinois has put it in these words: "The question is one of public policy — how far should a defendant's legal responsibility extend for conduct that did, in fact, cause the harm?

Public policy thus becomes a vehicle by which the court can deny recovery even though the plaintiff has proven that the defendant's negligence was the actual cause of his injury. Perhaps the following words from *Prosser and Keeton* can explain the concept of proximate cause/legal cause:

> In a philosophical sense, the consequences of an act go forward to eternity, and the causes of an event go back to the dawn of human events, and beyond. But any attempt to impose responsibility upon such a basis would result in infinite liability for all wrongful acts, and would "set society on edge and fill the courts with endless litigation. As a practical matter, legal responsibility must be limited to those causes which are so closely connected with the result and of such significance that the law is justified in imposing liability. Some boundary must be set to liability for the consequences of an act, upon the basis of some social idea of justice or policy.... [T]he legal limitation on the scope of liability is associated with policy — with our more or less inadequately expressed ideas of what justice demand, or of what is administratively possible and convenient[1] (§41, p. 264, footnotes omitted).

- **Foreseeability, Hindsight, Intervening Cause, and Intervening Superseding Cause**
The use of public policy in determining whether a defendant will be liable for having injured the plaintiff is facilitated in many instances by application of the concept of foreseeability. In this regard, the authors of *Prosser and Keeton* question the hypothetical: "[W]hat if one ... unreasonably fail[s] to guard against harm which one should foresee, and consequences which one could in no way have anticipated in fact follow? Suppose for example, that a defect in a railway platform offers at most the foreseeable possibility of a sprained ankle; but as a result of it a passenger dies of inflammation of the heart[.]"[1] (§43, p. 280). For some courts, the answer is that for there to be liability, the general as opposed to the exact consequences would have to be foreseeable. The Georgia Court of Appeals explained the basic nature of foreseeability and answered the foregoing questions in the following statement:

> To recover damages based upon a defendant's negligence, a plaintiff must show that the defendant's acts or omissions proximately caused the injury.
>
> [I]t is well established that a wrongdoer is not responsible for a consequence which is merely possible, according to occasional experience, but only for a consequence which is probable, according to ordinary and usual experience. The natural and probable consequences are those which human foresight can foresee, because they happen so frequently that they may be expected to happen again. The possible consequences are those which happen so infrequently that they are not expected to happen again. Thus, negligence is predicated on what should have been anticipated rather than on what happened.[174]

The North Carolina Court of Appeals put it in these words:

> Proximate cause is a cause which in natural and continuous sequence, unbroken by any new and independent cause, produced the plaintiff's injuries, and

without which the injuries would not have occurred, and one from which a person of ordinary prudence *could have reasonably foreseen* that such a result, or consequences of a generally injurious nature, was probable under all the facts as they existed. *Foreseeability is thus a requisite of proximate cause*, which is, in turn, a requisite for actionable negligence.

Thus, "'the test of proximate cause is whether the risk of injury, not necessarily in the precise form in which it actually occurs, is within the reasonable foresight of the defendant.'"[175]

Some legal authorities do not rely solely on foreseeability; they infuse hindsight into the proximate cause determination. The view taken by the Indiana Court of Appeals is an example. In a 1996 opinion, that court stated the following:

Foreseeability in the context of proximate cause involves evaluating the particular circumstances of an incident after the incident occurs. According to the American Law Institute, foreseeability for proximate cause purposes is determined from a perspective that is "after the event and looking back from the harm to the actor's negligent conduct." As stated in Indiana, "[a] negligent act or omission is the proximate cause of an injury if the injury is a natural and probable consequence which, *in light of the circumstances*, should reasonably *have been* foreseen or anticipated." Thus, when determining proximate cause, foreseeability is determined based on hindsight, and accounts for the circumstances that actually occurred.[176]

In Indiana, "foreseeability involves evaluating the particular circumstances *after*" negligence has caused injury.[177] In a 1985 case, the Arizona Supreme Court, while explaining the concept of intervening and intervening superseding causes, criticized the use of foresight and expressed the view that hindsight played a significant role in determining proximate cause:

An intervening cause is one which intervenes between defendant's negligent act and the final result and is a necessary component in bringing about that result. Given the complexity of life, there is little that can be attributed to any single act, and the law does not relieve a defendant from liability simply because of the intervening act of a third person. It is only when the intervening act is considered superseding cause that the original actor is relieved of liability for his negligence. The test for a superseding cause is simpler to articulate than it is to apply and has been a frequent source of litigation and confusion. In the final analysis, the question of superseding cause has been determined by asking whether the intervention of the later cause is a significant part of the risk involved in defendant's conduct, or so reasonably connected with it that the responsibility [of defendant] should not be terminated. It is therefore said that the defendant is to be held liable if, but only if, the intervening cause is "foreseeable."

But here, ... this overworked and undefined word covers a multitude of sins. It is at least clear that in many cases recovery has been allowed where the intervening cause was not one which any reasonable actor could be expected to anticipate or have in mind, but it is regarded as 'normal' to the situation which the actor has created. In other words, although the theory of the cases is one of foreseeability, a considerable element of hindsight may have entered into its practical application. Thus, the text writers and commentators generally acknowledge that an intervening force becomes a superseding cause only when its operation was both unforeseeable and when with the benefit of "hindsight" it may be described as abnormal or extraordinary.[178]

With the above 1985 Arizona Supreme Court explanation of intervening and intervening superseding causes as a starting point, we can look further into these two concepts. According to *Prosser and Keeton*:

> "Intervening cause," like "direct causation" is a term easier of general comprehension than of any exact definition. An intervening cause is one which comes into active operation in producing the result *after* the negligence of the defendant. "Intervening" is used in a time sense; it refers to later events. If the defendant sets a fire with a strong wind blowing at the time, which carries the fire to the plaintiff's property, the wind does not intervene, since it was already in operation; but if the fire is set first, and the wind springs up later, it is then an intervening cause.[179]

The *Prosser and Keeton* authors caution that "'intervening cause' is a highly unsatisfactory term, since we are dealing with problems of responsibility, and not physics."[1] (§44 at 302, footnote omitted)

Keep in mind the role that foreseeability plays in this aspect of causation. The Pennsylvania Superior Court has held that "[t]o determine if an intervening force is a superseding cause, 'the test is whether the intervening conduct was so extraordinary as not to have been reasonably foreseeable.'"[180] Other courts take a similar position. For example, the Supreme Court of Alabama has said that

> "The proximate cause of an injury is that cause which, in the natural and probable sequence of events, and without the intervention or coming in of some new or independent cause, produces the injury, and without which the injury would not have occurred." "[I]f a new, independent act breaks the chain of causation, it supersedes the original act, which thus is no longer the proximate cause of the injury." "[A]n [act] is superseding only if it is unforeseeable. A foreseeable intervening [act] does not break the causal relationship between the defendants' actions and the plaintiffs' injuries."[181]

The South Dakota Supreme Court has discussed the subject in the following words:

> [T]o determine whether an actor's liability is shifted to a third person, one must look to see if the intervening cause was foreseeable. The risk created by the original actor may include the intervention of the foreseeable negligence of others. Id. If such intervening negligence was foreseeable, the original actor remains liable because "[f]oreseeable intervening forces are within the scope of the original risk ...."[182]

Some courts make use of Section 442 of the *Restatement*[5]($442) to determine foreseeability. In a case involving the question of whether it was foreseeable that drunken teenagers, to whom the defendant store owner sold alcohol, would rape and kill two teenage girls, the Texas Supreme Court held that the plaintiff did not establish that the criminal conduct was foreseeable.[183] In coming to this decision, the court reasoned as follows:

> We conclude that a defendant who seeks to negate foreseeability on summary judgment must prove more than that the intervening third-party criminal conduct occurred. The defendant has the burden to prove that the conduct was not foreseeable. When a defendant presents evidence that the plaintiff's injuries resulted from intervening criminal conduct that rises to the level of a superseding cause based on considerations like those in Section 442, the defendant has negated the ordinary foreseeability element of proximate cause. The burden then shifts to the plaintiff to raise a fact issue by presenting controverting evidence that the criminal conduct was foreseeable. Our holding is based upon the [Section 442] factors considered in determining superseding cause, which presume that the intervening event and its resulting harm are unforeseeable.[184]

Section 442 of the *Restatement* provides the following:

> The following considerations are of importance in determining whether an intervening force is a superseding cause of harm to another:
>   (a) the fact that its intervention brings about harm different in kind from that which would otherwise have resulted from the actor's negligence
>   (b) the fact that its operation or the consequences thereof appear after the event to be extraordinary rather than normal in view of the circumstances existing at the time of its operation
>   (c) the fact that the intervening force is operating independently of any situation created by the actor's negligence, or, on the other hand, is or is not a normal result of such a situation
>   (d) the fact that the operation of the intervening force is due to a third person's act or to his failure to act
>   (e) the fact that the intervening force is due to an act of a third person which is wrongful toward the other and as such subjects the third person to liability to him
>   (f) the degree of culpability of a wrongful act of a third person which sets the intervening force in motion.[5] (citation is redundant)

- **Damages**

Damages are the fourth element of a cause of action for negligence. The *Restatement* defines damages as "a sum of money awarded to a person injured by the tort of another"[5] ($902), and states that damages serve the following four purposes: "(a) to give compensation, indemnity, or restitution for harms; (b) to determine rights; (c) to punish wrongdoers and deter wrongful conduct; and (d) to vindicate parties and deter retaliation or violent and unlawful self-help."[5]($901)

There are various types of damages. The *Restatement* lists out three types of damages, and compensatory damages, nominal damages, and punitive damages,[185] defines them as follows:

- "Compensatory damages are the damages awarded to a person as compensation, indemnity or restitution for harm sustained by him."[5] (§903)
- "Nominal damages are a trivial sum of money awarded to a litigant who has established a cause of action but has not established that he is entitled to compensatory damages."[5] (§907)
- "Punitive damages are damages, other than compensatory or nominal damages, awarded against a person to punish him for his outrageous conduct and to deter him and others like him from similar conduct in the future."[5] [§908(1)]

With regard to compensatory damages, the *Restatement* points out that there are four subtypes: general damages, special damages, nonpecuniary damages, and pecuniary damages.[186]

- *General Damages* "are compensatory damages for a harm so frequently resulting from the tort that is the basis of the action that the existence of the damages is normally to be anticipated and hence need not be alleged in order to be proved."[5] [§904(1)]
- *Special Damages* "are compensatory damages for a harm other than one for which general damages are given."[5] [§904(2)]
- *NonPecuniary Damages* are those "[c]ompensatory damages that may be awarded without proof of pecuniary loss [and] include compensation (a) for bodily harm, and (b) for emotional distress."[5] (§905)
- *Pecuniary Damages* are those "[c]ompensatory damages that will not be awarded without proof of pecuniary loss [and] include compensation for
  - Harm to property,
  - Harm to earning capacity, and
  - Creation of liabilities."[5] (§906)

As we shall see, some of these types of damages go by other names or are further broken down beyond subtypes. In a concurring opinion to a 2002 Hawaii Supreme Court case, one of the justices provided a lengthy explanation of the types of damages available to a plaintiff in a tort action. In part, his explanation consisted of the following:

> With respect to awards to a plaintiff for a tort action, it is axiomatic that three basic categories exist: (1) compensatory damages (general and specific); (2) punitive damages (also called "exemplary damages"); and (3) nominal damages. "Compensatory damages" are a broad range of damages that seek to restore a plaintiff to his or her position prior to the tortious act. Compensatory damages include "damages for pain and suffering, emotional distress, permanent injury, loss of enjoyment of life, medical expenses, lost wages, impairment of earning capacity, [and] damage to personal property."
>
> By contrast, "nominal damages" are "a small and trivial sum awarded for a technical injury due to a violation of some legal right and as a consequence of which some damages must be awarded to determine the right." . . .

[T]he aim of punitive damages is to punish the defendant, rather than to compensate the plaintiff. An award of punitive damages rests upon the egregious nature of a defendant's conduct, rather than the extent of proof of injury a plaintiff can show at trial.[187]

A 2004 Louisiana Court of Appeals case provides a helpful explanation of the nature of and the difference between general damages and special damages:

General damages involve mental or physical pain and suffering, inconvenience, loss of intellectual gratification or physical enjoyment, or other losses of life or lifestyle which cannot be definitively measured in monetary terms. There is no mechanical rule for determining general damages; the facts and circumstances of each case control....

Special damages are those which either must be specially pled or have a ready market value, that is, the amount of damages supposedly can be determined with relative certainty, such as the plaintiff's medical expenses incurred as a result of the tort. The discretion afforded the trier of fact to assess special damages is narrower or more limited than the discretion to assess general damages. Some special damages, such as medical and related expenses, are easily measured.[188]

Finally, when punitive damages are awarded, they serve as "a supplement to a compensatory damage award in egregious cases"and satisfy "a dual purpose — 'to punish wrongdoers and deter others from similar conduct.'"[189]

Defenses to a Cause of Action for Negligence

If a plaintiff is able to establish the elements to a cause of action for negligence, a defendant could nonetheless prevail if she were able to establish that she had a defense. The establishment of a defense would defeat the cause of action. There are two defenses that a defendant could assert against a negligence cause of action: contributory negligence and assumption of the risk.

The *Restatement* defines contributory negligence as "conduct on the part of the plaintiff which falls below the standard to which he should conform for his own protection, and which is a legally contributing cause co-operating with the negligence of the defendant in bringing about the plaintiff's harm."[5] (§463)

The Illinois Appellate Court defined and explained contributory negligence in the following words: "[c]ontributory negligence is ... a lack of due care for one's own safety as measured by an objective reasonable person standard. The test of such negligence is not the frequency with which the act has been safely completed by others, but whether plaintiff, at the time of the occurrence, used that degree of care which an ordinarily careful person would have used for his or her own safety under like circumstances."[190]

According to the North Carolina Court of Appeals "[c]ontributory negligence is 'negligence on the part of the plaintiff which joins, simultaneously or successively, with the negligence of the defendant ... to produce the injury of which the plaintiff complains.'"[191] The court also pointed out what a defendant must prove to establish that the plaintiff was contributorily negligent:

> "[T]wo elements, at least, are necessary to constitute contributory negligence[.]" The defendant must demonstrate: (1) a want of due care on the part of the plaintiff; and (2) a proximate connection between the plaintiff's negligence and the injury. "There must be not only negligence on the part of the plaintiff, but contributory negligence, a real causal connection between the plaintiff's negligent act and the injury, or it is no defense to the action."[191] (emphasis in original omitted)

Beginning in the nineteenth century[192] and well into the twentieth century,[193] a plaintiff who was contributorily negligent was completely barred from recovering against a negligent defendant who had caused injury to the plaintiff. As the Maryland Court of Special Appeals put it: "The traditional rule held that contributory negligence of a plaintiff, or the person from whom the plaintiff derived her claim, was a complete bar to the claim.[194] "Under the purest form of contributory negligence, an injured plaintiff could not recover any damages from a negligent defendant, if the defendant could prove that the plaintiff himself was also guilty of negligence, *however slight*."[195]

At some point in the twentieth century, the law began to acknowledge the harshness of the effect of the contributory doctrine. According to *Prosser and Keeton*, "there [had] been for many years an increasing dissatisfaction with the absolute defense of contributory negligence."[1] (§67) Enter comparative negligence — a concept that "ameliorate[s] the harshness of the complete bar resulting from common law contributory negligence.[196] Comparative negligence achieves this amelioration by "by mandating a comparison by the fact finder of the relative degrees of negligence of the plaintiff and the defendant."[197]

In a 1983 opinion, the Maryland Court of Appeals explained "the three general types" of comparative negligence:

> 1. "Slight/Gross": The plaintiff may recover that portion of his damages caused by the defendant's gross fault, unless the plaintiff's fault is not slight in contrast to the defendant's, in which case the plaintiff recovers nothing....
> 2. "Not As Great As": This form permits a plaintiff to recover only if his fault is less than that of the defendant....
> 3. "Not Greater Than": Under this form, if the plaintiff's fault is less than or equal to the defendant's fault, the plaintiff may recover damages reduced by the percentage of his own fault....[198]

We next need to consider the concept of comparative fault, which is to be distinguished from the concept of comparative negligence. As you should be able to surmise from the discussion in the introduction about the meaning of fault and the definition of negligence, fault is a broader term than negligence. Fault includes more wrongful acts than does negligence. Comparative fault therefore allows for consideration of wrongful acts by the plaintiff other than negligence.[199]

In a 1985 case, the Louisiana Supreme Court held that although comparative negligence could not be applied in a strict product liability case, comparative fault could:

> Contributory negligence as a complete bar to recovery does not apply in products liability cases because it is incompatible with that doctrine. The contributory negligence defense would permit the manufacturer to breach his duty to manufacture a reasonably safe product and escape liability simply because the fault of the user of the defective product contributed to the accident. Thus, in many instances the manufacturer would have no incentive to make and market a safer product, and the user who is usually less able to distribute the loss would be forced to absorb even the portion of the damages attributable to the unreasonably dangerous condition of the manufacturer's product. . . . The vast majority of the other state courts which have adopted the strict products liability doctrine do not permit the defense of ordinary contributory negligence to bar recovery.
>
> On the other hand, pure comparative fault principles would seem to coincide with and further the goals of products liability doctrine in some cases. Where the threat of a reduction in recovery will provide consumers with an incentive to use a product carefully, without exacting an inordinate sacrifice of other interests, comparative principles should be applied for the sake of accident prevention.[200]

The U.S. Court of Appeals for the Tenth Circuit explained the difference in the following words:

> [A]lthough the terms "comparative fault" and "comparative" negligence" are often used interchangeably by commentators and courts, the choice of the term "fault" and the express statement that Colorado's comparative negligence statute does not apply to product liability, suggests that the Colorado legislature intended some difference between "fault" and "negligence" in this context. From the statutory language alone then, we can discern an intention to draw some distinction between "fault" and "negligence"; however, the language itself does not define the precise nature of the distinction. Nevertheless, we are impressed with the breadth of the statute's word "fault" as it is employed in common usage, and with the breadth of the statute's strong language on the diminution of damages in "any product liability action."[201]

The courts of Tennessee appear to take a different view as to the nature and purpose of the difference between comparative fault and comparative negligence. As explained by the Tennessee Court of Appeals:

> The Tennessee Supreme Court has distinguished between "comparative negligence" and "comparative fault." Comparative negligence measures the plaintiff's negligence for the purpose of reducing the plaintiff's recovery. Comparative fault encompasses the allocation of recovery among multiple or joint tortfeasors according to their percentage of fault. The Court made this distinction on the theory that a plaintiff's recovery may only be reduced because

of the plaintiff's negligence, whereas a defendant's liability may be based on theories of liability other than negligence, for example, strict liability.[202]

Finally as to the difference between comparative fault and comparative negligence,
consideration should be given to the view that comparative fault can, in some circumstances, be inclusive of all tortious conduct on the part of those involved in circumstances
that results in injury.[203] For example, the Indiana Code defines fault as follows:

> (a) "Fault," ... means an act or omission that is negligent, willful, wanton, reck-
> less, or intentional toward the person or property of others. The term includes
> the following:
> (1) Unreasonable failure to avoid an injury or to mitigate damages.
> (2) A finding ... that a person is subject to liability for physical harm caused
> by a product, notwithstanding the lack of negligence or willful, wanton, or
> reckless conduct by the manufacturer or seller.
> (b) "Fault," for purposes of [compensatory damages] includes any act or omis-
> sion that is negligent, willful, wanton, reckless, or intentional toward the person
> or property of others. The term also includes unreasonable assumption of risk
> not constituting an enforceable express consent, incurred risk, and unreason-
> able failure to avoid an injury or to mitigate damages.[204]

Section 496 A of the *Restatement* states that "[a] plaintiff who voluntarily assumes a risk
of harm arising from the negligent or reckless conduct of the defendant cannot recover for
such harm." One of the definitions of "assume" is "to take over ... as one's own."[6](p. 110),
and for "assumption," the definition is "a taking to or upon oneself."[6] (p. 110)

In coming to an understanding of what assumption of the risk means, we should keep
in mind the definition of negligence, which is conduct that falls below the standard established by law for the protection of others against unreasonable *risks* of harm.[205] Remember
what was said earlier in this discussion on negligence about risks: A risk is a "[p]ossibility
[or probability] of loss or injury ... the chance of loss ...."[6](p. 1018) When one assumes a
risk, he/she takes over as his/her own the possibility or probability of injury. In other
words, when a person assumes a risk he/she accepts responsibility for any injury that
might befall him/her. When a person assumes the risk, he/she relieved the defendant of
any duty to him/her.[5] (§496A, cmt. c) In explaining the various meanings of assumption
of the risk, the *Restatement* explains that:

> [i]n its simplest form, assumption of risk means that the plaintiff has given his
> express consent to relieve the defendant of an obligation to exercise care for his
> protection, and agrees to take his chances as to injury from a known or possible
> risk. The result is that the defendant, who would otherwise be under a duty to
> exercise such care, is relieved of that responsibility, and is no longer under any
> duty to protect the plaintiff.[206]

Note in the foregoing quote the words "the plaintiff has given his *express* consent."[5]
(§496A, emphasis added) When a "plaintiff has given his express consent to relieve
the defendant of an obligation to exercise care"[5](§496A), we are dealing with express
assumption of the risk.[5] (§496B) As Section 496A of the *Restatement* states "[a] plaintiff

who voluntarily assumes a risk of harm arising from the negligent or reckless conduct of the defendant *cannot recover for such harm*."[5] (§496A, emphasis added)

In addition to "its simplest form," there are three additional forms of assumption of the risk. In the second form of assumption of the risk, referred to by the *Restatement* as a form of implied assumption of the risk, "the plaintiff has entered voluntarily into some relation with the defendant which he [the plaintiff] knows to involve the risk, and so is regarded as tacitly or impliedly agreeing to relieve the defendant of responsibility, and to take his own chances."[206] The effect of this second form of assumption of the risk is that like the simplest form of assumption of the risk "the defendant is relieved of his duty to the plaintiff."[206] With the third form of assumption of the risk, also referred to by the *Restatement* as a form of implied assumption of the risk, "the plaintiff, aware of a risk created by the negligence of the defendant, proceeds or continues voluntarily to encounter it.[206] With this form of assumption of the risk, the defendant also has no duty to the plaintiff.[206] Whichever form the implied assumed risk is, the cannot recover.[5] (§496C)

Some courts divide implied assumption of the risk into categories referred to as implied primary assumption of the risk and implied secondary assumption of the risk.

> Implied assumption of the risk has itself been subdivided into two forms: primary and secondary. Under implied primary assumption of the risk, the risk of harm plaintiff assumes is not created by defendant, but is inherent in the activity plaintiff has agreed to undertake. Primary implied assumption of the risk is not a true negligence defense since no cause of action for negligence is ever established. Obviously, if the doctrine of implied primary assumption of the risk is applicable to the facts of the case, the plaintiff would not be entitled to recover.
>
> Under the doctrine of secondary implied assumption of the risk, the risk of harm assumed by the plaintiff is created by the defendant's negligence. Implied secondary assumption of the risk is a fault-based concept which is functionally equivalent to contributory negligence, and like contributory negligence it should not operate as a complete bar in negligence cases.[207]

The fourth form of assumption of the risk spoken of in Section 496A of the *Restatement*.[5](§496A, cmt. c) can be confusing because it has the characteristics of contributory negligence. The *Restatement* explains the fourth form of assumption of the risk in the following words:

> To be distinguished from the [first, second, and third forms of assumption of the risk] is the fourth, in which the plaintiff's conduct in voluntarily encountering a known risk is itself unreasonable, and amounts to contributory negligence. There is thus negligence on the part of both plaintiff and defendant; and the plaintiff is barred from recovery, not only by his implied consent to accept the risk, but also by the policy of the law which refuses to allow him to impose upon the defendant a loss for which his own negligence was in part responsible.[206]

To the extent that the plaintiff's conduct constitutes the fourth form of assumption of the risk, application of comparative negligence principles precludes the plaintiff being barred from recovery.[208]

As you can see, we are faced with confusing categories when it comes to assumption of the risk. A 1977 decision of the Florida Supreme Court acknowledged the problem when it stated:

> At the outset, we note that assumption of risk is not a favored defense. There is a puissant drift toward abrogating the defense. The argument is that assumption of risk serves no purpose which is not subsumed by either the doctrine of contributory negligence or the common law concept of duty. It is said that this redundancy results in confusion and, in some cases, denies recovery unjustly. . . . At the commencement of any analysis of the doctrine of assumption of risk, we must recognize that we deal with a potpourri of labels, concepts, definitions, thoughts, and doctrines. The confusion of labels does not end with the indiscriminate and interchangeable use of the terms "contributory negligence" and "assumption of risk."[209]

Additional Matters

Res Ipsa Loquitur

Many books written about torts have a section on the concept of *res ipsa loquitur*, a Latin phrase that means "the thing speaks for itself."[14] (p. 1470) The Supreme Court of Nevada explained *res ipsa loquitur* in the following words:

> The general negligence rule is that a mere happening of an accident or injury will not give rise to the presumption of negligence. Res ipsa loquitur is an exception to the general negligence rule, and it permits a party to infer negligence, as opposed to affirmatively proving it, when certain elements are met . . . . The mere fact that there was an accident or other event and someone was injured is not of itself sufficient to predicate liability. Negligence is never presumed but must be established by substantial evidence.[210]

Many courts require that three conditions exist before a plaintiff will be allowed to apply this concept.[211] "In order to rely successfully upon the doctrine of *res ipsa loquitur*, a plaintiff must prove: (1) a casualty of a kind that does not ordinarily occur absent negligence, (2) that was caused by an instrumentality exclusively in the defendant's control, and (3) that was not caused by an act or omission of the plaintiff."[212]

Negligence Per Se

In understanding negligence *per se*, we should begin with the definition of *per se*, which means "by, of, or in itself."[6] (p. 877) As you will recall, there are four elements to a cause of action for negligence: duty, breach of duty, causation, and damages. Also recall that negligence itself consists of the first two elements of the cause of action for negligence. There are circumstances in which legislatures enact statutes that in effect establish that certain conduct in and of itself constitutes negligence; in other words, the legislation establishes a duty and declares what constitutes a breach of that duty. In explaining the Nevada law on negligence *per se*, the Federal District Court for the District of Nevada said the following:

> Nevada negligence jurisprudence has long-since recognized that "[t]he standard of conduct required of a reasonable man may be prescribed by legislative

enactment. When a statute provides that under certain circumstances particular acts shall or shall not be done, it may be interpreted as fixing a standard for all members of the community, from which it is negligence to deviate.). Commonly referred to as the doctrine of negligence per se, a duty and breach of duty may sometimes be established through evidence that a defendant failed to comply with a particular statute.[213]

The effect of negligence *per se* for a plaintiff is that she is relieved of having to establish that the defendant owed her a duty; she is also relieved of having to prove that the defendant's conduct breached the duty. As the Kentucky Court of Appeals put it: "With negligence *per se*, the standard of care is legislatively declared by statute and a jury only determines whether the specified act prohibited or required by statute was committed."[214] The plaintiff, however, must still prove the causation and damage elements. In this regard, the Kentucky Court of Appeals has also pointed out that: "As with common-law negligence, causation and injury must still be proved in negligence *per se* claims."[214]

Not every instance of a statutory violation constitutes negligence *per se*; certain circumstances must exist before a plaintiff can invoke this concept. The Connecticut Superior Court has stated that there are two required circumstances: "(1) the plaintiff must be a member of the class protected by the statute; and (2) the injury must be of the type the statute was intended to prevent."[215] The Federal District Court for the Eastern District of Pennsylvania has provided a convenient summary of the concept:

> "Negligence per se has been defined as conduct, whether of action or omission, which may be declared and treated as negligence without any argument or proof as to the particular surrounding circumstances." To prove a claim of negligence per se, a plaintiff must prove four elements:
> (1) The purpose of the statute must be, at least in part, to protect the interest of a group of individuals, as opposed to the public generally;
> (2) The statute or regulation must clearly apply to the conduct of the defendant;
> (3) The defendant must violate the statute or regulation;
> (4) The violation of the statute or regulation must be the proximate cause of the plaintiff's injuries.[216]

Negligent Infliction of Emotional Distress

As a final additional matter relative to negligence, we need to consider the concept of negligent infliction of emotional distress. Courts have described negligent infliction of emotional distress (NIED) in various ways. Applying Montana law, the U.S. District Court for the District of Montana defined NIED as "a tort claim where serious or severe emotional distress to the plaintiff was a reasonably foreseeable consequence of the defendant's negligent act or omission."[217] The Ohio Court of Appeals defined NIED as "a claim based upon the negligence of one party creating actionable emotional distress in another."[218] In a 1994 case, the U.S. Supreme Court described NIED in the following words:

> The term "negligent infliction of emotional distress" is largely self-explanatory, but a definitional point should be clarified at the outset. The injury we

contemplate when considering negligent infliction of emotional distress is mental or emotional injury, apart from the tort law concepts of pain and suffering. Although pain and suffering technically are mental harms, these terms traditionally "have been used to describe sensations stemming directly from a physical injury or condition." The injury we deal with here is mental or emotional harm (such as fright or anxiety) that is caused by the negligence of another and that is not directly brought about by a physical injury, but that may manifest itself in physical symptoms.[219]

In that same U.S. Supreme Court case, the Court discussed what it termed as the "[t]hree major limiting tests for evaluating claims alleging negligent infliction of emotional distress":

Three major limiting tests for evaluating claims alleging negligent infliction of emotional distress have developed in the common law. The first of these has come to be known as the "physical impact" test. It originated a century ago in some of the first cases recognizing recovery for negligently inflicted emotional distress . . . . Under the physical impact test, a plaintiff seeking damages for emotional injury stemming from a negligent act must have contemporaneously sustained a physical impact (no matter how slight) or injury due to the defendant's conduct. Most jurisdictions have abandoned this test, but at least five States continue to adhere to it.

The second test has come to be referred to as the "zone of danger" test. It came into use at roughly the same time as the physical impact test . . . . Perhaps based on the realization that "a near miss may be as frightening as a direct hit," the zone of danger test limits recovery for emotional injury to those plaintiffs who sustain a physical impact as a result of a defendant's negligent conduct, or who are placed in immediate risk of physical harm by that conduct. That is, "those within the zone of danger of physical impact can recover for fright, and those outside of it cannot." The zone of danger test currently is followed in 14 jurisdictions.

The third prominent limiting test is the "relative bystander" test, which was first enunciated in Dillon v. Legg. In Dillon, the California Supreme Court rejected the zone of danger test and suggested that the availability of recovery should turn, for the most part, on whether the defendant could reasonably have foreseen the emotional injury to the plaintiff. The court offered three factors to be considered as bearing on the question of reasonable foreseeability:

"(1) Whether plaintiff was located near the scene of the accident as contrasted with one who was a distance away from it. (2) Whether the shock resulted from a direct emotional impact upon plaintiff from the sensory and contemporaneous observance of the accident, as contrasted with learning of the accident from others after its occurrence. (3) Whether plaintiff and the victim were closely related, as contrasted with an absence of any relationship or the presence of only a distant relationship."

The courts of nearly half the States now allow bystanders outside of the zone of danger to obtain recovery in certain circumstances for emotional distress brought on by witnessing the injury or death of a third party (who typically must be a close relative of the bystander) that is caused by the defendant's negligence. Most of these jurisdictions have adopted the Dillon factors either verbatim or with variations and additions, and have held some or all of these factors to be substantive limitations on recovery.[220]

The Pennsylvania Superior Court has held that Pennsylvania recognizes all three of the NIED categories:

> Initially, the law of this Commonwealth only allowed recovery for injuries resulting from mental distress where they were accompanied by physical injury or physical impact. The impact rule was expanded by our Supreme Court in Niederman v. Brodsky wherein the court stated:
>
>> We today choose to abandon the requirement of a physical impact as a precondition to recovery for damages proximately caused by the tort in only those cases like the one before us where the plaintiff was in personal danger of physical impact because of the direction of a negligent force against him and where plaintiff actually did fear the physical impact.
>
> The Niederman ruling permitted recovery for infliction of emotional distress in the absence of physical injury or impact when the individual inflicted with emotional distress was in the "zone of danger" of injury or impact.
>
> A further expansion of this rule was adopted in Sinn v. Burd. In Sinn, our Supreme Court held that a mother who witnessed an automobile strike her child, causing fatal injury, could state a claim for emotional distress against the driver of the automobile, despite the fact that the mother had witnessed the accident from beyond the zone of danger. In creating this exception to the zone of danger rule, the Court reasoned that while the emotional distress suffered by an individual in the zone of danger typically results from a fear for his or her own safety, in the case of a parent witnessing his or her child's injury, "the emotional impact [is] most probably influenced by the event witnessed — serious injury to or death of the child — rather than the [parent's] awareness of personal exposure to danger." Accordingly, "the emotional impact upon a mother witnessing the sudden and violent death of her small child [from beyond the zone of danger] is unquestionably as traumatic as would have been the case if the mother had also been within the zone of danger." This exception has come to be known as the bystander rule.[221]

Strict Liability and Absolute Liability

The law is sometimes unclear when it comes to differentiating between the terms "strict liability" and "absolute liability," which are often spoken of as though they are the same thing. These terms are not the same and should not be used synonymously. An example of the lack of clarity can be seen in the following words of a 2003 federal district court case: "While the common law doctrine of absolute liability is less than fully settled in Pennsylvania ... the Superior Court of Pennsylvania, in several cases, has adopted section 519 ... of the *Restatement* (Second) of Torts for determining whether an activity is abnormally dangerous."[222] The confusion is demonstrated by the fact that Section 519 speaks in terms of strict liability as opposed to absolute liability.[223]

Strict Liability

Prosser and Keeton defines strict liability as "liability that is imposed on an actor apart from either (1) an intent to interfere with a legally protected interest without a legal justification for doing so, or (2) a breach of a duty to exercise reasonable care[1] (§75). The Wisconsin Supreme Court has defined strict liability as "a judicial doctrine which relieves a plaintiff from proving specific acts of negligence and protects him from certain defenses."[224] The Indiana Supreme Court has stated that "[s]trict liability ... assumes no negligence of the actor, but chooses to impose liability anyway."[225] The Louisiana Court of Appeal explains that "[s]trict liability is liability without personal fault."[226] The New Hampshire Supreme Court has said that "liability is said to be strict when it is imposed even though the defendant has committed no legal fault."[227] The conclusion that can be drawn from these definitions and explanations of strict liability is that strict liability relieves the plaintiff from having to prove that the defendant was at fault. In other words, the plaintiff is not required to prove that the defendant acted intentionally, negligently, or recklessly. Even if the plaintiff is allowed to use strict liability as the basis for the defendant's liability, the he/she nonetheless has to prove causation and damages.[228] We can also conclude that the defendant will be unable to assert certain defenses that can be asserted against causes of action based upon intent, recklessness, or negligence.[229]

Absolute Liability

As with strict liability, absolute liability relieves the plaintiff of having to prove that the defendant was at fault. Beyond that, the two concepts are different. In general, absolute liability is a more stringent form of liability without fault. In a 1972 case, the Michigan Court of Appeals explained the difference between the two concepts: "Strict liability is a term that has been used in product liability cases and absolute liability has been applied in cases involving persons who harbor dangerous animals or engage in abnormally dangerous activities."[230] Sections 504 and 507 of the *Restatement*, for example, provide for liability for injuries caused by certain animals and speak in terms of does not absolute liability, but rather of strict liability.[231] Section 519 of the *Restatement*, for example, provides for liability for injuries resulting from abnormally dangerous activities and does not speaks in terms of absolute liability, but rather in terms of strict liability.[5] (§519)

One area where the courts have distinguished between strict liability and absolute liability is product liability. Courts have specifically stated that in the area of product liability, there is a difference between strict liability and absolute liability. These courts have been reluctant to impose absolute liability in product liability cases, because to do so would be to make the manufacturer or seller of a product an insurer instead of a guarantor.[232] As an example, in a 1988 case, the New Hampshire Supreme Court said the following: "We limit the application of strict tort liability in this jurisdiction by continuing to emphasize that liability without negligence is not liability without fault. We do not impose what amounts to absolute liability on a manufacturer.[233]

As the Pennsylvania Superior Court has stated: "It is not the purpose of strict liability under §402A [of the *Restatement*] to impose absolute liability on the product's manufacturer or supplier since those entities are guarantors, not insurers, of the product's safety . . . ."[234]

Nuisance

According to *Prosser and Keeton*, "[t]here is perhaps no more impenetrable jungle in the entire law than that which surrounds the word 'nuisance.' It has meant all things to all people and has been applied indiscriminately . . . ."[1](§86, footnotes omitted) Despite this view, there are some basics to the tort concept of nuisance that provide a foundation for understanding what the word means.

To understand nuisance, we can begin with the observation that there are two categories of nuisance: a private nuisance and a public nuisance.[1](§86, 87, and 90) The Illinois Appellate Court has defined private nuisance in the following words:

> A private nuisance is a substantial invasion of another's interest in the use and enjoyment of his or her land. The invasion must be: substantial, either intentional or negligent, and unreasonable. The standard for determining if particular conduct constitutes a nuisance is the conduct's effect on a reasonable person. A nuisance is an interference with the interest in the private use and enjoyment of the land and does not require interference with possession.[235]

"[T]o recover damages for [a private] nuisance the plaintiff must prove the defendant's invasion of the plaintiff's interest in the use and enjoyment of the land was substantial, i.e., that it caused the plaintiff to suffer substantial actual damage. The interference must also be unreasonable. The test for determining whether the plaintiff has suffered an unreasonable interference with the use and enjoyment of his property is whether the gravity of the harm outweighs the social utility of the defendant's conduct[.]"[236]

Knowing the interest that is protected by the tort concept of nuisance is important in that nuisance can, to the unwary, be confused with trespass to land. The two are different, and the interest that is protected reveals that difference. Recall that the interest protected by trespass to land is the interest to be free from intentional interference with the right to possess real property. The interest that is protected by nuisance is the interest to be free from the interference "with the use and enjoyment of land."[1](§87 footnote omitted)

As for a public nuisance, the Wisconsin Supreme Court has provided a good definition while also explaining the interest that public nuisance protects, and how a public nuisance differs from a private nuisance:

> "[A] public nuisance is a condition or activity which substantially or unduly interferes with the use of a public place or with the activities of an entire community." In other words, "[a] public nuisance is an unreasonable interference with a right common to the general public." Therefore, the interest involved in a public nuisance is broader than that in a private nuisance because

"a public nuisance does not necessarily involve interference with use and enjoyment of land."[237]

Both private and public nuisances can be based upon the theories of intent, recklessness, negligence, strict liability, or absolute liability. With regard to private nuisances,
Section 822 of the *Restatement* provides the following:

> One is subject to liability for a private nuisance if, but only if, his conduct is a
> legal cause of an invasion of another's interest in the private use and enjoyment
> of land, and the invasion is either
> (a) intentional and unreasonable, or
> (b) unintentional and otherwise actionable under the rules controlling liability
> for negligent or reckless conduct, or for abnormally dangerous conditions or
> activities.[5] (§822)

A similar approach is taken as to public nuisances as evidenced by the comments to Section
821B of the *Restatement*:

> [B]y analogy to the rules stated in Section 822, [a] defendant is held liable for a
> public nuisance if his interference with the public right of way was intentional
> or was unintentional and otherwise actionable under the principles controlling
> liability for negligent or reckless conduct or for abnormally dangerous
> activities.[5] (§821B, cmt. e)

A defendant in a nuisance action that arises out of negligence may raise contributory
negligence.[5] (§840B) Assumption of the risk may also be raised as a defense.[5] (§840C)
Finally, if a plaintiff has "come to the nuisance," depending upon the circumstances, she
may be precluded from recovering against the owner of a pre-existing nuisance.[5] (§840D)

Notes

1. Page Keeton, W. et al., *Prosser and Keeton on Torts* (St. Paul, MN: West Publishing Co., 5th ed.
   1984) (hereinafter at times referred to as Prosser and Keeton).

2. See for example, Dan B. Dobbs, The Law of Torts §1, p. 1 (St. Paul, MN: West Publishing Co.,
   2000) and *Borchert v. Borchert*, 824 A.2d 293, 294 (N.J. Super. Ct. Ch. Div. 2002).

3. Miles, *Digest of English Civil Law*, Boston, MA: Boston Book Co., 1910, Book II, pp. xiv, xv;
   cited by Prosser and Keeton, §1, p. 1.

4. *U.S. v. Burke*, 504 U.S. 229, 234 (1992). In that the U.S. Supreme Court uses the same definition as does Prosser and Keeton; the other courts in the federal judiciary would be expected
   to use the same definition.

5. *Restatement* (Second) of Torts §1 (1965) (hereinafter referred to as the "*Restatement*"). The
   various restatements are published by the American Law Institute. The homepage of the
   American Law Institute (http://www.ali.org/) gives this account of the Institute's purpose:

   > The American Law Institute was established in 1923 "to promote the clarification and
   > simplification of the law and its better adaptation to social needs, to secure the better
   > administration of justice, and to encourage and carry on scholarly and scientific work."
   > The institute drafts for consideration by its Council and its membership and then publishes
   > Restatements of the Law, Model Codes, and other proposals of law reform

Professor David A. Thomas has said that "the Restatements were intended to 'restate' or clarify common law rules. Indeed, the Restatements were originally proposed because some feared the common law was becoming incomprehensible under the mass of case decisions that were not easily subject to research and analysis." David A. Thomas, *Restatements relating to property: why lawyers don't really care*, 38 Real Prop. Prob. & Tr. J. 655, 659 (2004).

6. *Webster's Ninth new Collegiate Dictionary* 452 (SpringField, MA: Merriam-Webster, Inc. 1988).

7. *Kitzig v. Nordquist*, 97 Cal. Rptr.2d 762, 775 (Cal. App. Ct.).

8. *Morris v. United Services Auto. Ass'n*, 756 So.2d 549, 559 (La. 2000) (citation omitted).

9. *Davis v. Marshall Homes, Inc.*, 576 S.E.2d 504, 510 (Va. 2003).

10. *Bourgeois v. A.P. Green Industries*, 841 So.2d 902, 02–713 (La. App. 5 Cir. 2/25/03) (citation omitted).

11. *Franc v. Bethel Holding Co.*, 807 A.2d 519, 534–535 (Conn. App. Ct. 2002).

12. *Regier ex rel. Regier v. Good Samaritan Hosp., Kearney*, 651 N.W.2d 210, 213 (Neb. 2002) (citation omitted).

13. *D.M. v. J.D.M. ex rel. C.F.*, 814 So.2d 1112 (Fla. Dist. Ct. App. 2002).

14. *Black's Law Dictionary* 613 (St. Paul, MN: West Publishing Co. rev 4th ed. 1968).

15. *Prosser and Keeton*, §8 p. 34 (footnotes omitted) (some emphasis deleted).

16. See *Helm v. K.O.G. Alarm Co.*, 5 Cal. Rptr.2d 615, 619 (Cal. Ct. App. 1992) [Stating that "the clearer and better course would be to refer to what we know as 'cause-in-fact' as either 'actual cause' or 'factual cause' while referring to what we know as 'proximate cause' — that is, cause-in-fact as qualified and tempered by . . . the 'social evaluative process,' that needed process by which the law seeks "to limit liability when cause and effect relationships logically continue to infinity" — as "legal cause."(citations omitted)].

17. *Kimberlein v. DeLong*, 637 N.E. 2d 121 (Ind. 1994).

18. BocKrath v. Aldrich Chemical Company, Inc., 74 Cal Rptr 2d 774, 780 (1998), citing Setliff v. E.Z. Du Pont de Nemours & Co., 38 Cal. Rptr. 2d 763 (1995).

19. Lombardo v. Huysentruyt, 110 Cal Rptr 2d, 699 (2002).

20. Lombardo v. Huysentruyt, 110 Cal Rptr 2d, 699 (2002).

21. *Tinkler v. Richter*, 295 N.W. 201, 203 (Mich. 1940).

22. *Smith v. John Deere Co.*, 614 N.E.2d 1148, 1154 (Ohio 1993) (citation omitted).

23. *Tancredi v. Cooper*, 2003 WL 22213699, at *4–5 (E.D.Pa.).

24. *Koffman v. Garnett*, 574 S.E.2d 258, 261 (Va. 2003) (citations omitted).

25. *State v. McMahon*, 81 P.3d 508, 510 (Mont. 2003).

26. If, on the other hand, the tortfeasor starts out with the intent only to cause apprehension of an imminent harmful and offensive contact (i.e., the intent only to cause an assault), but in fact causes a harmful or offensive contact, she could be found liable for battery. From either perspective, this is one example of the tort concept of "transferred intent." Unlike the intent element to a cause of action for tort and the intent element to a cause of action for battery are the same. For all of the other intentional tort causes of action, the intent element is different from all other intentional tort causes of action and are specific to the intentional tort involved. For all of the intentional tort causes of action, the intent element requires more than the fundamental tort definition of intent: the intent has to be particularized to the tort involved.

27. The term "black letter" is used because the portion of the section where the rule is stated is usually in bold black lettering.

28. Imminent is defined as "ready to take place." Webster's Ninth New Collegiate Dictionary 602 (1988).

29. *Kharmats v. Kasavin*, 2005 WL 460215, at *4 (Cal. Ct. App. 2005) (citations omitted).

30. *Bohrer v. DeHart*, 1996 WL 282293, at *2 (Colo. Ct. App. 1996).

31. *Holloway v. Wachovia Bank & Trust Co.*, N.A., 428 S.E.2d 453, 460 (N.C. Ct. App. 1993) (citation omitted).

32. *Doe v. Hartz*, 52 F. Supp.2d 1027, 1052 (N.D. Iowa 1999).

33. *Holloway v. Wachovia Bank & Trust Co.*, 428 S.E.2d 453, 459–460 (N. C. Ct. App. 1993).

34. See for example, *Bumgart v. Bailey*, 156 So.2d 823, 824 (Miss. 1963) (holding that "[t]he general rule is … as follows: 'Nominal damages may be awarded in an action for assault and battery where no actual damage has been inflicted, where the damage inflicted is very slight, or where there are strong mitigating circumstances, and even if the result of the assault and battery committed by the defendant was beneficial to the plaintiff.'") (citation omitted).

35. *Restatement* §10 cmt. c and §13 cmt. d.

36. *Bank v. Fritsch*, 39 S.W. 3d 474, 480 (Ky. Ct. App. 2001) (stating that "a showing of actual damages is not an element of assault or battery"). *See also Restatement* §§21 and 907 cmt. b and Prosser and Keeton §7 n. 18.

37. *Est. of Thurman v. City of Milwaukee*, 197 F.Supp.2d 1141, 1151 (E. D. Wis. 2002).

38. *Caudle v. Betts*, 512 So.2d 389, 391 (La. 1987) (citations omitted).

39. *Doe v. Johnson*, 817 F. Supp.1382, 1396 (W.D. Mich. 1993).

40. *Restatement* §§7 and 924. *See also Bank v. Fritsch*, 39 S.W. 3d 474, 480 (Ky. Ct. App. 2001) (stating that "a plaintiff need not prove actual damages in a claim for battery because a showing of actual damages is not an element of assault or battery and, when no actual damages are shown for a battery, nominal damages may be awarded.").

41. *Morgan v. Greenwaldt*, 786 So.2d 1037, 1043 (Miss. 2001).

42. *Tillman v. Nordon*, 771 N.Y.S.2d 670, 671 (2004) (citations omitted).

43. *Love v. City of Port Clinton*, 524 N.E. 2d 166, 167(Ohio 1988) (citations omitted).

44. *Levenson v. Souser*, 557 A.2d 1081, 1088 (Pa. Super. Ct. 1989) (citing Prosser and Keeton at 39).

45. *West Virginia Fire & Cas. Co. v. Stanley*, 2004 WL 1144050 at *27 (W. Va. May 21, 2004).

46. *Restatement* §10 cmt. c and §13 cmt. d.

47. *Banks v. Fritsch*, Excerpt from: 39 S.W.3d 474, 479 (Ky Ct. App. 2001) (footnote omitted).

48. *Restatement*, page 52; *See also Restatement* §35 cmt. h.

49. *Easton v. Sutter Coast Hosp.*, 95 Cal.Rptr.2d 316, 323 (Cal. Ct. App. 2000) (citation omitted).

50. *Moore v. City of Detroit*, 652 N.W.2d 688, 691 (Mich. Ct. App. 2002).

51. *Blaz v. Molin Concrete Products Co.*, 309 Minn. 382, 244 N.W.2d 277, 279 (Minn. 1976).

52. *Barnes v. Meijer Dept. Store*, 2004 WL 720906, at *3 (Ohio Ct. App. 2004) (citations omitted).

53. *Dyson v. City of Pawtucket*, 670 A.2d 233, 239 (R.I. 1996) (citation omitted).

54. *Carter v. May Dept. Store*, 853 A.2d 1037, 1040-1041 (Pa. Super. Ct. 2004). *See also Restatement* §§35 and 907 cmt. b and *Prosser and Keeton* §7 n. 18.

55. *Short v. Haywood Printing Co., Inc.*, 667 N.E. 2d 209, 214 (Ind. Ct. App.1996) (citations omitted) (footnote omitted). See also Case: *Kormi v. Kormi*, 1998 WL 126911, *3 (E.D.Pa. 1998) ("Intentional infliction of emotional distress has been defined as outrageous intentional or reckless conduct that causes severe emotional distress."). This tort is known in some states

as the "tort of outrage". See for example *Spoelstra v. Drainage* Dist. 2004 WL 737516, at *6 (Wash.App. Ct. 2004) ("The tort of outrage requires proof of three elements: (1) extreme and outrageous conduct; (2) intentional or reckless infliction of emotional distress; and (3) severe emotional distress. Such claims must be based on behavior 'so outrageous in character, and so extreme in degree, as to go beyond all possible bounds of decency, and to be regarded as atrocious, and utterly intolerable in a civilized community.'").

56. *Prosser and Keeton* §12 (footnote omitted).

57. See for example, R.D v. W.H., 875 P.2d 26, 32 (Wyo. 1994).

58. Subsection (2) of Section 46 allows for recovery by a third person:

> (2) Where such conduct is directed at a third person, the actor is subject to liability if he intentionally or recklessly causes severe emotional distress
> (a) to a member of such person's immediate family who is present at the time, whether or not such distress results in bodily harm, or
> (b) to any other person who is present at the time, if such distress results in bodily harm.

59. *Copeland v. Home and Community Health Services, Inc.*, 285 F. Supp.2d 144, 148 (D. Conn. 2003) (citation omitted). Whatever the state, (1) consent is not an element of the cause of action for intentional infliction of emotional distress (*Restatement* §§10 cmt. c and 13 cmt. d) and (2) damages are an element of the cause of action (*Prosser and Keeton* §7 n. 18.).

60. *Nagata v. Quest Diagnostics Inc.*, 303 F. Supp.2d 1121, 1125–1126 (D. Haw. 2004) (footnote omitted; citation omitted).

61. *Adams v. Sussman & Hertzberg, Ltd.*, 684 N.E.2d 935, 941 (Ill. App. Ct. 1997) (citations omitted).

62. *Watson v. Dixon*, 502 S.E.2d 15, 19 (N.C. Ct. App. 1998) (citations omitted).

63. *Worley v. Wyoming Bottling Co., Inc.*, 1 P.3d 615, 628 (Wyo. 2000) (citations omitted).

64. *Martin v. Reynolds Metals Co.*, 342 P.2d 790, 794 (Or. 1959).

65. *Silvester v. Spring Valley Country Club*, 543 S.E.2d 563, 566 (S.C. Ct. App. 2001).

66. *Adams v. Cleveland-Cliffs Iron Co.*, 602 N.W.2d 215, 222 (Mich. Ct. App. 1999).

67. *Restatement* (Second) of Torts §158. Unlike the law pertaining to the causes of actions for the intentional torts against the person, the law pertaining to a cause of action for trespass to land does not require that the plaintiff prove lack of consent. It is for the defendant to prove that the plaintiff consented to a trespass to her land. *Restatement* §§10 cmt. c and 13 cmt. d.

68. 342 P.2d 790, 704 (Or. 1959). In arriving at this holding, the court stated, among other things:

> [A] possessor's interest is not invaded by an intrusion which is so trifling that it cannot be recognized by the law. Inasmuch as it is not necessary to prove actual damage in trespass the magnitude of the intrusion ordinarily would not be of any consequence. But there is a point where the entry is so lacking in substance that the law will refuse to recognize it, applying the maxim de minimis non curat lex. Thus it would seem clear that ordinarily the casting of a grain of sand upon another's land would not be a trespass. And so too the casting of diffused light rays upon another's land would not ordinarily constitute a trespass. Conceivably such rays could be so concentrated that their entry upon the possessor's land would result in a trespassory invasion.... We think that a possessor's interest in land as defined by the considerations recited above may, under the appropriate circumstances, be violated by a ray of light, by an atomic particle, or by a particulate of fluoride and, contrariwise, if such interest circumscribed by these

considerations is not violated or endangered, the defendant's conduct, even though it may result in a physical intrusion, will not render him liable in an action of trespass. See *supra* note 68 at 795–797. See also Smith v. Carbide and Chemical Corp. 298 F.Supp.2d 561 (W. D. Ky. 2004).

69. *Restatement* §163. See also *Prosser and Keeton* §13, p 75.

70. *Restatement* §158, cmt. g and §159.

71. *Restatement* §158 cmts. h, I, and j.

72. *Restatement* §158 cmts. l and m.

73. *Bloodgood v. Organic Technologies Corp.*, 2001 WL 98656, at *9 (Iowa Ct. App. 2001).

74. *Adams v. Cleveland-Cliffs Iron Co.*, 602 N.W.2d 215, 223 (Mich. Ct. App. 1999). See also *Prosser and Keeton* §7 n.18.

75. *All American Foods, Inc. v. Aitkin County*, 266 N.W.2d 704, 705 (Minn. 1978) (citations omitted; internal quotations omitted).

76. *Hawkins v. City of Greenville*, 594 S.E.2d 557, 565–566 (S.C. Ct. App. 2004).

77. *Omnibus Int'l, Inc. v. AT & T, Inc.*, 111 S.W.3d 818, 826 (Tex. App. 2003).

78. *Poff v. Hayes*, 763 So.2d 234, 239 (Ala. 2000).

79. In re Marriage of Langham and Kolde, 106 P.3d 212, 218 (Wash. 2005) (citations omitted).

80. *Intel Corp. v. Hamidi*, 71 P.3d 296, 300 (Cal. 2003) (emphasis in original deleted).

81. *Intel Corp. v. Hamidi*, 1 P.3d 296, 303 (Cal. 2003).

82. *Restatement*, Trespass to Chattels Scope Note.

83. *eBay, Inc. v. Bidder's Edge, Inc.*, 100 F. Supp.2d 1058, 1069–1070 (N.D. Cal. 2000). As with the other causes of action involving torts against property, consent is not an element to the cause of action for trespass to chattels. *Restatement* §§10 cmt. c and 13 cmt. d.

84. *Atlantic Container Line AB v. Aref Hassan Abul, Inc.*, 281 F. Supp.2d 457, 468 (N.D. N.Y. 2003).

85. *Fordham v. Eason*, 521 S.E.2d 701, 704 (N.C. 1999) (citations omitted).

86. *Dryden v. Cincinnati Bell Tel. Co.*, 734 N.E.2d 409, 416 (Ohio Ct. App. 1999).

87. *Hawkins v. City of Greenville*, 594 S.E.2d 557, 566 (S.C. Ct. App. 2004).

88. *Maryland Staffing Services, Inc. v. Manpower, Inc.*, 936 F. Supp. 1494, 1507 (E.D. Wis. 1996).

89. Est. of Sigourney, 113 Cal. Rptr.2d 274, 282 (Cal. Ct. App. 2001).

90. *First Nat'l Bank of Omaha v. Acceptance Ins. Companies, Inc.*, 675 N.W.2d 689, 705 (Neb. Ct. App. 2004).

91. *Restatement* §§223, 221, and 222.

92. *Prosser and Keeton* §7 n.18 and *Restatement* §907 cmt. b.

93. *Restatement* §§10 cmt. c and 13 cmt. d.

94. *Oakdale Village Group v. Fong*, 50 Cal. Rptr.2d 810, 812 (Cal. Ct. App. 1996).

95. *Kentucky Ass'n of Counties v. McClendon*, 2005 WL 635019, at *8 (Ky. 2005).

96. *Manzer v. Sanchez*, 985 S.W.2d 936, 940 (Mo. Ct. App. 1999).

97. *Ahles v. Aztec Enterprises, Inc.*, 502 N.Y.S.2d 821, 822 (N.Y. App. Div. 1986) (citations omitted).

98. *Buono v. Scalia*, 843 A.2d 1120, 1124 (N.J. 2004).

99. *Buono v. Scalia*, 843 A.2d 1120, 1124 (N.J. 2004). In a 1997 case, the Arizona Supreme Court cited *Prosser and Keeton* for the proposition that "willful, wanton, and reckless conduct have commonly been 'grouped together as an aggravated form of negligence.'" *Williams v. Thude*, 934 P.2d 1349, 1351 (Ariz. 1997).

100. *Bauer v. Crotty*, 805 P.2d 392, 400 (Ariz. Ct. App. 1991) (citations omitted).

101. *Ward v. City of San Jose*, 737 F.Supp. 1502, 1513-1514 (N.D. Calif. 1990) (citations omitted).

102. *Henderson v. Romer*, 910 P.2d 48, 51 (Colo. Ct. App. 1995) (citation omitted).

103. *Est. of Despain v. Avante Group, Inc.*, 2005 WL 672090, at *2 (Fla. Dist. Ct. App. 2005).

104. *Martin v. Johns-Manville Corp.*, 494 A.2d 1088, 1097–1098 (Pa. 1985).

105. *Palsgraf v. Long Island R. Co.*, 162 N.E. 99, 99 (N.Y. 1928).

106. *Prosser and Keeton* §31; *Restatement* §282.

107. Webster's Ninth New Collegiate Dictionary 274 (SpringField, MA: Merriam-Webster, Inc., 1988).

108. See text accompanying footnote # 22–25.

109. Webster's Ninth New Collegiate Dictionary 1148 (SpringField, MA: Merriam-Webster, Inc., 1988).

110. Webster's Ninth New Collegiate Dictionary 207 (SpringField, MA: Merriam-Webster, Inc., 1988).

111. The T.J. Hooper, 60 F. 2d 737 (1932).

112. The T.J. Hooper, 60 F. 2d 737, 740 (1932) (citations omitted).

113. *Rossell v. Volkswagen of America*, 709 P. 2d 517, 522–524 (Ariz. 1985).

114. *Palsgraf v. Long Island R. Co.*, 162 N.E. 99, 99 (N.Y. 1928), quoting Pollock, Torts (11th ed.) p. 455. When you analyze the definition of negligence, you come to the realization that negligence itself consists of the first two elements of the cause of action for negligence: duty and breach. Proving that a person was negligent would be simply to prove that a person breached a duty of care; in other words, proving that a person was negligent would be proof of the first two elements of a cause of action for negligence.

115. *Williams v. Bear Stearns & Co.* 725 So.2d 397, 402 (Fla. Dist. Ct. App. 1998) (Harris, J., concurring and dissenting).

116. *Restatement* §281. The conduct that is spoken of in Subsection (d) is conduct on the part of a plaintiff that would constitute a defense such as contributory negligence. Defenses to a cause of action for negligence are a matter for the defendant to plead.

117. *Marchakov v. Champagne*, 2004 WL 1542227, *2 (R.I.Super. Ct.).

118. *Underwood v. Best Western Westbank, Inc.*, 2004 WL 1959912 (La. Ct. App. 5 Cir. Aug. 31, 2004).

119. *McNeal v. Thomas*, 2004 WL 1902745, at *5 (Tex. App. Aug. 26, 2004).

120. When we get to the discussion on causation, we will find that there are two components to the causation element.

121. *Wilkerson v. Harvey*, 2004 WL 2009280, at *2 (Ind. Ct. App. 2004).

122. *Stanley v. McCarver*, 92 P.3d 849, 851–852 (Ariz. 2004).

123. *Schmidt v. Courtney*, 592 S.E.2d 326, 334 (S.C. Ct. App. 2004).

124. *Asad v. Continental Airlines, Inc.*, 2004 WL 1752929 (N.D. Ohio June 4, 2004).

125. *Dillon v. Legg*, 441 P.2d 912, 916 (Cal. 1968).

126. *Investors Real Estate Trust Properties, Inc. v. Terra Pacific Midwest, Inc.*, 2004 WL 1933588, *2 (N.D. 2004) ("n a negligence action, the plaintiff has the burden of demonstrating (1) a duty ...."); *Simpson v. Boyd*, 2004 WL 1900815, *2 (Miss. 2004) ("[The plaintiff] bears the burden of producing evidence sufficient to establish the existence of ... [a] duty ...."); *Northwestern Mut. Life Ins. Co. v. Babayan*, 2004 WL 1902516, *20 (E.D.Pa. 2004) ("Under Pennsylvania law, [the plaintiff] only would succeed with her negligence claim should she demonstrate ... a duty, or obligation, recognized by the law, requiring the actor to

conform to a ceratin standard of conduct . . . ."); *Horridge v. St. Mary's County Dept. of Social Services*, 2004 ("[T]he plaintiff must allege facts demonstrating '. . . that the defendant was under a duty to protect the plaintiff from injury . . . .").

127. *Fultz v. Union-Commerce Assoc.*, 683 N.W. 2d 587, 591 (Mich. 2004).

128. 162 N.E. 99 (N.Y. 1928).

129. 162 N.E. 99, 99 (N.Y. 1928).

130. 162 N.E. 99, 99–100 (N.Y. 1928).

131. *Palsgraf v. Long Island R. Co.*, 162 N. E. 99, 100 (N. Y. 1928). This statement also demonstrates the theory of relationship as a basis for establishing a duty.

132. *Hamby v. State*, 2004 WL 1737390, at *3–4 (Tenn. Ct. App. 2004).

133. *Erickson v. Curtis Inv. Co.*, 447 N.W.2d 165, 166 (Minn. 1989).

134. *Erickson v. Curtis Inv. Co.*, 447 N.W.2d 165, 168–170 (Minn. 1989).

135. *Feld v. Merriam*, 485 A. 2d 742, 745 (Pa. 1984).

136. *Feld v. Merriam*, 485 A. 2d 742, 746 (Pa. 1984).

137. *Thing v. La Chusa*, 771 P. 2d 814, 821 (Cal. 1989).

138. *Thing v. La Chusa*, 771 P. 2d 814, 826 (Cal. 1989).

139. *Beck v. State*, 837 P.2d 105,110-111 (Alaska 1992).

140. *Gross v. Burt*, 2004 WL 1944382, *5 (Tex.App.2004) (citations omitted).

141. *Di Ponzio v. Riordan*, 679 N.E.2d 616–618 (N.Y. 1997) (citations omitted).

142. *Simmers v. Bentley Constr. Co.*, 597 N.E.2d 504, 507 (Ohio 1992). As you can see from this quote even when the relationship theory is used to establish duty, foreseeability comes into play. See also *Erickson v. Curtis Inv. Co.*, 447 N.W.2d 165, 168–169 (Minn. 1989):

> If the law is to impose a duty on A to protect B from C's criminal acts, the law usually looks for a special relationship between A and B, a situation where B has in some way entrusted his or her safety to A and A has accepted that entrustment. This special relationship also assumes that the harm represented by C is something that A is in a position to protect against and should be expected to protect against. . . .
> Whether a duty is imposed depends, therefore, on the relationship of the parties and the foreseeable risk involved.

143. *Davidson v. Univ. of North Carolina*, 543 S.E.2d 920, 926–927 (N. C. Ct. App. 2001) (citations omitted).

144. *Titus v. Canyon Lake Property Owners Assn.*, 13 Cal. Rptr.3d 807, 810 (Cal. Ct. App. 2004).

145. *Basso v. Miller*, 352 N. E. 2d 868 (N.Y. 1976).

146. *Basso v. Miller*, 352 N. E. 2d 868, 871 (N.Y. 1976).

147. *Basso v. Miller*, 352 N. E. 2d 868, 870 (N.Y. 1976).

148. *Basso v. Miller*, 352 N. E. 2d 868, 871–873 (N.Y. 1976) (footnote omitted; citations omitted).

149. 159 F. 2d 169 (2d Cir. 1947).

150. 159 F. 2d 169, 172–173 (2d Cir. 1947).

151. 159 F.2d 169, 173. (2d Cir. 1947). You can see that the BPL formula employs the foreseeability concept.

152. *Viar v. N.C. Department of Transp.* 590 S.E.2d 909, 916 (N. C. Ct. App. 2004) (citations omitted). As do other courts and commentators, the North Carolina Court of Appeals

mistakenly refers to this formula as one that "defines negligence." A careful reading of the Carroll Towing case demonstrates that Judge Hand proposed the formula as a method by which to determine whether a duty should be imposed on the defendant.

153. *Fultz v. Union-Commerce Assoc.*, 683 N.W. 2d 587, 591 (Mich. 2004); see supra text accompanying footnote 18.

154. *Fultz v. Union-Commerce Associates*, 683 N.W.2d 587, 591 (Mich. 2004).

155. *Clark v. Dalman, 150 N.W. 2d* 755, 759–760 (Mich. 1967).

156. *Holles v. Sunrise Terrace, Inc.*, 509 S.E.2d 494, 497–498 (Va. 1999).

157. *Webster's Ninth New Collegiate Dictionary* 176 (SpringField, MA: Merriam-Webster, Inc. 1983).

158. *Haney v. Bradley County Bd. of Educ.*, 2004 WL 2086327, 10 (Tenn. Ct. App. 2004).

159. *Prudhomme v. City of Iowa*, 758 So.2d 275, 278 (La. Ct. App.2000).

160. *Stibley v. Zimmerman*, 1998 WL 548755, at *9-*10 (Ohio Ct. App. 1998).

161. *People v. Zak*, 457 N.W. 2d 59, 63 (Mich. 1990); Vescio v. Merchants Bank, 272 B.R. 413, 435 (D. Vt. 2001).

162. *Frank O. Bowman*, III, Coping with "Loss": a re-examination of sentencing federal economic crimes under the guidelines, 51 *V and. L. Rev.* 461, 527–528. See also *Lidge v. Sears, Roebuck & Co.*, 318 F. Supp.2d 830, 835 (2004) ("[T]he point of . . . Swanson [v. Godwin, 327 S.W.2d 903 (Mo.1959)] . . .was that causation was established because there was no other logical cause for the plaintiff's fall."); and *Sensley v. Glenwood Regional Medical Center*, 873 So.2d 864, 868–869 (La. Ct. App. 2004) ("Dr. Einstein testified that Donnie was still under anesthesia when his endotracheal tube was removed and that, within a short time of the removal, he became critically ill. The most logical cause of this, according to Dr. Einstein, was an airway obstruction.").

163. *Lidge v. Sears, Roebuck & Co.*, 318 F. Supp.2d 830, 835 (2004)

164. 122 N.E. 389 (1919). Cited in *Tort and Accident Law: Cases and Materials* 332 (St. Paul, MN: West Publishing Co. 2d ed. 1989).

165. 122 N.E. at 390.

166. These theories, or rules are also sometimes referred to as "tests" See for example, *Viner v. Sweet*, 70 P.3d 1046 (Cal.), but see *Prosser and Keeton* §41, p. 267.

167. *Black' Law Dictionary*, (revised 4th ed., page 1556).

168. *Doe v. Garcia*, 895 P. 2d 1229 (Idaho Ct. App. 1229, 1233 (1995).

169. *People v. Bautista*, 2003 WL 21299975, at *11 (Cal. Ct. App. 2003) (citations omitted).

170. As we go further into this topic, we will see that the *Restatement* uses the term "legal cause" to include both aspects of causation.

171. *Coffey v. City of Milwaukee*, 247 N.W. 2d 132 (Wis. 1976).

172. *Coffey v. City of Milwaukee*, 247 N.W. 2d 132, 140 (Wis. 1976).

173. *Brown v. Hamilton County*, 26 S.W.3d 43, 50 (Tenn. Ct. App. 2004).

174. *Govea v. City of Norcross*, 2004 WL 2786361, at *6 (Ga. Ct. App. 2004) (footnotes omitted).

175. *Thomas v. Weddle*, 605 S.E.2d 244, 246–247 (N. C. Ct. App. 2004) (citations omitted).

176. *Goldsberry v. Grubbs*, 672 N.E.2d 475, 479 (Ind. Ct. App. 1996 (emphasis in original; citations omitted).

177. *Hammock v. Red Gold, Inc.*, 784 N. E. 2d 495, 500 n.8 (Ind. Ct. App. 2003) (emphasis added).

178. *Rossell v. Volkswagen of America*, 709 P. 2d 517, 525–526 (Ariz. 1985) (quoting the *Prosser and Keeton* §44 and citing the *Restatement* §435 cmt. d).

179. *Prosser and Keeton*, §44 at 301 (footnotes omitted; emphasis in original).

180. *Feeney v. Disston Manor Personal Care Home, Inc.*, 849 A.2d 590, 595 (Pa. Super. Ct. 2004) (footnote omitted).

181. *Alabama Power Co. v. Moore*, 2004 WL 1950304, at *2 (Ala. 2004) (citations omitted).

182. *Braun v. New Hope Tp.*, 646 N.W. 2d 737, 741 (S.D. 2002) (citations omitted).

183. *Phan Son Van v. Pena* 990 S.W. 2d 751, 752 (Tex 1999).

184. *Phan Son Van v. Pena* 990 S.W. 2d 751, 754 (Tex 1999).

185. *Restatement* §§903, 907, and 908(1) respectively.

186. *Restatement* §§904, 904, 905, and 906 respectively.

187. *Zanakis-Pico v. Cutter Dodge, Inc.*, 47 P.3d 1222, 1240–1243 (Haw. 2002) (Acoba, J. concurring; footnote omitted; citations omitted).

188. *Koehn v. Rhodes*, 882 So.2d 757, 762–763, (La. Ct. App. 2004) (citations omitted). There have been cases in which courts have referred to special damages in tort action as "consequential damages." For example in *Vanderbeek v. Vernon Corp.*, 50 P. 3d 866, 870 n.2, (1990), the Colorado Supreme Court said that "[i]n the context of economic torts, consequential damages and special damages are synonymous."

189. *Est. of Farrell ex rel. Bennett v. Gordon*, 770 A.2d 517, 521 (Del. 2001) (citation omitted).

190. *McCarthy v. Kunicki*, 2005 WL 265266, *11 (Ill. App. Ct. 2005) (citations omitted).

191. *Whisnant v. Herrera*, 603 S.E.2d 847, 850 (N.C. Ct. App. 2004) (citations omitted).

192. *Butterfield v. Forrester*, 103 Eng. Rep. 926, (K.B. 1809).

193. For example, *Hoffman v. Jones*, 280 So.2d 431, 438 (holding that in Florida "a plaintiff in an action based on negligence will no longer be denied any recovery because of his contributory negligence").

194. *Dehn v. Edgecombe*, 834 A.2d 146, 166 (Md. Ct. Spec. App. 2003) (emphasis in original omitted).

195. *Conroy v. City of Dickson*, 49 S.W.3d 868, 871 (Tenn. Ct. App. 2001) (emphasis added).

196. *Montgomery Elevator Co. v. Gordon*, 619 P.2d 66, 70 (1971). Prior to the development of the comparative negligence, the "last clear chance" doctrine was applied by the courts to ameliorate the harshness of the effect of contributory negligence. The Maryland Court of Special Appeals explained the concept in these words:

> The doctrine of last clear chance has been applied in this State for over 130 years and has remained relatively unchanged during that time. Essentially, the last clear chance doctrine is a plaintiff's defense to a defendant's allegation that the plaintiff was contributorily negligent. "[T]he doctrine of last clear chance permits a contributorily negligent plaintiff to recover damages from a negligent defendant if each of the following elements is satisfied: (i) the defendant is negligent; (ii) the plaintiff is contributorily negligent; and (iii) the plaintiff makes 'a showing of something new or sequential, which affords the defendant a fresh opportunity (of which he fails to avail himself) to avert the consequences of his original negligence.'" Nationwide Mut. Ins. Co. V. Anderson, 864 A.2d 201, 206 (Md. Ct. Spec. App. 2005) (internal quotation marks omitted)

197. *Sevigeny v. Dibble Hollow Condominium Ass'n, Inc.*, 819 A.2d 844, 857 (Conn. App. Ct. 2003).

198. *Harrison v. Montgomery County Bd. of Educ.*, 456 A. 2d 894, 896 n.3 (Md. Ct. App. 1983) (emphasis in original omitted; citation omitted).

199. Julie K. Weaver, Comment, jury instructions on joint and several liability in washington state, 67 *Wash. L. R.* 457 n.3 (1992).

200. *Bell v. Jet Wheel Blast, Div. of Ervin Indus.*, 462 So.2d 166, 171–172 (La. 1985) (citations omitted). See also Elizabeth K. Branned, Comment, *Daley v. General Motors, Corp: Comparative Negligence As A Defense to Strict Liability*, 17 Am. J. Trial Advoc. 555 n.40 (1993).

201. *Huffman v. Caterpillar Tractor Co.*, Excerpt from: 908 F. 2d 1470, 1476 (10th Cir. 1990) (footnote omitted).

202. *Grandstaff v. Hawks*, 36 S.W.3d 482, 491 n.12 (Tenn. Ct. App. 2000) (citations omitted).

203. Mary Jane Palmer, Case Comment, *Torts–Nelson v. Chester*: Weighing Gross Negligence on the Comparative Scale, 24 *Mem. St. U. L. R.* 587 n.68 (1994).

204. Ind. Code Ann. §34-6-2-45 (Lexis 1998).

205. Cite to earlier portion of the Negligence part where negligence is defined. (emphasis added).

206. *Restatement* §496A cmt. c; See also Prosser and Keeton §68.

207. *Hanke v. Wacker*, 576 N.E.2d 1113,118 (Ill. App. Ct. 1991) (citations omitted).

208. See for example, *Deas v. State*, 2004 WL 2715318, *6 (Tenn. Ct. App. 2004) (holding that "the contributory negligence doctrine, the last clear chance doctrine … and the doctrine of secondary implied assumption of the risk have been merged into the comparative fault scheme and are simply factors to consider when apportioning fault among the parties") and *Agbabian v. TST Colorado Ave.*, L.L.C., 2004 WL 1558293, *4 (Cal. Ct. App. 2004) (holding that "[u]nder secondary assumption of the risk, the defendant's does owe a duty of care to the plaintiff but the plaintiff knowingly encounters a risk of injury caused by the defendant's breach of that duty [and that] [l]iability under secondary assumption of the risk is apportioned by comparative fault").

209. *Blackburn v. Dorta*, 348 So.2d 287, 289, 290 (Fla. 1977) (footnotes omitted).

210. *Carver v. El-Sabawi*, 107 P.3d 1283, 1285–1286 (Nev. 2005) (citation omitted; footnotes omitted; internal quotation marks omitted).

211. See for example, *Norris v. Ross Stores, Inc.* 859 A. 2d 270–271 (Md. Ct. Spec. App. 2004).

212. *Norris v. Ross Stores, Inc.* 859 A. 2d 270–271 (Md. Ct. Spec. App. 2004) (internal quotation marks omitted).

213. *Doe v. Nevada*, 356 F. Supp.2d 1123, 1126 (D. Nev. 2004) (citations omitted).

214. *Stivers v. Ellington*, 140 S.W. 3d 599, 601 (Ky. Ct. App. 2004).

215. *McKiernan v. Green*, 2004 WL 2591891 at *4 (Conn. Super. Ct. 2004).

216. *Mest v. Cabot Corp.*, 2004 WL 1102754, *3 (E.D.Pa.) (footnote omitted).

217. *Nelson v. Hawkins*, 45 F. Supp.2d 1015, 1020 (D. Mont. 1999).

218. *Nadel v. Burger King Corp.*, 695 N.E.2d 1185, 1192 (Ohio 1997).

219. *Consolidated Rail Corp. v. Gottshall*, 512 U.S. 532, 544 (1994). (citations omitted).

220. *Consolidated Rail Corp. v. Gottshall*, 512 U.S. 532, 546–549 (1994) (citations omitted) (footnotes omitted). In a footnote, the Court noted that "[m]any jurisdictions that follow the zone of danger or relative bystander tests also require that a plaintiff demonstrate a "physical manifestation" of an alleged emotional injury, that is, a physical injury or effect that is the direct result of the emotional injury, in order to recover. *Consolidated Rail Corp. v. Gottshall* at 512 U.S. 532, 549 n.11.

221. *Shumosky v. Lutheran Welfare Services of Northeastern Pa, Inc.*, 784 A.2d 196, 199–200 (citations omitted).

222. *U.S. v. Union Corp.*, 277 F. Supp.2d 478, 493 (E.D. Pa. 2003) (footnotes omitted; internal quotation marks eliminated).

223. Section 519 provides.

> (1) One who carries on an abnormally dangerous activity is subject to liability for harm to the person, land or chattels of another resulting from the activity, although he has exercised the utmost care to prevent the harm.
> (2) This strict liability is limited to the kind of harm, the possibility of which makes the activity abnormally dangerous.

224. *Fandrey ex rel. Connell v. American Family Mut. Ins. Co.*, 680 N.W.2d 345, 350 (Wisc. 2004).

225. *Cook v. Whitsell-Sherman*, 796 N.E.2d 271, 276 (Ind. 2003).

226. *Cortez v. Zurich Ins. Co.*, 752 So.2d 957, 961 (La. Ct. App. 2000).

227. *Bruzga v. PMR Architects, P.C.*, 693 A.2d 401, 404 (N.H. 1997).

228. *Fandrey ex rel. Connell v. American Family Mut. Ins. Co.*, 680 N.W.2d 345, 351 (Wisc. 2004).

229. But see *McNeil v. Nissan Motor Co., Ltd.*, 365 F. Supp.2d 206, 211 (D. N.H. 2005) (stating that [t]he manufacturer or seller faced with an allegation of strict liability in tort for a defective design may have several defenses against liability, for example, product misuse or abnormal use ... and what was formerly termed contributory negligence or unreasonable assumption of the risk) and *Aguilar v. WEI Equipment*, 2004 WL 2367826, at*2 (E.D.Pa. 2004) (stating that "[u]nder Pennsylvania law, assumption of the risk is a complete defense to cases of both negligence and strict liability").

230. *Bradshaw v. Michigan Nat. Bank*, 197 N.W.2d 531, 532 (Mich. Ct. App. 1972). Sections 504–518 of the *Restatement* sets forth the principles under which a person is liable for injuries caused by animals. Sections 518–524A of the *Restatement* sets forth the principles under which a person is liable for injuries caused by abnormally dangerous activities.

231. *Restatement* §504 cmts e and g and §507 cmt. e.

232. See for example, *Davis v. Berwind Corp.*, 640 A.2d 1289 (Pa. Super. Ct. 1994).

233. *Simoneau v. South Bend Lathe, Inc.*, 543 A.2d 407, 409 (N.H. 1988) (citations omitted).

234. *Weiner v. American Honda Motor Co., Inc.*, 718 A.2d 305, 308 (Pa. Super. Ct. 1998).

235. *Schiller v. Mitchell*, 2005 WL 994914, *4 (Ill. App. Ct. 2005) (citations omitted).

236. *Fashion 21 v. Coalition for Humane Immigrant Rights of Los Angeles*, 12 Cal. Rptr. 3d 493, 504–505 (Cal Ct. App. 2004) (internal quotations omitted). Section 821F of the *Restatement* states that a defendant is liable for nuisance "only to those to whom it causes significant harm ...."

237. *Milwaukee Metro. Sewerage Dist. v. City of Milwaukee*, 691 N.W.2d 658, 670 (Wisc. 2005).

Product Liability

10

PATRICK LAVELLE

The term "product liability" simply stated means the liability for harm caused to a person or property by a defect in a product. Generally, liability is imposed upon the entity that manufactured, marketed, or otherwise introduced the defective product into the commercial stream of commerce. This seemingly straightforward definition might indicate to the uninitiated that advancing a case based upon a theory of product liability is a rather uncomplicated exercise. Yet, product liability has evolved into one of the most complicated and confusing areas of tort law.

In the Beginning, There Was Warranty

Product liability has its origins in the law of warranty. Early developments in the law in this country recognized the requirement of privity of contract in cases alleging harm caused by a product. This view was in line with the opinion of Lord Abinger, C.B., rendered in the case of *Winterbottom v. Wright, 10 M.&W. 109* (Exch. 1842). According to Lord Abinger, elimination of the rule of privity would open the door to an endless stream of plaintiffs claiming against sellers with whom they had no connection. This warranty approach limited the universe of plaintiffs in a product liability case. Under this rule, one could not recover for harm caused by a product, absent sufficient evidence to establish the existence of privity of contract between the injured buyer and the seller of the product. Basically, if you were not the one who bought it, you could not sue for harm caused by the product.

The often inequitable treatment of people injured by substandard product was first recognized as early as 1916 by the distinguished jurist, Benjamin Cardozo, in the case of *McPherson v. Buick Motor Co.*[1] In that case, Cardozo held that a person injured as a result of a defective automobile tire had a right of action against the manufacturer of the tire, despite the lack of privity. Cardozo's rationale was that the manufacturer expected that its product would be used in a certain manner, and the manufacturer was in a better position than the innocent consumer to know of the potential danger.[2] This decision has been regarded as the impetus for changes in the law, which were fueled by the ever-growing social pressures seeking protection of the consumer, and by the realization that liability would not unduly inhibit the enterprise of manufacturers as they were well placed both to profit from its lessons and to distribute its burdens.[3] More simply put, the rationale states that the law recognizes that the manufacturer of a product is in a better position to absorb the costs associated with injuries caused by his negligently made product, by spreading the cost over the entirety of his product line. The rule that has finally emerged in this regard states that the seller is liable for negligence in the manufacture or sale of any product which may reasonably be expected to be capable of inflicting harm if it is defective.[4]

All of the foregoing, however, should not be interpreted as abrogating a buyer's right to sue under a theory of warranty. Under the Uniform Commercial Code's (UCC) provisions regarding the sale of goods, the buyer of goods who is harmed by the product he buys may sue the seller for breach of the product warranty, either expressed or implied.[5] The same UCC warranty protections against harm caused by the product that are available to buyers are also extended to third persons in varying degrees. The UCC provisions set forth three alternative warranty provisions as applicable to third persons; however, those provisions leave the determination of the scope of such protections to the legislatures of the states.[6]

Under the present state of the UCC, a seller who markets a defective product is still liable to a buyer who is injured by the seller's product. This is an important aspect of the law from a practical point of view. In most jurisdictions, the statute of limitations for a breach of warranty claim is longer than that for a negligence claim, thereby giving longer life to certain product liability cases in situations which cause the typical two year negligence statute to run out.

From Warranty to Strict Liability

In the United States, the concept of strict product liability, in one form or another, has been generally accepted or adopted in all of the individual states. The development of the law of product liability in this country was a rather slow process. From the beginning of change in 1916 with Justice Cardozo's holding in *McPherson*, the practice of this theory revolved around issues in the negligence arena. One of the major issues that was litigated was the use of the concept of *res ipsa loquitor* to prove negligence on the part of a manufacturer. Such was the issue in the California case of *Escola v. Coca Cola.*[7] With respect to this issue the California Supreme Court stated that the doctrine of *res ipsa loquitor* may be applied upon the theory that the defendant had control of the product at the time of the negligent act, although not at the time of the accident, provided that the plaintiff first proves that the condition of the product had not been changed after it left the defendant's possession.[8]

The *Escola* case, however, has become historically significant not so much for its pronouncement on the theory of *res ipsa loquitor*, but for the *obiter dicta* comments contained in the concurring opinion written by Chief Justice Traynor.

Justice Traynor's opinion espousing the adoption of a theory of strict liability governing defective products was a harbinger of the future course of legal thought on the subject. In his opinion, Traynor outlined the social policy rationale for a strict liability approach as follows:

> Even if there is no negligence, however, public policy demands that responsibility be fixed wherever it will most effectively reduce the hazards to life and

health inherent in defective product that reach the market. It is evident that the manufacturer can anticipate some hazards and guard against the recurrence of others, as the public cannot. Those who suffer injury from defective product are unprepared to meet its consequences. The cost of an injury and the loss of time or health may be an overwhelming misfortune to the person injured, and a needless one, for the risk of injury can be insured by the manufacturer and distributed among the public as a cost of doing business. It is to the public interest to discourage the marketing of products having defects that are a menace to the public. If such product nevertheless find their way into the market it is to the public interest to place the responsibility for whatever injury they may cause upon the manufacturer, who, even if he is not negligent in the manufacture of the product, is responsible for its reaching the market. However intermittently such injuries may occur and however haphazardly they may strike, the risk of their occurrence is a constant risk and a general one. Against such a risk there should be general and constant protection and the manufacturer is best situated to afford such protection.[9]

With little variation, this social policy was recognized or adopted by all of the jurisdictions in the United States over the ensuing years.[10] Indeed, 16 years later, Justice Traynor himself had the opportunity, in the case of *Greenman v. Yuba Power Products*, to firmly establish strict liability in tort as a basis of a plaintiff's recovery for injuries caused by defective products.[11] In *Greenman*, the California Supreme Court reversed a ruling by the trial court granting judgment to a manufacturer based on the manufacturer's argument that the plaintiff had failed to provide mandated notice for the breach of a warranty under California's version of the UCC. Justice Traynor, writing for the majority and citing authority from numerous other jurisdictions, concluded:

"Although in these cases strict liability has usually been based on the theory of an express or implied warranty running from the manufacturer to the plaintiff, the abandonment of the requirement of a contract between them, the recognition that the liability is not assumed by agreement but imposed by law, and the refusal to permit the manufacturer to define the scope of its own responsibility for defective products make clear that the liability is not one governed by the law of contract warranties but by the law of strict liability in tort. Accordingly, rules defining and governing warranties that were developed to meet the needs of commercial transactions cannot properly be invoked to govern the manufacturer's liability to those injured by their defective product unless those rules also serve the purposes for which such liability is imposed."[12]

In 1965, the American Law Institute (ALI) completed and published its *Restatement (Second) of Torts*. Contained in that collection was its now famous, or infamous depending on your point of view, Section 402A, which attempted to codify the law of strict product liability in a uniform manner such that it would reflect the values supporting the underlying social policy identified and developed by Justice Traynor and others.

Section 402A reads as follows:

§402A. Special Liability of Seller of Product for Physical Harm to User or Consumer.

(1) One who sells any product in a defective condition unreasonably dangerous to the user or consumer or to his property is subject to liability for physical harm thereby caused to the ultimate user or consumer, or to his property, if

  (a) the seller is engaged in the business of selling such a product and
  (b) it is expected to and does reach the user or consumer without substantial change in the condition in which it is sold

(2) The rule stated in Subsection (1) applies although

  (a) the seller has exercised all possible care in the preparation and sale of his product, and
  (b) the user or consumer has not bought the product from or entered into any contractual relation with the seller

Product Defects

In the application of strict product liability under §402A, there are generally three theories of liability advanced by plaintiffs to establish that a product is defective. They are Manufacturing Defects, Design Defects, and Failure to Warn Defects.[13]

A manufacturing defect occurs when the product leaves the control of the manufacturer in a condition that does not conform with the original design of the product. The *Restatement Third of Torts: Product Liability* states that a manufacturing defect exists when a product departs from its intended design even though all possible care was exercised in the preparation and marketing of the product. In simple language, if a manufacturer's product does not comply with the design specifications for the product, and it leaves the plant containing the defect destined for commercial sale, then the manufacturer is liable for all harm caused by that defective product regardless of the extent of his efforts to prevent such manufacturing errors.

When it comes to the concept of a Design Defect, the discussion becomes much less straightforward. The perplexing question that always arises is how does one establish that a design is defective. The reporters of the *Restatement Third of Torts: Product Liability* have determined that a product will be found to have been defectively designed when the foreseeable risks of harm posed by the product could have been reduced or avoided by the adoption of a reasonable alternative design by the manufacturer, seller, or distributor, and the omission of the reasonable alternative design renders the product as not being reasonably safe.[14]

Other jurisdictions have determined that a product may be found to have been defectively designed if it is introduced into the stream of commerce lacking any element necessary to make it safe for its intended use, or possessing any feature that makes the product unsafe for its intended use.[15]

Comparing and contrasting the two definitions of design defect will clearly illuminate the inherent discrepancies in the different approaches, and the numerous questions raised in the context of such cases. With reference to the *Restatement (Third)* definition, one might ask how, in a practical sense, liability could be imposed on a seller or distributor of a manufacturer's product based upon proof of a failure to incorporate a reasonable alternative design in the manufacturing process of the product. Subsequent commercial sellers and distributors of a product have no input into the design choices made by a manufacturer. To expose such defendants to liability under the *Restatement Third* definition would impose on them an impossible burden of proof (i.e., supporting the design choices of the manufacturer) in defense of a product liability suit, or alternatively, force sellers and distributors to insist on indemnity clauses in contracts with their suppliers to protect themselves from product liability suits, or provide insurance against such suits themselves, thereby raising the cost of the product. It should be noted, however, that even the existence of insurance or an indemnity clause would do little to enhance the ability of a subsequent seller or distributor to defend against a product liability claim under the *Restatement (Third)*.

The underlying social policy supporting the existence of product liability law is that the manufacturer should be held as the guarantor of the safety of this product. This policy would appear to be the focus for the reporters in adopting the definition of design defect contained in the *Restatement Third*. Clearly, if there existed, at the time the product was manufactured, a feasible and available alternative design that would have resulted in a safer product, and the manufacturer failed to incorporate that design into his product, then it could easily be said that the manufacturer failed in its duty as the guarantor of the safety of the product.

The Courts and commentators have, however, noted a problem with the *Restatement Third* approach. The problem has been identified from two perspectives, the first being that the *Restatement Third* requirement of proof of a reasonable alternative design removes a design defect case from the realm of strict liability and places it squarely back into the arena of negligence. Proponents of this perspective would state that the reasonable alternative design approach to the proof of product defect focuses on the conduct of the manufacturer, and its actions in making its design choice.

The second perspective arises from the legal axiom that the focus of a strict product liability case should be on the product and not on the conduct of the manufacturer or the plaintiff. In determining whether a product is defective, one should look to the product as it exists in commerce, and judge the safety of the product based upon its present characteristics, as opposed to judging the safety of the product based upon what the manufacturer could or should have done relative to the basic design. Counter-arguments give rise to issues regarding distinctions to be made between the concepts of defect, and unreasonably dangerous. Some of these issues are discussed later.

The third major theory in support of product liability is a failure to warn. This theory is generally seen as a subset of a design defect theory.

To begin with, it should be made clear that the inclusion of warnings with a product that identifies a latent danger is not a universal method for avoiding liability for a defective product. In other words, a manufacturer may not avoid liability for harm caused by his defective product merely by slapping a warning label on the side of the product. A manufacturer has a duty to warn of latent dangers in his product when such dangers cannot be designed out of the product without destroying the utility of the product. The most obvious example of such a product is a prescription drug. Such products, when used as directed by a physician, provide a great benefit to society in preventing and curing illness. Yet, the same product, when misused, or used without warning and direction can have fatal results. Further, although such drugs are inherently dangerous, changing their design to eliminate the danger would render them ineffective for the purposes they are made, that is, treating illnesses. These are the types of product that require warnings to make them nondefective.

An exception to the foregoing general rule states that a manufacturer has no duty to warn people of obvious dangers. One of the most common examples of a product with an obvious danger is a kitchen knife. As it is with prescription drugs, kitchen knives generally possess an inherent latent danger in the form of a very sharp cutting blade. Further, designing the danger inherent in the sharp blade out of the knife would render it useless for its intended purpose, or in legal parlance, eliminating the risk would destroy the product's utility. Referencing our discussion regarding prescription drugs would, on its face, seem to require warnings with the knife. Yet, it is generally accepted that a knife requires no consumer warnings. In contrast with the warnings requirement associated with prescription drugs, no warnings about the sharp blade of the knife are needed or required because the danger inherent in kitchen knives is well known to people in general, and the dangers associated with the existence of the sharp blade on a knife should be obvious to the normal consumer.

The next obvious question deals with the contents of a warning. In order for a manufacturer to avoid liability by including warnings with his product, such warnings must amount to adequate warnings. What qualifies as an adequate warning is subject to interpretation; however, most jurisdictions would agree that an adequate warning is one that advises the user of the inherent danger, and instructs him how to avoid it.[16]

Important Issues in Strict Liability

The language of §402A of the *Restatement (Second)* of Torts has been the source of many and extended discussions regarding the practical application of the rule. One of the most confusing is the arguments revolving around the distinction to be made between the concepts of "unreasonably dangerous" and "defective."

The terms "unreasonably dangerous" and "defective" enter the law of strict product liability from the language set forth in §402A. The comments to the *Restatement (Second)* of Torts define defective condition of a product as being a condition not contemplated by the ultimate consumer, which will be unreasonably dangerous to him.[17] The comment defining unreasonably dangerous states, "The article must be dangerous to the extent beyond that which would be contemplated by the ordinary consumer who purchases it, with the ordinary knowledge common to the community as to its characteristics.[18] These definitions attempt to create a distinction between the two terms, yet it would be reasonable to argue that based upon these definitions, it is a distinction without a difference.

The distinction was explained by the reporter of the *Restatement (Second)* when he stated that the term "unreasonably dangerous" was added to the language in an effort to insure that the manufacturer would never be held to answer as an insurer of his product.[19]

The California Courts resolved the apparent dilemma with reference to the reporters clarification in the case of *Cronin v. J.B.E. Olson Corp.*, wherein they stated that:

> We recognize that the words "unreasonably dangerous" may also serve the beneficial purpose of preventing the seller from being treated as the insurer

of its product. However, we think that such protective end is attained by the necessity of proving that there was a defect in the manufacture or design of the product and that such defect was a proximate cause of the injuries. Although the seller should not be responsible for all injuries involving the use of its product, it should be liable for all injuries proximately caused by any of its product which are adjudged defective.[20]

Other jurisdictions have followed suit with California by concluding that the concept of unreasonably dangerous is related to the policy underlying strict product liability, and should serve to protect the manufacturer from being held liable as an insurer, while the concept of defective goes to the condition of the product, and is the element that must be proved by a plaintiff in asserting his cause of action.

Another conflict created by the language of §402A is that of "intended user" versus "intended use." This argument is ongoing and has become emotionally charged due to the fact that the "intended user" concept has, in many cases, been applied to prevent recovery under §402A to children who were seriously injured or killed by defective products. A majority of jurisdictions have held that a plaintiff who is not an intended user of the product may not recover under §402A for injuries caused by a defect in that product. Opponents of this view would state that such reasoning offends the rationale supporting the concepts of §402A. Specifically, they direct attention to the strict liability concept of focusing on the condition of the product, and not the conduct of any person associated with the product. They argue that regardless of any denomination as an intended user, a plaintiff should recover upon proof of product defect, coupled with proof that the injuries were caused by the defect in the product. They argue further that the concept of "intended user" creates an improper limitation on the universe of plaintiffs. Opponents insist that judicial determinations as to who was an intended user of a product are arbitrary, and can only be based upon some nebulous reference to evidence regarding the manufacturer's marketing strategy. These opponents suggest that before a defendant may avoid liability under §402A, they ought to assume the burden of proving that a plaintiff was not an intended user, and support that contention with evidence that establishes more than just the identity of the injured person.

Additional arguments have advanced the proposal of replacing in practice the concept of intended user with the concept of intended use. Proponents of this view hold that by changing over to a concept of intended use, focus once again is directed to the condition of the product and not on the conduct of any person. This they say is more in line with the concept of strict liability. Further, determinations as to whether or not any person was intended user of the product would have to be made with reference to the product, and not with reference to discretionary business decisions of the manufacturer.

References

1. *McPherson vs. Buick Motor Co.*, 217 N.Y. 382, 111 N.E. 1050, 1916.

2. *McPherson*, 217 N.Y. at 391, 111 N.E. at 1053.

3. James, *Product liability*, Tex. L. Rev. 34 (1955) 44.

4. Page Keeton, W. et al.; *Prosser and Keeton on the Law of Torts*, §96 at 683, 5th ed., 1984.

5. Uniform Commercial Code, §2-312–§2-315, 1999.

6. Uniform Commercial Code, §2-318, 1999.

7. *Escola v. Coca Cola Bottling Co.*, 150 P.2d 436, Ca. 1944.

8. *Escola v. Coca Cola Bottling Co.*, 150 P.2d at 438.

9. *Escola*, 150 P.2d at 440–41.

10. For a comprehensive compilation of the law of the states with respect to issues related to product liability, see Vargo, *The Emperor's New Clothes: The American Law Institute Adorns a "New Cloth"* for §402A *Product Liability Design Defects — A Survey of the States Reveals a Different Weave*, 26 U. Mem. L. Rev. 493, 1996.

11. *Greenman v. Yuba Power Product, Inc.*, 377 P.2d 897, Cal. 1962.

12. *Greenman v. Yuba Power Product, Inc.*, 377 P.2d at 901.

13. Plaintiffs may also assert a cause of action under theories of Crashworthiness and Malfunction; however, a discussion of these theories is beyond the scope of this article. For additional discussion on these theories See American Law Institute, *Restatement (Third) of Torts: Products Liability*, §3, §16, 1997.

14. American Law Institute, *Restatement (Third) of Torts: Products Liability*, §2(b).

15. *Lewis v. Coffing Hoist Div, Duff-Norton Co.*, 528 A.2d 590, 593, Pa. 1987.

16. See *Freund v. Cellofilm Properties, Inc.*, 87 N.J. 229, 243, 432 A.2d 925, 932, 1981. ("adequate warning is one that includes the directions, communications, and information essential to make the use of a product safe."); Compare with *Little v. P.P.G. Industries, Inc.*, 92 Wash 2d 118, 122, 594 P.2d 911, 914, 1979. ("The question is: Was the warning sufficient to catch the attention of persons who could be expected to use the product, to apprise them of its dangers and to advise them of the measures to take to avoid those dangers?"); *Cavers v. Cushman Motor Sales*, 95 Cal.App.3d 338, 342, 157 Cal.Rptr. 142, 144, 1979 (approving jury instruction: "An article otherwise appropriately made and maintained is defective if the manufacturer fails to adequately warn of dangerous propensities of such article which in the absence of an adequate warning renders the article substantially dangerous.").

17. Restatement (Second) of Torts, §402A, Cmt. g.

18. Restatement (Second) of Torts, §402A, Cmt. (I)

19. See Prosser, *Strict Liability to the Consumer in California*, 18 Hastings L.J. 9, 1966.

20. *Cronin v. J.B.E. Olson Corp.*, 501 P.2d 1153, 1162, Ca. 1972.

Forensic Medicine and Medical Negligence — Initial Case Investigation Applications

11

SUZANNE EDGETT COLLINS

Medical Negligence Litigation

Medical Errors and Adverse Events: A Fertile Field

"Errors are failures of planned actions to be completed as intended, or the use of the wrong plans to achieve what is intended. Adverse events are injuries caused by medical interventions, as opposed to the health care condition of the patient" (Institute of Medicine (IOM), 2004, p. 25). When the adverse event is caused by an error, it is referred to as a preventable adverse event (IOM, 2004). As defined by Leape, a heath care error is a nonintentional but preventable injury caused by health care treatment (Buerhaus, 1999).

In the context of medical and nursing care, human error has serious consequences. The well-publicized IOM study found that errors result in death for almost 100,000 Americans per year (IOM, 1999; Leape, 1994). Startling recent data reported by Reuters (2004), citing a study in Colorado from HealthGrades, Inc., indicate that many more, as many as 195,000 people a year, could be dying from easily prevented medical errors. The Agency for Health Care Policy Research (AHCPR), now known as Agency for Health Care Research and Quality (AHRQ), reports that errors causing injury in health care settings occur to as many as 1 out of 25 patients (AHCPR, 1998). The results of the Harvard Medical Malpractice Study suggest that, of approximately one million injuries caused by health care treatment every year, roughly two thirds are due to error (Leape, 1994). Although the Harvard study attempted to ascertain the incidence of error from a review of medical records only, more recent ethnographic studies of actual events of error in health care provision show that error incidence is much higher (Andrews et al., 1997). Investigative reporter, Michael Berens of the Chicago Tribune, analyzed three million state and federal computer records to create a data base that attempts to evaluate the "... hidden role registered nurses play in medical errors ..." and found that nursing mistakes kill, injure thousands..." (Berens, 2000). The premise of the Institute of Medicine's recent study, *Keeping Patients Safe, Transforming the Work Environment of Nurses* is that nursing is centrally and inseparably linked to patient safety (IOM, 2004), a link until recently, largely ignored in scientific research and litigation.

It is in this complex milieu of preventable adverse events that medical negligence cases arise and are defended. The publicity of the failings of medical and nursing care may be one reason for the increase in medical malpractice litigation over the years. The Insurance Information Institute (2004), citing a study by Aon Risk Services showing that medical malpractice claim costs have increased at a steady 9.7% since 2000, reports that the cost and frequency of claims continue to rise. In addition, it was reported that the number of claims is increasing at 3% a year with claim severity, increasing 6.5% per year. Hospital liability claim costs for 2004 are reported to be almost $150,000 per claim, compared with $79,000 per claim in 1996; claim costs against a physician is reported to be $178,000, compared with $120,000 in 1996 (Insurance Information Institute, 2004).

Medical Negligence Litigation and Forensic Medicine: A Necessary Alliance

Successful medical negligence litigation from both plaintiff and defense perspectives requires a congruent alliance with forensic medicine, especially in the investigation of potential and actual cases. The forensic exploration of the issues in the case begins with case intake investigation and necessarily continues throughout the duration of the case. Cawthon (2004) explores the phenomenon of the intertwining of law and medicine in the litigation of medical negligence cases in her book *Medicine on Trial*, and stresses the importance of forensic medical experts in making the ultimate resolutions. Zimmerly defines clinical forensic medicine as "...the collection and presentation of medical evidence for use in the civil and criminal law arena..." (Zimmerly, 1993, pp. 22–4). Wecht (2004) comments upon the necessity of forensic medical testimony for the integrity of the adversarial process, in that forensic medical evidence presented in the adversarial process supports the determination of truth. Clinical forensic medical experts are essential for the understanding of the complex medical issues in a medical negligence case that will lead to successful prosecution or defense.

The following discussion is a general introduction to medical negligence law and application of select issues in this practitioner's case investigation experience and is intended to introduce the new medical negligence investigator to the process of initial case evaluation. The medical–legal literature is full of treatises on the subject of medical negligence litigation. Complex case law across a multitude of jurisdictions is developing daily. A caution — the law of each jurisdiction regarding the substantive and procedural issues involved in medical negligence litigation varies significantly. Anecdotal examples in this application are composites of cases in this practitioner's experience, do not identify any specific parties in any specific case, and may only represent the state of the law at the time and place.

This application is dedicated to the memory of John R. Feegel, M.D., J.D., M.P.H. Dr. Feegel was one of the finest medical–legal practitioners in the medical negligence arena, a forensic pathologist–lawyer and, undeniably, a craftsman at forging beneficial alliances between forensic science and medical negligence litigation. Throughout his professional life of almost 40 years in the dual professions of law and forensic medicine (pathology), he was an avid proponent of the essential collaboration of forensics and law in the administration of both civil and criminal justice. Insights into his strategies for the initial and ongoing investigation of medical negligence cases are preserved here for the benefit of other investigators and legal practitioners.

The Social and Legal Context of Medical Malpractice

For the purposes of this discussion, medical malpractice will include all health-care professional (hereinafter HCP) malpractice. Medical malpractice in a global rather than strictly legal sense is professional health care provider misconduct that is manifest by an unreasonable lack of skill in fulfilling professional duties or an unreasonable lack of faithfulness in fulfilling fiduciary duties.

In this conceptual sense, medical malpractice may be described as unprofessional conduct as demonstrated in the four interrelated domains of the legal regulation of health care provider practice (see Figure 11.1):

1. Professional misconduct which is a violation of social policy, codes of ethics, or professional standards and is established by competencies and certifications by professional credentialing bodies with the result of quality assurance

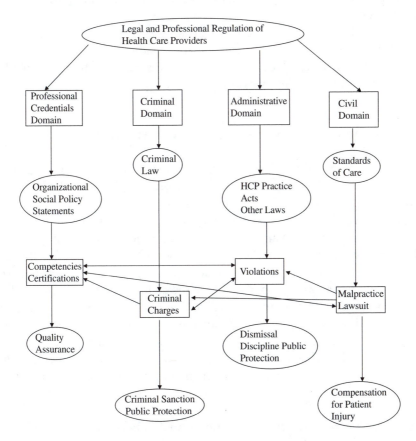

Figure 11.1 Concept map of legal and professional regulation of the health care professions. © Suzanne Edgett Collins.

2. Criminal misconduct which is a violation of criminal codes as demonstrated by criminal charges and which results in criminal sanction of the HCP and public protection
3. Administrative misconduct which is a violation of HCP professional practice acts as demonstrated by administrative complaint for rules violation and which results in licensure discipline and public protection
4. Professional negligence as demonstrated by the breach of professional duty through violation of the standards of care causing harm which results in a medical malpractice lawsuit and the award of money damages to compensate the patient for injury

Multiple and sometimes interrelated causes of action exist within these four domains, so that an action taken in one domain may result in collateral actions occurring in other domains. This may occur in medical malpractice litigation as follows: In some jurisdictions, the presuit investigation process or the filing of a complaint arising in medical negligence may result in required notification of the agency that regulates the individual or institutional provider or organization that certifies the provider's competency, thus precipitating the initiation of a licensure disciplinary investigation or professional certification body investigation. In cases of gross negligence with significant harm, or intentional tort such as battery, criminal charges may be filed, again with concurrent or subsequent licensure investigation, in addition to a civil action for damages and professional certification body investigation.

The investigation or litigation of any of these events is heavily dependent upon the discovery and reasonable interpretation of the medical facts. In any of the four domains, the forensic medical expert provides structure and direction in identifying, building, and sustaining the theory of the case.

Medical Negligence as a Subset of Medical Malpractice

There are many legal theories under which an HCP could be sued for medical malpractice. Many medical malpractice cases arise in professional negligence related to the action or inaction of an individual HCP. For the purposes of the following discussion of case investigation, individual HCP professional negligence will be the focus.

Different jurisdictions will vary as to what specific individual and institutional health care providers, and potential legal theories or causes of action fall under the auspices of the jurisdiction's medical negligence law. In addition, the laws of the various jurisdictions may determine who may be a proper party for the claim of damages as a result of health care provider negligence. Immunity or limited liability may apply to certain emergency situations, professions, or institutions under the law of the jurisdiction. Federal courts may borrow the States' substantive medical negligence law when a specific law does not exist, such as in claims that may be brought against the United States for the alleged negligent care of a veteran or a military dependant. The four elements required in an HCP professional negligence case are as follows:

1. The health care provider owes a professional duty of care to a patient
2. There is a breach of this duty
3. As a direct or proximate result of the breach of this duty an injury occurs
4. The injury may be compensated under the laws of the jurisdiction

All of these elements must be proven by a preponderance of the evidence. This equates to medical probability, more than mere possibility, but not absolute certainty. Medical negligence cases are subject to time limitations and must commence within those time limitations.

Brief Overview: Elements of and Defenses to Medical Negligence

Duty is created by the existence of the professional relationship of the HCP to the patient, and it requires that the HCP act in accordance with the reasonable and prudent expectations of that class of HCPs in similar circumstances.

These expectations are the *standards of care.* Existence of the duty relationship and its corresponding standards of care may be established in multiple cumulative or even confounding ways. The relationship and duties may exist by law such as a professional practice act, or through the laws regulating certain health care providing facilities such as hospitals, or laws regulating safety aspects of practice. They may exist by virtue of the norms of the profession as practiced by reasonable and prudent members of that pro-fession and the standards of practice published by professional or certifying organizations. They may be influenced by institutional policies and procedures and even by third party payer requirements. The medical forensic expert can help the investigator or the legal practitioner to identify and understand the implications of the input of the multiple facets of the standards of care on a particular case and help reduce them to language and applications understandable by the nonexpert *trier of fact*, either the jury or the judge in a nonjury trial.

It may be shown that an HCP failed in this duty by *commission* if the HCP did some-thing that the reasonable and prudent HCP in a similar situation would not have done, or by *omission* if the HCP failed to do something that the reasonable and prudent HCP in a similar situation would have done. The standard of care expected by a reasonable and prudent HCP may be established by the medical forensic experts for all parties to the litigation, but ultimately, it is the trier of fact who will determine the standard of care and whether the HCP upheld or violated the professional duty to adhere to the standard of care.

Breach of duty first requires that a duty to follow a certain standard of care existed. Breach of duty is when the HCP did not act in accordance with the professional duty relationship to adhere to the standard of care. Breach of duty, or adherence to duty, may be established by forensic clinical medical experts for all parties to the litigation.

Res ipsa loquitur, the thing speaks for itself, is invoked in some jurisdictions if the injury was caused by an instrumentality in the sole control of the HCP, that the patient did not voluntarily contribute to the injury, and that the injury is one that ordinarily does not occur in the absence of negligent health care provision. Jurisdictional variation exists as to whether the doctrine of *res ipsa loquitur* would be allowable to negate the need for expert testimony as to the breach of duty of an HCP. In the context of medical malpractice litigation, an example where *res ipsa loquitur* may apply is in the case of a surgical instrument that was unintentionally left within a patient in the course of an operation, and which would not have been left inside the patient but for the negligence of the HCPs involved in the operation.

Causation requires that a reasonably close causal connection must exist between the breach of the duty and the injury sustained and that as a direct or proximate result of the breach of duty an injury occurs. Simply put, causation in professional medical negligence addresses the process whereby conduct A led to result B. Legal causation involves two issues: (1) cause in fact and (2) foreseeability. Cause in fact is when injury would not have occurred but for the negligent act of the HCP. Foreseeability is that the injury must be such that would be foreseen by a reasonable and prudent HCP as a likely result of substandard care.

Causation may be the most difficult element of the medical negligence case to prove, or conversely, the easiest to defend. Establishing or defeating causation is a complex matter. Investigators and legal practitioners are well served to engage help from the forensic medical expert from the very beginning at the time of case intake and development. In a medical negligence case, this causal link between the breach of professional duty and the injury giving rise to damages must be established by a physician in most cases.

Damages relate to the harm that the patient has suffered as a result of the HCP's breach of duty. Damages are ultimately quantified by the trier of fact and encompass compensation to the injured patient for physical, mental, and financial injuries.

General damages are those that are noneconomic in nature and apply to the parties entitled under the law of the jurisdiction to compensation for pain and suffering, grief, mental anguish, and other emotional components generally attributed to the physical injury caused by the breach of duty of the HCP.

Special damages are economic in nature. They encompass the costs that flow from the injury caused by the breach of duty of the HCP, such as:

- Past and future medical expenses
- Past and future loss of income
- Past and future cost of services that the injured patient is no longer able to provide for himself
- Funeral expenses in the event of a death due to medical negligence

Punitive damages, in the event of extreme circumstances often defined by the law of the jurisdiction, may also be available. A claim of punitive damages may require judicial proceedings to establish the applicability to the particular medical negligence case.

Statutes of limitation and repose are the time limits in which a claim for medical negligence must be initiated. They refer to the time in which a plaintiff may bring a claim dependant on a variety factors. Wide jurisdictional variation exists for the time limits and procedures for noticing potential defendants of a potential claim, responding to the notice, filing, and service of legal claims. The actual event may be the start date for the running of the statutes of limitation, or sometimes the plaintiff's knowledge of the event. What constitutes the plaintiff's knowledge, and the burden on the plaintiff to be knowledgeable of the contents of his medical records are the subject of jurisdictional statutory and case law. *Statutes of repose* place a definite end to the time a plaintiff has in which to initiate a legal action for medical negligence, regardless of the plaintiff's knowledge of the event.

Cases arising in medical negligence resulting in death may have different limitation periods. The date of death may be the triggering event for the wrongful death part of the claim. Statutes of limitation and repose may be tolled in a variety of ways such as through the incompetence of the plaintiff, the age of the plaintiff, fraud or intentional concealment by the HCP as to the etiology or nature of the plaintiff's injury, continuing treatment by the HCP, through agreement of the parties, through statutory mechanisms, and are jurisdiction dependent.

Defenses to a medical negligence claim may be established to defeat the claim. If any one of the elements of medical negligence (duty, breach, causation, damages) is not established by a preponderance of the evidence by the plaintiff, the claim will be defeated.

The establishment by the defendant HCP that no duty existed will defeat the claim. For instance, two nurses named Susan Collins work in the same busy, one-day surgery center. Susan A. Collins was thought to be the nurse who administered a medication in error to a patient. Susan B. Collins was actually the nurse who administered the medication. Susan A. Collins was not even working on the day of the error and had no duty to the patient.

The establishment by the HCP that he or she complied with the standard of care will defeat the claim. For example, a pregnant patient is nearing the end of her term in an uncomplicated first pregnancy. She has been monitored and physically examined weekly by the nurse midwife. Her vital signs, weight gain, physical signs, and laboratory values are all in the normal range. The fetus has demonstrated apparent normal growth and placental development to ultrasound, and nonstress fetal heart monitoring shows a normal rate and variability. The patient presents to the labor and delivery suite complaining of loss of fetal movement three days after her last examination, and the ultrasound tests reveal fetal demise and upon induced labor it is determined that there is a true knot in the umbilical cord which cut off the blood supply to the baby. The jury determines on the basis of the forensic expert obstetrical testimony that the nurse midwife adhered to the standard of care.

The establishment by the HCP that the injury that the patient sustained was not legally caused by the HCP's breach of his or her duty will defeat the claim. A physician sees a female patient for the first time on October 1, 2002 for complaint of a palpable mass of the abdomen. A physical examination and radiology studies are performed with the resultant diagnosis of a benign uterine tumor on October 10, 2002. On October 25, 2002, the patient is admitted to the emergency department with abdominal pain. Additional studies are performed which reveal a very large and advanced ovarian cancer with multiple sites of metastatic spread, rather than the benign uterine tumor as diagnosed two weeks earlier. The patient dies of cancer several weeks later. The forensic expert oncologist testifies at trial on behalf of the examining physician, who contributed to the delay in diagnosis, that the misdiagnosis or the delay in the diagnosis had no significant effect on the treatment or outcome for the patient, and that her cancer was so far advanced at the time of the misdiagnosis that she was already essentially in a terminal condition. The jury finds no causal link between the misdiagnosis and the death of the patient.

A lack of damages attributable to the negligence will also defeat the claim. For instance, a patient who is allergic to aspirin visits a walk-in medical center complaining of back pain after moving a refrigerator. The patient tells the doctor he is allergic to aspirin (duty of patient–doctor relationship — established by forensic medical experts — the patient presents for treatment, the doctor accepts the patient and undertakes to treat him). Despite the known allergy, the doctor prescribes an injection for pain as a medication that has properties similar to aspirin (breach of duty — established by forensic medical experts — to prescribe medication to which the patient may be crossallergic to aspirin). Nothing happens to the patient (no causation of damages). The claim is defeated.

Other defenses to claims may be established to defeat the claim or apportion damages on the basis of the percentage of fault that parties may have. Three common affirmative defenses are as follows:

1. *Assumption of risk by the patient* wherein the patient knows that inherent risks accompany certain medical procedures but makes an informed choice to undergo the procedure. For example, this may be asserted in cases of complications following novel or experimental therapy to which the patient has given his informed consent.
2. *Comparative negligence of the patient* wherein the damages owned by the negligent HCP to the patient are reduced by the proportion of the patient's own negligence. Such might be the asserted defense when patients deliberately do not follow medical advice.
3. *Concurrent or intervening negligence of others* wherein a third party causes or contributes to the damages. For instance, the patient sues a physician for improperly casting his leg so that it does not heal properly but the patient was a victim of a car accident subsequent to casting in which his leg was re-injured.

The Critical Analysis of Potential Medical Negligence Cases

Initial Case Investigation

Case investigation is one key to successful litigation. Investigation from an open mindset is essential. Each medical negligence case presented to the investigator and legal practitioner, whether from the plaintiff's or the defendant's perspective, will be accompanied by a story. In the forensic medical investigation of the claim for medical negligence, it is imprudent to proceed in the investigation from the vantage of the accompanying story as being the truth. Proceeding from the story as truth closes the investigator's mind to potentially important information that does not or may not support the story. Dr. Feegel described this as his use of the "null hypothesis."

In scientific research, one starts with the premise that a hypothesis may not be proved and that it may only be disproved. The null hypothesis should be employed in the investigation of the facts, the application of the standards of care to the facts, and the scientific probability of the establishment of causation as supported or defeated by the forensic medical experts. Thus, if the story that comes with the case cannot be disproved, it might then be true. This critical reflective analysis should continue throughout the litigation of the case. This stimulates ongoing investigation and thus alerts the legal practitioner of the weaknesses and strengths of the case. Adversarial litigation provides frequent opportunity to attempt to disprove the story or case theory. In consciously doing so, the more likely it is that the most reasonable and scientifically sound explanation can be determined. This critical reflective analysis is visually aided through specific methods of the organization of the vast amounts of medical information that accompany medical negligence litigation. A thorough understanding of the forensic strengths and weakness of a medical negligence case begins with a thorough understanding of the medical information.

Information Organization Is Essential

Medical Records and Other Significant Information

Medical negligence cases are very costly to pursue and defend. The initial investigation of the case is often a balance between the costs of the investigation of possibly meritorious cases and reasonable appraisal of the potential for success for either plaintiff or defense. Investigation should start with gathering of the necessary medical records. The determination of what constitutes necessary medical records is dependent upon the nature of the case and the story that comes with it. For instance, the extent of records necessary to initially evaluate a failure to admit a 54-year-old male who presents to the emergency department (ED) with radiating chest pain, and who dies at home the same day of a myocardial infarction several hours after being released from the ED will be different from the extent of the records necessary to evaluate a case of a delayed diagnosis of breast cancer on the basis of negative findings on a several year series of mammograms and physical examinations by multiple HCPs. The medical forensic expert may help determine which are the essential records to obtain to promote efficacious initial review. Medical investigators and legal practitioners should evaluate whether a forensic medical consultant will need a business associate agreement in compliance with regulations protecting health information under the Health Insurance Portability and Accountability Act (HIPAA).

In the myocardial infarction case, minimal essential records for the preliminary evaluation of causation and negligence would be the complete ED records, the Medical Examiner's or Coroner's investigation file, autopsy report, and death certificate. Damage information should be obtained as to survivors and social factors related to the decedent such as occupation, employment, spouse, dependants, health history, and expenses. Information should be obtained regarding the potential defendants such as profession, degree, and board certifications. Classification of institutional providers (such as a public facility that holds immunity or statutory entitlement to limited liability; facility status such as primary, secondary, or tertiary care) should be obtained. This information is essential to the initial evaluation of the matter and may impact on whether to go forward on behalf of the plaintiff, or to strenuously defend or recommend settlement on behalf of the defendant.

These records will allow an educated estimation of the timeliness of the claim as to the applicable limitations periods; the existence or absence of the necessary elements of a negligence case: duty, breach, causation, damages; the existence or absence of proper parties to the case under the law of the jurisdiction; and the existence or absence of restraints of immunity or limited liability. The potential for the existence of other legal defenses such as comparative negligence of the patient (for instance, the records revealed that the patient left the ED against medical advice); or the existence of concurrent or intervening negligence of other HCPs (the ED physician wrote orders to admit the patient, but the patient's primary care physician determined that the patient did not need to be admitted and discharged the patient) may also be demonstrated.

In the delayed diagnosis of a breast cancer case, more medical extensive records would be required for the initial evaluation, in addition to the earlier damages described, to provide information records. One of the key issues in this case centers on causation and timeliness of the missed opportunities for treatment. Was the event of the probable opportunity for the cancer to have been discovered and treated within the period of the statutes of limitation or repose? In this series of physical examinations and mammography, when was the time that intervention, more likely than not, would have made a legally significant difference in the outcome for the patient? For instance, if the opportunity to discover the cancer occurred within the period of limitations when the cancer was small and amenable to treatment to a legally significant standard of better prognosis, the case may meet the legal requirements. If the only opportunity for the diagnosis occurred when the cancer was large and metastasized to other body structures, then the delayed diagnosis may have made no difference in the ultimate outcome. These are amazingly complex causation questions that require the expertise of forensic medical experts such as oncologists, radiologists, and practitioners who perform breast examination.

The records required for this evaluation would include all the treatment records and mammography films of the patient from all of the HCPs who participated in some way in the medical evaluation of the patient's breast. Conceivably this could span years. In addition, the records of the clinical investigation and treatment after the diagnosis was made will provide valuable forensic medical information as to the prognostic characteristics of the particular cancer that affects the patient. For instance, the aggressive nature of the cancer is a factor that can be evaluated by the forensic oncology and pathology experts as demonstrated by an assortment of tests and tissue studies.

Organizing the Information

Damages and information should be compiled for use in on-going evaluation of case strategy and disposition. Once the medical records have been obtained, the sequence of pertinent events must be discerned from the records to be of any practical value. This requires, at the very least, an individual who is familiar with medical terminology, medical record organization, and the cryptic encoding of medical practitioners. Registered nurses who are legal nurse consultants can function as forensic experts as they are skilled and can provide very cost effective services for this time-intensive process.

There are many different methods of organizing medical information. Some investigators and legal practitioners prefer exact translations of the medical records. Some use an assortment of templates or forms to discern pertinent information. Some scan medical information into computers for high tech manipulation of the medical information as data. The methods of organization of the information in initial investigations should reflect the time sequence of the story that comes with the case. If the critical event is acute and discreet, such as the myocardial infarction case mentioned earlier, a method of organizing the information should be used that allows for minute-by-minute evaluation, and yet is expandable for the addition of new information. If the critical event is not acute and discrete, such as in the delayed diagnosis of breast cancer case discussed earlier, a method of organizing the significant information is necessary so as to not muddle the analysis by an excess of insignificant details.

A caution, the records received for investigation should be treated as originals and protected as such! At this preliminary stage in case analysis, it is difficult to know how many iterations of copies of records exist and whether additional information may have been added to the original records after the first sets of copies were made. As an example, in a case in which a man being treated for hypertension was found dead at home, the widow obtained copies of her deceased husband's medical records from the primary care practitioner (PCP) who had been treating the decedent for hypertension.

This was accomplished in order to dispute a denial of life insurance benefits on the basis of pre-existent conditions that were not included on the application for life insurance. These early copies of the decedent's medical records were significantly different from the copies of medical records that were much later produced in response to discovery requests in the medical negligence lawsuit against the PCP. Records should not be highlighted or marked in any way, and the storage file should indicate the date of the receipt, from whom received, in response to what, and by what route. Comparison readings with the original records if possible and practical may sometimes reveal surprises!

In the myocardial infarction case, we need to organize information, which allows the investigator and the forensic medical expert consultants to see the sequence of events in multiple parameters. The investigator and forensic consultant have to be able to visualize through the organization of the records as to what was happening at the time the care was rendered. This helps to diminish the bias of retrospective evaluation when the information is organized in such a similar way to information that the actual care provider was evaluating at the time the care was actually provided.

One method of doing this is to plot the information on an *XY* axis wherein the *X* axis is the time, and multiple levels on the *Y* axis are the record events. This is a versatile "living" method because it is expandable over the course of the litigation to add new information obtained through discovery. It can be done by hand or can be entered into a computer program that is capable of generating charts and graphs that are expandable, such as an Excel spreadsheet. This method is also very helpful for organizing information for mediation presentation or trial preparation. Any number of content areas and times can be added so that multiple parameters can be visually/spatially oriented and evaluated. Other important information can be added to continually evaluate the strengths and weakness of a case as discovery progresses. Excerpts from depositions, policies, procedures, published standards of care, copies of EKG tracings, autopsy findings, cause of death are just a few examples. The actions of a specific individual can also be color coded so that the different threads of a case become very apparent. The exact location from where the information was retrieved can be added for enhanced credibility and easy referral. In one case in which this method was utilized very effectively, the counsel for one of the defendants remarked, "It's not easy being green!" (see Figure 11.2).

In the delayed diagnosis of the breast cancer case, we need to organize information so that the investigator and forensic consultants may be able to identify the time in the sequence of physical examinations and mammography, that appropriate intervention, more likely than not, would have made a legally significant difference in the outcome for the patient, and whether that time was within the statutes of limitation or repose, and if any circumstances that might lead to the tolling of the statute can be identified. In this method of organizing the medical information, a chart format is used. The rows represent the dates of the events, and the columns represent the events and findings of significance to the time/causation question.

The exemplar illustrated in Figure 11.3 does not include the specific details, but in real use, the chart would contain the quotations of the specific findings along with copies of the pertinent documents, ultrasound and mammography films, and pathology slides/block for the experts to come to their own independent conclusions. Originals are the best, but not always obtainable depending upon jurisdictional discovery rules and the record custodian's storage, destruction, retrieval protocols. A good feature of this method is that it is applicable for multiple forensic medical experts. The oncologist expert and

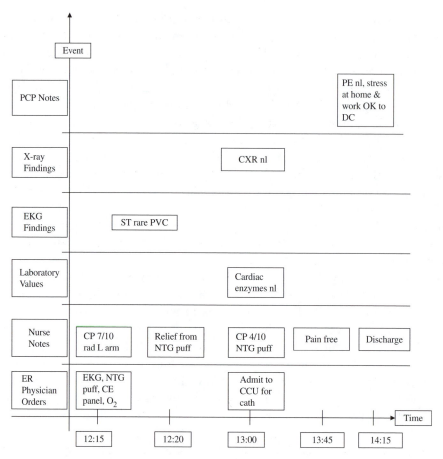

Figure 11.2 Example of medical information organization in an acute discreet event. © Suzanne Edgett Collins

radiologist expert will be better able to answer the time and causation questions with this type of format.

The foregoing are just two examples of the importance of the organization of the medical information to the critical discernment of the strongest theory of the case. Many other methods of information organization may be applicable to the kind of case or specific question to be answered. The most user-friendly organization methods are those that can be expanded as the information about the case grows. These summaries of information, while clearly not evidential, become important persuasive tools in the presentation of evidence as the case progresses through discovery, mediation or arbitration, pretrial proceedings, and trial.

A Changing Landscape: Reform Initiatives Focused on Medical Malpractice

Increasing costs and decreasing availability of medical malpractice insurance is causing a great deal of concern and has been the focus of on-going intense legislative efforts to

Date	Patient Complaint	HCP	Physical Exam Findings	Radiology Findings	Pathology Findings
4-27-96	Annual gyn exam	Jones	Age, weight, HX, PE, normal BE		
5-16-97	Annual gyn exam	Smith	Age, weight, HX, PE, normal BE		
5-3-98	Annual gyn exam	Smith	Age, weight, HX, PE, normal BE		
4-15-99	Annual gyn exam	Jones	Age, weight, HX, PE, abnormal L BE		
5-2-99		Johnson		Ultrasound report Mammography report	
6-1-99		Wilson			Biopsy L breast specimen gross, micro
5-15-00	Annual gyn exam	Smith	Age, weight, HX, PE, normal BE		
3-28-01	Tender L breast and L axilla	Jones	Age, weight, HX, PE, abnormal L BE		
4-30-01		Johnson		Ultrasound report Mammography	

Figure 11.3 Example of medical information organization in delayed diagnosis. © Suzanne Edgett Collins

deal with the problem in many of the States. Medical errors do in fact occur and the stigma associated with such errors may drive reporting of these errors underground. The legal system is a rather ineffective means of providing compensation, fostering great costs with relatively small returns, and few injured patients are actually fully compensated through a medical malpractice lawsuit. This results in cost shifting to both public and private insurance, Medicare, Medicaid, and to compensation programs such as sick leave, disability, and other programs.

The Council of State Governments (2003) identifies three prongs of the medical malpractice insurance crisis: (1) There are in fact medial care providers whose conduct results in medical negligence claims; (2) legal resolution of these claims involves a great deal of time, effort and money; and (3) the medical malpractice insurance industry is influenced by economic forces outside those of the physician's claims experience.

The Council of State Governments (2003) recognizes that response of industry and legislators to the crisis in the past has been what the Council has termed "first generation reforms." These reforms have consisted of insurance reforms such as the implementation of joint underwriting associations and patient compensation funds. Neither of these proved to survive the market forces. Other tort reforms attempted to diminish claim frequency and claim severity. More reform measures sought to restrict the ease of plaintiff victory through various statutory schemes such as limitation of attorney contingency fees, damage caps, utilization of periodic payment of settlement awards, abolition of joint and several liability, alterations to collateral source rules, restrictions of expert testimony, and prelitigation merit review. Challenges to the constitutionality of these measures continue. Jury awards seem to bear little correlation to the actual severity of the injury.

The Council of State Governments (2003) advocates a comprehensive approach to multisystem reform in three domains:

1. *Medical system reform*: Strengthening state licensing boards, promoting risk management programs, and advancing patient education and health literacy programs are all ways to address the occurrence of medical incidents that lead to medical malpractice suits.
2. *Alternative legal reforms*: A number of reform proposals seek to address the economic inefficiencies of the court system. Enterprise liability, summary trials and medical courts are aimed at improving efficiency in the legal system, while medical disciplinary tribunals and alternative dispute resolution seek to avoid the legal system.
3. *Insurance industry reforms*: Options for insurance reform include relatively simple actions such as rate regulation to nontraditional insurance schemes such as experience rating, no fault and patient-purchased medical malpractice protection.

Multiple reform measures have been entertained by the legislatures of the various States over the past year. What is clear is that the initiation of a medical negligence lawsuit and its defense will face increased scrutiny, and legal practitioners may face sanctions for unreasonable investigations. This will necessitate an even more careful initial case investigation, inclusive of forensic medical expertise to establish the validity of those claims brought forth, thus emphasizing the necessity for a congruent alliance with forensic medicine in the investigation and litigation of medical negligence cases.

References

Agency for Health Care Policy and Research (1998). *Research in Action: Reducing Errors in Health Care*. AHCPR Pub. No. 98-P018, September 21, 1998.

Andrews, L., Stocking, C., Krizek, T., Gottlieb, L., Krizek, C., Vargish, T., and Siegler, M. (1997). An alternative strategy for studying adverse events in medical care. *The Lancet*, 349, 309–313.

Berens, M.J. (2000). Nursing mistakes kill, injure thousands. *Chicago Tribune*, http://www.chicagotribune.com/news/nationworld/article/0,2669,2-46844,FF.html. Retrieved 9-22-00. Now available through *Chicago Tribune Archives* http://pqasb.pqarchiver.com/chicagotribune/.

Beurhaus, P.I. (1999). Lucian Leape on the causes and prevention of errors and adverse events in health care. *Image: J. Nurs. Scholarship*, 31(3), 281–286.

Cawthon, E.A. (2004). *Medicine on Trial*. ABC-CLIO, Inc., Santa Barbara, CA.

Council of State Governments (2003). *Trends Alert: Critical Information for State Decision Makers. Medical Malpractice Crisis*. http://www.csg.org/NR/rdonlyres/ek7ao3dfatxrcgh 656amm6vnlw2owndpku4rp3xhss32rzeche5ggb4j4mbwdozh4zsobfboqxysz3bnp5corc6rrae/ Medical+Malpractice+%28May+Revised%29.pdf. Retrieved 8-30-04.

Institute of Medicine (2004). *Keeping Patients Safe: Transforming the Work Environment of Nurses*. National Academy Press, Washington, D.C.

Institute of Medicine (1999). Committee on Quality of Health Care in America. *To Err is Human: Building a Better Health System*. (Kohn, L.T., Corrigan, J.M., and Donaldson, M.S., Eds.) National Academy Press, Washington, D.C.

Insurance Information Institute (2004). Medical Malpractice. http://www.iii.org/media/ hottopics/insurance/medicalmal/Retrieved 7-11-04.

Leape, L.L. (1994). The preventability of medical injury. In Bogner, M.S. (Ed.). *Human Error in Medicine*. (pp. 13–26) Lawrence Erlbaum Associates, Hillsdale, NJ.

Reuters. (2004). Report says 195,000 deaths due to hospital error. http://news.yahoo.com/ news?tmpl=story&u=/nm/20040727/hl_nm/health_mistakes_dc_1. Retrieved 7-29-04. (The original study may be accessed at http://www.healthgrades.com/media/english/ pdf/HG_Patient_Safety_Study_Final.pdf).

Wecht, C.H. (2004). Utilization of forensic science in the civil and criminal justice systems: Forensic use of medical information. In Sanbar, S. (Ed.). *American College of Legal Medicine. Legal Medicine*, 6th ed. Mosby (an affiliate of Elsevier), Philadelphia, PA.

Zimmerly, J.G. (1993). Clinical forensic medicine. In Wecht, C.H. (Ed.). *Forensic Sciences: Law/ Science Civil/Criminal*. Matthew Bender, New York, NY.

Construction Law

12

RICHARD F. PACIARONI and KEVIN J. STUBBLEBINE[1]

Introduction

It is a beautiful spring morning in Paris, the date is Sunday, May 23, 2004. Passengers are beginning to move through the new $900 million Terminal 2E at the Charles de Gaulle International Airport. The terminal has been open only 11 months. It is considered a jewel of French architecture and the "pride of the airport." As a few early morning travelers pass through the terminal, they hear a loud noise — looking up, they observe cracks in the ceiling and dust falling down. Minutes later a 150-foot-long section of the curved roof collapses, killing four people and injuring three. Terminal 2E is immediately closed, and will remain closed for an indefinite period of time. Its closure will severely disrupt international airline operations and divert 20,000 to 25,000 passengers per day to other terminals. Shares of stock in the two French construction companies responsible for the construction of the terminal drop 3% on the following Monday. French President Jacques Chirac calls for a swift investigation into the collapse. The spectre of having to raze the entire terminal looms large.

Who will investigate this construction disaster? What techniques will be employed? How will the investigation proceed? Was the collapse caused by a design flaw or a construction defect? Who is to blame? Who will pay damages to the dead and injured victims and compensate the airport for the property damage? The answers to these and other pressing questions surrounding this disaster and many others like it over the past century fall, in whole or in part, within the province of the "forensic engineer." It is on his or her shoulders that rests the responsibility of determining what went wrong, why it went wrong, and who the responsible party is.

The forensic engineer is now, more than ever, a key part of a legal team that is tasked by our judicial system to assist the finder of fact in assigning blame for these construction disasters. What then is a forensic engineer in the context of construction disasters? In simple terms, he or she is an engineer who seeks answers as to why structures fail.

There is no shortage of work for the modern construction forensic engineer; in fact, the list of infamous construction related disasters goes back a long way. Even in recent times, names such as the Kansas City Hyatt Regency Hotel skywalk collapse, the

L'Ambiance Plaza collapse, the Hartford Civic Center collapse, the Willow Island Cooling Tower collapse, and the famous "Galloping Gertie" (a/k/a the Tacoma Narrows Bridge) collapse all constitute construction disasters, which required the services of forensic engineers to sort out the cause of the failure and apportion blame.

The Legal Need for Forensic Engineers

Today, an entire industry exists whose sole purpose is to assist owners, engineers, architects, contractors, and lawyers in discovering why things that ought not to fall down do fall down. They work with instruments, experiments, photographs, videotape, 3D graphics, finite element analysis, and computer animation. They testify as expert witnesses in court for one side or the other in all types of construction disputes. As Lisa Shusto of Exponent, a leading failure analysis consulting firm, puts it, "Failure analysis is the Sherlock Holmes work of engineering — figuring out what went wrong is exciting and fascinating."

In simple terms, the legal system needs forensic engineers to communicate knowledge from one sphere of activity (engineering) to another (the law). This is a relatively new and emerging discipline for engineers. There is no television series showing the forensic engineer at work (unlike the hoards of programs depicting the practice of forensic medicine), and, in fact, the term "forensic engineer" cannot yet be found in the dictionary. The forensic engineer's role in the legal system is to analyze the failure or problem in such a manner so as to permit objective, impartial conclusions to be reached. At bottom, forensic engineering is a science concerned with the relation between engineering and the law.

Why do we care about that relationship in the context of construction failures? Simply put, the law requires proof of "causation," which refers to the relationship between an act and its consequences. With respect to proof of negligence, the forensic engineer can be expected to be called as an expert witness to establish the applicable standard of care in the industry (say, structural design, for instance) and whether that standard was met in the particular case under review. With respect to breach of contract actions, the forensic engineer can expect to be called upon to give expert testimony on whether the plans and specifications for a particular construction project complied with good industry practice and all applicable building and safety codes.

In other words, to demonstrate liability, a lawyer must show that the negligent act or breach of contract by the architect, engineer, contractor, or owner was the legal cause of an injury, whether physical or monetary. Without proof of a causal link between the act or breach and the injury, there is no entitlement to damages. Accordingly, it is the ability of the forensic engineer to link an action or failure to act to the cause of a construction disaster that forms the cornerstone of proof in a lawyer's case.

The Role of the Forensic Engineer

The Big Picture

If linking an act or failure to act to the cause of a construction disaster is the cornerstone of a lawyer's case, *what does it take to find that link*? A competent engineer, even one with impressive education, training, and experience, is not enough. It takes a sleuth, a scientist, a translator, a teacher, a storyteller, a diplomat, and a businessperson to make a great forensic engineer. Indeed, a forensic engineer must be able to play each of these roles if he or she expects to be able to "find the link" and provide the cornerstone of proof the lawyer needs to win a construction failure case.

As a *sleuth*, a forensic engineer must be ready to accept the challenge of a mysterious failure with no apparent cause. He or she must be able to:

- Assimilate unfamiliar information quickly
- Ask the right questions
- Request the right documents
- Talk to the right people
- Separate the important from the unimportant
- Piece together an answer to the mystery of a construction failure, even when pieces of the puzzle may be missing, confusing, or contradictory

As a *scientist*, the forensic engineer must be objective. He or she must:

- Analytically identify potential failure mechanisms
- Dispassionately consider all available facts
- Develop well-conceived hypotheses
- Fairly and thoroughly test each hypothesis
- Impartially arrive at and testify to a failure theory that accounts for all known facts and rationally explains the cause of the failure

As a *translator*, the forensic engineer must effectively bridge the terminology gap that exists between the construction world, the legal world, and a juror's world. Unless you are a trained structural engineer, being told that a building fell down because "the flexural stress at the extreme fiber of a wideflange beam exceeded its elastic limit" would be meaningless. A good forensic engineer avoids industry jargon and explains important points using terminology that his or her audience can readily understand.

As a *teacher and a story teller*, a forensic engineer must simplify and explain complex concepts and present opinions in a commonsense manner that is understandable, interesting, and persuasive. The specific challenge of the forensic engineer in this regard is to find everyday analogies that explain complex engineering and construction concepts. For example, an electrical engineering expert might analogize the flow of electricity through a wire to the flow of water through a garden hose. Just as water flow is limited by the diameter of a garden hose, the flow of electricity is limited by the diameter of the wire.

As a *diplomat*, a forensic engineer must be able to question and critique the work of peers without giving the appearance of being anything but an impartial investigator searching for the truth. A forensic engineer must also be able to maintain professional and ethical standards in the face of occasional pressure to do otherwise without, to the greatest extent possible, offending clients.

Last but not the least, as a *businessperson*, a forensic engineer must be able to perform all of the aforementioned roles in a timely, cost-effective, and yes, profitable manner.

The Process

Assuming that a forensic engineer is ready, willing, and able to fulfill each of the roles described above, what can a forensic engineer do to maximize the credibility of the investigations, analyses, and opinions associated with his or her work? A good forensic engineer, like a good scientist, must follow a disciplined and objective approach to conducting a forensic investigation to maximize the likelihood that the findings and opinions that result from his or her investigations are accepted as professionally credible. Fortunately, there exists a widely known process that, if properly followed, is generally recognized as yielding objective, reliable results. The process, which is applicable to every field of science including forensic engineering, is known as the scientific method.

A forensic engineer can apply the scientific method (and benefit from the indicia of reliability that comes from applying the scientific method) by following each of the steps generally outlined as follows:

- *Step 1:*   Observe as many relevant characteristics of the failure as is reasonably practicable to gain an insight into the cause of the failure
- *Step 2:*   Develop tentative explanations, referred to as hypotheses in the parlance of the scientific method, which are consistent with and appear to explain each observation
- *Step 3:*   Use the hypotheses to make predictions
- *Step 4:*   Test the predictions by experiments or further observations and, as necessary, revise the hypotheses to be consistent with the results of experiments and further observations
- *Step 5:*   Repeat Steps 3 and 4 as outlined before until there are no discrepancies between hypotheses and the results of experiments and further observations. Once all discrepancies are eliminated, the hypothesis becomes a theory. A theory accounts for all known facts and provides a rational explanation for the cause of an event[2]

Consider the following very simplified example. Assume that a small steel warehouse collapses for no apparent reason. Under Step 1 of the scientific method, the forensic engineer visits the site and observes as many relevant characteristics of the failure as practicable. Further assume that: (i) because the failure involved a simple steel structure and only a small section of the structure failed, there were a limited number of apparently relevant failure characteristics to observe; (ii) one of the characteristics that the forensic engineer observed was several bolts that had broken (sheared) away from a failed steel connection between a corner column and two supporting beams; and (iii) the failed connection appeared to be the point at which the structural failure of the warehouse was initiated.

Under Step 2 of the scientific method, the forensic engineer develops several tentative explanations or hypotheses to explain his or her observation that the bolts in the steel connection sheared and caused the building section to collapse. Based on the forensic engineer's education, training, and experience, he or she would likely formulate the following hypotheses: (i) the bolted connection was improperly designed; (ii) the bolted connection was improperly constructed; (iii) the material from which the bolts were fabricated was defective; and (iv) abnormally high winds may have overstressed the connection and caused the bolts to fail and the structure to collapse.

Under Step 3, the forensic engineer uses his or her hypotheses to make predictions. For example, the forensic engineer may make a prediction that any bolted connection designed as the connection in question was designed would always fail under the loading that the connection was intended to carry. The forensic engineer would then make similar predictions for each of his or her other applicable hypotheses.

Under Step 4, the forensic engineer would conduct tests and make further observations to test each hypothesis and modify his or her hypotheses to be consistent with the results of such testing and further observations. Assuming that the forensic engineer's tests and further observations *did not prove* that a bolted connection, designed as the connection in question was designed, would always fail under normal loading conditions, the forensic engineer would have to reject his or her hypothesis that the connection was defectively designed.

Under Step 5, the forensic engineer would continue to test his or her hypotheses and make further observations until such hypotheses were consistent with the results of all testing and observations. For the sake of discussion, assume that the forensic engineer confirmed that the connection was properly designed and constructed, using the proper quantity, size, and quality of bolts, and that no abnormal winds were present at the time of failure. It would appear that the forensic engineer was without an explanation for the failure. However, further assume, as is often the case, that the forensic engineer learned of a new fact while testing his or her initial hypotheses. Specifically, the forensic engineer learned from interviews with parties familiar with the failure that a large crane working on an adjacent project had struck the building in the immediate vicinity of the failed connection.

Based on the new information concerning the crane accident, the forensic engineer revises his or her hypotheses to state that the connection failure did not occur as the result of defective design, defective construction, defective bolts or high wind conditions. Instead, the forensic engineer hypothesizes that the crane collision weakened the bolted connection and caused it to fail. To test this hypothesis, the forensic engineer must arrange to analyze the failed connection to identify and document evidence of the alleged collision and to demonstrate that a crane collision such as the one described by eyewitnesses would weaken the bolted connection to the extent that failure would ultimately result.

Assuming that the forensic engineer's additional testing and observations supported his or her hypothesis that the crane collision caused the connection failure, the forensic engineer's revised hypothesis becomes consistent with all known information and becomes a theory that explains the cause of the connection failure.

Notice that there is nothing prejudiced about the forensic engineer's investigation or analysis of the facts. The forensic engineer (1) considered all reasonable possibilities for the connection failure; (2) tested each possibility; (3) ruled out potential causes not supported by testing or further observation; (4) identified a new hypothesis based on later acquired information; and (5) ultimately confirmed that the revised hypothesis was consistent with all available information. The advantage of the scientific method is that any reasonably qualified individual should be able to apply the method and arrive at the same results.

Unfortunately, competent forensic engineers, even when properly applying the scientific method, often arrive at different conclusions. In practice, differences of opinion concerning the interpretation of test results or other data frequently cause competent experts to arrive at different answers. Therefore, while it is imperative that a forensic engineer employs the scientific method to maximize the objectivity and quality of his or her investigation and analysis, application of the scientific method does not guarantee either a unanimous or a correct answer. Education, training, experience — and sometimes luck — all play a part in determining whether a forensic engineer will discover the true cause behind a construction failure.

Primary Tasks

The Investigation

It may have surprised you to read in the preceding section that luck plays a role in forensic engineering. Truth be told, some failures are so complex and involve such mountainous volumes of information that even a good forensic engineer sometimes needs a little luck to find the one or two elusive facts that hold the key to unlocking the mystery of a particularly complex construction failure. Short of carrying around a rabbit's foot, however, the best way for a forensic engineer to make his or her own good luck is to conduct a thorough investigation.

The particulars of any given investigation, of course, will depend upon the type of construction failure being investigated. As a general rule though, any reasonably complete forensic investigation will include a review of the following broad categories of information:

- The "as-planned" design documents
- The "as-built" construction documents
- Actual construction means and methods
- Requests for information submitted by the contractor during construction
- Change orders
- Daily diaries
- Inspector's records (labor, equipment, weather, etc.)
- Material delivery data
- All available photography
- Building codes, ordinances, and standards
- Test reports
- Published standards applicable to the type of construction at issue
- Meeting minutes
- Telephone logs
- Qualifications of all persons directly associated with the failed construction
- Weather reports
- All relevant government information available (e.g., geotechnical data)
- All historical information from prior projects performed in the same vicinity
- Copies of all applicable handwritten calculations and computer printouts
- Copies of all contracts and scopes of work related to the failed work
- All other required information specific to the type of failure involved

The Analysis

Just as a forensic engineer's investigation must be tailored to the type of failure being investigated, so too must a forensic engineer's method of analysis be tailored to the type of failure at issue. There is, however, a universal set of rules that apply to all types of forensic engineering analyses. Those rules, which determine whether a forensic engineer's testimony will survive long enough to see the inside of a courtroom, govern the admissibility and expert opinion testimony.

Although a thorough discussion of the rules that govern the admissibility of expert opinion testimony appears elsewhere in this text, it bears restating in this section that there are essentially two standards that determine whether an expert will be allowed to give his opinions to a jury. Determining which standard applies is normally as easy as determining the forum within which a dispute is being resolved. Typically, although not always, if a dispute is in a state court, an expert must base his or her expert opinion on an analytical methodology that has been generally accepted by the relevant professional community. In other words, state courts do not usually accept expert testimony unless it is based on an analytical method that has already been accepted by an expert's community of professional peers.

On the other hand, if a dispute is in a federal court, a different standard of admissibility can apply. In federal court, expert testimony is admissible if it is based on a reliable method, and the expert has reliably applied the method. Although the federal standard was intended to be more flexible than the "general acceptance" standard, in practice, it has been used with increasing regularity to exclude an expert's opinion before such testimony ever reaches a jury's ears.

Although a more detailed discussion of the standards that govern admissibility of expert testimony is beyond the scope of this section, experienced and novice forensic engineers alike would be well advised to become intimately familiar with such standards. In today's aggressive construction litigation environment, challenges to the admissibility of expert testimony are commonplace.

The Expert Report

Content. There is no universally prescribed format for a forensic engineer's expert report. However, Federal Rule of Civil Procedure 26(a)(2) provides a good outline of the minimum threshold of information that a good expert report should include. Rule 26, which applies to expert reports submitted in connection with matters in federal court, requires experts, including forensic engineers, to include the following information in a signed expert report:

- A complete statement of all opinions to be expressed in the expert's trial testimony and the basis and reasons thereof
- The data or other information considered by the witness in forming the opinions
- Any exhibits to be used as a summary of or support for the opinions
- A statement of the qualifications of the witness
- A list of all publications authored by the witness within the preceding ten years
- The compensation to be paid for the investigation and testimony
- A listing of all other cases in which the witness has testified as an expert at trial or by deposition within the preceding four years

Draft Reports: Considerations. The first question that a forensic engineer should ask before writing a draft report is whether the lawyer wants a draft report. Many lawyers prefer to have preliminary findings presented in an oral format instead of in writing.

Particularly in complex, factually intensive cases, a forensic engineer's oral presentation of draft findings avoids the problem of having a written record of findings that may be based on the type of inaccurate or incomplete understanding of a case that a forensic engineer may have in the early stages of an investigation.

Many forensic engineers have adopted a policy of overwriting draft reports with each successive draft and ultimately the final report. This policy avoids the inevitable questions that arise during depositions which seek to discover the reason for every difference between an expert's final report and prior draft reports. Although there is some merit to the argument that differences between draft and final expert reports may expose a lawyer's undue influence over an expert's ultimate opinions, overwriting of draft reports has become a common procedure. Note, however, that forensic engineers would again be well advised to consult with the lawyer who hired them to confirm local rules concerning the maintenance and use of draft reports. To the extent that local rules require draft reports to be maintained, destruction of such reports could have adverse consequences on the lawyer's case.

The Final Report: Rules of Thumb.   A good, final forensic engineering report should:

- Include an executive summary
- Properly disclose documents reviewed
- State qualifications of the expert
- Not overstate or inaccurately state professional credentials
- Define technical terms and abbreviations used in the report
- Stay within the forensic engineer's area of expertise
- Clearly and objectively express factual assumptions
- Avoid the appearance of advocacy or argumentativeness
- Express opinions in a clear, confident, and supportable manner
- State reasons for opinions
- Document methodologies used to reach opinions
- Cite to appropriate authorities to support opinions
- Disclose the help of colleagues and assistants
- Be proofread
- Avoid absolute words
- Avoid superfluous language
- Avoid hedging language
- Reserve the right to modify opinions upon receipt of new or updated information

In sum, a forensic engineer's final report must be a well supported, stand alone document that objectively and persuasively communicates the forensic engineer's theory of what caused a particular construction failure.

Attributes of an Effective Forensic Engineer

Qualifications/Expertise of a Construction Forensic Engineer

Codes of Ethics

The subject of ethical standards to be followed by a forensic engineer is a thorny one. At the current time, there is no national code of ethics for forensic engineers. What guidance there is, is only tangential and can be found in the ethics guidelines published by the American

Society of Civil Engineers (ASCE) and the National Society of Professional Engineers (NSPE). Generally speaking, experts and ethics fall between two poles: At one pole are those who will tell you what you want to hear no matter how bad they look. At the other pole is the scrupulously rigid expert who refuses to consider what is in the client's best interests and will not advocate for the client's position, no matter what. In between is where most experts lie, comfortable with the view that they can ethically take a position that is in the client's best interests so long as it is reasonable and supported by some evidence. For an excellent discussion of the forensic engineer's ethical issues, please refer to the ASCE publication, *Guidelines for Forensic Engineering Practice.*

Education

Of course, one would expect a qualified forensic engineer addressing construction-related problems to be formally trained in the discipline at issue in the case (structural, electrical, mechanical, etc.). From a qualifications perspective, it is usually preferable that the testifying expert hold one or more advanced degrees in his or her area of specialty.

Training

A well-qualified forensic engineer should have years of training in his or her field of specialty, through both formal education and ongoing continuing education in the profession via seminars, symposia, and so on.

Experience

Perhaps the most important consideration for an expert is his or her experience in practicing in the relevant field of engineering as well as experience in investigating the precise type of failure at issue. A top expert can be expected to have 20–30 years of experience in the field, much of which having been spent working as an expert witness, and authoring books or articles on the area of study at issue in a case.

Publications

It is becoming more and more critical for the testifying expert to have published articles, books, treatises, and so on, in the field of engineering, preferably in the area of inquiry for the assignment at hand. A well-qualified expert will be able to point to numerous articles and publications as proof of his/her pedigree and acceptance as an expert in industry.

Licensing

Although not a firm prerequisite to acting as a forensic engineer, a great amount of credibility is placed on the engineer who can say that he/she holds one or more professional licenses in the area of expertise at issue in the case.

Ability to Write

Although often overlooked and underappreciated, a good forensic engineer must be able to communicate effectively and clearly through a written expert report. The expert must also master the use of graphs and charts and be able to present complex ideas in a simple graphic fashion.

Ability to Teach

This is a critical factor for lawyers selecting experts. After all, our typical jurors know nothing of design, engineering, or construction principles so the ability to teach complex concepts in a simple, understandable way is vital to success. The best forensic experts will be able to get up out of the witness chair, approach the jury, and teach them what they need to know to come to the correct decision.

Objectivity and Truthfulness

No forensic engineer will hold that title long if he or she is not strictly objective and rigorous in the investigation and truthful in describing his or her findings. Once caught in a lie on the witness stand, all credibility is lost.

Compensation

A forensic engineer should always endeavor to arrange for fair and adequate compensation based strictly on an hourly rate plus reimbursement of reasonable expenses. Any expert who ventures into the arena of working on a contingency fee (they get paid if their side wins, or they get a percentage of the amount recovered) will have his or her objectivity and credibility extensively damaged by any good trial lawyer. Also, clients need to be sensitive to the expert's billing and pay the bills on time. You do not want an unhappy, unpaid expert working for you or giving testimony in your case.

Considerations for Lawyers Investigating Construction Failures

Types of Investigations

There are generally two types of investigations that the forensic engineer can be tasked to perform. First is the "wide open" investigation where a failure has just occurred and the cause is truly unknown. The question to be answered here is "What happened?" and all possible hypotheses for failure will be examined. The second type of investigation can be one where the lines have already been drawn, and the parties have taken positions on liability. In this type of investigation, the forensic engineer can be called upon to refute the specific allegations of the other parties and bolster the claims of the party retaining the expert. One might ask how two or more technically competent experts come to conflicting conclusions in a construction failure case. The answer lies in the circumstances postfailure where there is usually so much damage to the structure and the evidence that there is room for speculation and fertile ground for competing experts to propose an alternative hypothesis for the cause of the failure.

Protection of Evidence

In a major construction failure case, a key consideration is protection of the physical evidence. Often rescue and cleanup efforts cause key pieces of evidence to be removed from the accident site or destroyed. For this reason, it is critical for the lawyer to get his or her forensic experts out to the site as quickly as possible so as to preserve the best evidence which often is perishable. For example, often experts want to look at the fracture surfaces on steel members to determine whether the failure occurred at that member. Fracture surfaces on steel will corrode and become corrupted as evidence if left unprotected in the weather, so prompt identification and protection of such surfaces is critical to a proper failure investigation.

Coordination of Expert Investigations

In major failure cases, it is often the case that each party will retain its own experts, all of whom will need to investigate alongside local, state, and federal investigators. Such a plethora of investigators, all wanting to test the often limited set of physical exemplars, causes conflict and increases the risk of destruction of evidence. In circumstances such as these, it is beneficial to seek cooperation among the experts on what needs to be tested and the types of tests to be performed by an independent testing agency, whose results will be shared with and accepted by all parties. This test sharing should be noncontroversial on the simple tests that are normally done, like compression tests on concrete cylinders and tensile tests on steel coupons. In the case of more subjective tests such as petrography, there may be no agreement on a single test, so each expert may need to conduct his or her own tests.

Managing the Expert

Perhaps there is no more important task for the lawyer engaging a forensic expert witness than properly managing the expert during the course of the engagement. Proper expert management includes the following:

- Thoroughly check the expert's resume and verify education and work history. There is no more damaging cross of an expert than to expose lies in his/her resume. Along those lines, the lawyer must also request and review all prior deposition, trial, and arbitration testimony for statements made or positions taken by the expert that may be contradictory to the positions taken in the matter at hand
- Set a budget for the expert's work (if a client's liability is limited to $50,000 by contract, there is no need to spend $1 million on expert witness work)
- Agree on a schedule for the expert to complete the investigation, perform the analysis, and prepare a report
- Clearly define a scope of work for the expert, including identifying clear deliverables that will be produced
- Hold regular meetings with the experts to review progress, draft deliverables, and determine the status of the budget
- Provide the expert with all documents produced in the case. Do not attempt to filter the information the expert sees. This will only create a biased report that will likely be torn apart under cross-examination
- Tell the expert you want the bad news early. This will permit the lawyer to properly evaluate liability early on in the case and advise the client accordingly. There is nothing worse than spending millions of dollars on expert fees only to produce a report years down the line that is unfavorable to your position
- Do not ignore bad facts and produce a biased expert report. A biased report that does not cast a critical eye on all of the facts will be exposed in cross-examination

- Consider retaining two experts, one for testifying and one as a check on the testifying expert. The lawyer can use the latter as a sounding board for ideas and advice on unfavorable facts or theories without contaminating the testifying expert
- Take time to sit with the expert and learn the technical points of what the expert is doing. Develop a grasp of the basic engineering concepts the expert is using. This is needed to understand the report, the other side's report, and to take and defend depositions in the case
- Consider how much time the expert should spend refining his or her answer. If it is sufficient to say either A or B caused the failure (because your client is not responsible for either one), maybe you do not need to spend any more time or money on expert analysis to refine the answer down to only one of the two options
- Lastly, challenge the expert's methods and conclusions; test the strength of his or her views. Do not blindly or meekly accept what the expert says as gospel and trot off to the courtroom, only to be handed your head once the expert's theory falls apart under cross-examination. Make sure your expert has considered all of the evidence and tested alternative hypotheses before coming to his or her final conclusions

Types of Construction Failures[3]

Up to this point, this chapter has discussed the need for forensic engineers, the role of the forensic engineer, the attributes of an effective forensic engineer, and considerations for lawyers conducting investigations of construction failures. Each of the preceding sections, however, begs an important question — what is a "construction failure?" What does the term "construction failure" mean? For many people, the term "construction failure" invokes images of collapsing buildings and falling bridges. Undoubtedly, many people's perception of the term "construction failure" has been molded by such high-profile catastrophes as the 1981 Hyatt Regency Hotel skywalk collapse in Kansas City and the 1940 Tacoma Narrows Bridge collapse. Indeed, photos and film footage of a 2,800-foot span of the Tacoma Narrows Bridge twisting like a rubber band (shortly before disintegrating and plummeting 190 feet into the cold water below) have become infamous icons for the term "construction failure" (Figure 12.1 and Figure 12.2).

Although no one would seriously dispute that the Hyatt Regency Hotel skywalk and Tacoma Narrows Bridge disasters qualify as construction failures, such catastrophic events represent only one of the three major types of construction failures.

Before examining the generally recognized categories of construction failures, however, it is helpful to possess a working definition of the term "construction failure." One generally accepted definition of the term "construction failure" is the "inability of a component, structure, or facility to perform its intended function." Given such a broad definition, it is easy to see that construction failures are not necessarily limited to such catastrophic events as collapsing buildings and falling bridges. To the contrary, the term "construction failure" also includes such nonnewsworthy events as a leaky roof, schedule delays, and cost overruns.

Generally speaking, there are three recognized categories of construction failures: (i) safety failures, (ii) functional failures, and (iii) ancillary failures. Although the labels

Figure 12.1   Tacoma Narrows Bridge. An enlargement of a still from the Farguherson motion picture showing an abandoned car on a swaying bridge — November 7, 1940. Copyright © University of Washington Libraries.

used to describe each category are not particularly important, understanding the differences between each category is important.

Safety Failures

The first recognized category of construction failures is the "safety failure." This is characterized by conditions that result in loss of life, serious physical injury, or a substantial risk of either.

Figure 12.2   Tacoma Narrows Bridge. Bridge midsection crashing into the waters of the Tacoma Narrows — November 7, 1940. Copyright © University of Washington Libraries.

Examples of safety failures include:

- The rupture or impending rupture of a dam that places life at risk
- The collapse of an elevated walkway that results in loss of life and limb
- An inoperable or malfunctioning fire and smoke detection system that places the safety of the occupants of a facility at risk
- The absence of adequate steel reinforcing in a concrete column that places the column at risk of buckling and the lives of persons in the facility supported by such a column at risk

Functional Failures

The second recognized category of construction failure is the "functional" failure. This occurs when deficiencies associated with a project prevent the project from fulfilling the purpose it was intended to serve.

Examples of functional failures include:

- A commercial wastepaper recycling facility that does not meet specified output requirements because it is unable to properly process certain elements of the incoming wastepaper stream
- A leaky roof that prevents a facility owner from using affected portions of a facility for the purposes they were intended
- A defective facility design that did not take into account the nature of the work to be performed in the facility, causing significant inefficiencies in a manufacturing process intended to be carried out in the facility

A "functional" failure, unlike a "safety" failure, does not result in loss of life or create a danger that places life or limb at risk.

Ancillary Failures

The third and final recognized category of construction failure is referred to as an "ancillary" failure. This is characterized by events that materially prevent a project from being completed on time, on budget, or to specified levels of quality.

Examples of ancillary failures include any event that causes significant construction delays and cost overruns that interfere with a facility owner's ability to (i) begin using a facility for its intended purpose, (ii) in a timely manner, and (iii) for a reasonable cost. Examples of such events might include poor schedule management, late equipment delivery, inadequate planning to acquire required permits, and anything else that prevents a facility owner from gaining the use of its facility on time and within budget.

Ancillary failures, unlike safety failures and functional failures, do not result in loss of life or limb, place life or limb at risk of loss, or affect the functionality of a project.

Causes of Construction Failures

Construction failures are not, of course, always the result of defective construction. In fact, they often result from a number of other causes, including defective design, defective materials, improper operation and maintenance, poor planning or management, and any number of unforeseeable factors.

For illustration purposes, consider the following hypothetical situation: Ten months after the construction of a new school is completed, the general contractor responsible for constructing the school receives a letter from the school board's legal counsel. The letter places the contractor on notice that one of the school's primary heating, ventilating, and air conditioning ("HVAC") units is not properly cooling the school and must be repaired or replaced immediately. Because the HVAC unit is unable to perform its intended function, it qualifies as a "functional" construction failure.

The various categories of causes that might be responsible for the malfunctioning HVAC unit (or any type of construction failure for that matter) are briefly described below.

Defective Design

Defective design occurs when a design professional (i.e., an architect, an engineer, etc.) fails to exercise that degree of ordinary care and skill in the preparation of project plans (drawings and specifications) that would be exercised by a reasonable design professional under similar circumstances in a similar locality. In the case of a defective design, no amount of skill and competence exercised by a contractor in constructing a project will result in a satisfactory end product because the instructions for executing the construction (i.e., the project plans and specifications) are flawed.

In our hypothetical, defective design would exist if the design professional had mistakenly undersized the HVAC unit and, as a result, it was shutting down because its compressor was overheating in an attempt to provide more cooling than the unit was capable of providing.

Defective Construction

Defective construction occurs when a contractor fails to construct a project or portion of a project in accordance with a project's plans or specifications and the variance renders a project or portion of a project unable to serve its intended function.

In our scenario, defective construction could take any number of forms, including installation of an HVAC unit other than the unit specified, installation errors (e.g., defective wiring or piping), or improper calibration or balancing of the unit that renders it unable to operate as intended, just to name a few.

Defective Materials

Sometimes, construction failures occur despite proper design and construction. In such cases, defective materials are one of the two prime suspects that a forensic engineer should investigate. For purposes of our hypothetical, assume that the engineer who designed the malfunctioning HVAC unit specified a unit that was perfect for the school's cooling needs. Further assume that the contractor who installed the specified unit installed it perfectly. Under such a fact pattern, a reasonable forensic engineer would next investigate the materials used to fabricate and install the malfunctioning HVAC unit.

Although there are many potential material defects that could cause an HVAC unit to malfunction, one example of such a defect would be weaknesses in the walls of condenser coil piping that lead to hairline pipe wall fractures that, in turn, allow refrigerant to escape that, in turn, prevents an HVAC unit from operating as designed.

Improper Operation and Maintenance

The second of the two prime suspects that a forensic engineer should investigate in instances where a construction failure occurs despite the absence of design and construction defects is improper operation or maintenance. It is not uncommon for a facility owner to claim design or construction defects as the cause of equipment failures, only to later learn that the owner's equipment ceased operating because it was either improperly operated or inadequately maintained.

In our scenario, if the facility owner failed to perform routine preventative maintenance, such as changing air filters or scheduling annual service calls, it is likely that the failure of its HVAC unit was simply the result of improper operation and/or inadequate maintenance.

Poor Planning/Poor Management/Owner Interference

As noted above, construction failures do not always involve structures that fall down (safety failures) or structures that fail to perform their intended functions (functional failures). Construction failures also include a category of failures known as ancillary failures (which are characterized by substantial schedule delays and/or budget overruns).

Unlike our scenario, if a construction failure is characterized by substantial schedule delays and/or cost overruns, the obvious potential causes of such a failure that a forensic engineer would want to investigate would include poor project planning, poor project management, and owner interference in the construction contractor's execution of his or her work. In fact, there is an entire class of forensic engineers who specialize in analyzing the types of complex schedule delay and cost overrun issues that can frequently lead to protracted and expensive litigation.

Unforeseeable Factors

There are too many variables involved in design and construction to foresee every potential event that could cause a construction failure. Consider, for example, a freak snowstorm that dumps more snow on a roof in a single day than has ever been recorded on any preceding day for the last one hundred years. Notwithstanding the fact that a roof, at least in theory, could have been designed and constructed to support the freak snow load, because the event was not reasonably foreseeable, the failure cannot be attributed to a design or construction defect. As a result, the design professional who designed the roof and the contractor who constructed it would not generally be held liable for failing to anticipate the impact of such an unforeseeable event.

By way of summary, it is important to be able to recognize and distinguish between the different types of causes that lead to construction failures because that knowledge provides: (i) direction and guidance to ongoing failure investigations and (ii) a strong indication of the party that will be responsible for the damages that arise from a construction failure.

Case Studies of Infamous Construction Disasters

The following is a short discussion of a few of the most notorious construction and engineering failures in the past 25 years. In each of these accidents, forensic engineers were called upon to determine the cause and assess blame.

Kansas City Hyatt Regency Hotel Walkway Collapse[4-7]

The Hyatt Regency Hotel was built in Kansas City, Missouri, in 1979. A state-of-the-art facility, the hotel boasted a 40-story hotel tower with 750 rooms and conference facilities. These two components were connected by an open atrium. Within the atrium, three suspended walkways connected the hotel and conference facilities on the second, third, and fourth levels. Due to their suspension, these walkways were referred to as "floating walkways" or "skyways." The atrium boasted 17,000 square feet and was 50 feet high. The Hyatt Regency opened to the public in the summer of 1980.

On July 17, 1981, a catastrophe occurred. Approximately 2,000 people were gathered to watch a dance contest in the hotel's atrium lobby. Although the majority of the guests were on the ground level, some were dancing on the floating walkways on the second, third, and fourth levels. At approximately 7:05 P.M., a loud "crack" was heard as the fourth floor walkway collapsed onto the second floor walkway and then both fell onto the dance floor. The offset third floor walkway remained intact. The collapse resulted in the deaths of 114 people and injuries to more than 200 people, making this the United States' deadliest structural failure.

Immediately following the collapse, investigators from the National Bureau of Standards (NBS), as well as numerous forensic engineers hired by the hotel, the architect, the structural engineer, and the contractor began their investigation of the cause of the failure. Ultimately, they traced the cause of the walkway collapse to inadequate structural connections between the walkways and the hanger rods from which they were suspended. Originally, the design called for the box beam framing of the fourth and second floor walkways to be hung from a set of six 32-mm steel rods suspended from the lobby ceiling and running continuously through both walkways, which were not, however, built in accordance with the original plan. Instead, the fourth floor walkway hung from rods connected to the ceiling, and the second floor walkway hung from a second set of rods connected to the fourth floor walkway. That change effectively doubled the load on the fourth floor connection (Figure 12.3).

The investigation revealed that the structural engineer never completed the detail for the original rod to box beam connections at the fourth and second floors; instead, he left that detail to be designed by the structural steel fabricator as part of the "shop drawing" submittal process. Apparently, the contractor or construction manager decided that the single rod design was unbuildable (either they could not get 30-foot long rods or they did not want to thread half of the rod so the leveling nuts for the fourth floor could be used) and requested a change in the design to utilize two sets of rods. This change, which was shown in the shop drawings and apparently approved by the structural engineer, caused the nut under the fourth floor box beam to support the weight of two walkways, instead of one. In the end, the failure occurred when the overloaded nuts pulled through the fourth floor box beam, causing a progressive collapse of the walkways.

A grand jury was convened to probe criminal charges against the structural engineer, but it did not find evidence rising to the level of criminal negligence. The Missouri Board of Architects, Professional Engineers, and Land Surveyors, however, convened its own investigation and found the engineer of record and the project engineer guilty of gross negligence and unprofessional conduct for failing to check the load capacity of the changed hanger detail, and stripped them of their licenses to practice engineering.

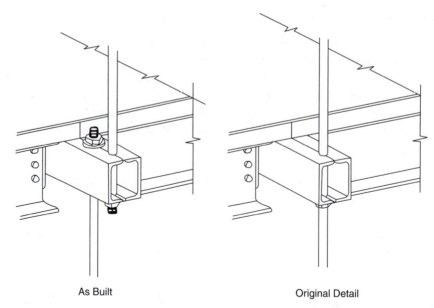

As Built   Original Detail

Figure 12.3 Comparison of interrupted and continuous hanger rod details. Copyright ©
National Bureau of Standards.

The Hartford Civic Center Collapse[8,9]

At about 4:00 A.M. on January 18, 1978, the huge space truss roof over the empty Hartford
Civic Center Coliseum in Hartford, Connecticut, collapsed under a load of snow and freezing rain. Just a few hours before, the building was occupied by thousands of basketball fans;
by the time of the collapse, however, the building was empty and no one was killed or
injured (Figure 12.4).

The roof structure for the building was a custom designed three-dimensional lattice
structure about 21 feet deep, supported on four pylons. The design of the space frame
truss had been based on innovative computer analysis techniques (for 1970). The roof
was built on the ground and jacked (lifted) to its final elevation.

The investigation of the failure was performed for the City of Hartford by the structural engineering firm Lev Zetlin Associates, Inc. (LZA). LZA's investigation consisted of
the following:

- Interviews and public hearings with the principal parties, firms, persons, and organizations involved in the planning, design, construction, and administration of the
  original construction of the Hartford Coliseum
- Technical investigations consisting of:
  (1) Field investigation
  (2) Metallurgical investigation performed on selected pieces of the trusses
  (3) Meteorological investigation of wind and snow and other precipitation in
      the Hartford area prior to the collapse
  (4) Review of relevant documents of the architect and engineers
  (5) Computer simulation of the failure of the roof structure

The LZA investigation revealed that, as a result of design deficiencies, the roof began to
fail (sag more than design allowables) as soon as it was completed. Interestingly, once

Figure 12.4   The Hartford Civic Center Collapse. Aerial view of collapsed Coliseum roof. Copyright © The Thornton Tomasetti Group and ASCE

erected, the deflection (sag) at the center of the space truss was 8.4 in. as compared to the engineer's expected deflection of 3.7 in. One might question why construction was allowed to continue despite this condition, but nevertheless, it did continue.

LZA determined that there were three major design deficiencies, which combined with an underestimation of the dead load by 20%, allowed the heavy snow load to collapse the roof. The principal LZA finding was that the top chord members of the east–west trusses were overstressed by as much as 852% and that lateral buckling of the top chord initiated the collapse. The computer model was blamed for the overstressed condition as it did not accurately represent the structure.

LZA's findings were challenged somewhat by the investigation performed by Loomis and Loomis, Inc. who, while agreeing with LZA that gross design errors were responsible for the roof collapse, believed that torsional buckling of the compression members initiated the collapse. Another structural consultant, Hannskarl Bandel, who was hired by the architect's insurance company, blamed the failure on a faulty weld connecting the scoreboard to the roof.

Six years after the collapse, all of the parties reached an out-of-court settlement. This ended the inquiry, and no one theory of failure was ever accepted or adopted by the courts or the engineering community.

The L'Ambiance Plaza Collapse[10–12]

The L'Ambiance Plaza was under construction in 1987 when it collapsed, killing 28 construction workers. It was to be a 16-story building and was to be constructed using a patented "lift-slab" method of construction. The "lift-slab" method required that the floor slabs for all 16 levels were constructed one on top of the other on the ground, then lifted into a temporary position using a hydraulic lifting apparatus located on the top of the columns and a pair of lifting rods extending down to lifting collars (the shearheads) cast in the slab. The slabs were to be lifted and held temporarily in place with steel wedges. Once positioned correctly, the slabs were to be permanently welded to the columns.

At the time of the collapse, the structure was about halfway completed. Workmen were tack welding wedges under the ninth, tenth, and eleventh floor slab package when they heard "a loud metallic sound followed by rumbling." The slabs fell onto the ones below them, which were unable to support the added weight, and they, in turn, fell, collapsing the entire structure. It was, by all accounts, the worst lift-slab construction accident on record. OSHA charged several contractors with violations and levied fines (Figure 12.5 and Figure 12.6).

Immediately after the collapse, and after rescue operations ceased, an investigation was begun into the cause of the collapse. The initial investigation was performed by NBS at the request of OSHA. NBS' initial theory in 1987 was that the most likely cause of the collapse was that a lifting nut slipped out from a certain shearhead, thereby causing the slab to lose support and fall. That theory was later challenged by other experts and, in 1993, the principal authors of the NBS theory withdrew their theory.

Subsequent work by investigators has led to a general consensus that the collapse was most likely caused by excessive clearance or "play" between the shearheads and the columns which permitted the wedge at the twelfth floor level to come loose, triggering the collapse. Support for the "excessive play in shearheads" theory is not, however, universal. Other experts have postulated that the collapse was caused by: (1) improper post-tensioning design, (2) substandard welds, (3) a column footing collapse, or (4) global instability of the tower. Although all of the theories appeared to be plausible, no one will ever know exactly what happened because a $41 million settlement among the 100 parties to the ensuing lawsuit ended the inquiry.

Willow Island Cooling Tower Collapse[13–23]

Shortly after 10:00 A.M. on April 27, 1978, at the coal-fired Pleasants Power Station in Willow Island, West Virginia, the top section of a partially built, reinforced concrete

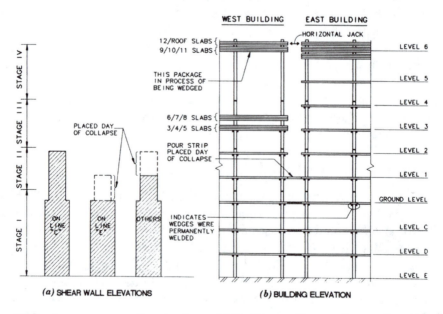

Figure 12.5 Status construction at time of L'Ambiance Plaza collapse. Copyright © The Thornton Tomasetti Group and ASCE.

Figure 12.6 The L'Ambiance Plaza Collapse. Copyright © The Thornton Tomasetti Group and ASCE.

hyperbolic cooling tower collapsed, along with the four-tier formwork and scaffolding it supported, killing all 51 construction workers (Figure 12.7).

The Occupational Safety and Health Administration (OSHA) immediately launched an investigation and requested the NBS to assist it in examining the cooling tower collapse and determine the most probable technical cause of the failure. Two days after the accident, the NBS began conducting its own in-depth investigation. The NBS analyzed data obtained

Figure 12.7 Willow Island Cooling Tower Collapse. Copyright © National Bureau of Standards.

from both OSHA and the contractor, as well as conducting its own field, laboratory, and analytical tests. Included in the NBS investigation were detailed studies on the construction method, site operations, concrete properties, components of the concrete hoisting and scaffolding system, loads acting at the time of collapse, and the forces generated in the concrete shell in relation to its strength.

A prominent focus of the investigation was the application of the patented lift-form construction method the contractor employed to construct the Willow Island cooling tower. This method involved anchor bolting the formwork and scaffolding system to the most recently poured top section of the concrete shell and progressively moving forms up the tower as it was built at a pace of one five-foot lift per day (Figure 12.8).

By the day of the collapse, the tower had reached an approximate height of 166 feet. Twenty-eight lifts had been placed, and workers were beginning construction of Lift 29. The necessary scaffolding and formwork was supported only by Lift 28, which had been cast 24 hours earlier. Accordingly, at the time of the collapse, Lift 28 was only one day old and had been exposed to an estimated average ambient temperature under 10°C due to the low night time temperatures the area had experienced during the construction process. As the third 2,500 pound bucket of concrete for Lift 29 was hoisted up to the working platform, the top five feet of the tower's shell collapsed inward. The shell's collapse

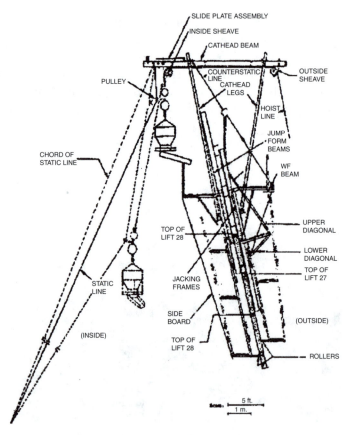

Figure 12.8 The patented lift-form method to construct the Willow Island Cooling Tower. Copyright © The Thornton Tomasetti Group.

triggered a chain reaction that brought down the four-level scaffolding system, which held the workers, work platforms, and safety nets. None of the workers survived the fall.

From the outset, it appears that NBS focused its attention on the strength of the 24-hour-old concrete in Lift 28. NBS Laboratory investigations included testing of concrete specimens under simulated field conditions to establish the strength (compressive, tensile, and bond) and stiffness of the concrete of Lift 28 at the time of collapse. The testing included an examination of the constituents of the concrete, such as cement content, fly ash content, fine and coarse aggregate content as well as testing for air-entraining admixtures. NBS also tested several components of the scaffolding and lift system, including the anchor bolts, hoist cables, and chain hoist and a grip hoist.

NBS concluded that the most probable cause of the collapse was the imposition of construction loads on the shell before the concrete of Lift 28 had gained sufficient strength to support the loads. Based on the NBS report, OSHA issued citations against the tower designer, tower contractor, general contractor, and the testing laboratory responsible for concrete cylinder testing.

The NBS findings did not, however, go unchallenged. The general contractor for the project, United Engineers & Constructors (UEC) retained Lev Zetlin Associates (LZA) to investigate the cause of the collapse. After undertaking an extensive field investigation and performing computer analysis of the cooling tower and forming system, LZA strongly disagreed with NBS' conclusions.

LZA found that NBS' focus on the strength of the concrete in Lift 28 to be misplaced because NBS apparently ignored the construction method statement issued by the tower's designer, Research-Cottrell, Inc. (RC) on how a tower was to be built. According to the LZA Report, RC never intended the formwork to be held in place by one-day-old concrete. Instead, the instructions for constructing the tower required the use of anchor bolts in the next lower level (in this case, Level 27) which was two to four days old. LZA's investigation determined that the primary cause of the failure was the premature removal of the anchor bolts at Lift 27 by inadequately trained and unsupervised workers who failed to understand the import of what they were doing. LZA determined that had the lower anchor bolts in Lift 27 not been prematurely removed, the failure would not have occurred.

The LZA findings, which were not published until 1997, caused a firestorm of controversy in the engineering world as it totally contradicted and undermined long-held beliefs as to the cause of this accident.

It appears now, however, that the controversy has subsided and that the NBS theory of failure is no longer valid.[23]

Notes

1. Mr. Paciaroni would like to acknowledge the assistance of his legal assistant, Ms. Roberta Cramer, who assisted with the preparation of this chapter.
2. See Appendix "A" for an outline of the phases of a failure investigation, courtesy of Mr. E. Velivasakis of LZA Technology, Inc.
3. David W. Fowler, Forensic Engineering: Detective Engineering, at www.ce.utexas.edu/prof/ fowlerd.
4. Pfaheicher, S.K.A., "The Hyatt Horror": Failure and Responsibility in American Engineering, *J. Perform. Constr. Facil.*, 2000, Volume 14, Number 2, Pages 62–66.
5. Rubin, R.A. and Banick, L.A., The Hyatt Regency Decision: One View, *J. Perform. Constr. Facil.*, 1987, Volume 1, Number 3, pages 161–167.

6. Luth, G.P., Chronology and Context of the Hyatt Regency Collapse, *J. Perform. Constr. Facil.*, 2000, Volume 14, Number 2, pages 51–61.

7. Martin, R., Hyatt Regency Walkway Collapse, at http://www.eng.uab.edu/cee/rev_nsf99/hyatt.htm.

8. Lev Zetlin Associates, Inc. (1978), Report of the Engineering Investigation Concerning the Causes of the Collapse of the Hartford Coliseum Space Truss Roof on January 18, 1978, Hartford, Connecticut.

9. Martin, R. and Delatte, N.J., Another Look at Hartford Civic Center Coliseum Collapse, *J. Perform. Constr. Facil.*, 2001, Volume 15, Number 1, pages 31–36.

10. Cuoco, D.A., Peraza, D.B., and Scarangello, T.Z., Investigation of L'Ambiance Plaza Building Collapse, *J. Perform. Constr. Facil.*, 1992, Volume 6, Number 4, pages 211–231.

11. Peraza, D.B., Lift-Slab Construction-Engineering Considerations, *Forensic Engineering Proceedings of the First Congress*, October 5–7, 1997, ASCE Publication.

12. Martin, R., Delatte, N.J., Another Look at the L'Ambiance Plaza Collapse, *J. Perform. Constr. Facil.*, 2000, ASCE Publications, Volume 14, Number 4, pages 160–165.

13. Lew, H.S., Fattal, S.G., Shaver, J.R., Reinhold, T.A., and Hunt, B.J., Investigation of Construction Failure of Reinforced Concrete Cooling Tower at Willow Island, National Bureau of Standards, September 1982.

14. Velivasakis, E.E., The Willow Island Cooling Tower Scaffold Collapse — America's Worst Construction Accident, *Forensic Engineering: Proceedings of the First Congress*, October 5–7, 1997, ASCE Publications.

15. "A black day, a very black day," at http://www.geocities.com/pburgwva2001/willow1.html.

16. Carino, N.J. and Lew, H.S., *The Maturity Method: From Theory to Application*, from the proceedings of the 2001 Structures Congress & Exposition, May 21–23, 2001, Washington, D.C., at fire.nist.gov/bfrlpubs/build01/art006.html.

17. Carper, K., Beware of Vulnerabilities During Construction, Construction & Equipment 2004 (Mar. 25, 2004), at http://www.djc.com/news/co/11155170.html.

18. Case Studies: Willow Island Cooling Tower, at http://www.eng.uab.edu/cee/faculty/ndelatte/case_studies_project/cases.htm.

19. Kennedy, E., The Tragedy at Tower No. 2, New York Times Magazine (Dec. 3, 1978), at http://www.maryellenmark.com/text/magazines/nytimes_magazine/904Z-000-006.html.

20. Nazario, C., Willow Island Cooling Tower Collapse (2000), at http://www.eng.uab.edu/cee/reu_nsf99/reu_nsf00/carlos/Willow%20Island%20Cooling%20Tower%20Collapse.htm.

21. Stirewalt, C., State Disasters Come in All Sizes, Charleston Daily Mail (Feb. 12, 1999), at http://www.daily mail.com/static/specialsections/lookingback/lb0212.htm.

22. Time Trail, West Virginia, April 1998 Programs, West Virginia Archives and History, at http://www.wvculture.org/history/timetrl/ttapr.html.

23. Richard N. Wright, Building and Fire Research at NBS/NIST 1975–2000 (Dec. 2003), at http://www2.bfrl.nist.gov/info/bfrl_history/Chapters%201-15%20BFRL%20History/chp%2015.pdf.

24. The LZA study was not published in 1978 because the case against UEC and RC was settled. It lay dormant for nearly 20 years, until the study's principal author, Mr. Emmanuel E. Velivasakis of LZA, determined that the industry needed to know of LZA's findings and he published those findings on his own.

Further Reading

Carper, K.L., Professor, School of Architecture, College of Engineering. *Construction Failures: Learning the Lessons*, BSCES/ASCE Structural Group Lecture Series, 1997.

Ratay, R., *Forensic Structural Engineering Handbook*, McGraw Hill, 2000.

Carper, K., Professor, School of Architecture, College of Engineering, *Forensic Engineering*, CRC Press.

American Society of Civil Engineers (ASCE), *Guidelines for Failure Investigation*, 1989.

American Society of Civil Engineers (ASCE), *Guidelines for Forensic Engineering Practice*, 2003.

American Society of Civil Engineers (ASCE), *Guide to Investigation of Structural Failures*, 1979, 1986.

Root Cause Analysis Guidance Document, DOE Guideline DOE-NE-STD-1004-92, U.S. Department of Energy, Office of Nuclear Energy, Office of Nuclear Safety Policy and Standards, February 1992.

Bell, G.R., *Structural Failure Investigations* (BSCES/ASCE Structural Group Lecture Series). 1997.

Appendix A: The Eight (8) Phases of a Failure Investigation

I. Phase I: The Field Investigation
- Securing the Site
  - Have site secured
  - Safety considerations, that is, danger of further collapse
  - Preserve evidence
  - Request police assistance
- Documentation of Failure
  - Photography
  - Video
  - Notes
  - Sketches
  - (Clearly identify each location and correlate photos to sketches of site and drawings)
- Gathering Physical Evidence
  - Data
  - Samples
  - Materials
  - Drawings, etc.
- Interview Eyewitnesses
  - Early efforts pay best dividends (people and parties tend to clam up later)
  - Speak to people informally; let them tell you their story
  - Take notes, recordings, etc.
  - Take names, addresses, etc.
- Identify Parties Involved
  - Through drawings, other documents
  - Town records, etc. (i.e., building department, tax rolls)

II. Phase II: Gathering of Documents and Other Information
- Applicable Codes and Standards
  - Standards *at time of design and construction*
  - Codes *at time of design and construction*
  - Papers, publications, trade journals, indicating standards of "Usual and Customary Practice" *at time of design and construction*

- Specific Project Documents
  - Drawings
  - Specifications
  - Shop drawings
  - Construction logs
  - Minutes of meetings
  - Construction photos

III. Phase III: Document Review
- Review Drawings and other Documentation
  - Review loading criteria
  - Review loading requirements
  - Review field data and other information
- Conduct Brainstorming Sessions
  - Keep an open mind
  - Do not box yourself into a corner!
  - Examine all options, no matter how absurd they may look, or sound!
  - Develop failure hypotheses

IV. Phase IV: Analytical Investigation
- Investigate each of the failure hypotheses
- Perform a preliminary analysis
  - Perform "an order of magnitude" evaluation
  - Analyze structure, or system, or components
  - Design-check structure or components
  - Correlate analyses with field data
- Perform a detailed analysis
  - Utilize computer assisted techniques
  - Finite element methods
  - Static vs. dynamic solutions
  - Time history vs. response spectra
  - Progressive collapse

V. Phase V: Materials and Component Testing
- *"Testing Labs"* cannot read your mind!
- You must know/understand materials!
- Simple tests work best!
- As much as possible, try to anticipate results *prior* to obtaining them
- Never over-test
- Obtain raw data for possible later use

VI. Phase VI: Technical Analysis and Evaluation
- Review relevant facts and data
- Correlate test results to analysis
- Develop "the failure scenario"
- Develop "roles and responsibilities"
- Develop remedial solutions
- Form conclusions and opinions as to "the most probable cause and origin"

VII.   Phase VII: Documentation and Reporting
- Consult with client/lawyer on need of report (*prior to writing one!*)
- Make verbal presentations
- Prepare documentation
- Prepare report

VIII. Phase VIII: Litigation Support
- Preparation for litigation support
- Carefully outline credentials
- Interrogatories
- Depositions
- Expert testimony

Bridging the Foundations

Experts and the Admissibility of Evidence Concerning Scientific, Technical, and Other Specialized Areas of Knowledge

13

RAYMOND F. SEKULA AND SARAH ECKEL HINTON

The aim of this chapter is to provide a general overview on how the rules of evidence apply to the use of expert witnesses regarding the admissibility of scientific, technical, or other specialized areas of knowledge. The Federal Rules of Evidence are used as a baseline for this chapter. It is important to note that each state has its own rules of evidence, which may differ from the federal rules. Thus, it is important for the reader to supplement the generalized discussion contained in this chapter by reviewing the evidentiary rules of a specific state. A comprehensive overview of the issues addressed here can be obtained by reviewing the authoritative list of references given at the end at this chapter.

Expert evidence is based upon scientific, technical, or other specialized knowledge acquired by an individual qualified to testify based upon experience, education, or training.[1] Scientific evidence is "fact or opinion evidence that purports to draw on specialized knowledge of a science or relies upon scientific principles for its value."[1] (p. 599) Technical or other specialized knowledge is similar to scientific evidence in that it is also based upon specialized knowledge of technology or other specialized fields. An expert is traditionally used to explain such evidence as well as its relevance to an issue in a case. To be admissible, such testimony must comply with certain evidentiary rules. These rules were formulated to assist the court in determining who can be qualified as an expert, what an expert may testify about, and how to determine if the alleged scientific, technical, or other specialized knowledge is reliable.

An Overview of the Rules of Evidence Concerning Witnesses in General

Testimonial evidence is all evidence presented to the jury through statements of witnesses. All testimonial evidence has specific requirements governing its admissibility. These requirements differ based upon the type of witness testifying and the manner in which the witness is testifying.

The competency of a witness is presumed unless it can be demonstrated to the trial judge that the witness lacks the ability to perceive, recollect, or narrate his firsthand knowledge or that he fails to understand that he has the duty to testify truthfully. This presumption is reflected in the general rule that all witnesses are competent to testify.[2] The ability to understand the duty to testify truthfully is manifested through the oath or affirmation of the witness, which is a condition precedent to the giving of testimony.[3]

Another interrelated but distinct rule of witness competency is that a lay witness must have had firsthand knowledge of the matter about which he intends to testify. This foundational requirement is met if the witness testifies that he was in a position to perceive and had firsthand knowledge regarding the matter about which he intends to testify. The most significant limitation imposed by the rules of evidence is that a lay witness may only testify to observed facts, and may not offer opinions regarding these facts, except in very specific circumstances.

An exception to this prohibition is that lay witnesses are competent to testify about opinions dealing with matters of common knowledge or experience. A form of this type of opinion testimony is called a collective fact or shorthand rendition, which is premised upon the inability of a witness to recount the actual facts underlying the basis for his opinion, such as age, speed, intoxication, mental state, or identification of the source of a smell.[4] A collective fact or shorthand rendition is an opinion that can be made reliably by a layperson because it is routinely made by the general population. For example, an opinion that the defendant was intoxicated could be made by a lay witness who had the opportunity to perceive the defendant's demeanor and behavior because most people know how an intoxicated person behaves.[5]

Another permissible lay witness opinion is that of a skilled lay observer who has specialized knowledge based upon firsthand observation, which in turn creates the witness's unique ability to state opinions about these observations. For example, a secretary may testify that a writing sample matches his/her boss's handwriting because he/she has been repeatedly exposed to his/her boss's handwriting. A skilled lay witness can also testify about the emotional state of a person who is well known to the witness.

To be admissible, an otherwise permissible lay witness opinion must be rationally based upon the perception of the witness and must be helpful in resolving any issue in question. Additionally, a lay witness will not be permitted to testify to an opinion when the jury is capable of drawing the same inference based upon the factual testimony of the witness. Therefore, any opinion testimony that would not be helpful or necessary for the jury to understand the facts observed by the witness is inadmissible. Although there are several exceptions to the general ban of opinion testimony offered by lay witnesses, these exceptions are generally interpreted and applied narrowly by the court.

Expert Testimony

Generally, as stated previously, a lay witness is incompetent to testify in opinion form. This rule is without exception when the opinion deals with scientific, technical, or other specialized areas of knowledge. On the other hand, experts are permitted to offer such opinions subject to the rules of evidence discussed later.

An expert may fulfill many different roles when testifying at trial and may testify as a custodian solely for establishing a chain of custody for physical evidence, or as an authenticator of demonstrative or documentary evidence. An expert may testify as a lay witness regarding his or her firsthand observations of a fact at issue, as a facilitator of admissibility of specialized facts or data, or as an educator to help the jury understand or evaluate technical evidence at issue in the case. An expert may be appointed by the court with specific duties, and may be called to testify or provide a deposition regarding such matters. Primarily, an expert is called to testify as a specialist to give an opinion or conclusion regarding facts that are at issue in a case.

Expert Qualifications

An expert is a person with specific training, education, experience, or understanding in an area which is beyond the common understanding of the public. By definition, an expert is "[a] person who, through education or experience, has developed skill or knowledge in a particular subject, so that he or she may form an opinion that will assist the fact finder."[6] There is no requirement that an expert has a specific educational degree or experience to qualify as an expert in the area and only has to have knowledge in a specific area that is greater than the understanding of the public. Generally, if he or she has more understanding of an issue or an area of specialty than the jury has, he or she will be considered an expert.

The court will determine that a witness is an expert based upon his knowledge, skill, training, experience, or education regarding a specialized matter. This standard uses a lay person as the basis for comparison to the expert's alleged expertise. Any person with greater knowledge, skill, experience, education, or training than a lay person regarding a specific matter can be determined by the court to be qualified as an expert. The witness's lack of formal education has no bearing on his ability to be qualified as an expert when practical skills or experience are better measures of expertise. The qualification of an expert is fact and subject matter specific to the issues litigated in a case.

Subject Matter

Expert testimony is only appropriate when such testimony would be necessary or helpful to the jury in understanding an issue presented in the case. This limitation recognizes that experts should not be permitted to testify regarding matters that are within common knowledge. Expert testimony is considered necessary when the subject matter is complex, technical, or scientific. Additionally, expert testimony will still be permissible if it is considered helpful to the jury. For expert testimony to be helpful, it must be offered for the purpose of aiding the jury's understanding of a fact which is at issue in the case. The court makes this subject matter determination with great latitude. Generally, expert testimony will not be excluded if reasonably connected to the goal of aiding the jury in making factual conclusions.

Opinion Validity and Admissibility

As stated before, the purpose of expert testimony is to aid the jury's understanding in making factual conclusions because the subject matter is beyond common experience. In addition, courts are concerned with the reliability of an expert's opinion because of its potential to mislead the jury. As a result, the court is required to determine that the expert's testimony is based on sufficient facts or data, is the product of reliable principles or methods, and that the expert's conclusions are reliable and relevant.

Theories, Methods, and Principles

The method, theory, or principle that supports the expert opinion is subject to a preliminary determination of admissibility. The court may ignore the preliminary determination of admissibility only when the theory utilized in formulating the opinion is deemed sufficiently reliable in the scientific or technical field to which it belongs, or is subject to judicial notice.[7] If the method, theory, or principle is determined to be sufficiently reliable in the field to which it belongs, the court will generally accept its use in the creation of scientific evidence or as the basis of expert opinions. The issue regarding how the court should make this reliability determination has undergone many historical changes. One of these three different approaches is still utilized in most of the state court systems, but in the federal system, the Federal Rules of Evidence provide a new and specific rule.[8] Four major cases that each provide a specific standard for evaluating scientific evidence and expert's opinions are *Frye*,[9] *Daubert*,[10] *Joiner*,[11] and *Kumho Tire Company*.[12]

The Frye Approach.   Originally, scientific evidence was uniformly reviewed under the *Frye* standard that required that the principle used in formulating it had "gained general acceptance in the specific field" to which it belonged, before any evidence based on the theory could be admitted.[13] This standard can be difficult to meet, especially if the scientific evidence that is in question is developing or is too new to have reached the level of "general acceptance." Although the majority of courts have abandoned the *Frye* approach, a minority of jurisdictions still follow it. As a result, in some jurisdictions, developing science, or opinions based on minority or alternative theories, may not be admissible. The *Frye* standard raises two issues that have not been uniformly resolved in the jurisdictions that still follow the *Frye* approach: (1) "What does 'general acceptance' require?" and (2) "What is the 'proper field' to which certain theories and techniques belong?"

The issue of "general acceptance" defines the degree to which scientific theory and technique must be accepted by a specific scientific community before it is admissible. The "general acceptance" standard allows the court to defer to the specialists within scientific communities to determine reliability. In theory, this deference is practical because scientists are the best individuals to determine scientific reliability. However, in practice, this standard has been difficult for courts to apply because "general acceptance" does not require all disciplines to agree. Some courts have determined that a clear majority of a particular field must believe that the theory or process is reliable.[14] Majority acceptance is not just a quantitative analysis made by the court, but requires a qualitative analysis of the opinions within the scientific community.[15]

The *Frye* analysis also questions which segment of the scientific community is the "particular field" that accepts the theory and technique as being reliable. This evaluation requires the court to categorically define the fields to which such evidence belongs.[16]

The court evaluates the community as a broad group because most theories are multidisciplinary in nature.[17] All relevant disciplines are evaluated as to their opinion regarding the reliability of the theory. As a result of this multidisciplinary approach under the *Frye* standard, general acceptance requires more than acceptance by the population that regularly uses such theories or techniques. This approach can result in the inadmissibility of theories, techniques, or principles that have not gained uniform acceptance within many disciplines. Problems with the standard, as well as its limited application to scientific evidence, resulted in the hallmark Supreme Court decision in *Daubert*.

The Daubert Approach and Its Trilogy. The *Daubert* decision established a two-part test, "reliability plus relevancy," to be employed when evaluating scientific evidence. The Court listed a number of factors, which are not exclusive or controlling of this determination. Those factors are as follows:

- Whether the scientific theory or technique can be or has been tested
- Whether the theory or technique has been subjected to peer review and publication
- Whether the theory or technique has a known or potential rate of error
- Whether the theory or technique is generally accepted.

The *Daubert* Court created a standard of review through this list that was flexible depending on the type of knowledge being reviewed. The standard could be applied to downplay or disregard factors that were inapplicable to the theory or technique reviewed, and allowed for new factors to be considered when appropriate. Under the *Daubert* standard, the courts may find certain theories to be so reliable that judicial notice of reliability is warranted.

The second question addressed under the *Daubert* analysis questions whether the knowledge will assist or could assist the jury in their deliberations. This standard recognized that the *Frye* test only concerns the admissibility of the theory or technique. *Daubert* expressly requires the court to evaluate the relevancy of the theory to the facts at issue in a case. This second test evaluates whether a sufficient nexus exists between the theory utilized and facts at issue which allowed the resulting opinion to be found relevant and reliable. If the theory could not be usefully applied to the facts of the case, it would be inadmissible. This evaluation applied the admissibility test by balancing the probative value of the opinion against the prejudicial effect of admitting the opinion into evidence, while also evaluating the usefulness of the theory to the jury's fact finding.[18] The *Daubert* decision effectively eliminated several issues that were problematic in *Frye*, but also raised new questions regarding the proper evaluation of conclusions generated by admissible theory, as well as how the court should evaluate nonscientific expert testimony for reliability. Two additional cases, *Joiner* and *Kumho Tire*, merged with the holding in *Daubert* to answer these questions, creating what is often referred to as the *Daubert* trilogy.

The case of *General Electric vs. Joiner* acknowledged that the conclusions, usually the ultimate opinion advanced by the expert, must also be evaluated for issues of relevancy and reliability before such conclusions can be admissible in the form of expert testimony. This holding recognized that opinions generated from reliable theory or process could still fail to be reliable. *Joiner* established the court's responsibility to evaluate the principles underlying scientific evidence or opinions, and whether the methodology was reliably applied to result in a specific conclusion. If the court determined that an "analytical gap" exists between the theory and the conclusion, the *Daubert* analysis will require such conclusions to be inadmissible. As a result, under *Joiner*, a *Daubert* analysis applies to all portions of an opinion before the opinion will be admissible, including the interaction between the opinion and the theory. Although an expert's conclusion had to be verifiable under *Joiner*, the question of how to evaluate nonscientific evidence remained until the Supreme Court decided the case of *Kumho Tire Co. vs. Carmichael.*

Kumho Tire held that a *Daubert* style evaluation is also appropriate for nonscientific theories, methods, or principles due to the flexibility of applying *Daubert* standards in addition to other pertinent factors. The Court expressly stated that this analysis is appropriate when technical or specialized knowledge is at issue. Therefore, an expert practicing in an area other than science must be held to the same standards of reliability as scientific experts. The Court created another problem by constructing this express rule because some theories used by experts can only be subjectively measured, and the resulting opinions lack sufficient external means of verification. This issue has been resolved by granting the trial court great discretion in determining admissibility by allowing the expert to justify his or her theories to satisfy the preliminary determination of reliability.

Federal Rules of Evidence 702.   The Daubert trilogy resulted in the amendment of the Federal Rules of Evidence in 2000.[19] Federal Rule of Evidence 702 expressly mandates that all expert testimony, not just scientific, shall be evaluated for reliability.[20] The rule provides that:

> If scientific, technical, or other specialized knowledge will assist the trier of fact to understand the evidence or to determine a fact in issue, a witness qualified as an expert by knowledge, skill, experience, training, or education, may testify thereto in the form of an opinion or otherwise, if (1) the testimony is based upon sufficient facts or data; (2) the testimony is the product of reliable principles and methods; and (3) the witness has applied the principles and methods reliably to the facts of the case.[20]

The legislative history underlying the Rules suggests additional considerations when reviewing the admissibility of a theory, method, or principle. These considerations include whether (1) the expert testimony is independently based on research not for the purposes of litigation; (2) it is from a commonly accepted discipline instead of one that has failed to gain general acceptance; (3) the opinion is sufficiently grounded in the method or principle applied; and (4) the consideration or accounting for viable alternative explanations is recognized within the discipline.[21] The Federal Rules also require some level of evaluation as to the relationship between a valid theory, sufficient underlying facts, and the conclusion offered by the expert.[20] This interrelated portion of the preliminary evaluation was never expressly required before the 2000 amendment Federal Rule of Evidence 702.

Sufficient Underlying Facts or Data

The underlying facts utilized in an expert's opinion are subject to two independent determinations regarding admissibility. The first analysis is a preliminary determination of whether the underlying data provides a sufficient basis for the opinion. The second evaluation focuses on the specific data utilized and questions whether the underlying fact itself is admissible.

The sufficiency determination focuses on (1) whether the facts relied upon can be supported by the evidence of record; (2) evaluates whether the data relied upon encompasses the issue in the case; and (3) measures the quantitative amount of data or facts utilized in formulating the expert opinion. Through this analysis, the court ensures that the opinion is sufficiently grounded in relevant facts of sufficient quantity to justify reliance.

The second analysis that is applied to the underlying data is not a preliminary determination, but is an evaluation of the admissibility of the facts or data underlying the opinion.[22] This analysis can result in the inadmissibility of the opinion as a whole, or serve to limit the permissible scope of disclosure of an expert on direct examination. Facts that provide the underlying basis for the expert's opinion may be inadmissible due to the application of other rules of evidence. When the data underlying the opinion is inadmissible, the opinion remains admissible only if those facts are of the type that is reasonably deemed reliable by the customary practices of the specialized field. For example, a physician who relies upon x-rays of a patient when making a diagnosis can testify to that diagnosis, even if the patient's x-rays are not a part of the record. This exception recognizes that if an expert can reasonably form an opinion based upon inadmissible evidence when performing his area of expertise, then the court should permit such an opinion to be sufficiently reliable to be presented to the trier of fact. However, if the underlying facts are not reasonably relied upon within the expert's specialty, an opinion premised on such facts will be inadmissible.[23]

When the underlying data is not admissible under other rules of evidence, specific procedural rules apply. The expert may not disclose the underlying evidence to the jury during direct examination because the jury could misapply the evidence to other issues in the case. The presumption that the evidence should not be disclosed can be overcome if the court determines that the probative value of disclosure substantially outweighs the prejudicial effect of disclosure.[22] For example, if disclosure was necessary for the jury to properly understand and weigh the expert opinion and a limiting instruction could resolve any issues of improper use of the evidence by the jury, then the court can permit disclosure of such facts. In contrast, when underlying facts are admissible in their own right as substantive evidence, these facts can be used by the jury for any purpose, and the full disclosure of such data is permissible. Finally, if the expert is questioned about inadmissible evidence by the opposing party, full disclosure of such data is then generally permissible.

An expert can utilize three sources of underlying facts or data to support his or her opinion. The first source of facts or data is the type received by firsthand observation by the expert, and is wholly admissible as firsthand knowledge of the expert. The second source is information gained by the expert during the presentation of evidence at trial. The expert who relies only on evidence presented at trial can disclose all underlying facts because these have already been disclosed to the jury. The final source of underlying facts is data received outside the court or as firsthand observation. When these outside facts are the basis of an expert opinion, the evaluation of admissibility and reasonable reliance will be required before an expert can testify as to either the facts or the opinion.

An expert can also form an opinion based upon assumed facts that are or will be part of the record. Assumed facts can be disclosed to the jury through a hypothetical question that is presented to the expert. A hypothetical question is poised by asking the expert to assume that the facts contained in the question are true before rendering an opinion based upon those assumed facts.[24] Hypothetical questions serve as a substitute for the expert's lack of firsthand knowledge.

The Expert's Conclusions

The conclusion reached by the expert must rationally relate to the theory and the underlying facts utilized in forming the expert's opinion. If an analytical gap exists between the opinion, the underlying facts, and the theory used by the expert the expert's opinion will be inadmissible.[25] Further, the expert's conclusion may be evaluated to determine if each stage of the analysis, technique, or process used was reliable. The court will disallow opinions that stray from the generally accepted cause and effect recognized within the specialty. The evaluation of an expert's conclusion will not require inadmissibility when competing, but reliable, principles within a discipline can result in different conclusions. The expert must only demonstrate to the trial judge that the conclusion fits the theory and underlying facts utilized by the expert. Some jurisdictions will permit the application of a recognized minority theory as long as reliability determinations are satisfied, and the theory is actually recognized by a minority within the specialty. However, the more subjective a theory utilized by the expert is, the greater is the likelihood that the conclusion is not verifiable and the opinion will be inadmissible. Additionally, an expert who bases an opinion only on experience must be able to validate why experience alone is an indicator of reliability.[26]

The preliminary determination of the admissibility of a conclusion weighs the interplay between the theory and the data. The court defers to the profession over the individual results of an expert, which requires the expert to follow professional standards. If the court is apprised that any step in the scientific, technical, or specialized process was unreliable, the entire opinion will be inadmissible regardless of whether the expert merely deviated from acceptable norms or misapplied the accepted process. A subjective process will be measured by determining whether the conclusion was well reasoned, properly grounded, and was not speculative. All conclusions must be sufficiently grounded in accepted learning or experience within the specialized field and must be adequately justifiable.

The Federal Rules of Evidence provide only one express limitation regarding expert conclusions. An expert cannot testify to an opinion regarding the mental state of a criminal defendant when the mental state is an element of a claim, charge, or defense.[27] A court also limits opinions that have purely legal connotations, but will generally allow opinions based on mixed issues of fact and law.[28] The rules of evidence do not expressly recognize this limitation on expert testimony, but the courts exclude legal conclusions by finding them to be neither necessary nor helpful, and as being beyond the permissible scope of the expert's field of specialty.

The final judicial safety net regarding the admissibility of expert opinions is not an exclusionary rule but the large scope of permissible questioning of an expert witness during cross-examination. The cross-examining attorney can ask the expert to disclose the underlying facts that were used in his or her opinion and challenge their validity. The theory, method, or principle can be challenged by the substantive introduction of reliable treatises, periodicals, or pamphlets to suggest that the expert employed an unreliable theory.[29] The expert's opinion can also be challenged by attacking the link between the theory, underlying data, and the conclusion. This would most likely occur by a battle of the experts, rather than by cross-examination.

Finally, cross-examination exposes the expert to an attack regarding many issues, including his or her opinions, qualifications, or character. The expert is subject to impeachment under the same guidelines as any witness, in addition to the supplementary considerations of the expert's qualifications. The trustworthiness of the opinion can be challenged by suggesting that the expert is not competent to give the opinion. An expert's education, skill, training, or knowledge is subject to attack during cross-examination to suggest incompetence to the jury even if the expert has satisfied the preliminary qualification determination. The expert's character is also subject to attack by opinion evidence or reputation evidence as to the expert's truthfulness or competence within his or her area of specialty. The expert may be subject to evidence that would suggest bias, as with the amount the expert's fee for testifying or the continued or past employment of the expert by the party for whom the expert is currently testifying. The expert's total income for testimony as compared to his or her professional salary can also be used to suggest bias. The expert's prior statements regarding the case and prior testimony in other cases can be used to impeach his or her opinions or credibility.

Notes

1. Black's Law Dictionary 597, 8th ed., 1999.
2. FED. R. EVID. 601.
3. FED. R. EVID. 603.
4. For example, to require that the underlying facts of the observation to be provided before the witness could testify that he or she "smelled marijuana" would require the witness to be able to articulate and identify all distinctive characteristics of the smell before testifying.
5. However, the statement that "the defendant was well over the legal limit when he got into his car" is an opinion that a layperson would not be competent to make because of the specific level of intoxication required legally. The fact not perceived by the witness, the BAC, would be necessary to support the opinion.
6. Black's Law Dictionary, at 619 (citing FED. R. EVID. 702).
7. See *Kumho Tire Co. v. Carmichael*, 119 S.Ct. 1167, 1176 (1999).
8. FED. R. EVID. 702.
9. *Frye v. United States*, 293 F. 1013 (D.C.Cir. 1923).
10. *Daubert v. Merrell Dow Pharmaceuticals*, 113 S.Ct. 2786 (1993).
11. *General Electric v. Joiner*, 522 U.S. 136 (1997).
12. *Kumho Tire Co.*, 119 S.Ct. 1167 (1999).
13. See *Frye*, 293 F. 1013.
14. See *People v. Guerra*, 690 P.2d 635 (Cal. 1984).
15. See *Hadden v. State*, 690 So.2d 573 (Fla. 1997).
16. See *Reed v. State*, 391 A.2d 364 (Md. 1978).
17. For example, polygraph evidence and opinions based on such theories relate to the fields of behavioral science, psychology, biological science, physiology, as well as other rationally related disciplines. See *United States vs. Alexander*, 526 F.2d 161 (8th Cir. 1975).

18. For example, a theory that failed to sufficiently affect a direct issue in the case would be inadmissible due to being a waste of time or leading to a confusion of the issues.

19. See FED. R. EVID. 701–704.

20. FED. R. EVID. 702.

21. FED. R. EVID. 702 cmt note.

22. FED. R. EVID. 703.

23. For example, a medical professional might reasonable rely on statements made by other professionals who have treated the patient, their records, the patient's own statements, or even the statements of a party on behalf of the patient. All of these underlying facts or data would be reasonably relied upon within the medical profession. Although these facts may be inadmissible in trial, they would be a valid basis for a medical opinion.

24. For example, "assuming that the patient was bleeding internally for five hours, would an operation performed during the first hour of bleeding have more success than an operation performed at the fifth hour?" The question suggests that the fact assumed is that the patient was bleeding internally for five hours.

25. See *Joines*, 522 US 136.

26. For example, if an individual would be recognized in his or her specialty as an expert because the individual has 20 years of experience, this status may be sufficient to warrant judicial deference to that specialty's standards for expertness.

27. FED. R. EVID. 704b.

28. For example, a question about whether an individual had the intent to act at the time of an event could be phrased to solicit a legal conclusion because intent is an element of an intentional tort whereas the lack of such intent allows recovery only in negligence.

29. See FED. R. EVID. 803(18).

Further Reading

J. Strong, *McCormick on* Evidence, 5th ed., Hornbook Series, Student ed., 1999.

J. Strong, *McCormick on Evidence*, 5th ed., Practitioner Treaties Series, 1992.

A. Moenssens, J. Starrs, C. Henderson, & F. Inbau, *Scientific Evidence in Civil and Criminal Cases*, 4th ed., 1995.

G. C. Lilly, *An Introduction to the Law of Evidence*, 3rd ed., 1996.

D. Leonard and V. Gold, *Evidence: A Structured Approach*, 2004.

Foundations of Forensic Science

Evidence and the Physical Sciences

A Critical Analysis of Selected Features of Fingerprinting

14

JAMES E. STARRS

Introduction: The Coverage

The scope of this section is not all-encompassing but is rather designedly selective. What is excluded are those challenges to fingerprinting and its interpretations whose likelihood is of infrequent occurrence. Among such exclusions are matters relevant to crime scene and crime laboratory efforts to visualize latent prints on both porous and nonporous surfaces.

Whether the failure to use a laser or an alternate light source is the cause for an inability to bring to light a latent print is of importance to the proficiency of fingerprint examinations, but in the forensic setting, it is more of theoretical significance than germane to what happens in a court of law concerning fingerprint evidence.

Occasionally, hopefully in only a rare instance, a document may be treated with the chemical ninhydrin by an inexperienced or careless fingerprint examiner who acts while failing to recognize that a document examiner's opportunity to glean identifying details from a document might be hampered or destroyed by the chemical reaction that ensues. Such incompetent spoliation of evidence is not the subject of this section for the reason that it is a statistical nonissue in contrast with others that go to the roots of fingerprint opinions relating to identifications of latent prints and other related matters. In fact, a search of the opinions of both state and federal courts fails to disclose any occasions when the processes of lifting fingerprints were the central focus of attention. That absence warrants a similar absence here.

In short, this section is directed to the fundamentals and the rubrics of fingerprint identification methods in all their configurations as well as the opinions of fingerprint examiners that go beyond fingerprint identifications to include opinions on the position or action of an identified individual at the time of the placement of a fingerprint.

Preposterous Claims

Since its first serious consideration for regular usage in law enforcement occurring at the end of the 19th century, fingerprinting has become the Holy Grail both of the courts and among the public, who bring their views into the jury room. From the time when fingerprint identifications were merely a corroboration for Alphonse Bertillon's method of identifying an individual through bodily measurements (termed anthropometry), fingerprinting has surpassed all else as the preferred and most assured method of personal identification. Whether that attitude and even conviction is justified is the gist of this section.

Even with the advent of Sir Alec Jeffries DNA identification system in the mid-1980s, fingerprinting has not lost its premier status. This purported elevated position among personal identifiers may be in part attributed to the established fact that unlike DNA identifications, the fingerprints of identical twins (monozygotes) differ sufficiently to distinguish one from the other. But there is more than that as well.

In the case of DNA identifications, bodily fluids or tissues are a must to start the identification process, but fingerprinting is not so limited. Indeed, in spite of the well-recognized capacity of fingerprinting to identify an individual, there are still those who deliberately commit their crimes without wearing gloves or who leave the gloves they were wearing at the crime scene to be reversed by a keen crime scene investigator to reveal the presence of fingerprint ridges inside the gloved fingers. Many residential burglaries are of this character as are a majority of daytime robberies of commercial establishments, either committed with ungloved hands or with gloves left behind.

It would appear, therefore, without the benefit of statistical studies and relying only on the anecdotal evidence of those practicing fingerprinting and DNA profiling, that quantitatively fingerprinting bulks larger as a usable tool in the arsenal of law enforcement than DNA profiling.

But even well before the emergence of DNA profiling, fingerprinting had garnered the reputation for being the most certain, most concrete, most definitive method of personal identification. Fingerprint identifications have thus come to be synonymous with absolute, even apodictic, certainty.

In proof of this assertion is the known fact that DNA arrived in the justice system courtesy of its coat-tailing on fingerprinting.[1] Even Jeffries in making a case for DNA's reliability characterized it in an early article by him as DNA fingerprinting. And article after article has followed suit, even in recent days, putting DNA on a pedestal of acceptability once occupied exclusively by fingerprinting.

The published opinions from the courts have not lagged behind journal articles, both scientific and nonscientific, to the extent that any new technique for identification can gain credence if it is dubbed as just another form of fingerprinting. So the voice spectrograph, now widely criticized as an identification medium, was once labeled by a court as a type of fingerprinting. And infrared spectroscopy, as far removed from fingerprinting as a mongoose is from a bicycle, has been given the designation in a court opinion of creating an infrared fingerprint.[2]

The band plays on with the refrain of fingerprint's linguistic usages. The databases in New York and Maryland of breech face markings from newly manufactured guns are said, in the media, to establish a data base of "ballistic fingerprints."[3] That phrasing is a misnomer of the worst order since firearms' identifications from breech face striae on spent cartridge cases are not even remotely related to ballistics, just as ballistics and fingerprinting are so divergent as to be antipodes.

One cannot read a magazine or a newpaper without being confronted with some device or activity being described as a fingerprint, if only since the work is seen to capture in the public's mind the notion of specificity, certainty, and uniqueness. Oncologists speak in terms of a genetic fingerprint, even though there are no data to support an assertion that the patters of arches, loops and whorls, or even the minutiae or Galton's details of fingerprints can be connected to one's ancestors' medical afflictions.[4]

Reviewers of dance routines find in them "stylistic fingerprints" distinguishing one from the other.[5] Why even terrorism leaves its fingerprints, so it is metaphorically said, so that Baathists in Syria can be clearly seen as participating "all over the violence in Iraq."[6]

The reason for this patently misleading use of fingerprinting is simple and straightforward. The acceptability, indeed the reliability, of a scientific or purported scientific technology is well-nigh guaranteed if it is misaligned with fingerprinting. In the public's and the judiciary's minds, fingerprinting identifications are confidently and regularly equated with a level of certainty next to Godliness. And who is daring enough to take God or His handiwork to task?

All of which makes challenging fingerprinting even more than an uphill battle on the order of that which confronted Sisyphus. It is also one that calls forth the wizardry of a Gandolf. In sum, to successfully challenge the received status of fingerprinting as nonetheless reeking with human and scientific fallibility, one must be in the presence of open-minded persons, not wedded to the view that fingerprinting is inviolate or untouchable.

The Fingerprint as an "Unforgeable Signature"

One of the least defensible encomiums in which fingerprinting is too often cloaked is its being described as an "unforgeable signature." The Virginia courts, both trial and appeal,[7] are particularly prone to propound this fallacy even though its first usage in the U.S. courts occurred in an Arizona appellate court opinion in 1921.[8] That decision cited as its principal precedent some unnamed "students of the science" of fingerprinting who were said to "claim that a finger print is 'an unforgeable signature.'"

It was not until 1968 that the origin of the phrasing "an unforgeable signature" became known. In a decision on an appeal from a burglary conviction to the Virginia Supreme Court, credit is given to *Parker v. Rex*,[9] a 1912 opinion from the High Court of Australia, for recognizing the "reality" that a fingerprint is an "unforgeable signature."

Even Mr. Justice Brennan, speaking for the U.S. Supreme Court in 1969, by implication, gave credence to the fingerprint as an "unforgeable signature." As he put it, "fingerprinting is an inherently more reliable and effective crime-solving tool than eye witness identifications or confessions and is not subject to such abuses as the improper line-up and the 'third degree.'"[10] One might rightly ask whether the abuse of forging a fingerprint was implicitly discounted by Mr. Justice Brennan since the possibility of a fingerprint forgery has been rejected quite expressly in court opinions parroting the "unforgeable signature" verbiage in Mississippi,[11] Nevada,[12] New York,[13] Pennslyvania,[14] Texas,[15] Virginia,[2] and Vermont.[16]

The phrasing of an "unforgeable signature" is redolent of handwriting analysis, a field in which document examiners are regularly and very conscientiously engaged. The connection of fingerprinting to document examination of handwriting is not entirely unwarranted, for document examinations, like fingerprint examinations, have stood the test of time, the mere passage of it, that is, and little else for more than one hundred years. In addition, it has been written by Frederick Cherrill, formerly the chief of New Scotland Yard's fingerprint bureau that "from time immemorial there seems to be abundant evidence that finger-marks and documents have had an inseparable affinity"[17] at least in the authentication of documents by the scrivener's placing his fingerprint on them. Currently, coinciding with legal efforts to bring a more thorough-going and honest appraisal of fingerprinting to the fore, handwriting analysis is also under intense scrutiny for its reliability. It seems only just therefore that both handwriting analysis and fingerprinting should stand or fall together.

The forgery of fingerprints, speaking expansively of all forms of the falsification of fingerprints, has been a subject of much, sometimes heated, discussion. Both before and after the ugly revelations of New York State's special prosecutor Nelson Roth in 1997[18] concerning the "reality" of the falsification of fingerprints by New York State troopers by planting, or testifying to having found, a person's fingerprints at a crime scene the forgery of fingerprints had been recognized in the courts.

In 1984 the travail of Gary W. Rank ended in a U.S. District Court in Pennsylvania[19] when a jury awarded Rank both compensatory and punitive damages in his civil rights action against three Pennsylvania state policemen alleging that his fingerprint had been planted at the scene of a burglary murder. Fortunately for Rank he had been acquitted after being tried in a Pennsylvania trial court for the murder which followed the breaking and entry. He was even more fortunate in being the beneficiary of a Pennsylvania court order expunging his arrest record which had been predicated on the false evidence of the planted fingerprint.

However, many of the victims of the falsification of fingerprints by the New York State troopers, which were highlighted in the Roth Report, were not graced with acquittals. Many of them were either unjustly convicted, because their convictions were based on testimony in support of the legitimacy of the falsified fingerprints, even though there was other more sustainable evidence of their guilt or were erroneously convicted solely resulting from the planted fingerprint evidence and nothing more incriminating.

The Roth Report and the tawdry disclosures that preceded it concerning the nefarious police conduct in New York State received wide and in depth coverage by both print and broadcast media. Such public attention even included a lengthy interview session on March 28, 1993, *CBS News program 60 Minutes*.[20]

In that program, David Harding, the *deus ex machina* of the corrupt fingerprint testimony elaborated upon in the Roth Report, was in a peculiarly confessional mood, both relating to his own involvement in the fingerprint chicanery and that of a number of his fellow police officers. At one point, he was asked by interviewer Lesley Stahl to provide the specifics as to how he would go about planting spurious fingerprints. His answer cast a long shadow, both on him and his superiors.

Harding cited a case "where the old man was beaten" inside the victim's house. Harding lifted a suspect's fingerprint from a beer bottle "outside the victim's house" and then lied by saying he had found the print on the kitchen sink in the house where the beating occurred.

Harding, however, was not willing to take the onus of responsibility for his misfeasance on his shoulders alone. "We're not talking about a loose cannon here," he said, "one person runs amok inside of an investigation. There are — there are far too many checks and balances, far too many bosses, far too many superiors overlooking your shoulders and so forth, that one person can run amok in all these cases and do all these things without somebody knowing what the score is."

What Harding was declaring was that the "checks and balances" do not always work to demonstrate that a fingerprint is not what it purports to be. The Roth Report recommended certain approaches to deter and discover such falsifications as occurred in the handling of the evidence by David Harding and others in the state police of his wrongdoing bent. Photographs should be taken of the fingerprint on the object and at the place from which it is said to be lifted. These are termed photos of the fingerprint *in situ*. As a result a, fingerprint on a beer bottle cannot be palmed off as a fingerprint lifted from a kitchen sink. Going further than this recommendation, the New York State police are said to have changed their policies "to require that two investigators confirm the gathering of a fingerprint" as well as to ensure that "photographs of fingerprints be taken."[21]

But the recommendation for photographs *in situ* and before lifting has long been a point of practical fingerprint processing according to the standards set forth in the FBI's booklet "The Science of Fingerprints."[22] At p. 187 of that document, it is said that "(I)n every case a print developed with powder should be photographed before lifting." The reason the FBI urges this practice is not to deter or disclose fingerprint misdeeds by crime scene investigators, although it most certainly will have that effect in a limited way, but to ensure that, if in the lifting process the latent print is rendered unusable to identify it to a suspect in a later laboratory comparison, the photograph will provide a fall back or second best opportunity to perform the comparison.

Yet with the sorry history of the Roth Report's disclosures still being aired in April of 2000 Judge Richard S. Bray of the Circuit Court of Newport News, Virginia, in a written opinion in *Watkins v. Com*[2] would be so out of touch with the new-found and much publicized reality of fingerprint forgery to repeat the old refrain that a fingerprint is "an unforgeable signature."

Worse yet in the burglary trial of Angel Morales in Brooklyn, New York's Supreme Court in February of 2000[23] the state's fingerprint expert, one Rosemarie Simonetti, when asked on crossexamination "is it true that fingerprints can be moved from one place to another?" she replied with an equivocal "Not to my knowledge."

The defense attorney, Mr. Sartori, however, was savvy enough to stay the course he had begun. "Are you familiar with the Roth report?" he asked, as he should since the Roth Report was replete with details concerning fingerprints being "moved from one place to another." Once again the fingerprint examiner (she called herself an "associate fingerprint technician") with ten years experience was ignorant of a matter integral to her own occupational calling. She said simply "No" indicating total unawareness of the Roth Report and the fingerprinting scandal underlying it.

But the defense attorney was tenacious enough not to take Ms. Simonetti's "No" for an answer. When the prosecutor, Mr. Kohler, interposed an objection to the defense's line of questioning, the Judge sided with Mr. Kohler in pointing out that "she said she's not familiar with it" which apparently means the subject was now off the charts.

But the defense, on the same issue, tried a different tack. "Are you familiar with the newspaper?", he inquired. To which Ms. Simonetti affirmed that she was, but the prosecutor was quick to object and the Judge was quicker yet in sustaining that objection without entertaining any argument from the defense.

Still the defense plodded on, "Are you familiar with New York State troopers —" but this time the prosecutor's objection cut off Ms. Simonetti's anwer. Yet, without giving a hint of being deterred or interrupted in his quest, the defense continued "being arrested and indicted for removing," to which the reply to the truncated question was "Only from reading it in the paper." That ended the exchange because the Judge chimed in with "Sustained. Sustained" causing Ms. Simonetti to say "I'm sorry." Meanwhile, the defense attorney sought to develop other matters with his continuing crossexamination.

Apparently not pleased with his treatment while crossexamining Ms. Simonetti, the defense attorney, Mr. Santori, returned to court two weeks later with a request designed to put the trial judge on the defensive, certainly on posttrial proceedings. On February 16, 2000, the defense attorney asked the trial judge, Lewis L. Douglass, for permission to call an expert witness on the fingerprint planting issue and another as well. He stated:

"The two witnesses that the people called with respect to the fingerprint evidence testified to two specific statements that I believe to be inaccurate, if not untrue."

He explained:

"One, that a print could not be messed up or destroyed in the lifting process, and secondly (Ms. Simonetti) that fingerprints couldn't be moved from one location to another."

The defense attorney requested the opportunity to call his expert for the purpose of attacking these two inaccuracies in the testimony of the prosecution's witnesses. But the court peremptorily stated, "That's denied" and elaborated, "I don't think there is any reasonable view of the evidence that a fingerprint was moved ... the movement from point A to point B seems irrelevant in the content of this case." And yet the police officer who lifted the print from the crime scene did not take any photographs *in situ*, as the FBI's manual urges, in part to protect the crime scene investigator from the wallop of a "You planted the print" argument. The fact that no photographs were taken made the falsification claim more than a distinct possibility and certainly a relevant issue. In a similarly abrupt manner, the trial judge determined that the truth of the matter whether fingerprint "tape will smudge a fingerprint" was "an irrelevant issue." Even a quick reference to the FBI's manual would have demonstrated its decided relevance.

But Mr. Sartori for the defense had managed to spread on the record his insistence, rejected by the trial judge, of his right to impugn the credibility of the prosecution's witnesses with the evidence from his own expert. He might also have urged that to deny his request was to short change his client's right to confront his accusers by presenting evidence in opposition to their testimony. That claim, I am led to believe, is a contention now being made in the Federal District Court in Brooklyn, New York, since Morales' appeal from his conviction was rejected by New York's Appellate Division, Second Judicial Department on September 8, 2003, without having addressed the issues raised by the defense's request to present the testimony of its fingerprint expert.

Paradoxically, the false notion that a fingerprint is an unforgeable signature found its origin in the Australian courts, and it is in Australia where the phrasing has met its donnybrook. It was in 1982 that the Royal Mint at Perth, Australia, suffered the theft of 2000 oz of gold bullion in a most daring criminal escapade. Shortly, the Mickelberg brothers, Raymond, Peter, and Brian, became the prime suspects. It was the right forefinger (index finger) of Raymond, found thrice on a check, that was his undoing.

However, in spite of the Australian criminal justice system's not siding with the Mickelbergs, an author Avon Lovell wrote a book *The Mickelberg Stitch*[24] claiming that the Mickelberg brothers, and particularly Raymond, had been the victims of a police frame-up when a detective Tony Lewandowski planted Raymond's fingerprint on the incriminating check. He was alleged to have used a rubber cast of Raymond's finger and to have impressed it three separate times on the check, all three prints being of the same finger at the same angle and otherwise suspiciously identical. Lovell's book was banned from sale in Australia until 2002. The dispute still resonates in Australia with a sharp division of views as to the question of whether Raymond's right forefinger was an unforgeable signature or a forged one.

There is yet another paradox in these tales of the fingerprints being the so-called "unforgeable signature." It would appear, as it did in the trial of Angel Morales in Brooklyn, New York, that a well-prepared and alert defense attorney had been given an angle of attack on fingerprint testimony because the forgery or, more generally, the falsification of fingerprints is an established fact. Especially when there is no corroboration by photographs or by independent witnessing by the police that there has been no odious hanky-panky in the lifting of the suspect's prints, there is open to the defense a case for a permissible introduction of the Roth Report, the Mickelberg incident, and other similar proofs that the reiteration of the claim that a fingerprint is "an unforgeable signature" is even less entitled to be intoned as a reality than an ephemeral will-o'-the-wisp.

More Fuel for the Defense Flame: The CSI Effect

Jurors are sometimes querulous but always unpredictable participants in criminal trials. Who could predict, for example, that Baltimore, Maryland's DeAndre Whitehead[25] would be acquitted of murder when the victim's 11-year-old daughter testified that she saw Whitehead shoot her father. At a posttrial interview, an alternate juror explained his being disturbed by the prosecution's not producing evidence that Whitehead's fingerprints were on the murder weapon. Such an unreasonably demanding attitude reflects current affairs in the courtroom courtesy of jurors being taken in by the flapdoodle of the various TV produced CSI programs.

That Baltimore juror's viewpoint typifies the unrealistic expectations spawned in the minds of the public by CSI producers who are seen to emote: "if it happens on CSI, it can and should happen in a real-life courtroom." But regardless of the bogus science displayed before the millions who watch and ingest the scientific hokum of CSI, fingerprints are rarely found on the guns used in homicides. The gun, especially the handgun, is just not generally suitable for the retention of prints of value. That is a well-regarded fact among fingerprint examiners but not to the public infected as it is by the CSI effect. Indeed, in Baltimore, the police crime laboratory's statistics show that it recovered fingerprints of value for comparison purposes in a paltry "0.3% of firearms and related evidence it processed" in 2003.[26]

The absence of fingerprints was also viewed as instrumental in moving the jury in the Ted Binion murder trial in Las Vegas, Nevada, recently to acquit the defendants, Sandy Murphy and Rick Tabish, of the fatal poisoning of their casino owner victim. At posttrial, the media commentators attributed the jury's verdict at this second trial, in largest part, to the failure of the prosecution's fingerprint experts to find the fingerprints of the accused on an empty Xanax bottle found next to Binion's dead body. If Binion was coerced by the two defendants to take a drug overdose, it was surmised that their fingerprints, or at least one of them, should have been on the Xanax bottle found at the death scene.[27]

Assuming it was the lack of fingerprints where they might be expected that brought the jury to acquit Murphy and Tabish, the absence of prints of value for comparison uses could easily be explained by the presentation of a fingerprint expert's testimony at the trial. The jury could be informed by the expert that, notwithstanding their instinctual reaction or that conveyed by CSI, fingerprints of a usable nature are very often not discovered at places and on objects which the general public and CSI think would be apt and even ideal for the visualization of fingerprints. The investigation of the kidnapping scene in the nursery of Charles Lindbergh's New Jersey home from which "Little Lindy" was spirited away to his death is a case in support of the lack of fingerprints in the nursery as having no significance to the guilt of the offender, here being Bruno Richard Hauptmann.

The prosecution's response to the CSI effect on jurors by which they will present the testimony of their own expert to obviate the fallacious impression that a lack of physical evidence is indicative of the innocence of the accused has been termed "negative evidence" and the experts presenting it "negative evidence witnesses."

In the summer of 2002, for example, Agapito Lao went to trial in Boston for strangling his estranged wife, Alicia. The prosecution called two witnesses to certify that Lao had been at the murder scene just a half hour before the body of his wife was found, but the defense, to counter that testimony, pointed to the absence of incriminating forensic evidence, such as fingerprints, at the crime scene to bolster the prosecution's position that the husband had in fact been present at the time of his wife's death.[28]

But the prosecution was not to be out-strategized.by the defense. A forensic chemist was summoned to testify that the lack of physical evidence, such as fingerprints, implicating the husband was meaningless since the defendant, Lao, "had been in and out of his wife's apartment before the murder."

Defense attorneys, on their part, have also had resort to "negative evidence witnesses" to give their opinions that the absence of evidence is suggestive of their client, the accused's, noninvolvement in the crime charged. But the tactic, successful for the prosecution, has not been equally fruitful for the defense since a trial judge may not acquiesce in its use. *United States v. Frazier*,[29] is a case in point. There a defense expert was prevented from testifying for a kidnap/rape defendant that the lack of hair and bodily fluids connecting the defendant to the sexual assaults were indications that the rape as reported by the victim did not in fact occur. Apparently, in criminal trials, what is sauce (allowable) for the goose (prosecution) is not always sauce for the gander (defense).

Of course both prosecution and defense can seek to neutralize the CSI effect by the opening statements they present to the jury as well as in the questions they pose to potential jurors at the *voir dire*, always assuming that the trial judge will be agreeable with that strategy. However, the double and misleading impact of CSI and the perceived sacrosanct status of fingerprinting may be too much to surmount.

But the reaction of fingerprint experts to the CSI effect upon their work-a-day routine may be much more ambivalent. On the downside, the CSI programing could add a burden on them at the crime scene and in the laboratory, to counteract any negativism from their failing to find prints of value. On the upside, it is always gratifying to fingerprint experts to know they are riding a tsunami of huge public acceptance of their work product, regardless of the fact that it may not be entirely justified.

Fingerprinting Testimony beyond the Expert's Qualifications

Just as a fingerprint expert who is an expert only in the Henry system of classification should not testify that a latent print from an unknown person is identifiable to an exemplar print from a known person on account of the expert's going beyond his/her expertise in doing so, so too a fingerprint expert qualified to identify prints should not indulge in opinions certifying to the activity of the person leaving the print at the time it was deposited there. That is not a subject within the expertise of the fingerprint expert by reason of either his/her training or experience.

To satisfy the judicially imposed need to associate a fingerprint found at a crime scene with the commission of a crime rather than the placement's being unconnected to the crime's commission, a prosecutor may produce evidence of "attendant circumstances," which do not have to be independent of the fingerprint. Such circumstances may be either scientific or of a nonscientific but convincing investigative nature. Among incriminating facts would be the location of the print, the character of the place of premises where it was found, and the accessibility of the general public to the object on which the print was impressed.

In addition, fingerprint experts have been qualified to aid the prosecutor in his evidentiary time dating of a crime scene fingerprint by giving testimony that the placement of the print is crime related. It is with respect to this claim of expertise, to buttress a sagging prosecution, that fingerprint experts have come acropper in speaking beyond the accepted and proved limits of dactyloscopy.

Intense pressure is sure to be brought to bear on fingerprint experts, particularly when appearing on behalf of the prosecution, to do more than simply identify a latent print to its owner. An identification does not necessarily incriminate a suspect, especially where the premises and the location of the print on them are open to public access. The prosecution needs an indication from the fingerprint expert that the print was placed at the crime scene contemporaneously with the commission of the crime and in pursuance of it. It is in this venture that the fingerprint expert too frequently strays from the straight and narrow path of scientific rectitude.

It is most especially on the issue of the presumed activity of a person at the time a fingerprint was impressed by him/her on an object that fingerprint experts have been invited to go beyond their more limited qualifications.

In this endeavor, fingerprint experts are generally not acting with neutral scientific pomp but rather with adversarial police investigative circumstance. They have become detectives who solve crimes more by a reliance on deduction than on the inductive process of a true scientist.

When a palm print was discovered on a countertop in an Arkansas establishment open to the public, a fingerprint expert was crowned with the untrammeled authority to say that the print was placed on the object while the person's hand was engaged in a twisting motion, "as distinguished from someone placing their hand on it in a normal manner," as if he were at the time of placement vaulting over the counter top. Guess what? The fingerprint expert's testimony, quite fortuitously I am sure, fits the description of the eyewitnesses to the crime who had seen the then unidentified robber hand vault over the counter using his hand to steady his leap.[30]

In a fingerprint-on-the-tub murder case from Hawaii,[31] a fingerprint comparison expert, as the court described him, who was a Sergeant with the Honolulu police, appeared for the prosecution to offset the accused's argument that his prints were implanted in the bathroom where the crime occurred while he was properly and legitimately using that public facility to relieve himself. The prosecution's expert found himself able to say that the prints on the tub and the toilet seat convinced him that they were impressed there by a person "apparently trying to pull himself forward at the time the prints were impressed" and that the accused's body was "fairly low in relation to the floor" when the prints were impressed there.

This testimony was tendered and received at the trial level over the accused's most ardent objection. This purportedly scientific evidence, the defendant protested, reeked of an expert's opinion that the prints were impressed when the accused "was in a prone position on top of the victim and was engaged in the act of rape at or about the time that the prints were made." Such an inference was said to beyond the ability of the fingerprint comparisons' expert to assert or even to insinuate.

The Hawaii Supreme Court, on review of the murder conviction, found "it somewhat difficult to agree with the trial court that (the expert) was qualified to give" those opinions. Nevertheless, the conviction was affirmed since the reviewing court thought the expert's opinions were not too far removed from the accused's claim that he planted his finger-prints at the murder scene when he lost his balance while removing a sandal in the act of lawfully using the facility. On that interpretation, no wrong had been done to him by the expert's testimony, so the court thought.

It remains to be seen how deep the wrong was that had been inflicted on the vaunted impartiality and competence of fingerprint identification experts, however, in the scientific community, by the testimony of one of their own who had strayed.

The Uniqueness Dilemma

Permanence and uniqueness are the twin linchpins upon which fingerprint identifications lay a claim to being the gold standard in the forensic sciences. But in 1905, Scotland's own Dr. Henry Faulds, cast a baleful eye on the proof that each person's fingerprint is unique. As he put it, "(A)n impression is produced ... that no two finger-prints can be identical ... this is not a practical conclusion to be accepted at once without further discussion."[32] Again in 1923, just seven years before his death in 1930, Faulds reiterated his views pointedly arguing against an Aristotelian-like "fictitious experience" and supporting a Galileo-like summons for empirical "evidence" to sustain the claimed uniqueness of fingerprints. "Unrelated fingers do chance to resemble," he said. In pursuing this theme, he wrote, "(I)t is useless to tell us that no two fingers can ever be found alike.

This is pure dogma, based on fictitious experience, and cannot be a true deduction from evidence . . . ."[33]

Since 1923, Dr. Faulds rightful summons for the "evidence" of empirical data has gone unanswered except for the twin studies which have been conducted and given unwarranted publicity and dominance after the fashion of Sir Cyril Burt's long renounced twin studies to establish the overweening power of genetics on traits of character and personality. This dearth of scientific support for the uniqueness of fingerprints has been recently reaffirmed in unambiguous terms. "The underlying scientific basis of fingerprint individuality has not been rigorously studied or tested," say Pankanti, et al. in their "*On the Individuality of Fingerprints*" (2002).[34]

On the contrary, in 1918, in the formative years of fingerprint acceptability, Wilder and Wentworth's text *Personal Identification* expressed the firm view of fingerprint uniqueness in a dramatic fashion. As they put it, a fingerprint's "numerous details . . . are as arbitrary in their occurrence and arrangement as are the pebbles on the beach . . . ." An Israel police report in 1996 presents quite a *contretemps* to Wilder and Wentworth's view.

In an article in *Fingerprint Whorld* in October 1996, Mark and Attias of the Israel National Police report[35] on an actual case where six "identical and continuous comparison points" were found in prints from two different people. They remark that such a situation could result in a "mistaken identity." Such an error is even more than likely in places where point counting has been completely downgraded and nothing better substituted for it, such as is at least the theory in the United States and in Great Britain.

What is sorely needed and is dramatically absent is the gathering of data, not through experiential posturing, but through controlled studies in blind and even double blind trials. It is entirely unconvincing to hear fingerprint examiners make their case for fingerprint uniqueness by the experience of one hundred years of such examinations. As SWGFAST puts the matter in its "Standards for Conclusions"[36] the individualization (of fingerprints) is supported by the . . . empirical data gained through more than one hundred years of operational experience." (Para. 1.2.2) It begs the question to ask us to believe that "the absence of disproof is the presence of proof." Just as the absence of evidence is well known not to be evidence of the absence of a suspect at a crime scene, so too one hundred years of anecdotal accounts of uniqueness is a wholly inadequate substitute for the hard data of scientifically based empirical studies.

When the U.S. Department of Justice's National Institute of Justice in 2000, echoing Dr. Faulds' call for empirical data on the status of fingerprinting, solicited proposals for its $5,000,000 grant to conduct studies on the validation of fingerprint examinations in which it stated that it "has identified the need for validation of the basis for friction ridge individualization and standardization of comparison criteria," there is once again a belated reminder of the written words of Dr. Faulds penned so many years before.

The upshot from the fingerprint community to the NIJ's solicitation was not a ready willingness to be scrutinized and tested but a concerted and successful effort to force the withdrawal of the NIJ solicitation. But the urgency of the need for data collection has not diminished since 2000. The National Institute of Justice has recently put forth another solicitation for a fingerprint research study, now titled "Quantitative Research on Friction Ridge Patterns." The objective is conservatively stated to be to obtain "a more comprehensive understanding of the empirical basis of friction ridge impression evidence to extend its use and facilitate the work of the fingerprint examiner. "There is nary a hint that any previous research was either undertaken or, if undertaken", was inadequate to the defined tasks. Nor is there any indication of the amount of government funds allocated for any proposals that are accepted, the submission date for proposal being February 25, 2005.

The Infallibility Equation

The infallibility of fingerprinting has been bandied about over the years in such a casual but assured way that one hesitates to explore, even to criticize, its legitimacy.[37] In that respect, it is comparable to permanence and uniqueness said to be the twin linchpins of fingerprinting, which have survived intact for more than one hundred years and are enshrined in the pantheon of fingerprinting as untouchables.

The mantra of fingerprinting infallibility has been stated as a given, even an axiom, without requiring verification by proof through hard physical data. In the Introduction to the FBI's 211 page handbook entitled *The Science of Fingerprints* (Revised in 1984), it is stated that "(o)f all the methods of identification, fingerprinting alone has proved to be both infallible and feasible."[22] (at iv) Of course, nothing is stated in this manual to buttress that opinion, and much is recommended to avoid a fingerprint examiner's falling afoul of error, even though the introduction eschews any concern for the possibility of fallibility in fingerprinting.

"Clearly fingerprint analysis is not the gold standard it is cracked up to be," so wrote the *New York Times* in an editorial on May 26, 2004, commenting upon the "shame over the mistaken arrest and jailing of (Brandon Mayfield)[38] a Muslim lawyer in Oregon." The skepticism expressed by the *New York Times* editorial toward the reliability of fingerprint examinations has been my frequently voiced credo for many years in articles penned by me and in my courtroom testimony. It is about time that the matter be given serious, conscientious, and impartial attention to insure that l'affair Brandon Mayfield is not the only face of fingerprint unreliability with more frequent infractions yet to surface.

As we have already discussed, there was a time when it was law enforcement officers who compromised fingerprint identifications by their fabricating the presence of a suspect's fingerprint at a crime scene. The 1997 report of Special Prosecutor Nelson E. Roth on the scandalous "almost routine" fabrication of fingerprint evidence by an Identification Unit of the New York State police over an eight year period grimly detailed the fact of such fabrication and an urgent call for remedies to forestall a recurrence.

But today, fingerprint identifications are being buffeted by storms from within the citadel of fingerprint examiners themselves, not as in the incidents in the Roth Report occurring at the lifting, investigative phase. That there is an international presence in fingerprint fallibility can be glaringly seen in the erroneous fingerprint identifications in cases such as that of Shirley McKie in Scotland where not only was police officer McKie's fingerprint misidentified as having been left at a murder scene after three experts concurred that it was hers but that of David Asbury, the alleged murderer in the same case, who also had his fingerprint misidentified.[39] Not even Scotland Yard has been untouched by fingerprint miscues as was revealed in 1997 when Andrew Chiory was cleared of leaving his fingerprint at the scene of the burglary of the home of Dr. Miriam Stoppard.[40]

The question to be assessed by deliberate and carefully designed studies is what remedies are mandated by such shocking disclosures and to what extent the fact of flawed fingerprint identifications is pandemic in the profession. In my view, it is no panacea for such disgraces to leave the corrective measures for them to the fingerprint community itself. In the first instance, it is imperative to ask what is the foundation for the current clamor over fingerprint identifications that has become a common refrain of late in the Federal and state courts in the United States. Surprising as it may seem, it was not until the retrial of Byron Mitchell in a Federal court in Philadelphia, Pennsylvania, in the late 1990s that the first concerted and full scale effort was made by a defense attorney to challenge the reliability of fingerprint examinations in courtroom proceedings.[41] That attack was buttressed by the U.S. Supreme Court's enunciation in its 1993 decision in *Daubert v Merrell Dow Pharmaceuticals, Inc.*[42] of standards governing the reliability of scientific evidence in Federal trial courts.

Although the first appellate court decision in the United States on the legitimacy of fingerprint identifications was handed down in 1911 in the Illinois murder trial of *People v. Jennings*[43] both in that trial and in subsequent trials, the opinions of fingerprint examiners were viewed as fact and accepted as a *fait accompli* without rigorous and adversarial courtroom testing. It has taken all these years and the prodding of the U.S. Supreme Court to put fingerprint identifications under the heat of the courtroom spit. What has the reaction been of the fingerprint community to the controversy that is raging in the courts and in the literature? In a word, stand-pat-ism. Complacency is no substitute, it bears reminding, for an open minded, objective, and truly scientific outlook.

Finally, a leading exponent of the status quo in fingerprint examinations has said, without empirical support, that "the error rate of the methodology (of fingerprinting) is zero."[44] In light of the FBI's now admitting that Portland, Oregon, lawyer Brandon Mayfield was the victim of three FBI misidentifications of a digital copy of the print found on a plastic bag in Madrid, Spain, maybe it is time to own up to the necessity to test the methodology as well as the examiner. Confronted by such an egregiously erroneous identification as that of Brandon Mayfield, the methodology of fingerprinting and the personnel conducting, it cannot so cavalierly be bifurcated into separate and unrelated camps. An error in a fingerprint identification can be so outrageous because so unexpected from the qualifications of the personnel conducting the identification and the method, they employ that the error is a distinct and direct challenge to the methodology as well as to the personnel as well. Was it only the three FBI examiners and the court appointed expert who are to be faulted in the Mayfield case or was it also an error attributable to a flawed methodology they utilized?[45]

I would propose a controlled study testing the efficacy of fingerprint examinations against that of DNA profiling, which has already shown the error in the way of microscopic hair analysis, bitemark evaluations, and lately in the ear print fiasco in the case of England's Mark Dallagher. Since it is well recognized by articles in the *Journal of Forensic Identification* and in other more scientific journals that DNA can be obtained from latent fingerprints, it seems to me overdue to arrange and to conduct blind trials to assess whether fingerprint examiners and molecular biologists will concur as to the donor of the same latent being examined. In fine I fear that the misidentifications by fingerprint analysts of the Brandon Mayfield is but the tip of the iceberg. Is fingerprinting so treasured as to be immune from a similar challenge through DNA profiling of the glandular secretions which are so large a part of a latent print?

Objectivity is the Watchword of Science

A nagging and continuing source of concern in fingerprint identifications is the litigation bias (lately termed a "context" bias)[46] that results from reversing the axiom that seeing is believing so as to become believing is seeing. The person suspected by one's law enforcement fellows should not be believed by the fingerprint examiner to be the culprit (in the vernacular of law enforcement "the perp") before the fingerprint examination has commenced.

As England has recently adopted the supposed remedy of trashing its sixteen point numeric,[47] fingerprint examiners in the United States have been similarly importuned to do the same since the 1973 edict of the International Association for Identification establishing a nonnumeric basis for fingerprint identifications for its membership.[48] Where does this leave fingerprint examiners in the search for, as the NIJ solicitation put it, the "standardization of comparison criteria" but only on the slippery and entirely subjective slope of sufficient match criteria according to the untested and unexamined experience of fingerprint examiners.

I am reminded in this connection of Benjamin Franklin's *Poor Richard's Almanac* in which he states "For want of a nail, the shoe is lost and for want of a shoe, the horse is lost and for want of a horse, the rider is lost." Just as Franklin linked the lack of a nail to the collapse of the rider, so too the lack of a better criterion for fingerprint identifications than "sufficiency" bodes ill for the reliability of fingerprint identifications. As I would phrase the situation in my linkage analysis, sufficiency leads to a reliance on individual experience which is personal and unstructured in nature leading to entirely personal and unverifiable conclusions fraught with the danger of built-in bias leading inexorably to erroneous conclusions.

The situation calls for new and imperious remedies to test the reliability of both the method of fingerprint identifications and the quality of the personnel conducting those examinations. On the latter score, I would strongly recommend the initiation of a review of all fingerprint identifications outside the confines of the agency first effecting the identification. Furthermore, I would urge the independent verification of identifications, if only selectively, of exclusions, and inconclusives and even those latents found to be unsuitable for analysis. The true scientist is concerned equally, it bears reminding, with false positives and false negatives, both of which sully the system with error. I would also maintain that the transcript of the trial testimony of fingerprint examiners should be part of the regular process of checks on the proficiency of such examiners if only to corral bonehead statements like "80% of people perspire," which appeared in the testimony of a fingerprint examiner on the trial and conviction of Boston's Stephan Cowans,[49] which conviction was lately overturned due to DNA profiling coming to Cowans' rescue.

A Method without Uniform Standards

A major flaw in the methods of fingerprinting rests in its nonstandardized approach to objectivity in the analytical process. Even the "Standards for Conclusions" adopted and promoted by SWGFAST fail to dispel the aura of subjectivity, which pervades fingerprint identifications. In its very first standard, SWGFAST pontificates that "The standard for individualization is agreement of *sufficient* friction ridge details . . . .[50] But what constitutes sufficient details is entirely left to the judgment of the fingerprint examiner giving subjectivism a central role in fingerprint identifications.

As the U.S. Supreme Court articulated it in its *Daubert v. Merrill Dow Pharmaceuticals, Inc.* opinion in 1993,[25] without standards, speculation becomes rampant creating individualized and unverifiable judgments as the order of the scientific day. I would propose that Karl Popper's falsification agenda[51] be instituted in fingerprint identifications. We then might be pleased and surprised to see verifications (second and independent opinions) occurring across the board including verification reports of inclusions, exclusions, and inconclusives. Such an unfocused and broad-based approach would reveal an equally concerned attempt to avoid false negatives setting the guilty free as well as false positives that can occasion the conviction of the innocent and, of course, to provide a safety net insuring that latents deemed not to be of value are in truth of such an unusable character.

Remedial Recommendations

I have a handful of modest proposals to uplift fingerprint identifications. First, proficiency testing should include monitoring, either through attendance or the occasional review of trial transcripts or otherwise of the courtroom testimony of fingerprint examiners. Then, it may well be that the shoemaker will be compelled to stick to his last avoiding testimony involving the discovery of "fresh prints" and other forms of bogus science exhibited in the trial testimony of fingerprint personnel such as that "only nervous persons (like criminals) leave fingerprints" or that "only 80% of people perspire."

Assuming one can discover a truly open-minded and concerned judge who will give a responsive ear to a defense entreaty to slow the runaway horse that fingerprinting has become in the eyes of the courts, the following additional possibilities for remedial action are proposed in descending order of intrusion on fingerprinting as presently received:

1. Exclude the testimony of a fingerprint individualization in its entirety as currently unreliable
2. Grant fingerprint testimony limited admissibility. The limitations to be either of the following
   a. No fingerprint opinion will be received identifying the latent print to a particular person, but the testimony concerning the various aspects of similarity to a known print will be admissible
   b. Permit an opinion on the aspects of similarity which point to a particular person as the donor of the latent print, but do not permit a statement of uniqueness assigning the latent to the known person to the exclusion of all other persons in the world
3. Require corroboration of the incriminating nature of the fingerprint found at the crime scene
4. Give an instruction to the jury at the end of the trial admonishing the jurors that they, not the experts, are to determine what weight, if any, they would ascribe to the experts' testimony

Who's in Charge?

Finally, I believe that Prime Minister Clemenceau's World War I injunction applies with equal vigor to fingerprint identifications. Whereas, as Clemenceau observed, "war is too important to be left to the generals," I would affirm that fingerprinting is too vital to the justice system to be left as the exclusive domain of fingerprint examiners. It is due time that others in the various realms of science be permitted to weigh in on the perplexities and uncertainties of fingerprinting.

Notes

1. Saks, M.J. and Koehler, J.J., *What DNA "fingerprinting" can teach the law about the rest of forensic science*, 13 *Cardozo L. Rev.* 361 (1991); Lander, E.S. and Budowle, B., DNA fingerprinting dispute laid to rest, 371 *Nature* 735 (Oct. 27, 1994); Jeffreys, A.J., Wilson, V., and Thein, S.L., Individual-specific 'fingerprints' of human DNA, Nature 318, no. 6046 (Dec. 12–18, 1985): 577–579; Gill, P., Jeffreys, A.J., and Werrett, D.J., Forensic application of DNA 'fingerprints,' Nature 316, no. 6023 (1985) and the latest, to my knowledge, is Epstein, E.S., Is the DNA fingerprint an infallible piece of evidence?, Litigation, Fall 2004, Vol. 31 (no. 1), pp. 25–32.

2. *State v. Tata*, 1981 Ohio App. Lexis 12077 where it was said that infra-red spectrometry (sic) gives a "fingerprint of the substance (drugs) that are present." Similarly see *Glaxo Inc. v. Novopharm Ltd.*, 931 F. Supp. 1280 (D. E.D. N.C. 1996) a patent dispute where the infra-red spectrograph said to give an "infra-red fingerprint." In *Woratzeck v. Stewart 118 F. 3d 648 (9th Cir. 1997)*, an expert stated that infra-red spectrophotometry is "as reliable as fingerprints."

3. Editorial, *Going Ballistic*, Wash. Post A 20, 1/31/05.

4. *Oncology Business Week*, p. 33, 2/6/05.

5. *Dance Magazine*, 2/1/05.

6. *Weekly Standard*, 1/31/05.

7. *Avent v. Comm.*, 164 S.E. 2d 655 (Va. 1968); *Turner v. Comm.*, 235 S.E. 2d 357 (Va. 1977); *Watkins v. Comm.*, Cir.Ct., Newport News, Va. (4/4/2000) http://caselaw.lp.funlaw.com/scripts/getcaserpl?court=Va.

8. *Moon v. State*, 198 p. 288 (Ariz. 1921).

9. 3 B.R.C. 68 (1912).

10. *Davis v. Mississippi*, 394 U.S. 721, 89 S.Ct. (1969).

11. *McLain v. State*, 24 So. 2d 15 (Miss. 1945).

12. *State v. Kuhl*, 175 p. 190, 3 A.L.R. 1694 (Nev. 1918).

13. *People v. Jones*, 12 N.Y.S. 2d 635 (N.Y. App. Div. 4th 1939).

14. *Comm. Albright*, 14 Pa. D. & C. 511 (C.P. Ct. Dauphin Pa. 1930).

15. *Grice v. State*, 151 S.W. 2d 211 (Tex. Cr. App. 1941).

16. *Davis v. Dunn*, 98 AS. 81 (Va. 1916); *State v. Lapan*, 141 A. 686 (Vt. 1928).

17. Quoted in Browne, D.G. and Brock, A. *Fifty Years of Scientific Crime Detection*, New York, NY: E.P. Dutton & Co., Inc, 1954.

18. *Report of special prosecutor Nelson Roth*, Feb. 1997.

19. *Rank v. Balshy, Shipe* et al., 590 F. Supp. 787 (D.M.D. Pa. 1984); other Pennsylvania decisions involving G.W. Rank's forged fingerprint complaint are *Balshy v. Rank*, 490 A. 2d 419

(Pa. 1985); *Comm. V. Rank*, 459 A. 2d 369 (Pa. Super 1981); *Rank v. Balshy*, 475 A. 2d 182 (Comm. Ct. Pa. 1984).

20. C.B.S. News, Vol. XXV, No. 27 Mar. 28, 1993.

21. Perez-Pena, R., *Supervision of troopers faulted in evidence-tampering scandal*, N.Y. Times, 2/4/97, sec. B, Page 1; Col. 3. N.Y. State Police Superintendent, McMahon, J., was also said to require that "any fingerprint match in a criminal case be referred to the central laboratory in Albany for confirmation." See article of Perez-Pena.

22. U.S. Dept. of Just., F.B.I. *The science of fingerprints: classification and uses*, Rev. 12–84, Stock N. 027-001-00035-5, Washington, D.C.: G.P.O.

23. The following references are to the trial transcript in the burglary et al. prosecution of Angel Morales in Kings County, N.Y. before Judge Lewis L. Douglass. Morales was convicted on March 15, 2000, and his appeal was denied, without comment on the fingerprint evidence, in *People v. Morales*, (9/8/03, App. Div. 2nd. N.Y.).

24. The book itself was for years banned from being sold in Australia but ultimately saw the light of freedom of the press and freedom of the public to read its claims of the falsification of Raymond Mickelberg's fingerprint through the use of a plastic (rubberized) cast of it by a law enforcement officer. See The West Australian (Perth) August 11, 2004. See also 86 ust. Law Rpts. 321 (High Court of Aust. 1989).

25. *Voir dire, Nat. Law J.* August 2, 2004; The Baltimore Sun, July 25, 2004.

26. The Baltimore Sun, July 25, 2004.

27. Puit, G., *Continuing deliberations: binion slaying testimony reheard*, Las Veg. Rev. J. (Nevada), Nov. 23, 2004. Pordum, M., *Tabish, Murphy not guilty of killing former casino boss Binion*, Scripps Howard News Service, Nov. 23, 2004.

28. Hempel, C., *TV's whodunit effect police dramas are having an unexpected impact in the real world: the public thinks every crime can be solved, and solved now — just like on television*, The Boston Globe, Feb. 9, 2003.

29. 2004 WL 2320339 (11th Cir. 10/15/04).

30. *Howard v. State*, 695 S.W. 2d 375, 376 (Ark. 1985).

31. *State v. Patrick*, 575 P.2d 448, 457 (Haw. 1978).

32. Faulds, H., *Guide to Finger-print Identification*, 15 (1905).

33. Faulds, H., *A Manual of Practical Dactylogaphy*, 31 (1923).

34. Pankanti, S., Prabhakar, S., and Jain, A.K. On the individuality of fingerprints, in 24 *IEEE Transactions on PAMI*, 1010 (2002).

35. Mark, Y. and Attias, D. *What is the minimum standard of characteristics for fingerprint identification?* "Fingerprint Whorld" Oct. 1996, pp. 148–150.

36. 54 *J. For. Ident.* 358–9 (3), 2004.

37. See *Corbin v. State*, 585 So. 2d 713 (Miss. 1991); *Murphy v. State*, 40 A. 2d 239 (Md. App. 1944) where a fingerprint was stated to be an "infallible means of identification"; *Jamison v. State*, 354 S.W. 2d 252, 255 (Tenn 1962) which was cited favorably in *Rutherford v. State*, 2000 Ten. Cr. App. Lexis 180 (2000); *State v. Quintana*, 103 P. 3d 168 (Utah 2004).

38. In *Stevenson v. United States*, 380 F. 2d 590, 592 (D.C. Cir. 1967) cert. denied, 88 S. Ct. 347 (1967) is was unequivocally and authoritatively stated that "The accuracy of fingerprint identification is a matter of common knowledge and no case has been cited, and we have found none, where identification so established has been rejected." That firm and assured declaration has since been proved to be deeply in error. See. Starrs, J.E., A miscue in fingerprint identification: causes and concerns, 12 (no. 3) *J. Pol. Sci. & Admin.* 287–296 (1984) detailing the erroneous

fingerprinting in the Elisabeth Congdon murder case in which Roger Sipe Caldwell was wrongfully charged with the killing based on fingerprint comparisons by a number of fingerprint examiners certified as qualified by the I.A.I.

39. Cole, S.A., *Suspect Identities: A History of Fingerprinting and Criminal Identification*, Cambridge, Massachusetts: Harvard University Press, 2001, p. 283.

40. Campbell, D., *Fingerprint proof 'flawed'*, The Guardian Home Page, p. 5, Apr. 7, 1997; Grey, S., *Yard in fingerprint blunder*, Times Newspapers Ltd, Apr. 6, 1997.

41. *United States v. Mitchell*, 365 F. 3d 215 (3d. Cir. 2004). More than a dozen cases have challenged fingerprint reliability since the Daubert decision in 1993. None have been successful on the merits. The decisions are listed in footnote 2 in Romandetti, K., Recognizing and responding to a problem with the admissibility of fingerprint evidence under Daubert, 45 *Jurimetrics* 41–58 (Fall 2004). See also Mnookin, J.L., Fingerprint evidence in an age of DNA profiling, 67 *Bklyn. L. Rev.* 13 (2001) and Cole, S.A., Grandfathering Evidence: Fingerprint Admissibility Rulings from Jennings to Llera Plaza and Back Again, 41 *Am. Crim. L. Rev.* 1089–1276 (2004).

42. *Daubert v. Merrell Dow Pharmaceuticals, Inc.*, 113 S. Ct. 2786 (1993).

43. *People v. Jennings*, 96 N.E. 1077 (Ill. 1911).

44. Meagher, S.B., F.B.I. Special Agent, Unit Chief, F.B.I. Latent Print Unit II.

45. The recommendations by an international review committee urged various changes in the policies at the F.B.I. and elsewhere which were designed to change the *method* of conducting fingerprint examinations at least in high profile cases such as the Madrid bombing. Two of the recommendations are particularly apt. The first was for a blind and independent verification of an initial conclusion, indicating apparently that that was not the *method* in place at the time of the Mayfield error. (But should not the method include a requirement that the fingerprint examination be made at all times separate "from the circumstances of the case" as is the reported protocol in Israel. See supra n. 27). Second, it was proposed that "a policy incorporating a definable quality and quantity standard, rather than the current 12-point standard, needs to be instituted … points … should be removed from any policy manual" including, I suppose the FBI's own *Science of Fingerprints*. See infra note 37.

46. In the report of an international review committee on the erroneous identification of Brandon Mayfield in the Madrid, Spain train bombing, the reporter, an F.B.I. agent, says the F.B.I. examiners were influenced by "confirmation bias (or context effect)" which he explains as a "mind-set in which the expectations with which people approach a task of observation will affect their perceptions and interpretations of what they observe." See Stacey, R.B., A report on the erroneous fingerprint individualization in the Madrid train bombing case, J. For. Ident. 54 (6) 706–718 (2004) Although this report does not identify the three F.B.I. examiners who erred nor the court appointed expert, we know, courtesy of The CACNews, 4th Quarter 2004 that two of the F.B.I. examiners were Wiener and Massey and the court appointed expert was Ken Moses. *The Proceedings of Lunch: Fingerprints in Print*, CACNews, 4th Quarter 2004, pp. 14–21.

47. The decision to adopt a nonnumeric standard for identification has been criticized, particularly since it follows on the heels of blunders in effecting fingerprint identifications under the strict 16 point standard, which has now been replaced with no fixed standard of any workable kind. Woffinden, B., *Thumbs down; Bob Woffinden asks why standards for fingerprinting are being abolished despite the recent McNamee appeal*, The Guardian Feature Page, p. 17, Jan. 12, 1999.

48. International Association for Identification (IAI), Standardization Committee Report, *FBI Law Enforcement Bulletin* (Oct. 1973) 3–18.

49. *Comm. V. Cowans*, 756 N.E. 2d 622 (Mass. App. 2001) which affirmed Cowans' conviction but that conviction was overturned in 2004 (Boston Globe, 2/2/04) when Cowns became the 141st person to be exonerated through DNA profiling.

50. SWGFAST, Standards for Conclusions, *J. For. Ident.* 54(3) 358 (2004).

51. Cited and quoted at p. 2797 of the opinion. See Supranote 25. As the U.S. Supreme Court put it Karl Popper in his *Conjectures and Refutations: The Growth of Scientific Knowledge* 37 (New York, NY: Basic Books, 5th ed. 1989) said "The criterion of the scientific status of a theory is its falsifiability, or refutability, or testability." Thus the rate of error becomes crucial to its reliability as does the fact that discrepancies (dissimilarities) were conscientiously sought between the known and unknown (latent) fingerprint.

SWGFAST Glossary

(Scientific Working Group on Friction Ridge Analysis, Study and Technology) Excerpted by Professor James E. Starrs from www.swgfast.org link to glossary

AFIS: Automated Fingerprint Identification System

ALPS: Automated Latent Print System — The latent print specific operations of an AFIS

Analysis: The methodical examination of friction skin impressions, separation into parts so as to determine the nature of the whole

APIS: Automated Palm Print Identification System — Computerized system for storage, searching and retrieval of known palm print records based on friction ridge detail

Arch-Plain: A fingerprint pattern in which the ridges enter on one side of the impression, and flow, or tend to flow, out the otherside with a rise or wave in the center

Arch-Tented: A type of fingerprint pattern that possesses either an angle, an upthrust, or two of the three basic characteristics of the loop

Artifact:

1. Any distortion or alteration not in the original friction ridge impression, produced by an external agent or action
2. Any information not present in the original object/image, inadvertently introduced by image capture, processing, compressions, transmission, display, or printing

Authentication:

1. Process used to determine whether a digital image has been altered in any way since its capture
2. Process used to determine whether an electric file has the correct association, name, unique identifier, friction ridge images, and criminal history record

Automated Latent System: The latent print specific operations of an AFIS

Bifurcation: The point at which one friction ridge divides into two friction ridges

Biometric Fingerprinting: Digital image capture of friction ridges and a template from friction ridges

Bridge: A connecting friction ridge between and at generally right angles to parallel running ridges

CA OR CAE: Cyanoacrylate ester (Superglue) — an adhesive used in a fuming method to develop friction ridge detail

Calcar Area: Area located at the heel of the foot

Carpal Delta Area: Area of the palm containing a delta formation nearest the wrist

Characteristics: Features of the friction ridges — commonly referred to as minutiae, Galtson detail, point, feature, ridge formation, ridge morphology

Clarity: Visual quality of a friction ridge impression

Class Characteristics: Characteristics used to put things into groups or classes, for example, arches, loops, whorls

Classification: Alpha/numeric formula of finger and palm print patterns used as a guide for filing and searching

Comparison: The observation of two areas of friction ridge impressions for finding similarities and differences

Core: The approximate center of a pattern

Crease: A line or linear depression; grooves at the joints of the phalanges, at the junction of the digits and across the palmar and plantar surfaces that accommodate flexion

Delta: That point on a ridge at or nearest to the point of divergence of two type lines, and located at or directly in front of the point of divergence

Dermal Papillae: Peg-like formations on the surface of the dermis

Dermis: The layer of skin beneath the epidermis

Digit: A toe or finger

Discrepancy: A difference in two friction ridge impressions due to different sources of the impressions (exclusion)

Dissimilarity: See *Discrepancy*

Distal: Farthest away from the center or point of attachment. The direction away from the body

Distortion: Variances in the reproduction of friction skin caused by pressure, movement, force, contact surface, etc

Divergence: The separation of two friction ridges that have been running parallel or nearly parallel

Dot: An isolated ridge unit whose length approximates its width in size

Dysplasia: Ridge units that did not form complete friction ridges due to a genetic cause

Eccrine Glands: Sweat glands that open on all surfaces of the skin

Ectrodactyly: Congenital absence of all or part of a digits

Edgeoscopy: Study of the morphological characteristics of friction ridges, contour or shape of the edges of friction ridges

Elimination Prints: Exemplars of friction fridge skin detail of persons known to have had access to the item examined for latent prints

Enclosure: A single friction ridge that bifurcates and rejoins after a short course and continues as a single friction ridge

Ending Ridge: A single friction ridge that terminates within the friction ridge structure

Epidermis: The outer layer of the skin

Erroneous Identification: The incorrect determination that two areas of friction ridge impressions originated from the same source

Evaluation: The determination of the significance, value, or clarity of a friction ridge impression by careful observation and study

Exemplar: Friction ridge record of an individual, recorded electronically, photographically, by ink or other medium

Exclusion: The determination that two areas of friction ridge impressions did not originate from the same source (nonidentification)

Finger: See *Phalange*

Fingerprint: An impression of the friction ridges of all or any part of the finger

Focal Points: Those areas that are enclosed within the pattern area of loops and whorls. They are also known as the core and the delta

Friction Ridge: A raised portion of the epidermis on the palmar or plantar skin, consisting of one or more connected ridge units of friction ridge skin

Friction Ridge Detail (Morphology): An area that comprises the combination of ridge flow, ridge characteristics, and ridge structure

Friction Ridge Identification: See *Individualization*

Friction Ridge Unit: Single section of friction ridge containing one pore

Fulcrum Area: The area between the thumb and the index finger on the palm

Furrows: Valleys or depressions between the friction ridges

Galton Details: Term referring to friction ridge characteristics attributed to the research of English fingerprint pioneer, Sir Francis Galton

Hallucal: A region which corresponds to the distal thenar and first interdigital region of the palm

Henry Classification: A system of fingerprint classification named after Sir Edward Richard Henry (1850–1931)

Hyperdactyly: See *Polydactyly*

Hypothernal Area: The friction ridge skin on the palm, below the interdigital area on the ulnar side of the palm

IAFIS: Integrated Automated Fingerprint Identification System. The FBI's national AFIS

Identification: See *Individualization*

Incipient Ridge: A friction ridge not fully developed that may be shorter and thinner in appearance than fully developed friction ridges (interstitial, nascent, rudimentary)

Individualization: The determination that corresponding areas of friction ridge impressions originated from the same source to the exclusion of all others (identification)

Inked Print (Finger, Palm, Foot): See *Exemplar*

Inked Print (Finger, Palm, Foot): See *Known Print*

Interdigital: Palmar area below the fingers and above the thenar and hypothenar areas

Intervening Ridges: The number of friction ridges between two characteristics

Known Print (Finger, Palm, Foot): A recording of an individual's friction ridges with black ink, electronic imaging, photography, or other medium on a contrasting background

Latent Print: Transferred impression of friction ridge detail not readily visible, generic term used for question friction ridge detail

Level 1 Detail: Friction ridge flow and general morphological information

Level 2 Detail: Individual friction ridge paths and friction ridge events, for example, bifurcations, ending ridges, dots

Level 3 Detail: Friction ridge dimensional attributes, for example, width, edge shape, and pores

Loop-Ulnar: A type of pattern in which one or more ridges enter upon either side, recurve, touch, or pass an imaginary line between delta and core pass out, or tend to pass out, on the same side the ridges entered. The flow of the pattern runs in the direction of the ulna bone of the forearm (toward the little finger)

Loop-Radial: A type of pattern in which one or more ridges enter upon either side, recurve, touch, or pass an imaginary line between delta and core and pass out, or tend to pass out, on the same side the ridges entered. The flow of the pattern runs in the direction of the radius bone of the forearm (toward the thumb)

Macrodactyly: Congenitally abnormal largeness of fingers or toes

Major Case Prints: A systematic recording of all of the friction ridge detail appearing on the palmar sides of the hands. This includes the extreme sides of the palms, and joints, tips, and sides of the fingers

Matrix: The substance that is deposited by the finger

Minutiae: See *Characteristics*

Missed Identification: The failure to make an identification (individualization) when, in fact, both friction ridge impressions are from the same source

Mottled Skin: Ridge detail is present, but is dissociated due to trauma or genetic causes. It lacks any continuous pattern flow

Nonidentification: See *Exclusion*

Orthodactyly: Fingers and toes cannot be flexed

Palm (Palmar Area): The friction ridge skin area on the side and underside of the hand

Palmar Zone: The interdigital area of the palm

Papillary Ridges: Orderly rows of eccrine glands positioned along the path of the friction ridge

Patent Print: Friction ridge impression of unknown origin, visible without development

Pattern Area (Classification): In the distal phalange of the fingers, the configuration of friction ridges that are utilized in classification

Pattern Formations: Friction ridge skin arrangements formed as early as the third month of gestation

Patterns: The designation of friction ridge skin into basic categories of general shapes

Pentadactyly: The occurrence of five fingers or toes on a hand or foot

Phalange (Phalanx): A finger or toe, with proximal, medical, and distal segments. Any bones in the fingers or toes

Plantar Area: The friction ridge skin area on the side and underside of the foot

Points/Points of Identification: See *Characteristics*

Polydactyly: A hand or foot having more than the normal number of fingers or toes

Pores: Small openings on friction ridges through which body fluids are released

Poroscopy: A study of the size, shape, and arrangement of pores

Primary: A numerical formula derived from the presence of any whorl pattern as they appear on the fingers

Proximal: Situated at the closest point of attachment, direction toward the body

Qualitative: The clarity of information contained within a friction ridge impression

Quantitative: The amount of information contained within a friction ridge impression

Radial: The smaller of the two bones of the forearm, on the same side as the thumb

Relative Position: Proximity of characteristics to each other

Ridge Aplasia: Congenital absence of friction ridge skin

Ridge Characteristics: See *Characteristics*

Ridge Flow: A series of adjacent friction ridges in a directional arrangement. See *Level 1 Detail*. Also see Classification Terms glossary

Ridge Hypoplasia: Underdeveloped ridges associated with an excess of creases

Ridge Path: The directional flow of a single friction ridge. See *Level 2 Detail*. Also see Classification Terms glossary

Ridgeology: The study of the uniqueness of friction ridge skin and its use for personal identification (individualization)

Sebaceous Gland: An oil-secreting gland generally associated with a hair follicle

Short Ridge: A single friction ridge beginning, traveling a short distance, and ending

Split Thumb: Thumb that has conjoined distal phalanges

Spur: A bifurcation with one short ridge branching off a longer ridge

Symphalangy: End-to-end fusion of the phalanges of the fingers or toes

Syndactyly: Refers to webbed fingers. Side-to-side fusion of digits

Thenar Area: The large cushion of the palm located at the base of the thumb

Tibia: A bone in the lower leg

Tibial Area: The plantar area situated on the big toe side of the foot

Trifurcation: The point at which one friction ridge divides into three ridges

Type Lines: The two innermost ridges associated with a delta that are parallel, diverge, and surround or tend to surround the pattern area

Ulna: The larger of the two bones of the forearm, on the palmar side of the little finger

Vacuum Cyanoacrylate Ester: Fuming method, conducted under vacuum conditions, in which cyanoacrylate polymerizes on friction ridge residue, used to visualize friction ridge detail

Verification: Confirmation of an examiner's conclusion by another qualified examiner

Volar: Related to the palmar and plantar surfaces

Volar Pads: Palmar and plantar fetal tissue growth that affects friction ridge skin development and patterns

Whorl-Accidental: A fingerprint pattern consisting of two different types of patterns, with the exception of the plain arch, with two or more deltas; or a pattern which possesses some of the requirements for two or more difficult types; or a pattern which conforms to none of the definitions

Whorl-Central Pocket Loop: A type of fingerprint pattern that has two details and at least one ridge which makes, or tends to make, one complete circuit, which may be spiral, oval, circular, or any variant of a circle. An imaginary line drawn between the two deltas must not touch or cross recurving ridges within the inner pattern area

Whorl-Double Loop: A type of fingerprint pattern that consists of two separate loop formations with two separate and distinct sets of shoulders and two details

Whorl-Plain: A type of fingerprint pattern that consists of one or more ridges, which make, or tend to make, a complete circuit, with two deltas, between which, when an imaginary line is drawn, at least one recurving ridge within the inner pattern area is cut or touched.

Trace Evidence Examination 15

PAMELA M. WOODS

Introduction

The collection and examination of trace evidence has largely developed due to the theory of Edmund Locard. His proposed theory, Locard's Exchange Principle, involves the transfer of evidence from one object or person to another object or person.[1] These ideas have become the basis for crime scene investigation. Popular culture is now more familiar with the transfer of evidence due to a surge in popularity of shows based on crime scene investigation. However, these television shows seem to focus audiences on the drama and glamor of the investigative process. Talk to those who work in the field of forensic science for a true opinion on crime scene investigation and the tedious task of examining the evidence. Although much attention is focused on the profession of Forensic Science, the public may be apt to have unreal expectations when it comes to the investigative process. Sensationalized television dramas are capable of solving a complicated homicide in one hour. The story line swiftly moves from a bloody crime scene to the hi-tech scientific examination of evidence and finally to a firm conclusion. A nice pat on the back for the forensic investigator and the case is solved ... next case, please.

Does an actual forensic investigation move so quickly and smoothly? Does every question that arise from the crime scene investigation have an answer? This would be highly unlikely. The time it takes to process a scene and the evidence would depend upon the depth of the crime scene and the items recovered. The primary task at both indoor and outdoor crime scenes is to evaluate the scene and determine what is valuable as trace evidence. Trace evidence may be less evident than a shell casing or footwear impression, but it is still very valuable to the investigation.

> For example, a burglar is prowling about the neighborhood looking for an easy target. Checking out the neighborhood houses, he finally spies an open window. As he tries to slide silently through the window, he hears a ripping noise. He has torn his favorite black acrylic sweater. Oh well, no time to lose, there are valuable items to steal. He cautiously creeps through the house, wearing gloves to eliminate the possibility of fingerprints. After gathering some jewellery

and cash, the robber exits through the open window. He feels sure he has left no evidence behind.

Investigating a scene such as this burglary scenario is usually an easy task. In this case, there is only one point of entry and exit, the open window. First, the window and the area surrounding the window is documented and photographed. Second, a sketch of the window is drawn including general measurements of the window and height from the ground. The third step is to examine the window and its frame closely for trace evidence. Since the burglar wore gloves, no fingerprints were left behind. However, on closely examining the frame of the window, a small nail is observed to have a few black fibers clinging to it. These few fibers provide enough evidence to do a fiber comparison and link the burglar to the crime scene. Of course, this link is dependent on finding the suspect and the torn black sweater.

This scenario represents a rather uncomplicated crime and therefore a simple investigation. More elaborate crime scenes require more time and a trained eye when searching for trace evidence. A fictitious homicide scene is used as a second example to illustrate the previous point.

A serial murderer cruises through a shabby part of town on a mission to find his next victim. He carefully selects a lone female prostitute standing on a darkened section of the street. Shortly after getting her into the car, he strikes her multiple times about the head and face with a crowbar he keeps stashed in the trunk. The crowbar is a handy tool. The killer used it once before to pry open a door at a previous victim's home. After the bludgeoning, he dumps the lifeless body of the prostitute into a stairwell a few blocks from where the victim was originally standing. He is confident he was not seen and left no evidence behind.

A few days later, a passerby discovers the body of the young female prostitute. Her body lies at the base of the stairwell, bloody and contorted from the fall. Although her face is not visible, dried blood is observed under the head and matted throughout the hair. She is wearing no clothing, and her only jewelry is a tarnished silver bracelet.

When forensic scientists arrive at the scene, they must carefully examine the stairwell and the region surrounding it to draw educated conclusions to posed questions:

- Where did the murder occur?
- How did the body get in this position?
- What are the best possible sources of trace evidence?

Once an investigator concludes that the body was dumped at the site, the examination would likely turn to the victim and immediate area surrounding the body. Nothing out of the ordinary is observed in the stairwell. The bracelet appears to hold no fibers or foreign matter within its links. However, it is noted that several fragments of blue colored material are observed in the bloody head wounds. Since no source for the blue colored substance is observed in the stairwell, it is collected as possible trace evidence.

Once the evidence is transferred to the laboratory, the traces of blue material are carefully examined and determined to be paint. The paint fragments recovered from the victim's head wound were transferred from the crowbar. In this case, if the suspect is apprehended and the crowbar is found with remaining paint residue, it may be possible to link the suspect to the murder and possibly other crimes using the paint fragments.

Investigating a homicide often requires more work in the areas of crime scene documentation, photography, and sketching. Detailed documentation and measurement of recovered trace evidence is essential to sketches. The sketches and photographs serve as a tool to preserve the scene in an investigator's mind, long after the victim has been removed and the blood has vanished. There is no difference between crime scenes when it comes to the necessity of careful evaluation for trace evidence.

Collection of Trace Evidence

The scale of trace evidence can range from a paint chip the size of a dime to a fiber fragment not visible to the human eye. The small size of trace items makes the collection techniques and preservation very important. There are various methods to consider at a crime scene when collecting trace evidence.[2] Three effective collection methods are the alternate light source, tape lifts, and the trace evidence vacuum. Precautions must always be taken to minimize loss of sample and decrease the risk of contamination when investigating a crime scene. Each case should be evaluated so that retrieval of the trace evidence is efficient and complete.

On occasion, a trace item is visible to the naked eye. In these cases, the item may be removed with forceps and placed into a clean envelope or a clean white paper. The paper is carefully folded, placed into a second sealed envelope, and then labeled with the appropriate information. Examples of visible material may include a loose fiber observed on the shirt of a victim or fibers embedded in a crust of blood. These can be removed with forceps, packaged, and labeled. Paint fragments can be carefully scraped from the surface of a suspect's vehicle with forceps or a clean blade, packaged, and labeled.

Many times, trace evidence is not visible to the human eye. If fibers or debris particles are too fine to be seen with the naked eye, the alternate light source may illuminate hidden materials. The light source has a flexible cable so that the light can be hand held. A range of wavelengths is used to illuminate fibers and biological materials for easy observation and collection.

Surface evidence may be collected using a trace evidence vaccuum or tape lifts. These methods are typically used when the evidence is not visible, or the item may be too large to package and return to the laboratory for analysis. Vacuumed debris and tape lifts are more easily packaged and transported to a laboratory for examination.

For large areas or vehicles, the trace evidence vacuum can remove all debris and fibers from a surface. It works like a regular hand held vacuum, except for a filter system attached to the suction tube that catches incoming materials. The filter compartment is opened after vacuuming a surface, and the contents caught on the filter are placed into a clean paper packet or an envelope (include the filter as well). All seams are sealed on the paper packet or envelope. The item is then placed in a second paper envelope or bag, sealed and labeled with the appropriate information. Vacuuming is effective for trace evidence collection; however, a good deal of worthless debris is also collected. This can make it difficult for examiners to isolate small items particularly if they have to sift through dirt and stones picked up from the vehicle.

A good procedure for an organized search process is to vacuum a crime scene in small sectioned areas. For example, if a vehicle is being vacuumed, first process the driver's seat. After going over the driver's seat, remove the filter and its contents and then package and label appropriately. Move on to the passenger seat using a clean filter. Continue with the rest of the vehicle, separately packaging each filter and vacuumed debris. Breaking a scene into smaller sections as you vacuum will give the best placement for any trace evidence found on the filter or in the debris. If a whole room is vacuumed all at once, there will be no way to pinpoint where specific evidence was located. This information may be important to the case when comparing victim versus suspect testimony.

This is apparent when the accounts of the victim and suspect are conflicting. If the suspect in a rape case stated that consensual sex took place in the back seat of his car, but the female victim has a different account, the placement of evidence is an important issue. The victim has further provided information that the assault occurred in the passenger seat, and that she was never in the back of the car. If no obvious evidence of a sex assault is present in the vehicle such as biological fluids, knowing what the victim was wearing at the time of the incident may be important information. If she were wearing a knit sweater that sheds fibers easily, such as wool, investigators would expect to find tiny wool fibers on the car seat. Provided the victim spent time in the front passenger seat, the wool fibers would likely be present there. However, fibers from the victim's clothing should be absent from the rear seat since no direct contact was made between the two according to the victim's statement. In this situation, it would be very important to document the location of recovered fibers. The presence or absence of trace evidence can support or refute the statements made by parties involved in a crime.

If vacuuming does not adequately represent the location of trace evidence, tape lifts are an effective way to document exact locations. Placing a strip of clear packing tape on a surface sticky side down and peeling it off pulls all loose materials from that surface. By carefully labeling the tape lifts, and working in an organized fashion, the investigator will have an excellent record of where recovered trace evidence was located. Once the lifts have been secured on a polyethylene bag or glass plate, they are packaged in a paper bag or envelope, which is then sealed and labeled.

Contamination of evidence is of major concern at all crime scenes[2] (pp. 105–106). Individuals collecting and packaging evidence should always be aware of compromising the value of that evidence. Clothing and objects collected from the suspect and the victim must be packaged separately. A cross transfer can easily occur between these items if they were packaged together. This would eliminate the value of a trace evidence examination since there is no way to tell exactly when the crosstransfer occurred. A second way to avoid contamination is to change latex gloves after packaging individual items. Any material retained on dirty gloves could be transferred to other items. In addition, use clean forceps for each sample collected to remove traces of debris from previous items. This is of primary concern when collecting fibers. For example, when collecting a clump of fibers from under the fingernail of a victim, the fibers are documented in scene notes, and then packaged and labeled. The forceps are rinsed with water or alcohol, then air dried or dried with lint-free wipes to remove traces of the collected fibers. A secondary source of contamination could result from wiping the forceps with a cloth rag or regular tissue. This will likely leave traces of fibers from those objects on the forceps. Fibers left behind by a drying cloth or tissue could contaminate the sample.

In all instances, the investigator must think ahead to the laboratory analysis, and take precautions to minimize contamination.

Packaging and Labeling Evidence

Extreme caution must be exercised to preserve any evidence present while packaging and transporting evidence to a laboratory for analysis. If an item is collected with the intention of looking for trace materials, it is to be handled by as few people as possible. Never hang or shake items, including wet or bloodstained clothing. Lay items flat to dry on large sheets of clean, white paper. When the item is dry, package it in the paper. Garments should be folded inward and wrapped in paper securing the paper with tape. Small items are placed in clean envelopes or folded white paper, making sure nothing can escape through the seams of the package. Place the paper package in a second paper bag and seal it. Glass or other sharp objects should be marked on the exterior of the bag with the words "caution" or "sharp." Items stained with blood and other biological fluids should be marked "biohazard." All exterior packaging of evidence must be labeled with the sufficient information.[3] The exterior of the bag is labeled with information to include at the minimum, the date and time when collected, item description, location of the item, initials of the person collecting the item, and a designation number or letter for purposes of an evidence log and scene documentation.

Questioned Materials and Known Materials

Once the evidence has been properly packaged and labeled, it is submitted to the laboratory for examination. Typically, a comparison of two or more items is requested. The items are often referred to as "questioned" and "known" samples. Usually, the forensic scientist seeks to link the questioned item to an item of known origin. For instance, if short dark fibers are observed on the white cotton socks of the victim, an investigator may request a comparison of these fibers to a known sample from a black shag carpet located in the suspect's home. The socks are submitted to the laboratory and examined for "target fibers."[2] (pp. 105–106) A target fiber may be defined as a fiber that has characteristics similar to the known sample. In this case, the target fibers would be those with an appearance similar to the black shag carpet. The target fibers are recovered from the socks and further analyzed as questioned fibers. A questioned fiber is thoroughly examined by the forensic scientist in an effort to find a match or rule out the possibility of a match to a known fiber. If questioned fibers recovered from the socks are determined to be consistent with the known fibers from the carpet, the sock may have been in contact with the carpet at some point in time.

"Target," "questioned," and "known" may be used to describe paint and glass items as well. Once back at the laboratory, target materials are removed from vacuumed debris and pulled from tape lifts. The target material may be a glass fragment from vacuumings or a paint chip recovered from the clothing of a hit and run victim. Since vacuumed debris and tape lifts often contain a lot of extraneous materials, a target material is essential when scanning the debris and lifts for useful trace evidence. If the target material is found, simply remove the material for comparison. Smaller pieces of trace evidence will require a more meticulous search using a magnifying glass or microscope.

Defining Trace Evidence

Fiber, glass, and paint are three types of trace evidence. The possibility of other types of trace evidence transfer may exist such as of hair and soil. Tape, plastics, and adhesives are also submitted for analysis in the trace section.

All people and animals easily shed hair. Hair comparisons and identifications consist of a microscopic examination that relies on the experience of the examiner. During a struggle between a suspect and a victim, hair is often pulled as a method of defense and may remain in the hands of the victim. This was evident in a past homicide where a woman was found stabbed in the neck in her bedroom. The witness reported that the victim was seen with a man while leaving a local bar earlier in the evening. As the scene was being documented, a short strand of dark hair was observed embedded in the prongs of the victim's ring. Hair can give important evidence since it may be long to the last person to see the victim alive.

Identifying a hair strand may be as easy as classifying it as a human's or an animal's. The task of comparing human hairs may be required in certain cases. Careful observations of hair characteristics are noted and generalized for all questioned and known hair samples. Microscopic comparisons determine if a questioned hair is similar or dissimilar to the known samples provided. Hair comparisons take time, but may prove valuable if other sources of evidence are exhausted.

Soil is present everywhere and when embedded in the tread of a sneaker it may be used to link a suspect or victim to a crime scene. Characteristics of soil such as color, mineral content, and pH can vary from region to region. The cause for a soil analysis would arise in specific cases. If a man is found shot in the Nevada dessert, yet he has dark colored mud in the tread of his shoes, it seems likely that he was not killed in the dessert. The conclusion may be that the man was transported there. A physical and chemical analysis of the soil may tell an investigator some information about the man's origin. Soil comparisons may also link the dirty clothing of a suspect to the scene of the crime.

Polymer materials such as adhesives and plastics can also be a source of information. The comparison of adhesive tapes such as duct tape was requested in the case of a past homicide. The body of a man was recovered from a local riverbed with duct tape bound to his legs and arms. Investigators found other pieces of duct tape at various locations including where the homicide was thought to have occurred. A request was made to examine the duct tape wrapped around the body for physical characteristics and compare it to the tape found at the crime scene.

Tape can be compared based on many physical characteristics including color and width. The adhesive material on the backing of the tape can also be examined. Although the comparison of tape seems trivial, a physical match of the tape found on a victim and a roll of tape found in custody of the suspect is a direct link between the two. Physical matching where two or more items fit together like the pieces of a puzzle is a definitive connection.

Trace evidence examination is a necessary part of the laboratory process that can link suspects to crime scenes and victims. The difficulty occurs when no suspect evolves, and as time passes, the possibility of recovering trace evidence such as fibers becomes less likely. Trace evidence is present at every crime scene in some form or another. The problem lies in finding this evidence and finding a valuable way to apply it to the case. Although there are many types of trace evidence to be examined, the analysis of fibers, glass, and paint are briefly discussed in the following sections.

Fiber Examination

Fiber analysis typically comprises a microscopic examination to observe the optical properties of a fiber and an instrumental technique to confirm fiber type. Chemical reagents and solubilities are a means to classify fibers (natural and synthetic).[4] Although chemical methods will help to identify a fiber, they are destructive. If a single fiber fragment is available, the forensic scientist cannot destroy it with solvents and chemical reagents.

Microscopic techniques are nondestructive and allow for a quick classification or comparison of fibers. Once a target fiber has been located on a tape lift or vacuum filter, it is carefully removed from the adhesive or debris with forceps and a nondestructive solvent such as "Histosolve™." Avoid pulling or squeezing the fiber to prevent altering the external appearance of the questioned sample. Finally, mount the fiber on a microscope slide and secure the sample with a cover slip. Once the fiber has been preserved and protected, the analysis can proceed. Numerous characteristics of fibers are gathered by examining them microscopically.[2] (pp.153–173) Some physical characteristics include diameter, color, cross-section, and length. Optical properties such as refractive index, birefringence, and sign of elongation are used to characterize synthetic fibers. A comparison microscope is also useful since it allows for a side by side view of questioned fibers and known fibers. This microscope has two stages and a bridge connecting them for separate or side by side viewing. The prepared slide of the questioned fiber is placed on one stage, and then a second slide of a known fiber is prepared and placed on the other stage. Placing the two samples next to each other gives the best indication of similarity between the two items with respect to color and diameter. A positive result, where the two samples are consistent with one another, can be digitally photographed to support conclusions of a fiber match.

Further confirmation of fiber type is achieved using instrumental analysis, specifically Fourier Transform Infrared Spectrometry (FTIR). One technique requires the use of a microscope attachment and reflective slides to obtain spectra. The microscope provides a magnified image of the fiber. The fiber is prepared for analysis and placed on a mirrored slide. As light is reflected through the sample, it interacts with the molecular structure of the fiber to produce a spectrum of energy vibrations and absorptions unique to that particular fiber. At this point, the questioned fiber type can be confirmed by searching a spectral library of numerous standard fibers. The spectra of questioned and known fiber samples may also be compared to one another visually, looking for the presence or absence of certain peaks.

Glass Evidence

Glass is often seen scattered about at crime scenes and is usually analyzed to determine the following:

- Where did the impact force originate?
- Does a physical match exist between two or more pieces?
- Are two or more glass samples consistent?

Glass evidence must be handled with care in all instances as sharp edges may be a concern. Glass should be packaged in puncture resistant envelopes or boxes and labeled "sharp" or "caution" to avoid injuries.

The value of glass is determined by the crime. If the glass has shattered as a result of an explosion or random gunfire, it may not hold as much value as a glass window broken by a vandal. In a situation where a building explodes, one would expect multiple windows to shatter assuming this is a high impact explosion. Since multiple windows have shattered, collecting random samples of glass from this scene would be futile. When the glass present at the scene is more isolated, it becomes more probative as trace evidence. For instance, if a series of churches are vandalized, the crime may point to a serial vandal. When a window is shattered in one of the churches, and the same window is thought to be the point of entry, the glass fragments become a possible link to a future suspect. These fragments can fall into jacket pockets or become embedded in the soles of sneakers.

If an investigator wants to determine whether the vandal broke the church window from inside or outside of the church, a simple approach exists in reconstructing the glass pane. If possible, place the pieces of a broken window together like a puzzle noting the inside of the glass versus the outside. Look for a point of impact where outward radiating fractures (radial fractures) and concentric circles converge. Fine lines called "rib" or "hackle" marks are present on the radial fractures closest to the point of impact. The rib marks indicate on what side of the glass the breaking force occurred.[5] (pp. 6–9)

It is also possible that glass items submitted as questioned and known may share a common fracture. If a piece of glass recovered from the scene can be connected to the broken headlight of a suspect's car, a physical match definitively links the suspect to the scene. The glass at the scene is like a key that only fits one lock. In this case, the lock is the headlight.

A comparison of glass items requires a questioned and known sample be submitted. A tablespoon of fragments is usually adequate. Several simple tests are done on submitted items to verify that a sample is glass. If the sample is pliable or dissolves in water, it is not glass. After concluding a sample is glass, physical properties such as color, thickness and fluorescence are observed. The refractive index is determined for glass particles using the "double variation" method. Temperature and specific wavelengths of light are variables plotted as data points on a graph. Refractive index is derived manually from the graph. A scanning electron microscope with an energy dispersive x-ray detector may be utilized to get an elemental profile of a glass particle.[5] (pp. 15–23) If the questioned sample is consistent to the known sample with respect to physical characteristics, optical properties, and elemental profiles, it is concluded that the two samples may have the same source of origin. Inconsistent samples do not have the same source of origin.

Paint Evidence

Paint evidence may be a factor in "hit and run" situations. A pedestrian struck down by a vehicle may have traces of paint on his or her clothing. Paint chips consisting of all possible layers are best for making conclusive matches, but partial paint chips and smears are also compared to known paint submissions. Although the larger the paint samples the better, it is possible to work with fragments smaller than a grain of rice, but testing will be very limited. Chemical extractions and testing were once widely used as a method to separate and analyze the components of paint. Today, less destructive techniques are available.

Questioned and known paint samples are examined visually, microscopically, and instrumentally to reach a conclusion. Physical characteristics such as color and metallic versus nonmetallic lustre can be described visually. A microscope is used to examine the sequence, number, and thickness of layers present in a paint fragment. A Scanning Electron Microscope can also be used to observe and measure the thickness of the layers. Additionally, the Energy Dispersive x-ray detector can examine the elemental profile of the layers. An effective instrumental method used to analyze the layers of a paint chip is FTIR[6] in which light interacts with the chemical components of the paint to produce a spectrum of the energy vibrations and absorptions characteristic to that substance. Comparing as many layers as possible between questioned and known paint samples confirms or disproves a match. If the questioned sample is consistent with the known sample with respect to physical characteristics and chemical structure, we can conclude that the two samples may have the same source of origin. Inconsistent samples do not have the same source of origin.

The Importance of Trace Evidence Collection

Trace evidence can provide a link between the suspect and the crime scene in many cases including homicides, burglaries, and rapes. Since the focus of crime scene investigation has turned to blood and DNA analysis for answers, trace evidence may be overlooked. There are many crime scenes where the victim is the only source of blood and body fluids found at the scene. When the suspect leaves behind no biological materials, DNA analysis may not be the answer. Bloodstain patterns may indicate a violent beating took place, but interpretation of the patterns can only provide an insight into the position and force used on the victim. Bloodstain patterns as they appear cannot link the responsible individual to a crime scene. In the absence of obvious pieces of evidence, such as blood and fingerprints, the alternative for investigators may lie within the unseen pieces of trace evidence.

Endnotes

1. Houck Max, Ed., *Mute Witness*, Academic Press, California: 2001, p. 49.

2. Robertson James and Grieve Michael, eds., *Forensic Examination of Fibres,* 2nd ed., Taylor and Francis Forensic Science Series, Pennsylvania: 1999, pp. 102–104.

3. The American Society for Testing and Materials, *Standard Practice for Collection and Preservation of Information and Physical Items by a Technical Investigator,* E 1188–95, vol. 14.02, ASTM Committee on Standards, Pennsylvania: 1995, pp. 326–327.

4. Kirk Paul, *Crime Investigation: Physical Evidence and the Police Laboratory*, Interscience Publishers Inc., New York, NY: 1953, pp. 632–635.

5. Curran James Michael, Hicks Tacha Natalie and Buckleton John., *Forensic Interpretation of Glass Evidence*, CRC Press, Florida: 2000, pp. 6–9.

6. Saferstein Richard, Ed., *Forensic Science Handbook*, Prentice Hall Regents, New Jersey: 1982, pp. 552–555.

Firearm and Toolmark Identification

16

DEBORAH L. CHAKLOS AND MICHELLE N. KUEHNER

Introduction

Firearms Identification is the branch of forensic science that is primarily concerned with determining whether an ammunition component was discharged by a particular firearm. It is a subspecialty of Toolmark Identification, which involves the examination of markings that are produced as a result of the action of a harder surface (tool) against a softer surface. With respect to Firearms Identification, the firearm is the "tool" that marks the ammunition.

Firearms Identification is often incorrectly referred to as "Ballistics." Ballistics, which is the study of a projectile in motion, is a complicated science involving mathematical calculations of velocities, trajectories, and pressures. Ballisticians are primarily concerned with a projectile's behavior in the barrel (internal ballistics), after it leaves the barrel (external ballistics), and once it impacts its target (terminal ballistics). Ballisticians study the forces acting upon the projectile, not the actual toolmarks that are made on the projectile during its travel down the barrel.

The science of Firearms and Toolmark Identification is based on the existence of random defects on the surfaces of various parts of the firearm. These random defects are created during the manufacturing process and arise through use or abuse. When a firearm is discharged, several parts of the firearm come into contact with the ammunition components and create markings that are individual in nature on the discharged bullets and cartridge cases.

The primary task of a Firearms Examiner is to examine and compare the markings left by the firearm on the discharged bullets and cartridge cases. Physical comparisons with the aid of a comparison microscope are performed in an effort to identify fired components to each other and to a specific firearm.

Casework involving firearms typically includes a safety check, followed by the test firing of the firearm to check its operability and to obtain test standards for comparison purposes. To that end, today's Firearms Examiners must have a working knowledge of the safeties and operating systems of a wide variety of firearms. Once test standards are obtained, the firearms examiner will use the comparison microscope to examine and compare the test fired components.

Casework involving only fired components will include a microscopic examination to determine the general rifling characteristics (caliber, number and width of lands and grooves, and the direction of twist) for bullets and the pattern of breech face and firing pin impressions, as well as extractor and ejector locations on cartridge cases. Using these characteristics, an experienced examiner may be able to render an opinion as to the make and model of the firearm involved.

In a majority of laboratories, the test fired components and submitted fired components are put into an automated comparison database. In some laboratories, examiners may also perform a manual search against an open case file, which is a collection of fired components recovered from a crime scene that have not yet been associated with a particular firearm.

In addition to examining discharged bullets and cartridge cases, Firearms Examiners may also perform any number of the following tasks:

- Restoration of obliterated serial numbers on firearms
- Detection and characterization of primer gunshot residue (PGSR)
- Distance determination, including detection and characterization of GSR and GSR patterns on clothing and around gunshot wounds
- Toolmark examination

There are a number of important terms that will be used throughout this chapter. For your convenience, a mini glossary of useful terms, as defined by the Association of Firearms and Toolmark Examiners (AFTE), is included at the end of this chapter.

Introduction to Firearms

Function testing of firearms in a forensic laboratory requires both a general and specific knowledge of how firearms operate. An understanding of firearm types, internal mechanisms, and safety features allows a Firearms Examiner to determine whether a firearm is in mechanical and safe operating condition.

There are two main categories of firearms: (1) *handguns*, which are designed to be held and fired using one hand, and (2) *longarms*, which are designed to be fired from the shoulder. Handguns can be subcategorized into pistols and revolvers, and longarms can be subcategorized into rifles and shotguns.

A *pistol* is a hand-held firearm in which the chamber (the area of the firearm designed to hold the ammunition cartridge) is part of the barrel. When a loaded magazine is inserted into a pistol and the slide (a movable top piece) is pulled rearward, a single cartridge is pushed from the magazine into the chamber (Figure 16.1).

A *revolver* is a hand-held firearm with a rotating cylinder that has several chambers, each of which can be discharged successively by the same firing mechanism. Revolver designs include "break open" type, "swing out" type, and "pin type," each of which describes the manner in which the cylinder is exposed for loading (Figure 16.2).

Figure 16.1 Semiautomatic pistol (sketch courtesy of the Bureau of Alcohol, Tobacco, Firearms, and Explosives).

A *rifle* is a firearm that has a rifled (spirally grooved) bore and is designed to be fired from the shoulder. Rifle designs include single-shot, lever-action, bolt-action, semiautomatic, and fully automatic. These terms are used to describe the manner in which the action is cycled (Figure 16.3).

A *shotgun* is a shoulder-fired weapon typically with a smooth bore that is designed to fire shotshells containing numerous pellets or a single projectile. There are, however, exceptions to this as some shotguns have rifled bores. Shotgun designs include slide or pump action, break-open, and semiautomatic. As with rifles, these terms are used to describe the manner in which the action is cycled (Figure 16.4).

In semiautomatic pistols, rifles, and shotguns, discharged cartridge cases or shotshell cases are automatically extracted and ejected from the firearm before the next cartridge or shotshell is loaded. The ejected cases can usually be found at crime scenes. In pistols, rifles,

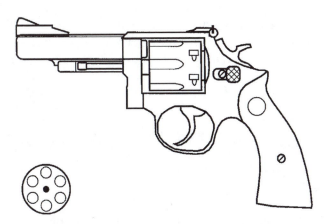

Figure 16.2 Revolver with a swing-out cylinder (sketch courtesy of the Bureau of Alcohol, Tobacco, Firearms, and Explosives).

Figure 16.3 Bolt-action rifle (sketch courtesy of the Bureau of Alcohol, Tobacco, Firearms, and Explosives).

and shotguns that are not semiautomatic, the discharged cartridge case or shotshell case will remain in the chamber until the chamber is manually opened to load a second cartridge or shotshell. In revolvers, the expended cartridge cases are stored in the revolving cylinder until they are manually extracted and ejected. Therefore, casings from revolvers and other manually operated firearms are less likely to be left behind at a scene.

Modern firearms operate in a similar manner, regardless of their type. When the trigger is pulled, a part of the firearm, usually called the firing pin or striker, is quickly forced against the primed area of the chambered cartridge by a hammer or spring. The rapid compression of the primer creates an internal spark that is sent into the cartridge to ignite the gunpowder. The rapid burning of the gunpowder causes a buildup of gasses, which in turn causes the cartridge case to expand against the chamber walls. When there is no more room for the gasses to expand, the projectile is forced to travel down the barrel, and the cartridge case or shotshell case is forced rearward against the breech face.

Introduction to Ammunition

A single unit of ammunition, called a cartridge, is made up of four components: (1) a cartridge case, (2) a projectile or projectiles, (3) gunpowder, and (4) a primer. Cartridges are often referred to as "rounds" or "bullets" by the general public. Use of the term "bullet," however, is incorrect because a bullet is only one component of a complete cartridge.

The head of the cartridge contains the primer and the headstamp markings. Head-stamps typically include the caliber designation and some type of manufacturer's information. The numerical portion of a caliber designation refers to the nominal diameter of the bullet. Some examples of caliber designations as they appear on a headstamp, are

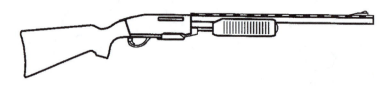

Figure 16.4 Slide-action or pump-action shotgun (sketch courtesy of the Bureau of Alcohol, Tobacco, Firearms, and Explosives).

22 LR (Long Rifle), 25 Auto, 32 S&WL (Smith & Wesson Long), 38 Special, 41 Rem Mag (Remington Magnum), 30-30 WIN (Winchester), and 7.62 × 39 mm.

Cartridges can be categorized as either rimfire or centerfire, based on their primer design. In *rimfire* cartridges, the priming mixture is in the rim of the cartridge head. To discharge a rimfire cartridge, such as those in the 22 caliber family, the firing pin must strike any part of the cartridge rim. *Centerfire* cartridges, on the other hand, have a primer located in the center of the head of the cartridge case. The firing pin must strike the centrally located primer to discharge the cartridge (Figure 16.5).

In addition to the primer design, the body design is also used to categorize cartridges. Revolvers use a rimmed cartridge in which the case head extends just beyond the case body. The extended rim allows the cartridge to properly sit in the cylinder and facilitates manual extraction. Semi-automatic pistols usually use cartridges where the head of the cartridge case is of the same diameter as that of the case body. This type of cartridge, called a rimless or semirimmed cartridge, has a groove adjacent to its rim that allows for the automatic extraction and ejection of the spent cartridge case.

The bullet component of a cartridge can also come in a variety of shapes and styles. One of the most common bullet styles is single projectile with a lead core and a metal jacket. Copper is the most common bullet jacket material, although brass, aluminum, nickel-plated brass, and copper-washed steel are also frequently used. Full metal jacketed and jacketed hollow point bullets are two common bullet designs for pistol, revolver, and rifle ammunition. Revolver ammunition is also often loaded with lead bullets. The nose design of a bullet, whether lead or jacketed, can be solid, flat, round, pointed, or hollow, to name a few. Some special use revolver cartridges, known as shot cartridges, are loaded with numerous projectiles.

Shotshells are similar to cartridges except that they typically hold numerous projectiles and are described by their gauge, rather than their caliber. Shotshells can also hold a single projectile known as a "slug." In addition, shotshells contain wadding, which is a plastic or cardboard component or number of components that hold the shot pellets in place and separate them from the powder (Figure 16.6).

Figure 16.5   9 mm caliber "Federal" cartridge loaded with Hydrashok™ bullet and discharged Hydrashok™ bullets.

Figure 16.6   Shotshells.

Firearms Identification

Theory of Firearms Identification

The microscopic markings that are produced incidental to manufacture and the general wear and tear on internal surfaces contribute to the individuality of a firearm. The individual or unique marks on the firearm are transferred to ammunition components during discharge. The marks left on the discharged ammunition components are unique to the firearm from which they were discharged.

Significant agreement of these unique marks allows for matches to be made between two bullets or two cartridge cases discharged by the same firearm. The unique quality of the marks also allows for a distinction to be made between bullets and cartridge cases discharged from two different firearms of the same make and model, even those that were consecutively manufactured.

Barrel Manufacturing Process

Barrel manufacturing methods are of special interest to firearm examiners because they affect the appearance of the individual characteristics found on discharged bullets. Most companies use their own set of procedures for barrel production; however, the same general production techniques have been used for decades.

Most manufacturers start with some type of solid steel or alloy bar stock. The stock is cut to a desired length and deep hole drilled. This process is also called gundrilling. Usually, the next step is reaming, which brings the bore up to a desired size and removes some of the gross surface marks from gundrilling. The bore of the reamed barrel blank may then be honed or lead lapped to bring it to a desired size or to remove the reaming marks. Some manufacturers perform several external machining operations next, including crowning the muzzle, and then rifle the bore. Others rifle the bore first and then machine the crown. The method of rifling used depends on the company and the make and model of the firearm. After rifling, additional cosmetic operations, such as polishing or bluing, may also be performed.

There are a variety of rifling methods that are used by modern barrel manufacturers. The most commonly used methods are broach rifling, button rifling, and hammer forging. The newest rifling method is electrochemical machining (ECM), also called electrochemical rifling (ECR).

Marks Produced on Bullets and Cartridge Cases: Class and Individual Characteristics

The marks that are produced on fired ammunition components have a general appearance, known as "class characteristics," and may have a unique appearance, known as an "individual characteristics."

Class characteristics refer to the features of a group of objects that are alike in some sense. Within each discipline of the forensic sciences, the term class characteristic takes on a more specific meaning. Examples of different class characteristics would be a cotton versus a synthetic fiber, a dog hair versus a human hair, a loop versus a whorl, or a 22 caliber bullet versus a 45 caliber bullet. In the field of firearms identification, class characteristics are a result of design specifications that are determined prior to manufacture. Examples of class characteristics include the caliber, number, width, and direction of twist of the barrel rifling (collectively known as the general rifling characteristics [GRCs]) or the size and shape of the firing pin.

Individual characteristics, on the other hand, are not an intentional result of the manufacturing process. In the broadest sense, individual characteristics can be defined as being of, by, for, or relating to a single person or thing. Examples of individual characteristics are the unique patterns of friction ridges on a person's fingertips or the unique DNA fingerprint of every individual (with the exception of identical twins). Individual characteristics, with respect to firearms identification, are imperfections or irregularities that are the accidental byproduct of the firearm manufacturing process. Imperfections on marking surfaces of a firearm can also occur over time from use, abuse, corrosion, or damage to the firearm itself. These individual imperfections make the firearm unique and allow it to be distinguished from all other firearms.

The marks that are produced on bullets differ from the marks that are produced on cartridge cases during discharge. The following sections detail the types of marks that are most commonly seen on discharged ammunition components.

Bullets

The rifling of the barrel is the primary component of the firearm that comes into contact with the bullet. Rifling is a series of spiral grooves inside a barrel that cause a bullet to spin as it leaves the muzzle. Like the spiral throw of a football, this spin helps to stabilize the bullet while it is in motion. The raised areas of the rifling are called "lands," and the lowered or indented areas, with respect to the lands, are called "grooves." On a bullet, the area marked by the land is called the "land impression" or "land engraved area" (LEA), and the area marked by the groove is called the "groove impression" or "groove engraved area" (GEA) (Figure 16.7).

As previously mentioned, the number, width, and direction of twist of the lands and grooves are collectively known as general rifling characteristics or GRCs. These measurable

Figure 16.7 Barrel rifling with six lands and grooves with a right-hand twist.

features can be useful in determining the make and model of the firearm from which a bullet was discharged, but they are not suitable for identifying the specific firearm that discharged the bullet.

The random imperfections on the surfaces of the lands and grooves in the barrel are imparted onto the bullet in the form of microscopic striations. These linear striations are found in the land impressions and can sometimes be found in the groove impressions, following the twist of the rifling. These microscopic striations are the individual or unique marks that are used for identification purposes (Figure 16.8).

Cartridge Cases

The cartridge case component of a cartridge is marked by a number of different parts inside the firearm during discharge. Each of the marks that are produced can potentially be identified as having been made by a specific firearm, to the exclusion of all others (Figure 16.9).

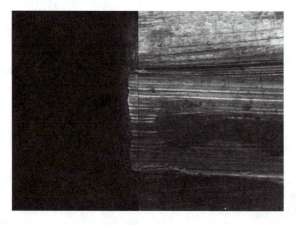

Figure 16.8 Comparison of striae in the land impressions of two bullets discharged from the same barrel. (Note dividing line down center of image.)

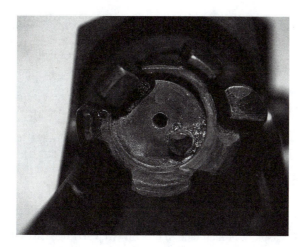

Figure 16.9 The bolt (breech) face supports the head of the cartridge during firing. The extractor is located in the upper left, the ejector in the lower right, and the firing pin aperture in the center of the bolt face.

The parts of the firearm that most frequently leave marks on discharged cartridge cases are the breech face, firing pin, extractor, and ejector. The magazine and chamber can also leave marks that may be useful for comparison purposes.

Breech Face Marks — The face of the breech of a firearm, known as the breech face, supports the head of the cartridge during discharge. When a cartridge is discharged, the rapid expansion of gasses pushes the cartridge case back against the breech face. As this happens, a negative impression of the markings from the breech face is made in the relatively soft metal of the cartridge case primer.

In some firearms, discharged cartridge cases may also display striated shearing marks on their primers. These shearing marks are produced as a small amount of metal from the primer is shaved off by the edge of the firing pin aperture, which is the hole in the breech face through which the firing pin protrudes. The size and shape of the firing pin aperture may also be observed as an impression in the primer area of the discharged cartridge case.

The various machining processes used to prepare the breech face leave behind both class and individual characteristics. A process known as face milling, for example, will leave circular or arced marks on the breech face of the firearm. Hand filing, on the other hand, will leave mostly parallel or slightly crosshatched markings. The general appearance of the marks can be considered to be a class characteristic and can be useful in determining the make and model of the firearm that discharged the cartridge case. The most typical breech face marks are parallel, circular, arced, granular, and crosshatched in appearance. These markings are found on the head of the cartridge case and are most prominent on the primer. The random imperfections found on the breech face that are transferred to the head of the cartridge case are considered to be individual characteristics and can be useful for identification purposes (Figure 16.10).

Firing Pin Impressions — The firing pin is the part of the firearm that strikes the primer and causes the discharge of a cartridge. When the firing pin strikes the soft metal of the primer, it leaves an indentation or impression that is a negative of its shape, contour, and surface detail.

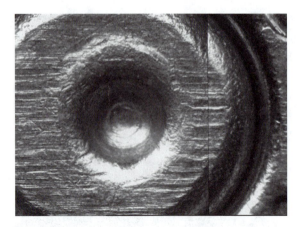

Figure 16.10   Comparison of breech face marks on two cartridge cases discharged by the same firearm. (Note dividing line down center of image.)

The general size and shape of the firing pin are class characteristics. Firing pins may be round, square, rectangular, or elliptical, to name a few. The end of the firing pin may be flat, hemispherical, pointed, or chiseled. As with the breech face marks, the manufacturing processes used to produce the firing pin will have an influence on the types of marks that will be transferred to the primer of a cartridge case during discharge. The striking end of a firing pin may have circular marks, parallel marks, a granular appearance, random marks, or they may be relatively smooth.

Like the breech face marks, the overall appearance of the firing pin impression may be useful for determining the make or model of the firearm that discharged the cartridge case. The random defects in the impression can be useful for identification purposes (Figure 16.11).

Extractor Marks — The extractor is the part of the firearm that withdraws the cartridge or discharged cartridge case from the chamber. It does this by hooking itself over the rim of the cartridge case, and engaging the extractor groove. When the slide or bolt travels

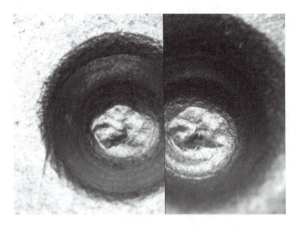

Figure 16.11   Comparison of firing pin marks on two cartridge cases discharged by the same firearm.

rearward, the extractor pulls the cartridge case from the chamber, and then the cartridge case is pushed free of the firearm by the ejector.

The size and the shape of the extractor vary among manufacturers but will usually have the general appearance of a wide crochet hook. The markings that are produced by the extractor can be striated or impressed toolmarks. The marks are typically produced on the underside of the rim of the cartridge case or on the wall of the extractor groove. Extractor marks can sometimes be found on the outer edge or the side of the cartridge case head. Typically, the extractor leaves only a small mark, so making an identification using this mark may be somewhat of a challenge.

Ejector Marks — The ejector is the part of the firearm that ejects or expels a cartridge or cartridge case from a firearm. The firing pin may act as the ejector, the ejector may be an integral part of the Frame, or it may be a separate part attached to the frame. Whatever the design, the ejector serves to push the cartridge or cartridge case out of the firearm as the slide or bolt moves rearward.

Ejector marks are typically impressed-type toolmarks found in the headstamp area or at the edge of the primer area of the cartridge case. Sometimes, however, the marks may be striated due to the movement of the cartridge case during ejection. Ejectors may be circular, square, rectangular, or irregularly shaped. The shape and position of the ejector relative to the extractor can be considered a class characteristic and may help in determining the make and model of the firearm in question. Like the extractor, using the small mark produced by the ejector can make identification somewhat of a challenge.

Magazine Marks — These narrow striated marks, if present, are typically located along the body of the cartridge or cartridge case. They are produced as a cartridge passes across the lips of a magazine, such as a detachable box or drum magazine. The marks that are produced are often so narrow that they lack sufficient detail for identification purposes.

Chamber Marks — These types of marks, if present, are located around the body of a discharged cartridge case. They can be impressed marks that are produced as the cartridge case expands in the chamber during discharge or they can be striated marks that are produced as the discharged and slightly expanded cartridge case is pulled from the chamber.

Laboratory Examination of Firearms and Fired Components

A drive-by shooting occurs on a busy neighborhood street. One victim is struck in the leg and is transported to the hospital. A second, less fortunate victim is fatally wounded and dies at the scene. Crime scene personnel recover several discharged cartridge cases from the street and sidewalk and are able to recover a number of bullets from the siding and framing of the nearby buildings. The body of the victim that died at the scene is transported to the Medical Examiner's or Coroner's Office for autopsy. Two bullets are recovered from the victim. Meanwhile, the medical personnel at the hospital are able to remove two more bullets from the other victim's leg. The cartridge cases and bullets collected at the scene and the bullets recovered from both victims are submitted to the Firearms Section for examination.

A month later, the three suspects that are believed to be involved in the shooting are pulled over for a routine traffic stop. During the stop, police observe the butt of a gun protruding from between the two front seats. After legally searching the vehicle, the police recover a firearm, several discharged cartridge cases, and two boxes of ammunition. The recovered items are submitted to the Firearms Section for examination.

This is a typical scenario for cases that come into the Firearms Section. Fired ammunition components are submitted to the laboratory with hopes that the Firearms Section can provide some information about the firearm that was used.

Conversely, firearms are submitted to the laboratory with the hope that they will be associated with an unsolved crime and also for the purpose of routine function testing. The criminal charges that can be filed for possession or discharge of a firearm may be dependent of the operability of the firearm.

This section outlines the routine examination of submitted firearms and fired components.

Laboratory Examination of Firearms

As with all forensic evidence, a chain of custody must be maintained when working with firearms-related evidence. When an examiner is ready to begin working on a case, the items of evidence are removed from a secure storage area, and the transfer of custody is recorded. If latent print examination is requested, the Firearms Examiner must make sure that it was completed before handling the firearm. Once the evidence is opened, the contents of the evidence package is inventoried and recorded in the examiner's notes.

A number of features including the make, model, caliber, general rifling characteristics, barrel length, and trigger pull of a submitted firearm are recorded. A field test is performed to ensure that the firearm will function during actual test firing. While following all safety rules, the firearm is loaded with live ammunition and is test fired into a water tank. Most laboratories use a water tank because the water in the tank slows the bullet with minimal damage. Another, less frequently used recovery system is a box filled with cotton filler. After test firing, the test bullets and cartridge cases are collected and are examined microscopically with the aid of a comparison microscope.

The *comparison microscope* is used in firearms examination to perform a side-by-side comparison of discharged bullets and cartridge cases. The design of the comparison microscope allows the user to view two objects through one split field of view. The dividing line between the two images can be moved back and forth to aid in direct comparison of two different objects or can be eliminated for viewing one object at a time. Oblique illumination from either a fluorescent bulb or fiber optic light source can be used with the comparison microscope (Figure 16.12).

Using the comparison microscope, the examiner will compare the test bullets to each other and the test cartridge cases to each other to evaluate the types of marks and the reproducibility of the marks that are present. The examiner may also measure the dimensions of the bullet's lands and grooves.

If the test fired components meet certain criteria, images of test cartridge cases and test bullets can be captured and entered into an automated comparison database. The test bullets and cartridge cases may also be manually compared to an open case file, which contains bullets and cartridge cases recovered from crime scenes that have not yet been associated with a particular firearm.

After all function testing and comparisons have been conducted, the examiner will properly seal and label the evidence for return to the submitting agency. The examiner

Figure 16.12   Comparison microscope.

will then issue a report on the operability of the firearm and, if applicable, open file and automated database search results.

Laboratory Examination of Fired Ammunition Components

After the chain of custody is recorded and the items of evidence are inventoried, fired components are examined, and several features are noted. For cartridge cases, the caliber, the headstamp information, the cartridge case type, and the types of marks that are left on the cartridge case, such as breech face, firing pin, extractor, and ejector marks, are recorded. For bullets, the design, bullet composition, general rifling characteristics, and any bullet damage or irregularities are recorded.

The fired components are microscopically examined, and individual characteristics are noted on the marked areas of the bullets and cartridge cases. A comparison between submitted bullets or between submitted cartridge cases allows the examiner to evaluate the reproducibility of the markings from one fired component to the next. The types of marks that are present can provide the examiner with information about the type of firearm from which the component was discharged. The examiner may then be able to provide the submitting agency with a list of possible firearms that could have been involved.

As with the test fired components from submitted firearms, images of suitable submitted ammunition components can be entered into the automated comparison database. The components can also be manually compared to the open case file and to test fires from submitted firearms. Any of these methods could potentially link the incident to another seemingly unrelated firearms-related incident.

> Let us continue the previously mentioned case scenario: During examination of the submitted evidence, it is found that two different caliber bullets were recovered from the victims. The cartridge cases collected from the scene are also found to be of two different calibers. This indicates that two different firearms were involved in the incident. After entering the casings into the automated search database and comparing them to the open case file, a link is made with a homicide that had occurred a month before the drive-by shooting. Also, after a comparison with the test fired components from the firearm submitted from the traffic stop, it is determined that one of the sets of bullets and cartridge cases from the crime scene was fired from that pistol. If the police had no suspects in the first homicide, they now have a lead and three potential suspects. Linking these seemingly unrelated cases could potentially help police solve each of the cases.

National Integrated Ballistic Information Network (NIBIN)

With the increased number of shooting incidents, it is difficult to maintain and manually search an open case file. Thanks to the Integrated Ballistics Identification System (IBIS^{TM}), gone are the days of posting Polaroid photographs on the wall and relying on memory during routine examinations of test fired bullets and cartridge cases to connect the two cases. The IBIS^{TM} technology was created by Forensic Technology, Inc. of Montreal, Canada, as a response to a request by a Firearms Examiner who wanted to automate the search of his open case file.

IBIS^{TM} works by capturing digital images of each of the toolmarked areas that can be found on the head of the cartridge case (breech face, firing pin, and extractor) and of the toolmarks made by the rifling in the barrel that can be found on the surface of the bullet. The images are then compared to those stored in a database using a sophisticated algorithm, and the results are displayed. The user can then compare the images of the high probability candidates and determine whether a manual comparison is necessary (Figure 16.13).

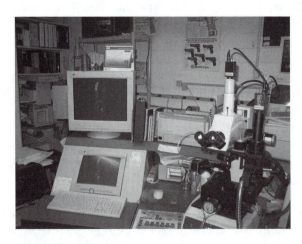

Figure 16.13   NIBIN/IBIS system.

In recent years, the Bureau of Alcohol, Tobacco, Firearms, and Explosives realized the potential of this technology and created the NIBIN program. ATF purchased the IBIS^{TM} technology and distributed it to local forensic laboratories. They then linked the individual IBIS^{TM} stations to create a national network. Examiners can now use IBIS^{TM} to search their own area databases and, if desired, any other NIBIN partner database they select in the United States. For example, if a person is arrested in one state with a gun but lives in another state, the examiner can enter the test bullets and cartridge cases into IBIS^{TM}, search the databases in their own region, and also search the databases in the state in which the actor lives. Routine use of NIBIN increases the likelihood of linking one gun or one incident to other seemingly unrelated incidents. This could potentially provide leads in a police investigation that may have been stalled because of lack of information. Before the advent of IBIS^{TM} and NIBIN, the detective would have had to have information that two incidents were linked and then physically transport the evidence to the out of state laboratory. Now, the images can be sent across the United States with just a few clicks of the computer mouse.

It is important to remember that IBIS^{TM} does not make identifications. The system only provides the examiner with a list of high probability candidates. A trained examiner must manually compare any high probability candidates before any conclusions are reached about an identification.

Other Types of Examinations

Serial Number Restoration

The restoration of obliterated serial numbers is another task commonly performed by the Firearms Section. A serial number is a sequence of alphabetical and numerical characters that is designed to be a unique identifier to a particular firearm, automobile, bicycle, electronic appliance, etc. In 1968, the federal Gun Control Act made it mandatory that all firearms manufactured in or imported into the United States be marked with a serial number on their frame or receiver. A serial number can be of use to investigative authorities in tracking the sales and ownership history of the firearm.

Attempts are often made to illegally remove the serial number from a firearm to thwart tracing efforts. Fortunately, the metal just below the obliterated serial number may be suitable for treatment with a few simple restoration techniques to reveal the original serial number.

Serial numbers of most modern firearms are stamped into the frame or receiver to a depth regulated by the ATF, which ensures that the stamping is sufficient enough to make a deep impression in the metal. When a serial number is stamped, the crystalline structure within the metal is altered beyond its elastic limit, and permanent deformation results. This deformation can extend well below the visibly stamped area. When a serial number is obliterated, one may remove the visible number but leave the plastically deformed crystals that are below the numbers.

There are numerous methods that have been used to obliterate serial numbers. Some of the most common methods are filing, grinding, scraping, gouging, peening, and drilling. Methods such as filing, grinding, and scraping tend to remove only the top surface of the metal, leaving behind the underlying deformed crystals. Cold working a metal surface by peening or hammering, however, tends to compress the underlying crystals in the same manner as the original stamping. This can make restoration difficult. As with filing and grinding, a drilled serial number may only remove the serial number just to the point where it is no longer visible. If, however, the underlying crystalline structure of the metal is removed or disrupted by the drill bit, restoration of the number may not be possible.

Restoration of an obliterated serial number can be accomplished using a variety of methods. One of the most common and most successful methods is a polishing and acid etching technique. In this method, a rough, obliterated surface is carefully polished to a smooth or nearly smooth finish, and the appropriate acid etching solution is applied to the polished area. After a period of time, the original serial number may appear. The examiner must be careful not to overpolish the area or leave the acid etchant on too long. If that happens, a successful serial number restoration may not be possible.

The theory behind the use of chemical etchants is that the deformed crystals in the metal will react with the chemicals in the etchant at a rate different from that of the crystals that had not been deformed during the original stamping of the serial number. The different reaction rates of the altered and unaltered crystalline structure allow a serial number to be restored. The type of acid etching solution applied is dependent on the metallic properties of the metal from which the serial number was removed.

A second restoration method employs the use of an electrolytic solution to raise the obliterated number. In this method, called the electrolytic method, the firearm acts as the anode, and a cotton swab dipped in a chemical etchant acts at the cathode of an electrochemical cell. Voltage is applied from an external source, and dissolution of the metal takes place. The chemical etching process is accelerated when an electrical potential is applied.

A third method that is used in serial number restoration is known as the magnetic particle method. In this technique, fine iron-rich particles are applied to the polished surface of a magnetized specimen. The altered crystalline structure will attract the particles differently than the unaltered crystals will. The magnetic particle method has an advantage over the other methods in that it is nondestructive.

Detection of Primer Gunshot Residue (PGSR)

The primer is considered the initiator of a cartridge. When it is struck, it starts the process of burning the gunpowder. The key ingredients of the priming compound typically contains the elements lead, barium, and antimony. The high temperatures produced during the ignition of the primes create spheroidal particles, which contain any combination of lead, barium, and antimony. Although these elements can be found separately in nature, a spheroidal particle containing lead, barium, and antimony or barium and antimony is considered to be characteristic of primer gunshot residue, or PGSR. In lead-free ammunition, any or all of the three main elemental components may be replaced with another element. The best way to determine the characteristic elemental composition for a specific lead-free brand would be to analyze a reference sample from a spent cartridge case.

When a firearm is discharged, the gasses from the burning gun powder along with partially burned and unburned particles emerge from the muzzle end of the firearm along with the projectile. Gasses can also escape through the ejection port of a pistol and through the cylinder gap of a revolver. These gasses and the minute particles that travel

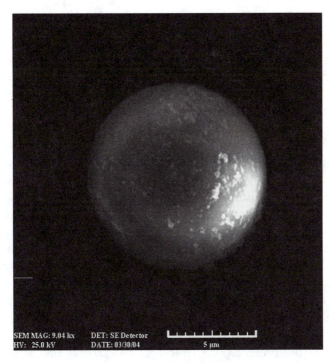

SEM MAG: 9.04 kx   DET: SE Detector
HV: 25.0 kV   DATE: 03/30/04   5 μm

Figure 16.14 Scanning electron microscope image of a spherical PGSR particle which contains lead, barium, and antimony.

with them can land on the firearm and on any surface near the firearm that has been discharged. The particles will remain there for a relatively short period of time. PGSR could be compared to a light dust on a person's hands. Any rubbing or washing will easily displace or remove the PGSR particles (Figure 16.14).

To determine whether someone has discharged a firearm, was near a recently discharged firearm, or handled a recently discharged firearm, samples can be taken from their hands or even their face. There are a few instrumental techniques that can be used to detect PGSR. The most common and least destructive instrumental method is Scanning Electron Microscopy/Energy Dispersive X-ray Spectroscopy (SEM/EDS).

Sampling for SEM/EDS analysis is done using a small circular stub that has an adhesive tape face. The face of the stub is dabbed on the designated areas (right hand, left hand, and sometimes face) until the adhesive loses its stickiness. The stub is then directly inserted into the SEM instrument for analysis.

The SEM uses a focused electron beam to excite the sample, which allows the shape of the particle to be observed, and the EDS determines the elemental composition of the particles. Spheroidal particles containing lead, barium, and antimony or barium and antimony are considered to be characteristic of PGSR. Some other combinations of particles such as lead/antimony, lead/barium, and lead are considered consistent with PGSR. Other elements such as copper, aluminum, and tin, to name a few, can also be seen in a PGSR particle. The source of these elements is most likely the ammunition components (bullet or cartridge case). Even if characteristic PGSR particles are found on a sample from a person, it is difficult to say whether a person discharged a firearm.

Distance Determination/Detection of Gunshot Residue on Clothing

The Firearms Section is routinely asked to examine a victim's clothing or other items of evidence to determine whether bullet holes and gunshot residues are present. The presence or the absence of residues may be useful in determining the distance between the muzzle of the firearm and the victim. Detection of gunshot residues may also be helpful in determining whether a bullet hole is an entrance hole or an exit hole.

As outlined in the previous section, gunshot residues and partially burned and unburned gunpowder particles ejected from a muzzle can be deposited onto nearby objects during discharge. At contact or near contact, hot gasses, smoke, and residues blown into the hole can leave a very dark, dense pattern inside the hole and may cause tears in the fabric. As the distance between the muzzle and the garment increases, the pattern of residues around the hole spreads out and becomes less dense. Tearing is no longer observed, and the margins of the hole tend to be more even. At a certain distance, residues will no longer be deposited onto the garment, with the possible exception of bullet wipe, which occurs when the residues adhering to a projectile transfer, or wipe, onto the rim of the entrance hole as the projectile passes through the object.

When conducting a gunshot residue examination, it is important to recognize that a positive reaction for certain residues does not mean that a hole in an item is a bullet hole, and vise versa. An examiner must take into account the overall position and pattern of the residues, as well as the presence or the absence of physical effects, such as ripping or tearing.

Gunshot Residue Examination

In a typical gunshot residue examination, the item of evidence is visually inspected for the presence of fabric separations or potential bullet holes. An examiner must be aware that it is possible that cuts made by medical personnel could transect and obscure a bullet hole. If a suspected bullet hole is observed, its general appearance is noted, and its margins and surrounding areas are examined microscopically for the presence of any melting, burning, residue deposits, and partially burned or unburned gunpowder particles. In some cases, a partial pattern of gunshot residues may be present without a bullet hole. This can occur if the bullet narrowly missed the item in question.

After a visual inspection, exhibits are chemically tested for the presence of deposited gunshot residues. The two chemical tests that are used give a color reaction in the presence of specific residues. The *Modified Griess Test* detects the presence of nitrite residues, which come from a component of the priming mixture and from the combustion of the nitrogen-based gunpowder. The Modified Griess Test is performed by placing the garment face-down on a sheet of chemically treated, desensitized photographic paper and covering it with an acetic-acid-soaked piece of cheese cloth or paper towel. The assembly of the photo paper, garment, and cheese cloth is then carefully ironed with a steam iron. Any nitrites that are present will produce a bright orange reaction on the chemically treated photo paper.

The *Sodium Rhodizonate Test* detects the presence of lead residues, which come from the bullet itself or a component of the priming mixture. This test is commonly performed by directly spraying the submitted item with a solution of Sodium Rhodizonate and distilled water followed by a spray of buffer solution. A bright pink color change indicates that lead residues *may* be present. Because the pink color is not specific for lead, an additional step is necessary to confirm the presence of lead. Overspraying the area with a dilute solution of hydrochloric acid will cause the pink areas to turn a blue–violet color if lead is *definitely* present.

Distance Determination

After a garment is visually examined and chemically processed for the presence of gunshot residues, a distance study may be performed to determine the muzzle-to-target or muzzle-to-garment distance. In this type of study, a series of test shots are fired at known distances using the suspected firearm and ammunition. The patterns are visually examined and chemically processed in the same manner as for the submitted garment. The patterns of residues on the test targets are compared to those on the victim's garment, and a possible distance range is determined (Figure 16.15).

For example, if a suspect claims that there was a close struggle over a firearm, the victim's clothing will be examined and test patterns will be produced at known distances using the suspect's firearm and ammunition. If the test patterns indicate that residue deposits like those present on the victim's shirt could be reproduced between four and five feet, then the suspect's claim will likely be called into question.

Shotgun Patterns

The procedure for determining the muzzle-to-target distance for shotguns is similar to that described before, with the addition of the analysis of the shot pellet pattern. As the muzzle-to-target distance increases, the diameter of the shot pattern increases. Test patterns are produced at known distances, and the physical dimensions of the patterns are compared to the pattern on the submitted garment (Figure 16.16).

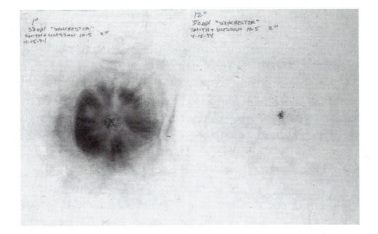

Figure 16.15 Gunshot residue pattern produced on a white cotton material using a 38 Special caliber Smith & Wesson revolver and 38 Special caliber "Winchester" ammunition. The patterns were produced at a muzzle-to-target distance of 1 inch (Left) and 12 inches (Right).

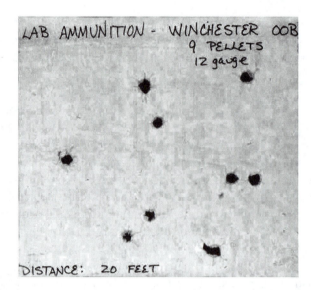

Figure 16.16 Shotgun pattern produced using a 12 Gauge shotshell containing nine 00 Buck shot pellets at a muzzle-to-target distance of 20 feet.

Toolmarks

Toolmark identification is the branch of forensic science that concentrates on the markings produced as a result of the action of a harder surface (tool) against a softer surface. Wire cutters used to cut telephone wire, bolt cutters used to cut the shackle of a padlock, and a knife used to puncture a tire are all examples of a harder surface acting against a softer surface. In each of these examples, the toolmarks that are made could potentially be identified back to the tool that was used.

Toolmarks can be broken down into two main types: (1) impressed marks and (2) striated marks. The surface that will receive the toolmark and the manner in which the tool is applied will determine the type of toolmark that is left behind. On a suitable marking surface, both class and individual characteristics may be present, which could allow for the identification of the toolmark and the individual tool.

Impressed toolmarks leave an impression of the shape of the tool as well as defects from the surface of the tool. Generally, the type of tool and some of the tool's physical characteristics can be determined from an impressed toolmark. An example of an impressed toolmark would be if a burglar used a screwdriver to pry open a door. If a good impression is left behind in the metal or wood, it may be possible to determine the width of the tip and the shape of the shaft on the screwdriver. Measurable features, such as width and shape, would be considered class characteristics of the tool.

Striated toolmarks occur when a tool is pushed or pulled against a softer surface. Pressure, direction, and angle all affect the appearance of the toolmark. Typically, flat pry-type tools (screwdrivers and crowbars), shearing-action tools (scissors and tin snips), pinching-action tools (bolt cutters and wire cutters), and slicing-action tools (knives and razors) can leave striated toolmarks (Figure 16.17a,b).

To continue with the previous example, let us say that the toolmarked areas of the door are collected from the scene, and a screwdriver is recovered from the suspect. The toolmark

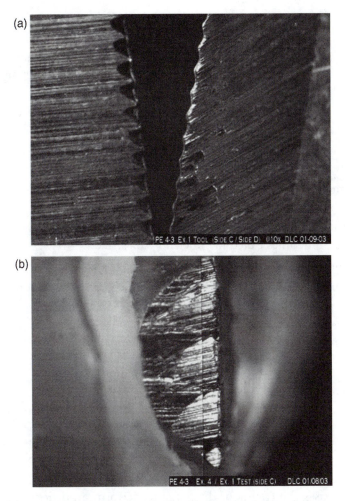

Figure 16.17 (a) Cutting surfaces on opposing blades of submitted sheet metal cutters and (b) Comparison of toolmarked surfaces. Cut end of submitted copper wire (Left) and test cut in copper wire, made with submitted sheet metal cutters (Right).

examiner will use the submitted screwdriver to make test toolmarks in a soft metal, such as lead, using different pressures, angles, and directions (pushing and pulling). The test toolmarks would then be microscopically compared to the toolmarks found at the crime scene with the possibility of linking the screwdriver to the pry-marks on the door.

Glossary of Terms

Automatic: A firearm design that feeds cartridges, fires, extracts, and ejects cartridge cases as long as the trigger is fully depressed and there are cartridges in the feed system. Also called full and machine gun.

Barrel: That part of a firearm through which a projectile or shot charge travels under the impetus of powder gasses, compressed air, or other like means. May be rifled or smooth.

Breech Face: That part of the breechblock or breech bolt that is against the head of the cartridge case or shotshell during firing.

Caliber: *Firearms:* The approximate diameter of the circle formed by the tops of the lands of a rifled barrel; *Ammunition:* A numerical term, without the decimal point, included in a cartridge name to indicate the nominal bullet diameter.

Chamber: The rear part of the barrel bore that has been formed to accept a specific cartridge. Revolver cylinders are multichambered.

Ejector: A portion of a firearm's mechanism that ejects or expels cartridges or cartridge cases from a firearm.

Extractor: A mechanism for withdrawing the cartridge or cartridge case from the chamber.

Firing Pin: That part of a firearm mechanism which strikes the primer of a cartridge to initiate ignition. Sometimes called hammer nose or striker.

Muzzle: The end of a firearm barrel from which the bullet or shot emerges.

Pistol: A handgun in which the chamber is part of the barrel. A term sometimes used for a handgun.

Revolver: A firearm, usually a handgun, with a cylinder having several chambers so arranged as to rotate around an axis and be discharged successively by the same firing mechanism.

Rifle: A firearm having rifling in the bore and designed to be fired from the shoulder.

Rifling: Helical grooves in the bore of a firearm barrel to impart rotary motion to a projectile.

Sear: A part which retains the hammer or striker in the cocked position until the trigger is pulled.

Semiautomatic: A repeating firearm requiring a separate pull of the trigger for each shot fired, and which uses the energy of discharge to perform a portion of the operating or firing cycle (usually the loading portion). Semiautomatic firearms are also referred to autoloading or are sometimes erroneously called automatic.

Shotgun: A smooth bore shoulder firearm designed to fire shotshells containing numerous pellets or sometimes a single projectile.

Trigger pull: The amount of force which must be applied to the trigger of a firearm to cause sear release.

References and Resources

Andrasko, J. and Maehly, A.C. Detection of gunshot residue by use of the scanning electron microscope, *J. Foren. Sci.*, 22, 279–287, 1977.

Brundage, D.J. The identification of consecutively rifled gun barrels, *AFTE J.*, 30(3), 438–444, 1998.

Dillon, J.H., "Modified Gneis Test: A Chemically Specific Chromophoric Test For Nitrite Compounds in Gunshot Residues," *AFTE J.*, 22(3), 243–250, 1990.

Dillon, J.H., "Protocol for Gunshot Residue Examinations in Muzzle-to-Target Distance Determinations," *AFTE J.*, 22(3), 257–274, 1990.

Dillon, J.H., "Sodium Rhodizonate Test: A Chemically Specific Chromophoric Test for Lead in Gunshot Residues," *AFTE J.*, 22(3), 251–256, 1990.

Glossary of the Association of Firearms and Toolmark Examiners, 3rd ed., Available Business Printing, Inc. Chicago, IL, 1994.

Hatcher, J.S., Jury, F.J., and Weller, J. 1957. *Firearms Investigation, Identification and Evidence*, Stackpole Books, Harrisburg, PA, 1957.

Heard, B.J. *Handbook of Firearms and Ballistics: Examining and Interpreting Forensic Evidence*, John Wiley & Sons, Chichester, England, 1997, p. 120.

Matanas, E.A. *Practical Gunsmithing*, Meredith Press, Published by Outdoor Life Books, New York, NY, 1990.

Mathews, J.H. *Firearms Identification, Vol. 1*, The University of Wisconsin Press, Madison, WI, 1962.

Papke, R.E. Electrochemical machining: A new barrel making process, *AFTE J.* 20(1), 1988.

Walker, J.R. *Machining Fundamentals*, Goodheart-Willcox Company, Inc., Tinley Park, IL, p. 508, 2000.

Walten, G.M., Nesbitt, R.S., Callaway, A.R., Loper, G.L., and Jones, P.F. Final report on particle analysis for gunshot residue detection, Report ATR-77(7915)-3. The Aerospace Corp., Sept. 1977.

The Investigation of Fire and Explosions

17

ROBERT M. HUSTON

The dynamics of the investigation of fire and explosion scenes has been rapidly evolving over the last decade from an "art" to "science". Skill, technology, knowledge, and science are utilized to determine the origin and cause. The scientific method is a systematic approach for the organizational and analytical process of investigation.

Principles of Ignition and Combustion

The principles of ignition and combustion will help in the interpretation of evidence at the fire scene and in the development of the conclusions regarding the origin and cause of the fire. The combustion reaction can be summarized by the four components of the fire tetrahedron: (1) the fuel, (2) the oxidizing agent, (3) the heat, and (4) the uninhibited chemical chain reaction. Fires can be prevented or suppressed by controlling or removing one or more of the sides of the tetrahedron.

The transfer of heat is a major factor in fires and has an effect on ignition, growth, spread, decay, and extinction. Heat is always transferred from the high-temperature mass to the low-temperature mass. Conduction, convection, and radiation are the mechanisms by which heat is transferred.

To be ignited, most materials, must be in a gaseous or vaporized state. These gases or vapors need to be present in the atmosphere in sufficient quantity to form a flammable mixture. Liquids with flash points below ambient temperatures do not require additional heat to produce a flammable mixture. Combustible substances in the gaseous state have an extremely low mass and require the least amount of energy for ignition. Self-heating is a process whereby a material undergoes an exothermic chemical reaction and increases in temperature without drawing heat from its surroundings. Most organic materials and metals capable of reacting with oxygen will oxidize at some critical temperature with evolution of heat.

The evolution of heat is also a result of organic materials undergoing polymerization reactions where liquids react to form solids. Self-heating and self-ignition are most commonly encountered in organic materials such as animal and vegetable fats and oils, because these materials contain polyunsaturated fatty acids, which react with oxygen to generate heat. Unsaturated molecules contain carbon-to-carbon double bonds, which are reactive. The most commonly encountered forms of self-heating and self-ignition are:

1. Polymerization of fatty acids (animal fats, cooking oils, and drying oils) in cellulose materials (wood, cloth, and paper).
2. Oxidation of carbonaceous materials (coal and charcoal).
3. Enzyme induced oxidation (hay bales and compost).
4. Heat induced oxidation of cellulose materials (wood fiber and cloth).
5. Polymerization reaction of plastics, rubbers, adhesives. Pyrophoric materials, such as white phosphorus, sodium, potassium, and some finely divided metals, that is, zirconium, spontaneously ignite when exposed to air.[1]

The chemical products of combustion can vary widely depending on the fuels involved and the amount of air available. Complete combustion of hydrocarbon fuels containing only hydrogen and carbon will produce carbon dioxide and water. Materials containing nitrogen, such as silk, wool, and polyurethane foam, produce nitrogen oxides and possibly hydrogen cyanide as combustion products. Hundreds of compounds have been identified as products of incomplete combustion of wood. The production of carbon monoxide increases, as does the production of soot and unburned fuels, as the availability of air decreases.

Combustion products exist in all three states of matter: solid, liquid, and gas. Solid material makes up the ash and soot products that represent the visible "smoke." Many other products of incomplete combustion exist as vapors or as extremely small droplets or aerosols, which often condense on surfaces that are cooler than the smoke, resulting in smoke patterns that can help determine the origin and spread of the fire. Smoke color is not necessarily an indicator of what is burning. Ventilation, materials being consumed, and fire suppression activities can all have an effect on the color of the smoke produced in a fire.

Processing the Fire Scene

The goal of documenting any fire or explosion investigation is to accurately record the investigation through media that will allow the investigator to recall and communicate their observations at a later date. Common methods of accomplishing this goal include the use of photographs, videotapes, diagrams, maps, overlays, tape recordings, notes, and reports. Thorough and accurate documentation of the investigation is critical because it is from this compilation of factual data that investigative opinions and conclusions can be supported and verified.

During the course of any fire investigation, the fire investigator is likely to be responsible for locating, collecting, identifying, storing, examining, and arranging for testing of physical evidence. Every attempt should be made to protect and preserve the fire scene as intact and undisturbed as possible, with the structure, contents, fixtures, and furnishings remaining in the prefire locations. The responsibility for the preservation of the fire scene and physical evidence does not lie solely with the fire investigator, but should begin with the arriving fire-fighting units and police authorities. Lack of preservation may result in the destruction, contamination, loss, or unnecessary movement of physical evidence.

Evidence at the fire scene should be considered in a criminal context, such as in traditional forensic evidence (e.g., weapons, bodily fluids, footprints) and it should not be limited to arson related evidence, items, artifacts, such as incendiary devices or containers.[4] Potential evidence at the fire scene and surrounding area can include the physical structure, the contents, the artifacts, and any material ignited or on which fire patterns appear.

Like improper preservation of the fire scene, any contamination of physical evidence may reduce the evidentiary value of the physical evidence. Contamination of physical evidence can occur from fire suppression, improper methods of collection, storage, or shipment. Every reasonable precaution to ensure that new and uncontaminated evidence containers are stored separately from used containers or contaminated areas. All evidence containers, including paint cans or glass jars, should be sealed immediately after receipt from the supplier. The containers are to remain sealed and only opened to obtain evidence at the time of collection, at which time it should remain sealed pending laboratory examination.

Most contamination of physical evidence occurs during its collection. The use of a new pair of disposable gloves for collection of each subsequent item of liquid or solid accelerant evidence prevents crosscontamination. All collection tools or overhaul equipment such as brooms and shovels need to be cleaned thoroughly between collections of each item of liquid or solid accelerant evidence to prevent similar crosscontamination. A 10–20% mixture of Dawn @ liquid detergent and water is good for decontamination. All waterless and other types of cleaners that may contain volatile solvents are to be avoided. The collection of physical evidence is an integral part of a properly conducted fire investigation. The method of collection of the physical evidence is determined by its physical state, physical characteristics, fragility, and volatility. Regardless of the method employed for collection, evidence collection is guided by the policies and procedures of the laboratory that will be examining or analyzing the physical evidence.

Physical evidence should be thoroughly documented before it is moved or disturbed. This documentation can include field notes, written reports, sketches, diagrams, with accurate measurements, and photographs. Traditional forensic physical evidence includes latent prints, bodily fluids, tool marks, footwear impressions, glass, paint, hair, fiber, and general types of trace evidence. Typically, this type of physical evidence may also become part of a fire or explosion investigation.

An accelerant is any fuel or oxidizer, often an ignitable liquid, used to initiate a fire or increase the rate of growth or speed the spread of fire. Liquid accelerants have unique characteristics in that they

- Are directly related to their collection as physical evidence
- Are readily absorbed by most structural components, interior furnishings, and other fire debris
- Have remarkable persistence when trapped within porous material
- Float when in contact with water — alcohol is a noted exception

When physical evidence is collected for examination and testing, it is often necessary to also collect comparison samples, which allow the laboratory to evaluate the possible contributions of volatile pyrolysis products to the analysis and also to estimate the flammability properties of the normal fuel present. For the purpose of identifying the presence of accelerant residue, the comparison sample should be collected from an area that is believed to be free of such accelerants, such as under furniture or in areas that have not been involved in the fire.

Properly trained and validated ignitable liquid detection canine/handler teams have proven their ability in locating samples for laboratory analysis to detect the presence of ignitable liquids. The proper use of detection canines is to assist with the location and selection of samples that will have a high probability of laboratory confirmation. Canine ignitable liquid detection should be used in conjunction with, and not in place of other fire investigation and analysis methods.

The selection of an appropriate evidence container depends on the physical state, physical characteristics, fragility, and volatility of the physical evidence. The evidence container should preserve the integrity of the evidence and should prevent any change to or contamination of the evidence. Evidence containers may be common items, such as envelopes, paper bags, glass or metal containers or they may be specifically designed for certain types of physical evidence. The policies and procedures of the laboratory that will analyze the physical evidence should guide the selection of an appropriate container.

All evidence should be labeled for identification at the time of collection. Identification includes (1) the name of the person collecting the physical evidence, (2) the date and time of collection, (3) an identification name or number, (4) the case number and item designation, (5) a description of the physical evidence, (6) where the physical evidence was located. (3) The value of physical evidence entirely depends on the security and integrity of that physical evidence from the time of its initial discovery and collection to it subsequent examination and testing.

Physical evidence should be stored in a secured location that is designed and designated for this purpose, and access to this storage location should be limited. When evidence is passed from one person to another, it should be done using a form on which the receiving person signs for the physical evidence, which is usually examined and tested in a laboratory. A wide variety of standardized tests are available, depending on the physical evidence and the hypothesis being tested.

The Nature and Role of Explosions

Fires and explosions so frequently accompany each other that no discourse on fire and its investigation would be complete without some special consideration of the nature and role of explosions. For fire and explosion investigations, an explosion is the sudden conversion of potential energy into kinetic energy with the production and release of gases under pressure.

There are two major types of explosions: mechanical and chemical.[2] The source or mechanism by which the explosive pressures are produced differentiates these two types. Mechanical explosions are those in which a high-pressure gas produces a purely physical reaction. These reactions do not involve changes in the basic chemical nature of the substances in the container. A purely mechanical explosion is the rupture of a gas storage tank or cylinder under high pressure resulting in the release of the stored high-pressure gas, such as compressed air, carbon dioxide, or oxygen.

Boiling Liquid Expanding Vapor Explosion (BLEVE) is the most frequent type of mechanical explosion encountered. A BLEVE can occur in containers as small as those of disposable lights or aerosol cans, and as large as tank cars and industrial storage tanks. A BLEVE frequently occurs when the temperature of the liquid and vapor within a confined tank or vessel is raised by an exposure to fire to the point where the increasing internal pressure can no longer be contained and the vessel explodes. This rupture of the confining vessel releases the pressurized liquid and allows it to vaporize almost instantaneously. If the contents are ignitable, there is almost always a fire ignited from the original external heat that caused the BLEVE or from some electrical or friction source. BLEVEs may also result from mechanical damage, overfilling, runaway reaction, overheating, vapor-space explosion, and mechanical failure.[1]

In chemical explosions, the generation of high pressure gas is the result of exothermic reactions wherein the fundamental chemical nature of the fuel is changed. Chemical explosions can involve solid combustibles or explosive mixtures of fuel and oxidizer, but more common to the investigator will be the propagating reactions involving gases, vapors, or dust mixed with air. Such combustion reactions are called propagation reactions because they occur progressively through the fuel, with a definable flame front separating the reacted and unreacted fuel. Combustion reactions, caused by the burning of hydrocarbon fuels, are classified as either deflagrations or detonations, depending on the velocity of the flame front propagation through the fuel.

Deflagration combustion reactions have a velocity less than the speed of sound; detonations are those that are greater than the speed of sound. The crater or area of greatest damage, located at the point of initiation of an explosion, is known as a seated explosion. The presence of a seat indicates the explosion of a concentrated fuel source in contact with or in close proximity to the seat. Nonseated explosions occur most often when the fuels are dispersed or diffused at the time of the explosion because the rates of pressure rise are moderate and the explosive velocities are subsonic. Explosives are any chemical compounds, mixtures, or devices, the primary purpose of which is to function by explosion. They are categorized into two main types: *low explosives* and *high explosives*. Low explosives are characterized by deflagration or slow reaction rate and low pressure development. Common low explosives are smokeless gunpowder, black powder, flash powder, and solid rocket fuel. High explosives are characterized by a detonation propagation mechanism. Common high explosives include dynamites, TNT, ANFO, RDX, and PETN.

Processing the Explosion Scene

The objectives of the explosion scene investigation are no different from those for a regular fire investigation. They involve:

- Determination of the origin
- Identification of the fuel and ignition source
- Determination of the cause
- Establishing the responsibility for the incident

A systematic approach to the scene examination is equally or even more important in an explosion investigation than in a fire investigation. Explosion scenes are often larger and more disturbed than fire scenes. Without a preplanned, systematic approach, explosion investigations become even more difficult and impossible to conduct effectively.

Fire and Explosions and Death Investigations

Fire and explosion injuries can lead to death hours, days, or even weeks after the event. Every fire and explosion that involves serious injuries should be investigated in the same way as a fire and explosion that has immediate fatalities. Any time a fire death occurs, or a death resulting from injuries received as a result of a fire or explosion occurs, an autopsy should be performed.

Fire suppression personnel should be made aware that the use of straight-stream hose streams can disturb fragile evidence such as clothing and can alter a badly charred body. As soon as a body is discovered, and it is determined that the victim is beyond medical aid, every effort should be made to minimize fire-fighting operations in close proximity to the victim, including foot traffic, hose lines, and equipment. It is beneficial to the entire death investigation if the body is left in place until it can be properly documented and examined. In death investigations, there are legal and procedural requirements for notifying the authorities, including the police, coroner, medical examiner, and the forensic laboratory that vary from jurisdiction to jurisdiction. A proper death investigation is a team effort and may involve the investigator, homicide detective, forensic scientist, and forensic pathologist. The search for evidence tends to focus on the body with the realization that, in any death investigation, critical evidence is often within arms reach of the body.

The body is a convenient reference point, but it should be remembered that the evidence may be elsewhere in the vicinity, so a careful search must be made of the entire room or area.

The sequence of events of death, fire, explosion, and collapse may be revealed by the sequence of layers in the debris and by noting where the fire damage occurred. The debris from each sector can be removed to a location where a more detailed search can be carried out. When the body is removed and placed in a new sealed body bag, debris associated with or adhering to the body should be transported in the body bag and preserved for trace evidence. The area under the body should then be carefully searched for evidence that has fallen loose while the body is being moved. There are a number of examinations that can be conducted on the victim that may yield information of value to an investigator. X-rays of anatomical features, toxicological levels of pyrolysis products, poisons, alcohol, pharmaceutical drugs, and drugs of abuse provide information relating to the cause of death. Evidence of soot in the lungs, bronchi, and trachea is one of the most significant factors in confirming that the victim was alive and breathing smoke during the fire.

Special Fire Investigation Scenarios

Vehicles are subject to arson motivated by a number of reasons. Setting fire to a modern vehicle does not require the use of an ignitable liquid accelerant. Any moderate size direct flame under the seat or under the instrument panel can result in a fast-spreading, destructive fire. As in structure fires, the investigator must treat every vehicle fire as a possible arson.

Wildland fires are those in open land covered with grass, brush, or timber. They begin like almost any other fire, with a suitable fuel and a small localized source of ignition. The investigation of a wildland fire, in some respects, is simpler than that of a structure fire, because the fuels involved are generally limited to naturally occurring vegetation.

They are ignited by some source of heat — natural, such as lightning; accidental, such as a discarded match; or incendiary, with an intentional ignition device. Some evidence of the source will remain, unless the source has been removed, as in a fire started with a lighter. The causes of wildland fires are more varied than for structure fires. Unlike structure fires, there are complications offered to retracing the course of the fire by variable environmental conditions, that is, wind, weather, and terrain. The investigator who understands fuels, fire behavior, and the effects of environmental conditions will be better able to identify the origin and cause, no matter what type of fire is involved.

Every fire deserves a careful and thorough investigation. Whether it is a small fire started by a light switch, a structure fire started by an arsonist, or a wildfire started by a careless camper, the cause and origin should be identified. With proper training, the investigator can apply a methodical, analytical approach to all fires and explosions. The investigator needs to have given the analysis and interpretation of his or her facts a great deal of consideration and be prepared to demonstrate to the court how the conclusion was reached, what the evidence was for each conclusion, and how other possible explanations were evaluated and eliminated. The investigator may be expected to prove how the methods used to investigate the fire and draw conclusions about it are soundly backed by acceptance within the investigation community as well as by scientific data, and not just by opinions drawn from recollections or from thin air.

References

1. NFPA 921. *Guide for Fire and Explosion Investigations*, National Fire Protection Association, Quincy, Massachusetts, 2004.
2. Dehaan, J.D. *Kirk's Fire Investigation*, 5th Edn, Upper Saddle River, NJ: Brady Publishing, Prentice Hall, 2002.
3. *A Pocket Guide to Accelerant Evidence Collection*. 2nd Edn, Massachusetts Chapter, International Association of Arson Investigators, Saugus: Massachusetts, 2000.
4. *Practical Fire and Arson Investigation*, New York, NY: Elsevier, 1987.

Questioned Document Examination

18

THOMAS W. VASTRICK

Introduction

Although most commonly recognized for handwriting examinations, questioned document examiners perform a litany of examinations far exceeding those of handwriting. Questioned document examination consists of the forensic comparison of handwriting, hand printing, or signatures of unknown authorship to comparable specimens of known authorship; examinations for alterations of documents and restoration of the original entries; indented writing restoration; ink and paper analyses; office machine classification and identification; and charred document examinations, just to name a few.

Questioned document examiners receive extensive training and the basis of experience through a standard two-year, full time, in-residence training program. Training consists of reading the various texts in the field, conducting individual research, and examining numerous designed and actual cases under the tutelage of an experienced, qualified examiner. Qualified questioned document examiners also undergo certification testing by the American Board of Forensic Document Examiners (ABFDE). In addition to requiring the successful completion of each phase of a three-phase test, ABFDE requires recertification every five years through participation in research and attendance at technical conferences and workshops. Many law enforcement crime laboratories require ABFDE certification to reach the journeyman level of examiner. Laboratories also require ABFDE certification of applicants for vacant posts. Currently, there are over 100 ABFDE-certified examiners in the United States.

Numerous national and regional organizations exist for the purpose of providing a forum for exchange of ideas and presenting the results of research and studies for peer review and verification. Notable of these organizations on the national level are the American Society of Questioned Document Examiners (ASQDE), the national chapter of the International Association for Identification, and the Questioned Document Section of the American Academy of Forensic Science. Notable among the regional organizations are the Northeastern Association of Forensic Science, the Mid-Atlantic Association of Forensic Science, the Southeastern Association of Forensic Document Examiners, The Midwestern

Association of Forensic Science, The Southwestern Association of Forensic Document Examiners, and the Northeastern Association of Forensic Science. Consistent among most of these organizations is the requirement of a baccalaureate degree in forensic science, science, criminal justice, or a related field and the completion of a minimum two-year, full-time training program as prescribed by standards within the discipline.

Albert S. Osborn is commonly recognized as the father of modern questioned document examination. He initially published his best-known text, *Questioned Documents*, in 1910 with a second edition printed in 1929 and was the driving force, founder, and first president of ASQDE, outlined methodologies that are still in use today. Osborn, and other leading questioned document examiners from across the country, testified in the trial of Bruno Richard Hauptmann, charged with the kidnapping of the infant son of aviator Charles Lindbergh. Although not the first case of significance within the field, it did provide many citizens with their first glimpse into the discipline.

A *document* is any medium on which a message has been in some way conveyed. Documents are commonly associated with paper, and this in fact is true in the vast majority of instances. However, it should be recognized that documents need not be only on paper. For example, one investigation involved the examination of writing on the torso of the body of a deceased female. As such, the body, by definition, would be considered a "document." For simplicity purposes, the remainder of this section will often refer to documents in paper form.

A *writing instrument* is a product that conveys a handwritten message onto the document, and it is commonly associated with pens and pencils since they comprise the most commonly used forms. Knives, eye pencils, lipstick, crayons, and paintbrushes have also been used as writing instruments.

Handwriting: Background Information

Foremost in the work of questioned document examiners is the examination of handwriting, whether in the form of printing, cursive, or signatures. The examinations conducted are comparison studies of entries with questioned authorship being compared to handwriting specimens of known authorship for purposes of identification or elimination. Some basic information about handwriting will assist in understanding the comparative process used by questioned document examiners.

Graphology is the study of personality assessment based on handwriting. Although graphology has made for interesting story lines in novels and movies, this field rightly takes its place next to palm reading, card reading, and other various voodoo and fortune telling practices as being without scientific basis and lacking in acceptance within the forensic sciences and courts. A surface review of this field clearly demonstrates its shortcomings. If one could assess personality from handwriting, then logic would dictate that all individuals with the same personality characteristics should then have the same type of handwriting. In addition, one should be able to submit a handwriting specimen to any graphologist in the country and get virtually the same reading. Test studies have shown these hypotheses not to be true. Qualified questioned document examiners in North America do not practice graphology.

Handwriting contains a combination of class and individual characteristics. The class characteristics of handwriting are those taught in school. Often "handwriting systems" are taught to students. A handwriting system is a series of upper and lower case letter designs. The most common handwriting systems in the United States are Zaner-Bloser, Palmer, and D'Nealian. Upon examination of the various handwriting systems, it will be noted that there are few differences between each of the systems. In addition to character designs, class characteristics will include grammatical structures such as paragraph indentation, margins, and punctuation usage.

Individual handwriting characteristics are those aspects of one's handwriting that deviate from the class characteristics. Although the term "individual" is a bit of a misnomer as no single such characteristic would be an adequate basis for an identification of a writer, statistical research has determined that handwriting can be identified to an individual.

The basis of handwriting comparisons are found in two statistically verified axioms of handwriting. The first, as previously discussed, is that no two people write exactly alike. This does not mean that different people cannot write in a strikingly similar way under limited circumstances. However, there will be distinct differences in the overall handwriting characteristics of the two writers. Studies into the individuality of handwriting have been conducted on the general population and on subgroups such as ethnic groups, classmates, and relatives, all supporting the statistical research that handwriting is unique to an individual.

The second statistically verified axiom of handwriting is that no one writes exactly the same way twice. Humans simply do not possess the machine-like precision of muscular movement that would be required to execute a complex series of detailed and subtle movements of the arm, wrist, and fingers that would be required to produce exact replications. The result is that characteristics of one's handwriting will contain variation, often manifesting itself as simplifications or exaggerations of the muscular movements. The results can be larger or smaller loops or taller or shorter strokes as two examples. Variation can also take the form of alternate letter designs — a surprisingly common occurrence.

Individual handwriting characteristics can be divided into eight categories to include:

- Spacing
- Letter height ratio
- Baseline habits
- Initial and terminal strokes
- Letter connections
- Pen pressure
- Letter design
- Slant

Spacing encompasses the amount of room between characters, words, lines, sentences, and paragraphs. Classroom education dictates that there should be equal spacing between characters; equal spacing between words; equal spacing between sentences (sometimes suggests that this spacing range from the equivalent in width of one to two characters); that lines are single, or in some instances, double spaced with this space being even and consistent; and paragraphs indented three spaces, five spaces, or no spaces. The left margin is taught to be along the vertical red line of rule paper or the approximate equivalent if such a line does not exist. The right margin is taught to exist at a point equivalent to the space between the left margin and the edge of the paper.

In practice, uniformity of spacing is not common (Figure 18.1). Variances in spacing should be charted in an effort to look for patterns. Spacing variances may occur at the start

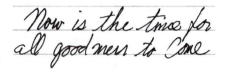

Figure 18.1   Examples of variation in spacing between characters and words.

or end of a word, or between certain characters such as a "t" and "h." Spacing variances can take the form of crowded or expanded forms.

Letter height ratio is the relative vertical position of one character to another (Figure 18.2). The class characteristic of letter height ratio dictates, in general, that upper case characters are of the same height. In addition, the body of lower case letters should be of a common height. Certain characters such as b, d, f, h, k, and t have upper extenders that rise to a height equivalent to or near the height of upper case characters. Height ratios of characters should be charted with particular note of the position of the characters involved to their position in a word. For example, a "th" combination may have a different letter height ratio between them in the word "think" than they would in the word "strength" due to the "th" combination being at the start of the word versus the end of the word. The "th" combination may even have a third letter height ratio, for instance in which the combination is located in the middle of the word.

A *baseline* is an actual or imaginary line along the bottom of the writing. Handwriting rarely follows the baseline with total consistency (Figure 18.3). Some portions of characters may cross the baseline, whereas other characters may float above the baseline. The examination of particular words or names and comparison with known specimens of the same word or name may reflect a habitual repetition of the position of certain characters to the baseline. The sum of these habitually repetitive deviations from the baseline constitutes the writer's *baseline habits*.

An *initial stroke* is the portion of a writing immediately following the contact of the writing instrument to the document. A *terminal stroke* is the portion of a writing immediately preceding the removal of the writing instrument from the paper. Initial and terminal strokes are examined for slope of the writing, length of the stroke, position relative to the baseline, and subtle changes in direction at the tip of the writing (Figure 18.4).

Letter connections are the strokes of cursive entries and signatures that terminate one character and become the initial stroke of the subsequent character. Handwriting

(a)   (b)

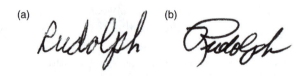

Figure 18.2   Differences in the relative heights of the (a) upper case R to the (b) lower case d.

Figure 18.3   Many strokes in this word cross below the baseline.

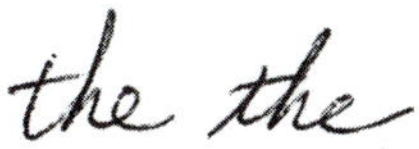

the the

Figure 18.4   Examples of variations in the initial and terminal strokes.

systems teach that symmetrical, rounded strokes should be used for connecting one character to another. Many of these strokes are designed to extend to the baseline. Examination and notation should be made of the degree of symmetry, degree of angularity, and the position of the strokes to the baseline (Figure 18.5). In addition, note should be taken of disconnections. If extended writing is involved in the questioned entries, examinations should be conducted as to whether disconnections are based on a particular character or combination of characters.

Pen pressure is the amount of downward force exerted on the writing instrument. Pen pressure manifests itself as indentations on paper; can be consistently heavy, consistently light, or vary (Figure 18.6); and can only be properly determined through the examination of original documents.

Letter design is the overall combination of strokes that create a character and is standardized in handwriting systems. However, this standardization is, at best, short lived (Figure 18.7). Students will immediately begin to inject their own variances into the letter designs. It is not unusual for teachers to be able to identify their student by their handwriting soon after lessons in cursive writing.

Letter designs can undergo significant changes over time, which are individualistic in both the extent of changes and the presence of changes. For this reason, comparison specimens should include samples from the same general time frame as that of the questioned entries.

Slant is a strong habit that is difficult to disguise or imitate (Figure 18.8). Extended writings with slight differences in slant between the same characters may well display a key feature of two different writers. It is common to find certain characters that will vary from the predominant slant of the writing. These characters should be charted when conducting a comparison examination.

One important aspect of many handwriting-related examinations involves the evaluation of the speed of execution of the writing. Slowness in execution could be a significant

is is

Figure 18.5   Examples of a rounded (right) and angular (left) connecting stroke between the i and s.

Figure 18.6   The upstroke of the loop at the top of the h shows clear evidence of a lightening of pen pressure.

Figure 18.7 Three different designs of the t.

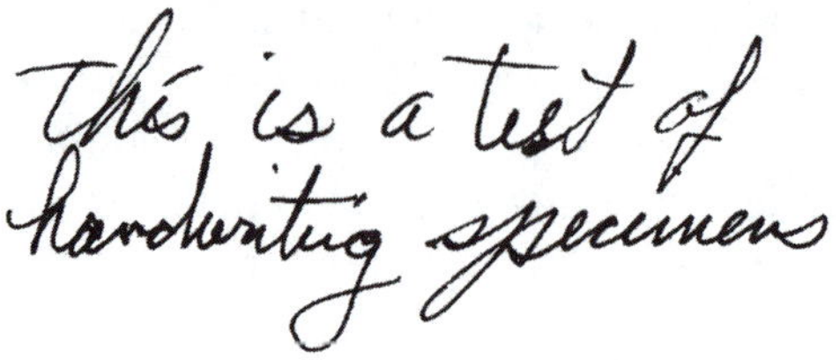

Figure 18.8 An example of variation in slant. Slant is not necessarily uniform within one's handwriting.

evidence of nongenuineness, disguise, outside influences, or deterioration. Features that provide evidence of speed of execution include line quality, blunt or flared initial and terminal strokes, breaks or hesitations in the writing line, and uniform heavy pen pressure throughout the writing (Figure 18.9).

Line quality is the smoothness of the writing stroke. At a normal writing speed, the writing line will be smooth and flowing. When writing is slowed to the speed of drawing, the writing line becomes very angular. Blunt initial and terminal strokes occur when the writing instrument comes to a complete stop before being lifted off the paper. This phenomenon occurs when the speed of execution is slowed significantly. Flared initial and terminal strokes occur when the writing instrument is lifted off the paper while in motion. Breaks and hesitations in the writing line can be a normal occurrence or a characteristic of something very different. The difference is based on whether breaks or hesitations are normal for the purported writer, in addition to the presence or absence of the other features of slowness of execution. Uniform heavy pen pressure is a natural result of a slow drawing.

Forgery

Forgery is a legal term. In general, laws specify forgery as requiring three aspects: (1) The signature is to be written by someone other than the purported writer (2) The signature is to be written without the consent of the purported writer (3) The signature is to be written with the intent to defraud. Questioned document examiners deal solely with the first of these three aspects. As such, examiners do not ordinarily use the term forgery. Henceforth,

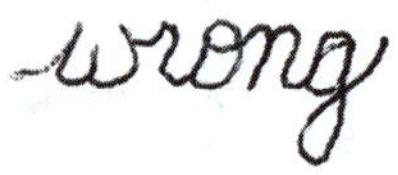

Figure 18.9 Some of the more common characteristics of slowness of execution include poor line quality, uniform heavy pen pressure, and blunt initial or terminal strokes.

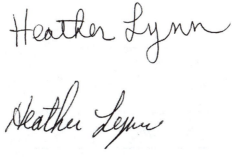

Figure 18.10   A genuine signature (top) and a simple forgery (bottom). Simple forgeries are characterized by obvious, overall design differences. Simple forgeries are the most common forms of forgery.

the word forgery will be used with the limited definition of a signature having been written by someone other than the purported writer.

There are four forms of forgery: A *simple forgery* is the writing of another's name in one's own normal, natural handwriting (Figure 18.10). The resulting forgery will not pictorially resemble the signature of the purported writer, but the forgery will be written at a normal writing speed. Hence, there will be no characteristics of slowness of execution present. Simple forgeries are the most common form of forgery.

A *simulated forgery*, or simulation, is the freehand copying of a model signature (Figure 18.11). The resulting product bears a pictorial similarity to some degree of signatures of the purported writer and may display a significant similarity to the specific signature from which it was modeled. Simulated forgeries may or may not have been slowly drawn depending on the method used. One method involves the slow, careful copying that will create closer design replication but will also include the common characteristics of slowness of execution. The other method of simulation is to write the name more rapidly. The result is a product that has less design replication but does not contain the common characteristics of slowness of execution.

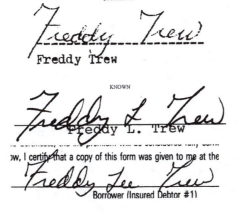

Figure 18.11   A simulated forgery (questioned) on a will and two genuine signatures (known). Characteristic of simulated forgeries is an overall design appearance similarity coupled with numerous specific design and characteristic differences.

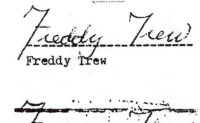

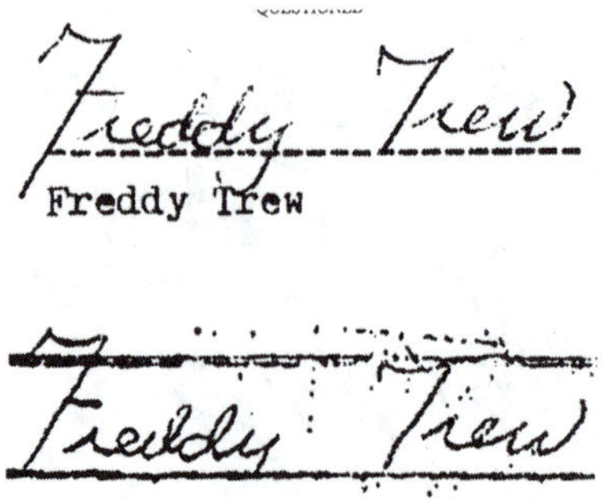

Freddy Trew

Figure 18.12 In an unusual twist to the will matter also demonstrated in Figure 18.11, another document (bottom) contained a traced forgery of the signature on the will (top) (i.e., a traced forgery of a simulated forgery). Characteristic of traced forgeries is a strong overall design appearance similarity coupled with few characteristic differences.

A *traced forgery*, as the name implies, is created through the tracing of a model signature (Figure 18.12). The resulting product bears a near exact replication of the model signature and the common characteristics of slowness of execution. It is not always possible to distinguish a tracing from a simulation. Direct tracings are created by placing the model signature behind the document onto which the forgery is to be placed. The "signature" is then directly traced onto the document. Indirect tracings are created by making a guide on the document onto which the forgery is to be placed. This guide is then traced again to create the finished product. The guide often takes the form of a light pencil line or an indentation. The presence of these guides is a distinctive evidence of tracing.

A *cut and paste forgery* is created by duplicating an existing genuine signature on a document and transferring the image to another document. This can be accomplished digitally through the use of a basic image enhancement software and a scanner. Cut and paste forgery can also be accomplished through the use of photocopiers, scissors, and glue. The resulting forgery is an exact replication of the model signature (Figure 18.13). Sloppy cut and paste work can leave outlines of the "cut" portion of the process. As such, the outlying region should be carefully reviewed for evidence of outlines while the signature should be carefully reviewed for remnants of intersecting lines from the original document that were not entirely separated and removed prior to the transfer. Cut and paste forgeries are characterized by the fact that an original ink signature does not exist. Since no one can write their name exactly the same way twice, the only way two alleged signatures could bear exact replication is if they are copies of the same signature. Once an original ink signature is found, one can determine the model document from the forged one. Without

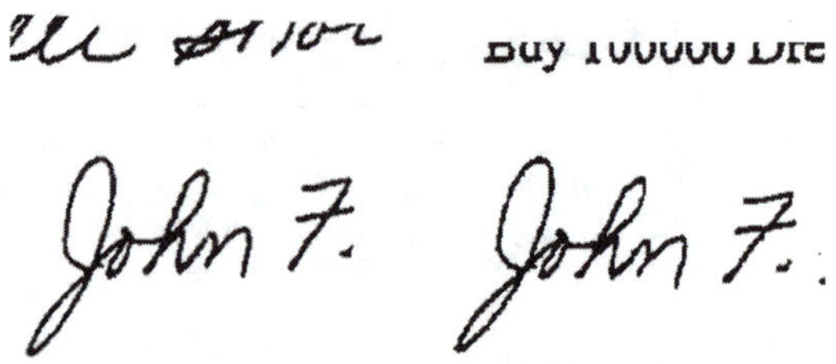

Figure 18.13 Partial signatures from two different documents. Characteristic of cut and paste forgeries is exact replication.

the original ink signature, it likely will not be possible to distinguish which is which based on the forensic examination.

Handwriting: Known Specimens

Handwriting examinations are comparison processes. The documents utilized for comparison purposes with the questioned writings are referred to as *known specimens*. Known specimens supply handwriting known to be from a particular writer. These specimens provide the basis on which any conclusions are drawn. As such, these specimens must meet certain criteria keeping in mind that scientific experimentation warrants that experimental cause and effect studies require only one variant. In handwriting comparisons, the variant is that of authorship. The introduction of any additional variances may prevent any meaningful conclusions. For example, known specimens should be contemporaneous to that of the questioned writings. Since handwriting can evolve over time, it is imperative that specimens are provided to illustrate the writing habits of the timeframe represented in the questioned writings.

Next, handwriting specimens should be comparable: Cursive writing should be compared to cursive specimens and printed ones should be compared to printed specimens. In addition, an "a" should be compared to an "a." It is even better to have letter combinations, words, phrases, and sentences that match verbatim to the entries in question. With these combinations, examiners have the opportunity to compare letter height ratios and other aspects of writing that may be affected by character interactions. In addition, the specimens should be on similar documents such that the writing space is comparable and the position of the signature space is in the same general location on the document. Again, these requirements are meant to limit the variances between the questioned writing and the known specimens.

Finally, handwriting specimens should be repetitive. Handwriting characteristics are habits, which by definition are repetitive actions. There would be no way to determine what a habit is and what it is not based on by reviewing just only one specimen. In addition, one specimen would not provide the examiner with any information concerning the range of variation of a writer. *Range of variation* is the extent to which writers alter their individual characteristics from one writing to the next. As previously stated, no one writes exactly the same way twice. However, the variation in writing will have a limited range that can be detected through the examination of numerous specimens. The extent of the range of variation will differ among writers.

The two forms of known specimens each having their strengths and weaknesses with regard to the requirements for specimens listed before are *request specimens* and *course-of-business specimens*. *Request specimens* are handwriting samples of known origin that are taken for the express purpose of being used for handwriting comparisons. These specimens have the advantage of control of content, and they can be (1) cursive or printed, (2) upper or lower case, (3) placed on a form that replicates the size and location of the writing space, (4) the written entries can repeat the questioned entries verbatim, (5) numerous repetitive specimens can be taken. The weakness of request specimens is the susceptibility of these specimens to attempts to disguise the writing. The U.S. Supreme Court has ruled that taking handwriting specimens do not violate any rights of the accused in criminal cases and is widely required by court order in civil matters in which authorship of entries is a legitimate issue. *Course-of-business specimens* are those documents provided for comparison that were not created for the express purpose of being used as known handwriting specimens. Common course-of-business specimen sources include cancelled checks, employment records, tax forms, applications, medical records, correspondences, greeting cards, and court records. The strength of course-of-business specimens is lessened likelihood of disguise, and its weakness is the lack of verbatim text. Examiners can avoid the potential weaknesses of each form of specimen by obtaining both forms. It should be noted that in most instances, either form of specimen will prove sufficiently adequate to perform a complete and thorough examination.

Taking request specimens from a subject is a process that requires a significant amount of preparation time and execution time. The underlying purpose of taking specimens is to provide repetitive specimens that reflect the writer's normal, natural handwriting and range of variation. In addition, the specimens should reflect the writer's habits under circumstances that, as close as possible, replicate the conditions in which the questioned entries were purportedly written. Again, these aspects are to limit any unnecessary variances that could preclude a scientifically based conclusion. Taking request specimens should utilize the following methodology:

1. Prepare an adequate number of specimen forms that replicate the questioned documents in size and writing area. As each form is completed, the form should be initialed, dated, and consecutively numbered.
2. Obtain course-of-business writings from the subject before taking the specimens. These writings can be obtained from numerous sources as previously outlined. If those cannot be obtained, the subject should be required to provide identification such as a driver's license that will contain a signature specimen.
3. Provide the subject with numerous writing instruments of the same form (ball point pen, pencil, etc.) consistent with that of the questioned writing. Allow the subjects to select which instrument they wish to use.
4. Directions should be written and read to the subject. These directions should then be included as part of the case notes. At no time should directions be given regarding letter design.
5. Allow the subject frequent breaks to avoid writers' cramps.
6. Initiate small talk with the subjects to mentally distract them from their efforts. This will not affect their normal, natural handwriting, but it will inhibit their ability to provide disguised writing.
7. The subject should never be shown the documents in question.
8. Begin by having the subjects write their signature or other writing consistent with the course-of-business writing previously obtained. A general review of the overall pictorial appearance of the initial request specimen and the course-of-business specimen should provide evidence as to whether the subject is cooperating or not.
9. Request completion of a one or two page general handwriting specimens form. The completion of this form permits the subject to shake off effects of nervousness and provides the examiner a chance to review the form for evidence of disguise as discussed later in this section. The extent of directions to be given to the subject should be limited to (1) providing normal, natural specimens, (2) hand printed or cursive depending on the form of the questioned entries, (3) upper

case, lower case, or a combination depending on the form of the questioned entries, and (4) not to obliterate any errors or misspellings.

10. Fifteen to twenty specimens on forms that replicate the questioned documents should be taken with one set of specimens per form. The entries should be dictated to the subject. Spellings should be at the discretion of the subject and if these differ from that of the questioned entry, the subject should be directed to the proper spelling after about five specimens have been taken. The case notes should clearly reflect the spelling direction and indicate on which document (based on the consecutive number) the direction began.

11. One additional specimen should be obtained with the other hand. If the writing appears fluent, a full set of specimens should be obtained with both hands. This step may also demonstrate that the subject was attempting to provide specimens with their awkward hand.

12. The subject should complete one more general handwriting form.

This list is a general guideline. Other specimens or other methods may be more appropriate for a specific case. Again, the underlying purpose of taking handwriting specimens should be kept in mind when determining whether the specimens taken are adequate or whether other specimens may be necessary.

Distorted Handwriting

Disguise

Disguise is the intentional attempt to delete one's individual characteristics from their handwriting. Disguise can take the form of change of slant, change of size, change of speed of execution, altered letter design, illegible scrawl, reversion to early schoolbook form, use of printing, use of the awkward hand, or any combination of the aforementioned. Since questioned document examiners cannot specifically and definitively determine intent from the examination of handwriting, definitive statements that handwriting is disguised are not scientifically based. However, experience will provide a basis on which a likelihood of disguise can be established.

Disguise can be recognized in a number of ways, dependent in part on the method used to disguise. Obtaining course-of-business specimens provide an excellent sample for overall comparison. Should the course-of-business specimens not pictorially resemble the request specimens, disguise is a likelihood. Another effective method is to look for evidence of slowness of execution. This will include watching the subject carefully while request specimens are being dictated. The fact that the subject is taking a great amount of time to complete simple sentences, could indicate the likelihood that the request specimens are being disguised. Finally, the request specimens can be reviewed for consistency. Handwriting is a very strong habit, and changing this involves a significant mental exercise and is rarely fully successful. As a result, examining letter designs, slant, and size of writing for internal consistency may shed significant light on the likelihood of disguise. Taking a handwriting specimen with the opposite hand will shed adequate light on the possibility that the subjects were using their awkward hand while providing request specimens (Figure 18.14). Obtaining a full set of request handwriting specimens with the other hand will solve that issue.

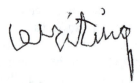

Figure 18.14 A sample of handwriting with the awkward hand. Common characteristics include the shape of the staff of the t; the shape of the lower extender of the g; and the angular movements of the writing line.

Once it has been determined that subjects are disguising their specimens, there are many avenues available to rectify the problem. First, the possibility of obtaining course-of-business specimens can be considered. Second, consideration can be given to getting a court order for taking specimens. The disguise of court ordered specimens constitutes contempt of court and can be dealt with accordingly. However, if a subject is accused of first degree murder, the threat of contempt of court charges ring hollow. For these and other instances in which course-of-business specimens or court orders are not available, more direct intervention in the taking of subsequent specimens is in the order as follows:

1. Terminate all breaks except for humanitarian bathroom breaks
2. Procure a book
3. Dictate pages of the book
4. Dictate at a pace consistent with normal writing speed
5. Remove each sheet upon completion of the page
6. Continue taking specimens for upwards of an hour or more observing the specimens and the internal consistencies
7. Continue initiating small talk and encouraging the subject to carry on a dialog

The purpose of this methodology is to utilize the strength of the writing habit against the subject. Since this habit is so strong, requiring the writing of long passages with no breaks will necessitate superhuman concentration in order to attempt to maintain the disguise. Eventually, when the disguise does break down, verbatim words and phrases can be interspersed into the dictation.

Outside Influences

Disguise is not the only reason that some handwriting entries will not be written in a normal, natural style. Writing can be affected by disease, injury, alcohol, recreational drugs, medication, cold, heat, unusual writing position, unusual writing instrument, mental distraction, emotional distress, nervousness, and vision problems. There are no specific ways in which outside influences will affect the writing of a specific person. Some persons may greatly change their handwriting after drinking alcohol, whereas others may have no changes in their handwriting. An alcoholic may actually write better while under the influence than while being sober. Some medications may result in one's handwriting becoming large and sloppy. Some medications of palsy-type conditions could actually improve one's writing. As a result, it is not possible to determine specifically that a particular outside influence had an effect on one's handwriting, though it may be possible to detect features that would indicate that the writing is not fully normal and natural in style.

Handwriting: The Comparison Process

Handwriting examination is a comparison process. A preliminary review of the submitted documents is the first part of the standard comparison. The examination of the original questioned document is highly recommended and, in some instances, vital for any meaningful conclusions. If the questioned documents are not of a quality that provides the basis for a meaningful examination, the case can be set aside until such time that the appropriate documents can be submitted. The known specimens can then be reviewed to determine whether they meet the requirements of being contemporaneous, comparable, and sufficient in quantity. Additionally, the known specimens should be of adequate clarity, either as original documents or good quality copies, for comparison purposes.

The next step in the process is to review the questioned documents for the purpose of determining the examinations requested and the possibility of other forensic evidence that may exist but were overlooked by the submitter. Once this stage has been completed, the known specimens should be examined separately for the purpose of insuring that the known specimens are truly the product of one writer. While rare, contamination of specimens by insertion of writings by other persons can create havoc in an examination.

Once the preliminary stages have been completed, a step-by-step comparison process can be undertaken, observing the characteristics of the questioned writings and comparing each significant feature with like characters among the known specimens. Examiners will chart these features and the results of the comparison point by point.

Once complete, the examiners, utilizing their training, experience, and expertise will reach a conclusion. Conclusions come in the form of unqualified findings of identification or elimination or qualified findings of levels of probability that the subject did or did not write the questioned entries. There are no set number of similarities or differences required for an identification or elimination as there is no statistical grounds on which to apply a statistical equation such as a certain form of the lower case "a" is only made by one person in ten. The reason for this is that one's writing changes over time and, as previously stated, no one writes the same way twice. As a result, handwriting is such a dynamic act that statistical rarity is not scientifically based.

Alterations to Documents

An alteration is an attempt to make an unauthorized substantive change to a document. When looking for evidence of alterations, it is important to take into account the location of potential points for alteration. For example, one would expect the potential locations of an alteration to a check to be either the amount entries or the payee name entry.

There are five types of alterations and many tools that can be used to determine the potential of alterations to documents. The different forms of alterations are erasures, additions, obliterations, pagination, and cut and paste. An *erasure* is a physical or chemical elimination of entries or portions thereof. The best way to examine a document for an erasure is to hold the document up to a window or a light box. Microscopically, physical erasure will show the significant paper fiber disturbance due to the abrasive action of erasure (Figure 18.15).

An *addition* is a noncontemporaneous entry that alters the meaning of a document or a portion therein. Additions can be to an entire document, an entire page, a paragraph, a

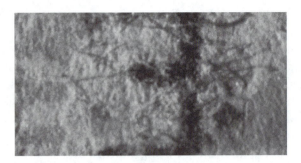

Figure 18.15   An example of paper fiber disturbance due to physical erasure.

line, a sentence, a word, a letter, or a part of a letter (Figure 18.16). A magnified examination can be conducted for entries of different size. Some individual letter may be noticeably larger or smaller than the other letters of the word, or a word or line may be smaller and crammed into available space between lines, at the end of paragraphs, at the end of margins, or at the top or bottom part of the page. These entries can also be examined for evidence of significant pen pressure differences. If consideration is being given to the possibility that a complete page has been replaced, the margin alignment of the pages can be reviewed, looking for commonality of folds or staple holes. Examiners can review the watermarks on the paper, review the alignment/spacing of the text, and examine the fonts for any differences in style. Any questioned page should be given the "Grammar Test." This test is simply reading the document to see whether the questioned entry is grammatically correct with the previous and subsequent entries.

Finally, additions are commonly examined for evidence of different inks. There are two categories of ink differentiation testing, namely nondestructive and destructive tests. Nondestructive tests consist of spectral analyses particularly in the infrared and ultraviolet regions of the electromagnetic spectrum. One such test is based on *reflected infrared* radiation. This test utilizes a light source rich in infrared light, a viewing scope such as a camera or video camera with low light capabilities, a viewing system such as a high speed infrared film for a camera or a television monitor for the video camera, and an infrared barrier filter located between the document and the camera. This system will permit the examiner to "see" the ink in the infrared range of the electromagnetic spectrum. The use of various infrared barrier filters will further subdivide the region that is viewed. Some ink will

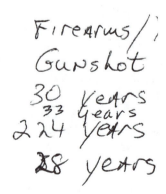

Figure 18.16   Two examples of additions — an added 2 and an added "33 years."

absorb the light, and other inks will reflect the light. Still other inks will partially absorb and partially reflect the light. This results in inks that are black, various shades of gray, and invisible. Different absorption or reflectance of inks on the same document under the same conditions is definitive evidence of different inks. However, just because the inks do not reflect/absorb the light in different ways does not necessarily mean that the inks are the same.

The other type of test in the infrared region of the electromagnetic spectrum is *infrared luminescence*, which entails electron excitation utilizing a law of physics known as *Stoke's Law*. This law states that absorbed light will be re-emitted with longer wavelengths. A blue–green light source is used to irradiate the document. The electrons of the ink absorb the light energy resulting in added energy, which allows the electrons to jump to a higher energy shell. Once much of the extra energy is used up, the electron will fall back to its natural energy shell. The moment the electron drops back to the original shell, it will expel what is left of the excess energy, and this can be detected as a glow in the infrared region of the electromagnetic spectrum. This process is repeated constantly while the blue–green light irradiates the document. A camera or video system like the one described for reflected infrared is used to record or visualize the glow. Some inks will glow, some will not. Some inks will disappear, and some will glow slightly. Differences in the result of this test will provide the basis to differentiate the inks (Figure 18.17). However, it does not necessarily mean that the inks are the same when there is no discernable difference.

The primary destructive test for differentiation of ink is thin layer chromatography (TLC), which requires that small portions of ink and paper be removed from the document. The inks are then placed in solution and applied to a silica gel plate and kept in a container with TLC chemicals at one end of the plate. The chemicals climb up the silica gel plate taking the ink with it. The ink will begin to separate creating a separation pattern indicative of the chemicals that constitute the ink.

Specific writing instruments are rarely identified with writing since there will normally be hundreds of thousands of pens with the same ink and many times more instruments with ink that may be so similar as to be indistinguishable. However, one possible avenue of associating a writing instrument with an entry or associating two entries as having been written with the same writing instrument is in defect patterns such as burr striations. These patterns are streaks of ink voids in lines written using ballpoint pens and are caused by defects in the ball system (Figure 18.18). It is common to find burr

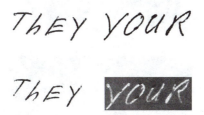

Figure 18.17 Examples of ink reactions under reflected infrared light (they — upper normal light, lower infrared reflected) and infrared luminescence (Your — upper normal light, lower infrared luminescence). Ink can also virtually disappear under such examinations. Differences in these reactions are evidence of different inks.

forgery

Figure 18.18 Burr striations show themselves as thin lines of ink void within the writing line.

striations while using ballpoint pens but not common to find striation patterns significantly complex to be considered unique.

Additions on *NCR* or *No Carbon Required* paper have a unique form of examination.
This paper is commonly found as two-, three-, or four-layer forms that require no carbon
for reproducing the entries on the top sheet on to the subsequent sheets. Usually, each
sheet is of a different color. Often, one or more sheets of the form will be separated
upon completion. As such, additions will require that each sheet be put back together
before making the alteration. Imperatively, the replacement of the sheets will not be
precise. As such, the alignment of the writing in relation to the printed portions of the
form will not coincide with other entries on the form.

Obliteration means the physical covering of entries. One of the most common forms of
obliteration is by using opaquing fluid, and the other is to cross out the writing with a
writing instrument. Opaquing fluid can be made temporarily transparent through application of a number of organic chemicals. In addition, the opaquing material can be physically removed by scraping. If these are not options, the best method of visualizing the
original entry is to use a strong fiber optic light to read through the material. Often, it
is helpful to view the document from the backside. There are two types of tests that can
be conducted for obliterations using writing instruments. One is the use of infrared technology: Reflected infrared and infrared luminescence may render the obliterated entry legible
(Figure 18.19). If infrared technology does not work, digital technology may provide an
avenue. The obliterated entry can be scanned at a very high resolution and viewed at
great magnification. Once patterns of obliteration such as back and forth lines or a
series of loops can be identified, they can slowly be erased rendering the underwritten
entry surprisingly legible. Although this method is slow and tedious, it has proved to be
an effective procedure. Digital image technology can also be used to enhance slight differences in color or hue through changing colors, hues, and contrasts.

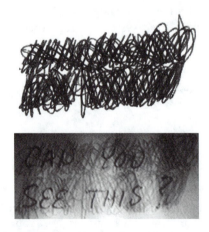

Figure 18.19 Reflected infrared (bottom) and infrared luminescence examinations can reveal
otherwise illegible obliterations (top).

Pagination is the addition or exchange of an entire page of a multipage document and is often found in contracts to which favorable changes have been added without the knowledge of one or more of the parties concerned with the contract. Pagination has also been found in medical record examinations though this form of alteration is not common for these types of cases. Key to the examination for pagination is consistency in the pages. Examiners will look at consistency in the paper, ink, printed font, handwriting, grammar, and staples.

Paper examinations take many forms of which one is by using reflected ultraviolet. Short wave and long wave ultraviolet light is irradiated onto the document and examined for the degree to which the paper glows. This glowing effect is primarily caused by the bleaching agents and coatings used in the paper. Different degrees of glow are indicative of different papers. Many quality papers will have a watermark, which is an dentifying label put into the paper during the early part of the papermaking process. As wet paper fiber is fed onto a wire mesh and pressed, large rolls bearing numerous watermark impressions are pressed into the paper. As the paper is pressed and dried, the watermark impression is still legible, but the embossment effect is eliminated. It is easy to see a watermark by holding the paper up to a light. A different watermark on one page, or even the inversion of the watermark on only one page of a multipaged document would be an inconsistency indicative of pagination.

If the document is stapled, a careful examination of the staple holes should be made to ascertain whether all hole patterns match. Occasionally, extra holes or sets of holes will appear near other holes. Sometimes, these holes are caused by the ends of staples re-entering the paper from the backside. Re-entry of staple holes can be found on a number of pages from the back but should appear consistently from the last page forward. The edges of paper can be examined for evidence of *guillotine blade defects*, caused by nicks in the blade of the device that cuts notebooks to their final size. These defects will appear as diagonal markings along the edge of notebooks and will appear as dimples or indentations along the edge of individual sheets of paper (Figure 18.20). Since the defect mark is diagonal, one must allow for some migration in the location of the defect on the page. The ink can be examined as described elsewhere in this section for consistency in writing instruments utilized.

The paper can also be examined for indented writings (see "Indented Writing" portion of this section). There should be a consistent pattern of indentations that may be present. If indentations of previous pages were present on all sheets below the first page, it would be logical to find the indentations on each page. Pagination is evident when one page does not have indentations or another page has indentations that are not consistent with entries from any previous pages. If tears, creases, or folds exist, each page should be examined for consistency in regard to these features. One page demonstrating an inconsistent pattern of any tears, creases, or folds could provide evidence of pagination.

Figure 18.20 The diagonal markings resulting from guillotine blade defects created during the final cutting portion of the manufacturing process.

If the document is typewritten or computer generated, the font can be examined for consistency. Typewriters have historically copied fonts from other manufacturers with minor differences that may escape detection from a cursory look. Numerous examples of each character in both the upper and lower case should be closely compared for similarities and differences. Numerous examples assist in differentiating design features or defects from accidental features that may result from inconsistencies on the surface of the paper. Included in the examination should be the spacing of the character, the size of the characters, and the space between lines. A microscopic examination of the printed entries may reflect different forms of computer printers (e.g., ink jet, dot matrix, laser jet) or typewriters (e.g., cloth ribbon, plastic ribbon). Individual defects of the particular typewriter or printer may be present and charted for purposes of associating the same office machine as the source of the different entries.

Cut and paste, although a form of alteration, is normally used for purposes consistent with forgery and was addressed in detail under the section on forgery.

Indented Writing

Indented writings are the indentations left on documents under the original ink document. The best example of this situation is paper in a notebook. Each time writing is placed on the top sheet, indented writings are left on numerous pages below. Some of the more common situations utilizing indented writings include ransom notes, bank robbery notes, and altered record cases such as medical records. Examiners use specialized scientific indentation detection devices to locate and make legible those, indentations that cannot be seen in any other way. The process utilized with these instruments is entirely nondestructive. A polymer film is placed over the document and suctioned down onto the document by vacuum holes. An electrostatic charge is rendered over the surface and toner is cascaded across the surface. This process creates a legible version of normally illegible or partially legible indentations from the paper (Figure 18.21).

Charred Documents

Charred documents are those documents that have lost pliability due to water loss upon exposure to heat or fire. Pliability can be restored to paper by soaking the document in a solution of water, alcohol, and glycerin. In emergency situations, hair spray has been

Figure 18.21   Electrostatic image of indentations from handwritten entry on previous page of an appointment calendar.

suggested as a widely available substitute. Decipherment of charred writing is a photographic technique. Various color filters and reflected infrared photography will often render charred, illegible remains into fully legible pieces of evidence.

Office Machine Examinations

In addition to typewriters and computer printers that have previously been discussed, other office machines, including checkwriters, staplers, photocopiers, and facsimile machines, are used in the creation of documents that are brought into question for a variety of reasons. As such, there are many types of examinations that can be conducted to glean information. Often, investigations are aided by knowing what to look for, and questioned document examiners are asked to supply any information concerning the make and model of a machine. Libraries of makes and possible model differentiation of various office machines are available to examiners. It may also be possible to run TLC examinations on typewritten or computer printer inks that may assist in manufacture identification. Photocopiers sometimes leave images or indentations of feeder bands or rollers of which the number, size, and location may provide sufficient information for make and model differentiation. Facsimile machines carry *transmitting terminal identifiers* (TTI) at the top of every fax containing information regarding the source of the transmission, though it should be kept in mind that one can prevent a TTI from being transmitted with the fax and a false TTI can also be sent.

Counterfeit Document Examination

The examination of documents for purposes of determining whether they are genuine or counterfeit requires that appropriate known specimens be available for comparison, which are contemporaneous, comparable in nature, and complete. Whether the documents being examined are currency, birth certificates, or immigration forms, they undergo periodic changes. As such, documents available at the time of the purported issuance are a necessary aspect of specimen collection, and they must be comparable in nature, as variations can exist between different types of forms being issued at the same time. Consideration should be given to how agencies deal with lapses in inventory: (1) Do the agencies issue copies? (2) Do they issue older versions of the form? (3) Do they create a generic form for use? Unless these questions are answered, no scientific basis can be established from which a determination of genuineness can be made. Finally, the specimens must be complete. It is common for countries to issue the same type of document in different forms depending on the specific source of the document. One need go no further than birth certificates in the United States to become aware of the variation in common forms.

The examination of documents for evidence of counterfeiting is a consistency comparison of the medium, whether paper or card, the ink, the print, the images, and the printing processes. Each should be consistent with the known specimens. One unexplainable difference is sufficient to warrant a finding of nongenuineness.

Evidence and the Biological Sciences

B

Forensic Pathology

19

CYRIL H. WECHT AND VICTOR W. WEEDN

Pathology and Forensic Pathology

"As pathology goes," remarked the pre-eminent late 19th century physician and medical educator Sir William Osler, "so goes medicine." Pathology developed as a subspecialty of medicine during Osler's time as "the study of disease," and the role of "pathologists" was to perform autopsies to find out what was really wrong with a patient. Without these raw data, medicine was largely anecdotal and speculative. Osler understood that physicians would have to better understand disease in order to treat it and that pathologists were the most important source of these new understandings, because they "studied disease."

As defined by the College of American Pathologists today, pathology is that branch of natural science concerned with the causes and nature of disease processes, together with the anatomic and functional changes that occur in conjunction with them. Furthermore, it is a medical specialty that may contribute to the understanding of diseases or medical conditions by means of information obtained through various types of laboratory examinations of the human body or any materials taken from the human body. In this context, the term "disease" is used quite broadly to involve anything and everything capable of altering the human body, from viruses and bacteria to metabolic and degenerative diseases, to tumors and injuries of all kinds.

Pathology as a discipline tends to conjure up conceptions among medically trained personnel that fall far short of an adequate explanation of the subspecialty of forensic pathology, although these thoughts would adequately apply to hospital pathology. Hospital pathology and forensic pathology, although sharing many training and scientific procedural factors, are significantly different in their approaches to death investigation.

Today, the professional practice of conventional pathology is that of the hospital pathologist who spends his or her time practicing either "anatomic" or "clinical" pathology. The former subspecialty involves looking at the anatomy of the cells, tissues, or organs for evidence of disease. Thus, the anatomic pathologist examines cell ("cytology") slide preparations, such as Pap smears and fine needle aspirations, and surgically resected specimens and tissue biopsies ("histology"). He or she may also occasionally perform autopsies, usually in hospitals. The primary instrument of the anatomic pathologist is the microscope, but a pathologist can tell much about a specimen by simple visual inspection without a microscope and, in fact, all examinations begin with this "gross pathology" inspection.

Clinical pathology, on the other hand, involves investigation of cells, tissues, and fluids of patients through laboratory testing. Thus, clinical pathologists typically direct hospital clinical chemistry laboratories, microbiology laboratories, hematology laboratories, blood banks, and molecular pathology/genetic laboratories. However, these laboratory functions are increasingly being taken over by Ph.Ds in other disciplines (e.g., hematologists running both the hematology service and the hematology diagnostic laboratory).

Whether anatomic or clinical, hospital pathologists are charged with ascertaining pathological findings and correlating them with the existing clinical data. In other words, they find morphological changes to explain particular clinical signs and symptoms. A hospital autopsy therefore seeks to verify the diagnosis made before death and evaluate the treatment rendered pursuant to that diagnosis. The purposes of this exercise are to increase the storehouse of medical knowledge and to provide a certain degree of quality control. Philosophically, therefore, hospital pathologists tend to approach their examinations with verification and academic discovery as their objectives. This predisposition can lead the hospital pathologist to overlook subtleties that contraindicate clinical background, diagnosis, and treatment rendered.

Forensic pathology, which was formally recognized as a subspecialty of pathology in 1959, is the application of pathology to medical–legal matters — specifically, the investigation of violent, sudden, suspicious, unexplained, unexpected, and medically unattended deaths for the purpose of determining the cause and manner of death. Forensic pathology now encompasses a large body of scientific knowledge.[1–6] The primary tool of the forensic pathologist is the autopsy. As hospital pathologists have stopped performing autopsies on a routine basis in recent years, the main expertise for autopsy examinations now resides within the forensic pathology community. Typically, forensic pathologists ply their trade as "medical examiners" or "coroners," though they may also practice as consultants to prosecutors and criminal defense attorneys, or as conventional pathologists performing some forensic autopsies as a minor part of their practice.

Whereas only patients of a hospital may be considered as falling within the purview of the traditional hospital-based pathologist, forensic pathology serves all members of society. The forensic pathologist must know traditional medicine and something about life in general to adequately deal with deaths at home, at work, during recreation, in public, and during transportation. Forensic pathologists will examine victims of heart attacks, therapeutic error, drugs, gunshots, motor vehicular accidents, and work-related injuries, to name but a handful of examples.

Only licensed physicians with formal training and expertise in the theory and practice of forensic pathology should perform medical–legal autopsies. After undergraduate study and four years of medical school, a forensic pathologist will matriculate through four years of pathology residency and one year of forensic pathology subspecialty training, as well as successful completion of an anatomic or combined anatomic/clinical pathology American Board of Pathology (ABP) certification examination and a forensic pathology subspecialty ABP certification examination. The American Council on Graduate Medical Education (ACGME) accredits forensic pathology residency programs and the American Board of Pathology, which is a member of the American Board of Medical Specialties, "board certifies" forensic pathologists.

The forensic pathologist approaches a death in an entirely different manner from the hospital pathologist. Frequently, the clinical history of the deceased does not exist or is not available, so that, even if forensic pathologists were intellectually disposed to match their findings with clinical observations, diagnosis or treatment, it often would be impossible to do so. More importantly, hospital and forensic pathologies are distinguished by their jurisdictional spheres. Forensic pathology goes beyond the hospital setting and investigates any sudden, unexpected, unexplained, violent, suspicious, or medically unattended death. The term "investigation" distinguishes these two disciplines because hospital pathologists usually limit themselves to an autopsy and review of available clinical data. Forensic pathologists, however, engage in investigations that routinely address the following:

1. Who is the deceased? This information, particularly in a criminal situation, is often unknown. Factors such as gender, race, age, and unique characteristics are evaluated.
2. Where did the injuries and ensuing death occur?
3. When did the death and injuries occur?
4. What injuries are present (type, distribution, pattern, cause, and direction)?
5. Which injuries are significant (major versus minor injuries, true versus artifactual or postmortem injuries)?
6. Why and how were the injuries produced? What were the mechanisms causing the injuries and the actual manner of causation?
7. What actually caused the death?

The scope of such a medical–legal investigation is necessarily broad and comprehensive. The information generated may determine whether a person is charged with a crime, is sued civilly for negligence, or receives insurance benefits, among other critical issues. These applications depend upon a general determination beyond the cause of death that is also alien to hospital pathology — that is, the *manner* of death.

Both hospital pathologists and forensic pathologists perform autopsies to determine the cause of death. Manner of death is a legal question that only forensic pathologists, armed with the results of their medical–legal investigations, are prepared to address. Hospital pathologists have little opportunity to develop a fair understanding, satisfactory appraisal, or high index of awareness of the medical, philosophical, and legal problems related to determination of the manner of death. For them, essentially every death is natural, and even medical negligence may go undetected or may be labeled as a natural complication of disease. Drafting and signing hospital death certificates is primarily the responsibility of the attending physician, which accentuates this trend. The hospital physician is often not inclined to include in the autopsy report a specific cause of death or the full causal chain of events, especially when a possible cause for litigation might be suggested or several causes of death may be present.

Autopsies should be undertaken as often as possible for many reasons, including a variety of benefits they confer upon the families of the deceased — for example, identifying familial disorders, assisting in genetic counseling, providing information for insurance and other death benefits, and indirectly helping to assuage grief. Benefits to the public welfare include discovering contagious diseases and environmental hazards, providing a source of organs and tissues for transplantation and scientific research, and furnishing essential data for quality control and risk assessment programs in hospitals and other health care facilities.

Autopsies also benefit the overall field of medicine through the teaching of medical students and residents, the discovery and elucidation of such new diseases as Legionnaires' Disease and acquired immunodeficiency syndrome [AIDS], and the ongoing education of surgeons and other physicians regarding the efficacy of particular operations and medications.[7] Additional benefits to the legal and judicial systems include determining when an unnatural death (accident, suicide, or homicide) has occurred, thereby enabling trial attorneys and judges to make valid decisions pertaining to the disposition of civil and criminal cases.

The idea that new technology and improved diagnostic skills have rendered autopsies obsolete is incorrect and naïve at best, and intellectually arrogant and scientifically dangerous at worst. Although certain death cases are so well understood and unequivocally documented that it is not necessary to perform an autopsy, many clinical questions still need to be asked and answered in a majority of deaths. Regardless of the treating physician's degree of competency and experience, and despite highly sophisticated equipment such as computed tomography scans and magnetic resonance imaging, no substitute exists for examining organs and tissues at autopsy in the documentation of definitive diagnoses.

The approach to the autopsy by these two subspecialties is also different. Forensic pathologists, who are frequently exposed to the pathology of trauma, recognize the importance of a careful external examination, including the clothing, to determine the pattern of injuries and their relationship to the identification of the injurious agent. Hospital pathologists, because their subjects usually die in the hospital, have generally no need to be concerned about these factors and are satisfied with a cursory and superficial external examination. Hospital pathologists, however, are more inclined to detect and diagnose microscopic changes of rare natural diseases because of the direction of their work and the academic environment in which they function. Forensic pathologists are more familiar with subtle microscopic changes caused by poisons, noxious substances, and environmental diseases — that is, with the microscopic profile of unnatural death.

Forensic pathologists also focus on the crime scene and the circumstances of death in the scientific reconstruction and understanding of the autopsy findings. Unlike hospital pathologists, forensic pathologists frequently visit the scene to determine possible inconsistencies with their scientific findings.

None of these comparisons should be construed as an assertion that hospital pathologists are somehow incompetent. Their approach is simply different from that of the forensic pathologist; hospital pathologists are not charged with determining the answers to many of the questions that forensic pathologists must routinely address. Also, hospital pathologists are not usually concerned with the determination of time of death or the timing of tissue injuries. For forensic pathologists, time of death and time of injuries may be crucial to civil and criminal legal matters, and thus must be specifically addressed.

Coroners and Medical Examiners

The medical–legal death investigation system of the United States is a patchwork quilt that loosely covers the societal landscape.[4,8] Our system was inherited from England, where coroners date back to the 11th century and were written into the law by King Richard I in the 12th century, at a time when suicides were considered crimes to be punished by forfeiture of the decedent's estate to the Crown. The term "coroner" comes from the Latin "corona," an appointee of the Crown. This individual, sometimes called the "crowner," was an officer who was dispatched to death scenes to protect the Crown's interest and collect any personal or real property that was deemed to have become the King's following certain types of deaths.

Coroner's inquests — preliminary hearings similar to those conducted by judges or magistrates — began in the United States in the early 1600s, with autopsy examinations being recorded as early as 1647. In 1877, Massachusetts replaced the coroner system with a limited form of a physician-based "medical examiner" system. New York City instituted the first true medical examiner system in 1918, and Maryland established the first true statewide medical examiner system in 1939.

Medical examiners are licensed pathologists, preferably forensic pathologists, officially responsible for performing medical–legal death investigations and conducting postmortem examinations and autopsies when appropriate to determine the cause and manner of death, along with fulfilling other jurisprudential and public health functions. This term includes government employees and private pathologists contracted to perform work for one or more jurisdictions. In some jurisdictions, however, the title "medical examiner" is used inappropriately for physicians who respond to initial notifications of death and are responsible for screening and referring appropriate cases to forensic pathologists who will perform autopsies. Such physicians function as local investigators ("physician investigators") within medical examiner systems. The term "medical examiner" is further confused by its use to describe physicians conducting physical examinations for insurance companies or worker's compensation boards as well as for physicians sitting on state boards that oversee medical licensure of physicians. In New Mexico, the title "medical investigator" is used instead of "medical examiner."

There are approximately 200 medical examiner jurisdictions in the United States, the vast majority of which, being mostly county based, serve populations of less than one million. Approximately 1% of a population will die in a given year, approximately half under medical care and between 20 and 40% requiring some degree of medical–legal investigation. Given this, most offices are severely underfunded, with total annual budgets of somewhere between $1 and $2 million. Funding for a medical examiner's office should be approximately $4 per capita.

Medical examiner offices vary greatly, but more than half are staffed by only a single pathologist. National Association of Medical Examiners (NAME) accreditation standards require that pathologists conduct fewer than 350 autopsies a year and recommend that they perform less than 250 per year. It is clear that many pathologists perform an excessive number of autopsies. In a typical office, approximately two thirds of the bodies are subjected to complete autopsies.

By contrast, coroners are elected officials who may or may not be physicians. In fact, most lay coroners are funeral home directors. Educational opportunities do exist for coroners, but funding for such programs is often problematic. In some jurisdictions, coroners are required to be physicians, but not board-certified forensic pathologists. They are responsible for initial receipt of notification of deaths, their certification, and the determination of whether or not to refer the cases for autopsy. In Texas counties where a formal medical examiner system has not been established, Justices of the Peace serve as coroners. In California, sheriffs often serve as coroners. Coroners' offices generally operate under more restrictive legislative authority (suspicious and violent deaths). Particularly in populous jurisdictions, forensic pathologists may fill coroner positions or work in coroners' offices, and in some jurisdictions, coroners must be physicians by legislative mandate.

Today, at least numerically, most jurisdictions are served by coroners. The coroner system is based on the county jurisdictional scheme of early English law. The result is a huge variation in the number of citizens served per office, with most offices serving only a small population base. Moreover, the emphasis on county systems has simply left many areas of the country uncovered by trained professional forensic pathologists. Some consolidation and regionalization is logical and necessary.

Medical–legal death investigators are nonphysician professional investigators who are used by medical examiners' offices to perform scene and circumstantial investigations in support of the medical examiner, who will file the case report. The American Board of Medical–legal Death Investigators registers and certifies such practitioners in the field based upon the knowledge and skills found in the National Institute of Justice National Guidelines for Death Investigation.

In states with coroners, lay coroners often function as medical–legal death investigators in rural jurisdictions. They perform investigations of deaths and determine whether cases should be referred to forensic pathologists for autopsy. However, coroners are independent and autonomous — neither under the supervision of, nor accountable to the forensic pathologists or medical examiners with whom they work. Thus, they do not answer for decisions not to refer cases for autopsy or for the death certificates they issue.

A good forensic pathologist is not necessarily a good politician, and thus may not win elections. It is difficult to bring in appropriate candidates from out of the jurisdiction as candidates for elected positions. Some argue that elected coroners are subject to elective pressures that are inappropriate to the unbiased scientific determination of the cause and manner of death, whereas others argue that community responsiveness is appropriate for the proper functioning of society. Elected officials do have a measure of independence that may shield them from pressures from law enforcement and prosecutors, which may not exist in the case of appointed government employees.

NAME is the primary organization for forensic pathologists in the United States, although it has a sizable international membership as well.[9,10] It was established in 1965 and currently has a membership of nearly 1,000 members, of which approximately 80% are physicians and 20% either lay death investigators or administrators working in medical examiners' offices. NAME has had an inspection and accreditation program since 1974. Approximately one quarter of the population of the United States is currently served by an accredited medical examiner's office. Additionally, NAME is currently professional practice standards.

Medical–Legal Death Investigation

In a typical medical examiner's system, a death is reported to the local police, who then notifies the appropriate medical examiner's office. If jurisdiction is accepted, a case number is generated, and the medical examiner's office takes charge of the body. Jurisdictional authority is determined by location, the absence of an attending physician, and local statutory responsibility (generally a listing of categories, such as violent deaths, deaths known or suspected to constitute a public threat, deaths occurring within 24 hours of hospital admission, and so on).

Medical–legal death investigators, and sometimes the forensic pathologist, are sent to investigate the scene of death and to write a short narrative, independently of the police investigators in accordance with the NIJ National Guidelines for Death Investigation. After a scene investigation, the body is placed in a body bag and transported to the medical examiner's morgue, where it is placed in a freezer until the time for examination.

The forensic pathologist reviews the investigative report and any available medical records prior to examination of the body. The decision is made either to administratively sign out the case and release the body, or to perform a postmortem examination, which may be an "inspection" (external examination only) or an autopsy (external and internal examination). Deaths generally requiring autopsy include known and suspected homicides or deaths caused by criminal violence, unexpected and unexplained deaths, deaths in custody and associated with police action, unidentified remains, vehicular drivers, occupational deaths, and deaths where litigation is anticipated, among others.

Dissection of the human body was performed as long ago as the third century B.C. for the purpose of obtaining medical knowledge. A postmortem examination of Julius Caesar concluded that only one of the 23 stab wounds inflicted by his fellow Roman senators was fatal. In 1247, the Chinese compiled a fascinating tome, *Hsi Yuan Yu* ("The Washing Away of Wrongs"), which set forth guidelines for medical investigators called upon to determine whether an individual found dead unexpectedly had died from unnatural causes. This remains today as one of the oldest classics on forensic medicine. Following the Dark Ages, autopsies were done for medical–legal purposes in several European cities, and in the 16th century, an extensive and detailed text on forensic medicine was written by Zacchia, an eminent Papal physician. Modern concepts of forensic pathology and toxicology as they apply to death investigation evolved in the latter part of the 18th and the early 19th centuries with the evolution of pathology into a true medical science. Morgagni and Rokitansky performed thousands of autopsies in which they correlated clinical signs and symptoms with postmortem findings, categorized various pathologic diagnoses, and established the importance of the autopsy to academic medicine and research.

Before a postmortem examination can be done, it is necessary to determine the sufficiency of the presumptive identification, if any. Standard identification procedures include a photograph of the face with a case number, fingerprints, and the obtaining of a DNA specimen. When identification cannot be made or questioned, additional procedures are undertaken, including the inventory of personal effects, full-body x-rays, charting and x-raying of dentition, and the performance of an autopsy.

The postmortem examination itself begins with a careful external examination. Often, this is the most important aspect of an autopsy. Bodies are generally photographed "as is" (clothed and with hospital appliances attached), weighed, and their lengths measured. A search for trace evidence is conducted, if warranted. The clothes are documented, removed, and sent for further forensic examination, if warranted. Postmortem changes, such as rigor mortis (muscle stiffness), livor mortis (pooling of the blood), and state of decomposition are noted.

Evidence of injury is described by type, location, size, shape, and pattern. The location of gunshot wounds and stab wounds is described by anatomic region and measured from two anatomic landmarks. These and other key injuries should be photographed with a special scale and described in a special section of the autopsy report.

The internal examination begins with opening the body with a Y-incision, in which incisions from the shoulders meet at the mid-chest and extend through the midline to the pubis. This allows the *in situ* examination and evisceration of the thoracic and abdominal organs by either the Virchow method (organ by organ) or the modified Rokitansky method (en bloc dissection). Each organ is examined, weighed, and serially sectioned. The head is examined by a coronal incision from behind each ear; the calvarium is removed, the brain evacuated, and dura stripped from the skull bone. The tongue and neck organs are removed last. Partial autopsies are to be eschewed. The brain and possibly the heart may be placed in fixative solution for a more careful examination at a later time, particularly with a neuropathology or cardiovascular specialist. Specimens are saved for immediate or potential later toxicological and histological studies. These procedures are performed in a manner that allows viewing at the subsequent funeral.

Special examinations are performed for specific circumstances. For instance, pubic combings, swabs and smears of the vaginal, anal, and oral orifices, and exemplar hairs are obtained for sexual assault victims, the eyes are taken in the case of suspected infant abuse, and cultures are taken in cases of pneumonia or other infectious disease pathology.

Vital organs may be harvested for transplant before an autopsy, and tissues may be taken before or, more often, after an autopsy. Corneal tissue is often harvested if no objection is known, although this practice, despite legal authorization, has resulted in liability in some jurisdictions. In general, the forensic pathologist accommodates organ and tissue harvest, if it will not interfere with his or her investigation.

The autopsy may be performed in approximately two to three hours — in multiple stab wound and other such complicated cases, several hours longer. However, the work of the forensic pathologist is far from over upon completion of the gross autopsy. The pathologist must next analyze the autopsy findings, dictate the preliminary autopsy report, fill out the death certificate, examine and interpret the microscopic slides, perform the neuropathology examination of the brain, incorporate the toxicology results and other consultation reports, perform further investigations and calls to others about the case, and prepare the final postmortem report. This process may take several weeks.

The Value of Forensic Pathologists to Society

Forensic pathologists accept a lower governmental salary compared to other pathology colleagues from a sense of satisfaction in performing an important societal function. They perform their professional duties for the living and, in a sense, speak for the dead playing important roles in law enforcement, public health and other forms of public service. In fact, the daily practice of the forensic pathologist extends far beyond questions related to medicine or forensic pathology and involves dealing with political entities, the media, law enforcement, the judicial system, the medical environment, and families of the deceased. Unfortunately, their value is not always obvious to others — coroner's offices and medical examiner's offices have all too often been invisible and considered by public officials as mere technicians that handle "bodies." Fortunately, some degree of visibility, even if distorted, has been provided by the media in recent years — for example, in the TV shows *Crossing Jordan, The X-Files, Forensic Files, CSI and NCIS*, as well as in Patricia Cornwell's fiction featuring Kay Scarpetta. Nonetheless, the role of the forensic pathologist sometimes seems marginalized by others, such as crime laboratories and departments of vital statistics.

Forensic Pathology and Criminal Justice

Forensic pathologists provide the public with unbiased, legally defensible determinations of the cause and manner of death. Their objective opinions provided in an open and free environment educates society and supplies answers to questions concerning suspicious deaths sensitive to the community. Forensic pathologists provide information to the media to ensure a timely exchange of truthful information to the community that reduces the potential for uninformed community reaction and civil unrest. Forensic pathologists investigate sudden, unexpected, and suspicious death occurring in institutional and police custody.

Forensic pathologists provide an important function to the criminal justice system through the application of medical science to death investigation. Sometimes, the forensic pathologist will recognize a seeming natural death as a homicide, and at other times, examination may reveal that a particular death is due to a suicide, natural disease, or other processes rather than from a homicidal act and thus prevent unnecessary legal actions. Forensic pathologists provide expert consultation to investigators, courts, prosecutors, and defense counsel. They are the custodians of the death records, maintaining the integrity, accessibility, and proper storage of the death records to be used in investigations. They can determine the cause and manner of death, collect evidence, and rule out natural disease processes that might be erroneously asserted by the defense. Identification of the deceased, range of fire of a gunshot wound, recognition of a patterned abrasion, may be important elements of a prosecution. Forensic pathologists are also sometimes asked about the role of an intoxicating substance, the order of death, or of pain that might have been experienced by the decedent. Perhaps most important is the ability to distinguish when facts seem to fit the mechanism of death and when they do not. Although neutral, as the expert on homicides, the forensic pathologist often provides the critical evidence in homicide prosecutions. In fact, it is the local forensic pathologist, rather than the local police detective, who will investigate more murders.

Forensic pathologists have also begun to use their expertise in wound recognition for examinations of the living. This has been a long standing practice in England by the so-called "police surgeons," but clinical forensic medicine is practiced by only a small segment of U.S. forensic pathologists.

The same reasons that make forensic pathology expertise important to criminal investigations of death apply to civil litigations over death. Forensic pathologists will match the injuries to the reported causes and mechanisms of death and then testify accordingly.

Forensic Pathology and Public Health

Forensic pathologists are front-line public health officials committed to preserving health and identifying causes of preventable and unnecessary deaths. Forensic pathologists identify potential threats to public welfare by providing valuable information on trends in activities such as drug and alcohol abuse, domestic and elderly abuse, child abuse, and other patterns of injury and disease that affect the community at large. Forensic pathologists provide surveillance for emerging infectious disease, dangerous work environments, environmental conditions, adverse drug reactions, defective products, medical therapy related deaths, and high-risk activities that have an impact on the nation's overall health and well-being.

Standardized death reporting allows for statistical medical research and epidemiological studies providing information on population-based disease, injury patterns, and for evaluating the effectiveness of therapy that benefits the population as a whole. These data will be used by public health officials, and by product manufacturers, by pharmaceutical companies, by OSHA, and by policy makers, among others.

By collaborating with public health officials, medical examiners ensure timely reporting and valid data collection to protect the health of the community. The National Vital Statistics System receives approximately one third of its information and all its nonnatural and sudden and unexplained deaths from medical examiner and coroner offices. The death certificates from forensic pathologists are generally considered to be of a higher quality than form other physicians. Moreover, forensic pathologists are specifically responsible for the reporting of nonnatural death statistics for the jurisdiction.

Examples of where forensic pathologists played key roles in the discovery of dangerous conditions and the development of preventive strategies are the "back-to-sleep" campaign in which infants are to sleep in a supine position and in the development of collapsible automotive steering wheels.

As the rate of hospital autopsies has continued to decline, forensic pathologists are the remaining bastions of autopsy expertise.[4] As such, they may become more involved with performing autopsies on hospital deaths. A recent Institute of Medicine (IOM) report noted that approximately 98,000 deaths occur in hospitals each year as a result of medical errors.[11] Medical examiner offices, as neutral governmental venues, should become the natural place for this activity.

Many of the organs and tissues harvested for transplantation come from accident fatalities. As such, forensic pathologists must decide whether to permit harvest. In most cases, harvest may proceed without jeopardizing a criminal investigation, and forensic pathologists are dedicated to assisting in the utilization of scarce organs and tissues for transplantation. Forensic pathologists assist families and organ procurement agencies in assessing the suitability of the decedent for organ/tissue donation.

Forensic Pathology and Homeland Security

Through their surveillance, monitoring, and investigation of deaths, forensic pathologists form an important sentinel for emerging infections, terrorist threats, and infectious epidemics.[12] The addition of public health responsibilities is one of the important aspects of progress from traditional coroner jurisdiction. Through the popular media, the general public has become more cognizant of the role of the medical examiner and has come to expect high quality death investigation.

Forensic pathologists are part of the fabric of a homeland security surveillance network. It is now clear that a victim of a biothreat agent may be first recognized at autopsy. CDC has awakened to the fact that death reporting is important to them and that they must work with medical examiners. Medical examiner offices have begun to hire "forensic epidemiologists."

Forensic Pathology Education and Research

Medical examiners are becoming increasingly recognized as an important resource of medical knowledge for law enforcement, the courts, and the medical profession. Forensic pathologists conduct research into the physiology and signs of disease and death. Forensic pathology research continues, but with little funding as the National Institutes of Health (NIH), the Centers for Disease Control and Prevention (CDC), and the National Institute of Justice (NIJ) generally do not fund forensic pathology research.

Forensic pathologists are involved in all aspects of medical education. Medical examiner's offices provide autopsy experience for medical students, pathology residents, and forensic pathology residents. In addition, forensic pathologists participate in the education of physicians in other specialties that interact with the functions of the medical examiner's office. Forensic pathologists provide medical education to nonphysicians involved in death investigation such as funeral directors, attorneys, law enforcement, and other allied health practitioners. In addition, forensic pathologists provide education in forensic sciences, forensic pathology, and medical science to death investigators and coroners.

The U.S. Supreme Court decision in the Daubert case, dealing with the admissibility of scientific evidence, is having a significant effect on the forensic sciences. This ruling (which is discussed in Chapter 4 of this book) is forcing a reconsideration of the scientific basis of forensic testimony. Forensic pathology has largely been spared, but it looms over us as dark clouds. Much of what is done is experienced based and anecdotal. Forensic pathologists should expect that they will receive routine and significant challenge as to the scientific underpinnings of their testimony.

Forensic pathologists often lead death review teams that look into pediatric deaths, deaths resulting from domestic violence, elderly abuse, and suicides. Forensic pathologists serve as valuable participants on injury boards, public health boards, mine safety boards, transportation safety boards, etc. and can provide and explain key data.

Forensic pathologists lecture to schools and public audiences on the consequences of drunk driving, on sexual assaults, and child abuse.

Forensic Pathology and the Federal Government

The federal government does not have a significant presence in traditional medical examiner operations. Medical examiners are not burdened by regulations. However, they have also not been supported by the federal funds that come with federal involvement.

The creation of a Department of Homeland Security (DHS) indicates federal emphasis on domestic security, and forensic pathologists are significant participants. Forensic pathologists have clearly been a major part of the World Trade Center effort. DHS has absorbed the NDMS that includes DMORT operations. Medical examiners may well see the first, sentinel case of a bioterrorist attack. I believe that the forensic science community can generally make a strong contribution to domestic security, and this should be seen as an opportunity.

The Armed Forces Medical Examiner System (AFMES), a department within the Armed Forces Institute of Pathology (AFIP) is the only federal medical examiner office. It performs medical–legal death investigation on service members dying on exclusive federal jurisdiction or in foreign countries according to Status of Forces Agreements and for top executives in the government according to Title XVIII congressional mandate. Their jurisdiction has also been expanded recently to cover some commercial air mishaps. Furthermore, when the FBI claims jurisdiction, for a terrorist event, they will often involve the AFMES.

The Disaster Mortuary Response Team, (DMORT), the element of the National Disaster Medical System that can be mobilized to assist state and local efforts in times of a declared disaster, has provided a valuable service to jurisdictions in need. Their services are most needed when a multiple fatality incident occurs in a coroner jurisdiction with no forensic pathology resources, training, or experience, but even well resourced offices often have a limited contingency capacity. Unfortunately, the DMORT has been limited to identification services only. They are being reorganized under the Department of Homeland Security (DHS).

Thus, the federal government has the ability to assist state and local assets in times of emergency on a limited basis and often at local expense. The federal government does not have a federal office equivalent to that of state and local jurisdictions. Moreover, there is no agency that provides a role model, leadership, or guidance or oversight of medical–legal death investigation in the United States.

Medical examiners fall between the cracks in an orphaned community, not truly owned by law enforcement, public health, or traditional medicine. Too often, community leadership equates funding forensic pathology as wasting money on the dead and does not recognize that the community exists for the living. One might conclude that crimes resulting in death are not given a high priority in criminal investigations. Certainly, dead victims will not bring suit or complain to newspapers.

Funding has remained at the paltry level of approximately one to two dollars per citizen per year in most jurisdictions over the last three decades.

There is no effective regulation of medical examiner offices. Theoretically, state medical licensure boards could oversee the medical practices, but in reality, they do not. Judicial scrutiny seems ineffective to weed out poor practice. Voluntary NAME accreditation standards have yet to be adopted by a majority of medical examiner offices. Medical examiners often lose their jobs over scandals, when longstanding poor practice or misunderstood practice becomes public. Other times, seemingly scandalous quality work by nonforensic pathologists seems to be tolerated.

The understanding of the neutral role of the medical examiner as an objective witness, autonomous from the prosecution or law enforcement, is an important aspect of their role.

Forensic pathologists promote the interests of the deceased and their families. Forensic pathologists provide impartial and accurate death certification, facilitate the grieving process, and provide closure for survivors. Forensic pathologists educate the family regarding health issues such as inherited diseases, risks of infection, and validate antemortem diagnosis and treatments. Forensic pathologists provide unbiased and accurate investigation of a death, which clarifies legal issues surrounding the sudden demise of a loved one, thereby providing documentation and information for families to complete necessary insurance and estate issues. This supports appropriate litigation and services to mitigate frivolous litigation. Forensic pathologists lead the efforts to identify remains in cases of mass disasters and ensure their return to their loved ones.

Forensic Science and the Forensic Pathologist

Forensic pathologists require the services of the crime laboratory, are themselves forensic scientists, and can conduct their own forensic investigations. Forensic pathologists need to be aware of the ability to process evidentiary material found on and submitted with bodies or that may be encountered at a crime scene discovered and analyzed by forensic scientific methods. Specifically, the forensic pathologist particularly should know how to conduct a thorough examination and how to collect, preserve, and document evidentiary material. This requires knowledge of forensic science principles and capabilities. The forensic sciences have been greatly expanding and maturing in recent years, and it has been difficult for forensic pathologists to keep current with this burgeoning field. Unfortunately, even though current forensic pathology residency requirements call for toxicology and crime laboratory training (perhaps more correctly called exposure), in reality, residents are often inadequately trained in this regard.

Historically, physicians have played important roles in the development of forensic science, particularly in the late nineteenth and early twentieth centuries. The scientific grounding in the medical tradition meant that physicians brought an analytic and technical background that typical detectives of the time did not have. Perhaps it is no accident that Sir Arthur Conan Doyle, creator of the legendary fictional sleuth Sherlock Holmes, was himself a physician, and that Sherlock Holmes' bungling assistant, Watson, was a physician as well.

References

1. Di Maio, V.J.M. and Dimaio, D. *Forensic Pathology*, 2nd edn., CRC Press, Boca Raton, NY, 2001.

2. Wecht, C.H. Ed. *Forensic Sciences*, Vol. 2., Matthew Bender & Co., Inc., New York, NY, 1993.

3. Froede, R.C. Ed., *Handbook of Forensic Pathology*, 2nd edn., College of American Pathologists, 2003.

4. *Medical–legal Death Investigation System: Workshop Summary*. Committee for the Workshop on Medical–legal Death Investigation System, Institute of Medicine, The National Academies Press, Washington, D.C., 2003.

5. Spitz, W.U. Ed., *Medical–legal Investigation of Death: Guidelines for the Application of Pathology to Crime Investigation*. Charles C. Thomas, Springfield, IL, 1993.

6. Baden, M.M. and Adler Hennessee, J. *Unnatural Death: Confessions of a Medical Examiner*. Ivy Books, New York, NY, 1989.

7. Lundberg, G.D., Medicine without the Autopsy, *Archiv. Pathol. Lab. Med.*, 108(6): 449–54, 1984.

8. Hanzlick, R., Combs, D., Medical examiner and coroner systems: History and Trends, *J. Amer. Med. Assn.*, 279(11): 870–4, 1998.

9. www.thename.org

10. Hanzlick, R., Name and its History: Implications for the future, *Am. J. For. Med. Pathol.*, 23(1): 90–5, 2002.

11. Institute of Medicine, *To Err is Human: Building a Safer Health System*, National Academy Press, Washington, D.C., 1999.

12. Nolte, K.B., Yoon, S.S., and Pestowski, C., Medical examiners, coroners, and bioterrorism, *Emerg. Infect. Dis.* 6(5): 559–60, 2000.

13. Pinckard, J.K., Hunsaker, D., and Weedn, V.W., A comprehensive analysis of forensic science training in forensic pathology fellowship programs, *J. Forensic Sci.*, 48(2), 1–6, 2003.

Forensic Toxicology

20

FREDERICK W. FOCHTMAN

Toxicology is generally considered as the study of poisons. Forensic toxicology is toxicology with medico-legal applications. Forensic toxicology studies are nearly always analytical in nature because the interpretation of the actions and effects of drugs and toxic substances require knowing what is present and how much is present. This is true regardless of whether the questions involve postmortem, human performance, or drug testing interpretations. These are the areas in which Forensic Toxicologists are routinely involved: Postmortem Forensic Toxicology, Human Performance Toxicology, and Forensic Drug Testing.[4]

Postmortem Forensic Toxicology

Postmortem forensic toxicology involves analyzing body fluids and organs from death cases and interpreting this information. Sudden unexpected and unexplained deaths become coroners' cases or fall under the jurisdiction of the medical examiner. Frequently in these cases toxicology studies are useful and necessary for the final decision regarding the cause and manner of death. In nearly every death that remains unexplained after postmortem examination, toxicology studies are sought to rule out poisoning, drug overdose, or therapeutic misadventure.

In some cases, there is a history or physical evidence to indicate an overdose or poisoning, such as intravenous drug use and drug paraphernalia at the death scene, presence of suicide notes or empty drug containers. A death from an accidental fire or arson, or exposure to incomplete combustion fumes (motor vehicle exhaust) will indicate that carbon monoxide poisoning should be suspected. In these instances, forensic toxicology studies are necessary to corroborate investigative findings. However, the problem presented when a young or middle aged therapeutic drug user, a nursing home patient, and a science researcher are found dead, all without a history or any physical evidence of overdose, may be solved by toxicology testing and interpretation.

Forensic toxicologists routinely test postmortem blood and urine specimens when available. Various other fluids, for example, eye fluid, stomach contents, and bile can also be analyzed. Samples of organ tissues may have to be tested when bodies are decomposed and fluids are not available. Some forensic laboratories will test both a heart blood sample and a peripheral (femoral) blood sample in order to evaluate postmortem changes in blood concentrations. It is important for toxicology specimens to be properly collected during the autopsy process. Care must be taken to ensure that specimens are not contaminated with fluids from other compartments of the body. It is also recommended that a portion of the blood specimens be preserved with fluoride to minimize postmortem degradation.

Analytical methodologies used by forensic laboratories vary, but most use a combination of immunoassay and chromatographic methods to identify and quantify drugs and poisons. Alcohol is routinely analyzed in forensic laboratories by gas chromatography. Enzymatic and colorimetric methods are occasionally used as an initial or screening test. Carbon monoxide testing can be tested by spectrophotometric differentiation between oxyhemoglobin, reduced hemoglobin, methemoglobin, and carboxyhemoglobin. Carbon monoxide analysis is also done by a diffusion and colorimetric method, and by gas chromatography. Cyanide testing is done by diffusion and by colorimetric quantitation. Immunoassay testing can be used for screening both blood and urine specimens for a variety of drugs and drug classes. Opiates, amphetamines, barbiturates, benzodiazepines, and cocaine metabolites are examples of immunoassay testing. Chromatographic methods such as thin layer chromatography (TLC), gas chromatography (GC), high performance liquid chromatography (HPLC), and chromatography interfaced with mass spectrometry (GC/MS, GC/MS/MS, LC/MS, LC/MS/MS) are used for qualitative analysis and quantitative testing of specimens for drugs and poisons. For heavy metal poisoning, specimens of arsenic, mercury, cadmium, lead, and so on can be analyzed by atomic absorption spectrophotometry.

For the results of toxicology testing to be scientifically valid, the methods and procedures used for analyzing specimens must be validated to ensure the accuracy, precision, and specificity of the method. The process includes identifying limits of detection and lower and upper limits of quantitation. The method of validation tests for possible interfering substances, evaluates carryover from previously tested samples. The method must be able to provide accurate results for reference specimens. The forensic toxicologist must understand the importance of validation and be able to evaluate the effectiveness of the process. Results from scientifically valid methods are necessary to support medico-legal circumstances of criminal or civil cases.

Most reference values for toxic and lethal concentrations of drugs and poisons appearing in the literature are from case reports. Reported reference values have a wide range and frequently have overlapping concentration ranges for toxic and lethal concentrations of drugs and poisons.[1] Accurate analytical reference values for scientific comparisons require experimental doses of substances under controlled conditions using validated procedures. Obviously, this type of information is not generally available for toxic and lethal doses in humans. The postmortem forensic toxicologist therefore must make interpretations based on information and data only from case reports. This emphasizes the importance of experience and training necessary for interpreting postmortem concentrations of drugs and poisons.

Interpretation of combined drug toxicity can be particularly challenging: If the combination includes several drugs that function with similar mechanisms, such as central nervous system depressant action, it may be somewhat easy to interpret its toxicity. However, when the combination includes drugs with different mechanisms or antagonistic mechanisms such as selective serotonin re-uptake inhibitor, central nervous system stimulant, and central nervous system depressant, the interpretation can be more difficult. This is an area where case reports involving combined drug toxicities can be helpful for interpretation, gaining experience, and for training of the forensic toxicologist.

Blood samples from fatalities of motor vehicle accidents are routinely tested by post-mortem forensic toxicologists for alcohol and also frequently for drugs. Alcohol (ethanol) and many different drugs can render a person incapable of safe driving. This is clearly shown by the yearly statistics issued by the National Traffic Safety Bureau on motor vehicle deaths involving alcohol and drugs. A forensic toxicologist's role in interpreting impairment from alcohol and drugs is emphasized in human performance toxicology.

Human Performance Toxicology

Human performance toxicology, which is an area of forensic toxicology that primarily deals with driving under the influence of drugs and alcohol, can also be referred to as behavioral toxicology dealing with an inability to perform in the workplace.

The forensic toxicologist is frequently asked to interpret blood alcohol concentration (BAC) and blood drug concentration and the relationship they have with impairment. In addition, since alcohol or drug testing is not done on a sample taken at the time of the accident or arrest, but only at a later time, it is often necessary for the toxicologist to extrapolate the person's BAC or drug level at the time of arrest or the accident. This type of interpretation of blood alcohol and drug concentration and the effect on an individual relies on an understanding and knowledge of the physiology and the pharmacology of ethyl alcohol and drugs.

Alcohol in the Body and Its Effects

Ethyl alcohol, or ethanol, is the active drug constituent in alcoholic beverages, and its concentration in beverages, varies from a low of 4–5% in beers, 7–12% in wines, 20–40% in cordials, to a high of 40–50% in most distilled beverages (whiskeys, vodkas, rums, etc.). Proof strength stated on labels of some beverages is a value that is double the percent strength. An example is a 100 proof beverage would be 50% alcohol. It is necessary for the forensic toxicologist to know the concentration of ethanol in beverages in order to interpret quantities consumed related to BAC.

For person drinking an alcoholic beverage, absorption of alcohol into the blood will not take place while the beverage is in the stomach. The stomach's function does not include absorption, but it merely prepares and liquefies swallowed contents for emptying into the small intestine. When the beverage passes from the stomach to the small intestine (duodenum), absorption into the blood will occur. This process takes approximately 20–30 minutes for complete absorption when the stomach is empty. When food is present in the stomach, the process takes a longer time due to the food causing the beverage to stay in the stomach longer, thus extending the time of absorption. Depending on the amount of food present in the stomach, the time for complete absorption of alcohol may take an hour or longer.

Once alcohol is absorbed into the blood, it will be distributed to all parts of the body. In the brain, alcohol has its primary pharmacological effect by producing central nervous system (CNS) depression. All of the impairment effects of alcohol are related to the depressant actions on the nervous system. These effects include increased reaction time, decreased visual acuity, decreased peripheral vision, poor judgment, and sensory–motor incoordination. The combined effects are referred to as "impairment" or "under the influence." Scientific studies have shown that impairment from alcohol can be related to a high concentration of alcohol in the blood. Various concentrations are used by the states and included in their statutes and regulations governing licensed drivers. A number of states use a concentration of 0.10% or greater in blood to indicate that a driver is impaired. However, allocation of federal highway funding has influenced many states to lower the concentration to 0.08%.

Once alcohol enters the blood and is distributed to the liver, it is metabolized first to acetaldehyde and then to acetate providing calories. Approximately 90–98% of alcohol is metabolized at a constant rate (zero order). A person's rate of metabolism depends on his/her experience and frequency of alcohol use. Heavy drinkers will metabolize more rapidly than do light or nondrinkers. Metabolism plus the amount of alcohol excreted unchanged represents elimination or dissipation rate, which averages 0.015–0.02% per hour.

A person's BAC can be estimated using the following formulae:

$$150/BW \times A/50 \times B \times 0.025\% = \text{maximum BAC},$$

where dissipation is the number of hours consuming beverage × elimination rate, maximum BAC minus dissipation the BAC, BW the body weight, A is the percent concentration of alcoholic beverage, and B, is the number of ounces of alcoholic beverage. It is necessary to know the person's body weight, the amount of beverage, and the percent alcohol content in the beverage. It is also necessary to know when the person started drinking and when he/she finished to make a meaningful estimation.

Rates of dissipation and absorption of alcohol are also used by the forensic toxicologist to extrapolate back to the time of arrest or accident. An example is an accident occurring at 8:00 pm. There is suspicion of driving under the influence of alcohol (DUI). The driver does not pass a field sobriety evaluation and is administered a breath test two hours after the accident at 10:00 pm. The result of the breath test is 0.095% BAC. The driver reports that he has not had anything to eat since lunch time and that he stopped drinking two hours earlier at 6:00 pm. Using the information provided and the range of average elimination rates, the driver's BAC at the time of the accident can be estimated. The driver's BAC would have been between 0.125 and 0.135%. These values were obtained by adding to the BAC at 10:00 pm the dissipation that occurred over two hours. Calculations become more complex when drivers eat their meals and continue to drink just before the accident or arrest takes place.

Drugs and Driving

For BACs and impairment, scientific studies similar to alcohol studies do not exist except for marijuana. Interpreting BACs and impairment while driving is more difficult than interpreting impairment with alcohol. Some states utilize trained police officers as drug recognition experts (DREs). The DRE evaluates a suspect by administering a series of tests that are more comprehensive than a field sobriety test as well as a breath test. In addition measurements of pulse, blood pressure, and body temperature are taken. After evaluation of all test information, the DRE forms an opinion on the drug or drug class that causes impairment. A blood or urine sample is also taken for toxicology testing to support the DRE's decision. Testing only a urine specimen provides for evidence of prior exposure but cannot provide a direct relationship to impairment. Opinions of forensic toxicology experts regarding impairment from drugs generally rely on blood concentrations and not on urine concentrations.

Forensic Drug Testing

In 1986, President Ronald Reagan issued Executive Order No. 12564 indicating that the federal government would be a drug-free workplace. Earlier in 1983, a study by the National Transportation Safety Board involving drugs and alcohol use in railway accidents prompted the Federal Railway Administration and the National Institute on Drug Abuse (NIDA) to begin developing drug regulations. Initially, the intent was to have guidelines for the Department of Transportation (DOT), but with Reagan's executive order, NIDA continued to investigate the appropriateness of drug testing through studies and conferences. In 1988, NIDA issued mandatory guidelines for federal drug testing programs. These guidelines were comprehensive including issues of confidentiality, choice of specimen and collection, chain of custody, procedures for testing, quality control, records, and reporting, and interpretation of results. The regulation guidelines provided for a medical review officer (MRO) to review results before final reporting. Also included were guidelines regarding accrediting laboratories, inspecting laboratories, and proficiency testing for laboratories to maintain accredited status. A National Laboratory Certification Program commenced in 1988 under the auspices of the Department of Health and Human Services through NIDA. Drug testing under the guidelines is applicable only to federal employees and federal agencies, but private sector drug testing quickly adopted many of the "NIDA guidelines" for their programs.[2]

Although forensic drug testing had been utilized much earlier in the military and in the Olympics, and also in a small segment of private industry before 1988, it was Reagan's executive order and subsequent NIDA guidelines that caused a tremendous growth in forensic testing. All types of industries both large Fortune 500 and smaller companies, commenced to develop drug-free workplace policies that included drug testing. In addition, many other organizations or specific populations instituted, modified, or increased their use of forensic drug testing to achieve certain objectives. Testing of professional, Olympic, and high school athletes; insurance testing; drug rehabilitation; probation and parole monitoring are examples of forensic drug testing. Drug testing in hospitals or clinical reference laboratories are generally done for medical purposes but may become forensic testing when involving legal questions.

Federal regulations recommend urine as the specimen for testing and allow testing of urine for five drugs or drug classes: cannabinoids (marijuana metabolites), cocaine (benzoylecgonine), amphetamines (amphetamine and methamphetamine), opiates (morphine and codeine), and phencyclidine (PCP). Nonfederal urine drug testing has been expanded to include barbituarates, benzodiazepines, methadone, LSD, and propoxyphene.

Two separate aliquots of a urine specimen are to be analyzed for a test to be reported as positive. An initial test on the first aliquot must be an immunoassay method. If the initial test is positive, a confirmatory test based on gas chromatography/mass spectrometry (GC/MS) is done on the second aliquot. Both the initial immunoassay test and the GC/MS confirmatory test are required to be validated by the laboratory. Validation criteria are discussed earlier in the postmortem forensic toxicology section.

For each test, the regulations provide cutoff concentrations to indicate a presumptive positive and a confirmed positive result. A specimen aliquot that tests negative on the initial test is reported as a negative and does not require any additional drug testing. The cutoff concentrations are chosen based on experience and recommendations of toxicologists involved with military, postmortem, and clinical testing for drugs. The Initial test cutoff values for cannabinoids and opiates were found to be inappropriate and have since been changed. Originally, the initial urine test cutoff for marijuana metabolites was 100 ng/ml. It was shown that this concentration was too high and likely resulted in many false negative reports. Many products promoted to "beat the drug test" that were based on drinking additional water were thought to be effective merely due to dilution of the urine. Subsequently, the cutoff for marijuana metabolites was lowered to 50 ng/ml, which was effective in decreasing the number of false negatives and is high enough to avoid a positive test due to passive inhalation.[3]

The original cutoff for opiates was 300 ng/ml. Foods containing poppy seeds were found to produce positive urine results for morphine. Poppy seeds contain enough morphine to produce urinary concentrations above 300 ng/ml. In addition, cough medicines containing codeine produced urinary concentrations greater than the cutoff for a positive. Prescription analgesics taken by many individuals contain codeine along with a nonopiate analgesics. Chronic use of these prescription analgesics can produce morphine in the urine as a metabolite of codeine. To avoid positives for unintentional exposure and medicinal therapy, the initial test for opiates and confirmatory test cutoff concentrations for morphine and codeine have been changed to 2,000 ng/ml for opiates.

Heroin use may be related to a positive result for morphine in the urine. Since heroin is diacetylmorphine and morphine is a heroin metabolite, the presence of morphine in the urine can indicate prior use of heroin. Since morphine present in the urine can be from sources other than heroin, the federal regulations allow for a definitive test for heroin use. Urine that is positive for morphine can be tested for mono-acetyl morphine, a metabolite that can only be produced in the urine by heroin use.

Nearly all workplace urine drug testing is done with unobserved collections. This has led to some problems because of numerous attempts to thwart the testing process. The collection process includes monitoring the temperature of freshly collected urine. If there is an attempt to substitute another urine sample, it is difficult to get the correct temperature. Various products referred to as adulterants are available for sale, and these can be added to the urine to interfere with testing. Some adulterants are very effective and are difficult to detect. In addition, individuals that are intent on "beating the test" will drink large amounts of water or other fluids prior to a test. This will dilute the urine and can cause a false negative when the concentration in the urine is less than the cutoff concentration.

Federal guidelines allow certified forensic laboratories to test for dilution, substitution, and adulteration of urine samples. There are guidelines established for dilution of urine based on creatinine and specific gravity, and for adulteration based on the pH. Most laboratories will test urine specimens for creatinine content and pH. Creatinine concentration in the urine and specific gravity can provide a measure of dilution. Adulteration of urine is frequently done by addition of an oxidizing substance such as a nitrite salt or pyridinium chromate. These issues pose a challenge for the forensic toxicologist.

Specimens other than urine are also being tested for evidence of drug use. Hair is being utilized for testing by some private sector companies. Oral fluid testing is also being used to detect illicit drug use. These alternative specimens are currently being evaluated as possible substitutes for urine drug testing.

References

1. Baselt, R.C., *Disposition of Toxic Drugs and Chemicals in Man*, 7th ed., Biomedical Publications, Foster City, CA, 2004.

2. Department of Health and Human Services, ADAMHA: Mandatory guidelines for federal workplace drug testing: Final guidelines, *Fed. Reg.*, 1988, 53(69), 11970–89.

3. Huestis, M.A., Mitchell, J.M. and Cone, E.J. Lowering the federally mandated cannabinoid immunoassay cutoff increases true-positive results, *Clin. Chem.*, 1994, 40(5), 729–33.

4. Klaasson, C.D., *Casarett and Doull's Toxicology: The Basic Science of Poisons*, 6th ed., McGraw-Hill, New York, NY, 2001.

THOMAS C. MEYERS

Serology

21

The Role of the Forensic Serologist

The role of the forensic serologist has shown a significant change over the last 10 year. With more and more forensic laboratories developing and implementing DNA methods, much less reliance has been placed on conventional genetic markers such as the cellular antigen and protein markers. The conventional antigenic and protein markers were much less stable and exhibited less specificity than their DNA counterparts. The shift away from serological genetic marker comparisons to evidence screening had followed suit.

In the first year of the twentieth century, Karl Landsteiner's observations that blood from different individuals could be categorized into distinguishable groups, later becoming known as the ABO Blood Group System, was the first reported successful attempt at distinguishing among individuals using biological properties of physiological fluids. Even though these findings were to be used to get a better understanding of the mechanics of blood transfusions, they would later form the basis of modern day forensic serologic comparisons. By 1916, use of the ABO Blood Group System had gained acceptance in Medico-Legal applications, and indeed was still in use in most forensic laboratories in the 1990s.

Forensic scientists, interested in expanding their ability to differentiate among individuals turned to serum and cellular protein markers in the early 1960s. Multiple forms of a single protein (enzyme), called an isozyme, could easily be separated into their various components (alleles) on a starch or agarose gel by electrophoretic methods. By the mid-1970s, forensic scientists multiplexed several protein markers on a single starch/agarose gel, thereby conserving the sample and increasing the specificity of the analysis.

These protein markers, like the ABO Blood Group Markers, are generally unstable in dried stains, require large sample volumes, and are easily degraded by environmental conditions such as heat, humidity, and sunlight. These characteristics, along with their inherent low specificity, made the decision to abandon the cellular antigen and protein markers much simpler once the newly identified DNA markers demonstrated their small sample needs, relative stability to environmental insults, and importantly, high specificity.

The modern forensic serologist no longer provides genetic marker comparisons, which previously had linked biological samples collected from crime scene evidence to a specific individual. Instead, their role is now focused on the identification of biological stains, documenting their appearance, determining body origin and species. Potentially probative samples are collected and preserved for DNA analysis.

This section is not intended to be a complete academic treatment of Forensic Serology, but instead, a practical guide to examining and screening crime scene evidence for the presence or absence of biological material.

Identification of Blood

Blood is a multicomponent fluid which circulates throughout the body while maintaining the homeostasis of tissue fluids. The proper balance of oxygen, pH, temperature, nutrients, and waste products is in part controlled by the blood. Blood accounts for approximately 8% of our total body weight.

Low speed centrifugation of fresh blood distributes this complex fluid into two parts: cells (or formed elements) and plasma. The former consists of erythrocytes (red blood cells), leukocytes (white blood cells), and thrombocytes (platelets), whereas the latter is made up of water, dissolved solids (proteins, cellular nutrients, cellular products, and waste), and gases.

The identification of blood merely requires the identification of one component that is unique to blood, the most obvious of this being the erythrocytes, or red blood cells, which account for approximately 99% of the elements formed. An erythrocyte, which has the characteristic shape of a biconcave disk, may be identified microscopically in fresh liquid blood. Most forensic blood samples, however, consist of dried stains. The erythrocytes are often lysed or deformed in the drying process, which makes microscopic identification generally unreliable.

The identification of blood may be made through the chemical identification of one of its components, namely hemoglobin, which is a globular tetrameric molecule consisting of four polypeptide chains, each bearing one heme prosthetic group. The heme group is responsible for the characteristic color of blood and exhibits certain catalytic properties based on a peroxidase-like activity. These catalytic properties along with the heme group's ability to form microcrystalline precipitates are the basis for the chemical identification of blood.

Catalytic Tests

All of the catalytic tests for blood rely upon the fact that the heme group in hemoglobin displays a peroxidase-like activity that catalyzes the breakdown of peroxides. Certain chemical compounds that appear colorless in a reduced state are oxidized by peroxides in the presence of hemoglobin to form a brightly colored or luminescing compound.

$$\text{Colorless compound} + \text{peroxide} \rightarrow \text{colored compound} + H_2O$$
$$\qquad\text{(reduced)}\qquad\qquad\qquad\qquad\qquad\text{(oxidized)}$$

Table 21.1   Sensitivity and Specificity of Catalytic Tests For Blood

Catalytic Test	Reported Sensitivity (whole blood in water)	False Positives	Advantages (Disadvantages)
Benzidine[1]	1×10^5	Iron, copper, vegetable peroxidases, bacterial metabolites	(Lack specificity, reported carcinogenic properties)
Tetramethyl benzidine[2]	1×10^6	Plant peroxidases, rust, bacterial metabolites	High sensitivity, not mutagenic
o-Tolidine[3]	1×10^6		(Mutagenic properties, reported carcinogenic properties)
Kastle–Meyer[2]	1×10^7	Sodium cobalt nitrate, potassium ferrilaamide, copper, nickel	High sensitivity, increased specificity
Leuco-malachite green[1]	1×10^5	Chemical oxidants	(Low sensitivity)
Luminol[1]	1×10^6	Copper salts, vegetable peroxidases	High sensitivity (Must be used in the dark)

The catalytic tests for blood are thus based upon the peroxidase mediated oxidation of a colorless compound to a colored or luminescent product catalyzed by hemoglobin.

The sensitivity of the catalytic tests used in forensic laboratories range from 1×10^5 to greater than 10^6 based on dilution of whole blood in water (see Table 21.1). These tests, however, suffer from a lack of specificity. For example, the heme prosthetic group, responsible for the catalytic activity, may also be found in cytochromes, plant peroxidases, and certain enzyme catalases. The presence of the heme group in molecules other than hemoglobin complicates the identification of blood. For this reason, most authorities consider the chemical identification of blood based upon the catalytic peroxidase-like activity of the heme group as a presumptive result. A positive result therefore indicates the presumed presence of blood but is not an absolute proof. A negative result is generally considered to indicate the absence of blood.

The catalytic blood tests are used in cases where sensitivity is needed or when screening of a large number of samples is required. The high sensitivity of these tests may be necessary where the sample size is extremely limited or when a perpetrator attempts to wash blood evidence away. Cases involving large numbers of possible bloodstains, particularly at crime scenes, are especially suited for these tests because of the ease with which a large number of stains may be processed. Positive results warrant additional tests back at the laboratory.

Crystal Tests

The catalytic blood tests, though extremely sensitive, lack the specificity forensic scientists need to conclusively identify blood in both liquid and dried states. Many laboratories rely upon microcrystal tests to confirm the presence of blood. The crystal tests used for blood identification center on attempts to crystallize hemoglobin derivatives. The two most common methods are based on the preparation of either hemins (heminchloride crystals) or hemochromogens (pyridine hemochromogen crystals).

Hemin (Teichmann Crystals)

In 1853, Teichmann described the formation of crystals in blood by the addition of glacial acetic acid and halide salts with gentle heating. These crystals, called hemin (hematin halide), became the basis for the identification of blood in forensic stains. The hemin crystals produced from blood are ferriprotoporphyrin halides. The Teichmann crystals, as they became known, were regarded by some as "a sure proof of the presence of blood in the suspected stain." Although the Teichmann crystals demonstrate specificity, they are difficult to produce when the blood is collected from wood or leather, presumably because the tannins found in these materials precipitate the blood proteins. Rust was also found to inhibit crystal growth. This test is susceptible to overheating.

Hemochromogen (Takayama crystals)

The hemochromagen crystals are coordinate complexes made up of the nitrogen atom of an organic base and a ferroprotoporphyrin prosthetic group (heme). In 1912, Masaro Takayama developed a hemochromogen test using pyridine as the organic base. Since then, the Takayama crystal test has become the most popular microcrystal test used to identify blood.

The sensitivity of the Teichmann and Takayama tests are about the same, but both are far less sensitive than the catalytic tests. Because of the low sensitivity of these tests, failure to produce crystals should not be considered indicative of the absence of blood. As noted earlier, plant peroxidases and bacterial catalases contain proteins with the heme prosthetic group (ferroprotoporphyrins). In their pure state, these proteins produce crystals indistinguishable from blood; however, in their natural plant or bacterial state, the level of heme bearing proteins is far below the detection limits of the crystal tests, significantly reducing false positive reactions.

Immunological Tests

Once the presence of blood has been established, say through the Takayama microcrystal test, the identity of the species from which the blood originated will need to be determined to maintain the probative value of the stain. The most commonly used forensic method to accomplish this result has been an immunological test based on an antigen–antibody precipitation reaction. As early as 1894, scientists realized that animals injected with bacteria produced specific bacterial antibodies which could then be used to precipitate other bacteria *in vitro*. In the same way, human serum proteins injected into the body of an animal responder, usually a goat, rabbit, or sheep, will produce specific antibodies capable of binding to and precipitating other human serum proteins. Antibodies capable of precipitating serum antigens of other animal species are made in the same way.

Two methods of detecting human serum proteins have gained wide acceptance in forensic laboratories: the ring test (tube technique) and the gel diffusion technique. Both methods rely on the fact that when human serum proteins meet antihuman serum proteins, a white precipitate will form at their interface. The tube technique, as its name implies, uses a clear tube into which a layer of antihuman serum is placed followed by carefully layering the blood stain extract on top. If the correct antigenic determinants are present, a white flocculant band (precipitate) will be produced at the liquid–liquid interface. A positive result indicates the presence of human serum proteins.

The gel diffusion technique relies on the fact that liquids added to a well punched in a gel will diffuse radially outward through the pores of the semisolid gel media. In the simplest case, using two wells, one containing antihuman antibody, the other a blood extract, the soluble component will diffuse into the gel, and a visible precipitate will form where they meet between the wells. This process became known as the two dimensional double diffusion technique (Ouchterlony test). The sensitivity of this technique is reported as 1 mg antigen/dl solution.

By placing the wells containing antibody and antigen opposite each other and applying a current to the gel, the electrophoretic mobility of the proteins can be used to cause them to migrate toward each other. A visible precipitin line will form between the wells if the antibody reacts specifically with the opposing antigen. This technique, crossover immunoelectrophoresis, was developed by Culliford for species determination of blood stains in 1964.

Immunoassay Test

Recently, immunoassay methods capable of extremely high sensitivity and specificity as well as ease of use are being used in forensic laboratories as one step human blood identification tests. The immunochromatographic method uses dye-conjugated mobile antihuman hemoglobin antibodies capable of complexing with human hemoglobin antigenic determinant sites to form a colored complex, which migrates through an absorbent layer to an immobilized antibody capture site where a dye-colored band appears.[4] The sensitivity of the test has been reported to be as low as 1×10^7 (whole blood diluted with Tris buffer),[5] which is superior to most of the presumptive catalytic tests. The test is primate specific with one reported exception, the domestic ferret.

Blood Stain Pattern Interpretation

Blood is the most frequently encountered type of biological evidence at the scene of a violent crime. The evidential impact of the blood evidence is demonstrated by its unique ability to link a suspect to a victim or a crime scene and to assist in reconstruction of the events of the crime. Linking is accomplished through genetic marker analysis (DNA), whereas crime scene reconstruction involves analysis of the physical properties of blood, the forces associated with the generating mechanism of the blood stains, and how they relate to environmental influences at the crime scene.

Through the analysis of blood stain patterns, the following may be established:

- Information relating to the point of origin of the bloodstains
- Minimum number of impacts needed to produce specific blood patterns
- Relative position of the victim or perpetrators at the time of the bloodshed
- Mechanism which generated the blood stains
- Movement of the victim or perpetrator after the bloodshed stops

This can be accomplished by observing the pattern of distribution, the location, general appearance, size, shape, quantity, and physical state of the blood stains. After all, blood stain evidence is the "static aftermath" of a dynamic event.[6]

Table 21.2   Generating Mechanisms for Blood Stain Patterns

Blood Stain or Distribution Patterns	Generating Mechanism
Blood droplet stains, random pattern	• Naturally occurring air-borne droplets affected by gravity
Blood droplet stains, linear pattern	• Air-borne droplets affected by gravity from an object moving in a linear fashion • Air-borne droplets propelled by an object moving in an arc or from an object undergoing a rapid change
Radial spatter pattern of blood	• Impact with blood or a bloody surface
Blood pools	• Excessive bleeding from a stationary open wound
Contact stains	• Stationary surface in contact with a bloody object
Smear (swipe/wipe) stains	• Stationary surface in contact with a moving bloody surface • Moving surface in contact with a moving or stationary bloody surface
Spurts	• Arterial bleeding

Blood stain patterns are the result of various generating mechanisms (see Table 21.2). Once outside the body, blood will behave in a predictable manner since shed blood has relatively uniform physical properties (density, surface tension, and viscosity) and follows the laws of physics. Although interpretation of blood stain patterns is more complex than a single blood stain, the same of analytical methods can be applied to more than one stain. A more precise estimate of the point of origin and generating mechanism can be obtained when information is gathered from numerous stains within the overall blood stain pattern.

Identification of Semen and Saliva

Semen

In cases of sexual assault, the identification of seminal material on physical evidence may assist the courts in rendering a verdict. Semen is composed of cellular material and seminal plasma. The latter functions as the transport medium for the male germ cells (spermatozoa). Fluids from the vas deferens, distal caudal epididymis, seminal vesicles, prostate gland, and bulbo urethral gland make up a major portion of the seminal plasma. The principal cells, spermatozoa, are found in great abundance in the normal neat ejaculate (60–100 million per ml).[7] Some physical limitations of the male suspect (i.e., oligospermia and aspermia) or a vasectomy could significantly reduce or eliminate spermatozoa from the seminal fluid.

Seminal material must first be located on the piece of physical evidence before any test for its absolute presence can be performed. Stains will appear crusty and off-white to yellow on nonabsorbent surfaces and will produce a stiff, starch-like appearance on absorbent fabrics. These stains may be difficult to detect with the naked eye on absorbent surfaces.

Semen stains often give a weak bluish-white fluorescence under ultraviolet light. This fluorescence is thought to be due to flavins, produced as a byproduct of the bacterium

Pseudomonas fluorescens.[8] This is not a test for semen because many other stains also fluoresce under ultraviolet light. However, this is an excellent method of screening large areas (i.e., bedsheets) or multiple items of clothing for the presence of stains.

Locating and determining which stains to perform microscopic analysis on is difficult on large items or on items displaying numerous stains (i.e., sheets, blankets). In addition to the ultraviolet light, quick presumptive screening tests can be performed on these stains to characterize positive semen stains and eliminate negative stains. Chemical and microcrystalline techniques have been developed to identify various components of the seminal plasma.

Acid Phosphatase Test

A high level of acid phosphatase activity was detected in seminal plasma as early as 1935. Acid phosphatase is a glycoprotein synthesized in secretory epithelial cells of the prostate gland and secreted into the seminal plasma. Studies by Sensabaugh demonstrated that acid phosphatase, though identified in other body fluids, is found at levels up to 900 times greater than in semen-free vaginal fluids.[9] The acid phosphatase test is the best known, most widely used chemical test for presumptive semen identification and is based on the enzymatic properties of this glycoprotein. A sample of the stain is treated with α naphthyl phosphate. Acid phosphatase cleaves the phosphate to produce α naphthol. The addition of Diazo Red RC salt will form an insoluble scarlet red precipitate in less than 10 seconds. A rapid, strong positive reaction is indicative of a semen stain.

Microcrystalline Test

Microcrystalline tests capable of detecting choline (Florence test) and spermine (Barberio test) were developed as a means of presumptively identifying semen stains. Neither test is specific for semen; however, positive results are a strong indication that seminal plasma is present.

Immunoassay Test

The microscopic identification of spermatozoa conclusively identifies seminal material, which may be present as a result of a sexual assault. In some instances, seminal material may be present; however, spermatozoa may be absent. These occurrences may be the result of a vasectomy or other physical condition which results in azoospermia. It is therefore necessary to identify a seminal component unique to semen.

Prostate specific antigen (p30 or PSA), a glycoprotein produced in the prostate, was identified by Sensabaugh in 1978. The protein has a molecular weight of 30,000 Da and was named p30.[10] Vasectomized males continue to secrete prostate specific antigen into seminal plasma. PSA is also found in blood serum and male urine. The level of PSA found in semen is approximately 200–5,500 μg/ml;[11] male blood serum was found to contain approximately 2.6 ng/ml, and male urine contained an average of 0.26 μg/ml.[12] PSA has not been found in females.

PSA can also be detected by using the Ouchterlony double diffusion, crossover electrophoresis, and ELISA methods. These methods suffer from low sensitivity or are time consuming. Immunoassay methods capable of extremely high sensitivity and specificity as well as ease of use are used in forensic laboratories as one step human semen identification tests. The method is immunochromatographic and uses a dye-conjugated antihuman p30 antibody capable of complexing with human p30 antigenic determinant sites to form a colored complex that migrates through an absorbent layer to an immobilized antibody capture site where a dye-colored band appears. The sensitivity of the tests has been reported to be as low as 1×10^6 (semen diluted in water) and requires 10 minutes to complete. The immunochromatographic method is as sensitive as the ELISA technique but is significantly less time consuming and labor intensive.

Microscopic Analysis

Spermatozoa, typically 50–60 μm in length, consist of a head, neck, midpiece, and cilia-like tail. The head is made up of the acrosome and nucleus, and measures approximately 2.6 μm in width, 4.6 μm in length, and 1.5 μm in thickness. When viewing spermatozoa under a microscope, the profile of the head is often described as porpoise-like. Microscopic examination of spermatozoa is carried out at a magnification range of 400× to 440×.

Finding spermatozoa in a stain through microscopic examination constitutes absolute proof of the presence of semen. The technique of microscopic identification of spermatozoa consists of (1) sample collection, (2) separation of spermatozoa from the substrate, (3) concentration through filtration or centrifugation, (4) contrast enhancement through histological staining using brightfield microscopy or phase contrast microscopy.

Biological stains have an affinity for specific structures that have different chemical compositions. The two most commonly used stains for the microscopic identification of spermatozoa are the Harris Hematoxylin–Eosin combination stain and the Nuclear Fast Red Picoindigocarmine stain (christmas tree stain). Structural members of the spermatozoa (i.e., acrosome, midpiece, tail) will be stained in different colors or shades of color, which enhances the contrast and facilitates sperm recognition.

Phase contrast microscopy is based on the theory that light passing through a specimen with a higher refractive index than the medium will result in diffracted light (specimen) contrasted against a background of undiffracted light (medium). Transparent structures, like spermatozoa or epithelial cells, with refractive indices different from the suspension medium, usually water or 0.1 N HCl, will be significantly contrasted making them to be easily detected. Unlike brightfield microscopy with histological stains, phase contrast microscopy requires no fixing of the sperm heads to the slide, heads can be rotated 360° allowing visualization of the profile, reduced eyestrain, and the enhanced contrast improves morphological imaging of the acrosome.

Saliva

Saliva is a complex, multicomponent fluid secreted from three pairs of salivary glands around the mouth (submaxillary, sublingual, and parotid). Adults secrete approximately 1–2 l of saliva per day. Of all the components which could be used to identify saliva, α-amylase is considered by most laboratories to be the best and therefore most extensively used. Amylase is an enzyme involved in the digestion of starch in the gastrointestinal tract.[13,14]

The α-amylase test is based on the enzymatic properties of this enzyme. A sample stain is allowed to react in a solution containing a cross-linked insoluble starch that is covalently bonded to a dye. In the presence of α-amylase, the insoluble starch/dye complex is hydrolyzed to soluble fragments containing the dye, and the resulting solution takes on the color of the dye. The test is both qualitative (specific for amylase activity) and quantitative. The optical density of the solution is a function of the level of α-amylase present in the stain.

Although the α-amylase test is specific for amylase, it is not entirely specific for saliva since amylase is found in other physiological fluids, including urine, blood plasma, semen, sweat, and tears.[15] The average level of amylase found in saliva is significantly higher than levels normally encountered in other physiological fluids. Amylase may also be found in high levels in feces, due to pancreatic secretions. Fecal stains are, however, easily recognized and should not be tested. In the absence of contamination with feces, an elevated level of amylase is a good indicator of saliva.

References

1. Grodsky, M., Wright, K., and Kirk, P., Simplified preliminary blood testing. An improved technique and comparative study of methods, *J. Crim. Law Criminol. Police Sci.*, 1951, 42.

2. Cox, M., A study of the sensitivity and specificity of four presumptive tests for blood, *J. For. Sci.*, 1991, 36(5).

3. Hunt, A.C., Corby, C., Dodd, B.E., and Camps, F.E., The identification of human blood stains. A critical survey, *J. For. Med.*, 1960, 7.

4. Product Literature. Abacus Diagnostics, Inc., West Hills, CA, ABAcard HemaTrace for the Forensic Identification of Blood, 1999.

5. Hochmeister, M., Budowle, B., Sparkes, R., Rudin, O., Gehrig, C., Thali, M., Schmidt, L., Cordier, A., and Dirnhofer, R., Validation studies of an immunochromatographic 1-step test for the forensic identification of human blood, *J. For. Sci.*, 1999, 33(3).

6. MacDonell, H., *Bloodstain patterns*, Laboratory of Forensic Science, Corning, NY, 1997.

7. Hafez, E.S.E., *Human semen and fertility regulation in men*, The C.V. Mosby Co., St. Louis, MO, 1976.

8. Gaensslen, R., The identification of semen, *Sourcebook in Forensic Serology, Immunology, and Biochemistry*, U.S. Department of Justice Publication, 1983.

9. Sensabaugh, G.F., The quantitative acid phosphatase test. A statistical analysis of endogenous and post coital AP levels in the vagina, *J. For. Sci.*, 1979, 24.

10. Sensabaugh, G.F., Isolation and characterization of a semen-specific protein for human seminal plasma: A potential new marker for semen identification, *J. For. Sci.*, 1978, 23.

11. Product Literature, Abacus Diagnostics, Inc., West Hills, CA, One step ABAcard p30 test for the forensic identification of semen, 1998.

12. Wang, M.C., Prostate antigen: A new potential marker for prostatic cancer, *The Prostate*, 1981, 2.

13. Willott, G.M., An improved test for the detection of salivary amylase in stains, *J. For. Sci. Soc.*, 1974, 14.

14. Baxter, S.J. and Rees, B., The identification of saliva, stains in forensic casework, *Med. Sci. Law*, 1975, 15(1).

15. Gaensslen, R.F., The identification of saliva, *Sourcebook in Forensic Serology, Immunology, and Biochemistry*, U.S. Department of Justice Publication, 1983.

DNA Analysis

22

VICTOR W. WEEDN

DNA testing is the most significant advance in forensic science in the century since fingerprints were first applied to the solution of crimes. Like fingerprints, DNA is a trace evidence deposit that, for practical purposes, positively identifies its source. The growth of the FBI's DNA effort is emblematic of the larger forensic DNA community — a team of six FBI analysts and technicians started the FBI's DNA section in 1988, and testing took six weeks; today, there are 100 scientists on the FBI's DNA team, and technology has shortened testing to as little as 24 hour. DNA testing has, in fact, heralded sweeping changes in forensic laboratories and within criminal justice and the law itself.

Historical Backdrop

In 1868, Friedrich Miescher discovered DNA when he detected an acidic phosphorus-containing substance from the nuclei of pus cells from surgical bandages that he named "nuclein."[1] In 1943, Oswald Avery, Colin MacLeod, and Maclyn McCarty demonstrated that DNA carried the genetic information that permitted the transformation of one form of pneumococcus to another. In 1952, Alfred Hershey and Martha Chase further demonstrated with radiotracer experiments that viruses replicate by injection of DNA into host cells. In 1953, James Watson, Francis Crick, and Rosalind Wilkins elucidated the structure of DNA using x-ray diffraction data, and postulated the mechanism by which genetic information may be passed on to the next generation. Molecular biologic techniques continued to improve, particularly after the introduction of recombinant DNA techniques in the mid-1970s. In 1985, Sir Alec Jeffreys published an article in *Nature* that is generally credited with the introduction of forensic DNA typing.[2,3]

Over the two decades since the advent of forensic DNA typing technology, the technology, methodology, instrumentation, and enzymatic reagents have evolved rapidly since and continues to progress. Restriction Fragment Length Polymorphism (RFLP) analysis dominated forensic typing in crime laboratories until the mid-1990s, when Polymerase Chain Reaction (PCR)-based testing replaced it as the dominant technology. PCR is a sample preparation method that harnesses cellular reproductive machinery to make copies of lengths of target DNA. The result is that with a large amount of high-quality target

DNA, testing can be sensitive, robust, automated, inexpensive, and rapid. Today, DNA typing is routinely performed worldwide using PCR-based STR testing (described later), with other genetic systems used adjunctively.

The importance of DNA to the modern criminal justice system can be seen in the policy arena. In 1998, the then Attorney General Janet Reno created a National Commission on the Future of DNA Evidence,[4,5] and on March 11, 2003, the current Attorney General John Ashcroft announced President Bush's "DNA Initiative" that called for over $1 billion over five years to further increase DNA testing in United States forensic science laboratories.[6] This has so dominated forensic science that all other non-DNA funding was zeroed out in the administration's budget proposed for the National Institute of Justice (NIJ).

What Is DNA?

DNA is the chemical *deoxyribonucleic acid*, which stores the genetic code of the human body — the hereditary blueprint imparted to us by our parents.

A bacterial cell, which is generally between 1 and 3 μm in length, may contain a DNA molecule that is 1000 times longer than its length. A human cell contains roughly 1000 times more DNA than a bacterial cell. If the DNA in a single human diploid cell were stretched out and laid end-to-end, it would measure more than 6 feet. The DNA (except mitochondrial DNA) is instead tightly coiled, supercoiled, and packed into 23 pairs of chromosomes (44 autosomes and the X and Y sex chromosomes) in the nucleus. This DNA weighs approximately 5–6 pg–five trillionth (10^{-12}) of a gram.

DNA has a ladder-like structure in which the sides are composed of a sugar phosphate scaffold, and the rungs are composed of pairs of nucleotides. There are four nucleotides in DNA: adenine (A), guanine (G), cytosine (C), and thymine (T). "As" are paired with "Ts" and "Cs" are paired with "Gs." The genetic information is present in the sequence of As, Gs, Cs, and Ts, similar to our use of the alphabet to form words, sentences, and paragraphs. Other chemical tests are basically "analog" as they generally depend upon mass equilibrium reactions, but DNA tests are "digital" in the sense that the biochemical tests result from the sequence of bases. This distinction is a key to the quality of information we obtain from DNA tests.

The ladder-like structure, known as double-stranded DNA (ds-DNA), can be split through the rungs to form two half-ladder-like structures, known as single-stranded DNA (ss-DNA) — a process known as "denaturation." Each ss-DNA strand has the complementary sequence to the other, for example, A–G–A–G–A is the complement of T–C–T–C–T.

The central dogma of biology is that DNA is replicated to create new generations of life, and it is transcribed into RNA and then translated into proteins. The stretches of DNA sequence that code for proteins are called *genes*. Sets of three nucleotide bases form "codons" that code for the amino acids that form the subunits of proteins — the so-called "genetic code." Proteins form the machinery of cells and may act as structural elements, as receptor and transport functions, or as "enzymes" that work on other molecules. An individual may inherit a given form of protein or another. The particular sequence corresponding to the protein type is known as an "allele." Because our DNA contains pairs of chromosomes, we inherit two alleles — one from our mother and one from our father.

There are three billion nucleotide base pairs that encode somewhere between 30,000 and 50,000 genes in each set of chromosomes. If each base was a letter, then human DNA in a cell at the tip of a pin contains the equivalent of 20 sets of Encyclopedia Britannica (44M words, 300M characters, and 2K illustrations).

Only a small fraction, between 2 and 3% of the DNA codes for proteins and the rest has been termed *junk DNA* by molecular biologists, because they were unable to ascribe any function to it. Of this noncoding DNA, approximately 70% is repetitive DNA. Most forensic DNA tests employ noncoding repetitive DNA. DNA that codes for genes is more highly conserved than the more variable noncoding regions because mutations in coding regions are often lethal. Specifically, forensic scientists look for the differences among individuals in the DNA known as "polymorphisms." Individual polymorphisms are most common as single nucleotide polymorphisms (SNPs), but differences in repeats of repetitive DNA sequences are also common. The human DNA sequence is 98–99% the same as that of a chimpanzee,[7] and there is even substantial homology between the gene sequences of worms and man. Differences among individuals of the *Homo sapien* species are on the order of 1 in a 1000 base pairs.

Thus, despite conservation of the genetic code among us, there is still tremendous individualizing information among the six billion base pairs of the human genome, but forensic scientists test only a very small fraction of the information in the genome.

Biological Evidence

Serological testing was the forerunner to current DNA tests, but was possible only upon certain biologic specimens (e.g., blood, saliva) and with sufficient quantity and state of preservation. Current DNA testing fulfills the promise of permitting identification of a perpetrator from virtually any biological specimen, even when present in trace amounts invisible to the eye, and even after prolonged environmental exposure. Saliva, skin cells, bone, teeth, tissue, urine, feces, and a host of other biological specimens, which may be found at crime scenes, are also sources of DNA. Saliva of a perpetrator may be found in chewing gum and on cigarette butts, envelope seals, and possibly drinking cups. Fingernail scrapings from a victim may reveal a perpetrator's DNA profile. Blood may be found on the broken glass of a window. DNA testing of urine may be used to establish whether an individual is, in fact, the source of the urine specimen, indicating drug use.

Forensic evidence usually links an object to a scene, but eyewitnesses, confessions, finger prints, and DNA provide evidence of identification. Clearly, other identifying biologic features exist such as dentition and ear morphology. Biologic variation is the basis for individuating characteristics. Facial features and fingerprints result from both genetic and environmental influence, but DNA testing is purely genetic and is not subject to environmental influence, save exceptional occurrences such as blood stain from an individual with a recent blood transfusion.

Because the DNA molecule is long lived, it is likely to be detectable for many years in bones or body fluid stains from older criminal cases in which questions of identity remain unresolved. The result is that DNA testing applies to a vastly wider array of specimens than conventional testing and is much more powerful in analyzing biological evidence than any previous technology. The longevity of the DNA molecule means its power extends to the present, future, and to the past. Specimens that are years or even decades old — dating to the time when DNA testing technology was not yet available — can be tested, resulting in overturned convictions and release of the innocent.

DNA is useful as an identity marker because: (1) it is different in every person (except identical twins), (2) does not change with time (except for the rare mutation), (3) it exists in all cells (except mature red blood cells), and (4) it is the same in all cells (except in eggs and sperm, where it is at half complement).

Biological evidence can be commonly found at crime scenes. Blood evidence was revealed in one study to be found in 60% of murders and in a similar percentage of assaults and batteries.[8] Hair was found at the scene of 10% of robberies and 6% of residential burglaries. However, despite the abundance of biological evidence that can be found at crime scenes and subjected to DNA testing, little of this evidence is recovered from crime scenes, less is submitted to crime laboratories, and still less is analyzed.

Rapes/Sexual Assaults

In the United States, DNA testing has been conducted on vaginal swabs and semen stains from sexual assaults cases. However, in the United States, less than half of rapes are investigated by the police, specimens are submitted to the crime laboratories in less than a third of these cases, and the crime laboratories do not process all specimens submitted; thus, in <10% of the 250,000 rape cases per year is the recovered DNA tested. Many rape kits remain on shelves unprocessed because crime laboratories have not had the resources to work on them. In 2003, the NIJ reported an estimated rape kit backlog of 350,000 in the United States. Significant amounts of funds were made available to crime laboratories to address the backlog through funding outsourcing, infrastructure, and in-house casework processing. The proposed President Bush's DNA Initiative ($1B/5 year) includes $76M for state casework backlogs, $90M to strengthen the capacity of crime laboratories, and $10M for improving DNA technology.[4]

Other Crimes

By contrast, the majority of DNA specimens typed in the United Kingdom involve burglaries, typically with blood found at sites of forced entry. The United States is beginning to follow the lead of the United Kingdom, isolated jurisdictions are focusing on crimes other than rape. However, testing in nonsexual assault cases opens the laboratories to greater work per case and to more difficulties.

Specimen Collection

Initial collection of evidence is a key link in the chain of events leading to successful testing, but it is also a vulnerable link. Specimen collection and preservation is being strengthened through more structured crime — scene teams and more formalized evidence collection procedures are being established in many jurisdictions to ensure that all potential evidence is recovered and properly preserved for testing, and especially to minimize the possibility of contamination.

Trace DNA

Recently, it has been reported that DNA could be recovered and typed from traditional fingerprint residues. This calls for sensitivity beyond normal testing techniques. This testing, termed "low copy number" (LCN) testing, may involve the typing of only a few molecules. This has permitted the DNA typing from the trigger of a gun and the handle of a knife. However, the potential to pickup spurious DNA from someone that handled or touched the surface is significant. To date, because of the contamination issues, LCN analysis has largely been used primarily for investigatory purposes.

Analytic Methods

Although DNA profiling began with a variety of methods, today, routine forensic DNA profiling is carried out in crime laboratories around the world using the same basic methodology — Short Tandem Repeats (STRs) typing based upon polymerase chain reaction (PCR). STRs have replaced older DNA tests. However, new genetic loci, new methods, and new instruments continue to be developed.

RFLP

The first widespread use of DNA tests in the criminal justice community involved Restriction Fragment Length Polymorphism (RFLP) analysis, which among individuals is based on the variation in the length of cut DNA fragments. This length variation arises from repetitive DNA sequence with Variable Number of Tandem Repeat loci (VNTR loci). Restriction enzymes are used to cut the DNA into specific fragments. The "Southern Blot technique" measures fragment sizes using radioactive isotopes exposing x-ray film, called an "autoradiogram." RFLP is informationally rich but is relatively insensitive and time consuming, taking about 6 weeks. Later, chemiluminescent and fluorescent methods replaced radioactive isotopes and permitted faster analysis. Nonetheless, RFLP testing has been supplanted by PCR-based technology which is faster, more automated, more sensitive, and produces less ambiguous results.

PCR

Virtually all currently used forensic DNA testing begins with amplifying the DNA target DNA sequence using the PCR technique. Kary Mullis won the Nobel prize for his invention of the PCR method in 1985, which has literally revolutionized the biological sciences by making DNA from cells accessible for investigation.[9] The PCR technique has proven to be a robust method that will not easily be displaced by alternative amplification systems (e.g., strand displacement assays, rolling circle technology).[10]

PCR is a method of preparing samples in which the target DNA is copied many times (amplified). PCR generates the copies of a DNA sequence, *amplicons*, in fashion analogous to a photocopier generating copies of a document. Two DNA molecules are produced from an original DNA molecule ("DNA template"); the procedure is repeated many times with a doubling of DNA fragments every time — resulting in the production of millions of amplicons. This makes PCR testing exquisitely sensitive, allowing successful testing of nanogram and even picogram quantities. However, this also means that PCR assays are sensitive to contamination. Laboratories have to be configured to separate preamplification from post-amplification areas.

PCR employs biologic machinery used by cells to reproduce. It is an iterative process in which temperature is controlled by an instrument known as a "thermal cycler." A "master mix" of DNA template, primers, polymerase, nucleotides, and buffer solution are incubated with the target DNA to produce amplicons, the amplified fragments of interest. After DNA is extracted from a specimen, in step 1 (denaturation), the DNA is melted (denatured) into two ssDNA strands by raising the temperature to a very high temperature ($\sim$94°C). In step 2 (annealing), the DNA is cooled ($\sim$54°C), allowing "primers" to attach ("hybridize" or "anneal"), which initiates the DNA replication. "Primers" are short ss-DNA fragments with a sequence complementary to a site with an invariable sequence which flanks the DNA target sequence of interest. In step 3 (extension), the temperature is raised ($\sim$72°C), and ds-DNA is generated. Cells use "polymerases" to replicate DNA. Polymerases are enzymes that insert a missing complementary nucleotide base at sites of transition between ds-DNA and ss-DNA. In PCR, the polymerase will extend the primers to generate ds-DNA. Thermostable polymerases (e.g., Taq polymerase), which can withstand high denaturation temperatures, are used in PCR assays. Since only a complement sequence is produced, a second primer is needed to attach to this complement sequence and replicates the base sequence. The process is repeated, resulting in a doubling of the DNA fragment of interest after each round of thermal cycling. In approximately 30 cycles, a million-fold amplification is achieved.

Fluorescent tags can be attached to the newly synthesized DNA fragments as they are produced. This is accomplished by the use of prelabeled primers before incorporation in the PCR master mix. A myriad of differently colored fluors can be used, permitting multiplexing of several systems simultaneously.

PCR technology was originally applied as a dot-blot technique in which the amplicons were allowed to hybridize with DNA probes bound to paper. One of the early genetic loci analyzed was the HLA DQ-alpha locus, which was useful for identification. This was commercialized and sold to the forensic community. Other systems were added and sold as the "polymarker system." These systems were based upon sequence variation. They were not powerful as identification systems, but were fast, easy, and sensitive. Mixtures were also problematic for dot-blot systems. The PCR technique was later applied to genetic systems with length polymorphisms (similar to RFLP VNTRs), the so-called amplified fragment length polymorphisms (AmpFLPs), that offered greater discriminatory power (i.e., D1S80). It became evident that smaller genetic loci were preferable for several technical reasons, eventuating in the current PCR-based STR systems. PCR is also used for Y-chromosome and mitochondrial typing.

STRs

Crime laboratories throughout the world use Short Tandem Repeat (STR) analysis as the standard method for DNA profiling.[11,12] STR loci, also called microsatellite regions, are scattered throughout the genome and have core repeats of 4 or 5 base pairs resulting in fragment sizes of approximately 100–350 base pairs. Core repeats of two or three bases yield substantial stutter, and larger core repeat regions are more susceptible to degradation and may demonstrate preferential amplification (such that shorter fragments may be amplified to the near exclusion of larger fragments).

STR testing is faster, easier, and less expensive than RFLP testing and amenable to automation. Furthermore, it is more sensitive and more resistant to sample degradation than RFLP tests. Moreover, unlike RFLP tests, it produces discrete, unambiguous results. Although less discriminating than RFLP genetic markers, STR analysis can be as discriminatorily powerful through the use of larger numbers of STR markers. The FBI convened a panel of forensic scientists in 1998 that chose a panel of 13 STR loci for use in the National DNA Index System (NDIS). This set of "13 Core loci" have become commercially available (through Applied Biosystems and Promega) and the basis for most forensic laboratories around the world. The commercial kits will often add a couple of addition loci as well. These commercial STR kits will typically yield discriminatory values of one in trillions to quadrillions.

STRs were first used in forensic casework during the first Persian Gulf War in 1991 for victim identification, but then applied to criminal cases by the Forensic Science Service in the United Kingdom in 1995. They were not widely adopted in the United States until the late 1990s.

Amelogenin

Amelogenin is a genetic locus used in the determination of gender. It is a gene that is located on the sex chromosomes in the region that is not shared between the X and Y chromosomes. The Amelogenin locus is six base pairs longer in the Y-chromosome than in the X-chromosome. Thus, males will have two differently sized fragments, whereas females will have only a single band of twice the height. The Amelogenin marker is incorporated in the commercial STR kits along with the 13 core loci.

Y-STRs

Y-chromosome markers are not gender markers, but rather are STRs found only in the male Y-chromosome. Thus, the DNA of a rapist can be directly typed from a vaginal swab without concern for the presence of the admixed female DNA. However, precisely because the Y-markers are inherited together, unlike STRs, individual allele frequencies cannot be multiplied together to obtain huge statistical inferences. Rather, the set of marker results form a "haplotype," and the number of times that such a haplotype is observed in the population constitutes its discriminatory power.

mtDNA

Approximately 99% of the DNA in a human cell is found in the chromosomes of the nucleus. On the other hand, mitochondrial DNA (mtDNA) is found in the mitochondria in the cytoplasm of the cell.[13,14] It neither participates in the sexual reproduction of the sperm and egg nor in the nuclear division cycles. Instead, mitochondrial DNA is passed directly from the mother to the offspring without any recombination events as in the nucleus. The mtDNA from the spermatozoa are destroyed by the enzyme *ubiquitin* in the egg. Thus, children will share exactly the same mtDNA sequence as their maternal grandmother. Because there may be hundreds to thousands of mitochondria per cell, there are hundreds to thousands of copies of mtDNA per cell — unlike nuclear DNA for which there will generally be only one copy per cell.

In humans, the DNA particle is a small circular DNA loop of 16,569 base pairs.[15] Forensic scientists typically sequence the DNA from only approximately 1,000 bases of the two hypervariable noncoding regions within the "displacement loop" (D-loop) or "control region," although polymorphisms outside the control region exist and are also useful. The mitochondrial DNA sequence is compared to the "revised Cambridge reference sequence." Similar to Y-chromosome markers, mtDNA polymorphisms are inherited as a haplotype set, the so-called "mitotype." Thus, mtDNA statistics involve counting of similar genotypes in a large database to derive a frequency statistic. Most mitotypes will have a rare haplotype frequency on the order of one in hundreds, but mitotypes with a significant presence in the population are not uncommon.

The normal state of mitochondria is one of homoplasmy, in which all the mtDNA has the same sequence. However, due to mutational events or otherwise, a state of heteroplasmy in which more than one MtDNA sequence is present in the same tissue or person may exist.[16] High-level heteroplasmy must generally be of the order of 30% of the mtDNA sequence before it is generally reported. Heteroplasmy appears to be somewhat tissue specific, so that it is not uniform throughout the body. Heteroplasmy may be lost rapidly in family lineages, because of the bottleneck phenomenon that occurs during reproduction from a single fertilized egg. Due to heteroplasmy, a single mismatch is not a basis for exclusion, and two mismatches may be an issue.

Because mtDNA testing is expensive, labor intensive, relatively slow, and highly sensitive to contamination, it is performed by only a few specialized laboratories, but state laboratories are beginning to implement this testing. A dot-blot technology has recently been commercialized, which will make screening mtDNA more accessible to most laboratories.

Mitochondrial DNA is used for testing shed hairs, which have essentially no nuclear DNA and bones from skeletal remains in which the DNA is severely degraded and because of the abundance of mtDNA is more likely to be recovered. Also, mtDNA may become important when only a distant relative is available for a reference specimen.

New Techniques

Other genetic loci are being investigated, including SNPs for specimens with degraded DNA and phenotypic markers (e.g., hair, eye, skin color) for investigatory purposes.[17] Also, new instrument platforms and technologies are being developed for forensic profiling purposes, such as mass spectrometers and microchips.

Databases

DNA databanking began in Virginia when it enacted authorizing legislation in 1989. The first Virginia "hit" came in 1993 when they had approximately 1300 specimens archived; they had their 1000th hit in 2002 when they had approximately 190,000 specimens archived. Now, all 50 states collect DNA specimens from certain convicted offenders. The databases are expanding to include all felons. Most include certain misdemeanor offenses of a sexual nature, but there is a push to include property crimes such as burglaries. Recently, the States of Virginia, Lousiana, and Texas authorized the collection of DNA specimens from mere arrested suspects.

The software that is used to match specimens locally or across jurisdictional borders is called "CODIS" (COmbined DNA Index System).[18,19] States have CODIS programs that are responsible for collecting, storing, DNA typing, and databasing test results. The National DNA Index System (NDIS) is the FBI network that permits information sharing. DNA profiles are matched, and then the involved local laboratories contact one another to discuss the specifics of the cases; the FBI does not see names or other case specifics.

Computerized searching converts crime laboratories into investigatory agencies. In crimes without suspects, evidentiary testing can do little more than link crimes together and is of little use in solving them without databases against which to compare results. In the same way that fingerprint registries and then automated fingerprint identification systems each dramatically enhanced the utility of fingerprint evidence, the development of DNA databases and CODIS software empower crime laboratories. In the United Kingdom, the chance of matching biologic evidence from a scene to an entry in their national database is approximately 50%. It is claimed that laboratory analysis is more cost effective than traditional police investigations in solving crimes.

DNA samples have been collected from more than 1.6 million criminals; each month, between 10,000 and 40,000 new samples are added across the nation. Databases include more than 80,000 DNA samples gathered from unsolved crime scenes. At the time of writing this in 2004, convicted offender databases have helped authorities identify suspects in more than 11,000 cases. Biologic evidence from more than 8000 unsolved cases has been matched to past or current convicts in the database and an additional 3000 samples have been matched to unidentified suspects in other cases that remain unsolved.

Field Testing

It is now possible to use portable DNA testing at the crime scene.[20] Suspects, witnesses, and physical evidence may disappear within a short time of the commission of a crime. Thus, immediate testing of biologic specimens may assist investigators to focus their efforts and enhance their effectiveness during this early and important period. DNA testing may help with scene reconstruction, by determining whether the bloodstain is from the victim or from someone else. The primary role of preliminary analysis in the field would be to eliminate certain individuals as suspects. On the other hand, an immediate CODIS comparison might point suspicion to a certain individual. This is particularly important when the States of Virginia, Texas, and Louisana have legislation authorization for collection of DNA from suspects. DNA specimens can be taken from individuals noninvasively by simply swabbing the inside of the cheek. It would be wise to confirm testing in the controlled environment of the laboratory.

QA/Accreditation

Forensic DNA testing is performed according to validated protocols and with substantial scientific literature support. All testing requires a technical and an administrative review. Forensic analysts must be trained and experienced to perform testing and should be competency tested. Some forensic scientists are voluntarily certified by the American Board of Criminalists (ABC);[21] ABC requires proficiency testing to maintain certification. Most laboratories are voluntarily accredited by the American Society of Crime Laboratory Directors/Laboratory Accreditation Board (ASCLD/LAB)[22] or by Forensic Quality Services (FQS).[23] Proficiency testing and laboratory audits are mandated by these accrediting organizations. The FBI has been regulating DNA operations since the 1994 legislation that gives them an oversight of laboratories participating in the NDIS; the FBI requires accreditation and conducts laboratory audits. The original FBI standards were developed by a DNA Advisory Board (DAB), but standard revisions have subsequently been made through their Scientific Working Group on DNA Analysis Methods (SWGDAM). Requirements and audits in the forensic community are rigorous. Of course, all forensic testing is also subject to judicial scrutiny.

Legal Challenges

The introduction of forensic DNA testing in courts resulted in such vitriolic debates that the early days of forensic DNA typing are referred to as the days of the "DNA wars." However, the underlying scientific basis of forensic DNA typing has never been successfully challenged. Advances in knowledge, methods, and technology have helped forensic DNA testing to overcome early objections. For instance, STRs permit discrete allele calling, and thus issues of measurement imprecision and "binning" inherent in RFLP tests have been obviated. Thus, despite early controversies and defense challenges, the admissibility of DNA test results in the courtroom has become routine. Questions of validity and reliability of forensic DNA test methods have essentially been addressed for most testing; however, there are new techniques and methods that will be scrutinized and challenged.

Forensic DNA identity tests did not receive significant legal challenge until the 1989 New York case of *People v. Castro* that resulted in a qualified success for the defense [afterwards the defendant admitted guilt].[27] By the 1995 O.J. Simpson trial, defense challenges to routine DNA tests had lost momentum. Despite O.J.'s "Dream Team" defense, admissibility of DNA was not challenged, but instead merely the weight of the evidence was challenged — largely on the theory police investigators had intentionally planted Mr. Simpson's blood. In 1998, testing of Monica Lewinsky's blue dress stain was not challenged at all by President Bill Clinton.

The most intense debates involved the statistical interpretation of test results rather than the test method. Resolution came from focused investigations by prominent population geneticists and statisticians and particularly with the publication of the first and second National Research Council (NRC I & II) publications that focused on statistical interpretation of forensic DNA testing.[28,29]

Today, most challenges involve adequacy of specimen collection and subsequent handling and preservation. Newer DNA methodologies and techniques will, of course, be exposed to increased scrutiny.

References

1. Lagerkvist, U., *DNA Pioneers and Their Legacy*, Yale University Press, New Haven, CT, 1998.
2. Jeffreys, A.J., Wilson, V., and Thein, S.L., Hypervariable "Minisatellite" regions in human DNA, *Nature*, 314: 67–73, 1985.

3. Jeffreys, A.J., Wilson, V., and Thein, S.L., Individual specific "fingerprints" of human DNA, *Nature*, 316: 76–9, 1985.

4. http://www.ojp.usdoj.gov/nij/topics/forensics/dna/commission/welcome.html

5. Reilly, P., Legal and public policy issues in DNA forensics, *Nature Reviews Genetics* 2(4): 313–17, 2001.

6. http://www.dna.gov/info/about.html

7. The Chimpanzee Sequencing and Analysis Consortium, Initial sequence of the chimpanzee genome and comparison with the human genome. *Nature* 437: 69–87, 2005.

8. Weedn, V.W. and Hicks, J., The Unrealized Potential of DNA testing, *Research in Action*, NIJ, Washington, DC, 1998.

9. http://nobelprize.org/chemistry/laureates/1993/mullis-lecture.html

10. McPherson, M.J. and Moller, S.G., *PCR: The Basics*, 2nd ed., Routledge, Taylor & Francis Group, Oxford, UK, 2005.

11. Butler, J.M. and Reeder, D.J., Short Tandem Repeat DNA Internet Database, NIST, http://www.cstl.nist.gov/div831/strbase/

12. Butler, J.M., *Forensic DNA Typing: Biology, Technology, and Genetics of STR markers*, 2nd ed., Elsevier Academic Press, London, UK, 2005.

13. Holland, M.M. and Parson, T.J., Mitochondrial DNA sequence analysis: Validation and use for forensic casework, 1999, *Forensic Science Review* 11: 25–51, 1999.

14. http://www.mitotyping.com/59859292811581/site/default.asp?5985Nav=|&NodeID=22

15. http://www.mitomap.org/

16. Melton, T., Mitochondrial DNA Heteroplasmy, *Forensic Science Review* 16: 1–20, 2004.

17. http://www.dnaprint.com/welcome/science/

18. http://www.fbi.gov/hq/lab/codis/index1.htm

19. http://www.fbi.gov/congress/congress01/dwight061201.htm

20. http://news.bbc.co.uk/1/hi/england/4545105.stm

21. http://www.criminalistics.com/

22. http://www.ascld-lab.org/

23. http://www.forquality.org/

24. http://www.fbi.gov/hq/lab/codis/forensic.htm

25. http://www.cstl.nist.gov/div831/strbase/dabqas.htm

26. Adams, D.E. and Lothridge, K., Scientific Working Groups, Forensic Science Communications, 2(3), 2000: http://www.fbi.gov/hq/lab/fsc/backissu/july2000/swgroups.htm

27. People v. Castro, 144 Misc. 2d 956, 545 N.Y.S.2d 985 (N.Y. Sup. Ct. 1989).

28. National Research Council, *DNA Technology in Forensic Science*, National Academy Press, Washington, DC, 1992.

29. National Research Council, *The Evaluation of Forensic DNA Evidence*, National Academy Press, Washington, DC, 1996.

The Science of Forensic Entomology

23

NEAL H. HASKELL

Forensic Entomology as a Concept

Entomologists who regularly testify can properly be termed "forensic entomologists," but, in fact, the term is largely reserved for those who primarily testify in criminal cases. These entomologists who are experts specializing in insects which get attracted to dead animals (carrion insects) must conduct the analysis related to cases when dead humans are found. Although it is true that there are basic and underlying general principles in all of entomology, these specific areas of entomology involve specific insects unique to that discipline. These specific insects require years of study, research, and experience to understand their behaviors, life cycles, growth, and their development. Furthermore, literally, life and death may hang in the balance. Therefore, only those individuals who are fully trained, educated, and possess a wealth of research knowledge and experience spread over years of studying carrion insects should take on this significant responsibility. It is no more correct to think that an economic entomologist, who studies corn or soybean insects, is qualified to conduct analysis and draw conclusions on insects that will be attracted to dead decomposing human remains than to think a dermatologist is qualified to conduct hip surgery. This procedure would require the expertise of an orthopedic surgeon, not a general practitioner.

Understanding the differences among these unique areas of entomology is imperative when calling upon the "entomologist" to appear in court to give an opinion. This is because they all come under the "umbrella" term "forensic entomologist," and to the lay person (even a judge or soliciting attorney), any entomologist may appear to have the knowledge necessary to offer an opinion in whatever case they are called upon. This simplified concept is far from the truth. The different areas and disciplines in entomology are unique within their areas (the specific experts). The courts, the judges, and the criminal justice system in general, must be aware of these differences in the field of entomology and strive to maintain the high level of expert integrity so necessary when the experts are involved in criminal murder cases where entomological evidence is present.

Historical Perspective of Forensic Entomology

The first documentation of the use of insects goes back even further by nearly half a millennia to 13th century China. The *Hsi Duan Yu* ("The Washing Away of Wrongs") is a fascinating collection of observations and anecdotal accounts regarding death, decomposition, and the processes by which human remains are subjected to when found in different environments; the author records century old observations which today are still in use by forensic scientists in drawing conclusions regarding circumstances of death (McKnight, 1981). One case in particular is of interest here:

> A local peasant from a Chinese village was found murdered, hacked to death by a hand sickle. The use of a sickle, a tool used by peasants to cut the rice at harvest time, suggested that another local peasant worker had committed the murder. The local magistrate began the investigation by calling all the local peasants who could be suspects into the village square. Each was to carry their hand sickles to the town square with them. Once assembled, the magistrate ordered the ten-or-so suspects to place their hand sickles on the ground in front of them and then step back a few yards. The afternoon sun was warm and as the villagers, suspects, and the magistrate waited, bright shiny metallic green flies began to buzz around them in the village square. The shiny metallic colored flies then began to focus in on one of the hand sickles lying on the ground. Within just a few minutes many had landed on the hand sickle and were crawling over in with interest. None of the other hand sickles had attracted any of these pretty flies. The owner of the tool became very nervous, and it was only a few more moments before all those in the village knew who the murderer was. With head hung in shame and pleading for mercy, the magistrate led the murderer away. The witnesses of the murder were the brightly metallic colored flies known as the blow flies which had been attracted to remaining bits of soft tissue, blood, bone and hair which had stuck to the hand sickle after the murder was committed. The knowledge of the village magistrate as to a specific insect group's behavior regarding their attraction to dead human tissue was the key to solving this violent act and justice was served in ancient China.

In the 17th century, Francesco Redi conducted early and particularly famous experiments to test the theory of spontaneous generation in which it was thought that maggots were *borne de novo* from rotten meats (Redi, 1668). He exposed meats directly to the open air and covered other containers of meats with cloth. The cloth prevented flies from laying their eggs, and he disproved the theory of spontaneous generation.

In the mid-19th century, French investigators applied their knowledge of a beetle's life cycle to clear current owners of a house where a dead infant was found behind a chimney. The time interval involved suggested, instead, that it had to be the previous owners who would have had information about the dead child. When the previous owners were contacted, they stated that they had delivered a child, but it had died of natural causes a few weeks after birth. They feared the police, and so they attempted to hide the dead child by wrapping it and placing it behind the fireplace (Bergeret, 1855).

By the late 1880s and early 1890s, Megnin, a French researcher completed a series of studies on the decomposition of the human body (Megnin, 1894). He soon discovered that as humans decompose, there is an orderly sequence in which this decomposition progresses. His design included fresh, bloat, decay, dry, and remains. As he studied this progression, he also observed and collected the insects throughout the progression of the decomposition. When he analyzed the insects, he discovered that there were certain specific insect groups (taxa) associated with the different stages of the decomposition. He then presented the idea that there could be a prediction of how old human remains could be dead by knowing which groups of insects are present on the body at the time the body is found. Thus, Megnin formulated the method of determining the time since death or the postmortem interval (PMI) of a dead human by using the insect succession method.

A few years later, an American working in Washington, D.C., disinterred 100 graves from a cemetery in the area (Motter, 1897). He built on the work of Megnin and found additional insects associated with the remains inside the coffins. In these two early studies, it appeared that the flies (Diptera) and the beetles (Coleoptera) were the primary insects to colonize dead, decomposing humans.

In the first half of the 20th century, research on insect fly and beetle groups expanded — not because of an interest in forensic applications, but because of an interest in the economic and welfare impact on society. Due to discoveries of insects vectoring many for primary human diseases as well as food-borne diseases, entomology was seen as important to human and animal health. Thus, federal funding was made available to study the biology, behavior, and taxonomy of flies — particularly blow files. In a monumental study by Knipling in the 1940s through the 1950s, the most successful biological control of a pest insect was accomplished. It is known as the sterile male eradication of the Primary Screw Worm from the southern latitudes of the United States (Florida, Georgia, Louisiana, Mississippi, Alabama, Texas, Arizona, New Mexico, and Southern California) to as far south as the isthmus of Panama. This work and complementary work of others at the time provided the fundamental base of knowledge which forensic entomologists use today. The majority of the data and knowledge which has been used through the end of the 20th century was derived from diligent and extensive research from the early decades of 20th century research. The primary authoritative publication on blow fly taxonomy (identification), life cycles, and species distribution (Hall, 1948) and identification keys of Knipling (1936) came from this economic insect crisis. Other important works on insect identification, biology, and behavior were from these sociological impacts and include Aldrich (1916), Knipling (1939), and Curan (1940). A historical review of this early work in forensic entomology is chronicled by Hall (1990) in *Entomology & Death*.

Current Forensic Entomology

Despite historical anecdotes and based upon sound scientific entomological principles, the application of forensic entomology to death investigations is relatively young.

A distinct body of forensic entomology literature has only developed since the mid-1960s (Payne, 1965; Payne et al., 1968a,b; Payne and King, 1969, 1970a,b; 1972; Payne and Mayson, 1971; Greenberg, 1971; Smith, 1975, 1986; Nuorteva, 1974, 1977, 1987, 1988) with an exception (Reed, 1958). However, publication from specific experiments regarding forensic entomology has only recently been expanding since the early 1980s.

Rodriguez and Bass (1983) were the first to look at insects on human remains from a study conducted at a unique research facility at the University of Tennessee's Anthropological Research Facility at Knoxville, Tennessee. This facility is the first and currently the only facility of its kind in the world where research studies can be conducted on freshly dead human remains where the remains are placed under field conditions. These field conditions may include: bodies in open areas, in wooded over story habitats, as burials, as victims in cars, or any number of other situations corresponding to real murder scenes where victims can be deposited. This research facility has led to establishing the domesticated pig as a model which will duplicate the human remains when studying the progression of decomposition and the insect fauna which will colonize human remains over periods of time. This positive correlation between the human and pig carcasses has proven essential in determining time of death based upon insect occurrence, growth, and development in several high profile trials in both the United States and Canada (Haskell et al., 2003).

A current listing of all forensic pertinent literature can be found in a publication through the FBI (Hockrein, 2004).

Entomologic evidence continues to be treated as novel scientific evidence; Frye and Daubert's hearings continue to be held in state and federal courts when encountering the forensic entomology expert. Entomologic evidence has for the most part been fully accepted. This author has testified and been accepted as an expert witness in 23 states in the United States and in provincial and regional courts (Ontario) in Canada. It is estimated by this author that nearly 3/4 of the states in the United States have accepted entomology as a reliable discipline of the overall forensic science field.

Time Since Death

Estimation of the time when a victim dies, or the postmortem interval (PMI), is the most often used application of forensic entomology today. This is because the time when a person dies or is murdered paramount to the investigation and ranks among the most important questions needing resolution. In cases when there is a delay in discovery of a body after death, the natural insect colonization of the decomposing remains can provide an accurate PMI. Once the PMI is determined and the identity is known, important questions surrounding the death, be it murder, suicide, accidental or natural, can be ascertained, and the circumstances surrounding the death can be learned. Witnesses and suspects who have been associated with the death can be cleared with respect to this time period or may become a focus of suspicion. Knowledge of the time a person died will enable investigators to link the victim with persons who had the last contact with the decedent. The basis of this estimation of the PMI is founded on accepted principles of entomology, which have been known and studied for several hundred years. The specific basis for PMI determinations comes from known insect biology, behavior, growth, and development relating to specific groups and species of insects known to colonize (establish their young) on decomposing animal carrion.

There are known specific insect groups which come to feed primarily on dead vertebrate animals, and it is with these specific groups that a time line of decomposition can be established. These colonizing groups come mainly from the Diptera (flies) and the Coleoptera (beetles), but other major taxa may also be involved in specific cases.

These groups may include the Hymenoptera (wasps, ants, and bees), Ephymeroptera (mayflies), and others where habitat specific groups may be found in connection with human remains. Of course, within each of these major insect Orders, there are many (potentially hundreds) of different kinds (species) of insects which may become involved.

The most often used group of insects for the determination of PMI is the family Calliphoridae (blow flies) of the Order Diptera. This is because species within this family are the first to find a dead body (often within seconds to minutes) and will establish a colony of offspring within the first hour is climatic and habitat conditions are favorable. Favorable conditions will include temperatures above 70F, no rain, full exposure of the remains to the out-of doors, and daylight hours. The PMI is based upon immediate discovery of the remains by the blow flies and then egg deposition shortly after. It must be recognized that there are many situations where there can be delays in the mother blow flies finding the body immediately, and so, a delay of a few hours can be expected. However, if these conditions are present, establishment of new offspring on a newly dead body will occur within minutes to just a couple of hours. For this very reason and variability within the developmental stages, a pin-point time of PMI estimation is usually neither obtainable nor provided from the analysis. It is preferable to provide a range of time, or window of opportunity, when the female blow flies most likely oviposited (laid eggs) on the remains. Thus, the prerequisite of death would be required before eggs would be deposited by the blow flies under most conditions. An exception would be maggot infestation of necrotic tissue on a living animal due to some prior infection or wound being present (myiasis).

Case Study on Time Since Death Estimation

The following case example will illustrate how the time since death estimation is determined:

The decomposing remains of a male were discovered under a pile of household items in the front side of a residence in a small town in central Oklahoma on Monday, August 8 at around noon. The coverings consisted of a bed comforter and a number of other items piled upon the comforter all of which were items found in a domicile. The residence was occupied by a married couple, and it was the husband who was later identified as the victim of a stabbing death who lay in the front yard under the comforter. The wife claimed that she had last seen her husband on the evening of Saturday, August 6, leaving with a couple of his friends to go out for a drink. Others interviewed stated that the last time anyone else had seen the husband was when he and his wife were leaving a local bar on Thursday evening, August 4, both engaged in a heated argument.

Investigators had collected insect larvae (maggots) from the body during the investigation of the death. The question requested of the forensic entomologist was to determine if it were possible that she had last seen her husband on the evening of August 6 or was August 4 a date which was more likely. Since the intervals in question would be either a 36-hour interval or nearly a 96-hour interval, the difference in the development of the blow fly larvae would be a sharp contrast.

The specimens collected from the body were examined by the forensic entomologist and were determined to be of two different calliphorid species, *Cochliomyia macellaria* (the Secondary Screw Worm) and *Phormia regina* (the Black Blow Fly), both very common species in Oklahoma. For this time of the year in Oklahoma, *C. macellaria* is the predominant species and would be expected to be found in the highest numbers on a dead human in this rural setting. A specific behavioral pattern for both these species is that, unlike other blow flies that come to a dead animal very quickly after death, these two species will delay from 12 to 24 hour depending on temperature. Thus, a person could be dead for 12–24 hour or more before these flies would lay their eggs on the body. The oldest life stage was determined to be mature third stage larvae (maggots). There were additional younger stages of the same species and some third stage larvae of *P. regina*. Figure 23.1 presents a typical blow fly life cycle with an egg stage, three larval stages first, second, and third; migrating larva, the puparial stage, and the adult blow fly which will consist of both male and female.

The next task of analysis is to determine how much energy in accumulated degree hours (ADH) is required for this primary indicator species (*C. macellaria*) to reach this mature third stage larva. The method of using energy units is one of several methods available to forensic entomologists for assessing the development over a time interval. This practitioner uses this method regularly in case work because it allows for fluctuations of temperature over time. It is derived from experimental research of the growth and development of the fly species at different temperatures to achieve different stages of its life cycle. These data are then converted to the energy units of either accumulated degree hours or accumulated degree days. In this case, with the short duration involved, ADH units apply. For the species *C. macellaria*, it takes between 950 and 1150 ADHs to reach the mature third stage larvae.

Once the energy requirements are determined, the weather records are examined for the period in questions. Two National Weather Service Stations were used due to their close proximity with the central Oklahoma town, and the hourly temperature data was combined and tabulated. The procedure begins with the date and time the insect specimens were collected (August 8 at 12:00 noon), and the energy units present were calculated

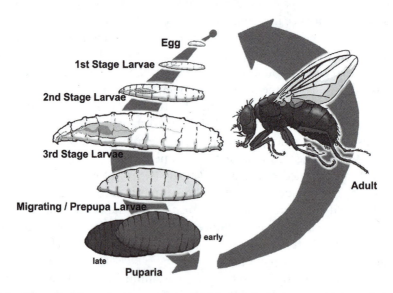

Figure 23.1   Blow fly life cycle. (From, B. Joel Haskell, after E.P. Catts, Entomology and Death. Clemson, S.C.: Joyce's Print Shop, 1990.)

for each hour figuring backwards to a period of time or range which these total units are reached (950 to 1150 ADHs). The result then gives us the time interval for which blow fly colonization (egg laying) occurred. Thus, this range will be found to span a period of time between sunrise on August 5 to sometime after sunset on August 5. Since the blow flies do not fly at night, colonization could only occur during the daylight hours, so the primary indicator blow fly laid eggs sometime during the day on August 5. This calculation, combined with their behavior of delaying their oviposition would put the PMI back into the night-time hours of August 4 or the early morning hours of August 5 during darkness. In addition, analysis of the case based upon the wife's statement of last seeing her husband on the evening of Saturday, August 6, is refuted by only having approximately 450 ADHs available for growth and development. This low number of energy units would only have facilitated eggs to hatch with small first instar larvae present.

This very argument was made at a suppression hearing just before trial. The defense argued that the temperatures were not known at the site of the discovery of the remains, even though there were two National Weather Service stations located 15 miles east of Stroud and 15 miles west of Stroud. The mean hourly temperatures were used for the energy unit analysis. The judge, who had a working knowledge of how weather patterns and temperatures varied in this area of Oklahoma was satisfied that a strong scientific basis had been established with the temperature analysis and overruled the objection by the defense to exclude the entomological evidence. Upon the forensic entomologist's testimony, a plea agreement was entered into the next day, due to the defendant realizing her story of when she had last seen her husband was not close to being realistic.

Determination of Victim Origin by Known Insect Species Distribution

Through the knowledge of a specific insect's species geographical range, it is sometimes possible to show that a victim was originally killed at one location of the country and later moved to a different geographic region. Knowledge of geographic distribution of a species is critical. The majority of insect species used for forensic applications have known geographic areas or ranges. Thus, by knowing these areas of distribution for the forensically important species, it may be concluded whether a remains actually came from the geographic area where it was found, or if the victim had been killed in another geographic location of the country and transported to the site where the remains were recovered. In a case from northern Florida, a body was found just off interstate 75. It was thought that the body was from the local area. However, carrion insects recovered from the remains were found only north of Tennessee, which suggested the body had been "dumped." In fact, the victim had been murdered in Detroit and driven to Florida for deposition.

In some cases, temporal distribution is involved. Certain aquatic insects, such as mayflies, will hatch as adults at very specific dates in the year, from very specific geographic location on waterways or lakes. This group (Order) is very short lived as adults, and when hatched, they quickly mate and then die. Most species in the group even lack mouthparts for feeding. Also typical, when they emerge as adults, they emerge in vast numbers often creating driving hazards due to the pile of dead adults on bridges and highways. Since they are airborne, vehicles will have them smashed into their grillwork and radiator.

If a perpetrator were to have deposited a victim after driving through an area or depositing the body along a body of water where these insects were emerging, a precise date and often a precise location can be established by knowing the geographic distribution and time of emergence of different species within the order.

Colonization of Areas on Remains to Identify Sites of Trauma

In still another use of forensic entomology, by knowing the specific sites where insect colonization is expected to occur on human remains, the forensic entomologist can assist the forensic pathologist in suggesting sites of trauma on the body when advanced decomposition has masked or destroyed the original evidence of the opening into deep body tissues.

The preferred sites of blow fly initial colonization centers on the mouth, the nose, and the eyes. This is due to direct openings into the body that are passageways for gases to escape internal portions of the body that are being generated by natural gut fauna present when there is life in the body. These gases contain many biochemical substances, some of which attract the blow flies to the corpse. As these gases are being produced by the decomposing body and the bacterial action upon the body tissues, they will leave the body through these natural openings. Gases also purge from the pelvic area of a dead body, but attraction is not immediate to this location of the body until a few hours have passed, or unless there has been some type of trauma to the rectal or vaginal openings.

If trauma has occurred to other parts of the body, such as a gunshot wound, stabbing, or blunt force trauma which penetrate or tear the skin and expose underlying muscle, fat, or organ tissue, these sites also will be attractive to early colonizing blow fly females. Human adult skin cannot be penetrated by blow fly maggots during the first several days of decomposition. It is only after degradation of the epidermis that the maggots will be able to feed through the keratinized outer skin layer. This attraction to exposed tissues will generate sites where eggs and later blow fly larvae will be feeding. Blood may enhance the blow fly attraction when in combination with soft body tissues, but blood itself is not a major attractant to the blow flies (Smith, 1986). When the remains are in an active state of decomposition with maggot masses in different locations of the body, sites where trauma may have occurred, but masked by the decomposition, can be identified by the forensic entomologist, thus directing the forensic pathologist to look deeper into the maggot infested area for signs of a wound. This could include tissues not yet fed upon by the blow fly larvae which could show evidence of being penetrated by some object, or it may include examination of bone tissue for cut marks or other trauma to the bone.

Other Applications of Forensic Entomology

The maggots and puparia of blow flies and other fly groups have been used to detect the presence or absence of drugs and other toxic chemicals (Beyer et al., 1980; Introna et al., 1990; 1996, 2001; Leclerq and Brahy, 1985). Many substances can be assimilated by the feeding larvae and then stored in the outer chitinous covering of the insect. Chitin is a protein-like substance whose molecular structure allows compounds to be "locked" into voids in a lattice-like arrangement. Once stored in the chitin, the chemical compounds may last for years with little or no degradation. In some cases years after the decedent had died cocaine has been detected in puparia left behind after the adult insects have matured and flown away. Nowadays, the presence or absence can be tested for, but new research helps detect if substance concentration levels in the humans can be correlated to substance levels in the larvae or puparia.

Identification of human DNA has recently been discovered in feeding blow fly maggots. Linville et al. (2004), and Wells et al. (2001) have recovered human DNA from tissues relating to the crop of the insect. Application of this cutting edge technique will have a profound impact on cases where the remains have been allowed to be colonized by flies and decomposed at a secluded site, then later removed and hidden away never to be found. The presence of a few remaining larvae, which can be analyzed for human DNA, will be proof that the persons identified as having their DNA in the maggots, would certainly be dead.

This application was offered as a test in court in a recent case in Florida where it was alleged by an examining forensic entomologist that larvae from a body were actually not the same maggots sent back after examination by the opposing expert, who emphatically deigned any such tampering of evidence and suggested that DNA sampling could prove from where the larvae had originated. When testing was attempted, it was found that preservation techniques by the original entomologist were not consistent with the conduction of human DNA sampling of maggots; thus, it was impossible to draw conclusions from these specific maggots.

Entomology in Civil Litigation

Experts trained in entomology may be called by a plaintiff or defendant to support their respective positions if civil legal action is required. For example, if a pest control operator has used insecticides to control a specific insect pest and the client does not see the intended results of the treatment, legal action may ensue. Both sides may call upon entomology experts from the chemical manufacturer or other entomologists knowledgeable in the insect to be controlled or the proper application of the insecticide at the appropriate time and in the appropriate location. In other examples, entomologists knowledgeable in medically important insects which carry diseases to man and animals may be called upon to testify in government hearings or inquiries regarding the proper emergency measures needed to be implemented to stop an impending outbreak. Still other entomologists may be called upon to testify regarding insect population outbreaks when large animal confinement production facilities are disposing of animal waste. In each of these examples, the areas of expert testimony and experience is very specific and very specialized within their fields of entomology and, in most instances, would not cross over into any of these other fields.

The estimation of the time since death is also used in answering questions in civil matters where a precise time of death is needed. For example, a person with a life insurance policy leaves his home and is never seen alive again. The life insurance policy expired during the time interval of their leaving to when the body is discovered after death. The local medical examiner will be called upon to answer whether the person died before or after the life insurance policy expiration date. Large sums of money are often at stake, thus obtaining a precise determination is important. In one case, a man left his home early in the week and was found dead at the end of the week. Court proceedings were underway regarding a divorce settlement between the man and his wife. The presiding judge signed the divorce papers during the middle of the week. After the body of the man was found, a court battle ensued over the estate — the wife argued that the man had died before the signing of the divorce decree and the children that the death had occurred after the official proceedings. Forensic entomologists were called into the case to answer the question of when the man died. The forensic entomology evidence indicated that death had occurred just before the signing of the divorce papers, and thus, the majority of the assets were awarded to the wife.

Conclusions

Forensic entomology has much to offer the courts, the investigating officers, and the public in general when used in conjunction with the criminal justice system. Knowledge is an ongoing evolutionary process which requires far-reaching ideas and concepts that can be integrated with new technologies being developed for forensic science in general. Yet, there are many areas that need to be revisited in our research endeavors to verify and validate what is being used at the moment to ensure that case studies are being done correctly. In the Introduction, it was pointed out that there have been occasions where individuals not qualified in forensic entomology have been allowed to give their opinions in death penalty murder trials. This is because the courts did not understand the necessity of using an expert with specific knowledge of these very special carrion insects. As a result, there were substantial differences between the qualified forensic entomologist and the witness claiming to have the required knowledge. These discrepancies are not just differences of opinion of the experts, but are omissions or misunderstandings of the basic scientific principles upon which our science is based due to the lack of training, knowledge, and understanding of those not qualified in the study of carrion insects. It is heartening that these errors are being recognized and addressed, and there is a new major effort being made internationally to set basic standards and protocols so as to eliminate the discordance that has pervaded court appearances from the few professional forensic entomologists practicing today.

References

Aldrich, J.M., 1916. *Sarcophaga and Allies in North America.* Thomas Say Foundation, LaFayette, IN.

Bergeret, M., 1855. Infanticide, momification du cadavre. Decouverte du cadavre d'un enfant nouveau-ne dans une dheminee ou il setait momifie. determination de l'epoque de la naissance par la presence de nymphes et de larves d'Insectes dans le cadvre et par l'Etude de leurs metamorphoses. (Homicide of a new-born child found in a chimney and its natural mummification. Determination of postmortem interval by the use of insect larvae and their metamophosis), *Ann. Hyg. Legal Med.,* 4, 442–452.

Beyer, J.C., Enos, W.F., and Stajic, M. 1980. Drug identification through analysis of maggots. *J. Foren. Sci.,* 25, 411–414 (also cited as 26, 411–412).

Curran, C.H., 1965. The Families and Genera of North American Dipthera. 2d Rev. ed. Henry Tripp, Woodhaven, NY.

Greenberg, B., 1971. Flies and disease, Vol. 1, *Ecology, Classification, and Biotic Associations.* Princeton University Press, Princeton, NJ.

Hall, D.G., 1948. *The Blowflies of North America*. The Thomas Say Foundation, Lafayette, IN.

Hall, R.D., 1990. Medicocriminal entomology. In *Entomology and Death: A Procedural Guide*, Ed., Catts E.P. and Haskell N.H., Joyces Print Shop, Inc., Clemson, pp. 1–8.

Haskell, N.H., et al. 2003. *Testing and Reliability of Animal Models in Research and Training Programs in Forensic Entomology* (http://www.ncjrs.org/rr/vol4_1/10.html).

Hochrein, M.J., 2004. A bibliography related to crime scene interpretation with emphases in geotaphonomic and forensic archaeological field techniques. U.S. Department of Justice, Federal Bureau of Investigation, FBI Print Shop, Washington, D.C.

Introna, F., Jr., Campobasso, C.P., and Goff, M.L., 2001 Entomotoxicology. *Foren. Sci. Int.*, 120(1-2), 42–47.

Introna, F., Jr., Candela, R.G., and Di Vella, G., 1996. Opiate analysis on empty puparia-positive results. *Proceedings of XX International Congress of Entomology*, Firenze, Italy, August 25–31, p. 755.

Introna, F., Jr., Lo Dico, C., Caplan, Y.H., and Smialek, J.E., 1990. Opiate analysis in cadaveric blow fly larvae as an indicator of narcotic intoxication. *J. Foren. Sci.*, 35, 118–122.

Knipling, E.F., 1936. A comparative study of the first-instar larvae of the genus *Sarcophaga*, with notes on the biology. *J. Parasitol.*, 22, 417–454 (also cited as, 427–454).

Knipling, E.F., 1939. A key for blowfly larvae concerned in wound and cutaneous myiasis. *Ann. Entomol. Soc. Amer.*, 32, 376–383.

Leclerq, M. and Brahy, G., 1985. Entomologie et medecine legale, datation de la mort. *J. Med. Leg. — Droit Med.*, 28, 271–278.

Linville, J.G., Hayes, J., and Wells, J.D., 2004. Mitochondrial DNA and STR analyses of maggot crop contents: effect of specimen preservation technique. *J. Foren. Sci.*, 49(2), 341–344.

McKnight, B.E., 1981. *The Washing Away of Wrongs: Forensic Medicine in the Thirteenth-Century China* by Sung T'zu. Center for Chinese Studies, University of Michigan, Ann Arbor, MI.

Megnin, J.P., 1894. La fauna des cadavares. application de L'entomologie a la medicine legale. *Encyclopedie Scientifique des Aide-Memoires*, Masson et Gauthiers, Villars, Paris.

Motter, M.G., 1897. Underground Zoology and Legal Medicine. *J. Amer. Med. Assoc.*, 29, 646, 810.

Nuorteva, P., 1974. Age determination of a blood stain in a decaying shirt by entomological means. *J. Foren. Sci.*, 3, 89–94.

Nuorteva, P., 1977. Sarcosaprophagous insects as forensic indicators. In: *Forensic Medicine: A Study in Trauma and Environmental Hazards*, Tedeschi, C.G., Eckert, W.G., and Tedeschi, L.G., Eds., W.B. Saunders, Philadelphia, pp. 1072–1095.

Nuorteva, P., 1987 Empty puparia of phormia terraenovae R.-D. (Diptera: Calliphoridae) as forensic indicators. *Ann. Entomol. Fennici.*, 53, 53–56.

Nuorteva, P., 1988 Medicolegal Entomology at the Meeting of Liege 1988 and Its Future. Synthesis and Conclusions of the Workshop 2. *Acta. Med. Leg. Soc.*, 38, 309–316.

Payne, J.A., 1965. A summer carrion study of the baby pig *Sus scrofa* Linnaeus. *Ecology*, 46, 592–602.

Payne, J.A. and King, E.W., 1969. Lepidoptera associated with pig carrion. *J. Lepidop. Soc.*, 23, 191–195.

Payne, J.A., 1970a. Coleoptera associated with pig carrion. *Nature*, 219, 1180–1181.

Payne, J.A., 1970b. Coleoptera associated with pig carrion. *Entomol. Mon. Mag.*, 105, 224–232.

Payne, J.A., 1972. Insect succession and decomposition of pig carcasses in water. *J. Georgia. Entomol. Soc.*, 7(3), 153–162.

Payne, J.A., King, E.W., and Beinhart, G., 1968a. Arthropod succession and decomposition of buried pigs. *Nature*, 219, 1180–1181.

Payne, J.A. and Mason, W.R.M., 1971. Hymenoptera associated with pig carrion. *Proceedings of the Entomological Society of Washington*, 73, 132–141.

Payne, J.A., Mead, F.W., and King, E.W., 1968b. Hermiptera associated with pig carrion, *Ann. Entomol. Soc. Amer.*, 61(3), 565–567.

Reed, H.B., 1958. A study of dog carcass communities in tennessee, with special references to the insects. *Amer. Midland. Natur.*, 59(1), 213–245.

Redi, F., 1668. Esperienze intorno alla generazione degl' insetti. Insegna della Stella, Florence, p. 228.

Rodriguez, W.C. and Bass, W.M., 1983. Insect activity and its relationship to decay rates of human cadavers in East Tennessee. *J. Foren. Sci.*, 28(2), 423–432.

Smith, K.G.V., 1975. The Faunal succession of insects and other invertebrates on a dead fox. *Entomol Gaz*, 26, 277–287.

Smith, K.G.V., 1986. *A Manual of Forensic Entomology*. Cornell University Press, Ithaca, New York, (ISBN: 0801419271).

Wells, J.D., Introna, Jr., F., Di Vella, G., Campobasso, C.P., Hayes, J., and Sperling, F.A.H., 2001. Human and insect mitochondrial DNA analysis from maggots. *J. Foren. Sci.*, 46(3), 685–687.

Forensic Odontology

24

MICHAEL N. SOBEL

Introduction

To most people, a dentist is a person who practices the specialty of health care relating to the promotion of good oral health and who helps maintain the various components of the oral cavity, for example, teeth, soft tissues, and bone. Today, the dentist goes even further by applying the principles of oral medicine in preventing, diagnosing, and treating oral disease. It is largely because of the progressive programs of study in the dental schools that the dentists practicing today are capable of reaching out into peripheral fields to apply their experiences.

The forensic sciences are involved in one such area known as forensic odontology (or its alternate term, forensic dentistry). In its most literal sense, forensic odontology is the application of the art and science of dental medicine to the resolution of matters pertaining to the law. Some of the diverse facets of this unique discipline can range from the identification of human remains to mass disaster management; from the assessment of bitemark and patterned skin injuries to the use of dental materials in the examination of evidence. As a vital part of the modern forensic science investigative team, forensic odontology contributes to, and has played, many significant roles.

Among the investigative contributions of the forensic odontologist are:

1. Dental identification
2. Mass disaster management
3. Bite mark and patterned injury assessment
4. Human abuse evaluation
5. Professional liability and civil litigation issues

A practicing dentist can be an important witness in civil cases involving dental injuries. Legal liabilities often arise in these cases as the result of trauma that causes injuries to the teeth, their supporting structures, and other portions of the dento-facial anatomy. A knowledge of oral anatomy and the functional relationships of these parts uniquely qualify the dentist to give testimony. However, testimony in many criminal cases, involving such matters as critical interpretations in human identification and bite marks, deserves the attention of a qualified forensic odontologist. This is so, because the expertise in these matters is a result of the additional training and experience required to achieve competency as a forensic odontologist.

To be formally accepted as a forensic odontologist, a dentist should have special training, especially in the areas of the forensic sciences, oral pathology, anthropology, the basic sciences, and law. Furthermore, he/she should be actively working in the field, preferably connected with a law enforcement agency or a coroner's/medical examiner's office. Additional evidence of qualification is indicated in achieving (1) certification by the American Board of Forensic Odontology (www.abfo.org), (2) membership or fellowship in the Odontology section of the American Academy of Forensic Sciences (www.aafs.org), and (3) membership in the American Society of Forensic Odontology (www.asfo.org). The dentist, who makes the effort to meet these requirements, and become a part of these active organizations, is greatly assisted in qualifying as an expert witness in the courts.

The entry level organization for those in dental medicine is the American Society of Forensic Odontology (ASFO). Membership is open to those with a genuine interest in forensic odontology, and this organization provides a forum for continuing education in this field. Through their periodically revised *ASFO Handbook* and their annual full day programs, those so motivated may begin to experience and "rub shoulders" with many people actively working in forensic odontology.

Membership in the American Academy of Forensic Sciences (AAFS), Odontology Section, represents the next level. Formal affiliation with a law enforcement agency and active experience on cases are a prior requirement. The AAFS offers the opportunity to advance to Fellow in the Academy through meeting participation and the presentation of papers at these annual meetings.

The American Board of Forensic Odontology is the official certifying board and is endorsed by the AAFS. To qualify to sit for the Board examination, evidence of participation in a mandated number of actual forensic cases involving dental identification, bite marks, and other dento-legal matters is required. There must be participation in sworn testimony, mass disaster incidents or drills, presentations of papers before valid forensic organizations, and formal forensic continuing education. There are additional requirements which may be found at www.abfo.org.

Once the dentist's application is accepted, he/she may proceed to challenge the Board examination. This is a rigorous test of knowledge involving dentistry, pathology, medicine, anthropology, basic sciences, and law, in addition to various other disciplines. Upon passing this examination, the applicant is awarded Diplomate status in the American Board of Forensic Odontology (DABFO). At present, there are approximately 100 Board certified forensic odontologists in the U.S. and Canada.

Every five years, the DABFO must be recertified based on continued good standing in forensic odontology, 50 hours of valid continuing forensic education, and presentation of a signed listing of all cases investigated in that time period, participation in sworn testimony, teaching, forensic writing, and forensic positions and offices held. These requirements serve to advance the skill level of the Diplomates so that they may work acceptably within the forensic community, and effectively mentor the next generation of forensic odontologists.

Basic Concept of Forensic Odontology

Forensic Odontology is a complex area of investigative procedures. The most basic concept is centered in applications of pattern recognition and comparisons of those patterns. The final conclusion ultimately arrives when a comparison of the unknown pattern with a known pattern determines the extent of similarity. For example, the dentition described in a set of dental records can exhibit a unique pattern against which one may evaluate the dentition of an unknown body. In mass disaster incidents, this problem solving experience is repeated, but on a much larger scale.

The same is true in bite mark evaluations. An accurate representation of the bite mark injury, as a pattern, is compared with an accurate representation of the suspect's dentition, both being similarly scaled in measurement. This procedure might also be observed in the activities of a criminalist investigating a tool mark case.

Of course, the pattern recognition analogy is a simplistic accounting of the core of forensic odontology. Investigator experience, knowledge of testing methodologies, and decision analysis abilities, among other issues, all contribute to successful evidence evaluation and assessment.

Dental Identification

The question might be asked as to why the teeth can be such a valuable aid in the body identification process? The dentition is significant in the human identification process primarily because teeth and the jaw structures can resist even the most severe environmental conditions and trauma. This is so, particularly for the teeth, because of the inherent durability of tooth enamel (the outermost covering of the crowns of the teeth) and of cementum (the outer covering of the roots of the teeth). As a result, aside from fingerprint analysis, one of the most legally reliable forms of identification of human remains is by comparison of dental structures with dental records. In fact, especially in the United States, there are many more dental records on file than fingerprint records due to the nature of our society which provides a wealth of readily accessible comparative material.

It has been observed that teeth and jaws are surprisingly able to resist environmental stress, such as even in the most severe fires. The oral cavity seems to be so well insulated against the high temperature of fires, that, often, even the supporting tissues surrounding the teeth within the oral cavity are also well preserved. In addition, the dental restorations and prosthetic replacements are frequently completely intact.

As a result of the durability of the human dentition, dental identification procedures have been useful in cases such as:

1. Skeletonized remains
2. Decomposed bodies
3. Burn victims
4. Drowning cases
5. Amnesia patients

Perhaps a short discussion would be in order to show how dental records are typically located for comparison with an unknown body that had been unearthed. Initially, the remains are examined for clues such as personal effects and clothing, general physical description, comparison with local and global missing persons' records, and timing, manner, and cause of death. These findings may lead investigators to potential identities and, it is these dental records which are requested under subpoena and compared first. If no positive match is possible after this initial activity, the general description and dental charting of the unknown remains are submitted to the FBI. National Crime Information Center (NCIC) computer system for searching, comparing, and archiving.

Identification Case Example 1

> A husband suspected his wife of infidelity. He confronted her in a bar with another man and shot them both. The shooter took off with the police in pursuit and returned to his trailer home. The police surrounded the trailer and his car, and the car erupted into flames. When the fire was extinguished, severely burned human remains were discovered. In particular, there was a mandible and only a part of the cranium attached to the maxilla. The question to be answered is "Was this the shooter they were after or someone else planted in the vehicle?" This author examined the skull and, finding that most of the dentition was intact, compared the antemortem dental records with the postmortem remains. There was complete concordance including a distinctive gold crown and several other dental restorations, thus confirming the identity of the shooter.

The inherent possibilities for uniqueness in the human dentition enable the forensic dentist to determine the degree of concordance between antemortem dental records and the oral structures of specific human remains under examination. The human adult dentition typically consists of 32 teeth, each with five surfaces, thus providing 160 possibilities for individual variations of surface anatomy and dental restorations in configuration, size, shape, material, and wear patterns. This does not even take into account, and is not limited to, such factors as decay, missing and extra teeth, alignment of the dental arches, individual tooth positioning, and prosthetic appliances. The experienced dental clinician can detect many subtleties in the observable detail of the teeth and jaws, which are most useful in confirming human identification. Among other distinctive characteristics for antemortem and postmortem comparisons are maxillary sinus patterns, bone trabeculation patterns, and orbital outlines.

A question often arises as to the number of points of concordance necessary to render a valid decision on a dental identification. However, this is not as significant as the singular quality, or exclusivity, of the points of comparison involved. In addition, when all of the points of concordance in a particular case are considered as a set of aggregate data, the investigator should be able to state, if possible, whether the identification is "positive within reasonable scientific certainty."

The following categories and terminology for body identification are suggested for use in communicating the results of a forensic odontology identification investigation:

Positive Identification: The antemortem and postmortem data match in sufficient detail to establish that they are from the same individual. In addition, there are no irreconcilable discrepancies.

Possible Identification: The antemortem and postmortem data have consistent features, but, due to the quality of either, the postmortem remains or the antemortem evidence, it is not possible to positively establish dental identification.

Insufficient Evidence: The available information is insufficient to form the basis for a conclusion.

Exclusion: The antemortem and postmortem data are clearly inconsistent. However, it should be understood that identification by exclusion is a valid technique in certain circumstances.

However, this warning from the American Board of Forensic Odontology should be noted: "The forensic dentist is not ordinarily in a position to verify that the antemortem records are correct as to the name, date, etc.; therefore, the report should state that the conclusions are based on records that are purported to represent a particular individual."[1]

In summary, the forensic odontologist can best be relied upon to render expert opinions concerning identifications based on postmortem evaluation of dental structures, while testing for concordance with antemortem dental records, which are as complete as can be obtained. The American Board of Forensic Odontology is continually updating and revising its ABFO Body Identification Guidelines, which are available online at www.abfo.org, and the reader is referred to that web site for the most recent information.

Identification Case Example 2

Two white males speeding on a highway ended their trip in a fiery crash. Tracing from the registration of the vehicle, the owner/driver was tentatively identified and witnesses indicated who the male passenger was alleged to be. Dental records were requested from the dentists of the victims for use by this author in the postmortem examinations and comparisons. The driver was readily identified by this process; however, the passenger did *not* match the dental chart furnished, although the family insisted that the passenger victim *had* to be their relative. Further investigation revealed that this victim had loaned his Medical Card to a friend so that the friend could receive unauthorized dental treatment at no charge. Ultimately, another set of dental records were located which did indeed match the passenger victim. Here is an example showing that, while people may lie, the dental evidence does not.

Mass Casualty Management

Perhaps mass casualty incident identifications are best appreciated as being a greatly expanded application of dental identifications as described previously. In fact, the most descriptive definition for a mass disaster or mass casualty incident would be: "... any situation, man-made or natural, which overtaxes the normal emergency resources available within a community."[2]

When the typical casualty incident is simultaneously multiplied many times over, and the local consulting forensic odontologist or the local dental ID team, is incapable of handling the incident because of the number of victims and lack of resources, outside help should be requested. For this reason, the Federal government has instituted a program under the National Disaster Medical System (NDMS) and Federal Emergency Management Agency (FEMA) called Disaster Mortuary Operations Response Team (DMORT). Currently, these programs are coordinated under the Department of Homeland Security.

These teams are set up regionally across the country and are composed of specialists, such as pathologists, anthropologists, forensic dentists, and funeral directors, who are trained in disaster operations. The DMORT units are prepared for rapid response, complete with supplies, in times of mass casualty incidents to bolster any community's resources when needed. Examples of DMORT mobilization were seen in the events of September 11, 2001. The DMORT website may be accessed at www.dmort.org.

It should be emphasized, however, that mass disaster incidents require some special management applications that differ from the typical unidentified body case. These differing methodologies may be necessary due to numerous fragmented and commingled body remains (e.g., an airplane crash or a building explosion). In some disasters, there may be complete disruption of the regional infrastructure such as water and power supplies (e.g., hurricanes or a war zone). For this reason, teamwork, integrating various specialists, equipment, and techniques, is mandated.

In identification situations, technology is playing an ever growing role. For example, computer programs, such as WinID, greatly aid the forensic odontologist in rapidly performing a "ballpark" comparison of the ante- and post-mortem dental records in large scale mass disasters.

Bite Mark Evidence

Another area which uses identifying characteristics of the teeth, although on a more functional level, is bitemark analysis. Bites on human tissue may be observed in violent incidents where the attacker may bite the victim or the victim may bite the attacker during defensive responses. In more passive incidents, a person may bite himself/herself or an inanimate object left at a scene, for example, an apple core.

Paramount is the ability to differentiate a patterned injury as a bitemark from a mark made by another source. Here, the forensic odontologist, through training and experience, is the individual most qualified to assess the injury pattern. To initially evaluate a patterned mark, this author has developed the CAPS System to help in the differentiation process to provide the direction for the investigation to proceed. The pattern should be viewed with the following characteristics in mind:

1. Configuration
2. Alignment or orientation
3. Pattern format
4. Size relationships

Teeth may be considered as tools leaving marks on the skin, food, or various other materials. However, there are often more characteristics involved in the analysis of bite marks than would occur from considering the teeth as merely simple tools. There are class characteristics to be considered, such as the type of the tooth that inflicted the bite, for example, incisor, cuspid. The biting surfaces of the individual groups of teeth are related to their function, such as teeth that incise, or tear, or grind. The incisors leave long rectangular imprints, whereas the cuspids can inflict diamond shaped, or pointy imprints. The bicuspids and molars are rarely observed in human bite mark patterns due to their distant placement far back in the oral cavity.

In addition, also observed are individual characteristics, such as rotations, fractures, missing, or extra teeth. The size relationships of the bitemark, as described by the width of the dental arches, could relate to a child or adult bite. Ability to open the mouth maximally may vary from individual to individual. It should be noted that bitemarks can also *exclude* a suspect by revealing a tooth pattern, or opening range, inconsistent with that of a particular person.

Once the class characteristics indicate where certain teeth are represented in a bite mark, the individual characteristics can come into play. Individual characteristics can relate to a unique description of a particular suspect's dentition by considering these characteristics as an aggregate description and literally "painting a distinctive picture."

The complex methodologies and guidelines for preserving, documenting, and comparing bite mark evidence are crucial to the proper and uniform objective analysis of patterned markings for legal substantiation. Further details may be accessed by reading the current *ABFO Bitemark Methodology Guidelines* at www.abfo.org.[3]

Bite Mark Case Example

An elderly woman was found unconscious, beneath a pile of concrete blocks, the victim of a brutal beating and rape. Investigators noticed what appeared to be a bitemark on the victim's right breast. A suspect was apprehended in the area and circumstantially linked to the crime. Permission was granted by the suspect for dental impressions and photographs to be taken. Comparison of a scaled photograph of the bite mark on the victim and plaster models poured from the suspect's dental impressions placed the accused at the scene of violence. Additional comparisons were performed using computer enhancements and overlays. The concordance of the suspect's dentition to the victim's bite mark was able to play a major role in the conviction of the perpetrator.

Patterned Mark Case Example

A nurse, checking on a middle aged female patient in a Critical Care Unit, discovered a patterned skin mark on the inner surface of the patient's left thigh. She questioned the patient, who was under sedation, about the marks. The nurse, getting "positive" responses to her questions, suggested that it was a bite mark. A report was filed, and the police were notified. The police photographed the patient's injury and made further inquiries which resulted in charges being filed against her physician on suspicion of molestation. A forensic odontologist was consulted by the police who took impressions on anyone who had contact with the patient during the estimated window of opportunity. All dental models obtained were compared by the prosecution forensic odontologist to the patterned skin mark photographs. As a result of the comparisons, the suspect physician was arrested and held for trial on criminal charges. This author was consulted by defense to evaluate the same materials and found that, although there were characteristics resembling a human bitemark, there were areas on the patterned markings to which the physician's dentition could not be matched positively. In addition, upon reviewing the patient's medical record, the defense odontologist found that an indwelling urinary catheter had been taped to the inner left thigh within the time range of the incident. An overlay of the catheter was then compared to the so-called "bitemark," and a near perfect outline accounted for all of the patterned marks. When the case came to trial, the judge's verdict (a bench trial) was in favor of the defendant, since the only conclusive evidence was that the urinary catheter was the culprit! ("The only truth that counts in court is that which can be proven.")[4]

Often, there are patterned markings observed in the course of assaults, rapes, homicides, and child abuse. Marks, such as fingernail scratches, imprints of hands, jewelry, or household objects, can be observed in many cases. This author participated in the first case of fingernail scratch identification admitted to and upheld by the U.S. courts.[5] In this case, deep fingernail scratches on the neck of a victim of homicide by manual strangulation were recorded by impressions and photography. The suspect was apprehended soon after the murder, and his fingernails were able to be matched to unusual curvatures and fractures captured in the marks on the victim's neck. The court admitted the evidence based on the same standards accorded tool marks. The guilty verdict survived appellate review.

Other cases have been reported in which markings on skin were recorded and matched to objects used to strike a victim. Therefore, the expertise of the forensic odontologist in interpreting bitemarks can be transferred to the evaluation of many other patterned injuries to the skin surface and inanimate objects at crime scenes.

Human Abuse Evidence

Another area relating to bites and patterned skin marks, in which the forensic odontologist is being consulted more frequently, is in cases of alleged human abuse, often in crimes involving children. Usually in cases of child abuse with apparent bitemarks, there are only a limited number of persons who could have been able to have intimate enough access to the child to have the opportunity to inflict a bite. This, then, greatly limits the suspect range for comparisons of dentition to the bitemark. Family members, friends of the family, siblings, paramours, and caregivers are most often high on the suspect list in child abuse bitemarks and patterned injuries.

To help determine the physical abuse status, the patterned injuries are usually categorized as, recent, healing, and healed injuries. This helps us to assess as to whether the abuse status is related to a solitary event or has been continuing over a period of time.

Other types of patterned injuries can be evaluated by the forensic odontologist to assist in determining the instrument of abuse. For example, victims beaten with coiled electric extension cords, belts (with or without buckles), household appliances (electric irons, hair curlers), or ropes can exhibit class and individual characteristics that can be revealing.

Cases involving elder, spousal, and political prisoner abuse could be examined in a like fashion for telling evidence of the instrument and timing of abuse.

Abuse Case Example

This author was called to a hospital emergency department to examine a two year old child with apparent multiple bite marks on the body. The mother had gone to work, leaving her daughter in the care of a 14 year old baby sitter. After examination, measurement, and photography of the bitemarks, a determination was made that the source of the bitemarks was the young baby sitter. She was questioned by the police and confessed to the biting activity, evidently a "normal" activity of interplay in the sitter's family. If prosecution, instead of only counseling of the perpetrator, had been pursued in this case, the correlation between biter and bitemarks could readily have been demonstrated in court with admissible legal certainty.

Analysis of Dental Evidence

The profession of dental medicine has become significantly more complex and varied within the past 50 year. Most recently, this is especially true because of the advent of the newer dental materials and technologies that have evolved. The presence of dental prosthetic tooth replacements (including dentures, bridges, partials, etc.) at a crime scene can be analyzed by the forensic odontologist. These materials can potentially yield information such as geography of origin, approximate dating of construction, and even linkage to a particular dentist or dental laboratory. Many unique characteristics and variations exist, "labeling" the type, quality, and socioeconomic levels of the dental restorations performed, both recently and in the past, in the victim's oral cavity. These factors and analyses can be helpful in a forensic investigation, both in opening avenues of exploration and for court expert testimony. In a number of cases, the finding of a single tooth or fragment of a tooth has been a pivotal point in assisting in an investigation.

Tooth Fragment Case Example

A portion of an upper right first molar was found adjacent to a badly beaten homicide victim on the shore of a river. The tooth fragment did *not* belong to this homicide victim. The appearance of the fractured crown was such that this author felt that the tooth fragment had sheared off as the outcome of a traumatic blow to the right side of the mandible, which probably fractured as a result. A bulletin was broadcast to check all treatment facilities for anyone requesting treatment for a mandibular fracture and broken molar. No leads developed until, several days later, another battered homicide victim was found in another area of the city. Upon examination, this victim had a fractured mandible and the tooth fragment matched the broken upper right first molar. Because of the evidence of a single tooth fragment, the two homicides were able to be linked to the same homicide case.

Developing Applications

Forensic odontology continues to advance as a science. Computers are being used more and more in many aspects, from assistance in identification matching (especially mass disaster incidents) to enhancement of x-ray films and bitemark evidence photographs.

The scanning electron microscope is being used to amplify details of individual components of bite mark evidence.

Reconstruction of the soft tissue layers of skulls can enable investigators to estimate the actual appearance of victims when they were alive. The caveat here is that certain features, such as eyebrows, eyelids, external nares, and external ears, are subject to extensive variation. In many cases, there may be little resemblance to these features in life.

Saliva washings from bitemarks can be serotypic indicators of blood group antigens and can also be a source of DNA for analysis and comparison with a suspect. The downside of saliva washings is that they can be easily contaminated (e.g., by medical treatment at a scene or in the hospital) before being adequately preserved.

Alternate light sources, such as UV range, infrared, can be helpful in the visualization of suspected healed skin injuries. These light sources, in various wave lengths, can penetrate the skin surface, or filter out overlying debris, to better document bite or patterned skin mark evidence photographically.

UV Light Case Example

An unknown intruder invaded a woman's apartment and kept her hostage for eight hours, brutalizing and sexually molesting her. After the incident, she called the police and was taken to the hospital emergency department where she was interviewed, photographed, and treated. One of the photographs showed an apparent bitemark on her left scapular area, which was confirmed by the victim. Five months later the suspect was identified, but by now, the bite mark had healed. In addition, the original hospital bitemark photograph did not have a reference scale and appeared to have little evidentiary value. Under court order, the suspect submitted to dental impressions and photographs of his dentition. The victim gave permission for new photographs of the healed bitemark site. This author and a colleague felt that reflective UV photography might be able to revisualize the original healed bitemark imprint. This was successfully accomplished with special equipment and a reference scale was included in the photographs. During trial, the court allowed the original hospital photograph to be introduced into evidence as there was demonstrated that there was a 7 mm piping border on the hospital gown the victim was wearing. Comparison of the original hospital photograph, the reflective UV photograph, and the dental models of the suspect indicated significant matching characteristics. A guilty verdict resulted which was upheld on all appeals.[6]

Conclusion

Forensic odontology, like most areas in contemporary forensic sciences, is constantly morphing and developing in usefulness within global justice systems and the world community. The resolution of a growing subset of forensic matters by qualified forensic odontologists, and their team interactions with law enforcement agencies, other specialities within the forensic sciences, and the legal community can be perceived as a rapidly developing and enhanced relationship.

References

1. American Board of Forensic Odontology: ABFO Body Identification Guidelines, www.abfo.org

2. Butman, A.M., *Responding to the Mass Casualty Incident. A Guide for EMS Personnel*, Emergency Training, Akron, OH, 1982.

3. American Board of Forensic Odontology, ABFO Bitemark Methodology Guidelines, www.abfo.org

4. Paraphrased from the 1997 Dutch film, *Character.*

5. Perper, J.A. and Sobel, M.N., Identification of fingernail markings in manual strangulation, *Am. J. Forensic Med. Pathol.*, 1981, 2(1): 45–8.

6. David, T.J. and Sobel, M.N., Recapturing a five-month old bite mark by means of reflective ultraviolet photography, *J. Forensic Sci.*, 1994, 39(6): 1560–7.

Forensic Anthropology 25

KATHLEEN J. REICHS

Introduction

Forensic anthropology is that branch of applied physical anthropology concerned with the identification of human remains in a legal context. It focuses on the analysis of otherwise unrecognizable remains, with a view to identifying the deceased and formulating opinions as to the circumstances surrounding death. Most physical anthropologists have knowledge of archeological field techniques, methods which serve well in crime scene recoveries involving buried or surface remains. Physical anthropologists are, in addition, experts in human biology. They are familiar with the range of biological variability present in human populations and with the causes of that variability. In addition, those trained in osteology have a thorough knowledge of skeletal anatomy and function. The blending of these skills, along with an appreciation for cultural diversity, combine to make forensic anthropology a unique specialty.

Although a relatively, newly recognized field of expertise, its formal beginnings dating only to World War II, forensic anthropology is today one of the select disciplines formally incorporated into the American Academy of Forensic Sciences (AAFS). As with other medical, scientific, and forensic fields, forensic anthropology has a certifying board, the American Board of Forensic Anthropology (ABFA), established to identify those qualified to provide professional services.

The forensic anthropologist rarely functions in a vacuum, but rather coordinates his/her efforts with those of other experts, particularly the pathologist and the odontologist. Forensic anthropologists are called upon in both civil and criminal contexts. Homicides, suicides, mass disasters (manmade and natural), the recovery and identification of military personnel, and of individuals killed due to human rights violations all pose problems most easily addressed through skeletal analysis.

Until recently, formal training in forensic anthropology was not available. Many professionals practicing today were schooled in osteology and entered the field via practical, case-in-hand experience. There are now institutions offering programs in forensic anthropology at both the graduate and undergraduate levels.

The role of the forensic anthropologist varies from region to region. Few are employed in full-time positions: Most work as consultants, and some are involved in their cases from the point of field recovery right through courtroom presentation. Others function strictly during the laboratory analysis phase of investigation. Some are on faculty at universities, and others work at medical examiners' offices. What one is asked to do varies with the problem at hand.

Generally, the cases brought to the attention of the forensic anthropologist fall into one of two categories: One type involves the recovery of completely unknown remains. Case reports in these instances are largely descriptive and involve a "narrowing of the field" process with regard to the broad biological categories of age, sex, race, and stature. Matching of missing persons' reports may then be attempted and a possible identification may be suggested. Should this occur, the case gets converted to one of the second type: a tentative identification.

Remains may be tentatively identified through the aforementioned process, by context, by materials on the body or associated at the death scene, or by informant reports. In such cases, it is the task of the forensic anthropologist to confirm or negate the presumed identity. This is often done in concert with a forensic odontologist, using antemortem dental records, with a pathologist using antemortem medical records, or with a DNA expert, using comparison samples.

Although anthropologists may work primarily with skeletons, a wide variety of materials pass through their laboratories, including burned, mutilated, mummified, or decomposed remains. Some specialize in histology, serology, the mechanics of trauma, the analysis of cut marks, or the interpretation of hand and footprints. Still others have expertise in facial reconstruction, and some work with photographs and anthropometrics. This author has been asked to assess the height of an assailant from knee and toe impressions left beside a rape/murder victim, to tie cut marks on moose meat to a butchered carcass found in the woods, and to determine the position of a victim before a vehicular accident.

A forensic investigation may involve all or any combination of the following phases:

- Stage One: Field recovery
- Stage Two: Laboratory analysis
- Stage Three: Report preparation and court testimony

Typically, a case study proceeds through a series of questions. It must first be determined that the remains are human. This established, a sorting process is initiated to determine the minimum number of individuals present (MNI). Commingling can be an especially difficult problem in situations involving multiple deaths, such as sites of mass disasters, scenes of war casualties, and cases of intentional criminal destruction.

Next, a biological profile is constructed for each individual, including age, sex, race, and stature. This process requires a sound knowledge of osteology and a familiarity with the variability present in the human skeleton. Any competent osteologist is capable of the analysis to this point. It is the process from here forward that sets the forensic anthropologist apart.

Forensic anthropologists do not simply describe remains in terms of demographic categories and descriptive features. Although this is sufficient for the bio-archaeologist working with prehistoric populations, the goal of forensic analysis is individuation. The forensic anthropologist works to identify a specific individual, to pinpoint a specific time of death, and to reconstruct as accurately as possible the circumstances surrounding a specific death episode. The latter may include information on manner of death and pattern of body disposal.

The forensic anthropologist relies on techniques little used by those not engaged in forensic work. In sum, every anthropologist with skeletal expertise is not a forensic anthropologist.

Stage I: Field Recovery

The success of any forensic identification depends to a large extent on what is recovered for analysis. Contextual information may be as critical as the remains themselves in reconstructing events surrounding death and body disposal.

Although law enforcement officials may be proficient at collecting, preserving, and processing physical evidence at crime scenes, they often do less well in skeletal recovery. Crime scene technicians may lack excavation skills, and may have little familiarity with bone. Forensic anthropologists are skilled at locating clandestine graves and are experts at recovering and processing human remains from surface locations, burials, burned areas, and scenes of manmade and natural disasters.

Stage II: Laboratory Analysis: The Biological Profile

Age

The accuracy with which age can be determined osteologically is inversely correlated with true age at death. With younger individuals, estimates are based on developmental processes, and more precise evaluations are possible. With older individuals, age-progressive and degenerative changes are observed, and estimated age ranges must be broader.

Determination of age in children and adolescents relies largely on dental development, eruption and replacement, on the appearance and fusion of ossification centers, and on the measurement of long bone growth.

In adults, following full epiphyseal fusion in the skeleton, the most useful standards are provided by the series of changes occurring at the pubic symphysis and at the costochondral junction at the (sternal) rib ends.

Age-related changes on the auricular surface of the ilium, cranial suture closure, arthritic development, and dental attrition may be broad indicators of adult age. In addition, methods exist based on microscopic and radiographic examination of bones and teeth, and these may prove particularly useful in the older adult ranges where reliable standards are largely lacking.

Each approach must be used with care. Dental eruption and replacement are subject to individual variability. Ossification centers in immature specimens are difficult to recognize and frequently lost. Long bone growth is subject to environmental influence, and the same may be true of dental microstructure. Cranial sutures exhibit wide ranges of variability in closure patterns. Pubic symphyseal changes may be affected by factors such as pregnancy and parturition. For a full discussion of aging techniques, see Burns (1999), Byers (2001), Galloway (2004), Krogman (1962), Nafte (2000), Reichs (1986, 1998), Rathbun and Buikstra (1984), Steadman (2002), Stewart (1979), or Ubelaker (1978).

Sex

Techniques for sex determination fall into two broad categories: metric and observational. These approaches are complementary and do not represent mutually exclusive analytical tools. Most forensic anthropologists employ a combination of procedures.

The standard morphological features useful in sex assessment are summarized in numerous anthropological texts written by Burns (1999), Byers (2001), Galloway (2004), Krogman (1962), Nafte (2000), Reichs (1986, 1998), Rathbun and Buikstra (1984), Steadman (2002), Stewart (1979), and Ubelaker (1978). They reflect, primarily, dimorphism in the pelvis and skull.

Metric data may be used in one of three ways: as raw measures of size and robusticity (i.e., diameter of head of femur or humerus), as ratios or indices indicating shape (i.e., ischiopubic index), or in discriminant function analysis.

One of the most important developments in forensic anthropology in the past two decades has been the establishment of the Forensic Anthropology Data Bank (FDB) at the University of Tennessee. The FDB is a unique resource for understanding morphometric variation among modern Americans.

The FDB makes it clear that sex (and ancestry) criteria derived from nineteenth century collections, and long relied upon by physical anthropologists, cannot be applied to modern skeletons. The data bank, containing information derived from approximately 2,500 sets of skeletal remains allowed the development of the Fordisc 3.0 program. Using Fordisc 3.0, sex (and ancestry) may now be evaluated by comparison of measurements taken from modern unknowns to standards established by the FDB.

Race

Categorization of an individual according to race or ancestry is perhaps the most problematical and least precise assessment in any forensic analysis. These difficulties are due to problems of inconsistency between social and biological definitions of racial categories, intermixture between groups, and the nature of the skeletal variation among populations. Nevertheless, this is an important aspect of any forensic report. Analysis depends, as in the determination of sex, on methods of observation and multivariate statistical analysis.

Traditional approaches emphasize variation in craniofacial features, including proportions of the orbital and nasal areas, characteristics of the nasal aperture and lower nasal border, lower facial prognathism, cheekbone contours, and palate form. Some dental features, such as shoveling in the incisors, are reliable. Few postcranial features have proven useful in anthroposcopic examination. Many texts, including those of Burns (1999), Byers (2001), Galloway (2004), Krogman (1962), Nafte (2000), Reichs (1986, 1998), Rathbun and Buikstra (1984), Steadman (2002), Stewart (1979), and Ubelaker (1978) provide overviews of features useful in determination of racial affiliation. All include warnings concerning the hazards involved.

As with sex estimation, racial evaluation is aided by anthropometrics. Ancestry may now be evaluated by comparison of measurements taken from modern unknowns to standards established by the FDB using Fordisc 3.0.

Stature

A number of formulas exist which enable the estimation of stature from long bones. In general, most calculations are based on the maximum length of limb bones. Outdated standards are to be avoided. Again, Fordisc 3.0 provides appropriate formulae for both sexes and for varying racial groups.

Individuation

Individuation is the process whereby a set of remains is matched with a specific personal identity. It is best accomplished by collaboration among the medical examiner, odontologist, and forensic anthropologist. Other specialists, such as fingerprint, blood, or hair analysis experts, may also be consulted. Individuation is accomplished via analysis of radiographs, medical or dental records, photographs, facial reconstruction, personal histories, or associated death scene materials.

In cases of tentative identification, radiographs may be consulted for evidence of anomalies, abnormalities, fractures, surgery, or unique structural properties (i.e., sinus or trabecular patterns). Life histories and descriptions may also prove useful. In cases in which radiographs are unavailable, photographic comparisons may be attempted.

All else failing, facial reproduction may be attempted as a last resort. Methods include the modeling of clay directly onto the skull (three dimensional), the construction of artists' drawings (two dimensional), and the use of computer-generated images. In cases of presumed identity, photo/portrait superimposition has occasionally proven useful.

Stage II: Laboratory Analysis: Time and Manner of Death

Time of Death

Cases coming to the forensic anthropologist are usually in an advanced stage of decomposition or already skeletonized. Pinpointing postmortem interval (PMI) can be difficult, especially when dealing with osseous materials alone. Under ideal conditions, a body can be reduced to bone in as little as two weeks, but decomposition rates vary tremendously with local conditions.

Many anthropologists are engaged in research that is adding to our knowledge of the decomposition process. Some have contributed information on the deterioration of associated death scene materials. Still others are focusing on correlations between time of death and amount of bone residuals, including total lipids, triglycerides, cholesterol, fatty acids, total proteins, zinc, iron, manganese, and phosphorous.

Much information on postmortem interval is contextual, but the bones also contain useful features, including the condition of adherent soft tissue, or the presence of blood vessels, ligament, or marrow cavity tissue. Skeletal elements may show weathering, staining, bleaching, cracking, mineralization, or animal damage.

The presence on scene of an anthropologist can ensure better understanding of the processes to which the remains have been subjected. In addition to body treatment (i.e., burial or exposure), factors affecting decomposition and bone degradation include climate, soil, water, vegetation, necrophagous insect activity, and animal scavenging. These forces are best understood by direct observation.

Manner of Death

Anthropologists use three terms to associate skeletal trauma with time of death. Antemortem injuries preceded, postmortem injuries followed, and perimortem injuries are related to a death event.

Antemortem vs. Perimortem

A sequence of physiological responses begins immediately after injury to bone. Upon disruption of the cortical surface, vascular damage leads to localized hematoma, and subsequent clotting. Additional fluid is generated at the injury site by plasma released by the injured vessels. Within days, a fibrous matrix is formed, providing a framework for the deposition of bony callus. Eventually, the callus is remodeled and replaced by lamellar bone.

Early osteogenic response can be seen as periostitis, callus formation, or etched lines denoting the extent of periosteal uplifting. Evidence of osseous remodeling is apparent on injured bone within one to two weeks of trauma (depending on the location of the injury, the health of the victim, and genetic variations).

Postmortem vs. Perimortem

Postmortem skeletal trauma can result from a number of things, including animal scavenging, mechanical or chemical factors, burial treatment, intentional mutilation, or improper handling during recovery.

Perimortem skeletal trauma can result from blunt or sharp instrument injuries, gunshot wounding, strangulation, or any insult causing skeletal damage.

Neither postmortem nor perimortem injury shows evidence of bone regeneration. Postmortem injury can be distinguished from perimortem injury by differences in fracture characteristics. Fresh or living bone contains fluid-filled vessels, grease, and collagen fibers, whereas dry bone does not. Therefore, fresh bone is significantly more pliable and has more tensile strength than does dry bone. Fresh bone fractures in a manner different from dry bone. A green stick versus a dried stick is a reasonable (though exaggerated) analogy.

The amount of time required for the loss of the organic content and moisture in bone and the concomitant change in the fracture characteristics after death is variable. This time interval is dependent upon the postmortem environment. Fire and heat accelerate the drying of bone and the deterioration of collagen and other organic components. Freezing and submersion retard the loss process. Fractures characteristic of fresh bone may persist for weeks after death.

In addition to differences in fracture patterning, differences in staining may also indicate that a bone was disrupted after death. Newly broken bone, (i.e., broken in recovery or transport) may show a color differential between a freshly fractured bone surface and the overall cortical surface. In other words, the recently broken surface is darker or lighter in color than the rest of the bone. Surfaces fractured perimortem will exhibit homogeneous coloration over all cortical surfaces.

For a fuller discussion of the timing of skeletal trauma relative to death, see Sauer (1998).

Trauma Analysis

Skeletal trauma rarely allows for the reconstruction of *cause* of death (i.e., the specific chain of physiological events that resulted in death), but, rather, provides clues as to *manner* of death. Trained in biomechanics, the forensic anthropologist is familiar with forces causing specific patterning in fractures and cuts.

Bone is a composite material, consisting of a collagen fiber (protein) matrix in which hydroxyapatite crystals (mineral) are embedded in alignment with the fiber axis.

The susceptibility of bone to fracture depends on extrinsic factors (direction, magnitude, and duration of the force, and the rate at which the force is applied) and on intrinsic factors, which include the bone's capacity to absorb energy, the bone's stiffness, density, and fatigue strength. Together the intrinsic and extrinsic factors determine the extent and patterning of bone fractures.

Being a viscoelastic material, bone is nearly twice as strong in compression as in tension. Bone deforms under a load and then, in the absence of that load, is restored to its original shape by its elastic component. If the load is sufficient, bone may exceed its elastic limits and enter the plastic phase of deformation. Once this happens, the bone will remain permanently deformed, even after removal of the load. When bone exceeds its elastic and plastic components, it fails (fractures). This relationship is referred to as a stress–strain curve.

Forensic anthropologists are competent in interpreting most common types of skeletal trauma, including damage resulting from blunt and sharp instruments, low and high velocity fire arms, strangulation, and fire.

For a fuller discussion of the biomechanics of bone fracture, see Berryman and Symes (1998). For an overview of the analysis and interpretation of blunt trauma injury to bone, see Galloway (1999).

Stage III: Report/Court Testimony

The final step in any forensic investigation is the writing of the case report and the presentation of evidence in court. Reports are generally submitted to the medical examiner or coroner and to all law enforcement agencies involved in the case. Copies should be retained for the anthropologist's own files.

A useful procedure is one in which a report is written on two levels: A summary report is sent to those in charge of the case with a statement that full details are on file and available upon request. A full report records the detailed analysis with photographs, radiographs, references, anthropometric and anthroposcopic data, diagrams, charts, appendices, and tables. Although the full report may not be of interest to law enforcement personnel, it proves invaluable when called upon to give depositional or courtroom testimony.

Some forensic anthropologists testify frequently, others rarely or never. In my experience, testimony has most often related to issues other than identity.

As an expert witness, an anthropologist should present testimony that is clear and unbiased. The jury should be made aware of one's precise role in the investigation, the procedures employed, and the conclusions reached. Visual data, including drawings, slides, photos, charts, or models, enhance mere verbal description.

Two caveats must be observed: (1) never overstep one's expertise, (2) remain unbiased, not an adversary for prosecution or defense.

Conclusion

Physical anthropologists have applied their knowledge of osteology and human variation to the analysis of unknown skeletons for almost a century. Since its emergence as a distinct subspecialty of anthropology more than 50 years ago, forensic anthropology has gained recognition in the broader forensic science network and has grown dramatically in the number of practitioners and of cases submitted to those practitioners.

More striking, however, is the expansion of forensic anthropology in terms of breadth of application. Forensic anthropologists are now applying their knowledge of human biology, skeletal anatomy, biochemistry, and biomechanics to a wider range of medicolegal problems. Forensic anthropologists are no longer restricting themselves to the reconstruction of biological profiles from skeletal remains. They are addressing questions, and qualifying as experts, in areas considered outside the boundaries of forensic anthropology just a few decades ago.

The increasing utilization of forensic anthropologists by law enforcement agencies and medical examiners has resulted in a tremendous growth in the field. This has stimulated an intensification of research into problems of human identification. The result has been improved accuracy in all stages of analysis, including the recovery, laboratory examination, and reporting phases. Collectively, these advances should be of great value to forensic anthropologists in the field, the laboratory, and the courtroom. Although knowledge of osteology continues as the foundation, forensic anthropologists today are engaged in more diverse areas of research and casework than ever before.

In 1977, the American Board of Forensic Anthropology was established to evaluate professional competence, and to promote adherence to high standards of ethics, conduct, and practice in forensic anthropology. The field is now self-regulating, through a process of examination and annual re-evaluation.

To obtain information, or to locate a board certified forensic anthropologist, visit the website of the American Board of Forensic Anthropology at www.csuchico.edu/anth/ABFA/.

References

Berryman, H.E. and Symes, S.A., Recognizing gunshot and blunt cranial trauma through fracture interpretation, In Reichs, K.J., Ed. *Forensic Osteology: Advances in the Identification of Human Remains.* Springfield, IL: Charles C. Thomas, 1998.

Burns, K.R., *The Forensic Anthropology Training Manual.* Upper Saddle River, NJ: Prentice Hall, 1999.

Byers, S.N., *Introduction to Forensic Anthropology: A Textbook.* Boston, Allyn and Bacon, 2001.

Galloway, A., *Broken Bones: Anthropological Analysis of Blunt Force Trauma.* Springfield, IL: Charles C. Thomas, 1999.

Galloway, A., *Theory and Practice in Forensic Anthropology.* Cambridge, England: Cambridge University Press, 2004.

Krogman, W.M., *The Human Skeleton in Forensic Medicine.* Springfield, IL: Charles C. Thomas, 1962.

Nafte, Myriam, *Flesh and Bone: An Introduction to Forensic Anthropology.* Carolina: Academic Press, 2000.

Rathbun, T.A. and Buikstra, J.E., Eds. *Human Identification: Case Studies in Forensic Anthropology.* Springfield, IL: Charles C. Thomas, 1984.

Reichs, K.J., Ed. *Forensic Osteology: Advances in the Identification of Human Remains.* Springfield, IL: Charles C. Thomas, 1986, 1998.

Steadman, D.W., *Hard Evidence*: *Case Studies in Forensic Anthropology*. Upper Saddle River, NJ: Prentice Hall, 2002.

Stewart, T.D., *Essentials of Forensic Anthropology*. Springfield, IL: Charles C. Thomas, 1979.

Sauer, N.J., The timing of injuries and manner of death: distinguishing among antemortem, perimortem, and postmortem trauma, In Reichs, K.J., Ed. *Forensic Osteology*: *Advances in the Identification of Human Remains*. Springfield, IL: Charles C. Thomas, 1998.

Ubelaker, D.H., *Human Skeletal Remains*. Chicago: Aldine, 1978.

Evidence and the Social and Applied Sciences: An Overview

JAGDEEP S. BHANDARI

This section contains five papers that illustrate and explain the applications of forensic techniques to areas that are not in the traditional fields of life sciences, but to social sciences(such as economics and linguistics), to business(accounting), to engineering, and to the newly developing area of digital analysis of computer "imprints."

Pollitt's paper contains a brief introduction to the field of digital evidence that is easily accessible to readers of all levels of expertise. As Pollitt observes, digital evidence consists of the ubiquitous binary fingerprints of zeroes and ones on digital devices, most of which are computers. The computer age itself is still less than a quarter century old, and it is not surprising that systematic examination of and training in digital fingerprint analysis is very recent. As Pollitt observes, in a section on the historical origins of digital forensics, the area and its potential for authentication and identification of digital footprints came to the attention of law enforcement (in particular, the Federal Bureau of Investigation) only in the early 1990s. And, it was not until the year 2000 at the earliest, that the field had become attractive enough for commercial exploitation, for example, by development of digital evidence kits such as "Encase" and others.[1] The Internal Revenue Service (IRS) acquired rights to use a digital investigative tool, ILOOK in 2002, and has commenced extensive training of its agents in the use of this software. Concomitantly with the commercialization of digital forensic products and their wider use in the last three years, various groups at both the national and international levels have begun to promulgate standards for "best practices." Although, not mentioned in the text, a new journal, *Digital Discovery and E-Evidence: Best Practices and Evolving Laws* has also recently commenced publication.[2]

In the second half of his contribution, Pollitt describes in layperson's terms the notion of digital evidence as being the imprint of a "process" (either static, if the data are stored or dynamic, in the case of movement of packets of information). He concludes his chapter by describing the steps involved in capturing and utilizing digital evidence, namely, acquisition, examination, analysis, and presentation.

If the analysis of digital evidence is to be useful at all in a legal context, it must withstand Daubert–Frye scrutiny and must be presented in a form consistent with the rules of evidence, in particular, those relating to expert testimony. Pollitt concludes his chapter by making these observations.

The next contribution in this section is by Batterman and Batterman, who are well recognized experts in the area of forensic engineering. Forensic techniques in engineering are conceptually similar to those in fields such as forensic accounting. In the broadest sense, forensic methods are diagnostic methods, usually employed after the fact of a failure or malfunction in a variety of contexts such as structural collapses, fire investigation, vehicular accidents, blasting, hail, wind or water damage, electrical and other explosions, and related physical failures. Much of the detailed analysis and reconstruction of a malfunction, especially in civil engineering or accident reconstruction contexts, involves principles of physics and higher mathematics. For example, vehicular accident reconstruction experts must be familiar with inferences regarding velocity, momentum, load shifting, skid marks, etc. and be conversant in principles of thermodynamics, mechanics, and related areas in physics.

The authors correctly observe that one of the principal tasks that may confront the forensic engineer is to be able to prepare a report suitable for use in litigation or even to testify, as an expert, as needed.[3] Hence, the usefulness of including this topic in a volume, such as this one, the audience for which is expected to include professionals in the legal community.

In view of the intended audience, the authors wisely eschew the inclusion of detailed materials employing higher mathematics and physics. The range of contexts in which forensic or diagnostic techniques may be employed is extremely wide, as noted earlier. In a short review of this type, the authors limit their discussion to vehicular accident reconstruction and engineering failures in physical structures. The section on engineering failures is made accessible to the general reader by a brief discussion of well publicized disasters such as the Hyatt Regency Skywalk in Kansas City, the Columbia and Challenger shuttle failures and, of course, the World Trade Center attacks of 2001.

Three sections of the paper are likely to prove to be of particular interest to the legal profession. These are the sections on biomechanics of injury, product liability, and slip and fall analysis. Biomechanic experts are involved in the design of medical devices, personal and industrial safety devices, protective sports and automotive safety equipment, as well as, the effects of trauma upon body tissue, cells, and other biological organs and systems.[4] In other words, biomechanical injury analysis requires successful interdisciplinary collaboration between engineers and medical researchers. To the extent that injury sustained in vehicular accidents can be quantified by objective scalar criteria, damage awards may become more predictable, which in turn could facilitate more speedy settlements.

Similar issues involving the measurement of trauma and its associated effects occur in Slip and Fall cases. As noted by the authors, a large proportion of persons over the age of 65 experience at least one serious slip and fall per year. The analogous concepts to "crashworthiness" in such cases are "tribometry" and measurement of slip resistance of walking surfaces (both of floors and shoes).[5] Whether or not a particular surface is dangerously defective in design or in manufacturing, is the centerpiece of product liability litigation.

The chapter is an effective bird's eye view of selected areas in forensic engineering and is suitable for the non-specialist reader. Space considerations limit discussion of other contexts in which forensic engineers make useful contributions. A short bibliography at the end of the chapter is intended to provide the reader with resources to pursue further interest in these areas.[6]

Forensic economics has been a skill among economists for at least two decades. Forensic accounting, although of much earlier vintage, has received a boost from the recent corporate scandals involving misstated earnings (e.g., Enron, Worldcom and others too numerous to mention). The next two chapters in this section deal with these areas, respectively.

Forensic economics in its broadest sense deals with the quantification of economic or pecuniary losses that may result from wrongful and actionable conduct on the part of another. A large portion of the work of the forensic economist is carried out in the context of actions for personal injury and wrongful death. However, business loss valuation, as, for example, in the contexts of wrongful discharge or discrimination, is also a common area of work for the forensic economist. In a wider commercial setting, the forensic expert may provide valuation services in the case of antitrust losses, loss of business opportunity, losses from theft or misappropriation of intellectual property (such as patents and trademarks) and a myriad of other contexts of business transactions gone awry.[7] In each instance, the forensic economist works closely with the attorney in the case.

Marlin's contribution focuses on losses resulting from personal injury and wrongful death. This chapter is especially useful as a survey and as a desk reference for forensic economists, as it also lists current sources of data for various economic magnitudes. The article will prove of value to both practicing forensic economists and to the legal professional wishing to gain an understanding of the work of his/her retained expert.

The principal ingredients of economic losses in an action for personal injury or wrongful death, are lost earnings (both from the date of injury or death to the present and prospectively) and other elements of lost compensation such as lost fringe benefits over the relevant work life of the injured party or decedent.[8] In addition, courts universally permit value of lost services performed in or for the home to be included in recoverable pecuniary losses. By contrast, nonpecuniary losses such as for pain and suffering, mental anguish, loss of companionship, guidance and counsel, and related elements comprising *in solatium* losses are not within the province of the forensic economist or of any expert.[9] Such nonpecuniary losses can be especially large (and may be the only losses) in certain cases, as, for example, in the case of the death of a child, but the dollar value of such losses is the unique prerogative of the fact finder (the jury or the judge in a bench trial).

In principle, the task of the forensic economist is to determine the extent of allowable economic losses, both past and prospective, that is, the elements of each type of permissible loss must be identified and computed using the most reliable data. Calculation of each element of economic loss carries its own set of complications and subtleties and these are well explicated by Marlin. For example, personal consumption expenditures of a decedent must be subtracted from net losses in a death action, but not for a personal injury claimant.[10] Another issue that must be considered is the effective expected work life of the personal injury plaintiff or decedent. Effective work life takes into account the expected age at retirement (which varies by gender and race) and the possibility of involuntary separation from the labor force for other reasons such as, layoffs, unemployment, or death due to other causes. Aside from the complications inherent in projection of losses of future income, even of regular wage earners, future dollars expected to be earned have to be added to current value dollars to arrive at a present value of the total loss. Courts in such cases do not retain jurisdiction (unlike alimony or child custody cases), and the current award by the court is the final one. Hence, the issue of discounting expected future losses to present value terms by means of a suitable discount rate. The choice of a suitable discount rate has been the subject of some controversy in the forensic economics literature and Marlin carefully discusses the issues with appropriate examples, toward the end of his contribution.[11]

In a short article of this type, it is difficult to cover all relevant topics. It may be of use, however, to briefly note certain selected issues not mentioned by the author, but which are likely to prove of some interest. Due to space constraints, I only comment on a handful of the myriad of other issues that could be discussed.

The elements of recoverable damages and how they may be acceptable measured depend upon both state case law and statutory law. Wrongful death is a creature purely of statute (the action being unknown at common law), and there is no uniform statute that applies. In other words, the statutory compilation of each state must be consulted. It is in this regard that the forensic economist must cooperate closely with the attorney in the case. State wrongful death laws exhibit a bewildering array of variety; some afford a remedy for the statutory beneficiaries only (i.e., the original Lord Campbell type statutes), whereas others are of the loss to estate variety. In some cases, for example, Florida, the statute authorizes recovery for both survivors and the estate.[12] At the same time, some state statutes contain relatively detailed guidance regarding the elements of recovery, whereas others merely authorize the fact finder to "just" damages, which may or may not include punitive awards, again depending upon the state.[13] State decisional law may provide additional guidance as to recoverable damages or as to methods of computation, especially when the relevant statute is broadly worded.

In contrast to wrongful death actions, actions for personal injury are common law actions, and the elements of damages are determined by canvassing recent state decisional law. Complicating these issues is the action that is governed by statute, known as the survival action. The term is an unfortunate misnomer and is often a source of confusion. Survival actions authorize recovery for pre-death damages only in the case of noninstantaneous death; the term "survival" only implies that the death of the injured party does not extinguish the action, as it did at common law. For reasons of lack of space, Marlin's contribution understandably omits discussion of these issues.

In certain instances, law other than the law of a particular state may apply, especially in instances of wrongful death. For example, federal maritime law applies in cases of death on navigable maritime waters. Cases of death in the high seas may be governed by a federal statute — Death on the High Seas by Wrongful Act (DOSHA) — with respect to both the extent of recovery and the identity of the beneficiaries.[14] In air crash disasters, particularly in international air space, liability may be governed by the Warsaw Convention and related international treaties.[15] The applicability of federal law in death actions may arise in garden variety wrongful death actions as well, under applicable state statutes. Under the *Erie Doctrine*, federal courts sitting in diversity (as is inevitable in state based causes of action for wrongful death) are to apply state substantive law, but are to apply federal procedural law. Commentators and courts have argued that, although the elements of recoverable damages for wrongful death is a substantive matter for *Erie* purposes, the computation of such damages is merely procedural. It is under this type of logic that some federal circuits authorize a deduction for taxes from the eventual award, while a state court could not do so.[16]

Other interesting factual variations also abound. In particular, in today's world of increased international commercial intercourse, decedents or injured plaintiffs may have derived part of all of their compensation from foreign sources, in foreign currency. Courts in the United States while authorized to award foreign currency judgments are reluctant to do so, and foreign currency amounts must by translated into U.S. dollars. Exchange rate forecasting is a particularly vexing business, especially when long time horizons are involved.[17] Currency units of countries may be redefined or redenominated.[18] National currencies may be abolished altogether, as, for example, with full entry into the European Union. Courts, lawyers, and forensic economists alike have paid scant attention thus far, to losses denominated in foreign currencies. Although a suit by a foreign plaintiff injured in the United States, say in New York, cannot normally be dismissed under *forum non conveniens*, questions arise as to choice of law and data. Should the elements of damages authorized by New York (the *situs* of the accident) apply, or those provided for under the law of the plaintiff's home country? Regardless of the answer to this conflicts issue, it is clear that data on wages, benefits, life spans, etc. must be obtained from foreign sources. Most forensic economists would find this endeavor to be a daunting task.

Returning to the domestic context, factual scenarios in which compensation is not primarily wage income, as, for example, in the case of a business owner or a corporate executive endowed with stock options, there are potentially interesting unresolved issues. For example, although the death of a key business owner or employee terminates that person's salary, is the loss to the business as a whole, also a compensable loss?[19] This issue gains more prominence when the business has publicly traded stock or has otherwise utilized capital markets to raise funds. Should the fall in corporate stock value or the increased cost of financing in capital markets following the death of a key person, also be a recoverable element of damages? Most jurisdictions have not addressed this issue to date.

There are other factual variations of interest even within the context of personal injury and wrongful death actions. For reasons of space constraints, Marlin has elected to focus his contribution on the most common cases involving regular wage earnings of U.S. workers.

Forensic accounting has come to the attention of the public in a big way since the corporate accounting fraud revealed since the 1990s. Fraud or investigative accounting is as old as accounting itself, but the spate of legal activity in the wake of the recent accounting scandals is unprecedented. Other than the myriad of lawsuits filed, one of the imposing pieces of new legislation in this context is the Sarbanes–Oxley Act.[20] The Act itself has been extensively discussed in the literature of various disciplines. The implications of defining the role and function of accounting in legal contexts, naturally requires accountants to cooperate closely with lawyers, both to forestall litigation and also, more importantly, after litigation has begun. The term forensic accountant (which is of relatively recent vintage) is meant to emphasize the role and function of the investigative accountant as a consultant or expert witness in an adversarial or legal context.

McCrory's chapter contains an overview of these functions of the investigative or forensic accountant. In view of the intended audience of the book, McCrory has appropriately chosen to devote most of his paper to the role of the forensic accountant in the legal process. As he highlights, one of the key differences between the roles of an auditor and a forensic accountant is that the latter may be called upon to testify in court or take part in settlement or mediation conferences. Therefore, communication skills, including interviewing skills (necessary in assisting preparation of deposition questions) are of much greater importance to the forensic accountant than an auditor *qua* auditor. In addition, the auditor usually confines his/her examination to past events, for example, historical or financial statements. In a legal setting, damages properly include both those that have occurred to date, as well as, expected future losses. Hence, forecasting skills are an important ingredient of the portfolio of the forensic accountant's desirable skills.

In the latter portion of his contribution, McCrory surveys the role and function of the forensic accountant in a variety of concrete factual contexts. These include breaches of contract in breach of construction contracts, or during purchase or sale of businesses, trademark, copyright and patent infringement, valuation of assets in bankruptcy, marital settlement, and in estate and probate matters. In the last section of his paper, the author discusses damages in the context of personal injury and wrongful death. To this extent, McCrory's discussion provides an interesting comparison with Marlin's treatment of these issues in the preceding chapter.

Each of the topics discussed or identified by McCrory is a subject in its own right that is capable of much more detailed analysis. Such analyses has in fact, been pursued in various other treatments of forensic accounting and the interested reader is referred to these additional sources.[21]

The next contribution in this section is by Carole Chaski, a well recognized expert, in the relatively new area of Forensic Linguistics. The paper provides both on introduction to linguistics as a science and also, an excellent survey of the forensic applications of linguistics in a legal setting. It will, therefore, be of interest to both linguists and the legal community.

Unlike instruction in language, grammar, style, and syntax, linguistics is the science of language and focuses on its positive, observational aspects rather than normative issues of correct style or grammar. It is a science in that it applies scientific methods for observation, hypothesis testing, and inference or prediction. For linguists, grammar is a description of observations of linguistic behaviors or rules, whether considered "good" or not, by grammarians or language scholars. Each grammar contains description of the language sound pattern, word patterns, syntax, conversation or discourse patterns, etc. Deviations from the available native pattern of any of these will appear "ungrammatical" to the listener, or will signal a nonnative language skill to the analyst. It is this signal that may permit the forensic examiner to pinpoint, or at least narrow down, authorship of the speech or writing by sociological or regional origin.[22]

Forensic Linguistics is a specialized application of linguistics to the legal process. This approach has generated a number of useful studies on the use of trial language, jury instructions, and the phraseology of interrogations and confessions.[23] In turn, forensic linguistics may be sub-categorized according to the uses to which it is put, such as linguistic profiling, discourse analysis, and authorship attribution. Linguistic profiling deduces demographic characteristics (race, gender, national or ethnic origin, occupation, etc.) from spoken words or written text. Discourse analysis in the forensic context is used by investigators to literally "crack codes," that is, deduce negotiated meanings of particular words or phrases. Often, this work takes place in the context of electronics surveillance or other interception. Finally, authorship attribution is similar to questioned document analysis and deduces the possible identity of the author. There is more than one approach to authorship attribution and one syntactic analysis has withstood Daubert's scrutiny.[24] Chaski has been a pioneer in this particular specialty.

In the second half of her article, Chaski focuses on describing the technique of syntactic analysis with respect to authorship attribution. The subsection is rich in practical suggestions for trial lawyers, complete with case citations and references to applicable rules of evidence. The reception by courts of authorship attribution evidence, when presented by experts, has been frosty, as noted by Chaski. But when interdisciplinary methods are used — as, for example, when forensic lingustic analysis is augmented with statistical techniques, such as discriminant analysis — the syntactic approach appears to have enjoyed a much warmer reception in recent court decisions and has been ruled to be fully admissible.

The concluding pages of the article contain a fascinating analysis of the possible authorship of the well publicized "anthrax letters."[25] Both expert and nonexpert readers will find this example interesting.

The final chapter in this section by Welner and Ramsland deals with forensic psychology.[26] Unlike the social sciences, such as economics (and possibly linguistics), psychology is one of the behavioral sciences, which are distinct in their methods from the "hard" sciences, such as engineering. Although, as noted previously, forensic linguistics is a relatively new area, forensic or investigative psychology is as old as crime itself.[27] As the authors point out, the forensic psychologist or psychiatrist has a different orientation and skill set than his/her clinical counterpart. For instance, the forensic examiner needs to be proficient in record review, witness interviews, examination of videos and phone call transcripts, crime scene visits, and above all, in effective presentation at trial. The clinician's primary focus is usually on diagnosis and treatment and his/her stance toward the examinee is likely to be non-judgmental and sympathetic. By contrast, the forensic examiner is not retained for purposes of treatment, time is short, and the orientation toward the subject or examinee needs to be objective or even somewhat cynical. Unlike his/her clinical counterpart, the forensic psychologist at trial must take a definite position or offer a firm opinion.[28]

The chapter is clearly organized into sections dealing with criminal matters, civil issues, workplace concerns, and a final section covering ethical responsibilities in practice. In each section, the authors offer the reader a sampling of issues and situations in which the services of a forensic psychologist are likely to be of use. In the criminal context, the context that is most well known relates to competency of the criminal accused. Competency includes competency to waive *Miranda* rights, to engage in *pro se* representation, to engage in plea bargaining, to be sentenced, and to be executed. Part of the task of the forensic examiner in these contexts is to rule out the possibility of malingering and deception. On some occasions, competency may be restored by education about the legal process, or more frequently, through medication. As a strategic matter, defense attorneys may resist both of these courses of action if they hamper their client's defense or ability to raise an insanity defense or to obtain a competency postponement. Most courts have ruled out, however, that criminal defendants have no absolute right to refuse medically appropriate treatment that is expected to restore competency. Competency to be executed is somewhat controversial and may raise complex ethical issues. Executing an incompetent person may implicate the Eighth Amendment; on the other hand, many persons may regard it as unethical or even unconstitutional to medicate a convict solely for the purpose of temporarily restoring competency to execute the prisoner. The U.S. Courts of Appeals that have considered the latter issue, have recently held that correctional officials may forcibly medicate a death row convict if that will enable him/her to gain sufficient competency to comprehend the fact of an impending and actual execution.

Two other examples offered in this section discuss behavioral profiling. In the investigative context, the type of profiling relevant is retrospective (i.e., after the commission of a crime) to assist detectives in narrowing the list of possible suspects (or more colorfully, "persons of interest"). The Behavioral Analysis Unit of the FBI was established both as an investigative unit for profiling in complex cases and as an educational arm for law enforcement authorities.

In the civil context too, the authors discuss various examples, and two may be briefly mentioned: Emotional injury is usually an important element of claimed damages in personal injury and wrongful death suits. It may also be relevant in certain situations involving toxic and other mass torts. In addition, emotional injury resulting in post-traumatic stress disorder may be relevant, as a defense in both civil and criminal actions. The behavioral psychologist has a useful role to play in assessing the type and degree of claimed emotional injury. Another example, all too familiar to most readers, is the use of behavioral or forensic experts in child custody and other domestic relations matters.

In the context of the workplace, forensic psychologists may be used to assess the degree of distress resulting from an alleged hostile environment (in Title VII discrimination suits). They may also be used in ADA cases that require an evaluation of fitness for particular duties, especially to weed out false claims motivated by malingering or shirking.

The reader will find this chapter to be a useful overview of the large variety of contexts in which forensic psychologists may play an important role.

Notes

1. Another such kit is known by the name "Biatchux." The Electronic Evidence Information Center maintains a web page with a host of resources in the area, including books, kits, and information on recent advances and inventions.

2. The journal is published by Pike and Fisher, a subsidiary of BNA. Other publications on digital evidence include books such as E. Casey, *Digital Evidence and Computer Crime*, Academic Press, 2001, and a more recent title, R. Slade, *Software Forensics: Collecting Evidence from the Scene of a Digital Crime*, McGraw Hill, 2004.

3. A report prepared by an expert may constitute hearsay, unless it is properly authenticated and introduced as one of the exceptions to the hearsay in the Federal Rules of Evidence, such as the exception for Business Records. One time reports prepared in anticipation of litigation may face special impediments under this exception. However, their principal use is for purposes of pre-trial settlement. The legal expert will also recognize that reports prepared by nontestifying experts are subject to specific protection from discovery in the Federal Rules of Civil Procedure. Many, if not most, states have modeled their rules of evidence and civil procedure based upon the federal rules.

4. In automotive safety, for example, there are several organizations such as the Association for the Advance of Automotive Medicine (AAAM) that have attempted to promulgate uniform standards for injury classification and measurement (e.g., the Abbreviated Injury Scale). In addition, federal legislation has established various threshold injury criteria with which automobile manufacturers must comply. See for example, Federal Motor Vehicle Safety Standards in 571 *et seq.*

5. Organizations such as the American Society for Testing of Materials (see www.astm.org) have been active in developing uniform standards in the measurement of slip resistance.

6. Aside from the references cited by Battman and Battman, the interested reader may also wish to consult, among others, R. Ratay, *Forensic Structural Engineering Handbook*, McGraw Hill, 2000, R. Noon, *Forensic Engineering Investigation*, CRC Press, 2000, J. Brown, K. Obenski and T. Osborn, *Forensic Engineering Reconstruction of Accidents*, Charles Thomas Publisher Inc., 2003, and R. Sherman, *Point of Impact: Case Studies of Forensic Engineering in Personal Injury Lawsuits*, Lawyers and Judges Publishing Co., 2000.

7. Some examples include termination of franchises, valuation of collateral or security interests in bankruptcy, foregone opportunities in mergers and acquisitions, losses from insider trading, and other inappropriate stock market activity, bond defaults, etc.

8. Many jurisdictions also recognize lost inheritance as an element of economic loss to statutory beneficiaries. Although Marlin does not discuss this element of loss explicitly, the careful reader can derive useful implications regarding its computation from a close reading of the paper.

9. Unfortunately, state laws are not uniform in their definition of pecuniary versus nonpecuniary losses. For example, Texas considers lost guidance and counsel to be a pecuniary loss, while loss of society and companionship is a nonpecuniary loss. It should also be noted that, the term "pecuniary" is not necessarily synonymous with "monetary" for purposes of state statutes.

10. Hence, the well-known tongue-in-cheek admonition to tort defendants: If you run over someone, be certain to reverse your car and run him over again to make sure he is dead.

11. The general consensus among forensic economists is that the chosen discount rate must be a risk-free rate (as e.g., on U.S. Treasury bonds), and its maturity is to coincide with the expected period of future losses in the case.

12. See FL. STAT ANN Section 768.21 Subsections (1)–(4) generally cover losses to survivors, while subsection (6) separately addresses loss to the estate.

13. In at least two states, New Mexico and Connecticut, there may be a possibility of also recovering "hedonic damages" (damages to the estate for loss of enjoyment of life). Hedonic damages were brought to the attention of the legal community in the well known civil rights case *Sherrod v Berry* 856 F.2d 802 (7th Cir., 1988).

14. See 46 USCA 761-768.

15. The Warsaw Convention is codified in the U.S. Code at 49 USCA 40105.

16. The Fifth Circuit, for example, has developed a practice of allowing a deduction of taxes from the wrongful death award.

17. In fact, forward or futures markets for foreign currencies (which might plausibly supply a forecast of the future exchange rate) simply do not exist for time horizons in excess of a few months.

18. For instance, the New Turkish Lira replaced the Turkish Lira on January 1, 2005, at a nominal parity of one to one million. Many commercial establishments in Turkey (which is an applicant to the European Union) quote prices simultaneously in old Turkish Lira, New Turkish Lira, U.S. Dollars, and in Euros.

19. For example, the business may lose a valuable customer base with the death or departure of a key employee. In other cases, financial markets may perceive a loss of leadership (say, by the death of a "key man") as a negative factor, which, in turn, may cause corporate stock prices to fall.

20. See Public Company Accounting Reform and Investor Protection (Sarbanes–Oxley) Act, *Pub. L. No. 107–204* (codified as amended in scattered sections of 15, 18 U.S.C.). Title VII of the Act is the Corporate and Criminal Fraud Accountability Act of 2002. § 801, 116 Stat., 800. Title IX

is White Collar Crime Penalty Enhancements Act of 2002. § 901, 116 Stat., 804. Title XI is the Corporate Fraud and Accountability Act of 2002. § 1101, 116 Stat., 807–10.

21. See for example, G. Murray, *Financial Investigation, and Forensic Accounting* CRC Press, 1999, L. Crumbley, *Forensic and Investigative Accounting*, Commerce Clearing House, 2003, J. Anastasi et al., *The New Forensics: Investigating Corporate Fraud and Theft of Intellectual Property* (Wiley, 2003), Z. Teloner and M. Mostek. *Expert Witnessing in Forensic Accounting: A Handbook for Lawyers and Accountants*, CRC Press, 2002, and James DiGabriele. *Forensic Accounting in Matrimonial Divorce*, R.T. Edwards, 2005, among several others.

22. A non-specialist, yet highly readable book on regional variations in enunciation and speech patterns in the U.S., is by R. MacNeil and W. Cran, *Do You Speak American?*, Doubleday, 2005.

23. See, for example, R. Shuy, *The Language of Confession, Interrogation and Deception*, Sage Publications, 1997, and S. Walters, *Principles of Kinesic Interview and Interrogation*, 2nd ed. CRC Press 2002, among others.

24. Another approach is forensic stylistics; see generally, G. Menamin (Ed.) *Forensic Linguistics: Advances in Forensic Stylistics*, CRC Press 2002. Some other useful references in the general area of forensic linguistics include J. Olsson, *Forensic Linguistics: An Introduction to Language, Crime and the Law*, Continuum International Publishing, 2004, J. Gibbons, *Forensic Linguistics: An Introduction to Language in the Justice System*, Blackwell, 2003, and M. Coulthard and J. Cotterill, *Introducing Forensic Linguistics*, Routledge, 2005.

25. The "anthrax letters" misspelled the word "pencillicin" as "penacilin." Chaski's view is that this misspelling, unless intentional, is not a predictable misspelling among native Arabic speakers as originally suspected by law enforcement. Another well known instance of authorship attribution is of course, the "Unabomber Case." Intentional misspelling by a person with some familiarity with forensic linguistics leads to a secondary set if issues, involving strategic game theory. As of this time, and to my knowledge, no one with training in higher mathematics, including game theory, has written in the area of forensic linguistics.

26. Although the authors have not provided follow up references, the following may be of use to interested readers; L. Wrightsman, M. Tuplinger, and M. Linsenman, *Forensic Psychology*, Wadsworth, 2000; G. Gudjonsson. L. Haward, and L.R.C. Haward *Forensic Psychology: A Guide to Practice* (Routledge, 1988); J. Jackson and E. Barkley (Eds.), *Offender Profiling*, Wiley, 1997; B. Turvey, *Criminal Profiling: An Introduction to Behavioral Evidence Analysis* (2nd ed. Academic Press 2002); A. Goldstein and E. Weiner, *Handbook of Psychology and Forensic Psychology*, Wiley, 2003; G. Melton, *Psychological Evaluation for the Courts*, Guilford Press, 1977, and T. Grisso, *Evaluating Competencies: Forensic Assessment and Instruments*, Plenum, 2002.

27. Investigative or forensic psychology plays an important and intriguing role, for example, in the many Sherlock Holmes' novels of Arthur Conan Doyle.

28. Forensic psychologists testifying at trial or in deposition would normally be classified as experts, for purposes of the Federal Rules of Evidence and are expected to offer opinion testimony. The Federal rules expressly prohibit the expert from testifying as to ultimate issues of fact (such as the existence of insanity) or from offering opinions as to legal conclusions (such as criminal intent). In exchange, the expert is given considerable leeway in forming his/her testimony (which may be in narrative form) and may rely upon inadmissible hearsay in forming the basis of opinion. See Federal Rules of Evidence 701–704. Most states have evidentiary rules closely patterned after the federal rules.

Behavioral Science and the Law

26

MICHAEL WELNER AND KATHERINE M. RAMSLAND

Introduction

The behavioral sciences interface with the law in numerous ways, reflecting a rich relationship unparalleled across the forensic sciences. Although the psychiatry/psychology and criminal law intersection is the most notorious, there are numerous civil, employment, and family court matters in which mental health consultation informs the court to a pivotal end.

Beyond the range of cases involving forensic psychiatry and psychology, the behavioral sciences address issues of vital policy interest. False confessions, sexual harassment, gay adoption, and securities fraud are a sampling of controversial disputes where mental health consultation elevates legal decision making above the pedestrian or salacious.

Forensic psychiatry and psychology extend beyond traditional notions of the behavioral sciences that activity is limited to the consultation room. Activities include record review, witness interviewing, house calls and crime scene visits, probing various forms of evidence ranging from videotaped interviews to cell phone records, tax returns to favorite Websites visited on the Internet. Psychological testing is used differently in forensic examination, and report writing is deliberate and detailed. And, of course, forensic matters also involve depositions and trial, embedding the behavioral sciences within the process of justice.

Interviews may be quite lengthy; the forensic mental health professional, unlike the clinical psychiatrist or psychologist, must form a complete opinion within a proscribed period and therefore does not have the luxury of saying, "See you next week."

One point of distinction of the clinical psychiatrist or psychologist from the forensic psychiatrist or psychologist is the orientation to the examinee. The clinical psychiatric examination reflects a climate of nonjudgmental presumption of trust. A treating doctor takes what a patient states at face value, with the sense that the patient's primary motivation is symptom relief.

People referred for forensic examination, however, have priorities that relate to their legal dispute. The forensic assessment therefore requires the presumption of skepticism that the examinee is influenced as to what to reveal by the pressures of the legal agenda.

This does not mean that all examinees lie, but does add a burden to the examiner of utilizing an understanding of behavioral science to exercise creative and complete diligence.

Criminal Matters

Competency

Competency questions should not be confused with the insanity defense. The former emphasizes mental functioning in a legal context at present and the latter, criminal responsibility associated with an accused person's mental state at the time of an offense.

Issues of competency can occur at several different junctures across the life cycle of a case. Although one's competency to stand trial is perhaps the most familiar, there are other types of competencies as well, and mental health professionals may be involved in assessing them. These include competency to: (1) waive *Miranda* rights, (2) represent one's self, (3) plea, (4) be sentenced, and (5) be executed.

In *Miranda v. Arizona*,[1] the constitutional privilege against self-incrimination was affirmed. Upon being arrested, suspects are advised of their *Miranda* rights to remain silent and to have an attorney present during interrogation. If suspects choose to waive these rights, they must do so knowingly, intelligently, and voluntarily. Mental illness and mental retardation can be factors, although the presence of either condition does not automatically make someone incompetent. If in the process of voluntarily responding to questions people confess to a crime, their competency to have done so may be raised prior to trial. To appraise competency in this issue requires consideration of both the circumstances of the police interview and the psychological characteristics of the person being questioned.

Since a high percentage of criminal cases are resolved through deals based on a guilty plea, the defendant must understand the nature of the charges, the associated penalties, and whatever rights he or she has waived upon entering the plea. A judge typically makes the determination of competency during the arraignment. In *Godinez v. Moran*,[2] which all federal jurisdictions and most states follow, the U.S. Supreme Court held that anyone found competent to stand trial is also competent to plead guilty.

In *Dusky v. U.S.*,[3] in 1960, the Supreme Court set standards for defining competency. According to the guidelines set forth, to be judged competent, a defendant must show a rational and factual understanding of the charges: he or she must possess sufficient present capacity to understand the criminal process, to function in that process, and to consult with counsel. That is, a defendant must clearly understand the roles played by the various participants and be able to plan or assist in the planning of his defense.

To decide on competency to stand trial, the evaluator must learn of the defendant's understanding of the charges against him. The examiner probes the defendant's understanding of the different court functionaries, including the attorneys, judge, jury, and witnesses. Furthermore, assessment also examines the defendant's sense of what will occur in the event of a guilty verdict, or acquittal; or, if a plea is involved, the examiner must examine the decision making related to plea discussions, as well as a defendant's willingness or ability to contribute to his defense. If competency is questioned because of a problem between defendant and defense attorney, the specifics of that incompatibility must be investigated. In addition, the competency examination must determine whether the defendant can conduct himself appropriately in court.

At any time during a proceeding that the defendant is thought to be unable to perceive the situation fully or realistically, he or she may be tested for competence. Either attorney may make a motion for a judicial order of examination, as may the court — even over the defendant's objections. One or more mental health professionals may then participate in the evaluation. Brief screenings may take place in jail early in the criminal processing, but more often full competency assessments are performed in a hospital setting.

The examining psychiatrist or psychologist may use a standardized intelligence test to measure intellectual deficiencies or may use diagnostic screening interviews. However, the presence of a diagnosis does not establish incompetency; rather, diagnosis may educate the court about why a specific defendant is or is not competent.

Several competency screening devices have been released for general use, and have attracted varying degrees of support. Nevertheless, a competency examination must focus first on gathering history specific to the particular case; standardized testing is useful, but not to the exclusion of tailoring an assessment specific to a given case. This also means soliciting information from collateral sources whenever possible.

Forensic assessment of competency must also account for the possibility of malingering. History and psychological testing may be useful for this purpose, and defendants are often referred for hospital observation when uncertainty lingers about a faking defendant. Corrections officers who observe the defendant away from mental health professionals, or taped telephone conversations, may be ideal sources of information to unearth malingered incompetency or validate one's incapacity.

The judge will then evaluate the facts to decide whether or not the accused is competent to the procedure at issue. A finding of incompetence, however, does not mean that the person is mentally ill. He or she may alternatively have neurological or intelligence deficits. If the defendant is found competent, the legal proceedings continue. If not, the proceedings are suspended until competency is restored.

A judgment of incompetency prompts the court to transfer the defendant to treatment facilities charged with restoring competency. Sometimes, competency can be restored with education about the legal process, but more often, treatment involves psychoactive medication.

But there are complications. Defendants may choose to resist treatment that could restore competency, especially if side effects are severe or irreversible. Some attorneys raise the issue that giving their clients a more rational demeanor for trial can actually hamper their efforts to get an insanity acquittal. However, many courts have found that defendants have no inherent right to refuse medically appropriate treatment, and in the event that treatment is the least intrusive means to achieving the state's goal, the state's interests generally supplant individual rights. Most psychotic, delusional, and affective disorders, such as depression or anxiety, which are not severely organic, can be treated well enough to restore competency. If the defendant is restored to competency, then the trial may proceed.

In *Jackson v. Indiana*[4] in 1972, the court decided that the state may not commit someone on the grounds of incompetency unless there was a substantial probability that competency could be restored. After a reasonable period, if competency was not restored, the person could only be detained if he or she was found to be a danger to self or others. In the event that attempts at restoration seem unfeasible without a constitutional deprivation of liberty, the evaluator should alert the court to the need for an alternative course of action.

Another consideration is the competency to proceed *pro se*, or to waive counsel and assume the task of self-representation. A finding of incompetency to do so may not be based on an inability to understand the technical aspects of the law. A judge, however, can allow a person to choose self-representation but also force him or her to proceed with standby counsel ready to take over should the need arise.

Plea agreements have their own complexities. Since freedom is directly impacted by a guilty plea, the defendant must understand the nature of the charges, the associated penalties, and whatever rights he or she has waived upon entering the plea.

Competency also becomes an issue at sentencing. Individuals found incompetent to be sentenced — that is, do not have an understanding of the sentencing proceedings — may not be sentenced to prison or executed. It is considered a violation of the Eighth Amendment, since they cannot participate in the legal process, as is their right.

Many mental health professionals sometimes have ethical difficulty with the evaluation of a convicted person for the purpose of judging them competent to be executed — especially if they must medicate the person for the purpose of rendering them competent. Yet, withholding treatment for mental illness is also unethical. Those mental health professionals whose beliefs may affect their objective judgment in capital cases must consider not participating in such evaluations.

Finding defendants incompetent to be executed raises other problems: inmates may malinger a mental illness as a way to avoid their sentence or simply refuse to be treated. The U.S. Court of Appeals for the Eight Circuit ruled in the case of Charles Singleton in 2003 that prison officials can force an inmate on death row to take medication that will restore sanity in preparation for execution.

Criminal Responsibility

The legal system recognizes that responsibility for committing a crime depends on two things: *actus reus*, which is evidence that the accused engaged in the act, and *mens rea*, the mental state required to have intended to commit the act and foresee its consequences.

The standard for determining criminal responsibility varies by state. However, insanity is not a diagnostic concept. It is a legal concept related to but not synonymous with mental illness. Nevertheless, there is no uniform standard for determining insanity, and a person found sane in one jurisdiction might be considered insane in another. In America today, federal and state courts use a variety of standards, generally grounded in knowledge of right and wrong, but sometimes including the ability to conform one's actions to the requirements of the law.

The insanity plea is used in a small minority of cases, and succeeds in very few of those. Although three states have no insanity defense, mental health practitioners in those jurisdictions may nevertheless be allowed to testify about criminal responsibility issues such as *mens rea*.

Beginning in 1975, some states instituted the legal standard of "guilty but mentally ill." This verdict means that the defendant committed the act, did not meet the insanity standard, but nevertheless is mentally ill. Convicted defendants receive the same sentence as if they were guilty, but may be confined where they can receive psychiatric treatment.

To make a determination of the mental state at the time of the offense (MSO), the clinician must examine the defendant's actions and perceptions leading up to the crime and coordinate these findings with police and medical examiner reports, as well as with documentation from witnesses and other informants about the presentation and progression of a condition. Mental health defenses to crime include insanity, automatism, diminished capacity, battered woman defenses, self-defense, delirium from medical conditions, and involuntary intoxication. All require an assessment of the client's mental state at the time the crime was committed.

History derives from investigative reports, interviews, crime scene evidence, toxicology reports, and medical examinations, for example. An insight into a person's mental state at the time of the crime can be derived from eyewitnesses and confidantes who observed or encountered the examinee before the offense. The most important of these informants can be identified from a survey of family and in-laws, telephone and email correspondence records, personal diaries and schedules, credit card, travel, and other records, acquaintances, and haunts. The common threads of information yielded from these investigations are communications and behaviors and their reflection on the mental state of the actor.

The MSO evaluation invariably appraises what motive was behind a crime; the more absent a rational motive, the more readily an examiner may consider an irrational motive that may herald impaired appreciation of wrong, impaired ability to conform conduct, or impaired appreciation of the nature and consequences of actions.

Mental illness defenses require confirmation of a diagnosis. Standardized testing instruments that assess personality and diagnosis may be helpful in this regard — although such instruments must account for the pressure that an examinee faces to exaggerate illness. To that end, self-report instruments are of less forensic evidentiary value than tests that can invalidate themselves if the examinee attempts to mislead the examiner.[5]

Tests should be administered according to the diagnosis in question. For example, the possibility of posttraumatic stress disorder can be explored with the Trauma Symptom Inventory (TSI),[6] while psychotic disorders can be further assessed with the MMPI-2.[7] Of course, even though diagnoses may manifest themselves in testing results, the possibility that the diagnosis is of different severity, or is different from the time of the crime, has to be explored through informants and history. Personality disorders, while often stated as diagnoses in psychiatric testimony, are not considered relevant to an insanity defense, although some personality disorders, such as paranoid or borderline, may manifest psychotic symptoms during periods of stress, to the degree that relevance to the insanity defense is understandable.[8]

Acquittals based on legal insanity are followed by evaluation of the need for commitment and treatment. Disposition is determined by level of dangerousness. A finding of dangerousness results in placement in a forensic hospital; lack of dangerousness in a civil hospital until signs of illness are resolved.

However, insanity is not the only issue covered in MSO evaluations. In certain states, a defendant can give evidence that focuses on *mens rea* without having to claim insanity. He or she can say they did not purposely or knowingly commit the crime, or that they could not have meaningfully premeditated it, and this could win a lesser verdict and sentence. For example, a defense of automatism may be raised in the context of sleep violence, such as sleep walking. A lack of *mens rea* may also be raised in the context of hypnotic suggestion, involuntary intoxication, and metabolic or brain disorders.

Some people voluntarily commit a crime and have the requisite *mens rea*, but claim they were not responsible due to compelling factors other than their mental state. This includes cases of self-defense, entrapment, acting under duress, and justification.

These defenses acknowledge the crime but offer reasons to acquit based on strong mitigating factors.

In homicide cases of some states, extreme emotional disturbance may be claimed for a possible reduced charge to manslaughter. It must be proven that the provocation would cause a reasonable person to violently react, the provocation actually caused the reaction, there was no time for a reasonable person to cool off between the provoking act and the reaction, and the defendant did not cool off. In situations such as significant assault (not deadly) or the discovery of something suddenly enraging such as adultery, reasonable people may not have taken time to think before acting.

When an unlawful threat causes a person to believe that he must take action to avoid serious harm or death and that action violates the law, the defendant can claim it was done under duress. Faced with a choice of evils, the defendant chose what would be considered the lesser of the two.

Specifying provocation or duress can involve a clinician as an expert on such situations as domestic abuse, coercion via brainwashing, dependent personality disorder, and intermittent explosive disorder, for example.

Presentencing

In nondeath penalty cases in many jurisdictions, the judge determines the sentence after the probation department's recommendations in a presentencing report. In preparing this report, the probation department incorporates all relevant information from the prosecutor, defendant, victims, defendant's family and employer, and anyone else who might offer relevant input.

With the possibility of rehabilitation in mind, mental health professionals can make treatment suggestions, provide information about the defendant's culpability and mitigating conditions, assess the defendant's remorse, and offer predictions about the future risk of criminal conduct. In a presentencing setting, the examiner may offer input on special considerations for housing, special hardships relating to adapting to the prison environment, suicidal risk, or impact on others such as the defendant's children.

Even when determinate sentencing leaves little room for discretion, a judge may still consider downward departure after reviewing input from a mental health professional. Examples of factors that may influence a judge to assign a lesser sentence include a non-pressured guilty plea, minor participation in the crime, a mental disorder that reduces capacity to appreciate the conduct's criminal nature, the defendant's youth, or the whether the defendant requires specialized treatment for a mental disorder. The defendant might also have acted under duress or provocation, or agrees to compensate the victim, and needs to work to do so.

Upward departure from the guidelines is also possible. A defendant with prior convictions, a history of violent offenses, or a high risk of recidivism may seem clearly established as a threat to society. In that case, the judge may extend the person's time in prison beyond what the guidelines suggest. Likelihood of risk may be responsible for upward departure.

Death penalty cases are divided into two phases: the *guilt phase* and the *sentencing phase*. During the sentencing phase, evidence is offered for aggravating or mitigating factors that can affect the sentencing. A defense attorney will invariably request a psychiatric assessment and psychological testing as a way to assist the defendant in accounting for any psychiatric condition, substance abuse, intellectual deficiency, relevant psychosocial history, or physical or sexual abuse that might influence a jury to avoid passing a death sentence. Once the defense introduces mental health issues, however, the prosecutor has a right to introduce rebuttal evidence. Under these circumstances, the examiner explores the legitimacy of the issues raised by the defense to see if they are indeed real or exaggerated, or if other issues are relevant to the determination of mitigation and aggravation. A jury considers the evidence and makes a decision as to whether the defendant will receive death or life in prison without the possibility of parole.

Forensic examiners are sometimes asked to offer assessments regarding the convicted person's potential danger to the community. Risk assessment methods have become increasingly sophisticated. The most highly regarded risk assessment instruments include *The Historical/Clinical/Risk Management Scale* (HCR-20),[9] which uses 20 items to gather information about the subject's background and personality, and the *Violence Risk Appraisal Guide* (VRAG), an actuarial instrument that uses 12 variables to arrive at an actuarial probability of re-offense.[10]

As the subdiscipline stands today, risk assessment data upon which judgments are to be made should meet the following criteria:

1. "Dangerousness" must be distinguished into clearly enumerating risk factors, nature of harm, and likelihood of occurrence
2. An array of risk factors must be assessed from multiple domains in the offender's life, across the offenders' life span
3. The probability estimate of risk must be acknowledged to change over time and context
4. More reliable predictions are available from actuarial research

At best, mental health professionals can make only recommendations about relative probability of risk, and should provide comprehensive information about the risk factors upon which they focus in a given case. Risk management, which involves devising programs to help a person avoid becoming dangerous, or criminal recidivism, focuses on those factors that may improve with intervention, such as drug treatment, assertiveness training, anger management, or medication interventions. Important factors in risk assessment include the quality of the individual's social support, living arrangements, and access to treatment.[10]

Corrections

The roles for mental health professionals in the correctional system are varied. They include classification of prisoners for mental health programs, assessment and treatment of mental illness, crisis intervention, consulting on mental health program design, screening of mental health unit staff, and designing or conducting research.

Offender classification is related to the results of psychological assessment tests, clinical interviews, structured questionnaires, and information about how well any given treatment works. The National Institute of Corrections offers a manual for mental health professionals working within correctional institutions to assist with deciding what tests and treatment procedures to use with each classification area.[11] Among those who get singled out from the general population for special treatment are repeat offenders (especially those who show a high degree of violence), the mentally ill, sexual offenders, substance abusers, and youthful offenders.

Mental health professionals have several aims. They hope to reduce risk in high-risk individuals, identify criminogenic factors, and focus on skills development that may offer a different type of life for offenders who will eventually be released. This approach has been shown to reduce the recidivism rate more effectively than focusing strictly on punishment and supervision — especially with juveniles. Recidivism, however, remains a problem nationwide.

Treating those who have a mental illness, mood disorder, or personality disorder inevitably involves medication. Antipsychotic drugs treat psychotic episodes and antidepressants assist with depression. The goals of drug therapy are to diminish acute episodes or prevent a relapse through maintenance. Careful supervision is often needed to prevent inmates from hoarding pills or selling them, particularly when those drugs are likely to be abused. Identifying and humanely addressing legitimate needs of patients with anxiety conditions, for example, is a particular challenge to mental health professionals behind bars.

People expecting to be released need to learn coping skills. Imprisonment itself will not correct the criminal tendencies. Although psychiatric treatment tends to be focused on the mentally ill, in fact, anyone can benefit. Many offenders show a certain amount of thought distortion and disinhibited impulse management, and quite a few have character disorders. The types of treatments most likely to be found in a correctional setting are:

1. Crisis intervention
2. Management of self-destructive behavior
3. Victim/offender interaction
4. Stress management and frustration tolerance skills training
5. Identity restructuring
6. Addiction counseling
7. Group therapy

Offenders with impulsivity issues and tendencies toward violence have to be handled carefully, especially during violent episodes. Mental health professionals who work with these inmates must take all precautions, such as knowing where the security personnel are, using calming influences, assessing the need to transfer the offender away from certain influences, and teaching alternatives to violence.

Sex offenders are generally grouped by the type of offense they commit, from pedophilia to rape to exhibitionism. Mental health professionals may guide them in accepting responsibility for their behavior, dealing with the cognitive distortions unique to sex offenders, developing empathy for victims, and reshaping sexual motivations. A long-term plan must be devised to prevent re-offending.

What counts for keeping any type of therapeutic program in force in a correctional setting is its effect on the recidivism rate. If a form of therapy cannot prevent an offender from repeating his crimes, then it may be revamped or abandoned.

Those offenders considered high risk in the community but not in need of incarceration may go into Intensive Supervision Programs (ISP) or Intensive Rehabilitation Supervision (IRS). These programs make frequent contact with the person and heavier demands for appropriate and responsible behavior. Targeting specific criminogenic needs for treatment is thought to help reduce recidivism.[12]

As people are downgraded from one type of program or supervision to another on the way to probation, mental health professionals may be called on for evaluation and risk assessment.

Behavioral Profiling

Over the past two decades, there has been an increased use of behavioral profiling in criminal investigation — that is, devising a hypothetical suspect portrait based on patterns and information derived from past cases. Criminal profiling, however, remains a controversial tool. Not everyone believes that devising a hypothetical portrait of a suspect makes a contribution to solving crimes, yet some profiles have been surprisingly accurate.

Profiling is an art, not a science. The idea is to use it as just one tool among many in police work. It can be a guide but should not be taken as the standard against which to measure all else.

There is also a difference between prospective and retrospective profiling. The former speculates about who might become violent, such as is done with potential terrorists or health-care serial killers. It relies on using personality traits and specific behaviors to flag suspicious people. However, such an approach risks targeting innocent people as well.

Mental health professionals engage in *retrospective profiling* after a crime by examining a specific crime scene or a series of crime scenes for certain elements that may yield information about the perpetrator. The point is to assist investigators in narrowing leads to specific types of individuals, based on the idea that people tend to be consistent in their behavior and may leave clues behind. Still, consultants caution that no one should be eliminated for failing to fit one or two of the identifiers.

Howard Teten, a special agent for the FBI, incorporated the methodology of successful profiling efforts into his abnormal psychology training program. Over the years, the FBI's Behavioral Science Unit (now called the Behavioral Analysis Unit) developed both an investigative and a teaching arm to assist local jurisdictions with difficult crimes. Mental health professionals may also work with police departments to help devise a criminal profile.

Examination includes factors relating to the:

- *Offense* — That is, time, location, and method of committing the crime
- *Crime scene*
  - Type of weapon used
  - Type of wounds inflicted
  - Evidence of fantasies or rituals that triggered the crime
  - Evidence that the perpetrator was experienced
  - Indications of intent or psychopathology
  - Evidence that the incident was staged to look like something else
  - Evidence of multiple perpetrators
- *Victim* — Age; occupation; risk of lifestyle; mental health, criminal, or substance abuse history; evidence of acquaintance with the perpetrator, for example, signs of compliance.

Profilers devise a timeline of the victim's known movements and frame of mind leading up until the crime, relying on journals, letters, phone and purchase records, and the input of acquaintances and witnesses.

Profiles work best when the offender displays obvious psychopathology, such as sadistic torture, postmortem mutilation, or pedophilia. Some killers leave a "signature" — a behavioral manifestation of an individualizing personality quirk, such as cutting a slit into the eyelids of a deceased victim, frenzied stabbing in a specific area, or tying several ligatures with the same complicated knot. This helps to link crime scenes and alert law enforcement to the presence of a serial offender.

What criminal profiles offer are the offender's general age range, probable racial identity, *modus operandi*, living situation, education level, travel patterns, and indications of a criminal or psychiatric record. A profile may also pinpoint an area where the offender probably resides. A responsible consultant will always caution investigators that profiles are valuable but limited. They are based on known data from other similar crimes, and there is always some chance of anomalous human behavior. Yet they still may be able to tell if the person will likely repeat this crime.

Even so, to assess the nuances of a crime scene, particularly to distinguish actual crimes from those that involve false allegations, or one type of crime from those staged to look like it, profilers must have knowledge of or experience with investigations. More than one professional, devising profiles from textbook concepts, has misled the police. And those who shoot from the hip during high profile investigations have misled the media and the public.

Most professionals would agree that profiling needs more research to determine its success rate, areas that need improvement, and the validity of its fundamental methods and assumptions about criminal behavior.

Psychological Autopsy

Victimology techniques are equally important in an investigative procedure known as equivocal death analysis or psychological autopsy. When the circumstances surrounding a death can be interpreted in more than one way and the manner of death is unclear, psychologists and psychiatrists can help to compile information about behavior, degree of lethal intent, and motive to distinguish between accident, homicide, and suicide.

A medical autopsy examines the body of the deceased, whereas a psychological autopsy considers the mental state. The results may be used to settle criminal cases, estate issues, malpractice suits, or insurance claims. First used formally in 1958 in Los Angeles, psychological autopsies are now a more standard resource, although not as developed in scientific methodology.

With this approach, mental health professionals examine numerous factors to make the proper determination. That may include the death scene, all documentation pertaining to the death, interviews with family members and associates, the subject's medical history and evidence of recent stressors, all relevant documents pertaining to the individual's life history, and any changes to that person's will or life insurance policies.

At times, the results will be clear, while at other times, the deceased's state of mind prior to death cannot be stated with certainty. If the psychological autopsy evidence is allowed in court, the methods supporting the opinion must be clarified. In the event that an apparent accident or suicide shows indications of homicide, the police must take over the investigation. The mental health examiner's primary role is to crystallize the psychological factors and help to lessen the interpretive ambiguity.

Civil Matters

The difference between forensic and clinical mental health practice is surprisingly significant. True, clinical acumen is the fundamental qualification for forensic expertise. However, forensic decision making is quite different from clinical decision making. Issues that interface with the law often transcend diagnostics and treatment planning. And then, there is the theatre of court proceedings. Mental health consultation is exactly that — meant to contribute and exist within a larger realm of case and trial strategy, without compromising the integrity of the science in any way.

Not surprisingly, many experienced psychiatry and psychology clinicians are inadequately suited to the specific realm of applied science to legal questions. Training in the behavioral sciences does not embrace the notion of collateral investigation, the nuances of decision making in areas as unrelated and broad ranging as criminal responsibility and drafting a will, or practical considerations such as report writing.

For most mental health professionals, the relationship between clinical and forensic decision making is greatest in forensic psychiatry and psychology matters attached to the hospital or treatment setting.

Involuntary Hospitalization and Treatment

Occasionally, concerns will be raised about whether a person may become violent to others at home, in the community, or at work. The emergency mental health worker or psychiatrist may be asked to assess an individual's need for involuntary hospitalization, if less restrictive measures are not available.

The prevailing standard for commitment requires a finding that the examinee be dangerous to self or to others in order to be hospitalized against his or her will.[13] Depending on the state, "dangerous" may include a passive danger to oneself through profound neglect.

In assessing future dangerousness, psychiatrists are often asked to appraise the likelihood of suicidality or homicidality. The best predictor of these outcomes is a past history.[14] Otherwise, some factors may increase the likelihood of future risk, as determined by available research, but otherwise do not definitively establish a person's imminent dangerousness. For this reason, determinations of dangerousness to self or to others rely heavily upon a professional's conclusions based on available history — using reasonable judgment that may nevertheless be tragically wrong. Decision making is dependent upon the accuracy of a patient's account, and that patient may be invested in avoiding hospitalization.

Likewise, unfortunately, the admitting psychiatrist may be invested in avoiding admission, either for being overworked, insurance denial of coverage, or overextended census.

Similar considerations, stated and unstated, influence disputes for treatment over objection. Patients may be quite disorganized and obviously impaired in court. Nevertheless, treatment teams must establish that a patient continues to represent a danger to self or to others, even in a protective hospital setting. Furthermore, the testifying doctor must impress the court that the medication recommended specifically targets the symptoms that perpetuate that dangerousness.[15]

Part of a court's decision to allow treatment over objection is driven by the hospital's ability to prove that a patient lacks capacity to give informed consent.[16] In reality, many who refuse treatment but need it retain their capacity to give informed consent and yet would remain dangerous if they refused medicines.

Increasing respect for the rights of the individual mandates that treatment may be administered only after informed consent is obtained. Included in an evaluation of a person's capacity to refuse or even accept treatment, therefore, is the capacity to provide informed consent in the first place. The psychiatrist verifies the patient's ability to understand the very reason for treatment, the actual treatment, the alternatives, and the risks, benefits, and side effects of each, as well as the risks of no intervention at all.

Informed consent has taken on more important significance in recent years. Side effects such as diabetes and hyperlipidemia were never before so closely attributed to psychotropics as they are now.[17] Suicides have been attributed to unanticipated reactions to antidepressants.[18] Weight gain and impaired sexuality are no longer so readily accepted for their consequences. At the same time, patient self-education and interactivity through the internet informs and occasionally inflames mental health consumers.

Malpractice attaches itself to informed consent, especially where psychotropic effects are concerned. Mental health malpractice, like other medical malpractice, requires:

1.   Damage
2.   Duty to care
3.   Deviation from standard
4.   Direct causation

At first blush, one might conclude that cases involving suicide and homicide are the only matters where damage might be sufficient to inspire a plaintiff's attorney — usually at his own expense in a contingency arrangement — to bring a malpractice action. Yet loss of consortium and loss of employment might have substantial and long-term personal and economic impact on the plaintiff. Thus, the nature of informed consent about potential risks, benefits, side effects, and alternatives of a treatment assumes importance in such later malpractice actions.

Not all mental health malpractice cases are rooted in prescribing choices and neglectful care, however. Inappropriate relationships, sexual or otherwise exploitative, are the dark side of psychotherapy's history. Breaches of confidentiality can have a far reaching impact on a person's life and welfare.

Mental health consultants in malpractice cases do well to speak to treatment staff whenever possible, in addition to reviewing medical records. Regrettably, sanitized medical charts and scant treatment notes are the rule in contemporary mental health treatment. Cynicism is not mandated — but diligence is, in the form of scrutiny beyond face value. The same investigation will expose spurious and opportunistic claims.

Emotional Injury

Despite the notoriety of criminal cases, the most frequent interface of behavioral sciences with the law emerges in personal injury cases. A legal finding of pain and suffering enhances the damages of civil cases. Such cases impose particular demands for erudition about trauma, malingering, effects of stress, and the assessment of function.

Posttraumatic stress disorder is a frequently claimed condition in civil cases, in part because attorneys are familiar with the diagnosis.[19] Nevertheless, definitions of posttraumatic stress disorder have evolved with emerging research on those exposed to workplace harassment[20] and other experiences of legal significance. Still predicated upon a sense of risk to body integrity, posttraumatic stress disorder is slowly being appreciated, however, in those beyond a natural zone of forseeability.[21]

The range of personality disorders and personality dynamics between victim and defendant confront the examiner who is assessing the possibility of emotional distress as an impact of an event. Adjustment disorders, delayed posttraumatic stress disorder, depression, and substance abuse conditions may present in particular in less obvious ways. Forensic examiners in emotional injury cases ascertain:

1. What has happened to a person emotionally (focusing on symptoms first, diagnosis second)?
2. What is causally responsible for the symptoms (was it the matter prompting the litigation, or some other stressor — family, relationship, financial, health, etc.)?
3. How is the person doing now, emotionally (symptoms and their severity) and functionally (social, interpersonal, marital and occupational)?
4. What is the examinee's prognosis (and if the prognosis is poor, what treatment or other interventions are needed to improve that prognosis)?

Clearly, the investigative burden required to resolve these questions is substantial. Forensic psychiatrists and psychologists will often find attorneys and even courts, let alone plaintiffs, resistant to allowing aggressive fact finding. But careful explanation of the relevance of multifaceted sources of information enhances truth in the court.

All personal injury examinations are better served by input on the presence or absence of symptoms from family or close acquaintances that interacted with an examinee before, during, and after an event or period in question. Access to actually speak to previous treating therapists is also helpful, for a treating professional may have many opinions he or she can share far beyond the often scant or illegible notes typically available through written records. The psychiatric-legal assessment of personal injury is not possible without an understanding of the context in which the event, the effect, and the complaint developed.

Assertions of brain injury are part of the emotional injury spectrum. In these cases, neuropsychological testing is pivotal to map specific functional capabilities and deficits. Correlation of testing results with school, employment, and previous testing records contributes to resolving questions of causation, should deficiencies manifest.

Complexity is fundamental to toxic tort cases. Because chemical sensitivity claims often arise in those individuals who express their emotions through physical complaints, careful teasing apart of different organ systems is essential, along with exquisite attention to chronology of complaints and potential psychological benefit from an examinee's embracing the sick role.

Elders and the Incapacitated

Dementing events such as stroke affect a person's capacity to meet his or her own needs. An otherwise capable person may no longer be able to keep track of needed medication regimen, have difficulty cleaning the home, or even finding one's address, for example. Although one logical alternative may be to refer a person to a nursing home, assessing for the utility of a guardian is a compassionate alternative.

Guardians are appointed to meet specific needs that a person has which otherwise interfere with independent living. Appropriately arranged guardianship, typically with the help of social service staff during an inpatient admission, facilitates an impaired person's continuing to live in the community in as autonomous a fashion as possible.

The evaluation for the need for guardianship extends beyond a mental status examination, or neuropsychological testing, and involves an inventory of one's functional challenges and daily demands, how those are met, and how accommodated when not met. Home visits by a member of the evaluating team are essential. Ultimately, the guardianship assessment enumerates the specific tasks for which the person requires a guardian, and what would enable the person to resume a more complete decision making independence.

Competency to draft a will invariably is raised with increasing age of the testatrix. With medical progress enhancing longevity, a person may warrant evaluation on several occasions; a will drafted at age 80 may be supplanted by a will drafted at age 88.

As in criminal cases, competency is task-specific. One may have Alzheimer's disease, and be perfectly competent to decline a CT scan, for example, but not competent to draft a will. The understandings required for competency to draft a will are different from those required for competency to invest, or to sign a contract.

Dementia does not preclude testamentary capacity. To establish competency to draft a will, the testatrix need demonstrate only an understanding of the nature of the assets of the estate, and the natural heirs. Along with resolving an examinee's competency, a responsible examiner observes for signs of undue influence by a concerned party that exploit an emotionally vulnerable individual who might otherwise be cognitively intact.

The testamentary capacity case is most frequently referred posthumously, when an aggrieved heir contests the will entered into probate. For this reason, studying the testatrix's cognition and intellect through videotape record of the drafting of the will, or by reviewing email, letters, and other records, is necessary.

As in criminal cases, competency is task-specific. One may have Alzheimer's disease, and be perfectly competent to decline a CT scan, for example, but not competent to draft a will. The understandings required for competency to draft a will are different from those required for competency to invest, or to sign a contract.

Review of medical records and antecedents to decisions, however, are likewise the foci of examinations relating to competency to invest. Security laws are very protective of the incapacitated investor, and transactions can be negated, to the liability of the investment house, if the appointed arbitration panel finds the investor was incapacitated when executing a trade.

Child Custody and Domestic Relations

The forensic mental health professional makes an important contribution to questions of custody determination. Similarly, in termination of parental rights proceedings, psychiatrists and psychologists may be called upon to assess a parent's abilities to care for a child. Many family courts place tremendous power in the hands of the examiner to assess the best interests of the child. Forensic consultants' recommendations strongly influence questions of visitation, and mandated supervision and treatment.

Child custody evaluations involve an evaluation of the parents and the children, incorporating information removed from the mudslinging of the parents' sometimes desperate efforts to secure children. The investigative tenacity to sort through the starkly differing representations, and appraisal through the experience of a child lends special qualification to those certified in child psychiatry and psychology, in addition to those experienced or certified in forensic psychiatry and psychology.

Because custody battles or parental rights cases may include questions about a parent's chemical dependency, sexual proclivities, or psychiatric illness, some cases require an assessment of the needs of the child and of the parent's health as well. The challenge of prognosticating the best parental scenario for a child's future demands that the examiner be conversant with family dynamics. In this regard, behavioral sciences and family law differs from other domains of the mental health–law interface. Family courts are tradition-ally more responsive to psychodynamic principles than other courts that more exclusively focus on symptom assessment exclusively.

Workplace Matters

Harassment and Discrimination

In recent years, mental health consultants have emerged in pivotal roles in labor and employment law. The proliferation of harassment and discrimination complaints, for example, have brought along complaints of emotional injury arising from the presence of a hostile work environment.

Psychiatrists and psychologists are precluded from offering opinion on whether an environment is hostile or abusive;[22] evaluations are usually focused on assessing the degree of emotional distress, its duration and causation, as well as its prognosis. However, psychiatric examination may introduce additional information that indirectly influences the determination of whether a hostile environment existed or corroborating that the examinee was reasonably experiencing the workplace as hostile or abusive.

Sensitivity to cultural issues — from black rage to traditional responses of Latina employees, to vulnerabilities of cancer survivors — improves the precision of the assessment and its conclusions.

Complicating assessments of workplace harassment is a paucity of physical evidence. Both sides become so polarized in their verbal recollections over the course of litigation that there may remain no reliable informants about words exchanged or feelings inspired. Engaging employees who are no longer with the defendant company and have no grudges or vested interest may enhance the collateral input available to the examiner.

The ADA and Disability, and Fitness for Duty

Legislation that enabled lawsuits over harassing or discriminating workplaces was oriented toward making opportunity equal to all.[23] In that vein, the Americans with Disabilities Act[24] focused on employer responsibilities for integrating the disabled employee alongside those without handicaps. Forensic psychiatrists and psychologists are called upon by human resource professionals to offer their opinion on whether individuals can perform the essential functions of their duties; whether they need accommodation for disabilities; what the disabilities are; and what prognosis can be expected.

Disability insurance companies often seek out mental health consultation as well, when policyholders claim they cannot work. Such evaluations are heavily focused on an examinee's diagnosis and prognosis. Applying forensic methodology, however, the interview is well suited for the examinee's home environment. Such proximity to the examinee's home turf minimizes a distorted picture of incapacitation that might present in the doctor's office, by observing the trappings of an examinee's day-to-day function. Conversely, latent dysfunction may be uncovered, particularly if pride or poor communication skill hinders an examinee from revealing just how limited he or she is.

A more complicated variant of disability examination arises in evaluations of those who carry own-occupation insurance policies. The forensic examiner must determine only if that person is unable to function in the duties of the specific position covered. A surgeon, for example, is fully covered if he is no longer able to perform surgery, but still able to practice medicine. Changes in medical economics have prompted many professionals with own-occupation policies to file claims because they are fed up with practicing medicine. Insurance companies, who do not consider occupational burnout a "disability," engage forensic mental health professionals to gauge the extent of illness versus loss of enthusiasm.

Somewhat related is the evaluation of fitness for duty. An employee suspended or disabled for behavior or substance abuse carries uncertainty as to when the time is right to return to the workplace. Forensic psychiatrists and psychologists who assess such individuals devise appropriate protocols for maintaining progress and alerting employers and employees to relapse. This involves a balancing between the essential demands of the position and the appropriate accommodations due to an ill and recovering employee.

Many professionals — from police and teachers, to health-care professionals and pilots — have specific character requirements for their position. Even if a prospective employee does not meet criteria for a diagnosable condition, that candidate may be unfit for duty because of impulsivity, poor anger management, poor judgment, or interpersonal difficulties. Pre-employment screening may require evaluation by a mental health professional to screen for history or behaviors that would later become problematic.

Workplace Risk

Mass homicides and a surge of workplace violence in the 1980s prompted aggressive research into methods of identifying and preventing such catastrophes. Employees who threaten others are referred for an assessment of whether they are likely to become dangerous, and under what circumstances. Out of respect for the individual concerned, these evaluations should involve a face to face examination. Examinations that do not afford this courtesy fall short of the humanism expected of forensic psychiatry and psychology. Questions of future workplace violence are delicate and require exceptional caution and discretion to avoid creating panic or provoking catastrophe.

Practice Issues

Ethics

No matter what role psychologists and psychiatrists play, they must uphold the general standards of their profession. Accordingly, mental health professionals in the legal arena should conduct themselves as competent representatives of the profession, both morally and legally. The range of issues mental health professionals face includes the following:

Remain within Limits of Expertise

In consulting or expert testimony, they should resist pressure to offer opinions on subjects about which they have little knowledge or experience. Likewise, they should not oversell themselves as experts on a subject or overstate a level of certainty on an issue that scientific research does not support. In addition, within their own range of expertise, they should seek to achieve the highest level of competence, including reliance upon the latest research in the area in which they are examining.

Confidentiality and Record Keeping

Confidentiality, in the forensic examination, exists between the examiner and the agency retaining that expert witness, be it attorney or court. Thus, the examiner is expected to report results of the examination to the agency retaining him or her — even if that agency is adversarial to the examinee. That aspect of the examination differs significantly from clinical practice. The examiner has an obligation to disclose that point at the outset of a forensic interview.

In some states, if an expert is retained by the criminal defense attorney but reaches a conclusion about the defendant that fails to support what the attorney hoped for, the results are privileged. However, some states have decided that, in the event that a psychiatric issue is raised for a defendant, the attorney–client privilege is no longer in effect, and the results are made available to the prosecutor. In all states, a court-ordered evaluation also goes to all parties.

Records of an evaluation should be kept and be legible. Although release of a forensic examiner's notes may occur only upon the direction of the court, destruction of notes is unethical practice.

Remain within the Parameters of the Assessment Issue

An evaluation must focus and remain within the parameters of the issue being assessed. Unless specified by the court, an assessment of competency to stand trial (and the defendant's current mental state) should not include an examination of criminal responsibility (mental state at the time of the offense). Reports should not extend beyond the psychiatric legal questions at hand to address other issues; for example, a presentencing report should not engage questions relating to the termination of parental rights.

The "Hired Gun"

No mental health professionals should conform their findings. Data may not be withheld simply because they reflect poorly on the examinee. Psychological tests cannot be administered contrary to standardized protocols, especially in a selective fashion designed to yield a result about the presence or absence of a given condition.

Although it is permissible for attorneys to request clarification of jargon, or correction of factual errors, it is not permissible to ask for the removal of material simply because it may hurt their case, or because an attorney deems it as "irrelevant." The dialogue between mental health consultant and attorney is predicated upon the understanding that the opinion offered is sought on the basis of expertise the mental health professional has, which the attorney does not.

In addition, a contingent fee arrangement should never be accepted, since that risks such compromises to ensure payment. Mental health professionals approached to do an evaluation must have a clearly written agreement to be paid for services, regardless of the assessment outcome or the verdict.

If mental health professionals suspect the attorney may be withholding relevant information about the client, they must address this issue. Missing information could lead to inadequate preparation and even a faulty diagnosis. For this reason, examiners should communicate little about their findings to the attorney or examinee before the inquiry is complete, to avoid contamination of the examination by an advocating attorney, or withholding of evidence in an effort to shape the outcome of the exam.

Furthermore, a forensic examiner should not offer an opinion on a matter in which inadequate material and history has been made available for review.

Malingering

The adversarial system lends itself to exaggerating or misstating psychiatric history for legal benefit. Forensic examinations, therefore, must establish whether or not this is taking place, and to what degree. A responsible forensic examination of any criminal or civil matter embraces the possibility of faked history by obtaining collateral information and employing objective testing measures when possible.

Malingering, or faking, psychiatric symptoms is to be distinguished from misstating personal history, or details of an event of importance. An examinee may prove to not be malingering psychiatric illness, but may intentionally be providing inaccurate history. The examiner has the burden to resolve the facts of a case by identifying and exploring confirming, impartial sources of information. Those sources who are not vested in the outcome of a case are preferred.

To that end, examiners should be familiar with standards for admissibility of hearsay evidence. A mental health professional may rely upon hearsay evidence if it is vital to arriving at diagnostic and forensic conclusions. Since use of collateral information is an essential component of reliable forensic examinations, every case should allow for the possibility for including hearsay evidence in a forensic examination and report.

The forensic evaluator may also sense that the examinee has been coached. Trying to get someone to feign symptoms is manufacturing evidence. Likewise, when hired to help prepare an examinee for trial, a forensic examiner must not coach the client to feign symptoms and perpetuate fraud.

The "Ultimate Issue"

The ultimate issue is the conclusion that the fact finders — judge or jury — must ultimately draw. It is the legal issue to be decided. The ultimate issue can be about competency, insanity, dangerousness, transfer from juvenile to adult court, or even parental fitness. Expert witnesses may provide contributing data, but it is controversial among practitioners as to whether they should make a pronouncement about legal issues. Some professionals fear that the expert may exert undue influence on the results. Yet mental health professionals are often pressured to draw those conclusions and, ethical standards notwithstanding, may have to make a statement of some type that addresses it. In that event, the opinion should be based on scientifically sound data and adequate history.

Psychological Testing

Some psychological testing, such as the MMPI-2,[25] offers the ability to validate itself so that examiners can objectively verify history they receive. In this manner, certain psychological tests may supplement the available history, along with documents from corroborating sources, to illuminate the psychological portrait of the examinee. Other tests, however, such as the Beck Depression Inventory, merely rely on an examinee's self-report. As the examinee may have a vested interest in being evaluated as sick in personal injury matters, or may not be psychologically self-aware, data gathered from self-report measures that afford no examination of their response style are unreliable. When such evidence is presented to the court as bolstering a claim, attorneys should suspect bad judgment or deliberate misrepresentation by the expert offering the opinion.

Working with the Psychiatrist and Psychologist

Within the behavioral sciences, subspecialization has given rise to further subspecialization. Expanded knowledge about the brain and behavior renders previously held "science" quickly obsolete. As important as board certification is to establishing the experience and familiarity of the expert witness, the most important qualification to the court is that the expert simply be an excellent psychiatrist or psychologist. A person who is certified in forensic psychiatry or psychology but does not practice in a treatment setting cannot possibly represent that he or she is as qualified to assist the court as is a person who sees patients and makes diagnostic and treatment decisions on a regular basis.

The forensic psychiatrist or psychologist should be prepared to assist the attorney in all aspects of case management, from recommending sources of information, to avenues of emphasis, to training for deposition, to the evaluation itself, to offering input on prospective jurors, to preparation for trial and for crossexamining opposing counsel's witnesses.

Still, it is the attorney's responsibility to determine the nature of the consultant's contribution. Additionally, the attorney bears the responsibility for preparing the consultant for deposition and for trial, by providing all pertinent documents and information and updating on the progress of the case in a timely manner.

Even with the camaraderie that naturally develops from working so closely, it is wise for the ethical forensic psychiatrist to maintain a distance so as to ensure one's objectivity will not be seduced by the bonds of friendship. Such distance need not compromise the quality of the consultation; on the contrary, it prompts the attorney to do one's best work and recognize the true strengths and weaknesses of the case. It is all about the case.

Notes

1. *Miranda v. Arizona*, 384 U.S. 436 (1966).
2. *Godinez v. Moran*, 509 U.S. 364 (1993).
3. *Dusky v. United States*, 362 U.S. 402 (1960).
4. *Jackson v. Indiana*, 406 U.S. 715 (1972).

5. Foley, P.F., Hartman, B.W., Dunn, A.B., Smith, J.E., and Goldberg, D.M. The utility of the State-Trait Anger Expression Inventory with offenders (2002). *Int. J. Offender Ther.* & Compar. Criminol., 46(3), 364–78.

6. Trauma Symptom Inventory Psychological Assessment Resources, Odessa, FL, 1996.

7. Butcher, J. MMPI-2 Regents of the University of Minnesota, Dist. By NCS Toronto, 1993.

8. Osran, H.C. and Weinberger, L.E. (1994). Personality disorders and "restoration" to sanity. *Bull. Amer. Acad. Psychia Law*, 22(2), 257–67.

9. Douglas, K.S., Ogloff, J.R.P., and Hart, S.D. (2003). Evaluation of a model of violence risk assessment among forensic psychiatric patients. *Psychiat. Serv.*, 54(10), 1372–9.

10. Quinsey, V., Harris, G., Rice, M., and Cormier, C. (2001). Violent Offenders: Appraising and Managing Risk, American Psychological Association, Washington, D.C.

11. National Institute of Corrections: http://nicic.org/

12. Ward, T. and Stewart, C. (2003). Criminogenic needs and human needs: A theoretical model. *Psychol. Crime Law*, 9(2), 125–43.

13. *The Lanterman-Petris — Short Act*, CA, 1969.

14. Simon, R. (1998). Murder masquerading as suicide: Postmortem assessment of suicide risk factors at the time of death, *J. Foren. Sci*, 43(6), 1119–23; Monahan, J. and Steadman, H. (1994). *Violence and Mental Disorder: Developments in Risk Assessment*, Chicago, IL: University of Chicago.

15. Melton, G., Petrila, J., Poythress, N., and Slobogin, C. (1997). *Psychological Evaluations for the Courts: A Handbook for Mental Health Professionals and Lawyers*, 2nd ed., Guilford Press, New York, NY: p. 323.

16. Schwartz, H.I. (1994). Informed consent and competency. In *Principles and Practice of Forensic Psychiatry*, Rosner, R. Ed., Chapman & Hall, New York, NY: p. 107.

17. Lund, B.C., Perry, P.J, Brooks, J.M., and Arndt, S. (2001). Clozapine use in patients with schizophrenia and the risk of diabetes, hyperlipidemia, and hypertension. *Arch. Gen. Psychiat.*, 58(12), 1172–76.

18. Healy, D. (2003). Lines of evidence on the risks of suicide with selective serotonin reuptake inhibitors. *Psychother. & Psychosom.*, 72(2), 71–9.

19. Slovenko, R. (1994). Legal aspects of post-traumatic stress disorder. *Psychiat. Clin. No. Am.* 17(2), 439–46.

20. Gold, L.H. (2003). PTSD in employment litigation. In *Posttraumatic Stress Disorder in Litigation: Guidelines For Forensic Assessment*, Simon, R.I. (Ed.), 2nd ed., American Psychiatric Publishing, Inc., Washington, DC, US, pp. 163–86.

21. Avina C. and O'Donohue W. (2002). USA. Sexual harassment and PTSD: is sexual harassment diagnosable trauma?. *Source J. Traum. Stress.* 15(1), 69–75.

22. *Harris v. Forklift Systems, Inc.* 114 S.Ct. 367 (1993).

23. *Title VII of the Civil Rights Act of 1964*, Equal Employment Opportunity Commission.

24. The American with Disabilities Act Public Law 101-336 July 26, 1990 104 Stat. 327.

25. Pope, H., Butcher, J., and Seelen, J. (1993). *The MMPI, MMPI-2, & MMPI-A in Court: A Practical Guide for Expert Witnesses and Attorneys*, American Psychological Association, Washington, DC.

Digital Forensics

27

MARK M. POLLITT

Introduction

DNA was the first really new forensic discipline in many years. Its impact on the criminal justice community has been truly revolutionary in that it has changed the way in which crimes against persons are investigated and fundamentally changed the value of biological evidence obtained from crime scenes. Now, there is an even newer and more powerful form of forensic evidence: digital evidence.

What Is Digital Evidence?

What is digital evidence? The best way to answer this question is to quote the definition published by the Scientific Working Group on Digital Evidence:[1]

> "Information of probative value stored or transmitted in digital form."

We go through our daily lives and give little thought to the information about us that is being stored in real, or near-real time. We routinely use electronic mail, visit websites, log into computer systems and computer applications. We "badge in and out" to access our workplaces. Our laptops, desktops, personal digital assistants, and the servers at our place of work contain a tremendous amount of information about us that is worth knowing. On our way to and from work, we use smart cards and radio frequency tags to pay our transit fares and highway tolls. Our phones are digital devices whose use creates records of our conversations, and in the case of cellular phones, can even provide geographical information concerning where we were physically located when we made the call.[2] Access cards are controlling our access to places of work, to the gas pumps and to mass transit. Records of each of these activities are being stored electronically, in digital form. These digital footsteps are a rich source of both incriminating and exculpatory information (Figure 27.1).[3]

But it is latent evidence: It cannot be seen, heard, tasted, or smelt. It is easily altered, damaged, or destroyed. It takes specialized tools and techniques to collect, examine, and

Figure 27.1 Digital storage media.

analyze. Because it is latent and its origins easily disputed, it takes specialized training to perform these tasks. Often, the complexity of the evidence or its obscure origins require the use of expert testimony. These characteristics of digital evidence are what make their study a forensic discipline. Digital forensics can be described as the application of science and engineering to the legal problem of evidence stored in digital form.[4] But it did not start out that way.

A Brief History of Digital Forensics

The early years of digital forensics are shrouded in the mists of time. No one knows for sure who first coined the phrase "computer forensics," but its origins may be earlier than might be thought. Parker wrote about collecting computerized evidence in his seminal 1962 book, *Crime by Computer*.[5]

The Internal Revenue Service and the Federal Bureau of Investigation trained a small number of agents to seize computerized records from mainframe and "mini" computers during the 1970s and early 1980s. However, the dawn of the personal computer, as heralded by the IBM PC in 1981, was greeted in the law enforcement community with a yawn. There were a few individuals in law enforcement who recognized the tremendous evidentiary potential that widespread adoption of these machines would present. Most had been involved in the early personal computers such as the TRS-80s, the Ataris, and the Commodore series of computers. Although some had some formal computer training, virtually always on mainframe computers, most were self-taught hobbyists who were forced to learn about the hardware by building it and about the software by writing it. There were few computer accessories (often called peripherals because they were placed outside the box that contained the main processor in the computer case). Getting these devices to work with the computer and with one another was not a simple matter. "Plug and play" was still years away. There were few programs written for these nonstandardized computers, so hobbyists often had to write their own software. Programing skills were often needed to make the computer do anything useful.

The mainstream of law enforcement virtually ignored what was taking place in the technology arena. As a result, it would be a number of years before criminal investigators would recognize that computers could potentially be sources of evidence. In the occasional instance when a computer was found at a crime scene or at the suspect's location, home, or office, investigators would sometimes wonder if they might have something "on them" that might be useful to their case. In rare cases, that wonder would translate into asking another officer, who was a computer hobbyist, to "take a look and tell me what's on it." These pioneers did the best that they could usually do using maintenance programs, called utilities, and some basic programing skills to tease the information from the seized evidence.

They subjectively realized that examining evidence on an *ad hoc* basis was not ideal and sought training from wherever they could get it. They would attend trade shows, product rollouts, and some of the early commercial training. There was little if any law enforcement specific training available until approximately 1990 when the Federal Law Enforcement Training Center at Glynco, Georgia, put on the first Seized Computer Evidence Recovery Specialist (SCERS) course. Some of the early graduates of this course went on to form the International Association of Computer Investigative Specialists (IACIS)[6] in 1991.

A small but dedicated group of law enforcement officers (and a few civilians) struggled to improve both their knowledge and skills in the fledgling discipline of digital forensics. At the same time, a few of these folks, who had excellent programing skills, worked hard to develop tools that would make the process quicker, easier, and more efficient. Some, like Gord Hama from the Royal Canadian Mounted Police, Andy Fried, and Dan Mares from the Internal Revenue Service selflessly gave of their time to help their colleagues. The FBI undertook a very ambitious program called ACES, standing for Automate Computer Examination System. Each of these had a very positive impact on those who were fortunate to have access to these programs.

Up until the late 1990s, commercial vendors ignored the law enforcement market, believing that the market was too small to support the development and maintenance of a major software product. This changed by 2000 with the introduction of several commercial forensic products, including Expert Witness, Encase, and Forensic Tool Kit. These products provided a graphical user interface, and the ability to organize the work-flow of the forensic examination of the evidence. By 2002, the Internal Revenue Service — Criminal Investigation Division acquired the rights to the ILOOK program, developed in the U.K., and provided both the software and the training for its use to law enforcement free of charge.

While this was going on, training was becoming more available and was of a higher quality. Much of the early computer forensic training was done by cooperative organiz-ations such as the Federal Computer Investigations Committee (FCIC) and the IACIS.[7] The SEARCH group[8] was one of the first government-funded training programs available to state and local officers on a regular basis. The National Institute of Justice funded the National White Collar Crime Center (NW3C),[9] which has provided thousands of law enforcement officers with a range of computer forensic and investigative training.

With the increase in the number of practitioners, the need for standards began to be felt. These standard helped ensure that one individual could understand work done by another individual and that evidence seized in one jurisdiction could be utilized in another. There was also the unspoken need to determine the competence of examiners.

Several groups undertook the fractious issue of standards. The Association of Chief Police Officers (ACPO) in the United Kingdom began by publishing their first ACPO

Best Practices document.[10] The G-8 High Tech Crime Subcommittee asked the International Organization for Computer Evidence (IOCE)[11] to develop a set of Principles that would assist in the "exchange of digital evidence" among nations. The IOCE worked with the European Network of Forensic Science Institutes (ENFSI),[12] the Scientific Working Group on Digital Evidence (SWGDE)[13] and other members of the community and in 2001, the G-8 adopted these definitions and principles.

With the proliferation of forensic software that hid much of its functionality behind the graphical user interface came a concern by the community that the Frye and Daubert doctrines concerning the admission of scientific evidence in court might require the validation or verification testing of the software's functionality. The Departments of Justice and Defense, along with the FBI and the National Institute of Science and Technology (NIST), initiated a project to perform validation testing of computer forensic software called the Computer Forensic Tool Testing (CFTT) program.[14]

Another step in the evolution of digital forensics from *ad hoc* investigative techniques into a recognized forensic discipline was the recognition, in 2003, of digital evidence as an accreditable discipline by the American Society of Crime Laboratory Directors — Laboratory Accreditation Board (ASCLD-LAB).[15] By traditional forensic standards, this recognition came extremely quickly. By early 2004, two laboratories had already been accredited under these standards.

In 2004, two more major steps were begun. To recognize the capabilities of qualified practitioners, a means of individual certification is needed. Under the leadership of the National Center for Forensic Science[16] at the University of Central Florida, a roundtable of representatives from industry, academia, and the government met to discuss this need. A high degree of unanimity was achieved, and the consensus was that a single certification body, which would be available to individuals regardless of employment, could seek a certification within a recognized framework of knowledge, skills, and abilities. Hopefully, this process will continue, and the professionalization of digital forensics will be raised to the level of many other, traditional, forensic science disciplines.

Whether certified by such a body or by an individual agency or organization, there is a need for independent testing of a person's skills. The traditional forensic community has used external competency and proficiency testing for years. In early 2004, Quality Forensics, Inc. announced that they would offer these tests in the digital evidence discipline.[17]

Digital Evidence as a Process

As described before, digital evidence is latent, and its secrets are hidden by a series of layers. Digital evidence takes two fundamental forms: static and dynamic. In the static form, information is stored in ones and zeros in a physical location either permanently, or for a period of time. The static form of digital evidence is best represented by floppy disks, optical disks, and hard drives as well as the ever-expanding forms of storage devices. One of the characteristics of this static form is the need for a system to organize and keep track of where the data are stored. Typically, this is done utilizing a file system, which is used to store files created by applications and organized into folders or directories by the user. The result can be notionally viewed using the example of the onion (Figure 27.2).

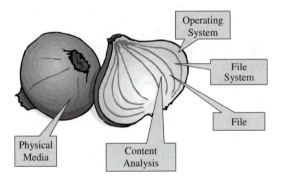

Figure 27.2 The onion analogy.

When the ones and zeros are in motion, transiting from place to place using copper wire, fiber optics, or radio frequency transmission, they are said to be dynamic. Like static digital evidence, we need a system to keep track of what information has been transmitted and received. A system that uses data communication protocols has evolved. This utilizes systems of packets that encapsulate data in a figurative "envelope" called a datagram, which also contains information about the data, the protocol, and the addressees.

Digital forensics peels back the layers of complexity to expose the data along with the information about how the data were created, stored, and manipulated. That forensic process starts with the acquisition of the data. Static forms of data may be seized in their native state. For example, an entire computer may be seized to examine the data stored on the hard drive contained in the computer's case. Alternatively, the hard drive itself may be seized. In some cases, it may be better to create a forensically exact copy of the data usually called an "image." In some circumstances, the creation of an image copy onsite may be a requirement mandated by the court or by practicality. For instance, it would not be prudent to shut down a hospital computer system to get e-mail information.

The analog for dynamic evidence is to capture the packets, while they are in transit, store them, arrange them in sequence, and examine both the contents and the metadata associated with the packets.

Once the data have been acquired, the examiner will:

- Design an examination, using forensic software, to document the contents of the media
- Determine if there is information of probative value contained in either the active or latent information in the examination specimen
- Export those results for investigative analysis and for presentation in the form of a report, testimony, or both

This process can be depicted as follows:

$$\text{Acquisition} \rightarrow \text{Examination} \rightarrow \text{Analysis} \rightarrow \text{Presentation}$$

Similarly, we work our way down from the physical media such as the *Hard Drive* through the *Operating System* (which acts as the interface between the hardware and the software) to the *File System* (which provides for the storage of files that have information stored by word processors applications) and finally down to the *Data* itself. Each of these layers provides us with opportunities and challenges. To the forensic examiner, each combination of hardware, operating system, file system, application set, and stored data provides a unique challenge. Not the least of the challenges is to process ever-increasing volumes of data and distill the pertinent material into a digestible form useful to the end user, investigator, attorney, or information security professional, while ensuring a complete examination that does not miss important data.

Acquisition

The first phase of any forensic examination is to collect the evidence in a manner that preserves its legal and scientific value. In the case of digital media (static evidence), the data can be seized in its entirety, or selective portions can be seized. It is generally acknowledged that seizure of the original media or an exact copy of it, commonly referred to as an "image" or "bit-stream copy," is preferable as it provides the complete context of the original data as well as allowing for the search of hidden or latent data.

In the context of dynamic data (network or Internet communications), the original packets are collected, from complete or filtered data streams. They are then re-assembled into the correct order and into data streams during the examination phase.

Investigators need to articulate the need for seizing original digital media when preparing search warrants. In cases where the original media cannot be seized, an on-site image should be prepared by qualified individuals. There are situations in which seizure of the entire original media would be impractical (such as seizing the entire reservations database of a major airline), inappropriate (shutting down a hospital to seize its computer system), or impermissible (such as cases involving privileged communications outside the scope of the warrant. There are few absolutes, however. The seizure of evidence is a balancing act between the interests of the parties and the state.

Examination

Examination is the forensic exploration of the original data to determine its content, origin, and characteristics. This is a scientific process that, while taking into account the investigative purpose, seeks only scientifically objective results.

To do this, the examiner begins by identifying an examination goal. This is then reviewed with the examination customer (end user). Without mutually understood goals, it is unlikely that an efficient or effective examination can be conducted. Once the goal is determined, the examiner will conduct documentation of the items to be examined:

- What media is to be examined?
- What operating systems are present?
- What file systems are being used to store the data?
- What is the volume of data present?

Once the media is documented, the examiner can effectively plan an examination.

Many examiners do not formally document their plan for conducting a given examination; however, it is a good practice to do so. Drafting an examination plan will allow the examiner to articulate what process was used and the rationale for using a particular methodology. Using the examination goals, which were agreed upon with the customer, the examiner can select tools and techniques, which will most effectively satisfy the examination goal. The order that these tools and techniques are applied can significantly impact both the efficiency of the examination as well as the results. So, it is important that examiners understand the impact of sequencing the use of different tools. The actual examination consists of the application of the selected tools and techniques. Some of the techniques include *data recovery*, where deleted files and directories are restored; *data reduction*, where files are excluded from further examination on the basis of a digital signature, header information, metadata, or content; and *content searches*, where strings of data, codes or keywords are matched.

After the tools are applied, it is very important for the examiner to review the results for accuracy, and to ensure that the results meet the desired outcomes for the individual stage of the examination and that it supports the accomplishment of the examination goal. This feedback loop is critical to quality assurance.

Analysis

The next phase of the digital evidence process is to analyze the examination results in the context of the case or investigation. In some ways, this is the most important phase of the process because it illuminates the case by answering such questions as: (1) "Does this information tend to prove or disprove the facts of the case?" (2) "Does this information corroborate what we currently know?" (3) "Is it testimonial or merely of lead value?" And while the examiner may do or assist in the analysis, it is not strictly a forensic process, but rather a part of the investigation.

Analysis has several vectors, and the same information can be viewed from several different perspectives. The most common view is to look at the information relative to the specific case for which it was collected. This is the most obvious and is the prime motive for the collection itself (vertical analysis). But much can be gained by seeing the similarities and differences to all other cases of this type and region (horizontal analysis). Horizontal analysis has both tactical and strategic value as it can identify other actors, organizations, or methods that impact the current case while providing a much clearer picture of organization and crime patterns from a strategic perspective. Failure to employ horizontal analysis disregards a substantial portion of the value of digital evidence.

Presentation

The examination product is typically a combination of written report and a set of data attached to the report in either paper or electronic form. Collectively, these are the presentation phase of the examination.

Report writing is an art form in itself. Reports must be complete, accurate, and understandable by nontechnical people, while providing the basis of the examiner's testimony.

This is very much a balancing act and requires training and experience to provide consistently good reports.

Testimony itself consists of three major elements: direct oral testimony, crossexamination testimony, and courtroom exhibits. As the testimony is based on latent evidence, there will often be a requirement for expert testimony. The Federal Rules of Evidence recognize the need for essentially two forms of "expert testimony," the most common form associated with scientific evidence being opinion testimony. In this form, the expert's training, education, and scientific process are evaluated, and if found admissible, the expert is allowed to form a conclusion which is presented to the finder of fact and is subject to crossexamination.

The other, less recognized form of expert testimony is the witness, who by education, training and experience, can provide information, which will help the trier of fact to understand the evidence presented. This form of expert testimony is essentially educating the jury so they can form their own conclusions regarding the evidence. The experience with digital evidence, thus far, has been that this latter form of expert testimony is more common.

In either case, the expert witness should be an objective, neutral party, who seeks to educate the jury on the facts, the science and the application of the science to the particular piece of physical evidence. Like writing clear, accurate, and understandable reports, this is also an art.

The Future

The examination of digital evidence is still in its infancy. It will need to become much more efficient, as the volume of data stored or transmitted grows exponentially every year. Daily, we rely on computers and data to make our lives comfortable and even possible. So, it is clear that digital forensics will have to grow and become more robust.

But capacity is not the only issue. Since this evidence is potentially as significant as DNA, we will have to ensure the quality of the science and the practice. Scientific working groups have been formed to monitor and facilitate the science. The accreditation of forensic laboratories that conduct this type of examinations has begun. But there is much more to do in the coming years. Certification of practitioners is one issue that is a likely next step. Following closely on the heels of individual certification will be the accreditation of training and educational programs which produce examiners.

Stay tuned, in the immortal words of Bachman Turner Overdrive: "You ain't seen nothing yet!"[18]

Notes

1. www.swgde.org
2. http://www.travelbygps.com/articles/tracking.php
3. Photographed by the author.
4. This definition began with Special Agent Stephen McFall, who served as the first Program Manager for the FBI's Computer Analysis Response Team. This author further refined it during his tenure in the FBI.

5. Parker, Donn B. *Crime by Computer.* New York, NY: Charles Scribner's Sons, 1976.

6. Personal knowledge of the author.

7. http://www.cops.org

8. http://www.search.org

9. http://www.nw3c.org

10. Association of Chief Police Officers of England, Wales, and Northern Ireland. *Good Practice Guide for Computer Based Evidence.* Manchester, United Kingdom, CISCOM, Ltd. 1999.

11. http://www.ioce.org

12. http://www.ensfi.org

13. http://www.swgde.org

14. http://www.cftt.nist.gov

15. http://www.ascld-lab.org/dual/aslabdualhistory.html

16. www.ncfs.org

17. Ed. Note: the author is the chair of the Quality Forensic, Inc. Digital Evidence Advisory Board.

18. http://www.canoe.ca/JamMusicPopEncycloPagesB/bachmanturner.html

Forensic Linguistics, Authorship Attribution, and Admissibility

28

CAROLE E. CHASKI

Language, Metalinguistic Ability, and Linguistic Expertise

All human beings are born with an innate propensity or genetic predisposition toward language; only the most severe brain damage or uninterrupted isolation can negate this genetic capacity, and even under such horrendous conditions, some linguistic ability survives (Pinker, 1994). In all languages, there are ways to discuss language, to declare that a statement is true or false, to deny making a statement, to ask for clarification; this kind of language about language is called *metalanguage*, and the ability to think about language in this way is called *metalinguistic ability*. As part of the human survival toolkit, metalinguistic ability helps us recognize people linguistically, helps us estimate demographic features of strangers by the language they produce, helps us identify people we know by voice on the telephone. Because all of us have language and metalinguistic ability to some degree or another, all of us can create descriptions of language. However, the contrast between metalinguistic ability in the general population (from which judges, jurors, and police are drawn) and metalinguistic ability of trained linguists in possession of the analytical tools of linguistic science is one justification for the development of forensic linguistics (Chaski, 2000; Rodman, 2002; Butters, 2005; Solan and Tiersma, 2005).

The Forensic Context

Investigators and attorneys often need to know the answers to questions such as:

- What can you tell me about the person who is speaking on this tape?
- What can you tell me about the person who authored this note?
- What can you tell me about the authenticity of this confession?
- What can you tell me about the genuineness of this negotiation or solicitation?
- Can you tell me whether the suspect did or did not author this note (or journal or e-mail)?

All of these questions ask someone to classify linguistic behavior and from this classification draw conclusions about the language user.

All native speakers of any language have some capability at making these kinds of classifications. Language is built into the human being in such a way that every native user of a language can make predictions about grammaticality (or language identification) and sociolinguistic variation (or dialect identification) regarding his or her own native language. For instance, if you overhear a conversation, you can tell immediately if you are hearing a foreign accent or foreign language. As you hear the sounds, the phonological-grammar umpire in your head is checking whether the sounds and sound combinations do or do not follow English patterns. If the sounds and sound combinations do not follow English patterns, you conclude that the speaker must be foreign or that you are hearing a foreign (non-English) language. A language expert who has specialized in the foreign language you overhear may be able to identify the language and tell you what is being said. But the professionally trained linguist knows how to identify the foreign-accented speaker's native language or the nonnative language which you are hearing, even if they do not know the foreign language. The "knowing-how" consists of applying the scientific method to language — of having observed language and specific languages to such a degree that hypotheses can be formulated and classifications of new phenomena can be made in a methodical and reproducible way.

Because language is structured in such a way that everyone has an internal grammar umpire which can make metalinguistic judgments about his or her native language, and because linguistics is almost invisible as a social science in most colleges and universities, there has been a burgeoning of language experts who are not trained in linguistics but have become associated with forensic linguistics. Fortunately, the difference between scientifically produced, reliable analysis and the nonlinguist's naïve intuitions are being distinguished in evidence hearings in Federal and State courts, due in large part to the interpretation of the Daubert decision which emphasizes normal science, replicability, error rate, and reliability (for some case discussions, see Solan and Tiersma, 2005).

Linguistics: The Scientific Approach to Language

In contrast to literary criticism, rhetoric, and English and foreign language instruction, linguistics takes a scientific approach to language. Linguistics is scientific because it follows the general scientific method of observation, description, hypothesis testing and prediction. Linguists observe what language users actually produce, and do not attend to opinions concerning what language users should or should not produce (the prescriptive or pedagogic approach). For linguists, grammars are descriptions of linguistic behaviors. Within each grammar, there are descriptions of the language's sound patterns (phonetics, phonology), word patterns (morphology, lexicon), phrase and sentential patterns (syntax, semantics), and paragraph and conversation patterns (discourse, pragmatics). These grammars describe the patterns which are available to the language user, and also by default the patterns which are not available. The available patterns are grammatical in the sense that any native language user comprehends and may even produce the patterns, whereas unavailable patterns are ungrammatical because the native language user does not comprehend or produce them.

Examples of these concepts are plentiful, but for brevity's sake, we consider just these few. In English, there are certain consonantal sounds that do combine with the sound [l] at the beginning of a word and certain sounds which do not. Grammatical combinations include [bl, cl, fl, gl, pl, sl], whereas ungrammatical combinations include [dl, hl, jl, ml, nl, tl]. The grammatical patterns are found in many English words [blare, clear, flare, glare, play, slay], but the ungrammatical patterns are not found at the beginning of any English words. When new words are introduced into English by advertising firms or borrowing from other languages, the new English words conform to the established English patterns. The native English user understands the grammatical patterns but does not understand the ungrammatical ones; in common parlance, the ungrammatical patterns sound "foreign" because they do indeed belong to a non-English grammar. Note that it is not that one should not produce a word such as [tlay] in English, as a prescriptive grammar might say, but that one cannot produce [tlay] and still be in English. From the observed patterns, linguists predict that [tlay] is not a possible English word.

Phrases are combinations of words. Languages differ on how words combine to make phrases. For instance, in English, the most common word order for the simple noun phrase is [determiner adjective noun], as in [the black dog], whereas in Spanish, the most common word order is [determiner noun adjective] as in [el perro negro]. Again, if a native English user hears [the computer laptop] or [the dog black], the phrase sounds "foreign" or ungrammatical, because the word order does not follow the common English pattern.

Connected sentences in texts and in conversations also pattern in particular ways. Certain formulaic phrases indicate typical types of texts and conversations; the phrase [once upon a time] correlates with fairy tales, while the phrase [sincerely yours] correlates with business letters. Again, if a native English user hears the phrase [once upon a time], followed rapidly by a [sincerely yours], the text's patterns sound confused and ungrammatical (or a kind soul may even say poetic).

Linguistic descriptions are rules in the sense that the grammatical umpire in our minds rules out language which violates the observed pattern and rules in language which follows the observed pattern. The grammar, or set of observed linguistic behaviors, can be seen as a theory of language because, like any theory, it is predictive. The grammar predicts what is and what is not possible within a language. Such a prediction can be tested by observing more language behavior which either verifies or falsifies the hypothetical linguistic pattern.

But there is another sense in which linguistics is a predictive science. Linguistic behaviors within one language illustrate patterns that are not shared productively by all the language users, but are still comprehended by all the language users. For instance, Language User A may say [he doesn't know anything] and Language User B may say [he don' know nothin']. Users A and B both comprehend each other, even if they do not produce each other's patterns. Users A and B speak different dialects of the same language. The social demographics of Users A and B typically differ in educational level attained, so that pattern A is correlated with a higher educational level than pattern B. Based on observable linguistic behavior of a particular person, linguists can predict such social demographics as education, socioeconomic status, geographic location, and race.

From the cognitive perspective, linguistics is predictive in that grammar in the universal sense predicts what is or is not understandable to any human being, whereas grammar in the particular sense predicts what is or is not understandable to any native language user of a particular language. From the social perspective, linguistics is predictive in that language-specific grammars are associated with particular demographic features within particular societies.

As in any science, prediction is the basis for classifying new phenomena. So in linguistics, English accents, words, phrases, sentences and discourses can be classified as grammatical or ungrammatical to English, or indicative of a native or nonnative language user, or indicative of a particular subpopulation within English users, or indicative of particular speech acts, or indicative of a particular author.

The Scope of Forensic Linguistics as an Application of Linguistics

In both its cognitive and social aspects, Language encompasses almost all of what humans experience. Therefore, linguistics as the science of language has very many aspects. Theoretical linguistics includes phonetics, phonology, morphology, syntax, semantics, discourse analysis, and pragmatics. Closely related to theoretical linguistics are interdisciplinary approaches that test theoretical hypotheses in particular ways; these include psycholinguistics, computational linguistics and sociolinguistics. Finally, there are applied fields in which linguistics can inform practice in nonlinguistics, such as educational linguistics and the acquisition of reading and second language instruction. Forensic linguistics is an application of linguistics, and has a very wide scope. In her bibliography, Levi (1994) notes that every branch of linguistics had been brought to bear on the many questions involving language and law.

In one aspect, forensic linguistics examines the way language functions within the legal context. Such an approach has produced studies of trial language, jury instructions, the language of judges, warning labels, and multilingualism in court (Berk-Seligson, 1990; Levi and Walker, 1990; Dumas, 1990, 2004; Solan, 1993; Gibbons, 1994, 2003; Cotterill, 2004). In another aspect, forensic linguistics produces methods for determining the answers to the kinds of questions which investigators and attorneys ask, the kinds of questions that focus on investigative leads and identification. As a result of responses to these questions, forensic linguistics is often associated with linguistic profiling, discourse analysis, and authorship attribution.

Linguistic profiling deduces demographic characteristics (gender, age, race, education, geographic location, religious orientation, occupation, etc.) from linguistic features in a document. Theoretically, linguistic profiling applies sociolinguistic research about the linguistic performance of demographic subpopulations. For instance, Shuy (2001) describes how a large database project in American English, the *Dictionary of American Regional English*, has been exploited in linguistic profiling. Different groups can be identified by linguistic features because clearly defined datasets of one dialect group can be compared to that of another dialect group; a person who exhibits such dialectal features can then be identified as a member of that particular group. Clearly defining subpopulations is a difficult task. For instance, the demographic feature "gender" is not obviously marked by particular linguistic features; rather, some scholars have argued that linguistic features associated with gender in early research are actually associated with powerlessness — a state of being for both men and women at certain points in life. Further, the ability to disguise dialect features by changing accent or adopting vocabulary obviously hinders the applicability of linguistic profiling to a degree. But even with these limitations, and as long as investigators are aware of these limitations, linguists can and do provide valuable investigative leads through empirically-founded identification of dialectal features.

Another approach to linguistic profiling has been developed by Pennebaker et al. (2003). Combining computational linguistics, syntactic tagging, and psychological assessment, Pennebaker et al. (2003) have been able to correlate syntactic patterns with psychological characteristics. Since syntax is an automated and unconscious behavior because our communication focuses on the meaning rather than the form of our messages, this approach to linguistic profiling analyzes linguistic features which are very difficult to disguise and thus can be the source of many investigative leads.

Discourse analysis in the forensic context deduces the negotiated meanings in surreptitiously taped conversations, confessions, and interrogations. Notionally, forensic discourse analysis applies theoretical principles and analytical methods for determining how two participants in a discourse say or do not say what they mean (Shuy, 1996, 1998). The structure of dialog — turn-taking, topic introductions, interruptions — can indicate differing levels of participation among the conversational participants. However, given the fact that metalinguistic ability is part and parcel of every native speaker's ability, analysis of conversation by a linguist or language expert may offend a judge or jury. Tiersma (1993) points out that "many courts are skeptical that linguistic analysis is necessary to assist the trier of fact (either judge or jury) in understanding conversation. Traditionally, courts consider the jury quite capable of understanding ordinary English without the aid of academics." Judges and lawyers may not discern the difference between documenting structure and interpreting a conversation, even when linguists are clearly documenting the structure from which conclusions related to the interpretation of events may be drawn, rather than an interpretation itself. But even with this potential limitation of judges' and lawyers' misconception of what discourse analysis provides, linguists can and do provide to law enforcement investigative leads which create alternative theories of a crime through the careful documentation of empirically-founded discourse strategies in forensically significant conversation. Even with this limitation, testimony based on discourse analysis has been admitted in more than 20 trials (Shuy, personal communication).

Authorship attribution deduces a document's author, given a group of potential authors, from linguistic patterns in the texts. Currently, there are two main approaches to authorship attribution: forensic stylistics (McMenamin, 1993, 2002; Foster, 2000) and the syntactic analysis method (Chaski, 1997, 2001, 2004, 2005; Kredens, 2000; cf. Stamatatos et al. 2001). Authorship attribution is, to my knowledge, the only forensic linguistic identification technique which has actually undergone the scrutiny of Daubert and other admissibility hearings. Therefore, the remainder of this chapter will focus on authorship attribution.

Authorship Evidence and Expertise

There are two basic strategies for introducing linguistic evidence. The first strategy is to simply introduce the document and hope that juries and judges are able to determine authorship based on language. The judicial record actually suggests that, for some jurisdictions, this might be the only option available.

Language-based author identification testimony has been proffered since the early 1900s, defended by the jurist Wigmore and questioned document examiners, and admitted by some courts. Table 28.1 shows the judicial record of admitting or not admitting

Table 28.1   Summary of Pre-Daubert Decisions Concerning Language-based Evidence

Date	Case Reference	Type of Linguistic Evidence	Admissible?
1901	*Throckmorton v. Holt* (1901) 180 U.S. 552, 45 L Ed 663, 21 S Ct 474	Punctuation, grammatical errors	Not admissible through expert opinion, but admissible for jury to decide
1909	*State vs. Kent* (1909) 83 Vt 28, 74 A 389	Punctuation	Yes
1914	*Josephs vs. Briant* (1914) 115 Ark 538, 172 SW 1002	Spelling, grammatical errors	Yes
1916	*Bartholomew vs. Walsh* (1916) 191 Mich 252, 157 NW 575	Punctuation	Yes
1919	Re Fleming's Estate (1919) 265 Pa 399, 109 A 265	Spelling	Implied admissible
1920	*Murphy vs. Murphy* (1920) 144 Ark 429, 222 SW 721	Spelling	Yes
1929	Re Creger's Estate (1929) 135 Okla 77, 274 P 30, 62 ALR 690	Spelling, vocabulary	Implied admissible
1934	Re Ridley's Will (1934) 151 Misc 474, 273 NYS 48	Spelling, grammatical errors	Yes
1935	*State vs. Hauptmann* (1935) 115 NJL 412, 180 A 809, cert den 296 U.S. 649, 80 L Ed 461, 56 S Ct 310	Spelling	Yes
1936	Re Bundy's estate (1936) 153 Or 234, 56 P2d 313	Punctuation	Yes
1943	Re Young's Estate (1943) 347 Pa 457, 32 A 2d 901, 154 ALR 643	Signature structure	Yes
1952	Re Cravens' Estate (1952) 206 Okla 174, 242 P2d 135, 34 ALR2d 615	Punctuation	Yes
1954	Succession of Prejean (1954) 224 La 921, 71 So 2d 328	Vocabulary	Implied admissible
1955	*New York vs. Henry and Armand Mulvey*, (1956) conviction rev'd, 1 App. Div. 541, 151 N.Y.S.2d 587	Sentence length (cf. Menicucci, 1977)	Yes
1963	*Hughes vs. United States* (1963, CA10 NM) 320 F2d 459, cert den 375 U.S. 966, 11 L Ed 2d 415, 84 S Ct 483	Spelling	Yes
1964	Cutler Estate (1964) 33 Pa D & C2d 682	Spelling	Yes
1973	Succession of Killingsworth (1973, La) 292 So 2d 536	Vocabulary	Implied admissible
1976	*United States vs. Pheaster* (1976, CA9 Cal(544 F2d 353, 2 Fed Rules Evid Serv 593, cert den 429 U.S. 1099, 51 L Ed 2d 546, 97 S Ct 1118	Spelling	Implied admissible

(Table continued)

TABLE 28.1 *Continued*

Date	Case Reference	Type of Linguistic Evidence	Admissible?
1976	*United States vs. Hearst* (1976, ND Cal) 412 F Supp 893	Vulgarity, breathing patterns and pauses, sentence beginnings (cf. Menicucci, 1977)	No — due to Frye criterion and materiality
1979	*United States vs. Larson* (1979, CA8 Minn) 595 F2d 759	Spelling	Yes
1982	Re estate of Ciaffoni (1982) 498 Pa 267, 446 A2d 225, 36 ALR4th 595, cert den 459 U.S. 1036, 74 L Ed 2d 602, 103 S Ct 447	Stylistic deviation	Admissible through expert testimony
1983	*United States vs. Clifford* (1983), CA3 Pa) 704 F2d 86, 12 Fed Rules Evid Serv 870	Spelling, punctuation, format, grammatical errors	District Court–no Court of Appeals — yes
1984	*United States vs. Campbell* (1984, CA1 Mass) 732 F2d 1017	Spelling	Implied admissible

language-based author identification as evidence. Donaldson's annotation (36 ALR4th 598, Donaldson, 1985) provides the bulk of the judicial record for both language-based and typewriting-based author identification; Table 28.1 includes only those cases related to language-based author identification. Menicucci (1977) mentions one case not in the annotation, and describes more fully the linguistic evidence offered in the Patricia Hearst case.

Table 28.1 demonstrates that the judicial record on admissibility of language-based author identification techniques is mixed. Historically, some courts admit expert testimony, some exclude expert testimony. Some courts allow lay experts with knowledge of the person whose writing is questioned to opine; for example, a husband might opine about a document ostensibly authored by his wife. Some courts acknowledge the language-based evidence in their rulings, other do not. State courts are apparently more liberal in admitting such testimony than Federal courts. Most courts already admit language-based evidence for the trier of fact to consider without expert testimony, either through a lay witness or the judge's or jurors' examination.

Depending on the jurisdiction, and the availability and cost of a language expert, the attorney might decide that the best strategy is just to let the trier of fact decide authorship based on language without any outside help. Based on the judicial record in Table 28.1, this would seem to be a firmly grounded strategy, at least from the legal perspective.

Scientifically, however, this strategy is not established. The scientific issue here is whether the trier of fact, without any special expertise in language analysis, can accurately assess language (Chaski, 2000; Solan and Tiersma, 2005). This is an empirical question, not a legal question and can only be answered by empirical testing, not by legal analysis or legal precedent. As discussed later, Chaski (2001) addresses this issue.

The second strategy is to argue that language experts should be allowed to testify regarding identification of authorship based on language in the same way that questioned document examiners are allowed to testify regarding handwriting or ink. FRE 901 b (3) states that a document can be authenticated by comparison between known documents, and the questioned document and this comparative authentication can be based on handwriting, typewriting or language.

When the comparison is based on handwriting or typewriter identification, typically the expertise of a Questioned Document Examiner (QDE) is utilized. Should the comparison be based on the habitual style of typewriting or language, *Black's Law Dictionary* (1991) defines two types of expertise: "comparative stylistics" (page 193) and "forensic linguistics" (page 448). It would seem then, as McMenamin (1993, 2002) argues, that the strategy of casting the language expert as a QDE may be legally appropriate.

There are a few obstacles, however, to pursuing the strategy of equating the language expert with the QDE as a way of getting language-based author identification testimony into court. These obstacles are the current status of QDE, the potentially prejudicial weight of academic affiliation, intellectual honesty, and the helpfulness of language experts.

Questioned Document Examination is having its own problems with admissibility. Recent attacks on questioned documents examination as impressionistic, without foundation, and probably not even a science but a skill have appeared in both legal commentary and judicial ruling (Risinger *et al.*, 1989; Risinger and Saks, 1996; Hansen, 1997; *United States v. Starzecpyzel*, 880 F. Supp. 1027; S.D.N.Y., 1995, and many cases following it). It seems clear then that attorneys should be cautious about aligning language experts with QDEs.

Language experts, unlike QDEs, typically have academic attributes that handwriting experts do not have. Academic degrees (M.A. and Ph.D.) and academic positions (professorships, chairmanships, editorial positions) could lead to undue weight being given to language experts, especially if the language experts are offering essentially what a QDE or a trier of fact, without any special expertise in linguistics, would already consider without an expert's help.

The academic affiliations and degrees of language experts cast as handwriting examiners also raise the question of intellectual honesty. Handwriting examiners do not currently have an academic discipline associated with its training via apprenticeship, whereas language experts with academic credentials but no apprenticeship are not permitted to join the questioned documents section of the American Academy of Forensic Sciences. So the language expert lacking the apprenticeship does not have the credentials to testify as a questioned document examiner, but the academic credentials which enable the language expert to pass *voir dire* and testify are actually irrelevant to testimony based on questioned document examination.

Under the Federal Rules of Evidence 702, expert testimony is admissible if it "assists the trier of fact to understand the evidence or to determine a fact in issue." Helpfulness from language experts is a controversial issue. If a lawyer presents a language expert to help the trier of fact determine authorship of a questioned document, the evaluative standard for language experts presenting authorship identification testimony is whether the language experts are presenting information which the jurors would not be able to come up with by themselves. In this light, Table 28.1 is especially interesting as it shows what has been proffered by experts as linguistic evidence: punctuation, grammatical errors, spelling errors, sentence beginnings, "stylistic deviation."

If the techniques draw on knowledge which can be safely assumed to be common knowledge based on American schools' grammar, writing, and literature instruction, then the expert testimony based on these techniques is not needed because they do not offer anything helpful to the average juror or judge. Table 28.1 shows that most of what has been offered as language-based evidence of authorship is exactly this kind of common knowledge based on American education: grammatical errors, vocabulary, spelling mistakes, and punctuation. But empirical research shows that these are not very reliable indicators of authorial identity (Chaski, 2001; Koppel and Schler, 2003).

Chaski (2001) tested hypotheses regarding authorship that have been offered by language experts, some of which are in Table 28.1. Specifically, Chaski (2001) reports the results of attempting to differentiate documents authored by four different women and to associate one unknown document with the actual writer among the four women. These hypotheses about language include as to what factors identify authors:

1. Vocabulary richness
2. *Hapax Legomena*
3. Readability measures
4. Content analysis identifies/discriminates between authors
5. Spelling errors
6. Grammatical errors
7. Sentential complexity
8. Punctuation marks

Table 28.2 states these ideas in nontechnical language and lists associated techniques for implementing these ideas in analyzing the texts of different authors.

Chaski (2001) reports that none of these techniques was able to differentiate the four writers from one another and associate the unknown document with the correct writer. In every one of the techniques, the four writers were confused with one another and/or the unknown document was assigned to the wrong writer. When spelling and punctuation techniques were extended to a larger sample of writers, the identification rates were still low.

Koppel and Schler (2003) also tested the forensic stylistics approach. Using almost 100 stylemarkers, including errors in spelling and punctuation, with two sophisticated classification algorithms, Koppel and Schler (2003) report that the highest accuracy rate for assigning documents to the correct authors was 72%.

Table 28.2 Common Conceptions of Language Use Related to Techniques

Common Conceptions of Language Use	Techniques
Individuals have distinct vocabularies	Type-token ratio Hapax legomena
Individuals use the same words over and over	Type-token ratio Hapax legomena
Individuals can be identified by the way each says things, that is, by the words each chooses	Type token ratio Hapax legomena Content analysis
Individuals can be identified by how sophisticated or simple their sentences are	Readability scores Sentence complexity
Individuals do not share spelling mistakes; spelling mistakes are so rare they can identify users	Spelling errors
Individuals do not share grammatical errors; grammatical errors are so rare they can identify users	Grammatical errors

An interesting example of how expertise affects analysis is punctuation. Chaski (2001) showed that just counting different types of punctuation marks is less able to correctly assign documents than classifying punctuation, regardless of the actual marks by the syntactic edge adjacent to the mark. Punctuation patterns are an obvious kind of textual phenomena which both the American high school graduate and the language expert would pay attention to, but the way that punctuation is used to accurately determine authorship requires knowledge of syntactic structures and statistics. Any juror or judge may notice that one document contains lots of hyphens while another does not, but any juror or judge may not notice — or even know to notice — that the hyphens in the one author's document are always syntactically conditioned in ways that occur significantly differently in the other author's document. In other words, even such an obvious feature as punctuation has to be handled in a nonobvious way in order to yield reliable results for author identification.

Whether these underlying ideas about language, listed in Table 28.2, are held by either the American high school graduate or the language expert, these common conceptions of language are not a reliable foundation for authorship identification in court. Indeed, the language experts who are proffered to present authorship evidence based on spelling mistakes or punctuation marks are distinctly not helpful to the trier of fact because they are using unreliable methods but allowed to opine as an expert witness. On the other hand, since these techniques are the very same that we might expect from the layperson, the trier of fact needs to be warned against depending on spelling and grammatical errors and punctuation when he or she decides an authorship issue without any expert help. From the experimental results in Chaski (2001) and Koppel and Schler (2003), these guidelines for authorship evidence are warranted:

1.   Do not let the trier of fact decide about the authorship of a document based on common conceptions of language such as spelling errors and vocabulary words
2.   Do not let language experts who are offering common conceptions evidence testify about the authorship of a document
3.   Use language experts to rebut language experts offering common conceptions evidence and to warn the trier of fact about error-based conclusions

Authorship Evidence and Admissibility Hearings

The third strategy for introducing linguistic evidence of authorship is to request a Daubert hearing into the techniques language experts use, whether the techniques are reliable, valid, and scientifically grounded and to introduce the language expert as a scientific expert. This strategy presupposes that there are actually methods grounded in or at least associated with a scientific community.

As noted earlier, forensic stylistics is grounded methodologically in questioned documents examination, but due to proponents' academic credentials and affiliations, it appears to be grounded within linguistics. McMenamin's "forensic stylistics" is a mixture of techniques which at first appear to have an academic basis in sociolinguistics but on further examination actually have more in common with Questioned Document Examination than linguistics. McMenamin (1993) devotes a chapter to laying a foundation for "stylistic analysis" within traditional questioned document examination. He quotes

Osborn (1910, p. 307) as emphasizing the "importance of composition, grammar, spelling, idioms, word division, spacing, margins, punctuation, use of capital letters, underscoring, and abbreviations," and expanding this direction in *The Problem of Proof* (Osborn, 1926) and *Questioned Documents* (Osborn, 1929), in which Osborn directs document examiners to consider subject matter; rhetoric, composition, and language; and errors (McMenamin, 1993, p. 113). In his review of other Questioned Document literature which directs the document examiner to consider spelling, punctuation, errors, "phraseology" and style, McMenamin also quotes Conway's (1959) *Evidential Documents*, Hilton's (1982) *Scientific Examination of Questioned Documents*, and Harrison's (1958) *Suspect Documents*. McMenamin's intellectual homebase has not changed in his 2002 publication. Although he includes a chapter on statistics, his chapter on methodology does not require the use of statistical testing. More importantly, empirical data regarding the method's error rate are not presented. Most importantly, there are still no empirical data supporting the essential claim of forensic stylistics that each individual has a cluster of stylemarkers which is different from everyone else's, actually unique to individuals. Further, there is no research that demonstrates the length of text necessary for the techniques to work properly.

In the early part of 2000, in the U.S. District Court, District of New Jersey, Roy Van Wyk was brought to trial for making threatening communications (*United States vs. Van Wyk*, 83 F.Supp.2d 515, D.N.J., 2000). The Government, represented by Assistant U.S. Attorney Charles B. McKenna, proposed that Special Agent James R. Fitzgerald of the Federal Bureau of Investigations be allowed to testify as an expert in forensic stylistics (later text analysis) about the authorship of the threatening letters.[1] The Government argued that Fitzgerald's testimony should be admitted because it relied on McMenamin's peer-reviewed publication (McMenamin, 1993), thus meeting at least one of the Daubert criteria which Federal judges must consider when determining the admissibility of evidence. Federal judges consider a variety of guidelines for admitting scientific and technical evidence; the Daubert criteria focus on the empirical reliability of a scientific technique.[2] Thus, the Government argued that Fitzgerald's technique should be admitted based on the fact that he relied on McMenamin (1993), which demonstrates the empirical reliability deducible from peer review before publication.

Defendant Van Wyk, represented by Assistant Federal Public Defender John H. Yauch, filed a motion *in limine* to exclude the proposed testimony of Agent Fitzgerald. The defense argued that the "proffered expert testimony is subjective, unreliable and lacks measurable standards" (Van Wyk, 83 F.Supp.2d 515, 521). Thus, the Defense argued that admitting forensic stylistics testimony would violate several other criteria of the Daubert standard of empirical reliability, such as falsifiability of the technique, known error rate, and standard operating procedures for performing the technique (see Note 2 for more discussion of admissibility factors). The Court did, in fact, recognize the "lack of scientific reliability of forensic stylistics":

> Although Fitzgerald employed a particular methodology that may be subject to testing, neither Fitzgerald nor the Government has been able to identify a known rate of error, establish what amount of samples is necessary for an expert to be able to reach a conclusion as to probability of authorship, or pinpoint any meaningful peer review. Additionally, as Defendant argues, there is no universally recognized standard for certifying an individual as an expert in forensic stylistics. (Van Wyk, 83 F.Supp.2d 515, 523).

Nonetheless, the Court recognized forensic stylistics as akin to questioned document examination, and so followed the Starczypyzel decision to allow the FBI agent to show similarities but not offer an opinion to the jury. McMenamin (2002) has argued that the van Wyk decision was due to the fact that the FBI did not have academic credentials in linguistics. But since the van Wyk decision, testimony based on the forensic stylistics method offered by experts with academic credentials has been completely excluded in criminal and civil trials in California and a criminal trial in Washington (*California vs. Flinner*, San Diego, 2003; *Beckman Coulter vs. Dovatron/Flextronics*, Santa Monica, 2003; *Washington vs. Preston*, Spokane, 2004). In the Flinner trial, Judge Alan Preckel referenced the van Wyk decision, calling it "a distinction without a difference." According to McMenamin's testimony in a family court trial, at least two courts have followed the van Wyk decision to the letter, restricting forensic stylistics testimony to showing similarities between documents but not stating an expert opinion regarding authorship (*Hargett vs. Hargett*, Placer County, CA, 2005).

Meanwhile, several different syntax-based author identification techniques have come forth from linguistics and computational linguistics. Svartik's (1968) work focused on sentence complexity and is perhaps the first example of forensic linguistics, since his data were the disputed confessions of Timothy Evans who was convicted and executed for murder. Svartik's work is also important because it sets forth what can realistically be expected from a linguistics-based approach: "we have already stated as a general requirement that the analysis should be maximally objective: in our case this means that the features can be unambiguously stated and open to outside inspection, and that they can be quantified and subjected to significance testing" (1968:24). The variable complexity of sentences is the central feature of Svartik's work.

Chaski (1997a,b, 1998a,b, 2001, 2004, 2005) has suggested that abstract syntactic structures can differentiate between authors and identify documents from one author. In Chaski's syntactic analysis method, the questioned documents and the known documents are analyzed for syntactic patterns in exactly the same way, using standard techniques from linguistics. The syntactic patterns in each document are then counted. These counts are then subjected to statistical testing to determine if these patterns do or do not come from a common origin, or in other words, can be classified together or separately. Each author's documents are tested first for internal consistency. Then known documents of Person A are tested against known documents of Person B to demonstrate that the method can correctly differentiate documents from different writers. Finally, the questioned document is tested against the known documents of Person A, and then against each potential author. All the statistical tests are pair-wise comparison (Person A to Person B, Questioned Document to Person A). The statistical results determine the conclusion about authorship. The conclusion about authorship indicates which author is excluded from the pool of potential authors based on being statistically differentiated and which author remains included in the pool of potential authors based on failing statistical differentiation.

Let me emphasize for a moment two features which in the syntactic analysis method (SAM) which differentiate it from other authorship identification methods. First, in SAM all the documents are processed in exactly the same way. Second, the comparisons are always pairwise in a pool of potential authors. Third, the method does not identify the one and only author of a questioned document; rather, the method concludes that the authors in the pool are either excluded based on statistical difference or included based on failing to find statistical difference.

Chaski (2001) showed the first error rate associated with the syntactic analysis method. In the four-writer experiment, syntactic structures parsed, counted ands statistically tested differentiated the four writers from one another, differentiated the unknown document from each of the nonwriters and, significantly, failed to differentiate the unknown writer from the actual writer. However, as Chaski (2001) states, even though this was a very promising an exciting result, 100% accuracy in one experiment merely means that this method should be seriously considered. Chaski (2004) reports an accuracy rate of 94% when 15 writers were tested against each other in pairwise comparisons. Importantly, the number of documents for each writer ranged from three to seven, and the total number of words for each writer ranged from 600 to 5,000 words. In the most robust analysis so far, Chaski (2005) reports an accuracy rate of 95% when syntactically classified punctuation, syntactic structures, and average word length variables are tested using crossvalidated discriminant function analysis. So Chaski's syntactic analysis method is showing a fairly high accuracy rate on the kinds of documents which are actually found in forensic cases.

Independent of Chaski, Stamatatos et al. (2000, 2001) have used a similar technique for determining authorship based on linguistic features and discriminant function analysis. Both approaches focus on the syntactic structures rather than vocabulary, punctuation, or errors in texts. The individual texts in Stamatatos' experiments are, on average, from 600 to 1,600 words in length. The total number of words for each author ranges from 17,000 to 50,000, with each author contributing 30 texts (20 for training and 10 for testing). Based on the discriminant function classification results, Stamatatos' nonlexical approach correctly classifies 1,000-word documents by author 81% of the time. Combining lexical features with the syntactic features, the method attained an accuracy rate of 87%. This is a very exciting result because it demonstrates the usefulness of both the syntactic approach and discriminant function analysis. Although 87% accuracy — or in Daubert terms error rate — may not be high enough for judicial purposes, it is certainly high enough to provide investigative leads worthy of consideration.

In addition to offering objective, replicable methods and statistical testing, the syntactic approaches of Svartik, Chaski, and Stamatatos et al. have some strong psycholinguistic evidence underlying them. First, it is a well-established principle in cognitive psychology that human memory consists of a short-term or working memory and a long-term or storage memory. The content of short-term memory fades within milliseconds, while some information is shunted to long-term memory. In language processing, it is again well-established and easily replicated that syntactic structure is processed in short-term memory but not shunted to long-term storage. In other words, people remember the gist of what is said, but not the exact form. Verbatim memory is extremely rare and typically found only in moment of great emotion which apparently freezes short-term memory.

Most people cannot be presumed to have the expertise to focus on, recognize and remember the syntactic forms of an author or message. Evidence based on the syntactic approach can thus be argued admissible based on the fact that this kind of evidence and conclusions drawn from syntactic analysis are not common knowledge and cannot be presumed of triers of fact.

Further, since natural language production is automatic for native speakers, syntactic details are in a sense unconsciously created. Thus, the possibility of false identification and elimination becomes slight. If person A seeks to write as person B, person A must first replicate syntactic details of B's language which are typically not remembered and second repress syntactic details of his own language which are typically automatized and not salient to native speakers.

Of these three syntax-based methods, only Chaski's has undergone the scrutiny of admissibility hearings. Chaski's syntactic analysis method has been ruled fully admissible, without restrictions, in State and Federal courts. In June 1998, Judge Lawrence H. Rushworth ruled that testimony of language-based author identification based on the Syntactic Method admissible without any restrictions (*Zarolia vs. Osborne*/Buffalo Environmental, Annapolis, MD). In June 2002, after a Daubert hearing in the trial *Greene vs. United States Navy*/Dalton, Judge Henry Kennedy of the U.S. District Court for the District of the District of Columbia ruled testimony of language-based author identification based on the Syntactic Analysis Method admissible without any restrictions. These rulings lead to the fourth guideline:

4. Do let language experts who offer something genuinely scientifically tested and helpful in terms of metalinguistic ability testify with an opinion to the trier of fact.

In conclusion, like any scientific endeavor, the current state of the art for language-based author identification is evolving. The direction for continued research in syntax-based methods is clear and the challenge for forensic stylistics to provide empirical evidence for its claims awaits.

Determining authorship from a fixed set of suspect documents is in no way the same as determining individuality in language. For language-based author identification to truly be developed, an entire database representative of an appropriate sample of the general population, or subpopulation, would have to be analyzed and quantified. No language expert will be able to answer the question "Did the defendant — and only this defendant — author the document in question?" until the population work has been completed. For now, the very best any language expert can rationally respond to such a question is that, given the limited set of comparison documents, there is a certain statistical chance that the defendant's comparison documents are similar or different from the document in question. Inclusion or exclusion is the best we can do.

Appendix A

Linguistic Profiling

Linguistic profiling exemplifies how the metalinguistic ability and tools of linguists and non-linguists differ radically. There is a qualitative and empirical difference between what a non-linguist and a linguist can produce. So even though non-linguists produce linguistic profiles which may not be helpful or in any way determinative, the baby of linguistic profiling as an investigative technique certainly should not be thrown out with the bathwater of linguistic speculation.

In the on-going Amerithrax case, the FBI has obtained a linguistic and behavioral profile. The burning question about the anthrax-laced letters sent to Senator Daschle, NBC anchorman Tom Brokaw, and the editor of the New York Post is who wrote them. Handwriting analysts readily admitted that they could do little with the block printing of these letters. Based on the text of the anthrax letters, Donald Foster, a professor of English literature, has suggested, at different times, that the author of the anthrax letters is foreign, a Pakistani, a speaker of Arabic, Persian, or Urdu, not an Arabic speaker, and a competent English speaker, as reported in articles in *The Washington Post, The London Times, The Hartford Courant*, and the *AP wire*. According to a February article in *The Hartford Courant*,

> "What we have here is a welter of contradictory and ambiguous evidence," he [Foster] said in an interview last week. (*The Hartford Courant*, February 6, 2002. Anthrax Mystery Turns Scholars Into Sleuths).

According to an October article in *The Washington Post*,

> One official said the only significant clue raising the possibility of foreign terrorist involvement is the conclusion of FBI behavioral scientists, who believe that whoever wrote the three letters delivered to Daschle, NBC News and the New York Post did not learn English as a first language. (*Washington Post*, October 27, 2001. *FBI and CIA* Suspect Domestic Extremists: Officials Doubt Any Links to Bin Laden).

Even though Professor Foster's analysis is self-contradictory, in November, the FBI broke through a front door in a raid on the house of two Pakistani brothers in West Chester, PA (*The Wall Street Journal*, November 15, 2001. Raids on Pakistan-Born Men Follow Fruitless Day on Anthrax Trail.). A few months later, however, according to *USA Today* (May 21, 2002) "The government has begun a strategy of focusing on possible sources of anthrax and casting a wide net, rather than identifying suspects from the few clues gained from the letters."

In Amerithrax, linguistic profiling has certainly not narrowed the list of potential suspects. This technique, however, has real potential use for law enforcement under two conditions: the sociolinguistic method, rather than intuition, is used and the linguistic profiler has documented training and proficiency as a linguist, shown by the appropriate credentials and research experience.

The Anthrax Letters: A Linguistic Analysis

Although spelling errors seem to jump out of the page to many people and may seem very odd to the point where one might think they are unique, spelling errors are not unique to individuals (Chaski, 2001). In the case of the anthrax letters, the misspelling of penicillin as "penacilin" is typical of groups rather than individuals. The spelling variation "penacilin" is common among American rap music aficionados. I have also found this spelling among native-American English speaking college graduates. But the spelling yields some profiling characteristics when it is contextualized within linguistic theory and sociolinguistics.

Second-language interference is a linguistic method examining the effect of the first language on the second; these effects are predictable from systematic differences between the two languages. Nonnative English speakers typically have phonetic interference from the native language; this accounts for the many different accents of foreign speakers of American English. Likewise, the nonnative English writer has orthographic interference, based on the native language, which will appear in spelling variations. On the hypothesis that the anthrax letters were written by a nonnative speaker of English, nonnative interference should show up depending on the spelling systems of different languages. In the anthrax letters, second-language interference actually suggests that the spelling variant "penacilin" is *not* predictable from Arabic and many other languages associated with terrorist groups.

Under the hypothesis of second-language interference, there are four interesting features of the spelling variant "penacilin" for "penicillin." The first spelling feature is the "p." In English, Korean, Indonesian, Thai, Russian, Hebrew and Farsi, penicillin is spelled with an initial "p." In Arabic, penicillin would be transliterated "benicillin." The "p" spelling aligns with a non-Arabic speller.

The second spelling feature is the "a" representing the unaccented vowel in the second syllable. All languages have a vowel which is used for unaccented syllables, known as the reduced vowel; in American English, the reduced vowel sounds like "uh" (as in "uh-huh"). This is also how we say the word "a" (as in "a letter"). What is interesting about "penacilin" is that the reduced vowel is spelled "a," representing the sound of the highly frequent word "a." But the pronunciation of "penicillin" in Arabic, Farsi, Russian, Korean, Indonesian, and Thai is notably without a reduced vowel in the second syllable. The fact that the second syllable is represented as having a reduced vowel indicates that the author is a native speaker of English.

A third interesting feature of "penacilin" is the "c" representing "s." In American English spelling, "c" has two phonetic values: "c" represents the "k" sound or the "s" sound depending on what follows it. In "penacilin," the "c" represents the "s" due to the following "i." In Pashto, Korean, Indonesian, Farsi, and Arabic, spelling interference would map the "c" onto "s" so that the expected spelling would be something like "penisilin." In Russian and Hebrew, spelling interference would map the "c" onto "tz" so the expected spelling would be something like "penitzilin." What is interesting is that the "c" is retained for the representation of "s." This indicates that the author is a native speaker of English.

The fourth feature of "penacilin" is the reduction of the double "ll" to single "l." American English spelling includes double consonants even though we do not lengthen our consonants when we speak. Because these double consonants are not phonetic, they are often reduced; for instance, we have "till" and "til" as spelling variants in American English. Arabic, Korean, and Thai do have double consonants, whereas Farsi, Russian and Hebrew do not. So, for instance, a native Russian speaker would be expected to reduce the consonant from a double "l" to a single "l," like a native American English speaker, while a native Arabic speaker would not.

These four features — the initial 'p,' the reduced vowel in the second unstressed syllable, the retention of 'c' to represent the 's' sound, and the reduction of the doubled consonant — plus the fact that the spelling variant "penacilin" is found among native American English speakers point to the conclusion that a native American English speaker authored the anthrax letter.

Endnotes

1. In an oral argument, the prosecution withdrew its proffer of Fitzgerald as an expert in forensic stylistics and instead proffered him as a text analysis expert; this change in title did not, however, change Fitzgerald's method based on forensic stylistics as represented by McMenamin (1993).

2. Recent rules and rulings on the admissibility of scientific and technical evidence through the testimony of expert witnesses include Federal Rule of Evidence 702 (FRE 702); Federal Rule of Evidence 403 (FRE 403), and the empirical reliability standard set by the U.S. Supreme

Court's opinion in *Daubert v. Merrell Dow Pharmaceuticals, Inc.*, 509 U.S. 593 (1993) and extended in *Kumho Tire Co. v. Carmichael*, 526 U.S. 137 (1999). FRE 702 requires that the expert must (a) qualify as an expert by knowledge, skill, experience, training, or education; (b) testify to scientific, technical, or other specialized knowledge; and (c) must assist the trier of fact. FRE 403 excludes testimony that may introduce the danger of unfair prejudice, confuse the issues or mislead the jury. The Daubert criteria include (1) whether a method consists of a testable hypothesis; (2) wither the method has been subject to peer review; (3) the known or potential rate of error; (4) the existence and maintenance of standards controlling the technique's operation; (5) whether the method is generally accepted; (6) the relationship of the technique to methods that have been established to be reliable; (7) the qualifications of the expert witness based on the methodology; (8) the nonjudicial uses of the method (Daubert, 509 U.S. 595). Berger (2000) admirably explains the legal complexity of these trends in admissibility; Solan (1999) indicates how these rulings may apply to linguistic experts.

References

Berger, M.A. (2000). The Supreme Court's trilogy on the admissibility of expert testimony. *Reference Manual on Scientific Evidence* (2nd ed.), Washington, DC: Federal Judicial Center.

Berk-Seligson, S. (1990). *The Bilingual Courtroom: Court Interpreters in the Judicial Process*. Chicago, University of Chicago Press.

Black's Law Dictionary (1991). St Paul, MN: West Publishing Co.

Butters, R. (2005). The credentials of linguists testifying in american trademark litigation. *The Law and Society Association Annual Conference*, Las Vegas, Nevada.

Chaski, C.E. (1997). who wrote it? steps toward a science of authorship identification. *Natnl. Inst. Justice J.*: 15–22.

Chaski, C.E. (2000). Linguistic authentication and reliability. *National Conference on Science and Law Proceedings*, San Diego, CA; Washington, DC: National Institute of Justice, U.S. Department of Justice. NCJ 179630.

Chaski, C.E. (2001). Empirical evaluations of language-based author identification techniques. *Foren. Ling. International Journal of Speech, Language and Law*, 8(1): 1–65.

Chaski, C.E. (2004). Recent validation results for the syntactic analysis method for author identification. *International Conference on Language and Law*, Cardiff, Wales.

Chaski, C.E. (2005). Who's at the Keyboard? Authorship attribution in digital evidence investigations. *International Journal of Digital Evidence*, Spring (2005), 4: 1. Available at www.ijde.org.

Chaski, C.E. and Chmelynski, H.J. (2005). Testing twenty variables for author attribution by discriminant function analysis, pending publication.

Conway, J.V.P. (1959). *Evidential Documents*. Springfield: Charles C. Thomas.

Cotterill, J., Ed. (2004). *Language in the Legal Process*. New York, NY: Palgrave MacMillan.

Donaldson, R.G. (1985). Admissibility of evidence as to linguistics or typing style (forensic linguistics) as basis of identification of typist or author. *Amer. Law. Rep., Annot* 36(ALR4th): 598.

Dumas, B.K. (1990). An analysis of the adequacy of federally mandated cigarette package warnings. *Language in the Judicial Process*. J.N. Levi, A.G. Walker (Eds.). New York, NY: Plenum, 302–42.

Dumas, B.K. (2004). Reasonable doubt about reasonable doubt: assessing jury instruction adequacy in a capital case. In Cotteril, J. (Ed). *Language in the Legal Process*. New York, NY: Palgrave MacMillan, pp. 246–259.

Foster, D. (2000). *Author Unknown: On the Trail of Anonymous*. New York, NY: Henry Holt and Co.

Gibbons, J., Ed. (1994). *Language and the Law*. New York, NY: Longman Publishing.

Gibbons, J. (2003). *Forensic Linguistics: An Introduction to Language in the Justice System*. Oxford: Blackwell Publishing.

Hansen, M. (1997). Evidence Section. *ABA J.* May 1997: 76–78.

Harrison, W.R. (1958). *Suspect Documents: Their Scientific Examination*. London: Sweet and Maxwell.

Hilton, O. (1982). *Scientific Examination of Questioned Documents*. Boca Raton, FL: CRC Press.

Koppel, M. and Schler, J. (2003). Exploiting stylistic idiosyncrasies for authorship attribution. Available at *www.cs.biu.ac.il/aaahtmlfiles/indexpeoplefiles/fmembers.html*.

Kredens, K. (2000). *Forensic Linguistics and the Status of Linguistic Evidence in the Legal Setting*. Ph.D. Dissertation. Lodz, Poland: University of Lodz.

Levi, J.N. (1994). *Language and Law: A Bibliographic Guide to Social Science Research in the USA*. Chicago, IL: American Bar Association.

Levi, J.N. and Walker, A.G. (1990). *Language in the Judicial Process*. New York, NY: Plenum.

McMenamin, G.R. (1993). *Forensic Stylistics*. Amsterdam: Elsevier Science Publishers.

McMenamin, G.R. (2002). *Forensic Linguistics; Advances in Forensic Stylistics*. Boca Raton, Florida: CRC Press.

Menicucci, J.D. (1977). Stylistics evidence in the trial of Patricia Hearst. *Ariz. State Law J.* 1977: 387.

Osborn, A. (1910). *Questioned Documents*. Rochester: Lawyer's Cooperative.

Osborn, A. (1926). *The Problem of Proof*. Newark: Essex.

Osborn, A. (1929). *Questioned Documents*. Albany: Boyd.

Pennebaker, J., Mehl, M.R., and Niederhoffer, K.G. (2003). Psychological aspects of natural language use: our words, our selves. *Ann. Rev. Psychol.* 54: 547–77.

Pinker, S. (1994). *The Language Instinct: How the Mind Creates Language*. New York, NY: William Morrow and Co.

Risinger, D.M., Denbeaux, M.P., and Saks, M.J. (1989). Exorcism of ignorance as a proxy for rational knowledge: the lessons of handwriting identification expertise. *Univ. Pennsyl. Law Rev.* 137: 731–87.

Risinger, D.M. and Saks, M.J. (1996). Science and nonscience in the courts: Daubert meets handwriting identification expertise. *Iowa Law Rev.* 82(1): 21–74.

Rodman, R.D. (2002). Linguistics and the law: How knowledge of, or ignorance of, elementary linguistics may affect the dispensing of justice. *Foren. Lingu.* 9(1).

Shuy, R.W. (1996). *Language Crimes: The Use and Abuse of Language Evidence in the Courtroom*. Oxford: Blackwell Publishers.

Shuy, R.W. (1998). *The Language of Confession, Interrogation and Deception*. Thousand Oaks, CA: Sage Publications.

Shuy, R.W. (2001). DARE's role in linguistic profiling. *DARE Newsletter*. 4: 1–5.

Solan, L.M. (1993). *The Language of Judges*. Chicago: University of Chicago Press.

Solan, L.M. (1999). Can the legal system use experts on meaning? *Tennessee Law Review*, 66: 4.

Solan, L.M., Tiersma, P.M. (2005). *Speaking of Crime: The Language of Criminal Justice*. Chicago: University of Chicago Press.

Stamatatos, E., Fakotakis, N., and Kokkinakis, G. (2000). Automatic text categorization in terms of genre and author. *Comput. Ling.* 26(4): 471–495.

Stamatatos, E., Fakotakis, N., and Kokkinakis, G. (2001). Computer-based authorship attribution without lexical measures. *Comp. Human.* 35: 193–214.

Svartik, J. (1968). *The Evans Statements: A Case for Forensic Linguistics*. Stockholm: Almqvist & Wiksell.

Tiersma, P.M. (1993). Linguistic issues in the law. *Language* 69(1): 113–37.

Forensic Accounting

29

KENNETH C. McCRORY

Introduction: The Role of the Forensic Accountant

Much of the legal process involves computation of monetary amounts. Accountants, particularly those specially trained, such as certified public accountants, certified fraud examiners, and certified valuation analysts are ideally suited to involvement in the legal process as forensic accountants.

Forensic accountants can play a variety of roles in the legal process including as:

- *Consultant* — wherein the forensic accountant advises an attorney and helps the attorney act as an advocate for the client's position.
- *Expert Witness* — wherein the forensic accountant helps the trier-of-fact arrive at a fair decision by providing unique and expert information and knowledge.
- *Other Roles* — such as trier-of-fact, special master, mediator, or arbitrator.

A forensic accountant acting as a *consultant* assists the attorney in understanding financial matters related to the case and helps the attorney act as an advocate for the client's position. As a consultant, the forensic accountant is usually engaged directly by the attorney, although payment may come directly from the client. When engaged as a consultant by the attorney, the forensic accountant's work is usually an attorney work-product privilege and is protected from discovery by opposing counsel. The forensic accountant, as consultant, will help the attorney understand the opponent's financial calculations, point out any weaknesses that may exist in the opponent's case and oftentimes help the attorney prepare questions for crossexamination of the opposing witnesses, particularly expert witnesses.

The forensic accountant's role as an *expert witness* usually calls for somewhat more objectivity than the consultant's role. An expert witness is expected to assist the trier-of-fact in understanding issues before the court by providing unique knowledge or insight into those issues. As an expert witness, the forensic accountant should not act as an advocate for the client's position. ". . . The client's attorney is the advocate, not the expert. CPA experts should take care to advocate their opinion, not the client's cause. This distinction means that the expert should objectively consider the case and develop his or her opinion of the facts."[1] The role of the expert witness is to act as a teacher and instruct the trier-of-fact about his or her opinion based on the unique knowledge of accounting that the expert possesses.

The accountant can play a role as a *trier-of-fact, special master, arbitrator, or mediator*. If the issue involves a dispute over financial matters or values, as opposed to matters of law or liability, then the forensic accountant is uniquely suited to act as an arbitrator or mediator. Forensic accountants can easily spot inflated values, over or understated profits, bogus financial claims, and overstated costs. Those forensic accountants who are also certified valuation analysts or accredited business valuators are particularly trained regarding comparative values or damages caused to business values.

The Difference between Accountants as Auditors and Forensic Accountants

One of the main differences between accountants as auditors and forensic accountants is that forensic accountants do not have a fixed set of rules. Auditors operate under generally accepted auditing standards promulgated by the American Institute of CPAs and others such as the Securities and Exchange Commission and the Public Companies Accounting Oversight Board. Forensic accountants generally have fewer professional rules for conducting their engagements but rather, are bound by legal rules and procedures. Auditors also give consideration to the materiality of an amount as it relates to the financial statements as a whole while forensic accountants may investigate even immaterial amounts.

An illustration of how standards and materiality differ for auditors and forensic accountants might be their approach to inventory. If the amount of inventory is material, an auditor is required under generally accepted auditing standards to perform various tests of the inventory and to observe the taking of a physical inventory. A forensic accountant, who, when conducting a fraud examination, does not suspect fraud in inventory, may ignore the inventory altogether. On the other hand, even though the inventory may be immaterial, a forensic accountant who suspects fraud in the inventory will examine it regardless of its materiality.

Another difference between accountants as auditors and forensic accountants is the language used in their reports and conclusions. Auditors tend to use language that is more qualified and less decisive than forensic accountants. For example, an auditor might conclude that "the income statement *appears* to include items that should be capitalized," whereas a forensic accountant would conclude "the income statement *includes items that, in my opinion, should be capitalized*." An auditor might also state "an equity percentage of 10% *may indicate* the company is undercapitalized," whereas a forensic accountant would state "an equity percentage of 10% *indicates* the company is undercapitalized." The reason forensic accountants use more affirmative language is to prevent opposing counsel from trying to give the impression that the forensic accountant is not certain about his opinion or conclusion.

What Forensic Accountants Bring to the Legal Process

Forensic accountants can use accounting and auditing techniques as well as data analysis to help prove or disprove a legal position.

There are a number of skills that forensic accountants have developed through their training and experience that can be used to assist the parties in a legal dispute. These include:

- Analytical skills
- Interviewing skills
- Investigatory skills
- Forecasting skills

Perhaps the major asset that a forensic accountant can bring to a legal proceeding is their ability to *analyze* financial statements, as well as financial and related data. Experienced accountants can look at a set of financial statements and almost immediately begin to identify any anomalies or unusual items should they exist in the financial statements. The ability to relate elements of a financial statement and do quick analyses is something that comes easily to accountants. For example, just scanning down the first few numbers on the balance sheet, an accountant will glance at the accounts receivable, and quickly look at annual sales volume to determine whether the company is slow in collecting its receivables. The accountant will note the amount of inventory and relate it to the cost of sales to determine whether inventory is turning over quickly or slowly in relation to the industry the company is in. The accountant will then begin to dig into even more detailed analyses, developing ratios and determining whether they appear to be in line with companies of this size and in this industry. From this analysis, the accountant can request additional information that will establish a complete financial picture of the subject business.

These analytical skills are supplemented by *interviewing* skills. The forensic accountant gathers evidence from financial statements, books and records, other documents, and from asking questions and making inquiries of people who have knowledge of the financial information. Oftentimes, forensic accountants will ask an individual to explain certain information not because they do not understand it, but because they want to see how the individual tries to interpret the data or what slant they might try to point out to the forensic accountant. This ability to ask questions relating to financial data of individuals is also useful in assisting the attorney to develop deposition questions and crossexamination questions, particularly for other experts. The forensic accountants' interviewing skills are a major component in allowing them to piece together the facts and the truth behind financial statements and documents.

Forensic accountants also possess strong *investigatory* skills. Accountants receive training as auditors, and many have spent a great deal of time developing significant expertise in auditing. Auditing is developing evidence, examining facts, confirming information, analyzing data, and drawing all of these elements together to arrive at a conclusion. During this process, the accountant will reconcile information from different sources and tie numbers together to form their opinion. There is a very close parallel between auditing and the work of a detective. Early in my career, in fact, a very experienced auditor drew the analogy by stating that "auditors and detectives do not believe in coincidences."

Another skill useful to the forensic accountant is their ability in *forecasting* future financial results. A forensic accountant can analyze existing data as well as industry and economic trends to prepare a forecast or projection of what might happen in the future, or what might have happened in the future if not for an intervening event. This is particularly useful in the legal process where an event has caused a business interruption, or one party has usurped the rights of another party (e.g., in patent or copyright infringement).

Services the Forensic Accountant Provides

A forensic accountant can provide a wide variety of services to those involved in the legal process. The services can be provided to either plaintiffs or defendants in both civil and criminal matters. Frequently, both sides use forensic accountants to prepare estimates of damage, to rebut each other, and to assist in crossexamination of each other. The services next described are those where a forensic accountant is most frequently engaged.

Business Damages

Business damages most often result from:

- Breach of contract
- A tort
- A business interruption

Breach of Contract

Breach of contract can occasionally lead to a business interruption, but this section will focus on the more narrow damages from the breach itself.

One of the more frequent causes of legal action are breaches relating to construction contracts. It has been said that the last step of any construction project is filing the lawsuit. Construction contract damages often involve pursuing or defending against a claim. Claims can take several forms but usually result from changes in the scope of the contract or construction delays. Changes in the scope of the contract involve increased costs due to redesign or different materials. The forensic accountant's role in these types of claims generally involves verifying costs and sometimes interpreting whether such costs were authorized. Claims resulting from delays are typically more complex than other types of claims. A delay in a construction project can be caused by weather, natural disasters, redesign, late supply of material, financial difficulties of the contractor or the owner, and a variety of other causes. From the owner's perspective, damages that can result from a construction delay include:

- Additional financing costs
- Lost sales for a retail project
- Lost production and sales for a manufacturing facility
- Lost rents, and perhaps lost tenants for a rental facility
- Overcrowding or inability to accommodate students for a school
- Court-imposed sanctions for a jail facility
- Higher cost from buying energy on the spot market for an electrical generating facility

Damages to a contractor caused by owner delays include:

- Missed opportunities for new work by having bonding or financial capacity tied up
- Unabsorbed overhead
- An increase in finance costs
- Higher prices for material used in the job
- Higher labor charges if a labor contract expires
- Inefficiency due to rescheduling other work

The forensic accountant will work with the attorney and his client to establish both the types of damages incurred and a proper calculation of them. The forensic accountant is also very important in advising on the type and quality of documentation necessary to convince the trier-of-fact of the legitimacy of the damages. In a claims situation, documentation is often the key to success.

Frequently, breaches of contract occur when a business is sold. Oftentimes, the buyer feels he has been misled or that a warranty was breached. The forensic accountant may be asked to compute damages from useless equipment, obsolete or damaged inventory, profits from customers who left or contracts that did not materialize, overstatement of assets or understatement of liabilities.

Breaches of employment contracts and covenants not to compete can also give rise to the need for a forensic accountant to compute damages. Unless the agreement specifies a formula, the computation is not often straightforward. There are usually no specific costs such as with bad inventory or increased material prices, and it is oftentimes difficult to draw a relationship between lost business and the breach of the employment contract or covenant not to compete. Of these two types of breaches, the covenant may be somewhat easier to analyze since the forensic accountant may, through the discovery process, gain access to the competing individuals' business records or know what business was diverted to the competing individual. In either case, the forensic accountant must exercise care to avoid overstated or false claims for damages.

Other types of contract breaches which may result in damage claims include: product warranties, stock sales, sales of real estate, and receipt of defective services.

Torts

A *tort* damage is one caused by the breach of a legal duty owed by one party to another. Torts related to fraud and theft are discussed next in more detail.

A frequent type of tort claim is that involving the infringement on a patent, trademark, servicemark, or copyright. Generally, infringements must provide that the damages are sufficient to compensate for the infringement, and damages should not be less than a reasonable royalty. In regard to the damages, the forensic accountant's approach must be to calculate not what the infringer made, or did not make, but what the injured party would have made had the infringement not occurred. In regard to the calculation of a reasonable royalty, the forensic accountant must be guided by the amount of royalty that would have resulted from a voluntary negotiation between the holder and the infringer before the infringement.

The *Georgia-Pacific Corporation v. U.S. Plywood Corporation* case (318 F. Supp. 1116, (S.D.N.Y. 1970), Modified 446 F.2d 295 (2d Cir. 1971), Cert. Denied 404 U.S. 870

(1971)) was one of the most significant cases in providing forensic accountants guidance on the important factors for calculating royalties in patent infringement cases. This case set forth 15 factors to consider. A follow up case to the *Georgia-Pacific Corporation v. U.S. Plywood Corporation* case is the *Panduit Corporation v. Stahlin Brothers Fibre Works, Inc.* case (575 F.2d 1152, 1156 [6th Cir. 1978]). This case establishes the so-called "Panduit Test" for assessing lost profits versus a reasonable royalty. As the Information or Technology Age replaces the Industrial Age, patents, trademarks, and other intellectual property are representing a greater percentage of business assets. The need for forensic accountants to understand these assets will grow accordingly.

Another tort that frequently involves forensic accounting is interference with business or contractual relationships. Common forms of this may be diversion of corporate opportunities (an employee conducts a business opportunity for himself rather than his employer), purposely luring away a competitor's employee who is bound by a business contract or providing false and disparaging information about a company to one of its customers. These interferences can result in the loss of customers, the loss of a valuable employee, or the loss of reputation. The forensic accountant will be asked to evaluate the damage to the business caused by these losses. The damage may be short term or specific (e.g., the loss of a given project or a single customer), or it may be very long-term (e.g., damage to the company's reputation). In many cases, there may be a combination of all of these factors. The forensic accountant will be called upon to determine the types of damages and a reasonable method of calculation of those damages.

Business Interruption

Both breach of contract and tort claims can lead to lost profits from business interruptions. Lost profits can also occur from fires, floods, other natural disasters, power outages, or breakdowns of equipment. Profits are lost due to a loss of revenue, an increase in costs, or a combination of both factors.

The principal elements that a forensic accountant must consider when calculating lost profits from a business interruption are:

- The effects of the interruption on revenue
- The effects of the interruption on expenses
- The time period of the interruption
- Any offsets to the lost profits

The first objective of the forensic accountant is to determine what the *revenue* would have been, absent the event that caused the loss. In a stable, consistent company, the forensic accountant can look to historical revenue as the best indicator of what revenue would have been. Although historical revenue might provide some guideline for a growth-oriented company, the forensic accountant must also consider the growth pattern and any new products or markets that may have become available to the company, absent the interruption. The forensic accountant can look to market studies or use similar companies for comparison. In a start-up company, a market study may indicate an ultimate volume, but the forensic accountant must also consider the "ramp up" period wherein the company has not achieved its full potential.

In determining *expenses* that would have been associated with lost revenue, it is necessary to consider which costs are variable and which are fixed. Variable costs are those which vary with the amount of revenue. Examples would include labor, material, and other costs of sales as well as sales commissions, supplies, and freight. Fixed costs are those that remain the same regardless of changes in volume. Examples of these might include rent, casualty insurance, professional fees, and administrative wages. Fixed expenses will, of course, only remain the same for a limited period of time. Ultimately, all costs will increase as the business grows.

It is important for the forensic accountant to make a determination of how long the *business interruption period* should be calculated. A company whose business has been interrupted has a responsibility to restore operations as quickly as possible since a damaged company cannot expect to receive lost profit payments for an infinite period of time. Occasionally, after a business interruption, a Company will never resume operations. For example, the owners may simply wish to retire. In these instances, the forensic accountant must make a reasonable determination of how long it would have taken the company to resume operation if it had chosen to do so.

A final area to consider is any *offsets* or mitigation of the lost profits incurred. Most often, these mitigating factors occur in companies that have multiple lines of business or multiple locations. For example, a business with four retail locations, one of which is closed due to a fire, may experience increases in business at the remaining three locations due to customers of the damaged location shifting their business to those locations. Any profits from the gain of this business should be used to reduce the calculated damages.

Calculating business damages is one of the most frequent reasons a forensic accountant is called upon. Calculation of these damages requires a knowledge of what losses are permitted by law and a broad understanding of business, a knowledge of how to calculate the losses, and an ability to present the calculations so they are understandable by the trier-of-fact.

Fraud

Perhaps the services the public most identifies with forensic accountants are those dealing with fraud. The forensic accountant can become involved in both civil and criminal fraud procedures and may work for the plaintiff or the defense. Criminal frauds are prosecuted by various government agencies. The objective of the government agency is to obtain a conviction against the defendant that will result in a prison sentence and some form of restitution to the victims. Civil trials result from a complaint filed by the victim against the defendant. The victim/plaintiff's objective is to seek monetary recovery from the defendant.

Fraud, in a business setting, usually consists of embezzlement, theft, or preparation of fraudulent financial statements. Embezzlement and theft typically involve an individual employee acting on their own. Fraudulent financial statements are more frequently the result of several high ranking individuals within an organization acting together.

There are generally three factors that merge in order for an individual to commit fraud. Often called the "fraud triangle," those factors are:

- *Financial pressure* (either real or imaginary) facing the individual
- The *opportunity* to commit fraud
- An *ability to rationalize* committing the fraud

Embezzlements can take many forms. There are literally thousands of types of embezzlements and thefts that employees perpetrate against businesses. The more common embezzlements involve diversion of cash receipts, fraudulent payments, payroll schemes, and minor chiseling involving expense reports, petty cash, and cash register thefts.

Diversion of cash receipts can be accomplished by opening checking accounts with names the same as, or similar to, the embezzler's employer. The embezzler then issues checks from the account to themselves.

Fraudulent payment schemes are more frequent than diversions of cash because they are generally easier to perpetrate. An embezzler who deals with disbursements can alter checks that have already been prepared to change the name of a payee to another business name which is under the control of the embezzler. For example, a check made payable to U.S. Bank may be altered after it has been signed to read "U.S. Bankers Supply Corporation." The embezzler will have set up an account with that name and thus be able to negotiate the checks. Occasionally, if the embezzler controls the disbursement process and the receipt of bank statements, they may be bold enough to make the checks payable to themselves while entering them into the books and records as payable to a legitimate vendor.

Another scheme frequently used is setting up phony vendors that appear to be legitimate. The embezzler will have invoices printed and will send them to their employer. If the embezzler is in a position to approve invoices, they will simply approve the phony invoices, mail the check to a post-office box where they will later collect, and deposit it to an account they control.

In larger corporations, an embezzler who works in the payroll department or the Human Resources department can conduct payroll schemes where they put phantom employees on the payroll. Such schemes are easier to conduct in corporations that have rapid employee turnover. The embezzler takes control of the phony payroll check and deposits it to an account or cashes it.

Other forms of employee dishonesty include cheating on expense reports, theft of petty cash, cash thefts from cash registers, theft of inventory, and theft of small or even large equipment.

A forensic accountant is usually called upon because management suspects fraud. Frequently in fraud investigations, the forensic accountant will work with corporate counsel or special counsel hired to investigate the fraud. Oftentimes, the forensic accountant will provide information to law enforcement authorities to assist them in prosecuting a criminal case.

The forensic accountant who has been engaged to investigate embezzlement or a theft will generally discuss the case with management and counsel to define what the objectives of the engagement are. They will then prepare a work program with various steps designed to ferret out all elements of the embezzlement or theft. The investigation will involve interviews with various employees as well as extensive review of documents and transactions. The forensic accountant will prepare workpapers and assemble documents necessary to support their conclusion. The last phase is the preparation of a report that will:

- Give the purpose of the engagement and the background of the investigation.
- Define each area of the embezzlement or theft and provide specific details of each instance of embezzlement or theft.
- Summarize the amount stolen.

- The forensic accountant may also make recommendations to prevent future fraud, although this is oftentimes done in a separate report.

In reporting on an embezzlement or theft, the forensic accountant should not pronounce an individual guilty. This is particularly true in a criminal case where that judgment is left to the trier-of-fact. The responsibility of the forensic accountant is to provide the facts in the case (including naming the individuals involved) and let management decide whether those individuals should be prosecuted, dismissed, or sued.

Bankruptcy

Another set of services forensic accountants frequently render to business is assisting them with the filing of a bankruptcy petition and providing services during the course of the bankruptcy. Bankruptcies are administered by the Federal Bankruptcy Court.

The bankruptcy code contains two types of bankruptcies applicable to business — Chapters 7 and 11. Under Chapter 7, the business is liquidated and any proceeds are used to pay creditors. Under Chapter 11, the business attempts to reorganize its financial affairs, settle with creditors, and emerge from the bankruptcy as a viable entity.

Forensic accountants can provide a variety of services both to the business in bankruptcy and to the creditors of that business. A forensic accountant generally works with the corporation and its bankruptcy counsel to determine the true and correct financial status of the business. Other services for the bankrupt estate will include:

- Preparation of reports to the court and the creditors including listing assets, debts, and other claims
- Preparation of reports identifying receipts and disbursements of the bankruptcy
- Preparation of forecasts and projections of how the business might operate if it is reorganized
- Preparation of information regarding the value of assets if the organization is liquidated
- Assisting in identifying and collecting assets that may have been improperly dissipated prior to, or during, the early stages of the bankruptcy

A forensic accountant may also be engaged by creditors to assist in protecting their interests. The creditors may develop a different plan of re-organization, or challenge the corporation's attempts to reorganize rather than liquidate. The creditors may also use a forensic accountant to challenge actions of the trustee in bankruptcy or the debtor in possession. This could include contesting the valuation of assets or liabilities and payment of various expenses.

Generally, in bankruptcy situations, the forensic accountant will be working under much more scrutiny than in other engagements. Usually, each step of the bankruptcy process, including payment of the forensic accountant, requires approval of the bankruptcy court.

Valuations

Business valuations involve a process and a set of computations designed to determine the fair market value of a portion of a business or an entire business. Most business valuations do not involve the legal process, but there are instances where valuations do become part of the legal process, most often in the following areas:

- Partnership and shareholder disputes
- Estate and gift valuations challenged by the Internal Revenue Service or heirs
- Divorce

A forensic accountant who becomes involved in valuation matters, usually must have specific training in business valuations and is well served to have the professional credentials of a Certified Valuation Analyst (National Association of Certified Valuation Analysts), Accredited Business Valuator (American Institute of CPAs) or an Accredited Senior Appraiser (American Society of Appraisers).

The valuation process includes the following elements:

- Determining what the definition of value is
- Determining the premise of value
- Defining what is to be valued
- Determining the valuation approach

The *definition of value* can vary depending on the situation and, in forensic situations, may direct what value is to be used. The most common value used for business valuations is fair market value. That value was defined by Internal Revenue Service, Revenue Ruling 59–60 as "... the amount at which property would change hands between a willing buyer and a willing seller when the former is not under compulsion to buy and the latter is not under compulsion to sell, both parties having reasonable knowledge of the relevant facts."

The *premise of value* is the fundamental principal underlying the valuation. Four commonly stated premises of value are:

- Value as a going concern
- Value as a group of assets
- Value in an orderly disposition
- Value in a forced liquidation

The usual premise used for a continuing business is value as a going concern.

The consideration of *what is to be valued* can be extremely varied depending on the purpose of the valuation. In a business situation, a forensic accountant can be called upon to value:

- An entire business
- A majority equity interest in the business
- A minority equity interest in the business
- Specific assets of the business
- Subsidiary entities of the business

This list is by no means exhaustive. The portion of a business being valued can have a significant effect on the value itself. For example, although an entire business might be worth $1 million, it does not necessarily follow that a 30% interest in that business is worth $300,000. A minority interest in a business is generally discounted since the person owning it does not control the business.

There are a number of *valuation approaches*. The three most common are:

- Asset-based approach
- Market approach
- Income approach

The *asset-based approach* is often used where a company is not profitable and has no discernable intangible value based on earnings. The highest value might be to dispose of the individual assets of the business.

The *market approach* is based on the theory that similar businesses in similar industries should be similarly valued. The difficulty of this approach, particularly with small businesses, is locating analogous companies whose value is determined either by a recent sale or in an open marketplace.

The most frequently used approach to valuation is the *income approach*. This is based on the theory that a potential buyer will pay the amount of future earnings discounted at a rate of interest that provides him with an acceptable return for the risk he takes. The most important elements in using the income approach are to determine what the future stream of earnings is going to be and what an appropriate risk-based discount rate is.

When a valuation is subject to the legal process, the forensic accountant must be prepared to defend the assumptions and estimates used in the valuation. It is almost certain that the other side to the dispute, whether it be a former partner, the Internal Revenue Service, or a spouse, is going to hire a valuator to challenge the assumptions used.

Divorce Proceedings

As noted before, forensic accountants are often called upon to provide valuation services in divorce proceedings. There are also a variety of other divorce related services that can be provided including:

- Determining a proper amount of alimony
- Determining a proper amount of child support
- Determining earning capacity of a spouse
- Tracing assets that a spouse may be hiding
- Calculating the tax effects of property settlements, alimony, and child support payments

Since over 50% of marriages in the United States end in divorce, this particular type of litigation is one with which the forensic accountant can frequently become involved.

Divorce proceedings are often characterized by the following:

- A great deal of personal, emotional antipathy between the parties to the dispute.
- Records may be harder to obtain than usual.
- Clients often become overinvolved rather than "letting the professionals handle it."

- The parties frequently attempt to deceive each other.
- It can be difficult to get paid since it frequently takes a good deal of effort to dispute relatively small amounts of money.

Perhaps one of the best services that the forensic accountant can render in divorce litigation is to help the parties reconcile their differences as quickly as possible and allow them to move on with their lives.

Personal Damages

Personal damages are those financial damages suffered by individuals as opposed to businesses. Forensic accountants are frequently called upon to calculate damages for wrongful death and personal injury which this section will discuss. Other personal damages includes:

- Employment discrimination
- Wrongful termination
- Defamation

Until more recently, personal damages were primarily calculated by economists, oftentimes university professors. More recently, forensic accountants have become involved because of their broader business background and analytical skills.

Wrongful Death

When a suit is brought because of wrongful death or personal injury, there are two aspects to the suit — liability and damages. If the trier-of-fact finds that the defendant is not liable, there is no need to determine damages.

The key elements involved in calculating damages from wrongful death for a person who is employed or could have been employed are:

- Determining work life expectancy
- Projecting future income
- Calculating future fringe benefits
- Calculating personal consumption expenses
- Calculating the value of household services
- Determining an appropriate rate for discounting earnings to present value

Work life expectancy is that period of time in an individual's life when they will be available for employment for compensation. The U.S. Department of Labor and various academic studies have analyzed the time the individual spends in the work force and variables that affect work life expectancy. A variety of factors can have an impact on an individual's work life including:

- Unemployment
- Time off for child rearing
- Injuries
- Work stoppages

All of these factors are evaluated in the tables used to determine work life expectancy.

Projecting income can be relatively simple or extremely complex depending on the nature of the individual's employment. A union worker who has been regularly employed and received steady raises can have a fairly predictable future income stream. On the other hand, an individual who is self-employed could have income that varies greatly from year to year. It is also difficult to calculate future income for executives and others who receive stock options and a wide variety of fringe benefits. Complexity is also added if the individual is a child, someone who has not yet decided on their career path, or someone who is changing jobs. At some point, the forensic accountant must make assumptions about future earnings which will be subject to challenge by the other side.

Today, *fringe benefits* both statutory (such as social security and unemployment) and employer voluntary comprise over 20% of the average person's income. Benefits can be quite straightforward, for example a union carpenter who receives contracted amounts for every hour worked, or extremely complex involving stock options, defined benefit pension plans, matching savings plans, complex life insurance arrangements, etc. Where benefits are complicated, it is important for the forensic accountant to talk to a human resources person from the client's employer.

The decedent's earnings are reduced by *personal consumption expenditures*. These are the expenses that an individual would have spent on himself over the period of time that the earnings were received. Different jurisdictions allow different types of expenses to be included as personal consumption expenditures. Some jurisdictions only consider basic expenses such as food, clothing, and shelter, while others allow a broader definition that includes all expenses (except income based taxes) that an individual may spend on himself. In determining personal consumption expenditures, it is important for a forensic accountant to understand what is allowed by the jurisdiction, as well as the individual's personal lifestyle.

Household services are those activities an individual conducts which result in a benefit to their household. The impetus for this type of computation is that a nonworking spouse or a spouse who is employed less than full time provides an economic benefit to the household despite the fact that no wages were brought into the household.

There are several factors a forensic accountant must consider relative to household services. First, while working individuals provide a certain level of economic benefit to the household from household services, they also consume a disproportionate amount of household services rendered by the nonworking spouse. Second, in evaluating the rate per hour that should be assigned to the hours spent in household services, it is important to remember that the person rendering the services generally is not trained in, or a professional in, those services. Just because an unskilled individual performs some plumbing services, does not mean that individual should be compensated at the rate of a professional, licensed plumber. A third point to consider is that it may cost the household significantly more money to replace the lost services by hiring outsiders to do the work.

Calculating the *present value* of future earnings is somewhat similar to the present value calculation discussed earlier under the income approach to valuations. The significant difference is that the discount rate used to discount future earnings for individuals is generally a fairly conservative rate. The Supreme Court stated in *Jones and Laughlin Steel Corp v. Pfeifer 462 U.S. 523 (1983)* that a worker "... is entitled to a risk-free stream of future income to replace his lost wages; therefore, the discount rate should not reflect the market's premium for investors who are willing to accept some risk ..." Some states, the largest of which is Pennsylvania, do not allow future wage projections to include inflation nor do they permit discounting to present value. The Pennsylvania Supreme Court has dictated the use of the "Net Offset Method," wherein the future effects of inflation are assumed to be offset by the discount to present value, and therefore neither is allowed. This type of computation tends to favor the plaintiff, resulting in higher wage and benefit damages than would otherwise be permitted.

Personal Injury

Personal injury calculations are similar in many ways to the wrongful death calculations detailed before. There are several differences, however, including:

- A period of injury replaces the work life expectancy
- There can be offsetting or mitigating earnings
- There are no personal consumption expenditures offset

Oftentimes, an injury only causes a person to be out of work for the period of time it takes to recover and rehabilitate. The loss of earnings is then calculated during this period. If the person is injured in such a manner as to prohibit their resuming their former occupation, but they are capable of some other occupation, then the forensic accountant must compute the mitigating earnings that the individual can earn in the new occupation. These earnings reduce the damages. No reduction of damages is allowed for consumption expenditures since the person is still consuming those expenditures.

Once a report is prepared, the forensic accountant may have to testify regarding the findings. As noted earlier, it is important to remember not to be an advocate for the client's position, but rather to represent and advance the opinion stated in the report.

Tax Matters

The forensic accountant may be called upon to assist in a variety of tax matters. We have already discussed the use of forensic accountants in gift and estate tax valuations in the "Valuation" section. In addition, forensic accountants can be called upon to:

- Serve as experts in determining taxable income or other forms of tax
- Assist in settling collection matters
- Provide services in criminal tax matters

Frequently forensic accountants are used in tax disputes because of their familiarity with legal procedures and their experience in providing testimony. An accountant who has prepared the tax return may have never testified in a legal proceeding and could find it a very daunting experience. Forensic accountants are then used because they know how to present facts in an organized manner, provide instruction and information to the trier-of-fact, and effectively respond to crossexamination.

The most frequent use of forensic accountants for tax matters is in criminal cases. There are a number of criminal violations of the Internal Revenue Code including:

- Tax evasion
- Failure to collect or pay over taxes

- Failure to file a tax return
- Making false statements or abetting preparation of a false return
- Filing a false return
- Interfering with administration of the Internal Revenue laws

The Internal Revenue Service can also impose civil penalties for fraud equal to 75% of the tax attributable to fraud.

To prove tax evasion, the government must show:

- There was additional tax due
- There was an attempt to evade that tax
- The evasion was willful

For failure to file a tax return, the government must also show that a tax return was in fact due. A person without sufficient gross receipts is not required to file a tax return.

The forensic accountant is used to show that there was no income, or no additional income, and thus a tax return was not required or there is no additional tax due. Other defenses that the forensic accountant may assist with include that:

- The taxpayer relied on advice given by a professional or the Internal Revenue Service itself.
- The taxpayer was an innocent spouse who had no knowledge of the business affairs of the other spouse.
- The taxpayer was a sloppy recordkeeper, and the errors were due to negligence, not an intentional disregard of the law.

It can be very difficult to defend against government charges of tax crimes. The Internal Revenue Service does not bring such charges lightly and is very meticulous and thorough in their investigation. They have access to vast resources and typically spend a good deal of time and effort in putting the case together. For all these reasons, the conviction rate in criminal tax cases is well over 90%. Forensic accountants defending against criminal tax charges certainly have their work cut out for them.[1]

It is important for forensic accountants to remember that their engagement letter should be addressed to the attorney, and they should be engaged by the attorney, instead of the client. In this manner, communications between the attorney and the forensic accountant as well as the forensic accountant's workpapers are protected by the attorney–client privilege. This principle was first laid down in a 1960 case *U.S. v. Kovel*, 296 F. 2d 918, 922 (2d CIR. 1961); hence, engagement letters like this are frequently referred to as "Kovel Letters."

Murder and Arson for Profit

One of the most unusual areas in which forensic accountants can become involved are the criminal activities of murder and arson. Individuals are frequently suspected of murder because of a financial motive, often involving being a beneficiary of a life insurance policy, beneficiary of an inheritance, or involving a business deal. The forensic accountant is engaged to show that the suspect was financially well off and had sufficient income that financial matters could not have been a motivating factor. The forensic accountant must assemble the suspect's income and a statement of financial position for the period prior to the murder to show a financial motive is unlikely. It may also be necessary for the forensic accountant to establish that the suspects had good financial prospects for the future, even though they were not currently in a strong financial position.

Frequently, arson is used to destroy business property or rental property that is not sufficiently profitable and cannot be sold. If these conditions exist and the fire investigators determine that the cause of fire was arson, then a forensic accountant can be used to show that finances were not sufficiently bad to be a motivating factor for arson. The forensic accountant may prepare financial projections for a business that has not been profitable to show that it had good profitability prospects for the future. For rental property, the forensic accountant, by referring to property sales, may be able to demonstrate that the property destroyed was indeed saleable at a good price or could have been profitably rented.

For these criminal cases, as with all criminal tax matters, it is important for the forensic accountant to be engaged by the attorney to have privileged communication.

How to Use Forensic Accountants

Oftentimes, attorneys will hire forensic accountants later in the legal process, perhaps hoping to lessen the fees to their client. This is usually a mistake, and it rarely results in significantly lower fees. Forensic accountants should be involved very early in the litigation process since they can provide a variety of services, not the least of which is making a preliminary determination whether litigating is financially worthwhile.

The forensic accountant should be involved in all phases of discovery including:

- *Interrogatories* — the forensic accountants are well positioned to provide financial interrogatories since they will have usually been involved in this type of litigation before and may well be quite familiar with the industry involved.
- *Document requests* — Forensic accountants will know from experience what financial documents they should have and what these documents will contain. The ability to obtain these documents and analyze them early in the case can be significant to a favorable outcome.
- *Depositions* — The attorney should involve the forensic accountant in drafting financial questions for some of the witnesses. This is particularly true if other experts are to be deposed.

In summary, the early involvement of the forensic accountant in the case can avoid duplicate work, missed opportunities to obtain information, and provide an early insight into the financial aspects of the case.

Conclusion

This chapter has discussed the myriad types of matters where forensic accountants participate in the legal process, and the wide variety of roles they can play. It is often said that accounting is the language of business and money. If litigants, or their lawyers, are not fluent in that language, it is extremely important to have a good interpreter. That is the role the forensic accountant plays — translating monetary and financial concepts used in the legal system for those less fluent in such matters.

Reference

Guide to Litigation Support Services, Fort Worth, TX: Practitioners Publishing Company, 8th Edition, July 2003.

Forensic Economics in Instances of Wrongful Death and Injury[1]

30

MATTHEW R. MARLIN

Introduction to Forensic Economics

The role of the forensic economist (FE) in cases of personal injury of wrongful death is to determine how large a financial settlement is necessary to make a plaintiff — either the injured party or his or her survivors — financially whole. The FE will compare the economic status of the plaintiff, as a result of an incident, to the status that would have existed "but for" the incident in question.

Despite the best attempts at determining the value of economic damages, and despite the relative standardization of forensic economics as a science, these determinations can never be exact. No one can possibly know exactly how much a person would have worked, earned, or spent *but for* the incident in question. Different FEs might use different assumptions, and different assumptions will give rise to different estimates of the true value. For this reason, it is often advisable for defense attorneys to engage the services of an FE to evaluate the underlying assumptions in the plaintiff's FE report, assess its accuracy, and assist in preparing for a potential crossexamination of the FE.

At first glance, it would seem that the FE has a simple task. For example, the survivors of a decedent who was making $50,000 per year and had 10 years of work-life remaining would need 10 times $50,000, or $500,000, to compensate for his or her lost earnings. But things are not as simple as they may seem:

- Would the decedent's earnings remain the same over his or her work-life or would they decline or grow?
- How can one determine the expected years of work-life?
- What is the value of lost employer-paid fringe benefits?

541

- Did the decedent or injured party work around the house doing chores that must now be done by someone else or remain undone?
- How much of the family's income would have been consumed by the decedent had he or she lived?
- If an injured worker cannot continue in the same type of work, what opportunities are available for mitigating earnings?

Finding the correct answers to the above questions is the job of the FE. The best source of information is the injured individual or his or her survivors; and just as it is essential that the plaintiff disclose all pertinent information to the attorney, it is essential that the FE be provided with all the information he or she needs. This may include such things as tax returns, pay stubs, union contracts, and a copy of an employer's benefit plan. In the absence of such information and for projecting such things as inflation, wage growth, and earnings in alternative employment, the FE will often rely on local, regional, or national averages and statistics to arrive at the best estimate of the economic loss.

The following sections of this chapter provide a very broad and general description of how an FE arrives at estimates of the following economic values:

- Earnings, earning capacity, and mitigating earnings
- Fringe benefits
- Worklife, retirement, and life expectancies
- Household services
- Personal maintenance and consumption.

The last part of the chapter explains the concept of *present value*, why it is essential, and how different discount rate assumptions made by the FE can result in significantly different estimates. Attached as an Appendix is the code of ethics adopted by the National Association of Forensic Economists; although it is not necessary that your FE be a member of this organization, it is nonetheless important that he or she abides by these, or similar, ethical standards.

It should be noted at the outset that the FE ordinarily will not generate an estimate of hedonic losses, place a value on pain and suffering, nor estimate the appropriate level of punitive damages. Despite various attempts to do so, especially in the instance of hedonic losses, the Courts have generally accepted the doctrine that such estimates are too inconsistent to be considered scientifically determined. For example, although different FEs will arrive at similar estimates for the value of lost earnings, benefits, and household services, estimates of the actual value of a life or of life's pleasures will vary widely from one economic analyst to another.

The legal rules guiding economic evaluation for wrongful death and personal injuries vary considerably among the states and the federal courts depending on the nature of the action. Although the legal parameters may vary, the basic procedures and assumptions outlined later are generally accepted by the forensic economics community throughout the United States.

Economic Estimates and Valuation

At the time of trial, economic losses will have occurred in two time periods, from the date of the incident to the date of the trial and from the date of the trial into the future. Economic valuation therefore is usually done for two time frames — *losses to date* and *future losses.* An estimate of losses from the date of the incident to the present (or trial date) is often necessary because prejudgment interest may be assessed on losses to date. Estimates of losses to date are usually very accurate because they can be based on actual, historic values. Future losses extend from the present through work-life or life expectancy, depending on the nature of the economic loss. Because the future is unknown and must be predicted, estimates of future losses are less exact than estimates of losses to date.

Earning Capacity, Earnings, and Mitigating Earnings

Individuals' total compensation includes wages and salaries plus employer-paid fringe benefits. Although both are technically *earned income*, this chapter will refer to wage and salary income simply as *earnings* or *income*, and use the term *total compensation* to refer to the combined amount of money earned and fringe benefits.

Earning Capacity

Although nearly all forensic analysis concerns itself with the *actual* earnings of an individual, the correct amount to be estimated is the *earning capacity* or *earning potential* of an individual — the amount he or she could potentially earn "but for" the incident. In most instances, an individual will choose to maximize his or her earnings, and therefore, actual earnings and earning capacity are one and the same. In some instances, however they will differ. For example, a master plumber who is self-employed may earn $40,000 per year from operating his own business while, at the same time, master plumbers in the same region earn $60,000 as employees of plumbing, heating and cooling, or construction companies. As long as he or she had the option of working for someone else at a higher rate of pay, then estimates of lost earnings must take this into consideration. As another example, suppose that an attorney had passed the bar exam and had practiced law for a number of years earning $100,000 per year. At the time of his or her death or injury, however, he or she had elected to teach disadvantaged children in an inner city school for $40,000. If the incident prevents her from returning to any kind of work, her lost *earning capacity* is $100,000 per year.

Earnings

Estimating the loss of *earning to date* can be a simple process of examining past earnings history and projecting it to the present. Union contracts, the employer's past history of raises, and the wage rates or salaries of employees in the same position at the same firm can provide guidance as to the appropriate rate of increase to apply to the actual earnings before the incident. If no information is available from these sources, the FE can turn to a plethora of data prepared by the Bureau of Labor Statistics (BLS) and the Office of the Actuary of the Social Security Administration (SSA).[2] Alternatively, estimating lost earnings to date can be more difficult in instances where the decedent or injured party (1) was self-employed, (2) worked irregular hours, (3) was employed on a seasonal basis, (4) worked on commission, (5) earned overtime or premium pay for different shifts, (6) received income from more than one source, or (7) had been out of work for periods in the past due to illness, layoff, or job loss. In these cases, the FE must work with the injured party or survivors to arrive at a fair estimate of lost earnings to date.

Another complication involves ascertaining which forms and sources of income are collateral and which are not. Although this may vary from state to state, the general criteria is that medical and insurance benefits received by the plaintiff from sources independent of the defendant are collateral and should not be included as income for the purpose of estimating lost or mitigating income. Such sources would include (but are not limited to) unemployment and workers' compensation, Social Security retirement and disability income, other government disability and benefit programs, veterans' benefits, and proceeds from plaintiff-paid life, auto, and health insurance policies.

In federal court cases and in most state courts, the FE must estimate the growth in *future earnings*. A number of different and acceptable procedures may be used. The first approach is to use a historical trend of past earnings, assuming that enough history is available to do so. Projecting from only three or four data points can be challenged as not being statistically valid. If such a history is not available, or to validate the projection, the Social Security Administration (SSA) publishes long range forecasts of changes in inflation, productivity, and average annual wages. Along with these forecasts, the SSA publishes historical data for these variables, and the resulting Table is therefore very useful for both past and future adjustments to earning potential. The SSA actually prepares three forecasts for three different growth scenarios: one each for low, intermediate (the most likely scenario), and high economic growth. Some of the data extracted from the 2002 intermediate forecast are shown in Table 30.1. As can be seen, the annual wage increase usually exceeds the Consumer

Table 30.1 Extracted Portions from the Social Security Administration's Principle Economic Assumptions (Annual Percentage Changes)

(1) Calendar Year	(2) Productivity (Total U.S. Economy)	(3) Average Annual Wage	(4) Consumer Price Index (CPI-U)	(5) Real Wage Differential $[(3) - (4)]$
Historical Data				
1980–1985	1.7	6.7	5.2	1.4
1985–1990	1.3	4.7	3.8	0.9
1990–1995	1.1	3.6	3.0	0.6
1995–2000	2.1	5.3	2.4	2.9
2001	2.0	2.0	2.7	−0.8
2002	3.2	0.4	1.4	−1.0
2003	3.5	2.6	2.2	0.4
2004	3.3	3.8	2.6	1.2
Intermediate Forecast				
2005	2.0	4.2	2.2	2.1
2006	2.0	4.3	2.2	2.2
2007	1.8	4.4	2.6	1.8
2008	1.8	4.3	2.8	1.5
2009	1.8	4.1	2.8	1.3
2010	1.7	4.1	2.8	1.3
2011	1.7	4.1	2.8	1.3
2012	1.7	4.2	2.8	1.4
2013	1.6	4.0	2.8	1.2
2014	1.6	3.9	2.8	1.1
2015–2080	1.6	4.0	2.8	1.2

Source: 2005 OASDI Trustees Report, PART V. ASSUMPTIONS AND METHODS UNDERLYING ACTUARIAL ESTIMATES, SECTION B. *ECONOMIC ASSUMPTIONS AND METHODS* Table VB.1 http://www.ssa.gov/OACT/TR/TR05/V economic.html#wp180099 Downloaded September 3, 2005. With permission.

Price Index (CPI), the most common inflation measure; therefore, inflating wages only by the rate of inflation tends to understate actual wage gains in the past and in the future.

Mitigation

In cases where an injury has rendered an individual unable to continue working in his or her past occupation, the FE must estimate mitigating future earnings in alternative employment. The input of a vocational expert is often relied upon to determine the types of jobs that the individual might be able to obtain. After determining the types of jobs, the FE can obtain information on corresponding earnings from a number of sources. A primary source for these data is the BLS, which maintains an extensive hardcopy and on-line data bases which includes the *Occupational Outlook Handbook* (OOH), the *National Compensation Survey* (NCS), the *Occupational Employment Statistics* (OES) program, and the *Current Population Survey* (CPS). Other sources include on-line services such as salary.com and salaryexpert.com, private businesses that earn their profits by providing information to human resource departments and job seekers.[3]

When the litigation involves a minor who has not yet begun a career, the FE must estimate potential future earnings based on a number of factors including ethnicity, gender, and projected educational attainment. The Current Population Survey provides extensive estimates of gross earnings by all three of these characteristics (white, black, and Hispanic for ethnicity).[4] Although a child's gender and ethnic background are obviously known, the future educational attainment cannot be known for certain. Because of its extreme importance in determining income, an accurate estimate of educational attainment is critical in forecasting future earning potential. For example, Table 30.2 shows that race and gender have a significant effect on the average level of education a person will receive. Although only 7.3% of the Hispanic population had completed college in 2000, the number jumps to 17.3% for the white population. Then looking at Table 30.3, it can be seen that education and income are highly correlated. Although high school dropouts will, on average, earn between $15,000 and $23,000, those with a college degree will earn between $35,000 and $65,000 per year.

A number of studies have empirically estimated the probability that a child will attain a specified level of education based on ethnic background, parents' education, and a number of other demographic and socioeconomic characteristics.[5] When faced with the problem of

Table 30.2 Educational Attainment (Highest Level) by Select Characteristics in 2000 (Percentage of the Population)

Category	Not a High School Graduate	High School Graduate	Some College	Associate's Degree	Bachelor's Degree	Advanced Degree
Male	15.8	31.9	17.4	7.1	17.8	10.0
Female	16.0	34.3	17.7	8.4	16.3	7.3
White	15.1	33.4	17.4	8.0	17.3	8.8
Black	21.5	35.2	20.0	6.8	11.4	5.1
Hispanic	43.0	27.9	13.5	5.0	7.3	3.3
Northeast	15.0	35.8	13.5	7.7	18.0	10.5
Midwest	13.1	35.5	18.2	8.3	16.8	8.0
South	18.3	34.0	17.1	7.0	15.7	7.8
West	15.7	27.4	21.1	8.6	18.6	8.6

Source: Extracted from the 2002 Statistical Abstract of the United States, Table 210. With permission.

Table 30.3   Average Income by Education, Gender and Ethnicity

	White Males	White Females	Black Males	Black Females	Hispanic Males	Hispanic Females
High school dropout	$22,773	$14,747	$18,682	$16,480	$21,437	$15,460
High school graduate	$33,545	$20,866	$25,037	$18,683	$26,745	$17,786
Associate's degree	$43,121	$27,696	$38,714	$26,157	$37,148	$25,117
Bachelor's degree	$65,046	$36,698	$46,511	$35,448	$45,445	$35,142
Master's degree	$80,793	$48,089	$63,489	$44,328	$65,273	$43,891
Professional degree	$122,560	$64,668	$86,632	$65,704	$104,106	$60,272

Source: Bureaus of Labor Statistics and the Census. *Current Population Survey*, Table PINC-04. Educational Attainment — People 18 Years Old and Over, by Total. With permission.

projecting education and then earnings, the FEE uses these estimates to provide a set of different earning scenarios based upon different levels of educational attainment. The jury can then decide for itself which level of education and its associated earnings provides the best estimate in that specific case.

Fringe Benefits

After lost income, lost employer-paid fringe benefits represent the largest economic loss in the majority of tort actions. In December 2004 full-time civilian workers averaged $18.07 per hr in earnings and another $7.50 per hr in benefits that included paid vacation, insurance, retirement plans, and government mandated contributions to Social Security, workers' compensation and unemployment compensation trust funds. On average, benefits equaled over 40% of earnings and accounted for 29.3% of total compensation. Benefits tend to be higher than average for union workers and state and local employees and lower than average for service workers.[6] They also increase with the size of the firm, with larger businesses offering higher valued benefits and a wider variety of benefits, including day care, physical fitness facilities, and educational reimbursement programs.

The Bureau of Labor Statistics constructs and annually updates the *Employment Cost Index* (ECI), which measures the cost of hiring employees. The current index in based on June 1989 costs, and has a value equal to 100 as of then. In September 2003, it reached 168.0 for all civilian workers, indicating that employer costs in this sector had increased 68.0% since June 1989. However, the wage and salary index equaled 161.7, whereas the benefit index was at 182.3. The obvious interpretation is that the value of employee benefits is rising faster than the value of wages and salaries.

Not all benefits lost due to death or injuries that prevent continued employment are recoverable. Care must be taken to avoid benefits that do not represent losses to survivors or the employee and to avoid double counting. Workers' compensation, unemployment compensation, and sickness and accident insurance should be excluded from the FE's estimates. These are benefits paid by the employer to the employee only if he or she is hurt on the job, loses the job, or becomes ill. They do not represent economic gains to the employee while on the job so they therefore cannot be counted as economic losses associated with death or the inability to continue work because of injury.

Although paid vacations are an important benefit, they should be excluded from estimates of economic loss because their inclusion would amount to double counting.

If an employee earned $52,000 per year and had a two-week paid vacation, then $2000 will appear in the employee's paycheck during the two weeks that he or she was on vacation. Adding another $2000 ($1000 per week for two weeks) would result in counting the vacation pay twice.

The three most important benefits that the FE will usually evaluate are healthcare insurance, pension plans, and Social Security retirement contributions made by the employer.

Medical Insurance

It should come as no surprise that medical insurance is the most costly benefit for a worker or his or her survivors to replace. One cannot open a newspaper or listen to a news broadcast without hearing about the rising cost of health insurance and the growing number of Americans without it. The Consolidated Omnibus Budget Reconciliation Act of 1985 (COBRA) mandates that employers with group health insurance must make coverage available at the group rate for former employees and their families. The COBRA coverage is limited to 36 months at the maximum; after this, the FE must estimate what a similar coverage will cost in the marketplace. Given the specifics of the former plan, it is not too difficult to use the Internet to obtain premium quotes for a similar coverage. Care must be taken, however, to determine how much of the premium was paid by the employer and how much was paid for by the employee. Projecting the costs into the future is somewhat more complicated as the costs for medical care and health insurance have been increasing at a much faster rate than the overall rate of inflation. The BLS does provide special price indices for medical care, and these can be used to derive estimates of future costs.

Pension Plans

After health insurance, the most valuable foregone benefit is the employer's contributions to the employee's private retirement or pension plan. About 55% of private sector employees and nearly all public sector employees are covered by some type of retirement income plan. Although declining in use, *defined benefit* plans specify a formula, typically based on earnings and length of service, for determining an employee's retirement annuity. Determining the value of a lost defined benefit plan requires that the FE obtain a copy of the plan details and project an estimate of the foregone annuity. This in turn requires estimates of both the employee's projected earnings at retirement and the length of time that the employee could have been expected to remain on the job.

Employers that offer defined benefit pension plans are required by law to insure the plans through the Pension Benefit Guarantee Corporation (PBGC). In a growing number of instances (especially in the steel industry), the PBGC has taken over private pension plans when companies have entered bankruptcy or are unable to make pension payments as promised. The monthly amount it pays, however, is limited to $28,000 per year, and some pensioners may have to settle for an amount less than that indicated by the plan's formula.

Much more common in today's workplace are *defined contribution* plans that specify a percentage of earnings that the employee contributes to a specified account and that the employer matches at a specified rate. The value of the pension is simply the total amount accrued at the end of the work-life. Estimating the value of a defined contribution plan is a fairly straightforward task once lost earnings have been estimated. For example, if the employee was contributing 5.0% of earnings and the employer was matching employee contributions at a 50% rate, then the value of the foregone employer contribution is simply 2.5% of total earnings plus the compounded interest earnings until the projected retirement date.

In instances where employer data regarding the value of benefits is lacking, the FE may rely on data provided by the BLS in its *Employer Costs for Employee Compensation* Tables that show average employer costs for all aspects of employee compensation based upon the cost per employee hour worked.[6] The tables provide estimates for various categories of employment (e.g., white or blue collar, private or government, union or nonunion) and different geographic regions.

Social Security

Although the employer's contribution to the Social Security Trust Fund is equal to 7.65% of the employee's earned income, only 6.2% goes to the Social Security retirement and disability funds, and the remaining 1.45% goes toward the Medicare Trust Fund. There is an earnings cap on the amount taxed for the retirement fund ($87,900 in 2004), but there is no limit on the amount taxed for Medicare. Once a plaintiff has worked 10 year, he or she becomes fully qualified for Medicare benefits, and contributing more will not increase the benefit level. Therefore, in cases where the injured party had more than 10 year on the job, the 1.45% of earnings that go to Medicare coverage does not represent an additional economic loss. One method for calculating the lost value of Social Security benefits is therefore to take 6.20% of lost earnings on all income up to the specified limit.

Alternatively, lost Social Security benefits can be calculated by estimating the value of the Social Security retirement benefit. In cases of wrongful death, there can be a significant difference in the value of the benefit when it is estimated as a percentage of lost earnings rather than as the lost postretirement Social Security benefit. The Social Security Administration (SSA) provides on-line calculators that can be used to estimate monthly retirement benefits.[7] The more complete a decedent's earning history and the more time available to the FE, the more accurate the estimate of what the monthly retirement benefit "would have been" absent the incident and "what it will be" due to the incident.

In total, the sum of lost recoverable benefits including health insurance, pension benefits, and Social Security contributions usually average between 20 and 25% of the employee's earnings. As always, the FE will examine the specific details of the person and employment in question before arriving at an estimate of the value of lost benefits. The 20–25% range does, however, provide a benchmark for defense attorneys. Although certainly possible, estimates in excess of these values should raise a red flag.

Work Life, Retirement, and Life Expectancy

Work Life Expectancy

Once estimates of future income and benefits have been estimated, it is necessary to estimate the work life horizon over which the total compensation will be earned. Although some individuals might continue to work well into their seventies, existing data indicate that most will permanently exit the labor force (retire) well before the end of their life expectancy. In addition, many workers will temporarily leave (*decrements*) and then re-enter the labor force (*increments*). For example, workers may leave the labor force due to lay-offs, job changes, illness or injury, premature death, or to raise a family. Decrements are usually highest for women during their child-bearing years. The number of years in the work life expectancy (WLE) therefore is usually less than the number of years until retirement.

Models that incorporate the above factors into estimates of actual years of work life remaining at a given age are consequently known as increment–decrement models. Increment–decrement estimates of WLE were first constructed by the BLS in the early 1980s using data from the *Current Population Survey.* For a given age, the estimates are derived from the probability that an individual will be alive in the following year, in the labor force ("active"), and employed. Individuals not in the labor force at the time of the death or injury are considered to be "inactive." Each of these probabilities is different for people of different work status, gender, and educational background, and the BLS estimates vary accordingly.

Although the BLS no longer computes WLE estimates, it has turned the data over to a number of different private analysts who have continued to produce new and more detailed estimates. For example, the BLS estimates included only three categories of education — less than high school, high school to 14 year, and 15 or more years of schooling. In contrast, a 1997 study by Tamorah Hunt, Joyce Pickersgill, and Herbert Rutemiller included six levels of education, from less than high school through an advanced degree. The study also included estimates of median years to retirement as well the mean expected years of WLE.[8] As an example, Table 30.4 shows some extracts from the Hunt *et al.* study. According to their estimates, a 35-year-old woman with a bachelor's degree has a WLE of 23.1 years and a "median years to retirement" equal to 27.5 years. The implication is that her "decrement" will be equal to 4.4 years. Notice that a man of the same age with the same education will have a WLE of 27.3 years and a decrement of

Table 30.4 Median Years to Retirement (MYR), Work Life Expectancy, and Years of "Decrement" for Active Men and Women with Bachelor's Degrees

	Males			Females		
Age	MYR	WLE	Decrement	MYR	WLE	Decrement
30	33.1	31.9	1.2	32.2	27.0	5.2
31	32.1	30.9	1.2	31.2	26.2	5.0
32	31.1	30.0	1.1	30.3	25.4	4.9
33	30.1	29.1	1.0	29.4	24.7	4.7
34	29.1	28.2	0.9	28.3	23.9	4.4
35	28.1	27.3	0.8	27.5	23.1	4.4
36	27.1	26.4	0.7	26.4	22.4	4.0
37	26.2	25.5	0.7	25.4	21.6	3.8
38	25.1	24.6	0.5	24.4	20.8	3.6
39	24.2	23.7	0.5	23.3	20.0	3.3
40	23.3	22.8	0.5	22.2	19.2	3.0
50	13.8	13.9	−0.1	12.4	11.2	1.2
60	5.6	6.5	−0.9	4.8	4.8	0.0
70	4.0	3.4	0.6	4.1	3.2	0.9

Source: Extracted from Hunt, Tamorah, Joyce Pickersgill, and Herbert Rutemiler, "Median years to retirement and worklife expectancy for the civilian U.S. population," *Journal of Forensic Economics* 10(2), 1997. With permission.

Table 30.5 Comparative WLE Estimates from Different Studies for An Active 30-year-Old College Graduate

Study	Men		Women	
	All	Active	All	Active
BLS	31.9	32.3	24.3	25.2
Hunt *et al.*	31.8	31.9	26.4	27.0
Richards	32.4	32.5	27.1	27.6
Skoog and Ciecka	N/A	32.2	N/A	28.0

Source: Hunt, Tamorah, Joyce Pickersgill, and Herbert Rutemiler, "Median years to retirement and worklife expectancy for the civilian U.S. population," *Journal of Forensic Economics* 10(2), 1997; H. Richards, *Life and Worklife Expectancies*. Lawyers and Judges Publishing Company, 1999; G.R. Skoog and J. Ceicka, "The Markov (increment-decrement) model of labor force activity: new results beyond work-life expectancies," *Journal of Legal Economics* 11(1), 2001. With permission.

only 0.8 years. (One should also be aware that WLE estimates can generate inconsistent results as age approaches retirement age.)

Other WLE estimates worth noting include those constructed by Hugh Richards (which disaggregate the data by characteristics such as race, occupation, and smoking), and by Gary Skoog and James Ciecka (which include probability intervals for retirement ages).[9] Selected estimates from these two studies, the Hunt et al. study, and the original BLS study are shown in Table 30.5 (Skoog and Ciecka's study includes estimates for "active" and "inactive" persons only). With the exception of WLE estimates for women in the original BLS study, there is little variation in the estimates. The following patterns are consistent in all the studies: WLE increases with education, it is higher for men than for women, and it is higher for those in the labor force than for those not presently active.

The tables in all the studies mentioned are straightforward and easy to understand. Nonetheless, there remains substantial room for interpretation. For example, the tables generally refer to degrees earned or total years of education.

Should apprenticeships be considered as years of education, or should certification as a master in a specific trade (e.g., plumbers or electricians) be considered as equivalent to an Associate's degree? Because WLEs increase with education, the interpretation may have significant consequences for the total estimate of economic loss. Another issue is that the CPS tables that the estimates are based on primarily use data for employees rather than self-employed individuals. Estimates for the self-employed, especially those who own or operate their own businesses, may vary substantially from those constructed for employees.

Retirement

It is often necessary to obtain an estimate of an individual's retirement age as opposed to actual years of work remaining in instances where pension income is an important component of the earnings horizon. In addition, the change in employment status often impacts other factors such as the nonmarket amount of household services a person produces or the amount of a family's income that the person will use for their personal maintenance or consumption (these items will be discussed later in the chapter).

Most people think of 65 as the "normal" retirement age, probably because for many years that was the age that an individual could begin to collect full Social Security retirement benefits. However, between 75 and 80% of all Americans retire before age 65, and the average age has declined steadily to about 62 in 2000.[10] Estimates based on national averages can be obtained from studies such as the Hunt *et al.* work cited before. For example, adding the first two columns in Table 30.4 yields an estimate of the expected retirement age for men and women of different ages.

Factors leading to earlier retirement ages include increased wealth and the growing number of retirement communities that make retirement more attractive. Factors that might cause retirement to occur at a later age include better overall health, the increasing age limits for receiving full Social Security benefits, and laws prohibiting age discrimination.

Life Expectancy

Pension incomes, certain fringe benefits, and the production of household services can continue beyond retirement age and throughout a person's entire lifetime. Accurate estimation of the economic value of these items requires an estimate of the plaintiff's life expectancy. Remaining years of life expectancy, for all ages and disaggregated by race and gender, are published periodically by the U.S. Department of Health and Human Services in *Vital Statistics of the United States, Life Tables.*[11]

Household Services

The Concept of Household Services

The productivity and economic contributions of an individual extend beyond his or her earnings in the marketplace. Activities such as child care, household repairs, washing windows, mowing the lawn, auto repairs, grocery shopping, cooking, etc., all have economic value. The death of the person who at one time provided these services, or an injury that limits the person's ability to provide the services at his or her prior level, imposes real costs upon the former recipients of the service.

Consider, for example, a man injured in an automobile accident who can no longer climb a ladder to wash the windows at his house. There are three possible outcomes:

1. Someone must be hired to do the work at a market wage
2. Another family member or a friend can wash the windows
3. The windows stay unwashed

In the first case, the family is clearly less well off because they must now pay the market price to hire someone else to provide the service that a household member used to provide. In the second case, someone else must sacrifice his or her time and effort to provide the service. Even if not compensated monetarily, it is obvious that the injury is imposing real costs on someone else. In the third case, the windows stay unwashed. No explicit cost is involved, but the family is clearly worse off than they were before because now they must live with dirtier windows than they had before.

The point to be made is that failure to include the value of the nonmarket household services provided by a deceased or injured individual into the economic loss experienced due to death or injury is to significantly understate the value of the loss. One of the more difficult tasks faced by the FE, however, is trying to estimate the economic value of that loss. First, it must be determined how many hours the injured party would have spent producing and providing household services, and then the hourly value of the services must be estimated. Both estimates are often challenged by FEs working for the opposing side.

Hours Spent Producing Household Services

Time spent producing and providing household services varies with marital status. Marriage increases the time spent working at home, although the amount increases more for women than for men. The presence of children in the home will also increase the amount of time spent doing chores around the house. Job status will also affect the number of hours; full-time workers spend less time working around the home than do single or retired individuals. Not surprisingly, most studies have shown that married women who do not work outside the home spend the most time providing household services and that unmarried men spend the least. Retirement dramatically increases the time spent doing household tasks for both men and women.

Martin summarized the results of eight studies that have estimated the time spent in household work performed by married couples using data from the 1970s and early 1980s.[12] The hours spent by married men varied from 10.5 to 14.2 hour per week with an average of 12.4 hour. The hours for married women ranged from 33.8 to 47.6 hour, with an average of 41.5 hour.

A more recent estimate of the hours spent producing household services is *The Dollar Value of a Day* (DVD), by John Ward and Kurt Krurger.[13] This work uses data obtained from 1992 through 1994 by the *National Human Activity Pattern Survey* (NHAPS).[14] The DVD provides estimates of the number of hours spent in household production for a wide variety of demographic categories, including gender, age, number and age of children, marital status, and work status (student, working, unemployed, homemaker, and retired). It provides hourly estimates for various categories of Household Production including such things as Housework, Food Cooking and Cleanup, Outdoor Chores, Home and Auto Maintenance, Obtaining Goods and Services (Shopping), Child Care, Child Guidance, Playing with Children, Transporting Children, and Providing Care to Others.

Some samples from the DVD are shown in Table 30.6. As can be seen there, the hours per week spent working around the house increase as a person moves through the cycle of

Table 30.6   Average Hours per Week in Household Work by Different Classifications (Dollar Value of a Day)

	Men		Women	
Children Present?	Yes	No	Yes	No
Single and working	15.7	16.7	26.7	21.8
Married and working	19.3	18.1	30.1	22.2
Married homemaker	–	–	48.0	43.2
Married and retired	–	27.3	–	36.4
Single and retired	–	25.6	–	31.0
Married and unemployed	–	23.8	–	35.3

Source: Extracted from Expectancy Data, *The Dollar Value of a Day: 1999 Dollar Valuation.* Shawnee Mission, KS, 2001. With permission.

being single, married, and then retired. Similar to the earlier studies cited by Martin, women in each category spend more time providing household services than do men. Nonetheless, the DVD and other more recent studies show a gradual trend toward fewer hours spent in household work by women and more spent by men.

It is important for the FE to keep in mind that the estimates included in the preceding studies are based on national averages. More so than with other values to be estimated, the time spent working around the house will vary from individual to individual. Some people can and do build decks, add rooms, do most auto, plumbing, and electrical repairs, sew all the family's clothes, reupholster furniture, etc. Others have trouble changing a light bulb or frying an egg. It is extremely important for the FE to take the time to learn all that can be learned about the type and amount of services that the injured party provided.

Hourly Value of Household Services

A considerable amount of controversy surrounds the most appropriate method to use when valuing of household services. An often cited study by W. Bryant, Cathleen Zick, and Hyoshin Kim released by Cornell University in 1993 provided three alternative methodologies:

1. *Offered Wage Rate*: The wage rate the individual commands in the labor market or could command if she or he were to enter the labor market
2. *Asked Wage Rate*: The lowest after-tax rate an individual will accept to do one or more hour of work in the labor market
3. *Market Alternative Cost*: The rate one would have to pay someone in the market-place to do that work[15]

Regardless of which rate is most theoretically precise, data for the market alternative cost are most easily obtainable and most often used by the FE. The sources for earnings by occupation indicated earlier in the chapter can be used to estimate wages for the type of services that the injured/deceased party once produced and provided. As wages vary by region, the FE must be careful to use regional data when and if it is available.

Ward and Krueger applied wage data from the BLS's *Occupational Employment Statistics* (OES) survey to the hourly amounts of household production discussed earlier and given in Table 30.6. A sample of the values they report are shown in Table 30.7. An FE using these data as a baseline would need to adjust the values for inflation

Table 30.7 Average value of Household Work by Different Classifications (Dollar Value of a Day)

	Nonworking Married Woman: With Children	Single Working Women: No Children	Married Working Men: With Children	Married Retired Men: No Children
Weekly hours	48.0	21.8	19.3	27.3
Annual hours	2,496	1,134	1,004	1,420
Annual value	$22,408	$10,058	$8,739	$13,059
Average hourly rate	$8.98	$8.87	$8.70	$9.20

Source: Extracted from Expectancy Data, *The Dollar Value of a Day: 1999 Dollar Valuation*. Shawnee Mission, KS, 2001. With permission.

(the numbers reflect 1999 hourly rates), regional wage variations, and for variations from the average due to individual circumstances. What is clear from these estimates is that the value of household services can be substantial, and the omission of such services in estimates of economic loss will result in an understatement of the actual loss.

Adjustments to the total value of household services must be made in both personal injury and wrongful death cases. In a personal injury case, the FE will need an estimate of the diminished capacity to provide the services that has resulted from the injury. For example, if an injury has reduced a single working woman's capacity by 20%, then the lost value of household services might be ($10,058 × 0.20) = $2,012 per year. In wrongful death cases, it must be recognized that a portion of the services provided by the decedent were for his or her own benefit: a married working man with children who cooked, did laundry, and mowed the lawn enjoyed the meals, clean clothes, and neat yard, along with the rest of the family. Although FEs disagree on the appropriate reduction, most will use a value between 20 and 30% that is consistent with the reduction used for personal consumption/maintenance.

Personal Consumption or Maintenance

At the same time that an individual's death results in an economic loss to his or her survivors, it must be recognized that a certain percentage of the family's income would have been allocated to his or her personal consumption or maintenance. For example, expenses would have been incurred for his or her transportation, food, clothes, toiletries, entertainment, medical expenses, etc. Other expenditures such as the rent or mortgage, property taxes, furniture, a DVD player, the cable bill, newspaper subscription, and home maintenance expenses are jointly determined and will not change with the passing of one family member.

It is a generally accepted practice to estimate the total earnings loss resulting from the loss of a life, and then to subtract estimated personal expenditures from this total. Estimating the appropriate amount of income to allocate to this category of expenditures, however, is one of the areas where FEs may disagree and estimates may be challenged. An often cited early study by Earl Cheit in 1961 found that jointly determined expenses accounted for approximately 30% of family income and that the remaining income used by the head of the household (the only person included in this study) declined steadily with the number of children in the home.[16] A number of later studies have found results that differ very little from Cheit's original findings. Martin has summarized a number of these studies and concluded that joint expenditures account for 38% of family income and the consumption factors for each parent decline from 31.0% down to 23.9% with one child, 20.1% with two children, 15.1% with three children, and 12.4% with four children.[12]

Making the computations simpler are state laws or rulings that specify what is to be included in the deductions. For example, some states specify that the FE is only to deduct the amount necessary to *maintain* the individual so that he or she is able to earn an income. This would be a smaller amount than that deducted for personal *consumption* for two reasons. First, consumption might include spending on hobbies such as golf, fishing, or boating that is significantly above the rudiments necessary to keep a person on the job. Second, deducting only the amount necessary to maintain employment implies that no deductions are made from estimates of lost retirement income. Another area of contention is whether or not the above percentages are applied to the decedent's income only, or in the case where both spouses earn an income, to the total family income. As in the case of consumption versus maintenance, most states stipulate which income measure is to be used.

Consumption patterns vary with the income of the household. It makes intuitive sense that a low income family on a tight budget will spend a higher proportion of their income on consumption than will a higher income family (assuming that savings is not considered to be a part of consumption). The Consumer Expenditure Survey provides an extensive data base that can be used to estimate consumption patterns by age, gender, family size, etc. For example, in the $20,000–$29,000 annual income range, each adult in a two-person household spends about 45% of their income on personal consumption, whereas the percentages decrease to about 18% when income exceeds $70,000.

Present Value

The Concept of Present Value

Lost income is usually estimated as a stream of estimated payments over time stretching from the time of the incident for a number of years into the future. This presents a problem in that the value of $100.00 five years from now does not have the same value as $100.00 in one's hand today. One way to understand why this is so is to ask yourself how much you would have needed to put in the bank five years ago at 5% interest in order to have $100.00 today. The answer is $78.35. With compounding,

$$\$78.35 \times (1.05) \times (1.05) \times (1.05) \times (1.05) \times (1.05) = \$100.00.$$

Alternatively, if you had $100.00 and you put it into the bank today earning 5% interest and left it there for five years, you would have:

$$\$100.00 \times (1.05) \times (1.05) \times (1.05) \times (1.05) \times (1.05) = \$127.63.$$

The *present value* of $100.00 five years from now is therefore equal to $78.35, and the present value of $127.63 five years from today is $100.00. Another way to look at this is to note that if the interest rate is 5%, then an individual will be indifferent among $78.35 five years ago, $100.00 today, or $127.63 five years in the future.

In the context of lost future earnings, the present value is the lump-sum amount that needs to be invested today, at a specified interest rate, to generate enough income to replace a foregone stream of income. Consider the example of an accountant who has established a loss of $200,000 per year for five years due to the negligence of another. The implication of the above is that the loss is not equal to $1,000,000. Table 30.8 shows that if he or she received a lump-sum award of $1,000,000, invested it at 5.0%, and withdrew $200,000 annually for five years, he or she would end up with $171,155 still in the bank at the end of five years! This is obviously overcompensation. If the accountant instead was awarded $865,895.33 (the present value of $200,000 per year for five years at 5.0%), he or she could invest it at 5.0% per year, withdraw $200,000 per year, and have zero left in the bank after five years. This would exactly replace the lost $200,000 per year

Table 30.8   The Allocation of $1,000,000 Invested at 5.0% for Five Years

Year	(1) Principal Balance	(2) Annual Interest Received [(1) ×.05]	(3) Principal Plus Interest [(1) + (2)]	(4) Annual Withdrawal	(5) New Principal [(3) − (4)]
1	$1,000,000	$50,000	$1,050,000	$200,000	$850,000
2	$850,000	$42,500	$892,500	$200,000	$692,500
3	$692,500	$34,625	$727,125	$200,000	$527,125
4	$527,125	$26,356	$553,481	$200,000	$353,481
5	$353,481	$17,674	$371,155	$200,000	$171,155
Total		$171,155		$1,000,000	

income stream [the reader can prove this to himself or herself by replicating Table 30.8 and inserting $865,893.33 in the first row of Column (1)].

The Appropriate Interest (Discount) Rate

Once the annual loss, number of years (life or work life expectancy), and interest rate are known, it is relatively straightforward to calculate the present lump-sum value using a scientific calculator, Excel, or other easily obtainable software. The process of estimating the first two values was explained earlier in this chapter. The process of determining the correct interest rate, or *discount rate*, is inexact and open to challenge by the opposition, primarily because different rates can result in wide variations in the size of awards. As shown in Table 30.9, the undiscounted value of $50,000 over 20 years is $1,000,000 (20 × $50,000), but the present value discounted at 8% is under $500,000. The choice of 4% rather than 6% results in an award that is over $100,000 greater. Clearly, there is much to be gained through challenging the value of the discount rate. Plaintiffs will prefer a low discount rate, and defendants will argue for a high rate.[17] The basic idea behind using present values is that the injured party, or survivors, should be able to invest a lump-sum award and generate a stream of income that exactly replicates the stream of income that was lost. A successful plaintiff could invest the lump sum in risky stocks and earn a much greater — or smaller — income. What the FE should be seeking is a no-risk, or low-risk, investment that will generate the desired income

Table 30.9   The Present Value of $50,000 for 20 years Using Different Interest Rates

Interest Rate (%)	Present Value ($)
0.0	1,000,000
1.0	902,278
2.0	817,572
3.0	743,874
4.0	679,516
5.0	623,111
6.0	573,496
7.0	529,701
8.0	490,907

stream. Because of this, the yields on U.S. government bonds are commonly used as the appropriate discount rate, that is, it is assumed that the recipient of the award will put the award into government bonds.

Three questions still remain: First, which maturity should be used? One year treasury bills are currently yielding between 1 and 2%, 10-year bonds are around 4%, and 20 year bonds are yielding about 5%. The easiest answer is use the rate that most closely corresponds to time horizon involved in the case. Second, should the FE use current or historical yields? For example, the 10-year bond rate is currently at a 40 year low (around 4%), but in the early 1980s, the rate exceeded 15%. Estimates using current rates in 2004 would likely overcompensate plaintiffs, whereas estimates made in 1982 using the then current rates would surely undercompensate them. For this reason, FEs will sometimes take an average over a period of years. For example, the 30 year average of 10-year bond yields is a little over 8%. This however is open to the criticism that the plaintiff cannot take the lump-sum to the bank and demand the historic average interest rate. The Social Security Administration's actuaries must project future interest rates to estimate future expenses and income, and their estimates extend to 2080. Although such forecasts are subject to debate, they are arguably as good as any others.

The final question is whether to use inflation adjusted rates (*real rates*) or the unadjusted market rates (*nominal rates*). As a rule of thumb, the answer depends on whether or not future losses are or are not increased by some projected rate of inflation. If future earning estimates include a growth in wages that, in turn, includes an inflation component, then it is appropriate to use the higher nominal rate. For example, if the yield on 20 year bonds is 8% and wages are projected to grow at 5.0% per year, then future wages will be inflated at 5% per year and then discounted at 8%. Alternatively, assume that the future inflation rate will be 2%. The FE will subtract the inflation rate from both the interest rate and wage growth rate (8%–2% = 6% and 5%–2% = 3.0%), and then use the resulting values to inflate future wage rates and then discount back to present value.[18] The results will be essentially the same in either case.

Summary

This chapter provided a brief overview of the types of analyses and data used by forensic economists to estimate the economic loss that results from wrongful death or injury. The objective of the economist is to arrive at an estimate that will fully compensate the injured party (or the survivors) for the financial losses resulting from the tort. Most of these damages are centered on the losses associated with lost employment opportunities. Hedonic losses, valuations of pain and suffering, and the value of punitive damages are generally beyond the realm of forensic economic analysis.

The increased availability of electronic data, increased communication among FEs through professional organizations and professional journals, and continuing research in all aspects of the field have all contributed to the growth and evolution of forensic economics into a distinct and well defined field of scientific inquiry. As a result, the economic loss estimates generated by two independent FEs who have been given the same information will be surprisingly similar.

A large part of the forensic economist's analysis relies on the use of statistical averages, actuarial tables, and national data that are very general in their nature. Nonetheless, it must always be recognized that the loss being estimated is the loss associated with an individual, and no two individuals are alike and no person is exactly average. Whenever feasible, the FE must take into account all the personal data at his or her disposal. The statistical data, whether it is from national, regional, or state sources, is a starting point — it is the job of the FE to blend these data with individual circumstances to arrive at a fair estimate of economic loss.

Although noted in the Appendix, it is well worth restating in closing that, whether working for the plaintiff or the defense, "Practitioners of forensic economics should strive to provide impartial and accurate economic analysis related to any litigation for which they are engaged, improve the science of forensic economics, and protect the integrity of the profession. . ."

Notes

1. This Chapter draws heavily on Marlin, Matthew and Reuben Slesinger. Forensic economics: estimating economic loss in wrongful death, permanent disability, and discriminatory discharge cases' Chapter 39C, in C. Wecht, Ed. *Forensic Sciences*, 2003: New York, NY, Matthew Bender & Co.

2. The BLS provides a wealth of national and regional data that describe current and past wage rates by occupation, gender, ethnicity, etc. The interested reader can surf their site beginning with the home page at http://www.bls.gov The Actuary of the Social Security Administration produces the estimates necessary earnings necessary for the SSA to plan for the future revenue and expenditures of the SSA. The estimates are published annually in the Principal Economic Assumptions Table of the "Annual Report of the Board of Trustees, the Federal Old-Age and Survivors Insurance and Disability Trust Funds." The most recent Table as of this writing is at http://www.ssa.gov/OACT/TR/TR03/V_economic.html#wp159107.

3. http://www.bls.gov/bls/blswage.htm (BLS); http://www.bls.gov/oco/home.htm (Occupational Outlook Handbook); http://www.bls.gov/ncs/home.htm (National Compensation Survey); http://www.bls.gov/oes/home.htm (Occupational Employment Statistics); www.salary.com, and www.salaryexpert.com. Salary.com data is used by the popular job search site, Monster.com

4. Bureaus of Labor Statistics and the Census. *Current Population Survey*, Table PINC-04. Educational attainment — people 18 year old and over, by total money earnings in 2001, work experience in 2001, age, race, hispanic origin and sex http://www.ccpr.ucla.edu/ccprwpseries/ccpr_004_00.pdf

5. Four such studies appear in T. Ireland, J. O. Ward, *Assessing Damages in Injuries and Deaths of Minor Children* Tuscan: Lawyers and Judges Publishing Company, 2002.

6. Bureau of Labor Statistics, *Employer Costs for Employee Compensation*. December 2004, http://www.bls.gov/news.release/ecec.t01.htm

7. http://www.ssa.gov/planners/calculators.htm

8. T. Hunt, J. Pickersgill, and H. Rutemiller, Median years to retirement and work-life expectancy for the civilian U.S. population. *J. Foren. Econ.*, 1997, pp. 171–205.

9. H. Richards, Life and Worklife Expectancies. Lawyers and Judges Publishing Company, 1999. G.R. Skoog, J. Ciecka, The Markov (increment-decrement) model of labor force activity: new results beyond work-life expectancies. *J. Legal Econ.*, 11(1), 2001.

10. P.J. Purcell, Older workers: employment and retirement trends. *Mon. Lab. Revi.*, October 2000, pp. 19–30; Gendell, Murray, Retirement age declines again in the 1990s. *Mon. Lab. Revi.*, 2001, pp. 12–21.

11. The most current tables as of early 2005 were published in February 2004 and can be found at http://www.cdc.gov/nchs/data/nvsr/nvsr52/nvsr52_14.pdf.

12. G. Martin, *Determining Economic Damages* (James Publishing, Revision 16, June 2004).

13. Expectancy Data, *The Dollar Value of a Day: 1999 Dollar Valuation*. Shawnee Mission, Kansas, 2001.

14. Although the data used in the DVD were originally obtained in order to assess peoples' activities and their potential exposure to pollutants, it provides very useful estimates to forensic economists because it is disaggregated across so many dimensions.

15. W.K. Bryant, C.D. Zick, and H. Kim, The Dollar Value of Household Work. Ithaca, NY: Cornell Coop. Extension Pub. 323IB228. Rev. Ed., 1993.

16. E. Cheit, *Injury and Recovery in the Course of Employment*, John Wiley & Sons, 1961.

17. As a result, many FEs will provide a range of potential awards based on different discount rate scenarios.

18. Technically, the rates are found by $[(1 + .08)/(1 + .02) - 1] = 5.88\%$ and $[(1 + .05)/(1 + .02)] = 2.94\%$

Appendix A: Ethics and the Forensic Economist

There is no requirement that the forensic economist be a member of the National Association of Forensic Economists (NAFE), nor any requirement that the he or she follow any specified code of ethics. However, many forensic economists voluntarily comply with the following code of ethics adopted by the members of NAFE in 2002. However, the code is reproduced here in its entirety.

National Association of Forensic Economics

Preamble: The primary missions of the National Association of Forensic Economics (NAFE) are research and education in the field of forensic economics. NAFE is not a credentialing organization that has assessed whether its members have met certain qualifications or whether those wanting to become members meet certain qualifications. NAFE does not require its members to pledge to follow a particular code of professional or ethical conduct, nor does it have a formal mechanism to sanction those who might violate such a code. However, because NAFE members are interested in protecting and elevating the integrity of the profession, they have voted to adopt and promulgate the following statement of ethical principles and tenets of practice.

Statement of Ethical Principles and Tenets of Practice

Practitioners of forensic economics should strive to provide impartial and accurate economic analysis related to any litigation for which they are engaged, improve the science of forensic economics, and protect the integrity of the profession through adherence to the following:

1. Employment Practitioners of forensic economics should decline involvement in any litigation when they are asked to assume invalid representations of fact or alter their methodologies without foundation or compelling reason.

2. Compensation Practitioners of forensic economics should not accept contingency fee arrangements, or fee amounts associated with the size of a court award or out-of-court settlement in a legal proceeding.

3. Diligence, Objectivity, and Accuracy Practitioners of forensic economics should strive to ensure that proffered opinions are based upon theoretically sound methodologies and unbiased, valid, and reliable economic information. They should also strive to be accurate, objective, and thorough in their analyses and refrain from submitting to any party in the litigation any information, through commission or omission, that they know to be misleading, biased, or inaccurate.

4. Disclosure Practitioners of forensic economics should stand ready to provide sufficient detail to allow replication of all numerical calculations, with reasonable effort, by other competent forensic economics experts, and be prepared to provide sufficient disclosure of sources of information and assumptions underpinning their opinions to make them understandable to others.

5. Consistency While it is recognized that practitioners of forensic economics may be given a different assignment when working for the plaintiff than when working for the defense, for any given assignment, the basic assumptions, sources, and methods should not change regardless of the party who employs the expert to perform the assignment. There should be no change in methodology for purposes of favoring any party's claim. This tenet is not meant to preclude methodological changes as new knowledge evolves, nor is it meant to preclude performing requested calculations based upon a hypothetical.

6. Knowledge Practitioners of forensic economics should strive to maintain a current knowledge base of their discipline.

7. Discourse NAFE supports the preservation of open, uninhibited discussion at conference sessions related to the profession of forensic economics. It is NAFE policy to discourage the citation of oral remarks made by participants in professional conference sessions.

8. Responsibility Practitioners of forensic economics are encouraged to make known the existence of, and their adherence to, these principles and tenets to those retaining them to perform economic analyses and to other participants in litigation. In addition, it is appropriate for practitioners of forensic economics to offer criticisms of breaches of these principles and tenets.

Forensic Engineering and Science

31

STEVEN C. BATTERMAN AND SCOTT D. BATTERMAN

Introduction

Forensic engineering has been a rapidly growing field of forensic practice and shall likely continue as such into the 21st century and beyond. By definition, engineering is the practical application of scientific and mathematical principles and has traditionally been divided into the well-known disciplines of civil, mechanical, chemical, electrical, and metallurgical engineering. Furthermore, the latter portion of the 20th century, saw the emergence of forensic engineering as a separate specialty and the advent of additional engineering specialties known by such names as bioengineering or biomedical engineering, computer and information science, and materials science, to name a few. Hence, forensic engineering, which is defined as engineering applied toward the purposes of the law, is an extremely broad field encompassing all of the traditional and emerging engineering disciplines, and obviously cannot be covered comprehensively in a short chapter. It is also emphasized at the outset that engineering is largely quantitative in nature and often relies heavily on the use of higher mathematics. However, to appeal to a wider audience, this chapter will be qualitative in nature and shall not focus on the use of mathematics. A bibliography is provided that will direct readers to more in-depth treatments, including mathematical analyses, of some of the topics discussed herein.

It is also worth noting at this juncture that the majority of forensic engineering investigations are carried out in a civil litigation context rather than a criminal context. This is a major difference from most of the topics covered in this volume and is certainly different from the common perception of forensic science where crime scene investigations and DNA considerations are often dominant, to the exclusion of other scientific fields. We emphasize, however, that in today's world, criminal and civil considerations can arise from the same incident. For example, consider the September 11, 2001 attack on America by terrorists who used fully fueled commercial airliners as effective, deadly weapons. Obviously, there is no question that the terrorists, and their accomplices, are guilty of perpetrating a crime of horrific, epic proportions. However, the fact that the terrorists were able to pass through security at the various airports from which they departed may imply that the security screening procedures were negligent and deficient. Moreover, the fact that the two World Trade Center (WTC) towers catastrophically collapsed, may imply civil liability due to design defects, as some have alleged. More will be said about the collapses of the WTC towers in a subsequent section of this chapter but is mentioned here to note that civil litigation considerations may also appear in an obvious criminal situation. An already litigated example is the terrorist bombing of Pan Am 103, which occurred over Lockerbie, Scotland, on December 21, 1988. This was a criminal act, resulting in convictions, but also led to civil verdicts against Pan American World Airways for violations of Federal Aviation Administration directives concerning baggage inspection, particularly unaccompanied baggage that might contain explosives. It is noted that the authors of this chapter were involved in analyzing aspects of the biomechanics of the passengers' injuries and deaths resulting from the breakup of Pan Am 103 at 31,000 feet and its subsequent fall to the ground.

Subsequent sections of this chapter will mainly focus on areas of interest to the authors. Apologies are extended in advance to practitioners of other forensic engineering specialties that are not covered in this short review.

Accident Reconstruction

Accident reconstruction is typically thought of as only applying to vehicular accident reconstruction, but it does indeed encompass all types of accidents including vehicular, electrical, industrial, chemical, structural collapses, fire cause and origin investigations, etc. However, for definiteness, further attention in this section will be focused on vehicular accidents.

Vehicular accident reconstruction may be defined as the scientific process of analyzing an accident using the physical facts and data left at an accident scene, and all relevant data such as weights and dimensions of vehicles, in conjunction with the appropriate natural laws of physics, that is, the laws of classical mechanics stated by Sir Isaac Newton in 1687. General statements of Newton's laws, which are formulated for a particle, are stated next with more detailed information given in some of the references (Greenwood, 1977; Beer and Johnston, 1977; Yeh and Abrams, 1960):

First Law: Every material body continues in its state of rest, or of constant velocity motion in a straight line, unless acted upon by external forces that cause it to change its state of rest or motion.

Second Law: The time rate of change of linear momentum (product of mass times velocity) of a particle is proportional to the external force acting on the particle and occurs in the direction of the force. An alternate form of this law, which is the more commonly stated form, is that the resultant force acting on a particle is equal to the mass times the acceleration.

Third Law: To every action there is an equal and opposite reaction. Or equivalently, the mutual forces of two bodies acting upon each other are equal in magnitude and opposite in direction.

Although Newton's laws appear to be simple statements, it must be emphasized that there are significant concepts and sophisticated philosophy embedded in the laws, which are essential to their understanding and proper application. The significance of this statement is that only qualified engineers and physical scientists should be retained to do accident reconstructions, since they are generally thoroughly educated in understanding and properly applying the laws of physics. This is noted herein since the advent of various "cookbook" manuals, as well as user-friendly computer programs have seen many unqualified individuals enter into the accident reconstruction field. The danger of this is that it can, and has, lead to miscarriages of justice in both criminal and civil cases where accident reconstructions become a central issue in a case (as an example, see Manning and Bentson, 1984). A general discussion of the significant concepts embedded in Newton's laws can be found in Batterman, et al. (2004a) as well as the other references previously cited.

The general philosophy employed in accident reconstruction is to work backward from the final positions of the vehicles, to the points of impact or beginning of the occurrence, and if sufficient information exists, before the impacts or occurrence. Calculations can be performed either by hand or by computer using the available data in conjunction with Newton's laws. Sometimes Newton's laws are cast in other forms for convenience, such as the work–energy principle or impulse–momentum principle (see references previously cited). In collision problems at the moment of impact, the impulse–momentum principle is particularly useful since the resultant external force acting on the system of colliding bodies is zero. This then leads to the principle of conservation of linear momentum (product of mass times velocity), which states that the linear momentum of a system of colliding bodies is conserved at impact. This principle combined with the information left at the accident scene and the vehicle data is often sufficient to solve for the velocities of the vehicles at impact. Examples of the application of the principle of conservation of linear momentum, along with the associated vector concepts and mathematics, are given in Batterman and Batterman (2000), Beer and Johnston (1977), and the SAE Accident Reconstruction Technology Collection. It should also be mentioned that numerous, commercially available, computer programs exist for accident reconstruction calculations, and these programs shall not be discussed herein. The programs are based on Newton's laws, as they must be, and many of them contain algorithms specialized for accident reconstruction, for example, crush damage considerations. As indicated earlier, some of the programs are so user friendly that it is possible for unqualified people, who do not have an adequate educational background and who do not understand their own limitations as well as those of the programs, to obtain solutions which may not be valid for a particular accident.

Another aspect of accident reconstruction, and undoubtedly the most difficult, is occupant kinematics, that is, to determine how an occupant moves with respect to the crashing vehicle. The determination of an occupant's kinematics is often critically related to the injuries that may have been sustained by the occupant. To determine the complete occupant kinematics, an enormous amount of physical information is required in addition to the mathematical complexities of solving a very difficult problem in dynamics. This physical information includes knowing the properties of the vehicle interior structures which may be contacted by the occupants, the actual contact points in the interior of the vehicle and on the occupant's body since this will then change the direction of motion of the occupant, the dynamic response of the human body to impact, and the details of how the vehicle is moving as a function of time. To completely solve an occupant's kinematics problem throughout the entire crash duration, an enormous amount of information is required along with many assumptions, which may influence or bias the outcome.

Often, only the initial occupant kinematics may be significant in an injury analysis, and this can sometimes be determined without a complete occupant kinematics analysis. For example, an occupant initially tends to move toward the impact, which is opposite the change in velocity (delta-v) of the vehicle, or equivalently is opposite the resultant vehicle acceleration (see Batterman et al., 2000). Hence, it follows that (a) In a frontal crash, occupants will tend to move forward with respect to the vehicle. If the occupants are unrestrained, front seat occupants can impact the interior front structure such as the steering wheel, dashboard, or windshield, whereas rear seat occupants can impact the backs of the front seats. It is noted, however, in a moderate to severe frontal crash, that is, high delta-v, even restrained occupants can contact the interior structure in front of them. (b) In a rear end crash, occupants will tend to initially move backward toward/into their seats followed by a forward rebound phase. If unrestrained, occupants can rebound forward into the vehicle structure in front of them. Restrained occupants will not exhibit such large excursions and will often be prevented from, or sustain only limited, contact, with the interior vehicle structure. Another important aspect of rear end collisions is that front seat backs can fail causing occupants to tumble into the rear of a vehicle and thus sustain serious injuries. The special and interesting case of serious injuries that can occur in low delta-v rear end collisions has been analyzed by Batterman, et al. (2002b). (c) In a lateral crash, nearside occupants to the crash will move toward the impact and may physically contact the impacting vehicle or a roadside object, such as a pole or a tree. Lap-shoulder belts worn by nearside occupants may not be effective in preventing injuries in this type of crash, but lateral or curtain airbags would offer some protection. However, a restrained farside occupant to a lateral crash may derive benefit from wearing a lap-shoulder belt, which would then limit occupant excursions toward the impact.

Biomechanics of Injury

The general field of biomechanics is concerned with the application of Newtonian mechanics to biology. Biomechanics is a subfield of the broader field of bioengineering, which is defined as the application of engineering principles and methodology to biological systems. Bioengineering is a huge and rapidly developing field in the United States and worldwide with burgeoning numbers of degree programs at the bachelors, masters, and doctorate levels. The field of biomechanics is likewise vast with applications beyond the considerations discussed in this article. For example, to name a few, biomechanicians are involved in the design of artificial organs, prostheses, bioinstrumentation, medical devices, safety devices such as protective sports equipment, automobile design, and restraint system design to minimize injuries in a crash, as well as with understanding the response of tissues, cells, and biological systems to mechanical loading.

Biomechanics of injuries has already been briefly mentioned when initial occupant kinematics was discussed. As a complete discussion of injury biomechanics is beyond the scope of this review, only a few key ideas and concepts will be mentioned. The interested reader is referred to the bibliography, in particular the Stapp Car Crash Conference Proceedings and extensive literature available from the Society of Automotive Engineers.

A concept that has already been noted, and which frequently appears in automotive injury biomechanics, is that of delta-v, which is often correlated with the injury producing potential of a crash. Delta-v is defined as the *change in velocity* (not speed) of a vehicle from its immediate preimpact velocity to its immediate postimpact velocity. Delta-v is a *vector quantity*, which has both magnitude and direction, and it is generally incorrect to merely subtract speeds, which are *scalar quantities*, to determine delta-v (e.g., see Batterman et al. 2000). The major reason delta-v is correlated with injury potential is that delta-v is closely related to the vehicle accelerations in a crash and, by Newton's second law, it is accelerations which determine the resultant forces acting on a system. However, it is emphasized that an occupant's body or body segments, in general, will not experience the same delta-v as the vehicle. This is because vehicle and body segment rotations can, and do, greatly influence the velocities and velocity changes an occupant may undergo in a crash.

Correlations of injury with delta-v appear in the biomechanics literature (Mills and Hobbs, 1984) and are continuously being collected and updated. It should be noted at the outset that the correlations are statistical in nature, that is, they give the probability of a certain type of injury occurring as a function of delta-v. Furthermore, to ensure uniformity and standardization of reporting, injuries are typically described using the Abbreviated Injury Scale (AIS) promulgated by the Association for the Advancement of Automotive Medicine (AAAM). The AIS is based on anatomical injury immediately following the accident and does not score impairments or disabilities that may result from the injuries over time. A severity code is used in the AIS, which ranges from 0 (no injury) to 6 (currently untreatable, fatal), and the reader is referred to the AIS manual for details. Furthermore, other injury classification systems exist and are discussed by Pike.

It is again worth emphasizing that injury correlations are statistical and are not absolute. For example, a 60% probability of a certain type and injury severity occurring means that in the same crash, there is a 40% probability of not sustaining that injury. In addition, a person can be critically injured (AIS 5) or killed (AIS 6) in a moderate delta-v accident, say 15 to 20 mph, but can walk away uninjured (AIS 0) or with minor injuries (AIS 1) in a high delta-v accident, say 35–40 mph. Hence, care and discretion must be used when the injury correlation data are to be used in an attempt to predict injuries in a given crash.

It is also worthwhile to briefly mention a few other ideas in the field of injury biomechanics. The concept of threshold injury criteria refers to those combinations of kinematics variables, that is, related to geometry and motion, and kinetic variables, that is, related to forces that cause the motion, which can cause a traumatic injury to various body tissues. These variables include, but are not necessarily limited to, forces, moments or torques (rotational effect of forces), accelerations, stresses, strains, and their associated time histories. Time duration of loading (impulses and vibrations) can be very significant and, for example, forces and accelerations applied for a short time period may not cause injury, whereas the same forces applied for a longer time period may be injury producing. In determining threshold injury criteria, an implicit assumption is made that such criteria do indeed uniquely exist which apply across the spectrum of the human population. This should be interpreted with caution since not only is there expected biological variability between individuals, but factors such as age, disease, gender, pre-existing conditions, and other variables can and do influence the response of whole tissues and single cells to mechanical loading.

The concept of threshold injury criteria has entered into the law. The National Traffic and Motor Vehicle Safety Act of 1966 introduced the concept of vehicle crashworthiness, that is, the ability of a motor vehicle to protect its occupants in a crash. This Act led to the creation of the Federal Motor Vehicle Safety Standards (FMVSS), which require a minimum level of crashworthiness for all cars sold in the United States. The FMVSS contain essentially three threshold injury criteria (see Pike, 1990), which manufacturers must comply with. The first, known as the Head Injury Criterion (HIC), requires that a certain mathematical expression, that is, an integral containing the resultant acceleration–time history measured at the center of gravity of the head of a restrained ATD (anthropomorphic test device) in a crash test, cannot exceed a value of 1000 or else the vehicle fails the test. The second criterion refers to a force measurement made in the femur of the restrained ATD. The vehicle fails the test if the force in the femur exceeds 10.0 kN (2250 pounds). The third threshold injury criterion refers to the resultant acceleration measured at the center of gravity of the thorax of the ATD. A vehicle passes this test if the acceleration does not exceed 60 g (sixty times the acceleration due to gravity) for intervals whose cumulative duration is not more than 3 msec (0.003 sec). This criterion is an example of where the time duration of loading is significant.

The preceding three criteria are not absolute and have many known deficiencies. These include, but are not necessarily limited to (a) The use of a surrogate such as an ATD may not be biofidelic, that is, does not faithfully reproduce human response, and accurately reflect conditions to cause human injury. (b) The HIC does not distinguish among types of head injuries such as skull fractures, subdural hematoma, diffuse axonal injury (see Newman). In addition, it is possible for a person to walk away uninjured from an accident with an HIC greater than 1000 while a person can die from a head injury in a crash where the HIC was significantly less than 1000. (c) Loads to fracture human femora can be less than 2250 pounds for a significant portion of the population, that is, normal biological variation across the population spectrum is not accounted for. [d] In addition to normal biological variability, the thorax criterion does not distinguish types of thoracic trauma such as a transected aorta, fractured ribs, etc.

This section shall be closed noting that other injury criteria have been proposed, and still others are undergoing intense research investigation. Biomechanics injury research, with its spin-offs to forensic engineering applications, requires the collaboration of engineers, medical researchers, and forensic scientists working toward the goal of understanding whole body and tissue responses to traumatic loading conditions.

Engineering Failures

The ultimate goal of engineering is to design safely and to minimize or eliminate the probability of failures. Failure has a meaning that depends on the system and may mean loss of function of a component or a total disaster, such as the complete loss of the system. To name a few, when an engineering system does fail — such as a building or major structural collapse, chemical plant toxic vapor leak, dam burst, space shuttle explosion or breakup, aircraft malfunction leading to a crash, nuclear reactor malfunction leading to an escape of radiation, or overdoses from a cancer irradiation device — thousands of people can be injured or killed. In fact, since engineering systems are typically designed to interface with a large number of people, the potential for disaster with mass injury or loss of life is a major distinguishing feature between engineering and other professions. Once the reasons for the failure are ultimately diagnosed and understood, engineering knowledge is thereby advanced enormously, that is, engineers can and often do learn more from analyzing a failure than by successfully designing systems which do not fail. In the 21st century, the role of forensic engineering will be essential to understanding the causes of particular failures. Some notable engineering failures include the following.

Tacoma Narrows Bridge, November 17, 1940

This slender and narrow, two lane center span suspension bridge, which came to be known as "Galloping Gertie," collapsed into Puget Sound in a 42 mph wind only a few months after it had been opened. The failure was the result of aerodynamic or wind induced vibrations. Fortunately, the swaying of the bridge leading to the collapse was anticipated, and there was no traffic crossing the bridge at the time of the collapse. The spectacular and large (huge) amplitude of the vibrations, resulting in roadway undulations and twisting of the bridge, are dramatically shown in videos of the bridge that are available from several sources, including the Internet. During the design of the bridge, engineers simply did not consider the aerodynamic effects of the wind as a possible cause of a failure, although wind-loading effects have long been considered in building design. As a result of the analysis of the collapse, engineers learned about aerodynamic wind effects on slender bridges and applied these lessons to the design of subsequent narrow profile, long span suspension bridges.

Kansas City Hyatt Regency Skywalk Collapse, July 17, 1981

This failure of a suspended concrete catwalk or walkway, on which people were dancing, resulted in 114 deaths, and more than 200 people were injured. Analysis of the failure indicated that the original suspension rods for the suspended walkways were underdesigned but would likely not have failed, even under the dynamic load of people dancing. However, a design change made to the suspension rods at their connections to the walkway box beam supports caused one of the rods to pull through its box beam connection thus leading to the disaster. This failure is an example of where a small but critical change in a design detail, simply to facilitate construction of the walkway, apparently went unchecked or was mistakenly not found to be deficient. Further comments on this disaster can be found in Petroski (1985) and on the Internet.

Space Shuttle Failures Challenger Explosion, January 28, 1986, and Columbia Breakup, February 1, 2003

These failures, the Challenger occurring during lift-off and the Columbia during re-entry, resulted in the loss of both crews (14 astronauts). Analysis of the Challenger explosion, which occurred at 73 sec into the flight, revealed the basic cause of the disaster to be a failure of one of the O-rings for the right solid propellant rocket booster. The explosion occurred when the hot 3315°C (6000°F) exhaust gases and flames from the booster's defective O-ring seal breached the external tank and ignited the hydrogen contained in the tank (the external tank provides the necessary liquid fuel to the shuttle's aft engines to achieve orbit after which time the tank is jettisoned). In addition to the defective O-ring design, which did not properly seal the segments of the solid rocket boosters, the launch was attempted in cold weather conditions, which adversely affected the mechanical behavior and sealing qualities of the O-rings. Furthermore, it was revealed afterward, that engineers, acting in accord with their ethical responsibilities, tried in vain to stop the launch since they felt disaster was impending because of previous shuttle problems and the nonoptimum launch conditions. However, NASA officials rebuffed the engineers in their attempts, and the resulting tragedy occurred.

The Columbia disaster occurred during re-entry when the space shuttle was only about 16 min from landing. This failure occurred when a chunk of insulating foam fell off the external tank 82 second and after lift-off and unknowingly damaged the thermal tiles of the leading edge of the left wing of the shuttle. Columbia did achieve a successful orbit but, upon re-entry, superheated air entered the damaged left wing, weakened the structure, and aerodynamic forces then caused the ensuing loss of control and breakup. Videos of the launch did reveal that foam had fallen off the external tank and impacted the wing, but engineers did not properly consider the damage potential of a chunk of even lightweight foam (weighing less than 2 pounds) moving at a high velocity (425–570 mph) relative to the wing. Impact testing after the accident, based on forensic evidence of the most likely impact or strike area on the wing, demonstrated that the impact could cause damage ranging from cracks to a 16–17 in. hole.

Collapse of the World Trade Center (WTC) Towers, September 11, 2001; Remarks on the Murrah Federal Building, Oklahoma City, July 19, 1995

It should be stated at the outset that the WTC towers did not collapse, tip, or topple over as a result of the impact forces, which they withstood extremely well. Furthermore, the ensuing fires were not hot enough, and did not burn long enough, to melt the steel perimeter columns or the core columns. However, the fires were intense enough to cause thermal weakening of the exterior columns and core columns, many of which obviously sustained structural damage in the immediate impact areas. Eventually, the thermally weakened columns buckled and could not support the weight of the towers above the impact areas, whereas the columns below the impact areas could not support the dynamic loading caused by the sequential and cascading collapsing floors after the tower collapses were initiated. Although analyses of the collapses are still ongoing, the collapses of the WTC towers are examples of progressive collapse where the floors pancaked into one another as each floor was sequentially subjected to increased loading from above, beyond the ultimate capacity of the remaining structure to sustain loads.

A recent, comprehensive, draft report concerning the WTC tower collapses was issued on April 5, 2005 by the National Institute of Standards and Technology (NIST) for public comment, with the final report expected in September 2005. The NIST report, which is available for download from the Internet (wtc.nist.gov), is entitled Design, Construction, and Maintenance of Structural and Life Safety Systems. Among other items, the report concludes that the towers withstood the initial aircraft impacts and would have remained standing but for the subsequent fires. Furthermore, a very significant conclusion is that the aircraft impacts caused fireproofing to be dislodged, which exacerbated the thermal weakening of the columns that eventually caused the global collapse.

Although the total collapses of the towers appear to be disproportionate to the initial structural damage done by the aircraft impacts, the presently available evidence indicates that the WTC towers may not have been defective in structural design within the framed tube design concept used for very tall buildings, that is, perimeter columns, load bearing external walls, internal load bearing core structure. The towers were designed with excessive redundant column capacity, which did indeed allow for load redistribution when perimeter and core columns failed due to the initial impacts (see the NIST report). It does not appear based on available evidence and analyses that simple structural design changes to the WTC framed tube design concept would have significantly, if at all, altered the outcome. However, the controversy concerning the tower collapses is likely to continue since aircraft impacts to tall buildings are foreseeable, and have indeed occurred long before the advent of 9/11 terrorism and even before the WTC was designed. For example, to name a few, a B-25 bomber crashed into the Empire State Building on July 28, 1945; 10 months later an Army C-45 Beechcraft crashed into the Bank of Manhattan Building in New York City on May 20, 1946; and an El Al 747 cargo plane crashed into an apartment complex in Amsterdam on October 4, 1992. Hence, the initial engineering and architectural choice of the WTC framed tube design concept, along with the fireproofing used and the lack of other fire protection features, may be open to criticism even though the towers were more than strong enough to resist design loads and did indeed resist the initial aircraft impacts.

The terrorist bombing of the Murrah Federal Building in Oklahoma City, built in 1976, is also an example of progressive collapse. In this reinforced concrete building, the collapse damage was disproportionate to the size of the truck bomb that caused damage to columns on the lower levels of the building. However, because of the design of the building, and lack of reinforcing steel in critical areas, the upper floors underwent a progressive, sequential collapse. It has been estimated that if the building had been built or retrofitted to the seismic standards of the 1990s, as much as 50–80% of the damage, and perhaps some of the resulting injuries/fatalities, could have been prevented.

In closing this section, it is noted that 21st century engineers will have a critical role to play in counterterrorism activities ranging from techniques to assess risk and vulnerability to effective systems design to prevent or mitigate casualties and damage from terrorist acts.

Products Liability

Products liability is a burgeoning area of forensic engineering investigation. Products liability investigations revolve around the issue of whether a product is defective and whether the defects are causally related to any injuries that may have occurred to the users or people in the vicinity of the product. Essentially, the following three types of product defects are recognized in the law, but this may vary according to the jurisdiction of the lawsuit: (1) design defects, that is, the product lacks those elements that are necessary for its safe and foreseeable uses; (2) manufacturing defects, that is, the product was not manufactured according to the manufacturer's own specifications or standards; and (3) failure to properly warn or instruct the user in the proper and safe use of the product. Examples of design defects, manufacturing defects, and considerations of failure to warn can be found in Batterman et al. (2002a, 2004a) and Weinstein et al. (1978).

As already noted in Section IV, the goal of design engineering is to design safe products and systems, which are free of hazards caused by defects. Engineers must be able to identify hazards in advance, or prospectively, and then design out the hazards, if it is practical and feasible to do so, before the product or system leaves their control. Once an accident due to a design defect occurs, the injured person has essentially identified the design defect, and it is too late for a prospective hazard identification analysis. Several hazard identification analysis procedures and variations of procedures exist, which should be part of the normal design process that engineers routinely employ in the design stages of a product or system to eliminate defects and improve system reliability. Three of the commonly used identification procedures are as follows:

Failure Modes and Effects Analysis (FMEA)

The FMEA is a bottom to top basic procedure where the system is examined component by component, and a failure or malfunction of any component is traced throughout the entire system. Flow sheets and computer programs are available to assist the engineering design team in this procedure that screens the entire system. If the component failure results in a hazard that can cause injury, it is identified, and necessary design changes should be made to remove the hazard and protect the user.

Fault-Tree Analysis (FTA)

The FTA is a top to bottom procedure where the undesirable outcome (top event or fault condition) is the starting point. This top event is then traced down through the system, and the failures of individual components or events, which can lead to the undesirable outcome, are identified. Design changes are then made as required, eliminating or minimizing the probability of the occurrence of the fault condition. The FTA is a complicated procedure, which is used to analyze complex systems, for example, a space shuttle, and relies heavily on Boolean algebra techniques and symbols and is most often done on a digital computer.

Product Safety Audit (PSA)

The PSA is basically a checklist containing hundreds, if not thousands, of questions concerning the design of the product. The questions are framed in a manner such that a negative answer triggers further investigation that may lead to a design change. The major drawback, as with any checklist procedure, is that if the list of questions is incomplete, a defect can be easily overlooked. Once the hazards in a product or system are identified by a proper hazard identification analysis, the engineer follows a codified procedure known as the "safety hierarchy" to prevent or minimize the probability of personal injury (see Batterman et al. 2004a).

Slips and Falls

Traumatic injuries and deaths resulting from slip, trip, and fall accidents are a significant public health problem in the United States. It is reported that in the year 2000, there were approximately 8.1 million visits to emergency rooms as a result of accidental falls, which constitutes approximately 12% of the total number of reported emergency room visits in that year. Amongst the elderly, it is reported that approximately 30% of those over the age of 65 fall each year, and for those over 80 years old, the rate is approximately 40%. Others estimate that, on average, more than 16,000 people die each year as a result of fall related injuries. As a result of this epidemic in slip, trip, and fall related injuries, numerous measures have been undertaken in an attempt to reduce the number of slip and fall accidents including, but not limited to, the use of slip resistant materials on walkway surfaces and prescribed shoe outsole materials and patterns.

Many forensic engineers are involved in the area of walkway and floor safety with much of the current work concentrated in the area of tribometry and the characterization and measurement of slip resistance. In addition, the American Society for Testing and Materials (ASTM) has developed, and continues to propose and develop, consensus standards intended to promote uniformity in the characterization and measurement of slip resistance. Although numerous tribometers are currently in use by practitioners to assess slip resistance (see Batterman et al. 2005), it is well known that the different types of tribometers yield different results on the same wet or dry walkway surfaces, although each is supposedly measuring the "slip resistance" of the subject surface. Some of the differences in the results appear to arise, at least in part, from the fact that the different tribometers are apparently measuring static effects, others are measuring dynamic effects, while others do not rigorously consider the effect of wet surfaces. Differences also arise relating to the manner and time interval between the application of the loads to the surface (see Batterman et al., 2004b, 2005) for a discussion of the aforementioned effects).

The lack of uniformity in testing devices, results, and procedures raises serious questions about current testing methodologies and tribometers, and whether or not it is sufficient to consider a walkway as safe or unsafe without considering the interaction of the walkway surface with the manner in which a person negotiates the surface. A rigorous engineering model and analysis by Batterman et al. (2004b) for wet and dry surfaces, incorporating anthropometric and gait related factors, demonstrates that the onset of slip is dependent upon the chosen measure of slip resistance and strongly dependent on walking speed and stride, or step, length in addition to an Anthropometric Gait Index (AGI), that can vary significantly among individuals. When analyzing a slip and fall accident, it is not enough to simply attempt to characterize the slip resistance of the shoe/walkway interface, but individual gait characteristics must also be taken into consideration. For example, some people may be able to negotiate a walkway surface without any incident, whereas others attempting to negotiate the same walkway in the same, or substantially similar footwear may be caused to slip and fall. Even if a consensus was to be reached as to which tribometer or testing method most accurately characterizes the slip resistance of a given walkway, that number alone would have only limited utility in determining those individuals prone to slip and fall.

The biomechanical analysis of slip and fall accidents is a vast topic and is the subject of ongoing research. The major purpose of this brief introduction is to indicate that in order to properly understand why and how a person slips on a given floor, several factors have to be considered, which include (1) the slip resistance of the footwear/walkway surface system, (2) the manner in which a person walks across the surface (stride or step length, velocity), and (3) the anthropometry of the person.

Conclusion

The purpose of this short chapter is twofold: (1) to expose the reader to the exciting and rapidly developing field of forensic engineering by briefly introducing a few representative areas that are current and topical; (2) to encourage forensic scientists to use the expertise and services of forensic engineers in injury and death investigation cases. The topics discussed in this chapter are necessarily limited in scope, and the interested reader is referred to the bibliography for references to further applications and in-depth treatments. The bibliography is provided for representative coverage of the field without endorsement of any publication. An attempt has been made to generally group the bibliography by subject matter, as discussed in the chapter, although there is considerable overlap.

Bibliography

Forensic Engineering

Batterman, S.C. and Batterman, S.D. Forensic engineering. Legal medicine, 6th ed., Chap. 66, Mosby, 2004a.

Batterman, S.C. and Batterman, S.D. Forensic engineering. McGraw-Hill Yearbook of Science & Technology, 115–117, 2002a, pp. 115–117, McGraw-Hill.

Carper, K.L., Ed. Forensic engineering. 2nd ed., CRC Press, 2001.

Putchat, N. Forensic engineering — a definition. *J. Forensic Sci.*, 1984; 29: 375–378.

Newton's Laws and Principles of Classical Dynamics

Beer, F.P. and Johnston, E.R. Vector mechanics for engineers: statics and dynamics. McGraw-Hill, 1977.

Greenwood, D.T. Classical dynamics. McGraw-Hill, 1977.

Yeh, H. and Abrams, J.I. Principles of mechanics of solids and fluids: particle and rigid body mechanics. McGraw-Hill, 1960.

Accident Reconstruction

Accident reconstruction technology collection (2004). CD-ROM, *Soc. Auto Engineers*.

Accident reconstruction: human, vehicle and environmental factors; SAE SP-814. *Soc Auto Engineers*, 1990.

Batterman, S.C. and Batterman, S.D. Accident investigation/motor vehicle (accident reconstruction and biomechanics of injuries). In J.A. Siegel et al. (Eds.), Encyclopedia of forensic sciences, Academic Press, 2000.

Batterman, S.D. and Batterman, S.C. Delta-v, spinal trauma, and the myth of the minimal damage accident. *J. Whiplash & Related Disorders*, 2002b.

Bohan, T.L. and Damask, A.C., Eds. Forensic accident investigation: motor vehicles. Michie Butterworth, 1995.

Brach, R.M. Mechanical impact dynamics: rigid body collisions. Wiley, 1991.

Limpert, R. Motor vehicle accident reconstruction and cause analysis, 2nd ed. Michie, 1984.

Mathematical simulation of occupant and vehicle kinematics, SAE P-146. *Soc Auto Engineers*, 1984.

Biomechanics of Injury

Stapp Car Crash Conference Proceedings (2002). CD-ROM. *Soc. Auto Engineers*.

Mills, P.J. and Hobbs, C.A. The probability of injury to car occupants in frontal and side impacts. In: Proceedings of Twenty-eighth Stapp Car Crash Conference, paper 841652. *Soc Auto Engineers* 1984: 223–235.

The abbreviated injury scale, 1990 revision. Des Plaines, IL: Assoc Adv Auto Medicine (AAAM), 1990.

Newman, J.A. Head injury criteria in automotive crash testing. In: Proceedings of Twenty-Fourth Stapp Car Crash Conference. paper 801317, *Soc Auto Engineers*, 1980; 703–747.

Pike, J.A. Automotive safety: anatomy, injury, testing and regulation, *Soc Auto Engineers,* 1990.

Yamada, H. Strength of biological materials. Krieger, 1973.

Evans, F.G. Mechanical properties of bone. Thomas, 1973.

Human tolerance to impact conditions as related to motor vehicle design, SAE J885. Soc Auto Engineers, 1986.

Damask, A.C. and Damask, J.N. Injury causation analyses: case studies and data sources. Michie, 1990.

McElhaney, J.H., Roberts, V.L., and Hilyard, J.F. Handbook of human tolerance, Japan Auto Res Institute, 1976.

Nahum, A.M. and Melvin, J., Eds. The biomechanics of trauma. Appleton-Century-Crofts, 1985.

Biomechanics of impact injury and injury tolerances of the head-neck complex, SAE PT-43. *Soc Auto Engineers*, 1993.

Biomechanics of impact injury and injury tolerances of the thorax-shoulder complex, SAE PT-45. *Soc. Auto Engineers*, 1994.

Engineering Failures

Petroski, H. To engineer is human: the role of failure in successful design. St. Martin's Press, 1985.

Tens of thousands of Internet articles that can be accessed using a variety of search engines and entering the name of the failed system or topic under consideration.

Products Liability

Phillips, J.J. Products Liability. 3rd ed. West Publishing Co., 1988.

Thorpe, J.F. and Middendorf, W.H. What every engineer should know about product liability. Marcel Dekker, 1979.

Weinstein, A.S., Twerski, A.D., Piehier, H.R., and Donaher, W.A. Products liability and the reasonably safe product: a guide for management, design and marketing. Wiley, 1978.

Dhillon, B.S. and Singh, C. Engineering reliability, new techniques and applications. Wiley, 1981.

Brown, D.B. Systems analysis and design for safety. Prentice-Hall, 1976.

Slips and Falls

Batterman, S.D., Batterman, S.C., and Medoff, H.P. Mechanics of Macroslip: A New Phenomenological Theory, International Symposium on Slips, Trips and Falls, Annual Conference of the Ergonomics Society, University of Wales, Swansea, April 2004, published in Contemporary Ergonomics 2004, CRC Press, 2004b.

Batterman, S.D. and Batterman, S.C. Biomechanical Analysis of Slip, Trip and Fall Accidents. In J. Rich et al. (Eds.), Forensic medicine of the lower extremity: Human identification and trauma analysis from the thigh, leg and foot, Humana Press, 2005, Chapter 11, pp. 343–355.

Special series on walkway safety. *J. Forensic Sci.* 1996; 41: 731–785.

Topics in the Practice of Forensic Science

Crime Scene Management

32

HENRY C. LEE AND TIMOTHY M. PALMBACH

Introduction

Historically, criminal investigations were dependent on the ability of the investigator to extract information from witnesses and suspects, or on the use of informants or under-cover operations. If interviews or interrogations failed to provide the required investigative information, or if false information were obtained, often the wrongful person was arrested, or cases remained unsolved.

In contrast, contemporary law enforcement has greatly expanded its ability to solve crimes by adopting techniques and procedures that recognize the importance of combined powers of crime scenes, physical evidence, data mining, and witnesses in successful criminal investigations. Today's crimes are most often solved by a system that focuses on teamwork, advanced investigative skills, and the ability to process a crime scene properly, recognizing, collecting, and preserving all relevant physical evidence and information at the crime scene and from the suspect.

However, numerous routine and high profile cases have demonstrated the harsh reality that, despite available current crime scene technologies and specialized personnel, the effectiveness of crime scene functions are only as good as the crime scene management system that supports those functions. Moreover, the expertise and advanced abilities of the Forensic Science Laboratory that will conduct testing on the evidence can not undue or compensate for subpar crime scene management system and procedures.

Crime Scene Management Components

Successful crime scene management systems require five separate but interconnected sub-components: (1) manpower management, (2) technology management, (3) evidence management, (4) information management, and (5) logistics management.

A deficiency in any one of these areas, or an overemphasis on one component and neglect of another, will result in a system that is out of balance, jeopardizing the overall crime scene investigation process. As stated, there are five necessary components for an effective crime scene evidence management system (see Figure 32.1).

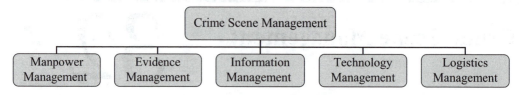

Figure 32.1 Components of a crime scene management system.

Manpower Management

Manpower management is a very important aspect of any criminal investigation. It is essential that sufficient manpower be allocated for an investigation, and the assigned personnel have sufficient technical skill and experience to complete the assigned task. There are many tasks to be performed at a given crime scene. The scope and the variety of tasks depend on the nature and the complication of the case. The crime scene investigation team should comprise personnel who share certain duties and responsibilities that will always be part of any major investigation. They must work as a team. To conduct a thorough, coordinated, and successful investigation, all participants must know their duties, importance, and limitations. It is important to note that, in many investigations, it is not always possible to have only one person assigned to a duty, and it is common that one individual will perform more than one assignment. Regardless of the number of team members and their respective duties, each team member, from first responder to the investigating detective, from the laboratory scientist to the prosecuting attorney, must work with one another to do their best in solving the case.

There are many different crime scene investigation models, such as the local agency's crime scene technician concept; the federal, state, or county major crime squad concept; and the uniformed officer/detective concept. These various concepts are widely used, but the most effective model for conducting a crime scene investigation is the team concept. In this concept, individuals of the team are assigned to specific duties, dependent upon their specific experiential training, producing the most efficient and successful results in the crime scene investigation. For all positions on the team, training and experience are important, but interest and attitude can be significant, given the human aspect of crime scene investigation. The complete criminal investigation team should consist of all of the following members:

1. *First Responder*: police officer, fire department — rescue worker, medical personnel — emergency medical technician (EMT)
2. *Crime Scene Investigators*: team leader, photographer, videographer, sketcher, note taker, evidence technician
3. *Forensic Science Laboratory Personnel*: fingerprint examiner, bloodstain expert, serologist, chemist, trace analyst
4. *Medical Examiner*: hospital physician (if required)
5. *Forensic Consultants*: anthropologist, odontologist, computer analyst — forensic data examiner, entomologist, etc.
6. Prosecutor's Office Personnel

Each of these team members should carry out their respective duties and responsibilities. The most important aspects of the team concept are cooperation, coordination, and communication. Investigators should work together to avoid any "tunnel vision" problem, that is, when a team member or the entire team begins to focus or limit their activities based on certain assumptions that may or may not ultimately be established as correct.

It is not possible for one very experienced and multitalented crime scene investigator to adequately process a crime scene alone. In addition, as the complexity of the case increases so do the requisite man-hours necessary to complete the many crime scene functions. In most cases, where available resources and workload permit, crime scene units should consist of at least four investigators and one supervisor.

All of these investigators and the supervisor may have certain strengths or skills, but they should strive to expand their skill bases and become generalists in scope. Obviously, some more technical or complex tasks such as blood stain pattern interpretation and crime scene reconstruction, or advanced latent print processing methods may be within the expertise of none or only one of the team members. If that skill level is not present within the team, it is incumbent upon the supervisor to recognize the need and obtain outside expertise before critical mistakes or oversights occur.

There are basic skills or training objectives that a crime scene investigator should possess. All aspects of scene documentation need to be fully covered at a scene. These methods include still photography in a variety of formats, videotaping, and preparation of sketch maps and diagrams. A wide variety of searching methods and techniques must be included in the available procedures. These include organized manual search grids and technology-based methods involving the use of metal detectors, flammable vapor detectors, portable lasers, and forensic light sources (see Figure 32.2). Specialized skills in a wide variety of disciplines will often be needed to enhance pattern evidence or to develop potential evidence located at the scene.

Investigators must be proficient in recognizing, collecting, and preserving:

- Fingerprints
- Footprints
- Tire tracks
- Bloodstains and other biological specimens
- Entomology specimens

Figure 32.2   Using an alternate light source to examine evidence.

- Trace evidence
- Narcotics and chemicals
- Firearms
- Explosive residues
- Botanical and soil samples

Finally, even if the crime scene unit does not possess expertise to conduct a full-scale scene reconstruction, its members must be sufficiently trained so as to understand the process and basic requirements for a subsequent successful reconstruction.

Regardless of the size of a particular jurisdiction, these personnel demands will be realized during a major investigation. The only truly effective method to manage these conflicting personnel demands is through the establishment of a team concept.

Evidence Management

A central purpose of crime scene investigation is to find evidence either linking a suspect to the case or eliminating the person from the case. Therefore, it is essential to establish a crime scene evidence management system to assure that all evidence collected meets legal and scientific requirements.

Any crime scene must be thoroughly documented or recorded by notes, photography, sketching, audiotaping, and videotaping. Photography, videotaping, and sketching will provide a permanent graphic record of the appearance and position of victims, patterns, physical evidence, and their relationship to one another. Notes and audio taping will provide necessary descriptive details, such as names, numbers, time, date, weather, condition, locations, and other nonphotographable information at the crime scene. The documentation techniques support testimony from crime scene investigators as to what was found, its location, nature, and condition at the crime scene, and they provide crucial information for possible future reconstruction, case analysis, and courtroom presentation.

After the crime scene has been thoroughly documented, the scene should be searched systematically. Crime scene searches involve both the surrounding ancillary areas as well as the primary target areas of the scene. A principal focus of crime scene searching is the recognition, and collection, and preservation of physical evidence. Unless potential physical evidence can be recognized and collected, there is no forensic testing that can be conducted. Searching of the areas and the scene should be carefully planned. Various crime scene search models and methods have been developed. Figure 32.3 depicts the most commonly used crime scene search methods. Special crime scene procedures should be developed for scenes involving underwater scenes, clandestine drug laboratories, fire scenes, and excavations that require extra attention.

Physical evidence located at a scene comes in different forms requiring different methods to properly recognize, collect, and preserve it. Physical evidence is what we generally perceive to be as forensic evidence, such as the homicide weapon, or spent bullet or casing. However, in any given case, any particular object may prove to be the crucial piece of physical evidence necessary to solve the case. Thus, physical evidence can best be described as any evidence that can provide useful information for investigators in solving cases. Investigators should be assigned as physical evidence collectors, and given the responsibility to collect, mark, preserve, and package the evidence found at the scene. There are many and

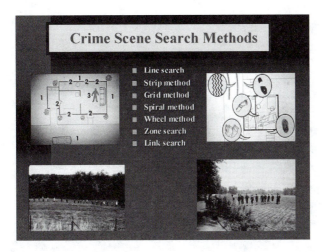

Figure 32.3 Crime scene search methods.

diverse possible types of physical evidence that can be found at a crime scene. These types of evidence generally fall into one of the five following categories.

Transient Evidence

Transient evidence is a type of evidence that is, by its very nature, temporary and can be easily changed or lost. Commonly encountered transient evidence includes odors, temperatures, color, and some biological and physiological phenomena such as lucidity or coagulation of blood evidence. This type of evidence, because it is temporary in nature, has to be documented as soon as the evidence is observed. Moreover, documentation may be the only mechanism to capture and preserve the evidentiary nature.

Conditional Evidence

Conditional evidence is generally produced by a set of actions or inactions, or an event. If conditional evidence is not observed and documented while at the crime scene, that information will also be lost forever. Examples of commonly encountered conditional evidence include lighting conditions of the scene, location and color of smoke or fire, condition of the victim's body, or precise location of specific pieces of evidence within the scene.

Pattern Evidence

There are a variety of patterns that can be found at crime scenes; most of these patterns are in the form of imprints, indentations, striations, and other markings, fractures, or depositions. The patterns commonly found at different crime scenes are blood spatter or stain patterns, glass fracture patterns, fire burn patterns, furniture position patterns, projectile trajectory patterns, track-trail patterns, clothing or article patterns, tire or skid mark patterns, *modus operandi* patterns, powder or residue patterns. Pattern analysis is a critical component in crime scene reconstruction and may be observed in a variety of different formats (see Figure 32.4).

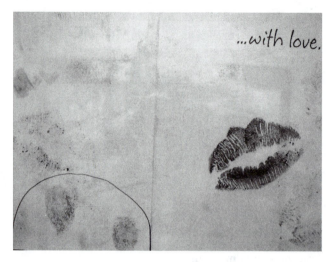

Figure 32.4 Pattern evidence may consist of various forms of imprint evidence. This photograph depicts latent fingerprints developed with ninhydrin as well as patent lip prints.

Transfer Evidence

Transfer evidence, also referred to as trace evidence, is generally produced by physical contact of persons, objects, or between persons or objects. Locard's Theory of Exchange best states this phenomenon by declaring that any time two or more surfaces come into contact with one another there is a mutual exchange of trace matter between those surfaces. Some commonly found types of transfer evidence include blood, fingerprint, hair, fiber, body fluids, soil, glass, and chemicals.

Associative Evidence

Specific items located at a crime scene or during an investigation may be used as evidence to associate a victim or suspect with a particular scene or to each other. Examples of associative evidence include a suspect's vehicle parked at the crime scene, a wallet found at the crime scene, the victim's ring, or other personal belongings of the suspect. The 4-Way Linkage Theory underscores the importance of associations (see Figure 32.5).

Information Management

For centuries, crimes have been solved traditionally through the effective gathering of investigative leads by investigators. However, since the early 1970s, many court decisions have severely constrained investigators in their use of traditional interrogation techniques. With new developments in forensic technology, the investigator has realized that information can be obtained from the witness, from the crime scene, physical evidence, and through data mining. Information can often link a suspect to a crime scene, prove or disprove an alibi, or develop investigative leads. Information can be in oral form, visual form, as written statements, documents, or electronic means. Information can be derived from individuals at the scene, forensic evidence located or remarked absent from the scene, or pattern evidence located within the scene, or through a search of the sex offender data base.

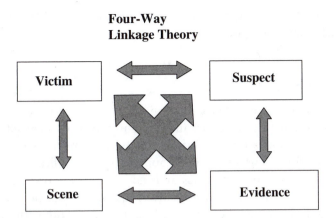

Figure 32.5 Four-way linkage theory.

The sooner the information can be recognized, analyzed, collected, and preserved, the better the chance that the case will be solved.

There are various types of information that can be used for solving crimes, as described next.

Information from Victims

Information can be obtained directly from a victim. The victims' information can originate from the victims' body, their vehicles, or their belongings. Also, discovering the victim's activity, particularly within the 24-hour period preceding the crime, can be helpful to the investigation. This comprehensive background investigation may be conducted by contact with business, family, or personal associates. An extended victim background will include an inquiry into the business and financial affairs, the victim's credit card or bank accounts, background information on family members or close associates of the victim, and habitual behavior that the victim demonstrated.

Information from Witnesses

Witnesses come from a wide variety of sources; therefore, a potential witness source should not be overlooked or ignored. However, history has shown that, all too often, individuals' perception of a particular act or event they witness by one or more of their five senses is not totally consistent with reality. Any witness that actually perceived some portion of an incident with any of these senses should be questioned in great detail. A witness's ability to relate minute details, which can only be corroborated through physical evidence, helps to bolster the credibility of that witness.

Since even under the best of circumstances crime scene processing is difficult and challenging, any information which may help illuminate the underlying facts or sequence of events should not be overlooked. The information obtained from these individuals should not determine the scope of crime scene functions. Yet, one of the objectives of the process should be to try and find physical evidence or corroborating facts, which either tends to prove or disprove a witness's statements. The following list of people describes potential witnesses that should be interviewed. This group of witnesses may have a direct knowledge about the crime scene, victim, or facts of the crime. Specifically, interview the first responding police officer, fire fighter, EMT members, family members, general public, or the informant.

Information from Suspects

Linking the suspect to the scene, the victim, or physical evidence associated with the investigation is vital to solving the case. Traditionally, police focus their efforts regarding a suspect on obtaining a confession or incriminating statements. Recent advances in behavioral science and criminology have made apparent the significance of determining a potential suspect's motives, opportunities and *modus operandi*, or method of operation patterns. Generally, the same basic investigative inquiries should be conducted into the suspect's background. However, there may be legal restraints with gathering or searching for some of the suspect related information. The 24-hour activities of the suspect are critical and need to be thoroughly studied. Moreover, a time line and comprehensive financial analysis is often beneficial. Thereafter, a more extensive background can be conducted focusing on information that would associate the suspect with the victim, or help in establishing a reasonable motive and opportunity. Also, it may be beneficial merely to place the suspect at the scene of the crime or in contact with a piece of significant physical evidence.

Behavioral science and criminal profiling research and analysis have identified specific general patterns or methods of operation that can be deduced from a systematic and thorough crime scene analysis. Once a particular *modus operandi* pattern has been identified, generalizations can be established that may help identify a limited class of likely suspects. Moreover, in cases involving serial criminals, identification of these patterns may help link separate cases and associate the known previous behavior of a suspect to those cases. Typical cases where this type of analysis is beneficial are those cases involving serial killers, serial rapists, or serial arsonists. However, caution should be exercised to avoid placing too much emphasis on behavioral profiling as that may result in a tunnel vision or a misguided investigation. In addition to behavioral science based profiling, ancestry based DNA profiling is being developed. This type of DNA profiling will provide investigators with the probabilities that a suspect belongs to a particular racial or ethnic group. As with any form of investigative information, *modus operandi* patterns should be evaluated in conjunction with other investigative information and physical evidence.

Information from Databases

Tremendous advances in forensic science and recent implementation of artificial intelligence and forensic databases have also expanded the potential pool of information available from a suspect. Records pertaining to an individual's identification vary in the degree of individualization and in the accessibility to law enforcement. With the advent of forensic databases, forensic laboratories are employing artificial intelligence methods that can actually identify potential suspects and link previously unconnected cases.

Currently, these databases include CODIS-DNA database, fingerprints — Automated Fingerprint Identification System (AFIS), and bullet and cartridge casing characteristics (NIBIN) database systems. Each of these systems has accomplished significant successes and helped to solve no-suspect homicides, sexual assaults, burglaries, and other criminal offenses. This ability to search no-suspect cases against offender databases has greatly enhanced the value of forensic analysis in a preponderance of criminal investigations. Some of these databases are created and maintained locally, but many jurisdictions are in the process of linking their databases to national databases, thus greatly expanding the size of the database.

DNA Databases

Some of the most individualizing records are DNA profiles obtained within a sexual offender or felony database. With the discriminating power of current DNA systems such as the short-tandom repeat (STR) multiplex system, the identification ability or discrimination index is extremely high.

Many state and federal jurisdictions have enacted legislation that allows for the collection of known blood samples from all individuals convicted of a felony. These blood samples are then analyzed, and DNA profiles are obtained and stored within an offender database. No-suspect cases in which suspect DNA profiles have been obtained can then be compared to the offender database profiles. This technology has solved many no-suspect cases and identified several serial rapists. Nationwide, there are more than 20,000 investigations that have been aided by DNA database hits. Yet the potential value for these databases has just been realized since most jurisdictions have only implemented their offender databases within the past five years, and the relative size of these databases compared to all known offenders is still small. As these backlogs get cleared, the solve rates associated with these expanded DNA databases are likely to be astonishing.

In an effort to balance the privacy interests and concerns associated with an individual's DNA profile, many American states have implemented stringent regulations concerning the accessibility to and use of the database profiles. Moreover, in a general sense, the type of data generated and stored in a DNA offender database will not yield prejudicial or personal information about the donor. As technologies continue to expand and become increasingly more common and accepted, the use of individualizing records, such as DNA databases, will likely expand.

Fingerprint Databases

Automated fingerprint identification systems have been used to solve crimes and associate unknown fingerprints to an individual for many years. The success of these systems is mainly due to large databases. Many states have fingerprint files in the million range, including known inked fingerprint impressions from persons arrested for a wide variety of offenses, military and government employees, special license applicants, and other various sources. Many of these individual fingerprint databases are connected to adjacent or nationally linked databases.

Once an individual's known fingerprints are entered into the automated fingerprint system, those fingerprints can be checked against a file of unidentified latent prints associated with a criminal investigation, or checked against the known file to determine whether the person is using an alias or is wanted for a crime under a different name.

New developments include the implementation of the IAFIS system. IAFIS has much key advancement including higher resolution and a mechanism to store and search a palm print database. Laboratories using IAFIS have developed hits from prints that had been previously entered into AFIS, but no identification was made until the higher resolution of the newer system made the match possible. The implementation of a palm print database will be beneficial in that a significant number of latent prints submitted for examination are from palm surfaces, not the tips of fingers, which were the source of traditional database systems. As new technology and better trained crime scene personnel become more prevalent, more fingerprint evidence will be located and recovered from crime scenes, thus further enhancing the success rate of automated fingerprint identification systems.

Casing and Bullet Databases

Violent crime involving the use of weapons, particularly drug and gang related offenses, prompted the introduction of database systems that can store individual characteristics associated with firearms evidence and help solve many of these violent crimes. With many of the all-too-common drive-by shootings or street crimes associated with the illegal drugs trade, the only available evidence has been a few cartridge cases recovered from the shooting scene. Until the advent of these databases, this evidence was of little value unless the police were able to recover the weapon used in the shooting. Currently, these databases can be used to associate cartridge cases from one crime scene to another, or associate those cases to a particular gun from which a known cartridge case sample has been obtained. Known databases consist of test shots obtained from any weapon submitted to the firearms unit of the laboratory as well as from guns seized by police and ordered to be destroyed.

Following the success of databases that stored individualizing information on casings, new databases are being developed to store and search individualizing characteristics identified on the bullets themselves. This technology is helpful in those instances where the casings were not recovered and a bullet was recovered and determined to be identifiable.

Information from Records

Records and data available for investigative purposes have grown exponentially during the past decade. Many of the traditional law enforcement databases have been expanded while entirely new databases have been developed and implemented. In addition, our computer-dominated culture has spawned an entire network of personal databases that often provide invaluable information to investigators. A vast majority of that data is readily available as public records or can be located relatively easily through Internet domain searches. The following are some of the most commonly searched records:

A. NCIC criminal record
B. Firearms sale and transfer records
C. Judicial and correction records
D. Motor vehicle related file
E. Financial records
F. Social security and related records

Technology Management

Advances in technology mandate the continual acquisition of new and often expensive equipment and supplies to maximize the potential for effective crime scene processing.

The amount of resources allocated to purchasing and upgrading equipment should be appropriate for the variety and volumes of crime scenes encountered by that unit.

Crime scene supervisors must take a detailed inventory of their unit's equipment, keep abreast of available technologies, and be aware of their unit's limitations due to a lack of equipment. In addition, personnel must be provided with adequate training to properly use any new technology or equipment. The following categories of equipment are essential:

- *Support Vehicles* — Commonly, customized cube vans specifically constructed for crime scene purposes.
- *Communications* — Two-way radio with channels for the police jurisdictions serviced by the crime scene unit, cellular telephones, fax machines, and laptop computers with modem. Currently, tele-forensics and telecommunication technologies are being developed. Tele-forensics involves the use of portable instrumentation and technology that can transmit data or digitized images directly to a laboratory for further analysis, while the crime scene processing is being conducted.
- *Tools and Search Equipment* — Hand tools, yard/garden tools, power saws and drills, auxiliary lighting and generators, forensic light sources, metal detectors.
- *Specialized Crime Scene Kits* — For example, GSR collection kits, latent print kits, trajectory reconstruction dowels and accessories, casting kits for tool marks and footwear impressions.
- *Chemicals and Reagents* — For example, Bloody print enhancement reagent, presumptive blood testing reagents, latent print chemical developers.
- *Evidence Packaging:* Materials and related forms.
- *Portable Instrumentation* — For example, portable lasers, portable gas chromatography, ground-penetrating radar, night vision equipment.

Management of Logistics

Logistical concerns must be properly addressed or managed to ensure that the maximum information possible is obtained from the crime scene and during the critical first 24 hour of a major investigation. Organization and efficient allocation of resources must be established early in the investigation. The following elements should be established (see Figure 32.6).

Command Posts

First responders and their supervisors must do everything possible to secure the integrity of the crime scene. However, to maintain the integrity, crime scene managers need to establish outer perimeters and a command post. A command post has to be outside the perimeters of the working crime scene, where evidence may be located and investigators can have the space to document the scene properly. However, the command post must be so located as to be convenient enough to the crime scene to logistically support the crime scene personnel as well as provide a center for accurately and quickly disseminating relevant information to and from the crime scene. During the initial portion of the investigation, when crime scene processing is a primary function, a mobile or temporary command post is ideal as it can be located near the outer perimeter of the scene. If possible, this command post should not be at the same vehicle or structure where the crime scene

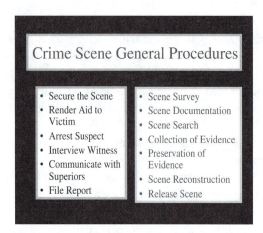

Figure 32.6 Crime scene general procedures.

processing equipment and personnel are located as the command post functions may interfere with the crime scene functions.

As the investigation evolves and crime scene functions diminish, a longer term command post may be established. This command post should focus on supporting the investigative personnel and provide a facility to establish a task force office or long-term investigative center.

Media Relations

Care should be taken to restrict access to the command post and identify a separate area for members of the public or media to gather. It is always beneficial to establish a specific media area and have a department public information officer available to the media. Whether we like it or not, the media will exercise their right to gather information and publicize the event. It is to our advantage to control this portion of a major criminal investigation. If the public information officer is constantly updated and portrays an honest and timely dissemination of information to the media, the vast majority of media representatives will gladly comply with reasonable requests to protect the scene or sensitive investigative information. The media area should be close enough to the actual crime scene so that they can obtain some file footage for their newscasts. Again, by controlling the placement of that location we can carefully protect sensitive information or views from the cameras. Periodic news conferences should be scheduled and conducted by PIO officers during major case investigations.

Interagency Liaison

Even in large agencies with significant resources, there are occasions when an investigation will involve multiple agencies. This situation may arise when crimes occur in more than one jurisdiction, or when the investigating jurisdiction realizes that it lacks the necessary resources, personnel, expertise, or equipment. In either scenario, the key to a successful investigation is complete cooperation and a team approach to solving the case. One way to build up the team spirit is by establishing a formal liaison between the involved agencies.

An effective liaison relationship involves a commitment by all involved agencies to cooperate and share information and resources readily. Despite cooperation, it is necessary to establish the lead investigating agency and any chain of command within the individual agencies. The biggest obstacle often involves inadequate communication between the agency members. By assigning a liaison officer or staff, a system can be established to funnel all information through the liaison in a timely manner. It is the responsibility of the liaison personnel to keep all interested parties informed of developments, problems, and needs. If this model is followed, the probability of success will be greater and the future interagency cooperation and relations will also be enhanced.

Resource Allocation

Recent advances in forensic science and crime scene technology are astounding. When all of these innovative resources are properly integrated into a criminal investigation, in a timely manner, the probability for success is high. Unfortunately, very few jurisdictions have the individual financial resources or demands to justify possessing the full array of these resources. In addition, many of these new high-tech methods or instruments require operation by specially trained personnel. Thus, it is often more beneficial for a law enforcement agency to identify the spectrum of available services within their jurisdictions and establish mutual exchange or support agreements with agencies that offer needed services. They will access the availability of newer crime-solving technology without needlessly depleting their personnel or fiscal resources.

Technology/Procedures

Merely obtaining each of the aforementioned four key components is not enough to ensure that the crime scene is managed to its utmost potential. Developing organized and comprehensive procedures is imperative to any type of crime scene management system, from the most basic to a highly technical and innovative model. To a great extent, this is an area lacking in many jurisdictions tasked with crime scene processing. Most likely, the lack of a comprehensive written crime scene management procedure can be attributed to one of the following reasons.

First, a particular agency may feel that it has survived thus far relying on the expertise and guidance of a select few individuals to individually access the crime scenes. Second, those specific crime scene managers may be the dwindling few who have not endured the public disgrace and reality of a failed criminal investigation due largely to an ineffective crime scene process. Third, the importance of crime scenes in the overall success of a criminal investigation has not been identified; thus, the managers do not know what they do not know.

Some agencies have the benefit of a few key crime scene investigators or technicians who have accumulated sufficient training and years of experience. Despite their reliance on written guidelines or procedures, these investigators frequently perform professional and high-quality functions based on their individual expertise. Yet even these most experienced individuals risk the possibility of making a crucial mistake or omission because they fail to realize the value of a systematic approach to crime scene processing. Moreover, these local crime scene experts can fail to realize the need to pass on their expertise and help train newly developing personnel.

In the light of the on-the-job aspect of acquiring crime scene expertise, it is too late to adequately prepare a new crime scene investigator once the experienced personnel have retired. However, if these experienced crime scene investigators and their managers commit to preparing some form of written procedures, many of these potential problems can be minimized or averted altogether.

How many times must we, as professionals in the criminal investigative and forensic science community, live with the daily public scrutiny of a high profile criminal case that remains unsolved or unable to be successfully tried in court due mainly to inept or insufficient evidence and information obtained from the crime scene? Problems with many high profile cases from the past, such as Sacco or Venzetti, the John F. Kennedy assassination, were equally aggravating but far easier to accept. Clearly, investigators in those days did not have even a fraction of the technological and scientific advances available to today's crime scene personnel. Yet despite our tremendous gains, we continue to see these basic critical errors occurring at the initial crime scene. Vincent Foster, O.J. Simpson, and Jon Bonnet Ramsey are but a few examples.

Every agency must accept the reality that is also susceptible to these problems and embarrassments unless it adopts a philosophy that recognizes and commits to the importance of quality crime scene management. No longer will good old-fashioned police work and a confession be the necessary and complete ingredients for the resolution of a case in today's physical evidence oriented criminal trials. Regardless of the reasons why, the reality in almost every modern legal system is that physical evidence, forensic examination of that evidence, and the crime scene analysis related to that evidence are integral and desired components of the process.

Simply, juries want to hear about and see demonstrative evidence detailing the crime scene and evidence located at that scene. Thus, an overall criminal investigation plan must incorporate a crime scene management model that is realistic for the available resources, and yet is effective.

Selecting an Appropriate Crime Scene Investigation Model

There are many major crime scene investigative models available to choose as the backbone of a criminal investigative approach that recognizes the value of crime scenes in criminal investigations. Each model has its own positive and negative attributes. Selecting the appropriate model requires a careful consideration of many key factors, which include (1) available resources, (2) manpower and qualifications, (3) types of crimes, (4) the crime rate and need for crime scene services, (5) degree of scientific and legal system requirements of the jurisdiction, and (6) support services available for analysis of the gathered physical evidence. Ultimately, each jurisdiction should evaluate these criteria against the different models and select the one model or combination of several models that best suits the needs of the criminal justice system in their community.

Traditional

A traditional approach to crime scene management uses regular patrol officers and detectives from local detective units as the primary crime scene personnel. This model is beneficial in jurisdictions where there are limited law enforcement resources and the demand for crime scene processing functions is relatively low. Also, if alternative models are not available, this becomes a default model, as police services will always need to be in place. Some of the negative features of this model include the use of personnel with limited scientific training and technical experience, and minimal crime scene experience. Moreover, the time commitment needed for effective crime scene processing may conflict with daily patrol, investigative and public service functions.

Crime Scene Technicians

This concept uses full-time crime scene, civilian personnel. This system allows for continuity and specialization. Often, these personnel have special scientific and technical training. However, sometimes this category of crime scene personnel has minimal investigative experience.

General investigative experience is invaluable for assisting a crime scene processor in identifying and recognizing relevant evidence for a particular crime or *modus operandi*. Often, these personnel lack a global perspective to the criminal investigation, for which their role as crime scene technicians is essential.

Scene-of-the-Crime/Major Crime Squad

Scene-of-the-crime units comprise sworn officers specifically assigned to full-time crime scene processing and investigation duties. Unlike members of a traditional approach, these individuals can focus only on criminal investigations and on crime scenes. This allows for increased experience, less distractions, and an opportunity to obtain supplemental scientific and technical training.

One major drawback is the very nature of most police agencies that will transfer personnel in and out of the unit due to promotions or shifting agency priorities. Although they often possess more scientific and technical skills than do most traditional personnel, they still lack many of the skills associated with the recent technological advances in forensic science. Also, using sworn personnel to conduct the technical functions of crime scene processing may deplete resources needed to actually conduct the criminal investigation.

Laboratory Based Crime Scene Scientists

Laboratory scientists usually have superior technical and scientific skills over all the previous models. These individuals, by nature of their job and exposure to the forensic academic and research communities, will often have to stay more up to date with the changes that may affect crime scene technology. This model is also advantageous in that the crime scene field and laboratory examination functions are closely integrated. Some negative features of this model include personnel who have no investigative experience and are thus prone to problems with evidence recognition. Some laboratory scientists lack motivation for crime scene work due to inadequate training and resources; therefore, they respond to only a select few types of crime scenes and are thus often somewhat limited in their experience. Finally, assigning laboratory scientists to time consuming field assignments will deplete laboratory resources needed to analyze the seized physical evidence.

Collaborative Team Approach

In most cases, this is the best overall crime scene investigative model. However, this model requires extensive resources in diverse areas: police, laboratory, crime scene personnel, medical examiners, and prosecuting authorities. Further, the success of this model mandates a comprehensive crime scene procedure to be implemented and followed by each participating member of the cohesive team. In this model, advanced scientific, technical and investigative resources are available.

Demanding crime scene responsibilities are shared among the team components, and this team approach enhances the future abilities of each individual member. As with other models, there are some obstacles to overcome. The team must work together to develop and integrate a plan for crime scene processing and the recognition, collection, and preservation of physical evidence. This model requires cooperation, not competition.

The Roles of Public Attorneys in the Practice of Forensic Science

33

LAURA ANN DITKA AND MICHAEL J. MACHEN

The Role of the Prosecutor in the Practice of Forensic Science

A prosecutor's job is to prosecute those who have committed a wrong against society, a crime. To that end, a prosecutor has to determine three things:

1. Whether a crime has been committed
2. Who committed the crime
3. How the crime happened

Television and movies lead us to believe that the prosecutor must prove "why" a crime occurred, which is most often unimportant to the prosecution of a crime. Forensic science is essential to a prosecution because it answers the questions of whether there was a crime, how it happened, who did it and, in some cases, why the crime occurred.

Determination of Criminal Occurrence

It seems prudent to begin our discussion with how forensic science helps a prosecutor determine whether a crime occurred. This most basic question can often not be answered without the aid of a forensic scientist. Let us examine some everyday examples and review how forensic science is absolutely essential in the determination of whether or not a crime occurred.

On a rainy night, a police officer follows a vehicle down a highway and notices that the vehicle continues to cross the lane line and weave onto the berm. The officer effectuates a stop of the vehicle, approaches the driver, and then observes a woman who is pale, sweaty, and somewhat confused. The officer does not notice any odor of alcohol. The area inside the vehicle appears to be in order. The officer asks the woman why she is swerving and she responds she does not feel well and is trying to get home to bed. The officer believes she is under the influence of a drug or narcotic.

How do we know whether a crime has occurred? How do we know whether this is just an unfortunate case of a woman with the flu, or a woman coming down from a heroin or OxyContin high?

The officer will make an arrest and take the woman to a local hospital for drawing out blood which will then be sent to a forensic laboratory, where a toxicologist will test it to determine whether there are any drugs in her blood. The scientist can also determine what drugs are present and whether they are above or below the therapeutic level — the level expected on taking a prescribed drug at the recommended medical dosage.

In our example, if the woman tests positive to opiates, then a crime has been committed because she was operating her vehicle under the influence of a narcotic. If the blood tests reveal a drug that is typically prescribed (and, in fact, has been prescribed for her) and it is within the therapeutic range, then the officer would determine that she may have been careless but did not violate the more serious law of driving under the influence after imbibing. If the toxicologist finds nothing in the woman's blood, then the officer knows she is suffering from the flu and that a crime has not been committed.

In another common circumstance, police are patrolling an area known for frequent drug sales and drug use. After observing what they believe to be a drug sale, they chase and catch the person they believe to be the seller. A search of the suspect reveals some money and a bag of pills the suspect claims are health supplements. Without forensic science, the police and prosecutor cannot proceed in the prosecution of the suspect for either the possession or the sale of drugs. The seized pills are sent to a forensic laboratory, where they are tested for their contents. If the pills are controlled substances, which one cannot possess without a prescription, then a crime is thought to have been committed. If the pills are a nutritional supplement, the conclusion is that no crime has been committed.

Let us now turn to a more serious case. Two police officers are called to a home where the boyfriend finds his woman in a pool of blood. The woman is incoherent and, though covered in blood, shows no visible signs of injury. The police call for paramedics to take the woman to the hospital. They then search the woman's home for answers as to what had happened to her and enter the bathroom and find a newborn infant in the tub — covered in blood and lifeless. The police again call paramedics, and the infant is taken to the hospital, where he or she is pronounced dead. At the hospital, it is also discovered that the woman, whose health is fine, has recently given birth to a full-term infant. When questioned about these findings, the woman says that she was unaware that she was pregnant until she went into labor and states that before she could seek help, the child was beginning to be born. The woman recounts that the child was stillborn in the bathtub and that she was so drained after the birth that she did not call for help.

The infant's body is sent for an autopsy, where forensic science experts will once again determine whether a crime has occurred. The forensic pathologist will observe everything about the body. If the pathologist finds that the infant was alive (e.g., if there is air in the child's lungs), then a crime has been committed and the woman is lying. Further tests and observations may determine how the infant died, which brings us to our next consideration. However, without the aid of forensic science in any of these situations, it would be impossible for the prosecutor to determine the answer to the most basic question: Was a crime committed?

Determination of Criminal Mechanism

The next question the prosecutor will attempt to answer is: "How was the crime committed?" A judge or jury will not accept a bold allegation that a crime has occurred without the details of what the crime was and how it was carried out. Here, too, forensic science can provide the answers.

If we return to the previous example of the deceased infant, we tread into an area where forensic science is most important — murder. If we are to believe the old saying, "dead men tell no tales"; but in the area of forensic pathology, nothing could be further from the truth. A forensic pathologist can get a dead man to tell the tale of his own death, to refute the testimony of witnesses, and, as we will see in our next section, even to point out the killer.

A prosecutor always uses evidence from witnesses, but witnesses can be unreliable. They operate under a number of motivations, including fear, hatred, regret, self-preservation, and simple human nature. Science, fortunately, does not suffer the same shortcomings, and a good forensic scientist can objectively tell the tale of a crime.

In our previous example of the deceased infant, a forensic pathologist determined that the infant was born alive. Now, he must determine the cause of death. The forensic pathologist will review all hospital records and will determine whether the child had a medical condition that would have led to immediate death. If no such evidence exists, then other causes of death must be examined. In our example, upon examining the body, the forensic pathologist observes retinal hemorrhages, bleeding in the brain, and a clear impact on the back of the head. The conclusion could be drawn that upon birth, this child was shaken and thrown into the tub, causing a contusion of the brain that resulted in death. The forensic pathologist would then find the cause of death to be blunt force trauma. The child's death would now be explained; through science, the infant could tell the tale of his death. The prosecution would now have the facts to refute the mother's story that the child was born alive, facts that could be taken to a jury or a judge. The initial information, without the benefit of forensic science, would simply not be enough to prove a case.

In another example, a shooting occurs as a result of a robbery. The police arrive to find a body and some witnesses. One witness recounts an argument between the victim and another man and the others, say that after hearing shouting, they heard shots and came to the street to find the victim. Some of the witnesses recognized the voice of the person with whom the victim was arguing. The police find this person, who denies all involvement in the crime. They then obtain a warrant to seize the gun, which they take to a forensic science laboratory, where it is test fired and the bullets compared to those found in the victim. The forensic scientist finds a match. The police arrest the suspect, and now the suspect changes his story to self-defense — he shot the victim because the victim was going to shoot him. Once again, a forensic pathologist helps a dead man tell his tale. The forensic pathologist can also observe that these were not contact wounds at close range. The dead man is now telling the tale of his death through forensic science. An examination of the scientific facts shows us that the victim was not attacking his assailant but was running away and was shot in the back. This was not self-defense, but murder.

There are countless other examples of how forensic science gives us the mechanism of the crime — how the crime occurred. A prosecution could not go forward without this evidence.

Suspect Identification

Finally, forensic science often tells us who has commited a crime. In many instances, prosecutors have a wealth of information, including the fact that a crime has been committed and how it happened, but might not know who committed it. For years, forensic science has been the front-runner in the area of suspect identification, where it continues to expand its scientific ability today through the growing application and constant refinement of DNA testing.

In one last example, a couple goes on vacation. When they return home, they find their house burglarized. The police are unable to secure any witness testimony to aid them in finding the identity of the thief, but they do find fingerprints on the window that was pried open to allow entry into the home. The evidence is taken to the crime laboratory, and the prints are identified by running them through a database and a match is made.

As this example illustrates, the solving, clearing, and prosecution of criminal cases would be a far more difficult task if not for the continuing advances in forensic science. The use of tested and reliable scientific methods allows prosecutors to explain the unexplainable and imagine the unimaginable. Forensic science provides answers for the important questions of how, when, and where a crime occurred. It is fortunate for lawyers, perhaps, that the "why" cannot always be explained, leaving at least that task to them.

The Role of the Public Defender in the Practice of Forensic Science

The Responsibility and Structure of a Public Defender's Office

In my jurisdiction of Allegheny County, Pennsylvania — as elsewhere — the Office of the Public Defender (hereafter referred to as the Office) is responsible for furnishing competent and effective legal counsel to any person who lacks sufficient funds to hire private counsel. The Office uses the Federal Poverty Guidelines to determine eligibility for our legal services. If an individual qualifies, legal counsel will be provided in any proceeding "where representation is constitutionally required."[1] This is known as the "Public Defender Act," which details that legal counsel be provided in the following matters:

- Juvenile delinquency
- Pretrial identification (i.e., line-up procedures)
- Preliminary hearings where the commonwealth is required to present a *prima-facie* case against the client
- State *habeas corpus* proceedings
- Trial
- Superior Court appeals, which include those appeals where the public defender is appointed by the Court of Common Pleas
- Supreme Court appeals
- Postconviction hearings at the trial and appellate levels
- Criminal extradition hearings
- Probation and parole hearings
- Involuntary commitment under the Mental Health Procedures Act
- Indirect criminal contempt

The Office is divided into five divisions — Intake/Investigations, Pretrial, Adult Trial, Juvenile Trial, and Appeals — each with its own unique set of responsibilities.

Intake/Investigations Division

The responsibilities of this division include initial interviews with clients for the purpose of gathering facts, which initiates the client files. In addition, investigators from this division interview witnesses, take crime scene photographs, obtain records, and serve subpoenas.

Pretrial Division

This division represents clients in preliminary hearings, for most clients their first — and hopefully only — court appearance. The Office averages 18,000 preliminary hearings a year, with approximately 50% of them settled at that level. This is the first "critical stage" where counsel is mandated.

Adult Trial Division

Through this division, the Office represents adult clients in anywhere between 9,000 and 10,000 trials per year, ranging from misdemeanor simple assault to homicide.

Juvenile Trial Division

This division represents children under the age of 18 who are charged with delinquency proceedings, at both the adjudication and disposition phases of the proceedings. The counseling continues in the postadjudication phase to include violation of probations, commitment reviews, probation hearings, and detention hearings.

Appellate Division

This division handles appeals, along with many cases referred by private attorneys due to their clients' exhaustion of funds or incarceration. The appellate work is demanding and, due to time limits set by the Superior Court and Supreme Court, extremely time sensitive.

Forensic Science in the Public Defender's Office

The Public Defender's Office has seen an explosion in forensic expert consultations in recent years. A simplistic yet accurate statement is that the high visibility of forensic themes in television and the movies is most probably the basis for the increase.[2]

Television shows and movies have found that forensic themes draw the masses and keep them coming back for more. *CSI* and *Forensic Files* consistently rank among the top 10 television shows, and the trend continues to spread with *CSI* "spin-offs" such as *CSI: Miami*, *CSI: New York*, to mention such shows as *Cold Case*, *Without a Trace*, *NCIS*, and *Medical Investigation*. These shows do not escape the attention of clients of this office.

Increasingly, these clients want forensic experts to find the "smoking gun." But they often make the mistake of viewing forensic experts as detectives, which they are not. They are neutral to prosecution and defense. They perform analytical tests, interpret results, and render opinions that benefit either the prosecution or defense. There is no way to skew the results.

This office utilizes forensic science in the following types of applications: DNA testing, bite-mark analysis, psychiatric evaluation, identification of saliva, determination of the direction of gunshot fire, toxicology, engineering (accident reconstruction), and fingerprint analysis.

A Case Study in Forensic Consultation

A good example of how forensic science is used by a public defender's office would be the application of forensic toxicology to estimate a client's blood alcohol content, or BAC. "A forensic toxicologist is a scientist with basic training and education in chemistry, pathophysiology, and pharmacology, and frequently the holder of a graduate degree."[3] (p. 635) In this example, the Office needs a forensic toxicologist to testify that its client was so highly intoxicated that he was overwhelmed "to the point of losing faculties and sensibilities that he/she could not form specific intent to kill."[4] This testimony, if accepted by the trier of fact, would reduce a charge of first degree murder to one of third degree murder.[5]

The two-part process is, first, an analytical one and second, a matter of expert opinion. The analytical process is initiated with the Office providing the following data:

- The client's weight, which may have fluctuated since the time of arrest, so the earliest measure of a client's weight is crucial
- A detail of foods consumed, including specific names of foods, for example, a Burger King Whopper and a small Coke, not a burger and a drink
- A timeline documenting when the client began and finished drinking
- The specific amounts (number of drinks) and proofs of the alcohol consumed, along with the order of consumption
- The client's history of alcohol abuse and treatments

These factors are plugged into the Widmark Formula,[3] (p. 637) which was developed to estimate BAC levels. A derivative of this formula[3] (p. 637) — with "BW" connoting body weight, A the percent concentration of alcoholic beverage, and B, the number of ounces of alcoholic beverage consumed — is as follows:

A. $150/BW + A/50 \times B \times 0.025\% = $ Maximum BAC
B. Dissipation $=$ number of hours after consuming beverage $\times$ elimination rate
C. Maximum BAC $-$ Dissipation $=$ BAC

A forensic toxicologist also frequently employs a computer program based upon the Widmark Formula as a check and balance.[2] This BAC estimate is verbally forwarded to the public defender, who will decide whether it is a viable defense tactic. Based on this information, the public defender will ask the forensic toxicologist to render an opinion as follows: "That the alcohol's effect produced central nervous system depression, decreased visual acuity, decreased peripheral vision, [rendered] poor judgment, decreased sensory motor coordination to the degree that the client lost faculties and sensibility that he/she could not form a specific intent to kill."[3,4]

It is important to note that a forensic toxicologist rendering this opinion would have both the knowledge of, and experience with the pharmacology of alcohol necessary to do so. If he forensic toxicologist answers unequivocally "yes," then the preparation for his/her estimony must begin.

The need for forensic experts will not subside once the television shows are cancelled. The trier of fact, the defense lawyer, and, most importantly, the client will continue to demand their assistance — the only caveat being the economic impact on the Office.

Notes

1. Public Defender Act.
2. Fochtman F.W., Ph.D., DABT, DABFT, Director, Allegheny County Crime Laboratories.
3. Legal Medicine, 6th ed.
4. *Commonwealth of Pennsylvania v. Lytle.*
5. 18 PA CSA §308.

Forensic and Legal Nursing 34

L. KATHLEEN SEKULA AND ANN WOLBERT BURGESS

Overview and History of Forensic Nursing

Forensic nursing is one of the newest specialty areas in nursing practice. Although nurses have long performed duties that interface with the legal community, it is only in recent years that leaders in the nursing community have formally identified a specialty area of practice in nursing that brings together components of nursing, health care, and law to serve victims (or perpetrators) of violence who present in a health care setting. As defined by the International Association of Forensic Nurses (IAFN):

> *Forensic nursing* involves the application of the forensic aspects of health care combined with the biopsychosocial education of the registered nurse in the scientific investigation and treatment of trauma and/or death related medical-legal issues   (1997, p. 30).

By the very nature of the profession, nurses have long provided care for victims and perpetrators in settings such as emergency departments, trauma settings, and outpatient clinics. However, the focus of the nurse's role in these settings has traditionally been primarily on meeting physical and psychological needs. The nurse was expected to assess for injury but not to have knowledge of assessment strategies for identifying victims of violence, evidence collection, or preservation of evidence techniques. The American Public Health Association's 1984 paper identifying violence as a major public health issue, as well as the 1985 Surgeon General's Workshop on Violence and Public Health, which focused on sexual and physical assault, stimulated the health care community to begin to develop protocols to address issues of violence as they relate to care of victims (Cammuso et al., 2001).

Much progress has been made in public health and medicine since the United States first embarked on the national planning process for the Healthy People initiative in 1979, resulting in the publication: *Healthy People: The Surgeon General's Report on Health Promotion and Disease Prevention. Healthy People 2000* followed in 1990. *Healthy People 2010* represents the third time that the U.S. Department of Health and Human Services (HHS) has identified 10-year health objectives for the nation.

Two major goals in *Healthy People 2010* reflect the nation's changing demographics. The first goal, which addresses the fact that we are growing older as a nation, is focused on increasing the quality and years of healthy life. The second goal, which addresses the diversity of our population, is focused on eliminating health disparities. And, for the first time, a set of "leading health indicators" provides a framework to assist individuals and communities in targeting actions to improve health. These indicators also help communities track the success of these actions. *Healthy People 2010* identifies 467 objectives in 28 focus areas. Focus Area 15 addresses injury and violence prevention, with objectives 15–32 through 15–39 specifically targeting violence and abuse prevention (Services, 2000). The goal of Focus Area 15 is to reduce injuries, disabilities and deaths due to unintentional injuries and violence (Table 34.1).

Forensic, a word derived from the Latin word "forensis" that refers to a forum wherein legal disputes were argued and settled, is defined as "belonging to courts of justice" (Black, 1990). "Forensics" encompasses legal issues of debate and discourse as these issues help to address and settle approaches to the judicial management of criminal behavior (Burrow, 1998). Forensic medicine refers to that science which teaches the application of every branch of medical knowledge to the purpose of law; hence, its limits are, on the one hand, the requirements of the law, and, on the other, the entire range of medicine (Black, 1990). The term *forensic* has most often been associated with death or murder because, until recent years, forensic pathology and death investigation were the most recognized areas of forensic work.

Forensic nursing is then, an area of health care in which nurses work with patients who are, at the same time, either victims or perpetrators of criminal acts (Sekula et al., 2001). Forensic practice involves the application of nursing science as it relates to legal proceedings or courts of law. In response to violence in society and the need to care for both victims of violence and perpetrators of violence, the specialty of forensic nursing focuses on specialized care of both victims and perpetrators. Forensic nurses may practice in clinical settings as well as in community settings in roles in which they focus on identification of victims and the collection of evidence from living victims (patients) or perpetrators. Forensic nursing practice has developed in direct response to the increase in criminal and interpersonal violence in society (Lynch, 1995a).

There is an urgent need for well-trained health-care professionals to recognize, assess, evaluate, and treat victims of violence, as well as the perpetrators of violence. The Joint Commission on Accreditation of Health Care Organizations (JCAHCO) first began to recommend screening for family violence in hospitals and clinics in 1992. In 1998, the Centers for Disease Control and Prevention (CDC) supported efforts to improve violence

Table 34.1

Healthy People 2010 — Focus Area 15 — injury and violence prevention

15–32. Reduce homicides
15–33. Reduce maltreatment and maltreatment fatalities of children
15–34. Reduce the rate of physical assault by current or former intimate partners
15–35. Reduce the annual rate of rape or attempted rape
15–36. Reduce sexual assault other than rape
15–37. Reduce physical assaults
15–38. Reduce physical fighting among adolescents
15–39. Reduce weapon carrying by adolescents on school property

screening and issued the publication *Intimate Partner Violence and Sexual Assault: A Guide to Training Materials and Programs for Health Care Providers*. JCAHO now requires that policies and procedures for family violence screening in hospitals and clinics be utilized in all health care settings (Initiative, 2003).

Several nursing organizations have published position statements on violence as it occurs within the nursing practice area, including the American Nurses' Association (1991) and the Association of Emergency Nurses (1996).

In response to an increase in violence within all of society, and specifically an increase in violence against women, the American Nurses' Association (ANA) strengthened its 1991 position statement in 2000 to address this specific issue. The statement stresses that violence against women is pervasive and cuts across all ethnic, racial, religious, and socioeconomic groups. However, there appear to be differences in the rates of violence experienced by race. American Indian and Alaskan natives report significantly higher rates, whereas Asian and Pacific Islander women report very low rates.

- The rate of domestic violence suffered by black women is 50% higher than for white women
- The poorer you are, the higher the rate of domestic violence
- Slightly more than half the women victims of domestic violence live in households with children under 12

The ANA supports:

- Universal, routine assessment and documentation of abuse for all women in any health care facility or community setting
- Principles of intervention and care that include partnership between the clinician and the victim, assurance of confidentiality, culturally sensitive care, and problem solving within a framework of choice and safety planning
- Education of all nurses and health care providers in the skills necessary for detection, prevention, or initial intervention in situations of violence against women
- Inclusion of content related to violence against women in all undergraduate nursing curricula
- Targeted assessment of women at increased risk of abuse including pregnant women and women presenting in emergency rooms or outpatient settings
- Development of coordinated community systems to address abuse which include an interdisciplinary approach and the voice of the women survivors of violence
- Education of all women as to the cycle of violence, the potential for homicide, and community resources for primary, secondary, and tertiary prevention and care
- Education of school age children and adolescents in public schools about building relationships without violence and community resources available for help
- Research on violence against women, including the development and evaluation of nursing models for preventive assessment, intervention, and treatment for abused women, their children, and perpetrators of violence
- Expanded education and use of Sexual Assault Nurse Examiners (SANE)

Guidelines for Practice

The focus on forensic nursing as a specialty area brings with it the demand for clarification of roles, educational requirements, certification requirements, standards of practice and research initiatives. Levels of entry into forensic practice vary by educational preparation and certification. Nurses who have the RN licensure, prepared at the associate degree, diploma, or baccalaureate levels, may practice in various settings in forensic roles and advance their practice through continuing education, specialty courses, and mentorship experiences. Nurses with forensic educational preparation at the master's and Ph.D. levels bring a different standard of practice. Practice guidelines determine the scope of practice. Standards set forth by the professional nursing association serve as the guidelines for what is expected of a nurse in any given situation. Therefore, forensic nurses must be familiar with the ANA general standards of practice for all nurses (ANA, 1991). The ANA officially recognized the specialty area of forensic nursing in 1997 and published the scope and standards for forensic practice (I.A.o.F.N.a.A.N. Association, 1997).

Violence is increasingly recognized as a major public health problem, affecting individuals of all ethnic and socioeconomic backgrounds. Although battered women make up 20–30% of ambulatory care patients, barely one in 20 victims of violence is identified as a victim when seen in the health care setting. Efforts to change these statistics have been successful largely due to the education of health care clinicians in identifying and caring for victims of violence. Clinicians are encouraged to routinely inquire about domestic violence, to provide sensitive and nonpunitive support, address patient safety, document abuse, report as appropriate, and offer referrals (Hyman et al., 1995).

In addition, *The Scope and Standards of Forensic Nursing Practice* (Table 34.2), the result of a collaborative effort by the ANA and IAFN, guides practice for the specialty of forensic nursing. It is these standards by which a nurse practicing in the area of forensics may be measured or judged in legal proceedings. As the discipline develops, established standards are used as guidelines to further develop and implement protocols that will guide role development.

The entry level forensic nurse is expected to maintain the basic standards of forensic care, as defined in Table 34.2.

Table 34.2   Standards of Forensic Care

Standard I. Assessment
  The forensic nurse shall provide an accurate assessment, based upon data collected, of the physical or psychological issues of the client as related to forensic nursing or forensic pathology

Standard II. Diagnosis
  The forensic nurse shall analyze the assessment data to determine a diagnosis pertaining to forensic issues in nursing.

Standard III. Outcome Identification
  The forensic nurse will identify expected individual outcomes based on the forensic diagnoses of the client.

Standard IV. Planning
  The forensic nurse develops a comprehensive plan of action of the forensic client appropriate to forensic interventions to attain expected outcomes.

Standard V. Implementation
  The forensic nurse implements a plan of action based on forensic issues derived from assessment data, nursing diagnoses, and medical diagnoses, when applicable, and scientific knowledge.

Standard VI. Evaluation
  The forensic nurse evaluates and modifies the plan of action to achieve expected outcomes.

The advance practice registered nurse (APRN) is a registered nurse who has received advanced education in a master's or postmaster's certificate program (Berry and Mackay, 2001). The required number of hours must be completed in a preceptored setting, at which time the advance practice nurse may sit for board certification (APRN-BC). The APRN-BC, when practicing independently, is most often in a collaborative relationship with a physician.

Practice/Specialty Areas

Four distinct areas of forensic nursing practice were first identified in 1995:

- *Clinical Forensic Nursing*, which involves the application of clinical and scientific knowledge to questions of law and the criminal and civil investigation of survivors of traumatic injury and for patient treatment related to the legal system
- *The Sexual Assault Nurse Examiner*, who examines the sexually assaulted victim and directs follow-up care
- *The Forensic Psychiatric Nurse*, who assesses and intervenes with criminal defendants before court hearings
- *The Forensic Correctional/Institutional Nurse*, who specializes in the care, treatment and rehabilitation of individuals who have violated criminal law and have been committed for therapy to hospitals within prisons (Lynch, 1995b)

Since 1995, the roles of the forensic nurse have expanded to include broader and more clearly defined practice roles, including the sexual assault nurse examiner, the forensic clinical nurse specialist, the forensic nurse practitioner, the legal nurse consultant, expert witness, and the nurse lawyer, among others. Within many of the broader roles, nurses may specialize by population (pediatric, adult, geriatric, victim versus perpetrator, bioterrorism) or by clinical or community site (i.e., hospital versus prison, occupational health).

Sexual Assault Nurse Examiner

The entry level role of the SANE, or sexual assault forensic examiner (SAFE), terms used interchangeably, is the most widely recognized role in forensic nursing practice and is responsible for forensic nursing first becoming recognized for its unique role. A landmark research study on rape trauma syndrome provided the impetus for the development of the role of the sexual assault nurse examiner (Burgess and Holstrum, 1974). The study motivated a group of concerned nurses to begin to evaluate strategies to meet the needs of victims of rape. It was recognized that victims of sexual assault were not receiving appropriate care in the health care system. Patients were not being seen in a timely manner which had the potential to seriously impact the collection of evidence in a case. Health-care personnel questioned their own competency in collecting and preserving evidence. And the possibility of having to testify in court impacted the clinician's decision in caring for the sexual assault victim. All of these variables worked together in giving sexual assault victims the message that they were not a priority for care in the health system as it existed. The psychological and social impact of this standard of care served to convey the message that sexual assault victims may have a difficult time traversing through the health care system which in turn caused victims to hesitate in reporting. It is estimated that more than 60% of all sexual assaults go unreported (U.S. Department of Justice, 1999; *World report on violence and health: Summary*).

In response, nurses who were advocates for women's rights convened and determined protocols that could be established to change the standards of care for victims of sexual assault. The first procedures were in place in the late 1970s. The SANE (SAFE) is a registered nurse specially trained in the comprehensive care of victims of sexual assault. The SANE recognizes trauma, collects forensic evidence, and may provide expert testimony in a court of law (Evans and Wells, 2001). The use of the SANE (1) enhances the care of the rape victim by decreasing the amount of time before examination (SANEs are often hired for the specific role of rape examiner within a clinical setting, or can be called to a clinical setting); (2) examination time is decreased because of the expertise of the SANE; and (3) the quality of the examination is improved significantly because of their expertise (Ledray and Simmelink, 1997).

The goals of sexual assault examiners in practice are to:

- Protect the sexual assault victim from further harm
- Provide crisis intervention
- Provide timely, thorough, and professional forensic evidence collection documentation, and preservation of evidence
- Evaluate and treat prophylactically for sexually transmitted diseases (STDs)
- Evaluate pregnancy risk and offer prevention
- Assess, document, and seek care for injuries
- Appropriately refer victims for immediate and follow-up medical care and follow-up counseling (Ledray, 1996)

The use of standard protocols and guidelines can significantly improve the quality of treatment and psychological support of victims, as well as the evidence that is collected. Comprehensive protocols and guidelines for female victims of assault should include:

- Recording a full description of the incident, listing all the assembled evidence
- Listing the gynecological and contraceptive history of the victim
- Documenting the results of a full physical examination in a standard way
- Assessment of the risk of pregnancy
- Testing for and treating STDs, including, where appropriate, testing for HIV
- Providing emergency contraception and, where legal, counseling on abortion
- Providing psychological support and referral (Krug et al., 2002)

Over the past 15 years, guidelines for training programs for SANEs have been established through the International Association of Forensic Nurses (IAFN). Accredited courses consist of 40 hour of didactic content related to all aspects of training necessary to prepare a nurse to function as a sexual assault examiner. The course content includes information related to theories of violence, psychology of offenders, the medical advocacy role, community education, assessment skills, specifics related to the collection, and preservation of evidence using sexual assault evidence kits, maintaining the chain of possession, psychiatric and health responses to victimization, and legal implications, along with many other important educational concepts. SANE preparation courses are made available throughout the country at various times throughout the year. Courses are now being offered online as well as in the live classroom. Following the 40 hour of classroom education, the nurse is expected to be preceptored by experts in the field until the nurse and the preceptor agree that the nurse is an expert in the process of the forensic examination of the sexual assault victim. At that time, the nurse may sit for the certification examination through IAFN and become certified (SANE-C). Continuing education is a requirement for recertification. As a result of the increased number of nurses becoming SANE certified, more victims are receiving expert care throughout the country.

Pediatric Sexual Assault Nurse Examiner

A nurse certified as an adult sexual assault nurse examiner may further their practice by preparing as a pediatric sexual assault examiner (SANE-P). These examiners are in a position to significantly impact the care of child victims of sexual abuse, as well as to help educate others in the health care system about risk factors, signs of abuse, and assessment and treatment techniques. Nurses who function in the role of pediatric sexual assault examiners provide an important service to children as well as to the medical community, in general.

Child sexual abuse constitutes almost 10% of substantiated child maltreatment cases (approximately 88,000 in the year 2000). Risk factors include (1) gender, (2) age, (3) disabilities, and (4) parental dysfunction (Putnam, 2003). Victims of child abuse are at significant risk for psychopathology, especially depression and substance abuse. Child abuse is reported by 13.5% of women and 2.5% of men (Molnar et al., 2001). Although reporting of sexual abuse of children is mandated in every state, child sexual abuse remains seriously underreported. Problems related to assessment skills, identification, and collection of evidence impact the care of such victims.

Because of their expertise in identification of abuse as well as their ability to educate others as to the risk factors and warning signs, more incidences are now identified, and children are provided with proper care, including evidence collection.

Sexual Assault Response Team

As the number of SANEs has grown, the needs of the community have been highlighted. Nurses recognize the need to offer consistent standards of care for all victims regardless of the hospital to which they report. Nurses and community leaders have therefore regrouped to set standards for educating the public on assault prevention techniques and for establishing comprehensive care to victims through Sexual Assault Response Teams (SART), which utilize a collaborative model in providing care. SANEs are involved in the formation of SARTs in many communities throughout the United States. Among those who may assist in the formation of a team include community representatives from the health department, law enforcement and advocacy groups, the department of family and children services, District Attorneys' offices, local hospitals, victim-assistant programs, and other service areas, as pertinent.

The team approach provides a standard of care that includes expert care in the acute setting, advocacy for the acute and long-term needs of the victim, and referral for counseling for the survivors in an effort to decrease long-term effects resulting from the assault (Antognoli-Toland, 1985; Ledray, 1992). The response team usually includes a SANE, an advocate, and a police officer. The primary advantages of the team approach to sexual assault include:

- A comprehensive approach that should encompass most of the victim's needs that arise from the crisis situation incurred by the sexual assault
- Efficient care where more data related to the sexual assault can be gleaned by merging and pooling efforts and talents, and where communication is facilitated among all members of the team and sharing of necessary information and ideas is the norm
- And compassionate care is delivered because key members have a good working relationship with one another and can help decrease the stressors on the victim by filling in the gaps of care and facilitation of the criminal justice system experience (Crowley, 1999)

Approximately 400 SANE/SAFE/SART Programs (in the United States and Canada) were registered with the International Association of Forensic Nurses in the year 2004. Response teams vary with the needs of the community. Variables such as the area served (rural versus urban), size of the population to be served, politics of the hospitals involved, and participation within the communities helps guide the process and the type of team that is established. A primary goal of SANE practice is to enhance the process of identification and detection of violent crimes and collection of evidence related to sexual assault resulting in an increase in the number of convictions (Ledray, 1998; Hutson, 2002). The SART helps to deliver the services in a cost effective and comprehensive manner.

Forensic Clinical Nurse Specialist

The role of the forensic clinical nurse specialist (CNS) varies among hospitals. However, consistent within this role is the need to be knowledgeable in the areas of assessment and treatment of victims of violence, evidence collection and preservation, proper documentation, the legal system, and setting standards of care for victims and perpetrators (Evans and Stagner, 2003). The CNS may work as a general resource person for the hospital or may work in a specialty department such as the emergency room, trauma team, critical care, or outpatient women's health clinic. The CNS serves as a resource for others within the hospital when faced with caring for a patient who has been a victim of violence (care of the perpetrator will be discussed in "Corrections"). Nurses have long focused on physical and psychological care of all patients, but many are not prepared to identify and care for the patient who is a victim of violence, when evidence should be collected and preserved (Wick, 2000). Nurses are often neither prepared, nor cognizant of the need to assess for violence and to collect evidence. The forensic clinical nurse specialist provides expertise to cope with the increasing complexity of the health care system in an attempt to provide care within a society where violence is increasing. In this role, nurses must have knowledge related to how to identify victims of violence wherever they appear within the system, and then to provide care that takes into consideration the changing society and the legal system (Goll-McGee, 1999).

The critical care environment, as well as all other health care settings, challenges the skills of any clinician. Within the health care setting, the forensic nurse enhances patient care management, resulting in clinical service, legal order, and forensic protocol (Goll-McGee, 1999). Among the many issues that face any clinician is the issue of advance directives. Do not resuscitate orders (DNR), advance declarations, and health care power of attorneys (proxies), describe processes by which a patient may ensure respect for their wishes at end-of-life. The Patient Self-Determination Act (PSDA) of 1985 assures the rights of patients to state their wishes in the form of an Advance Directive. The PSDA requires all facilities that accept Medicare and Medicaid to advise patients of their rights, provide education for the community, and demand that health care clinicians respect these rights.

In addition, issues related to organ donation often present similar dilemmas. Although the physician declares death, the nurse is often in a position to notify the family. The forensic nurse is in a position to educate health care workers as to the protocol for requesting donors, ways to humanely approach survivors, and the legal implications of the process (Goll-McGee, 1999).

Ideally, the CNS has advanced education programs at the Masters or Ph.D. level in psychiatric assessment and intervention skills, death investigation, forensic wound identification, domestic violence, and sexual assault of all types and in varied populations, introductory law, and principles of criminal justice, and forensic science (Wick, 2000). It is this expertise and the resulting skills that make this role a valuable asset to all health care personnel.

In a 1995 study of emergency departments, one out of nine emergency room visits were related to domestic violence, whereas less than 3% of patients admitted to an emergency department were screened for domestic violence by health care providers in those settings (Abbott et al., 1995). There is an opportunity for proactive forensic nursing practice in primary care and emergency room settings when nurses are prepared in the medicolegal process of violence screening, evidence collection, and forensic documentation (McCracken, 1999). At one time, violence was dealt with primarily through the criminal justice system; however, it is now regarded as both a preventable and predictable public health problem requiring that health care providers be prepared to identify traumatized individuals and their perpetrators.

A major impact of the development of the field of forensic nursing is the emphasis on proper treatment of the victim of violence or the perpetrator of violence. Health care personnel can no longer opt out of involvement in the process of assessing for victimization, proper collection of evidence, documentation of cases, and preservation of the chain of custody of evidence. With the steady increase in violence in the society, health care personnel are seeing increasing numbers of victims and perpetrators in the clinical settings. With the clear focus of *Healthy People 2010* on injury and violence prevention, health care personnel are faced with the challenge to increase their expertise in these areas of practice. Forensic nurses must be prepared to assess for and identify injuries resulting from violent acts, gather physical evidence, and interview the patient and document facts appropriately. The ability to collaborate with law enforcement personnel and others in the legal system is required.

Forensic Psychiatric Nurse

Those who advocate the specialty of forensic psychiatric nursing view this role as being unique from the general nursing role (Lynch, 1993; Burrow, 1998). Nurses who work with mentally ill clients and forensic prisoners must have a knowledge of their state nursing practice act, as well as the ANA Statement on Psychiatric-Mental Health Clinical Nursing Practice and the Standards of Psychiatric-Mental Health Clinical Nursing Practice (A.N.A., 1994). Nurses must also be familiar with the mental health statute in the state in which they practice, as well as agency policies and procedures.

Nurses function in the generalist role and the advance practice role when caring for mentally ill clients. In the generalist role, they function as direct care providers and client advocates and are prepared at the entry level as a college/university, associate degree or diploma graduate (Weiss-Kaffie and Purtell, 2001).

Nurses who practice at the advance practice level require education at the graduate level, which prepares them to function as psychiatric clinical nurse specialists or psychiatric nurse practitioners. In addition to the competencies of the generalist, the advance practice psychiatric nurse may function as a psychotherapist, providing individual, family, and group therapies. Some advance practice nurses, depending on educational preparation and individual state statutes, have prescriptive privileges and can initiate psychopharmacology treatment along with psychotherapy. Advance practice psychiatric nurses serve the entire community of nurses by serving as clinical nurse specialists, providing a constant source of education and support, including providing consultation to assist with special circumstances involving care of mentally ill patients.

Forensic psychiatric nurses are prepared to conduct therapy with various patients, including those who have been victims of violence and with perpetrators. Efficacious treatments exist that are known to improve psychological symptoms in all mentally ill populations, such as adults and children who have experienced sexual abuse (Molnar et al., 2001). Both the SANE-A and the SANE-P have impacted the early identification and treatment of victims of abuse and help with referrals to clinicians who can intervene early with appropriate therapy, thus impacting the long-term outcomes of abuse. Posttraumatic Stress Disorder is a major diagnosis within which the forensic psychiatric nurse functions.

Psychiatric nurses can also practice in unique roles such as criminal profilers. Although developing the psychodynamics of a case requires time and thoughtful consideration, the insights gleaned are usually critical for diagnosis and treatment. The following case study presents an introduction to this type of forensic profiling.

Case Study 1

To better understand the psychodynamics of a case formulation, a complex case of a serial sexual killer of 11 young women will be described. This case is presented for several reasons. First, the repetitive pattern of this man's killing had its origins of development in early childhood experiences. The dynamics set into play in those early experiences shaped his views of himself and others in relationship to his world. What emerged in his lifeline of relationships was a deep preoccupation with sex and power related to the social experience of humiliation and shame. A forensic psychiatric nurse specialist in profiling of violent sex offenders examined the man for trial and testified as to his mental illness, childhood history, and development of obsessional murderous fantasies.

Two critical factors in understanding this man are:

- The early formative dynamic life events that shaped his thinking and fantasies about sex, aggression, and females
- The life stresses that weakened his psychological defenses and triggered the acting on his murderous fantasies

Early Formative Events When HB finished describing in detail his killing of the 11 women over 18 months in his March 1992 taped confession, he spontaneously added:

> "There is no way that I can say why I did what I did because I really don't know. Like when I was a little kid, my Mom used to ask why I would steal and I couldn't explain it... I could never say that it was abuse from childhood because I don't think that I was abused no more or no less than any other kid who grew up the way I grew up. I got my ass cut up (by mother) sometimes on a daily basis, sometimes for things I didn't do. You just learn to expect that, but I was first sexually active way before I even knew about sex. I was about four or five years old and the women that I was having intercourse with were like sixteen and I really didn't know what I was doing... I really didn't experience sex until my junior year in high school... I remember when I was about eight years old seeing several guys rape a girl and they got off scot-free. They walked away and the charges were dropped in court... then the first time I'd ever heard something about somebody being raped and killed was that same girl's sister. She was raped and strangled to death... It was her husband or boyfriend and it seems like ever since I heard that, raped and strangled to death, it always stuck in my mind, raped and strangled to death."

In this brief soliloquy, HB identifies key formative events:

- Physical abuse by mother
- Sexual abuse by teenage girls
- Seeing a gang rape
- Hearing of the rape-strangulation of the rape victim's sister

History HB, a 31-year-old African American, was the second child born to his mother, LB, and her married lover, JL. A high school science teacher, JL was 20 years older than LB and never provided financial support for the children. When JL learned of the second pregnancy, he said he could understand one mistake but not two. He left town and his teaching position shortly after the birth of HB.

HB was raised in abject poverty and in an oppressive matriarchal environment. He lived with his mother, great-grandmother, and sister in a four-room shack with no running water, indoor plumbing, or electricity. A bucket that served as a toilet was kept in his bedroom, and he had the task of emptying the bucket in the outhouse, a task he was ashamed of doing in front of other children.

In analyzing the intricate dynamics between mother and son, it is important to note the chain of disappointments that the mother suffered at the hands of the men in her life. Beginning with her own father who abandoned her at birth, LB was later robbed of the only person with whom she was able to bond, her mother. Her mother's marriage to a new stepfather and the resulting birth of her youngest brother proved tragic. LB was replaced by this newest brother as the favored child, and within three months, her mother died of a massive coronary when LB was 13 years old. LB was told not to grieve or express her loss and to take over the mother's duties. Her emotional development was stymied; her older brother was physically abusive to her and one of his friend's tried to rape her.

Within two years of her mother's death, at age 15, LB was seduced by her teacher, who filled the role of surrogate father and lover in exchange for a vow of silence not unlike relationships involving fathers and daughters. Even at the time of HB's birth, the father's name was withheld, despite the midwife saying that everyone knew JL was the father. When LB was again abandoned by a parental figure it was yet again because of a male child.

HB's earliest memories are of his toilet training and his mother beating him when he failed to "make potty." She needed him trained so she could place him in daycare in order that she could work. The beatings were inconsistent and inflicted at random; the children were beaten with anything the mother could get her hands on including extension cords, water hose, and tree limbs. There was a pattern to the beatings where the children would lie on the bed, trapped in such a manner to avoid escape. Sometimes, HB knew the trigger to the beating; other times, he would not. He had trouble controlling bowel movements; his mother thought he soiled on purpose and would beat him. He recalled rushing to get home before his mother, so he could wash his underwear before she found them; this soiling continued until age 10 or 11. HB's mother was proud of her control over her children, stating they were scared of no one but lightening and their mama.

HB's sexual exposure began around age 4 when an 11-year-old girl forced him under a car, where she removed her underclothes and had him lay on top of her. They were caught, and HB remembered the girl being whipped, and while he too expected a beating, his mother only laughed at him because the "girl was so ugly." That sexual encounter led to many others. Girls ranging from seven to twelve years older than HB exploited him over a ten-year period. The activities included oral sex and fondling. His mother recounted that the girls would come over and that they had made up rhymes, "We have the buns, and HB makes our buns rise." The mother's boyfriend's comment was that HB was the only boy in the neighborhood and it was natural for him to "service the girls."

HB's preoccupation with sex, aggression, and females was evidenced by the many magazines that he was exposed to from a young boy through adolescence. He described reading his mother's magazines including confession, detective, and pornographic magazines. In addition to the molestation, HB witnessed a high school girl gang raped by a group of high school boys when he was 8 years old; this girl's sister was raped and strangled several months later.

HB molested a 5-year-old girl when he was 13 years old in the same way the older girls had abused him. The girl's mother told LB, who acted as though it was no big deal, stating, "He gotta get it from somewhere."

To the outside world, HB presented a picture of buoyancy, a contradiction to the inner turmoil he felt. School was a place where HB did fairly well. His mother was less successful in controlling him in school activities. When she tried to keep him from playing school sports because of a prior shoulder injury, he joined the cheerleading squad, as the only male. It provided an opportunity to travel with the team and independence from his mother. A former teacher and coach of the cheerleading squad remembered HB's deportment as exemplary, of his camaraderie with the members of the squad and that he "was like a big brother to the girls." He was said to have a good sense of responsibility and was hard working. His school grades fluctuated, but when he graduated, he ranked 80 in a class of 126, completing high school with a cumulative grade point average of 2.02. During his high school years, HB was involved in a number of school activities. These included participation in the School Bus Driver Program, involvement in the 4-H program and he served on the Vocational Center Student Council. He served as a newspaper staff photographer and was commended for his outstanding service to his community.

HB's military record was excellent. He enlisted in the Navy on December 1984. All reports describe him as an outstanding seaman, and he was ranked above average. He was selected for advancement to third class petty officer and qualified for a sea service ribbon. He reported witnessing the deaths of seven persons who lost their lives in an aircraft crash. He left the service in December 1988 and had earned an overall trait average of 3.76 out of a possible 4. HB's exemplary career was cut short when he broke into a garden supply store, thus losing his security clearance. He was given the option of being honorably discharged or facing criminal charges. He chose to be discharged.

HB's employment history from 1988 to his arrest in 1992 shows a steady decline from his military performance. He was fired from his first job at a radio station for stealing tape recorders and CD's. He then worked as a security guard at a department store where he was fired for suspected larceny. At his next employment, he worked 18 months but was fired for excessive absenteeism. His remaining jobs were at fast food restaurants and he had been unemployed several weeks before his capture.

Partnerships HB's first romantic involvement began in tenth grade. This first girlfriend and first sexual partner was to become his wife. During high school, HB was sexually active with other girls. His relationship with his girlfriend fluctuated, and during one separation, he met another woman whom he decided to marry; however, his mother discouraged him, stating the girl did not have a promising future. He returned to the first girlfriend, who, in the interim, had a child that she claimed was conceived during a rape. They married; HB declared he wanted a child of his own, but his wife refused and the relationship deteriorated. His wife asserted that whenever they had had sex, she was reminded of the rape. He suggested they go for marriage counseling and she refused; the couple separated.

Upon dissolution of his marriage, HB returned to his mother's new house, one that he had helped pay for. HB's mother stated that for the first time, HB began answering her back, and this caused problems. HB attempted reconciliation with his wife, but when this failed, he took an overdose of pills. He was not encouraged to seek professional help; rather, HB recalled his mother slapping him on the face because he stayed in his room moping over the breakup of his marriage.

HB began dating again, but his mother constantly discouraged him, referring to his girlfriends as "whores and sluts." She also searched his car, wallets, and his drawers. LB complained that HB did not play around with her as they once did, for example, she would hold him down and playfully try to kiss him. He had told her to get herself a man because he was tired of playing that role. She was dismayed with his attitude because she said she was the one who was supporting him since he was not working steadily. Other people interviewed commented on the inappropriateness of the intimacy LB shared with her son.

HB, during childhood, suffered four accidents in which he was unconscious for a short period of time. Around age 7 or 8, he fell out of a tree; at age 10 he was hit on the head with a bat; at age 13, he was in a bicycle accident, and at age 14, he was in a skateboard accident. He reported a history of polydrug abuse, including abuse of LSD, cocaine, and marijuana; and at a very young age, up until age 30, he drank an average of 16 to 18 beers a day. While in the service, he was treated for secondary syphilis, and he was circumcised as treatment for painful erections.

Intellectual testing indicated a full scale IQ of 92 on the WAIS-R, which is in the average range of functioning. Neurological testing indicated impairment on measures of sustained auditory attention and cognitive flexibility consistent with evidence of mild frontal lobe impairment. This impairment was believed to be consistent with a history of possible multiple mild closed head injuries in addition to a significant history of alcohol and drug abuse.

The Consequences By age 14, HB had the beginning awareness of his sexually aggressive fantasies. Part of these secret fantasies were grounded in the sexual acts from his own exploitation and the gang rape he witnessed and part comes from his ruminations over the visual images he retains from the magazines he coveted.

His confessions to the murders have a patterned script. He methodically repeated how he administered the choke hold; he rendered the victim unconscious; he performed sexual acts and had intercourse. But there was no detailing of the sexual acts, in contrast to the killings and robberies. He comes back to the crime scenes of his first four victims, an example of the unreality of what he did. He questioned himself: "Did it really happen; did I really kill them?"

HB was a mass of contradictions. He said he raped his victims, but forensic evidence was inconclusive or absent, and he left all except one of his victims totally dressed. He said he wiped the crime scene for fingerprints, but he left many footprints. He left the biggest clue, the victim; he left his signature, the ligatures. He took a taxi and pawned stolen jewelry giving his own name. He denied involvement in the crimes but talked to the police and admitted to two murders the police knew nothing about.

In summary, HB's method of committing his crimes reflected the abusive events in his early life with females; however, in the repetition of the traumatic events he switches his role from victim to perpetrator and puts the females in the role of victim. He is alert for any behavior that is reminiscent of the control that the girls had over him when he was younger, such as calling him names, criticizing, or teasing him. His crimes were like a map to his personal history with cross streets and landmarks. HB was streetwise and one of the women he dated (HB's term for a prostitute) told the police, after the first murder, that they should make HB a prime suspect. The police discredited her because of her work. But she was streetwise and knew what HB was capable of, given the structure of his fantasies. HB admitted that, while in the service, he visited many prostitutes and raped and did not pay them. He also had a rape charge pending at the time of his first murder; a charge that he strongly denied. Clearly, there were early warnings that if addressed might have spared 11 lives.

Diagnosis The diagnostic clues led to the evaluation of presenting symptoms that met or did not meet criteria for the *Diagnostic and Statistics Manual of Mental Disorders -IV-TR*. The primary outcome of multiaxis assessment was that of Personality Disorder Not Otherwise Specified. At trial, testimony was given that HB was diagnosed as having a severe mental illness given the nature of his murderous fantasies and acts; that there was no specific category for him in the DSM as he was an emotional condition unto himself. That he, in fact, contained many pieces of the DSM, specifically features of various personality traits and disorders to include the following.

- *Obsessive–Compulsive Personality*: HB was preoccupied with control. The obsessions drove the compulsion to kill. The obsession was noted in the crime scene patterns. The victims were known black women, with whom he had a psychological connection and even an emotional bond and where he was in a position of control. This fantasy did not include women who had control over him, for example, mother, sister, ex-wife, girl friend.

  HB provided no logic for the killings. He had an elaborate ritual of killing that was built on an irrational perception. He had to kill the same each time. The obsession or fantasy drove the behavior or killing. The rage broke through and he could not control it; it controlled him. He could not stop. He had intent and could plan the killing, but he did not have the choice not to kill. In his confession, he repeatedly said, "It was like a switch was turned; I couldn't stop." It was like the compulsive hand washer, who could not stop the washing.

- *Borderline Personality*: HB described unstable interpersonal relationships, mood swings, and impulsivity. He exhibited great sensitivity to slight rejection. He described a victim teasing him; he exploded and killed her.

- *Antisocial Personality*: HB showed a pattern of disregard for and violation of the rights of others. He stole from his employers. There was the breakdown of inhibition to steal and take from people where value was not the issue.

- *Schizoid Personality*: There was a pattern of detachment from social relationships and a restricted range of emotional expression. HB also exhibited bizarre thinking in the content of his fantasies.

- *Paranoid Personality*: There was a pattern of distrust and suspiciousness in other's motives. Some of this suspicion was heightened because of the drug abuse, whereas some was grounded in reality that he was afraid of being caught. He did not know whom he could trust.

- *Narcissistic Personality*: There was a pattern of grandiosity, a need for admiration and a lack of empathy that was manifested in his self-aggrandizement, sense of entitlement, and sensitivity if people said no to him or did not give him what he wanted. He was offended by his wife saying she was raped; he felt betrayed and preoccupied with himself rather than have any concern for her feelings.

In conclusion, an understanding of psychodynamics for case formulation is important for several reasons: (1) Such an understanding is a window to how behavior is repeated in various relationships. (2) From a forensic behavioral standpoint, it suggests characterological footprints in crime behavior and crime scene factors. Psychiatric nurses can serve as profilers of specific perpetrators because of their experience in psychiatry and in the care of both victims and perpetrators.

Forensic Correctional Nurse

Nursing with prisoners and care of the perpetrator presents challenges to the way nurses think about the patient. The number of incarcerated individuals in the United States has increased significantly for both men and women over the last two decades. Incarcerated men and women have increased rates of serious and chronic physical and mental illnesses requiring enormous health care efforts (Maeve and Vaughn, 2001). Within a social climate that does not encourage caring behavior toward perpetrators, nurses often find that caring for prisoners is difficult and often unrewarding. In the U.S. the idea of caring for the victim is much more accepted than caring for the perpetrator. In contrast, forensic nurses in the United Kingdom are very much focused on the care of the perpetrator (Hambridge, 1995; Mason, 1999; Mercer et al., 2001). The majority of research conducted in the area of care of prisoners has been conducted by practitioners in the U.K.

In the year 2003, federal and state prisons and local jails housed more than two million prisoners in the U.S. (Harrison and Karberg, 2004). Adult men (88%) comprise the majority of prisoners with women making up about 12% of the population. Persons of color are dramatically overrepresented among incarcerated individuals (Tonry, 1995). With the increased use of life without parole, the number of elderly inmates in the prison population will steadily grow (LaMere et al., 1996). Pregnancy in inmates, both adolescent and adult, presents unique problems in care (Hufft, 2004).

Within this large population, there are diverse health care needs. Rates of confirmed AIDS cases are three times higher among prison inmates than in the U.S. general population. Approximately 49 in every 10,000 prison inmates have confirmed AIDS. Axis I and Axis II mental illness criteria are met at increased rates in the prison population (Maeve and Vaughn, 2001). It is projected that 10% of the prison population report sick each day, a rate eight times higher than the number of individuals who see their primary care physicians each day. Health care problems inside corrections settings are similar to those outside prison; however, they are in a higher proportion than would be expected in people of the same age group in the community (Dale and Woods, 2002).

Nurses function in various health care roles within the corrections setting caring for psychological and health care needs. In addition to providing health care, nurses by virtue of their position are often placed in a powerful position with respect to the patient (prisoner). Listed as reasons why corrections settings are traditionally difficult to staff and do not provide attractive employment for health care providers include:

- Society places less value on prisoners' health care. Most nurses in the corrections settings have associate degrees versus baccalaureate masters, or doctoral degrees
- Most corrections settings are located in remote areas where pay is commonly lower and where professionals interested in career development do not choose to live
- The caliber of physicians who work in corrections settings is frequently called into question
- Because of the relative isolation of a majority of corrections settings, nurses who practice in those sites have fewer resources when needed
- The professional stigma associated with working in corrections settings contributes to a lesser value being placed on the care of prisoners versus those who follow the law (Dabney and Vaughn, 2000; Maeve and Vaughn, 2001)

Because the idea of "caring" with the corrections population often leads to ethical issues regarding this concept, many nurses may question the value of their role. Caring involves the reciprocal relationship between a patient and the nurse. Prisoners can severely test a nurse's ability to develop a caring relationship (Nodding, 1984).

Can a nurse remain caring while at the same time collecting evidence on a prisoner when needed? As the National Commission on Correctional Health Care notes, health-care professionals cannot gather evidence to be used against a prisoner while at the same time maintain a caring relationship with a patient (Northrop and Kelly, 1987). The role of the nurse in corrections is often conflicting.

As stated previously, the role of the forensic nurse is evolving, and specific to the cor-rections settings, the role has not been clearly defined. Nurses may function in a general medical surgical unit in a corrections setting or in the psychiatric corrections setting — two very different roles. Forensic psychiatric nursing is a commonly discussed forensic role and involves the evaluation and treatment of the mentally ill who have committed crimes. Such nurses are often involved in the decision making process as corrections teams decide the safety of their return to society (Maeve and Vaughn, 2001). Once again, the issue of educational experience, or lack thereof, impacts the performance of the forensic nurse in the corrections setting. Is it enough to say that any nurse who works in a corrections setting is a forensic nurse? Or is the forensic nurse (psychiatric or otherwise) one who has advance education which prepares them to care for the prisoner in a way that is advantageous to both the prisoner and the society?

Currently, nurses who practice in the corrections' settings are not generally educated in the advance practice forensic role. As the number of forensic nurses with advanced edu-cation grows, it is hoped that more will choose to practice in corrections setting. However, only if the barriers to practice, mentioned before, are addressed will society benefit. Defining the exact role of the forensic nurse and what impact the forensic com-ponent has on the caring relationship is an important area for research.

Nurse Coroner/Death Investigator

The coroner role for nurses was first recognized in the mid-1990s. This previously non-traditional role for nurses involves assessing clients in a new way, through understand-ing, discovery, preservation, and use of evidence. The coroner is a public official who is primarily charged with the duty of determining how and why people under the coroner's jurisdiction die (Cumming, 1995). In the role of coroner, nurses are prepared as death investigators/deputy coroners. Nurses can practice as death investigators in Medical Examiners' or Coroners' offices or can practice independently in private offices.

A coroner should possess medical knowledge to make expert judgments based on observations of history, symptomatology, autopsy results, toxicology, other diagnostic studies, and evidence revealed in other areas of the case. Areas in which nurse coroners practice are dependent on county regulations. In recent years, the value of employing a nurse as coroner has been highlighted (Cumming, 1996). Nurses are knowledgeable about anatomy and physiology, pathophysiology, pharmacology, grief and grieving, growth and development, interviewing, outcomes measurement, and many other valuable areas of nursing/medical practice (Wooten, 2003). Who better to lead the death investi-gation team? Nursing provides an excellent background for death investigation. Nurses have proven that they can improve on and expand the role of the coroner by identifying ways to improve services provided to families, health care agencies, and communities. Nurses bring a broad perspective of the patient to include the family and the larger society.

An area to be addressed as nurses move forward in the role of the coroner is the question of adequate compensation. How will expert nurses be attracted to this new role unless adequate compensation for the professionalism that nursing has to offer this role is rewarded?

Legal Nurse Consultant/Nurse as Expert Witness/Nurse Attorney

Attorneys and other officers of the court have consulted with nurses regarding medical–legal matters for years. However, nurses first began to gain recognition as legal nurse consultants in the early 1970s (Magnusson et al., 2003). Nurses began to be recognized in the legal arena as expert witnesses in nursing malpractice cases. As nursing malpractice litigation and medical malpractice expanded in the 1980s, the role of the nurse as an expert witness came to be recognized as essential. Nurses were valued as cost effective alternatives to physician consultants. Law firms began to employ nurses for their expertise in personal injury and criminal cases, in addition to medical and nursing negligence cases. The broader role as experts continues to evolve.

Role of the Legal Nurse Consultant

The American Association of Legal Nurse Consultants (AALNC) was founded in 1989. The major goal was to promote the professional advancement of registered nurses practicing in a consultant capacity in the legal field. The education of legal professionals as well as nursing professionals as to how this role could function was a priority (Magnusson et al., 2003).

The legal nurse consultant (LNC) is identified as a specialist unique in the profession of nursing and as someone whose practice is of value in the legal field and is distinct from the role of the paralegal and legal assistant. The role of the LNC is to evaluate, analyze, and render informed opinions on the delivery of health care and the resulting outcomes (A.A.O.L.N. Consultants, 1995a,b). Although the practice of each legal nurse consultant varies with respective practice opportunities and experience levels, certain commonalities prevail. Parameters of the practice may include, but are not limited to:

- Facilitating communications and thus strategizing with the legal professional for successful resolutions between parties involved in health care-related litigation or other medical–legal or health care–legal matters
- Educating attorneys and others involved in the legal process regarding the health care facts and issues of a case or a claim
- Researching and integrating health care and nursing literature as it relates to the health care facts and issues of a case or a claim
- Reviewing, summarizing, and analyzing medical records and other pertinent health care and legal documents and comparing and correlating them to the allegations
- Assessing issues of damages and causation relative to liability within the legal process
- Identifying, locating, evaluating, and conferring with expert witnesses
- Interviewing witnesses and parties pertinent to the health care issues in collaboration with legal professionals
- Drafting legal documentations in medically related cases under the supervision of an attorney

- Developing collaborative case strategies with those practicing within the legal system
- Providing support during discovery, depositions, trial, and other legal proceedings
- Supporting the process of adjudication of legal claims (Iyer, 2003)

The fact that nurses do not practice law (unless prepared educationally as both a nurse and a lawyer) and lawyers do not practice nursing, provides the impetus for the unique services that nurse consultants bring to the legal arena (Steinhardt, 2003). An entry level LNC does not require additional education in a formal program; however, in recent years, masters programs in forensic nursing offer education that encompasses both principles of advance practice for nursing and legal education components. Whether reviewing a case, writing a report, or testifying in court, the validity of the nurse's work is dependent on the nurse's qualifications as determined by education, training, and experience in order to provide an opinion about a specific subject matter, such as nursing standards of care (Steinhardt, 2003). It is anticipated that future studies will reveal expanded roles and practice environments for the legal nurse consultant.

The following case is an example of a case and the forensic issues involved in a case where forensic psychiatric nurses are often called to testify as to standards of nursing practice in institutional settings:

Case Study 2 JB, a 30-year-old unemployed homeless man, was admitted to a psychiatric unit by the police after completing a detoxification treatment program. On admission he said that sometimes his "mood makes him explode." A thorough history indicated a troubled childhood, use of alcohol by age 12, and juvenile delinquency arrests. Admission diagnoses using the *Diagnostic and Statistics Manual of Mental Disorders -IV-TM* included:

- Axis I, Posttraumatic Stress Disorder, alcohol dependence, Impulse Control (not otherwise specified)
- Axis II, deferred
- Axis III, deferred
- Axis IV, deferred
- Axis V, highest level of functioning — 30 (a scale of 0–100).

JB was restless and agitated much of his hospitalization, stating he wanted to leave treatment and kill himself. He was put on special precautions and elopement precautions. Commitment papers were completed due to the severity of suicidal intent. Three days after being placed on special observation/checks he was placed in locked seclusion for physically threatening a staff RN.

Nursing staff described JB as having an explosive disorder from his alcohol abuse, having a poor tolerance for frustration and minimal insight; was contrite, and at times out of control, throwing temper tantrums. He had poor hygiene, took few showers, dressed in the same clothes, had a neglected scalp infection, and was ambivalent about getting better. He had a history of assaulting staff, was devious, and had an extreme fascination with an actress on a television program. He had a labile personality, vacillated between being sweet and pleasant and being verbally violent and aggressive. He swore frequently when he did not get his own way.

On the day of the incident, JB was at the nurse's station, threatening and stating he wanted to leave against medical advice. He then went to his room and slammed the door. The charge nurse stated she called for extra help as a show of force. He said he wanted a cup of tea, to try to calm down and was escorted to the kitchen by a staff member. He drew five cups of water and then broke a faucet in the sink.

Because the staff feared JB would burn himself, he was told to go to the seclusion room. He asked to take some books to the seclusion room. When told to take only one he became highly agitated and broke out of his room. Security were called and a "hands on" was called for, and JB was held with his hands at his side. During the incident, JB kicked at a staff member who then fell on JB. JB was then restrained, placed on a litter, and moved to the seclusion room. It was subsequently learned that he had fractured his pelvis.

The incident was reported to the risk management department and investigated. Questions to be considered are:

- Was the standard of care breached during the take down?
- Was it a factor that only one staff person directed JB to the seclusion room although other staff members were present and had responded to the incident?
- Were the Policy and Procedures of the Clinic for the Management of the Aggressive Patient followed in terms of notification of the incident to the Program Coordinator and the charge nurse?
- Were other staff members available and present to assist in the management of the patient?
- Did staff use a supportive and a directive approach to JB to help him control his aggressive behavior?

The answers to these questions would factor into the hospital and staff's exposure regarding liability and possible lawsuit.

Role of the Legal Nurse Expert

Three types of witnesses can be used in the courtroom trial: (1) the principals (plaintiffs and defendants), (2) fact witnesses, and (3) expert witnesses. Each witness has a specific role in the presentation of the case and establishing the required burden of proof (Matthews, 2001). The nurse may serve in any one of these roles as a witness depending on his/her involvement in the case. The *fact witness* is now used routinely in medical malpractice cases as an individual who is considered by the court to be capable and qualified to summarize and explain complex and voluminous medical records and medical terminology to the jury (Matthews, 2001).

In serving as an *expert witness* nurses have only formally been accepted by the courts since 1980 (Josberger and Ries, 1985). In many instances, the nurse as an expert witness presents the nursing standard that was in force at the time of the incident and gives an opinion as to whether the standard was adhered to by the defendant clinician. The standard is viewed in relationship to what any reasonable and prudent clinician would have done in the same circumstance.

Based upon the level of education, clinical expertise, research activities, publications, and professional involvement, many nurses serve as witnesses in trials. The level of education and experience in practice can seriously impact any nurse's ability to serve as a witness in a trial. Nurses are often identified as experts by peers.

Education

The IAFN adopted a resolution in 2001 calling for the development and implementation of comprehensive forensic nursing content at all levels of formal nursing education. Specific targeted activities include:

- The development of an international forensic nursing core curriculum
- Collaboration with nursing accreditation bodies such as the AACN, the Canadian Nurses Association, the NLN, and the U.K. Nursing Council
- The development and implementation of comprehensive forensic nursing content into the nursing curricula
- Advocacy for certification/qualification standards that require forensic nursing education provided or sponsored by colleges and schools of nursing
- The development of quality educational programs is the precursor to certification/qualification standards

In order for forensic nursing to establish itself as a viable practice area, schools of nursing were mandated to address the need for students to be prepared to meet the needs of victims of violence and perpetrators of violence. Forensic content is mandated at all levels of nursing education:

- Continuing education courses provide ongoing education for practicing nurses. Many states require continuing education credits to fulfill renewal criteria for state licensure
- Certification programs provide specific content in the area of forensics and provide the awarding of a certificate once all requirements are met
- A minor or focus in forensics is offered as part of some undergraduate and graduate programs in nursing
- Doctor of Philosophy (Ph.D.), Doctor of Nursing Practice (DNP), and masters degrees with a forensic focus are awarded at the graduate level

Graduate level preparation should ideally be built on the foundation of the baccalaureate program, facilitating the growth from generalist to specialist (Burgess et al., 2004). Nurses designated as specialists in a particular area are required to meet a higher standard of care when providing services (Hanson and Hamric, 2003). Graduate level forensic nursing practice requires a solid foundation in nursing enhanced by interdisciplinary courses that provide expertise in working collaboratively with other disciplines such as law, medicine, social services, public health, public policy, psychology, education, and research.

The growth of graduate forensic nursing programs reflects the changes occurring and the need for nurses prepared to care for such victims and perpetrators. A multidisciplinary approach to providing education has been adopted. Programs include courses that reflect content from the legal, social sciences, and medical disciplines.

The preparation of the forensic nurse at the advance practice level varies. Before the establishment of Master's programs specifically in forensic nursing, many nurses who had acquired a Master's degree in nurse practitioner programs, critical care, mental health, or gerontology programs, who interfaced with forensic patients in a variety of settings, often identified themselves as forensic nurses. However, without a background in theories of violence, clinical practice in specialty areas of forensic practice, and a thorough understanding of social policy related to forensic practice, clinicians are not adequately prepared as experts to interface with forensic patients (both victims and perpetrators).

Research

In recent years, forensic nurses have addressed the need to establish guidelines for practice through rigorous research. An in-depth body of knowledge in the area of forensic nursing practice needs to be developed. Although much of the knowledge base in forensic nursing comes from other disciplines at this time, integration of "borrowed" theory into a nursing framework through rigorous nursing research is needed to establish evidence based forensic nursing practice. Some of the initial areas to be addressed in forensic nursing research were in the areas of Rape Trauma Syndrome, elder abuse, child abuse, and corrections, among others.

The *Violence Against Women Act* of 1994 called for research addressing interpersonal violence. This national act called attention to the need to look at theories of violence, methods of assessment, treatment outcomes for victims, and prosecution of perpetrators. It is only by documenting outcomes of practice that forensic nurses can validate their practice.

Burgess and Holstrom (1974) identified the concept of Rape Trauma Syndrome (RTS), which they used to describe the short term and long-term effects of sexual assault. RTS is identified as a subtype of PostTraumatic Stress Disorder (PTSD). In this groundbreaking study, the researchers studied 146 victims of sexual assault. They identified an acute phase (disorganization phase) characterized by expressive or guarded interviews following the assault. During the period between the acute phase and the long-term process of re-organization the victims experience physical, emotional, social, and sexual reactions. RTS is a nursing diagnosis that addresses the sequelae related to sexual assault and addresses recovery strategies specific to this type of PTSD. Other studies have built upon the original study to research the recovery process and implications for practice (Ledray and Arndt, 1994).

Elder abuse is an important area of research interest at this time (Adams and Johnson, 1998; Safarik et al., 2000; Brown et al., 2004). Although there is much debate as to legal and ethical implications on mandatory reporting, most clinicians agree that identifying elder abuse remains a difficult task. Much current research by forensic nurses and others is focused on identifying the markers of elder abuse and identifying procedures by which clinicians can better assess for this type of abuse.

Other areas of current research include studies on domestic violence, child abuse, corrections nursing, and workplace violence, among others.

Professional Organizations and Journals

The number of professional organizations is as large as the number of practice areas. Major sources of information for all forensic nurses include:

- The International Association of Forensic Nurses (IAFN) http://www.forensicnurse.org/ which has two publications: the newsletter *On the Edge* and the peer reviewed *Journal of Forensic Nursing*
- The American Psychiatric Nurses Association (APNA) http://www.apna.org/
- The International Society of Psychiatric Mental-Health Nurses, http://www.ispn-psych.org/which has a newsletter *Connections* and peer reviewed journals *Archives of Psychiatric Nursing, Journal of Child and Adolescent Psychiatric Nursing,* and *Perspectives in Psychiatric Care*
- The American Association of Nurse Attorneys (TAANA) which has the publication
- The American Association of Legal Nurse Consultants (AALNCA) which has *The Journal of Legal Nurse Consulting*

References

Abbott, J., Johnson, R., Koziol-McLain, J., and Lowenstein, S.R. (1995). Domestic violence against women: Incidence and prevalence in an emergency department population. *J. Amer. Med. Assoc.,* 273(22), 1763–1767.

Adams, J. and Johnson, J. (1998). Nurses' perceptions of gross self-neglect amongst older people living in a community. *J. Clin. Nurs.* 7(6), 547–552.

American Nurses Association (1991). Scope and standards of clinical nursing practice. Washington, DC: American Nurses Publishing.

Antognoli-Toland, P. (1985). Comprehensive program for examination of sexual assault victims by nurses: A hospital-based project in Texas. *J. Emerg. Nurs.* 11(3), 132–135.

A.N.A. (1994). Statement on psychiatric-mental health clinical nursing practice and standards of psychiatric-mental health clinical nursing practice. Washington, DC: American Nurses Publishing.

Bastian, L. (1995). *Criminal Victimization 1993.* Bureau of Justice Statistics Bulletin Washington, DC: NCJ, U.S. Department of Justice.

Berry, V. and Mackay, T.R. (2001). Advanced practice nursing. In: O'Keefe, M.E. (Ed.), *Nursing Practice and the Law,* Vol. 1, pp. 301–316, Philadelphia: F.A. Davis.

Bouton, K. (1990). The *prosecutor: Linda Fairstein vs. rape.* New York Times Magazine. pp. 21–23, 58–60.

Briere, J.N. and Elliott, D.M. (1994). Immediate and long term impacts of child sexual abuse. *The Future of Children,* 4, 54–69.

Brown, K., Streubert, G., and Burgess, A. (2004). Effectively detect and manage elder abuse. *Nurse Practi.,* 29(8), 22–43.

Burgess, A., Berger, A.D., and Boersma, R.R. (2004). Forensic nursing: Investigating the career potential in this emerging graduate specialty. *American Journal of Nursing,* 104(3), 58–64.

Burgess, A. and Holstrum, L.L. (1974). Rape trauma syndrome. *Amer. J. Psychiat.,* 131, 981–986.

Burrow, S. (1998). Therapy versus security: reconciling healing and damnation. In: Mason, T. and Mercer, D. (Eds.), *Critical Perspectives in Forensic Care*, pp. 171–187, London: Macmillan.

Buvinic, M. and Morrison, A. (1999). Economic and social consequences of violence (Technical Note 4). Violence as an obstacle to development Washington, DC: Inter-American Development Bank. pp. 1–8.

Cammuso, B.S., Madden, B.P., and Wallen, A.J. (2001). Forensic nursing. In M.E. O'Keefe (Ed.), *Nursing Practice and the Law*, pp. 397–415, Philadelphia: F. A. Davis.

Consultants, American Association of Legal Nurse (1995a). *AALNC Scope of Practice for the Legal Nurse Consultant.* Glenview, IL.

Consultants, American Association of Legal Nurse (1995b). *Standards of Legal Nurse Consulting Practice and Professional Performance.* Glenview, IL.

Crowell, N.A. and Burgess, A.W. (1996). Introduction. In: Crowell, N.A., and Burgess, A.W. (Eds.), *Understanding Violence Against Women*, Washington, DC: National Academy Press, pp. 7–21.

Crowley, S.R. (1999). *Sexual Assault: The Medical-Legal Examination.* Stamford, Conn.: Appleton and Lange.

Cumming, M. (1996). Nurse-coroner to forensic consultant: one emergency nurse's experience. *J. Emerg. Nurs.*, 22(6), 494–497.

Cumming, M.F. (1995). The vision of the nurse-coroner: A "protector of the living through the investigation of death". *J. Psychosoc. Nurs.* 33(5), 29–33.

Dabney, D. and Vaughn, M.S. (2000). Incompetent jail and prison doctors. *Prison J.*, 80(2), 151–183.

Dale, C. and Woods, P. (2002). Caring for prisoners: Their professional, educational, and occupational needs. *Nurs. Mgmt.*, 9(6), 16–21.

Douglas, J.E. and Olshaker, M. (2001). Perpetrators. In: Olshaker, J.S., Jackson, M.C., and Smock, W.S. (Eds.), *Forensic Emergency Medicine*, p. 299, Philadelphia: Lippincott Williams and Wilkins.

Ellis, C.A. (2001). The victims of violence. In: Olshaker, J.S., Jackson, M.C., and Smock, W.S. (Eds.). *Forensic Emergency Medicine*, Philadelphia: Lippincott Williams and Wilkins, p. 299.

Emergency Nurses Association (1998). Emergency nurses association position statement. *Journal of Emergency Nursing*, 24(5), 38A.

Evans, A.M. and Wells, D. (2001). Scope of practice issues in forensic nursing. *J. Psychos. Nurs. Mental Hlth. Serv.*, 39(1), 38–46.

Evans, M.M. and Stagner, P. (2003). Maintaining the chain of custody: Evidence handling in forensic cases. *AORN Online*, 78(4), 563–569.

Garner, B.A. (Ed.) (2000). Black's Law Dictionary (7th ed.): West Publishing Company.

Goll-McGee, B. (1999). The role of the clinical forensic nurse in critical care. *Crit. care Nurs. Quar.*, 22(1), 8–18.

Hambridge, J.A. (1995). Mentally abnormal killers in the UK health care system: Issues facing the multidisciplinary team. *J. Foren. Sci.* 40: 69–73.

Hanson, C.M. and Hamric, A.B. (2003). Reflections on the continuing evolution of advanced practice nursing. *Nurs. Outlook*, 51(5), 203–211.

Harrison, P.M. and Karberg, J.C. (2004). Prison and jail inmates at midyear 2003 (No. NCJ 203947). Washington, DC: U.S. Department of Justice, Office of Justice Programs.

Health, W.G.C.o.V.a. (1996). *Violence: a Public Health Priority.*

Healthy people (2001): the Surgeon General's report on health promotion and disease prevention. Publication 79–55071 Washington, DC: U.S. Department of Health, Education, and Welfare, Public Health Service, Office of the Assistant Secretary for Health and Surgeon General.

Hufft, A.G. (2004). Supporting psychosocial adaptation for the pregnant adolescent in corrections. *Amer. J. Matern./Child Nurs.*, 29(2), 122–127.

Hutson, L.A. (2002). Development of sexual assault nurse examiner programs. *Nurs. Clini. North Amer.*, 37(1), 79–88.

Hyman, A., Schillinger, D., and Lo, B. (1995). Laws mandating reporting of domestic violence: Do they promote patient well-being? *J. Amer. Med. Assoc.*, 273(22), 1781–1787.

Initiative, J.C.o.A.o.H.O.s. P.P. (2003). Health care at the crossroads: Strategies for creating and sustaining community-wide emergency preparedness systems (White paper 2). Oak Brook Terrace, IL: JCAHO.

I.A.o.F.N.a.A.N. Association (1997). Scope and standards of forensic nursing practice. Washington, DC: American Nurses Publishing.

Iyer, P.W. (Ed.). (2003). *Legal Nurse Consulting: Principles and Practice* 2nd ed. Boca Raton: CRC Press.

Josberger, M.C. and Ries, D.T. (1985). Nurse experts. *Trial*, 68–71.

Krug, E.G. et al., Eds. (2002). *World Report on Violence and health.* Geneva: World Health Organization, p. 372.

LaMere, S., Smyer, T., and Gragert, M. (1996). The aging inmate. *J. Psychosoc. Nurs.*, 34(4), 25–29.

Ledray, L.E. (1992). The sexual assault nurse clinician: A fifteen-year experiment in Minneapolis. *J. Emerg. Nurs.* 18(3), 218–221.

Ledray, L.E. (1996). *Sexual Assault Nurse Examiner, SANE: Development and Guide.* Washington, DC: U.S. Department of Justice, Office of Justice.

Ledray, L.E. (1998). SANE development and operation guide. *J. Emerg. Nurs.*, 24(2), 197–198.

Ledray, L.E. and Arndt, S. (1994). Examining the sexual assault victim: a new model for nursing care. *J. Psychosoc. Nurs. and Mental Hlth. Serv.*, 32(2), 7–12.

Ledray, L.E. and Simmelink, K.A. (1997). Efficacy of SANE evidence collection: A Minnesota study. *J. Emerg. Nurs.*, 23(1), 75–77.

Lynch, V. (1993). Forensic aspects of health care: new roles, new responsibilities. *J. Psychosoc. Nurs. Mental Hlth. Serv.*, 31(11), 5–6.

Lynch, V.A. (1995a). Clinical forensic nursing: a new perspective in the management of crime victims from trauma to trial. *Crit. Care Nurs. Clin. North Amer.*, 7(3), 489–507.

Lynch, V.A. (1995b). Forensic nursing: what's new? *J. Psychosoc. Nurs. Mental Hlth Serv.*, 33(9), 6–8.

Maeve, M.K. and Vaughn, M.S. (2001). Nursing with prisoners: the practice of caring, forensic nursing or penal harm nursing? *Adv. Nurs. Sci.*, 24(2), 47–64.

Magnusson, J.K., Joos, B., Pike, J.B., Janes, R., and Beerman, J. (2003). The history and evolution of legal nurse consulting. In: Iyer, P.W. (Ed.), *Legal Nurse Consulting: Principles and Practice*, 2nd ed., Vol. 1, pp. 145–164, New York, NY: CRC Press.

Mason, T. (1999). The psychiatric "supermax"?: Long-term, high-security psychiatric services. *Int. J. Law Psychia.* 22: 155–166.

Matthews, M.D. (2001). The nurse and the legal system. In: O'Keefe, M.E. (Ed.), *Nursing Practice and the Law.* Philadelphia: F. A. Davis Company.

McCracken, L.M. (1999). Living forensics: a natural evolution in emergency care. *Accid. Emerg. Nurs.* 7: 211–216.

Mercer, D., Mason, T., and Richman, J. (2001). Professional convergence in forensic practice. *Aust. N. Zealand J. Mental Hlth. Nurs.* 10: 105–115.

Mian, M. (2004). World report on violence and health: What it means for children and pediatricians. *J. Pediat.*, July.

Molnar, B.E., Buka, S.L., and Kessler, R.C. (2001). Child sexual abuse and subsequent psychopathology: Results from the national co morbidity survey. *Amer. J. Pub. Hlth.*, 91(5), 753–760.

Nodding, N. (1984). *Caring: A Feminine Approach to Ethics and Moral Education.* Los Angeles: University of California Press.

Northrop, C. and Kelly, M. (1987). Nursing practice in correctional facilities. In C. Northrop (Ed.), *Legal issues in nursing.* St. Louis: CV Mosby.

Putnam, F. (2003). Ten-year research update review: Child sexual abuse. *J. Amer. Acad. Child Adolesc. Psychiat.*, 42(3), 269–278.

Safarik, M., Jarvis, J., and Nussbaum, K. (2000). Elderly female serial sexual homicide. *Homicide Stud.*, 4(3), 294–301.

Sekula, K., Holmes, D., Zoucha, R., DeSantis, J., and Olshansky, E. (2001). Forensic psychiatric nursing. Discursive practices and the emergence of a specialty. *J. Psychosoc. Nurs. Mental Hlth. Serv.*, 39(9), 51–57.

Services, U.S.D.o.H.a.H. (2000). *Healthy People* 2010, 2nd ed., Vol. 2., Washington, DC: U.S. Government Printing Office.

Steinhardt, T.A. (2003). Entry into specialty practice of legal nurse consulting. In P.W. Iyer (Ed.), *Legal Nurse Consulting: Principles and Practice*, Vol. 1, pp. 165–180, New York, NY: CRC Press.

Tonry, M. (1995). *Malign Neglect: Race, Crime, and Punishment in America.* New York, NY: Oxford.

U.S. Department of Justice, F.I., Laboratory Division. (1999). *Handbook of Forensic Services*, 2nd ed., Boca Raton: CRC Press.

Weiss-Kaffie, C.J. and Purtell, N.E. (2001). Psychiatric Nursing. In: O'Keefe, M.E. (Ed.), *Nursing Practice and the Law*, Vol. 1, pp. 352–371, Philadelphia: F.A. Davis.

Wick, J.M. (2000). "Don't Destroy the Evidence." *AORN J.*, 75(5), 805–836.

Wooten, R. (2003). Applying the nursing process to death investigation. www.forensicnursemag.com

Appendix A

Violence

In the first *World Report on Violence and Health*, the World Health Organization (WHO) in Geneva made a major contribution to our understanding of violence and its impact on societies (2002). Statistics were revealed that challenged those who care to address the fact that 1.6 million people worldwide lose their lives to violence: self-directed (suicide), interpersonal, and collective (societal). The WHO challenged us to review our part in preventing violence as well as in caring for victims of violence. The report strengthens legitimate claims to resources, whether national, regional, or local; governmental, institutional, or private; monetary or humanitarian (Mian, 2004). Academia, lawmakers, the media, and communities were called upon to address this important issue. In addition, we were challenged to consider that what we find acceptable and unacceptable relates to the way we relate to others, is influenced by culture, and deserves to be viewed through a lens that is sensitive to values and social norms.

Violence is a nebulous concept, with its definition being a matter of judgment rather than an exact science. The WHO defines violence as "the intentional use of physical force or power, threatened or actual, against oneself, another person, or... a group or community that either results in injury, death, psychological harm, maldevelopment or deprivation" (Health, 1996). This definition includes interpersonal violence as well as suicidal behavior and armed conflict. Two subcategories define interpersonal violence:

- *Family and Intimate Partner Violence* — violence between family and intimate partners, occurring most commonly in the home
- *Community Violence* — violence between individuals who are unrelated, and who may be familiar with one another, and usually occurring outside the home

Although the statistics that 1.6 million people worldwide lost their lives to violence (one half of those deaths are due to suicide, almost one third were homicides, and about one fifth were casualties of war) is astounding, these statistics tell only a part of the story. Physical, sexual, and psychological abuse occurs in every country on a daily basis. Abuse of all kinds undermines the health and well-being of millions of people, impacting economies in health care costs, legal costs, absenteeism from work and lost productivity (Briere and Elliott, 1994; Buvinic and Morrison, 1999).

The Surgeon General of the United States of America was the first to clearly delineate the impact of violence on victim health and the burden it places on health care institutions (1979). In its 1979 report, *Healthy People*, the consequences of violent behavior were highlighted in an effort to improve the nation's health, making tackling the roots of violence a top priority for the health care community.

Violence is a universal phenomenon that impacts all communities and threatens the life, health, and happiness of all who inhabit those communities. Because it is so pervasive, we sometimes label it as part of the human condition. The purpose of the first *World Report on Violence and Health* (2002) was to challenge the secrecy, taboos, and feelings of inevitability that surround violent behavior, and to encourage debate that will increase our understanding of a very complex human tragedy.

A key requirement for addressing violence in a comprehensive manner that will impact all of society is for people to work together in partnerships of all kinds, and at all levels, to develop effective responses (2002). Forensic nurses were among the first to respond to the international problem of interpersonal violence, beginning with educating nurses to be experts in caring for victims of sexual assault and continuing to the present time, when nurses are being educated at the advance practice level to provide expert care for all victims of violence, along with the perpetrators. Forensic nurses are at the forefront in developing collaborative programs to protect those who are victims — from our most vulnerable populations, children, and elders, to the more obvious violence related to war and social conflict.

Rape

Rape is a crime of violence where sex is the weapon (Bouton, 1990). Regardless of the ongoing debate involving health care clinicians, law enforcement, and members of the women's movement concerning the issue of whether rape should be classified as a crime of sex or violence, there is a fair amount of agreement that whatever the debate, anger is almost always a key component (Douglas and Olshaker, 2001).

Within the overall picture of violence in our society, men and women both experience the devastation. Although men are more likely than women to be victims of violent crimes — 61 per 1,000 men, 42.6 per 1,000 women — patterns of victimization differ (Bastian, 1995). Women are more likely to be victimized by intimate partners or someone known to the victim (Crowell and Burgess, 1996). But everyone from male and female children and adolescents, to adult men and women, to elderly men and women, are victims of sexual assault. The Illinois Criminal Sexual Assault Statute is considered the national model for broadly defining rape:

- Rape is defined as "gender neutral," which broadens the earlier definition of rape so that it now includes men as well as women.
- It includes acts of sexual penetration other than vaginal penetration by a penis.
- It distinguishes types of sexual abuse on the basis of the degree or threat of force, similar to the "aggravated" versus "simple" distinction of physical assaults.
- In addition, a new category of rape victim, "taking advantage of an incapacitated victim" is included. This category includes the mentally ill as well as victims under the influence of drugs or alcohol. (Some states require that the perpetrator had to give the victim the intoxicant in order to obtain sexual access.) (Ellis, 2001)

A wide range of sexually violent acts can take place in different circumstances and settings. These include, for example:

- Rape within marriage or dating relationships
- Rape by strangers
- Systematic rape during armed conflict
- Unwanted sexual advances or sexual harassment, including demanding sex in return for favors
- Sexual abuse of mentally or physically disabled people
- Sexual abuse of children
- Forced marriage or cohabitation, including the marriage of children
- Denial of the right to use contraception or to adopt other measures to protect against STDs
- Forced abortion

Nurses are often the first people to come in contact with victims. Forensic nurses can, and do, help all health care clinicians understand the importance of assessing every person in the health care system for potential abuse, and ultimately to provide both legal and medical care that is required for positive outcomes. The WHO provides an impetus for us to improve care for victims of violence and also challenges us to provide primary prevention. Forensic nurses are again at the forefront as architects of prevention programs.

Forensic Science and Public Health — The Role of Enabling Statutes, Reporting Obligations, and Privacy Laws

35

JACK W. SNYDER

Public health activities can be defined as "preventing or controlling disease, injury, or disability, including but not limited to, the reporting of disease, injury, vital events . . . , and the conduct of public health surveillance, . . . investigations, and . . . interventions" and receiving child abuse and neglect reports. Such disclosure may be authorized to public health authorities, an official of a foreign government acting in collaboration with a domestic public health authority, or a person exposed to or at risk of contracting or spreading disease if the public health authority is authorized by law to notify such persons. A public health authority can be defined as "an agency or authority of the United States, a State, a territory, a political subdivision of a State or territory, or an Indian tribe, or a person, entity acting under a grant of authority from or contract with such public agency or its contractors or persons or entities to whom it has granted authority, that is responsible for public health matters as part of its official mandate." See, for example, Standards for Privacy of Individually Identifiable Health Information, 45 C.F.R. §512(b)(1)(i) (2002).

Practitioners of the various disciplines of forensic science play an important role in the protection of public health. Consequently, forensic professionals must acquire and maintain a basic knowledge of laws that require, encourage, or permit disclosure and reporting of communicable diseases, hazardous conditions, and injuries that are of public health significance. In many jurisdictions, reporting duties transcend an individual's right to privacy and a health care provider's obligation to protect the patient's confidential information.

The constitutionality of reporting laws has been upheld by the U.S. Supreme Court. In a case involving the reporting of controlled substance prescriptions, the Court addressed many of the concerns about public health reporting. The Court first noted that common law did not recognize the right to withhold medical information from the state. Such a right of physician–patient confidentiality arises from state or federal law and is subject to limitations such as public health reporting. The Court then held that although some individuals' concern for their own privacy may lead them to avoid or to postpone needed medical attention, disclosures of private medical information to doctors, hospital personnel, insurance companies, and public health agencies nevertheless are often an essential part of modern medical practice, even when disclosure may reflect unfavorably on the character of the patient. Requiring such disclosures to representatives of the State having responsibility for the health of the community, does not automatically amount to an impermissible invasion of privacy. See, for example, *Whalen v. Roe, 429 U.S.* 589, 602 (1977).

All states have laws that require physicians to report certain diseases and injuries to a local or state health officer.[1] Many jurisdictions extend this requirement to nurses, dentists, veterinarians, laboratories, school officials, administrators of institutions, and police officials. For some conditions, health care providers must report only the number of cases they see. For other conditions, health care providers must give identifying information, such as name, address, occupation, and birth date, as well as information on the disorder and how it might have been acquired.

In 2004, there are approximately 60 diseases that are commonly reportable in all jurisdictions. State health departments typically provide information on which diseases to report and to whom the reports should be directed. Most health departments accept reports for diseases that are not on the state list of reportable diseases, but acceptance of information does not then require these agencies to take action. Importantly, health care providers rarely, if ever, risk legal liability for making reports that are not required. HIV is the only disease where there is a significant difference in state reporting procedures. All 50 states require that the names of persons with AIDS be reported to local or state health departments. The reporting of individuals infected with the HIV antibody, however, is a far more contentious matter. Although most health experts believe that HIV reporting is important for providing treatment and preventing future infection among others, HIV advocates argue that name based HIV reporting violates patient confidentiality and deters people from being tested. Some groups also oppose HIV reporting because of the fear that public health officials will not protect the confidentiality of the reports and will use the information for improper purposes. Although there is no evidence that this has ever happened, there are still states that do not require HIV reporting. Some states have attempted to find middle ground by devising systems in which patients are assigned a unique identifier code in place of a name. Others have gone further by using a hybrid system of collecting names and transferring them to unique identifiers while yet others are using patient initials or simply removing names from HIV-positive test results and recording cases anonymously.

Legally required disease control reporting is not subject to informed consent. Health care providers do not need medical record releases for disease reporting because neither they nor their patients have the right to refuse the release of the information. Although patients do not have a legal right to be informed that they are being reported to the health department, it is good practice to inform them regarding diseases such as syphilis or measles, for which the health department will contact them for additional information.

Health care providers must never knowingly report false information to public health authorities, and they are liable for any injuries, such as transmission of HIV or tuberculosis, occasioned by false reports. Although health care providers are not required to personally investigate the information that patients provide, they must truthfully report what is known to them. In reality, very few health care providers do not know their patients' correct names and addresses, because few patients pay cash for medical care or never need a prescription or other order that requires a correct identity. Health care providers who provide information in good faith are not liable if the information is incorrect.

Disease registries are a special class of reporting laws. Most disease registries are state-wide and involve either cancer or occupational illness. Some, such as the CDC registry of cases of toxic shock syndrome, are national. Reporting cases to the registry may be mandatory or voluntary. Because the objective is not to control a communicable disease, there is often no penalty for failing to report to a disease registry. However, it is always desirable to have a complete registry because registries are used to determine the extent of certain problems in the community and to try to determine causes. If they are inaccurate, they may give false correlations and become useless for research and prevention.

Every jurisdiction requires health care providers to report certain types of injuries to law enforcement officials or protection agencies, generally including assaults, family violence, and criminal activity. Although the victim may have a plausible explanation of the injury and be anxious to avoid reporting for fear of reprisals or because he is under investigation already, proper reports should be made despite the victim's wishes. It is not up to the health care provider to investigate the incident before reporting it; that is the job of the law enforcement agency that receives the report.

Whenever health care providers suspect that a child has been abused or neglected, they should report this immediately to the child protective agency.[2] Child abuse is not a diagnosis, however, but a legal finding, and medical personnel who try to investigate this crime may confuse the evidence to the point that the law enforcement agency cannot protect the child.[3] Health care providers should defer to experts in child abuse and neglect rather than attempting to make an independent determination of abuse.[4] The experts will also act as consultants to the courts and protective services.

Generally, health care providers have a responsibility to report violent or suspicious injuries to the local law enforcement agency. These include all gunshot wounds, knifings, poisonings, serious motor vehicle injuries, and any other wounds that seem suspicious. The legal assumption is that anyone who has knowledge that a crime may have been committed has a duty to report it to the police. If the patient is brought to the hospital in the custody of the police or from the scene of a police investigation, then the health care provider may safely assume that the police have been notified. In all other cases, however, the health care provider should call the police and make the report.

Pennsylvania Enabling Statutes

To provide the forensic practitioner with a sampling of laws within a single jurisdiction that may involve reporting, registration, or disclosure activities, this section summarizes relevant enabling statutes in the Commonwealth of Pennsylvania.

Sections 2101 to 2121 of the Administrative Code of 1929 (71 P.S. §§531–551) and provisions ancillary to the Administrative Code (71 P.S. §§1401–1435) establish the general authority for the Pennsylvania Department of Health and the Secretary of Health. A frequently cited section of the Administrative Code states that "the Department of Health shall have the power, and its duty shall be: (a) to protect the health of the people of this Commonwealth, and to employ the most efficient and practical means for the prevention and suppression of disease." (71 P.S. §532[a]).

Reporting of Diseases (Including Cancer)

The *Disease Prevention and Control Law of 1955* (35 P.S. §§521.1 to 521.21) addresses the prevention and control of communicable and noncommunicable diseases in all areas of the Commonwealth that do not have an effective local board or department of health.

The *Local Health Administration Law* (16 P.S. §§12001 to 12026) approves the establishment of local departments of health and provides grants to local health departments that conduct public health activities and offer health services in accordance with Department of Health regulations.

The *Vital Statistics Law of 1953* (35 P.S. §§450.101 to 450.1003) requires the development and maintenance of a statewide system of vital statistics (e.g., live births and deaths) designed to protect the public health and preserve completeness and integrity of records.

The *Pennsylvania Cancer Control, Prevention, and Research Act* (35 P.S. §§5631 to 5637) establishes a statewide cancer registry and enables the awarding of grants and contracts for cancer control, prevention, education, training, and research.

The *Cancer Law* (35 P.S. §§5601 to 5610) requires investigation and reporting to appropriate authorities any cancer treatment provided by persons not authorized by law to do so.

As of 2004, the *Pennsylvania Department of Health List of Reportable Diseases* includes:

1. AIDS (Acquired Immune Deficiency Syndrome)[a]
2. Amebiasis[a,b]
3. Animal bite[c]
4. Anthrax[b,c]
5. An unusual cluster of isolates[b,d]
6. Arboviruses[b,c]
7. Botulism (All forms)[b,c]
8. Brucellosis[a,b]
9. Campylobacterosis[a,b]
10. Cancer[a,b]
11. CD4 T-lymphocyte test result with a count <200 cells/μl, or a CD4 T-lymphocyte % of <14% of total lymphocytes[a,b]
12. Chancroid[a,b]
13. Chickenpox (Varicella) + (Effective 01-26-05)
14. Chlamydia trachomatis infections[a,b]
15. Cholera[b,c]
16. Congenital adrenal hyperplasia (CAH) (<5 year old)[a,b]
17. Creutzfeldt–Jakob disease[a,b]
18. Cryptosporidiosis[a,b]
19. Diphtheria[b,c]
20. Encephalitis[a]
21. Enterohemorrhagic *E. coli*[b,c,d]
22. Food poisoning outbreak[c]
23. Giardiasis[a,b]
24. Gonococcal infections[a,b]
25. Granuloma inguinale[a,b]
26. Guillain–Barre syndrome[a]
27. *Haemophilus influenzae* invasive disease[a,b,d]
28. Hantavirus pulmonary syndrome[b,c]
29. Hemorrhagic fever[c]

(Table Continued)

(Table Continued)

30.	Hepatitis, viral, acute and chronic cases[a,b]
31.	Histoplasmosis[a,b]
32.	HIV[a,b]
33.	Influenza[a,b]
34.	Lead poisoning[b,c]
35.	Legionellosis[b,c]
36.	Leprosy (Hansen's disease)[a,b]
37.	Leptospirosis[a,b]
38.	Listeriosis[a,b]
39.	Lyme disease[a,b]
40.	Lymphogranuloma venereum[a,b]
41.	Malaria[a,b]
42.	Maple syrup urine disease (MSUD) (<5 year old)[a,b]
43.	Measles (rubeola)[b,c]
44.	Meningitis (all types not caused by either invasive *Haemophilus influenzae* or *Neisseria meningitides*)[a]
45.	Meningococcal invasive disease[b,c,d]
46.	Mumps[a,b]
47.	Pertussis (whooping cough)[a,b]
48.	Phenylketonuria (PKU) (<5 year old)[a,b]
49.	Plague[b,c]
50.	Poliomyelitis[b,c]
51.	Primary congenital hypothyroidism (<5 year old)[a,b]
52.	Psittacosis (ornithosis)[a,b]
53.	Rabies[b,c]
54.	Respiratory syncytial virus[b]
55.	Rickettsial diseases/infections[a,b]
56.	Rubella (German measles) and congenital rubella syndrome[a,b]
57.	Salmonellosis[a,b,d]
58.	Severe acute respiratory syndrome (SARS)[c]
59.	Shigellosis[a,b,d]
60.	Sickle cell hemoglobinopathies (<5 year old)[a,b]
61.	Smallpox[c]
62.	Staphylococcus aureus, vancomycin resistant (VRSA) or intermediate (VISA) invasive disease[a,b]
63.	Streptococcal invasive disease (Group A)[a]
64.	*Streptococcus pneumoniae*, drug resistant invasive disease[a,b]
65.	Syphilis (all stages)[a,b]
66.	Tetanus[a,b]
67.	Toxic shock syndrome[a]
68.	Toxoplasmosis[a,b]
69.	Trichinosis[a,b]
70.	Tuberculosis, suspected or confirmed active disease (all sites) including the results of drug susceptibility[a,b]
71.	Tularemia[a,b]
72.	Typhoid fever[b,c]

[a]Health care practitioners and health care facilities must report within five working days.
[b]Clinical laboratories must report by next working day.
[c]Health care practitioners and health care facilities must report within 24 hours.
[d]Clinical laboratories must submit isolates to the state laboratory within five working days of isolation.

Pennsylvania's Electronic Disease Reporting Project (PA-NEDSS)

Recognizing the current surveillance systems' inefficient response to infectious disease incidents, and outbreaks, the Centers for Disease Control and Prevention (CDC) established a vision for the National Electronic Disease Surveillance System (NEDSS). Started in October 1999, this vision included the use of the Internet and other advanced information technologies to improve the systematic collection analysis, interpretation, and dissemination of data regarding health-related events. In addition, the CDC desired more timely, complete and useful data that could be utilized by public health staff as they take action to reduce morbidity and mortality, and to improve public health in general. Further, it was envisioned that data disseminated by the public health surveillance system could be used for immediate public health action, program planning and evaluation, and formulating research hypotheses.

As the CDC was laying the foundation for NEDSS, the events of September 11th and the increased threats of bioterrorism called attention to the need for a new generation of disease surveillance systems to be developed and implemented. The Pennsylvania Department of Health (DOH) understood the importance of the NEDSS initiative. The DOH leadership group oversaw an aggressive campaign to arm their public health officials and providers with critical information technology tools to help them improve public health decision making. The Commonwealth became the first state to develop and implement a Web-based application in which hospitals, laboratories, and physicians enter disease reports online and public health staff, based on program area and jurisdiction, review and begin investigation of reportable diseases.

Pennsylvania's Electronic Disease Reporting project, PA-NEDSS, is Pennsylvania's response to this national initiative. PA-NEDSS is a new way to report diseases and investigative findings to the Pennsylvania DOH via the Internet. It replaces the card and form-based methods. As of November 16, 2003, PA-NEDSS is the mandatory electronic disease reporting application for Pennsylvania. For more information about electronic disease reporting regulation, please review [33 Pa.B 2439] www.pabulletin.com/secure/data/vol33/33-20/941.html.

PA-NEDSS Functionality

PA-NEDSS establishes a near real-time, secure communication link between laboratories, hospitals, individual medical practices, and the Pennsylvania DOH. Although the reporting process remains unchanged, PA-NEDSS seeks to improve the timeliness and accuracy of disease reporting and expand the public health infrastructure to improve response to possible bioterrorism attacks. PA-NEDSS provides the following core features:

1. Web-based reporting for laboratories, hospitals, and physicians
2. Integrated electronic lab reporting (ELR)
3. Integrated Health Alert Network (HAN)
4. Morbidity and Mortality Weekly Report (MMWR) and report extracts for CDC
5. Graphical reporting/analytical tools
6. Geographical Information System (GIS) mapping tools used to plot cases on a map
7. Comprehensive and integrated system for all program areas including Case Management for Epidemiology (EPI), Tuberculosis (TB), Sexually Transmitted Disease (STD), and Elevated Blood Lead Level (Lead) program areas

Reporting of Drugs

The *Controlled Substance, Drug, Device, and Cosmetic Act* (35 P.S. §§780–101 to 780–144) regulates the schedules of controlled substances and requires the registration of manufacturers, distributors, and retailers of controlled substances, other drugs, and devices.

The *Pennsylvania Wholesale Prescription Drug Distributors' Act* (63 P.S. §§391.1 to 391.15) requires the licensing of all wholesale distributors of prescription drugs who deal in interstate commerce.

The *Noncontrolled Substances Reporting and Registration Act* (35 P.S. §§881 to 888) mandates additions to the list of drugs identified in the statute that could be used in the illegal manufacture or sale of controlled substances. This act also requires the registration of persons engaged in the sale, distribution, or transfer of any substance that could be used in the illegal manufacture or sale of controlled substances.

The *Pennsylvania Drug and Alcohol Abuse Control Act* (71. P.S. §§1690.101 to 1690.115) mandates the development and adoption of a comprehensive state plan for the control, prevention, intervention, treatment, rehabilitation, research, education, and training aspects of drug and alcohol abuse and dependence problems.

Act 152 of 1988 (71 P.S. §§611.14 and 611.115) addresses nonhospital residential detoxification and rehabilitation by requiring availability and administration (by the DOH) of Medical Assistance funds for detoxification and substance abuse rehabilitation offered in nonhospital residential settings.

Reports of sales by wholesalers (35 P.S. §823) states that "it shall be the duty of all wholesale dealers to make quarterly reports of their sales to other dealers, wholesalers, or retailers, of cocaine or its salts, derivatives, or compounds, or any substance or preparation containing cocaine, its salts, derivatives, or compounds, to the State Pharmaceutical Examining Board (now the State Board of Pharmacy), upon blanks to be provided for this purpose by the said Board." Under *Punishment for violations* (35 P.S. §824), "any person violating any of the provisions of this act [§§821–826] shall be sentenced to pay a fine of not more than $500, and undergo an imprisonment of not more than two years, or both, or either, at the discretion of the court."

Reporting of Impaired Drivers

The Pennsylvania Department of Transportation (PennDOT) has adopted physical and mental criteria for licensing drivers of motor vehicles. In accordance with Section 1518(b) of Title 75 of the Pennsylvania Vehicle Code, all physicians and other persons authorized to diagnose or treat disorders and disabilities must report to PennDOT any patient over 15 years of age who is diagnosed as having a condition that could impair his or her ability to drive safely. This reporting by physicians assists PennDOT in determining whether those individuals applying for drivers' licenses or those individuals already possessing drivers' licenses are medically qualified to safely operate a motor vehicle.

Reportable Conditions are those that must be reported to PennDOT and include impaired vision, seizure disorders, and other general disqualifications.

Impaired Vision

Certain conditions of impaired vision must be reported to PennDOT. For example, a person with visual acuity of less than 20/70 with the best correction is not authorized to drive.

Epilepsy

A person suffering from epilepsy may not drive unless their personal licensed physician reports that the person has been free from seizure for a period of one year or more immediately preceding, with or without medication.

Driver's License Applicants — 16–18 years of Age

Applicants between 16 and 18, applying for their first license, shall have been free from seizure for a period of at least two years immediately preceding, with or without medication.

Waiver

A physician specializing in neurology or neurosurgery may recommend waiver of the freedom of seizure requirement for the person if:

A. A strictly nocturnal pattern of the condition has existed for more than three years immediately preceding, with or without medication
B. A specific, prolonged aura accompanied by "sufficient warning" was established over a period of at least five years immediately preceding, with or without medication

Other Disqualifications

A person afflicted by any of the following conditions may not drive if, in the opinion of the examining health care provider, the conditions are likely to interfere with the ability to control and safely operate a motor vehicle.

A. Unstable or brittle diabetes or hypoglycemia, unless the individual for a continuous period of at least six months has not experienced any related syncopal attack
B. Cerebral vascular insufficiency or cardiovascular disease, including hypertension, with accompanying signs and symptoms
C. Periodic loss of consciousness, attention, or awareness from whatever cause
D. Loss or impairment of the use of a foot, leg, finger, thumb, hand, or arm as a functional defect or limitation
E. Rheumatic, arthritic, orthopedic muscular, or neuromuscular disease
F. Mental or emotional disorders, whether organic or functional
G. Use of any drug or substance, including alcohol, known to impair skill or functions, regardless of whether the drug or substance is medically prescribed
H. Another condition which, in the opinion of the examining licensed physician, could interfere with the ability to control and safely operate a motor vehicle
I. Mental deficiency or marked mental retardation in accordance with the International Classification of Diseases. For diagnostic categories, terminology, and concepts to be used in classification, the health care provider should refer to the *Diagnostic and Statistical Manual* of the American Psychiatric Association and the *Manual on Terminology and Classification in Mental Retardation* of the American Association on Mental Deficiency

Reporting Procedure

The Pennsylvania Vehicle Code requires physicians (and other persons authorized to diagnose or treat the disorders and disabilities discussed before) to report, in writing, the full name, date of birth, and address of individuals, age 15 or older, having a specified disorder or disability. The report must be made within 10 days of the health care provider's contact with the individual, and it must be sent to the following address:

PennDOT
Bureau of Driver Licensing
Driver Qualifications Section
P.O. Box 68682
Harrisburg, PA 17106-8682, U.S.
Tel.: +1-717-787-9662

By law, these reports must remain confidential. They must be used solely by PennDOT and solely to determine the competency of any person to operate a motor vehicle in Pennsylvania. The health care provider's duty to report supersedes patient–physician confidentiality.

Reporting of Errors

The *Medical Care Availability and Reduction of Error Act* (40 P.S. §§1303.101 to 1303.901) mandates: (1) investigation and collection of reports of serious events and infrastructure failures from hospitals, ambulatory surgical facilities, and birth centers; (2) assessment and collection of a surcharge on facilities' license fees to be deposited in the Patient Safety Fund; (3) review and approval of patient safety plans submitted by facilities; (4) analysis and evaluation of existing health care procedures and approval of recommendations issued by the Patient Safety Authority; and (5) promulgation of regulations when it is determined that patient safety recommendations should be required as conditions of licensure.

Reporting of Health Care Institutions and Practitioners

The *Health Care Facilities Act* (35 P.S. §§448.101 to 448.904b) addresses the licensure and regulation of hospitals, nursing homes, ambulatory surgical facilities, home health agencies, birth centers, and cancer treatment centers, while the *Prescribed Pediatric Extended Care Centers Act* (35 P.S. §§449.61 to 449.77) addresses the licensure and regulation of pediatric extended care centers.

The *Federal Nursing Home Reform Act* (42 U.S.C. §1395i-3) establishes a nurse aide registry and mandates periodic hearing on nurse aide abuse, neglect, and misappropriation of resident property.

The *Health Maintenance Organization Act* (40 P.S. §§1551 to 1568) enables the PA Department of Health and the PA Department of Insurance to regulate jointly to ensure quality, accessibility, and adequacy of health services provided through HMOs, whereas the *Professional Health Services Plan Corporations (Blue Shield) Act* enables the same two agencies to ensure quality, accessibility, and adequacy of health services provided through professional health services plan corporations.

Section 764a of the Pennsylvania Insurance Code (concerning preferred provider organizations) (40 P.S. § 764a) seeks to regulate PPOs and to ensure adequate quality and utilization controls for PPOs that assume financial risk that may lead to undertreatment or poor quality care.

Article XXI of the Insurance Company Law of 1921, relating to health care accountability and protection (40 P.S. §§991.2101 to 991.2193), requires managed care organizations (MCOs) to assure the availability and accessibility of adequate and timely health care services for their enrollees. This law also requires MCOs to properly credential health care providers, to provide complaint and grievance systems, to follow utilization review procedures, to pay claims promptly, to ensure continuity of care, and to ensure access to emergency care.

The *Emergency Medical Services Act* (P.S. §§6921 to 6938) mandates planning, guidance, assistance, and improvement of local emergency medical service systems and coordination of these systems into a unified statewide system. This act also provides for inspection, approval, and regulation of the components of the statewide EMS system, and establishes the Catastrophic Medical Rehabilitation Fund to provide medical, rehabilitation, and attendant care services to trauma victims through the Head Injury Program.

The *Clinical Laboratory Act* (35 P.S. §§6700-101 to 6700-802) mandates licensure of laboratories to ensure minimum standards for adequacy of equipment and facilities, the accuracy of results, and ethical practice and advertising.

The *Pennsylvania Blood Bank Act* (35 P.S. §§6501 to 6523) seeks to safeguard the health and well-being of citizens with reference to use of blood and blood products.

Reporting of Crimes and Criminal Activities

In the aftermath of the death of Jeanne Clery, a 19-year-old Lehigh University freshman, who was assaulted and murdered in her dorm room in April 1986, her parents began lobbying state lawmakers for statutes requiring colleges to publicize their crime statistics. In May 1988, Pennsylvania Governor Robert Casey signed the first such bill, mandating that all state colleges and universities publish three years' worth of campus crime statistics. President George Bush signed a similar federal bill, the Student Right-To-Know and Campus Security Act, into law on November 8, 1990. The 1998 amendments to the law formally renamed the act in memory of Clery.

The Jeanne Clery Disclosure of Campus Security Policy and Campus Crime Statistics Act (20 U.S.C. §1092(f)) is a federal law that requires colleges and universities to disclose information about crime on and around their campuses. The requirements of the Clery Act are straightforward. Colleges and universities must perform the following:

1. Publish and distribute an annual campus security report by October 1 of each year. This report should provide on- and off-campus crime statistics for the prior three years, policy statements, campus crime prevention program descriptions, and procedures to be followed in the investigation and prosecution of alleged sex offenses
2. By October 1 of each year, distribute to all current students and employees a copy of the annual security report, or a notice including a brief description of the

report's contents that announces the report's availability on the Internet, the exact electronic address for the report, and a statement on how to obtain a paper copy if desired

3. Inform prospective students and employees about the existence of the campus security report and how to access it on the Internet or request a paper copy
4. Provide timely notice to the campus community of crimes considered threats to the public safety
5. Maintain a public log of all crimes reported to the institution's campus police or security departments, if any

The U.S. Department of Education is charged with enforcing the Clery Act and may level civil penalties, up to $25,000 per violation, against institutions of higher education or may suspend those in violation from participating in federal student financial aid programs. Regulations effective as of July 1, 2003, can be found at 34 C.F.R. §668.46 *et seq.*

What Is a "Reported" Crime?

According to the Clery Act, a crime is "reported" when a victim or witness brings it to the attention of the local police or a campus security authority. A crime report does not have to be made to, or be investigated by, the police or a security officer, nor must a finding of guilt or criminal responsibility be made.

Debate rages, however, over what is meant by "on campus." A good operative definition for "on campus" is property within a reasonably contiguous geographic area of the college or university that is owned by the institution but is:

- Controlled by another person or institution
- Frequently used by students or supports institutional purposes, such as a restaurant or retail business frequented by students

Crimes that occur in student residence halls, apartments, and houses operated by officially recognized student groups are considered "on campus" crimes, and crimes that occur on all public property that passes through or is adjacent to campus must be reported in a separate "public property" category. This important provision of the act means that crimes committed on any thoroughfares, streets, sidewalks, or parking facilities that are within the campus, or immediately adjacent to and accessible from the campus, must be counted as campus crimes.

If a college or university is in doubt about whether a crime has been reported or whether the crime occurred "on campus," the institution should defer to the judgment of recognized law enforcement professionals.

Compliance and Prevention

Compliance with the Clery Act is far more than just a data collection exercise. Campuses are expected to use the information to better understand crime and violence at and around their institutions. The information collected can give details on prevention efforts and lead to policy changes that will enable colleges and universities to improve their responses to campus community crime and violence generally. The data also provide important consumer information to families and students in the process of selecting a college or university.

Since no campus security or police department is big enough to do the job alone, promoting campus safety requires the involvement and cooperation of students, faculty, and staff. For example, students can help make the campus a safer place by assuming responsibility for their own safety and by looking out for their friends and other classmates. Campus officials can organize safe-ride and campus-escort services at night and ensure that doors to residence halls are secure. Those students who drink alcoholic beverages can protect themselves by never accepting an open container at a party or in other social settings.

In addition, by conducting frequent campus safety audits — including walks around the campus by trained crime prevention specialists — colleges and universities can identify areas of the campus that may require enhanced lighting at night or physical redesign to reduce the risk of pedestrians becoming crime victims.

Among the campus security Web resources available to assist campuses both to understand the requirements of the Clery Act, and to make their environments safer for students, faculty, staff, and community members, are the following:

- The Council on Law in Higher Education (CLHE), a nonprofit, independent educational organization dedicated to identifying and explaining important legal issues to the higher education community and policymakers: http://www.clhe.org/issues/security.htm
- The International Association of Campus Law Enforcement Administrators, established to advance public safety for educational institutions by providing educational resources, advocacy, and professional development: http://www.iaclea.org
- Security On Campus, Inc., "Jeanne Clery Act Information Page," committed to maintaining the most comprehensive resource on this law: http://www.campussafety.org/schools/cleryact
- U.S. Department of Education Office of Postsecondary Education campus security page: http://www.ed.gov/offices/OPE/PPI/security.html.

Under the *Clery Act*, colleges and universities are required to report crimes in the following categories:

- Criminal homicide
  - Murder and nonnegligent manslaughter
  - Negligent manslaughter
- Sex offenses — forcible
- Sex offenses — nonforcible
- Robbery
- Aggravated assault
- Burglary
- Arson
- Motor vehicle theft
- Arrest and disciplinary referrals for
  - Liquor-law violations
  - Drug-law violations
  - Illegal weapons possession.

Reporting of Abortions

To protect the health and safety of women having abortions and of premature infants aborted alive, the *Abortion Control Act* (18 Pa.C.S. §§ 3201 to 3218) establishes standards regarding abortions and facilities in which abortions are performed. This Act also mandates development and dissemination of materials that may assist women in making decisions about abortion. The Act further directs the PA Department of Health to (1) receive various reports relating to abortions, (2) develop annual reports of statistical data for review by the PA General Assembly, and (3) establish and enforce standards applicable to the sale and use of fetal tissue and organs.

Reporting of Child Care and Abuse

The *Children's Health Care Act* (40 P.S. §§991.2301 to 991.2361 and 62 P.S. §§5001.1303 to 5001.1304) increases the availability of primary health practitioners in medically underserved areas through various grants to improve training, recruitment, and retention of such practitioners, through loan repayment programs for practitioners who agree to practice in medically underserved areas, and by linking efforts of the Departments of Health and Insurance to coordinate and supervise outreach activities for enrolling children in the Children's Health Insurance Program (CHIP).

The *Childhood Immunization Insurance Act* (40 P.S. §§3501 to 3508) determines the immunizations of children that must be covered by insurance carriers.

The *School Health Code* (24 P.S. §14-1401 *et seq.* and §25-2501.1) enables approval or direction of modified school health programs, and provides a basis for reimbursement for school health services that comply with minimum statutory and regulatory requirements for basic medical and dental services.

Section 1303a of the Public School Code (24 P.S. §§13-1303a) authorizes an Advisory Health Board to make and review a list of diseases against which children must be immunized, as the Secretary may direct, before being admitted to school for the first time. This section also authorizes issuance of certificates of immunization, by which schools are to determine whether immunization has occurred.

The *Federal Child Nutrition Act of 1966* (42 U.S.C.A. §§1786 to 1788) establishes the WIC Program administered through the states, while the *State Women's, Infants', and Children's Nutrition Improvement Act* (62 P.S. §§2951 to 2955) authorizes the provision of state funds to expand participation in the WIC Program in Pennsylvania.

The *Newborn Child Testing Act* (35 P.S. §§621–625), as amended by language amending the *Administrative Code in Act 47 of 2003* (71 P.S. §531), establishes a newborn screening program requiring testing of newborns for diseases which, if undetected, may cause mental retardation, permanent disability, or death. The amendment provides that the DOH shall permit any CLIA-certified laboratory using normal pediatric reference ranges to perform the specimen analyses required by the Act. The testing performed by such a laboratory must include testing for the newborn diseases as established by law or regulation and shall provide test results and reports consistent with policies, procedures, law, and regulations.

The *Infant Hearing Education, Assessment, Reporting, and Referral (IHEARR) Act* (11.P.S. §§876-1 to 876-9) authorizes the DOH to plan, establish, administer, and evaluate a comprehensive IHEARR program of appropriate screening and other services for newborns, infants, and children who have hearing loss.

The *Infant Crib Safety Act* (35 P.S. §§991 to 999) authorizes a public–private collaboration to provide public education materials to individuals and organizations regarding risks posed by second hand, hand-me-down, or heirloom cribs that do not conform to modern safety standards or which have dangerous features or characteristics.

Child Abuse Reporting Statutes

All 50 states and the District of Columbia have enacted statutes that mandate the reporting of suspected child abuse. States are required to enact statutes that provide for the reporting of known and suspected child abuse and neglect, and that provide for certain procedures and programs relating to child abuse to qualify for federal grant monies under the Child Abuse Prevention and Treatment Act, 42 U.S.C. §5101–5106 (West 1997).

Many of these statutes were patterned after a model statute promulgated by the U.S. Department of Health, Education, and Welfare in 1963, which requires physicians to report suspected cases of child abuse, and which makes the failure to make such a report a misdemeanor.[5] Since 1963, however, the statutes have been amended to expand both the circumstances that give rise to the duty to report abuse and the class of persons who are required to report abuse. The statutes have also been expanded to include civil liability as well as criminal liability. See generally the works of Besharov[6] (discussing the civil liability of health-care professionals for the failure to report child abuse), Deed[7] (discussing the duty of a psychotherapist to report child abuse), Wesley et al.[8] (discussing the duty of a psychotherapist to report child abuse) and Veilleux.[9]

As to the persons who must report child abuse, the statutes may be divided into four categories. First, there are those statutes that require a particular and exclusive class of persons to report suspected cases of child abuse that do *not* include attorneys. Generally, the class comprises health care practitioners and child custodians. These states include Alabama, Alaska, Arizona, Arkansas, California, Colorado, Connecticut, District of Columbia, Georgia, Hawaii, Illinois, Iowa, Kansas, Louisiana, Maine, Maryland, Massachusetts, Michigan, Minnesota, Missouri, Montana, New York, North Dakota, South Carolina, South Dakota, Vermont, Virginia, Washington, and West Virginia. It has been generally held that where the statute does not mandate that attorneys report suspected cases of child abuse, then the attorney has no duty to report under the criminal law, and the attorney–client privilege remains intact. (e.g., *D.A.S. v. Colorado*, 863 P.2d 291 [Colo. 1993]).

Second, there are those statutes that require a particular and exclusive class of persons to report suspected cases of child abuse that *do* include attorneys. These states include Mississippi and Nevada.

Third, there are those statutes that require *any* person to report suspected cases of child abuse, *including attorneys*, either explicitly or implicitly by not providing for an exception based on attorney–client privilege. These states include Idaho, Indiana, Nebraska, New Mexico, North Carolina, Oklahoma, Pennsylvania, Texas, and Utah.

Fourth, there are those statutes that require *any* person to report suspected cases of child abuse, *but which then specifically excludes attorneys from reporting by preserving the attorney–client privilege*. These states include Delaware, Florida, Kentucky, New Hampshire, New Jersey, Ohio, Oregon, Rhode Island, Tennessee, and Wyoming.

The following is a summary for each state of who must report suspected cases of child abuse and neglect:

(1) *Alabama*: Ala. Code §26-14-3 (Supp. 1997): Mandatory reporting by hospitals, clinics, sanitariums, doctors, physicians, surgeons, medical examiners, coroners, dentists, osteopaths, optometrists, chiropractors, podiatrists, nurses, school teachers and officials, peace officers, law enforcement officials, pharmacists, social workers, day care workers or employees, mental health professionals, or any other person called upon to render aid to medical assistance to any child. Ala. Code § 26-14-10 specifically provides that attorney–client privilege is not abrogated by the reporting statute.

(2) *Alaska*: Alaska Stat. §47-17.020 (Michie 1996): Mandatory reporting by practitioners of the healing arts, school teachers and administrators, social workers, peace officers and officers of the Department of Corrections, administrative officers of institutions, child care providers, employees of domestic violence and sexual assault programs, and substance abuse counselors. Alaska Stat. §47.17.060 makes no mention of attorney–client privilege, but abrogates physician–patient and husband–wife privilege in cases of abuse.

(3) *Arizona*: Ariz. Rev. Stat. Ann. §13-3620(A) (West Supp. 1997): Mandatory reporting by any physician, hospital intern or resident, surgeon, dentist, osteopath, chiropractor, podiatrist, county medical examiner, nurse, psychologist, school personnel, social worker, peace officer, parent, counselor, clergyman or priest, or any other person having responsibility for the care or treatment of children. Ariz. Rev. Stat. Ann. §13-3620(F) specifically preserves attorney–client privilege.

(4) *Arkansas*: Ark. Code Ann. §12-12-507(b) (1995): Mandatory reporting by any physician, surgeon, coroner, dentist, osteopath, resident intern, licensed nurse, medical personnel of a hospital, teacher, school official, school counselor, social worker, family service worker, day care center worker, foster care worker, mental health professional, peace officer, law enforcement official, prosecuting attorney, or judge. Ark. Code Ann. § 12-12-507(c) provides that no privilege shall relieve anyone required to make a notification of the requirement to make a notification. Ark. Code Ann. §12-12-518(1) specifically preserves attorney–client privilege.

(5) *California*: Cal. Penal Code §11166 (West Supp. 1998): Mandatory reporting by any child care custodian, health practitioner, employee of a child protective agency, child visitation monitor, firefighter, animal control officer, humane society officer, clergy member, or commercial film and photographic print processor.

(6) *Colorado*: Colo. Rev. Stat. Ann. §19-3-304(2) (West 1997): Mandatory reporting by any physician or surgeon, child health associate, medical examiner or coroner, dentist, osteopath, optometrist, chiropractor, chiropodist or podiatrist, registered nurse or licensed practical nurse, hospital personnel, Christian Science practitioner, public or private school official or employee, social worker, mental health professional, dental hygienist, psychologist, physical therapist, veterinarian, peace officer, pharmacist, commercial film processor, firefighter, or victim's advocate. Colo. Rev. Stat. Ann. §19-3-311 does not mention abrogation of the attorney–client privilege.

(7) *Connecticut*: Conn. Gen. Stat. Ann. §17a-101 (West Supp. 1998): Mandatory reporting by any physician or licensed surgeon, resident physician or intern in any hospital, nurse, licensed practical nurse, medical examiner, dentist, dental hygienist, psychologist, school teacher, school principal, school guidance counselor, school paraprofessional, social worker, police officer, clergyman, pharmacist, physical therapist, osteopath, optometrist, chiropractor, podiatrist, mental health professional, physician assistant, licensed

substance abuse counselor, licensed marital and family therapist, sexual assault counselor, battered women's counselor, or any person paid to care for a child in any public or private facility, day care center, or family day care home.

(8) *Delaware*: Del. Code Ann. tit. 16, §903 (1995): Mandatory reporting by any physician, any other person in the healing art, intern, resident, nurse, school employee, social worker, psychologist, medical examiner, *or any other person who knows or reasonably suspects child abuse.* Del. Code Ann. tit. 16, §908 specifically preserves attorney–client privilege.

(9) *District of Columbia*: D.C. Code Ann. §2-1352(b) (1994): Mandatory reporting by any physician, psychologist, medical examiner, dentist, chiropodist, registered nurse, licensed practical nurse, person involved in the care and treatment of patients, law enforcement officer, school official, teacher, social service worker, day care worker, or any mental health professional. D.C. Code Ann. §2-1355 does not mention the attorney–client privilege.

(10) *Florida*: Fla. Stat. Ann. §415.504 (West 1998): Any person, including but not limited to, physician, osteopathic physician, medical examiner, chiropractor, nurse, hospital personnel, health or mental health professional, practitioner who relies on spiritual means for healing, school teacher or other school official or personnel, social worker, day care center worker, or other professional child care, foster care, residential, or institutional worker, or law enforcement officer. Fla. Stat. Ann. §415.512 specifically provides that attorney–client confidences shall be a defense to failure to report.

(11) *Georgia*: Ga. Code Ann. §19-7-5 (Supp. 1997): Mandatory reporting by physicians, hospital or medical personnel, dentists, licensed psychologists, podiatrists, registered professional nurses, licensed practical nurses, professional counselors, social workers, marriage and family therapists, school teachers, school administrators, school guidance counselors, child welfare agency personnel, child counseling personnel, child service organization personnel, or law enforcement personnel.

(12) *Hawaii*: Haw. Rev. Stat. Ann. §350-1.1 (Michie 1994): Mandatory reporting by any licensed or registered professional in the healing arts or any health related profession, employees or officers of any public or private school, employees or officers of any public or private agency or institution providing health care, employees or officers of any law enforcement agency, providers of child care, medical examiners and coroners, employees of any agency providing recreational or sports activities. Haw. Rev. Stat. Ann. §350-5 does not mention attorney–client privilege.

(13) *Idaho*: Idaho Code §16-1619(a) (Supp. 1997): Mandatory reporting by any physician, resident, intern, nurse, coroner, school teacher, day care personnel, social worker, *or any other person having reason to believe that a child has been abused.* Idaho Code §16-1619(c) exempts duly ordained ministers of a religion.

(14) *Illinois*: 325 Ill. Comp. Stat. Ann. 5/4 (West Supp. 1998): Mandatory reporting by any physician, resident, intern, hospital, hospital administrator and personnel engaged in examination, care and treatment of persons, surgeon, dentist, dental hygienist, osteopath, chiropractor, podiatrist, physician assistant, substance abuse treatment personnel, Christian Science practitioner, funeral home director, coroner, medical examiner, emergency medical technician, acupuncturist, crisis line or hotline personnel, school personnel, educational advocates, truant officer, social worker, social services administrator, domestic violence program personnel, registered nurse, licensed practical nurse, director or staff assistant of nursery school, or child day care center, recreational program or facility personnel, law enforcement officer, registered psychologist or assistant thereto, psychiatrist,

field personnel of Illinois government agencies, probation officer, foster parent, home-maker, or child care worker.

(15) *Indiana*: Ind. Code Ann. §31-33-5-1 (Michie 1997): Mandatory reporting by *any individual who has reason to believe that a child is a victim of abuse or neglect.*

(16) *Iowa*: Iowa Code Ann. §232.69 (West Supp. 1998): Mandatory reporting by any health care practitioner, social worker, employee or operator of a health care facility, psychologist, school employee, employee or operator of child care facility, employee of the department of human services, employee of a substance abuse program, employee of a juvenile detention center, employee of a foster care facility, peace officer, dental hygienist, counselor, or mental health professional. Iowa Code Ann. §232.74 does not mention attorney–client privilege.

(17) *Kansas*: Kan. Stat. Ann. §38-1522 (Supp. 1998): Mandatory reporting by persons licensed to practice the healing arts, dentistry, or optometry, licensed psychologists, licensed practical nurses, teachers, school administrator, officers of medical care facilities, marriage and family therapists, child care providers, social workers, firefighters, emergency medical services personnel, mediators, juvenile officers, and law enforcement officers. Kan. Stat. Ann. §38-1554 does not mention attorney–client privilege.

(18) *Kentucky*: Ky. Rev. Stat. Ann. §620.030 (Michie 1990): Mandatory reporting by any person, including but not limited to, physician, osteopathic physician, nurse, teacher, school personnel, social worker, coroner, medical examiner, child-caring personnel, resident, intern, chiropractor, dentist, optometrist, emergency medical technician, paramedic, health professional, mental health professional, or peace officer. Ky. Rev. Stat. Ann. §620.050 specifically preserves the attorney–client privilege.

(19) *Louisiana*: La. Children's Code Ann. art. 603 (1995): Mandatory reporting by health practitioner, mental health/social service practitioner, teaching or child care provider, police officer or law enforcement official, or commercial film and photographic print processor.

(20) *Maine*: Me. Rev. Stat. Ann. tit. 22, §4011 (Supp. 1997): Mandatory reporting by medical or osteopathic physician, resident, intern, emergency medical services person, medical examiner, physician's assistant, dentist, dental hygienist, dental assistant, chiropractor, podiatrist, registered or licensed practical nurse, teacher, guidance counselor, school official, social worker, court appointed special advocate, guardian *ad litem*, homemaker, home health aide, medical or social service worker, psychologist, child care personnel, mental health professional, law enforcement official, state fire inspector, municipal code enforcement official, municipal fire inspector, commercial film and print processor, and clergy member (except when received as the result of confession). Me. Rev. Stat. Ann. tit. 22, §4015 does not mention attorney–client privilege.

(21) *Maryland*: Md. Code Ann., Family Law §5-704 (Supp. 1997): Mandatory reporting by any health practitioner, police officer, educator, or human service worker.

(22) *Massachusetts*: Mass. Gen. Laws Ann. ch. 119, §51A (West Supp. 1998): Mandatory reporting by any physician, medical intern, hospital personnel, medical examiner, psychologist, emergency medical technician, dentist, nurse, chiropractor, podiatrist, optometrist, osteopath, public or private school teacher, educational administrator, guidance or family counselor, day care worker, any person paid to care for or work with a child in any public or private facility or home program, probation officer, clerk/magistrate of the district court, parole officer, social worker, foster parent, fire fighter, policeman, office for children licensor, school attendance officer, allied mental health and human services professional, drug and alcoholism counselor, psychiatrist, clinical social worker.

(23) *Michigan*: Mich. Comp. Laws §722.623 (West Supp. 1998); Mich. Stat. Ann. §25.248(3) (Law. Co-op. 1992 & Supp. 1998): Mandatory reporting by physician, coronor, dentist, registered dental hygienist, medical examiner, nurse, person licensed to provide emergency medical care, audiologist, psychologist, marriage and family therapist, licensed professional counselor, certified social worker, social worker, social work technician, school administrator, school counselor or teacher, law enforcement officer, or regulated child care provider. No privilege other than the attorney–client privilege will constitute grounds for failure to report.

(24) *Minnesota*: Minn. Stat. Ann. §626.556(3) (West Supp. 1998): Mandatory reporting by any person who practices the healing arts, social services, hospital administration, psychological or psychiatric treatment, child care, education, or law enforcement, or member of the clergy who is performing ministerial as opposed to confessional duties.

(25) *Mississippi*: Miss. Code Ann. §43-21-353 (Supp. 1997): Mandatory reporting by any *attorney*, physician, dentist, inter, resident, nurse, psychologist, social worker, child care giver, minister, law enforcement officer, public or private school employee. No exception based on attorney–client privilege.

(26) *Missouri*: Mo. Ann. Stat. §210.115 (West 1996): Mandatory reporting by any physician, medical examiner, coroner, dentist, chiropractor, optometrist, podiatrist, resident, intern, nurse, hospital or clinic personnel, any other health practitioner, psychologist, mental health professional, social worker, day care center worker, child care worker, juvenile officer, probation or parole officer, teacher, principal, Christian Science practitioner, peace officer or law enforcement official, or other person with the responsibility for children.

(27) *Montana*: Mont. Code Ann. §41-3-201(2) (1997): Mandatory reporting by physician, resident, intern, member of hospital staff, nurse, osteopath, chiropractor, podiatrist, medical examiner, coroner, dentist, optometrist, health or mental health professional, Christian Science practitioner, school teacher, school official, social worker, operator or employee of day care center, foster care, residential care, or institutional worker, peace officer, clergy (if information obtained not from confession), guardian *ad litem* or court appointed advocated who is authorized to investigate a report of abuse or neglect. No mention of attorney–client privilege.

(28) *Nebraska*: Neb. Rev. Stat. §28-711 (1995): Mandatory reporting by physician, medical institution, nurse, school employee, social worker, or *other person who has reason to believe that a child has been abused or neglected.* Nev. Rev. Stat. §28-714 does not mention attorney–client privilege.

(29) *Nevada*: Nev. Rev. Stat. Ann. §432B.220 (Michie 1996): Mandatory reporting by physician, dentist, dental hygienist, chiropractor, optometrist, podiatrist, medical examiner, resident, intern, nurse, physician's assistant, psychiatrist, psychologist, marriage and family therapist, substance abuse counselor, advanced emergency medical technician, hospital personnel, coroner, clergyman, Christian Science practitioner (except if knowledge comes from confession), social worker or administrator, teacher, school counselor, school librarian, operator or employee of child care facility, foster home operator, law enforcement personnel, or an *attorney* (unless he has knowledge of abuse from a client who is or may be accused of abuse or neglect).

(30) *New Hampshire*: N.H. Rev. Stat. Ann. §169-C:29 (1994): Mandatory reporting by any physician, surgeon, county medical examiner, psychiatrist, resident, intern, dentist, osteopath, optometrist, chiropractor, psychologist, therapist, registered nurse, hospital personnel, Christian Science practitioner, teacher, school official, school nurse, school

counselor, social worker, day care worker, child or foster care worker, law enforcement official, priest, minister, rabbi, or *any other person having reason to suspect that a child has been
abused or neglected.* N.H. Rev. Stat. Ann. §169-C:32 specifically preserves attorney–client
privilege.

(31) *New Jersey:* N.J. Stat. Ann. §9:6-8.10 (West 1993): Mandatory reporting by *any
person having reasonable cause to believe that a child has been subjected to child abuse.*
The attorney–client privilege is preserved.

(32) *New Mexico:* N.M. Stat. Ann. §32A-4-3 (Michie Supp. 1998): Mandatory reporting by *any person,* including but not limited to physicians, law enforcement officers, judges,
nurses, teachers, and social workers, who knows or has reason to know that a child
is abused or neglected. N.M. Stat. Ann. §32A-4-5 provides that a report shall not be
inadmissible because of physician-patient privilege "or similar privilege or rule against
disclosure."

(33) *New York:* N.Y. Soc. Serv. Law §413 (McKinney Supp. 1998): Mandatory reporting
by any physician, registered physician assistant, surgeon, medical examiner, coroner,
dentist, dental hygienist, osteopath, optometrist, chiropractor, podiatrist, resident,
intern, psychologist, registered nurse, hospital personnel, Christian Science practitioner,
school official social services worker, day care worker, mental health professional, substance
abuse counselor, alcoholism counselor, peace officer, police officer, district attorney, assistant district attorney, investigator employed by the district attorney's office, or other law
enforcement official.

(34) *North Carolina:* N.C. Gen. Stat. §7A-543 (1995): Mandatory reporting *by any
person who has cause to suspect that a child is abused. No exception for attorneys stated.*

(35) *North Dakota:* N.D. Cent. Code §50-25.1-03 (Supp. 1997): Mandatory reporting
by any physician, nurse, dentist, optometrist, medical examiner, coroner, medical or mental
health professional, religious practitioner of healing arts, schoolteacher or administrator,
school counselor, addiction counselor, social worker, day care center worker, police or
law enforcement officer, or member of clergy (except of knowledge comes from confession).

(36) *Ohio:* Ohio Rev. Code Ann. §2151.421 (Anderson Supp. 1997): Mandatory
reporting by an *attorney,* physician, dentist, podiatrist, practitioner of a limited branch
of medicine, registered nurse, licensed practical nurse, visiting nurse, other health care
professional, licensed psychologist, licensed school psychologist, speech pathologist,
audiologist, coroner, administrator or employee of day care center or child care agency,
school teacher, school employee, school authority, person engaged in social work, or person
rendering spiritual treatment through prayer. An attorney, however, is not required to
make a report concerning any communication as the result of an attorney–client
relationship.

(37) *Oklahoma:* Okla. Stat. Ann. tit. 10, §7103 (1998): Mandatory reporting by any
physician or surgeon, nurse, teacher, *or any other person who has reason to believe that a
child is abused or neglected. No privilege or contract shall relieve any person from the reporting
requirement.*

(38) *Oregon:* Or. Rev. Stat. § 419B.005, §419B.010 (1995): Mandatory reporting by any
public or private official having reason to believe that a child has suffered abuse. Public or
private official is defined as any physician, dentist, school employee, nurse, employee of
DHR, peace officer, psychologist, clergyman, licensed clinical social worker, optometrist,
chiropractor, day care provider, *attorney,* naturopathic physician, licensed professional
counselor, licensed marriage and family therapist, and firefighter or emergency medical

technician. Or. Rev. Stat. §419B.010(1) provides, however, *that an attorney shall not be required to report such information communicated by a person if the communication is privileged.*

(39) *Pennsylvania*: 23 Pa. Cons. Stat. §6311 (Supp. 1998): Mandatory reporting by persons *who, in the course of their employment, occupation or practice of their profession, come into contact with children.* Moreover, the privileged communication between any professional person required to report and the patient or client of that person shall not apply. Persons required to report include, but are not limited to, any licensed physician, osteopath, medical examiner, coroner, funeral director, dentist, optometrist, chiropractor, podiatrist, intern, registered nurse, licensed practical nurse, hospital personnel, Christian Science practitioner, member of the clergy, school administrator, school nurse, school teacher, social services worker, day care worker, mental health professional, peace officer, or law enforcement official.

(40) *Rhode Island*: R.I. Gen. Laws §40-11-3 (1997): Mandatory reporting by *any person who has reasonable cause to know or suspect that any child has been abused or neglected.* R.I. Gen. Laws § 40-11-11, however, *provides that attorney–client privilege constitutes an excuse for failure to report.*

(41) *South Carolina*: S.C. Code Ann. §20-7-510 (Law Co-op. Supp. 1997): Mandatory reporting by any physician, nurse, dentist, optometrist, medical examiner, coroner, or any other medical, emergency medical services, mental health professional, Christian Science practitioner, religious healer, school teacher, counselor, principal, assistant principal, social or public assistance worker, substance abuse treatment staff, child care worker, police or law enforcement officer, undertaker, funeral home director, person responsible for processing film, or any judge. S.C. Code Ann. §20-7-550 specifically provides that the privileged quality of a communication is abrogated for purposes of the reporting statute, except between an attorney and client and between a priest and penitent.

(42) *South Dakota*: S.D. Codified Laws §26-8A-3 (Michie Supp. 1998): Mandatory reporting by any physician, dentist, doctor of osteopathy, chiropractor, optometrist, mental health professional or counselor, podiatrist, psychologist, religious healing practitioner, social worker, hospital intern or resident, parole or court services officer, law enforcement officer, teacher, school counselor, school official, nurse, licensed or registered child welfare provider, employee or volunterr of a domestic abuse shelter, chemical dependency counselor, or coroner. S.D. Codified Laws § 26-8A-15 does not mention attorney–client privilege.

(43) *Tennessee*: Tenn. Code Ann. §37-1-403 (1996): Mandatory reporting by *any person*, including but not limited to, any physician, osteopathic physician, medical examiner, chiropractor, nurse, hospital personnel, health or mental health professional, spiritual healer, school teacher or other school official or personnel, judge of any court of the state, social worker, day care center worker, professional child care worker, foster care worker, law enforcement officer, neighbor, relative, friend of any other person. Tenn. Code Ann. §37-1-614 provides that privilege does not apply, *except as to between an attorney and client.*

(44) *Texas*: Tex. Fam. Code §261.101 (West Supp. 1998): Mandatory reporting by a person having cause to believe that a child's physical or mental health or welfare has been or may be adversely affected by abuse. The requirement to report applies without exception to an individual whose personal communications may otherwise be privileged,

including an attorney, member of the clergy, medical practitioner, social worker, or mental health professional.

(45) *Utah*: Utah Code Ann. §62A-4a-403(1) (1997): Mandatory reporting by *any person who has reason to believe that a child has been abused or neglected*. An exception is made for a clergyman or priest. *No exception is stated for an attorney*.

(46) *Vermont*: Vt. Stat. Ann. tit. 33, §4913 (Supp. 1997): Mandatory reporting by any physician, surgeon, osteopath, chiropractor, physician's assistant, resident, intern, hospital administrator, nurse, medical examiner, dentist, psychologist, any health care provider, school superintendent, school teacher, school librarian, day care worker, school principal, school guidance counselor, mental health professional, social worker, probation officer, police officer, camp owner, camp administrator, or camp counselor.

(47) *Virginia*: Va. Code Ann. §63.1-248.3 (1995): Mandatory reporting by any person licensed to practice medicine or any of the healing arts, any hospital intern, resident, nurse, social worker, probation officer, teacher or school employee, child care provider, Christian Science practitioner, mental health professional, law enforcement officer, mediator eligible to receive court referrals, any professional staff person of a facility to which children have been placed for care, any person associated with or employed by any private organization responsible for the care, custody, or control of children.

(48) *Washington*: Wash. Rev. Code Ann. §26.44.030(1)(a) (West 1997): Mandatory reporting by any coroner, medical examiner, law enforcement officer, professional school personnel, nurse, social service counselor, psychologist, pharmacist, child care provider, juvenile probation officer, department of corrections personnel, or any adult relative to a child who lives with that adult.

(49) *West Virginia*: W. Va. Code Ann. §49-6A-2 (1996): Mandatory reporting by medical, dental, or mental health professional, Christian Science practitioner, religious healer, school teacher or other school personnel, social service worker, child care or foster care worker, emergency medical services personnel, peace officer or law enforcement official, member of the clergy, circuit court judge, family law master or magistrate.

(50) *Wisconsin*: Wis. Stat. Ann. §48.981 (1997): Mandatory reporting by a physician, coroner, medical examiner, nurse, dentist, chiropractor, optometrist, acupuncturist, other medical or mental health professional, social worker, marriage and family therapist, professional counselor, public assistance worker, school teacher or administrator, mediator, child care worker, day care provider, alcohol or substance abuse counselor, physical therapist, occupational therapist, dietician, speech language pathologist, audiologist, emergency medical technician, or law enforcement officer. *An attorney may make a report but is not required to*.

(51) *Wyoming*: Wyo. Stat. Ann. §14-3-205(a) (Michie 1997): Mandatory reporting by *any person who knows or has reasonable cause to believe or suspect that a child has been abused or neglected*. Wyo. Stat. Ann. §14-3-210 provides that *evidence of abuse may be excluded on the basis of attorney–client privilege*.

Public Health Surveillance Laws

Although the public health activity for which information is to be disclosed must be "authorized by law," the activity does not need to be specified by the law. General authority to conduct traditional or innovative public health surveillance for known organisms or diseases, for previously uncharacterized diseases or conditions, for covert deliberate terrorist events, or for "syndromic surveillance" can be found in the broadly worded language of many state public health statutes.[10] The following is a summary for each state of the pertinent general language that could be relied upon to authorize public health agencies to obtain ongoing or "real-time" data on relevant symptoms.

Alabama, Ala. Admin. Code r. 420-4-1-.04(7)(d) (2002), cases of diseases of potential public health significance.

Alaska, Alaska Admin. Code title 7, §27.005(a) (2002), epidemic outbreaks and an unusual incidence of infectious disease.

Arizona, Ariz. Admin. Code R9-6-202 (2002), Outbreaks of foodborne/waterborne illness.

Arkansas, Ark. Reg. 007 05 003 (2002), Occurrences which threaten the welfare, safety, or *health* of the *public* such as epidemic outbreaks.

California, Cal. Code Regs. title 17, §2500 (2002), the Occurrence of any unusual disease and outbreaks of any disease.

Colorado, 6 Colo. Code Regs. §1009-1 (2002), any unusual illness, or outbreak, or epidemic of illnesses which may be of *public* concern.

Connecticut, Conn. Agencies Regs. §19a-36-A1 (2002), other condition of *public health* significance.

Delaware, Del. Code Ann. title 16, §130 (2002), all cases of persons who harbor any illness or *health* condition that may be potential causes of a *public health* emergency.

Florida, Fla. Admin. Code Ann. r. 64D-3.002 (2002), Any disease outbreak in a community, a hospital, or other institution, or a foodborne, or waterborne outbreak.

Georgia, Ga. Comp. R. & Regs. r. 290-5-3-.02 (2001), Outbreaks or unusual clusters of disease (infectious and noninfectious).

Hawaii, Haw. Admin. Rules §11-156-3 (b) (2002), Any communicable disease ... occurring beyond usual frequency, or of unusual or uncertain etiology, including diseases which might be caused by a genetically engineered organism.

Idaho, Idaho Admin. Code 16.02.10.004 (2002), Rare diseases and unusual outbreaks of illness which may be a risk to the *public*.

Illinois, Ill. Admin. Code title 77, §690.295 (2002), Any unusual case or cluster of cases; and Ill. Admin. Code title, 77, §690.800 (2002), any suspected bioterrorist threat or events.

Indiana, Ind. Admin. Code. title 410, r. 1-2.3-47 (2002), Unusual occurrence of disease and any disease ... considered a bioterrorism threat.

Iowa, Iowa Admin. Code r. 641-1.3 (139A) (2002), Outbreaks of any kind, unusual syndromes, or uncommon diseases.

Kansas, Kan. Admin. Regs. 28-1-2 (2002), Any exotic or newly recognized disease, and any disease unusual in incidence or behavior, known or suspected to be infectious or contagious and constituting risk to the *public health* and The occurrence of a single case of any unusual disease or manifestation of illness that the *health* care provider determines or suspects may be caused by or related to a bioterrorist agent or incident.

Kentucky, 902 Ky. Admin. Regs. 2:020 (2002), an extraordinary number of cases or occurrences of disease or condition.

Louisiana, Sanitary Code Ch. 2 §2:003 (2002), all cases of rare or exotic communicable disease, unexplained death, unusual cluster of disease and all outbreaks.

Maine, 10-144 Code ME R. Ch. 258 §2 (2002), Any pattern of cases or increased incidence of illness beyond the expected number of cases in a given period, or cases which may indicate a newly recognized infectious agent, or an outbreak or related *public health* hazard.

Maryland, Md. Regs. Code title 10, §06.01.03 (2002), Outbreaks and Single Cases of Diseases of *Public Health* Importance.

Massachusetts, Mass. Regs. Code title 105 §300.122 (2002), Illness Believed to be Part of an Outbreak or Cluster.

Michigan, Mich. Admin. Code r. 325.173 (2002), the unusual occurrence of any disease, infection, or condition that threatens the *health* of the *public*.

Minnesota, Minn. R. 4605.7050 (2002), Any pattern of cases, suspected cases, or increased incidence of any illness beyond the expected number of cases in a given period.

Mississippi, Miss. Reg. 12 000 028 (2002), Any Suspected Outbreak.

Missouri, Mo. Code Regs. title 19, §20-20.020(3) (2002), The occurrence of an outbreak or epidemic of any illness, disease or condition which may be of *public health* concern ... [and] *public health* threats that could result from terrorist activities such as clusters of unusual diseases or manifestations of illness and clusters of unexplained deaths.

Montana, Mont. Admin. R. 37.114.203 (2002), Any unusual incident of unexplained illness or death in a human or animal.

Nebraska, 173 Neb. Admin. Code Ch. 1 §003 (2002), Clusters, outbreaks or epidemics of any *health* problem, infectious or other, including food poisoning, influenza or possible bioterroristic attack; increased disease incidence beyond expectations; unexplained deaths possibly due to unidentified infectious causes; any unusual disease or manifestations of illness.

Nevada, Nev. Admin. Code ch. 441A, §225 (2002), Extraordinary occurrence of illness.

New Hampshire, N.H. Code Admin. R. Ann. [He-P] 301.02 (2002), Unusual occurrence or cluster of illness which may pose a threat to the *public's health*.

New Jersey, N.J. Admin. Code title 8, §57-1.3 (2002), Any outbreak or suspected outbreak, including, but not limited to, foodborne, waterborne, or nosocomial disease or a suspected act of bioterrorism.

New Mexico, N.M. Admin. Code title 7 §4.3 (2002), Illnesses suspected to be caused by the intentional or accidental release of biologic or chemical agents, Acute illnesses of any type involving large numbers of persons in the same geographic area, and Other conditions of *public health* significance.

New York, N.Y. Comp. Codes R. & Regs. title 10 §2.1 (2002), Any disease outbreak or unusual disease.

North Carolina, N.C. Admin. Code title 15A, r. 19A.0102 (2002), all outbreaks or suspected outbreaks of foodborne illness; and N.C. Admin. Code title 15A, r. 19A.0103 (2002), a cluster of cases of a disease or condition ... which represents a significant threat to the *public health*.

North Dakota, N.D. Admin. Code §33-06-01-01 (2002), Unusual cluster of severe or unexplained illnesses or deaths.

Ohio, Ohio Admin. Code §3701-3-02 (2002), Any unexpected pattern of cases, suspected cases, deaths or increased incidence of any other disease of major *public health* concern, because of the severity of disease or potential for epidemic spread, which may indicate a newly recognized infectious agent, an outbreak, epidemic, related *public health* hazard or act of bioterrorism.

Oklahoma, Okla. Admin. Code §3701-3-02 (2002), Outbreaks of apparent infectious disease.

Oregon, Or. Admin. R. 333-018-0015 (2002), Any known or suspected common-source outbreaks; any Uncommon Illness of Potential *Public Health* Significance.

Pennsylvania, 28 Pa. Code §27.3 (2002), Unusual occurrence of a disease, infection or condition.

Rhode Island, R.I. Code R. 14 040 002 (2002), an outbreak of infectious disease or infestation, or a cluster of unexplained illness, infectious or noninfectious . . . Exotic diseases and unusual group expressions of illness which may be of *public health* concern.

South Carolina, S.C. Code Ann. §44-29-10 (2002), all cases of known or suspected contagious or infectious diseases . . . all cases of persons who harbor any illness or *health* condition that may be caused by chemical terrorism, bioterrorism, radiological terrorism, epidemic or pandemic disease, or novel and highly fatal infectious agents and might pose a substantial risk of a significant number of human fatalities or incidents of permanent or long-term disability.

South Dakota, S.D. Admin. R. 44:20:01:03 (2001), Epidemics or outbreaks . . . and Unexplained illnesses or deaths of humans or animals.

Tennessee, Tenn. Comp. R. & Regs.1200-14-1.02 (2002), Disease outbreaks, foodborne, waterborne, and all other.

Texas, 25 Tex. Admin. Code §97.3 (2002), any outbreak, exotic disease, and unusual group expressions of disease which may be of *public health* concern.

Utah, Utah Admin. Code 386-702 (2002), Any sudden or extraordinary occurrence of infectious or communicable disease and Any disease occurrence, pattern of cases, suspect cases, or increased coincidence of any illness which may indicate an outbreak, epidemic or related *public health* hazard, including but not limited to suspected or confirmed outbreaks of foodborne or waterborne disease, newly recognized or re-emergent diseases or disease producing agents.

Vermont, Vt. Code R. 13 140 007 (2002), Any unexpected pattern of cases, suspected cases, deaths or increased incidence of any other illness of major *public health* concern, because of the severity of illness or potential for epidemic spread, which may indicate a newly recognized infectious agent, an outbreak, epidemic, related *public health* hazard or act of bioterrorism.

Virginia, 12 Va. Admin. Code §5-90-80 (2002), Outbreaks, all (including foodborne, nosocomial, occupational, toxic substance-related, waterborne, and other outbreaks).

Washington, Wash. Admin. Code §246-101-301 (2002), Disease of suspected bioterrorism origin and Other rare disease of *public health* significance.

West Virginia, W. Va. Code St. R. §64-7-3 (2002), An outbreak or cluster of any illness or condition — suspect or confirmed and Unexplained or ill-defined illness, condition, or *health* occurrence of potential *public health* significance.

Wisconsin, Wis. Admin. Code Ch. HFS 145, App. A (2002), Suspected outbreaks of . . . acute or occupationally related diseases.

Wyoming, WY Rules and Regulations HLTH CHI Ch 1 s 5 (2002) and (http://wdhfs.state.wy.us/epiid/reportlist.pdf), A cluster of unusual or unexplained illnesses or deaths and suspected biological incidents.

The Clash between Compliance with Reporting Obligations and Compliance with Privacy Laws

In a nutshell, the recent Privacy Rule, promulgated pursuant to the Health Insurance Portability and Accountability Act of 1996 (HIPAA), is intended to protect the public from unauthorized access to, use of, and disclosure of individually identifiable health information. An undesirable consequence of the implementation of this Privacy Rule has been an increased reluctance of some practitioners to meet various public health reporting obligations. Some entities covered by HIPAA may use the Privacy Rule as an excuse to avoid the demands of public health reporting, especially the requirement of tracking disclosures that are not made for purposes of treatment, payment, or operations. Others may knowingly violate the law by refusing to disclose, and then invoke the Privacy Rule as a defense. The perceived conflict, however, between the HIPAA Privacy Rule and public health reporting obligations is unwarranted and cannot withstand even modest scrutiny. Although the language of the Privacy Rule does not require public health disclosures, it also does not prevent an entity from complying with relevant reporting laws.

> "In response to comments arguing that the provision (defining public health authority) is too broad we [Office of Civil Rights] note that section 1178(b) of the [HIPAA] Act, as explained in the NPRM [notice of proposed rulemaking], explicitly carves out protection for state public health laws. This provision states that: '[N]othing in this part shall be construed to invalidate or limit the authority, power, or procedures established under any law providing for the reporting of disease or injury, child abuse, birth or death, public health surveillance, or public health investigation or intervention.' In light of this broad congressional mandate not to interfere with current public health practices, we [OCR] believe the broad definition of 'public health authority' is appropriate to achieve that end."
>
> See 65(250) *Federal Register* 86264, December 28, 2000.

Clearly, the language of the Privacy Rule specifically excludes disclosures for public health activities from the requirement for individual authorization. Consequently, the sharing of protected health information (PHI) for public health purposes is permitted as long as the agency to which the information is provided is legally authorized to receive and collect the information. The Privacy Rule permits disclosures of PHI without patient authorizations — when the disclosures are required by law or when a public health authority is authorized by law to collect or receive information for preventing or controlling disease, injury, or disability. The specific exclusion for public health reporting (mandatory or voluntary) was allowed because public health authorities have a legitimate need for PHI to ensure public health and safety, and because public health agencies have a track record of protecting the confidentiality of PHI. The HIPAA Privacy Rule attempts to strike a reasonable balance between individual privacy rights and the need for public protection, and forensic professionals who engage in good-faith public health disclosures have little to fear from the HIPAA Privacy Rule in the way of civil or criminal liability.

References

1. Chorba, T.L., Berkelman, R.L., Safford, S.K., Gibbs, N.P., and Hull, H.E., Mandatory reporting of infectious diseases by clinicians. *JAMA*, 262, 3018–3026, 1989.

2. Gaus, S.M., Reporting child abuse. "Whistle blower protection" and physician responsibility. *Mich. Med.*, 87(4), 191–193, 1988.

3. Johnson, C.F., and Showers, J., Injury variables in child abuse. *Child Abuse Negl.*, 9(2), 207–215, 1985.

4. Morris, J.L., Johnson, C.F., and Clasen, M., To report or not to report. Physicians' attitudes toward discipline and child abuse. *Am. J. Dis. Child.*, 139(2), 194–197, 1985.

5. Children's Bureau, U.S. Department of Health, Education, and Welfare, *The Abused Child: Principles and Suggested Language of Legislation on Reporting of the Physically Abused Child*, 1963.

6. Douglas, J., Besharov, D.J., Child abuse and neglect: liability for failing to report, 22 Trial 67 (August 1986).

7. Deed, M.L., Mandated reporting revisited, *Law and Policy*, 14, 219, April/July 1992.

8. Crenshaw, W.B., and Lichtenberg, J.W., Child abuse and the limits of confidentiality: forewarning practices, *Behav. Sci. Law*, 11, 181, 1993.

9. Veilleux, D.R., Annotation, Validity, Construction, and Application of State Statute Requiring Doctor or Other Person to Report Child Abuse, 73 A.L.R. 4th 782 (1989).

10. Broome, C.V., Horton, H.H., Tress, D., Lucido, S.J., Koo, D., Statutory basis for public health reporting beyond specific diseases. *J. Urban Hlth: Bull NY Acad Med.*, 80(2) (Suppl 1), i14–22, 2003.

Forensic Science and Public Health — The Role of Forensic Epidemiology

36

STEVEN KOEHLER

Introduction

Forensic epidemiology is the convergence of two fields sharing a common goal: the application of epidemiological principles to forensic issues. Traditionally, the science of epidemiology has concentrated on the study of the distribution, causation, and control of disease in the human population, along with the risk factors that influence those patterns. The epidemiologist is primarily interested in the occurrence of disease by time, place, and individual. Epidemiology is the application of the scientific method to the study of disease in populations for the purpose of prevention or control. Epidemiologists (detectives) play a fundamental role in public health and preventive medicine by identifying variabilities in human situations that may have a critical influence on the occurrence of disease within populations.

The discipline provides the means of describing and predicting patterns of disease from a select group to an entire population by surveillance and research. Epidemiologic methods are designed to gather unbiased evidence from groups of people to test hypotheses and to characterize the health of populations. Epidemiological methods include the description of the frequency and determinants of a disease in a defined population, evaluation of factors that may cause a disease, and conducting experimental studies of the effects of modifying risk factors on the subsequent frequency of a disease. Epidemiologic data provide a quantitative foundation for public health policy and clinical research, as well as a basis for the implementation and evaluation of prevention and control approaches in medicine and public health.

The science is interested in distinguishing personal, biological, or socioeconomic characteristics that increase or decrease the risk of disease and death. Basically, the rationale behind epidemiology is to determine statistically the probability, association, causation, and risk between certain characteristics and particular disease processes, and then derive a biological, socioeconomic, or behavioral inference from such a pattern. Epidemiologists study the variation in the occurrence of disease to identify and understand the reasons for this variation. In so doing, epidemiologists strive to identify factors that cause disease, with the broader goal of identifying opportunities for prevention to reduce and eventually eliminate the burden of disease in human populations.

Epidemiologists are also interested in genetic and environmental factors affecting human health. Their areas of study include cancer, infectious diseases, cardiovascular diseases, renal diseases, vision, aging, AIDS, tuberculosis, occupational and environmental health, and the genetics of disease. More recently, epidemiologists have begun looking at injury and the biological, behavioral, and environmental characteristics that increase or decrease the risk of injury or death.

The term "forensic," on the other hand, defines the application of science to law. Typically, forensic science concerns the investigation of unnatural deaths, such as homicide, suicide, accidents, and those from natural causes. In addition, the field of forensic science can be applied to the investigation of nonfatal events such as the analysis of bloodstains, DNA, biological fluids, trace evidence, fingerprints, firearms, the examination of questionable documents, tool marks, cyber-technology, and criminal profiling to list a few.

The Emergence of a New Science

Recently, a new field of science has emerged — namely, forensic epidemiology. As previously stated, this discipline involves the application of epidemiological principles to forensic issues. More specifically, forensic epidemiology has been defined by Goodman et al. as the use of epidemiologic methods in the investigation of public health problems in which there is suspicion of, or evidence regarding possible intentional acts of criminal behavior as factors contributing to health problems. The forensic epidemiologist concentrates on a select population of individuals and examines the patterns and distribution of unnatural deaths (homicide, suicide, accidents) and natural diseases and the associated risk factors that influence those patterns.

For example, a forensic epidemiologist would be interested in the distribution of homicide cases by time and place and the motive of the individual committing the homicide. He or she would also be interested in distinguishing personal, biological, or socioeconomic characteristics that place certain individuals at an increased risk of disease. Does living in proximity to a chemical facility increase the likelihood of dying of cancer, or are those individuals who develop cancer more genetically susceptible to cancer? Basically, the *modus operandi* of epidemiology is to determine whether there is a statistical association between various characteristics and a particular disease process, and then derive a biological inference from such a pattern.

This relatively new specialty will increase our knowledge of intentional and unintentional injuries and death and thereby improve the health and safety of the community. The field of forensic epidemiology also has the potential to bridge the wide gap between science and public health and the civil and criminal justice systems. However, there is a bleak side to this evolving and expanding profession. At present, novice forensic epidemiologists are poorly trained and ill prepared for the careers they have chosen. Although a few graduate programs are offering a degree in forensic epidemiology, the curriculum, while teaching the fundamentals of epidemiology, does not provide exposure to the legal environment. Unfortunately, once inexperienced forensic epidemiologists are released from their carefully controlled ivory towers, they find themselves ill prepared for the legal arena they had just entered. Individuals who choose a career in forensic epidemiology will ultimately become employed in one of the following professional capacities: forensic consultant, expert witness, forensic epidemiologist in a coroner/medical examiner's office, or in a county or state health department.

Forensic Consulting

The primary role of a forensic consultant is the evaluation of scientific, forensic, and legal information determine whether further investigation is warranted. A practicing private forensic consultant is customarily contacted by the next of kin of the decedent to review medical records, autopsy reports, and police reports to provide a written report indicating whether further investigation or other actions are necessary. Cases range from family members who refuse to accept the cause of death listed on the death certificate (usually suicide) to cases of alleged infidelity. Most forensic consultants gain their experience by working in the field, including death scene investigation and postmortem examination, or by obtaining an advanced educational degree to provide a comprehensive and creditable review of the medical and scientific evidence. This type of experience and education is difficult to obtain, and locations where such a background can be acquired are scarce. Logically, it would be most beneficial for an individual interested in a career as a forensic consultant to begin his or her training as a death scene investigator (e.g., deputy coroner), followed by formal education leading to a doctorate in forensic epidemiology. Unfortunately, the majority of forensic consultants obtain their doctorates first, without any formal practical field training. This places them at a disadvantage as consultants and as expert witnesses (a further discussion is given later). Forensic consultants are normally hired by both prosecutors and defense attorneys to review and answer questions regarding the medical and scientific aspects of cases. The consultant then provides written opinions for the attorneys to use. This action is conducted outside of the courtroom.

Expert Witnesses

An expert witness, in contrast to a forensic consultant, is hired by either a prosecutor or a defense attorney to testify in a court of law as to his/her opinions regarding a particular aspect of a case. Before proceeding further, we must first describe what defines an expert witness. According to the Federal Rules of Evidence (Rule 702), anyone with scientific, technical, or other specialized knowledge who can assist in the court's understanding of the evidence or determine the facts in an issue in which witness qualifies as an expert by knowledge, skill, experience, training, or education, may testify in the form of an opinion.

In the courtroom, the expert witness from the academic world collides with the legal world. The expert witness encounters a totally different procedural and intellectual milieu from academia and science. There is no direct overlap between science and the legal system. A short account of the unique experiences an expert witness may face in a court of law is given next.

The first novel experience comes in the form of a crossexamination. The purpose of a crossexamination of the expert witness is twofold: First, to elicit facts from the expert that are only favorable to his or her client's theory. Within the academic and scientific setting, it is the accepted practice to present all aspects of a theory. By contrast, in a crossexamination, the expert witness would only be allowed to provide opinions regarding limited aspects of a particular issue. The sequence of questioning, the phrasing, and the limits placed on the answers are in contrast to the open ended format that usually prevails during scientific conferences and symposia. The use of a "yes–no" response does not afford the expert an opportunity to explain all possible explanations.

Second, the examiner tries to destroy the expert's credibility by bringing out any facts that would tend to lessen the weight of the expert's opinion. This is accomplished by attempting to show that the witness is overcompensated, biased in favor of the party's cause, not really knowledgeable in his or her field, or holds a different view from that of other experts generally recognized as authorities in the field. This attempt to destroy one's creditability is totally foreign to expert witnesses coming from the academic and scientific universe. Within the academic world, one's credibility is determined by educational degrees, number of publications, and faculty appointments. These are rarely questioned. In contrast, when a forensic epidemiologist takes the witness stand, every grade (back to high school) and every published paper (especially with conflicting views), may be examined and called into question. Academics rarely find it necessary to defend their scholarly positions. In a court of law, every opinion may be subjected to a blistering dissection on crossexamination.

Third, the examiner attempts to cast doubt on the expert's theories while trying to have the expert admit that an alternative explanation can be possible. This is done by intensity, rapidity, and sometimes adversarial questioning during the crossexamination. Academic and scientific debates are designed to determine facts and separate out fiction or mere assumptions to support a hypothesis. In contrast, in the courtroom, opposing counsel attempts to have the expert admit the possibility that a particular event could have occurred in a different manner, or that the conclusions expressed by the witness could have an alternative explanation. The end result is to cast doubt on the truthfulness and credibility of that particular witness. This goal is diametrically opposed to the training of epidemiologists and basic science theory.

Coroners'/Medical Examiners' Offices and Health Departments

Forensic epidemiologists are also employed in coroners' and medical examiners' offices, as well as in county and state health departments. In these positions, they have the greatest impact as advocates for social change. Their role is the information collection, analysis, and evaluation of the health of the communities they serve, and alerting them to present and emerging health risks. After the risk has been identified, they support the advocates with epidemiological data and identify the risk factors that warrant action.

A forensic epidemiologist in a metropolitan coroner's or a medical examiner's office can best appreciate how forensic data constitute the starting point to trigger social change that can alter behavior and result in the saving of lives. A case in point is the Sudden Infant Death Syndrome (SIDS). Only through the compilation of forensic epidemiological data was the relationship between the risks of a face-down sleeping position and death determined. Based primarily upon such epidemiological data, the American Academy of Pediatrics policy, "Infant Positioning and SIDS," was adopted, recommending that healthy term infants be placed on their sides or backs to sleep. Recent data show that the original policy appears to have had a positive effect in significantly decreasing the prevalence of prone sleeping and simultaneously lowering the SIDS rate in the United States.

Forensic Epidemiologists are also called upon to examine food poisoning outbreaks in restaurant chains. Prior to the terrorist attacks, these outbreaks were investigated simply to determine the specific etiological agent that caused the outbreak. The results of the investigation would end in changes in food handling procedures and fines. The investigation is nowadays also focused on the possibility of a deliberate tainting of the food products either at the restaurant site or at the product distribution center. These investigations would end in arrests, court trials, and jail, time.

Two Different Worlds

One must ask, "Why is there such a wide gap between the world of science and the medical community and that of the legal system?" The explanation is rooted in the fact that the two disciplines serve different purposes and share no overlapping grounds. The law is concerned with ordering human conduct in accordance with certain standards, values, and societal goals. Science, on the other hand, is designed to describe and explain occurrences and data in neutral objective terms. (This discordance was clearly evident during the recent National Conference on Science and the Law, at which the scientist attendees sat on one side of the hall and the lawyers on the other as witnessed by the author.)

The reasons for this are threefold:

1. There is a purposeful difference between science/medicine and the law. The goal of science is to follow objective methodology to find the cause or multiple causes of a condition. The purpose of the legal system is to settle disputes
2. The scientist or physician and the attorney speak two different languages. The term "causation" illustrates this point the best. The law assumes that the expert can quantify his/her opinion in such terms as "reasonable medical certainty" or "reasonable probability." This is driven by the fact that causation in the legal world is testimony that is sufficient to support a verdict in favor of the plaintiff even though it may not meet the scientific level of causation
3. Students in law schools have no exposure to the basics of scientific methodology, statistics, and the evaluation of scientific studies. In turn, forensic epidemiologists and physicians in their training programs have no exposure as to how to prepare and present one's opinion for court, the verbal mechanics of testifying, and the handling of crossexamination

To eliminate this gap between the legal and medical and scientific communities, the two sides cannot simply meet at the middle of the chasm. They need to cross the bridge to the other side and understand the world at the other side.

Examples of Forensic Epidemiology

Forensic epidemiology investigations have played key roles in establishing epidemiological causation and legal causation. The concepts of the former involve the calculation of risk that an agent caused a disease (relative risk) and reliability has both scientific and legal perspectives. Forensic epidemiologists provide the concept of causation in issues of law and epidemiology. Several examples include deaths from drug overdoses, the risk of silicone breast implant, the risk associated with motor vehicle accidents, to list a few.

Forensic epidemiologists employed in coroners'/medical examiners' offices play a key role in providing information to agencies such as the Drug Enforcement Administration (DEA), Food and Drug Administration (FDA), Federal Bureau Investigation (FBI), Fatal Accident Reporting System (FARS), pharmacological companies, school of public health, and the Consumer Product Safety Commission (CPSC). The forensic epidemiologist has an in-depth understanding of the data and is in a position to evaluate and provide a clear picture of categories of deaths. Agencies such as the DEA and FDA are provided information of deaths relating to drug overdoes. These agencies are provided not only with the total number of drug-related deaths, but also with the number and types of drugs involved and the populations at greatest risk of dying, by age, sex and race. In addition, they are provided geographical mapping showing areas of heavy drug deaths and, more importantly, where drug deaths are emerging. Pharmacological companies are required to monitor adverse reactions to their products, including deaths. More than just the death certificate, forensic epidemiologists play a key role by providing the pharmacological companies with information such as the toxicological level of their drug, the circumstances surrounding the death, and the past medical history of the individual.

The collection of epidemiological data plays an important role in the understanding of the relationship between silicon breast implants and cancer. The chronology of the development of the implant, the collection of epidemiological data between the time of implant and occurrence of cancer, provided the FDA the data to set regulations regarding this and other medical devices.

Aside from providing the FARS, the government agency that analyzes motor vehicle accidents, the forensic epidemiologist provides the local Department of Transportation (DOT) information highlighting dangerous intersection, sections of roadway, and other hazards. The forensic epidemiologist also provides supplementary information to the FARS report. This includes the type of vehicles involved, the past medical history of the fatalities, and the use of safety devices.

Forensic epidemiologists also have a role in public health. Epidemiological data collected from coroners'/medical examiners' offices in the United States provide critical information illustrating the risks associated with the facedown sleeping position, co-sleeping, non-crib sleeping placement, and SIDS. The forensic epidemiologist daily reviews the circumstances and manner of death in order to help identify consumer products that may pose a public health threat.

The science of forensic epidemiology can also act as a community advocate for social change by assessing the needs of a community, the use of epidemiological data, and the development and organization of social advocacy. Social advocacy for change can take many forms. For example, program and policies of Mothers Against Drunk Drivers (MADD) has three main goals are public awareness, legal advocacy, and victim assistance.

A second example of social change is the Needle Exchange Program (NEP) started in response to epidemiological data pertaining to the increased spread of HIV infections and the sharing of needles. Epidemiological data linked HIV and AIDS to the sharing of needles, and the community activism to establish NCP was formed.

Conclusion

The field of forensic epidemiology is still in its infancy, and its true potential in bridging the gap between the scientific, health, and legal communities is yet to be realized. The knowledge, expertise, and assistance offered by forensic epidemiologists practicing as expert witnesses or consultants should increasingly be sought out by forensic pathologists and attorneys.

References

Wecht, C.H. and Koehler, S.A., Case studies in forensic epidemiology. *J. Legal Med.*, 24: 587–94, 2003.

Loue, S., *Case Studies in Forensic Epidemiology*. New York, NY: Kluwer Academic/Plenum Publisher, 2002.

Goodman, R.A., Munson, J.W., Dammers, K., Lazzarini, Z., and Barkley, J.P., Forensic epidemiology: Law at the intersection of public health and criminal investigations. *J. Law Med. & Ethics*, 31: 684–700, 2003.

Lawyers, Ethics, and the Forensic Professional

37

MARK D. YOCHUM

Introduction

Forensic professionals, regardless of their underlying disciplines, whether in science, sociology, medicine, accountancy, or other pursuits, must inevitably deal with the lawyer. In fact, dealing with lawyers and the court processes is fundamental to the meaning of "forensic." This chapter will explore the forensic professional's dealings with a lawyer as constrained by the lawyers' ethical rules and duties under codes of professional responsibility. The forensic professional when acting in association with a lawyer, is, in fact, surprisingly bound by those rules of professional conduct as well. Even though the forensic professional's own society or licensing agency may have its own rules with respect to ethical behavior, the lawyer rules will have a real effect on how the forensic professional must perform his job. Understanding lawyers' ethics necessarily improves the forensic professional's ability to work effectively with the lawyer. The principal topics covered in this chapter are the authority to enforce rules of lawyers' ethics against the nonlawyer forensic professional, issues with respect to the confidentiality of information learned in the forensic process, conflicts of interest, fairness or candor in the litigation process, and, finally, fees.

Authority to Enforce Rules of Lawyers' Ethics against the Nonlawyer Forensic Professional

Ethical rules with respect to the practice of law have developed fitfully over the past 200 years. Originally, a lawyer's practice was regulated on a court-by-court basis as individual judges reviewed the activities of lawyers before them, sanctioning conduct which was unbecoming to the practice of law." In the latter part of the 19th century, science and rationality in the professions led to the development of formal professional societies (not just in law), state licensing and institutional accrediting processes. For lawyers, bar examinations began as the 19th century turned to the 20th. At this time, as well, the American Bar Association (ABA) was formed to elevate the character of the profession ostensibly. For half a century, the ABA has been involved in creating Model Rules of Professional Conduct culminating most recently in the 2003 Model Rules of Professional Conduct. These Model Rules have been created pursuant to the ABA's Ethics 2000 Project, an extensive re-examination of modern ethical principles in law. Much of the following discussion will refer to the Rules promulgated by the ABA in this fashion.

The ABA Model Rules of Professional Conduct, however, are just that, model rules. Each state has its own rules with respect to professional practice by lawyers that may, in some detail, vary from these model rules. Further, states have different methodologies for creating and enforcing these rules. The majority approach in the United States is that rules of professional conduct governing lawyer behavior (and governing behavior of those associating with lawyers) are solely within the power of the supreme court of that state. Some jurisdictions permit the legislature to pass laws regulating the practice of law in conjunction with the supreme court but subject to the supreme court's ultimate review. Some states permit the legislature without such review to pass rules governing law practice. This mix of authority and source of law creates some differences throughout the United States with respect to some of the issues discussed herein. Key to this analysis everywhere is the question, "What is the practice of law?"

Other rules can also affect the forensic professional when acting in concert with lawyers: rules with respect to judicial conduct, rules of evidence, federal statutes and regulations governing particular parts of the profession (such as securities lawyers, patent attorneys, or tax professionals) and certain rules dealing with the criminal justice system and family law. The focus of this chapter, however, will be on those rules of professional conduct that govern all lawyers that, in turn, affect the forensic professional.

The forensic professional is most likely to have a professional society that itself is concerned with ethical issues. Frequently "ethical" issues are not moral ones, but rather in the nature of almost commercial regulations such as appropriate advertising or the appropriate fee to be charged. Nonetheless, the guidance and inspiration provided by these rules is without a doubt helpful and elevating to that professional. Nonetheless, these sorts of rules, including the rules of lawyers for professional responsibility, may be divided into two styles: aspirational or enforceable. For example, the ABA's Model Rule with respect to service to the public by lawyers, *pro bono publico service*, is aspirational in the sense that the rule does not mandate charitable service by lawyers but rather reflects a hope that they will engage in it. Many of the lawyers' rules however, unlike the rules of the forensic professional society, are, in fact, enforceable. Further, these rules may be enforced against the forensic professional when working in concert with the lawyer.

Enforcement may occur against the lawyer by suspension or disbarment or by public or private reprimand. Additionally, the conduct of the lawyer or the forensic professional may be enjoined, that is prevented, by a court on protest from a complaining party. The forensic professional may be prevented from working for a particular client or a particular lawyer because of a conflict of interest. Additionally, as well, economic sanctions are available for violations of rules, the principal sanction being the loss of fees. Most of the rules discussed later are practical in nature to insure that the forensic professional will be acting in an economically sound and professional manner. This chapter will not explore the aspirational rules of professional conduct.

What does the practice of law entail? The forensic professional necessarily must deal with lawyers, and violations of the lawyer rules may lead to sanction. A problematic occurrence in America today is the growth of what lawyers term the unauthorized practice of law. The opportunity to engage in the unauthorized practice of law (a misdemeanor in most states as well as enjoinable conduct) is seductively presented to the forensic professional. After sufficient education in the forensic aspects of their discipline, forensic professionals may be tempted to engage in advisement or other counseling with respect to clients as to legal matters without the participation of a lawyer. A forensic professional might engage in a business relationship with a lawyer, yet, nonetheless be unsupervised with respect to the advisement given the ultimate client. The growth of this troublesome issue of professionalism in America over the last decade has been astounding, particularly with regard to accountancy professionals, professionals in family law areas, financial advisors in bankruptcy, but also many other nonlawyer disciplines. The Model Rules of Professional Conduct restrict lawyers themselves from assisting an individual in the unauthorized practice of law. The lawyer rules also prohibit fee sharing, the sharing of legal shares with a nonlawyer. The rules also preclude a lawyer from entering into a partnership for the practice of law with an individual who is not a lawyer. The most frequently articulated goal of unauthorized practice of law restrictions is to protect the public through ensuring competence. It may go without saying that many competing professionals view these restrictions as a device to ensure that lawyers complete franchise over matters that other professionals could more cheaply address.

What more does the practice of law entail? Courts throughout the country have been unable to settle on a definition after a century of trying. Most recently, the ABA has proposed, although not adopted, the following definition: "The application of legal principles and judgment with regard to the circumstances and objectives of a person that require knowledge and skill of a person trained in law." A person is practicing law when "giving advice or counsel to persons as to their legal rights and responsibility or to those of others." Many American states take a view that is even broader than the proposed ABA definition. For example, suppose you are handling a workers' compensation claim wherein the only issue is whether the employee has been injured. One might believe that a forensic medical professional might be able to complete the simple forms associated with such a proceeding and provide all the necessary evidence and expertise to accomplish the hearing process successfully. In Pennsylvania, for example, this activity would be considered unauthorized practice of law. The Commonwealth of Pennsylvania's definition, such as it is, is that "if there is argument over facts or law, if legal decisions may be made," is the practice.

As you can see from the foregoing, there is a great risk in legal advice coming from the forensic professional without a lawyer's participation. More frequently, the experience of the forensic professional is that he engages in a contractual relationship with the participation of the lawyer. In modern practice, the forensic professional might be employed by the lawyer for use with respect to a particular client of the lawyer. The forensic professional and the lawyer may be in a contractual relationship jointly with the client. Or, we see increasingly that robust forensic professional organizations may employ lawyers to interface with the client. This latter structure is most problematic as it looks as if the lawyer is improperly sharing legal fees with the forensic professional. Further, as the growth of the forensic professional industry increases, we see possibilities of new relationships between the forensic professional and the lawyer. For example, a lawyer and a forensic professional might develop a law-related service, independent of the lawyer's practice. Currently, many states have rules of professional conduct that regulate law-related services in which a lawyer partners with others. The key to these rules is that the client of the law-related service must be informed that the law-related service is not legal service, and consequently, the client is not afforded the protections of lawyers' rules of professional conduct with respect to such issues as confidentiality of information and conflict of interest.

Typically, however, the forensic professional is employed by the lawyer (properly in the litigation context, with an arrangement that, ultimately, the fee is to be paid by the client). In this situation, we begin to see how the lawyer's supervision of the nonprofessional forensic expert creates for the forensic expert a welter of lawyer professional responsibility concerns. It is an awareness of the lawyer's responsibility that allows the forensic professional to work effectively in this setting.

ABA Model Rule 5.3 governs the responsibilities of the lawyer regarding nonlawyer "assistance." This rule provides that a partner or lawyer who has managerial authority, and the law firm itself shall "make reasonable efforts to ensure that the firm has in effect measures giving reasonable assurance that the person's conduct is compatible with the professional obligations of the lawyer." This rule takes the anomalous position that the nonprofessional (i.e., nonlawyer) working with the lawyer shall be judged with respect to professional responsibility matters as if he were a lawyer. Thus, failure to follow lawyers' rules with respect to ethics must necessarily lead to the discharge of the nonlawyer assistant and, perhaps, additional sanctions. Note that to violate the aforementioned rule, the law firm does not actually have to commit a violation. The rule mandates that the firm must keep in place a system to insure that violations will not occur. The term "law firm" includes legal departments of corporations and other entities and governmental legal offices. The rule provides that a lawyer having "direct supervisory authority over the nonlawyer" must make reasonable efforts to insure compatibility in practice with lawyers' rules. Finally, and most importantly, for the forensic professional, the lawyer can be held responsible for the conduct of a nonlawyer if that conduct would be a violation of lawyers' rules of professional conduct if committed by a lawyer. Lawyers' responsibilities for the professional acts of the forensic expert comes when the lawyer orders or ratifies inappropriate conduct or learns of inappropriate conduct when its consequences may be avoided but fails to take remedial action. Thus, within the law firm, the forensic professional has the responsibility to become aware of lawyers' restrictions, and the good forensic professional will attempt to follow them.

Initially, it is apparent that the foregoing rules can cover a wide range of defalcations by subordinates. In the context of the unauthorized practice of law, these and other related rules require that the lawyer participate in the giving of legal advice and has ultimate responsibility for the work product. As is probably not unexpected, the most frequent complaint to boards of professional conduct with respect to lawyer behavior is competence and communication. The job was done badly and my lawyer does not talk with me. Too frequently, unauthorized practice of law rules are violated by lawyers who engage nonprofessional assistants who are the only interface with the client. For example, the forensic health professional who is an expert in asbestosis meets with the perspective client, fills out the necessary forms to commence the action, and, in fact, the lawyer himself never meets the client. This activity is a violation of the unauthorized practice of law restrictions because although lawyers are permitted to engage others to aid in the practice of law, they are not permitted to abdicate their responsibility to consider and render independent judgment with respect to the particular problem of a client. Lawyers may appropriately delegate work to nonprofessionals if the lawyer maintains a direct relationship with the client, supervises the ultimate work, and has complete professional responsibility for that work.

Issues with Respect to the Confidentiality of Information Learned in the Forensic Process

The foregoing rules create the obligation of the forensic professional in terms of compliance with all of the requirements of the lawyers' professional responsibility rules. Key to an attorney's obligation with respect to any client is confidentiality of information. This duty is equally important for the forensic professional. In fact, the term "confidential information" is a misleading statement of law. The lawyer's obligation with respect to information learned during the course of representation of a client is far broader than merely the preservation of confidences. In the past, lawyers were only obliged to keep secret confidential information — that is, information given to them with the specific understanding of its confidential nature. For over a quarter of a century, that obligation has been expanded to include all information learned during the course of a representation whether confidential or not. In fact, even information known to the general public or published, cannot be commented upon or mentioned by the lawyer if he learned that information in the course of representation.

There are certain instances in which a lawyer may reveal a confidence or information learned during the course of representation. However, those permissive revelations are extremely limited. The purpose of the rule on confidentiality of information is for lawyers as it is with many other professionals with the same ethical rule: to encourage free communication even as to embarrassing or, in this instance, legally damaging subject matter. This requirement extends to information learned during the course of representation, with respect to the existence of the representation itself. For example, your representation of a particular client cannot occur on your resume absent permission from the client. Good practice in this area might even impinge on ordinary family life. Dinner table chatter cannot include particulars about the day's work if it has the effect of revealing this sort of information.

There are a number of instances in which information learned during the course of representation may be revealed at the option of the lawyer. For example, a lawyer (and thereby the forensic professional) may disclose information impliedly authorized to be disclosed to carry out the representation. For example, it is obvious that you can reveal your relationship with the client in order to participate in court processes. Of particular interest to the forensic professional community has been the notion of exchange of information, especially within the scientific community. Science thrives on the free exchange information that is produced by the individual experiences of the scientists. Recently, the ABA has been concerned with a similar issue concerning the education of lawyers. Lawyers would profit in their community by an exchange of stories that had occurred in their practice. The rule preserving confidences has inhibited such exchanges. The ABA now permits lawyers to use for educational objectives incidents from their practice so long as the auditor cannot determine whom the particular story is about. Nonetheless, this rule of secrecy versus forensic science will be long debated. But for now, the participation by a scientist in the representation of a lawyer's client will render him silent, in the absence of the client's permission.

There is a great deal of disparity among various state rules on the ability of the lawyer to reveal information without client permission to prevent harm. The Model Rules of Professional Conduct allow a lawyer (but do not mandate a lawyer) to reveal information relating to the representation if the lawyer reasonably believes it is necessary to prevent the client from committing a criminal act that is likely to result in reasonably certain death or substantial bodily harm. This exception in some states (and, as of August, 2003, by the ABA Model Rules) is further supplemented by an ability to reveal such information if it will cause substantial economic injury. Particularly troublesome to the medical forensic professional is the requirement that, for permissive revelation, some jurisdictions require that the client must be prevented from committing a criminal act or that the lawyer's services be used in the commission of that act. In those jurisdictions, if during the course of your work as a forensic professional, you discover that the other side's client is more seriously injured than he even knows, you are not permitted to reveal that information. While the revelation may prevent serious bodily harm, the revelation would not prevent the client from committing a crime. Remember, always, that revelation is always permitted if the client consents after full disclosure of his rights. The obvious difficulty is that sometimes the client does not consent.

Permissive revelation of information is also available to secure advice about compliance with the rules of professional conduct. Further, in actions against the lawyer in a controversy between the lawyer and the client, the information may also be revealed. Additionally, information may be revealed to comply with a specific law or court order. For example, during the course of litigation, the forensic professional may be ordered to reveal specific information.

How long does the obligation of the rule on preserving information last? The answer is forever. This obligation extends beyond the representation. In fact, it extends beyond the death of the client and, further, beyond the death of the professional himself.

As noted before, this rule of ethics for lawyers (and for forensic professionals working with lawyers) differs from the rule dealing with the attorney–client privilege. Although the privilege will be discussed in this text, the key difference between the privilege and the ethical rule is that the attorney–client privilege only applies to communications (i.e., writing, speech) and only those communications that are intended to be and actually held in confidence. Thus, revelation of information by either the client or the attorney or their agents outside of that group will destroy the attorney–client privilege.

One of the most troublesome interactions in the rules of professional conduct generally is between the obligation of the confidentiality of information and the obligation of candor toward the tribunal. This troublesome interaction is produced when the professional knows or believes that his client or witness is lying or intends to lie in the litigation context. First, a comment upon knowledge and belief. For purposes of these rules, the term knowledge means *actual knowledge*, not that the lawyer or the professional merely has reason to know. It is an unfortunate comment on the professional life of lawyers that they frequently attempt to avoid knowledge of information that may be problematic. For example, the prudent criminal defense lawyer will not ask his client whether he committed the crime or not. If the client says that he did commit it but intends to tell the court he did not, the lawyer is in an ethical dilemma, the perplexing "solution" to which is described in the following. Consequently, lawyers sometimes decide not to ask those questions to which they do not want to know the answer.

A lawyer, under the Model Rules, shall not knowingly offer evidence that the lawyer knows to be false. A lawyer may refuse to offer evidence that the lawyer reasonably believes is false. Note that the first rule is a mandate. If there is knowledge of falsity, the lawyer may not offer the evidence. And, if the lawyer discovers that falsity after it has been offered, he must take remedial measures. (It should be noted that this obligation to correct a known falsity terminates at the end of the proceeding.) If a lawyer simply believes the evidence is false, he has the option of whether to allow the testimony or not.

Unfortunately, clients do lie on the stand, and we surmise that, with microscopic frequency, other witnesses, including a forensic professional, might lie. What is the lawyer's obligation with respect to known falsity? The lawyer is required to bring the falsity to the attention of the court and seek his own withdrawal from representation or some correction of the false statements or evidence. States differ, but the prevailing rule is that this is necessary even if doing so involves the lawyer in the revelation of protected information. Additionally, the lawyer is instructed first to importune the witness to come forward on his own to correct the falsity. As a last resort, the lawyer is instructed to withdraw from the case. Such withdrawal, however, in the litigation setting can only occur with the permission of the court. All of the foregoing remedial measures are particularly troublesome when the liar is a criminal defendant. States and federal courts differ with respect to how remedial measures should be taken against the lying criminal defendant. The problem at root is that the criminal defendant may learn that lying delays his case as his lawyer, upon discovering the lie, must withdraw with court permission. The typical solution, however, has been to not allow the lawyer to withdraw but simply to allow the jury to be a check on the falsity of the criminal's testimony. There is great faith (and it is just faith) that the jury will still be able to identify the lie.

Although the client described in the preceding story is evil and adept, too often our clients are individuals with no mental or physical capacity. One of the problems of dealing with clients who have diminished capacity is that they are less capable of making judgments about the conduct of their case. At root, the client is the boss and should make critical decisions with respect to the course of representation. Unfortunately, sometimes during the course of the representation, it becomes apparent that the client does not have the mental or physical capacity to do so. Although, there are legal mechanisms such as guardianships and trustees that are available as a substitute for client direction, the rules on confidentiality of information inhibit the professionals from seeking this advice, medical or other professional, during the pendency of representation. The ABA has recently considered the interaction of our rules on confidentiality and incapacitated clients, and a new rule is proposed which may allow for the revelation of information about the client to other professionals to seek assistance with the handicapped client.

The obligation to preserve confidential information is obviously broad. For the forensic professional and the lawyer, it applies to those in the current employment situation and requires the preservation of confidences with respect to former employees. Consequently, forensic professionals should experience in their relationship with lawyers contractual obligations to maintain confidentiality, both now and in the future, with respect to information learned during the course of the representation. Additionally, the forensic professional should have in place (and the lawyer should demand) mechanisms within the forensic professional's firm to maintain the confidentiality required by the legal rule. This requirement would also mean contracts or other forms of writing that bring home to the employees of the forensic professional the obligation to keep information secret. The prudent law firm is instructed by the ABA to audit compliance with confidential information rules. Once again, the ABA properly points out that this concern applies to lawyers and forensic professionals, experts of all sorts, paralegals, secretaries, in-house accountants, witnesses, computer and technological advisors, and even to the garbage men.

Conflicts of Interest

Hand-in-hand with the restrictions imposed upon legal professionals and lawyers on the preservation of confidences is the requirement that lawyers avoid conflicts of interest. The concept of both confidentiality and conflicts of interest are somewhat foreign to the scientist. The scientist has an ethic to disseminate information that has been learned in the course of a scientific investigation to promote general scientific knowledge and development. Similarly, it is difficult for a scientist to adopt the idea that their pursuit is only for the benefit of a particular client. Perhaps the pursuit of the general scientific objective of the advance of knowledge is inhibited by rules imposing limitations on advocacy based upon conflicts of interest. Nonetheless, the forensic professional (scientist or not) will be bound by lawyers' ethical restrictions in this area as well. Lawyers are ethically constrained from representing conflicting interests. A conflicting interest is one where "there is a significant risk that the representation of one or more clients will be materially limited by the lawyer's responsibilities to another client, a former client or a third person or by a personal interest of the lawyer." Further, conflicts of interest occur when the representation of one client is "directly adverse to another client."

One of the difficulties in analyzing the existence of conflicts of interest from a legal perspective is that analysis requires substantive legal knowledge. Frequently, this knowledge is necessary for an analysis of whether a conflict of interest exists or not. Direct adversity in representation in many cases is straightforward: a lawyer cannot be both the prosecutor and the defense attorney; a lawyer cannot represent both the landlord and the tenant; the lawyer cannot represent both the tax collector and the taxpayer.

The lawyer (and the forensic professional) may obtain a waiver of the conflict from clients affected. Lawyers are permitted to seek a waiver of such conflicts if they reasonably believe that their representation will not be adversely affected by the conflict, the representation does not involve assertion of claims by one client against the other in litigation, and the representation is not prohibited otherwise by law. A waiver can be effected by the client giving a written waiver after the client has been informed of the nature of the conflict and its implications. (Not all states require the waiver to be in writing.) This sort of waiver frequently occurs in a lawyer's practice. For example, a single lawyer might represent three parties interested in forming a business entity. Even though, in some sense, the interests of the three parties might conflict with respect to management or division of profits, the lawyer usually can reflect the wishes of all the parties and still provide competent representation. The issue for the forensic professional becomes more complex as the professional might in one case represent the plaintiff's interests with respect to a forensic conclusion and yet be sought to support a defense position at a different time. Further in this discussion, we will explore how to judge whether that presents a conflict of interest. It should be noted, however, at this point that not all conflicts are waivable, only those in which diligent representation can be provided to the not too conflicting positions.

You should also note that conflicts of interest are created by representation of clients and former clients and include responsibilities to a third person or to the personal interest of the professional. With respect to third parties and their interests, this conflict comes into play frequently in litigation wherein the forensic professional is involved. For example, insurance companies are often interested participants in litigation that the forensic professional is working on, not just through payment ultimately for damage but also through their payment of lawyers and professional fees for the insured. The insurance company may wish the forensic professional to take a position in a particular matter that is to the insurance company's advantage, generally concerning a wide range of insureds, but such a position may not be beneficial to the particular client. Additionally, a professional's own interest can create a conflict, sometimes financial with a client in terms of business dealings. In fact, even romantic involvement between the professional and a client is viewed in legal ethics as a problem of conflict of interest. For example, the romantically involved client may be inhibited from discharging his professional or otherwise criticizing the professional's advice or suggested course of action.

As noted previously, the rules of professional conduct for lawyers are almost universally enforced through a disciplinary process, a violation of the rules leading to lawyer suspension, disbarment, or other forms of censure. In the area of conflicts of interest, however, this rule is enforceable by trial courts. A charge of conflict of interest is brought before a trial court to disqualify from representation the other side's professional, including experts. (It is perhaps a sad comment on legal ethics that claims of conflict of interest are not brought to elevate the profession, but are used as a tactical device to make the representation or litigation more costly for the opposing side.)

Additionally, and importantly, the conflict of interest rules also apply to former clients. There is an on-going obligation to avoid conflicts with respect to the interests of clients that you have previously represented. This conflict is measured by whether the matter is the same between the present and former client or is substantially related and materially adverse. (Again, materially adverse representation may go forward with consent from the former client. Obviously, in contested matters, this consent is impossible to come by.) Many states additionally have a rule concerning "imputed disqualification." This means that if one professional in the law firm is not permitted by reason of these rules from representing a client, the entire firm is disqualified from representation as well.

The issue with respect to the forensic professional is how these rules affect their practice. Forensic professionals when working with lawyers are bound by legal ethics. Thus, the issue becomes: Can the forensic professional be subject directly to these rules on conflicts and consequently be precluded from representation of particular clients or worse, create a conflict of interest that would disqualify an entire law firm? The law on this issue is developing in the United States, but the prevailing view is that the employee of a law firm or independent contractor — be it secretary, paralegal, or forensic professional — will be tested for adversity of interest just as if they were a lawyer. The ABA has reviewed the issue of whether the lawyer can hire or associate with someone (not a lawyer) who produces a conflict and if you have hired such an employee or independent contractor with a conflict, can the firm avoid the problem of imputed disqualification. The ABA concluded that the ordinary tests with respect to conflicts of interest apply even to the employee. However, with respect to imputed disqualification, principally produced by the representation of a client in the past whose interests are adverse to a current client of the firm, the ABA suggests that the rule for nonlawyers should be modified. The nature of that modification is to allow for screening devices.

A short interlude is appropriate here on the idea of screening devices. Although many people think that the rules on conflicts of interest are imposed to insure zealous representation not tainted by conflict, in fact, the basic purpose of the conflict of interest rules is to preserve confidential information. The idea is this — in a conflict situation, you may be required to give information learned from one client to the other to provide competent representation. But obviously, the disclosure of that information would be a violation of your obligation to preserve confidences. Thus, the key factor in determining whether a conflict of interest exists is whether there is information learned in the course of representation of one client that would be useful in the representation of the conflicted client. Screening devices, in ancient days called Chinese walls or cones of silence, are internal office mechanisms to screen the tainted professional (or forensic professional) from receiving or disseminating information about the particular client at issue. Some states allow screening devices to avoid imputed disqualification when the incoming professional is a lawyer, but many states do not. The ABA felt that screening devices would be useful in conflicts produced by nonlawyers because of its uncertainty in its ability to restrict hiring practices of nonlawyers. Nonetheless, to avoid imputed disqualification of the entire firm, the screening device must be put into place immediately upon entry of the new employee or independent contractor.

The existence of these rules on conflict of interest also suggest and, in fact the ABA mandates, that there be in place in the firm, mechanisms for determining whether conflicts of interest exist. Thus, for example, it is typical to require of the incoming professional a list of clients represented, matters worked upon, and other pertinent data to evaluate whether the entry of the professional in the firm will create conflict. Even this process is fraught with difficulty as you will recall lawyers are precluded from disclosing who they have represented without the consent of the particular client. Additionally, you will note that firms should have in place a mechanism to review new clients for conflicts with existing clients.

Determination of whether a client conflict exists is not always simple. The key issue is the preservation of confidences, but courts are also concerned with what may be termed as systemic propriety, that is, the system looks good. Before the 1970s, lawyers' ethics were tested under an "appearance of impropriety" standard. This is no longer the rule; lawyers may appear to be improper so long as they are not improper. Nonetheless, there is a flavor of this old notion that continues in the cases and decisions on conflicts of interest. The principal test to determine whether there is a conflict or not is a threefold analysis: Evaluate the scope of the prior representation; what did you and your firm do? Could one reasonably infer that confidential information was obtained during that course of representation? If so, would that information be relevant to the new representation? If so, the courts conclude a disqualifying conflict exists. Note that as a part of this process of determining conflict, the actual receipt of information is not relevant. The courts will not explore whether the professional actually received any confidential information but rather whether he could have during the course of the prior representation. This analysis in virtually all jurisdictions is not rebuttable. By that it is meant that the forensic professional or other professional cannot even offer evidence that, though it may appear that he/she could have received confidential information, he/she did not. Courts have determined that an exploration of the course of the prior representation and the information disclosed therein would defeat the purpose of the rule to preserve confidences. Thus, courts only look at the structural possibilities of obtaining that information and if that structure suggests that the information could have been exchanged, it is irrebuttably assumed that it was exchanged.

Fees

Another way in which conflicts of interests can actually arise is by fee. The payment of the fee, or, in fact, the sophistication of the fee agreement itself, may set up a conflict among the forensic professional, the lawyer, and your client. Additionally, lawyers' ethical rules circumscribe how you, as a forensic professional, may be paid and to some degree, how much.

In the popular perception, it seems that all lawyers these days charge on a contingency fee basis. Contingency fees are simply fees generated based upon some contingency, typically success in litigation. The lawyer's advertisement that "you pay us nothing unless you collect" is everywhere. Although this method of charging is acceptable for attorneys, except in cases of family law and criminal defense work, it is generally not permitted for experts in any situation. The notion, of course, is this: the forensic professional will act as an expert in XYZ Toxic Tort litigation. He could charge a flat fee based on the service or charge an hourly rate. Or he may be tempted to ask for 10% of the proceeds of the litigation. ABA Model Rule 3.4(b), however, limits lawyers' ability to pay anybody to testify. In sum, the forensic expert can be paid for time and expenses. But experts may not be compensated on the contingency basis. The reason is actually in a sense protection of the client. If the expert is being paid on a contingency basis, the perception of the veracity or reliability of the forensic professional's opinion is reduced for the fact finder because of the expert's interest in the outcome.

Lawyers are also not permitted to support litigation financially. This principle is an ancient rule based upon concepts that are called barratry and other sorts of common law crimes. In the modern era, these rules of conduct mean that the client has to be ultimately responsible for the payment of all sorts of fees associated with litigation. The appropriate contract for employment of an outside expert is a three-party contract (i.e., the lawyer, the client, and the expert), wherein the client agrees that the expert will be paid by the client. (This rule also applies in arrangements where the lawyer changes on a contingency fee basis.) This rule has been particularly troublesome with respect to the representation of poorer people. You may know that one of the unfortunate litigation techniques is "starve them out." In order to live, the client might need medical assistance. He may not be able to afford even transportation to his medical assistance. He may need forensic examination and ordinary living expenses. The longer the litigation goes on, the less the likelihood that the client is going to be able to survive economically, and then, the defense lawyer will be able to make a lower settlement offer.

There are ethical obligations on a lawyer not to engage in dilatory tactics. But, as we have seen already, the rules of professional conduct are not always bright in their lines. There are a number of cases in the United States where sympathetic lawyers have provided and to indigent clients, bus transportation to medical assistance, food, presents for the children at Christmas time. Frequently, the attorney will be reported to the local disciplinary board and, almost uniformly, these lawyers have been sanctioned for improper assistance in litigation. Some states have permitted, in the representation of indigents, that the lawyer may be responsible for litigation costs. The requirements for this assistance (in very few states) are that (1) the individual is being represented is indigent; (2) ultimately the client is responsible (i.e., the lawyer must retain a right to receive the money from the client sometime in the future); and (3) the lawyer cannot advertise the fact that he is engaging in this sort of assistance.

Experts' fees may be affected by statute or regulation. For example, in administrative hearings, where experts may be required, administrative agencies may be empowered to look at the experts' fees. Otherwise, the notion of what is the appropriate fee for an expert is folded in with the notion of what is an appropriate fee for a lawyer. In spite of the terms of engagements, courts are empowered in reviewing fee agreements, to modify the compensation if the court finds the fee charged unfair or unreasonable. The manner of charging must be in a fee agreement, which should be in writing. (Not all states mandate writings, but, as a matter of practice, it is unwise to function without one.) Many lawyers and experts have an hourly rate, minimum increments for billing must be explicit, and the professional must be specific with respect to the expenses directly charged to the client. Those sorts of expenses may be test costs, mailing and delivery, long distance phone calls, use of computer assisted data based research that can be separately charged, and a range of other sources. Be aware that sophisticated purchasers of legal service (particularly insurance companies) are greatly concerned by these costs.

In establishing a fee, the rules also permit consideration of "The likelihood apparent to the client that the acceptance of the particular employment will preclude other employment...." This provision goes hand-in-hand with the conflicts of interests rule. If a client hires an expert witness, that means others who want to sue the client cannot hire the expert because it would set up a conflict of interest. Thus, even for lawyers, one can collect a fee simply to be conflicted out of working for some other party.

This chapter is meant as an introduction to the interaction between a lawyer's professional ethics and the work of the nonlawyer forensic professional. The key objective is to make the forensic professional aware that when working with lawyers, it is the lawyers' codes of conduct that will impose restrictions on how the forensic professional must operate. An understanding of these obligations is important for the development of a competent and successful forensic professional.

Index

A

AAAM. *see* Association for the Advancement of Automotive Medicine (AAAM)

AAFS. *see* American Academy of Forensic Sciences (AAFS)

AALNC. *see* American Association of Legal Nurse Consultants (AALNC)

Abbreviated Injury Scale (AIS), 565

ABFA. *see* American Board of Forensic Anthropology (ABFA)

ABFDE. *see* American Board of Forensic Document Examiners (ABFDE)

A-B-O blood grouping, 55, 409

Abraham (Biblical), 68

Absolute liability, 217–218

Accident reconstruction
  injury biomechanics, 564–566
  occupant kinematics, 563–564

Accumulated degree hours (ADH), 436–437

Acid phosphatase test, 415

ACPO. *see* Association of Chief Police Officers (ACPO)

Actual cause, 169, 200
  theories proving, 200–201

Actus reus, 139, 478

ADA. *see* Americans with Disabilities Act (ADA)

Adequate remedy at law, 163

ADH. *see* Accumulated degree hours (ADH)

Adhesives
  identification, 328

Administrative misconduct, 242

Admissibility, 292–293
  hearings, 514–518

Advance directive for health care, 128–129

Adverse events, 239–241

Affidavit, 87

AFIP. *see* Armed Forces Institute of Pathology (AFIP)

AFMES. *see* Armed Forces Medical Examiner System (AFMES)

AFTE. *see* Association of Firearms and Toolmark Examiners (AFTE)

Agbabian v. TST Colorado Ave., 228

Age
  forensic anthropology, 457

Agency for Health Care Policy Research (AHCPR), 239

Agency for Health Care Research and Quality (AHRQ), 239

Age of Chaos, 8

Aggrieved party, 162

AGI. *see* Anthropometric Gait Index (AGI)

Agreements
  vs. forensic agreements, 158

AHCPR. *see* Agency for Health Care Policy Research (AHCPR)

AHRQ. *see* Agency for Health Care Research and Quality (AHRQ)

AIS. *see* Abbreviated Injury Scale (AIS)

Alcohol
  abuse, 395
  analysis, 402
  body effects, 403–404
  central nervous system, 403–404

Alexander the Greek, 70

ALI. *see* American Law Institute (ALI)

AMA. *see* American Medical Association (AMA)

Amelogenin
  DNA testing, 425

American Academy of Forensic Sciences (AAFS), 444, 455

American Association of Legal Nurse Consultants (AALNC), 618

American Board of Forensic Anthropology (ABFA), 455

American Board of Forensic Document Examiners (ABFDE), 365

American criminal justice system
  philosophical basis, 71–82

American Law Institute (ALI), 82, 219, 233

American Medical Association (AMA)
  domestic violence guidelines, 113

American Society of Civil Engineers (ASCE), 262–263

American Society of Crime Laboratory Directors — Laboratory Accreditation Board (ASCLD-LAB), 498

American Society of Questioned Document Examiners (ASQDE), 365

Americans with Disabilities Act (ADA), 489–490

Ammunition, 336–337
  markings
    class characteristics, 339
    individual characteristics, 339

Amphetamines
  analysis, 402
  urine testing, 405

Amylase test, 416–417
Analogy, 23–24
  examples of, 25–26
  vs. induced generalizations, 25–26
Anatomic pathology, 387–388
Ancient civilization, 68
Ancient tradition, 3–8
Andrews, Tommy Lee, 56
Answer
  civil justice proceeding, 144–145
Antemortem *vs.* perimortem
  forensic anthropology, 460
Anthrax letters, 519–520
Anthropometric Gait Index (AGI), 571
Antifederalists, 72
Antisocial personality, 615
Appeal
  civil justice proceeding, 147–148
Appropriate interest (discount) rate
  wrongful death and injury, 556–557
Arbiter
  forensic accounting, 524
Argument
  defined, 12
Argumentum ad nauseum, 32–33
Arizona
  recklessness case law, 188
Armed Forces Institute of Pathology
      (AFIP)
  Armed Forces Medical Examiner
      System, 397
Armed Forces Medical Examiner System
      (AFMES)
  Armed Forces Institute of Pathology, 397
Asbury, David, 310
ASCE. *see* American Society of Civil Engineers
      (ASCE)
ASCLD-LAB. *see* American Society of Crime
      Laboratory Directors — Laboratory
      Accreditation Board (ASCLD-LAB)
Ashcroft, John, 420
Ashforth, Dawn, 43–44
ASQDE. *see* American Society of
      Questioned Document Examiners
      (ASQDE)
Assault
  case law, 172–173
  defined, 170
  elements of the cause of action, 171–172
  interest protected, 170
Asset-based approach, 533
Association for the Advancement of Automotive
      Medicine (AAAM), 472, 565
Association of Chief Police Officers (ACPO),
      497–498

Association of Firearms and Toolmark
      Examiners (AFTE), 334
Associative evidence, 582
Assumption of risk, 211
  patient, 246
Astronomers, 5
Athens
  homicide punishment law, 69
Authorship
  evidence and admissibility hearings, 514–518
  evidence and expertise, 509–514
Autopsy, 388–390
  forensic pathologists, 396
    vs. hospital pathologists, 390
  psychological, 484
Avery, Oswald, 419

B

BAC. *see* Blood alcohol concentration (BAC)
Ballistic fingerprints, 300
Bandel, Hannskarl, 273
Barberio test, 415
Barbiturates
  analysis, 402
Barrel rifling, 340f
Battered spouse syndrome, 118–119
Battery, 174–175
  case law, 175
  defined, 174
  elements of the cause of action, 174–175
  interest protected, 174
Beckman Coulter vs. Dovatron/Flextronics, 516
Beetles (Coleoptera)
  human body decomposition, 433
  life cycle, 432
  time since death, 434–435
Behavioral profiling, 483–484
  crime scene, 483
Behavioral science, 475–493
  civil matters, 485–489
  criminal matters, 476–484
  practice issues, 490–493
  workplace, 489–490
Behavioral toxicology, 403
Beneficiary
  trust, 125
Benzodiazepines
  analysis, 402
Bertillon, Alphonse, 300
Beyond a reasonable doubt
  standard of proof, 79
Biatchux, 472
Biblical times, 68

Bill of Rights, 72
Binion murder trial, 306
Biological materials
    preserve and locate, 38
Biomechanics, 466
Black Blow Fly (*Phormia regina*), 435–436
Black letter, 220
Blake, Edward, 44
BLEVE. *see* Boiling Liquid Expanding Vapor
        Explosion (BLEVE)
Blood
    identification, 410
    immunological tests, 412–413
    stain pattern investigation, 413–414
Blood alcohol concentration (BAC), 403
    determination of, 404
Blood drug concentration, 403
Blooding, 39–45
Bloodsworth, Kirk Noble, 39–43, 46,
        48, 49, 51
    interviews, 54
    remarried, 58
Blow flies
    colonization sites on victims, 438
    drug detection, 438–439
    life cycle, 436
    time since death, 435
Boiling Liquid Expanding Vapor Explosion
        (BLEVE), 360–361
Bolt face, 341f
Bolt-action rifle, 336f
Borderline personality, 615
Bradshaw v. Michigan Nat. Bank, 229
Brady, 95
Breach
    contract law, 162
    immaterial
        contract law, 162
Breach of contract
    forensic accountants, 526–527
Breach of duty
    medical negligence, 243
Breech face marks, 341, 342f
Bullets
    databases, 586
    jacket, 337
    markings, 339–340
Burgess, Ann, 116
Burglary
    DNA testing, 422
Burt, Cyril, 309
Bush, George W., 47
Business interruption
    forensic accountants, 528–529
But-for theory, 200

C

Calendars, 5
California
    assault case law, 172
    conversion case law, 186
    false imprisonment case law, 177
    recklessness case law, 188
    trespass to chattels case law, 184
California vs. Flinner, 516
Campbell, Joseph, 6
Cannabinoids
    urine testing, 405
Capel, Robert, 41, 42
Carbon monoxide
    analysis, 402
Cardozo, Benjamin, 231
Carstairs, Jonathan, 19
Cartridges
    case markings, 340–343
    components, 336–337
        headstamp markings, 336
Casing databases, 586
Catalytic blood tests, 410–413
    sensitivity, 411
Catholic Church
    Luther's revolt against, 70
Causation
    construction failures, 256, 267–270
    intentional torts, 169
    intervening, 203–206
    medical negligence, 243–244
Cause-in-fact, 169, 200
Cause of action
    tort liability, 166–167
Centerfire cartridges, 337
Central nervous system (CNS)
    alcohol effects, 403–404
CFTT. *see* Computer Forensic Tool Testing (CFTT)
Chain of custody
    evidence, 92–93
Challenger explosion, 567–568
Chamber marks, 343
Charred documents, 382–383
Chase, Martha, 419
Chattels. *see* Trespass to chattels
Checkwriters
    examination, 383
Chemical explosions, 360
Cherrill, Frederick, 302
Cheung vs. Maddock, 96
Child abuse
    forensic pathologists, 395
Child custody, 114–115
    mental health professionals, 488–489

China
  historical insect use, 432
Chiory, Andrew, 310
Choline
  detection, 415
Circuit courts, 141–142
Citizen soldier, 69
City-state
  emergence, 5
Civil claims, 140
Civil discovery, 151–155
  history, 151–152
Civil injury, 140
Civil justice proceeding
  answer, 144–145
  appeal, 147–148
  closing arguments, 147
  complaint, 144
  phases, 143–148
  post trial phase, 147–148
  pretrial phase, 144–145
  trial phase, 146
Civil justice system, 139–148
  elements, 140
Claim preclusion, 144
Class characteristics
  ammunition markings, 339
Clinical pathology, 387–388
Clinton, William, 428
Closing arguments
  civil justice proceeding, 147
CNS. see Central nervous system (CNS)
Cocaine
  analysis, 402
  urine testing, 405
Cochliomyia macellaria, 435–436
Codeine
  urine testing, 405
Coffin vs. United States, 76
Coleoptera
  human body decomposition, 433
  life cycle, 432
  time since death, 434–435
Collaborative team approach, 592
Collateral estoppel, 145
Collective fact, 286
Collins, Susan, 62
Colorado
  assault case law, 172
  recklessness case law, 188
Columbia breakup, 567–568
Combined DNA Index System Program
    (CODIS)
  FBI, 53, 427
Combustion, 357–358

Command posts, 587–588
Common knowledge, 286
Common law jury, 74
Common man, 70
Commonwealth vs. Phoenix, 95
Commonwealth vs. Smith, 105
Commonwealth vs. Webster, 77
Comparative fault
  vs. comparative negligence, 210–211
Comparative negligence, 209
  vs. comparative fault, 210–211
  patient, 246
Comparison microscope, 344, 345f
Compensation to family
  for homicide, 69
Compensatory damages, 207
Competency
  to draft will, 488
  mental health professionals, 476–478
  witnesses, 286
Complaint
  civil justice proceeding, 144
Computer Forensic Tool Testing (CFTT), 498
Computer printers
  examination, 383
Conclusion, 15
  defined, 12
Conditional evidence, 581
Confession, 80
Confidentiality
  mental health professionals, 491
Connecticut
  intentional infliction of emotional distress
      case law, 178–179
Consent searches, 90
Constitution, 72
  criminal procedure, 85–92
Construction failure
  materials and component testing, 280
Construction failures
  analytical investigation, 280
  ancillary failures, 267
  case studies, 270–277
  causation, 256, 267–270
  defective construction, 269
  defective design, 269
  defective materials, 269
  documentation, 281
  experts, 265–266
  field investigation, 279
  functional failures, 267
  improper operation and maintenance, 270
  investigation
    phases, 279–281
  lawyers investigating, 264–266

litigation support, 281
materials and component testing, 280
owner interference, 270
poor management, 270
poor planning, 270
safety failures, 267
types, 266–268
unforeseeable factors, 270
Construction law, 255–281
   forensic engineers, 256–262
Contact wounds, 24
Contraband
   dogs detecting, 90–91
Contract law, 157–164, 158–159
   breach, 162
   interpretation, 161–162
   material breach, 162
   purpose, 162–164
Contract remedies, 162–164
Contractual claim, 140
Contributory negligence, 210, 228
Converse fallacy of accident, 29
Conversion, 185–187
   case law, 186–187
   defined, 185
   elements of the cause of action, 185–186
   interest protected, 185
Convicted by Juries, Exonerated by Science,
   44–45
Convicting the Innocent, 49
Conviction. *see* Wrongful conviction
Copernicus, 6
Coroners, 390–392
   educational opportunities, 391–392
   inquests, 391
Corrections
   mental health professionals, 481–482
Cough medicine
   drug testing, 406
Council of State Governments, 251
Counterfeit document examination, 383
Course-of-business specimens
   handwriting, 373–374
Court
   finding the right one, 142
Court of Appeals, 141
Court system, 140–143
Courts of last resort, 141
Crick, Francis, 39, 419
Crime Bill, 111
Crime by Computer, 496
Crime scene
   behavioral profiling, 483
   investigation model selection, 589–592
   investigators, 578

management, 577–592
   components, 577–582
   evidence management, 580–582
   information management, 582–586
   manpower management, 578–580
scientists
   laboratory based, 591–592
technicians, 591
Crime squad
   major, 591
Criminal defense lawyers, 81
Criminal justice reform, 47
Criminal laws, 67–107
   historical perspective, 68–71
   need for clearly defined, 73–74
   precision in writing and administration,
      73–74
   sources, 82–83
Criminal mechanism
   determination of, 595
Criminal misconduct, 242
Criminal occurrence
   determination of, 593–594
Criminal procedures, 67–107
   historical perspective, 68–71
Criminal responsibility, 37–38
   mental health professionals,
      478–479
Criminals
   number of, 67
   risk assessment, 481
Cronin v. J.B.E. Olson Corp., 236
Crusades, 70
Cruzan, 128
Crystal blood tests, 411–412
Custodial interrogations
   Fifth Amendment, 91–92
Cut and paste forgery, 372
Cyanide
   analysis, 402

D

DABFO. *see* Diplomat status in the American
      Board of Forensic Odontology (DABFO)
Dallagher, Mark, 311
Damages
   calculations, 163
   compensatory, 207
   general, 207, 244
   medical negligence, 244
   nominal, 207
   nonpecuniary, 207
   pecuniary, 207

Damages (*Continued*)
  personal, 534–536
  punitive, 207, 244
  special, 207, 244
Databases
  bullets, 586
  DNA, 585
  fingerprints, 585–586
  information from, 584–585
Daubert v. Merrell Dow Pharmaceuticals, Inc.,
    288, 289–290, 311, 313, 397
Davis vs. Pitchess, 96
Deas v. State, 228
Death. *see also* Time since death; Wrongful death
  manner of, 389
  time of, 459
Death on the High Seas by Wrongful Act
    (DOSHA), 468
Death investigations
  fire and explosions, 362
  forensic *vs.* hospital pathologist, 389
  forensic pathologists, 395
Death penalty, 52
  guilt phase, 480–481
  sentencing phase, 480–481
Death records
  forensic pathologists, 395
Death review teams
  forensic pathologists, 397
Deceased
  family, 398
Decedents' property
  default system for administering and
    distributing, 123–124
Declaration of Independence
  jury trial, 74
Deductive reasoning, 15–16
  in forensic science, 19–21
  vs. inductive reasoning, 14, 21–22, 24–25
Defective, 236
Defendant's case in chief
  civil justice proceeding, 146
Defense motions
  civil justice proceeding, 146
Defenses, 245
Defined contribution plans, 547–548
Definition of value, 532
Delahunt, Bill, 62
Delta-v, 564–565
Dementia
  testamentary capacity, 488
Democracy, 69
Dental evidence
  analysis, 451
Dental identification, 445–447

Department of Homeland Security (DHS)
  forensic pathologists, 396, 397
Depositions, 153–154
  forensic accountants, 539
Desaguliers, John Theophilus, 7
DHS. *see* Department of Homeland
    Security (DHS)
Dicto simpliciter, 29
Digital Discovery and E-Evidence, 465
Digital evidence, 466, 495–496
  acquisition, 500
  analysis, 501
  examination, 500–501
  future, 502
  presentation, 501–502
  as process, 498–500
Digital forensics, 495–502
  history, 496–498
Digital storage media, 496
Dillon v. Legg, 215
Diplomat status in the American Board of
    Forensic Odontology (DABFO), 444
Diptera
  human body decomposition, 433
  time since death, 434–435
Disability
  mental health professionals, 489–490
Disaster Mortuary Response Team (DMORT),
    398, 448
Discovery
  forms, 153
  tools, 153
Discretionary cases, 141
Distributed term, 15
Divorce
  defined, 110
DMORT. *see* Disaster Mortuary Response Team
    (DMORT)
DNA
  analysis, 419–428
    historical backdrop, 419–420
  databases, 585
  exonerations, 51
  fingerprinting, 40
    immigration case, 40
    murder, 40
  identification
    blow flies, 439
  identification system, 300
  junk, 421
  profiling, 40
  structure, 420–421
  testing, 97
    amelogenin, 425
    analytic methods, 423–426

biological evidence, 421–422
burglary, 422
databases, 426–427
familial relationship, 56
field testing, 427
legal challenges, 428
new techniques, 426
QA/accreditation, 427–428
review, 55
specimen collection, 422
survey, 45
DNA Sexual Assault Justice Act, 48
Doctrine of last clear chance, 227
Documents
addition, 377–378
alterations, 377–382
charred, 382–383
construction failure, 279–280
defined, 366
erasure, 377
fonts, 382
guillotine blade defects, 381
obliteration, 380
pagination, 381
Dogs
detecting contraband, 90–91
Domestic relations
mental health professionals, 488–489
Domestic violence, 111–114
American Medical Association
guidelines, 113
Emergency Nurses Association,
113–114
forensic pathologists, 395
DOSHA. see Death on the High Seas by
Wrongful Act (DOSHA)
Double variation, 330
Double-stranded DNA (ds-DNA), 420
Doubt
reasonable
instructions on, 79, 101
Douglass, Lewis L., 304
Doyle, Arthur Conan, 11, 399
DRE. see Drug recognition experts
(DRE)
Driving
drugs, 404–405
Drug recognition experts (DRE), 404–405
Drugs
abuse, 395
and driving, 404–405
ds-DNA, double-stranded DNA (ds-DNA)
Durable power of attorney for financial matters,
127
Dusky v. U.S., 476

Duty, 192–198
contractual relationship, 197–198
fitness for, 489–490
medical negligence, 243
relationship, 194–195
special relationship, 195–196

E

Earnings
wrongful death and injury, 543–545
ECE. see Electrochemical machining (ECM)
Economic estimates and valuation
wrongful death and injury, 542–543
Economic organization, 157
ECR. see Electrochemical rifling (ECR)
Ejector marks, 343
Elderly
abuse, 395, 622
law, 121–130
planning for autonomy, 121–130
mental health professionals, 487–488
Electrochemical machining (ECM), 339
Electrochemical rifling (ECR), 339
Embezzlement
forensic accountants, 530
Emergency Nurses Association (ENA)
domestic violence, 113–114
Emotional distress. see Intentional infliction of
emotional distress
Emotional injury
mental health professionals, 486–487
ENA. see Emergency Nurses Association (ENA)
Encase, 497
ENFSI. see European Network of Forensic Science
Institutes (ENFSI)
England
statute of frauds, 161
Enlightenment, 71
Entrapment, 84
Equivocation, 31
Erickson v. Curtis Inv. Co., 225
Erie Doctrine, 468
Erythrocytes (red blood cells), 410
Escola v. Coca Cola, 232
Ethanol
body effects, 403–404
Ethics
mental health professionals, 490–491
Ethyl alcohol
body effects, 403–404
Euphrates River, 5
European Network of Forensic Science Institutes
(ENFSI), 498

Evidence. *see also* Digital evidence; Physical
      evidence
   associative, 582
   authentication, 92–93
   authorship, 509–514
   chain of custody, 92–93
   conditional, 581
   construction failures, 264–265
   contamination, 326
   contract law, 159–160
   crime scene management, 580–582
   dental
      analysis, 451
   dogs detecting, 90–91
   excluded, 81
   glass, 329–330
   hearings
      authorship, 514–518
   known materials, 327
   language-based
      pre-Daubert decisions, 510–511
   light sources, 579
   packaging and labeling, 327
   paint, 330–331
   pattern, 581
   preserving and producing in discovery, 93–96
   preserving for trial, 92–93
   questioned materials, 327
   scientific, 285
   testimonial, 286
   trace
      collection, 325–327
      defined, 328
      examination, 323–331
      importance, 331
   transfer, 582
   transient, 581
Ewell, Brenda, 58
Expert testimony
   methods, 288
   principles
      Frye approach, 288–289
   scientific and technical evidence, 287–293
   theories, 288
Expert witness
   nurse as, 618–619
Expert witnesses, 146, 497
   conclusions, 292–293
   forensic accounting, 523
   underlying facts, 290–292
Experts
   authorship, 509–514
   linguistics, 505
   mental health professionals, 491
   scientific and technical evidence, 285–294

Explosions, 360–361
   death investigations, 362
Exponent, 256
Extortion, 84
Extractor marks, 342–343
Eyewitness identification, 62

F

Facsimile machines
   examination, 383
Fact witnesses, 146
Factual cause, 169, 200
Failure modes and effects analysis (FMEA), 570
Failure to warn, 235
Fallacies, 26–33
   miscellaneous informal, 29
Fallacies of distraction, 28–29
Fallacy of amphibology, 31
Fallacy of composition, 31–32
Fallacy of division, 32
Fallacy of irrelevance, 28
Fallacy of vicious abstraction, 32
False cause, 29–30
False imprisonment, 176–177
   case law, 177
   defined, 176
   elements of the cause of action, 176–177
   interest protected, 176
   Prosser and Keeton on Torts, 176
Family, 109–130
   of deceased
      forensic pathologists, 398
   homicide compensation, 69
   law, 109–111
Faulds, Henry, 308–310
Fault
   tort liability, 166
Fault-tree analysis (FTA), 570
FBI. *see* Federal Bureau of Investigation (FBI)
FCIC. *see* Federal Computer Investigations
      Committee (FCIC)
Federal Bureau of Investigation (FBI)
   Behavioral Science Unit, 41, 483
   CODIS, 53, 59, 427
   computerized records, 496
Federal cartridge, 337f
Federal Computer Investigations Committee
      (FCIC), 497
Federal court system, 141–142
Federal district courts, 141–142
Federal Emergency Management Agency
      (FEMA), 448
Federal mail fraud statute, 102

Federal maritime law, 468
Federal Motor Vehicle Safety Standards
    (FMVSS), 565–566
Federal Rules of Criminal Procedure, 93
Federal Rules of Evidence, 285, 290, 292
    witnesses, 286
Federalism, 72
Feegel, John R., 240
FEMA. *see* Federal Emergency Management
    Agency (FEMA)
Fiber
    examination, 329
Fifth Amendment, 80
    custodial interrogations, 91–92
Fingerprint Whorld, 309
Fingerprinting
    critical analysis, 299–322
    CSI, 305–306
    DNA, 40
    infallibility equation, 310–311
    objectivity, 312
    preposterous claims, 300–301
    recommendations, 313
    testimony beyond the expert's
        qualifications, 307–308
    uniform standards, 312–313
    uniqueness dilemma, 308–310
Fingerprints, 95
    ballistic, 300
    databases, 585–586
    as unforgeable signature, 301–305
Fire
    death investigations, 362
    investigations, 357–363
    scene processing, 358–360
    special scenarios, 362–363
Firearms
    fired components
        laboratory examination, 343–346
    identification, 333–355
        barrel manufacturing process,
            338–339
        glossary of terms, 353–354
        serial number restoration, 347–348
        theory, 338
    laboratory examination, 343–345
Firing pin
    impressions, 341
    marks, 342f
First responders, 578
Fitness for duty
    mental health professionals,
        489–490
Fitzgerald, James R., 515
Fletcher, Conrad, 19

Flies (Diptera)
    human body decomposition, 433
    time since death, 434–435
Flippo vs. West Virginia, 89
Florence test, 415
FMEA. *see* Failure modes and effects analysis (FMEA)
FMVSS. *see* Federal Motor Vehicle Safety
    Standards (FMVSS)
Ford v. Trident Fisheries Co., 200
Foreign linguistics, 505–521
Forensic accountants
    vs. accountants as auditors, 524
    analytical skills, 525
    bankruptcy, 531
    breach of contract, 526–527
    business damages, 526–530
    business interruption, 528–529
    cash receipts diversion, 530
    depositions, 539
    divorce proceedings, 533–534
    document requests, 539
    embezzlement, 530
    expenses, 529
    forecasting future financial results, 525
    fraud, 529–531
    fraudulent payment schemes, 530
    interviewing skills, 525
    investigatory skills, 525
    legal process, 524–526
    murder and arson for profit, 537–538
    personal damages, 534
    personal injury, 536
    revenue, 528
    services, 526–538
    tax matters, 536–537
    utilization of, 539
    valuations, 531–533
Forensic accounting, 469–470, 523–538
    arbiter, 524
    consultant, 523
    mediator, 524
    special master, 524
    trier-of-fact, 524
Forensic agreements, 157–164
    discipline, 158–159
Forensic anthropology, 455–462
    age, 457
    biological profile, 457–460
    court testimony, 461
    field recovery, 457
    individuation, 459
    laboratory analysis, 457–461
    manner of death, 459–460
    race, 458
    stature, 458–459

Forensic anthropology (*Continued*)
time of death, 459
trauma analysis, 460–461
Forensic clinical nurse specialist, 608–609
Forensic consultants, 578
case study in, 598–599
Forensic correctional nurse, 615–617
Forensic crime labs
DNA testing, 52
Forensic drug testing, 405–407
Forensic economics, 467–468
wrongful death and injury, 541–568
Forensic engineering and science, 466–467,
561–573
accident construction, 562–564
products liability, 569–570
Forensic engineers
analysis, 260–261
attributes, 262–264
business person, 257
codes of ethics, 262–263
compensation, 264
diplomat, 257
draft reports, 261–262
education, 263
experience, 263
expert report, 261–262
final report, 262
investigation, 260
licensing, 263
objectivity, 264
primary tasks, 260–261
process, 258–260
publications, 263
qualifications, 262–264
role, 256–262
teaching ability, 257, 264
training, 263
translator, 257
truthfulness, 264
writing ability, 263
Forensic entomology, 431–440
civil litigation, 439–440
current, 433–434
historical perspective, 432–433
time since death, 434–435
Forensic epidemiologists, 396
Forensic *vs.* hospital pathologist
death investigations, 389
Forensic linguistics, 470–471
scope, 508–509
Forensic medicine, 239–278
Forensic nursing, 601–628
education, 621–622
practice guidelines, 603–605

practice/specialty areas, 605–621
professional organizations and
journals, 623
research, 622–623
Forensic odontology, 443–452
bite mark evidence, 448–450
examples, 449–450
dental identification, 445–447
developing applications, 451–452
human abuse, 450–451
mass casualty management, 447–448
tooth fragments
example, 451
UV light case example, 452
Forensic pathologists
child abuse, 395
criminal justice, 395
death investigations, 395
death records, 395
death review teams, 397
Department of Homeland Security, 396, 397
domestic abuse, 395
drug and alcohol abuse, 395
education and research, 396–397
elderly abuse, 395
federal government, 397–398
forensic science, 398–399
portrayed in fiction, 394
portrayed in TV shows, 394
public health, 395–396
societal value, 394–397
transplantation, 396
wound recognition, 395
Forensic pathology, 387–399
Forensic psychiatric nurse, 609–616
case studies, 610–615, 619–629
Forensic psychology, 471–472
Forensic science and law, 3–8
engineering failures, 566–569
logistics, 587–590
slips and falls, 570–571
technology management, 586–587
Forensic Science Associates (FSA), 44
Forensic Science Laboratory Personnel, 578
Forensic stylistics, 474
Forensic Tool Kit, 497
Forensic toxicology, 401–407
reference values, 402
Foreseeability, 203–206
Forgery, 370
cut and paste, 372
simple, 371
simulated, 371
traced, 372
Formal fallacies, 26–27

Forum non conveniens, 469
Fourier transform infrared spectrometry
    (FTIR), 329
Fourteenth Amendment, 80, 85–86, 114–115
    custodial interrogations, 91–92
Fourth Amendment, 81, 85–86
    search warrants, 87
    state courts, 91
Four-way linkage theory, 583
Fraud
    England statute, 161
Freedom, 35–63
French revolution, 71
Freund v. Cellofilm Properties, Inc., 238
Fringe benefits
    wrongful death, 535
    wrongful death and injury, 546–547
Frye, 288
FSA. *see* Forensic Science Associates (FSA)
FTA. *see* Fault-tree analysis (FTA)
FTIR. *see* Fourier transform infrared
    spectrometry (FTIR)
Full Faith and Credit Clause, 110
Future, 8

G

Gel diffusion technique, 412–413
Gender bias
    imprisonment, 60
General damages, 207
    medical negligence, 244
General Electric vs. Joiner, 288, 289
Genes, 420
*Georgia-Pacific Corporation v. U.S. Plywood
    Corporation*, 527–528
Gideon, 80
Glass evidence, 329–330
Glass particles
    refractive index, 330
God (Yahweh), 68
Godinez v. Moran, 476
Godschalk, Bruce, 60
Grand Jury, 75
Graphology, 366
Gray, Richard, 43
Greene vs. United States Navy, 518
Greenman v. Yuba Power Products, 233
Guardian of the person, 128
Guardianship, 124
    evaluation for, 488
    limited, 124
Guillotine blade defects
    documents, 381

Gun Control Act, 347
Gunshots
    distance determination, 351
    distant wounds, 24
    intermediate range wounds, 24
    near contact wounds, 24
    residue examination, 350–351

H

Habeas corpus, 46, 61
Hair
    drug testing, 407
    identification, 328
Hama, Gord, 497
Hamilton, Alexander, 74
Hamilton, Dawn, 40–45
Handguns, 334
Handwriting, 366–370
    baseline, 368
    comparison process, 377
    course-of-business specimens,
        373–374
    disguise, 375–376
    distorted, 375–376
    individual characteristics, 367
    initial stroke, 368
    known specimens, 373–375
        comparable, 373
        range of variation, 373
        repetitive, 373
    letter connections, 368
    letter design, 369
    letter height ratio, 368
    line quality, 370
    outside influences, 376
    pen pressure, 369
    request specimens, 373
    slant, 369
    spacing, 367–368
    system, 367
    terminal stroke, 368
Hanger rod
    details, 272f
Harassment
    mental health professionals, 489
Harding, David, 302
Hargett vs. Hargett, 516
Hartford Civic Center collapse, 272–273,
    273f
Harvard Medical Malpractice Study,
    239
Hasty generalization, 29
Hauptmann, Bruno Richard, 366

Hawaii
  intentional infliction of emotional distress
    case law, 179
HCR-20. *see* Historical/Clinical/Risk
    Management Scale (HCR-20)
Head Injury Criterion (HIC), 566
Health Insurance Portability and Accountability
    Act (HIPAA), 247
Health-care professionals
  domestic violence injuries, 113
  regulation of, 241f
Healthy People, 601–602
Heating, ventilating, and air conditioning
    (HVAC), 269
Heirs
  default identification system, 122–123
  identification, 122–123
Hemin (Teichmann crystals), 412
Hemochromogen (Takayama crystals), 412
Heroin
  drug testing, 406
Hershey, Alfred, 419
HIC. *see* Head Injury Criterion (HIC)
High explosives, 361
Hill, David Jayne, 72
Hindsight, 203–206
Hinkel, J. William, 42
HIPAA. *see* Health Insurance Portability and
    Accountability Act (HIPAA)
Historical/Clinical/Risk Management Scale
    (HCR-20), 481
Hobbs Act, 84
Hohfeldian jurisprudence, 7
Holmes, Sherlock, 11, 18, 399
Holmstrom, Lynda, 116
Homicide
  Athenian law, 69
  compensation to family, 69
  DNA fingerprints, 40
  Pennsylvania law, 82
Honaker, Edward, 59
Hospitalization
  involuntary, 485–486
Household services, 551–554
  hourly value, 553–554
  hours spent producing, 552–553
  wrongful death, 535
Hsi Duan Yu (Washing Away of Wrongs), 432
Human body
  decomposition, 432–433
  dissection, 393
Human performance toxicology, 403
Hutcheson, Joseph C., 12
HVAC. *see* Heating, ventilating, and air
    conditioning (HVAC)

I

IACIS. *see* International Association of Computer
    Investigative Specialists (IACIS)
IBIS. *see* Integrated Ballistics Identification System
    (IBIS)
Ignition, 357–358
Ignoratio elenchi, 28
Illinois
  intentional infliction of emotional distress
    case law, 179
ILOOK, 465
Immaterial breach
  contract law, 162
Immigration case
  DNA testing, 40, 56
Immunoassay test, 413, 415–416
Impressed toolmarks, 352
Imprisonment. *see also* False imprisonment
  gender bias, 60
  number of, 67
  race bias, 60
Incapacitated
  mental health professionals, 487–488
Income approach, 533
Incompetency
  personal decision making, 124
Indented writing, 382
Individual rights
  primacy, 72
Individuation
  forensic anthropology, 459
Inductive enumeration, 22–23
Inductive generalization, 22–23
  in forensic science, 24–25
Inductive reasoning, 21–22
  vs. deductive reasoning, 14, 21–22,
    24–25
Inference
  defined, 13
Informal (material) fallacies, 27–28
Information
  management at crime scene, 582–586
  prior to trial, 93
Informed consent, 486
Infrared luminescence, 379
Ink
  differentiation, 379
Innocence
  presumption of, 39, 50, 75–76
    threatening, 79
Innocence Project, 52, 60
Innocence Protection Act, 47, 62, 63
Innocence reforms, 37–39, 38, 46–47
In re: Winship, 78

In re Brown, 96
Insanity
    legal, 479
Insanity plea, 478
Insects
    China's historical use, 432
    time since death, 434–435
Institute of Medicine (IOM), 239–240
Insurance crisis, 251
Insurance industry reforms, 252
Integrated Ballistics Identification System (IBIS),
        346–347
Intensive rehabilitation supervision, 482
Intensive supervision programs (ISP), 482
Intentional infliction of emotional distress,
        177–179
    case law, 178–179
    defined, 177
    elements of the cause of action, 178
    interest protected, 177–178
Intentional torts, 167–187
    act, 167–168
    against person, 170–179
    against property, 179–181
    causation, 169
    intent, 168–169
    preliminary considerations, 167–169
Interagency liaison, 588–589
Internal Revenue Service (IRS)
    computerized records, 496
    ILOOK, 465
International Association of Computer
        Investigative Specialists (IACIS), 497
International Organization for Computer
        Evidence (IOCE), 498
Interrogatories, 154–155
    forensic accountants, 539
Intervening cause, 203–206
Intervening superseding cause, 203–206
Inter vivos, 125
Intestacy, 122–123
Intestate succession, 122
*Intimate Partner Violence and Sexual
        Assault*, 603
Investigatory system of justice, 80
Involuntary hospitalization and treatment
    mental health professionals, 485–486
IOCE. *see* International Organization for
        Computer Evidence (IOCE)
IOM. *see* Institute of Medicine (IOM)
Iowa
    assault case law, 173
    trespass to land case law, 180–181
IRS. *see* Internal Revenue Service (IRS)
Isozymes, 409

ISP. *see* Intensive supervision programs
        (ISP)
Israel of biblical times, 68
Issue preclusion, 145

J

Jackson v. Indiana, 477
James, William, 54
Jefferson, Thomas, 72
Jeffreys, Alec, 40
Jeffries, Alec, 300
Jesus
    freedom and truth, 50
Johnson, Herbert, 68
Joint accounts, 126
Joint property arrangements, 125
Joint tenants with right of survivorship,
        126
Jones and Laughlin Steel Corp v. Pfeifer, 535
Junk DNA, 421
Jury
    instructions
        civil justice proceeding, 147
    and militia, 75
    trial, 74–75
Justice for All Act of 2004, 47, 48, 62

K

Kansas City Hyatt Regency skywalk collapse,
        266, 271, 567
Kennedy, Henry, 518
Kentucky
    conversion case law, 186
Knock and announce, 88
Kumho Tire Company, 288, 289
Kyle vs. Whitley, 94
Kyllo vs. United States, 86

L

LaHood, Ray, 62
L'Ambiance Plaza collapse, 273–274,
        274f, 275f
Land. *see* Trespass to land
Landsteiner, Karl, 409
Language, 505
Language-based evidence
    pre-Daubert decisions, 510–511
Law
    emergence, 4
Lay witness, 286

LCN. *see* Low copy number (LCN) testing
Leahy, Patrick, 47, 62
Legal cause, 169, 201–203
Legal insanity, 479
Legal nurse consultant (LNC),
        618–619
Legal nurse expert, 620–621
Legal profession
    response to errors, 46–47
Legal reforms
    alternative, 252
Leukocytes (white blood cells), 410
Lev Zetlin Associates (LZA), 272, 277
Lewinsky, Monica, 428
Liability
    absolute, 217–218
    product, 231–238
    strict, 217, 236–237
    strict *vs.* absolute liability, 216–218
    strict product, 232–233
    tort
        categories, 165–166
        cause of action, 166–167
        fault, 166
Liberty
    structural protection, 72
Liberum judicium, 36
Liebman, James S., 50
Life expectancy
    wrongful death and injury, 551
Life-prolonging treatment, 129
Limited guardianship, 124
Lindbergh, Charles, 306, 366
Linguistics, 506–508
    expertise, 505
    fallacies, 30–32
    foreign, 505–521
    profiling, 508–509, 518–519
Living wills, 127–128, 128–129
Lloyd, E.J., 59
LNC. *see* Legal nurse consultant (LNC)
Locard's Exchange Principle, 323
Locke, John, 71
Logic
    in forensic science, 11–33
    helping you, 33
    language of, 12–14
Logical cause, 169
Logical form, 15
Logical validity, 16–19
Longarms, 334
Loomis and Loomis, Inc., 273
Lovell, Avon, 305
Low copy number (LCN) testing, 423
Low explosives, 361

Luther, Martin
    Catholic Church revolt, 70
LZA. *see* Lev Zetlin Associates (LZA)

M

Machine regime, 6–7
MacLeod, Colin, 419
Madison, James, 100
Magazine marks, 343
Maggots
    spontaneous generation, 432
Magna Carta
    jury trial, 74
Mail fraud
    federal statute, 102
Major crime squad, 591
Major premises, 17
Malingering
    mental health professionals, 492
Malpractice, 486
    claim costs, 240
Mandatory cases, 141
Manner of death
    forensic anthropology, 459–460
Manpower management
    crime scene management, 578–580
Mapp vs. Ohio, 85
Mares, Dan, 497
Marijuana
    urine testing, 405
Maritime law
    federal, 468
Market approach, 533
Markings
    ammunition
        class characteristics, 339
        individual characteristics, 339
    bullets, 339–340
    cartridge cases, 340–343
Marriage
    defined, 110
Material breach
    contract law, 162
Material fallacies, 27–28
Mayfield, Brandon, 310, 311, 316
McCarty, Maclyn, 419
McFall, Stephen, 502
McKenna, Charles B., 515
McKie, Shirley, 310
McNeil v. Nissan Motor Co., Ltd., 229
McPherson v. Buick Motor Co., 231, 232
Mechanical explosions, 360
Media relations, 588

Medical errors, 239–241
Medical examiner offices
  regulation, 398
Medical examiners, 390–392, 578
Medical information organization, 247–254, 250f
  delayed diagnosis, 251f
Medical insurance
  wrongful death and injury, 547
Medical investigator, 391
Medical malpractice
  reform initiatives, 250–251
  social and legal context, 241–242
Medical negligence, 239–278
  breach of duty, 243
  causation, 243–244
  commission, 243
  concurrent or intervening negligence of
    others, 246
  damages, 244
  defenses to, 243–244
  duty, 243
  general damages, 244
  litigation, 239–241
    and forensic medicine, 240–241
  omission, 243
  res ipsa loquitor, 243
  special damages, 244
  standards of care, 243
  as subset of medical malpractice, 242–246
  trier-of-fact, 243
Medical records, 247–248
Medical review officer (MRO), 405
Medical system reform, 252
Medical-legal death investigation, 392–394
Medicine on Trial, 240
Melias, Robert, 56
Mens rea, 139, 478–479
Mental health professionals
  child custody, 488–489
  competency, 476–478
  confidentiality, 491
  corrections, 481–482
  criminal responsibility, 478–479
  disability, 489–490
  discrimination, 489
  domestic relations, 488–489
  elders, 487–488
  emotional injury, 486–487
  ethics, 490–491
  expertise, 491
  fitness for duty, 489–490
  harassment, 489
  incapacitated, 487–488
  involuntary hospitalization and treatment,
    485–486

  malingering, 492
  presentencing, 480–481
Mental state at the time of the offense (MSO),
    478–479
Metalanguage, 505
Metalinguistic ability, 505
Methamphetamines
  urine testing, 405
Michael H. v. Gerald D., 120
Michigan
  false imprisonment case law, 177
  trespass to land case law, 181
Mickelberg Stitch, 305
Microcrystalline test, 415
Microscope
  comparison, 344, 345f
  phase contrast
    spermatozoa, 416
Miescher, Friedrich, 419
Mincey vs. Arizona, 89
Minimum number of individuals present
    (MNI), 456
Minnesota
  trespass to land case law, 181
Minor premises, 15, 17
Miranda v. Arizona, 476
Miranda warnings, 80, 91–92
Mississippi
  battery case law, 175
Mitigation
  wrongful death and injury, 545–546
MNI. see Minimum number of individuals
    present (MNI)
Model Penal Code, 82
Modified Griess Test, 350
Modified Rokitansky method
  postmortem examination, 394
Montesquieu, 71
Montgomery Elevator Co. v. Gordon,
    227
Moral certainty, 76, 77
Morales, Angel, 303, 305
Morin, Robert E., 44
Morphine
  urine testing, 405
Morrison, 112
Motor vehicle accidents
  blood samples, 403
MRO. see Medical review officer (MRO)
MSO. see Mental state at the time of the
    offense (MSO)
MtDNA
  DNA testing, 425–426
Murder. see Homicide
Murphy, Sandy, 306

Murrah Federal Building
  Oklahoma City, 568–569

N

NAME. see National Association of Medical
      Examiners (NAME)
Narborough Village murders, 43–44
Narcissistic personality, 615
National Association of Medical Examiners
      (NAME)
  accreditation standards, 391
  establishment, 392
National Disaster Medical System
      (NDMS), 448
National DNA Index System (NDIS), 427
National Forensic Science Commission, 47
National Institute of Justice (NIJ), 44, 498
National Institute of Standards and Technology
      (NIST), 568
National Institute on Drug Abuse (NIDA)
  federal drug testing guidelines, 405
National Integrated Ballistic Information
      Network (NIBIN), 346–347
National Traffic and Motor Vehicle Safety
      Act of 1966, 565
National Vital Statistics System
  forensic pathologists, 396
National White Collar Crime Center
      (NW3C), 497
NDIS. see National DNA Index System (NDIS)
NDMS. see National Disaster Medical System
      (NDMS)
Negligence, 189–199. see also Medical negligence
  breach of duty, 198–199
  case law, 191–192
  causation, 199
  comparative, 209
    vs. comparative fault, 210–211
    patient, 246
  contributory, 210, 228
  damages, 206–208
  defenses to cause of action for, 208–213
  defined, 189–190
  duty, 192–198
  elements of the cause of action, 191–199
  elements considered individually, 192–199
  interest protected, 191
  professional, 242
  proof of
    construction failures, 256
Negligence per se, 197, 213–214
Negligent infliction of emotional distress (NIED),
      194, 214–216
Neolithic period, 5–6

New York
  battery case law, 175
  conversion case law, 187
Newton, Isaac, 6–7, 562
Newton's laws, 562–563
NIBIN. see National Integrated Ballistic
      Information Network (NIBIN)
NIDA. see National Institute on Drug Abuse
      (NIDA)
NIED. see Negligent infliction of emotional
      distress (NIED)
NIJ. see National Institute of Justice (NIJ)
Nile, 5
NIST. see National Institute of Standards and
      Technology (NIST)
No Carbon Required paper, 380
Nominal damages, 207
Non causa pro causa, 29
Non sequitur (it does not follow), 30
Nonpecuniary damages, 207
North Carolina
  assault case law, 172–173
  intentional infliction of emotional distress
      case law, 179
  trespass to chattels case law, 184–185
Notice
  civil justice proceeding, 144
Nucleotide base pairs, 421
Nurse attorney, 618–619
Nurse coroner/death investigator, 617–618
Nurse as expert witness, 618–619
NW3C. see National White Collar Crime
      Center (NW3C)

O

Obiter dicta, 232
Obsessive–compulsive personality, 615
Offenders
  coping skills, 482
Offense
  behavioral profiling, 483
Office machines
  examination, 383
Offsets
  forensic accountants, 529
Ohio
  battery case law, 175
  false imprisonment case law, 177
  trespass to chattels case law, 185
Oklahoma City
  Murrah Federal Building, 568–569
On the Individuality of Fingerprints, 309
Opening statements
  civil justice proceeding, 146

Opiates
  analysis, 402, 406
  urine testing, 405
Opinion validity and admissibility
  expert testimony, 288
Oral fluids
  drug testing, 407
Organized criminal conduct, 69
Osborn, Albert S., 366
Osler, William, 387

P

Paint evidence, 330–331
Palsgraf v. Long Island Railroad Company,
    189, 192, 224
*Panduit Corporation v. Stahlin Brothers Fibre
    Works, Inc.*, 528
Paranoid personality, 615
Parens patriae, 110, 124
Parentage testing, 119–121
Parker v. Rex, 301
Parole, 67
Paternity index, 120–121
Pathology
  defined, 387
Patient
  assumption of risk, 246
  comparative negligence, 246
Pattern evidence, 581
PBGC. *see* Pension Benefit Guarantee
      Corporation (PBGC)
PCP. *see* Phencyclidine (PCP)
PCR. *see* Polymerase chain reaction (PCR)
      testing
Pecuniary damages, 207
Pediatric sexual assault nurse examiner
      (SANE-P), 607
Pennsylvania
  battery case law, 175
Pension Benefit Guarantee Corporation
      (PBGC), 547
Pension plans
  wrongful death and injury, 547–548
People v. Castro, 428
People v. Jennings, 311
Personal damages
  wrongful death, 534–536
Personal Identification, 309
Personal injury
  forensic accountants, 536
Personal jurisdiction, 142–143
Personal prerogative, 72
Personal privacy, 105

Personal representative
  probate, 123
Personality
  antisocial, 615
  borderline, 615
  narcissistic, 615
  obsessive–compulsive, 615
  paranoid, 615
  schizoid, 615
Petitio principii (begging the question), 30
PGSR. *see* Primer gunshot residue (PGSR)
Phase contrast microscopy
  spermatozoa, 416
Phencyclidine (PCP)
  urine testing, 405
Phormia regina, 435–436
Photocopiers
  examination, 383
Photographs, 95
  surveillance, 96
Phrases, 507
Physical evidence
  fire scene, 359–360
    contamination, 359
    documentation, 359
Physical impact test, 215
Pirates
  mindset, 69
Pistol, 334
Pitchfork, Colin, 43, 56
Plaintiff's case in chief
  civil justice proceeding, 146
Plaintiff's motions
  civil justice proceeding, 147
Plasma, 410
Plastics
  analysis, 328
Platelets, 410
Pleistocene epoch, 4–5
PMI. *see* Postmortem interval (PMI)
Poisonous tree doctrine, 103
Poling, Jackie, 40, 42
Polymerase chain reaction (PCR) testing,
    44, 419
  DNA testing, 423–424
Polysyllogisms, 13
Pope John Paul II, 36, 49
Poppy seeds
  drug testing, 406
Post hoc ergo propter hoc, 29
Post trial motions
  civil justice proceeding, 147
Postconviction DNA testing, 60
  learning moment, 37–38
  legislation, 52

Postmortem examination
   internal, 394
   Julius Caesar, 393
   modified Rokitansky method, 394
   procedure, 393–394
   Virchow method, 394
Postmortem forensic toxicology, 401–403
Postmortem interval (PMI), 434–435
Postmortem *vs.* perimortem
   forensic anthropology, 460
Posttraumatic stress disorder (PTSD), 116, 622
Potential medical negligence cases
   critical analysis, 246–250
   initial investigation, 246
Powers of attorney for financial matters,
       125, 126–127
   agent, 126
   principal, 126
Powers of attorney for health care, 127–128,
       129–130
Preclaim personal jurisdiction, 143
Preliminary objections
   civil justice proceeding, 144
Premise, 15
   defined, 12–13
   major, 17
   minor, 15, 17
Premise of value, 532
Prescription analgesics
   drug testing, 406
Presentencing
   mental health professionals, 480–481
Presumption of innocence, 39, 50, 75–76
   threatening, 79
Pretrial
   disclosure, 93
   discovery, 105
Primary Screw Worm, 433
Primer gunshot residue (PGSR), 348–349
   electron microscopy, 349f
Printers
   computer
      examination, 383
Privacy
   personal, 105
Private law, 140
Probate
   administrator, 123
   estate, 122
   executor, 123
Probation, 67
Product defects, 234–236
Product liability, 231–238
Product safety audit, 570
Professional misconduct, 241

Professional negligence, 242
Proof
   standard of
      beyond a reasonable doubt, 79
Proof beyond a reasonable doubt, 39, 75–76
Proof of negligence
   construction failures, 256
Prosecutors, 593–596
Prosser and Keeton on Torts, 165
   false imprisonment, 176
   fault, 166
Prostate specific antigen (PSA), 415–416
Protective sweep, 89
Protein markers, 409
Proximate cause, 169, 199, 201–203
PSA. *see* Prostate specific antigen (PSA)
Pseudomonas fluorescens, 415
Psychiatrists
   working with, 493
Psychological autopsy, 484
Psychological testing, 493
Psychologists
   working with, 493
PTSD. *see* Posttraumatic stress disorder (PTSD)
Public attorneys, 593–599
Public defenders, 596–599
Public defenders office
   adult trial division, 597
   appellate division, 597
   intake/investigative division, 597
   juvenile trial division, 597
   pretrial division, 597
   structure, 596–597
   television shows portraying, 597
Public law, 140
Public policy
   response to errors, 46–47
Punctuation, 514
Punitive damages, 207
   medical negligence, 244

Q

Questioned document examination, 365–383
Questioned Document Examiner (QDE), 512
Questioned Documents, 366
Quinlan, 128

R

Race
   forensic anthropology, 458
   imprisonment, 60
Raiders, 68

Ramsey, William, 41
Rank, Gary W., 302
Rape, 40–45, 627–628
  DNA testing, 422
Rape trauma syndrome (RTS),
      116–117, 622
Reagan, Ronald
  drug-free workplace, 405
Reason, 71
Reasonable doubt
  instructions on, 79, 101
Recklessness
  case law, 188–189
  defined, 187
  elements to the cause of action and
      defense to the cause of action,
      187–188
  interest protected, 187
Records
  information from, 586
  mental health professionals, 491
Red blood cells, 410
Redi, Francesco, 432
Reflected infrared radiation, 378, 380
Regime of fire over ice, 4–5
Rehill, David, 43
Relative bystander test, 215
Reno, Janet, 420
Request for admissions, 155
Requests to produce or examine documents
      and things, 154
Research-Cottrell, Inc., 277
Res ipsa loquitor, 197, 213, 232
  medical negligence, 243
Res judicata, 144, 145
Resource allocation, 589
Restatement (Second) of Torts, 233
Restatement Third of Torts, 234, 235
Restriction fragment length polymorphisms
      (RFLP), 55, 56, 419
  DNA testing, 423
Retirement
  wrongful death and injury, 550–551
Retrospective profiling, 483
Revolver, 334, 335f
RFLP. *see* Restriction fragment length
      polymorphisms (RFLP)
Rhode Island
  false imprisonment case law, 177
Rifle, 335
Rimfire cartridges, 337
Ring test (tube technique), 412–413
Risk
  assumption of, 211
    patient, 246

Rokitansky method
  modified
      postmortem examination, 394
Roman law
  death penalty, 69
Roman theory, 69
Roth Report, 302
RTS. *see* Rape trauma syndrome (RTS)

S

SAFE. *see* Sexual assault forensic examiner (SAFE)
Saliva
  testing, 416–417
SAM. *see* Syntactic analysis method (SAM)
SANE. *see* Sexual assault nurse examiners (SANE)
SANE-P. *see* Pediatric sexual assault nurse
      examiner (SANE-P)
Sarbanes–Oxley Act, 469
Scanning Electron Microscopy/Energy Dispersive
      X-ray Spectroscopy (SEM/EDS), 349
Scene-of-the-crime units, 591
SCERS. *see* Seized Computer Evidence Recovery
      Specialist (SCERS) course
Scheck, Barry, 63
Schizoid personality, 615
Science of Fingerprints, 310
Scientific evidence, 285
Scientific Working Group on Digital Evidence
      (SWGDE), 498
Scientific Working Group on Friction Ridge
      Analysis, Study and Technology
      (SWGFAST)
  glossary, 317–322
Scientist
  forensic engineer, 257
Scoggins vs. State, 95
*Scope and Standards of Forensic Nursing
      Practice*, 604
Searches
  consent, 90
  exigent circumstances, 89
  incident to valid arrest, 88
  plain view exception, 90
  and seizure, 85–86
    by government, 85
    privacy, 86
SEARCH group, 497
Search warrants
  exceptions to, 88–89
  Fourth Amendment, 87
  requirements of, 86–87
Secondary Screw Worm *(Cochliomyia macellaria)*,
      435–436

Second of Torts, 233
Seized Computer Evidence Recovery Specialist
    (SCERS) course, 497
Self-heating, 358
Self-ignition, 358
SEM/EDS. *see* Scanning Electron Microscopy/
    Energy Dispersive X-ray Spectroscopy
    (SEM/EDS)
Semen
    identification, 414–416
Semiautomatic pistol, 335, 335f
Separation of powers, 72
Serology, 409–417
Settlor
    trust, 125
Sex
    forensic anthropology, 458
Sex offenders, 482
Sexual assault
    DNA testing, 422
    semen identification, 414–416
    wrongful conviction, 97
Sexual assault forensic examiner (SAFE),
    605–607
Sexual assault nurse examiners (SANE),
    117, 605–607
    pediatric, 607
Sexual assault response team, 607–608
Shipley, Chris, 40, 42
Short tandem repeat (STR)
    analysis
        DNA testing, 424–425
    markers, 55
Shorthand rendition, 286
Shotgun, 335
    patterns, 351–352
Shotshells, 337, 338f
Shusto, Lisa, 256
Simmers v. Bentley Constr. Co., 225
Simonetti, Rosemarie, 303
Simpson, O.J., 428
Single nucleotide polymorphisms
    (SNP), 421
Single-stranded DNA (ss-DNA), 420
Sinn v. Burd, 216
Sleuth
    forensic engineer, 257
Slide-action shotgun, 336f
Slugs, 337
Smith, Adam, 7
Smith, Debbie, 48
Smith, Gordon, 63
SNP. *see* Single nucleotide polymorphisms
    (SNP)
Social and applied sciences, 465–493

Social security
    wrongful death and injury, 548
Sodium Rhodizonate Test, 350
Soil
    analysis, 328
South Carolina
    trespass to land case law, 181
Sovereignty of the people, 72
Space shuttle failures, 567–568
Special damages, 207
    medical negligence, 244
Spermatozoa
    microscopic analysis, 416
Spermine
    detection, 415
ss-DNA. *see* Single-stranded DNA (ss-DNA)
St. Thomas, 36
    freedom and truth, 50
Standard of proof
    beyond a reasonable doubt, 79
Standards of care
    medical negligence, 243
Staplers
    examination, 383
Staples
    documents, 381
State vs. Baur, 95
State vs. Hawkins, 95
State constitutions
    jury trial, 74
State court system, 141
Statute of frauds
    England, 161
Stature
    forensic anthropology, 458–459
Statutes of limitation and repose
    medical negligence, 244–245
Stellar regime, 5–6
Stevenson v. United States, 315
Stoke's Law, 379
Stoppard, Miriam, 310
Story teller
    forensic engineer, 257
STR. *see* Short tandem repeat (STR)
Striated toolmarks, 352
Strickler vs. Greene, 94
Strict liability, 217, 236–237
    vs. absolute liability, 216–218
Strict product liability, 232–233
Study in Scarlet, 11, 18
Subject matter
    expert testimony
        scientific and technical evidence, 287
Substantial factor theory, 200–201
Substitution of judgment, 128

Summary judgment
    civil justice proceeding, 145–146
Supreme Court, 141
    presumption of innocence, 76
Surveillance photographs, 96
Suspects
    identification, 596
    information from, 584
SWGDE. *see* Scientific Working Group on
        Digital Evidence (SWGDE)
SWGFAST. *see* Scientific Working Group on
        Friction Ridge Analysis, Study and
        Technology (SWGFAST)
Syllogism, 17
Syndromes, 115–116
Syntactic analysis, 471
Syntactic analysis method (SAM), 516

T

Tabish, Rick, 306
Tacoma Narrows Bridge collapse, 266, 267f, 567
Takayama crystals, 412
Talmadge, Florence, 19
Tape
    analysis, 328
Taxes
    forensic accountants, 536–537
Technical analysis
    construction failure, 280
Teichmann crystals, 412
Television
    forensic scientists, 11
Terry stop doctrine, 90
Testamentary capacity
    dementia, 488
Testamentary intent, 125
Testimonial evidence, 286
Teten, Howard, 483
Thin layer chromatography (TLC)
    ink differentiation, 379
Thomson vs. Louisiana, 89
Thrombocytes (platelets), 410
Thucydides, 68
Tigris River, 5
Time of death
    forensic anthropology, 459
Time since death
    case study, 435–437
    civil litigation, 439–440
    insects, 434–435
TLC. *see* Thin layer chromatography (TLC)
Toolmarks
    identification, 333–355

    impressed, 352
    striated, 352
Tort law
    negligence, 189–216
    nuisance, 218–219
    principles, 165–229
    protected interests, 165
    recklessness, 187–189
Tort liability
    categories, 165–166
    cause of action, 166–167
    fault, 166
Torts, 140. *see also* Intentional torts
    defined, 165
    forensic accountants, 527–528
Torture, 80
Trace DNA, 423
Trace evidence
    collection, 325–327
    defined, 328
    examination, 323–331
    importance, 331
Transfer evidence, 582
Transferred intent, 220
Transient evidence, 581
Transmitting terminal identifiers (TTI), 383
Transplantation
    forensic pathologists, 396
Trauma, 466
    analysis
        forensic anthropology, 460–461
Trauma Symptom Inventory (TSI), 479
Trespass to chattels, 181–185
    case law, 184–185
    defined, 181–182
    elements of the cause of action, 182–184
    interest protected, 182
Trespass to land, 179–181
    case law, 180–181
    defined, 179
    elements of the cause of action, 180
    interest protected, 180
Trial
    preparation for, 92–96
    preparing case for, 92–96
Trier of law
    civil justice proceeding, 146
Trier-of-fact
    civil justice proceeding, 146
    forensic accounting, 524
    medical negligence, 243
Trusts, 125, 126
    beneficiary, 125
Truth, 15–16, 35–63
TSI. *see* Trauma Symptom Inventory (TSI)

TTI. *see* Transmitting terminal identifiers (TTI)
Tube technique, 412–413
Twelve Tables, 69
Typewriters
  examination, 383

U

UCC. *see* Uniform Commercial Code (UCC)
UMDA. *see* Uniform Marriage and Divorce Act
    (UMDA)
Undistributed term, 15
Uniform Commercial Code (UCC), 232
Uniform Marriage and Divorce Act (UMDA), 115
Uniform Parentage Act (UPA), 119–120
United States v. Carroll Towing Co., 196–197
United States v. Frazier, 306
United States vs. Leon, 88
United States vs. Van Wyk, 515
Universal proposition, 15
Unreasonably dangerous, 236
UPA. *see* Uniform Parentage Act (UPA)
Urine testing, 405–406
  amphetamines, 405
  cannabinoids, 405
  cocaine, 405
  codeine, 405
  marijuana, 405
  methamphetamine, 405
  morphine, 405
U.S. Supreme Court, 141

V

Vacuuming, 326
Valuation approaches, 533
Van Wyk, Roy, 515
Variable number of random repeats
    (VNTR), 40
VAWA. *see* Violence Against Women Act (VAWA)
Vehicles
  change in velocity, 565
  searches, 90
Venue, 143
Verdict
  civil justice proceeding, 147
Victims
  behavioral profiling, 483
  information from, 583
  insect trauma site identification, 438
  origin determination by known insect species
    distribution, 437–438
Victorian age, 70
Violence, 626–627

Violence Against Women Act (VAWA), 111, 622
Violence Against Women Civil Rights Restoration
    Act of 2000, 112
Violence Risk Appraisal Guide (VRAG), 481
Virchow method
  postmortem examination, 394
VNTR. *see* Variable number of random repeats
    (VNTR)
Voir dire, 306
VRAG. *see* Violence Risk Appraisal Guide (VRAG)

W

Wambaugh, Joseph, 43
Warrant requirement exceptions
  exigent circumstances, 89
  protective sweep, 89
Warranty, 231–232
Warrior tradition, 68
Watkins v. Com, 303
Watson, James D., 39, 419
Watson, John H., 11, 399
Weeks vs. United States, 85
West Virginia
  battery case law, 175
White blood cells, 410
Whitehead, DeAndre, 305
Wilde, Oscar, 98
Wilkins, Rosalind, 419
Willing, Richard, 63
Willow Island Cooling Tower collapse, 274–277,
    275f, 276f
Wills, 125
  competency to draft, 488
  living, 127–128, 128–129
  substitutes, 125
Wilson, Colin, 68, 70
Winterbottom v. Wright, 231
Witnesses
  competency, 286
  Federal Rules of Evidence, 286
  information from, 583–584
Work life expectancy
  wrongful death, 534–535, 548–550
Workplace
  behavioral science, 489–490
  drug testing, 406
  risk, 490
World Trade Center (WTC), 568–569
Writing
  indented, 382
Writing instrument
  defined, 366
  identification, 379
Writ of certiorari, 141

Wrongful conviction, 37–38, 58, 96–99, 107
    sexual assault, 97
Wrongful death and injury, 468
    earnings, 543–545
    economic estimates and valuation,
        542–543
    future earnings estimate, 544
    future earnings present value, 535
    future losses, 543
    household services, 551–554
    income projection, 535
    life expectancy, 551
    losses to date, 543
    medical insurance, 547
    mitigation, 545–546
    pension plans, 547–548
    personal consumption expenditures, 535
    personal consumption or maintenance,
        554–555
    present value, 555–557
    retirement, 550–551

Wrongful injury. *see* Wrongful death
        and injury
WTC. *see* World Trade Center (WTC)
Wyoming
    intentional infliction of emotional distress
        case law, 179

Y

Yahweh, 68
Yauch, John H., 515
Y-STRs
    DNA testing, 425

Z

Zacchia, 393
Zarolia vs. Osborne, 518
Zone of danger test, 215